Algebra and Trigonometry

SIXTH EDITION

KEEDY
BITTINGER

Instructor's Solutions Manual

Judith A. Penna

Addison-Wesley Publishing Company

Reading, Massachusetts • Menlo Park, California • New York
Don Mills, Ontario • Wokingham, England • Amsterdam • Bonn
Sydney • Singapore • Tokyo • Madrid • San Juan • Milan • Paris

TABLE OF CONTENTS

Special thanks are extended to Patsy Hammond for her
excellent typing and to Pam Smith for her careful
proofreading. Their patience, efficiency, and good
humor made the author's work much easier.

Exercise Set 1.1

1. - 6. Consider the numbers

$-6, 0, 3, -\frac{1}{2}, \sqrt{3}, -2, -\sqrt{7}, \sqrt[3]{2}, \frac{5}{8}, 14, -\frac{9}{4},$

$8.53, 9\frac{1}{2}, \sqrt{16}, -\sqrt[3]{8}$

1. Natural numbers: $3, 14, \sqrt{16}$ $(\sqrt{16} = 4)$

2. Whole numbers: $0, 3, 14, \sqrt{16}$

3. Irrational numbers: $\sqrt{3}, -\sqrt{7}, \sqrt[3]{2}$

4. Rational numbers: $-6, 0, 3, -\frac{1}{2}, -2, \frac{5}{8}, 14, -\frac{9}{4},$

$8.53, 9\frac{1}{2}, \sqrt{16}, -\sqrt[3]{8}$

5. Integers: $-6, 0, 3, -2, 14, \sqrt{16},$

$-\sqrt[3]{8}$ $(-\sqrt[3]{8} = -2)$

6. Real numbers: All of them

7. $-\frac{6}{5}$ can be expressed as $\frac{-6}{5}$, a quotient of integers. Thus, $-\frac{6}{5}$ is <u>rational</u>.

8. Rational

9. -9.032 is an ending decimal. Thus, -9.032 is <u>rational</u>.

10. Rational

11. $4.\overline{516}$ is a repeating decimal. Thus, $4.\overline{516}$ is <u>rational</u>.

12. Rational

13. $4.303003000300003...$ has a pattern but not a pattern formed by a repeating block of digits. The numeral is an unending nonrepeating decimal and thus <u>irrational</u>.

14. Irrational

15. $\sqrt{6}$ is <u>irrational</u> because 6 is not a perfect square.

16. Irrational

17. $-\sqrt{14}$ is <u>irrational</u> because 14 is not a perfect square.

18. Irrational

19. $\sqrt{49}$ is <u>rational</u> because 49 is a perfect square.

$\sqrt{49} = \sqrt{7^2} = 7 = \frac{7}{1}$ (Quotient of integers)

20. Rational

21. $\sqrt[3]{5}$ is <u>irrational</u> because 5 is not a perfect cube.

22. Irrational

23. "$-x$" means "find the opposite of x." If $x = -7$, then we are finding the opposite of -7.

$-(-7) = 7$ (The opposite of -7 is 7.)

"$-1 \cdot x$" means "find negative one times x." If $x = -7$, then we are finding -1 times -7.

$-1 \cdot (-7) = 7$ (The product of two negative numbers is positive.)

24. $\frac{10}{3}, \frac{10}{3}$

25. "$-x$" means "find the opposite of x." If $x = 57$, then we are finding the opposite of 57.

$-(57) = -57$ (The opposite of 57 is -57.)

"$-1 \cdot x$" means "find negative one times x." If $x = 57$, then we are finding -1 times 57.

$-1 \cdot 57 = -57$ (The product of a negative number and a positive number is negative.)

26. $-\frac{13}{14}, -\frac{13}{14}$

27. $-(x^2 - 5x + 3)$

$= -(12^2 - 5 \cdot 12 + 3)$ (Substituting 12 for x)

$= -(144 - 60 + 3)$

$= -87$

28. $-(x^2 - 5x + 3)$

$= -[(-8)^2 - 5(-8) + 3]$

$= -(64 + 40 + 3)$

$= -107$

29. $-(7 - y)$

$= -[7 - (-9)]$ (Substituting -9 for y)

$= -[7 + 9]$

$= -16$

30. $-(7 - 19)$

$= -(-12)$

$= 12$

31. $-3.1 + (-7.2)$

The sum of two negative real numbers is a negative real number.

$-3.1 + (-7.2) = -10.3$

32. -416

33. $\frac{9}{2} + \left(-\frac{3}{5}\right)$

    The positive number $\left(\frac{9}{2}\right)$ is farther from 0 on a number line than $-\frac{3}{5}$ is, so the answer is positive.

    $\frac{9}{2} + \left(-\frac{3}{5}\right) = \frac{39}{10}$

34. -20

35. $-7(-4) = 28$

    The product of two negative numbers is positive.

36. $-\frac{8}{3}\left(-\frac{9}{2}\right) = \frac{72}{6} = 12$

37. $(-8.2) \times 6 = -49.2$

    The product of a negative number and a positive number is negative.

38. -48

39. $-7(-2)(-3)(-5)$

    $= 14 \cdot 15$ (The product of two negative numbers is positive.)

    $= 210$

40. 16.33

41. $-\frac{14}{3}\left(-\frac{17}{5}\right)\left(-\frac{21}{2}\right)$

    $= -\frac{17}{5}\left[\left(-\frac{14}{3}\right)\left(-\frac{21}{2}\right)\right]$ (Using associativity and commutativity)

    $= -\frac{17}{5} \cdot \frac{294}{6}$ (The product of two negative numbers is positive.)

    $= -\frac{17}{5} \cdot 49$

    $= -\frac{833}{5}$ (The product of a negative number and a positive number is negative.)

42. $-\frac{13}{4}\left(-\frac{16}{5}\right)\left(\frac{23}{2}\right)$

    $= -\frac{13}{4}\left(-\frac{184}{5}\right)$

    $= \frac{2392}{20}$

    $= \frac{598}{5}$

43. $\frac{-20}{-4} = 5$ (The quotient of two negative numbers is positive.)

44. -7

45. $\frac{-10}{70}$

    $= -\frac{10}{70}$ (The quotient of a negative number and a positive number is negative.)

    $= -\frac{1}{7}$ (Simplifying)

46. -5

47. $\frac{2}{7} \div \left(-\frac{14}{3}\right)$

    $= \frac{2}{7} \cdot \left(-\frac{3}{14}\right)$ (Multiplying by the reciprocal)

    $= -\frac{6}{98}$

    $= -\frac{3}{49}$

48. $-\frac{3}{5} \div \left(-\frac{6}{7}\right) = -\frac{3}{5}\left(-\frac{7}{6}\right) = \frac{21}{30} = \frac{7}{10}$

49. $-\frac{10}{3} \div \left(-\frac{2}{15}\right)$

    $= -\frac{10}{3} \cdot \left(-\frac{15}{2}\right)$ (Multiplying by the reciprocal)

    $= \frac{150}{6}$

    $= 25$

50. $-\frac{12}{5} \div (-0.3) = -\frac{12}{5}\left(-\frac{1}{0.3}\right) = \frac{12}{1.5} = 8$

51. $11 - 15$

    $= 11 + (-15)$ $[a - b = a + (-b)]$

    $= -4$

52. -29

53. $12 - (-6)$

    $= 12 + 6$ $[a - b = a + (-b)]$

    $= 18$

54. -9

55. $15.8 - 27.4$

    $= 15.8 + (-27.4)$ $[a - b = a + (-b)]$

    $= -11.6$

56. -34.8

57. $-\frac{21}{4} - \left(-\frac{7}{8}\right)$

    $= -\frac{21}{4} + \frac{7}{8}$ $[a - b = a + (-b)]$

    $= -\frac{42}{8} + \frac{7}{8}$

    $= -\frac{35}{8}$

58. $\frac{2}{3} - \left(-\frac{17}{4}\right) = \frac{8}{12} + \frac{51}{12} = \frac{59}{12}$

59. a) $(1.4)^2 = 1.96$
           $(1.41)^2 = 1.9881$
           $(1.414)^2 = 1.999396$
           $(1.4142)^2 = 1.999962$
           $(1.41421)^2 = 1.999990$

    b) $\sqrt{2}$

60. a) $(2.1)^3 = 9.261000$
           $(2.15)^3 = 9.938375$
           $(2.154)^3 = 9.993948$
           $(2.1544)^3 = 9.999517$
           $(2.15443)^3 = 9.999935$

    b) $\sqrt[3]{10}$

61. $k + 0 = k$ Additive identity property

62. Commutative law of multiplication

63. $-1(x + y) = (-1x) + (-1y)$
    Distributive law of multiplication over addition

64. Associative law of addition

65. $c + d = d + c$ Commutative law of addition

66. Multiplicative identity property

67. $4(xy) = (4x)y$ Associative law of multiplication

68. Distributive law of multiplication over addition

69. $y\left(\dfrac{1}{y}\right) = 1$, $y \neq 0$ Multiplicative inverse property

70. Additive inverse property

71. $a + (b + c) = a + (c + b)$
    Commutative law of addition

72. Commutative law of multiplication

73. $a(b + c) = a(c + b)$
    Commutative law of addition

74. Distributive law of multiplication over addition

75. $7 - 5 \neq 5 - 7$
    $7 - 5 = 2$
    $5 - 7 = -2$
    $2 \neq -2$

76. $16 \div 8 \neq 8 \div 16$
    $16 \div 8 = 2$
    $8 \div 16 = \dfrac{1}{2}$
    $2 \neq \dfrac{1}{2}$

77. $16 \div (4 \div 2) \neq (16 \div 4) \div 2$
    $16 \div (4 \div 2) = 16 \div 2 = 8$
    $(16 \div 4) \div 2 = 4 \div 2 = 2$
    $8 \neq 2$

78. $7 - (5 - 2) \neq (7 - 5) - 2$
    $7 - (5 - 2) = 7 - 3 = 4$
    $(7 - 5) - 2 = 2 - 2 = 0$
    $4 \neq 0$

79. $\pi = 3.1415926535...$
    $3.14 = 3.14$
    $\dfrac{22}{7} = 3.\overline{142857}$

    $\dfrac{3927}{1250} = 3.1416$

    Of these three, $\dfrac{3927}{1250}$ is the best approximation to π.

80. $\dfrac{22}{7}$ differs from π at the third decimal place. (See Exercise 79.)

81. Let $n = 0.\overline{9} = 0.999...$

    Then $10n = 9.999...$
    $\underline{\quad\quad n = 0.999\quad}$
    $\quad 9n = 9$ Subtracting
    $\quad\quad n = 1.$

82. Let $n = 3.\overline{74} = 3.7474...$

    Then $100n = 374.7474...$
    $\underline{\quad\quad n = \quad\; 3.7474...}$
    $\quad 99n = 371$
    $\quad\quad n = \dfrac{371}{99}.$

83. Let $n = 18.3\overline{245} = 18.3245245...$

    Then $10,000n = 183,245.245...$
    $\underline{\quad\; 10n = \quad\quad 183.245...}$
    $\quad 9990n = 183,062$ Subtracting
    $\quad\quad n = \dfrac{183,062}{9990}.$

84. Let $n = 12.34\overline{7652}$.

Then $1{,}000{,}000n = 12347652.76527652\ldots$

$100n = 1234.76527652\ldots$

$999{,}900n = 12346418$

$n = \dfrac{12{,}346{,}418}{999{,}900}.$

85. Prove: $(b + c)a = ba + ca$

Proof: $(b + c)a = a(b + c)$ Commutative law of multiplication

$ = ab + ac$ Distributive law

$ = ba + ca$ Commutative law of multiplication, used twice

86. Let a be a positive number. Then by the definition of subtraction,

$a - 0 = c$ if and only if $0 + c = a$.

Now $0 + c = c$ (identity property of addition), so $c = a$ and $a - 0 = a$ where a is a positive number. Then $a - 0$ is positive, so

$0 < a$ or $a > 0$.

Exercise Set 1.2

1. $2^3 \cdot 2^{-4} = 2^{3+(-4)} = 2^{-1} = \dfrac{1}{2}$

2. $3^4 \cdot 3^{-5} = 3^{-1} = \dfrac{1}{3}$

3. $b^2 \cdot b^{-2} = b^{2+(-2)} = b^0 = 1$

4. $c^3 \cdot c^{-3} = c^0 = 1$

5. $4^2 \cdot 4^{-5} \cdot 4^6 = 4^{2+(-5)+6} = 4^3$

6. 5^3

7. $2x^3 \cdot 3x^2 = 2 \cdot 3 \cdot x^{3+2} = 6x^5$

8. $12y^7$

9. $(5a^2b)(3a^{-3}b^4) = 5 \cdot 3 \cdot a^{2+(-3)} \cdot b^{1+4} = 15a^{-1}b^5$

$\phantom{(5a^2b)(3a^{-3}b^4)} = \dfrac{15b^5}{a}$

10. $(4xy^2)(3x^{-4}y^5) = 12x^{-3}y^7 = \dfrac{12y^7}{x^3}$

11. $(2x)^3(3x)^2 = 2^3x^3 \cdot 3^2x^2 = 8 \cdot 9 \cdot x^{3+2} = 72x^5$

12. $(4y)^2(3y)^3 = 16y^2 \cdot 27y^3 = 432y^5$

13. $(6x^5y^{-2}z^3)(-3x^2y^3z^{-2})$

$= 6 \cdot (-3) \cdot x^{5+2}y^{-2+3}z^{3+(-2)}$

$= -18x^7yz$

14. $-10x^6yz$

15. $\dfrac{b^{40}}{b^{37}} = b^{40-37} = b^3$

16. a^7

17. $\dfrac{x^2y^{-2}}{x^{-1}y} = x^{2-(-1)}y^{-2-1} = x^3y^{-3} = \dfrac{x^3}{y^3}$

18. $\dfrac{x^3y^{-3}}{x^{-1}y^2} = x^4y^{-5} = \dfrac{x^4}{y^5}$

19. $\dfrac{9a^2}{(-3a)^2} = \dfrac{9a^2}{9a^2} = 1$

20. $\dfrac{16y^2}{(-4y)^2} = \dfrac{16y^2}{16y^2} = 1$

21. $\dfrac{24a^5b^3}{8a^4b} = 3a^{5-4}b^{3-1} = 3ab^2$

22. $6x^3y^2$

23. $\dfrac{12x^2y^3z^{-2}}{21xy^2z^3} = \dfrac{12}{21}x^{2-1}y^{3-2}z^{-2-3} = \dfrac{4}{7}xyz^{-5} = \dfrac{4xy}{7z^5}$

24. $\dfrac{15x^3y^4z^{-3}}{45xyz^5} = \dfrac{x^2y^3z^{-8}}{3} = \dfrac{x^2y^3}{3z^8}$

25. $(2ab^2)^3 = 2^3a^3b^{2 \cdot 3} = 8a^3b^6$

26. $16x^2y^6$

27. $(-2x^3)^4 = (-2)^4x^{3 \cdot 4} = 16x^{12}$

28. $81x^8$

29. $-(2x^3)^4 = -2^4x^{3 \cdot 4} = -16x^{12}$

30. $-81x^8$

31. $(6a^2b^3c)^2 = 6^2a^{2 \cdot 2}b^{3 \cdot 2}c^2 = 36a^4b^6c^2$

32. $25x^6y^4z^2$

33. $(-5c^{-1}d^{-2})^{-2} = (-5)^{-2}c^{-1(-2)}d^{-2(-2)} = \dfrac{1}{25}c^2d^4$

$$\left[(-5)^{-2} = \dfrac{1}{(-5)^2} = \dfrac{1}{25}\right]$$

34. $(-4x^{-1}z^{-2})^{-2} = 4^{-2}x^2z^4 = \dfrac{1}{16}x^2z^4$

35. $\dfrac{4^{-2} + 2^{-4}}{8^{-1}} = \dfrac{\dfrac{1}{4^2} + \dfrac{1}{2^4}}{\dfrac{1}{8}} = \dfrac{\dfrac{1}{16} + \dfrac{1}{16}}{\dfrac{1}{8}} = \dfrac{\dfrac{2}{16}}{\dfrac{1}{8}} =$

$\dfrac{\dfrac{1}{8}}{\dfrac{1}{8}} = 1$

36. $\dfrac{3^{-2} + 2^{-3}}{7^{-1}} = \dfrac{\frac{1}{9} + \frac{1}{8}}{\frac{1}{7}} = \dfrac{\frac{17}{72}}{\frac{1}{7}} = \dfrac{17}{72} \cdot \dfrac{7}{1} = \dfrac{119}{72}$

37. $\dfrac{(-2)^4 + (-4)^2}{(-1)^8} = \dfrac{16 + 16}{1} = \dfrac{32}{1} = 32$

38. $\dfrac{(-3)^2 + (-2)^4}{(-1)^6} = \dfrac{9 + 16}{1} = 25$

39. $\dfrac{(3a^2b^{-2}c^4)^3}{(2a^{-1}b^2c^{-3})^2}$

$= \dfrac{3^3a^6b^{-6}c^{12}}{2^2a^{-2}b^4c^{-6}}$

$= \dfrac{27}{4} a^{6-(-2)}b^{-6-4}c^{12-(-6)}$

$= \dfrac{27}{4} a^8b^{-10}c^{18}$

$= \dfrac{27a^8c^{18}}{4b^{10}}$

40. $\dfrac{(2a^3b^{-3}c^3)^3}{(3a^{-1}b^{-3}c^{-5})^2} = \dfrac{8a^9b^{-9}c^9}{9a^{-2}b^{-6}c^{-10}} = \dfrac{8a^{11}b^{-3}c^{19}}{9} =$

$\dfrac{8a^{11}c^{19}}{9b^3}$

41. $\dfrac{6^{-2}x^{-3}y^2}{3^{-3}x^{-4}y} = \dfrac{3^3}{6^2} x^{-3-(-4)}y^{2-1} = \dfrac{27}{36}xy = \dfrac{3}{4}xy$

42. $\dfrac{5^{-2}x^{-4}y^3}{2^{-3}x^{-5}y} = \dfrac{2^3xy^2}{5^2} = \dfrac{8}{25}xy^2$

43. $\left[\dfrac{24a^{10}b^{-8}c^7}{3a^6b^{-3}c^5}\right]^5 = \left(\dfrac{8a^4c^2}{b^5}\right)^5 = \dfrac{8^5a^{20}c^{10}}{b^{25}} =$

$\dfrac{32,768a^{20}c^{10}}{b^{25}}$

44. $\left[\dfrac{125p^{12}q^{-14}r^{22}}{25p^8q^6r^{-15}}\right]^{-4} = (5p^4q^{-20}r^{37})^{-4} =$

$5^{-4}p^{-16}q^{80}r^{-148} = \dfrac{q^{80}}{625p^{16}r^{148}}$

45. When $x = 5$, $-x^2 = -5^2 = -25$
and $(-x)^2 = (-5)^2 = 25$

46. $-7^2 = -49$, $(-7)^2 = 49$

47. When $x = -1.08$, $-x^2 = -(-1.08)^2 = -1.1664$
and $(-x)^2 = [-(-1.08)]^2 = (1.08)^2 = 1.1664$

48. $-(\sqrt{3})^2 = -3$, $(-\sqrt{3})^2 = 3$

49. 5.8,000,000.

7 moves

Since the number to be converted is large, the exponent is positive.

$58,000,000 = 5.8 \times 10^7$

50. 2.7,000.

4 moves

Since the number to be converted is large, the exponent is positive.

$27,000 = 2.7 \times 10^4$

51. 3.65,000.

5 moves

Since the number to be converted is large, the exponent is positive.

$365,000 = 3.65 \times 10^5$

52. 3.645.

3 moves

Since the number to be converted is large, the exponent is positive.

$3645 = 3.645 \times 10^3$

53. 0.000002.7

6 moves

Since the number to be converted is small, the exponent is negative.

$0.0000027 = 2.7 \times 10^{-6}$

54. 0.00006.58

5 moves

Since the number to be converted is small, the exponent is negative.

$0.0000658 = 6.58 \times 10^{-5}$

55. 0.02.7

2 moves

Since the number to be converted is small, the exponent is negative.

$0.027 = 2.7 \times 10^{-2}$

56. 0.003.8

3 moves

Since the number to be converted is small, the exponent is negative.

$0.0038 = 3.8 \times 10^{-3}$

57. 0.0000000000000000000000000009.11

28 moves

Since the number to be converted is small, the exponent is negative.

$0.000000000000000000000000000911 = 9.11 \times 10^{-28}$

58. 9.3,000,000.

    |‾‾‾‾‾‾‾‾|
    7 moves

Since the number to be converted is large, the exponent is positive.

$93,000,000 = 9.3 \times 10^7$

59. 3.664,000,000.

    |‾‾‾‾‾‾‾‾|
    9 moves

Since the number to be converted is large the exponent is positive.

$3,664,000,000 = 3.664 \times 10^9$

60. 0.000000001.

    |_____|
    9 moves

Since the number to be converted is small, the exponent is negative.

$0.000000001 = 10^{-9}$

61. $4 \times 10^5 = 400,000$

62. 0.0005

63. $6.2 \times 10^{-3} = 0.0062$

64. $7,800,000$

65. $7.69 \times 10^{12} = 7,690,000,000,000$

66. 0.000000854

67. $5.67 \text{ E} - 7 = 0.000000567$

68. $1,314,000,000,000$

69. $9.46 \times 10^{12} = 9,460,000,000,000$

70. 0.000066

71. $7.69 \text{ E} - 8 = 0.0000000769$

72. 0.0000000008603

73. $2.567 \text{ E } 8 = 256,700,000$

74. $111,300,000,000$

75. $(3.1 \times 10^5)(4.5 \times 10^{-3})$

    $= (3.1 \times 4.5) \times (10^5 \times 10^{-3})$

    $= 13.95 \times 10^2$

    $= (1.395 \times 10) \times 10^2$

    $= 1.395 \times 10^3$

76. $(9.1 \times 10^{-17})(8.2 \times 10^3) = 74.62 \times 10^{-14}$

    $= (7.462 \times 10) \times 10^{-14}$

    $= 7.462 \times 10^{-13}$

77. $\dfrac{6.4 \times 10^{-7}}{8.0 \times 10^6} = \dfrac{6.4}{8.0} \times \dfrac{10^{-7}}{10^6}$

    $= 0.8 \times 10^{-13}$

    $= (8 \times 10^{-1}) \times 10^{-13}$

    $= 8 \times 10^{-14}$

78. $\dfrac{1.1 \times 10^{-40}}{2.0 \times 10^{-71}} = 0.55 \times 10^{31}$

    $= (5.5 \times 10^{-1}) \times 10^{31}$

    $= 5.5 \times 10^{30}$

79. The amount of water discharged in one hour is the amount discharged per second times the number of seconds in one hour.

    $4,200,000 \times 3600$

    $= (4.2 \times 10^6) \times (3.6 \times 10^3)$ Using scientific notation

    $= (4.2 \times 3.6) \times (10^6 \times 10^3)$

    $= 15.12 \times 10^9$ Multiplying

    $= (1.512 \times 10) \times 10^9$

    $= 1.512 \times 10^{10}$

In one hour the discharge of water is 1.512×10^{10} cubic feet.

80. $(3 \times 10^6) \times (3.65 \times 10^2) = 10.95 \times 10^8$

    $= (1.095 \times 10) \times 10^8$

    $= 1.095 \times 10^9$ gallons

81. We begin by expressing one billionth as a fraction.

    $\dfrac{1}{1,000,000,000} = \dfrac{1}{10^9}$ Using scientific notation

    $= 10^{-9}$

Scientific notation for 1 nanosecond is 10^{-9} sec.

82. $2 \times \pi \times (9.3 \times 10^7) \approx 2 \times 3.14 \times 9.3 \times 10^7$

    $= 58.404 \times 10^7$

    $= (5.8404 \times 10) \times 10^7$

    $= 5.8404 \times 10^8$ mi

83. The distance light travels in 13 weeks is the portion of a year in 13 weeks times the number of miles that light travels in one year. (See Example 23.) We will use 52 weeks for 1 year. Then 13 weeks is $\dfrac{13}{52}$, or 0.25 of a year.

    $0.25 \times (5.88 \times 10^{12})$

    $= (2.5 \times 10^{-1}) \times (5.88 \times 10^{12})$ Using scientific notation

    $= (2.5 \times 5.88) \times (10^{-1} \times 10^{12})$

    $= 14.7 \times 10^{11}$

    $= (1.47 \times 10) \times 10^{11}$

    $= 1.47 \times 10^{12}$

Light travels 1.47×10^{12} miles in 13 weeks.

84. $1 \text{ m} \times 30 \text{ m} \times (0.8 \times 10^{-3} \text{ m})$

  $= 24 \times 10^{-3} \text{ m}^3$

  $= 2.4 \times 10^{-2} \text{ m}^3$, or $2.4 \times 10^7 \text{ mm}^3$

85. $3 \cdot 2 + 4 \cdot 2^2 - 6(3 - 1)$

  $= 3 \cdot 2 + 4 \cdot 2^2 - 6 \cdot 2$ Working inside parentheses

  $= 3 \cdot 2 + 4 \cdot 4 - 6 \cdot 2$ Evaluating 2^2

  $= 6 + 16 - 12$ Multiplying

  $= 22 - 12$ Adding in order

  $= 10$ from left to right

86. $3[(2 + 4 \cdot 2^2) - 6(3 - 1)]$

  $= 3[(2 + 4 \cdot 4) - 6 \cdot 2]$

  $= 3[(2 + 16) - 6 \cdot 2]$

  $= 3[18 - 6 \cdot 2]$

  $= 3[18 - 12]$

  $= 3[6]$

  $= 18$

87. $\dfrac{4(8 - 6)^2 + 4 \cdot 3 - 2 \cdot 8}{3^1 + 19^0}$

  $= \dfrac{4 \cdot 2^2 + 4 \cdot 3 - 2 \cdot 8}{3 + 1}$ Calculating in the numerator and in the denominator

  $= \dfrac{4 \cdot 4 + 4 \cdot 3 - 2 \cdot 8}{4}$

  $= \dfrac{16 + 12 - 16}{4}$

  $= \dfrac{28 - 16}{4}$

  $= \dfrac{12}{4}$

  $= 3$

88. $\dfrac{[4(8 - 6)^2 + 4](3 - 2 \cdot 8)}{2^2(2^3 + 5)}$

  $= \dfrac{[4 \cdot 2^2 + 4](3 - 16)}{2^2(8 + 5)}$

  $= \dfrac{[4 \cdot 4 + 4](-13)}{2^2 \cdot 13}$

  $= \dfrac{[16 + 4](-13)}{4 \cdot 13}$

  $= \dfrac{20(-13)}{52}$

  $= \dfrac{-260}{52}$

  $= -5$

89. $16 \div 4 \cdot 4 \div 2 \cdot 256$

  $= 4 \cdot 4 \div 2 \cdot 256$ Multiplying and dividing in order from left to right

  $= 16 \div 2 \cdot 256$

  $= 8 \cdot 256$

  $= 2048$

90. $2^6 \cdot 2^{-3} \div 2^{10} \div 2^{-8}$

  $= 2^3 \div 2^{10} \div 2^{-8}$

  $= 2^{-7} \div 2^{-8}$

  $= 2$

91. $\left[\dfrac{5^2}{8} + 5(5) - \dfrac{5^3}{12}\right] - \left[\dfrac{(-4)^2}{8} + 5(-4) - \dfrac{(-4)^3}{12}\right]$

  $= \left[\dfrac{25}{8} + 5(5) - \dfrac{125}{12}\right] - \left[\dfrac{16}{8} + 5(-4) - \dfrac{-64}{12}\right]$

  $= \left[\dfrac{25}{8} + 25 - \dfrac{125}{12}\right] - \left[2 - 20 + \dfrac{16}{3}\right]$

  $= \dfrac{425}{24} - \left[-\dfrac{38}{3}\right]$

  $= \dfrac{729}{24}$

  $= \dfrac{243}{8}$

92. $\left[\dfrac{2^2}{8} + \dfrac{2}{2} - \dfrac{2^3}{12}\right] - \left[\dfrac{(-1)^2}{8} - \dfrac{1}{2} - \dfrac{(-1)^3}{12}\right]$

  $= \left[\dfrac{4}{8} + \dfrac{2}{2} - \dfrac{8}{12}\right] - \left[\dfrac{1}{8} - \dfrac{1}{2} - \dfrac{-1}{12}\right]$

  $= \left[\dfrac{1}{2} + 1 - \dfrac{2}{3}\right] - \left[\dfrac{1}{8} - \dfrac{1}{2} + \dfrac{1}{12}\right]$

  $= \dfrac{5}{6} - \left[-\dfrac{7}{24}\right]$

  $= \dfrac{27}{24}$

  $= \dfrac{9}{8}$

93.   The distance of 12 from 0 is 12, so $|12| = 12$.

94.   2.56

95.   The distance of -47 from 0 is 47, so $|-47| = 47$.

96.   0

97. $|-7a| = |-7| \cdot |a| = 7|a|$

98. $10|m| \, |n|$

99. $|-8x^6| = |-8| \cdot |x^6| = 8x^6$

100. $5x^4y^8$

101. $|9xy| = |9| \cdot |xy| = 9|xy|$ or $9|x| \, |y|$

102. y^4

103. $|3a^2b| = |3| \cdot |a^2| \cdot |b| = 3a^2|b|$

104. $\dfrac{4|a|}{b^2}$

105. $(x^t \cdot x^{3t})^2 = (x^{4t})^2 = x^{4t \cdot 2} = x^{8t}$

106. $(x^y \cdot x^{-y})^3 = (x^0)^3 = 1^3 = 1$

107. $(t^{a+x} \cdot t^{x-a})^4 = (t^{2x})^4 = t^{2x \cdot 4} = t^{8x}$

108. $(m^{x-y} \cdot m^{3y-x})^t = (m^{2y})^t = m^{2yt}$

109. $(x^a y^b \cdot x^b y^a)^c = (x^{a+b} y^{a+b})^c = x^{ac+bc} y^{ac+bc}$

$$= (xy)^{ac+bc}$$

110. $(m^{x-b} \cdot n^{x+b})^x (m^b n^{-b})^x$

$$= (m^{x^2-bx} n^{x^2+bx})(m^{bx} n^{-bx})$$

$$= m^{x^2} n^{x^2}$$

$$= (mn)^{x^2}$$

111. $\left[\dfrac{(3x^a y^b)^3}{(-3x^a y^b)^2}\right]^2 = \left[\dfrac{27x^{3a} y^{3b}}{9x^{2a} y^{2b}}\right]^2$

$$= \left[3x^a y^b\right]^2$$

$$= 9x^{2a} y^{2b}$$

112. $\left[\left(\dfrac{x^r}{y^t}\right)^2 \left(\dfrac{x^{2r}}{y^4 t}\right)^{-2}\right]^{-3}$

$$= \left[\left(\dfrac{x^{2r}}{y^2 t}\right)\left(\dfrac{x^{-4r}}{y^{-8} t}\right)\right]^{-3}$$

$$= \left(\dfrac{x^{-2r}}{y^{-6} t}\right)^{-3}$$

$$= \dfrac{x^{6r}}{y^{18} t}$$

113. $P = \$92{,}000 - \$14{,}000 = \$78{,}000$, $n = 12 \cdot 25 = 300$

$$M = P\left[\dfrac{\dfrac{i}{12}\left(1 + \dfrac{i}{12}\right)^n}{\left(1 + \dfrac{i}{12}\right)^n - 1}\right]$$

$$M = 78{,}000\left[\dfrac{\dfrac{0.1075}{12}\left(1 + \dfrac{0.1075}{12}\right)^{300}}{\left(1 + \dfrac{0.1075}{12}\right)^{300} - 1}\right] \text{(Substituting)}$$

$$= \$750.43 \qquad \text{(Using a calculator)}$$

114. $n = 12 \cdot 20 = 240$

$$M = 78{,}000\left[\dfrac{\dfrac{0.1075}{12}\left(1 + \dfrac{0.1075}{12}\right)^{240}}{\left(1 + \dfrac{0.1075}{12}\right)^{240} - 1}\right]$$

$$= \$791.88$$

$n = 12 \cdot 30 = 360$

$$M = 78{,}000\left[\dfrac{\dfrac{0.1075}{12}\left(1 + \dfrac{0.1075}{12}\right)^{360}}{\left(1 + \dfrac{0.1075}{12}\right)^{360} - 1}\right]$$

$$= \$728.12$$

115. $x^4(x^3)^2 = x^4 \cdot x^5 = x^9$

Exponents were added instead of multiplied.
$x^4(x^3)^2 = x^4 \cdot x^6 = x^{10}$ (Correct)

116. Exponents were added instead of subtracted; $\dfrac{x^6}{y^{12}}$

117. $(2x^{-4} y^6 z^3)^3 = 6x^{-1} y^3 z^6$
① ② ③ ④   ① ② ③ ④

Four errors were made.

① $2 \cdot 3$ instead of 2^3

② Exponents were added instead of multiplied.

③ Exponents were subtracted instead of multiplied.

④ Exponents were added instead of multiplied.

$(2x^{-4} y^6 z^3)^3 = 2^3 x^{-4 \cdot 3} y^{6 \cdot 3} z^{3 \cdot 3} = 8x^{-12} y^{18} z^9 =$

$$\dfrac{8y^{18} z^9}{x^{12}} \quad \text{(Correct)}$$

Exercise Set 1.3

1. $-11x^4 - x^3 + x^2 + 3x - 9$

Term	Degree	
$-11x^4$	4	
$-x^3$	3	
x^2	2	
$3x$	1	$(3x = 3x^1)$
-9	0	$(-9 = -9x^0)$

The degree of a polynomial is the same as that of its term of highest degree.

The term of highest degree is $-11x^4$. Thus, the degree of the polynomial is 4.

2. 3, 2, 1, 0; 3

3. $y^3 + 2y^6 + x^2 y^4 - 8$

Term	Degree	
y^3	3	
$2y^6$	6	
$x^2 y^4$	6	$(2 + 4 = 6)$
-8	0	$(-8 = -8x^0)$

The terms of highest degree are $2y^6$ and $x^2 y^4$. Thus, the degree of the polynomial is 6.

4. 2, 5, 7, 0; 7

5. $a^5 + 4a^2b^4 + 6ab + 4a - 3$

Term	Degree	
a^5	5	
$4a^2b^4$	6	$(2 + 4 = 6)$
$6ab$	2	$(1 + 1 = 2)$
$4a$	1	$(4a = 4a^1)$
-3	0	$(-3 = -3a^0)$

The term of highest degree is $4a^2b^4$. Thus, the degree of the polynomial is 6.

6. 6, 8, 4, 2, 0; 8

7. $(5x^2y - 2xy^2 + 3xy - 5)+(-2x^2y - 3xy^2 + 4xy + 7)$
= $(5 - 2)x^2y + (-2 - 3)xy^2 + (3 + 4)xy + (-5 + 7)$
= $3x^2y - 5xy^2 + 7xy + 2$

8. $2x^2y - 7xy^2 + 8xy + 5$

9. $(-3pq^2 - 5p^2q + 4pq + 3)+(-7pq^2 + 3pq - 4p + 2q)$
= $(-3 - 7)pq^2 - 5p^2q + (4 + 3)pq - 4p + 2q + 3$
= $-10pq^2 - 5p^2q + 7pq - 4p + 2q + 3$

10. $-9pq^2 - 3p^2q + 11pq - 6p + 4q + 5$

11. $(2x+3y+z-7) + (4x-2y-z+8) + (-3x+y-2z-4)$
= $(2+4-3)x + (3-2+1)y + (1-1-2)z + (-7+8-4)$
= $3x + 2y - 2z - 3$

12. $7x^2 + 12xy - 2x - y - 9$

13. $\left[7x\sqrt{y} - 3y\sqrt{x} + \frac{1}{5}\right] + \left[-2x\sqrt{y} - y\sqrt{x} - \frac{3}{5}\right]$
= $(7 - 2)x\sqrt{y} + (-3 - 1)y\sqrt{x} + \left[\frac{1}{5} - \frac{3}{5}\right]$
= $5x\sqrt{y} - 4y\sqrt{x} - \frac{2}{5}$

14. $7x\sqrt{y} - 5y\sqrt{x} + 1$

15. The opposite of $5x^3 - 7x^2 + 3x - 6$ can be symbolized as
$-(5x^3 - 7x^2 + 3x - 6)$ (With parentheses)
or
$-5x^3 + 7x^2 - 3x + 6$ (Without parentheses)

16. $-(-4y^4 + 7y^2 - 2y - 1)$, $4y^4 - 7y^2 + 2y + 1$

17. $(3x^2 - 2x - x^3 + 2) - (5x^2 - 8x - x^3 + 4)$
= $(3x^2 - 2x - x^3 + 2) + (-5x^2 + 8x + x^3 - 4)$
= $(3 - 5)x^2 + (-2 + 8)x + (-1 + 1)x^3 + (2 - 4)$
= $-2x^2 + 6x - 2$

18. $-4x^2 + 8xy - 5y^2 + 3$

19. $(4a - 2b - c + 3d) - (-2a + 3b + c - d)$
= $(4a - 2b - c + 3d) + (2a - 3b - c + d)$
= $(4 + 2)a + (-2 - 3)b + (-1 - 1)c + (3 + 1)d$
= $6a - 5b - 2c + 4d$

20. $8a - 8b - 2c + 6d$

21. $(x^4 - 3x^2 + 4x) - (3x^3 + x^2 - 5x + 3)$
= $(x^4 - 3x^2 + 4x) + (-3x^3 - x^2 + 5x - 3)$
= $x^4 - 3x^3 + (-3 - 1)x^2 + (4 + 5)x - 3$
= $x^4 - 3x^3 - 4x^2 + 9x - 3$

22. $2x^4 - 5x^3 - 7x^2 + 10x - 5$

23. $(7x\sqrt{y} - 4y\sqrt{x} + 7.5) - (-2x\sqrt{y} - y\sqrt{x} - 1.6)$
= $(7x\sqrt{y} - 4y\sqrt{x} + 7.5) + (2x\sqrt{y} + y\sqrt{x} + 1.6)$
= $(7 + 2)x\sqrt{y} + (-4 + 1)y\sqrt{x} + (7.5 + 1.6)$
= $9x\sqrt{y} - 3y\sqrt{x} + 9.1$

24. $13x\sqrt{y} - 5y\sqrt{x} + \frac{5}{3}$

25. $(0.565p^2q - 2.167pq^2 + 16.02pq - 17.1)$
$+ (-1.612p^2q - 0.312pq^2 - 7.141pq - 87.044)$
= $(0.565 - 1.612)p^2q + (-2.167 - 0.312)pq^2 +$
$(16.02 - 7.141)pq + (-17.1 - 87.044)$
= $-1.047p^2q - 2.479pq^2 + 8.879pq - 104.144$

26. $2859.6xy^{-2} - 6153.8xy + 7243.4\sqrt{xy} - 10,259.12$

Exercise Set 1.4

1.
$$\begin{array}{r} 2x^2 + 4x + 16 \\ 3x - 4 \\ \hline -8x^2 - 16x - 64 \\ 6x^3 + 12x^2 + 48x \\ \hline 6x^3 + 4x^2 + 32x - 64 \end{array}$$
(Multiplying by -4)
(Multiplying by $3x$)
(Adding)

2.
$$\begin{array}{r} 3y^2 - 3y + 9 \\ 2y + 3 \\ \hline 9y^2 - 9y + 27 \\ 6y^3 - 6y^2 + 18y \\ \hline 6y^3 + 3y^2 + 9y + 27 \end{array}$$

3.
$$\begin{array}{r} 4a^2b - 2ab + 3b^2 \\ ab - 2b + 1 \\ \hline 4a^2b - 2ab + 3b^2 \\ -8a^2b^2 + 4ab^2 - 6b^3 \\ 4a^3b^2 - 2a^2b^2 \qquad\qquad +3ab^3 \\ \hline 4a^3b^2 - 10a^2b^2 + 4ab^2 - 6b^3 + 4a^2b - 2ab + 3b^2 + 3ab^3 \end{array}$$

4.
$$
\begin{array}{r}
2x^2 + \ \ y^2 - 2xy \\
x^2 - 2y^2 - \ xy \\
\hline
-2x^3y - \ xy^3 + 2x^2y^2 \\
-2y^4 \qquad + 4xy^3 - 4x^2y^2 \\
2x^4 \qquad\quad - 2x^3y \qquad\quad + x^2y^2 \\
\hline
2x^4 - 2y^4 - 4x^3y + 3xy^3 - \ x^2y^2
\end{array}
$$

5.
$$
\begin{array}{r}
a^2 + ab + b^2 \\
a - b \\
\hline
-a^2b - ab^2 - b^3 \\
a^3 + a^2b + ab^2 \\
\hline
a^3 \qquad\qquad\quad - b^3
\end{array}
$$

The product is $a^3 - b^3$.

6.
$$
\begin{array}{r}
t^2 - t + 1 \\
t + 1 \\
\hline
t^2 - t + 1 \\
t^3 - t^2 + t \\
\hline
t^3 \qquad\qquad + 1
\end{array}
$$

7. $(2x + 3y)(2x + y)$
   = $4x^2 + 2xy + 6xy + 3y^2$ (FOIL)
   = $4x^2 + 8xy + 3y^2$

8. $4a^2 - 8ab + 3b^2$

9. $\left[4x^2 - \frac{1}{2} y\right]\left[3x + \frac{1}{4} y\right]$

   = $12x^3 + x^2y - \frac{3}{2} xy - \frac{1}{8} y^2$ (FOIL)

10. $6y^4 - \frac{1}{2} xy^3 + \frac{3}{5} xy - \frac{1}{20} x^2$

11. $(2p^2q^3 - r^2)(5pq - 2r)$
    = $10p^3q^4 - 4p^2q^3r - 5pqr^2 + 2r^3$ (FOIL)

12. $9y^3 - 3xy^2 - 6y + 2x$

13. $(2x + 3y)^2$
    = $(2x)^2 + 2(2x)(3y) + (3y)^2$
    $\qquad\quad \left[(A + B)^2 = A^2 + 2AB + B^2\right]$
    = $4x^2 + 12xy + 9y^2$

14. $25x^2 + 20xy + 4y^2$

15. $(2x^2 - 3y)^2$
    = $(2x^2)^2 - 2(2x^2)(3y) + (3y)^2$
    $\qquad\quad \left[(A - B)^2 = A^2 - 2AB + B^2\right]$
    = $4x^4 - 12x^2y + 9y^2$

16. $16x^4 - 40x^2y + 25y^2$

17. $(2x^3 + 3y^2)^2$
    = $(2x^3)^2 + 2(2x^3)(3y^2) + (3y^2)^2$
    $\qquad\quad \left[(A + B)^2 = A^2 + 2AB + B^2\right]$
    = $4x^6 + 12x^3y^2 + 9y^4$

18. $25x^6 + 20x^3y^2 + 4y^4$

19. $\left[\frac{1}{2} x^2 - \frac{3}{5} y\right]^2$

    = $\left[\frac{1}{2} x^2\right]^2 - 2\left[\frac{1}{2} x^2\right]\left[\frac{3}{5} y\right] + \left[\frac{3}{5} y\right]^2$
    $\qquad\quad \left[(A - B)^2 = A^2 - 2AB + B^2\right]$

    = $\frac{1}{4} x^4 - \frac{3}{5} x^2y + \frac{9}{25} y^2$

20. $\frac{1}{16} x^4 - \frac{1}{3} x^2y + \frac{4}{9} y^2$

21. $(0.5x + 0.7y^2)^2$
    = $(0.5x)^2 + 2(0.5x)(0.7y^2) + (0.7y^2)^2$
    $\qquad\quad \left[(A + B)^2 = A^2 + 2AB + B^2\right]$
    = $0.25x^2 + 0.7xy^2 + 0.49y^4$

22. $0.09x^2 + 0.48xy^2 + 0.64y^4$

23. $(3x - 2y)(3x + 2y)$
    = $(3x)^2 - (2y)^2$ $\qquad \left[(A - B)(A + B) = A^2 - B^2\right]$
    = $9x^2 - 4y^2$

24. $9x^2 - 25y^2$

25. $(x^2 + yz)(x^2 - yz)$
    = $(x^2)^2 - (yz)^2$ $\qquad \left[(A + B)(A - B) = A^2 - B^2\right]$
    = $x^4 - y^2z^2$

26. $4x^4 - 25x^2y^2$

27. $(3x^2 - \sqrt{2})(3x^2 + \sqrt{2})$
    = $(3x^2)^2 - (\sqrt{2})^2$ $\qquad \left[(A - B)(A + B) = A^2 - B^2\right]$
    = $9x^4 - 2$

28. $25x^4 - 3$

29. $(2x + 3y + 4)(2x + 3y - 4)$
    = $(2x + 3y)^2 - 4^2$ $\qquad \left[(A + B)(A - B) = A^2 - B^2\right]$
    = $4x^2 + 12xy + 9y^2 - 16$

30. $(5x + 2y + 3)(5x + 2y - 3)$
    = $(5x + 2y)^2 - 3^2$
    = $25x^2 + 20xy + 4y^2 - 9$

31. $(x^2 + 3y + y^2)(x^2 + 3y - y^2)$
    = $(x^2 + 3y)^2 - (y^2)^2$ $\qquad \left[(A + B)(A - B) = A^2 - B^2\right]$
    = $x^4 + 6x^2y + 9y^2 - y^4$

32. $(2x^2 + y + y^2)(2x^2 + y - y^2)$
$= (2x^2 + y)^2 - (y^2)^2$
$= 4x^4 + 4x^2y + y^2 - y^4$

33. $(x + 1)(x - 1)(x^2 + 1)$
$= (x^2 - 1)(x^2 + 1)$
$= x^4 - 1$

34. $(y - 2)(y + 2)(y^2 + 4)$
$= (y^2 - 4)(y^2 + 4)$
$= y^4 - 16$

35. $(2x + y)(2x - y)(4x^2 + y^2)$
$= (4x^2 - y^2)(4x^2 + y^2)$
$= 16x^4 - y^4$

36. $(5x + y)(5x - y)(25x^2 + y^2)$
$= (25x^2 - y^2)(25x^2 + y^2)$
$= 625x^4 - y^4$

37. $(0.051x + 0.04y)^2$
$= (0.051x)^2 + 2(0.051x)(0.04y) + (0.04y)^2$
$= 0.002601x^2 + 0.00408xy + 0.0016y^2$

38. $1.065024x^2 - 5.184768xy + 6.310144y^2$

39. $(37.86x + 1.42)(65.03x - 27.4)$
$= 2462.0358x^2 - 1037.364x + 92.3426x - 38.908$
$= 2462.0358x^2 - 945.0214x - 38.908$

40. $169.625105x^2 - 711.87827x - 546.525$

41. $(y + 5)^3$
$= y^3 + 3 \cdot y^2 \cdot 5 + 3 \cdot y \cdot 5^2 + 5^3$
$= y^3 + 15y^2 + 75y + 125$

42. $t^3 - 21t^2 + 147t - 343$

43. $(m^2 - 2n)^3$
$= [m^2 + (-2n)]^3$
$= (m^2)^3 + 3(m^2)^2(-2n) + 3(m^2)(-2n)^2 + (-2n)^3$
$= m^6 - 6m^4n + 12m^2n^2 - 8n^3$

44. $27t^6 + 108t^4 + 144t^2 + 64$

45. $(\sqrt{2}\ x^2 - y^2)(\sqrt{2}\ x - 2y)$
$= 2x^3 - 2\sqrt{2}\ x^2y - \sqrt{2}\ xy^2 + 2y^3$ (FOIL)

46. $3y^3 - \sqrt{3}\ xy^2 - 2\sqrt{3}\ y + 2x$

47. $(a^n + b^n)(a^n - b^n)$
$= (a^n)^2 - (b^n)^2$
$= a^{2n} - b^{2n}$

48. $t^{2a} - 3t^a - 28$

49. $(x^m - t^n)^3$
$= [x^m + (-t^n)]^3$
$= (x^m)^3 + 3(x^m)^2(-t^n) + 3(x^m)(-t^n)^2 + (-t^n)^3$
$= x^{3m} - 3x^{2m}t^n + 3x^mt^{2n} - t^{3n}$

50. $y^{3n+3}z^{n+3} - 4y^4z^{3n}$

51. $(x - 1)(x^2 + x + 1)(x^3 + 1)$
$= (x^3 - 1)(x^3 + 1)$
$= (x^3)^2 - 1^2$
$= x^6 - 1$

52. $a^{2n} + 2a^nb^n + b^{2n}$

53. $[(2x - 1)^2 - 1]^2$
$= [4x^2 - 4x + 1 - 1]^2$
$= [4x^2 - 4x]^2$
$= (4x^2)^2 - 2(4x^2)(4x) + (4x)^2$
$= 16x^4 - 32x^3 + 16x^2$

54. $[(a + b)(a - b)][5 - (a + b)][5 + (a + b)]$
$= [a^2 - b^2][5^2 - (a + b)^2]$
$= (a^2 - b^2)(25 - a^2 - 2ab - b^2)$
$= -a^4 - 2a^3b + 25a^2 + 2ab^3 + b^4 - 25b^2$

55. $(x^{a-b})^{a+b}$
$= x^{(a-b)(a+b)}$
$= x^{a^2-b^2}$

56. $(t^{m+n})^{m+n} \cdot (t^{m-n})^{m-n}$
$= t^{m^2+2mn+n^2} \cdot t^{m^2-2mn+n^2}$
$= t^{2m^2+2n^2}$

57. $(a + b + c)^2$
$= (a + b + c)(a + b + c)$
$= a^2 + ab + ac + ba + b^2 + bc + ca + cb + c^2$
$= a^2 + b^2 + c^2 + 2ab + 2ac + 2bc$

58. $[(a + b) + c]^3$
$= (a + b)^3 + 3(a + b)^2c + 3(a + b)c^2 + c^3$
$= a^3 + 3a^2b + 3ab^2 + b^3 + 3a^2c + 6abc + 3b^2c + 3ac^2 + 3bc^2 + c^3$

59. $(a + b)^4$
$= (a + b)(a + b)^3$
$= (a + b)(a^3 + 3a^2b + 3ab^2 + b^3)$
$= a^4 + 3a^3b + 3a^2b^2 + ab^3 + a^3b + 3a^2b^2 + 3ab^3 + b^4$
$= a^4 + 4a^3b + 6a^2b^2 + 4ab^3 + b^4$

60.
$$x^4 + x^3y + x^2y^2 + xy^3 + y^4$$
$$\underline{\hspace{4cm} x \quad - y}$$
$$-x^4y - x^3y^2 - x^2y^3 - xy^4 - y^5$$
$$\underline{x^5 + x^4y + x^3y^2 + x^2y^3 + xy^4 \hspace{1cm}}$$
$$x^5 \hspace{4cm} - y^5$$

61. $(m + t)(m^4 - m^3t + m^2t^2 - mt^3 + t^4)$

$= m^5 - m^4t + m^3t^2 - m^2t^3 + mt^4 +$

$\qquad m^4t - m^3t^2 + m^2t^3 - mt^4 + t^5$

$= m^5 + t^5$

62. $(a-b)(a^7+a^6b+a^5b^2+a^4b^3+a^3b^4+a^2b^5+ab^6+b^7)$

$= a^8 + a^7b + a^6b^2 + a^5b^3 + a^4b^4 + a^3b^5 + a^2b^6 +$

$\quad ab^7 - a^7b - a^6b^2 - a^5b^3 - a^4b^4 - a^3b^5 - a^2b^6 -$

$\quad ab^7 - b^8$

$= a^8 - b^8$

63. $(3a + b)^2 = 3a^2 + b^2$

The first term is $9a^2$, not $3a^2$.
The middle term, $2 \cdot 3a \cdot b$, is missing.
$(3a + b)^2 = (3a)^2 + 2 \cdot 3a \cdot b + b^2$

$\qquad = 9a^2 + 6ab + b^2$ \qquad (Correct)

64. The middle term, $-12xy$, is missing; $-9y^2$ should
be $+9y^2$; correct answer is $4x^2 - 12xy + 9y^2$.

65. $2x(x + 3) + 4(x^2 - 3)$

$= 2x^2 + 3x + 4x^2 - 3$ \qquad (1)

The $3x$ should be $6x$; the 2 and 3 were not
multiplied. Similarly, -3 should be -12; the
4 and -3 were not multiplied.

$= 6x^2 + x$

$3x - 3$ is not x since they are not like terms.

$\quad 2x(x + 3) + 4(x^2 - 3)$

$= 2x^2 + 6x + 4x^2 - 12$

$= 6x^2 + 6x - 12$ \qquad (Correct)

66. In (1) the middle term, $-5ab$, is missing; in going
from (1) to (2) the factor 6 has been omitted;
correct answer is $6a^2 - 5ab - 6b^2$.

67. Using the results of Exercises 60 and 62 we might
conclude that the product is $x^n - y^n$. We can
confirm this by multiplying as follows:

$$x^{n-1} + x^{n-2}y + x^{n-3}y^2 + \cdots + x^2y^{n-3} + xy^{n-2} + y^{n-1}$$
$$\underline{\hspace{6cm} x - y}$$
$$-x^{n-1}y - x^{n-2}y^2 - \cdots - x^2y^{n-2} - xy^{n-1} - y^n$$
$$\underline{x^n + x^{n-1}y + x^{n-2}y^2 + \cdots + x^2y^{n-2} + xy^{n-1} \hspace{1cm}}$$
$$x^n \hspace{6cm} - y^n$$

The product is $x^n - y^n$.

Exercise Set 1.5

1. $p^2 + 6p + 8$

We look for factors of 8 whose sum is 6. By
trial we determine the factors to be 4 and 2.
$p^2 + 6p + 8 = (p + 4)(p + 2)$

2. $(w - 5)(w - 2)$

3. $2n^2 + 9n - 56$

We look for binomials $an + b$ and $cn + d$ for which
the product of the first terms is $2n^2$. The
product of the last terms must be -56. When we
multiply the inside terms, then the outside terms,
and add, we must have $9n$. By trial, we determine
the factorization to be

$\qquad (2n - 7)(n + 8)$.

4. $(3y - 5)(y + 4)$

5. $y^4 - 4y^2 - 21$

Think of this polynomial as $u^2 - 4u - 21$, where
we have mentally substituted u for y^2. Then we
look for factors of -21 whose sum is -4. By trial
we determine the factors to be -7 and 3, so

$\qquad u^2 - 4u - 21 = (u - 7)(u + 3)$.

Then, substituting y^2 for u, we obtain the
factorization of the original trinomial.

$\qquad y^4 - 4y^2 - 21 = (y^2 - 7)(y^2 + 3)$

6. $(m^2 - 10)(m^2 + 9)$

7. $18a^2b - 15ab^2$

$= 3ab \cdot 6a - 3ab \cdot 5b$

$= 3ab(6a - 5b)$

8. $4xy(x + 3y)$

9. $a(b - 2) + c(b - 2)$

$= (a + c)(b - 2)$

10. $(a - 2)(x^2 - 3)$

11. $x^3 + 3x^2 + 6x + 18$

$= x^2(x + 3) + 6(x + 3)$

$= (x^2 + 6)(x + 3)$

12. $3x^3 + x^2 - 18x - 6$

$= x^2(3x + 1) - 6(3x + 1)$

$= (x^2 - 6)(3x + 1)$

13. $y^3 - 3y^2 - 4y + 12$

$= y^2(y - 3) - 4(y - 3)$

$= (y^2 - 4)(y - 3)$

$= (y + 2)(y - 2)(y - 3)$

14. $p^3 - 2p^2 - 9p + 18$
$= p^2(p - 2) - 9(p - 2)$
$= (p^2 - 9)(p - 2)$
$= (p + 3)(p - 3)(p - 2)$

15. $9x^2 - 25$
$= (3x)^2 - 5^2$
$= (3x + 5)(3x - 5)$

16. $(4x - 3)(4x + 3)$

17. $4xy^4 - 4xz^2$
$= 4x(y^4 - z^2)$
$= 4x[(y^2)^2 - z^2]$
$= 4x(y^2 + z)(y^2 - z)$

18. $5xy^4 - 5xz^4$
$= 5x(y^4 - z^4)$
$= 5x(y^2 + z^2)(y^2 - z^2)$
$= 5x(y^2 + z^2)(y + z)(y - z)$

19. $y^2 - 6y + 9$
$= y^2 - 2 \cdot y \cdot 3 + 3^2$
$= (y - 3)^2$

20. $(x + 4)^2$

21. $1 - 8x + 16x^2$
$= 1^2 - 2 \cdot 1 \cdot 4x + (4x)^2$
$= (1 - 4x)^2$

22. $(1 + 5x)^2$

23. $4x^2 - 5$
$= (2x)^2 - (\sqrt{5})^2$
$= (2x + \sqrt{5})(2x - \sqrt{5})$

24. $(4x - \sqrt{7})(4x + \sqrt{7})$

25. $x^2y^2 - 14xy + 49$
$= (xy)^2 - 2 \cdot xy \cdot 7 + 7^2$
$= (xy - 7)^2$

26. $(xy - 8)^2$

27. $4ax^2 + 20ax - 56a$
$= 4a(x^2 + 5x - 14)$
$= 4a(x + 7)(x - 2)$

28. $21x^2y + 2xy - 8y$
$= y(21x^2 + 2x - 8)$
$= y(7x - 4)(3x + 2)$

29. $a^2 + 2ab + b^2 - c^2$
$= (a + b)^2 - c^2$
$= [(a + b) + c][(a + b) - c]$
$= (a + b + c)(a + b - c)$

30. $x^2 - 2xy + y^2 - z^2$
$= (x - y)^2 - z^2$
$= (x - y + z)(x - y - z)$

31. $x^2 + 2xy + y^2 - a^2 - 2ab - b^2$
$= (x^2 + 2xy + y^2) - (a^2 + 2ab + b^2)$
$= (x + y)^2 - (a + b)^2$
$= [(x + y) + (a + b)][(x + y) - (a + b)]$
$= (x + y + a + b)(x + y - a - b)$

32. $r^2 + 2rs + s^2 - t^2 + 2tv - v^2$
$= r^2 + 2rs + s^2 - (t^2 - 2tv + v^2)$
$= (r + s)^2 - (t - v)^2$
$= (r + s + t - v)(r + s - t + v)$

33. $5y^4 - 80x^4$
$= 5(y^4 - 16x^4)$
$= 5(y^2 + 4x^2)(y^2 - 4x^2)$
$= 5(y^2 + 4x^2)(y + 2x)(y - 2x)$

34. $6y^4 - 96x^4$
$= 6(y^4 - 16x^4)$
$= 6(y^2 + 4x^2)(y^2 - 4x^2)$
$= 6(y^2 + 4x^2)(y + 2x)(y - 2x)$

35. $x^3 + 8$
$= x^3 + 2^3$
$= (x + 2)(x^2 - 2x + 4)$

36. $(y - 4)(y^2 + 4y + 16)$

37. $3x^3 - \dfrac{3}{8}$
$= 3\left[x^3 - \dfrac{1}{8}\right]$
$= 3\left[x^3 - \left(\dfrac{1}{2}\right)^3\right]$
$= 3\left[x - \dfrac{1}{2}\right]\left[x^2 + \dfrac{1}{2}x + \dfrac{1}{4}\right]$

38. $5y^3 + \dfrac{5}{27}$
$= 5\left[y^3 + \dfrac{1}{27}\right]$
$= 5\left[y + \dfrac{1}{3}\right]\left[y^2 - \dfrac{1}{3}y + \dfrac{1}{9}\right]$

39. $x^3 + 0.001$
$= x^3 + (0.1)^3$
$= (x + 0.1)(x^2 - 0.1x + 0.01)$

40. $(y - 0.5)(y^2 + 0.5y + 0.25)$

41. $3z^3 - 24$
     $= 3(z^3 - 8)$
     $= 3(z^3 - 2^3)$
     $= 3(z - 2)(z^2 + 2z + 4)$

42. $4t^3 + 108$
     $= 4(t^3 + 27)$
     $= 4(t + 3)(t^2 - 3t + 9)$

43. $a^6 - t^6$
     $= (a^3)^2 - (t^3)^2$
     $= (a^3 + t^3)(a^3 - t^3)$
     $= (a + t)(a^2 - at + t^2)(a - t)(a^2 + at + t^2)$

44. $(4m^2 + y^2)(16m^4 - 4m^2y^2 + y^4)$

45. $16a^7b + 54ab^7$
     $= 2ab(8a^6 + 27b^6)$
     $= 2ab[(2a^2)^3 + (3b^2)^3]$
     $= 2ab(2a^2 + 3b^2)(4a^4 - 6a^2b^2 + 9b^4)$

46. $24a^2x^4 - 375a^8x$
     $= 3a^2x(8x^3 - 125a^6)$
     $= 3a^2x(2x - 5a^2)(4x^2 + 10a^2x + 25a^4)$

47. $x^2 - 17.6$
     $= x^2 - (\sqrt{17.6})^2$
     $= (x + \sqrt{17.6})(x - \sqrt{17.6})$
     $= (x + 4.19524)(x - 4.19524)$

48. $(x + 2.8337)(x - 2.8337)$

49. $37x^2 - 14.5y^2$
     $= 37(x^2 - 0.391892y^2)$
     $= 37[x^2 - (0.626y)^2]$
     $= 37(x + 0.626y)(x - 0.626y)$

50. $1.96x^2 - 17.4y^2$
     $= 1.96(x^2 - 8.876y^2)$
     $= 1.96(x + 2.980y)(x - 2.980y)$

51. $(x + 3)^2 - 2(x + 3) - 35$
     Think of this polynomial as $u^2 - 2u - 35$, where we have mentally substituted u for x + 3. Then we look for factors of -35 whose sum is -2. By trial we determine the factors to be -7 and 5, so
     $$u^2 - 2u - 35 = (u - 7)(u + 5).$$
     Then, substituting x + 3 for u, we obtain the factorization of the original trinomial.
     $(x + 3)^2 - 2(x + 3) - 35 = (x + 3 - 7)(x + 3 + 5)$
     $ = (x - 4)(x + 8)$

52. $(y - 4)^2 + 5(y - 4) - 24$
     $= u^2 + 5u - 24$ \qquad Substituting u for y - 4
     $= (u + 8)(u - 3)$
     $= (y - 4 + 8)(y - 4 - 3)$ \quad Substituting y - 4 for u
     $= (y + 4)(y - 7)$

53. $3(a - b)^2 + 10(a - b) - 8$
     Think of this polynomial as $3u^2 + 10u - 8$, where we have mentally substituted u for a - b. Then we look for binomials ax + b and cx + d for which the product of the first terms is $3u^2$ and the product of the last terms is -8. When we multiply the inside terms, then the outside terms, and add, the sum must be 10u. By trial, we determine the factorization to be
     $$(3u - 2)(u + 4).$$
     Then, substituting a - b for u, we obtain the factorization of the original trinomial.
     $3(a - b)^2 + 10(a - b) - 8$
     $= [3(a - b) - 2](a - b + 4)$
     $= (3a - 3b - 2)(a - b + 4)$

54. $6(2p + q)^2 - 5(2p + q) - 25$
     $= 6u^2 - 5u - 25$ \qquad Substituting u for 2p + q
     $= (3u + 5)(2u - 5)$
     $= [3(2p + q) + 5][2(2p + q) - 5]$ \quad Substituting 2p + q for u
     $= (6p + 3q + 5)(4p + 2q - 5)$

55. $(x + h)^3 - x^3$
     $= [(x + h) - x][(x + h)^2 + x(x + h) + x^2]$
     $= (x + h - x)(x^2 + 2xh + h^2 + x^2 + xh + x^2)$
     $= h(3x^2 + 3xh + h^2)$

56. $(x + 0.01)^2 - x^2$
     $= (x + 0.01 + x)(x + 0.01 - x)$
     $= 0.01(2x + 0.01)$
     $= 0.02(x + 0.005)$

57. $y^4 - 84 + 5y^2$
     $= y^4 + 5y^2 - 84$
     $= u^2 + 5u - 84$ \qquad Substituting u for y^2
     $= (u + 12)(u - 7)$
     $= (y^2 + 12)(y^2 - 7)$ \qquad Substituting y^2 for u

58. $11x^2 + x^4 - 80$
     $= x^4 + 11x^2 - 80$
     $= u^2 + 11u - 80$ \qquad Substituting u for x^2
     $= (u + 16)(u - 5)$
     $= (x^2 + 16)(x^2 - 5)$, \quad Substituting x^2 for u
     or $(x^2 + 16)(x + \sqrt{5})(x - \sqrt{5})$

59. $y^2 - \frac{8}{49} + \frac{2}{7}y$

$= y^2 + \frac{2}{7}y - \frac{8}{49}$

$= \left(y + \frac{4}{7}\right)\left(y - \frac{2}{7}\right)$

60. $\left(x + \frac{4}{5}\right)\left(x - \frac{1}{5}\right)$, or $\frac{1}{25}(5x + 4)(5x - 1)$

61. $t^2 - 0.27 + 0.6t$

$= t^2 + 0.6t - 0.27$

$= (t + 0.9)(t - 0.3)$

62. $(m - 0.1)(m + 0.5)$

63. $x^{2n} + 5x^n - 24$

$= (x^n)^2 + 5x^n - 24$

$= (x^n + 8)(x^n - 3)$

64. $(2x^n - 3)(2x^n + 1)$

65. $x^2 + ax + bx + ab$

$= x(x + a) + b(x + a)$

$= (x + b)(x + a)$

66. $bdy^2 + ady + bcy + ac$

$= dy(by + a) + c(by + a)$

$= (by + a)(dy + c)$

67. $\frac{1}{4}t^2 - \frac{2}{5}t + \frac{4}{25}$

$= \left(\frac{1}{2}t\right)^2 - 2 \cdot \frac{1}{2}t \cdot \frac{2}{5} + \left(\frac{2}{5}\right)^2$

$= \left(\frac{1}{2}t - \frac{2}{5}\right)^2$

68. $\frac{4}{27}r^2 + \frac{5}{9}rs + \frac{1}{12}s^2 - \frac{1}{3}rs$

$= \frac{4}{27}r^2 + \frac{2}{9}rs + \frac{1}{12}s^2$ Collecting like terms

$= \frac{1}{3}\left(\frac{4}{9}r^2 + \frac{2}{3}rs + \frac{1}{4}s^2\right)$

$= \frac{1}{3}\left(\frac{2}{3}r + \frac{1}{2}s\right)^2$

Other forms of the answer are $\frac{1}{108}(4r + 3s)^2$ and $\left(\frac{1}{9}r + \frac{1}{12}s\right)\left(\frac{4}{3}r + s\right)$.

69. $25y^{2m} - (x^{2n} - 2x^n + 1)$

$= (5y^m)^2 - (x^n - 1)^2$

$= [5y^m + (x^n - 1)][5y^m - (x^n - 1)]$

$= (5y^m + x^n - 1)(5y^m - x^n + 1)$

70. $4x^{4a} + 12x^{2a} + 10x^{2a} + 30$

$= 2(2x^{4a} + 6x^{2a} + 5x^{2a} + 15)$

$= 2[2x^{2a}(x^{2a} + 3) + 5(x^{2a} + 3)]$

$= 2(x^{2a} + 3)(2x^{2a} + 5)$

71. $3x^{3n} - 24y^{3m}$

$= 3(x^{3n} - 8y^{3m})$

$= 3[(x^n)^3 - (2y^m)^3]$

$= 3(x^n - 2y^m)(x^{2n} + 2x^ny^m + 4y^{2m})$

72. $(x^{2a} - t^b)(x^{4a} + x^{2a}t^b + t^{2b})$

73. $(y - 1)^4 - (y - 1)^2$

$= (y - 1)^2[(y - 1)^2 - 1]$

$= (y - 1)^2[y^2 - 2y + 1 - 1]$

$= (y - 1)^2(y^2 - 2y)$

$= y(y - 1)^2(y - 2)$

74. $x^6 - 2x^5 + x^4 - x^2 + 2x - 1$

$= x^4(x^2 - 2x + 1) - (x^2 - 2x + 1)$

$= (x^4 - 1)(x^2 - 2x + 1)$

$= (x^2 + 1)(x^2 - 1)(x - 1)^2$

$= (x^2 + 1)(x + 1)(x - 1)(x - 1)^2$

$= (x^2 + 1)(x + 1)(x - 1)^3$

75. $5x - 9 = 5 \cdot x - 5 \cdot \frac{9}{5}$

$= 5\left(x - \frac{9}{5}\right)$

76. $\frac{2}{3}\left(x - \frac{21}{2}\right)$

77. a)

$$
\begin{array}{r}
x^2 - x + 1 \\
x^3 + x^2 - 1 \\
\hline
-x^2 + x - 1 \\
x^4 - x^3 + x^2 \\
x^5 - x^4 + x^3 \\
\hline
x^5 \qquad\qquad + x - 1
\end{array}
$$

The product is $x^5 + x - 1$.

b) We use the result in part (a).

$x^5 + x - 1 = (x^2 - x + 1)(x^3 + x^2 - 1)$

Exercise Set 1.6

---

1. $\frac{3x - 3}{x(x - 1)}$

Since division by zero is not defined, any number that makes the denominator zero is not a meaningful replacement. When x is replaced by 0 or 1, the denominator is 0. Thus, all real numbers except 0 and 1 are meaningful replacements.

2. $\frac{(x^2 - 4)(x + 1)}{(x + 2)(x^2 - 1)} = \frac{(x^2 - 4)(x + 1)}{(x + 2)(x - 1)(x + 1)}$

All real numbers except -2, 1, and -1 are meaningful replacements.

3. We first factor the denominator completely.

$$\frac{7x^2 - 28x + 28}{(x^2 - 4)(x^2 + 3x - 10)} = \frac{7x^2 - 28x + 28}{(x+2)(x-2)(x+5)(x-2)}$$

We see that $x + 2 = 0$ when $x = -2$, $x - 2 = 0$ when $x = 2$, and $x + 5 = 0$ when $x = -5$. Thus, all real numbers except -2, 2, and -5 are meaningful replacements.

4. $\dfrac{7x^2 + 11x - 6}{x(x^2 - x - 6)} = \dfrac{7x^2 + 11x - 6}{x(x - 3)(x + 2)}$

All real numbers except 0, 3, and -2 are meaningful replacements.

5. $\dfrac{3x - 3}{x(x - 1)} = \dfrac{3\cancel{(x - 1)}}{x\cancel{(x - 1)}}$

$= \dfrac{3}{x}$

All real numbers except 0 are meaningful replacements in the simplified expression.

6. $\dfrac{(x^2 - 4)(x + 1)}{(x + 2)(x^2 - 1)} = \dfrac{\cancel{(x + 2)}(x - 2)\cancel{(x + 1)}}{\cancel{(x + 2)}(x - 1)\cancel{(x + 1)}}$

$= \dfrac{x - 2}{x - 1}$

All real numbers except 1

7. $\dfrac{7x^2 - 28x + 28}{(x^2 - 4)(x^2 + 3x - 10)} = \dfrac{7(x^2 - 4x + 4)}{(x+2)(x-2)(x+5)(x-2)}$

$= \dfrac{7\cancel{(x - 2)^2}}{(x+2)(x+5)\cancel{(x-2)^2}}$

$= \dfrac{7}{(x + 2)(x + 5)}$

All real numbers except -2 and -5 are meaningful replacements in the simplified expression.

8. $\dfrac{7x^2 + 11x - 6}{x(x^2 - x - 6)} = \dfrac{(7x - 3)\cancel{(x + 2)}}{x(x - 3)\cancel{(x + 2)}}$

$= \dfrac{7x - 3}{x(x - 3)}$

All real numbers except 0 and 3

9. $\dfrac{25x^2y^2}{10xy^2} = \dfrac{5xy^2 \cdot 5x}{5xy^2 \cdot 2}$

$= \dfrac{5x}{2}$

All real numbers are meaningful replacements in the simplified expression.

10. $\dfrac{x^2 - 4}{x^2 + 5x + 6} = \dfrac{(x + 2)(x - 2)}{(x + 3)\cancel{(x + 2)}}$

$= \dfrac{x - 2}{x + 3}$

All real numbers except -3

11. $\dfrac{x^2 - 3x + 2}{x^2 + x - 2} = \dfrac{(x - 2)\cancel{(x - 1)}}{(x + 2)\cancel{(x - 1)}}$

$= \dfrac{x - 2}{x + 2}$

All real numbers except -2 are meaningful replacements in the simplified expression.

12. $\dfrac{a^2 + 2a + 4}{(a^3 - 8)(a + 5)} = \dfrac{\cancel{(a^2 + 2a + 4)} \cdot 1}{(a - 2)\cancel{(a^2 + 2a + 4)}(a + 5)}$

$= \dfrac{1}{(a - 2)(a + 5)}$

All real numbers except 2 and -5.

13. $\dfrac{x^2 - y^2}{(x - y)^2} \cdot \dfrac{1}{x + y}$

$= \dfrac{(x^2 - y^2) \cdot 1}{(x - y)^2(x + y)}$

$= \dfrac{\cancel{(x + y)}\cancel{(x - y)} \cdot 1}{\cancel{(x - y)}(x - y)\cancel{(x + y)}}$

$= \dfrac{1}{x - y}$

14. $\dfrac{r - s}{r + s} \cdot \dfrac{r^2 - s^2}{(r - s)^2} = \dfrac{(r - s)(r^2 - s^2)}{(r + s)(r - s)^2}$

$= \dfrac{\cancel{(r - s)}\cancel{(r - s)}\cancel{(r + s)} \cdot 1}{\cancel{(r + s)}\cancel{(r - s)}\cancel{(r - s)}}$

$= 1$

15. $\dfrac{x^2 - 2x - 35}{2x^3 - 3x^2} \cdot \dfrac{4x^3 - 9x}{7x - 49}$

$= \dfrac{\cancel{(x - 7)}(x + 5)\cancel{(x)}(2x + 3)\cancel{(2x - 3)}}{\cancel{x} \cdot x\cancel{(2x - 3)}(7)\cancel{(x - 7)}}$

$= \dfrac{(x + 5)(2x + 3)}{7x}$

16. $\dfrac{x^2 + 2x - 35}{3x^3 - 2x^2} \cdot \dfrac{9x^3 - 4x}{7x + 49}$

$= \dfrac{\cancel{(x + 7)}(x - 5)\cancel{(x)}(3x + 2)\cancel{(3x - 2)}}{\cancel{x} \cdot x\cancel{(3x - 2)}(7)\cancel{(x + 7)}}$

$= \dfrac{(x - 5)(3x + 2)}{7x}$

17. $\dfrac{a^2 - a - 6}{a^2 - 7a + 12} \cdot \dfrac{a^2 - 2a - 8}{a^2 - 3a - 10}$

$= \dfrac{\cancel{(a - 3)}(a + 2)\cancel{(a - 4)}\cancel{(a + 2)}}{\cancel{(a - 4)}\cancel{(a - 3)}(a - 5)\cancel{(a + 2)}}$

$= \dfrac{a + 2}{a - 5}$

18. $\dfrac{a^2 - a - 12}{a^2 - 6a + 8} \cdot \dfrac{a^2 + a - 6}{a^2 - 2a - 24}$

$= \dfrac{\cancel{(a - 4)}(a + 3)(a + 3)\cancel{(a - 2)}}{\cancel{(a - 2)}\cancel{(a - 4)}(a - 6)(a + 4)}$

$= \dfrac{(a + 3)^2}{(a - 6)(a + 4)}$

19. $\dfrac{m^2 - n^2}{r + s} \div \dfrac{m - n}{r + s}$

$= \dfrac{m^2 - n^2}{r + s} \cdot \dfrac{r + s}{m - n}$

$= \dfrac{(m + n)\cancel{(m - n)}\cancel{(r + s)}}{\cancel{(r + s)}\cancel{(m - n)}}$

$= m + n$

20. $\dfrac{a^2 - b^2}{x - y} \div \dfrac{a + b}{x - y}$

$= \dfrac{a^2 - b^2}{x - y} \cdot \dfrac{x - y}{a + b}$

$= \dfrac{(a + b)(a - b)\cancel{(x - y)}}{\cancel{(x - y)}\cancel{(a + b)} \cdot 1}$

$= a - b$

21. $\dfrac{3x + 12}{2x - 8} \div \dfrac{(x + 4)^2}{(x - 4)^2}$

$= \dfrac{3x + 12}{2x - 8} \cdot \dfrac{(x - 4)^2}{(x + 4)^2}$

$= \dfrac{3\cancel{(x + 4)}\cancel{(x - 4)}(x - 4)}{2\cancel{(x - 4)}\cancel{(x + 4)}(x + 4)}$

$= \dfrac{3(x - 4)}{2(x + 4)}$

22. $\dfrac{a^2 - a - 2}{a^2 - a - 6} \div \dfrac{a^2 - 2a}{2a + a^2}$

$= \dfrac{a^2 - a - 2}{a^2 - a - 6} \cdot \dfrac{2a + a^2}{a^2 - 2a}$

$= \dfrac{\cancel{(a - 2)}(a + 1)\cancel{(a)}\cancel{(2 + a)}}{(a - 3)\cancel{(a + 2)}\cancel{(a)}\cancel{(a - 2)}}$

$= \dfrac{a + 1}{a - 3}$

23. $\dfrac{x^2 - y^2}{x^3 - y^3} \cdot \dfrac{x^2 + xy + y^2}{x^2 + 2xy + y^2}$

$= \dfrac{\cancel{(x + y)}\cancel{(x - y)}\cancel{(x^2 + xy + y^2)} \cdot 1}{\cancel{(x - y)}\cancel{(x^2 + xy + y^2)}\cancel{(x + y)}(x + y)}$

$= \dfrac{1}{x + y}$

24. $\dfrac{c^3 + 8}{c^2 - 4} \div \dfrac{c^2 - 2c + 4}{c^2 - 4c + 4}$

$= \dfrac{c^3 + 8}{c^2 - 4} \cdot \dfrac{c^2 - 4c + 4}{c^2 - 2c + 4}$

$= \dfrac{\cancel{(c + 2)}\cancel{(c^2 - 2c + 4)}(c - 2)(c - 2)}{\cancel{(c + 2)}\cancel{(c - 2)}\cancel{(c^2 - 2c + 4)} \cdot 1}$

$= c - 2$

25. $\dfrac{(x - y)^2 - z^2}{(x + y)^2 - z^2} \div \dfrac{x - y + z}{x + y - z}$

$= \dfrac{(x - y)^2 - z^2}{(x + y)^2 - z^2} \cdot \dfrac{x + y - z}{x - y + z}$

$= \dfrac{\cancel{(x - y + z)}(x - y - z)\cancel{(x + y - z)}}{(x + y + z)\cancel{(x + y - z)}\cancel{(x - y + z)}}$

$= \dfrac{x - y - z}{x + y + z}$

26. $\dfrac{(a + b)^2 - 9}{(a - b)^2 - 9} \cdot \dfrac{a - b - 3}{a + b + 3}$

$= \dfrac{\cancel{(a + b + 3)}(a + b - 3)\cancel{(a - b - 3)}}{(a - b + 3)\cancel{(a - b - 3)}\cancel{(a + b + 3)}}$

$= \dfrac{a + b - 3}{a - b + 3}$

27. $\dfrac{3}{2a + 3} + \dfrac{2a}{2a + 3}$

$= \dfrac{3 + 2a}{2a + 3}$

$= 1$

28. $\dfrac{a - 3b}{a + b} + \dfrac{a + 5b}{a + b} = \dfrac{2a + 2b}{a + b}$

$\qquad\qquad\qquad = \dfrac{2\cancel{(a + b)}}{1 \cdot \cancel{(a + b)}}$

$\qquad\qquad\qquad = 2$

29. $\dfrac{y}{y - 1} + \dfrac{2}{1 - y}$

$= \dfrac{y}{y - 1} + \dfrac{-1}{-1} \cdot \dfrac{2}{1 - y}$

$= \dfrac{y}{y - 1} + \dfrac{-2}{y - 1}$

$= \dfrac{y - 2}{y - 1}$

30. $\dfrac{a}{a - b} + \dfrac{b}{b - a} = \dfrac{a}{a - b} + \dfrac{-b}{a - b}$

$\qquad\qquad\qquad = \dfrac{a - b}{a - b}$

$\qquad\qquad\qquad = 1$

31. $\dfrac{x}{2x - 3y} - \dfrac{y}{3y - 2x}$

$= \dfrac{x}{2x - 3y} - \dfrac{-1}{-1} \cdot \dfrac{y}{3y - 2x}$

$= \dfrac{x}{2x - 3y} - \dfrac{-y}{2x - 3y}$

$= \dfrac{x + y}{2x - 3y} \qquad\qquad [x - (-y) = x + y]$

32. $\dfrac{3a}{3a - 2b} - \dfrac{2a}{2b - 3a} = \dfrac{3a}{3a - 2b} - \dfrac{-2a}{3a - 2b}$

$\qquad\qquad\qquad\qquad = \dfrac{5a}{3a - 2b}$

33. $\dfrac{3}{x + 2} + \dfrac{2}{x^2 - 4}$

$= \dfrac{3}{x + 2} + \dfrac{2}{(x + 2)(x - 2)}, \quad$ LCD is $(x + 2)(x - 2)$

$= \dfrac{3}{x + 2} \cdot \dfrac{x - 2}{x - 2} + \dfrac{2}{(x + 2)(x - 2)}$

$= \dfrac{3x - 6}{(x + 2)(x - 2)} + \dfrac{2}{(x + 2)(x - 2)}$

$= \dfrac{3x - 4}{(x + 2)(x - 2)}$

34. $\dfrac{5}{a-3} - \dfrac{2}{a^2-9}$

    $= \dfrac{5}{a-3} - \dfrac{2}{(a+3)(a-3)}$, LCD is $(a+3)(a-3)$

    $= \dfrac{5(a+3)-2}{(a+3)(a-3)}$

    $= \dfrac{5a+15-2}{(a+3)(a-3)}$

    $= \dfrac{5a+13}{(a+3)(a-3)}$

35. $\dfrac{y}{y^2-y-20} + \dfrac{2}{y+4}$

    $= \dfrac{y}{(y+4)(y-5)} + \dfrac{2}{y+4}$,   LCD is $(y+4)(y-5)$

    $= \dfrac{y}{(y+4)(y-5)} + \dfrac{2}{y+4} \cdot \dfrac{y-5}{y-5}$

    $= \dfrac{y}{(y+4)(y-5)} + \dfrac{2y-10}{(y+4)(y-5)}$

    $= \dfrac{3y-10}{(y+4)(y-5)}$

36. $\dfrac{6}{y^2+6y+9} - \dfrac{5}{y+3}$

    $= \dfrac{6}{(y+3)^2} - \dfrac{5}{y+3}$,   LCD is $(y+3)^2$

    $= \dfrac{6-5(y+3)}{(y+3)^2}$

    $= \dfrac{6-5y-15}{(y+3)^2}$

    $= \dfrac{-5y-9}{(y+3)^2}$

37. $\dfrac{3}{x+y} + \dfrac{x-5y}{x^2-y^2}$

    $= \dfrac{3}{x+y} + \dfrac{x-5y}{(x+y)(x-y)}$,   LCD is $(x+y)(x-y)$

    $= \dfrac{3}{x+y} \cdot \dfrac{x-y}{x-y} + \dfrac{x-5y}{(x+y)(x-y)}$

    $= \dfrac{3x-3y}{(x+y)(x-y)} + \dfrac{x-5y}{(x+y)(x-y)}$

    $= \dfrac{4x-8y}{(x+y)(x-y)}$

38. $\dfrac{a^2+1}{a^2-1} - \dfrac{a-1}{a+1}$

    $= \dfrac{a^2+1}{(a+1)(a-1)} - \dfrac{a-1}{a+1}$, LCD is $(a+1)(a-1)$

    $= \dfrac{a^2+1-(a-1)(a-1)}{(a+1)(a-1)}$

    $= \dfrac{a^2+1-a^2+2a-1}{(a+1)(a-1)}$

    $= \dfrac{2a}{(a+1)(a-1)}$

39. $\dfrac{9x+2}{3x^2-2x-8} + \dfrac{7}{3x^2+x-4}$

    $= \dfrac{9x+2}{(3x+4)(x-2)} + \dfrac{7}{(3x+4)(x-1)}$,

              LCD is $(3x+4)(x-2)(x-1)$

    $= \dfrac{9x+2}{(3x+4)(x-2)} \cdot \dfrac{x-1}{x-1} + \dfrac{7}{(3x+4)(x-1)} \cdot \dfrac{x-2}{x-2}$

    $= \dfrac{9x^2-7x-2}{(3x+4)(x-2)(x-1)} + \dfrac{7x-14}{(3x+4)(x-1)(x-2)}$

    $= \dfrac{9x^2-16}{(3x+4)(x-2)(x-1)}$

    $= \dfrac{\cancel{(3x+4)}(3x-4)}{\cancel{(3x+4)}(x-2)(x-1)}$

    $= \dfrac{3x-4}{(x-2)(x-1)}$

40. $\dfrac{3y}{y^2-7y+10} - \dfrac{2y}{y^2-8y+15}$

    $= \dfrac{3y}{(y-2)(y-5)} - \dfrac{2y}{(y-5)(y-3)}$,

              LCD is $(y-2)(y-5)(y-3)$

    $= \dfrac{3y(y-3)-2y(y-2)}{(y-2)(y-5)(y-3)}$

    $= \dfrac{3y^2-9y-2y^2+4y}{(y-2)(y-5)(y-3)}$

    $= \dfrac{y^2-5y}{(y-2)(y-5)(y-3)}$

    $= \dfrac{y\cancel{(y-5)}}{(y-2)\cancel{(y-5)}(y-3)}$

    $= \dfrac{y}{(y-2)(y-3)}$

41. $\dfrac{5a}{a-b} + \dfrac{ab}{a^2-b^2} + \dfrac{4b}{a+b}$

    $= \dfrac{5a}{a-b} + \dfrac{ab}{(a+b)(a-b)} + \dfrac{4b}{a+b}$,

              LCD is $(a+b)(a-b)$

    $= \dfrac{5a}{a-b} \cdot \dfrac{a+b}{a+b} + \dfrac{ab}{(a+b)(a-b)} + \dfrac{4b}{a+b} \cdot \dfrac{a-b}{a-b}$

    $= \dfrac{5a^2+5ab}{(a+b)(a-b)} + \dfrac{ab}{(a+b)(a-b)} + \dfrac{4ab-4b^2}{(a+b)(a-b)}$

    $= \dfrac{5a^2+10ab-4b^2}{(a+b)(a-b)}$

42. $\dfrac{6a}{a-b} - \dfrac{3b}{b-a} + \dfrac{5}{a^2-b^2}$

    $= \dfrac{6a}{a-b} - \dfrac{-3b}{a-b} + \dfrac{5}{(a+b)(a-b)}$,

              LCD is $(a+b)(a-b)$

    $= \dfrac{6a(a+b)+3b(a+b)+5}{(a+b)(a-b)}$

    $= \dfrac{6a^2+6ab+3ab+3b^2+5}{(a+b)(a-b)}$

    $= \dfrac{6a^2+9ab+3b^2+5}{(a+b)(a-b)}$

43. $\dfrac{7}{x + 2} - \dfrac{x + 8}{4 - x^2} + \dfrac{3x - 2}{4 - 4x + x^2}$

$= \dfrac{7}{x + 2} - \dfrac{x + 8}{(2 + x)(2 - x)} + \dfrac{3x - 2}{(2 - x)^2}$

$\qquad\qquad$ LCD is $(2 + x)(2 - x)^2$

$= \dfrac{7}{2 + x} \cdot \dfrac{(2 - x)^2}{(2 - x)^2} - \dfrac{x + 8}{(2 + x)(2 - x)} \cdot \dfrac{2 - x}{2 - x} +$

$\qquad\qquad\qquad \dfrac{3x - 2}{(2 - x)^2} \cdot \dfrac{2 + x}{2 + x}$

$= \dfrac{28 - 28x + 7x^2 - (16 - 6x - x^2) + 3x^2 + 4x - 4}{(2 + x)(2 - x)^2}$

$= \dfrac{28 - 28x + 7x^2 - 16 + 6x + x^2 + 3x^2 + 4x - 4}{(2 + x)(2 - x)^2}$

$= \dfrac{11x^2 - 18x + 8}{(2 + x)(2 - x)^2}$

44. $\dfrac{6}{x + 3} - \dfrac{x + 4}{9 - x^2} + \dfrac{2x - 3}{9 - 6x + x^2}$

$= \dfrac{6}{x + 3} - \dfrac{x + 4}{(3 + x)(3 - x)} + \dfrac{2x - 3}{(3 - x)^2}$,

$\qquad\qquad$ LCD is $(3 + x)(3 - x)^2$

$= \dfrac{6(3 - x)^2 - (x + 4)(3 - x) + (2x - 3)(3 + x)}{(3 + x)(3 - x)^2}$

$= \dfrac{54 - 36x + 6x^2 + x^2 + x - 12 + 2x^2 + 3x - 9}{(3 + x)(3 - x)^2}$

$= \dfrac{33 - 32x + 9x^2}{(3 + x)(3 - x)^2}$

45. $\dfrac{1}{x + 1} + \dfrac{x}{2 - x} + \dfrac{x^2 + 2}{x^2 - x - 2}$

$= \dfrac{1}{x + 1} + \dfrac{x}{2 - x} + \dfrac{x^2 + 2}{(x + 1)(x - 2)}$

$= \dfrac{1}{x + 1} + \dfrac{-1}{-1} \cdot \dfrac{x}{2 - x} + \dfrac{x^2 + 2}{(x + 1)(x - 2)}$

$= \dfrac{1}{x + 1} + \dfrac{-x}{x - 2} + \dfrac{x^2 + 2}{(x + 1)(x - 2)}$,

$\qquad\qquad$ LCD is $(x + 1)(x - 2)$

$= \dfrac{1}{x + 1} \cdot \dfrac{x - 2}{x - 2} + \dfrac{-x}{x - 2} \cdot \dfrac{x + 1}{x + 1} + \dfrac{x^2 + 2}{(x + 1)(x - 2)}$

$= \dfrac{x - 2}{(x + 1)(x - 2)} + \dfrac{-x^2 - x}{(x + 1)(x - 2)} + \dfrac{x^2 + 2}{(x + 1)(x - 2)}$

$= \dfrac{x - 2 - x^2 - x + x^2 + 2}{(x + 1)(x - 2)}$

$= \dfrac{0}{(x + 1)(x - 2)}$

$= 0$

46. $\dfrac{x - 1}{x - 2} - \dfrac{x + 1}{x + 2} - \dfrac{x - 6}{4 - x^2}$

$= \dfrac{x - 1}{x - 2} - \dfrac{x + 1}{x + 2} - \dfrac{x - 6}{(2 + x)(2 - x)}$

$= \dfrac{1 - x}{2 - x} - \dfrac{x + 1}{x + 2} - \dfrac{x - 6}{(2 + x)(2 - x)}$,

$\qquad\qquad$ LCD is $(2 + x)(2 - x)$

$= \dfrac{(1 - x)(2 + x) - (x + 1)(2 - x) - (x - 6)}{(2 + x)(2 - x)}$

$= \dfrac{2 - x - x^2 + x^2 - x - 2 - x + 6}{(2 + x)(2 - x)}$

$= \dfrac{6 - 3x}{(2 + x)(2 - x)}$

$= \dfrac{3(2 - x)}{(2 + x)(2 - x)}$

$= \dfrac{3}{2 + x}$

47. $\dfrac{\dfrac{x^2 - y^2}{xy}}{\dfrac{x - y}{y}} = \dfrac{x^2 - y^2}{xy} \cdot \dfrac{y}{x - y}$

$\qquad\qquad = \dfrac{(x + y)(x - y)y}{xy(x - y)}$

$\qquad\qquad = \dfrac{x + y}{x}$

48. $\dfrac{\dfrac{a - b}{b}}{\dfrac{a^2 - b^2}{ab}} = \dfrac{a - b}{b} \cdot \dfrac{ab}{(a + b)(a - b)}$

$\qquad\qquad = \dfrac{ab(a - b)}{b(a + b)(a - b)}$

$\qquad\qquad = \dfrac{a}{a + b}$

49. $\dfrac{a - a^{-1}}{a + a^{-1}} = \dfrac{a - \dfrac{1}{a}}{a + \dfrac{1}{a}} = \dfrac{a \cdot \dfrac{a}{a} - \dfrac{1}{a}}{a \cdot \dfrac{a}{a} + \dfrac{1}{a}}$

$\qquad\qquad = \dfrac{\dfrac{a^2 - 1}{a}}{\dfrac{a^2 + 1}{a}}$

$\qquad\qquad = \dfrac{a^2 - 1}{a} \cdot \dfrac{a}{a^2 + 1}$

$\qquad\qquad = \dfrac{a^2 - 1}{a^2 + 1}$

50. $\dfrac{a - \dfrac{a}{b}}{b - \dfrac{b}{a}} = \dfrac{\dfrac{ab - a}{b}}{\dfrac{ab - b}{a}}$

$\qquad\qquad = \dfrac{a(b - 1)}{b} \cdot \dfrac{a}{b(a - 1)}$

$\qquad\qquad = \dfrac{a^2(b - 1)}{b^2(a - 1)}$

51. $\dfrac{c + \dfrac{8}{c^2}}{1 + \dfrac{2}{c}} = \dfrac{c \cdot \dfrac{c^2}{c^2} + \dfrac{8}{c^2}}{1 \cdot \dfrac{c}{c} + \dfrac{2}{c}}$

$= \dfrac{\dfrac{c^3 + 8}{c^2}}{\dfrac{c + 2}{c}}$

$= \dfrac{c^3 + 8}{c^2} \cdot \dfrac{c}{c + 2}$

$= \dfrac{\cancel{(c + 2)}(c^2 - 2c + 4)\cancel{c}}{\cancel{c} \cdot c\cancel{(c + 2)}}$

$= \dfrac{c^2 - 2c + 4}{c}$

52. $\dfrac{x^{-1} + y^{-1}}{x^{-3} + y^{-3}} = \dfrac{\dfrac{1}{x} + \dfrac{1}{y}}{\dfrac{1}{x^3} + \dfrac{1}{y^3}}$

$= \dfrac{\left(\dfrac{1}{x} + \dfrac{1}{y}\right)(x^3 y^3)}{\left(\dfrac{1}{x^3} + \dfrac{1}{y^3}\right)(x^3 y^3)}$

$= \dfrac{x^2 y^3 + x^3 y^2}{y^3 + x^3}$

$= \dfrac{x^2 y^2 \cancel{(y + x)}}{\cancel{(y + x)}(y^2 - yx + x^2)}$

$= \dfrac{x^2 y^2}{y^2 - yx + x^2}$

53. $\dfrac{x^2 + xy + y^2}{\dfrac{x^2}{y} - \dfrac{y^2}{x}} = \dfrac{x^2 + xy + y^2}{\dfrac{x^2}{y} \cdot \dfrac{x}{x} - \dfrac{y^2}{x} \cdot \dfrac{y}{y}}$

$= \dfrac{x^2 + xy + y^2}{\dfrac{x^3 - y^3}{xy}}$

$= (x^2 + xy + y^2) \cdot \dfrac{xy}{x^3 - y^3}$

$= \dfrac{\cancel{(x^2 + xy + y^2)}xy}{(x - y)\cancel{(x^2 + xy + y^2)}}$

$= \dfrac{xy}{x - y}$

54. $\dfrac{\dfrac{a^2}{b} + \dfrac{b^2}{a}}{a^2 - ab + b^2} = \dfrac{\dfrac{a^3 + b^3}{ab}}{a^2 - ab + b^2}$

$= \dfrac{(a + b)\cancel{(a^2 - ab + b^2)}}{ab} \cdot \dfrac{1}{\cancel{a^2 - ab + b^2}}$

$= \dfrac{a + b}{ab}$

55. $\dfrac{\dfrac{x}{y} - \dfrac{y}{x}}{\dfrac{1}{y} + \dfrac{1}{x}} = \dfrac{\dfrac{x}{y} - \dfrac{y}{x}}{\dfrac{1}{y} + \dfrac{1}{x}} \cdot \dfrac{xy}{xy}$, LCM is xy

$= \dfrac{\left(\dfrac{x}{y} - \dfrac{y}{x}\right)(xy)}{\left(\dfrac{1}{y} + \dfrac{1}{x}\right)(xy)}$

$= \dfrac{x^2 - y^2}{x + y}$

$= \dfrac{\cancel{(x + y)}(x - y)}{\cancel{(x + y)} \cdot 1}$

$= x - y$

56. $\dfrac{\dfrac{a}{b} - \dfrac{b}{a}}{\dfrac{1}{a} - \dfrac{1}{b}} = \dfrac{a^2 - b^2}{b - a}$ $\left[\text{Multiplying by } \dfrac{ab}{ab}\right]$

$= \dfrac{(a + b)(a - b)}{b - a}$

$= \dfrac{(a + b)\cancel{(a - b)}}{-1 \cdot \cancel{(a - b)}}$

$= -a - b$

57. $\dfrac{x^2 y^{-2} - y^2 x^{-2}}{xy^{-1} + yx^{-1}} = \dfrac{\dfrac{x^2}{y^2} - \dfrac{y^2}{x^2}}{\dfrac{x}{y} + \dfrac{y}{x}}$, LCM is $x^2 y^2$

$= \dfrac{\dfrac{x^2}{y^2} - \dfrac{y^2}{x^2}}{\dfrac{x}{y} + \dfrac{y}{x}} \cdot \dfrac{x^2 y^2}{x^2 y^2}$

$= \dfrac{x^4 - y^4}{x^3 y + xy^3}$

$= \dfrac{(x^2 + y^2)(x + y)(x - y)}{xy(x^2 + y^2)}$

$= \dfrac{(x + y)(x - y)}{xy}$

58. $\dfrac{a^2 b^{-2} - b^2 a^{-2}}{ab^{-1} - ba^{-1}} = \dfrac{\dfrac{a^2}{b^2} - \dfrac{b^2}{a^2}}{\dfrac{a}{b} - \dfrac{b}{a}}$

$= \dfrac{a^4 - b^4}{a^3 b - ab^3}$ $\left[\text{Multiplying by } \dfrac{a^2 b^2}{a^2 b^2}\right]$

$= \dfrac{(a^2 + b^2)\cancel{(a + b)}\cancel{(a - b)}}{ab\cancel{(a + b)}\cancel{(a - b)}}$

$= \dfrac{a^2 + b^2}{ab}$

59. $\dfrac{\dfrac{a}{1 - a} + \dfrac{1 + a}{a}}{\dfrac{1 - a}{a} + \dfrac{a}{1 + a}} = \dfrac{\dfrac{a}{1 - a} \cdot \dfrac{a}{a} + \dfrac{1 + a}{a} \cdot \dfrac{1 - a}{1 - a}}{\dfrac{1 - a}{a} \cdot \dfrac{1 + a}{1 + a} + \dfrac{a}{1 + a} \cdot \dfrac{a}{a}}$

$= \dfrac{\dfrac{a^2 + (1 - a^2)}{a(1 - a)}}{\dfrac{(1 - a^2) + a^2}{a(1 + a)}}$

$= \dfrac{1}{a(1 - a)} \cdot \dfrac{a(1 + a)}{1}$

$= \dfrac{1 + a}{1 - a}$

60. $\dfrac{\dfrac{1 - x}{x} + \dfrac{x}{1 + x}}{\dfrac{1 + x}{x} + \dfrac{x}{1 - x}} = \dfrac{\dfrac{1 - x^2 + x^2}{x(1 + x)}}{\dfrac{1 - x^2 + x^2}{x(1 - x)}}$

$= \dfrac{1}{x(1 + x)} \cdot \dfrac{x(1 - x)}{1}$

$= \dfrac{\cancel{x}(1 - x)}{\cancel{x}(1 + x)}$

$= \dfrac{1 - x}{1 + x}$

61. $\dfrac{\frac{1}{a^2} + \frac{2}{ab} + \frac{1}{b^2}}{\frac{1}{a^2} - \frac{1}{b^2}} = \dfrac{\frac{1}{a^2} + \frac{2}{ab} + \frac{1}{b^2}}{\frac{1}{a^2} - \frac{1}{b^2}} \cdot \dfrac{a^2b^2}{a^2b^2}$, LCM is a^2b^2

$\qquad = \dfrac{b^2 + 2ab + a^2}{b^2 - a^2}$

$\qquad = \dfrac{\cancel{(b + a)}(b + a)}{\cancel{(b + a)}(b - a)}$

$\qquad = \dfrac{b + a}{b - a}$

62. $\dfrac{\frac{1}{x^2} - \frac{1}{y^2}}{\frac{1}{x^2} - \frac{2}{xy} + \frac{1}{y^2}} = \dfrac{y^2 - x^2}{y^2 - 2xy + x^2}$

$\qquad\qquad\qquad\left[\text{Multiplying by } \dfrac{x^2 y^2}{x^2 y^2}\right]$

$\qquad = \dfrac{(y + x)\cancel{(y - x)}}{(y - x)\cancel{(y - x)}}$

$\qquad = \dfrac{y + x}{y - x}$

63. $\dfrac{(x + h)^2 - x^2}{h} = \dfrac{x^2 + 2xh + h^2 - x^2}{h}$

$\qquad = \dfrac{2xh + h^2}{h}$

$\qquad = \dfrac{\cancel{h}(2x + h)}{\cancel{h} \cdot 1}$

$\qquad = 2x + h$

64. $\dfrac{\frac{1}{x + h} - \frac{1}{x}}{h} = \dfrac{\frac{x - x - h}{x(x + h)}}{h}$

$\qquad = \dfrac{-h}{x(x + h)} \cdot \dfrac{1}{h}$

$\qquad = \dfrac{-1 \cdot \cancel{h}}{x\cancel{h}(x + h)}$

$\qquad = \dfrac{-1}{x(x + h)}$

65. $\dfrac{(x + h)^3 - x^3}{h} = \dfrac{x^3 + 3x^2h + 3xh^2 + h^3 - x^3}{h}$

$\qquad = \dfrac{3x^2h + 3xh^2 + h^3}{h}$

$\qquad = \dfrac{\cancel{h}(3x^2 + 3xh + h^2)}{\cancel{h} \cdot 1}$

$\qquad = 3x^2 + 3xh + h^2$

66. $\dfrac{\frac{1}{(x + h)^2} - \frac{1}{x^2}}{h} = \dfrac{\frac{x^2 - x^2 - 2xh - h^2}{x^2(x + h)^2}}{h}$

$\qquad = \dfrac{-2xh - h^2}{x^2(x + h)^2} \cdot \dfrac{1}{h}$

$\qquad = \dfrac{\cancel{h}(-2x - h)}{x^2\cancel{h}(x + h)^2}$

$\qquad = \dfrac{-2x - h}{x^2(x + h)^2}$

67. $\left[\dfrac{\frac{x + 1}{x - 1} + 1}{\frac{x + 1}{x - 1} - 1}\right]^5 = \left[\dfrac{\frac{(x + 1) + (x - 1)}{x - 1}}{\frac{(x + 1) - (x - 1)}{x - 1}}\right]^5$

$\qquad = \left[\dfrac{2x}{x - 1} \cdot \dfrac{x - 1}{2}\right]^5$

$\qquad = \left[\dfrac{2x\cancel{(x - 1)}}{1 \cdot 2\cancel{(x - 1)}}\right]^5$

$\qquad = x^5$

68. $1 + \dfrac{1}{1 + \dfrac{1}{1 + \frac{1}{1 + \frac{1}{x}}}} = 1 + \dfrac{1}{1 + \dfrac{1}{1 + \frac{1}{\frac{x + 1}{x}}}}$

$\qquad = 1 + \dfrac{1}{1 + \dfrac{1}{1 + \frac{x}{x + 1}}}$

$\qquad = 1 + \dfrac{1}{1 + \dfrac{1}{\frac{2x + 1}{x + 1}}}$

$\qquad = 1 + \dfrac{1}{1 + \frac{x + 1}{2x + 1}}$

$\qquad = 1 + \dfrac{1}{\frac{3x + 2}{2x + 1}}$

$\qquad = 1 + \dfrac{2x + 1}{3x + 2}$

$\qquad = \dfrac{5x + 3}{3x + 2}$

69. $\dfrac{a}{b} \div \left(\dfrac{a}{3} + \dfrac{b}{4}\right)$

$= \dfrac{a}{b} \cdot \left(\dfrac{3}{a} + \dfrac{4}{b}\right)$ (1) Step (1) uses the wrong reciprocal. The reciprocal of a sum is not the sum of the reciprocals.

$= \dfrac{a}{b} \cdot \left(\dfrac{3b + 4a}{ab}\right)$ (2) Step (2) would be correct if step (1) had been correct.

$= \dfrac{a(3b + 4a)}{ab^2}$ (3) Step (3) would be correct if steps (1) and (2) had been correct.

$= \dfrac{4a + 3b}{b}$ (4) Step (4) has an improper simplification of the b in the denominator.

$\dfrac{a}{b} \div \left(\dfrac{a}{3} + \dfrac{b}{4}\right) = \dfrac{a}{b} \div \left(\dfrac{4a + 3b}{12}\right)$

$\qquad\qquad = \dfrac{a}{b} \cdot \dfrac{12}{4a + 3b}$

$\qquad\qquad = \dfrac{12a}{b(4a + 3b)}$ (Correct answer)

70. In step (1) the $\frac{5x^2}{4xy}$ should be $\frac{10x^2}{4xy}$.

Step (2) would be correct if step (1) had been.

In going from step (2) to step (3) the quantity x is not a factor of both terms in the numerator of (2).

In going from step (3) to step (4) the quantity y is not a factor of both terms in the numerator of (3).

The correct answer is $\frac{10x^2 + 3y^2}{4xy}$.

71. $\frac{n(n + 1)(n + 2)}{2 \cdot 3} + \frac{(n + 1)(n + 2)}{2}$

$= \frac{n(n + 1)(n + 2)}{2 \cdot 3} + \frac{(n + 1)(n + 2)}{2} \cdot \frac{3}{3}$, LCD is $2 \cdot 3$

$= \frac{n(n + 1)(n + 2) + 3(n + 1)(n + 2)}{2 \cdot 3}$

$= \frac{(n + 1)(n + 2)(n + 3)}{2 \cdot 3}$ (Factoring the numerator by grouping)

72. $\frac{n(n + 1)(n + 2)(n + 3)}{2 \cdot 3 \cdot 4} + \frac{(n + 1)(n + 2)(n + 3)}{2 \cdot 3}$

$= \frac{n(n + 1)(n + 2)(n + 3) + 4(n + 1)(n + 2)(n + 3)}{2 \cdot 3 \cdot 4}$,

$\text{LCD is } 2 \cdot 3 \cdot 4$

$= \frac{(n + 1)(n + 2)(n + 3)(n + 4)}{2 \cdot 3 \cdot 4}$

Exercise Set 1.7

1. $\sqrt{x - 3}$

We substitute -2 for x in x - 3: -2 - 3 = -5. Since the radicand is negative, -2 is not a meaningful replacement.

We substitute 5 for x in x - 3: 5 - 3 = 2. Since the radicand is not negative, 5 is a meaningful replacement.

2. $2 \cdot 3 - 5 = 1$; yes

$2 \cdot 2 - 5 = -1$; no

3. $\sqrt{3 - 4x}$

We substitute -1 for x in 3 - 4x: 3 - 4(-1) = 7. Since the radicand is not negative, -1 is a meaningful replacement.

We substitute 1 for x in 3 - 4x: 3 - 4·1 = -1. Since the radicand is negative, 1 is not a meaningful replacement.

4. $0^2 + 3 = 3$; yes

$(4.3)^2 + 3 = 21.49$; yes

5. $\sqrt{1 - x^2}$

We substitute 1 for x in $1 - x^2$: $1 - 1^2 = 0$. Since the radicand is not negative, 1 is a meaningful replacement.

We substitute 3 for x in $1 - x^2$: $1 - 3^2 = -8$. Since the radicand is negative, 3 is not a meaningful replacement.

6. $(-3)^2 + 2(-3) + 1 = 4$; yes

$4^2 + 2 \cdot 4 + 1 = 25$; yes

7. $\sqrt[3]{2x + 7}$

Since every real number, positive, negative, or zero, has a cube root, -4 and 5 are both meaningful replacements.

8. $3 - 5 \cdot 1 = -2$; no

$3 - 5 \cdot 2 = -7$; no

9. $\sqrt{(-11)^2} = |-11| = 11$

10. 1

11. $\sqrt{16x^2} = \sqrt{(4x)^2} = |4x| = 4|x|$

12. $6|t|$

13. $\sqrt{(b + 1)^2} = |b + 1|$

14. $|2c - 3|$

15. $\sqrt[3]{-27x^3} = \sqrt[3]{(-3x)^3} = -3x$

16. $-2y$

17. $\sqrt{x^2 - 4x + 4} = \sqrt{(x - 2)^2} = |x - 2|$

18. $\sqrt{y^2 + 16y + 64} = \sqrt{(y + 8)^2} = |y + 8|$

19. $\sqrt[5]{32} = \sqrt[5]{2^5} = 2$

20. -2

21. $\sqrt{180} = \sqrt{36 \cdot 5} = \sqrt{36} \cdot \sqrt{5} = 6\sqrt{5}$

22. $\sqrt{48} = \sqrt{16 \cdot 3} = 4\sqrt{3}$

23. $\sqrt[3]{54} = \sqrt[3]{27 \cdot 2} = \sqrt[3]{27} \cdot \sqrt[3]{2} = 3\sqrt[3]{2}$

24. $\sqrt[3]{135} = \sqrt[3]{27 \cdot 5} = 3\sqrt[3]{5}$

25. $\sqrt{128c^2d^4} = \sqrt{64c^2d^4 \cdot 2} = |8cd^2|\sqrt{2} = 8|c|d^2\sqrt{2}$

26. $\sqrt{162c^4d^6} = \sqrt{81c^4d^6 \cdot 2} = 9c^2|d^3|\sqrt{2}$

27. $\sqrt{3}\sqrt{6} = \sqrt{18} = \sqrt{9 \cdot 2} = 3\sqrt{2}$

28. $\sqrt{6} \cdot \sqrt{8} = \sqrt{48} = \sqrt{16 \cdot 3} = 4\sqrt{3}$

29. $\sqrt{2x^3y}\sqrt{12xy} = \sqrt{24x^4y^2} = \sqrt{4x^4y^2 \cdot 6} = 2x^2y\sqrt{6}$

30. $\sqrt{3y^4z}\ \sqrt{20z} = \sqrt{60y^4z^2} = \sqrt{4y^4z^2 \cdot 15} = 2y^2z\ \sqrt{15}$

31. $\sqrt[3]{3x^2y}\ \sqrt[3]{36x} = \sqrt[3]{108x^3y} = \sqrt[3]{27x^3 \cdot 4y} = 3x\ \sqrt[3]{4y}$

32. $\sqrt[5]{8x^3y^4}\ \sqrt[5]{4x^4y} = \sqrt[5]{32x^7y^5} = 2xy\ \sqrt[5]{x^2}$

33. $\sqrt[3]{2(x+4)}\ \sqrt[3]{4(x+4)^4} = \sqrt[3]{8(x+4)^5}$
$$= \sqrt[3]{8(x+4)^3 \cdot (x+4)^2}$$
$$= 2(x+4)\ \sqrt[3]{(x+4)^2}$$

34. $\sqrt[3]{4(x+1)^2}\ \sqrt[3]{18(x+1)^2} = \sqrt[3]{72(x+1)^4}$
$$= \sqrt[3]{8(x+1)^3 \cdot 9(x+1)}$$
$$= 2(x+1)\ \sqrt[3]{9(x+1)}$$

35. $\dfrac{\sqrt{21ab^2}}{\sqrt{3ab}} = \sqrt{\dfrac{21ab^2}{3ab}} = \sqrt{7b}$

36. $\dfrac{\sqrt{128ab^2}}{\sqrt{16a^2b}} = \sqrt{\dfrac{8b}{a}} = 2\ \sqrt{\dfrac{2b}{a}} = \dfrac{2\sqrt{2ab}}{a}$

37. $\dfrac{\sqrt[3]{40m}}{\sqrt[3]{5m}} = \sqrt[3]{\dfrac{40m}{5m}} = \sqrt[3]{8} = 2$

38. $\sqrt{5y}$

39. $\dfrac{\sqrt[3]{3x^2}}{\sqrt[3]{24x^5}} = \sqrt[3]{\dfrac{3x^2}{24x^5}} = \sqrt[3]{\dfrac{1}{8x^3}} = \dfrac{1}{2x}$

40. $\dfrac{\sqrt[3]{40xy^3}}{\sqrt[3]{8x}} = \sqrt[3]{5y^3} = y\ \sqrt[3]{5}$

41. $\dfrac{\sqrt{a^2-b^2}}{\sqrt{a-b}} = \sqrt{\dfrac{a^2-b^2}{a-b}} = \sqrt{\dfrac{(a+b)\cancel{(a-b)}}{\cancel{a-b}}}$
$$= \sqrt{a+b}$$

42. $\dfrac{\sqrt{x^3-y^3}}{\sqrt{x-y}} = \sqrt{\dfrac{\cancel{(x-y)}(x^2+xy+y^2)}{\cancel{(x-y)} \cdot 1}} =$
$\sqrt{x^2+xy+y^2}$

43. $\sqrt{\dfrac{9a^2}{8b}} = \sqrt{\dfrac{9a^2}{8b} \cdot \dfrac{2b}{2b}} = \sqrt{\dfrac{9a^2}{16b^2} \cdot 2b} = \dfrac{3a\sqrt{2b}}{4b}$

44. $\sqrt{\dfrac{5b^2}{12a}} = \sqrt{\dfrac{5b^2}{12a} \cdot \dfrac{3a}{3a}} = \sqrt{\dfrac{15ab^2}{36a^2}} = \dfrac{b\sqrt{15a}}{6a}$

45. $\sqrt[3]{\dfrac{2x^2y^3}{25z^4}} = \sqrt[3]{\dfrac{2x^2y^3}{25z^4} \cdot \dfrac{5z^2}{5z^2}} = \sqrt[3]{\dfrac{y^3}{125z^6} \cdot 20x^2z^2}$
$$= \dfrac{y\ \sqrt[3]{20x^2z^2}}{5z^2}$$

46. $\sqrt[3]{\dfrac{24x^3y}{3y^4}} = \sqrt[3]{\dfrac{8x^3}{y^3}} = \dfrac{2x}{y}$

47. $\dfrac{\left[\sqrt[3]{32x^4y}\right]^2}{\left(\sqrt[3]{xy}\right)^2} = \left[\sqrt[3]{\dfrac{32x^4y}{xy}}\right]^2 = \left[\sqrt[3]{32x^3}\right]^2$
$$= \left[\sqrt[3]{2^5x^3}\right]^2$$
$$= \sqrt[3]{(2^5x^3)^2}$$
$$= \sqrt[3]{2^{10}x^6}$$
$$= \sqrt[3]{2^9x^6 \cdot 2}$$
$$= 2^3x^2\ \sqrt[3]{2}$$
$$= 8x^2\ \sqrt[3]{2}$$

48. $\dfrac{\left(\sqrt[3]{16x^2y}\right)^2}{\left(\sqrt[3]{xy}\right)^2} = \left(\sqrt[3]{16x}\right)^2 = \sqrt[3]{256x^2} = \sqrt[3]{64 \cdot 4x^2} =$
$4\ \sqrt[3]{4x^2}$

49. $\dfrac{3\sqrt{a^2b^2}\ \sqrt{4xy}}{2\sqrt{a^{-1}b^{-2}}\ \sqrt{9x^{-3}y^{-1}}} = \dfrac{3}{2}\ \sqrt{\dfrac{a^2b^2}{a^{-1}b^{-2}}}\ \sqrt{\dfrac{4xy}{9x^{-3}y^{-1}}}$
$$= \dfrac{3}{2}\ \sqrt{a^3b^4}\ \sqrt{\dfrac{4}{9}\ x^4y^2}$$
$$= \dfrac{3}{2} \cdot ab^2\ \sqrt{a} \cdot \dfrac{2}{3}\ x^2y$$
$$= ab^2x^2y\sqrt{a}$$

50. $\dfrac{4\sqrt{xy^2}\ \sqrt{9ab}}{3\sqrt{x^{-1}y^{-2}}\ \sqrt{16a^{-5}b^{-1}}} = \dfrac{4}{3}\ \sqrt{x^2y^4}\ \sqrt{\dfrac{9a^6b^2}{16}}$
$$= \dfrac{4}{3} \cdot \dfrac{3}{4}xy^2a^3b$$
$$= xy^2a^3b$$

51. $9\sqrt{50} + 6\sqrt{2} = 9\sqrt{25 \cdot 2} + 6\sqrt{2}$
$$= 9 \cdot 5\sqrt{2} + 6\sqrt{2}$$
$$= 45\sqrt{2} + 6\sqrt{2}$$
$$= (45+6)\sqrt{2}$$
$$= 51\sqrt{2}$$

52. $11\sqrt{27} - 4\sqrt{3} = 33\sqrt{3} - 4\sqrt{3} = 29\sqrt{3}$

53. $8\sqrt{2} - 6\sqrt{20} - 5\sqrt{8}$
$$= 8\sqrt{2} - 6\sqrt{4 \cdot 5} - 5\sqrt{4 \cdot 2}$$
$$= 8\sqrt{2} - 6 \cdot 2\sqrt{5} - 5 \cdot 2\sqrt{2}$$
$$= 8\sqrt{2} - 12\sqrt{5} - 10\sqrt{2}$$
$$= -2\sqrt{2} - 12\sqrt{5}$$

54. $\sqrt{12} - \sqrt{27} + \sqrt{75} = 2\sqrt{3} - 3\sqrt{3} + 5\sqrt{3} = 4\sqrt{3}$

55. $2\sqrt[3]{8x^2} + 5\sqrt[3]{27x^2} - 3\sqrt[3]{x^3}$

$= 2\cdot2\sqrt[3]{x^2} + 5\cdot3\sqrt[3]{x^2} - 3x$

$= 4\sqrt[3]{x^2} + 15\sqrt[3]{x^2} - 3x$

$= 19\sqrt[3]{x^2} - 3x$

56. $5a\sqrt{(a+b)^3} - 2ab\sqrt{a+b} - 3b\sqrt{(a+b)^3}$

$= 5a(a+b)\sqrt{a+b} - 2ab\sqrt{a+b} - 3b(a+b)\sqrt{a+b}$

$= (5a^2 + 5ab - 2ab - 3ab - 3b^2)\sqrt{a+b}$

$= (5a^2 - 3b^2)\sqrt{a+b}$

57. $3\sqrt{3y^2} - \dfrac{y\sqrt{48}}{\sqrt{2}} + \sqrt{\dfrac{12}{4y^{-2}}}$

$= 3\sqrt{3y^2} - y\sqrt{24} + \sqrt{3y^2}$

$= 3y\sqrt{3} - 2y\sqrt{6} + y\sqrt{3}$

$= 4y\sqrt{3} - 2y\sqrt{6}$

58. $\sqrt[3]{x^5} - \dfrac{2\sqrt[3]{x}}{\sqrt[3]{x^{-1}}} + 3\sqrt{\dfrac{8}{x^{-5}}} = \sqrt[3]{x^5} - 2\sqrt[3]{x^2} + \sqrt[3]{8x^5}$

$= x\sqrt[3]{x^2} - 2\sqrt[3]{x^2} + 2x\sqrt[3]{x^2}$

$= (3x - 2)\sqrt[3]{x^2}$

59. $\left(\sqrt{3} - \sqrt{2}\right)\left(\sqrt{3} + \sqrt{2}\right)$

$= \left(\sqrt{3}\right)^2 - \left(\sqrt{2}\right)^2$

$= 3 - 2$

$= 1$

60. $(\sqrt{8} + 2\sqrt{5})(\sqrt{8} - 2\sqrt{5}) = 8 - 4\cdot5 = -12$

61. $(1 + \sqrt{3})^2 = 1^2 + 2\cdot1\cdot\sqrt{3} + (\sqrt{3})^2$

$= 1 + 2\sqrt{3} + 3$

$= 4 + 2\sqrt{3}$

62. $(\sqrt{2} - 5)^2 = 2 - 10\sqrt{2} + 25 = 27 - 10\sqrt{2}$

63. $\left(\sqrt{t} - x\right)^2$

$= \left(\sqrt{t}\right)^2 - 2\cdot\sqrt{t}\cdot x + x^2$

$= t - 2x\sqrt{t} + x^2$

64. $\left(\sqrt{a} + \dfrac{1}{\sqrt{a}}\right)^2 = a + 2 + \dfrac{1}{a}$, or

$a + 2 + a^{-1}$, or $\dfrac{(a+1)^2}{a}$

65. $5\sqrt{7} + \dfrac{35}{\sqrt{7}}$

$= 5\sqrt{7} + \dfrac{35}{\sqrt{7}} \cdot \dfrac{\sqrt{7}}{\sqrt{7}}$

$= 5\sqrt{7} + \dfrac{35\sqrt{7}}{7}$

$= 5\sqrt{7} + 5\sqrt{7}$

$= 10\sqrt{7}$

66. $(\sqrt{a^2b} + 3\sqrt{y})(2a\sqrt{b} - \sqrt{y})$

$= 2a\cdot ab - \sqrt{a^2by} + 6a\sqrt{by} - 3y$

$= 2a^2b - a\sqrt{by} + 6a\sqrt{by} - 3y$

$= 2a^2b + 5a\sqrt{by} - 3y$

67. $\left(\sqrt{x+3} - \sqrt{3}\right)\left(\sqrt{x+3} + \sqrt{3}\right)$

$= \left(\sqrt{x+3}\right)^2 - \left(\sqrt{3}\right)^2$

$= (x + 3) - 3$

$= x$

68. $(\sqrt{x+h} - \sqrt{x})(\sqrt{x+h} + \sqrt{x}) = x + h - x = h$

69.   We substitute 90 for L in the formula.

$r = 2\sqrt{5L}$

$= 2\sqrt{5\cdot90}$

$= 2\sqrt{450}$

≈ 42.43 Using a calculator

The speed of the car was about 42.43 mph.

70. $r = 2\sqrt{5\cdot110} = 2\sqrt{550} \approx 46.90$ mph

71.   We use the Pythagorean theorem to find b, the airplane's horizontal distance from the airport. We have a = 3700 and c = 14,200.

$c^2 = a^2 + b^2$

$14{,}200^2 = 3700^2 + b^2$

$201{,}640{,}000 = 13{,}690{,}000 + b^2$

$187{,}950{,}000 = b^2$

$13{,}709.5 \approx b$ Using a calculator

The airplane is about 13,709.5 ft horizontally from the airport.

72.

2 mi = 2·5280 ft = 10,560 ft

2 mi + 2 ft = 10,562 ft

Then b = $\frac{1}{2}$ · 10,560 ft = 5280 ft and c =

$\frac{1}{2}$ · 10,562 ft = 5281 ft.

$a^2 = c^2 - b^2$

$a^2 = (5281)^2 - (5280)^2$

$a^2 = 10,561$

$a \approx 102.8$ ft

73. a) $h^2 + \left[\frac{a}{2}\right]^2 = a^2$ (Pythagorean theorem)

$h^2 + \frac{a^2}{4} = a^2$

$h^2 = \frac{3a^2}{4}$

$h = \sqrt{\frac{3a^2}{4}}$

$h = \frac{a}{2}\sqrt{3}$

b) Using the result of part (a) we have

$A = \frac{1}{2}$ · base · height

$A = \frac{1}{2}a \cdot \frac{a}{2}\sqrt{3}$ $\left[\frac{a}{2} + \frac{a}{2} = a\right]$

$A = \frac{a^2}{4}\sqrt{3}$

74. $c^2 = s^2 + s^2$

$c^2 = 2s^2$

$c = s\sqrt{2}$ (Length of third side)

75.

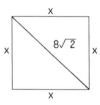

$x^2 + x^2 = (8\sqrt{2})^2$ (Pythagorean theorem)

$2x^2 = 128$

$x^2 = 64$

$x = 8$

76.

$(2x)^2 = 100$

$4x^2 = 100$

$x^2 = 25$

$x = 5$

$A = y^2 = x^2 + x^2 = 5^2 + 5^2 = 25 + 25 = 50$ ft^2

77. $\frac{6}{3 + \sqrt{5}} = \frac{6}{3 + \sqrt{5}} \cdot \frac{3 - \sqrt{5}}{3 - \sqrt{5}}$

$= \frac{6(3 - \sqrt{5})}{9 - 5}$

$= \frac{6(3 - \sqrt{5})}{4}$

$= \frac{3(3 - \sqrt{5})}{2}$

78. $\frac{2}{\sqrt{3} - 1} = \frac{2}{\sqrt{3} - 1} \cdot \frac{\sqrt{3} + 1}{\sqrt{3} + 1}$

$= \frac{\cancel{2}(\sqrt{3} + 1)}{\cancel{2}\cdot 1}$

$= \sqrt{3} + 1$

79. $\sqrt[3]{\frac{16}{9}} = \sqrt[3]{\frac{16}{9} \cdot \frac{3}{3}} = \sqrt[3]{\frac{48}{27}} = \sqrt[3]{\frac{8}{27} \cdot 6} = \frac{2\sqrt[3]{6}}{3}$

80. $\frac{\sqrt[3]{3}}{\sqrt[3]{6}} = \sqrt[3]{\frac{3}{6}} = \sqrt[3]{\frac{1}{2}} = \frac{1}{\sqrt[3]{2}} = \frac{1}{\sqrt[3]{2}} \cdot \frac{\sqrt[3]{4}}{\sqrt[3]{4}} = \frac{\sqrt[3]{4}}{2}$

81. $\frac{4\sqrt{x} - 3\sqrt{xy}}{2\sqrt{x} + 5\sqrt{y}} = \frac{4\sqrt{x} - 3\sqrt{xy}}{2\sqrt{x} + 5\sqrt{y}} \cdot \frac{2\sqrt{x} - 5\sqrt{y}}{2\sqrt{x} - 5\sqrt{y}}$

$= \frac{8x - 20\sqrt{xy} - 6x\sqrt{y} + 15y\sqrt{x}}{4x - 25y}$

82. $\frac{5\sqrt{x} + 2\sqrt{xy}}{3\sqrt{x} - 2\sqrt{y}} = \frac{5\sqrt{x} + 2\sqrt{xy}}{3\sqrt{x} - 2\sqrt{y}} \cdot \frac{3\sqrt{x} + 2\sqrt{y}}{3\sqrt{x} + 2\sqrt{y}}$

$= \frac{15x + 10\sqrt{xy} + 6x\sqrt{y} + 4y\sqrt{x}}{9x - 4y}$

83. $\dfrac{8\sqrt{2} + 5\sqrt{3}}{5\sqrt{3} - 7\sqrt{2}} = \dfrac{8\sqrt{2} + 5\sqrt{3}}{5\sqrt{3} - 7\sqrt{2}} \cdot \dfrac{5\sqrt{3} + 7\sqrt{2}}{5\sqrt{3} + 7\sqrt{2}}$

$= \dfrac{40\sqrt{6} + 56 \cdot 2 + 25 \cdot 3 + 35\sqrt{6}}{25 \cdot 3 - 49 \cdot 2}$

$= \dfrac{40\sqrt{6} + 112 + 75 + 35\sqrt{6}}{75 - 98}$

$= \dfrac{187 + 75\sqrt{6}}{-23}$

84. $\dfrac{4\sqrt{6} - 5\sqrt{3}}{2\sqrt{3} + 7\sqrt{6}} = \dfrac{4\sqrt{6} - 5\sqrt{3}}{2\sqrt{3} + 7\sqrt{6}} \cdot \dfrac{2\sqrt{3} - 7\sqrt{6}}{2\sqrt{3} - 7\sqrt{6}}$

$= \dfrac{8\sqrt{18} - 28 \cdot 6 - 10 \cdot 3 + 35\sqrt{18}}{4 \cdot 3 - 49 \cdot 6}$

$= \dfrac{24\sqrt{2} - 168 - 30 + 105\sqrt{2}}{12 - 294}$

$= \dfrac{-198 + 129\sqrt{2}}{-282}$

$= \dfrac{-66 + 43\sqrt{2}}{-94}$, or $\dfrac{66 - 43\sqrt{2}}{94}$

85. $\dfrac{p - q\sqrt{s}}{q + \sqrt{s}} = \dfrac{p - q\sqrt{s}}{q + \sqrt{s}} \cdot \dfrac{q - \sqrt{s}}{q - \sqrt{s}}$

$= \dfrac{pq - p\sqrt{s} - q^2\sqrt{s} + qs}{q^2 - s}$

86. $\dfrac{c\sqrt{t} + d}{c - d\sqrt{t}} = \dfrac{c\sqrt{t} + d}{c - d\sqrt{t}} \cdot \dfrac{c + d\sqrt{t}}{c + d\sqrt{t}}$

$= \dfrac{c^2\sqrt{t} + cdt + cd + d^2\sqrt{t}}{c^2 - d^2 t}$

87. $\dfrac{\sqrt{2} + \sqrt{5a}}{6} = \dfrac{\sqrt{2} + \sqrt{5a}}{6} \cdot \dfrac{\sqrt{2} - \sqrt{5a}}{\sqrt{2} - \sqrt{5a}}$

$= \dfrac{2 - 5a}{6(\sqrt{2} - \sqrt{5a})}$

88. $\dfrac{\sqrt{3} + \sqrt{5y}}{4} = \dfrac{\sqrt{3} + \sqrt{5y}}{4} \cdot \dfrac{\sqrt{3} - \sqrt{5y}}{\sqrt{3} - \sqrt{5y}}$

$= \dfrac{3 - 5y}{4(\sqrt{3} - \sqrt{5y})}$

89. $\dfrac{\sqrt{x + 1} + 1}{\sqrt{x + 1} - 1} = \dfrac{\sqrt{x + 1} + 1}{\sqrt{x + 1} - 1} \cdot \dfrac{\sqrt{x + 1} - 1}{\sqrt{x + 1} - 1}$

$= \dfrac{(x + 1) - 1}{(x + 1) - 2\sqrt{x + 1} + 1}$

$= \dfrac{x}{x - 2\sqrt{x + 1} + 2}$

90. $\dfrac{\sqrt{x + 4} - 2}{\sqrt{x + 4} + 2} = \dfrac{\sqrt{x + 4} - 2}{\sqrt{x + 4} + 2} \cdot \dfrac{\sqrt{x + 4} + 2}{\sqrt{x + 4} + 2}$

$= \dfrac{x + 4 - 4}{x + 4 + 4\sqrt{x + 4} + 4}$

$= \dfrac{x}{x + 8 + 4\sqrt{x + 4}}$

91. $\dfrac{\sqrt{a + 3} - \sqrt{3}}{3} = \dfrac{\sqrt{a + 3} - \sqrt{3}}{3} \cdot \dfrac{\sqrt{a + 3} + \sqrt{3}}{\sqrt{a + 3} + \sqrt{3}}$

$= \dfrac{(a + 3) - 3}{3(\sqrt{a + 3} + \sqrt{3})}$

$= \dfrac{a}{3(\sqrt{a + 3} + \sqrt{3})}$

92. $\dfrac{\sqrt{a + h} - \sqrt{a}}{h} = \dfrac{\sqrt{a + h} - \sqrt{a}}{h} \cdot \dfrac{\sqrt{a + h} + \sqrt{a}}{\sqrt{a + h} + \sqrt{a}}$

$= \dfrac{a + h - a}{h(\sqrt{a + h} + \sqrt{a})}$

$= \dfrac{h \cdot 1}{h(\sqrt{a + h} + \sqrt{a})}$

$= \dfrac{1}{\sqrt{a + h} + \sqrt{a}}$

93. $\dfrac{\sqrt{x + h} - \sqrt{x}}{h} = \dfrac{\sqrt{x + h} - \sqrt{x}}{h} \cdot \dfrac{\sqrt{x + h} + \sqrt{x}}{\sqrt{x + h} + \sqrt{x}}$

$= \dfrac{x + h - x}{h(\sqrt{x + h} + \sqrt{x})}$

$= \dfrac{\cancel{h} \cdot 1}{\cancel{h}(\sqrt{x + h} + \sqrt{x})}$

$= \dfrac{1}{\sqrt{x + h} + \sqrt{x}}$

94. $\dfrac{\sqrt{p + 7} - \sqrt{p}}{7} = \dfrac{\sqrt{p + 7} - \sqrt{p}}{7} \cdot \dfrac{\sqrt{p + 7} + \sqrt{p}}{\sqrt{p + 7} + \sqrt{p}}$

$= \dfrac{p + 7 - p}{7(\sqrt{p + 7} + \sqrt{p})}$

$= \dfrac{\cancel{7} \cdot 1}{\cancel{7}(\sqrt{p + 7} + \sqrt{p})}$

$= \dfrac{1}{\sqrt{p + 7} + \sqrt{p}}$

95. $\dfrac{\sqrt{x} + \sqrt{y}}{\sqrt{x} - \sqrt{y}} = \dfrac{\sqrt{x} + \sqrt{y}}{\sqrt{x} - \sqrt{y}} \cdot \dfrac{\sqrt{x} - \sqrt{y}}{\sqrt{x} - \sqrt{y}}$

$= \dfrac{x - y}{x - \sqrt{xy} - \sqrt{xy} + y}$

$= \dfrac{x - y}{x - 2\sqrt{xy} + y}$

96. $\dfrac{\sqrt{a} - \sqrt{b}}{\sqrt{a} + \sqrt{b}} = \dfrac{\sqrt{a} - \sqrt{b}}{\sqrt{a} + \sqrt{b}} \cdot \dfrac{\sqrt{a} + \sqrt{b}}{\sqrt{a} + \sqrt{b}}$

$= \dfrac{a - b}{a + 2\sqrt{ab} + b}$

97. $\sqrt{1 + x^2} + \dfrac{1}{\sqrt{1 + x^2}}$

$= \sqrt{1 + x^2} \cdot \dfrac{1 + x^2}{1 + x^2} + \dfrac{1}{\sqrt{1 + x^2}} \quad \dfrac{\sqrt{1 + x^2}}{\sqrt{1 + x^2}}$

$= \dfrac{(1 + x^2)\sqrt{1 + x^2}}{1 + x^2} + \dfrac{\sqrt{1 + x^2}}{1 + x^2}$

$= \dfrac{(2 + x^2)\left(\sqrt{1 + x^2}\right)}{1 + x^2}$

98. $\sqrt{1 - x^2} - \dfrac{x^2}{2\sqrt{1 - x^2}}$

$= \sqrt{1 - x^2} - \dfrac{x^2 \sqrt{1 - x^2}}{2(1 - x^2)} \qquad$ (Rationalizing the denominator)

$= \dfrac{2(1 - x^2)\sqrt{1 - x^2} - x^2 \sqrt{1 - x^2}}{2(1 - x^2)}$

$= \dfrac{(2 - 3x^2)\sqrt{1 - x^2}}{2(1 - x^2)}$

99. Let $a = 16$ and $b = 9$.

Then $\sqrt{a + b} = \sqrt{16 + 9} = \sqrt{25} = 5$

and $\sqrt{a} + \sqrt{b} = \sqrt{16} + \sqrt{9} = 4 + 3 = 7$.

100. $\left(\sqrt{5 + \sqrt{24}}\right)^2 = 5 + \sqrt{24} = 5 + 2\sqrt{6}$

$\left(\sqrt{2} + \sqrt{3}\right)^2 = \left(\sqrt{2}\right)^2 + 2\sqrt{2}\sqrt{3} + \left(\sqrt{3}\right)^2$

$= 2 + 2\sqrt{6} + 3$

$= 5 + 2\sqrt{6}$

101. We substitute 0.1 for h, 0.03 for d, and 0.6 for v_0 in the formula.

$w = d\sqrt{\dfrac{v_0}{\sqrt{v_0^2 + 19.6h}}}$

$= 0.03\sqrt{\dfrac{0.6}{\sqrt{(0.6)^2 + 19.6(0.1)}}}$

$= 0.03\sqrt{\dfrac{0.6}{\sqrt{0.36 + 1.96}}}$

$= 0.03\sqrt{\dfrac{0.6}{\sqrt{2.32}}}$

$\approx 0.0188 \qquad$ (Using a calculator)

The width of the stream is about 0.0188 m.

102. $10\sqrt{26} - 51 \approx -0.0098$

$51 - 10\sqrt{26} \approx 0.0098$

$18 - 5\sqrt{13} \approx -0.0278$

$3\sqrt{11} - 10 \approx -0.0501$

$10 - 3\sqrt{11} \approx 0.0501$

The smallest positive number is $51 - 10\sqrt{26}$.

103. a) We substitute 6.672×10^{-11} for G, 5.97×10^{24} for M, 6.37×10^6 for R in the formula.

$V_0 = \sqrt{\dfrac{2GM}{R}}$

$= \sqrt{\dfrac{2 \times 6.672 \times 10^{-11} \times 5.97 \times 10^{24}}{6.37 \times 10^6}}$

$\approx 11{,}183 \qquad$ (Using a calculator)

The escape velocity is about 11,183 m/sec.

b) We substitute 6.672×10^{-11} for G, 6.27×10^{23} for M, and 3.3917×10^6 for R in the formula.

$V_0 = \sqrt{\dfrac{2GM}{R}}$

$= \sqrt{\dfrac{2 \times 6.672 \times 10^{-11} \times 6.27 \times 10^{23}}{3.3917 \times 10^6}}$

$\approx 4967 \qquad$ (Using a calculator)

The escape velocity is about 4967 m/sec.

Exercise Set 1.8

1. $x^{3/4} = \sqrt[4]{x^3}$

2. $\sqrt[5]{y^2}$

3. $16^{3/4} = (16^{1/4})^3 = \left(\sqrt[4]{16}\right)^3 = 2^3 = 8$

4. $4^{7/2} = (\sqrt{4})^7 = 2^7 = 128$

5. $125^{-1/3} = \dfrac{1}{125^{1/3}} = \dfrac{1}{\sqrt[3]{125}} = \dfrac{1}{5}$

6. $32^{-4/5} = \left(\sqrt[5]{32}\right)^{-4} = 2^{-4} = \dfrac{1}{16}$

7. $a^{5/4} b^{-3/4} = \dfrac{a^{5/4}}{b^{3/4}} = \dfrac{\sqrt[4]{a^5}}{\sqrt[4]{b^3}} = \dfrac{a\sqrt[4]{a}}{\sqrt[4]{b^3}}$, or $\dfrac{a\sqrt[4]{ab}}{b}$

8. $x^{2/5}y^{-1/5} = \sqrt[5]{\dfrac{x^2}{y}} = \dfrac{\sqrt[5]{x^2y^4}}{y}$

9. $\sqrt[3]{20^2} = 20^{2/3}$

10. $17^{3/5}$

11. $\left(\sqrt[4]{13}\right)^5 = \sqrt[4]{13^5} = 13^{5/4}$, or $\sqrt[4]{13^5} = 13\sqrt[4]{13}$

12. $12^{4/5}$

13. $\sqrt[3]{\sqrt{11}} = \left(\sqrt{11}\right)^{1/3} = (11^{1/2})^{1/3} = 11^{1/6}$

14. $\sqrt[3]{\sqrt[4]{7}} = (7^{1/4})^{1/3} = 7^{1/12}$

15. $\sqrt{5}\,\sqrt[3]{5} = 5^{1/2} \cdot 5^{1/3} = 5^{1/2 + 1/3} = 5^{5/6}$

16. $\sqrt[3]{2}\,\sqrt{2} = 2^{1/3} \cdot 2^{1/2} = 2^{5/6}$

17. $\sqrt[5]{32^2} = 32^{2/5} = (32^{1/5})^2 = 2^2 = 4$

18. $\sqrt[3]{64^{-2}} = (\sqrt[3]{64})^{-2} = 4^{-2} = \dfrac{1}{16}$

19. $\sqrt[3]{8y^6} = (8y^6)^{1/3} = (2^3y^6)^{1/3} = 2^{3/3}y^{6/3} = 2y^2$

20. $2c^2d^3$

21. $\sqrt[3]{a^2 + b^2} = (a^2 + b^2)^{1/3}$

22. $(a^3 - b^3)^{1/4}$

23. $\sqrt[3]{27a^3b^9} = (3^3a^3b^9)^{1/3} = 3^{3/3}a^{3/3}b^{9/3} = 3ab^3$

24. $3x^2y^2$

25. $\sqrt[6]{\dfrac{m^{12}n^{24}}{64}} = \left[\dfrac{m^{12}n^{24}}{2^6}\right]^{1/6} = \dfrac{m^{12/6}n^{24/6}}{2^{6/6}} = \dfrac{m^2n^4}{2}$

26. $\dfrac{m^2n^3}{2}$

27. $(2a^{3/2})(4a^{1/2}) = 8a^{3/2 + 1/2} = 8a^2$

28. $(3a^{5/6})(8a^{2/3}) = 24a^{3/2} = 24a\sqrt{a}$

29. $\left[\dfrac{x^6}{9b^{-4}}\right]^{-1/2} = \left[\dfrac{x^6}{3^2b^{-4}}\right]^{-1/2} = \dfrac{x^{-3}}{3^{-1}b^2} = \dfrac{3}{x^3b^2}$

30. $\left[\dfrac{x^{2/3}}{4y^{-2}}\right]^{-1/2} = \dfrac{x^{-1/3}}{4^{-1/2}y} = \dfrac{2}{y\sqrt[3]{x}} = \dfrac{2\sqrt[3]{x^2}}{xy}$

31. $\dfrac{x^{2/3}y^{5/6}}{x^{-1/3}y^{1/2}} = x^{2/3-(-1/3)}y^{5/6-1/2} = xy^{1/3} = x\sqrt[3]{y}$

32. $\dfrac{a^{1/2}b^{5/8}}{a^{1/4}b^{3/8}} = a^{1/4}b^{1/4} = \sqrt[4]{ab}$

33. $\sqrt[3]{6}\,\sqrt{2} = 6^{1/3}2^{1/2} = 6^{2/6}2^{3/6}$
$= (6^2 2^3)^{1/6}$
$= \sqrt[6]{36 \cdot 8}$
$= \sqrt[6]{288}$

34. $\sqrt{2}\,\sqrt[4]{8} = 2^{1/2}(2^3)^{1/4} = 2^{1/2}2^{3/4} = 2^{5/4} =$
$= \sqrt[4]{2^5} = 2\sqrt[4]{2}$

35. $\sqrt[4]{xy}\,\sqrt[3]{x^2y} = (xy)^{1/4}(x^2y)^{1/3} = (xy)^{3/12}(x^2y)^{4/12}$
$= \left[(xy)^3(x^2y)^4\right]^{1/12}$
$= [x^3y^3x^8y^4]^{1/12}$
$= \sqrt[12]{x^{11}y^7}$

36. $\sqrt[3]{ab^2}\,\sqrt{ab} = (ab^2)^{1/3}(ab)^{1/2} = (ab^2)^{2/6}(ab)^{3/6} =$
$\sqrt[6]{(ab^2)^2(ab)^3} = \sqrt[6]{a^5b^7} = b\sqrt[6]{a^5b}$

37. $\sqrt[3]{a^4\sqrt{a^3}} = \left[a^4\sqrt{a^3}\right]^{1/3} = (a^4a^{3/2})^{1/3}$
$= (a^{11/2})^{1/3}$
$= a^{11/6}$
$= \sqrt[6]{a^{11}}$
$= a\sqrt[6]{a^5}$

38. $\sqrt{a^3\sqrt[3]{a^2}} = (a^3 \cdot a^{2/3})^{1/2} = (a^{11/3})^{1/2} = a^{11/6} =$
$\sqrt[6]{a^{11}} = a\sqrt[6]{a^5}$

39. $\dfrac{\sqrt{(a+x)^3}\,\sqrt[3]{(a+x)^2}}{\sqrt[4]{a+x}} = \dfrac{(a+x)^{3/2}(a+x)^{2/3}}{(a+x)^{1/4}}$
$= \dfrac{(a+x)^{26/12}}{(a+x)^{3/12}}$
$= (a+x)^{23/12}$
$= \sqrt[12]{(a+x)^{23}}$
$= (a+x)\sqrt[12]{(a+x)^{11}}$

40. $\dfrac{\sqrt[4]{(x+y)^2}\,\sqrt[3]{x+y}}{\sqrt{(x+y)^3}} = \dfrac{(x+y)^{2/4}(x+y)^{1/3}}{(x+y)^{3/2}} =$
$= (x+y)^{-2/3} = \dfrac{1}{\sqrt[3]{(x+y)^2}} = \dfrac{\sqrt[3]{x+y}}{x+y}$

41. $\left[\sqrt[4]{13}\right]^5 = 13^{5/4} = 13^{1.25} \approx 24.685$

42. 8.372

43. $12.3^{3/2} = 12.3^{1.5} \approx 43.138$

44. 2.098

45. $105.6^{3/4} = 105.6^{0.75} \approx 32.942$

46. 11.671

47. $L = \dfrac{0.000169d^{2.27}}{h}$
$= \dfrac{0.000169(180)^{2.27}}{4}$
$\approx 5.56 \text{ ft}$

48. $L = \dfrac{0.000169(100)^{2.27}}{4} \approx 1.46 \text{ ft}$

49. $L = \dfrac{0.000169d^{2.27}}{h}$

    $L = \dfrac{0.000169(200)^{2.27}}{4}$

    ≈ 7.07 ft

50. $L = \dfrac{0.000169(300)^{2.27}}{4} \approx 17.74$ ft

51. $T = 34\,x^{-0.41}$

    When $x = 1$:   When $x = 6$:
    $T = 34(1)^{-0.41}$ $T = 34(6)^{-0.41}$
    $= 34$ hr ≈ 16.3 hr

    When $x = 8$:   When $x = 10$:
    $T = 34(8)^{-0.41}$ $T = 34(10)^{-0.41}$
    ≈ 14.5 hr ≈ 13.2 hr

    When $x = 32$:   When $x = 64$:
    $T = 34(32)^{-0.41}$ $T = 34(64)^{-0.41}$
    ≈ 8.2 hr ≈ 6.2 hr

52. 25.6 hr, 21.7 hr, 17.6 hr, 13.8 hr, 12.7 hr, 10.2 hr, 5.1 hr

53. $a^{-2}b^5 - a^3b^{-5}$

    a) The variables common to both terms involve powers of a and b.

    b) a^{-2} has a smaller exponent than a^3.
       b^{-5} has a smaller exponent than b^5.

    c) $a^{-2}b^{-5}$ factored out of $a^{-2}b^5$ leaves $a^{-2-(-2)}b^{5-(-5)} = a^0b^{10} = b^{10}$.
       $a^{-2}b^{-5}$ factored out of a^3b^{-5} leaves $a^{3-(-2)}b^{-5-(-5)} = a^5b^0 = a^5$.

    d) Thus,
       $a^{-2}b^5 - a^3b^{-5} = a^{-2}b^{-5}(b^{10} - a^5) = \dfrac{b^{10} - a^5}{a^2b^5}$.

54. $p^8q^{-2} + p^{-5}q^4 = q^{-2}p^{-5}(p^{13} + q^6) = \dfrac{p^{13} + q^6}{q^2p^5}$

55. $5a^{2/3}b^{-1/2} + 2a^{-1/3}b^{1/2}$

    a) The variables common to both terms involve powers of a and b.

    b) $a^{-1/3}$ has a smaller exponent than $a^{2/3}$.
       $b^{-1/2}$ has a smaller exponent than $b^{1/2}$.

    c) $a^{-1/3}b^{-1/2}$ factored out of $5a^{2/3}b^{-1/2}$ leaves $5a^{2/3-(-1/3)}b^{-1/2-(-1/2)} = 5a^1b^0 = 5a$.
       $a^{-1/3}b^{-1/2}$ factored out of $2a^{-1/3}b^{1/2}$ leaves $2a^{-1/3-(-1/3)}b^{1/2-(-1/2)} = 2a^0b^1 = 2b$.

56. $p^{4/5}q^{-2} + 2p^{-1/5}q^2 = p^{-1/5}q^{-2}(p + 2q^4) = \dfrac{p + 2q^4}{p^{1/5}q^2}$

57. $x^{-1/3}y^{3/4} - x^{2/3}y^{-1/4}$

    a) The variables common to both terms involve powers of x and y.

    b) $x^{-1/3}$ has a smaller exponent than $x^{2/3}$.
       $y^{-1/4}$ has a smaller exponent than $y^{3/4}$.

    c) $x^{-1/3}y^{-1/4}$ factored out of $x^{-1/3}y^{3/4}$ leaves $x^{-1/3-(-1/3)}y^{3/4-(-1/4)} = x^0y^1 = y$.
       $x^{-1/3}y^{-1/4}$ factored out of $x^{2/3}y^{-1/4}$ leaves $x^{2/3-(-1/3)}y^{-1/4-(-1/4)} = x^1y^0 = x$.

    d) Thus,
       $x^{-1/3}y^{3/4} - x^{2/3}y^{-1/4} = x^{-1/3}y^{-1/4}(y - x) = \dfrac{y - x}{x^{1/3}y^{1/4}}$.

58. $4a^{1/2}b^{-3/4} - 6a^{-1/2}b^{1/4} = 2a^{-1/2}b^{-3/4}(2a - 3b) = \dfrac{2(2a - 3b)}{a^{1/2}b^{3/4}}$

59. $\quad (2x - 3)^{-3}(x + 1)^{5/4} + (2x - 3)^{-2}(x + 1)^{1/4}$

    $= (2x - 3)^{-3}(x + 1)^{1/4}[(x + 1) + (2x - 3)]$

    $\hspace{6cm}$ Factoring

    $= (2x - 3)^{-3}(x + 1)^{1/4}(3x - 2)$ $\quad$ Simplifying

    $= \dfrac{(x + 1)^{1/4}(3x - 2)}{(2x - 3)^3}$

60. $\quad 2x(5x + 3)^{2/3} + 3x^2(5x + 3)^{-1/3}$

    $= x(5x + 3)^{-1/3}[2(5x + 3) + 3x]$

    $= x(5x + 3)^{-1/3}(13x + 6)$

    $= \dfrac{x(13x + 6)}{(5x + 3)^{1/3}}$

61. $\quad 2(x+1)^{1/2}(3x+4)^{-3/4} - 10(x+1)^{-1/2}(3x+4)^{1/4}$

    $= 2(x + 1)^{-1/2}(3x + 4)^{-3/4}[(x + 1) - 5(3x + 4)]$

    $\hspace{6cm}$ Factoring

    $= 2(x + 1)^{-1/2}(3x + 4)^{-3/4}(x + 1 - 15x - 20)$

    $\hspace{6cm}$ Simplifying

    $= 2(x + 1)^{-1/2}(3x + 4)^{-3/4}(-14x - 19)$

    $= \dfrac{2(-14x - 19)}{(x + 1)^{1/2}(3x + 4)^{3/4}}$, or $\dfrac{-2(14x + 19)}{(x + 1)^{1/2}(3x + 4)^{3/4}}$

62. $-4(2x - 5)^{-3}(3x + 1)^{1/3} + 8(2x + 5)^{-2}(3x + 1)^{-2/3}$

$= -4(2x - 5)^{-3}(3x + 1)^{-2/3}[3x + 1 - 2(2x - 5)]$

$= -4(2x - 5)^{-3}(3x + 1)^{-2/3}(-x + 11)$

$= \dfrac{-4(-x + 11)}{(2x - 5)^3(3x + 1)^{2/3}}$, or $\dfrac{4(x - 11)}{(2x - 5)^3(3x + 1)^{2/3}}$

63. $3(x^2 + 1)^3 + 3(3x - 5)(x^2 + 1)^2(2x)$

$= 3(x^2 + 1)^2[(x^2 + 1) + (3x - 5)(2x)]$ Factoring

$= 3(x^2 + 1)^2(x^2 + 1 + 6x^2 - 10x)$ Simplifying

$= 3(x^2 + 1)^2(7x^2 - 10x + 1)$

64. $3x^2(x - 1)^4 + x^3(4)(x - 1)^3$

$= x^2(x - 1)^3[3(x - 1) + 4x]$

$= x^2(x - 1)^3(7x - 3)$

65. $\dfrac{x^3(2x) - (x^2 + 1)(3x^2)}{x^6}$

$= \dfrac{2x^4 - 3x^4 - 3x^2}{x^6}$

$= \dfrac{-x^4 - 3x^2}{x^6} = \dfrac{x^2(-x^2 - 3)}{x^2 \cdot x^4}$

$= \dfrac{-x^2 - 3}{x^4}$

66. $\dfrac{1}{2}x^{-1/2}(x^3 - 4) + x^{1/2}(3x^2)$

$= x^{-1/2}\left[\dfrac{1}{2}(x^3 - 4) + x \cdot 3x^2\right]$

$= x^{-1/2}\left[\dfrac{x^3}{2} - 2 + 3x^3\right]$

$= x^{-1/2}\left[\dfrac{7}{2}x^3 - 2\right]$

$= \dfrac{7x^3 - 4}{2x^{1/2}}$

67. $\dfrac{x^2(x^2 + 1)^{-1/2}(x) - (2x)(x^2 + 1)^{1/2}}{x^4}$

$= \dfrac{x(x^2 + 1)^{-1/2}[x^2 - 2(x^2 + 1)]}{x^4}$

$= \dfrac{x(x^2 + 1)^{-1/2}(x^2 - 2x^2 - 2)}{x^4}$

$= \dfrac{x(x^2 + 1)^{-1/2}(-x^2 - 2)}{x \cdot x^3}$

$= \dfrac{-x^2 - 2}{x^3(x^2 + 1)^{1/2}}$

68. $\dfrac{(x - 1)^{1/2} - (x + 1)\left[\dfrac{1}{2}\right](x - 1)^{-1/2}}{x - 1}$

$= \dfrac{(x - 1)^{-1/2}\left[x - 1 - \dfrac{1}{2}(x + 1)\right]}{x - 1}$

$= \dfrac{(x - 1)^{-1/2}\left[\dfrac{1}{2}x - \dfrac{3}{2}\right]}{(x - 1)}$

$= \dfrac{x - 3}{2(x - 1)^{3/2}}$

69. $\left[\sqrt{a^{\sqrt{a}}}\right]^{\sqrt{a}} = \left[a^{\sqrt{a}/2}\right]^{\sqrt{a}} = a^{a/2}$

70. $\dfrac{(2a^3b^{5/4}c^{1/7})^4}{(54a^{-2}b^{2/3}c^{6/5})^{-1/3}} = \dfrac{16a^{12}b^5c^{4/7}}{54^{-1/3}a^{2/3}b^{-2/9}c^{-2/5}}$

$= 16\sqrt[3]{54}\, a^{34/3}b^{47/9}c^{34/35}$

$= 48 \cdot 2^{1/3} \cdot a^{34/3} \cdot b^{47/9} \cdot c^{34/35}$

Exercise Set 1.9

1. 36 ft $\cdot \dfrac{1 \text{ yd}}{3 \text{ ft}}$

$= \dfrac{36}{3} \cdot \dfrac{\text{ft}}{\text{ft}} \cdot \text{yd}$

$= 12$ yd

2. 6 lb $\cdot \dfrac{16 \text{ oz}}{1 \text{ lb}} = 6 \cdot 16$ oz $\cdot \dfrac{\text{lb}}{\text{lb}} = 96$ oz

3. 6 kg $\cdot 8\dfrac{\text{hr}}{\text{kg}}$

$= 6 \cdot 8 \cdot \dfrac{\text{kg}}{\text{kg}} \cdot \text{hr}$

$= 48$ hr

4. $9\dfrac{\text{km}}{\text{hr}} \cdot 3$ hr $= 9 \cdot 3$ km $\dfrac{\text{hr}}{\text{hr}} = 27$ km

5. 3 cm $\cdot \dfrac{2g}{2 \text{ cm}}$

$= \dfrac{3 \cdot 2}{2} \cdot \dfrac{\text{cm}}{\text{cm}} \cdot g$

$= 3$ g

6. $\dfrac{9 \text{ km}}{3 \text{ days}} \cdot 6$ days $= \dfrac{9 \cdot 6}{3}$ km $\dfrac{\text{days}}{\text{days}} = 18$ km

7. $6m + 2m$

$= (6 + 2)m$

$= 8$ m

8. 10 tons $+ 6$ tons $= (10 + 6)$ tons $= 16$ tons

9. 5 ft^3 $+ 7$ ft^3

$= (5 + 7)$ ft^3

$= 12$ ft^3

10. 10 yd^3 $+ 17$ yd^3 $= (10 + 17)$ yd^3 $= 27$ yd^3

11. $\dfrac{3 \text{ kg}}{5m} \cdot \dfrac{7 \text{ kg}}{6m}$

$= \dfrac{3 \cdot 7}{5 \cdot 6} \cdot \dfrac{\text{kg}}{m} \cdot \dfrac{\text{kg}}{m}$

$= \dfrac{7 \text{ kg}^2}{10 \text{ m}^2}$

12. 3 acres $\times 60\dfrac{1}{\text{acre}} = 3 \cdot 60 \cdot \dfrac{\text{acre}}{\text{acre}} = 180$

13. $$\frac{2000 \text{ lb} \cdot (6 \text{ mi/hr})^2}{100 \text{ ft}}$$

    $$= 2000 \text{ lb} \cdot \frac{36 \text{ mi}^2}{\text{hr}^2} \cdot \frac{1}{100 \text{ ft}}$$

    $$= \frac{2000 \cdot 36}{100} \cdot \text{lb} \cdot \frac{\text{mi}^2}{\text{hr}^2} \cdot \frac{1}{\text{ft}}$$

    $$= 720 \frac{\text{lb-mi}^2}{\text{hr}^2\text{-ft}}$$

14. $\dfrac{7 \text{ m} \cdot 8 \text{ kg/sec}}{4 \text{ sec}} = \dfrac{7 \cdot 8}{4} \text{ m} \cdot \dfrac{\text{kg}}{\text{sec}} \cdot \dfrac{1}{\text{sec}} = 14 \dfrac{\text{m-kg}}{\text{sec}^2}$

15. $$\frac{6 \text{ cm}^2 \cdot 5 \text{ cm/sec}}{2 \text{ sec}^2/\text{cm}^2 \cdot 2\frac{1}{\text{kg}}}$$

    $$= 6 \text{ cm}^2 \cdot \frac{5 \text{ cm}}{\text{sec}} \cdot \frac{\text{cm}^2}{2 \text{ sec}^2} \cdot \frac{\text{kg}}{2}$$

    $$= \frac{6 \cdot 5}{2 \cdot 2} \cdot \frac{\text{cm}^2 \cdot \text{cm} \cdot \text{cm}^2 \cdot \text{kg}}{\text{sec} \cdot \text{sec}^2}$$

    $$= \frac{15}{2} \frac{\text{cm}^5\text{-kg}}{\text{sec}^3}$$

16. $$\frac{320 \text{ lb} \cdot (5 \text{ ft/sec})^2}{2 \cdot 32 \frac{\text{ft}}{\text{sec}^2}}$$

    $$= \frac{320 \cdot 5^2}{2 \cdot 32} \cdot \text{lb} \cdot \frac{\text{ft}^2}{\text{sec}^2} \cdot \frac{\text{sec}^2}{\text{ft}}$$

    $$= 125 \text{ ft-lb}$$

17. $72 \text{ in.} = 72 \text{ in.} \cdot \dfrac{1 \text{ ft}}{12 \text{ in.}}$

    $$= \frac{72}{12} \cdot \frac{\text{in.}}{\text{in.}} \cdot \text{ft}$$

    $$= 6 \text{ ft}$$

18. $17 \text{ (hr)} = 17 \text{ (60 min)} = 1020 \text{ min}$

19. $2 \text{ days} = 2 \text{ days} \cdot \dfrac{24 \text{ hr}}{1 \text{ day}} \cdot \dfrac{60 \text{ min}}{1 \text{ hr}} \cdot \dfrac{60 \text{ sec}}{1 \text{ min}}$

    $$= 2 \cdot 24 \cdot 60 \cdot 60 \cdot \frac{\text{day}}{\text{day}} \cdot \frac{\text{hr}}{\text{hr}} \cdot \frac{\text{min}}{\text{min}} \cdot \text{sec}$$

    $$= 172,800 \text{ sec}$$

20. $360 \text{ (sec)} = 360 \left[\dfrac{1}{3600} \text{ hr}\right] = 0.1 \text{ hr}$

21. $60 \dfrac{\text{kg}}{\text{m}} = 60 \dfrac{\text{kg}}{\text{m}} \cdot \dfrac{1000 \text{ g}}{1 \text{ kg}} \cdot \dfrac{1 \text{ m}}{100 \text{ cm}}$

    $$= \frac{60 \cdot 1000}{100} \cdot \frac{\text{kg}}{\text{kg}} \cdot \frac{\text{m}}{\text{m}} \cdot \frac{\text{g}}{\text{cm}}$$

    $$= 600 \frac{\text{g}}{\text{cm}}$$

22. $44 \dfrac{\text{ft}}{\text{sec}} = 44 \dfrac{\left[\frac{1}{5280} \text{ mi}\right]}{\left[\frac{1}{3600} \text{ hr}\right]} = 30 \dfrac{\text{mi}}{\text{hr}}$

23. $216 \text{ m}^2 = 216 \cdot \text{m} \cdot \text{m}$

    $$= 216 \cdot 100 \text{ cm} \cdot 100 \text{ cm}$$

    $$= 2,160,000 \text{ cm}^2$$

24. $60 \dfrac{\text{lb}}{\text{ft}^3} = 60 \cdot \dfrac{\left[\frac{1}{2000} \text{ ton}\right]}{\left[\frac{1}{3} \text{ yd}\right]^3} = 0.81 \dfrac{\text{ton}}{\text{yd}^3}$

25. $\dfrac{\$36}{\text{day}} = \dfrac{\$36}{\text{day}} \cdot \dfrac{100\text{¢}}{\$1} \cdot \dfrac{1 \text{ day}}{24 \text{ hr}}$

    $$= \frac{36 \cdot 100}{24} \cdot \frac{\$}{\$} \cdot \frac{\text{day}}{\text{day}} \cdot \frac{\text{¢}}{\text{hr}}$$

    $$= 150 \frac{\text{¢}}{\text{hr}}$$

26. $1440 \text{ man (hr)} = 1440 \text{ man} \left[\dfrac{1}{24} \text{ day}\right] = 60 \text{ man-days}$

27. $1.73 \dfrac{\text{mL}}{\text{sec}} = 1.73 \dfrac{\text{mL}}{\text{sec}} \cdot \dfrac{1 \text{ L}}{1000 \text{ mL}} \cdot \dfrac{60 \text{ sec}}{1 \text{ min}} \cdot \dfrac{60 \text{ min}}{1 \text{ hr}}$

    $$= \frac{1.73 \cdot 60 \cdot 60}{1000} \cdot \frac{\text{mL}}{\text{mL}} \cdot \frac{\text{sec}}{\text{sec}} \cdot \frac{\text{min}}{\text{min}} \cdot \frac{\text{L}}{\text{hr}}$$

    $$= 6.228 \frac{\text{L}}{\text{hr}}$$

28. $1800 \cdot \dfrac{\text{g}}{\text{L}} = 1800 \cdot \dfrac{100 \text{ cg}}{1000 \text{ mL}} = 180 \dfrac{\text{cg}}{\text{mL}}$

29. $186,000 \dfrac{\text{mi}}{\text{sec}}$

    $$= 186,000 \frac{\text{mi}}{\text{sec}} \cdot \frac{60 \text{ sec}}{1 \text{ min}} \cdot \frac{60 \text{ min}}{1 \text{ hr}} \cdot \frac{24 \text{ hr}}{1 \text{ day}} \cdot \frac{365 \text{ days}}{1 \text{ yr}}$$

    $$= 186,000 \cdot 60 \cdot 60 \cdot 24 \cdot 365 \frac{\text{sec}}{\text{sec}} \cdot \frac{\text{min}}{\text{min}} \cdot \frac{\text{hr}}{\text{hr}} \cdot \frac{\text{day}}{\text{day}} \cdot \frac{\text{mi}}{\text{yr}}$$

    $$= 5,865,696,000,000 \frac{\text{mi}}{\text{yr}}$$

30. $1100 \dfrac{\text{ft}}{\text{sec}} = 1100 \dfrac{\frac{1}{5280} \text{ mi}}{\frac{1}{60} \cdot \frac{1}{60} \cdot \frac{1}{24} \cdot \frac{1}{365} \text{ yr}}$

    $$= 6,570,000 \frac{\text{mi}}{\text{yr}}$$

31. $89.2 \dfrac{\text{ft}}{\text{sec}} = 89.2 \dfrac{\text{ft}}{\text{sec}} \cdot \dfrac{1 \text{ m}}{3.3 \text{ ft}} \cdot \dfrac{60 \text{ sec}}{1 \text{ min}}$

    $$= \frac{89.2(60)}{3.3} \cdot \frac{\text{ft}}{\text{ft}} \cdot \frac{\text{sec}}{\text{sec}} \cdot \frac{\text{m}}{\text{min}}$$

    $$\approx 1621.8 \frac{\text{m}}{\text{min}}$$

32. $1013 \text{ yd}^3 = 1013 \text{ yd}^3 \left[\dfrac{1 \text{ m}}{1.1 \text{ yd}}\right]^3$

    $$= \frac{1013}{(1.1)^3} \text{ m}^3 \cdot \frac{\text{yd}^3}{\text{yd}^3}$$

    $$\approx 761.08 \text{ m}^3$$

33. $640 \text{ mi}^2 = 640 \text{ mi}^2 \left[\dfrac{1 \text{ km}}{0.62 \text{ mi}}\right]^2$

    $$= \frac{640}{(0.62)^2} \text{ km}^2 \cdot \frac{\text{mi}^2}{\text{mi}^2}$$

    $$\approx 1664.93 \text{ km}^2$$

34. $312.2 \dfrac{\text{kg}}{\text{m}} = 312.2 \left[\dfrac{2.2 \text{ lb}}{3.3 \text{ ft}}\right] \approx 208.13 \dfrac{\text{lb}}{\text{ft}}$

35. $3 \text{ cm} \cdot \dfrac{5 \text{ g}}{2 \text{ cm}} = \dfrac{3 \cdot 5}{2} \text{ g} \cdot \dfrac{\text{cm}}{\text{cm}} = 7.5 \text{ g}$

    A steel rod 3 cm long weighs 7.5 g.

    $5 \text{ m} \cdot \dfrac{100 \text{ cm}}{1 \text{ m}} \cdot \dfrac{5 \text{ g}}{2 \text{ cm}} = \dfrac{5 \cdot 100 \cdot 5}{2} \text{ g} \cdot \dfrac{\text{m}}{\text{m}} \cdot \dfrac{\text{cm}}{\text{cm}} = 1250 \text{ g}$

    A steel rod 5 m long weighs 1250 g.

36. $4.3 \text{ g} \cdot \dfrac{2 \text{ cm}}{5 \text{ g}} = \dfrac{4.3(2)}{5} \text{ cm} \cdot \dfrac{\text{g}}{\text{g}} = 1.72 \text{ cm}$

    $20 \text{ cg} \cdot \dfrac{1 \text{ g}}{100 \text{ cg}} \cdot \dfrac{2 \text{ cm}}{5 \text{ g}} = \dfrac{20 \cdot 2}{100 \cdot 5} \text{ cm} \cdot \dfrac{\text{cg}}{\text{cg}} \cdot \dfrac{\text{g}}{\text{g}} =$
    0.08 cm

37. 1 mole of oxygen is 32 grams.

    $\begin{aligned} 50 \text{ moles} &= 50 \cdot 1 \text{ mole} \\ &= 50 \cdot 32 \text{ g} \\ &= 1600 \text{ g} \end{aligned}$

    50 moles of oxygen is 1600 grams of oxygen.

38. $44 \text{ moles} = 44(20.2 \text{ g}) = 888.8 \text{ g}$

39. $303 \text{ g} = 303 \text{ g} \cdot \dfrac{1 \text{ mole}}{20.2 \text{ g}}$

    $\qquad = \dfrac{303}{20.2} \text{ moles} \cdot \dfrac{\text{g}}{\text{g}}$

    $\qquad = 15 \text{ moles}$

    303 grams of neon is 15 moles of neon.

40. $(377.6 \text{ g}) \cdot \dfrac{1 \text{ mole}}{32 \text{ g}} = \dfrac{377.6}{32} \text{ moles} \cdot \dfrac{\text{g}}{\text{g}} = 11.8 \text{ moles}$

41. $E = mc^2$

    Substitute 5000 g for m and 2.9979×10^8 m/sec for c.

    $\begin{aligned} E &= 5000 \text{ g}(2.9979 \times 10^8 \text{ m/sec})^2 \\ &\approx 44{,}937 \times 10^{16} \text{ g} \cdot \text{m}^2/\text{sec}^2 \\ &= (4.4937 \times 10^4) \times 10^{16} \text{ g} \cdot \text{m}^2/\text{sec}^2 \\ &= 4.4937 \times 10^{20} \text{ g} \cdot \text{m}^2/\text{sec}^2 \end{aligned}$

42. $18 \text{ mL} \cdot \dfrac{0.86 \text{ g}}{1 \text{ mL}} = (18)(0.86) \text{ g} \dfrac{\text{mL}}{\text{mL}} = 15.48 \text{ g}$

43. From Exercise 41 we know that the speed of light is 2.9979×10^8 m/sec. We convert m/sec to m/nanosecond.

    $2.9979 \times 10^8 \dfrac{\text{m}}{\text{sec}} \cdot \dfrac{10^{-9} \text{ sec}}{1 \text{ nanosecond}} =$

    $2.9979 \times 10^{-1} \dfrac{\text{m}}{\text{nanosecond}}, \text{ or } 0.29979 \dfrac{\text{m}}{\text{nanosecond}}$

    Light travels 0.29979 m in one nanosecond.

Exercise Set 2.1

1. $4x + 12 = 60$

    $4x + 12 - 12 = 60 - 12$

    $4x = 48$

    $\frac{1}{4} \cdot 4x = \frac{1}{4} \cdot 48$

    $x = 12$

    The solution set is {12}.

2. $2y - 11 = 37$

    $2y = 48$

    $y = 24$

    The solution set is {24}.

3. $4 + \frac{1}{2} x = 1$

    $4 + \frac{1}{2} x - 4 = 1 - 4$

    $\frac{1}{2} x = -3$

    $2 \cdot \frac{1}{2} x = 2(-3)$

    $x = -6$

    The solution set is {-6}.

4. $4.1 - 0.2y = 1.3$

    $-0.2y = -2.8$

    $y = 14$

    The solution set is {14}.

5. $y + 1 = 2y - 7$ or $y + 1 = 2y - 7$

    $1 + 7 = 2y - y$ $\quad$ $y - 2y = -7 - 1$

    $8 = y$ $\quad\quad\quad$ $-y = -8$

    $\quad\quad\quad\quad\quad\quad$ $y = 8$

    The solution set is {8}.

6. $5 - 4x = x - 13$

    $18 = 5x$

    $\frac{18}{5} = x$

    The solution set is $\left\{\frac{18}{5}\right\}$.

7. $5x - 2 + 3x = 2x + 6 - 4x$

    $8x - 2 = 6 - 2x$

    $8x + 2x = 6 + 2$

    $10x = 8$

    $x = \frac{8}{10}$

    $x = \frac{4}{5}$

    The solution set is $\left\{\frac{4}{5}\right\}$.

8. $5x - 17 - 2x = 6x - 1 - x$

    $3x - 17 = 5x - 1$

    $-2x = 16$

    $x = -8$

    The solution set is {-8}.

9. $1.9x - 7.8 + 5.3x = 3.0 + 1.8x$

    $7.2x - 7.8 = 3.0 + 1.8x$

    $7.2x - 1.8x = 3.0 + 7.8$

    $5.4x = 10.8$

    $x = \frac{10.8}{5.4}$

    $x = 2$

    The solution set is {2}.

10. $2.2y - 5 + 4.5y = 1.7y - 20$

    $6.7y - 5 = 1.7y - 20$

    $5y = -15$

    $y = -3$

    The solution set is {-3}.

11. $7(3x + 6) = 11 - (x + 2)$

    $21x + 42 = 11 - x - 2$

    $21x + 42 = 9 - x$

    $21x + x = 9 - 42$

    $22x = -33$

    $x = -\frac{33}{22}$

    $x = -\frac{3}{2}$

    The solution set is $\left\{-\frac{3}{2}\right\}$.

12. $4(5y + 3) = 3(2y - 5)$

    $20y + 12 = 6y - 15$

    $14y = -27$

    $y = -\frac{27}{14}$

    The solution set is $\left\{-\frac{27}{14}\right\}$.

13. $2x - (5 + 7x) = 4 - [x - (2x + 3)]$

    $2x - 5 - 7x = 4 - x + 2x + 3$

    $-5x - 5 = 7 + x$

    $-5 - 7 = x + 5x$

    $-12 = 6x$

    $-\frac{12}{6} = x$

    $-2 = x$

    The solution set is {-2}.

14. $y - (9y - 8) = 5 - 2y - 3(2y - 3) + 29$

 $y - 9y + 8 = 5 - 2y - 6y + 9 + 29$

  $-8y + 8 = -8y + 43$

   $8 = 43$ False equation

The solution set is $\emptyset$.

15. $(2x - 3)(3x - 2) = 0$

 $2x - 3 = 0$ or $3x - 2 = 0$

 $2x = 3$ or $3x = 2$

 $x = \frac{3}{2}$ or $x = \frac{2}{3}$

The solution set is $\left\{\frac{3}{2}, \frac{2}{3}\right\}$.

16. $(5x - 2)(2x + 3) = 0$

 $x = \frac{2}{5}$ or $x = -\frac{3}{2}$

The solution set is $\left\{\frac{2}{5}, -\frac{3}{2}\right\}$.

17. $x(x - 1)(x + 2) = 0$

 $x = 0$ or $x - 1 = 0$ or $x + 2 = 0$

 $x = 0$ or $x = 1$ or $x = -2$

The solution set is $\{0, 1, -2\}$.

18. $x(x + 2)(x - 3) = 0$

 $x = 0$ or $x = -2$ or $x = 3$

The solution set is $\{0, -2, 3\}$.

19. $3x^2 + x - 2 = 0$

 $(3x - 2)(x + 1) = 0$

 $3x - 2 = 0$ or $x + 1 = 0$

  $x = \frac{2}{3}$ or $x = -1$

The solution set is $\left\{\frac{2}{3}, -1\right\}$.

20. $10x^2 - 16x + 6 = 0$

 $2(5x - 3)(x - 1) = 0$

 $x = \frac{3}{5}$ or $x = 1$

The solution set is $\left\{\frac{3}{5}, 1\right\}$.

21. $(x - 1)(x + 1) = 5(x - 1)$

   $x^2 - 1 = 5x - 5$

  $x^2 - 5x + 4 = 0$

 $(x - 4)(x - 1) = 0$

 $x - 4 = 0$ or $x - 1 = 0$

  $x = 4$ or $x = 1$

The solution set is $\{4, 1\}$.

22. $6(y - 3) = (y - 3)(y - 2)$

 $6y - 18 = y^2 - 5y + 6$

  $0 = y^2 - 11y + 24$

  $0 = (y - 8)(y - 3)$

 $y = 8$ or $y = 3$

The solution set is $\{8, 3\}$.

23. $x[4(x - 2) - 5(x - 1)] = 2$

 $x(4x - 8 - 5x + 5) = 2$

   $x(-x - 3) = 2$

   $-x^2 - 3x = 2$

    $0 = x^2 + 3x + 2$

    $0 = (x + 2)(x + 1)$

 $x + 2 = 0$ or $x + 1 = 0$

  $x = -2$ or $x = -1$

The solution set is $\{-2, -1\}$.

24. $14\left[(x - 4) - \frac{1}{14}(x + 2)\right] = (x + 2)(x - 4)$

 $14\left[x - 4 - \frac{1}{14}x - \frac{1}{7}\right] = x^2 - 2x - 8$

  $14\left[\frac{13}{14}x - \frac{29}{7}\right] = x^2 - 2x - 8$

   $13x - 58 = x^2 - 2x - 8$

    $0 = x^2 - 15x + 50$

    $0 = (x - 5)(x - 10)$

 $x = 5$ or $x = 10$

The solution set is $\{5, 10\}$.

25. $(3x^2 - 7x - 20)(2x - 5) = 0$

 $(3x + 5)(x - 4)(2x - 5) = 0$

 $3x + 5 = 0$ or $x - 4 = 0$ or $2x - 5 = 0$

  $x = -\frac{5}{3}$ or $x = 4$ or $x = \frac{5}{2}$

The solution set is $\left\{-\frac{5}{3}, 4, \frac{5}{2}\right\}$.

26. $(8x + 11)(12x^2 - 5x - 2) = 0$

 $(8x + 11)(4x + 1)(3x - 2) = 0$

 $x = -\frac{11}{8}$ or $x = -\frac{1}{4}$ or $x = \frac{2}{3}$

The solution set is $\left\{-\frac{11}{8}, -\frac{1}{4}, \frac{2}{3}\right\}$.

27. $16x^3 = x$

  $16x^3 - x = 0$

  $x(16x^2 - 1) = 0$

 $x(4x + 1)(4x - 1) = 0$

 $x = 0$ or $4x + 1 = 0$ or $4x - 1 = 0$

 $x = 0$ or $x = -\frac{1}{4}$ or $x = \frac{1}{4}$

The solution set is $\left\{0, -\frac{1}{4}, \frac{1}{4}\right\}$.

28.
$$9x^3 = x$$
$$9x^3 - x = 0$$
$$x(3x + 1)(3x - 1) = 0$$
$$x = 0 \quad \text{or} \quad x = -\frac{1}{3} \quad \text{or} \quad x = \frac{1}{3}$$
The solution set is $\left\{0, -\frac{1}{3}, \frac{1}{3}\right\}$.

29.
$$2x^2 = 6x$$
$$2x^2 - 6x = 0$$
$$2x(x - 3) = 0$$
$$2x = 0 \quad \text{or} \quad x - 3 = 0$$
$$x = 0 \quad \text{or} \quad x = 3$$
The solution set is $\{0, 3\}$.

30.
$$18x + 9x^2 = 0$$
$$9x(2 + x) = 0$$
$$x = 0 \quad \text{or} \quad x = -2$$
The solution set is $\{0, -2\}$.

31.
$$3y^3 - 5y^2 - 2y = 0$$
$$y(3y^2 - 5y - 2) = 0$$
$$y(3y + 1)(y - 2) = 0$$
$$y = 0 \quad \text{or} \quad 3y + 1 = 0 \quad \text{or} \quad y - 2 = 0$$
$$y = 0 \qquad y = -\frac{1}{3} \quad \text{or} \quad y = 2$$
The solution set is $\left\{0, -\frac{1}{3}, 2\right\}$

32.
$$3t^3 + 2t = 5t^2$$
$$3t^3 - 5t^2 + 2t = 0$$
$$t(t - 1)(3t - 2) = 0$$
$$t = 0 \quad \text{or} \quad t = 1 \quad \text{or} \quad t = \frac{2}{3}$$
The solution set is $\left\{0, 1, \frac{2}{3}\right\}$.

33.
$$(2x - 3)(3x + 2)(x - 1) = 0$$
$$2x - 3 = 0 \quad \text{or} \quad 3x + 2 = 0 \quad \text{or} \quad x - 1 = 0$$
$$x = \frac{3}{2} \quad \text{or} \quad x = -\frac{2}{3} \quad \text{or} \quad x = 1$$
The solution set is $\left\{\frac{3}{2}, -\frac{2}{3}, 1\right\}$.

34.
$$(y - 4)(4y + 12)(2y - 1) = 0$$
$$y = 4 \quad \text{or} \quad y = -3 \quad \text{or} \quad y = \frac{1}{2}$$
The solution set is $\left\{4, -3, \frac{1}{2}\right\}$.

35.
$$(2 - 4y)(y^2 + 3y) = 0$$
$$2(1 - 2y)y(y + 3) = 0$$
$$1 - 2y = 0 \quad \text{or} \quad y = 0 \quad \text{or} \quad y + 3 = 0$$
$$y = \frac{1}{2} \quad \text{or} \quad y = 0 \quad \text{or} \quad y = -3$$
The solution set is $\left\{\frac{1}{2}, 0, -3\right\}$.

36.
$$(y^2 - 9)(y^2 - 36) = 0$$
$$(y + 3)(y - 3)(y + 6)(y - 6) = 0$$
$$y = -3 \quad \text{or} \quad y = 3 \quad \text{or} \quad y = -6 \quad \text{or} \quad y = 6$$
The solution set is $\{-3, 3, -6, 6\}$.

37.
$$x + 4 = 8 + x$$
$$-x + x + 4 = -x + 8 + x$$
$$4 = 8$$
We get a false equation. There are no solutions, so the solution set is $\varnothing$.

38.
$$x - 7 = 9 + x$$
$$-7 = 9 \quad \text{False equation}$$
The solution set is $\varnothing$.

39.
$$7x^3 + x^2 - 7x - 1 = 0$$
$$x^2(7x + 1) - (7x + 1) = 0$$
$$(x^2 - 1)(7x + 1) = 0$$
$$(x + 1)(x - 1)(7x + 1) = 0$$
$$x + 1 = 0 \quad \text{or} \quad x - 1 = 0 \quad \text{or} \quad 7x + 1 = 0$$
$$x = -1 \quad \text{or} \quad x = 1 \quad \text{or} \quad x = -\frac{1}{7}$$
The solution set is $\left\{-1, 1, -\frac{1}{7}\right\}$.

40.
$$3x^3 + x^2 - 12x - 4 = 0$$
$$x^2(3x + 1) - 4(3x + 1) = 0$$
$$(3x + 1)(x^2 - 4) = 0$$
$$(3x + 1)(x + 2)(x - 2) = 0$$
$$x = -\frac{1}{3} \quad \text{or} \quad x = -2 \quad \text{or} \quad x = 2$$
The solution set is $\left\{-\frac{1}{3}, -2, 2\right\}$.

41.
$$y^3 + 2y^2 - y - 2 = 0$$
$$y^2(y + 2) - (y + 2) = 0$$
$$(y^2 - 1)(y + 2) = 0$$
$$(y + 1)(y - 1)(y + 2) = 0$$
$$y + 1 = 0 \quad \text{or} \quad y - 1 = 0 \quad \text{or} \quad y + 2 = 0$$
$$y = -1 \quad \text{or} \quad y = 1 \quad \text{or} \quad y = -2$$
The solution set is $\{-1, 1, -2\}$.

42. $t^3 + t^2 - 25t - 25 = 0$
$t^2(t + 1) - 25(t + 1) = 0$
$(t + 1)(t^2 - 25) = 0$
$(t + 1)(t + 5)(t - 5) = 0$
$t = -1$ or $t = -5$ or $t = 5$

The solution set is $\{-1, -5, 5\}$.

43. $11 + x = x + 11$
$-x + 11 + x = -x + x + 11$
$11 = 11$

We get a true equation. The solution set is the set of all real numbers.

44. $0 \cdot x = 0$
$0 = 0$

The solution set is the set of all real numbers.

45. $x + 6 < 5x - 6$ or $x + 6 < 5x - 6$
$6 + 6 < 5x - x$ $x - 5x < -6 - 6$
$12 < 4x$ $-4x < -12$
$\dfrac{12}{4} < x$ $x > \dfrac{-12}{-4}$
$3 < x$ $x > 3$

The solution set is $\{x \mid x > 3\}$.

46. $3 - x < 4x + 7$
$-5x < 4$
$x > -\dfrac{4}{5}$

The solution set is $\left\{x \mid x > -\dfrac{4}{5}\right\}$.

47. $3x - 3 + 2x \geqslant 1 - 7x - 9$
$5x - 3 \geqslant -7x - 8$
$5x + 7x \geqslant -8 + 3$
$12x \geqslant -5$
$x \geqslant -\dfrac{5}{12}$

The solution set is $\left\{x \mid x \geqslant -\dfrac{5}{12}\right\}$.

48. $5y - 5 + y \leqslant 2 - 6y - 8$
$6y - 5 \leqslant -6y - 6$
$12y \leqslant -1$
$y \leqslant -\dfrac{1}{12}$

The solution set is $\left\{y \mid y \leqslant -\dfrac{1}{12}\right\}$.

49. $14 - 5y \leqslant 8y - 8$ or $14 - 5y \leqslant 8y - 8$
$14 + 8 \leqslant 8y + 5y$ $-5y - 8y \leqslant -8 - 14$
$22 \leqslant 13y$ $-13y \leqslant -22$
$\dfrac{22}{13} \leqslant y$ $y \geqslant \dfrac{22}{13}$

The solution set is $\left\{y \mid y \geqslant \dfrac{22}{13}\right\}$.

50. $8x - 7 < 6x + 3$
$2x < 10$
$x < 5$

The solution set is $\{x \mid x < 5\}$.

51. $-\dfrac{3}{4}x \geqslant -\dfrac{5}{8} + \dfrac{2}{3}x$
$\dfrac{5}{8} \geqslant \dfrac{3}{4}x + \dfrac{2}{3}x$
$\dfrac{5}{8} \geqslant \dfrac{9}{12}x + \dfrac{8}{12}x$
$\dfrac{5}{8} \geqslant \dfrac{17}{12}x$
$\dfrac{12}{17} \cdot \dfrac{5}{8} \geqslant \dfrac{12}{17} \cdot \dfrac{17}{12}x$
$\dfrac{15}{34} \geqslant x$

The solution set is $\left\{x \mid x \leqslant \dfrac{15}{34}\right\}$.

52. $-\dfrac{5}{6}x \leqslant \dfrac{3}{4} + \dfrac{8}{3}x$
$-\dfrac{21}{6}x \leqslant \dfrac{3}{4}$
$x \geqslant -\dfrac{3}{14}$

The solution set is $\left\{x \mid x \geqslant -\dfrac{3}{14}\right\}$.

53. $4x(x - 2) < 2(2x - 1)(x - 3)$
$4x(x - 2) < 2(2x^2 - 7x + 3)$
$4x^2 - 8x < 4x^2 - 14x + 6$
$-8x < -14x + 6$
$-8x + 14x < 6$
$6x < 6$
$x < \dfrac{6}{6}$
$x < 1$

The solution set is $\{x \mid x < 1\}$.

54. $(x + 1)(x + 2) > x(x + 1)$
$x^2 + 3x + 2 > x^2 + x$
$2x > -2$
$x > -1$

The solution set is $\{x \mid x > -1\}$.

55. $\{x \mid x > 2.5\}$

56. $\{y \mid y \leqslant -7\}$

57. $2t^2 = 10$

   $t^2 = 5$

   The solution set is $\{t \mid t^2 = 5\}$.

58. $\{m \mid m^3 + 3 = m^2 - 2\}$

59. $\sqrt{x - 3}$

   The radicand must be nonnegative. We set
   $x - 3 \geqslant 0$ and solve for x.

   $x - 3 \geqslant 0$

   $x \geqslant 3$

   The meaningful replacements are $\{x \mid x \geqslant 3\}$.

60. $2x - 5 \geqslant 0$

   $2x \geqslant 5$

   $x \geqslant \dfrac{5}{2}$

   The meaningful replacements are $\left\{x \mid x \geqslant \dfrac{5}{2}\right\}$.

61. $\sqrt{3 - 4x}$

   The radicand must be nonnegative. We set
   $3 - 4x \geqslant 0$ and solve for x.

   $3 - 4x \geqslant 0$

   $-4x \geqslant -3$

   $x \leqslant \dfrac{3}{4}$

   The meaningful replacements are $\left\{x \mid x \leqslant \dfrac{3}{4}\right\}$.

62. $x^2 + 3 \geqslant 0$ for all real values of x. The
   meaningful replacements are
   $\{x \mid x$ is a real number$\}$.

63. $2.905x - 3.214 + 6.789x = 3.012 + 1.805x$

   $9.694x - 3.214 = 3.012 + 1.805x$

   $9.694x - 1.805x = 3.012 + 3.214$

   $7.889x = 6.226$

   $x = \dfrac{6.226}{7.889}$

   $x \approx 0.7892$

   The solution set is $\{0.7892\}$.

64. $\{-1.3053, 1.9892\}$

65. $3.12x^2 - 6.715x = 0$

   $x(3.12x - 6.715) = 0$

   $x = 0$ or $3.12x - 6.715 = 0$

   $x = 0$ or $\qquad 3.12x = 6.715$

   $x = 0$ or $\qquad\qquad x \approx 2.1522$

   The solution set is $\{0, 2.1522\}$.

66. $9.25x^2 + 18.03x = 0$

   $x(9.25x + 18.03) = 0$

   $x = 0$ or $x \approx -1.9492$

   The solution set is $\{0, -1.9492\}$.

67. $1.52(6.51x + 7.3) < 11.2 - (7.2x + 13.52)$

   $9.8952x + 11.096 < 11.2 - 7.2x - 13.52$

   $9.8952x + 11.096 < -7.2x - 2.32$

   $9.8952x + 7.2x < -2.32 - 11.096$

   $17.0952x < -13.416$

   $x < -\dfrac{13.416}{17.0952}$

   $x < -0.7848$

   The solution set is $\{x \mid x < -0.7848\}$.

68. $4.73(5.16y + 3.62) \geqslant 3.005(2.75y - 6.31)$

   $24.4068y + 17.1226 \geqslant 8.26375y - 18.96155$

   $16.14305y \geqslant -36.08415$

   $y \geqslant -2.2353$

   The solution set is $\{y \mid y \geqslant -2.2353\}$.

69. $(x + 1)^3 = (x - 1)^3 + 26$

   $x^3 + 3x^2 + 3x + 1 = x^3 - 3x^2 + 3x - 1 + 26$

   $x^3 + 3x^2 + 3x + 1 = x^3 - 3x^2 + 3x + 25$

   $6x^2 - 24 = 0$

   $6(x^2 - 4) = 0$

   $6(x + 2)(x - 2) = 0$

   $x + 2 = 0$ or $x - 2 = 0$

   $x = -2$ or $\qquad x = 2$

   The solution set is $\{-2, 2\}$.

70. $(x - 2)^3 = x^3 - 2$

   $x^3 - 6x^2 + 12x - 8 = x^3 - 2$

   $0 = 6x^2 - 12x + 6$

   $0 = 6(x - 1)^2$

   $x = 1$

   The solution set is $\{1\}$.

71. $(x^2 - x - 20)(x^2 - 25) = 0$

   $(x - 5)(x + 4)(x + 5)(x - 5) = 0$

   $x - 5 = 0$ or $x + 4 = 0$ or $x + 5 = 0$ or $x - 5 = 0$

   $x = 5$ or $\quad x = -4$ or $\quad x = -5$ or $\quad x = 5$

   The solution set is $\{5, -4, -5\}$.

72. $(x^3 - 3x^2 - 16x + 48)(x^3 + x^2 - 9x - 9) = 0$

   $[x^2(x - 3) - 16(x - 3)][x^2(x + 1) - 9(x + 1)] = 0$

   $(x^2 - 16)(x - 3)(x^2 - 9)(x + 1) = 0$

   $(x + 4)(x - 4)(x - 3)(x + 3)(x - 3)(x + 1) = 0$

   $x = -4$ or $x = 4$ or $x = 3$ or $x = -3$ or $x = -1$

   The solution set is $\{-4, 4, 3, -3, -1\}$.

Exercise Set 2.2

1. $3x + 5 = 12$ $3x = 7$

       $3x = 7$ $x = \frac{7}{3}$

         $x = \frac{7}{3}$

                  The solution set is $\left\{\frac{7}{3}\right\}$.

The solution set is $\left\{\frac{7}{3}\right\}$.

The equations are equivalent.

2. $x^2 = -7x$ $x = -7$

   $x^2 + 7x = 0$ The solution set is $\{-7\}$.

$x(x + 7) = 0$

The solution set is
$\{0, -7\}$.

The equations are not equivalent.

3. $x = 3$ $x^2 = 9$

The solution set is $\{3\}$. $x = \pm\, 3$

               The solution set is
               $\{-3, 3\}$.

The equations are not equivalent.

4. $2y + 1 = -3$ $8y + 4 = -12$

      $y = -2$ $y = -2$

The solution set   The solution set
is $\{-2\}$.   is $\{-2\}$.

The equations are equivalent.

5. $\dfrac{(x - 3)(x + 9)}{(x - 3)} = x + 9$,   Note: $x \neq 3$

         $x + 9 = x + 9$

            $9 = 9$

The solution set is the set of all real numbers
except 3.

$x + 9 = x + 9$

     $9 = 9$

The solution set is the set of all real numbers.
Thus, the equations are not equivalent.

6. $x^2 + x - 20 = 0$ $x^2 - 25 = 0$

$(x + 5)(x - 4) = 0$ $(x + 5)(x - 5) = 0$

The solution set is   The solution set is
$\{-5, 4\}$. $\{-5, 5\}$.

The equations are not equivalent.

7. $\dfrac{1}{4} + \dfrac{1}{5} = \dfrac{1}{t}$,   LCM is 20t

      $20t\left(\dfrac{1}{4} + \dfrac{1}{5}\right) = 20t \cdot \dfrac{1}{t}$

$20t \cdot \dfrac{1}{4} + 20t \cdot \dfrac{1}{5} = 20t \cdot \dfrac{1}{t}$

          $5t + 4t = 20$

             $9t = 20$

               $t = \dfrac{20}{9}$

Check:

$$\dfrac{1}{4} + \dfrac{1}{5} = \dfrac{1}{t}$$

$\dfrac{1}{4} + \dfrac{1}{5}$	$\dfrac{1}{\frac{20}{9}}$
$\dfrac{5}{20} + \dfrac{4}{20}$	$1 \cdot \dfrac{9}{20}$
$\dfrac{9}{20}$	$\dfrac{9}{20}$ TRUE

The solution set is $\left\{\dfrac{20}{9}\right\}$.

8. $\dfrac{1}{3} - \dfrac{5}{6} = \dfrac{1}{x}$,   LCM is 6x

$2x - 5x = 6$

    $-3x = 6$

       $x = -2$

-2 checks.   The solution set is $\{-2\}$.

9. $\dfrac{3}{x - 8} = \dfrac{x - 5}{x - 8}$,   LCM is $x - 8$

$(x - 8) \cdot \dfrac{3}{x - 8} = (x - 8) \cdot \dfrac{x - 5}{x - 8}$ Check:

              $3 = x - 5$ $\dfrac{3}{x - 8} = \dfrac{x - 5}{x - 8}$

              $8 = x$

The solution set is $\emptyset$.

$\dfrac{3}{8 - 8}$	$\dfrac{8 - 5}{8 - 8}$
$\dfrac{3}{0}$	$\dfrac{3}{0}$

Division by
zero is
undefined.

10. $\dfrac{23}{y} = -\dfrac{5}{y}$,   LCM is y

$23 = -5$ False equation

The solution set is $\emptyset$.

11. $\dfrac{x + 2}{4} - \dfrac{x - 1}{5} = 15$,   LCM is 20

   $20\left(\dfrac{x + 2}{4} - \dfrac{x - 1}{5}\right) = 20 \cdot 15$

$5(x + 2) - 4(x - 1) = 300$

    $5x + 10 - 4x + 4 = 300$

            $x + 14 = 300$

                 $x = 286$

The solution set is $\{286\}$.

12. $\dfrac{t + 1}{3} - \dfrac{t - 1}{2} = 1$,   LCM is 6

All replacements are meaningful.

$2t + 2 - 3t + 3 = 6$

          $-t = 1$

            $t = -1$

The solution set is $\{-1\}$.

13. $\dfrac{3x}{x+2} + \dfrac{6}{x} = \dfrac{12}{x^2 + 2x}$

$\dfrac{3x}{x+2} + \dfrac{6}{x} = \dfrac{12}{x(x+2)}$,   LCM is $x(x+2)$

Note that -2 and 0 are not meaningful replacements.

$x(x+2)\left[\dfrac{3x}{x+2} + \dfrac{6}{x}\right] = x(x+2) \cdot \dfrac{12}{x(x+2)}$

$3x \cdot x + 6(x+2) = 12$

$3x^2 + 6x + 12 = 12$

$3x^2 + 6x = 0$

$3x(x+2) = 0$

$3x = 0$ or $x + 2 = 0$

$x = 0$ or $\quad\quad x = -2$

Since we noted at the outset that -2 and 0 are not meaningful replacements, the solution set is $\emptyset$.

14. $\dfrac{5x}{x-4} - \dfrac{20}{x} = \dfrac{80}{x^2 - 4x}$

$\dfrac{5x}{x-4} - \dfrac{20}{x} = \dfrac{80}{x(x-4)}$,   LCM is $x(x-4)$

Note that 4 and 0 are not meaningful replacements.

$5x^2 - 20x + 80 = 80$

$5x^2 - 20x = 0$

$5x(x-4) = 0$

$x = 0$ or $x = 4$ Not meaningful replacements

The solution set is $\emptyset$.

15. $\dfrac{x+2}{2} + \dfrac{3x+1}{5} = \dfrac{x-2}{4}$,   LCM is 20

$20\left[\dfrac{x+2}{2} + \dfrac{3x+1}{5}\right] = 20 \cdot \dfrac{x-2}{4}$

$10(x+2) + 4(3x+1) = 5(x-2)$

$10x + 20 + 12x + 4 = 5x - 10$

$22x + 24 = 5x - 10$

$22x - 5x = -10 - 24$

$17x = -34$

$x = -2$

The solution set is $\{-2\}$.

16. $\dfrac{2x-1}{3} - \dfrac{x-2}{5} = \dfrac{x}{2}$,   LCM is 30

All replacements are meaningful.

$20x - 10 - 6x + 12 = 15x$

$2 = x$

The solution set is $\{2\}$.

17. $\dfrac{1}{2} + \dfrac{2}{x} = \dfrac{1}{3} + \dfrac{3}{x}$,   LCM $= 6x$

$6x\left[\dfrac{1}{2} + \dfrac{2}{x}\right] = 6x\left[\dfrac{1}{3} + \dfrac{3}{x}\right]$

$3x + 12 = 2x + 18$

$3x - 2x = 18 - 12$

$x = 6$

Check:

$\dfrac{1}{2} + \dfrac{2}{x} = \dfrac{1}{3} + \dfrac{3}{x}$

$\dfrac{1}{2} + \dfrac{2}{6} \ \bigg| \ \dfrac{1}{3} + \dfrac{3}{6}$

$\dfrac{1}{2} + \dfrac{1}{3} \ \bigg| \ \dfrac{1}{3} + \dfrac{1}{2}$ TRUE

The solution set is $\{6\}$.

18. $\dfrac{1}{t} + \dfrac{1}{2t} + \dfrac{1}{3t} = 5$,   LCM is $6t$

$6 + 3 + 2 = 30t$

$11 = 30t$

$\dfrac{11}{30} = t$

$\dfrac{11}{30}$ checks. The solution set is $\left\{\dfrac{11}{30}\right\}$.

19. $\dfrac{4}{x^2 - 1} - \dfrac{2}{x-1} = \dfrac{3}{x+1}$,

$\quad\quad\quad\quad\quad$ LCM is $(x+1)(x-1)$

$(x+1)(x-1)\left[\dfrac{4}{(x+1)(x-1)} - \dfrac{2}{x-1}\right] = (x+1)(x-1) \cdot \dfrac{3}{x+1}$

$4 - 2(x+1) = 3(x-1)$

$4 - 2x - 2 = 3x - 3$

$2 - 2x = 3x - 3$

$2 + 3 = 3x + 2x$

$5 = 5x$

$1 = x$

Check:

$\dfrac{4}{x^2 - 1} - \dfrac{2}{x-1} = \dfrac{3}{x+1}$

$\dfrac{4}{1^2 - 1} - \dfrac{2}{1-1} \ \bigg| \ \dfrac{3}{1+1}$

$\dfrac{4}{0} - \dfrac{2}{0} \ \bigg| \ \dfrac{3}{2}$

Division by zero is undefined.

The solution set is $\emptyset$.

20. $\dfrac{3y+5}{y^2 + 5y} + \dfrac{y+4}{y+5} = \dfrac{y+1}{y}$

$\dfrac{3y+5}{y(y+5)} + \dfrac{y+4}{y+5} = \dfrac{y+1}{y}$,   LCM is $y(y+5)$

Note that 0 and -5 are not meaningful replacements.

$3y + 5 + y^2 + 4y = y^2 + 6y + 5$

$y = 0$ Not a meaningful replacement

The solution set is $\emptyset$.

21.
$$\frac{490}{x^2 - 49} = \frac{5x}{x - 7} - \frac{35}{x + 7}$$

$$\frac{490}{(x + 7)(x - 7)} = \frac{5x}{x - 7} - \frac{35}{x + 7},$$

LCM is $(x + 7)(x - 7)$

Note that -7 and 7 are not meaningful replacements.

$$(x+7)(x-7)\left[\frac{490}{(x+7)(x-7)}\right] = (x+7)(x-7)\left[\frac{5x}{x-7} - \frac{35}{x+7}\right]$$

$$490 = 5x(x + 7) - 35(x - 7)$$

$$490 = 5x^2 + 35x - 35x + 245$$

$$0 = 5x^2 - 245$$

$$0 = 5(x + 7)(x - 7)$$

$x + 7 = 0$ or $x - 7 = 0$

$x = -7$ or $x = 7$

Since we noted at the outset that -7 and 7 are not meaningful replacements, the solution set is Ø.

22.
$$\frac{3}{m + 2} + \frac{2}{m - 2} = \frac{4m - 4}{m^2 - 4}$$

$$\frac{3}{m + 2} + \frac{2}{m - 2} = \frac{4m - 4}{(m + 2)(m - 2)},$$

LCM is $(m + 2)(m - 2)$

Note that -2 and 2 are not meaningful replacements.

$$3m - 6 + 2m + 4 = 4m - 4$$

$$m = -2 \qquad \text{Not a meaningful replacement}$$

The solution set is Ø.

23.
$$\frac{4}{x} - \frac{4}{x - 6} = \frac{24}{6x - x^2}$$

$$\frac{4}{x} - \frac{4}{x - 6} = \frac{24}{x(6 - x)}$$

$$\frac{4}{x} - \frac{4}{x - 6} = \frac{-1}{-1} \cdot \frac{24}{x(6 - x)}$$

$$\frac{4}{x} - \frac{4}{x - 6} = \frac{-24}{x(x - 6)} \qquad [-1 \cdot (6 - x) = -6 + x, \text{ or } x - 6]$$

Note that 0 and 6 are not meaningful replacements.

$$x(x - 6)\left[\frac{4}{x} - \frac{4}{x - 6}\right] = x(x - 6) \cdot \frac{-24}{x(x - 6)}$$

$$4(x - 6) - 4x = -24$$

$$4x - 24 - 4x = -24$$

$$0 = 0$$

We get an equation that is true for all meaningful replacements. Since we noted at the outset that 0 and 6 are not meaningful replacements, the solution set is the set of all real numbers except 0 and 6.

24.
$$\frac{24}{4 - x^2} = \frac{6}{x + 2} - \frac{3x}{x - 2}$$

$$\frac{24}{(2 + x)(2 - x)} = \frac{6}{x + 2} - \frac{3x}{x - 2},$$

LCM is $(x + 2)(x - 2)$

Note that -2 and 2 are not meaningful replacements.

$$-24 = 6x - 12 - 3x^2 - 6x$$

$$3x^2 - 12 = 0$$

$$3(x + 2)(x - 2) = 0$$

$x = -2$ or $x = 2$ Not meaningful replacements

The solution is Ø.

25.
$$\frac{11 - t^2}{3t^2 - 5t + 2} = \frac{2t + 3}{3t - 2} + \frac{t - 3}{1 - t}$$

$$\frac{11 - t^2}{(3t - 2)(t - 1)} = \frac{2t + 3}{3t - 2} + \frac{t - 3}{1 - t}$$

$$\frac{11 - t^2}{(3t - 2)(t - 1)} = \frac{2t + 3}{3t - 2} + \frac{-1}{-1} \cdot \frac{t - 3}{1 - t}$$

$$\frac{11 - t^2}{(3t - 2)(t - 1)} = \frac{2t + 3}{3t - 2} + \frac{-t + 3}{t - 1},$$

LCM is $(3t - 2)(t - 1)$

$$(3t-2)(t-1) \cdot \frac{11 - t^2}{(3t-2)(t-1)} = (3t-2)(t-1)\left[\frac{2t+3}{3t-2} + \frac{-t+3}{t-1}\right]$$

$$11 - t^2 = (t-1)(2t+3) + (3t-2)(-t+3)$$

$$11 - t^2 = 2t^2 + t - 3 - 3t^2 + 11t - 6$$

$$11 - t^2 = -t^2 + 12t - 9$$

$$11 = 12t - 9$$

$$20 = 12t$$

$$\frac{20}{12} = t$$

$$\frac{5}{3} = t$$

The value checks. The solution set is $\left\{\frac{5}{3}\right\}$.

26.
$$\frac{1}{3y^2 - 10y + 3} = \frac{6y}{9y^2 - 1} + \frac{2}{1 - 3y}$$

$$\frac{1}{(3y - 1)(y - 3)} = \frac{6y}{(3y + 1)(3y - 1)} + \frac{2}{1 - 3y},$$

LCM is $(3y - 1)(y - 3)(3y + 1)$

$$3y + 1 = 6y^2 - 18y - 6y^2 + 16y + 6$$

$$5y = 5$$

$$y = 1$$

1 checks. The solution set is {1}.

27. $\dfrac{7x}{x-3} - \dfrac{21}{x} + 11 = \dfrac{63}{x^2-3x}$,   LCM is $x(x-3)$

Note that 0 and 3 are not meaningful replacements.

$$x(x-3)\left[\dfrac{7x}{x-3} - \dfrac{21}{x} + 11\right] = x(x-3) \cdot \dfrac{63}{x(x-3)}$$

$$7x^2 - 21(x-3) + 11x(x-3) = 63$$

$$7x^2 - 21x + 63 + 11x^2 - 33x = 63$$

$$18x^2 - 54x = 0$$

$$18x(x-3) = 0$$

$18x = 0$ or $x - 3 = 0$

$\quad x = 0$ or $\quad\quad x = 3$

Since we noted at the outset that 0 and 3 are not meaningful replacements, the solution set is ∅.

28. $\dfrac{3x}{x-5} - \dfrac{15}{x+5} = \dfrac{150}{x^2-25}$,   LCM is $(x+5)(x-5)$

Note that 5 and -5 are not meaningful replacements.

$$3x^2 + 15x - 15x + 75 = 150$$

$$3x^2 - 75 = 0$$

$$3(x+5)(x-5) = 0$$

$x = -5$ or $x = 5$ Not meaningful replacements

The solution set is ∅.

29. $\qquad\dfrac{2.315}{y} - \dfrac{12.6}{17.4} = \dfrac{6.71}{7} + 0.763,$

$\qquad\qquad\qquad\qquad$ LCM is $7(17.4)y$

$$7(17.4)y\left[\dfrac{2.315}{y} - \dfrac{12.6}{17.4}\right] = 7(17.4)y\left[\dfrac{6.71}{7} + 0.763\right]$$

$$281.967 - 88.2y = 116.754y + 92.9334y$$

$$281.967 - 88.2y = 209.6874y$$

$$281.967 = 297.8874y$$

$$0.94656 \approx y$$

The value checks. The solution set is {0.94656}.

30. $\dfrac{6.034}{x} - 43.17 = \dfrac{0.793}{x} + 18.15$

$$\dfrac{5.241}{x} = 61.32,\quad \text{LCM is } x$$

$$5.241 = 61.32x$$

$$0.0855 \approx x$$

The solution set is {0.0855}.

31. $\dfrac{2x^2}{x-3} + \dfrac{4x-6}{x+3} = \dfrac{108}{x^2-9}$,   LCM is $(x+3)(x-3)$

Note that 3 and -3 are not meaningful replacements.

$$(x+3)(x-3)\left[\dfrac{2x^2}{x-3} + \dfrac{4x-6}{x+3}\right] = (x+3)(x-3) \cdot \dfrac{108}{(x+3)(x-3)}$$

$$2x^2(x+3) + (x-3)(4x-6) = 108$$

$$2x^3 + 6x^2 + 4x^2 - 18x + 18 = 108$$

$$2x^3 + 10x^2 - 18x + 18 = 108$$

$$2x^3 + 10x^2 - 18x - 90 = 0$$

$$2(x^3 + 5x^2 - 9x - 45) = 0$$

$$2[x^2(x+5) - 9(x+5)] = 0$$

$$2(x^2 - 9)(x+5) = 0$$

$$2(x+3)(x-3)(x+5) = 0$$

$x + 3 = 0$ or $x - 3 = 0$ or $x + 5 = 0$

$\quad x = -3$ or $\quad\quad x = 3$ or $\quad\quad x = -5$

We noted at the outset that the numbers -3 and 3 are not meaningful replacements. The number -5 checks. The solution set is {-5}.

32. $\dfrac{3x^2}{x+2} + \dfrac{48}{x^2-4} = \dfrac{2x+8}{x-2}$,   LCM is $(x+2)(x-2)$

Note that -2 and 2 are not meaningful replacements.

$$3x^3 - 6x^2 + 48 = 2x^2 + 12x + 16$$

$$3x^3 - 8x^2 - 12x + 32 = 0$$

$$x^2(3x-8) - 4(3x-8) = 0$$

$$(x^2-4)(3x-8) = 0$$

$x = -2$ or $x = 2$ or $x = \dfrac{8}{3}$

-2 and 2 are not meaningful replacements. $\dfrac{8}{3}$ checks. The solution set is $\left\{\dfrac{8}{3}\right\}$.

33. $\dfrac{24}{x^2-2x+4} = \dfrac{3x}{x+2} + \dfrac{72}{x^3+8}$

$\qquad\qquad\qquad$ LCM is $(x+2)(x^2-2x+4)$

Note that -2 is not a meaningful replacement.

$(x+2)(x^2-2x+4) \cdot \dfrac{24}{x^2-2x+4} =$

$\qquad (x+2)(x^2-2x+4)\left[\dfrac{3x}{x+2} + \dfrac{72}{(x+2)(x^2-2x+4)}\right]$

$$24(x+2) = 3x(x^2-2x+4) + 72$$

$$24x + 48 = 3x^3 - 6x^2 + 12x + 72$$

$$0 = 3x^3 - 6x^2 - 12x + 24$$

$$0 = 3(x^3 - 2x^2 - 4x + 8)$$

$$0 = 3[x^2(x-2) - 4(x-2)]$$

$$0 = 3(x^2-4)(x-2)$$

$$0 = 3(x+2)(x-2)(x-2)$$

$x + 2 = 0$ or $x - 2 = 0$ or $x - 2 = 0$

$\quad x = -2$ or $\quad\quad x = 2$ or $\quad\quad x = 2$

We noted at the outset that -2 is not a meaningful replacement. The number 2 checks. The solution set is {2}.

34. $\dfrac{90}{x^2 - 3x + 9} - \dfrac{5x}{x + 3} = \dfrac{405}{x^3 + 27}$,

$$\text{LCM is } (x + 3)(x^2 - 3x + 9)$$

Note that -3 is not a meaningful replacement.

$$90x + 270 - 5x^3 + 15x^2 - 45x = 405$$
$$-5x^3 + 15x^2 + 45x - 135 = 0$$
$$-5(x^3 - 3x^2 - 9x + 27) = 0$$
$$-5[x^2(x - 3) - 9(x - 3)] = 0$$
$$-5(x - 3)(x^2 - 9) = 0$$

$$x = 3 \text{ or } x = -3$$

-3 is not a meaningful replacement. 3 checks.
The solution set is {3}.

35. $\dfrac{5}{x - 1} + \dfrac{9}{x^2 + x + 1} = \dfrac{15}{x^3 - 1}$

$$\text{LCM is } (x - 1)(x^2 + x + 1)$$

Note that 1 is not a meaningful replacement.

$$(x-1)(x^2+x+1)\left[\dfrac{5}{x-1} + \dfrac{9}{x^2+x+1}\right] =$$

$$(x-1)(x^2+x+1) \cdot \dfrac{15}{(x-1)(x^2+x+1)}$$

$$5(x^2 + x + 1) + 9(x - 1) = 15$$
$$5x^2 + 5x + 5 + 9x - 9 = 15$$
$$5x^2 + 14x - 4 = 15$$
$$5x^2 + 14x - 19 = 0$$
$$(5x + 19)(x - 1) = 0$$

$$5x + 19 = 0 \quad \text{or} \quad x - 1 = 0$$
$$5x = -19 \quad \text{or} \quad x = 1$$
$$x = -\dfrac{19}{5} \quad \text{or} \quad x = 1$$

The number $-\dfrac{19}{5}$ checks. We noted at the outset
that -1 is not a meaningful replacement. The
solution set is $\left\{-\dfrac{19}{5}\right\}$.

36. $\dfrac{7}{x + 2} + \dfrac{5}{x^2 - 2x + 4} = \dfrac{84}{x^3 + 8}$,

$$\text{LCM is } (x + 2)(x^2 - 2x + 4)$$

Note that -2 is not a meaningful replacement.

$$7x^2 - 14x + 28 + 5x + 10 = 84$$
$$7x^2 - 9x - 46 = 0$$
$$(7x - 23)(x + 2) = 0$$

$$x = \dfrac{23}{7} \text{ or } x = -2$$

$\dfrac{23}{7}$ checks. -2 is not a meaningful replacement.
The solution set is $\left\{\dfrac{23}{7}\right\}$.

37. $\dfrac{7}{x - 9} - \dfrac{7}{x} = \dfrac{63}{x^2 - 9x}$,   LCM is $x(x - 9)$

Note that 9 and 0 are not meaningful replacements.

$$x(x - 9)\left[\dfrac{7}{x - 9} - \dfrac{7}{x}\right] = x(x - 9) \cdot \dfrac{63}{x(x - 9)}$$
$$7x - 7(x - 9) = 63$$
$$7x - 7x + 63 = 63$$
$$63 = 63$$

We get an equation that is true for all
meaningful replacements. We noted at the outset
that 9 and 0 are not meaningful replacements. The
solution set is the set of all real numbers except
9 and 0.

38. $\dfrac{26}{x + 13} - \dfrac{14}{x + 7} = \dfrac{12x}{x^2 + 20x + 91}$,

$$\text{LCM is } (x + 13)(x + 7)$$

Note that -13 and -7 are not meaningful
replacements.

$$26x + 182 - 14x - 182 = 12x$$
$$12x = 12x$$

The equation is true for all meaningful
replacements. The solution set is the set of
all real numbers except -13 and -7.

39. $\dfrac{(x - 3)^2}{x - 3} = x - 3$,   LCM is $x - 3$

Note that 3 is not a meaningful replacement.

$$(x - 3) \cdot \dfrac{(x - 3)^2}{x - 3} = (x - 3)(x - 3)$$
$$(x - 3)^2 = (x - 3)^2$$

We get an equation that is true for all meaningful
replacements. We noted at the outset that 3 is
not a meaningful replacement. The solution set
is the set of all real numbers except 3.

40. $\dfrac{x^2 + 6x - 16}{x - 2} = x + 8$,   LCM is $x - 2$

Note that 2 is not a meaningful replacement.

$$x^2 + 6x - 16 = x^2 + 6x - 16$$

The equation is true for all meaningful
replacements. The solution set is the set of
all real numbers except 2.

41. $\dfrac{x^3 + 8}{x + 2} = x^2 - 2x + 4$,   LCM is $x + 2$

Note that -2 is not a meaningful replacement.

$$(x + 2) \cdot \dfrac{x^3 + 8}{x + 2} = (x + 2)(x^2 - 2x + 4)$$
$$x^3 + 8 = x^3 + 8$$

We get an equation that is true for all
meaningful replacements. We noted at the outset
that -2 is not a meaningful replacement. The
solution set is the set of all real numbers
except -2.

42. $\dfrac{x + 8}{x - 2} = \dfrac{8 + x}{-2 + x}$,   LCM is $x - 2$

Note that 2 is not a meaningful replacement.

$x + 8 = 8 + x$

The equation is true for all meaningful replacements. The solution set is the set of all real numbers except 2.

43. Find the solution set of each equation.

Equation (1): $x^2 - x - 20 = x^2 - 25$

$$-x = -5$$
$$x = 5$$

The solution set is $\{5\}$.

Equation (2): $(x - 5)(x + 4) = (x - 5)(x + 5)$

$$x^2 - x - 20 = x^2 - 25$$

Multiplying, we get equation (1), so the solution set of equation (2) is also $\{5\}$.

Equation (3): $x + 4 = x + 5$

$$4 = 5 \qquad \text{Adding } -x$$

We get a false equation, so the solution set is $\emptyset$.

Equation (4): $4 = 5$

This is a false equation, so the solution set is $\emptyset$.

(1) and (2) have the same solution set, so they are equivalent; (2) and (3) do not have the same solution set, so they are not equivalent; (3) and (4) have the same solution set, so they are equivalent.

44. Identity (See Exercise 40.)

45. $x + 4 = 4 + x$

Adding $-x$ to both sides, we get $4 = 4$, a true equation. Thus, the equation is an identity.

46. $(x - 1)(x^2 + x + 1) = x^3 - 1$

$$x^3 - 1 = x^3 - 1$$
$$-1 = -1$$

Identity

47.
$$\dfrac{x^3 + 8}{x^2 - 4} = \dfrac{x^2 - 2x + 4}{x - 2}$$

$$\dfrac{x^3 + 8}{(x + 2)(x - 2)} = \dfrac{x^2 - 2x + 4}{x - 2}$$

$$(x+2)(x-2) \cdot \dfrac{x^3 + 8}{(x+2)(x-2)} = (x+2)(x-2) \cdot \dfrac{x^2-2x+4}{x - 2}$$

$$x^3 + 8 = (x + 2)(x^2 - 2x + 4)$$
$$x^3 + 8 = x^3 + 8$$
$$8 = 8$$

We get an equation that is true for all meaningful replacements of the variables. Thus, the equation is an identity.

48. $(x + 7)^2 = x^2 + 49$

$$x^2 + 14x + 49 = x^2 + 49$$
$$14x = 0$$
$$x = 0$$

There is only one replacement that makes the equation true, even though all real numbers are meaningful replacements. The equation is not an identity.

49. $\sqrt{x^2 - 16} = x - 4$

The set of meaningful replacements is $\{x \mid x \leqslant -4 \text{ or } x \geqslant 4\}$. Substitute 5, a meaningful replacement, for x in the equation.

$$\sqrt{5^2 - 16} = 5 - 4$$
$$\sqrt{9} = 1$$
$$3 = 1$$

We get a false equation. Thus, the equation is *not* true for all meaningful replacements. It is not an identity.

50. $\dfrac{x + 3}{x + 2} - \dfrac{x + 4}{x + 3} = \dfrac{x + 5}{x + 4} - \dfrac{x + 6}{x + 5}$,

LCM is $(x + 2)(x + 3)(x + 4)(x + 5)$

Note that -2, -3, -4, and -5 are not meaningful replacements.

$x^4 + 15x^3 + 83x^2 + 201x + 180 - x^4 - 15x^3 - 82x^2 - 192x - 160 = x^4 + 15x^3 + 81x^2 + 185x + 150 - x^4 - 15x^3 - 80x^2 - 180x - 144$

$$x^2 + 9x + 20 = x^2 + 5x + 6$$
$$4x = -14$$
$$x = -\dfrac{7}{2}$$

The solution set is $\left\{ -\dfrac{7}{2} \right\}$.

Exercise Set 2.3

1.
$$P = 2\ell + 2w$$
$$P - 2\ell = 2w$$
$$\dfrac{P - 2\ell}{2} = w$$

2. $r = \dfrac{C}{2\pi}$

3. $A = \dfrac{1}{2}bh$

$$2A = bh$$
$$\dfrac{2A}{h} = b$$

4. $\pi = \dfrac{r^2}{A}$

5. $d = rt$

$$\dfrac{d}{t} = r$$

6. $a = \dfrac{F}{m}$

7. $E = IR$

$\dfrac{E}{R} = I$

8. $m_2 = \dfrac{Fd^2}{km_1}$

9. $\dfrac{P_1V_1}{T_1} = \dfrac{P_2V_2}{T_2}$

$T_1T_2 \cdot \dfrac{P_1V_1}{T_1} = T_1T_2 \cdot \dfrac{P_2V_2}{T_2}$

$T_2P_1V_1 = T_1P_2V_2$

$\dfrac{T_2P_1V_1}{P_2V_2} = T_1$

10. $V_2 = \dfrac{T_2P_1V_1}{T_1P_2}$

11. $S = \dfrac{H}{m(v_1 - v_2)}$ or $\qquad S = \dfrac{H}{m(v_1 - v_2)}$

$m(v_1 - v_2)S = H \qquad\qquad m(v_1 - v_2)S = H$

$mSv_1 - mSv_2 = H \qquad\quad v_1 - v_2 = \dfrac{H}{mS}$

$mSv_1 = H + mSv_2$

$v_1 = \dfrac{H + mSv_2}{mS} \qquad\qquad v_1 = \dfrac{H}{mS} + v_2$

12. Using an intermediate step of Exercise 11 we have the following:

$mSv_1 = H + mSv_2$ or $v_1 - v_2 = \dfrac{H}{mS}$

$mSv_1 - H = mSv_2 \qquad v_1 - \dfrac{H}{mS} = v_2$

$\dfrac{mSv_1 - H}{mS} = v_2$

13. $\dfrac{1}{F} = \dfrac{1}{m} + \dfrac{1}{p}$

$Fmp \cdot \dfrac{1}{F} = Fmp\left(\dfrac{1}{m} + \dfrac{1}{p}\right)$

$mp = Fp + Fm$

$mp - Fp = Fm$

$p(m - F) = Fm$

$p = \dfrac{Fm}{m - F}$

14. From the third line of Exercise 13, we have the following:

$mp = Fp + Fm$

$mp = F(p + m)$

$\dfrac{mp}{p + m} = F$

15. $(x + a)(x - b) = x^2 + 5$

$x^2 - bx + ax - ab = x^2 + 5$

$ax - bx = 5 + ab$

$x(a - b) = 5 + ab$

$x = \dfrac{5 + ab}{a - b}$

16. $(c + d)x + (c - d)x = c^2$

$cx + dx + cx - dx = c^2$

$2cx = c^2$

$x = \dfrac{c}{2}$

17. $10(a + x) = 8(a - x)$

$10a + 10x = 8a - 8x$

$10x + 8x = 8a - 10a$

$18x = -2a$

$x = -\dfrac{2a}{18}$

$x = -\dfrac{a}{9}$

18. $4(a + b + x) + 3(a + b - x) = 8a$

$4a + 4b + 4x + 3a + 3b - 3x = 8a$

$x = a - 7b$

19. Familiarize: We restate the situation.

The amount invested plus the interest is \$702. We let x = the amount originally invested.

Translate:

Invested amount	plus	8% of invested amount	is	\$702.
↓	↓	↓	↓	↓
x	+	8%·x	=	702

Carry out:

$x + 8\%x = 702$

$x + 0.08x = 702$

$(1 + 0.08)x = 702$

$1.08x = 702$

$x = 650$

Check:

\$650 + 8% of \$650 = \$650 + \$52 = \$702

State:

The amount originally invested was \$650.

20. Solve: $x + 0.09x = 926.50$

$x = \$850$

21. Familiarize: We make a drawing.

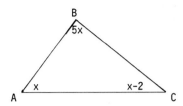

We let x represent the measure of angle A. Then 5x represents angle B, and x - 2 represents angle C. The sum of the angle measures is 180°.

Translate:

Carry out:

$x + 5x + x - 2 = 180$

$7x - 2 = 180$

$7x = 182$

$x = 26$

If x = 26, then 5x = 5·26, or 130, and x - 2 = 26 - 2, or 24.

Check:

The measure of angle B, 130°, is five times the measure of angle A, 26°. The measure of angle C, 24°, is 2° less than the measure of angle A, 26°. The sum of the angle measures is 26° + 130° + 24°, or 180°.

State:

Angle A measures 26°. Angle B measures 130°, and angle C measures 24°.

22. Solve: $x + 2x + x + 20 = 180$

$x = 40°$, so $2x = 80°$, and $x + 20 = 60°$

23. Familiarize: We make a drawing.

We let x represent the width. Then x + 25 represents the length.

Translate:

Perimeter = 2 × length + 2 × width

$322 = 2(x + 25) + 2(x)$

Carry out:

$322 = 2x + 50 + 2x$

$322 = 4x + 50$

$272 = 4x$

$68 = x$

If x = 68, then x + 25 = 68 + 25, or 93.

Check:

The length is 25 m more than the width: 93 = 68 + 25. The perimeter is 2·93 + 2·68, or 186 + 136, or 322 m.

State:

The length is 93 m; the width is 68 m.

24. Solve: $2·2w + 2·w = 39$

$w = 6.5$ m, so $2w = 13$ m

25. Familiarize:

We let x represent the score on the fourth test. Then the average of the four scores is

$$\frac{87 + 64 + 78 + x}{4}.$$

Translate:

The average must be 80.

$$\frac{87 + 64 + 78 + x}{4} = 80$$

Carry out:

$87 + 64 + 78 + x = 4·80$

$229 + x = 320$

$x = 91$

Check:

The average of 87, 64, 78, and 91 is

$$\frac{87 + 64 + 78 + 91}{4}, \text{ or } \frac{320}{4}, \text{ or } 80.$$

State:

The score on the fourth test must be 91%.

26. Solve: $\dfrac{74 + 55 + 68 + x}{4} = 70$

$x = 83\%$

27. Familiarize: We make a drawing.

We let x represent the length of a side of the square in each corner. Then the length and width of the resulting base are represented by 20 - 2x and 10 - 2x.

Translate:

The area of the base is 96 cm².

$(20 - 2x)(10 - 2x) = 96$

Carry out:

$200 - 60x + 4x^2 = 96$

$4x^2 - 60x + 104 = 0$

$x^2 - 15x + 26 = 0$

$(x - 13)(x - 2) = 0$

$x - 13 = 0$ or $x - 2 = 0$

$x = 13$ or $x = 2$

Since the length and width of the base cannot be negative, we only consider x = 2.

Check:

If x = 2, then 20 - 2x = 16 and 10 - 2x = 6. The area of the base is 16·6, or 96 cm².

State:

The length of the sides of the squares is 2 cm.

28. Solve: (28 - 2x)(32 - 2x) = 192
$$x = 8 \text{ cm}$$

29. Familiarize and Translate:

Let x = the former population.

Carry out:

x + 0.02x = 826,200

1.02x = 826,200

$$x = \frac{826,200}{1.02}$$

x = 810,000

Check:

2%·810,000 = 0.02·810,000 = 16,200. The present population is 810,000 + 16,200, or 826,200.

State:

The former population was 810,000.

30. Solve: x + 0.03x = 741,600
$$x = 720,000$$

31. Familiarize:

We first make a drawing. We let r represent the speed of the boat in still water. Then the speed downstream is r + 3, and the speed upstream is r - 3. The time to go downstream is the same as the time to go upstream. We call it t.

t hours   Downstream
⊢————————————————————————————————————→
50 km   r + 3 km/h

      t hours   Upstream
      ←————————————————————————————————⊣
      30 km   r - 3 km/h

We organize the information in a table.

	Distance	Speed	Time
Downstream	50	r + 3	t
Upstream	30	r - 3	t

Translate:

Using t = d/r we can get two expressions for t from the table.

$$t = \frac{50}{r + 3} \qquad \text{and} \qquad t = \frac{30}{r - 3}$$

Thus

$$\frac{50}{r + 3} = \frac{30}{r - 3}$$

Carry out:

$$(r + 3)(r - 3) \cdot \frac{50}{r + 3} = (r + 3)(r - 3) \cdot \frac{30}{r - 3}$$

(Multiplying by the LCM)

50(r - 3) = 30(r + 3)

50r - 150 = 30r + 90

50r - 30r = 90 + 150

20r = 240

r = 12

Check:

If r = 12, the speed downstream is 12 + 3, or 15 km/h, and thus the time downstream is 50/15, or 3.$\overline{3}$ hr. If r = 12, the speed upstream is 12 - 3, or 9 km/h, and thus the time upstream is 30/9 or 3.$\overline{3}$ hr. The times are equal; the value checks.

State:

The speed of the boat in still water is 12 km/h.

32. Solve: $\frac{50}{16 + r} = \frac{30}{16 - r}$

$$r = 4 \text{ km/h}$$

33. Familiarize:

We organize the information in a table. We let r represent the speed of train B. Then the speed of train A is r - 12. The time, t, is the same for each train.

	Distance	Speed	Time
Train A	230	r - 12	t
Train B	290	r	t

Translate:

Using t = d/r we get two expressions for t from the table.

$$t = \frac{230}{r - 12} \qquad \text{and} \qquad t = \frac{290}{r}$$

Thus

$$\frac{230}{r - 12} = \frac{290}{r}$$

Carry out:

$$r(r - 12) \cdot \frac{230}{r - 12} = r(r - 12) \cdot \frac{290}{r}$$

230r = 290(r - 12)

230r = 290r - 3480

3480 = 60r

58 = r

Check:

If r = 58, then the speed of train A is 58 - 12, or 46 mph. Thus the time for train A is 230/46, or 5 hr. If the speed of train B is 58 mph, the time for train B is 290/58, or 5 hr. The times are the same; the value checks.

State:

The speed of train A is 46 mph; the speed of train B is 58 mph.

<u>34.</u>   Solve: $\dfrac{400}{f + 14} = \dfrac{330}{f}$

$f = 66$ mph, so $f + 14 = 80$ mph

<u>35.</u>   Familiarize:

We first make a drawing.

```
 Chicago                    Cleveland
•————————————→      ←————————————•
 475 mph                    500 mph

 t hours                    t - 1/3 hours

 d₁ miles                   d₂ miles
←————————————350 miles————————————→
```

We organize the information in a table.

	Distance	Speed	Time
From Chicago	d_1	475	t
From Cleveland	d_2	500	$t - \frac{1}{3}$

Translate:

Using d = rt we get two equations from the table.

$d_1 = 475t$ $d_2 = 500\left(t - \frac{1}{3}\right)$

We also know that $d_1 + d_2 = 350$. Thus

$475t + 500\left(t - \frac{1}{3}\right) = 350$

Carry out:

$475t + 500t - \dfrac{500}{3} = 350$

$975t = \dfrac{1050}{3} + \dfrac{500}{3}$

$975t = \dfrac{1550}{3}$

$2925t = 1550$

$t = \dfrac{1550}{2925}$

$t = \dfrac{62}{117}$

Substitute $\dfrac{62}{117}$ for t and solve for d_2.

$d_2 = 500\left(t - \frac{1}{3}\right)$

$d_2 = 500\left(\dfrac{62}{117} - \dfrac{1}{3}\right) = 500 \cdot \dfrac{23}{117} \approx 98.3$

Check:

If $t = \dfrac{62}{117}$, then $d_1 = 475 \cdot \dfrac{62}{117}$, or ≈ 251.7. The sum of the distances is 98.3 + 251.7, or 350 miles. The value checks.

State:

When the trains meet, they are 98.3 miles from Cleveland.

<u>36.</u>   Solve: $180(t + 2) = 900t$

$t = \dfrac{1}{2}$, so $900t = 450$ km

<u>37.</u>   Familiarize:

A does $\dfrac{1}{3}$ of the job in 1 hr.

B does $\dfrac{1}{5}$ of the job in 1 hr.

C does $\dfrac{1}{7}$ of the job in 1 hr.

Together they do $\dfrac{1}{3} + \dfrac{1}{5} + \dfrac{1}{7} = \dfrac{71}{105}$ of the job in 1 hr. Together they do $2\left(\dfrac{1}{3}\right) + 2\left(\dfrac{1}{5}\right) + 2\left(\dfrac{1}{7}\right) = \dfrac{142}{105}$ or $1\dfrac{37}{105}$ in 2 hr. But $1\dfrac{37}{105}$ would represent more than 1 job.

We let t = the number of hours required for A, B, and C, working together, to do the job.

Translate:

$t\left(\dfrac{1}{3}\right) + t\left(\dfrac{1}{5}\right) + t\left(\dfrac{1}{7}\right) = 1$, or

$\dfrac{t}{3} + \dfrac{t}{5} + \dfrac{t}{7} = 1$

Carry out:

$\dfrac{t}{3} + \dfrac{t}{5} + \dfrac{t}{7} = 1$, LCM = 3·5·7, or 105

$105\left(\dfrac{t}{3} + \dfrac{t}{5} + \dfrac{t}{7}\right) = 105 \cdot 1$

$35t + 21t + 15t = 105$

$71t = 105$

$t = \dfrac{105}{71}$

$t = 1\dfrac{34}{71}$

Check:

In $1\dfrac{34}{71}$ hr, A will do $\left(\dfrac{1}{3}\right)\left(\dfrac{105}{71}\right)$, or $\dfrac{35}{71}$ of the job. Then B will do $\dfrac{1}{5}\left(\dfrac{105}{71}\right)$, or $\dfrac{21}{71}$ of the job and C will do $\dfrac{1}{7}\left(\dfrac{105}{71}\right)$, or $\dfrac{15}{71}$, or the job. Together they will $\dfrac{35}{71} + \dfrac{21}{71} + \dfrac{15}{71}$, or 1 complete job.

We have another partial check in noting from the familiarization step that the entire job can be done between 1 hr and 2 hr.

State: It will take $1\dfrac{34}{71}$ hr for A, B, and C to do the job together.

38. Solve: $t\left(\frac{1}{4}\right) + t\left(\frac{1}{10}\right) + t\left(\frac{1}{12}\right) = 1$

$$t = \frac{30}{13} \text{ hr}$$

39. Familiarize: Let t = the amount of time it takes B to do the job, working alone. In 1 hr A can do $\frac{1}{3.15}$ of the job and B can do $\frac{1}{t}$ of the job. Then in 2.09 hr A can do $2.09\left(\frac{1}{3.15}\right)$ of the job and B can do $2.09\left(\frac{1}{t}\right)$ of the job. If we add these fractional parts we get the entire job, represented by 1.

Translate: We add as described in the previous step and set the result equal to 1.

$$2.09\left(\frac{1}{3.15}\right) + 2.09\left(\frac{1}{t}\right) = 1, \text{ or } \frac{2.09}{3.15} + \frac{2.09}{t} = 1$$

Carry out: We first multiply by the LCM, 3.15t.

$$3.15t\left(\frac{2.09}{3.15} + \frac{2.09}{t}\right) = 3.15t(1)$$
$$2.09t + 6.5835 = 3.15t$$
$$6.5835 = 1.06t$$
$$6.21 \approx t$$

Check: In 2.09 hr A will do $\frac{2.09}{3.15}$ of the job and B will do $\frac{2.09}{6.21}$ of the job. Together they will do $\frac{2.09}{3.15} + \frac{2.09}{6.21} \approx 0.66 + 0.34$, or 1 complete job. The answer checks.

State: It would take B about 6.21 hr to do the job, working alone.

40. In one hour, B emits p particles and A emits 2.13p particles. Then $(p + 2.13p)(16.3) \approx 51.02p$ is the combined pollution in 16.3 hr.

A alone would need $\frac{51.02p}{2.13p} \approx 23.95$ hr, and

B alone would need $\frac{51.02p}{p} = 51.02$ hr.

41. a) $A = P(1 + i)^t$
     $A = 1000(1 + 0.0875)^1$
     $= \$1087.50$

   b) $A = P\left(1 + \frac{i}{2}\right)^{2t}$
     $A = 1000\left(1 + \frac{0.0875}{2}\right)^2$
     $= \$1089.41$

   c) $A = P\left(1 + \frac{i}{4}\right)^{4t}$
     $A = 1000\left(1 + \frac{0.0875}{4}\right)^4$
     $= \$1090.41$

   d) $A = P\left(1 + \frac{i}{365}\right)^{365t}$
     $A = 1000\left(1 + \frac{0.0875}{365}\right)^{365}$
     $= \$1091.43$

   e) $A = P\left(1 + \frac{i}{8760}\right)^{8760t}$
     $A = 1000\left(1 + \frac{0.0875}{8760}\right)^{8760}$
     $= \$1091.44$

42. a) $\$1000(1 + 0.075)^5 = \$1435.63$

   b) $\$1000\left(1 + \frac{0.075}{2}\right)^{2\cdot5} = \$1445.04$

   c) $\$1000\left(1 + \frac{0.075}{4}\right)^{4\cdot5} = \$1449.95$

   d) $\$1000\left(1 + \frac{0.075}{365}\right)^{365\cdot5} = \$1454.94$

   e) $\$1000\left(1 + \frac{0.075}{365\cdot24}\right)^{365\cdot24\cdot5} = \$1454.99$

43. Familiarize:
We let r represent the speed for the slow trip and t the time for the slow trip. Then r + 4 and $t - \frac{1}{2}$ represent the speed and time respectively for the fast trip. We organize the information in a table.

	Distance	Speed	Time
Slow trip	144	r	t
Fast trip	144	r + 4	$t - \frac{1}{2}$

Translate:
Using t = d/r we get two equations from the table.

$$t = \frac{144}{r} \quad \text{and} \quad t - \frac{1}{2} = \frac{144}{r + 4}$$
$$\text{or } t = \frac{144}{r + 4} + \frac{1}{2}$$

This gives us the following equation:
$$\frac{144}{r} = \frac{144}{r + 4} + \frac{1}{2}$$

Carry out:

$$2r(r + 4) \cdot \frac{144}{r} = 2r(r + 4)\cdot\left(\frac{144}{r + 4} + \frac{1}{2}\right)$$
                      (Multiplying by the LCM)
$$288(r + 4) = 288r + r(r + 4)$$
$$288r + 1152 = 288r + r^2 + 4r$$
$$0 = r^2 + 4r - 1152$$
$$0 = (r + 36)(r - 32)$$
$$r + 36 = 0 \quad \text{or} \quad r - 32 = 0$$
$$r = -36 \quad \text{or} \quad r = 32$$

Check:

We only consider r = 32 since the speed in this problem cannot be negative. If r = 32, then the time for the slow trip is $\frac{144}{32}$, or 4.5 hr. If r = 32, then r + 4 = 36. Thus, the time for the fast trip is $\frac{144}{36}$, or 4 hr. The time for the fast trip is $\frac{1}{2}$ hr less than the time for the slow trip. The value checks.

State:

The car's speed is 32 mph.

44. Solve: $\frac{280}{r + 5} = \frac{280}{r} - 1$

$r = 35$ mph

45. Familiarize:

Freeway: d = rt

$d = 55 \cdot 3$, or 165

City: $t = \frac{d}{r}$

$t = \frac{10}{35}$, or $\frac{2}{7}$

We organize the information in a table.

	Distance	Speed	Time
Freeway	165	55	3
City	10	35	$\frac{10}{35}$, or $\frac{2}{7}$
Totals	175		$3\frac{2}{7}$ or $\frac{23}{7}$

Translate:

Average speed = $\frac{\text{Total distance}}{\text{Total time}}$

Average speed = $\frac{175}{\frac{23}{7}}$

Carry out: We simplify.

Average speed = $\frac{175}{\frac{23}{7}}$

$= 175 \cdot \frac{7}{23}$

$= \frac{1225}{23}$, or $53\frac{6}{23}$

Check: At $53\frac{6}{23}$ mph, the distance traveled in $3\frac{2}{7}$ hr is $\left(53\frac{6}{23}\right) \cdot \left(3\frac{2}{7}\right) = \frac{1225}{23} \cdot \frac{23}{7} = 175$ mi.

This is the total distance the student traveled, so the answer checks.

State: The average speed was $53\frac{6}{23}$ mph.

46. For the whole trip, $t = \frac{100}{40} + \frac{100}{60} = \frac{25}{6}$ hr.

Then $r = \frac{d}{t} = \frac{200}{\frac{25}{6}} = 48$ km/h.

47. Familiarize:

Making a drawing is helpful.

40 mph	$\frac{d}{40}$ hours	r mph	$\frac{d}{r}$ hours
	d miles		d miles

$\longleftarrow$————————2d miles————————$\longrightarrow$

We let d represent the distance of the first half of the trip. Then 2d represents the total distance. We also let r represent the speed for the second half of the trip. The times are represented by $\frac{d}{40}$ and $\frac{d}{r}$. The total time is $\frac{d}{40} + \frac{d}{r}$.

Translate:

Average speed = $\frac{\text{Total distance}}{\text{Total time}}$

Substituting we get

$45 = \frac{2d}{\frac{d}{40} + \frac{d}{r}}$.

Carry out:

$45 = \frac{2d}{\frac{d}{40} + \frac{d}{r}}$

$45\left(\frac{d}{40} + \frac{d}{r}\right) = 2d$

$45\left(\frac{1}{40} + \frac{1}{r}\right)d = 2d$

$\frac{45}{40} + \frac{45}{r} = 2$

$\frac{45}{r} = 2 - \frac{45}{40}$

$\frac{45}{r} = \frac{35}{40}$

$40 \cdot 45 = r \cdot 35$

$1800 = 35r$

$\frac{1800}{35} = r$

$51\frac{3}{7} = r$

Check: This value checks.

State: The speed for the second half of the trip would have to be $51\frac{3}{7}$ mph.

48. At the final time, the minute hand will be x minutes from top of clock and the hour hand will be 20 + (x)$\left(\frac{1}{12}\right)$ minutes from top of clock.

Then $x = 20 + \frac{x}{12}$ gives $x = 21\frac{9}{11}$ minutes (after 4 o'clock).

49. Familiarize:

It is helpful to make drawings.

At 10:30 the minute hand is 30 units after the 12. The hour hand is $52\frac{1}{2}$ units after the 12. Let x represent the number of units the minute hand moves before the hands are perpendicular for the first time. When the minute hand moves x units, the hour hand moves $\frac{1}{12}$ x units. Then the minute hand is 30 + x units after the 12, and the hour hand is $52\frac{1}{2} + \frac{1}{12}$ x units after the 12. When the hands are perpendicular, they must be 15 units apart.

Translate: We subtract to find the number of units between the hands. This difference must be 15 units.

$$\left(52\frac{1}{2} + \frac{1}{12}x\right) - (30 + x) = 15$$

Carry out:

$$\left(52\frac{1}{2} + \frac{1}{12}x\right) - (30 + x) = 15$$

$$52\frac{1}{2} + \frac{1}{12}x - 30 - x = 15$$

$$-\frac{11}{12}x + 22\frac{1}{2} = 15$$

$$\frac{15}{2} = \frac{11}{12}x$$

$$\frac{12}{11} \cdot \frac{15}{2} = x$$

$$8\frac{2}{11} = \frac{90}{11} = x$$

Check: This answer checks:

State: After 10:30, the hands will first be perpendicular in $8\frac{2}{11}$ minutes, or at 10:38 $\frac{2}{11}$.

50. Solve: $\frac{1}{t+1} + \frac{1}{t+6} + \frac{1}{t+t} = 1$

$$t = \frac{2}{3} \text{ hr}$$

51. a) Familiarize: We organize the information in a table. We let d = the distance from Los Angeles at which it takes the same amount of time to return to Los Angeles as it does to go on to Honolulu. We let t = the time for either part of the trip.

	Distance	Speed	Time
Return to L.A.	d	750 – 50, or 700	t
Go on to Honolulu	2574 – d	750 + 50, or 800	t

Translate: Using the formula t = d/r and the rows of the table we get two equations:

$$t = \frac{d}{700} \quad \text{and} \quad t = \frac{2574 - d}{800}$$

Thus,

$$\frac{d}{700} = \frac{2574 - d}{800}.$$

Carry out:

$$\frac{d}{700} = \frac{2574 - d}{800}$$

$$700(800) \cdot \frac{d}{700} = 700(800) \cdot \frac{2574 - d}{800}$$

$$800d = 700(2574 - d)$$

$$800d = 1,801,800 - 700d$$

$$1500d = 1,801,800$$

$$d = 1201.2$$

Check: This answer checks.

State: At a distance of 1201.2 mi from Los Angeles it takes the same amount of time to return to Los Angeles as it does to go on to Honolulu.

b) Since 1187 mi < 1201.2 mi, less time is required to return to Los Angeles.

52. Solve: $\frac{d}{45} + \frac{1}{60} = \frac{d}{40} - \frac{1}{60}$

$$d = 12 \text{ mi}$$

53. Familiarize: Let m = the amount of money in your father's pocket at the outset. After giving your mother half of his money, your father has $\frac{1}{2} \cdot m$, or $\frac{m}{2}$ left. After giving your sister one-fourth of $\frac{m}{2}$, he has $\frac{3}{4} \cdot \frac{m}{2}$, or $\frac{3m}{8}$, left. After giving your brother one-third of $\frac{3m}{8}$, he has $\frac{2}{3} \cdot \frac{3m}{8}$, or $\frac{m}{4}$, left. After giving you one-half of $\frac{m}{4}$, he has $\frac{1}{2} \cdot \frac{m}{4}$, or $\frac{m}{8}$, left. This final amount is $2.

Translate:

Final amount	is	$2.
$\frac{m}{8}$	=	2

Carry out:

$$\frac{m}{8} = 2$$

$$m = 16$$

Check: This value checks.

State: Your father had $16 at the outset.

<u>54.</u> Let p = the number of pies in the bakery at the outset. Then after the first purchase the number of pies left is $p - \left[\frac{1}{2}p + \frac{1}{2}\right]$, or $\frac{1}{2}p - \frac{1}{2}$. After the second purchase the number of pies left is $\left[\frac{1}{2}p - \frac{1}{2}\right] - \left[\frac{1}{2}\left(\frac{1}{2}p - \frac{1}{2}\right) + \frac{1}{2}\right]$, or $\frac{p}{4} - \frac{3}{4}$. And after the third purchase the number of pies left is $\left[\frac{p}{4} - \frac{3}{4}\right] - \left[\frac{1}{2}\left(\frac{p}{4} - \frac{3}{4}\right) + \frac{1}{2}\right]$, or $\frac{p}{8} - \frac{7}{8}$. This number is exactly one. Solving $\frac{p}{8} - \frac{7}{8} = 1$ gives p = 15.

Exercise Set 2.4

<u>1.</u> $\sqrt{-15} = \sqrt{-1 \cdot 15} = \sqrt{-1}\,\sqrt{15} = i\sqrt{15}$

<u>2.</u> $i\sqrt{17}$

<u>3.</u> $\sqrt{-81} = \sqrt{-1 \cdot 81} = \sqrt{-1}\,\sqrt{81} = 9i$

<u>4.</u> $5i$

<u>5.</u> $-\sqrt{-12} = -\sqrt{-1 \cdot 4 \cdot 3} = -\sqrt{-1}\,\sqrt{4}\,\sqrt{3} = -2i\sqrt{3}$

<u>6.</u> $-\sqrt{-20} = -\sqrt{-4 \cdot 5} = -2i\sqrt{5}$

<u>7.</u> $\sqrt{-16} + \sqrt{-25} = i\sqrt{16} + i\sqrt{25} = 4i + 5i = 9i$

<u>8.</u> $\sqrt{-36} - \sqrt{-4} = 6i - 2i = 4i$

<u>9.</u> $\sqrt{-7} - \sqrt{-10} = i\sqrt{7} - i\sqrt{10} = (\sqrt{7} - \sqrt{10})i$

<u>10.</u> $\sqrt{-5} + \sqrt{-7} = i\sqrt{5} + i\sqrt{7} = (\sqrt{5} + \sqrt{7})i$

<u>11.</u> $\sqrt{-5}\,\sqrt{-11} = i\sqrt{5} \cdot i\sqrt{11} = i^2\sqrt{5}\,\sqrt{11} = -\sqrt{55}$

<u>12.</u> $\sqrt{-7}\,\sqrt{-8} = i\sqrt{7} \cdot 2i\sqrt{2} = 2i^2\sqrt{14} = -2\sqrt{14}$

<u>13.</u> $-\sqrt{-4}\,\sqrt{-5} = -(i\sqrt{4} \cdot i\sqrt{5}) = -(i^2 \cdot 2 \cdot \sqrt{5})$
$$= -(-1)2\sqrt{5}$$
$$= 2\sqrt{5}$$

<u>14.</u> $-\sqrt{-9}\,\sqrt{-7} = -3i \cdot i\sqrt{7} = -3i^2\sqrt{7} = 3\sqrt{7}$

<u>15.</u> $\dfrac{-\sqrt{5}}{\sqrt{-2}} = \dfrac{-\sqrt{5}}{i\sqrt{2}} = \dfrac{-\sqrt{5}}{i\sqrt{2}} \cdot \dfrac{i}{i} = \dfrac{-i\sqrt{5}}{i^2\sqrt{2}}$
$$= \dfrac{-i\sqrt{5}}{-1\sqrt{2}}$$
$$= \sqrt{\dfrac{5}{2}}\,i$$

<u>16.</u> $\dfrac{\sqrt{-7}}{-\sqrt{5}} = \dfrac{i\sqrt{7}}{-\sqrt{5}} = -\sqrt{\dfrac{7}{5}}\,i$

<u>17.</u> $\dfrac{\sqrt{-9}}{-\sqrt{4}} = \dfrac{3i}{-2} = -\dfrac{3}{2}\,i$

<u>18.</u> $\dfrac{-\sqrt{25}}{\sqrt{-16}} = \dfrac{-5}{4i} = \dfrac{-5i}{4i^2} = \dfrac{5}{4}\,i$

<u>19.</u> $\dfrac{-\sqrt{-36}}{\sqrt{-9}} = \dfrac{-i\sqrt{36}}{i\sqrt{9}} = -\dfrac{6}{3} = -2$

<u>20.</u> $\dfrac{\sqrt{-25}}{-\sqrt{-16}} = \dfrac{5i}{-4i} = -\dfrac{5}{4}$

<u>21.</u> $i^{18} = (i^2)^9 = (-1)^9 = -1$

<u>22.</u> $i^{14} = (i^2)^7 = (-1)^7 = -1$

<u>23.</u> $i^{15} = (i^2)^7 \cdot i = (-1)^7 \cdot i = -1 \cdot i = -i$

<u>24.</u> $i^{16} = (i^2)^8 = (-1)^8 = 1$

<u>25.</u> $i^{39} = (i^2)^{19} \cdot i = (-1)^{19} \cdot i = -1 \cdot i = -i$

<u>26.</u> $i^{40} = (i^2)^{20} = (-1)^{20} = 1$

<u>27.</u> $i^{46} = (i^2)^{23} = (-1)^{23} = -1$

<u>28.</u> $i^{72} = (i^2)^{36} = (-1)^{36} = 1$

<u>29.</u> $(2 + 3i) + (4 + 2i) = 2 + 4 + 3i + 2i = 6 + 5i$

<u>30.</u> $11 + i$

<u>31.</u> $(4 + 3i) + (4 - 3i) = 4 + 4 + 3i - 3i = 8$

<u>32.</u> 0

<u>33.</u> $(8 + 11i) - (6 + 7i) = 8 + 11i - 6 - 7i$
$$= 8 - 6 + 11i - 7i$$
$$= 2 + 4i$$

<u>34.</u> $5 - 7i$

<u>35.</u> $2i - (4 + 3i) = 2i - 4 - 3i = -4 - i$

<u>36.</u> $-5 + i$

<u>37.</u> $(1 + 2i)(1 + 3i) = 1 + 3i + 2i + 6i^2$
$$= 1 + 5i - 6 \qquad (i^2 = -1)$$
$$= -5 + 5i$$

38. $(1 + 4i)(1 - 3i) = 1 - 3i + 4i - 12i^2 = 13 + i$

39. $(1 + 2i)(1 - 3i) = 1 - 3i + 2i - 6i^2$
$$= 1 - i + 6 \qquad (i^2 = -1)$$
$$= 7 - i$$

40. $(2 + 3i)(2 - 3i) = 4 - 9i^2 = 13$

41. $3i(4 + 2i) = 12i + 6i^2 = 12i - 6, \text{ or } -6 + 12i$

42. $5i(3 - 4i) = 15i - 20i^2 = 20 + 15i$

43. $(2 + 3i)^2 = 4 + 12i + 9i^2$
$$= 4 + 12i - 9 \qquad (i^2 = -1)$$
$$= -5 + 12i$$

44. $(3 - 2i)^2 = 9 - 12i + 4i^2 = 5 - 12i$

45. $4x^2 + 25y^2 = (2x + 5yi)(2x - 5yi)$

Check by multiplying:
$(2x + 5yi)(2x - 5yi) = 4x^2 - 25y^2i^2 = 4x^2 + 25y^2$

46. $(4a + 7bi)(4a - 7bi)$

47.

$$\begin{array}{r|l} x^2 - 2x + 5 = 0 \\ \hline (1 + 2i)^2 - 2(1 + 2i) + 5 & 0 \\ 1 + 4i + 4i^2 - 2 - 4i + 5 & \\ 4i^2 + 4 & \\ -4 + 4 & \\ 0 & \end{array}$$

The number $1 + 2i$ is a solution.

48.

$$\begin{array}{r|l} x^2 - 2x + 5 = 0 \\ \hline (1 - 2i)^2 - 2(1 - 2i) + 5 & 0 \\ 1 - 4i + 4i^2 - 2 + 4i + 5 & \\ 4 + 4i^2 & \\ 4 - 4 & \\ 0 & \end{array}$$

The number $1 - 2i$ is a solution.

49. $4x + 7i = -6 + yi$

We equate the real parts and solve for x.
$$4x = -6$$
$$x = -\frac{3}{2}$$

We equate the imaginary parts and solve for y.
$$7i = yi$$
$$7 = y$$

50.
$$5x = x - 4 \qquad\qquad y - 3 = 6y$$
$$4x = -4 \qquad\qquad\quad -3 = 5y$$
$$x = -1 \qquad\qquad -\frac{3}{5} = y$$

51. $\dfrac{4 + 3i}{1 - i} = \dfrac{4 + 3i}{1 - i} \cdot \dfrac{1 + i}{1 + i}$
$$= \dfrac{4 + 7i + 3i^2}{1 - i^2} = \dfrac{1 + 7i}{2} = \dfrac{1}{2} + \dfrac{7}{2}i$$

52. $\dfrac{2 - 3i}{5 - 4i} = \dfrac{2 - 3i}{5 - 4i} \cdot \dfrac{5 + 4i}{5 + 4i} = \dfrac{22 - 7i}{41} = \dfrac{22}{41} - \dfrac{7}{41}i$

53. $\dfrac{\sqrt{2} + i}{\sqrt{2} - i} = \dfrac{\sqrt{2} + i}{\sqrt{2} - i} \cdot \dfrac{\sqrt{2} + i}{\sqrt{2} + i}$
$$= \dfrac{2 + 2\sqrt{2}\,i + i^2}{2 - i^2} = \dfrac{1 + 2\sqrt{2}\,i}{3} = \dfrac{1}{3} + \dfrac{2\sqrt{2}}{3}i$$

54. $\dfrac{\sqrt{3} + i}{\sqrt{3} - i} = \dfrac{\sqrt{3} + i}{\sqrt{3} - i} \cdot \dfrac{\sqrt{3} + i}{\sqrt{3} + i} = \dfrac{2 + 2\sqrt{3}\,i}{4}$
$$= \dfrac{1}{2} + \dfrac{\sqrt{3}}{2}i$$

55. $\dfrac{3 + 2i}{i} = \dfrac{3 + 2i}{i} \cdot \dfrac{-i}{-i}$
$$= \dfrac{-3i - 2i^2}{-i^2} = \dfrac{2 - 3i}{1} = 2 - 3i$$

56. $\dfrac{2 + 3i}{i} = \dfrac{2 + 3i}{i} \cdot \dfrac{-i}{-i} = \dfrac{-2i + 3}{1} = 3 - 2i$

57. $\dfrac{i}{2 + i} = \dfrac{i}{2 + i} \cdot \dfrac{2 - i}{2 - i}$
$$= \dfrac{2i - i^2}{4 - i^2} = \dfrac{1 + 2i}{5} = \dfrac{1}{5} + \dfrac{2}{5}i$$

58. $\dfrac{3}{5 - 11i} = \dfrac{3}{5 - 11i} \cdot \dfrac{5 + 11i}{5 + 11i} = \dfrac{15 + 33i}{146}$
$$= \dfrac{15}{146} + \dfrac{33}{146}i$$

59. $\dfrac{1 - i}{(1 + i)^2} = \dfrac{1 - i}{1 + 2i + i^2} = \dfrac{1 - i}{2i}$
$$= \dfrac{1 - i}{2i} \cdot \dfrac{-2i}{-2i} = \dfrac{-2i + 2i^2}{-4i^2}$$
$$= \dfrac{-2 - 2i}{4} = -\dfrac{1}{2} - \dfrac{1}{2}i$$

60. $\dfrac{1 + i}{(1 - i)^2} = \dfrac{1 + i}{-2i} = \dfrac{1 + i}{-2i} \cdot \dfrac{2i}{2i} = \dfrac{2i - 2}{4} = -\dfrac{1}{2} + \dfrac{1}{2}i$

61. $\dfrac{3 - 4i}{(2 + i)(3 - 2i)} = \dfrac{3 - 4i}{6 - i - 2i^2}$
$$= \dfrac{3 - 4i}{8 - i} \cdot \dfrac{8 + i}{8 + i}$$
$$= \dfrac{24 - 29i - 4i^2}{64 - i^2}$$
$$= \dfrac{28 - 29i}{65} = \dfrac{28}{65} - \dfrac{29}{65}i$$

62. $\dfrac{(4 - i)(5 + i)}{(6 - 5i)(7 - 2i)} = \dfrac{21 - i}{32 - 47i}$
$$= \dfrac{21 - i}{32 - 47i} \cdot \dfrac{32 + 47i}{32 + 47i}$$
$$= \dfrac{719 + 955i}{3233} = \dfrac{719}{3233} + \dfrac{955}{3233}i$$

63. $\dfrac{1+i}{1-i} \cdot \dfrac{2-i}{1-i} = \dfrac{2+i-i^2}{1-2i+i^2}$

$= \dfrac{3+i}{-2i} \cdot \dfrac{2i}{2i}$

$= \dfrac{6i+2i^2}{-4i^2}$

$= \dfrac{-2+6i}{4} = -\dfrac{1}{2} + \dfrac{3}{2}i$

64. $\dfrac{1-i}{1+i} \cdot \dfrac{2+i}{1+i} = \dfrac{3-i}{2i} = \dfrac{3-i}{2i} \cdot \dfrac{-2i}{-2i} = \dfrac{-6i-2}{4}$

$= -\dfrac{1}{2} - \dfrac{3}{2}i$

65. $\dfrac{3+2i}{1-i} + \dfrac{6+2i}{1-i} = \dfrac{3+6+2i+2i}{1-i}$

$= \dfrac{9+4i}{1-i} \cdot \dfrac{1+i}{1+i}$

$= \dfrac{9+13i+4i^2}{1-i^2}$

$= \dfrac{5+13i}{2} = \dfrac{5}{2} + \dfrac{13}{2}i$

66. $\dfrac{4-2i}{1+i} + \dfrac{2-5i}{1+i} = \dfrac{6-7i}{1+i} = \dfrac{6-7i}{1+i} \cdot \dfrac{1-i}{1-i}$

$= \dfrac{-1-13i}{2} = -\dfrac{1}{2} - \dfrac{13}{2}i$

67. The reciprocal of $4+3i$ is $\dfrac{1}{4+3i}$, or

$\dfrac{1}{4+3i} \cdot \dfrac{4-3i}{4-3i} = \dfrac{4-3i}{16-9i^2} = \dfrac{4-3i}{25} = \dfrac{4}{25} - \dfrac{3}{25}i$.

68. $\dfrac{1}{4-3i} = \dfrac{1}{4-3i} \cdot \dfrac{4+3i}{4+3i} = \dfrac{4+3i}{25} = \dfrac{4}{25} + \dfrac{3}{25}i$

69. The reciprocal of $5-2i$ is $\dfrac{1}{5-2i}$, or

$\dfrac{1}{5-2i} \cdot \dfrac{5+2i}{5+2i} = \dfrac{5+2i}{25-4i^2} = \dfrac{5+2i}{29} = \dfrac{5}{29} + \dfrac{2}{29}i$.

70. $\dfrac{1}{2+5i} = \dfrac{1}{2+5i} \cdot \dfrac{2-5i}{2-5i} = \dfrac{2-5i}{29} = \dfrac{2}{29} - \dfrac{5}{29}i$

71. The reciprocal of i is $\dfrac{1}{i}$, or

$\dfrac{1}{i} \cdot \dfrac{-i}{-i} = \dfrac{-i}{-i^2} = \dfrac{-i}{1} = -i$.

72. $\dfrac{1}{-i} = \dfrac{1}{-i} \cdot \dfrac{i}{i} = \dfrac{i}{1} = i$

73. The reciprocal of $-4i$ is $\dfrac{1}{-4i}$, or

$\dfrac{1}{-4i} \cdot \dfrac{4i}{4i} = \dfrac{4i}{-16i^2} = \dfrac{4i}{16} = \dfrac{1}{4}i$.

74. $\dfrac{1}{5i} = \dfrac{1}{5i} \cdot \dfrac{-5i}{-5i} = \dfrac{-5i}{25} = -\dfrac{1}{5}i$

75. $(3+i)x + i = 5i$

$(3+i)x = 4i$

$x = \dfrac{4i}{3+i}$

$x = \dfrac{4i}{3+i} \cdot \dfrac{3-i}{3-i}$

$x = \dfrac{12i-4i^2}{9-i^2} = \dfrac{4+12i}{10}$

$x = \dfrac{2}{5} + \dfrac{6}{5}i$

76. $(2+i)x - i = 5+i$

$(2+i)x = 5+2i$

$x = \dfrac{5+2i}{2+i}$

$x = \dfrac{5+2i}{2+i} \cdot \dfrac{2-i}{2-i} = \dfrac{12-i}{5}$

$x = \dfrac{12}{5} - \dfrac{1}{5}i$

77. $2ix + 5 - 4i = (2+3i)x - 2i$

$5 - 4i + 2i = (2+3i)x - 2ix$

$5 - 2i = (2+i)x$

$\dfrac{5-2i}{2+i} = x$

$\dfrac{2-i}{2-i} \cdot \dfrac{5-2i}{2+i} = x$

$\dfrac{8-9i}{5} = \dfrac{10-9i+2i^2}{4-i^2} = x$

$\dfrac{8}{5} - \dfrac{9}{5}i = x$

78. $5ix + 3 + 2i = (3-2i)x + 3i$

$(-3+7i)x = -3+i$

$x = \dfrac{-3+i}{-3+7i}$

$x = \dfrac{-3+i}{-3+7i} \cdot \dfrac{-3-7i}{-3-7i} = \dfrac{16+18i}{58}$

$x = \dfrac{8}{29} + \dfrac{9}{29}i$

79. $(1+2i)x + 3 - 2i = 4 - 5i + 3ix$

$(1+2i)x - 3ix = 4 - 5i - 3 + 2i$

$(1-i)x = 1 - 3i$

$x = \dfrac{1-3i}{1-i}$

$x = \dfrac{1-3i}{1-i} \cdot \dfrac{1+i}{1+i}$

$x = \dfrac{1-2i-3i^2}{1-i^2} = \dfrac{4-2i}{2}$

$x = 2 - i$

80. $(1 - 2i)x + 2 - 3i = 5 - 4i + 2x$

$(-1 - 2i)x = 3 - i$

$x = \dfrac{3 - i}{-1 - 2i}$

$x = \dfrac{3 - i}{-1 - 2i} \cdot \dfrac{-1 + 2i}{-1 + 2i} = \dfrac{-1 + 7i}{5}$

$x = -\dfrac{1}{5} + \dfrac{7}{5} i$

81. $(5 + i)x + 1 - 3i = (2 - 3i)x + 2 - i$

$(5 + i)x - (2 - 3i)x = 2 - i - 1 + 3i$

$(3 + 4i)x = 1 + 2i$

$x = \dfrac{1 + 2i}{3 + 4i}$

$x = \dfrac{1 + 2i}{3 + 4i} \cdot \dfrac{3 - 4i}{3 - 4i}$

$x = \dfrac{3 + 2i - 8i^2}{9 - 16i^2} = \dfrac{11 + 2i}{25}$

$x = \dfrac{11}{25} + \dfrac{2}{25} i$

82. $(5 - i)x + 2 - 3i = (3 - 2i)x + 3 - i$

$(2 + i)x = 1 + 2i$

$x = \dfrac{1 + 2i}{2 + i}$

$x = \dfrac{1 + 2i}{2 + i} \cdot \dfrac{2 - i}{2 - i} = \dfrac{4 + 3i}{5}$

$x = \dfrac{4}{5} + \dfrac{3}{5} i$

83. For example, $\sqrt{-1}\,\sqrt{-1} = i^2 = -1$
but $\sqrt{(-1)(-1)} = \sqrt{1} = 1$.

84. For example, $\sqrt{\dfrac{4}{-1}} = \sqrt{-4} = 2i$, but $\dfrac{\sqrt{4}}{\sqrt{-1}} = \dfrac{2}{i} = -2i$

85. Let $z = a + bi$. Then $z \cdot \bar{z} = (a + bi)(a - bi) =$ $a^2 - b^2i^2 = a^2 + b^2$. Since a and b are real numbers, so is $a^2 + b^2$. Thus $z \cdot \bar{z}$ is real.

86. Let $z = a + bi$. Then $z + \bar{z} = (a + bi) + (a - bi)$ $= 2a$. Since a is a real number, $2a$ is real. Thus $z + \bar{z}$ is real.

87. Let $z = a + bi$ and $w = c + di$. Then $\overline{z + w} =$ $\overline{(a + bi) + (c + di)} = \overline{(a + c) + (b + d)i} =$ $(a + c) - (b + d)i$. Now $\bar{z} + \bar{w} =$ $\overline{a + bi} + \overline{c + di} = (a - bi) + (c - di) =$ $(a + c) - (b + d)i$, the same result as before. Thus $\overline{z + w} = \bar{z} + \bar{w}$.

88. Let $z = a + bi$ and $w = c + di$. Then $\overline{z \cdot w} =$ $\overline{(a + bi)(c + di)} = \overline{(ac - bd) + (ad + bc)i} =$ $(ac - bd) - (ad + bc)i$. Now $\bar{z} \cdot \bar{w} =$ $\overline{(a + bi)} \cdot \overline{(c + di)} = (a - bi)(c - di) =$ $(ac - bd) - (ad + bc)i$, the same result as before. Thus $\overline{z \cdot w} = \bar{z} \cdot \bar{w}$.

89. By definition of exponents the conjugate of z^n is the conjugate of the product of n factors of z. Using the result of Exercise 88, the conjugate of n factors of z is the product of n factors of $\bar{z}$. Thus $\overline{z^n} = \bar{z}^n$.

90. If z is a real number, then $z = a + 0i = a$ and $\bar{z} = a - 0i = a$. Thus $\bar{z} = z$.

91. $\overline{3z^5 - 4z^2 + 3z - 5}$

$= \overline{3z^5} - \overline{4z^2} + \overline{3z} - \overline{5}$ By Exercise 87

$= \overline{3}\,\overline{z^5} - \overline{4}\,\overline{z^2} + \overline{3}\,\overline{z} - \overline{5}$ By Exercise 88

$= 3\,\overline{z^5} - 4\,\overline{z^2} + 3\,\overline{z} - 5$ By Exercise 90

$= 3\bar{z}^5 - 4\bar{z}^2 + 3\bar{z} - 5$ By Exercise 89

92. Let $z = a + bi$. Then $\bar{z} = a - bi$

$z + 6\bar{z} = 7$

$a + bi + 6(a - bi) = 7$

$a + bi + 6a - 6bi = 7$

$7a - 5bi = 7$

Then $7a = 7$, so $a = 1$, and $-5b = 0$, so $b = 0$. Then $z = 1$.

93. Solve $5z - 4\bar{z} = 7 + 8i$ for z.

Let $z = a + bi$. Then $\bar{z} = a - bi$.

$5z - 4\bar{z} = 7 + 8i$

$5(a + bi) - 4(a - bi) = 7 + 8i$

$5a + 5bi - 4a + 4bi = 7 + 8i$

$a + 9bi = 7 + 8i$

Equate the real parts.

$a = 7$

Equate the imaginary parts.

$9b = 8$

$b = \dfrac{8}{9}$

Then $z = 7 + \dfrac{8}{9} i$.

94. $\dfrac{1}{2}(z + \bar{z}) = \dfrac{1}{2}(a + bi + a - bi) = \dfrac{1}{2} \cdot 2a = a$

95. Let $z = a + bi$. Then $\bar{z} = a - bi$.

$\frac{1}{2}(\bar{z} - z) = \frac{1}{2}[(a - bi) - (a + bi)]$

$\qquad\qquad = \frac{1}{2}(-2bi) = -bi$

96. $(a + bi)^2 = -2i$, or $a^2 - b^2 + 2abi = -2i$

Solve: $a^2 - b^2 = 0$,
$\qquad\quad 2ab = -2$

$a = 1, b = -1$ or $a = -1, b = 1$

$z = 1 - i$ or $z = -1 + i$

97. $\frac{(a + bi)^2}{4} = i$, or $a^2 - b^2 + 2abi = 4i$

Solving $\begin{array}{l} a^2 - b^2 = 0, \\ 2ab = 4 \end{array}$, we get $a = \sqrt{2}$, $b = \sqrt{2}$ or

$a = -\sqrt{2}$, $b = -\sqrt{2}$. Then $z = \sqrt{2} + i\sqrt{2}$ or
$z = -\sqrt{2} - i\sqrt{2}$.

98. $\frac{1}{z} = \frac{1}{a + bi} \cdot \frac{a - bi}{a - bi} = \frac{a}{a^2 + b^2} + \frac{-b}{a^2 + b^2}i$

99. $\frac{w}{z} = \frac{c + di}{a + bi} \cdot \frac{a - bi}{a - bi} = \frac{ac + bd}{a^2 + b^2} + \frac{ad - bc}{a^2 + b^2}i$

Exercise Set 2.5

1. $3x^2 = 27$
$\quad x^2 = 9$ Multiplying by $\frac{1}{3}$
$\quad x = 3$ or $x = -3$ Taking square roots
The solution set is $\{3, -3\}$, or $\{\pm 3\}$.

2. $5x^2 = 80$
$\quad x^2 = 16$
$\quad x = 4$ or $x = -4$
$\{4, -4\}$, or $\{\pm 4\}$

3. $x^2 = -1$
$\quad x = \sqrt{-1}$ or $x = -\sqrt{-1}$ Taking square roots
$\quad x = i$ or $x = -i$ Simplifying
The solution set is $\{i, -i\}$, or $\{\pm i\}$.

4. $x^2 = -4$
$\quad x = 2i$ or $x = -2i$
$\{2i, -2i\}$, or $\{\pm 2i\}$

5. $4x^2 = 20$
$\quad x^2 = 5$
$\quad x = \sqrt{5}$ or $x = -\sqrt{5}$
The solution set is $\{\pm\sqrt{5}\}$.

6. $3x^2 = 21$
$\quad x^2 = 7$
$\quad x = \sqrt{7}$ or $x = -\sqrt{7}$
$\{\pm\sqrt{7}\}$

7. $10x^2 = 0$
$\quad x^2 = 0$
$\quad x = 0$
The solution set is $\{0\}$.

8. $9x^2 = 0$
$\quad x^2 = 0$
$\quad x = 0$
$\{0\}$

9. $2x^2 - 3 = 0$
$\quad 2x^2 = 3$
$\quad x^2 = \frac{3}{2}$

$x = \sqrt{\frac{3}{2}}$ or $x = -\sqrt{\frac{3}{2}}$

$x = \sqrt{\frac{3}{2} \cdot \frac{2}{2}}$ or $x = -\sqrt{\frac{3}{2} \cdot \frac{2}{2}}$

$x = \frac{\sqrt{6}}{2}$ or $x = -\frac{\sqrt{6}}{2}$

The solution set is $\left\{\pm\frac{\sqrt{6}}{2}\right\}$.

10. $3x^2 - 7 = 0$
$\quad x^2 = \frac{7}{3}$

$x = \sqrt{\frac{7}{3}}$ or $x = -\sqrt{\frac{7}{3}}$

$x = \frac{\sqrt{21}}{3}$ or $x = -\frac{\sqrt{21}}{3}$

$\left\{\pm\frac{\sqrt{21}}{3}\right\}$

11. $2x^2 + 14 = 0$
$\quad 2x^2 = -14$
$\quad x^2 = -7$
$x = \sqrt{-7}$ or $x = -\sqrt{-7}$
$x = i\sqrt{7}$ or $x = -i\sqrt{7}$
The solution set is $\{\pm i\sqrt{7}\}$.

12. $3x^2 + 15 = 0$
$\quad x^2 = -5$
$x = i\sqrt{5}$ or $x = -i\sqrt{5}$
$\{\pm i\sqrt{5}\}$

13. $ax^2 = b$

$x^2 = \dfrac{b}{a}$

$x = \pm\sqrt{\dfrac{b}{a}}$

The solution set is $\left\{\pm\sqrt{\dfrac{b}{a}}\right\}$.

14. $\pi x^2 = k$

$x^2 = \dfrac{k}{\pi}$

$x = \sqrt{\dfrac{k}{\pi}}$ or $x = -\sqrt{\dfrac{k}{\pi}}$

$\left\{\pm\sqrt{\dfrac{k}{\pi}}\right\}$

15. $(x - 7)^2 = 5$

$x - 7 = \pm\sqrt{5}$

$x = 7 \pm\sqrt{5}$

The solution set is $\{7 \pm\sqrt{5}\}$.

16. $(x + 3)^2 = 2$

$x + 3 = \pm\sqrt{2}$

$x = -3 \pm\sqrt{2}$

$\{-3 \pm\sqrt{2}\}$

17. $\dfrac{4}{9}x^2 - 1 = 0$

$\dfrac{4}{9}x^2 = 1$

$x^2 = \dfrac{9}{4}$

$x = \sqrt{\dfrac{9}{4}}$ or $x = -\sqrt{\dfrac{9}{4}}$

$x = \dfrac{3}{2}$ or $x = -\dfrac{3}{2}$

The solution set is $\left\{\pm\dfrac{3}{2}\right\}$.

18. $\dfrac{16}{25}x^2 - 1 = 0$

$x^2 = \dfrac{25}{16}$

$x = \dfrac{5}{4}$ or $x = -\dfrac{5}{4}$

$\left\{\pm\dfrac{5}{4}\right\}$

19. $(x - h)^2 - 1 = a$

$(x - h)^2 = a + 1$

$x - h = \pm\sqrt{a + 1}$

$x = h \pm\sqrt{a + 1}$

The solution set is $\{h \pm\sqrt{a + 1}\}$.

20. $y = a(x - h)^2 + k$

$\dfrac{y - k}{a} = (x - h)^2$

$\pm\sqrt{\dfrac{y - k}{a}} = x - h$

$h \pm\sqrt{\dfrac{y - k}{a}} = x$

$\left\{h \pm\sqrt{\dfrac{y - k}{a}}\right\}$

21. $x^2 + 6x + 4 = 0$

$x^2 + 6x + 9 - 9 + 4 = 0$ $\qquad\left[\dfrac{1}{2}\cdot 6 = 3,\ 3^2 = 9;\right.$
$\left.\text{thus we add } 9 - 9.\right]$

$(x + 3)^2 - 5 = 0$

$(x + 3)^2 = 5$

$x + 3 = \pm\sqrt{5}$

$x = -3 \pm\sqrt{5}$

The solution set is $\{-3 \pm\sqrt{5}\}$.

22. $x^2 - 6x - 4 = 0$

$x^2 - 6x + 9 - 9 - 4 = 0$

$(x - 3)^2 = 13$

$x = 3 \pm\sqrt{13}$

$\left\{3 \pm\sqrt{13}\right\}$

23. $y^2 + 7y - 30 = 0$

$y^2 + 7y + \dfrac{49}{4} - \dfrac{49}{4} - 30 = 0$ $\qquad\left[\dfrac{1}{2}\cdot 7 = \dfrac{7}{2},\ \left(\dfrac{7}{2}\right)^2 = \dfrac{49}{4};\right.$
$\left.\text{thus we add } \dfrac{49}{4} - \dfrac{49}{4}\right]$

$\left(y + \dfrac{7}{2}\right)^2 - \dfrac{169}{4} = 0$

$\left(y + \dfrac{7}{2}\right)^2 = \dfrac{169}{4}$

$y + \dfrac{7}{2} = \pm\sqrt{\dfrac{169}{4}} = \pm\dfrac{13}{2}$

$y = -\dfrac{7}{2} \pm\dfrac{13}{2} = \dfrac{-7 \pm 13}{2}$

$y = \dfrac{-7 + 13}{2}$ or $y = \dfrac{-7 - 13}{2}$

$y = 3$ or $y = -10$

The solution set is $\{3, -10\}$.

24. $y^2 - 7y - 30 = 0$

$y^2 - 7y + \dfrac{49}{4} - \dfrac{49}{4} - 30 = 0$

$\left(y - \dfrac{7}{2}\right)^2 = \dfrac{169}{4}$

$y = \dfrac{7}{2} \pm\dfrac{13}{2}$

$y = 10$ or $y = -3$

$\{10, -3\}$

25.
$$5x^2 - 4x - 2 = 0$$
$$x^2 - \frac{4}{5}x - \frac{2}{5} = 0 \quad \left[\text{Multiplying by } \frac{1}{5}\right]$$
$$x^2 - \frac{4}{5}x + \frac{4}{25} - \frac{4}{25} - \frac{2}{5} = 0 \quad \left[\text{Adding } \frac{4}{25} - \frac{4}{25}\right]$$
$$\left(x - \frac{2}{5}\right)^2 - \frac{14}{25} = 0$$
$$\left(x - \frac{2}{5}\right)^2 = \frac{14}{25}$$
$$x - \frac{2}{5} = \pm\sqrt{\frac{14}{25}} = \pm\frac{\sqrt{14}}{5}$$
$$x = \frac{2}{5} \pm \frac{\sqrt{14}}{5} = \frac{2 \pm \sqrt{14}}{5}$$

The solution set is $\left\{\dfrac{2 \pm \sqrt{14}}{5}\right\}$.

26.
$$12y^2 - 14y + 3 = 0$$
$$y^2 - \frac{7}{6}y + \frac{1}{4} = 0$$
$$y^2 - \frac{7}{6}y + \frac{49}{144} - \frac{49}{144} + \frac{1}{4} = 0$$
$$\left(y - \frac{7}{12}\right)^2 = \frac{13}{144}$$
$$y = \frac{7}{12} \pm \frac{\sqrt{13}}{12}$$

$$\left\{\frac{7 \pm \sqrt{13}}{12}\right\}$$

27.
$$2x^2 + 7x - 15 = 0$$
$$x^2 + \frac{7}{2}x - \frac{15}{2} = 0 \quad \left[\text{Multiplying by } \frac{1}{2}\right]$$
$$x^2 + \frac{7}{2}x + \frac{49}{16} - \frac{49}{16} - \frac{15}{2} = 0 \quad \left[\text{Adding } \frac{49}{16} - \frac{49}{16}\right]$$
$$\left(x + \frac{7}{4}\right)^2 - \frac{169}{16} = 0$$
$$\left(x + \frac{7}{4}\right)^2 = \frac{169}{16}$$
$$x + \frac{7}{4} = \pm\sqrt{\frac{169}{16}} = \pm\frac{13}{4}$$
$$x = -\frac{7}{4} \pm \frac{13}{4} = \frac{-7 \pm 13}{4}$$

$$x = \frac{-7 + 13}{4} \quad \text{or} \quad x = \frac{-7 - 13}{4}$$
$$x = \frac{3}{2} \quad \text{or} \quad x = -5$$

The solution set is $\left\{\dfrac{3}{2}, -5\right\}$.

28.
$$9x^2 - 30x = -25$$
$$x^2 - \frac{10}{3}x = -\frac{25}{9}$$
$$x^2 - \frac{10}{3}x + \frac{25}{9} - \frac{25}{9} = -\frac{25}{9}$$
$$\left(x - \frac{5}{3}\right)^2 = 0$$
$$x = \frac{5}{3}$$

$$\left\{\frac{5}{3}\right\}$$

29.
$$x^2 + 4x = 5$$
$$x^2 + 4x - 5 = 0$$
$$a = 1, \quad b = 4, \quad c = -5$$
$$x = \frac{-b \pm \sqrt{b^2 - 4ac}}{2a}$$
$$x = \frac{-4 \pm \sqrt{4^2 - 4(1)(-5)}}{2(1)} = \frac{-4 \pm \sqrt{16 + 20}}{2}$$
$$x = \frac{-4 \pm \sqrt{36}}{2} = \frac{-4 \pm 6}{2}$$
$$x = \frac{-4 + 6}{2} \quad \text{or} \quad x = \frac{-4 - 6}{2}$$
$$x = 1 \quad \text{or} \quad x = -5$$

The solution set is $\{1, -5\}$.

30.
$$x^2 = 2x + 15$$
$$x^2 - 2x - 15 = 0$$
$$x = \frac{-(-2) \pm \sqrt{(-2)^2 - 4(1)(-15)}}{2 \cdot 1}$$
$$x = \frac{2 \pm \sqrt{64}}{2} = \frac{2 \pm 8}{2}$$
$$x = 5 \quad \text{or} \quad x = -3$$
$$\{5, -3\}$$

31. $2y^2 - 3y - 2 = 0$
$$a = 2, \quad b = -3, \quad c = -2$$
$$y = \frac{-b \pm \sqrt{b^2 - 4ac}}{2a}$$
$$y = \frac{-(-3) \pm \sqrt{(-3)^2 - 4(2)(-2)}}{2(2)} = \frac{3 \pm \sqrt{9 + 16}}{4}$$
$$y = \frac{3 \pm \sqrt{25}}{4} = \frac{3 \pm 5}{4}$$
$$y = \frac{3 + 5}{4} \quad \text{or} \quad y = \frac{3 - 5}{4}$$
$$y = 2 \quad \text{or} \quad y = -\frac{1}{2}$$

The solution set is $\left\{2, -\dfrac{1}{2}\right\}$.

32. $5m^2 + 3m - 2 = 0$
$$m = \frac{-3 \pm \sqrt{3^2 - 4(5)(-2)}}{2 \cdot 5} = \frac{-3 \pm \sqrt{49}}{10}$$
$$m = \frac{-3 \pm 7}{10}$$
$$m = \frac{2}{5} \quad \text{or} \quad m = -1$$

$$\left\{\frac{2}{5}, -1\right\}$$

33. $3t^2 + 8t + 3 = 0$

    $a = 3, \qquad b = 8, \qquad c = 3$

    $t = \dfrac{-b \pm \sqrt{b^2 - 4ac}}{2a}$

    $t = \dfrac{-8 \pm \sqrt{8^2 - 4\cdot3\cdot3}}{2\cdot3} = \dfrac{-8 \pm \sqrt{64 - 36}}{6}$

    $t = \dfrac{-8 \pm \sqrt{28}}{6} = \dfrac{-8 \pm 2\sqrt{7}}{6} = \dfrac{2(-4 \pm \sqrt{7})}{6}$

    $t = \dfrac{-4 \pm \sqrt{7}}{3}$

    The solution set is $\left\{\dfrac{-4 \pm \sqrt{7}}{3}\right\}$.

34. $\qquad 3u^2 = 18u - 6$

    $3u^2 - 18u + 6 = 0$

    $\quad u^2 - 6u + 2 = 0$

    $u = \dfrac{-(-6) \pm \sqrt{(-6)^2 - 4\cdot1\cdot2}}{2\cdot1} =$

    $\qquad \dfrac{6 \pm \sqrt{28}}{2}$

    $u = \dfrac{6 \pm 2\sqrt{7}}{2} = 3 \pm \sqrt{7}$

    $\{3 \pm \sqrt{7}\}$

35. $\qquad 3 + u^2 = 12u$

    $u^2 - 12u + 3 = 0$

    $a = 1, \quad b = -12, \quad c = 3$

    $u = \dfrac{-b \pm \sqrt{b^2 - 4ac}}{2a}$

    $u = \dfrac{-(-12) \pm \sqrt{(-12)^2 - 4\cdot1\cdot3}}{2\cdot1} = \dfrac{12 \pm \sqrt{144 - 12}}{2}$

    $u = \dfrac{12 \pm \sqrt{132}}{2} = \dfrac{12 \pm 2\sqrt{33}}{2}$

    $u = \dfrac{2(6 \pm \sqrt{33})}{2} = 6 \pm \sqrt{33}$

    The solution set is $\{6 \pm \sqrt{33}\}$.

36. $40 + 30p + 5p^2 = 0$

    $\quad p^2 + 6p + 8 = 0$

    $p = \dfrac{-6 \pm \sqrt{6^2 - 4\cdot1\cdot8}}{2\cdot1} = \dfrac{-6 \pm \sqrt{4}}{2}$

    $p = \dfrac{-6 \pm 2}{2} = -3 \pm 1$

    $p = -2 \ $ or $\ p = -4$

    $\{-2, -4\}$

37. $x^2 - x + 1 = 0$

    $a = 1, \qquad b = -1, \qquad c = 1$

    $x = \dfrac{-b \pm \sqrt{b^2 - 4ac}}{2a}$

    $x = \dfrac{-(-1) \pm \sqrt{(-1)^2 - 4\cdot1\cdot1}}{2\cdot1}$

    $x = \dfrac{1 \pm \sqrt{1 - 4}}{2} = \dfrac{1 \pm \sqrt{-3}}{2}$

    $x = \dfrac{1 \pm i\sqrt{3}}{2}$

    The solution set is $\left\{\dfrac{1 \pm i\sqrt{3}}{2}\right\}$.

38. $x^2 + x + 2 = 0$

    $x = \dfrac{-1 \pm \sqrt{1^2 - 4\cdot1\cdot2}}{2\cdot1} = \dfrac{-1 \pm \sqrt{-7}}{2}$

    $x = \dfrac{-1 \pm i\sqrt{7}}{2}$

    $\left\{\dfrac{-1 \pm i\sqrt{7}}{2}\right\}$

39. $\qquad x^2 + 13 = 4x$

    $x^2 - 4x + 13 = 0$

    $a = 1, \qquad b = -4, \qquad c = 13$

    $x = \dfrac{-b \pm \sqrt{b^2 - 4ac}}{2a}$

    $x = \dfrac{-(-4) \pm \sqrt{(-4)^2 - 4\cdot1\cdot13}}{2\cdot1}$

    $x = \dfrac{4 \pm \sqrt{16 - 52}}{2} = \dfrac{4 \pm \sqrt{-36}}{2}$

    $x = \dfrac{4 \pm 6i}{2} = \dfrac{2(2 \pm 3i)}{2} = 2 \pm 3i$

    The solution set is $\{2 \pm 3i\}$.

40. $\qquad 2x + 1 = -5x^2$

    $5x^2 + 2x + 1 = 0$

    $x = \dfrac{-2 \pm \sqrt{2^2 - 4\cdot5\cdot1}}{2\cdot5} = \dfrac{-2 \pm \sqrt{-16}}{10}$

    $x = \dfrac{-2 \pm 4i}{10} = \dfrac{-1 \pm 2i}{5}$

    $\left\{\dfrac{-1 \pm 2i}{5}\right\}$

41.
$$5x^2 = 13x + 17$$
$$5x^2 - 13x - 17 = 0 \quad \text{Standard form}$$
$$a = 5, \ b = -13, \ c = -17$$
$$x = \frac{-b \pm \sqrt{b^2 - 4ac}}{2a}$$
$$x = \frac{-(-13) \pm \sqrt{(-13)^2 - 4(5)(-17)}}{2 \cdot 5}$$
$$x = \frac{13 \pm \sqrt{169 + 340}}{10}$$
$$x = \frac{13 \pm \sqrt{509}}{10}$$
The solution set is $\left\{ \dfrac{13 \pm \sqrt{509}}{10} \right\}$.

42.
$$x^2 = \frac{5}{3}x + \frac{4}{3}$$
$$x^2 - \frac{5}{3}x - \frac{4}{3} = 0$$
$$3x^2 - 5x - 4 = 0$$
$$x = \frac{-(-5) \pm \sqrt{(-5)^2 - 4(3)(-4)}}{2 \cdot 3}$$
$$= \frac{5 \pm \sqrt{73}}{6}$$
$$\left\{ \frac{5 \pm \sqrt{73}}{6} \right\}$$

43. $0.03 + 0.08v = v^2$
$$0 = v^2 - 0.08v - 0.03 \quad \text{Standard form}$$
$$a = 1, \ b = -0.08, \ c = -0.03$$
$$v = \frac{-b \pm \sqrt{b^2 - 4ac}}{2a}$$
$$v = \frac{-(-0.08) \pm \sqrt{(-0.08)^2 - 4(1)(-0.03)}}{2 \cdot 1}$$
$$v = \frac{0.08 \pm \sqrt{0.0064 + 0.12}}{2} = \frac{0.08 \pm \sqrt{0.1264}}{2}$$
$$v = \frac{0.08 \pm \sqrt{0.0016 \cdot 79}}{2} = \frac{0.08 \pm 0.04\sqrt{79}}{2}$$
$$v = \frac{2(0.04 \pm 0.02\sqrt{79})}{2} = 0.04 \pm 0.02\sqrt{79}$$
The solution set is $\{0.04 \pm 0.02\sqrt{79}\}$.

44. $3x^2 - 2x - 5\frac{1}{3} = 0$
$$x = \frac{-(-2) \pm \sqrt{(-2)^2 - 4(3)\left(-\frac{16}{3}\right)}}{2 \cdot 3} =$$
$$\frac{2 \pm \sqrt{68}}{6}$$
$$x = \frac{2 \pm 2\sqrt{17}}{6} = \frac{1 \pm \sqrt{17}}{3}$$
$$\left\{ \frac{1 \pm \sqrt{17}}{3} \right\}$$

45.
$$\frac{1}{x} + \frac{1}{x + 3} = 7, \ \text{LCM is } x(x + 3)$$
$$x(x + 3)\left[\frac{1}{x} + \frac{1}{x + 3} \right] = x(x + 3) \cdot 7$$
$$x + 3 + x = 7x^2 + 21x$$
$$2x + 3 = 7x^2 + 21x$$
$$0 = 7x^2 + 19x - 3 \quad \text{Standard form}$$
$$a = 7, \ b = 19, \ c = -3$$
$$x = \frac{-b \pm \sqrt{b^2 - 4ac}}{2a}$$
$$x = \frac{-19 \pm \sqrt{19^2 - 4(7)(-3)}}{2 \cdot 7}$$
$$x = \frac{-19 \pm \sqrt{361 + 84}}{14} = \frac{-19 \pm \sqrt{445}}{14}$$
Both values check.
The solution set is $\left\{ \dfrac{-19 \pm \sqrt{445}}{14} \right\}$.

46. $\dfrac{1}{x - 2} - \dfrac{1}{x + 2} = 5, \quad \text{LCM is } (x - 2)(x + 2)$
$$x + 2 - x + 2 = 5x^2 - 20$$
$$0 = 5x^2 - 24$$
$$x = \frac{-0 \pm \sqrt{0^2 - 4(5)(-24)}}{2 \cdot 5} = \pm \frac{\sqrt{480}}{10}$$
$$x = \pm \frac{4\sqrt{30}}{10} = \pm \frac{2\sqrt{30}}{5}$$
Both values check.
$$\left\{ \pm \frac{2\sqrt{30}}{5} \right\}$$

47.
$$1 + \frac{x + 5}{(x + 1)^2} - \frac{2}{x + 1} = 0, \ \text{LCM is } (x + 1)^2$$
$$(x + 1)^2 \left[1 + \frac{x + 5}{(x + 1)^2} - \frac{2}{x + 1} \right] = (x + 1)^2 \cdot 0$$
$$(x + 1)^2 + x + 5 - 2(x + 1) = 0$$
$$x^2 + 2x + 1 + x + 5 - 2x - 2 = 0$$
$$x^2 + x + 4 = 0$$
$$a = 1, \ b = 1, \ c = 4$$
$$x = \frac{-b \pm \sqrt{b^2 - 4ac}}{2a}$$
$$x = \frac{-1 \pm \sqrt{1^2 - 4 \cdot 1 \cdot 4}}{2 \cdot 1} = \frac{-1 \pm \sqrt{1 - 16}}{2}$$
$$x = \frac{-1 \pm \sqrt{-15}}{2} = \frac{-1 \pm \sqrt{-1 \cdot 15}}{2}$$
$$x = \frac{-1 \pm i\sqrt{15}}{2}$$
Both values check.
The solution set is $\left\{ \dfrac{-1 \pm i\sqrt{15}}{2} \right\}$.

48. $\dfrac{x^2}{x + 11} + 1 = 0$,   LCM is $x + 11$

    $x^2 + x + 11 = 0$

    $$x = \frac{-1 \pm \sqrt{1^2 - 4\cdot1\cdot11}}{2\cdot1} = \frac{-1 \pm \sqrt{-43}}{2}$$

    $$x = \frac{-1 \pm i\sqrt{43}}{2}$$

    $\left\{\dfrac{-1 \pm i\sqrt{43}}{2}\right\}$

49. $x^2 - 6x + 9 = 0$

    $a = 1$, $b = -6$, $c = 9$

    We compute the discriminant.

    $b^2 - 4ac = (-6)^2 - 4\cdot1\cdot9$

    $\qquad\qquad = 36 - 36$

    $\qquad\qquad = 0$

    Since $b^2 - 4ac = 0$, there is just one solution, and it is a real number.

50. $b^2 - 4ac = 0$; one real solution

51. $x^2 + 7 = 0$

    $a = 1$, $b = 0$, $c = 7$

    We compute the discriminant.

    $b^2 - 4ac = 0^2 - 4\cdot1\cdot7$

    $\qquad\qquad = -28$

    Since $b^2 - 4ac < 0$, there are two nonreal solutions.

52. $b^2 - 4ac = -8$; two nonreal solutions

53. $x^2 - 2 = 0$

    $a = 1$, $b = 0$, $c = -2$

    We compute the discriminant.

    $b^2 - 4ac = 0^2 - 4\cdot1\cdot(-2)$

    $\qquad\qquad = 8$

    Since $b^2 - 4ac > 0$, there are two real solutions.

54. $b^2 - 4ac = 20$; two real solutions

55. $4x^2 - 12x + 9 = 0$

    $a = 4$, $b = -12$, $c = 9$

    We compute the discriminant.

    $b^2 - 4ac = (-12)^2 - 4\cdot4\cdot9$

    $\qquad\qquad = 144 - 144$

    $\qquad\qquad = 0$

    Since $b^2 - 4ac = 0$, there is just one solution, and it is a real number.

56. $b^2 - 4ac = 144$; two real solutions

57. $x^2 - 2x + 4 = 0$

    $a = 1$, $b = -2$, $c = 4$

    We compute the discriminant.

    $b^2 - 4ac = (-2)^2 - 4\cdot1\cdot4$

    $\qquad\qquad = 4 - 16$

    $\qquad\qquad = -12$

    Since $b^2 - 4ac < 0$, ther are two nonreal solutions.

58. $b^2 - 4ac = -7$; two nonreal solutions

59. $9t^2 - 3t = 0$

    $a = 9$, $b = -3$, $c = 0$

    We compute the discriminant.

    $b^2 - 4ac = (-3)^2 - 4\cdot9\cdot0$

    $\qquad\qquad = 9 - 0$

    $\qquad\qquad = 9$

    Since $b^2 - 4ac > 0$, there are two real solutions.

60. $b^2 - 4ac = 49$; two real solutions

61. $y^2 = \dfrac{1}{2}y + \dfrac{3}{5}$

    $y^2 - \dfrac{1}{2}y - \dfrac{3}{5} = 0$ (Standard form)

    $a = 1$, $b = -\dfrac{1}{2}$, $c = -\dfrac{3}{5}$

    We compute the discriminant.

    $b^2 - 4ac = \left(-\dfrac{1}{2}\right)^2 - 4\cdot1\cdot\left(-\dfrac{3}{5}\right)$

    $\qquad\qquad = \dfrac{1}{4} + \dfrac{12}{5}$

    $\qquad\qquad = \dfrac{53}{20}$

    Since $b^2 - 4ac > 0$, there are two real solutions.

62. $b^2 - 4ac = 7$; two real solutions

63. $4x^2 - 4\sqrt{3}\,x + 3 = 0$

    $a = 4$, $b = -4\sqrt{3}$, $c = 3$

    We compute the discriminant.

    $b^2 - 4ac = (-4\sqrt{3})^2 - 4\cdot4\cdot3$

    $\qquad\qquad = 48 - 48$

    $\qquad\qquad = 0$

    Since $b^2 - 4ac = 0$, there is just one solution, and it is a real number.

64. $b^2 - 4ac = 36$; two real solutions

65. The solutions are -11 and 9.

$$x = -11 \text{ or } \quad x = 9$$
$$x + 11 = 0 \text{ or } x - 9 = 0$$
$$(x + 11)(x - 9) = 0$$
$$x^2 + 2x - 99 = 0$$

66. $(x + 4)(x - 4) = 0$
$$x^2 - 16 = 0$$

67. The solutions are both 7.
$$x = 7 \text{ or } \quad x = 7$$
$$x - 7 = 0 \text{ or } x - 7 = 0$$
$$(x - 7)(x - 7) = 0$$
$$x^2 - 14x + 49 = 0$$

68. $\left(x + \dfrac{2}{3}\right)\left(x + \dfrac{2}{3}\right) = 0$
$$x^2 + \dfrac{4}{3}x + \dfrac{4}{9} = 0, \text{ or } 9x^2 + 12x + 4 = 0$$

69. The solutions are $-\dfrac{2}{5}$ and $\dfrac{6}{5}$.

$$x = -\dfrac{2}{5} \text{ or } \quad x = \dfrac{6}{5}$$
$$x + \dfrac{2}{5} = 0 \quad \text{ or } x - \dfrac{6}{5} = 0$$
$$\left(x + \dfrac{2}{5}\right)\left(x - \dfrac{6}{5}\right) = 0$$
$$x^2 - \dfrac{4}{5}x - \dfrac{12}{25} = 0$$
or
$$25x^2 - 20x - 12 = 0$$

70. $\left(x + \dfrac{1}{4}\right)\left(x + \dfrac{1}{2}\right) = 0$
$$x^2 + \dfrac{3}{4}x + \dfrac{1}{8} = 0, \text{ or } 8x^2 + 6x + 1 = 0$$

71. The solutions are $\dfrac{c}{2}$ and $\dfrac{d}{2}$.

$$x = \dfrac{c}{2} \text{ or } \quad x = \dfrac{d}{2}$$
$$x - \dfrac{c}{2} = 0 \text{ or } x - \dfrac{d}{2} = 0$$
$$\left(x - \dfrac{c}{2}\right)\left(x - \dfrac{d}{2}\right) = 0$$
$$x^2 - \left(\dfrac{c + d}{2}\right)x + \dfrac{cd}{4} = 0$$
or
$$4x^2 - 2(c + d)x + cd = 0$$

72. $\left(x - \dfrac{k}{3}\right)\left(x - \dfrac{m}{4}\right) = 0$
$$x^2 - \left(\dfrac{k}{3} + \dfrac{m}{4}\right)x + \dfrac{km}{12} = 0, \text{ or }$$
$$12x^2 - (4k + 3m)x + km = 0$$

73. The solutions are $\sqrt{2}$ and $3\sqrt{2}$.
$$x = \sqrt{2} \text{ or } \quad x = 3\sqrt{2}$$
$$x - \sqrt{2} = 0 \text{ or } x - 3\sqrt{2} = 0$$
$$(x - \sqrt{2})(x - 3\sqrt{2}) = 0$$
$$x^2 - 4\sqrt{2}\,x + 6 = 0$$

74. $(x + \sqrt{3})(x - 2\sqrt{3}) = 0$
$$x^2 - \sqrt{3}\,x - 6 = 0$$

75. The solutions are $3i$ and $-3i$.
$$x = 3i \text{ or } \quad x = -3i$$
$$x - 3i = 0 \text{ or } x + 3i = 0$$
$$(x - 3i)(x + 3i) = 0$$
$$x^2 - 9i^2 = 0$$
$$x^2 + 9 = 0$$

76. $(x - 4i)(x + 4i) = 0$
$$x^2 + 16 = 0$$

77. $x^2 - 0.75x - 0.5 = 0$

$a = 1, \quad b = -0.75, \quad c = -0.5$

$$x = \dfrac{-(-0.75) \pm \sqrt{(-0.75)^2 - 4(1)(-0.5)}}{2(1)}$$

$$x = \dfrac{0.75 \pm \sqrt{0.5625 + 2}}{2} = \dfrac{0.75 \pm \sqrt{2.5625}}{2}$$

$$x = \dfrac{0.75 + \sqrt{2.5625}}{2} \text{ or } x = \dfrac{0.75 - \sqrt{2.5625}}{2}$$

$$x \approx 1.1754 \qquad \text{ or } x \approx -0.4254$$

The solution set is $\{1.1754, -0.4254\}$.

78. $5.33x^2 - 8.23x - 3.24 = 0$

$$x = \dfrac{-(-8.23) \pm \sqrt{(-8.23)^2 - 4(5.33)(-3.24)}}{2(5.33)}$$

$$x = \dfrac{8.23 \pm \sqrt{136.8097}}{10.66}$$

$$x \approx 1.8693 \text{ or } x \approx -0.3252$$

$\{1.8693, -0.3252\}$

79. $$x + \dfrac{1}{x} = \dfrac{13}{6}, \quad \text{LCM is } 6x$$

$$6x\left(x + \dfrac{1}{x}\right) = 6x \cdot \dfrac{13}{6}$$

$$6x^2 + 6 = 13x$$

$$6x^2 - 13x + 6 = 0$$

$$(3x - 2)(2x - 3) = 0$$

$$3x - 2 = 0 \text{ or } 2x - 3 = 0$$

$$x = \dfrac{2}{3} \text{ or } \quad x = \dfrac{3}{2}$$

Both values check.

The solution set is $\left\{\dfrac{2}{3}, \dfrac{3}{2}\right\}$.

80.
$$\frac{3}{x} + \frac{x}{3} = \frac{5}{2}, \quad \text{LCM is } 6x$$
$$18 + 2x^2 = 15x$$
$$2x^2 - 15x + 18 = 0$$
$$(2x - 3)(x - 6) = 0$$
$$x = \frac{3}{2} \text{ or } x = 6$$

Both values check.

$\left\{\frac{3}{2}, 6\right\}$

81. $x^2 + x - \sqrt{2} = 0$

$a = 1, \quad b = 1, \quad c = -\sqrt{2}$

$$x = \frac{-1 \pm \sqrt{1^2 - 4(1)(-\sqrt{2})}}{2 \cdot 1} = \frac{-1 \pm \sqrt{1 + 4\sqrt{2}}}{2}$$

The solution set is $\left\{\frac{-1 \pm \sqrt{1 + 4\sqrt{2}}}{2}\right\}$.

82. $x^2 + \sqrt{5}\, x - \sqrt{3} = 0$

$$x = \frac{-\sqrt{5} \pm \sqrt{(\sqrt{5})^2 - 4(1)(-\sqrt{3})}}{2 \cdot 1}$$

$$x = \frac{-\sqrt{5} \pm \sqrt{5 + 4\sqrt{3}}}{2}$$

$\left\{\frac{-\sqrt{5} \pm \sqrt{5 + 4\sqrt{3}}}{2}\right\}$

83.
$$(2t - 3)^2 + 17t = 15$$
$$4t^2 - 12t + 9 + 17t = 15$$
$$4t^2 + 5t - 6 = 0$$
$$(4t - 3)(t + 2) = 0$$
$$4t - 3 = 0 \text{ or } t + 2 = 0$$
$$t = \frac{3}{4} \text{ or } \quad t = -2$$

The solution set is $\left\{\frac{3}{4}, -2\right\}$.

84. $2y^2 - (y + 2)(y - 3) = 12$
$$2y^2 - y^2 + y + 6 = 12$$
$$y^2 + y - 6 = 0$$
$$(y - 2)(y + 3) = 0$$
$$y = 2 \text{ or } y = -3$$
$$\{2, -3\}$$

85. $(x + 3)(x - 2) = 2(x + 11)$
$$x^2 + x - 6 = 2x + 22$$
$$x^2 - x - 28 = 0$$

$a = 1, \quad b = -1, \quad c = -28$

$$x = \frac{-(-1) \pm \sqrt{(-1)^2 - 4(1)(-28)}}{2 \cdot 1}$$

$$x = \frac{1 \pm \sqrt{1 + 112}}{2} = \frac{1 \pm \sqrt{113}}{2}$$

The solution set is $\left\{\frac{1 \pm \sqrt{113}}{2}\right\}$.

86. $9t(t + 2) - 3t(t - 2) = 2(t + 4)(t + 6)$
$$9t^2 + 18t - 3t^2 + 6t = 2t^2 + 20t + 48$$
$$4t^2 + 4t - 48 = 0$$
$$t^2 + t - 12 = 0$$
$$(t + 4)(t - 3) = 0$$
$$t = -4 \text{ or } t = 3$$
$$\{-4, 3\}$$

87.
$$2x^2 + (x - 4)^2 = 5x(x - 4) + 24$$
$$2x^2 + x^2 - 8x + 16 = 5x^2 - 20x + 24$$
$$0 = 2x^2 - 12x + 8$$
$$0 = x^2 - 6x + 4$$

$a = 1, \quad b = -6, \quad c = 4$

$$x = \frac{-(-6) \pm \sqrt{(-6)^2 - 4 \cdot 1 \cdot 4}}{2 \cdot 1} = \frac{6 \pm \sqrt{36 - 16}}{2}$$

$$x = \frac{6 \pm \sqrt{20}}{2} = \frac{6 \pm 2\sqrt{5}}{2}$$

$$x = \frac{2(3 \pm \sqrt{5})}{2} = 3 \pm \sqrt{5}$$

The solution set is $\{3 \pm \sqrt{5}\}$.

88. $(c + 2)^2 + (c - 2)(c + 2) = 44 + (c - 2)^2$
$$c^2 + 4c + 4 + c^2 - 4 = 44 + c^2 - 4c + 4$$
$$c^2 + 8c - 48 = 0$$
$$(c + 12)(c - 4) = 0$$
$$c = -12 \text{ or } c = 4$$
$$\{-12, 4\}$$

89. a) $\dfrac{-b + \sqrt{b^2 - 4ac}}{2a} + \dfrac{-b - \sqrt{b^2 - 4ac}}{2a} = \dfrac{-2b}{2a} = -\dfrac{b}{a}$

b) $\dfrac{-b + \sqrt{b^2 - 4ac}}{2a} \cdot \dfrac{-b - \sqrt{b^2 - 4ac}}{2a}$

$= \dfrac{b^2 - (b^2 - 4ac)}{4a^2}$

$= \dfrac{4ac}{4a^2}$

$= \dfrac{c}{a}$

90. a) $k(3)^2 - 17(3) + 33 = 0$

$$9k = 18$$
$$k = 2$$

b) $\quad 2x^2 - 17x + 33 = 0$

$$(2x - 11)(x - 3) = 0$$
$$x = \frac{11}{2} \ \text{ or } \ x = 3$$

The other solution is $\frac{11}{2}$.

91. a) $\qquad kx^2 - 2x + k = 0$

$k(-3)^2 - 2(-3) + k = 0 \qquad$ (Substituting -3 for x)

$$9k + 6 + k = 0$$
$$10k = -6$$
$$k = -\frac{3}{5}$$

b) $\quad -\frac{3}{5}x^2 - 2x - \frac{3}{5} = 0 \quad \left[\text{Substituting} -\frac{3}{5} \text{ for } k\right]$

$\quad 3x^2 + 10x + 3 = 0 \quad$ (Multiplying by -5)

$$(3x + 1)(x + 3) = 0$$
$$3x + 1 = 0 \quad \text{ or } \quad x + 3 = 0$$
$$3x = -1 \quad \text{ or } \qquad x = -3$$
$$x = -\frac{1}{3} \quad \text{ or } \qquad x = -3$$

The other solution is $-\frac{1}{3}$.

92. a) $(1 + i)^2 - k(1 + i) + 2 = 0$

$$1 + 2i - 1 - k - ki + 2 = 0$$
$$2 + 2i = k + ki$$
$$2(1 + i) = k(1 + i)$$
$$2 = k$$

b) $x^2 - 2x + 2 = 0$

$$x = \frac{-(-2) \pm \sqrt{(-2)^2 - 4 \cdot 1 \cdot 2}}{2 \cdot 1} = $$
$$\frac{2 \pm \sqrt{-4}}{2}$$
$$x = \frac{2 \pm 2i}{2} = 1 \pm i$$

The other solution is $1 - i$.

93. a) $x^2 - (6 + 3i)x + k = 0$

$3^2 - (6 + 3i) \cdot 3 + k = 0 \qquad$ (Substituting 3 for x)

$$9 - 18 - 9i + k = 0$$
$$k = 9 + 9i$$

b) $x^2 - (6 + 3i)x + 9 + 9i = 0$

$$x = \frac{-[-(6+3i)] \pm \sqrt{[-(6+3i)]^2 - 4(1)(9+9i)}}{2 \cdot 1}$$
$$x = \frac{6 + 3i \pm \sqrt{36 + 36i - 9 - 36 - 36i}}{2}$$
$$x = \frac{6 + 3i \pm \sqrt{-9}}{2} = \frac{6 + 3i \pm 3i}{2}$$
$$x = \frac{6 + 3i + 3i}{2} \quad \text{ or } \quad x = \frac{6 + 3i - 3i}{2}$$
$$x = \frac{6 + 6i}{2} \quad \text{ or } \quad x = \frac{6}{2}$$
$$x = 3 + 3i \quad \text{ or } \quad x = 3$$

The other solution is $3 + 3i$.

94. $kx^2 - 4x + (2k - 1) = 0$

$a = k, \ b = -4, \ c = 2k - 1$

From Exercise 89, we know that the product of the solutions is c/a.

$$\frac{2k - 1}{k} = 3$$
$$2k - 1 = 3k$$
$$-1 = k$$

95. Write $ax^2 + bx + c = 0$ as $x^2 - \left(-\frac{b}{a}\right)x + \frac{c}{a} = 0$.

From Exercise 89 we know that $-b/a$ is the sum of the solutions and c/a is the product of the solutions. Then we have $x^2 - \sqrt{3}x + 8 = 0$.

96. Write $ax^2 + bx + c = 0$ as $x^2 - \left(-\frac{b}{a}\right)x + \frac{c}{a} = 0$. From Exercise 89 we know that $-b/a$ is the sum of the solutions and c/a is the product of the solutions.

a) $\frac{2 + \sqrt{3}}{2} + \frac{2 - \sqrt{3}}{2} = \frac{4}{2} = 2$

$\left(\frac{2 + \sqrt{3}}{2}\right)\left(\frac{2 - \sqrt{3}}{2}\right) = \frac{4 - 3}{4} = \frac{1}{4}$

Then we have $x^2 - 2x + \frac{1}{4} = 0$, or $4x^2 - 8x + 1 = 0$.

b) $\frac{g}{h} - \frac{h}{g} = \frac{g^2 - h^2}{hg}$

$\frac{g}{h}\left(-\frac{h}{g}\right) = -1$

Then we have $x^2 - \frac{g^2 - h^2}{hg}x - 1 = 0$, or

$hgx^2 - (g^2 - h^2)x - hg = 0$.

c) $(2 - 5i) + (2 + 5i) = 4$

$\quad (2 - 5i)(2 + 5i) = 4 + 25 = 29$

Then we have $x^2 - 4x + 29 = 0$

97. $3x^2 - hx + 4k = 0$

$a = 3$, $b = -h$, $c = 4k$

From Exercise 89 we know that the sum of the solutions is $-b/a$, or $-(-h)/3 = h/3$ and the product of the solutions is c/a, or $4k/3$. Then we have

$\dfrac{h}{3} = -12$ and $\dfrac{4k}{3} = 20$

$h = -36$ and $4k = 60$

$h = -36$ and $k = 15$.

98. Substitute 2 for y in the given equation and obtain $p = \dfrac{qr}{3r - 2q}$. Then, in the given equation, substitute $\dfrac{qr}{3r - 2q}$ for p and obtain $y^2 - 3y + 2 = 0$. Thus the other solution is 1.

99. Let $1 \cdot x^2 + 2kx - 5 = 0$ have solutions r and s.

Then $r + s = \dfrac{-2k}{1}$, or $-2k$ and $rs = -5/1$, or -5. Adding $2rs = -10$ and $r^2 + s^2 = 26$ we obtain $r^2 + 2rs + s^2 = 16$ so that $r + s = \pm 4$. Then $r + s = -2k = \pm 4$, so $k = -2$ or $k = 2$, or $|k| = 2$.

100. $ax^2 + bx + c = 0$ has solution set

$S_1 = \left\{ \dfrac{-b + \sqrt{b^2 - 4ac}}{2a}, \dfrac{-b - \sqrt{b^2 - 4ac}}{2a} \right\}$.

$cy^2 + by + a = 0$ has $y = \dfrac{-b \pm \sqrt{b^2 - 4ac}}{2c}$.

Then $\dfrac{1}{y} = \dfrac{2c}{-b \pm \sqrt{b^2 - 4ac}} \cdot \dfrac{-b \mp \sqrt{b^2 - 4ac}}{-b \mp \sqrt{b^2 - 4ac}}$

$= \dfrac{-b \mp \sqrt{b^2 - 4ac}}{2a}$, so that the

reciprocals of the solutions of the second equation form the set

$S_2 = \left\{ \dfrac{-b - \sqrt{b^2 - 4ac}}{2a}, \dfrac{-b + \sqrt{b^2 - 4ac}}{2a} \right\}$ which is

the same as S_1.

Exercise Set 2.6

1. $F = \dfrac{kM_1 M_2}{d^2}$

$Fd^2 = kM_1 M_2$

$d^2 = \dfrac{kM_1 M_2}{F}$

$d = \sqrt{\dfrac{kM_1 M_2}{F}}$ (Taking the positive square root)

2. $c = \sqrt{\dfrac{E}{m}}$

3. $S = \dfrac{1}{2} at^2$

$2S = at^2$

$\dfrac{2S}{a} = t^2$

$\sqrt{\dfrac{2S}{a}} = t$ (Taking the positive square root)

4. $r = \sqrt{\dfrac{S}{4\pi}}$ or $\dfrac{1}{2}\sqrt{\dfrac{S}{\pi}}$

5. $s = -16t^2 + v_0 t$

$0 = -16t^2 + v_0 t - s$

$a = -16$, $b = v_0$, $c = -s$

$t = \dfrac{-v_0 \pm \sqrt{v_0^2 - 4(-16)(-s)}}{2(-16)}$

$t = \dfrac{-v_0 \pm \sqrt{v_0^2 - 64s}}{-32}$

or

$t = \dfrac{v_0 \pm \sqrt{v_0^2 - 64s}}{32}$

6. $A = 2\pi r^2 + 3\pi rh$

$0 = 2\pi r^2 + 3\pi rh - A$

$r = \dfrac{-3\pi h \pm \sqrt{(3\pi h)^2 - 4(2\pi)(-A)}}{2 \cdot 2\pi}$

$r = \dfrac{-3\pi h \pm \sqrt{9\pi^2 h^2 + 8\pi A}}{4\pi}$, or just

$r = \dfrac{-3\pi h + \sqrt{9\pi^2 h^2 + 8\pi A}}{4\pi}$ since the negative square root would result in a negative solution.

7. $d = \dfrac{n^2 - 3n}{2}$

$2d = n^2 - 3n$

$0 = n^2 - 3n - 2d$

$a = 1$, $b = -3$, $c = -2d$

$n = \dfrac{-(-3) \pm \sqrt{(-3)^2 - 4(1)(-2d)}}{2 \cdot 1}$

$n = \dfrac{3 \pm \sqrt{9 + 8d}}{2}$, or just

$n = \dfrac{3 + \sqrt{9 + 8d}}{2}$ since the negative square root would result in a negative solution.

8. $\sqrt{2}t^2 + 3k = \pi t$

$\sqrt{2}t^2 - \pi t + 3k = 0$

$t = \dfrac{-(-\pi) \pm \sqrt{(-\pi)^2 - 4 \cdot \sqrt{2} \cdot 3k}}{2\sqrt{2}}$

$t = \dfrac{\pi \pm \sqrt{\pi^2 - 12k\sqrt{2}}}{2\sqrt{2}}$

9.
$$A = P(1 + i)^2$$
$$\frac{A}{P} = (1 + i)^2$$
$$\pm \sqrt{\frac{A}{P}} = 1 + i$$
$$-1 \pm \sqrt{\frac{A}{P}} = i, \text{ or just}$$

$-1 + \sqrt{\frac{A}{P}} = i$ since the negative square root would result in a negative solution.

10.
$$A = P\left(1 + \frac{i}{2}\right)^2$$
$$\frac{A}{P} = \left(1 + \frac{i}{2}\right)^2$$
$$\pm \sqrt{\frac{A}{P}} = 1 + \frac{i}{2}$$
$$-1 \pm \sqrt{\frac{A}{P}} = \frac{i}{2}$$

$2\left(-1 \pm \sqrt{\frac{A}{P}}\right) = i$, or just $2\left(-1 + \sqrt{\frac{A}{P}}\right) = i$ since the negative square root would result in a negative solution.

11.
$$A = P(1 + i)^t$$
$$7290 = 6250(1 + i)^2 \qquad \text{(Substituting)}$$
$$\frac{7290}{6250} = (1 + i)^2$$
$$\pm \sqrt{\frac{729}{625}} = 1 + i$$
$$\pm \frac{27}{25} = 1 + i$$
$$-1 \pm \frac{27}{25} = i$$
$$-1 + \frac{27}{25} = i \quad \text{or} \quad -1 - \frac{27}{25} = i$$
$$\frac{2}{25} = i \quad \text{or} \quad -\frac{52}{25} = i$$

Since the interest rate cannot be negative, $i = \frac{2}{25} = 0.08 = 8\%$.

12. Solve: $6760 = 6250(1 + i)^2$
$i = 0.04$ or $i = -2.04$
Only 0.04 makes sense in the original problem, so $i = 0.04 = 4\%$.

13.
$$A = P(1 + i)^t$$
$$4410 = 4000(1 + i)^2 \qquad \text{(Substituting)}$$
$$\frac{4410}{4000} = (1 + i)^2$$
$$\pm \sqrt{\frac{4410}{4000}} = 1 + i$$
$$-1 \pm 1.05 = i$$
$$-1 + 1.05 = i \quad \text{or} \quad -1 - 1.05 = i$$
$$0.05 = i \quad \text{or} \qquad -2.05 = i$$

Since the interest rate cannot be negative, $i = 0.05 = 5\%$.

14. Solve: $4840 = 4000(1 + i)^2$
$i = 0.1$ or $i = -2.1$
Only 0.1 makes sense in the original problem, so $i = 0.1 = 10\%$.

15.
$$d = \frac{n^2 - 3n}{2}$$
$$27 = \frac{n^2 - 3n}{2} \qquad \text{(Substituting 27 for d)}$$
$$54 = n^2 - 3n$$
$$0 = n^2 - 3n - 54$$
$$0 = (n - 9)(n + 6)$$
$$n - 9 = 0 \text{ or } n + 6 = 0$$
$$n = 9 \text{ or } \qquad n = -6$$

The number of sides must be positive. Thus the number of sides is 9.

16. Solve: $44 = \frac{n^2 - 3n}{2}$

$n = 11$ or $n = -8$
Only 11 makes sense in the original problem.

17. Familiarize: We make a drawing and label it with the known and unknown data.

Translate: We use the Pythagorean theorem. From the taller triangle we get
$$h^2 + 7^2 = 25^2. \qquad (1)$$
From the other triangle we get
$$(h - d)^2 + 9^2 = 25^2. \qquad (2)$$
Carry out: We solve equation (1) for h and get h = 24. Then we substitute 24 for h in equation (2).
$$(24 - d)^2 + 9^2 = 25^2, \text{ or}$$
$$d^2 - 48d + 32 = 0$$

Using the quadratic formula, we get

$$d = \frac{48 \pm \sqrt{2176}}{2} = \frac{48 \pm 8\sqrt{34}}{2} = 24 \pm 4\sqrt{34}.$$

Check and State: The length $24 + 4\sqrt{34}$ is not a solution since it exceeds the original length. The number $24 - 4\sqrt{34} \approx 0.7$ checks and is the solution. Therefore, the top of the ladder moves down the wall about 0.7 ft when the bottom is moved 2 ft.

<u>18.</u>

Solve $h^2 + 4^2 = 15^2$,

$\quad\quad\quad (h - d)^2 + 7^2 = 15^2.$

We get $h = \sqrt{209}$, so $d = \sqrt{209} \pm \sqrt{176}$. Only $\sqrt{209} - \sqrt{176}$ makes sense in the original problem. The top of the ladder moves $\sqrt{209} - \sqrt{176} \approx 1.2$ ft.

<u>19.</u> Familiarize and Translate:

Using the Pythagorean theorem we determine the length of the other leg.

$10^2 = 6^2 + a^2$

$100 = 36 + a^2$

$64 = a^2$

$8 = a$

We let x represent the amount the ladder is pulled away and pulled down. The legs then become $6 + x$ and $8 - x$. Then we again use the Pythagorean theorem.

$10^2 = (6 + x)^2 + (8 - x)^2$

Carry out:

$100 = 36 + 12x + x^2 + 64 - 16x + x^2$

$100 = 2x^2 - 4x + 100$

$0 = 2x^2 - 4x$

$0 = x^2 - 2x$

$0 = x(x - 2)$

$x = 0$ or $x - 2 = 0$

$x = 0$ or $\quad\quad x = 2$

We only consider $x = 2$ since $x \neq 0$ if the ladder is pulled away.

Check and State:

When $x = 2$, the legs of the triangle become $6 + 2$, or 8, and $8 - 2$, or 6. The Pythagorean relationship still holds.

$8^2 + 6^2 = 10^2$

$64 + 36 = 100$

The ladder is pulled away 2 ft and pulled down 2 ft.

<u>20.</u>
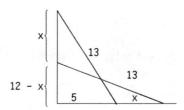

Solve: $(12 - x)^2 + (5 + x)^2 = 13^2$

$x = 0$ or $x = 7$

Only 7 ft makes sense in the original problem.

<u>21.</u> Familiarize:

We make a drawing. We let h represent the height and $h + 3$ represent the base.

Translate:

$A = \frac{1}{2} \cdot$ base $\cdot$ height   (Area of triangle)

$18 = \frac{1}{2}(h + 3)h$ (Substituting)

Carry out:

$36 = h^2 + 3h$

$0 = h^2 + 3h - 36$

$a = 1, \quad b = 3, \quad c = -36$

$h = \dfrac{-3 \pm \sqrt{3^2 - 4(1)(-36)}}{2 \cdot 1}$

$h = \dfrac{-3 \pm \sqrt{9 + 144}}{2} = \dfrac{-3 \pm \sqrt{153}}{2}$

$h = \dfrac{-3 + \sqrt{153}}{2}$ (h cannot be negative)

$h \approx 4.7$

Check and State:

When $h = 4.7$, $h + 3 = 7.7$ and the area of the triangle is $\frac{1}{2}(4.7)(7.7) \approx 18.1$.

The height is 4.7 cm.

<u>22.</u> Solve: $d^2 = 90^2 + 90^2$

$d = \pm 90\sqrt{2}$

Only $90\sqrt{2} \approx 127.3$ ft makes sense in the original problem.

23. Familiarize: We make a drawing.

We let r represent the speed of train A. Then
r + 5 represents the speed of train B. The
distances they travel in 2 hours are 2r and
2(r + 5). After 2 hours they are 50 miles apart.

Translate:

Using the Pythagorean theorem we have an
equation.

$(2r)^2 + [2(r + 5)]^2 = 50^2$

Carry out:

$$4r^2 + 4(r + 5)^2 = 2500$$
$$r^2 + (r + 5)^2 = 625$$
$$r^2 + r^2 + 10r + 25 = 625$$
$$2r^2 + 10r - 600 = 0$$
$$r^2 + 5r - 300 = 0$$
$$(r + 20)(r - 15) = 0$$

$$r + 20 = 0 \quad \text{or } r - 15 = 0$$
$$r = -20 \text{ or} \qquad r = 15$$

Check and State:

Since speed in this problem must be positive, we
only check 15. If r = 15, then r + 5 = 20. In
2 hours train A will travel 2·15, or 30 miles, and
train B will travel 2·20, or 40 miles.

We now calculate how far apart trains A and B
will be after 2 hours.

$$30^2 + 40^2 = d^2$$
$$900 + 1600 = d^2$$
$$2500 = d^2$$
$$50 = d$$

The value checks.

The speed of train A is 15 mph; the speed of
train B is 20 mph.

24.

Solve: $(5r)^2 + [5(r + 14)] = 130^2$

r = -24 or r = 10; r must be positive.

Then the speed of train A is 10 + 14, or 24 km/h,
and the speed of train B is 10 km/h.

25. a) $s = 4.9t^2 + v_0t$

$75 = 4.9t^2 + 0·t$ (Substituting 75 for
s and 0 for v_0)

$$75 = 4.9t^2$$
$$\frac{75}{4.9} = t^2$$
$$\sqrt{\frac{75}{4.9}} = t$$
$$3.9 \approx t$$

It takes 3.9 sec to reach the ground.

b) $s = 4.9t^2 + v_0t$

$75 = 4.9t^2 + 30t$ (Substituting 75 for s
and 30 for v_0)

$$0 = 4.9t^2 + 30t - 75$$

$$a = 4.9, \quad b = 30, \quad c = -75$$

$$t = \frac{-30 \pm \sqrt{30^2 - 4(4.9)(-75)}}{2(4.9)}$$

$$t = \frac{-30 \pm \sqrt{900 + 1470}}{9.8}$$

$$t = \frac{-30 + \sqrt{2370}}{9.8} \quad \text{(t must be positive)}$$

$$t \approx 1.9$$

It takes 1.9 sec to reach the ground.

c) $s = 4.9t^2 + v_0t$

$s = 4.9(2)^2 + 30(2)$ (Substituting 2 for t
and 30 for v_0)

$$s = 19.6 + 60$$
$$s = 79.6$$

The object will fall 79.6 m.

26. a) $500 = 4.9t^2 + 0t$ gives t ≈ 10.1 sec.

b) $500 = 4.9t^2 + 30t$ gives t ≈ 7.5 sec.

c) $s = 4.9(5)^2 + 30(5)$ gives s = 272.5 m

27. Familiarize and Translate:

It helps to make a drawing.

We let s represent the length of the side. Then
s + 1.341 represents the diagonal. Using the
Pythagorean theorem we have an equation.

$$s^2 + s^2 = (s + 1.341)^2$$

Carry out:

$$2s^2 = s^2 + 2.682s + 1.798281$$

$$s^2 - 2.682s - 1.798281 = 0$$

$$s = \frac{-(-2.682) \pm \sqrt{(-2.682)^2 - 4(1)(-1.798281)}}{2 \cdot 1}$$

$$s = \frac{2.682 \pm \sqrt{7.193124 + 7.193124}}{2}$$

$$s = \frac{2.682 + \sqrt{14.386248}}{2}$$

$$s \approx 3.2$$

Check and State:

The value checks. The length of the side is 3.2 cm.

28. Solve: $x^2 + (10.23 - x)^2 = (8.312)^2$

$x = 8.01$ or $x = 2.22$

Choosing either value for x, we find that $10.23 - x$ is the other solution of the equation. Thus, the lengths of the legs are 8.01 cm and 2.22 cm.

29. Familiarize and Translate: From the drawing in the text we see that the area of the original garden is $80 \cdot 60$ and the area of the new garden is $(80 - 2x)(60 - 2x)$, where x is the width of the sidewalk. We know the area of the new garden is 2/3 of the original area, so we can write an equation.

$$(80 - 2x)(60 - 2x) = \frac{2}{3} \cdot 80 \cdot 60, \text{ or}$$

$$x^2 - 70x + 400 = 0$$

Carry out: Using the quadratic formula, we get

$$x = \frac{70 \pm \sqrt{3300}}{2} = \frac{70 \pm 10\sqrt{33}}{2} = 35 \pm 5\sqrt{33}.$$

Check and State: The number $35 + 5\sqrt{33}$ is not a solution since twice that number exceeds both the original length and width of the garden. The number $35 - 5\sqrt{33} \approx 6.3$ checks and is the solution. Therefore, the sidewalk is about 6.3 ft wide.

30. Let r represent the speed of the current.

Solve: $\dfrac{24}{20 - r} + \dfrac{24}{20 + r} = 10$

$r = \pm \sqrt{304}$

Only $\sqrt{304}$ makes sense in the original problem. The speed of the current is $\sqrt{304} \approx 17.4$ mph.

31. Familiarize: We make a drawing, letting x represent the length of a side of the square cut from each corner.

The dimensions of the resulting base are $10 - 2x$ and $20 - 2x$.

Translate: The area of the resulting base is 90 cm², so we can write an equation.

$$(20 - 2x)(10 - 2x) = 90, \text{ or}$$

$$2x^2 - 30x + 55 = 0$$

Carry out: Using the quadratic formula, we get

$$x = \frac{30 \pm \sqrt{460}}{4} = \frac{30 \pm 2\sqrt{115}}{4} = \frac{15 \pm \sqrt{115}}{2}.$$

Check and State: The number $\dfrac{15 + \sqrt{115}}{2}$ is not a solution since twice that number exceeds the width of the piece of tin. The number $\dfrac{15 - \sqrt{115}}{2} \approx 2.1$ checks and is the solution. Therefore, the length of the sides of the squares is about 2.1 cm.

32. Let x represent the width of the frame.

Solve: $(32 - 2x)(28 - 2x) = 200$

$x = 15 \pm \sqrt{51}$

Only $15 - \sqrt{51}$ makes sense in the original problem. The width of the frame is $15 - \sqrt{51} \approx 7.9$ cm.

33. Familiarize: We can use the formula $d = rt$ in the form $t = \dfrac{d}{r}$. Let x represent the speed on the first part of the trip. Then $x - 10$ represents the speed on the second part of the trip. The time for the first part of the trip is $\dfrac{50}{x}$, and the time for the second part is $\dfrac{80}{x - 10}$.

Translate: We know that the total time for the trip is 2 hr, so we can write an equation.

$$\frac{50}{x} + \frac{80}{x - 10} = 2, \text{ or}$$

$$x^2 - 75x + 250 = 0 \quad \text{Clearing fractions and simplifying}$$

Carry out: Using the quadratic formula, we get

$$x = \frac{75 \pm \sqrt{4625}}{2} = \frac{75 \pm 5\sqrt{185}}{2}.$$

Check and State: The number $x = \frac{75 - 5\sqrt{185}}{2}$ is
not a solution since $x - 10 < 0$. The number
$x = \frac{75 + 5\sqrt{185}}{2} \approx 71.5$ mph checks and is the
solution. This is the speed on the first part
of the trip. The speed on the second part is
approximately 71.5 - 10, or 61.5 mph.

34. Let r represent the speed.

Solve: $\frac{120}{r} - 2 = \frac{120}{r + 10}$

$r = -30$ or $r = 20$

Only 20 makes sense in the original problem.
The speed is 20 mph.

35. Familiarize: We will use the formula $t = \frac{d}{r}$
as we did in Exercise 33. Let x represent the
speed of the boat in still water. Then the time
to travel upstream is $\frac{12}{x - 3}$ and the time to
travel downstream is $\frac{12}{x + 3}$.

Translate: We know the total time for the round
trip is 2 hr, so we can write an equation.

$\frac{12}{x - 3} + \frac{12}{x + 3} = 2$, or

$x^2 - 12x - 9 = 0$ Clearing fractions and
simplifying

Carry out: Using the quadratic formula, we get

$x = \frac{12 \pm \sqrt{180}}{2} = \frac{12 \pm 6\sqrt{5}}{2} = 6 \pm 3\sqrt{5}$

Check and State: The number $6 - 3\sqrt{5}$ is not a
solution, because the speed cannot be negative.
The number $6 + 3\sqrt{5} \approx 12.7$ checks and is the
solution. The speed of the boat in still water
is $6 + 3\sqrt{5} \approx 12.7$ mph.

36. Let t represent the time it would take person B
to do the job, working alone.

Solve: $\frac{4}{x + 5} + \frac{4}{x} = 1$

$x = \frac{3 \pm \sqrt{89}}{2}$

Only $\frac{3 + \sqrt{89}}{2}$ makes sense in the original problem.
It would take person B $\frac{3 + \sqrt{89}}{2} \approx 6.2$ hr to do
the job, working alone.

37. Familiarize and Translate:

We let x represent the number of students in the
group at the outset. Then $x - 3$ represents the
number of students at the last minute.

Total cost = (Cost per person)·(Number of
persons)

$\frac{\text{Total cost}}{\text{Number of persons}} = \text{Cost per person}$

Using this formula we get the following:

Cost per person
at the outset $= \frac{140}{x}$

Cost per person at
the last minute $= \frac{140}{x - 3}$

The cost at the last minute was $15 more than the
cost at the outset. This gives us an equation.

$\frac{140}{x - 3} = 15 + \frac{140}{x}$

Carry out:

$x(x - 3) \cdot \frac{140}{x - 3} = x(x - 3)\left[15 + \frac{140}{x}\right]$

(Multiplying by the LCM)

$140x = 15x(x - 3) + 140(x - 3)$

$140x = 15x^2 - 45x + 140x - 420$

$0 = 15x^2 - 45x - 420$

$0 = x^2 - 3x - 28$

$0 = (x - 7)(x + 4)$

$x - 7 = 0$ or $x + 4 = 0$

$x = 7$ or $x = -4$

Check and State:

Since the number of people cannot be negative, we
only check $x = 7$. When $x = 7$, the cost at the
outset is 140/7, or $20. When $x = 7$, the cost at
the last minute is 140/(7 - 3), or 140/4, or $35
and $35 is $15 more than $20. The value checks.

Thus, 7 students were in the group at the outset.

38. Let x = the number of lots. Then

$\left[\frac{8400}{x} + 350\right] \cdot (x - 4) = 8400$

$\begin{bmatrix}\text{Selling}\\\text{price}\\\text{per lot}\end{bmatrix} \cdot \begin{bmatrix}\text{Lots}\\\text{sold}\end{bmatrix} = \text{Total selling price.}$

$x = 12$

39. Familiarize and Translate:

Let x represent the number of shares bought. Then
$\frac{720}{x}$ represents the cost of each share. When the
cost per share is reduced by $15, the new cost is
$\frac{720}{x} - 15$. When the number of shares purchased is
increased by 4, the new number of shares is
$x + 4$. The total cost remains the same.

$720 = \left[\frac{720}{x} - 15\right] \cdot (x + 4)$

Carry out:

$$720 = 720 + \frac{2880}{x} - 15x - 60$$

$$60 = \frac{2880}{x} - 15x$$

$$60x = 2880 - 15x^2$$

$$15x^2 + 60x - 2880 = 0$$

$$x^2 + 4x - 192 = 0$$

$$(x + 16)(x - 12) = 0$$

$$x + 16 = 0 \quad \text{or} \quad x - 12 = 0$$

$$x = -16 \quad \text{or} \quad x = 12$$

Check and State:

The number of shares must be positive. We only check x = 12. The cost per share when x = 12 is 720/12, or $60. The cost per share when the number is increased by 4 is 720/16, or $45, and $45 is $15 less than $60. The value checks.

Thus, 12 shares of stock were bought.

40. Let x = the original number of students. Then $\frac{112}{x} - 4 = \frac{112}{x + 14}$ gives x = 14. Hence $\frac{\$112}{14} = \$8$, the original cost per student.

41. $kx^2 + (3 - 2k)x - 6 = 0$

$a = k, \quad b = 3 - 2k, \quad c = -6$

$$x = \frac{-(3 - 2k) \pm \sqrt{(3 - 2k)^2 - 4(k)(-6)}}{2k}$$

$$= \frac{-3 + 2k \pm \sqrt{4k^2 + 12k + 9}}{2k}$$

$$= \frac{-3 + 2k \pm \sqrt{(2k + 3)^2}}{2k}$$

$$= \frac{-3 + 2k \pm (2k + 3)}{2k}$$

$$x = \frac{-3 + 2k + 2k + 3}{2k} \quad \text{or} \quad x = \frac{-3 + 2k - 2k - 3}{2k}$$

$$x = \frac{4k}{2k} \quad \text{or} \quad x = \frac{-6}{2k}$$

$$x = 2 \quad \text{or} \quad x = -\frac{3}{k}$$

The solution set is $\left\{2, -\frac{3}{k}\right\}$.

42. $$x^2 - 2x + kx + 1 = kx^2$$

$$(1 - k)x^2 + (-2 + k)x + 1 = 0$$

$$x = \frac{-(-2 + k) \pm \sqrt{(-2 + k)^2 - 4(1 - k)(1)}}{2(1 - k)}$$

$$x = \frac{2 - k \pm \sqrt{4 - 4k + k^2 - 4 + 4k}}{2 - 2k}$$

$$x = \frac{2 - k \pm k}{2 - 2k}$$

$$x = \frac{2}{2 - 2k} \quad \text{or} \quad x = \frac{2 - 2k}{2 - 2k}$$

$$x = \frac{1}{1 - k} \quad \text{or} \quad x = 1 \qquad \left\{\frac{1}{1 - k}, 1\right\}$$

43. $$(m + n)^2x^2 + (m + n)x = 2$$

$$(m + n)^2x^2 + (m + n)x - 2 = 0$$

$$a = (m + n)^2, \quad b = m + n, \quad c = -2$$

$$x = \frac{-(m + n) \pm \sqrt{(m + n)^2 - 4(m + n)^2(-2)}}{2(m + n)^2}$$

$$= \frac{-(m + n) \pm \sqrt{9(m + n)^2}}{2(m + n)^2}$$

$$= \frac{-(m + n) \pm 3(m + n)}{2(m + n)^2}$$

$$x = \frac{2(m + n)}{2(m + n)^2} \quad \text{or} \quad x = \frac{-4(m + n)}{2(m + n)^2}$$

$$x = \frac{1}{m + n} \quad \text{or} \quad x = \frac{-2}{m + n}$$

The solution set is $\left\{\frac{1}{m + n}, -\frac{2}{m + n}\right\}$.

44. $$x^2 - 3xy - 4y^2 = 0$$

$$(x + y)(x - 4y) = 0$$

a) $x = -y \quad \text{or} \quad x = 4y$

The solution set is $\{-y, 4y\}$.

b) $y = -x \quad \text{or} \quad y = \frac{x}{4}$

The solution set is $\left\{-x, \frac{x}{4}\right\}$.

45. $$A = P(1 + i)^t$$

$$13,704 = 9826(1 + i)^3 \qquad \text{(Substituting)}$$

$$\frac{13,704}{9826} = (1 + i)^3$$

$$\sqrt[3]{\frac{13,704}{9826}} = 1 + i$$

$$-1 + \sqrt[3]{\frac{13,704}{9826}} = i$$

$$0.117 \approx i$$

The interest rate is 11.7%.

46.

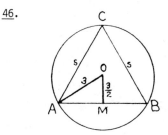

C = 6π, so r = 3. Since O is a trisection point of CM, OM = $\frac{3}{2}$. Then AM = $\frac{3}{2}\sqrt{3}$ and s = $3\sqrt{3}$. The area of Δ ABC = $\frac{1}{2}\left[3\sqrt{3}\right]\left[3 + \frac{3}{2}\right]$, or $\frac{27}{4}\sqrt{3} \approx 11.7$.

47. Familiarize:
We first make a drawing.

  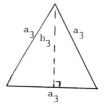

We find the height of the first triangle.

$$\left(\frac{a_1}{2}\right)^2 + (h_1)^2 = a_1^2$$

$$(h_1)^2 = a_1^2 - \frac{a_1^2}{4} = \frac{3a_1^2}{4}$$

$$h_1 = \frac{a_1\sqrt{3}}{2}$$

Next we find the area of the first triangle.

$$A_1 = \frac{1}{2} \cdot a_1 \cdot \frac{a_1\sqrt{3}}{2} = \frac{a_1^2\sqrt{3}}{4}$$

Similarly we find the areas of the other two triangles:

$$A_2 = \frac{a_2^2\sqrt{3}}{4} \quad \text{and} \quad A_3 = \frac{a_3^2\sqrt{3}}{4}.$$

Translate:
The sum of the areas of the first two triangles equals the area of the third triangle.

$$\frac{a_1^2\sqrt{3}}{4} + \frac{a_2^2\sqrt{3}}{4} = \frac{a_3^2\sqrt{3}}{4}$$

Carry out:

$$\frac{\sqrt{3}}{4}(a_1^2 + a_2^2) = \frac{\sqrt{3}}{4} \cdot a_3^2$$

$$a_1^2 + a_2^2 = a_3^2$$

$$\sqrt{a_1^2 + a_2^2} = a_3 \quad \text{Taking the positive square root}$$

Check and State: The answer checks.

Thus the length of a side of the third triangle is $\sqrt{a_1^2 + a_2^2}$.

48.

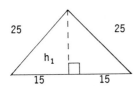

$$h_1^2 = 25^2 - 15^2 = 400$$
$$h_1 = 20$$
$$A = \frac{1}{2} \cdot 30 \cdot 20 = 300 \text{ ft}^2$$

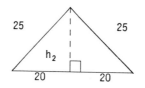

$$h_2^2 = 25^2 - 20^2 = 225$$
$$h_2 = 15$$
$$A = \frac{1}{2} \cdot 40 \cdot 15 = 300 \text{ ft}^2$$

The triangles have the same area.

49.

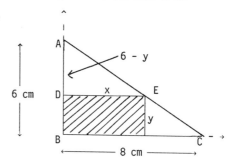

Familiarize:
Triangle ABC is similar to triangle ADE.

Translate:
The area of the rectangle is 12 cm², so we have
$$xy = 12, \quad \text{or} \quad y = \frac{12}{x}.$$

Using similar triangles, we have
$$\frac{6-y}{x} = \frac{6}{8}, \quad \text{or} \quad 48 - 8y = 6x.$$

Carry out:
$$48 - 8y = 6x$$
$$48 - 8\left(\frac{12}{x}\right) = 6x \quad \left[\text{Substituting } \frac{12}{x} \text{ for } y\right]$$
$$48 - \frac{96}{x} = 6x, \quad \text{LCM is } x$$
$$48x - 96 = 6x^2 \quad \text{(Multiplying by } x\text{)}$$
$$0 = 6x^2 - 48x + 96$$
$$0 = 6(x-4)^2$$
$$0 = (x-4)^2 \quad \left[\text{Multiplying by } \frac{1}{6}\right]$$
$$0 = x - 4$$
$$4 = x$$

When $x = 4$, $y = \frac{12}{4} = 3$.

Check and State: The answer checks.
The dimensions of the rectangle are 4 cm by 3 cm.

50. $s = \frac{1}{2}gt^2 + v_0t$ gives $175 = \frac{1}{2}(32)t^2 + 0t$ for s in feet.

$$t = \pm\frac{5\sqrt{7}}{4}$$

Since t must be positive, we have $t = \frac{5\sqrt{7}}{4} \approx 3.3$ sec.

Exercise Set 2.7

1. $\sqrt{3x - 4} = 1$ Check:

$(\sqrt{3x - 4})^2 = 1^2$ $\begin{array}{c|c} \sqrt{3x - 4} = 1 \\ \hline \sqrt{3 \cdot \frac{5}{3} - 4} & 1 \\ \sqrt{5 - 4} \\ \sqrt{1} \\ 1 & \text{TRUE} \end{array}$

$\qquad 3x - 4 = 1$

$\qquad\quad 3x = 5$

$\qquad\quad x = \frac{5}{3}$

The solution set is $\left\{\frac{5}{3}\right\}$.

2. $\sqrt[3]{2x + 1} = -5$

$\quad 2x + 1 = -125$

$\quad\quad 2x = -126$

$\quad\quad x = -63$

The answer checks. The solution set is {-63}.

3. $\sqrt[4]{x^2 - 1} = 1$ Check:

$(\sqrt[4]{x^2 - 1})^4 = 1^4$ $\begin{array}{c|c} \sqrt[4]{x^2 - 1} = 1 \\ \hline \sqrt[4]{(\pm\sqrt{2})^2 - 1} & 1 \\ \sqrt[4]{2 - 1} \\ \sqrt[4]{1} \\ 1 & \text{TRUE} \end{array}$

$\quad\quad x^2 - 1 = 1$

$\quad\quad\quad x^2 = 2$

$\quad\quad\quad x = \pm\sqrt{2}$

The solution set is $\{\pm\sqrt{2}\}$.

4. $\sqrt{m + 1} - 5 = 8$

$\quad\quad \sqrt{m + 1} = 13$

$\quad\quad m + 1 = 169$

$\quad\quad\quad m = 168$

The answer checks. The solution set is {168}.

5. $\sqrt{y - 1} + 4 = 0$

$\quad\quad \sqrt{y - 1} = -4$

Note:

The principal square root is never negative.
Thus, there is no solution.

If we do not observe the above fact, we can
continue and reach the same answer.

$(\sqrt{y - 1})^2 = (-4)^2$ Check:

$\quad\quad y - 1 = 16$ $\begin{array}{c|c} \sqrt{y - 1} + 4 = 0 \\ \hline \sqrt{17 - 1} + 4 & 0 \\ \sqrt{16} + 4 \\ 4 + 4 \\ 8 & \text{FALSE} \end{array}$

$\quad\quad\quad y = 17$

Since 17 does not check, there is no solution.
The solution set is Ø.

6. $5 + \sqrt{3x^2 + \pi} = 0$

$\quad\quad \sqrt{3x^2 + \pi} = -5$

The principal square root is never negative. The
solution set is Ø.

7. $\sqrt{x - 3} + \sqrt{x + 2} = 5$

$\quad\quad \sqrt{x + 2} = 5 - \sqrt{x - 3}$

$\quad (\sqrt{x + 2})^2 = (5 - \sqrt{x - 3})^2$

$\quad\quad x + 2 = 25 - 10\sqrt{x - 3} + (x - 3)$

$\quad\quad x + 2 = 22 - 10\sqrt{x - 3} + x$

$\quad 10\sqrt{x - 3} = 20$

$\quad\quad \sqrt{x - 3} = 2$

$\quad (\sqrt{x - 3})^2 = 2^2$

$\quad\quad x - 3 = 4$

$\quad\quad\quad x = 7$

Check: $\begin{array}{c|c} \sqrt{x - 3} + \sqrt{x + 2} = 5 \\ \hline \sqrt{7 - 3} + \sqrt{7 + 2} & 5 \\ \sqrt{4} + \sqrt{9} \\ 2 + 3 \\ 5 & \text{TRUE} \end{array}$

The solution set is {7}.

8. $\sqrt{x} - \sqrt{x - 5} = 1$

$\quad\quad \sqrt{x} = \sqrt{x - 5} + 1$

$\quad\quad x = x - 5 + 2\sqrt{x - 5} + 1$

$\quad\quad 2 = \sqrt{x - 5}$

$\quad\quad 4 = x - 5$

$\quad\quad 9 = x$

The answer checks. The solution set is {9}.

9. $\sqrt{3x - 5} + \sqrt{2x + 3} + 1 = 0$

$\quad\quad \sqrt{3x - 5} + \sqrt{2x + 3} = -1$

Note:

The principal square root is never negative. Thus
the sum of two principal square roots cannot equal
-1. There is no solution. The solution set is Ø.

10. $\sqrt{2m - 3} = \sqrt{m + 7} - 2$

$\quad 2m - 3 = m + 7 - 4\sqrt{m + 7} + 4$

$\quad m - 14 = -4\sqrt{m + 7}$

$\quad m^2 - 28m + 196 = 16m + 112$

$\quad m^2 - 44m + 84 = 0$

$\quad (m - 2)(m - 42) = 0$

$\quad m = 2 \quad \text{or} \quad m = 42$

Only 2 checks. The solution set is {2}.

11. $\sqrt[3]{6x + 9} + 8 = 5$ Check:

$\sqrt[3]{6x + 9} = -3$

$(\sqrt[3]{6x + 9})^3 = (-3)^3$

$6x + 9 = -27$

$6x = -36$

$x = -6$

	$\sqrt[3]{6x + 9} + 8 = 5$
$\sqrt[3]{6(-6) + 9} + 8$	5
$\sqrt[3]{-27} + 8$	
$-3 + 8$	
5	TRUE

The solution set is {-6}.

12. $\sqrt[5]{3x + 4} = 2$

$3x + 4 = 32$

$3x = 28$

$x = \dfrac{28}{3}$

The answer checks. The solution set is $\left\{\dfrac{28}{3}\right\}$.

13. $\sqrt{6x + 7} = x + 2$

$(\sqrt{6x + 7})^2 = (x + 2)^2$

$6x + 7 = x^2 + 4x + 4$

$0 = x^2 - 2x - 3$

$0 = (x - 3)(x + 1)$

$x - 3 = 0$ or $x + 1 = 0$

$x = 3$ or $x = -1$

Both values check. The solution set is {3, -1}.

14. $\sqrt{6x + 7} - \sqrt{3x + 3} = 1$

$\sqrt{6x + 7} = \sqrt{3x + 3} + 1$

$6x + 7 = 3x + 3 + 2\sqrt{3x + 3} + 1$

$3x + 3 = 2\sqrt{3x + 3}$

$9x^2 + 18x + 9 = 12x + 12$

$9x^2 + 6x - 3 = 0$

$3(3x - 1)(x + 1) = 0$

$x = \dfrac{1}{3}$ or $x = -1$

Both values check. The solution set is $\left\{\dfrac{1}{3}, -1\right\}$.

15. $\sqrt{20 - x} = \sqrt{9 - x} + 3$

$(\sqrt{20 - x})^2 = (\sqrt{9 - x} + 3)^2$

$20 - x = (9 - x) + 6\sqrt{9 - x} + 9$

$20 - x = 18 - x + 6\sqrt{9 - x}$

$2 = 6\sqrt{9 - x}$

$1 = 3\sqrt{9 - x}$

$1^2 = (3\sqrt{9 - x})^2$

$1 = 9(9 - x)$

$1 = 81 - 9x$

$9x = 80$

$x = \dfrac{80}{9}$

The value checks. The solution set is $\left\{\dfrac{80}{9}\right\}$.

16. $\sqrt{n + 2} + \sqrt{3n + 4} = 2$

$\sqrt{n + 2} = 2 - \sqrt{3n + 4}$

$n + 2 = 4 - 4\sqrt{3n + 4} + 3n + 4$

$4\sqrt{3n + 4} = 2n + 6$

$2\sqrt{3n + 4} = n + 3$

$12n + 16 = n^2 + 6n + 9$

$0 = n^2 - 6n - 7$

$0 = (n - 7)(n + 1)$

$n = 7$ or $n = -1$

Only -1 checks. The solution set is {-1}.

17. $\sqrt{x} - \sqrt{3x - 3} = 1$

$\sqrt{x} = \sqrt{3x - 3} + 1$

$(\sqrt{x})^2 = (\sqrt{3x - 3} + 1)^2$

$x = (3x - 3) + 2\sqrt{3x - 3} + 1$

$2 - 2x = 2\sqrt{3x - 3}$

$1 - x = \sqrt{3x - 3}$

$(1 - x)^2 = (\sqrt{3x - 3})^2$

$1 - 2x + x^2 = 3x - 3$

$x^2 - 5x + 4 = 0$

$(x - 4)(x - 1) = 0$

$x = 4$ or $x = 1$

The number 4 does not check, but 1 does. The solution set is {1}.

18. $\sqrt{2x + 1} - \sqrt{x} = 1$

$$\sqrt{2x + 1} = \sqrt{x} + 1$$
$$2x + 1 = x + 2\sqrt{x} + 1$$
$$x = 2\sqrt{x}$$
$$x^2 = 4x$$
$$x^2 - 4x = 0$$
$$x(x - 4) = 0$$

x = 0 or x = 4

Both values check. The solution set is {0, 4}.

19. $\sqrt{2y - 5} - \sqrt{y - 3} = 1$

$$\sqrt{2y - 5} = \sqrt{y - 3} + 1$$
$$(\sqrt{2y - 5})^2 = (\sqrt{y - 3} + 1)^2$$
$$2y - 5 = (y - 3) + 2\sqrt{y - 3} + 1$$
$$y - 3 = 2\sqrt{y - 3}$$
$$(y - 3)^2 = (2\sqrt{y - 3})^2$$
$$y^2 - 6y + 9 = 4(y - 3)$$
$$y^2 - 6y + 9 = 4y - 12$$
$$y^2 - 10y + 21 = 0$$
$$(y - 7)(y - 3) = 0$$

y = 7 or y = 3

Both numbers check. The solution set is {7, 3}.

20. $\sqrt{4p - 5} - \sqrt{p - 2} = 3$

$$\sqrt{4p - 5} = \sqrt{p - 2} + 3$$
$$4p - 5 = p - 2 + 6\sqrt{p - 2} + 9$$
$$3p - 12 = 6\sqrt{p - 2}$$
$$p - 4 = 2\sqrt{p - 2}$$
$$p^2 - 8p + 16 = 4p - 8$$
$$p^2 - 12p + 24 = 0$$
$$p = 6 \pm 2\sqrt{3} \quad \text{(Using the}$$
quadratic formula)

Only $6 + 2\sqrt{3}$ checks. The solution set is $\{6 + 2\sqrt{3}\}$.

21. $\sqrt{7.35x + 8.051} = 0.345x + 0.067$

$$(\sqrt{7.35x + 8.051})^2 = (0.345x + 0.067)^2$$
$$7.35x + 8.051 = 0.119025x^2 + 0.04623x +$$
$$0.004489$$
$$0 = 0.119025x^2 - 7.30377x -$$
$$8.046511$$

$$x = \frac{-(-7.30377) \pm \sqrt{(-7.30377)^2 - 4(0.119025)(-8.046511)}}{2(0.119025)}$$

$x \approx 62.4459$ or $x \approx -1.0826$

Since -1.0826 does not check and 62.4459 does check, the solution set is {62.4459}.

22. $\sqrt{1.213x + 9.333} = 5.343x + 2.312$

$$1.213x + 9.333 = 28.547649x^2 + 24.706032x +$$
$$5.345344$$
$$0 = 28.547649x^2 + 23.493032x -$$
$$3.987656$$

$x \approx 0.1444$ or $x \approx -0.9673$ (Using the quadratic formula)

Only 0.1444 checks. The solution set is {0.1444}.

23. $x^{1/3} = -2$

$$(x^{1/3})^3 = (-2)^3 \qquad (x^{1/3} = \sqrt[3]{x})$$
$$x = -8$$

The value checks. The solution set is {-8}.

24. $t^{1/5} = 2$

$$t = 32$$

The value checks. The solution set is {32}.

25. $t^{1/4} = 3$

$$(t^{1/4})^4 = 3^4 \qquad (t^{1/4} = \sqrt[4]{t})$$
$$t = 81$$

The value checks. The solution set is {81}.

26. $m^{1/2} = -7$

The principal square root is never negative. The solution set is $\emptyset$.

27. $8 = \dfrac{1}{\sqrt{x}}$

$$8\sqrt{x} = 1$$
$$\sqrt{x} = \frac{1}{8}$$
$$(\sqrt{x})^2 = \left(\frac{1}{8}\right)^2$$
$$x = \frac{1}{64}$$

The value checks. The solution set is $\left\{\frac{1}{64}\right\}$.

28. $3 = \dfrac{1}{\sqrt{y}}$

$$3\sqrt{y} = 1$$
$$9y = 1$$
$$y = \frac{1}{9}$$

The value checks. The solution set is $\left\{\frac{1}{9}\right\}$.

29. $\sqrt[3]{m} = -5$

$$(\sqrt[3]{m})^3 = (-5)^3$$
$$m = -125$$

The value checks. The solution set is {-125}.

30. $\sqrt[4]{t} = -5$

    The principal fourth root is never negative. The solution set is Ø.

31. For L: $T = 2\pi \sqrt{\dfrac{L}{g}}$ For g: $T = 2\pi \sqrt{\dfrac{L}{g}}$

    $\dfrac{T}{2\pi} = \sqrt{\dfrac{L}{g}}$ $\dfrac{T}{2\pi} = \sqrt{\dfrac{L}{g}}$

    $\left[\dfrac{T}{2\pi}\right]^2 = \left[\sqrt{\dfrac{L}{g}}\right]^2$ $\left[\dfrac{T}{2\pi}\right]^2 = \left[\sqrt{\dfrac{L}{g}}\right]^2$

    $\dfrac{T^2}{4\pi^2} = \dfrac{L}{g}$ $\dfrac{T^2}{4\pi^2} = \dfrac{L}{g}$

    $\dfrac{gT^2}{4\pi^2} = L$ $gT^2 = 4\pi^2 L$

    $\qquad\qquad\qquad g = \dfrac{4\pi^2 L}{T^2}$

32. $\qquad H = \sqrt{c^2 + d^2}$

    $\qquad H^2 = c^2 + d^2$

    $H^2 - d^2 = c^2$

    $\sqrt{H^2 - d^2} = c$ (Taking the positive square root)

33. $V = 1.2\sqrt{h}$

    $V = 1.2\sqrt{30,000}$ (Substituting)

    ≈ 208

    You can see about 208 miles to the horizon.

34. $V = 1.2\sqrt{72} \approx 10$ mi

35. $\qquad V = 1.2\sqrt{h}$

    $144 = 1.2\sqrt{h}$ (Substituting)

    $\dfrac{144}{1.2} = \sqrt{h}$

    $120 = \sqrt{h}$

    $14,400 = h$

    The airplane is 14,400 ft high.

36. $11 = 1.2\sqrt{h}$

    $121 = 1.44h$

    $84 \approx h$

    The mast is about 84 ft high.

37. $\qquad (x - 5)^{2/3} = 2$

    $\sqrt[3]{(x - 5)^2} = 2$

    $(\sqrt[3]{(x - 5)^2})^3 = 2^3$

    $\qquad (x - 5)^2 = 2^3$

    $x^2 - 10x + 25 = 8$

    $x^2 - 10x + 17 = 0$

    $a = 1, \quad b = -10, \quad c = 17$

    $x = \dfrac{-(-10) \pm \sqrt{(-10)^2 - 4\cdot1\cdot17}}{2\cdot1}$

    $= \dfrac{10 \pm \sqrt{100 - 68}}{2} = \dfrac{10 \pm \sqrt{32}}{2}$

    $= \dfrac{10 \pm 4\sqrt{2}}{2} = 5 \pm 2\sqrt{2}$

    Both values check. The solution set is $\{5 \pm 2\sqrt{2}\}$.

38. $(x - 3)^{2/3} = 2$

    $x^2 - 6x + 9 = 8$

    $x^2 - 6x + 1 = 0$

    $\qquad x = 3 \pm 2\sqrt{2}$

    Both values check. The solution set is $\{3 \pm 2\sqrt{2}\}$.

39. $\dfrac{x + \sqrt{x + 1}}{x - \sqrt{x + 1}} = \dfrac{5}{11}$

    $11(x + \sqrt{x + 1}) = 5(x - \sqrt{x + 1})$

    $11x + 11\sqrt{x + 1} = 5x - 5\sqrt{x + 1}$

    $6x = -16\sqrt{x + 1}$

    $(6x)^2 = (-16\sqrt{x + 1})^2$

    $36x^2 = 256(x + 1)$

    $36x^2 - 256x - 256 = 0$

    $9x^2 - 64x - 64 = 0$

    $(9x + 8)(x - 8) = 0$

    $9x + 8 = 0$ or $x - 8 = 0$

    $x = -\dfrac{8}{9}$ or $x = 8$

    Only $-\dfrac{8}{9}$ checks. The solution set is $\left\{-\dfrac{8}{9}\right\}$.

40. $\sqrt{\sqrt{x + 25} - \sqrt{x}} = 5$

    $\sqrt{x + 25} - \sqrt{x} = 25$

    $\sqrt{x + 25} = \sqrt{x} + 25$

    $x + 25 = x + 50\sqrt{x} + 625$

    $-12 = \sqrt{x}$

    The principal square root is never negative. The solution set is Ø.

41.
$$\sqrt{x + 2} - \sqrt{x - 2} = \sqrt{2x}$$
$$(\sqrt{x + 2} - \sqrt{x - 2})^2 = (\sqrt{2x})^2$$
$$x + 2 - 2\sqrt{(x + 2)(x - 2)} + x - 2 = 2x$$
$$-2\sqrt{(x + 2)(x - 2)} = 0$$
$$\sqrt{(x + 2)(x - 2)} = 0$$
$$(\sqrt{(x + 2)(x - 2)})^2 = 0^2$$
$$(x + 2)(x - 2) = 0$$

$x + 2 = 0$ or $x - 2 = 0$

$x = -2$ or $x = 2$

Only 2 checks. The solution set is {2}.

42.
$$2\sqrt{x + 3} = \sqrt{x} + \sqrt{x + 8}$$
$$4x + 12 = x + 2\sqrt{x^2 + 8x} + x + 8$$
$$2x + 4 = 2\sqrt{x^2 + 8x}$$
$$x + 2 = \sqrt{x^2 + 8x}$$
$$x^2 + 4x + 4 = x^2 + 8x$$
$$4 = 4x$$
$$1 = x$$

The value checks. The solution set is {1}.

43.
$$\sqrt[4]{x + 2} = \sqrt{3x + 1}$$
$$(\sqrt[4]{x + 2})^4 = (\sqrt{3x + 1})^4$$
$$x + 2 = (3x + 1)^2$$
$$x + 2 = 9x^2 + 6x + 1$$
$$0 = 9x^2 + 5x - 1$$

$a = 9$, $b = 5$, $c = -1$

$$x = \frac{-5 \pm \sqrt{5^2 - 4(9)(-1)}}{2 \cdot 9} = \frac{-5 \pm \sqrt{25 + 36}}{18}$$
$$= \frac{-5 \pm \sqrt{61}}{18}$$

Only $\frac{-5 + \sqrt{61}}{18}$ checks. The solution set is $\left\{\frac{-5 + \sqrt{61}}{18}\right\}$.

44.
$$\sqrt[3]{2x - 1} = \sqrt[6]{x + 1}$$
$$4x^2 - 4x + 1 = x + 1$$
$$4x^2 - 5x = 0$$
$$x(4x - 5) = 0$$

$x = 0$ or $x = \frac{5}{4}$

Only $\frac{5}{4}$ checks. The solution set is $\left\{\frac{5}{4}\right\}$.

45.
$$\frac{14}{3 + \sqrt{7 + x}} - \frac{\sqrt{7 + x}}{2} = 0, \text{ LCM is } 2(3 + \sqrt{7 + x})$$
$$2(3 + \sqrt{7 + x})\left[\frac{14}{3 + \sqrt{7 + x}} - \frac{\sqrt{7 + x}}{2}\right] =$$
$$2(3 + \sqrt{7 + x}) \cdot 0$$
$$28 - 3\sqrt{7 + x} - (7 + x) = 0$$
$$21 - x = 3\sqrt{7 + x}$$
$$(21 - x)^2 = (3\sqrt{7 + x})^2$$
$$441 - 42x + x^2 = 9(7 + x)$$
$$441 - 42x + x^2 = 63 + 9x$$
$$x^2 - 51x + 378 = 0$$
$$(x - 9)(x - 42) = 0$$

$x = 9$ or $x = 42$

Only 9 checks. The solution set is {9}.

46.
$$\frac{\sqrt{10 + x}}{4} = \frac{6}{2 + \sqrt{10 + x}},$$
$$\text{LCM is } 4(2 + \sqrt{10 + x})$$
$$2\sqrt{10 + x} + 10 + x = 24$$
$$2\sqrt{10 + x} = -x + 14$$
$$40 + 4x = x^2 - 28x + 196$$
$$0 = x^2 - 32x + 156$$
$$0 = (x - 26)(x - 6)$$

$x = 26$ or $x = 6$

Only 6 checks. The solution set is {6}.

47.
$$\sqrt{3x + 1} - \sqrt{2x} = \frac{5}{\sqrt{3x + 1}},$$
$$\text{LCM is } \sqrt{3x + 1}$$
$$\sqrt{3x + 1}(\sqrt{3x + 1} - \sqrt{2x}) = \sqrt{3x + 1} \cdot \frac{5}{\sqrt{3x + 1}}$$
$$(3x + 1) - \sqrt{6x^2 + 2x} = 5$$
$$3x - 4 = \sqrt{6x^2 + 2x}$$
$$(3x - 4)^2 = (\sqrt{6x^2 + 2x})^2$$
$$9x^2 - 24x + 16 = 6x^2 + 2x$$
$$3x^2 - 26x + 16 = 0$$
$$(3x - 2)(x - 8) = 0$$

$x = \frac{2}{3}$ or $x = 8$

Only 8 checks. The solution set is {8}.

48. $\sqrt{3 + x} + \sqrt{x} = \dfrac{5}{\sqrt{x}}$,   LCM is $\sqrt{x}$

$$\sqrt{3x + x^2} + x = 5$$
$$\sqrt{3x + x^2} = 5 - x$$
$$3x + x^2 = 25 - 10x + x^2$$
$$13x = 25$$
$$x = \frac{25}{13}$$

The value checks. The solution set is $\left\{\dfrac{25}{13}\right\}$.

49. $\sqrt{15 + \sqrt{2x + 80}} = 5$

$$\left[\sqrt{15 + \sqrt{2x + 80}}\right]^2 = 5^2$$
$$15 + \sqrt{2x + 80} = 25$$
$$\sqrt{2x + 80} = 10$$
$$(\sqrt{2x + 80})^2 = 10^2$$
$$2x + 80 = 100$$
$$2x = 20$$
$$x = 10$$

This number checks. The solution set is $\{10\}$.

50. $\sqrt{x + 5} + 1 = \dfrac{6}{\sqrt{x + 5}}$,   LCM is $\sqrt{x + 5}$

$$x + 5 + \sqrt{x + 5} = 6$$
$$\sqrt{x + 5} = 1 - x$$
$$x + 5 = 1 - 2x + x^2$$
$$0 = x^2 - 3x - 4$$
$$0 = (x - 4)(x + 1)$$

$x = 4$ or $x = -1$

Only -1 checks. The solution set is $\{-1\}$.

Exercise Set 2.8

1. $x - 10\sqrt{x} + 9 = 0$

We substitute u for $\sqrt{x}$.
$$u^2 - 10u + 9 = 0$$
$$(u - 9)(u - 1) = 0$$

$u - 9 = 0$ or $u - 1 = 0$
      $u = 9$ or $u = 1$

Now we substitute $\sqrt{x}$ for u and solve for x.
$\sqrt{x} = 9$ or $\sqrt{x} = 1$
   $x = 81$ or $x = 1$

Check:
For 81:   For 1:

$x - 10\sqrt{x} + 9 = 0$		$x - 10\sqrt{x} + 9 = 0$	
$81 - 10\sqrt{81} + 9$	0	$1 - 10\sqrt{1} + 9$	0
$81 - 10 \cdot 9 + 9$		$1 - 10 + 9$	
$81 - 90 + 9$			0
0			

The solutions are 81 and 1. The solution set is $\{81, 1\}$.

2. $2x - 9\sqrt{x} + 4 = 0$
$$2u^2 - 9u + 4 = 0$$
$$(2u - 1)(u - 4) = 0$$
$$u = \frac{1}{2} \quad \text{or} \quad u = 4$$
$$\sqrt{x} = \frac{1}{2} \quad \text{or} \quad \sqrt{x} = 4$$
$$x = \frac{1}{4} \quad \text{or} \quad x = 16$$

Both values check. The solution set is $\left\{\dfrac{1}{4}, 16\right\}$.

3. $x^4 - 10x^2 + 25 = 0$

We substitute u for x^2.
$$u^2 - 10u + 25 = 0$$
$$(u - 5)(u - 5) = 0$$

$u - 5 = 0$ or $u - 5 = 0$
   $u = 5$ or $u = 5$

Now we substitute x^2 for u and solve for x.
$x^2 = 5$ or $x^2 = 5$
   $x = \pm\sqrt{5}$ or $x = \pm\sqrt{5}$

The solutions are $\pm\sqrt{5}$. The solution set is $\{\pm\sqrt{5}\}$.

4. $x^4 - 3x^2 + 2 = 0$
$$u^2 - 3u + 2 = 0$$
$$(u - 1)(u - 2) = 0$$

$u = 1$ or $u = 2$
$x^2 = 1$ or $x^2 = 2$
   $x = \pm 1$ or $x = \pm\sqrt{2}$

$\{\pm 1, \pm\sqrt{2}\}$

5. $t^{2/3} + t^{1/3} - 6 = 0$

We substitute u for $t^{1/3}$.

$u^2 + u - 6 = 0$

$(u + 3)(u - 2) = 0$

$u + 3 = 0$ or $u - 2 = 0$

$u = -3$ or $u = 2$

We now substitute $t^{1/3}$ for u and solve for t.

$t^{1/3} = -3$ or $t^{1/3} = 2$

$t = (-3)^3$ or $t = 2^3$

$t = -27$ or $t = 8$

The solutions are -27 and 8. The solution set is {-27, 8}.

6. $w^{2/3} - 2w^{1/3} - 8 = 0$

$u^2 - 2u - 8 = 0$

$(u - 4)(u + 2) = 0$

$u = 4$ or $u = -2$

$w^{1/3} = 4$ or $w^{1/3} = -2$

$w = 64$ or $w = -8$

{64, -8}

7. $z^{1/2} = z^{1/4} + 2$

$z^{1/2} - z^{1/4} - 2 = 0$

We substitute u for $z^{1/4}$.

$u^2 - u - 2 = 0$

$(u - 2)(u + 1) = 0$

$u - 2 = 0$ or $u + 1 = 0$

$u = 2$ or $u = -1$

Next we substitute $z^{1/4}$ for u and solve for z.

$z^{1/4} = 2$ or $z^{1/4} = -1$

$z = 2^4$ or $z = (-1)^4$

$z = 16$ or $z = 1$

The number 16 checks, but 1 does not. The solution set is {16}.

8. $6 = m^{1/3} - m^{1/6}$

$0 = m^{1/3} - m^{1/6} - 6$

$0 = u^2 - u - 6$

$0 = (u - 3)(u + 2)$

$u = 3$ or $u = -2$

$m^{1/6} = 3$ or $m^{1/6} = -2$

$m = 729$ or   No solution

{729}

9. $(x^2 - 6x)^2 - 2(x^2 - 6x) - 35 = 0$

We substitute u for $x^2 - 6x$.

$u^2 - 2u - 35 = 0$

$(u - 7)(u + 5) = 0$

$u - 7 = 0$ or $u + 5 = 0$

$u = 7$ or $u = -5$

Next we substitute $x^2 - 6x$ for u and solve for x.

$x^2 - 6x = 7$ or $x^2 - 6x = -5$

$x^2 - 6x - 7 = 0$ or $x^2 - 6x + 5 = 0$

$(x - 7)(x + 1) = 0$ or $(x - 5)(x - 1) = 0$

$x - 7 = 0$ or $x + 1 = 0$ or $x - 5 = 0$ or $x - 1 = 0$

$x = 7$ or $x = -1$ or $x = 5$ or $x = 1$

The solutions are 7, -1, 5, and 1. The solution set is {7, -1, 5, 1}.

10. $(1 + \sqrt{x})^2 + (1 + \sqrt{x}) - 6 = 0$

$u^2 + u - 6 = 0$

$(u + 3)(u - 2) = 0$

$u = -3$ or $u = 2$

$1 + \sqrt{x} = -3$ or $1 + \sqrt{x} = 2$

$\sqrt{x} = -4$ or $\sqrt{x} = 1$

No solution   or $x = 1$

{1}

11. $(y^2 - 5y)^2 + (y^2 - 5y) - 12 = 0$

We substitute u for $y^2 - 5y$.

$u^2 + u - 12 = 0$

$(u + 4)(u - 3) = 0$

$u + 4 = 0$ or $u - 3 = 0$

$u = -4$ or $u = 3$

Next we substitute $y^2 - 5y$ for u and solve for y.

$y^2 - 5y = -4$ or $y^2 - 5y = 3$

$y^2 - 5y + 4 = 0$ or $y^2 - 5y - 3 = 0$

$(y - 4)(y - 1) = 0$ or $y = \dfrac{-(-5) \pm \sqrt{(-5)^2 - 4(1)(-3)}}{2 \cdot 1}$

$y - 4 = 0$ or $y - 1 = 0$ or $y = \dfrac{5 \pm \sqrt{25 + 12}}{2}$

$y = 4$ or $y = 1$ or $y = \dfrac{5 \pm \sqrt{37}}{2}$

The solutions are 4, 1, and $\dfrac{5 \pm \sqrt{37}}{2}$. The solution set is $\left\{4, 1, \dfrac{5 \pm \sqrt{37}}{2}\right\}$.

12. $(2t^2 + t)^2 - 4(2t^2 + t) + 3 = 0$

$$u^2 - 4u + 3 = 0$$

$$(u - 1)(u - 3) = 0$$

$u = 1$ or $\qquad$ $u = 3$

$2t^2 + t = 1$ or $\qquad$ $2t^2 + t = 3$

$2t^2 + t - 1 = 0$ or $\qquad$ $2t^2 + t - 3 = 0$

$(2t - 1)(t + 1) = 0$ or $(2t + 3)(t - 1) = 0$

$t = \frac{1}{2}$ or $t = -1$ or $t = -\frac{3}{2}$ or $t = 1$

$\left\{\frac{1}{2}, -1, -\frac{3}{2}, 1\right\}$

13. $w^4 - 4w^2 - 2 = 0$

First we substitute u for w^2.

$u^2 - 4u - 2 = 0$

$$u = \frac{-(-4) \pm \sqrt{(-4)^2 - 4(1)(-2)}}{2 \cdot 1}$$

$$u = \frac{4 \pm \sqrt{16 + 8}}{2} = \frac{4 \pm \sqrt{24}}{2}$$

$$u = \frac{4 \pm 2\sqrt{6}}{2} = 2 \pm \sqrt{6}$$

Next we substitute w^2 for u and solve for w.

$w^2 = 2 + \sqrt{6}$ $\quad$ or $w^2 = 2 - \sqrt{6}$

$w = \pm\sqrt{2 + \sqrt{6}}$ or $w = \pm\sqrt{2 - \sqrt{6}}$

The solutions are $\pm\sqrt{2 + \sqrt{6}}$ and $\pm\sqrt{2 - \sqrt{6}}$.

The solution set is $\left\{\pm\sqrt{2 + \sqrt{6}}, \pm\sqrt{2 - \sqrt{6}}\right\}$.

14. $t^4 - 5t^2 + 5 = 0$

$u^2 - 5u + 5 = 0$

$u = \frac{5 + \sqrt{5}}{2}$ $\qquad$ or $\quad$ $u = \frac{5 - \sqrt{5}}{2}$

$t^2 = \frac{5 + \sqrt{5}}{2}$ $\qquad$ or $\quad$ $t^2 = \frac{5 - \sqrt{5}}{2}$

$t = \pm\sqrt{\frac{5 + \sqrt{5}}{2}}$ or $\quad$ $t = \pm\sqrt{\frac{5 - \sqrt{5}}{2}}$

$\left\{\pm\sqrt{\frac{5 + \sqrt{5}}{2}}, \pm\sqrt{\frac{5 - \sqrt{5}}{2}}\right\}$

15. $x^{-2} - x^{-1} - 6 = 0$

We substitute u for x^{-1}.

$u^2 - u - 6 = 0$

$(u - 3)(u + 2) = 0$

$u - 3 = 0$ or $u + 2 = 0$

$u = 3$ or $\qquad$ $u = -2$

Then we substitute x^{-1} for u and solve for x.

$x^{-1} = 3$ or $x^{-1} = -2$

$\frac{1}{x} = 3$ or $\quad$ $\frac{1}{x} = -2$

$x = \frac{1}{3}$ or $\quad$ $x = -\frac{1}{2}$

The solutions are $\frac{1}{3}$ and $-\frac{1}{2}$. The solution set is $\left\{\frac{1}{3}, -\frac{1}{2}\right\}$.

16. $4x^{-2} - x^{-1} - 5 = 0$

$4u^2 - u - 5 = 0$

$(4u - 5)(u + 1) = 0$

$u = \frac{5}{4}$ or $u = -1$

$\frac{1}{x} = \frac{5}{4}$ or $\frac{1}{x} = -1$

$x = \frac{4}{5}$ or $x = -1$

Both values check. The solution set is $\left\{\frac{4}{5}, -1\right\}$.

17. $2x^{-2} + x^{-1} = 1$

$2x^{-2} + x^{-1} - 1 = 0$

We substitute u for x^{-1}.

$2u^2 + u - 1 = 0$

$(2u - 1)(u + 1) = 0$

$2u - 1 = 0$ or $u + 1 = 0$

$u = \frac{1}{2}$ or $\qquad$ $u = -1$

Next we substitute x^{-1} for u and solve for x.

$x^{-1} = \frac{1}{2}$ or $x^{-1} = -1$

$\frac{1}{x} = \frac{1}{2}$ or $\frac{1}{x} = -1$

$x = 2$ or $\quad$ $x = -1$

The solutions are 2 and -1. The solution set is {2, -1}.

18. $10 - 9m^{-1} = m^{-2}$

$0 = m^{-2} + 9m^{-1} - 10$

$0 = u^2 + 9u - 10$

$0 = (u + 10)(u - 1)$

$u = -10$ $\quad$ or $\quad$ $u = 1$

$\frac{1}{m} = -10$ $\quad$ or $\quad$ $\frac{1}{m} = 1$

$m = -\frac{1}{10}$ $\quad$ or $\quad$ $m = 1$

Both values check. The solution set is $\left\{-\frac{1}{10}, 1\right\}$.

19. $x^4 - 24x^2 - 25 = 0$

We substitute u for x^2.

$u^2 - 24u - 25 = 0$

$(u - 25)(u + 1) = 0$

$u - 25 = 0$ or $u + 1 = 0$

$u = 25$ or $u = -1$

Then we substitute x^2 for u and solve for x.

$x^2 = 25$ or $x^2 = -1$

$x = \pm 5$ or $x = \pm i$

The solutions are ± 5 and $\pm i$. The solution set is $\{\pm 5, \pm i\}$.

20. $x^4 - 5x^2 - 36 = 0$

$u^2 - 5u - 36 = 0$

$(u - 9)(u + 4) = 0$

$u = 9$ or $u = -4$

$x^2 = 9$ or $x^2 = -4$

$x = \pm 3$ or $x = \pm 2i$

$\{\pm 3, \pm 2i\}$

21. $\left(\dfrac{x^2 - 2}{x}\right)^2 - 7\left(\dfrac{x^2 - 2}{x}\right) - 18 = 0$

We first substitute u for $\dfrac{x^2 - 2}{x}$.

$u^2 - 7u - 18 = 0$

$(u - 9)(u + 2) = 0$

$u - 9 = 0$ or $u + 2 = 0$

$u = 9$ or $u = -2$

Then we substitute $\dfrac{x^2 - 2}{x}$ for u and solve for x.

$\dfrac{x^2 - 2}{x} = 9$ or $\dfrac{x^2 - 2}{x} = -2$

$x^2 - 2 = 9x$ or $x^2 - 2 = -2x$

$x^2 - 9x - 2 = 0$ or $x^2 + 2x - 2 = 0$

$x = \dfrac{-(-9) \pm \sqrt{(-9)^2 - 4(1)(-2)}}{2 \cdot 1}$ or $x = \dfrac{-2 \pm \sqrt{2^2 - 4(1)(-2)}}{2 \cdot 1}$

$x = \dfrac{9 \pm \sqrt{89}}{2}$ or $x = \dfrac{-2 \pm 2\sqrt{3}}{2}$

or $x = -1 \pm \sqrt{3}$

The solutions are $\dfrac{9 \pm \sqrt{89}}{2}$ and $-1 \pm \sqrt{3}$. The solution set is $\left\{\dfrac{9 \pm \sqrt{89}}{2}, -1 \pm \sqrt{3}\right\}$.

22. $\left(\dfrac{x^2 + 1}{x}\right)^2 - 8\left(\dfrac{x^2 + 1}{x}\right) + 15 = 0$

$u^2 - 8u + 15 = 0$

$(u - 5)(u - 3) = 0$

$u = 5$ or $u = 3$

$\dfrac{x^2 + 1}{x} = 5$ or $\dfrac{x^2 + 1}{x} = 3$

$x^2 - 5x + 1 = 0$ or $x^2 - 3x + 1 = 0$

$x = \dfrac{5 \pm \sqrt{21}}{2}$ or $x = \dfrac{3 \pm \sqrt{5}}{2}$

All four values check. The solution set is $\left\{\dfrac{5 \pm \sqrt{21}}{2}, \dfrac{3 \pm \sqrt{5}}{2}\right\}$.

23. $\dfrac{x}{x - 1} - 6\sqrt{\dfrac{x}{x - 1}} - 40 = 0$

We substitute u for $\sqrt{\dfrac{x}{x - 1}}$.

$u^2 - 6u - 40 = 0$

$(u - 10)(u + 4) = 0$

$u - 10 = 0$ or $u + 4 = 0$

$u = 10$ or $u = -4$

We then substitute $\sqrt{\dfrac{x}{x - 1}}$ for u and solve for x.

$\sqrt{\dfrac{x}{x - 1}} = 10$ or $\sqrt{\dfrac{x}{x - 1}} = -4$

$\dfrac{x}{x - 1} = 100$ No solution

$x = 100x - 100$

$100 = 99x$

$\dfrac{100}{99} = x$

The solution is $\dfrac{100}{99}$. The solution set is $\left\{\dfrac{100}{99}\right\}$.

24. $\dfrac{2x + 1}{x} - 30 = 7\sqrt{\dfrac{2x + 1}{x}}$

$\dfrac{2x + 1}{x} - 7\sqrt{\dfrac{2x + 1}{x}} - 30 = 0$

$u^2 - 7u - 30 = 0$

$(u - 10)(u + 3) = 0$

$u = 10$ or $u = -3$

$\sqrt{\dfrac{2x + 1}{x}} = 10$ or $\sqrt{\dfrac{2x + 1}{x}} = -3$

$\dfrac{2x + 1}{x} = 100$ or No solution

$2x + 1 = 100x$

$1 = 98x$

$\dfrac{1}{98} = x$

The value checks. The solution set is $\left\{\dfrac{1}{98}\right\}$.

25.
$$5\left(\frac{x + 2}{x - 2}\right)^2 = 3\left(\frac{x + 2}{x - 2}\right) + 2$$

$$5\left(\frac{x + 2}{x - 2}\right)^2 - 3\left(\frac{x + 2}{x - 2}\right) - 2 = 0$$

Substitute u for $\frac{x + 2}{x - 2}$.

$$5u^2 - 3u - 2 = 0$$

$$(5u + 2)(u - 1) = 0$$

$5u + 2 = 0 \quad$ or $\quad u - 1 = 0$

$\quad u = -\frac{2}{5}$ or $\quad u = 1$

Then substitute $\frac{x + 2}{x - 2}$ for u and solve for x.

$\frac{x + 2}{x - 2} = -\frac{2}{5} \quad$ or $\frac{x + 2}{x - 2} = 1$

$5(x + 2) = -2(x - 2)$ or $x + 2 = x - 2$

$5x + 10 = -2x + 4 \quad$ or $\quad 2 = -2$

$7x = -6 \qquad\qquad$ No solution

$\quad x = -\frac{6}{7}$

The solution is $-\frac{6}{7}$. The solution set is $\left\{-\frac{6}{7}\right\}$.

26.
$$\left(\frac{x + 1}{x + 3}\right)^2 + \left(\frac{x + 1}{x + 3}\right) - 6 = 0$$

$$u^2 + u - 6 = 0$$

$$(u + 3)(u - 2) = 0$$

$\quad u = -3 \qquad$ or $\qquad u = 2$

$\frac{x + 1}{x + 3} = -3 \qquad$ or $\quad \frac{x + 1}{x + 3} = 2$

$x + 1 = -3x - 9$ or $x + 1 = 2x + 6$

$\quad 10 = -4x \qquad$ or $\qquad -5 = x$

$-\frac{5}{2} = x$

Both values check. The solution set is $\left\{-\frac{5}{2}, -5\right\}$.

27.
$$\left(\frac{x^2 - 1}{x}\right)^2 - \left(\frac{x^2 - 1}{x}\right) - 2 = 0$$

Substitute u for $\frac{x^2 - 1}{x}$.

$$u^2 - u - 2 = 0$$

$$(u - 2)(u + 1) = 0$$

$u - 2 = 0$ or $u + 1 = 0$

$\quad u = 2$ or $\quad u = -1$

Then substitute $\frac{x^2 - 1}{x}$ for u and solve for x.

$\frac{x^2 - 1}{x} = 2 \quad$ or $\qquad \frac{x^2 - 1}{x} = -1$

$x^2 - 1 = 2x$ or $\quad x^2 - 1 = -x$

$x^2 - 2x - 1 = 0 \quad$ or $x^2 + x - 1 = 0$

$x = \frac{-(-2) \pm \sqrt{(-2)^2 - 4(1)(-1)}}{2 \cdot 1}$ or $x = \frac{-1 \pm \sqrt{1^2 - 4(1)(-1)}}{2 \cdot 1}$

$x = \frac{2 \pm \sqrt{8}}{2} \qquad\qquad x = \frac{-1 \pm \sqrt{5}}{2}$

$x = \frac{2 \pm 2\sqrt{2}}{2}$

$x = 1 \pm \sqrt{2}$

The solutions are $1 \pm \sqrt{2}$ and $\frac{-1 \pm \sqrt{5}}{2}$. The solution set is $\left\{1 \pm \sqrt{2}, \frac{-1 \pm \sqrt{5}}{2}\right\}$.

28.
$$\left(\frac{x + 8}{x - 8}\right)^2 - 6 = 5\left(\frac{x + 8}{x - 8}\right)$$

$$\left(\frac{x + 8}{x - 8}\right)^2 - 5\left(\frac{x + 8}{x - 8}\right) - 6 = 0$$

$$u^2 - 5u - 6 = 0$$

$$(u - 6)(u + 1) = 0$$

$\quad u = 6 \qquad$ or $\qquad u = -1$

$\frac{x + 8}{x - 8} = 6 \qquad$ or $\quad \frac{x + 8}{x - 8} = -1$

$x + 8 = 6x - 48$ or $x + 8 = -x + 8$

$\quad 56 = 5x \qquad$ or $\qquad 2x = 0$

$\frac{56}{5} = x \qquad$ or $\qquad x = 0$

Both values check. The solution set is $\left\{\frac{56}{5}, 0\right\}$.

29. Familiarize and Translate:

We let t_1 represent the time it takes for the object to fall to the ground and t_2 represent the time it takes the sound to get back. The total amount of time, 3 sec, is the sum of t_1 and t_2. This gives us an equation.

$\quad t_1 + t_2 = 3 \qquad\qquad$ (1)

We use the formula $s = 16t^2 + v_0 t$ to find an expression for t_1. Since the stone is dropped, v_0 is 0.

$$s = 16t_1^2$$

$$\frac{s}{16} = t_1^2$$

$$\sqrt{\frac{s}{16}} = t_1$$

$$\frac{\sqrt{s}}{4} = t_1 \qquad\qquad (2)$$

We use $d = rt$ (here we use $s = rt$) to find an expression for t_2.

$\quad s = 1100 \cdot t_2 \qquad$ (Substituting 1100 for r)

$$\frac{s}{1100} = t_2 \qquad\qquad (3)$$

We substitute (2) and (3) in (1) and obtain

$$\frac{\sqrt{s}}{4} + \frac{s}{1100} = 3$$

Carry out:

$$275\sqrt{s} + s = 3300 \quad \text{(Multiplying by 1100)}$$

$$s + 275\sqrt{s} - 3300 = 0$$

Substitute u for $\sqrt{s}$.

$$u^2 + 275u - 3300 = 0$$

Using the quadratic formula, we get $u \approx 11.52$. Then $u = \sqrt{s} \approx 11.52$ and $s \approx 132.7$.

Check and State:

The value checks. The cliff is 132.7 ft high.

30. Use $s = 16t^2$. Then solve:

$$\frac{\sqrt{s}}{4} + \frac{s}{1100} = 4$$

$$s \approx 229.9 \text{ ft}$$

31. Familiarize: We will use the formula $A = P(1 + i)^t$. At the beginning of the third year the $2000 investment has grown to $2000(1 + i)^2$ and the $1200 investment has grown to $1200(1 + i)$.

Translate: We know the total in both accounts is $3573.80, so we can write an equation.

$$2000(1 + i)^2 + 1200(1 + i) = 3573.80, \text{ or}$$

$$2000(1 + i)^2 + 1200(1 + i) - 3573.80 = 0$$

Carry out: This equation is reducible to quadratic with $u = 1 + i$. Substituting, we get

$$2000u^2 + 1200u - 3573.80 = 0.$$

Using the quadratic formula and taking the positive solution, we get $u = 1.07$. Substituting $1 + i$ for u, we get

$$1 + i = 1.07$$

$$i = 0.07.$$

Check: We check by substituting 0.07 for i back through the related equations.

State: The interest rate is 0.07, or 7%.

32. Solve: $3500(1 + i)^2 + 4000(1 + i) = 8518.35$ The positive solution is 0.09, or 9%.

33.

$$6.75x = \sqrt{35x} + 5.36$$

$$6.75x - \sqrt{35}\sqrt{x} - 5.36 = 0 \quad (\sqrt{35x} = \sqrt{35}\sqrt{x})$$

Substitute u for $\sqrt{x}$.

$$6.75u^2 - \sqrt{35}u - 5.36 = 0$$

$$u = \frac{-(-\sqrt{35}) \pm \sqrt{(-\sqrt{35})^2 - 4(6.75)(-5.36)}}{2(6.75)}$$

$$= \frac{\sqrt{35} \pm \sqrt{35 + 144.72}}{13.5}$$

$$= \frac{\sqrt{35} \pm \sqrt{179.72}}{13.5}$$

$$u \approx 1.4313 \text{ or } u \approx -0.5548$$

Substitute $\sqrt{x}$ for u and solve for x.

$$\sqrt{x} \approx 1.4313 \text{ or } \sqrt{x} \approx -0.5548$$

$$x \approx 2.05 \qquad \text{No solution}$$

The value checks. The solution set is {2.05}.

34.

$$\pi x^4 - \sqrt{99.3} = \pi^2 x^2$$

$$\pi x^4 - \pi^2 x^2 - \sqrt{99.3} = 0$$

$$\pi u^2 - \pi^2 u - \sqrt{99.3} = 0$$

$$u = \frac{\pi^2 + \sqrt{\pi^4 + 4\pi\sqrt{99.3}}}{2\pi} \quad \text{or} \quad u = \frac{\pi^2 - \sqrt{\pi^4 + 4\pi\sqrt{99.3}}}{2\pi}$$

$u \approx 3.9455$	or $u \approx -0.8039$
$x^2 \approx 3.9455$	or $x^2 \approx -0.8039$
$x \approx \pm 1.99$	or $x \approx \pm 0.90i$

$$\{\pm 1.99, \pm 0.90i\}$$

35.

$$9x^{3/2} - 8 = x^3$$

$$0 = x^3 - 9x^{3/2} + 8$$

Substitute u for $x^{3/2}$.

$$0 = u^2 - 9u + 8$$

$$0 = (u - 8)(u - 1)$$

$$u - 8 = 0 \text{ or } u - 1 = 0$$

$$u = 8 \text{ or } \quad u = 1$$

Substitute $x^{3/2}$ for u and solve for x.

$$x^{3/2} = 8 \quad \text{or} \quad x^{3/2} = 1$$

$$x^{1/2} = 2 \quad \text{or} \quad x^{1/2} = 1 \quad \text{(Taking cube roots)}$$

$$x = 4 \quad \text{or} \quad x = 1$$

Both values check. The solution set is {4, 1}.

36.

$$\sqrt[3]{2x + 3} = \sqrt[6]{2x + 3}$$

$$\sqrt[3]{2x + 3} - \sqrt[6]{2x + 3} = 0$$

$$u^2 - u = 0$$

$$u(u - 1) = 0$$

$$u = 0 \qquad \text{or} \qquad u = 1$$

$$\sqrt[6]{2x + 3} = 0 \quad \text{or} \quad \sqrt[6]{2x + 3} = 1$$

$$2x + 3 = 0 \quad \text{or} \quad 2x + 3 = 1$$

$$x = -\frac{3}{2} \quad \text{or} \qquad x = -1$$

Both values check. The solution set is $\left\{-\frac{3}{2}, -1\right\}$.

37. $\sqrt{x - 3} - \sqrt[4]{x - 3} = 2$

Substitute u for $\sqrt[4]{x - 3}$.

$$u^2 - u - 2 = 0$$

$$(u - 2)(u + 1) = 0$$

$$u - 2 = 0 \text{ or } u + 1 = 0$$

$$u = 2 \text{ or } \quad u = -1$$

Substitute $\sqrt[4]{x-3}$ for u and solve for x.

$\sqrt[4]{x-3} = 2$ or $\sqrt[4]{x-3} = -1$

$\quad x - 3 = 16$ No solution

$\qquad\quad x = 19$

The value checks. The solution set is {19}.

38. $a^3 - 26a^{3/2} - 27 = 0$

$\qquad u^2 - 26u - 27 = 0$

$\quad (u - 27)(u + 1) = 0$

$\qquad u = 27$ or $u = -1$

$\quad a^{3/2} = 27$ or $a^{3/2} = -1$

$\qquad a = 9$ or   No solution

$\{9\}$

39. $x^6 - 28x^3 + 27 = 0$

Substitute u for x^3.

$\quad u^2 - 28u + 27 = 0$

$(u - 27)(u - 1) = 0$

$u = 27$ or $u = 1$

Substitute x^3 for u and solve for x.

$\qquad\qquad x^3 = 27$ or $\qquad x^3 = 1$

$\qquad\qquad x^3 - 27 = 0$ or $\qquad x^3 - 1 = 0$

$(x-3)(x^2 + 3x + 9) = 0$ or $(x-1)(x^2 + x + 1) = 0$

Using the principle of zero products and, where necessary, the quadratic formula, we find that the solution set is

$\left\{ 3, \dfrac{-3 \pm 3i\sqrt{3}}{2}, 1, \dfrac{-1 \pm i\sqrt{3}}{2} \right\}.$

40. $\qquad x^6 + 7x^3 = 8$

$\qquad x^6 + 7x^3 - 8 = 0$

$\qquad u^2 + 7u - 8 = 0$

$\quad (u + 8)(u - 1) = 0$

$\quad u = -8$ or $u = 1$

$\quad x^3 = -8$ or $x^3 = 1$

$\qquad\qquad x^3 + 8 = 0$ or $\qquad x^3 - 1 = 0$

$(x+2)(x^2 - 2x + 4) = 0$ or $(x-1)(x^2 + x + 1) = 0$

Using the principle of zero products and, where necessary, the quadratic formula, we find that the solution set is

$\left\{ -2, 1 \pm i\sqrt{3}, 1, \dfrac{-1 \pm i\sqrt{3}}{2} \right\}.$

41. $(x^2 - 5x - 2)^2 - 5(x^2 - 5x - 2) + 4 = 0$

Substitute u for $x^2 - 5x - 2$.

$\quad u^2 - 5u + 4 = 0$

$(u - 4)(u - 1) = 0$

$u = 4$ or $u = 1$

Substitute $x^2 - 5x - 2$ for u and solve for x.

$x^2 - 5x - 2 = 4$ or $x^2 - 5x - 2 = 1$

$x^2 - 5x - 6 = 0$ or $x^2 - 5x - 3 = 0$

$(x + 1)(x - 6) = 0$ or $x = \dfrac{-(-5) \pm \sqrt{(-5)^2 - 4(1)(-3)}}{2 \cdot 1}$

$x + 1 = 0$ or $x - 6 = 0$ or $x = \dfrac{5 \pm \sqrt{25 + 12}}{2}$

$\quad x = -1$ or $\quad x = 6$ or $x = \dfrac{5 \pm \sqrt{37}}{2}$

The solution set is $\left\{-1, 6, \dfrac{5 \pm \sqrt{37}}{2}\right\}.$

42. $\qquad x^{1/2} + \dfrac{1}{x^{1/2}} = \dfrac{13}{6},$ LCM is $6x^{1/2}$

$\qquad\qquad 6x + 6 = 13x^{1/2}$

$\qquad 6x - 13x^{1/2} + 6 = 0$

$\qquad 6u^2 - 13u + 6 = 0$

$\quad (3u - 2)(2u - 3) = 0$

$\qquad u = \dfrac{2}{3}$ or $u = \dfrac{3}{2}$

$\quad x^{1/2} = \dfrac{2}{3}$ or $x^{1/2} = \dfrac{3}{2}$

$\qquad x = \dfrac{4}{9}$ or $x = \dfrac{9}{4}$

Both values check. The solution set is $\left\{\dfrac{4}{9}, \dfrac{9}{4}\right\}.$

43. $\qquad \left(y + \dfrac{2}{y}\right)^2 + 3y + \dfrac{6}{y} = 4$

$\left(y + \dfrac{2}{y}\right)^2 + 3\left(y + \dfrac{2}{y}\right) - 4 = 0$

Substitute u for $y + \dfrac{2}{y}$.

$\quad u^2 + 3u - 4 = 0$

$(u + 4)(u - 1) = 0$

$u = -4$ or $u = 1$

Substitute $y + \dfrac{2}{y}$ for u and solve for y.

$\quad y + \dfrac{2}{y} = -4$ or $\qquad y + \dfrac{2}{y} = 1$

$\quad y^2 + 2 = -4y$ or $\quad y^2 + 2 = y$

$y^2 + 4y + 2 = 0$ or $y^2 - y + 2 = 0$

$y = \dfrac{-4 \pm \sqrt{4^2 - 4 \cdot 1 \cdot 2}}{2 \cdot 1}$ or $y = \dfrac{-(-1) \pm \sqrt{(-1)^2 - 4 \cdot 1 \cdot 2}}{2 \cdot 1}$

$y = \dfrac{-4 \pm \sqrt{8}}{2}$ or $y = \dfrac{1 \pm \sqrt{-7}}{2}$

$y = \dfrac{-4 \pm 2\sqrt{2}}{2}$ or $y = \dfrac{1 \pm i\sqrt{7}}{2}$

$y = -2 \pm \sqrt{2}$ or $y = \dfrac{1 \pm i\sqrt{7}}{2}$

The solution set is $\left\{-2 \pm \sqrt{2}, \dfrac{1 \pm i\sqrt{7}}{2}\right\}.$

44. $x^2 + 3x + 1 - \sqrt{x^2 + 3x + 1} = 8$

$x^2 + 3x + 1 - \sqrt{x^2 + 3x + 1} - 8 = 0$

$u^2 - u - 8 = 0$

$u = \dfrac{1 + \sqrt{33}}{2}$ or $\quad u = \dfrac{1 - \sqrt{33}}{2}$

$\sqrt{x^2 + 3x + 1} = \dfrac{1 + \sqrt{33}}{2}$ or $\sqrt{x^2+3x+1} = \dfrac{1 - \sqrt{33}}{2}$

$x^2 + 3x + 1 = \dfrac{34 + 2\sqrt{33}}{4}$ or $x^2+3x+1 = \dfrac{34 - 2\sqrt{33}}{4}$

$x^2 + 3x + \dfrac{-15 - \sqrt{33}}{2} = 0 \quad$ or $\quad x^2 + 3x + \dfrac{-15 + \sqrt{33}}{2} = 0$

$x = \dfrac{-3 \pm \sqrt{39 + 2\sqrt{33}}}{2}$ or $x = \dfrac{-3 \pm \sqrt{39 - 2\sqrt{33}}}{2}$

Only $\dfrac{-3 \pm \sqrt{39 + 2\sqrt{33}}}{2}$ checks. The solution set is

$\left\{ \dfrac{-3 \pm \sqrt{39 + 2\sqrt{33}}}{2} \right\}$.

45. $\dfrac{2x + 1}{x} = 3 + 7\sqrt{\dfrac{2x + 1}{x}}$

$\dfrac{2x + 1}{x} - 7\sqrt{\dfrac{2x + 1}{x}} - 3 = 0$

Substitute u for $\sqrt{\dfrac{2x + 1}{x}}$.

$u^2 - 7u - 3 = 0$

$u = \dfrac{-(-7) \pm \sqrt{(-7)^2 - 4(1)(-3)}}{2 \cdot 1}$

$u = \dfrac{7 \pm \sqrt{61}}{2}$

Substitute $\sqrt{\dfrac{2x + 1}{x}}$ for u and solve for x.

$\sqrt{\dfrac{2x + 1}{x}} = \dfrac{7 + \sqrt{61}}{2} \quad$ or $\sqrt{\dfrac{2x + 1}{x}} = \dfrac{7 - \sqrt{61}}{2}$

$\left[\sqrt{\dfrac{2x + 1}{x}} \right]^2 = \left[\dfrac{7 + \sqrt{61}}{2} \right]^2 \qquad$ No solution since $\dfrac{7 - \sqrt{61}}{2} < 0$

$\dfrac{2x + 1}{x} = \dfrac{49 + 14\sqrt{61} + 61}{4}$

$8x + 4 = 110x + 14x\sqrt{61}$

$4 = 102x + 14x\sqrt{61}$

$4 = (102 + 14\sqrt{61})x$

$\dfrac{4}{102 + 14\sqrt{61}} = x$

Rationalizing the denominator, we get

$x = \dfrac{-51 + 7\sqrt{61}}{194}$. The solution set is

$\left\{ \dfrac{-51 + 7\sqrt{61}}{194} \right\}$.

46. $\$2000\left[1 + \dfrac{i}{2}\right]^{2 \cdot 1} + \$956.80 = \$3000\left[1 + \dfrac{i}{2}\right]^{2 \cdot \frac{1}{2}}$.

Let $x = \left[1 + \dfrac{i}{2}\right]$. Then $2000x^2 - 3000x + 956.80 = 0$

gives $x = 1.04$ and then $i = 8\%$.

Exercise Set 2.9

1. $y = kx$

$0.6 = k(0.4) \qquad$ (Substituting)

$\dfrac{0.6}{0.4} = k$

$\dfrac{3}{2} = k$

The equation of variation is $y = \dfrac{3}{2} x$.

2. $y = kx$

$125 = k \cdot 32$

$\dfrac{125}{32} = k$

$y = \dfrac{125}{32} x$

3. $y = \dfrac{k}{x}$

$125 = \dfrac{k}{32} \qquad$ (Substituting)

$4000 = k$

The equation of variation is $y = \dfrac{4000}{x}$.

4. $y = \dfrac{k}{x}$

$0.4 = \dfrac{k}{0.8}$

$0.32 = k$

$y = \dfrac{0.32}{x}$

5. $y = kx$

$8.6 = k(1.6) \qquad$ (Substituting)

$\dfrac{8.6}{1.6} = k$

$5.375 = k$

The equation of variation is $y = 5.375x$.

6. $y = \dfrac{k}{x}$

$5.4 = \dfrac{k}{3.8}$

$20.52 = k$

$y = \dfrac{20.52}{x}$

7. $y = \dfrac{k}{x^2}$

$0.15 = \dfrac{k}{(0.1)^2} \qquad$ (Substituting)

$0.15 = \dfrac{k}{0.01}$

$0.01(0.15) = k$

$0.0015 = k$

The equation of variation is $y = \dfrac{0.0015}{x^2}$.

8. $y = kxz$
    $56 = k \cdot 7 \cdot 10$
    $0.8 = k$
    $y = 0.8xz$

9. $y = k \cdot \dfrac{xz}{w}$

    $\dfrac{3}{2} = k \cdot \dfrac{2 \cdot 3}{4}$ (Substituting)

    $\dfrac{3}{2} = k \cdot \dfrac{6}{4}$

    $\dfrac{4}{6} \cdot \dfrac{3}{2} = k$

    $1 = k$

    The equation of variation is $y = \dfrac{xz}{w}$.

10. $y = kxz^2$
    $105 = k \cdot 14 \cdot 5^2$
    $0.3 = k$
    $y = 0.3xz^2$

11. $y = k \cdot \dfrac{xz}{w^2}$

    $\dfrac{12}{5} = k \cdot \dfrac{16 \cdot 3}{5^2}$ (Substituting)

    $\dfrac{12}{5} = k \cdot \dfrac{48}{25}$

    $\dfrac{25}{48} \cdot \dfrac{12}{5} = k$

    $\dfrac{5}{4} = k$

    The equation of variation is $y = \dfrac{5}{4} \cdot \dfrac{xz}{w^2}$.

12. $y = k \cdot \dfrac{xz}{wp}$

    $\dfrac{3}{28} = k \cdot \dfrac{3 \cdot 10}{7 \cdot 8}$

    $\dfrac{1}{5} = k$

    $y = \dfrac{1}{5} \cdot \dfrac{xz}{wp}$

13. $y = kx$

    We double x.
    $y = k(2x)$
    $y = 2 \cdot kx$

    Thus, y is doubled.

14. $y = \dfrac{k}{x}$

    Triple x.

    $y = \dfrac{k}{3x} = \dfrac{1}{3} \cdot \dfrac{k}{x}$

    y is multiplied by $\dfrac{1}{3}$.

15. $y = \dfrac{k}{x^2}$

    We multiply x by n.

    $y = \dfrac{k}{(nx)^2}$

    $y = \dfrac{k}{n^2x^2}$

    $y = \dfrac{1}{n^2} \cdot \dfrac{k}{x^2}$

    Thus, y is multiplied by $\dfrac{1}{n^2}$.

16. $y = kx^2$
    Multiply x by n.
    $y = k(nx)^2$
    $y = n^2 \cdot kx^2$
    y is multiplied by n^2.

17. $A = kN$
    $42{,}600 = k \cdot 60{,}000$ (Substituting)
    $0.71 = k$

    The equation of variation is $A = 0.71N$.
    $A = 0.71N$
    $A = 0.71(750{,}000)$ (Substituting)
    $A = 532{,}500$

    Thus, 532,500 tons will enter the atmosphere.

18. $V = k \cdot \dfrac{T}{P}$

    $231 = k \cdot \dfrac{420}{20}$

    $11 = k$

    $V = 11 \cdot \dfrac{T}{P}$

    $V = 11 \cdot \dfrac{300}{15}$

    $V = 220 \text{ in}^3$

19. $L = \dfrac{kwh^2}{\ell}$

    The width and height are doubled, and the length is halved.

    $L = \dfrac{k \cdot 2w \cdot (2h)^2}{\dfrac{\ell}{2}}$

    $L = k \cdot 2w \cdot 4h^2 \cdot \dfrac{2}{\ell}$

    $L = 16 \cdot \dfrac{kwh^2}{\ell}$

    Thus, L is multiplied by 16.

20. $\overline{PA} = \dfrac{k}{\overline{AQ}}$

    $64 = \dfrac{k}{16}$

    $1024 = k$

    $\overline{PA} = \dfrac{1024}{\overline{AQ}}$

    $4 = \dfrac{1024}{\overline{AQ}}$

    $\overline{AQ} = 256$

21. $d = k\sqrt{h}$

    $28.97 = k\sqrt{19.5}$ (Substituting)

    $\dfrac{28.97}{\sqrt{19.5}} = k$

    $d = \dfrac{28.97}{\sqrt{19.5}}\sqrt{h}$ (Equation of variation)

    $54.32 = \dfrac{28.97}{\sqrt{19.5}}\sqrt{h}$ (Substituting)

    $\dfrac{54.32\sqrt{19.5}}{28.97} = \sqrt{h}$

    $\left[\dfrac{54.32\sqrt{19.5}}{28.97}\right]^2 = (\sqrt{h})^2$

    $68.6 \approx h$

One must be about 68.6 m above sea level.

22. $R = k \cdot \dfrac{\ell}{d^2}$

    $0.112 = k \cdot \dfrac{15.24}{(0.254)^2}$

    $0.000474 \approx k$

    $R = 0.000474 \cdot \dfrac{\ell}{d^2}$

    $R = 0.000474 \cdot \dfrac{608.7}{(0.478)^2}$

    $R \approx 1.26$ ohms

23. $A = ks^2$

    $168.54 = k(5.3)^2$ (Substituting)

    $168.54 = 28.09k$

    $6 = k$

    $A = 6s^2$ (Equation of variation)

    $A = 6(10.2)^2$ (Substituting)

    $A = 624.24$

The area is 624.24 m².

24. $\ell = k \cdot \dfrac{1}{d^2}$

    $90 = k \cdot \dfrac{1}{5^2}$

    $2250 = k$

    $\ell = 2250 \cdot \dfrac{1}{d^2}$

    $\ell = 2250 \cdot \dfrac{1}{10^2}$

    $\ell = 22.5$ W/m²

25. $A = \dfrac{kR}{I}$

    $2.92 = \dfrac{k \cdot 85}{262}$ (Substituting)

    $2.92 \cdot \dfrac{262}{85} = k$

    $9 \approx k$

    $A = \dfrac{9R}{I}$ (Equation of variation)

    $2.92 = \dfrac{9R}{300}$ (Substituting)

    $\dfrac{2.92(300)}{9} = k$

    $97 \approx k$

He would have given up 97 runs.

26. $V = k \cdot \dfrac{T}{P}$

    $40 = k \cdot \dfrac{60}{24}$

    $16 = k$

    $V = 16 \cdot \dfrac{T}{P}$

    $V = 16 \cdot \dfrac{30}{5}$

    $V = 96$ cm³

27. If p varies directly as q,
then $p = kq$.

Thus, $q = \dfrac{1}{k}p$,
so q varies directly as p.

28. $u = \dfrac{k}{v}$ gives $v = \dfrac{k}{u}$; and $u = \dfrac{k}{v}$ gives $\dfrac{1}{u} = \left(\dfrac{1}{k}\right)v$
or $\dfrac{1}{u} = (k_2)v$, where $k_2 = \dfrac{1}{k}$.

29. $A = kd^2$

    $\pi r^2 = kd^2$

    $\pi\left(\dfrac{d}{2}\right)^2 = kd^2$

    $\dfrac{\pi}{4} \cdot d^2 = kd^2$

    $\dfrac{\pi}{4} = k$

__30.__ Solving for t we have $t = \left[\dfrac{1}{\sqrt{k}}\right] \cdot \sqrt{P}$ so that
t varies directly as $\sqrt{P}$.

__31.__ a)
$$N = \frac{kP_1P_2}{d^2}$$

$$11{,}153 = \frac{k(741{,}952)(364{,}040)}{(174)^2}$$

$$\frac{(11{,}153)(174)^2}{(741{,}952)(364{,}040)} = k$$

$$0.001 \approx k$$

The equation of variation is $N = \dfrac{0.001P_1P_2}{d^2}$.

b) $N = \dfrac{0.001(741{,}952)(1{,}027{,}974)}{(446)^2}$

$N \approx 3834$

The average number of daily phone calls is
about 3834.

c) $4270 = \dfrac{0.001(741{,}952)(7{,}322{,}564)}{d^2}$

$d^2 = \dfrac{0.001(741{,}952)(7{,}322{,}564)}{4270}$

$d \approx 1128$

The distance is about 1128 km.

d) Division by 0 is undefined.

Exercise Set 3.1

<u>1</u>. The origin has coordinates (0,0). The x-coordinate of each ordered pair tells us how far to move to the left or right of the y-axis. The y-coordinate tells us how far to move up or down from the x-axis.

<u>2</u>.

<u>3</u>.

<u>4</u>.

<u>5</u>.

<u>6</u>.

<u>7</u>.

<u>8</u>.

<u>9</u>.

$$\begin{array}{c|c} y = 2x - 3 \\ \hline -1 & 2 \cdot 1 - 3 \\ & 2 - 3 \\ & -1 \end{array}$$

We substitute 1 for x and -1 for y (alphabetical order of variables).

The equation -1 = -1 is true, so (1,-1) is a solution.

$$\begin{array}{c|c} y = 2x - 3 \\ \hline 3 & 2 \cdot 0 - 3 \\ & 0 - 3 \\ & -3 \end{array}$$

The equation 3 = -3 is false, so (0,3) is not a solution.

<u>10</u>.

$$\begin{array}{c|c} y = 3x - 1 \\ \hline 5 & 3 \cdot 2 - 1 \\ & 5 \end{array}$$
$$\begin{array}{c|c} y = 3x - 1 \\ \hline -7 & 3(-2) - 1 \\ & -7 \end{array}$$

(2, 5) is a solution.   (-2, -7) is a solution.

<u>11</u>.

$$\begin{array}{c|c} 3s + t = 4 \\ \hline 3 \cdot 3 + 4 & 4 \\ 9 + 4 & \\ 13 & \end{array}$$

We substitute 3 for s and 4 for t (alphabetical order of variables).

The equation 13 = 4 is false, so (3,4) is not a solution.

$$\frac{3s + t = 4}{3(-3) + 5 \quad | \quad 4}$$
$$-9 + 5$$
$$-4$$

The equation -4 = 4 is false, so (-3,5) is not a solution.

12. $$\frac{2p + q = 5}{2 \cdot 2 + 3 \quad | \quad 5}$$
$$7$$

$$\frac{2p + q = 5}{2(-5) + (-15) \quad | \quad 5}$$
$$-25$$

(2, 3) is not a solution.

(-5, -15) is not a solution.

13. $$\frac{2a + 5b = 3}{2 \cdot 0 + 5 \cdot \frac{3}{5} \quad | \quad 3}$$
$$0 + 3$$
$$3$$

$$\frac{2a + 5b = 3}{2\left(-\frac{1}{2}\right) + 5\left(-\frac{4}{5}\right) \quad | \quad 3}$$
$$-1 - 4$$
$$-5$$

$\left(0, \frac{3}{5}\right)$ is a solution.

$\left(-\frac{1}{2}, -\frac{4}{5}\right)$ is not a solution.

14. $$\frac{3f + 4g = 6}{3 \cdot 0 + 4 \cdot \frac{3}{2} \quad | \quad 6}$$
$$6$$

$$\frac{3f + 4g = 6}{3 \cdot \frac{2}{3} + 4 \cdot 1 \quad | \quad 6}$$
$$6$$

$\left(0, \frac{3}{2}\right)$ is a solution.

$\left(\frac{2}{3}, 1\right)$ is a solution.

15. $$\frac{r^2 - s^2 = 3}{2^2 - (-1)^2 \quad | \quad 3}$$
$$4 - 1$$
$$3$$

$$\frac{r^2 - s^2 = 3}{(-0.75)^2 - (2.75)^2 \quad | \quad 3}$$
$$0.5625 - 7.5625$$
$$-7$$

(2, -1) is a solution.

(-0.75, 2.75) is not a solution.

16. $$\frac{5w + 2z^2 = 70}{5 \cdot 2 + 2(-4)^2 \quad | \quad 70}$$
$$10 + 32$$
$$42$$

$$\frac{5w + 2z^2 = 70}{5 \cdot 4 + 2(-5)^2 \quad | \quad 70}$$
$$20 + 50$$
$$70$$

(2, -4) is not a solution.

(4, -5) is a solution.

17. $y = x$

We select numbers for x and find the corresponding values for y.

x	y	(x,y)
-4	-4	(-4,-4)
-2	-2	(-2,-2)
0	0	(0,0)
1	1	(1,1)
3	3	(3,3)

Plot these points and draw the line.

The graph shows the relation $\{(x,y) | y = x\}$.

18.

19. $y = -2x$

We select numbers for x and find the corresponding values for y.

x	y	(x,y)
-2	4	(-2,4)
0	0	(0,0)
1	-2	(1,-2)
3	-6	(3,-6)

Plot these points and draw the line.

The graph shows the relation $\{(x,y) | y = -2x\}$.

20.

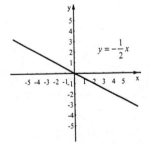

21. y = x + 3

   We select numbers for x and find the corresponding
   values for y.

x	y	(x,y)
0	3	(0,3)
2	5	(2,5)
-3	0	(-3,0)
-5	-2	(-5,-2)

   Plot these solutions and draw the line.

   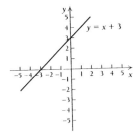

   The graph shows the relation {(x,y)|y = x + 3}.

22.

   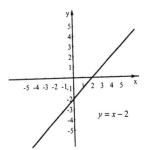

23. y = 3x - 2

   We select numbers for x and find the corresponding
   values for y.

x	y	(x,y)
2	4	(2,4)
0	-2	(0,-2)
-1	-5	(-1,-5)

   Plot these solutions and draw the line.

   The graph shows the relation {(x,y)|y = 3x - 2}.

24.

   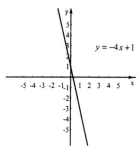

25. y = x²

   We select numbers for x and find the corresponding
   values for y.

x	y	(x,y)
-2	4	(-2,4)
-1	1	(-1,1)
0	0	(0,0)
1	1	(1,1)
2	4	(2,4)

   Plot these ordered pairs and connect the points
   with a smooth curve.

   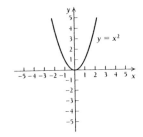

   The graph shows the relation {(x,y)|y = x²}.

26.

27. y = x² + 2

   We select numbers for x and find the corresponding
   values for y.

x	y
-2	6
-1	3
0	2
1	3
2	6

   We plot these ordered pairs and connect the points
   with a smooth curve.

The graph shows the relation $\{(x,y)|y = x^2 + 2\}$.

28.

29. $x = y^2 + 2$

Here we select numbers for y and find the corresponding values for x.

x	y
6	-2
3	-1
2	0
3	1
6	2

We plot these points and connect them with a smooth curve.

The graph shows the relation $\{(x,y)|x = y^2 + 2\}$.

30.

31. $y = |x + 1|$

We find numbers that satisfy the equation.

x	y
-5	4
-3	2
-1	0
2	3
4	5

We plot these points and connect them.

The graph shows the relation $\{(x,y)|y = |x + 1|\}$.

32.

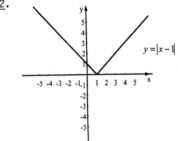

33. $x = |y + 1|$

Here we choose numbers for y and find the corresponding values for x.

x	y
4	-5
1	-2
0	-1
1	0
4	3
5	4

We plot these points and connect them.

The graph shows the relation $\{(x,y)|x = |y + 1|\}$.

34.

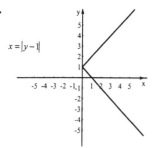

$x = |y - 1|$

35. xy = 10

We find numbers that satisfy the equation. We then plot these points and connect them. Note that neither x nor y can be 0.

x	y
-6	$-\frac{5}{3}$
-5	-2
-3	$-\frac{10}{3}$
-2	-5
-1	-10

x	y
1	10
2	5
3	$\frac{10}{3}$
5	2
6	$\frac{5}{3}$

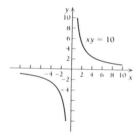

$xy = 10$

The graph shows the relation {(x, y)⏐xy = 10}.

36.

$xy = -18$

37. $y = \frac{1}{x}$

We find numbers that satisfy the equation. We then plot these points and connect them. Note that neither x nor y can be 0.

x	y
-5	$-\frac{1}{5}$
-3	$-\frac{1}{3}$
-2	$-\frac{1}{2}$
-1	-1
$-\frac{1}{2}$	-2
$-\frac{1}{4}$	-4

x	y
$\frac{1}{4}$	4
$\frac{1}{2}$	2
1	1
2	$\frac{1}{2}$
3	$\frac{1}{3}$
5	$\frac{1}{5}$

$y = \frac{1}{x}$

The graph shows the relation $\left\{(x, y)\middle| y = \frac{1}{x}\right\}$.

38.

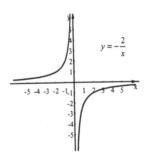

$y = -\frac{2}{x}$

39. $y = \frac{1}{x^2}$

We find numbers that satisfy the equation. We plot these points and connect them. Note that neither x nor y can be 0.

x	y
-3	$\frac{1}{9}$
-2	$\frac{1}{4}$
-1	1
$-\frac{1}{2}$	4
$-\frac{1}{4}$	16

x	y
3	$\frac{1}{9}$
2	$\frac{1}{4}$
1	1
$\frac{1}{2}$	4
$\frac{1}{4}$	16

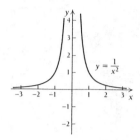

The graph shows the relation $\left\{(x, y)\,\middle|\,y = \dfrac{1}{x^2}\right\}$.

40.

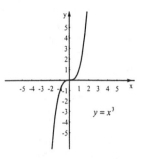

41. $y = \sqrt{x}$

The meaningful replacements for x are x ⩾ 0. We choose meaningful replacements for x and find corresponding values of y.

x	y
0	0
2	1.414
4	2
6	2.449
9	3

We plot these points and connect them.

The graph shows the relation $\{(x, y)\,|\,y = \sqrt{x}\}$.

42.

43. $y = 8 - x^2$

We choose numbers for x and find the corresponding values of y.

x	y
-3	-1
-2	4
-1	7
0	8
1	7
2	4
3	-1

We plot these ordered pairs and connect the points with a smooth curve.

The graph shows the relation $\{(x, y)\,|\,y = 8 - x^2\}$.

44.

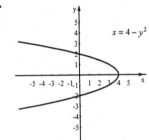

45. $y = x^2 + 1$

x	y
0	1
1	2
-1	2
2	5
-2	5

$y = (-x)^2 + 1$

x	y
0	1
1	2
-1	2
2	5
-2	5

The graphs are the same. The equations are equivalent.

46. $y = x^2 - 2$ $y = 2 - x^2$

 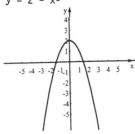

The graphs are not the same. The equations are not equivalent.

47. To determine the domain, think of drawing vertical lines to the x-axis from the left and right extremities of the relation. (In this case the extreme points lie on the x-axis.) The domain consists of the numbers where the lines cross the x-axis and all numbers in between.

To determine the range, think of drawing horizontal lines to the y-axis from the upper and lower extremities of the relation. (In this case the extreme points lie on the y-axis.) The range consists of the numbers where the lines cross the y-axis and all numbers in between.

Range = {y | -2 ⩽ y ⩽ 4}

Domain = {x | -2 ⩽ x ⩽ 5}

48.

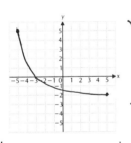

Range = {y | -2 ⩽ y ⩽ 5}

Domain = {x | -5 ⩽ x ⩽ 5}

49. a)

b) Domain: {x | 2 ⩽ x ⩽ 6}

c) Range: {y | 1 ⩽ y ⩽ 5}

50. a)

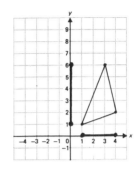

b) Domain: {x | 1 ⩽ x ⩽ 4}

c) Range: {y | 1 ⩽ y ⩽ 6}

51. $y = -x^2$

Domain: The set of real numbers

Range: {y | y ⩽ 0}

52. Domain: The set of real numbers

Range: The set of real numbers

53. $x = |y + 1|$

Domain: {x | x ⩾ 0}

Range: The set of real numbers

54. Domain: {x | x ≠ 0}

Range: {y | y ≠ 0}

55. $y = \sqrt{x}$

Domain: {x | x ⩾ 0}

Range: {y | y ⩾ 0}

56. Domain: The set of real numbers

Range: The set of real numbers

57. $y = 8 - x^2$

Domain: The set of real numbers

Range: {y | y ⩽ 8}

58. Domain: {x | x ⩽ 4}

Range: The set of real numbers

59.

x	y
-1	0
$-\frac{1}{2}$	$\pm\frac{1}{2}$
0	± 1
$\frac{1}{2}$	$\pm\frac{1}{2}$
1	0

$|x| + |y| = 1$

<u>60.</u> The graph of {(x, y)| |x| ⩽ 1 and |y| ⩽ 2}
consists of the interior <u>and</u> boundary of the
rectangle shown:

$$\{(x,y)\,\big|\,|x|\le 1 \text{ and } |y|\le 2\}$$

<u>61.</u> $y = |x| + x$

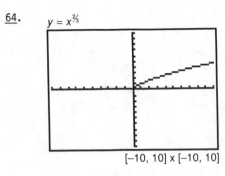

<u>64.</u> $y = x^{2/3}$

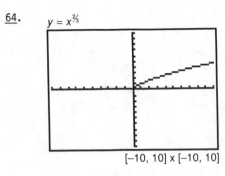

$[-10, 10]$ x $[-10, 10]$

<u>65.</u> $y = x^2|x|$

$[-10, 10]$ x $[-5, 15]$

<u>61.</u> $y = |x| + x$

$[-10, 10]$ x $[-10, 10]$

<u>62.</u> $y = x|x|$

$[-10, 10]$ x $[-10, 10]$

<u>66.</u> $y = |x^3|$

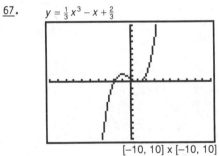

$[-10, 10]$ x $[-5, 15]$

<u>63.</u> $y = |x^2 - 4|$

$[-10, 10]$ x $[-5, 15]$

<u>67.</u> $y = \frac{1}{3}x^3 - x + \frac{2}{3}$

$[-10, 10]$ x $[-10, 10]$

<u>68.</u> $y = -\frac{1}{3}x^3 + \frac{1}{2}x^2 + 2x - 1$

$[-10, 10]$ x $[-10, 10]$

96

69. $y = 1 + \sqrt{2 - x}$

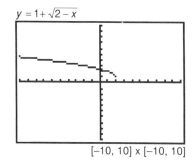

[−10, 10] x [−10, 10]

70. $y = 1 + \dfrac{2}{x + 1}$

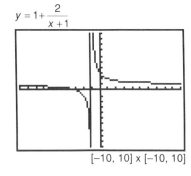

[−10, 10] x [−10, 10]

Exercise Set 3.2

1. We substitute into the distance formula.

$d = \sqrt{(x_2 - x_1)^2 + (y_2 - y_1)^2}$

$d = \sqrt{[1 - (-3)]^2 + [1 - (-2)]^2}$

$d = \sqrt{4^2 + 3^2} = \sqrt{16 + 9}$

$d = \sqrt{25} = 5$

2. $d = \sqrt{(-1 - 5)^2 + (6 - 9)^2} = \sqrt{36 + 9} = \sqrt{45} =$

$3\sqrt{5} \approx 6.708$

3. We substitute into the distance formula.

$d = \sqrt{(x_2 - x_1)^2 + (y_2 - y_1)^2}$

$d = \sqrt{(3 - 0)^2 + [-4 - (-7)]^2}$

$d = \sqrt{3^2 + 3^2} = \sqrt{9 + 9}$

$d = \sqrt{18} = \sqrt{9 \cdot 2}$

$d = 3\sqrt{2} \approx 4.243$

4. $d = \sqrt{(-2 - 2)^2 + (-2 - 2)^2} = \sqrt{16 + 16} =$

$\sqrt{32} = 4\sqrt{2} \approx 5.657$

5. $d = \sqrt{(x_2 - x_1)^2 + (y_2 - y_1)^2}$ (Distance formula)

$d = \sqrt{(2a - a)^2 + [5 - (-3)]^2}$ (Substituting)

$d = \sqrt{a^2 + 8^2}$

$d = \sqrt{a^2 + 64}$

6. $d = \sqrt{(-3 - 5)^2 + (k - 2k)^2} = \sqrt{64 + k^2}$

7. $d = \sqrt{(x_2 - x_1)^2 + (y_2 - y_1)^2}$ (Distance formula)

$d = \sqrt{(a - 0)^2 + (b - 0)^2}$ (Substituting)

$d = \sqrt{a^2 + b^2}$

8. $d = \sqrt{(0 - \sqrt{2})^2 + (0 - \sqrt{3})^2} = \sqrt{2 + 3} = \sqrt{5} \approx 2.236$

9. $d = \sqrt{(x_2 - x_1)^2 + (y_2 - y_1)^2}$ (Distance formula)

$d = \sqrt{(-\sqrt{a} - \sqrt{a})^2 + (\sqrt{b} - \sqrt{b})^2}$ (Substituting)

$d = \sqrt{(-2\sqrt{a})^2 + 0^2} = \sqrt{4a}$

$d = 2\sqrt{a}$

10. $d = \sqrt{[c + f - (c - f)]^2 + [f - c - (c + f)]^2} =$

$\sqrt{(2f)^2 + (-2c)^2} = \sqrt{4f^2 + 4c^2} = 2\sqrt{f^2 + c^2}$

11. $d = \sqrt{(x_2 - x_1)^2 + (y_2 - y_1)^2}$ (Distance formula)

$d = \sqrt{(18.9431 - 7.3482)^2 + [-17.9054 - (-3.0991)]^2}$

(Substituting)

$d = \sqrt{(11.5949)^2 + (-14.8063)^2}$

$d \approx \sqrt{134.4417 + 219.2265}$

$d \approx \sqrt{353.6682} \approx 18.806$

12. $d = \sqrt{[275.34 - (-25.414)]^2 + (-95.144 - 175.31)^2} =$

$\sqrt{163,598.3346} \approx 404.473$

13. First we find the squares of the distances between the points:

Between (9, 6) and (-1, 2):

$d_1^2 = (-1 - 9)^2 + (2 - 6)^2 = 100 + 16 = 116$

Between (-1, 2) and (1, -3):

$d_2^2 = [1 - (-1)]^2 + (-3 - 2)^2 = 4 + 25 = 29$

Between (9, 6) and (1, -3):

$d_3^2 = (1 - 9)^2 + (-3 - 6)^2 = 64 + 81 = 145$

Since 116 + 29 = 145, it follows from the Pythagorean theorem that the points are the vertices of a right triangle.

14. $d_1^2 = [1 - (-5)]^2 + [6 - (-8)]^2 = 36 + 196 = 232$

$d_2^2 = (5 - 1)^2 + (-4 - 6)^2 = 16 + 100 = 116$

$d_3^2 = [5 - (-5)]^2 + [-4 - (-8)]^2 = 100 + 16 = 116$

232 = 116 + 116, so the points are the vertices of a right triangle.

15. $\left[\dfrac{x_1 + x_2}{2}, \dfrac{y_1 + y_2}{2}\right]$ (Midpoint formula)

$\left[\dfrac{-4 + 3}{2}, \dfrac{7 + (-9)}{2}\right]$ (Substituting)

$\left[\dfrac{-1}{2}, \dfrac{-2}{2}\right]$

The midpoint is $\left[-\dfrac{1}{2}, -1\right]$.

16. $\left[\dfrac{4 + 6}{2}, \dfrac{5 - 7}{2}\right]$, or $(5, -1)$

17. $\left[\dfrac{x_1 + x_2}{2}, \dfrac{y_1 + y_2}{2}\right]$ (Midpoint formula)

$\left[\dfrac{a + a}{2}, \dfrac{b + (-b)}{2}\right]$ (Substituting)

$\left[\dfrac{2a}{2}, \dfrac{0}{2}\right]$

The midpoint is $(a, 0)$.

18. $\left[\dfrac{-c + c}{2}, \dfrac{d + d}{2}\right]$, or $(0, d)$

19. $\left[\dfrac{x_1 + x_2}{2}, \dfrac{y_1 + y_2}{2}\right]$ (Midpoint formula)

$\left[\dfrac{-3.895 + 2.998}{2}, \dfrac{8.1212 + (-8.6677)}{2}\right]$

                   (Substituting)

$\left[\dfrac{-0.897}{2}, \dfrac{-0.5465}{2}\right]$

The midpoint is $(-0.4485, -0.27325)$.

20. $\left[\dfrac{4.1112 + 5.1928}{2}, \dfrac{6.9898 + 6.9143}{2}\right]$, or

$(4.652, 6.95205)$

21. We write standard form.
$(x - 0)^2 + (y - 0)^2 = 6^2$
The center is $(0, 0)$, and the radius is 6.

22. $(x - 0)^2 + (y - 0)^2 = 5^2$
Center: $(0, 0)$; radius: 5

23. We write standard form.

$(x - 3)^2 + (y - 0)^2 = (\sqrt{3})^2$

The center is $(3, 0)$, and the radius is $\sqrt{3}$.

24. $(x - 4)^2 + (y - 1)^2 = (\sqrt{2})^2$

Center: $(4, 1)$; radius: $\sqrt{2}$

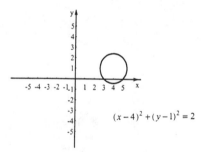

25. We write standard form.
$[x - (-1)^2] + [y - (-3)]^2 = 2^2$
The center is $(-1, -3)$, and the radius is 2.

26. $(x - 2)^2 + [y - (-3)]^2 = 1^2$
Center: (2, -3); radius: 1

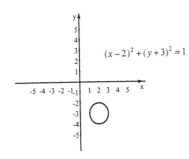

$(x-2)^2 + (y+3)^2 = 1$

27. $(x - 8)^2 + (y + 3)^2 = 40$
$(x - 8)^2 + [y - (-3)]^2 = (\sqrt{40})^2 = (2\sqrt{10})^2$

Center: (8, -3),   Radius: $2\sqrt{10}$

28. $[x - (-5)]^2 + (y - 1)^2 = (\sqrt{75})^2 = (5\sqrt{3})^2$
Center: (-5, 1),   Radius: $5\sqrt{3}$

29. $(x - 3)^2 + y^2 = \frac{1}{25}$

$(x - 3)^2 + (y - 0)^2 = \left[\frac{1}{5}\right]^2$

Center: (3, 0),   Radius: $\frac{1}{5}$

30. $(x - 0)^2 + (y - 1)^2 = \left[\frac{1}{2}\right]^2$

Center: (0, 1),   Radius: $\frac{1}{2}$

31. $x^2 + y^2 + 8x - 6y - 15 = 0$
We complete the square twice to get standard form:
$(x^2 + 8x \quad) + (y^2 - 6y \quad) = 15$
We take half the coefficient of the x-term and square it, obtaining 16. We add 16 - 16 in the first parentheses. Similarly, we add 9 - 9 in the second parentheses.
$(x^2 + 8x + 16 - 16) + (y^2 - 6y + 9 - 9) = 15$
Next we rearrange and factor:
$(x^2 + 8x + 16) + (y^2 - 6y + 9) - 16 - 9 = 15$
$(x + 4)^2 + (y - 3)^2 = 40$
$[x - (-4)]^2 + (y - 3)^2 = (2\sqrt{10})^2$

Center: (-4, 3),   Radius: $2\sqrt{10}$

32. $\left[x^2 + 25x + \frac{625}{4}\right] + (y^2 + 10y + 25) =$
$-12 + \frac{625}{4} + 25$

$\left[x + \frac{25}{2}\right]^2 + (y + 5)^2 = \frac{677}{4}$

Center: $\left[-\frac{25}{2}, -5\right]$,   Radius: $\frac{\sqrt{677}}{2}$

33. $x^2 + y^2 + 6x = 0$
$(x^2 + 6x \qquad) + y^2 = 0$
$(x^2 + 6x + 9 - 9) + y^2 = 0$ Completing the square once
$(x^2 + 6x + 9) + y^2 - 9 = 0$
$(x + 3)^2 + y^2 = 9$
$[x - (-3)]^2 + (y - 0)^2 = 3^2$

Center: (-3, 0),   Radius: 3

34. $(x^2 - 4x + 4) + y^2 = 0 + 4$
$(x - 2)^2 + y^2 = 4$
Center: (2, 0),   Radius: 2

35. $x^2 + y^2 + 8x = 84$
$(x^2 + 8x \qquad) + y^2 = 84$
$(x^2 + 8x + 16 - 16) + y^2 = 84$ Completing the square once
$(x^2 + 8x + 16) + y^2 - 16 = 84$
$(x + 4)^2 + y^2 = 100$
$[x - (-4)]^2 + (y - 0)^2 = 10^2$

Center: (-4, 0),   Radius: 10

36. $x^2 + (y^2 - 10y + 25) = 75 + 25$
$x^2 + (y - 5)^2 = 100$
Center: (0, 5),   Radius: 10

37. $x^2 + y^2 + 21x + 33y + 17 = 0$
$(x^2 + 21x \qquad) + (y^2 + 33y \qquad) = -17$
$\left[x^2 + 21x + \frac{441}{4} - \frac{441}{4}\right] + \left[y^2 + 33y + \frac{1089}{4} - \frac{1089}{4}\right] = -17$
                Completing the square twice
$\left[x^2 + 21x + \frac{441}{4}\right] + \left[y^2 + 33y + \frac{1089}{4}\right] - \frac{441}{4} - \frac{1089}{4} = -17$
$\left[x + \frac{21}{2}\right]^2 + \left[y + \frac{33}{2}\right]^2 = \frac{1462}{4}$
$\left[x - \left[-\frac{21}{2}\right]\right]^2 + \left[y - \left[-\frac{33}{2}\right]\right]^2 =$
$\left[\frac{\sqrt{1462}}{2}\right]^2$

Center: $\left[-\frac{21}{2}, -\frac{33}{2}\right]$,   Radius: $\frac{\sqrt{1462}}{2}$

38. $\left[x^2 - 7x + \frac{49}{4}\right] + \left[y^2 + 3y + \frac{9}{4}\right] = 10 + \frac{49}{4} + \frac{9}{4}$
$\left[x - \frac{7}{2}\right]^2 + \left[y + \frac{3}{2}\right]^2 = \frac{98}{4}$

Center: $\left[\frac{7}{2}, -\frac{3}{2}\right]$,   Radius: $\frac{7\sqrt{2}}{2}$

39. $x^2 + y^2 + 8.246x - 6.348y - 74.35 = 0$

   $(x^2 + 8.246x \qquad) +$

   $(y^2 - 6.348y \qquad) = 74.35$

   $(x^2 + 8.246x + 16.999 - 16.999) +$

   $(y^2 - 6.348y + 10.074 - 10.074) = 74.35$

   $(x^2 + 8.246x + 16.999) + (y^2 - 6.348y + 10.074) -$

   $16.999 - 10.074 = 74.35$

   $(x + 4.123)^2 + (y - 3.174)^2 = 101.423$

   $[x - (-4.123)]^2 + (y - 3.174)^2 = (10.071)^2$

   Center: $(-4.123, 3.174)$,   Radius: 10.071

40. $(x^2 + 25.074x + 157.176369) +$

   $(y^2 + 10.004y + 25.020004) =$

   $-12.054 + 157.176369 + 25.020004$

   $(x + 12.537)^2 + (y + 5.002)^2 = 170.142373$

   Center: $(-12.537, -5.002)$, Radius: 13.044

41. $9x^2 + 9y^2 = 1$

   $x^2 + y^2 = \frac{1}{9}$ Multiplying by $\frac{1}{9}$

   $(x - 0)^2 + (y - 0)^2 = \left[\frac{1}{3}\right]^2$

   Center: $(0, 0)$,   Radius: $\frac{1}{3}$

42. $x^2 + y^2 = \frac{1}{16}$ $\left[\text{Multiplying by } \frac{1}{16}\right]$

   Center: $(0, 0)$,   Radius: $\frac{1}{4}$

43.   Since the center is $(0, 0)$, we have

   $(x - 0)^2 + (y - 0)^2 = r^2$ or $x^2 + y^2 = r^2$

   The circle passes through $(-3, 4)$. We find
   r^2 by substituting -3 for x and 4 for y.

   $(-3)^2 + 4^2 = r^2$

   $9 + 16 = r^2$

   $25 = r^2$

   Then $x^2 + y^2 = 25$ is an equation of the circle.

44. $(x - 3)^2 + (y + 2)^2 = r^2$;

   $(11 - 3)^2 + (-2 + 2)^2 = r^2$, and $r^2 = 64$.

   $(x - 3)^2 + (y + 2)^2 = 64$.

45.   Since the center is $(-4, 1)$, we have

   $[x - (-4)]^2 + (y - 1)^2 = r^2$, or

   $(x + 4)^2 + (y - 1)^2 = r^2$.

   The circle passes through $(-2, 5)$. We find r^2
   by substituting -2 for x and 5 for y.

   $(-2 + 4)^2 + (5 - 1)^2 = r^2$

   $4 + 16 = r^2$

   $20 = r^2$

   Then $(x + 4)^2 + (y - 1)^2 = 20$ is an equation of
   the circle.

46. $(x + 3)^2 + (y + 3)^2 = r^2$;

   $(1.8 + 3)^2 + (2.6 + 3)^2 = r^2$, and $r^2 = 54.4$

   $(x + 3)^2 + (y + 3)^2 = 54.4$

47.

Between $(x, 0)$ and $(1, 3)$:

$d = \sqrt{(1 - x)^2 + (3 - 0)^2}$

$= \sqrt{1 - 2x + x^2 + 9} = \sqrt{x^2 - 2x + 10}$

Between $(x, 0)$ and $(8, 4)$:

$d = \sqrt{(8 - x)^2 + (4 - 0)^2}$

$= \sqrt{64 - 16x + x^2 + 16} = \sqrt{x^2 - 16x + 80}$

Thus,

$\sqrt{x^2 - 2x + 10} = \sqrt{x^2 - 16x + 80}$

$x^2 - 2x + 10 = x^2 - 16x + 80$

$14x = 70$

$x = 5$

The point on the x-axis equidistant from the
points $(1, 3)$ and $(8, 4)$ is $(5, 0)$.

48.   Let $(0, y)$ be the required point. We set the
   distance between $(-2, 0)$ and $(0, y)$ equal to
   the distance between $(4, 6)$ and $(0, y)$ and
   solve for y.

   $\sqrt{[0 - (-2)]^2 + (y - 0)^2} = \sqrt{(0 - 4)^2 + (y - 6)^2}$,
   or $y = 4$. Hence the point is $(0, 4)$.

49.   If the circle with center $(2, 4)$ is tangent to the
   x-axis, the radius is 4. We substitute 2 for h,
   4 for k, and 4 for r.

   $(x - h)^2 + (y - k)^2 = r^2$

   $(x - 2)^2 + (y - 4)^2 = 4^2 = 16$

50. $r = 3$, so $(x + 3)^2 + (y + 2)^2 = 9$

51.

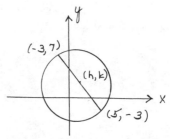

The center of the circle is the midpoint of the
line segment with endpoints $(5, -3)$ and $(-3, 7)$:

$\left[\frac{5 + (-3)}{2}, \frac{-3 + 7}{2}\right]$, or $(1, 2)$

r^2 is the square of the distance from (1, 2) to (5, -3) (or to (-3, 7)):

$r^2 = (5 - 1)^2 + (-3 - 2)^2 = 16 + 25 = 41$

The equation of the circle is
$$(x - 1)^2 + (y - 2)^2 = 41.$$

52. Center: $\left(\dfrac{9 - 4}{2}, \dfrac{8 - 3}{2}\right)$, or $\left(\dfrac{5}{2}, \dfrac{5}{2}\right)$

$r^2 = \left(\dfrac{5}{2} - 9\right)^2 + \left(\dfrac{5}{2} - 8\right)^2 = \dfrac{290}{4} = \dfrac{145}{2}$

$\left(x - \dfrac{5}{2}\right)^2 + \left(y - \dfrac{5}{2}\right)^2 = \dfrac{145}{2}$

53. $C = 2\pi r$
$10\pi = 2\pi r$
$5 = r$

Then $[x - (-8)]^2 + (y - 5)^2 = 5^2$, or
$(x + 8)^2 + (y - 5)^2 = 25.$

54. $\pi r^2 = 36\pi$
$r^2 = 36$

$(x + 3)^2 + (y + 8)^2 = 36$

55.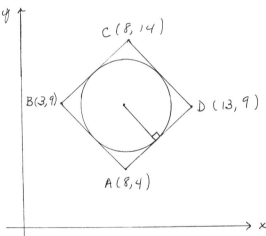

The center is the midpoint of AC or BD. We use AC:

$\left(\dfrac{8 + 8}{2}, \dfrac{4 + 14}{2}\right)$, or (8, 9)

The radius is the distance from the center to the midpoint of a side of the square. We will use side AD. The midpoint of AD is

$\left(\dfrac{8 + 13}{2}, \dfrac{4 + 9}{2}\right)$, or $\left(\dfrac{21}{2}, \dfrac{13}{2}\right)$. Then

$r = \sqrt{\left(8 - \dfrac{21}{2}\right)^2 + \left(9 - \dfrac{13}{2}\right)^2} = \sqrt{\dfrac{25}{2}} = \dfrac{5\sqrt{2}}{2}.$

56. Label the drawing with additional information and lettering.

Find b using the Pythagorean Theorem.
$b^2 + 10^2 = 20^2$
$b^2 + 100 = 400$
$b^2 = 300$
$b = 10\sqrt{3}$
$b \approx 17.32$

Find a_1:
$a_1 = 20 - b \approx 20 - 17.32 \approx 2.68$ ft

Find a_2:
$a_2 = 2b + a_1 \approx 2(17.32) + 2.68 \approx 37.32$ ft

57. $\dfrac{x^2 + y^2 = 1}{\begin{array}{c|c} (-1)^2 + 0^2 & 1 \\ 1 & \end{array}}$

(-1, 0) lies on the unit circle.

58. $\dfrac{x^2 + y^2 = 1}{\begin{array}{c|c} \left(\dfrac{\sqrt{3}}{2}\right)^2 + \left(-\dfrac{1}{2}\right)^2 & 1 \\ \dfrac{3}{4} + \dfrac{1}{4} & \\ 1 & \end{array}}$

$\left(\dfrac{\sqrt{3}}{2}, -\dfrac{1}{2}\right)$ lies on the unit circle.

59. $\dfrac{x^2 + y^2 = 1}{\begin{array}{c|c} (0.838670568)^2 + (-0.544639035)^2 & 1 \\ 0.703368321 + 0.296631678 & \\ 1 & \end{array}}$

(0.838670568, -0.544639035) lies on the unit circle.

60. $\dfrac{x^2 + y^2 = 1}{\begin{array}{c|c} \left(\dfrac{\pi}{3}\right)^2 + \left(\dfrac{3}{\pi}\right)^2 & 1 \\ \dfrac{\pi^2}{9} + \dfrac{9}{\pi^2} & \\ \dfrac{\pi^4 + 81}{9\pi^2} & \\ 0.9231 & \end{array}}$

$\left(\dfrac{\pi}{3}, \dfrac{3}{\pi}\right)$ does not lie on the unit circle.

61.
$$\frac{x^2 + y^2 = 1}{\left[\frac{\sqrt{2}}{2}\right]^2 + \left[\frac{\sqrt{2}}{2}\right]^2 \;\Big|\; 1}$$
$$\frac{2}{4} + \frac{2}{4}\;\Big|$$
$$1\;\Big|$$

$\left[\frac{\sqrt{2}}{2}, \frac{\sqrt{2}}{2}\right]$ lies on the unit circle.

62.
$$\frac{x^2 + y^2 = 1}{\left[\frac{1}{4}\right]^2 + \left[-\frac{3}{4}\right]^2 \;\Big|\; 1}$$
$$\frac{1}{16} + \frac{9}{16}\;\Big|$$
$$\frac{5}{8}\;\Big|$$

$\left[\frac{1}{4}, -\frac{3}{4}\right]$ does not lie on the unit circle.

63.
$$\frac{x^2 + y^2 = 1}{0^2 + 2^2 \;\Big|\; 1}$$
$$4\;\Big|$$

(0, 2) does not lie on the unit circle.

64.
$$\frac{x^2 + y^2 = 1}{\left[\frac{1}{2}\right]^2 + \left[-\frac{\sqrt{3}}{2}\right]^2 \;\Big|\; 1}$$
$$\frac{1}{4} + \frac{3}{4}\;\Big|$$
$$1\;\Big|$$

$\left[\frac{1}{2}, -\frac{\sqrt{3}}{2}\right]$ lies on the unit circle.

65. See the answer section in the text.

66. For two points on a vertical line, (x, y_1) and (x, y_2), $d = \sqrt{(x - x)^2 + (y_2 - y_1)^2} = |y_2 - y_1|$. For two points on a horizontal line, (x_1, y) and (x_2, y), $d = \sqrt{(x_2 - x_1)^2 + (y - y)^2} = |x_2 - x_1|$.

67. The result of combining the graphs is a circle with center (0, 0) and radius 2.

68. Graph $y = \sqrt{9 - x^2}$ and $y = -\sqrt{9 - x^2}$ on the same set of axes.

Exercise Set 3.3

1. This is not a function. There are two members of the range, Mets and Giants, that correspond to New York. There are other instances that also show that this is not a function, but only one case is necessary.

2. This is a function. Each member of the domain corresponds to exactly one member of the range.

3. This is a function. Each member of the domain corresponds to exactly one member of the range.

4. This is not a function because 16 corresponds to both 4 and -4. There are other instances that also show that this is not a function, but only one case is necessary.

5. This is a function, because no two ordered pairs have the same first coordinate and different second coordinates.

6. This is not a function, because the ordered pairs (-3, 5) and (-3, -5) have the same first coordinates and different second coordinates.

7. This is not a function, because the ordered pairs (-4,-4) and (-4,4) have the same first coordinate and different second coordinates.

8. This is not a function, because the ordered pairs (4, 2) and (4, -9) have the same first coordinate and different second coordinates.

9. This is a function, because no two ordered pairs have the same first coordinate and different second coordinates.

10. This is not a function, because there are ordered pairs that have the same first coordinate, q, and different second coordinates, r, t, and w.

11. $f(x) = 5x^2 + 4x$

   a) $f(0) = 5 \cdot 0^2 + 4 \cdot 0 = 0 + 0 = 0$

   b) $f(-1) = 5(-1)^2 + 4(-1) = 5 - 4 = 1$

   c) $f(3) = 5 \cdot 3^2 + 4 \cdot 3 = 45 + 12 = 57$

   d) $f(t) = 5t^2 + 4t$

   e) $f(t - 1) = 5(t - 1)^2 + 4(t - 1)$
   $$= 5(t^2 - 2t + 1) + 4(t - 1)$$
   $$= 5t^2 - 10t + 5 + 4t - 4$$
   $$= 5t^2 - 6t + 1$$

   f) $f(a + h) = 5(a + h)^2 + 4(a + h)$
   $$= 5(a^2 + 2ah + h^2) + 4(a + h)$$
   $$= 5a^2 + 10ah + 5h^2 + 4a + 4h$$

   $f(a) = 5a^2 + 4a$
   $$\frac{f(a + h) - f(a)}{h} = \frac{(5a^2+10ah+5h^2+4a+4h)-(5a^2+4a)}{h}$$
   $$= \frac{10ah + 5h^2 + 4h}{h}$$
   $$= \frac{h(10a + 5h + 4)}{h}$$
   $$= 10a + 5h + 4$$

12. $g(x) = 3x^2 - 2x + 1$

   a) $g(0) = 3 \cdot 0^2 - 2 \cdot 0 + 1 = 1$

   b) $g(-1) = 3(-1)^2 - 2(-1) + 1 = 6$

   c) $g(3) = 3 \cdot 3^2 - 2 \cdot 3 + 1 = 22$

   d) $g(t) = 3t^2 - 2t + 1$

   e) $g(a + h) = 3(a + h)^2 - 2(a + h) + 1 =$
     $3a^2 + 6ah + 3h^2 - 2a - 2h + 1$

   f) $\dfrac{g(a + h) - g(a)}{h} =$

     $\dfrac{3a^2 + 6ah + 3h^2 - 2a - 2h + 1 - (3a^2 - 2a + 1)}{h} =$

     $\dfrac{6ah + 3h^2 - 2h}{h} = 6a + 3h - 2$

13. $f(x) = 2|x| + 3x$

   a) $f(1) = 2|1| + 3 \cdot 1 = 2 + 3 = 5$

   b) $f(-2) = 2|-2| + 3(-2) = 4 - 6 = -2$

   c) $f(-4) = 2|-4| + 3(-4) = 8 - 12 = -4$

   d) $f(2y) = 2|2y| + 3(2y) = 4|y| + 6y$

   e) $f(a + h) = 2|a + h| + 3(a + h)$
     $= 2|a + h| + 3a + 3h$

   f) $\dfrac{f(a + h) - f(a)}{h}$

     $= \dfrac{(2|a + h| + 3a + 3h) - (2|a| + 3a)}{h}$

     $= \dfrac{2|a + h| - 2|a| + 3h}{h}$

14. $g(x) = x^3 - 2x$

   a) $g(1) = 1^3 - 2 \cdot 1 = -1$

   b) $g(-2) = (-2)^3 - 2(-2) = -4$

   c) $g(-4) = (-4)^3 - 2(-4) = -56$

   d) $g(3y) = (3y)^3 - 2 \cdot 3y = 27y^3 - 6y$

   e) $g(2 + h) = (2 + h)^3 - 2(2 + h) =$
     $8 + 12h + 6h^2 + h^3 - 4 - 2h =$
     $4 + 10h + 6h^2 + h^3$

   f) $\dfrac{g(2 + h) - g(2)}{h} =$

     $\dfrac{4 + 10h + 6h^2 + h^3 - (2^3 - 2 \cdot 2)}{h} =$

     $\dfrac{10h + 6h^2 + h^3}{h} = 10 + 6h + h^2$

15. $f(x) = \dfrac{x}{2 - x}$

   a) $f(1) = \dfrac{1}{2 - 1} = \dfrac{1}{1} = 1$

   b) $f(2) = \dfrac{1}{2 - 2} = \dfrac{1}{0}$; division by 0 is not
     defined, so $f(2)$ does not exist.

   c) $f(-3) = \dfrac{-3}{2 - (-3)} = \dfrac{-3}{5}$, or $-\dfrac{3}{5}$

   d) $f(-16) = \dfrac{-16}{2 - (-16)} = \dfrac{-16}{18} = -\dfrac{8}{9}$

   e) $f(x + h) = \dfrac{x + h}{2 - (x + h)} = \dfrac{x + h}{2 - x - h}$

   f) $\dfrac{f(x + h) - f(x)}{h} = \dfrac{\dfrac{x + h}{2 - x - h} - \dfrac{x}{2 - x}}{h}$

     $= \dfrac{\dfrac{x+h}{2-x-h} - \dfrac{x}{2-x}}{h} \cdot \dfrac{(2-x-h)(2-x)}{(2-x-h)(2-x)}$

     $= \dfrac{(x+h)(2-x) - x(2-x-h)}{h(2-x-h)(2-x)}$

     $= \dfrac{2x - x^2 + 2h - hx - 2x + x^2 + xh}{h(2-x-h)(2-x)}$

     $= \dfrac{2h}{h(2 - x - h)(2 - x)}$

     $= \dfrac{2}{(2 - x - h)(2 - x)}$

16. $g(x) = \dfrac{x - 4}{x + 3}$

   a) $g(5) = \dfrac{5 - 4}{5 + 3} = \dfrac{1}{8}$

   b) $g(4) = \dfrac{4 - 4}{4 + 7} = 0$

   c) $g(-3) = \dfrac{-3 - 4}{-3 + 3} = \dfrac{-7}{0}$; division by 0 is not
     defined, so $g(-3)$ does not exist.

   d) $g(-16.25) = \dfrac{-16.25 - 4}{-16.25 + 3} = \dfrac{-20.25}{-13.25} = \dfrac{81}{53}$

   e) $g(x + h) = \dfrac{x + h - 4}{x + h + 3}$

   f) $\dfrac{g(x + h) - g(x)}{h} = \dfrac{\dfrac{x + h - 4}{x + h + 3} - \dfrac{x - 4}{x + 3}}{h}$

     $= \dfrac{(x+h-4)(x+3) - (x-4)(x+h+3)}{h(x+h+3)(x+3)}$

     $= \dfrac{7h}{h(x + h + 3)(x + 3)}$

     $= \dfrac{7}{(x + h + 3)(x + 3)}$

17. $f(x) = \dfrac{x^2 - x - 2}{2x^2 - 5x - 3}$

   a) $f(0) = \dfrac{0^2 - 0 - 2}{2 \cdot 0^2 - 5 \cdot 0 - 3} = \dfrac{-2}{-3} = \dfrac{2}{3}$

   b) $f(4) = \dfrac{4^2 - 4 - 2}{2 \cdot 4^2 - 5 \cdot 4 - 3} = \dfrac{10}{9}$

   c) $f(-1) = \dfrac{(-1)^2 - (-1) - 2}{2(-1)^2 - 5(-1) - 3} = \dfrac{0}{4} = 0$

   d) $f(3) = \dfrac{3^2 - 3 - 2}{2 \cdot 3^2 - 5 \cdot 3 - 3} = \dfrac{4}{0}$

   Division by 0 is not defined, so $f(3)$ does
   not exist.

   e) $f(2 - h) = \dfrac{(2 - h)^2 - (2 - h) - 2}{2(2 - h)^2 - 5(2 - h) - 3}$

     $= \dfrac{4 - 4h + h^2 - 2 + h - 2}{2(4 - 4h + h^2) - 10 + 5h - 3}$

     $= \dfrac{-3h + h^2}{8 - 8h + 2h^2 - 10 + 5h - 3}$

     $= \dfrac{-3h + h^2}{-5 - 3h + 2h^2}$, or $\dfrac{h^2 - 3h}{2h^2 - 3h - 5}$

f) $f(a + b) = \dfrac{(a + b)^2 - (a + b) - 2}{2(a + b)^2 - 5(a + b) - 3}$

$= \dfrac{a^2 + 2ab + b^2 - a - b - 2}{2(a^2 + 2ab + b^2) - 5a - 5b - 3}$

$= \dfrac{a^2 + 2ab + b^2 - a - b - 2}{2a^2 + 4ab + 2b^2 - 5a - 5b - 3}$

18. $s(x) = \sqrt{\dfrac{3x - 4}{2x + 5}}$

a) $s(10) = \sqrt{\dfrac{3 \cdot 10 - 4}{2 \cdot 10 + 5}} = \sqrt{\dfrac{26}{25}} = \dfrac{\sqrt{26}}{5}$

b) $s(2) = \sqrt{\dfrac{3 \cdot 2 - 4}{2 \cdot 2 + 5}} = \sqrt{\dfrac{2}{9}} = \dfrac{\sqrt{2}}{3}$

c) $s(1) = \sqrt{\dfrac{3 \cdot 1 - 4}{2 \cdot 1 + 5}} = \sqrt{\dfrac{-1}{7}}$; $s(1)$ does not exist as a real number.

d) $s(-1) = \sqrt{\dfrac{3(-1) - 4}{2(-1) + 5}} = \sqrt{\dfrac{-7}{3}}$; $s(-1)$ does not exist as a real number.

e) $s(3 + h) = \sqrt{\dfrac{3(3 + h) - 4}{2(3 + h) + 5}} = \sqrt{\dfrac{5 + 3h}{11 + 2h}}$

f) $s(a - b) = \sqrt{\dfrac{3(a - b) - 4}{2(a - b) + 5}} = \sqrt{\dfrac{3a - 3b - 4}{2a - 2b + 5}}$

19. $f(x) = x^2$

$f(a + h) = (a + h)^2 = a^2 + 2ah + h^2$

$f(a) = a^2$

$\dfrac{f(a + h) - f(a)}{h} = \dfrac{(a^2 + 2ah + h^2) - (a^2)}{h}$

$= \dfrac{2ah + h^2}{h} = \dfrac{h(2a + h)}{h}$

$= 2a + h$

20. $f(x) = x^3$

$f(a + h) = (a + h)^3 = a^3 + 3a^2h + 3ah^2 + h^3$

$f(a) = a^3$

$\dfrac{f(a + h) - f(a)}{h} = \dfrac{a^3 + 3a^2h + 3ah^2 + h^3 - a^3}{h}$

$= 3a^2 + 3ah + h^2$

21. $f(x) = x + \sqrt{x^2 - 1}$

$f(0) = 0 + \sqrt{0^2 - 1} = 0 + \sqrt{-1}$

Since $\sqrt{-1}$ is not a real number, $f(0)$ does not exist as a real number.

$f(2) = 2 + \sqrt{2^2 - 1} = 2 + \sqrt{4 - 1} = 2 + \sqrt{3}$

$f(10) = 10 + \sqrt{10^2 - 1} = 10 + \sqrt{100 - 1} =$

$10 + \sqrt{99} = 10 + \sqrt{9 \cdot 11} = 10 + 3\sqrt{11}$

22. $g(x) = \dfrac{x}{\sqrt{1 - x^2}}$

$g(0) = \dfrac{0}{\sqrt{1 - 0^2}} = 0$

$g(3) = \dfrac{3}{\sqrt{1 - 3^2}} = \dfrac{3}{\sqrt{-8}}$; $g(3)$ does not exist as a real number

$g\left(\dfrac{1}{2}\right) = \dfrac{\frac{1}{2}}{\sqrt{1 - \left(\frac{1}{2}\right)^2}} = \dfrac{\frac{1}{2}}{\sqrt{\frac{3}{4}}} = \dfrac{\frac{1}{2}}{\frac{\sqrt{3}}{2}} = \dfrac{1}{\sqrt{3}}$, or $\dfrac{\sqrt{3}}{3}$

23. $f(x) = 7x + 4$

There are no restrictions on the numbers we can substitute into this formula. Thus, the domain is the entire set of real numbers.

24. All real numbers

25. $f(x) = 4 - \dfrac{2}{x}$

Division by 0 is undefined. Thus, $x \neq 0$. The domain is all real numbers except 0, or $\{x | x \neq 0\}$.

26. $y = \dfrac{1}{x^4}$

Division by 0 is undefined. Then $x \neq 0$.

$\{x | x \neq 0\}$

27. $f(x) = \sqrt{7x + 4}$

Since this formula is meaningful only if the radicand is nonnegative, we want the replacements for x which make the following inequality true.

$7x + 4 \geqslant 0$

$\quad 7x \geqslant -4$

$\quad\ x \geqslant -\dfrac{4}{7}$

The domain is $\left\{x \middle| x \geqslant -\dfrac{4}{7}\right\}$.

28. $f(x) = \sqrt{x - 3}$

$x - 3 \geqslant 0$

$\quad x \geqslant 3$

$\{x | x \geqslant 3\}$

29. $f(x) = \dfrac{1}{x^2 - 4}$

This formula is meaningful as long as a replacement for x does not make the denominator 0. To find those replacements which do make the denominator 0, we solve $x^2 - 4 = 0$.

$x^2 - 4 = 0$

$(x + 2)(x - 2) = 0$

$x = -2$ or $x = 2$

Thus the domain consists of all real numbers except -2 and 2. This set can be named $\{x | x \neq -2 \text{ and } x \neq 2\}$.

30. $f(x) = \dfrac{1}{9 - x^2}$

    $9 - x^2 = 0$

    $(3 + x)(3 - x) = 0$

    $x = -3$ or $x = 3$

    $\{x \mid x \neq -3$ and $x \neq 3\}$

31. Since $(-1,2)$ is in the function, $f(-1) = 2$.

    Since $(7,9)$ is in the function, $f(7) = 9$.

    Since $(5,-6)$ is in the function, $f(5) = -6$.

    Since $(-3,4)$ is in the function, $f(-3) = 4$.

    The domain is $\{-1,-3,5,7\}$.

    The range is $\{2,4,-6,9\}$.

32. $g(8) = -7$, $g(6) = -7$, $g(-4) = 5$, $g(2) = -3$;

    domain: $\{2,-4,6,8\}$; range: $\{-3,5,-7\}$

33. $f(z) = z^2 - 4z + i$

    $f(3 + i) = (3 + i)^2 - 4(3 + i) + i$

    $\qquad = 9 + 6i + i^2 - 12 - 4i + i$

    $\qquad = i^2 + 3i - 3$

    $\qquad = -1 + 3i - 3$

    $\qquad = -4 + 3i$

34. $g(2 - i) = 2(2 - i)^2 + (2 - i) - 2i =$

    $8 - 8i - 2 + 2 - i - 2i = 8 - 11i$

35. $f(x) = \dfrac{1}{x}$ $\qquad\qquad$ $f(x + h) = \dfrac{1}{x + h}$

    $\dfrac{f(x + h) - f(x)}{h} = \dfrac{\dfrac{1}{x + h} - \dfrac{1}{x}}{h}$

    $\qquad = \dfrac{\dfrac{1}{x + h} \cdot \dfrac{x}{x} - \dfrac{1}{x} \cdot \dfrac{x + h}{x + h}}{h}$

    $\qquad = \dfrac{\dfrac{x - (x + h)}{x(x + h)}}{h}$

    $\qquad = \dfrac{-h}{x(x + h)} \cdot \dfrac{1}{h}$

    $\qquad = \dfrac{-1}{x(x + h)}$

36. $\dfrac{f(x + h) - f(x)}{h} = \dfrac{\dfrac{1}{(x + h)^2} - \dfrac{1}{x^2}}{h}$

    $\qquad = \dfrac{x^2 - (x + h)^2}{hx^2(x + h)^2}$

    $\qquad = \dfrac{-2xh - h^2}{hx^2(x + h)^2}$

    $\qquad = \dfrac{-2x - h}{x^2(x + h)^2}$

37. $f(x) = \sqrt{x}$ $\qquad\qquad$ $f(x + h) = \sqrt{x + h}$

    $\dfrac{f(x + h) - f(x)}{h} = \dfrac{\sqrt{x + h} - \sqrt{x}}{h}$

    $\qquad = \dfrac{\sqrt{x + h} - \sqrt{x}}{h} \cdot \dfrac{\sqrt{x + h} + \sqrt{x}}{\sqrt{x + h} + \sqrt{x}}$

    $\qquad = \dfrac{(x + h) - x}{h(\sqrt{x + h} + \sqrt{x})}$

    $\qquad = \dfrac{h}{h(\sqrt{x + h} + \sqrt{x})}$

    $\qquad = \dfrac{1}{\sqrt{x + h} + \sqrt{x}}$

38. Since $(0, 3)$ and $(0, -3)$ are both in the relation, the relation is not a function.

39. $\left\{ x \mid x \neq -\dfrac{3}{4}$ and $x \neq 2 \right\}$

40. $\{x \mid x \neq 0$ and $x \neq -2$ and $x \neq 2\}$

41. $\{x \mid x \neq 0$ and $x \neq -2$ and $x \neq 1\}$

42. All real numbers

43. $\{x \mid x \neq 2$ and $x \neq -1$ and $x \geqslant -3\}$

44. $\left\{ x \mid x \neq \dfrac{5}{2}$ and $x \geqslant 0 \right\}$

45. All real numbers

46. $\{x \mid x > 0\}$

Exercise Set 3.4

1. Graph: $8x - 3y = 24$

   First find two of its points. Here the easiest points are the intercepts.

   y-intercept: Set $x = 0$ and find y.

   $8x - 3y = 24$

   $8 \cdot 0 - 3y = 24$

   $\qquad -3y = 24$

   $\qquad\quad y = -8$

   The y-intercept is $(0, -8)$.

   x-intercept: Set $y = 0$ and find x.

   $8x - 3y = 24$

   $8x - 3 \cdot 0 = 24$

   $\qquad 8x = 24$

   $\qquad\quad x = 3$

   The x-intercept is $(3, 0)$.

   Plot these two points and draw a line through them.

A third point should be used as a check.

Set x = 2 and find y.

$8x - 3y = 24$

$8 \cdot 2 - 3y = 24$

$16 - 3y = 24$

$-3y = 8$

$y = -\frac{8}{3}$

The ordered pair $\left(2, -\frac{8}{3}\right)$ is also a point on the line.

2. $5x - 10y = 50$

3. Graph: $3x + 12 = 4y$

First find two of its points. Here the easiest points to find are the intercepts.

y-intercept: Set x = 0 and find y.

$3x + 12 = 4y$

$3 \cdot 0 + 12 = 4y$

$12 = 4y$

$3 = y$

The y-intercept is (0, 3).

x-intercept: Set y = 0 and find x.

$3x + 12 = 4y$

$3x + 12 = 4 \cdot 0$

$3x + 12 = 0$

$3x = -12$

$x = -4$

The x-intercept is (-4, 0).

Plot these points and draw a line through them. A third point should be used as a check.

4. $4x - 20 = 5y$

5. Graph: y = -2

The equation y = -2 says that the second coordinate of every ordered pair of the graph is -2. Below is a table of a few ordered pairs that are solutions of y = -2. (It might help to think of y = -2 as $0 \cdot x + y = -2$.)

x	y	
-3	-2	(x can be any number,
0	-2	but y must be -2)
1	-2	
4	-2	

Plot these points and draw the line through them.

6. $2y - 3 = 9$

7. Graph: $5x + 2 = 17$
$$5x = 15$$
$$x = 3$$

The equation $5x + 2 = 17$ is equivalent to $x = 3$. The equation $x = 3$ says that the first coordinate of every ordered pair of the graph is 3. Below is a table of a few ordered pairs that are solutions of $x = 3$. (It might help to think of $x = 3$ as $x + 0 \cdot y = 3$.)

x	y
3	0
3	-2
3	4
3	-1

(y can be any number, but x must be 3)

Plot these point and draw a line through them.

8. $19 = 5 - 2x$

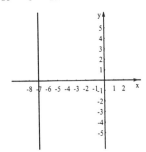

9. Find the slope of the line containing $(6, 2)$ and $(-2, 1)$.

$$m = \frac{\text{change in } y}{\text{change in } x} = \frac{2 - 1}{6 - (-2)} = \frac{1}{8}$$
$$\text{or} = \frac{1 - 2}{-2 - 6} = \frac{-1}{-8} = \frac{1}{8}$$

Note that it does not matter in which order we choose the points, so long as we take the differences in the same order. We get the same slope either way.

10. $m = \dfrac{-2 - 1}{-4 - (-2)} = \dfrac{-3}{-2} = \dfrac{3}{2}$

11. Find the slope of the line containing $(2, -4)$ and $(4, -3)$. Let $(4, -3)$ be (x_1, y_1) and $(2, -4)$ be (x_2, y_2).

$$m = \frac{y_2 - y_1}{x_2 - x_1} = \frac{-4 - (-3)}{2 - 4} = \frac{-1}{-2} = \frac{1}{2}$$

12. $m = \dfrac{8 - (-3)}{-5 - 5} = -\dfrac{11}{10}$

13. Find the slope of the line containing $(\pi, 5)$ and $(\pi, 4)$. Let $(\pi, 4)$ be (x_1, y_1) and $(\pi, 5)$ be (x_2, y_2).

$$m = \frac{y_2 - y_1}{x_2 - x_1} = \frac{5 - 4}{\pi - \pi} = \frac{1}{0}$$

The slope is not defined, because we cannot divide by 0.

14. $m = \dfrac{-4 - (-4)}{\pi - \sqrt{2}} = 0$

15. $m = \dfrac{920.58}{13,740} = 0.067$

The road grade is 6.7%.

We can think of an equation giving the height y as a function of the horizontal distance x as an equation of variation where y varies directly as x and the variation constant is 0.067. The equation is $y = 0.067x$.

16. $m = \dfrac{50}{1250} = 0.04$

The grade is 4%.

The equation is $y = 0.04x$.

17. We express the slope of the treadmill, 8%, as a decimal quantity. Let $h =$ the height of the vertical end of the treadmill.

$$0.08 = \frac{h}{5}$$
$$0.4 = h$$

The end of the treadmill is 0.4 ft high.

18. $0.12 = \dfrac{f}{250}$

$$30 \text{ ft} = f$$

19. Find an equation of the line through $(3, 2)$ with $m = 4$.

$$(y - y_1) = m(x - x_1) \quad \text{(Point-slope equation)}$$
$$(y - 2) = 4(x - 3) \quad \text{(Substituting)}$$
$$y - 2 = 4x - 12$$
$$y = 4x - 10$$

20. $y - 7 = -2(x - 4)$
$$y = -2x + 15$$

21. Find an equation of the line with y-intercept -5 and $m = 2$.

$$y = mx + b \quad \text{(Slope-intercept equation)}$$
$$y = 2x + (-5) \quad \text{(Substituting)}$$
$$y = 2x - 5$$

22. $y = \dfrac{1}{4}x + \pi$

23. Find an equation of the line through (-4, 7) with $m = -\frac{2}{3}$.

$(y - y_1) = m(x - x_1)$ (Point-slope equation)

$(y - 7) = -\frac{2}{3}[x - (-4)]$ (Substituting)

$y - 7 = -\frac{2}{3}(x + 4)$

$y - 7 = -\frac{2}{3}x - \frac{8}{3}$

$y = -\frac{2}{3}x + \frac{13}{3}$

24. $y - (-5) = \frac{3}{4}[x - (-3)]$

$y = \frac{3}{4}x - \frac{11}{4}$

25. Find an equation of the line through (5, -8) with $m = 0$.

$(y - y_1) = m(x - x_1)$ (Point-slope equation)

$[y - (-8)] = 0(x - 5)$

$y + 8 = 0$

$y = -8$

26. $x = 5$

27. Find an equation of the line containing (1, 4) and (5, 6). Let $(x_1, y_1) = (1, 4)$ and $(x_2, y_2) = (5, 6)$.

$y - y_1 = \frac{y_2 - y_1}{x_2 - x_1}(x - x_1)$ (Two-point equation)

$y - 4 = \frac{6 - 4}{5 - 1}(x - 1)$ (Substituting)

$y - 4 = \frac{2}{4}(x - 1)$

$y - 4 = \frac{1}{2}x - \frac{1}{2}$

$y = \frac{1}{2}x + \frac{7}{2}$

28. $y - 0 = \frac{3 - 0}{2 - (-2)}[x - (-2)]$

$y = \frac{3}{4}(x + 2)$

$y = \frac{3}{4}x + \frac{3}{2}$

29. Find an equation of the line containing (-2, 5) and (-4, -7). Let $(x_1, y_1) = (-2, 5)$ and $(x_2, y_2) = (-4, -7)$.

$y - y_1 = \frac{y_2 - y_1}{x_2 - x_1}(x - x_1)$ (Two-point equation)

$y - 5 = \frac{-7 - 5}{-4 - (-2)}[x - (-2)]$ (Substituting)

$y - 5 = \frac{-12}{-2}(x + 2)$

$y - 5 = 6x + 12$

$y = 6x + 17$

30. $y - \left(-\frac{4}{5}\right) = \frac{8.2 - \left(-\frac{4}{5}\right)}{-\frac{1}{2} - \frac{2}{3}}\left(x - \frac{2}{3}\right)$

$y + \frac{4}{5} = \frac{9}{-\frac{7}{6}}\left(x - \frac{2}{3}\right)$

$y = -\frac{54}{7}x + \frac{152}{35}$

31. Find an equation of the line containing (3, 6) and (-2, 6). Let (x_1, y_1) be (3, 6) and (x_2, y_2) be (-2, 6).

$y - y_1 = \frac{y_2 - y_1}{x_2 - x_1}(x - x_1)$ (Two-point equation)

$y - 6 = \frac{6 - 6}{-2 - 3}(x - 3)$ (Substituting)

$y - 6 = \frac{0}{-5}(x - 3)$

$y - 6 = 0$

$y = 6$

32. Since $x_1 = x_2$, m is undefined and the line is vertical.

$x = -\frac{3}{8}$

33. $y = 2x + 3$

$\uparrow\uparrow$

$y = mx + b$ (Slope-intercept equation)

The slope is 2, and the y-intercept is 3.

34. $m = -1$, $b = 6$

35. $2y = -6x + 10$

$y = -3x + 5$

$\uparrow\uparrow$

$y = mx + b$ (Slope-intercept equation)

The slope is -3, and the y-intercept is 5.

36. $-3y = -12x + 9$

$y = 4x - 3$

$m = 4$, $b = -3$

37. $3x - 4y = 12$

$-4y = -3x + 12$

$y = \frac{3}{4}x - 3$

$\uparrow\phantom{\frac{3}{4}x }\uparrow$

$y = mx + b$ (Slope-intercept equation)

The slope is $\frac{3}{4}$, and the y-intercept is -3.

38. $5x + 2y = -7$

$y = -\frac{5}{2}x - \frac{7}{2}$

$m = -\frac{5}{2}$, $b = -\frac{7}{2}$

39. $3y + 10 = 0$

$\qquad 3y = -10$

$\qquad y = -\dfrac{10}{3}$

or

$\qquad y = 0 \cdot x + \left(-\dfrac{10}{3}\right)$

$\qquad\qquad \uparrow \qquad\qquad \uparrow$

$\qquad y = mx \quad + \quad b \qquad$ (Slope-intercept equation)

The slope is 0, and the y-intercept is $-\dfrac{10}{3}$.

40. $m = 0$, $b = 7$

41. Graph $y = -\dfrac{3}{2}x$.

First we plot the y-intercept $(0, 0)$. We think of the slope as $\dfrac{-3}{2}$. Starting at the y-intercept and using the slope, we find another point by moving 3 units down and 2 units right. We get to a new point $(2, -3)$. By thinking of the slope as $\dfrac{3}{-2}$ we can start again at the y-intercept and find another point by moving 3 units up and 2 units left. We get to another point on the line, $(-2, 3)$. We draw the line through these points.

42.

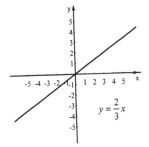

43. Graph $y = -\dfrac{5}{2}x - 2$.

First we plot the y-intercept $(0, -2)$. We think of the slope as $\dfrac{-5}{2}$. Starting at the y-intercept and using the slope, we find another point by moving 5 units down and 2 units right. We get to a new point, $(2, -7)$. By thinking of the slope as $\dfrac{5}{-2}$ we can start again at the y-intercept and find another point by moving 5 units up and

2 units left. We get to another point on the line, $(-2, 3)$. We draw the line through these points.

44.

45. Graph $y = \dfrac{1}{2}x + 1$.

First we plot the y-intercept $(0, 1)$. We consider the slope $\dfrac{1}{2}$. Starting at the y-intercept and using the slope, we find another point by moving 1 unit up and 2 units right. We get to a new point, $(2, 2)$. By thinking of the slope as $\dfrac{-1}{-2}$ we can start again at the y-intercept and find another point by moving 1 unit down and 2 units left. We get to another point on the line, $(-2, 0)$. We draw the line through these points.

46.

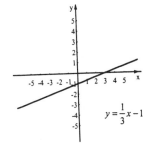

47. Graph $y = \frac{4}{3} - \frac{1}{3}x$, or $y = -\frac{1}{3}x + \frac{4}{3}$.

First we plot the y-intercept $\left(0, \frac{4}{3}\right)$. We think of the slope as $\frac{-1}{3}$. Starting at the y-intercept and using the slope, we find another point by moving 1 unit down and 3 units right. We get to a new point, $\left(3, \frac{1}{3}\right)$. By thinking of the slope as $\frac{1}{-3}$ we can start again at the y-intercept and find another pont by moving 1 unit up and 3 units left. We get to another point on the line, $\left(-3, \frac{7}{3}\right)$. We draw the line through these points.

48.

49.
$$y - y_1 = m(x - x_1) \quad \text{(Point-slope equation)}$$
$$y - (-2.563) = 3.516(x - 3.014) \quad \text{(Substituting)}$$
$$y + 2.563 = 3.516x - 10.597224$$
$$y = 3.516x - 13.1602$$

50.
$$y - 2.443 = \frac{11.012 - 2.443}{8.114 - 1.103}(x - 1.103)$$
$$y - 2.443 = 1.2222(x - 1.103)$$
$$y = 1.2222x + 1.0949$$

51. $T(d) = 10d + 20$

a)
$$T(5 \text{ km}) = 10 \cdot 5 + 20 = 50 + 20 = 70°C$$
$$T(20 \text{ km}) = 10 \cdot 20 + 20 = 200 + 20 = 220°C$$
$$T(1000 \text{ km}) = 10 \cdot 1000 + 20 = 10{,}000 + 20 = 10{,}020°C$$

b) This is a linear function. We plot the points (5, 70), (20, 220), and (1000, 10,020) and draw the graph.

c) The depth must be nonnegative, so $d \geqslant 0$. If we go more than 5600 km into the earth, we begin to emerge on the other side. Thus $d \leqslant 5600$.

The domain of the function is $\{d | 0 \leqslant d \leqslant 5600\}$.

52. $T(L) = 0.143L - 1.18$

a)
$$T(0 \text{ mm}) = 0.143(0) - 1.18 = 0 - 1.18 = -1.18 \text{ mm}$$
$$T(50 \text{ mm}) = 0.143(50) - 1.18 = 7.15 - 1.18 = 5.97 \text{ mm}$$
$$T(80 \text{ mm}) = 0.143(80) - 1.18 = 11.44 - 1.18 = 10.26 \text{ mm}$$

b) This is a linear function. We plot the points (50, 5.97) and (80, 10.26) and draw the graph.

c) Since tail length must be nonnegative, we solve:
$$0.143L - 1.18 \geqslant 0$$
$$L \geqslant 8.25$$

We can assume there is no upper bound on the tail length, so the domain of the function is $\{L | L \geqslant 8.25\}$.

53. $V(t) = \$5200 - \$512.50t$

a)
$$V(0) = \$5200 - \$512.50(0) = \$5200 - \$0 = \$5200$$
$$V(1) = \$5200 - \$512.50(1) = \$5200 - \$512.50 = \$4687.50$$
$$V(2) = \$5200 - \$512.50(2) = \$5200 - \$1025 = \$4175$$
$$V(3) = \$5200 - \$512.50(3) = \$5200 - \$1537.50 = \$3662.50$$
$$V(8) = \$5200 - \$512.80(8) = \$5200 - \$4100 = \$1100$$

b) This is a linear function. We plot the
    points (0, $5200) and (8, $1100) and draw
    the graph.

54. a) M(45) = 2.97(45) + 73.6 = 207.25 cm

     b) F(45) = 3.14(45) + 65.0 = 206.3 cm

     c) For each function, x > 0. The upper bound
         of the domains depends on the maximum
         height of men and women in the population
         from which the bone came.

55. Solve each equation for y.

$$2x - 5y = -3 \qquad\qquad 2x + 5y = 4$$
$$-5y = -2x - 3 \qquad\qquad 5y = -2x + 4$$
$$y = \frac{2}{5}x + \frac{3}{5} \qquad\qquad y = -\frac{2}{5}x + \frac{4}{5}$$

The slopes are $\frac{2}{5}$ and $-\frac{2}{5}$. The slopes are not
equal. The product of the slopes is not -1.
Thus, the lines are <u>neither</u> parallel nor
perpendicular.

56. $x + 2y = 5 \qquad\qquad 2x + 4y = 8$
$$y = -\frac{1}{2}x + \frac{5}{2} \qquad\qquad y = -\frac{1}{2}x + 2$$

$m_1 = m_2, \quad b_1 \neq b_2;$ parallel

57. Solve each equation for y.

$$y = 4x - 5 \qquad\qquad 4y = 8 - x$$
$$y = -\frac{1}{4}x + 2$$

The slopes are 4 and $-\frac{1}{4}$. Their product is -1,
so the lines are <u>perpendicular</u>.

58. $m_1 m_2 = (-1)(1) = -1;$ perpendicular

59. We first solve for y.
$$3x - y = 7$$
$$-y = -3x + 7$$
$$y = 3x - 7$$

The slope of the given line is 3. The line
parallel to the given line will have slope 3.
Since the line contains the point (0, 3), we
know that the y-intercept is 3. We use the
slope-intercept equation.

$$y = mx + b$$
$$y = 3x + 3$$

The perpendicular line has slope $-\frac{1}{3}$ and
y-intercept 3. We use the slope-intercept
equation again.

$$y = mx + b$$
$$y = -\frac{1}{3}x + 3$$

60. $2x + y = -4$
$$y = -2x - 4$$
$$m = -2, \quad -\frac{1}{m} = \frac{1}{2}$$

Parallel line: $y + 5 = (-2)(x + 4)$
$$y = -2x - 13$$
Perpendicular line: $y + 5 = \frac{1}{2}(x + 4)$
$$y = \frac{1}{2}x - 3$$

61. We first solve for y.
$$5x - 2y = 4$$
$$-2y = -5x + 4$$
$$y = \frac{5}{2}x - 2$$

The slope of the given line is $\frac{5}{2}$. The line
parallel to the given line will have slope $\frac{5}{2}$.
We use the point-slope equation to write an
equation with slope $\frac{5}{2}$ and containing the point
(-3, -5).

$$y - y_1 = m(x - x_1)$$
$$y - (-5) = \frac{5}{2}[x - (-3)]$$
$$y + 5 = \frac{5}{2}x + \frac{15}{2}$$
$$y = \frac{5}{2}x + \frac{5}{2}$$

The slope of the perpendicular line is $-\frac{2}{5}$.

$$y - y_1 = m(x - x_1) \qquad \text{(Point-slope equation)}$$
$$y - (-5) = -\frac{2}{5}[x - (-3)] \quad \left[\begin{array}{l}\text{Substituting -3 for} \\ x_1, \text{ -5 for } y_1, \text{ and} \\ -\frac{2}{5} \text{ for m}\end{array}\right]$$

$$y + 5 = -\frac{2}{5}(x + 3)$$
$$y + 5 = -\frac{2}{5}x - \frac{6}{5}$$
$$y = -\frac{2}{5}x - \frac{31}{5}$$

62. $3x + 4y = 5$

$$y = -\frac{3}{4}x + \frac{5}{4}$$

$$m = -\frac{3}{4}, \quad -\frac{1}{m} = \frac{4}{3}$$

Parallel line: $\quad y + 2 = -\frac{3}{4}(x - 3)$

$$y = -\frac{3}{4}x + \frac{1}{4}$$

Perpendicular line: $\quad y + 2 = \frac{4}{3}(x - 3)$

$$y = \frac{4}{3}x - 6$$

63. $x = -1$ is the equation of a vertical line. The line parallel to the given line is a vertical line containing the point $(3, -3)$, or $x = 3$.

The line perpendicular to the given line is a horizontal line containing the point $(3, -3)$, or $y = -3$.

64. $y = -1$ is a horizontal line.

Parallel line: $\quad y = -5$

Perpendicular line: $\quad x = 4$

65.
$$f(x) = mx + b \qquad \text{(Linear function)}$$
$$f(3x) = 3f(x) \qquad \text{(Given)}$$
$$m(3x) + b = 3(mx + b)$$
$$3mx + b = 3mx + 3b$$
$$b = 3b$$
$$0 = 2b$$
$$0 = b$$

Thus, if $f(3x) = 3f(x)$, then

$$f(x) = mx + 0$$
$$f(x) = mx$$

66.
$$f(x) = mx + b \qquad \text{(Linear function)}$$
$$f(x + 2) = f(x) + 2 \qquad \text{(Given)}$$
$$m(x + 2) + b = mx + b + 2$$
$$mx + 2m + b = mx + b + 2$$
$$2m = 2$$
$$m = 1$$

Thus, if $f(x + 2) = f(x) + 2$, then

$$f(x) = 1 \cdot x + b$$
$$f(x) = x + b$$

67. $f(x) = mx + b \qquad \text{(Linear function)}$

$f(c + d) = m(c + d) + b = mc + md + b$

$f(c) + f(d) = (mc + b) + (md + b) = mc + md + 2b$

$mc + md + b \neq mc + md + 2b$, for example, when $m = 0$, $b = 1$

Thus, $f(c + d) = f(c) + f(d)$ is false.

68. Assume true; then $m(cd) + b = (mc + b)(md + b)$ which fails, for example, when $m = 0$, $b = 2$. Thus $f(cd) = f(c) \, f(d)$ is false.

69. $f(x) = mx + b \qquad \text{(Linear function)}$

$f(kx) = m(kx) + b = mkx + b$

$kf(x) = k(mx + b) = mkx + kb$

$mkx + b \neq mkx + kb$, for example, when $m = 0$, $b = 1$, $k = 2$

Thus, $f(kx) = kf(x)$ is false.

70. Assume true; then

$m(c - d) + b = (mc + b) - (md + b)$ leads to $b = 0$.

Thus $f(c - d) = f(c) - f(d)$ is false for $b \neq 0$.

71. If $A(9, 4)$, $B(-1, 2)$, and $C(4, 3)$ are on the same line, then the slope of the segment $\overline{AB}$ must be the same as the slope of the segment $\overline{BC}$. (Note that B is a point of each segment.)

Slope of $\overline{AB} = \dfrac{4 - 2}{9 - (-1)} = \dfrac{2}{10} = \dfrac{1}{5}$

Slope of $\overline{BC} = \dfrac{2 - 3}{-1 - 4} = \dfrac{-1}{-5} = \dfrac{1}{5}$

Since the slopes are the same, and B is on both lines, A, B, and C are on the same line.

72. Slope of $\overline{AB} = \dfrac{2 - (-1)}{2 - (-1)} = 1$

Slope of $\overline{BC} = \dfrac{-4 - 2}{-3 - 2} = \dfrac{6}{5}$

Since the slopes are different, the points are not on a line.

73.

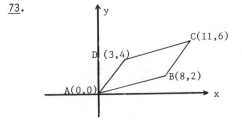

Slope of $\overline{AB} = \dfrac{2 - 0}{8 - 0} = \dfrac{2}{8} = \dfrac{1}{4}$

Slope of $\overline{CD} = \dfrac{6 - 4}{11 - 3} = \dfrac{2}{8} = \dfrac{1}{4}$

Slope of $\overline{BC} = \dfrac{6 - 2}{11 - 8} = \dfrac{4}{3}$

Slope of $\overline{DA} = \dfrac{4 - 0}{3 - 0} = \dfrac{4}{3}$

$\overline{AB}$ and $\overline{CD}$ have the same slope.
$\overline{BC}$ and $\overline{DA}$ have the same slope.

74.

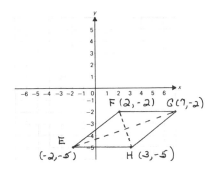

$F(2, -2)$ $G(7, -2)$

E $(-2, -5)$ $H(3, -5)$

m_1 = slope of $\overline{EG}$ = $\frac{-2 - (-5)}{7 - (-2)}$ = $\frac{1}{3}$

m_2 = slope of $\overline{FH}$ = $\frac{-5 - (-2)}{3 - 2}$ = -3

$m_1 m_2 = -1$, or $m_1 = -\frac{1}{m_2}$, or $m_2 = -\frac{1}{m_1}$

75. Consider a line containing the ordered pairs (0, 32) and (100, 212).

The slope of the line is $\frac{212 - 32}{100 - 0}$, or $\frac{9}{5}$.

$F(C) = mC + b$ (Linear function)

$F(C) = \frac{9}{5} C + b$ [Substituting $\frac{9}{5}$ for m]

We now determine b.

$32 = \frac{9}{5} \cdot 0 + b$ (Substituting 0 for C and 32 for F)

$32 = b$

The linear function is

$F(C) = \frac{9}{5} C + 32$.

76. $m = \frac{100 - 0}{212 - 32} = \frac{5}{9}$

$C = \frac{5}{9} F + b$

$0 = \frac{5}{9} \cdot 32 + b$ (Substituting 32 for F and 0 for C)

$-\frac{5}{9} \cdot 32 = b$

$C = \frac{5}{9} F - \frac{5}{9} \cdot 32$

$C = \frac{5}{9}(F - 32)$

77. $P = mQ + b$, $m \neq 0$ (Linear function)

We solve for Q.

$P - b = mQ$

$\frac{P - b}{m} = Q$

$\frac{P}{m} - \frac{b}{m} = Q$ (Linear function)

78. By definition, $y = kx$. Thus, y is a linear function of x.

79. The slope of the line containing (-1, 4) and (2, -3) is $\frac{4 - (-3)}{-1 - 2}$, or $-\frac{7}{3}$. The slope of the line parallel to this line and containing (4, -2) is also $-\frac{7}{3}$.

$y - y_1 = m(x - x_1)$ (Point-slope equation)

$y - (-2) = -\frac{7}{3}(x - 4)$ [Substituting 4 for x_1, -2 for y_1, and $-\frac{7}{3}$ for m]

$y + 2 = -\frac{7}{3} x + \frac{28}{3}$

$y = -\frac{7}{3} x + \frac{22}{3}$

The slope of the line perpendicular to the given line is $\frac{3}{7}$.

$y - y_1 = m(x - x_1)$ (Point-slope equation)

$y - (-2) = \frac{3}{7}(x - 4)$ (Substituting)

$y + 2 = \frac{3}{7} x - \frac{12}{7}$

$y = \frac{3}{7} x - \frac{26}{7}$

80. Parallel line: $y - 3 = m(x + 1)$ where $m = \frac{-5 - (-7)}{3 - (-2)} = \frac{2}{5}$.

Then $y = \frac{2}{5} x + \frac{17}{5}$.

Perpendicular line: $y - 3 = -\frac{5}{2}(x + 1)$, or

$y = -\frac{5}{2} x + \frac{1}{2}$

81. The slope of the line containing (-3, k) and (4, 8) is

$\frac{8 - k}{4 - (-3)} = \frac{8 - k}{7}$.

The slope of the line containing (6, 4) and (2, -5) is

$\frac{-5 - 4}{2 - 6} = \frac{-9}{-4} = \frac{9}{4}$.

The lines are parallel when their slopes are equal:

$\frac{8 - k}{7} = \frac{9}{4}$

$32 - 4k = 63$

$-4k = 31$

$k = -\frac{31}{4}$

82. Use the slopes computed in Exercise 81. Then

$\frac{8 - k}{7}\left(\frac{9}{4}\right) = -1$, and $k = \frac{100}{9}$.

83. The slope of the line segment with endpoints
(-1, 3) and (-6, 7) is $\frac{3 - 7}{-1 - (-6)} = -\frac{4}{5}$.

The midpoint of the given line segement is
$\left[\frac{-1 + (-6)}{2}, \frac{3 + 7}{2}\right]$, or $\left[-\frac{7}{2}, 5\right]$.

The perpendicular bisector of the given line
segment has slope $\frac{5}{4}$ and contains the point
$\left[-\frac{7}{2}, 5\right]$.

$$y - y_1 = m(x - x_1)$$
$$y - 5 = \frac{5}{4}\left[x - \left[-\frac{7}{2}\right]\right]$$
$$y - 5 = \frac{5}{4}x + \frac{35}{8}$$
$$y = \frac{5}{4}x + \frac{75}{8}$$

84. $m = \frac{0 - (-12)}{1 - (-7)} = \frac{3}{2}$

Midpoint: $\left[\frac{1 - 7}{2}, \frac{0 - 12}{2}\right]$, or (-3, -6)

Then $y + 6 = -\frac{2}{3}(x + 3)$, or $y = -\frac{2}{3}x - 8$.

85. See the answer section in the text.

86. $x^2 + y^2 = a^2$ gives $b^2 + c^2 = a^2$
or $c^2 = -(b^2 - a^2)$. Also

slope of $\overline{AB}$ · slope of $\overline{BC} = \frac{c - 0}{b - (-a)} \cdot \frac{c - 0}{b - a}$

$$= \frac{c^2}{b^2 - a^2} = \frac{-(b^2 - a^2)}{b^2 - a^2}$$
$$= -1.$$

Then $\overline{AB}$ is perpendicular to $\overline{BC}$, so $\angle ABC$ is a
right angle.

Exercise Set 3.5

---

1. $f(x) = |x| + 2$

We compute some function values.
$f(-3) = |-3| + 2 = 3 + 2 = 5$
$f(-1) = |-1| + 2 = 1 + 2 = 3$
$f(0) = |0| + 2 = 0 + 2 = 2$
$f(2) = |2| + 2 = 2 + 2 = 4$
$f(4) = |4| + 2 = 4 + 2 = 6$

x	f(x)	(x, f(x))
-3	5	(-3,5)
-1	3	(-1,3)
0	2	(0,2)
2	4	(2,4)
4	6	(4,6)

We plot these points, look for a pattern,
and sketch the graph.

2.

3. $g(x) = 4 - x^2$

We compute some function values.
$g(-3) = 4 - (-3)^2 = 4 - 9 = -5$
$g(-2) = 4 - (-2)^2 = 4 - 4 = 0$
$g(0) = 4 - 0^2 = 4 - 0 = 4$
$g(1) = 4 - 1^2 = 4 - 1 = 3$
$g(2) = 4 - 2^2 = 4 - 4 = 0$

x	g(x)	(x, g(x))
-3	-5	(-3,-5)
-2	0	(-2,0)
0	4	(0,4)
1	3	(1,3)
2	0	(2,0)

We plot these points, look for a pattern, and
sketch the graph.

4.

5. $f(x) = \frac{2}{x}$

We compute some function values. Note that x cannot be 0.

$f(-4) = \frac{2}{-4} = -\frac{1}{2}$ $f\left(\frac{1}{2}\right) = \frac{2}{\frac{1}{2}} = 4$

$f(-2) = \frac{2}{-2} = -1$ $f(2) = \frac{2}{2} = 1$

$f\left(-\frac{1}{2}\right) = \frac{2}{-\frac{1}{2}} = -4$ $f(4) = \frac{2}{4} = \frac{1}{2}$

x	f(x)	(x, f(x))
-4	$-\frac{1}{2}$	$\left(-4, -\frac{1}{2}\right)$
-2	-1	(-2, -1)
$-\frac{1}{2}$	-4	$\left(-\frac{1}{2}, -4\right)$
$\frac{1}{2}$	4	$\left(\frac{1}{2}, 4\right)$
2	1	(2, 1)
4	$\frac{1}{2}$	$\left(4, \frac{1}{2}\right)$

We plot these points, look for a pattern, and sketch the graph.

6.

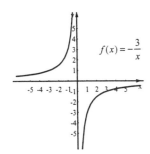

7. $f(x) = x^2 - 3$

We compute some function values.

$f(-3) = (-3)^2 - 3 = 9 - 3 = 6$

$f(-1) = (-1)^2 - 3 = 1 - 3 = -2$

$f(0) = 0^2 - 3 = 0 - 3 = -3$

$f(2) = 2^2 - 3 = 4 - 3 = 1$

$f(3) = 3^2 - 3 = 9 - 3 = 6$

We plot these points, look for a pattern, and sketch the graph.

8.

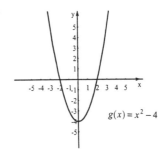

9. $g(x) = 3$

The function value is 3 for every value of x. For example,

g(-5) = 3,   g(1) = 3,
g(-3) = 3,   g(2) = 3,
g(0) = 3,   g(4) = 3.

The graph is a horizontal line 3 units above the x-axis. We sketch the graph.

10.

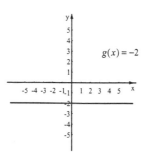

11. f(x) = x³ - 3x

We compute some function values.

f(-3) = (-3)³ - 3(-3) = -27 + 9 = -18
f(-2) = (-2)³ - 3(-2) = -8 + 6 = -2
f(-1) = (-1)³ - 3(-1) = -1 + 3 = 2
f(0) = 0³ - 3·0 = 0 - 0 = 0
f(1) = 1³ - 3·1 = 1 - 3 = -2
f(2) = 2³ - 3·2 = 8 - 6 = 2
f(3) = 3³ - 3·3 = 27 - 9 = 18

We plot these points, look for a pattern, and sketch the graph.

12.

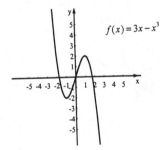

13. f(x) = |x| + x

We compute some function values.
f(-4) = |-4| + (-4) = 4 - 4 = 0
f(-2) = |-2| + (-2) = 2 - 2 = 0
f(0) = |0| + 0 = 0 + 0 = 0
f(1) = |1| + 1 = 1 + 1 = 2
f(3) = |3| + 3 = 3 + 3 = 6

We plot these points, look for a pattern, and sketch the graph.

14.

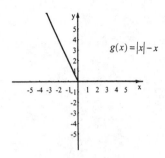

15. f(x) = √(x + 3)

We compute some function values. Note that the meaningful replacements for x are x ⩾ -3.

f(-3) = √(-3 + 3) = √0 = 0

f(-2) = √(-2 + 3) = √1 = 1

f(1) = √(1 + 3) = √4 = 2

f(6) = √(6 + 3) = √9 = 3

We plot these points, look for a pattern, and sketch the graph.

16.

17. This is not the graph of a function, because it fails the vertical line test. We can find a vertical line which intersects the graph at more than one point.

18. This is the graph of a function. This is no vertical line which intersects the graph at more than one point.

19. This is the graph of a function. There is no vertical line which intersects the graph at more than one point.

20. This is the graph of a function. There is no vertical line which intersects the graph at more than one point.

21. This is not the graph of a function. We can find a vertical line which intersects the graph in more than one point.

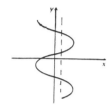

22. This is the graph of a function. There is no vertical line which intersects the graph at more than one point.

23. This is the graph of a function. There is no vertical line which intersects the graph in more than one point.

24. This is the graph of a function. There is no vertical line which intersects the graph at more than one point.

25. The endpoints 0 and 5 are not included in the interval, so we use parentheses. Interval notation is (0,5).

26. [-1,2]

27. The endpoint -9 is included in the interval, so we use a bracket before the -9. The endpoint -4 is not included, so we use a parenthesis after the -4. Interval notation is [-9,4).

28. (-9,-5]

29. Both endpoints are included in the interval, so we use brackets. Interval notation is [x, x + h].

30. (x, x + h]

31. The endpoint p is not included in the interval, so we use a parenthesis before the p. The interval is of unlimited extent in the positive direction, so we use the infinity symbol ∞. Interval notation is (p,∞).

32. (-∞,q]

33. This is a closed interval, so we use brackets. Interval notation is [-3,3].

34. (-4,4)

35. This is a half-open interval. We use a bracket on the left and a parenthesis on the right. Interval notation is [-14,-11).

36. (6,20]

37. This interval is of unlimited extent in the negative direction, and the endpoint -4 is included. Interval notation is (-∞,-4].

38. (-5,∞)

39. This interval is of unlimited extent in the negative direction, and the endpoint 3.8 is not included. Interval notation is (-∞, 3.8).

40. [$\sqrt{3}$,∞)

41. a) Increasing, b) Neither
    c) Decreasing, d) Neither

42. a) Neither, b) Decreasing
    c) Increasing, d) Neither

43. Graph $f(x) = \begin{cases} 1 & \text{for } x < 0 \\ -1 & \text{for } x \geqslant 0. \end{cases}$

    We graph $f(x) = 1$ for inputs less than 0. Note that $f(x) = 1$ only for numbers less than 0. We use an open circle at the point (0, 1).

    We graph $f(x) = -1$ for inputs greater than or equal to 0. Note that $f(x) = -1$ only for numbers greater than or equal to 0. We use a solid circle at the point (0, -1).

44.

$$f(x) = \begin{cases} 2 & \text{for } x \text{ an integer} \\ -2 & \text{for } x \text{ not an integer} \end{cases}$$

45. $f(x) = \begin{cases} 3 & \text{for } x \leqslant -3 \\ |x| & \text{for } -3 < x \leqslant 3 \\ -3 & \text{for } x > 3 \end{cases}$

We graph f(x) = 3 for inputs less than or equal to -3. Note that f(x) = 3 <u>only</u> for numbers less than or equal to -3.

We graph f(x) = |x| for inputs greater than -3 and less than or equal to 3. Note that f(x) = |x| <u>only</u> on the interval (-3, 3]. We use a solid circle at the point (3, 3).

We graph f(x) = -3 for inputs greater than 3. Note that f(x) = -3 <u>only</u> for numbers greater than 3. We use an open circle at the point (3, -3).

46.

$f(x) = \begin{cases} -2x - 6 & \text{for } x \leq -2 \\ 2 - x^2 & \text{for } -2 < x < 2 \\ 2x - 6 & \text{for } x \geq 2 \end{cases}$

47. $f(x) = \begin{cases} \dfrac{x^2 - 1}{x - 1}, & \text{for } x \neq 1 \\ -2, & \text{for } x = 1 \end{cases}$

When x ≠ 1, the denominator of $\dfrac{x^2 - 1}{x - 1}$ is nonzero, so we can simplify.

$$\frac{x^2 - 1}{x - 1} = \frac{(x + 1)(x - 1)}{x - 1} = x + 1$$

Thus, f(x) = x + 1 for x ≠ 1. The graph of this part of the function consists of a line with a hole at the point (1,2). At x = 1, f(1) = -2, so the point (1,-2) is plotted below (1,2).

48. $f(x) = \begin{cases} \dfrac{x^2 - 9}{x + 3} & \text{for } x \neq -3 \\ 4 & \text{for } x = -3 \end{cases}$

49.

$p(x) = \begin{cases} 29¢ & \text{if } 0 < x \leqslant 1 \\ 52¢ & \text{if } 1 < x \leqslant 2 \\ 75¢ & \text{if } 2 < x \leqslant 3 \\ 98¢ & \text{if } 3 < x \leqslant 4 \\ \$1.21 & \text{if } 4 < x \leqslant 5 \\ \$1.44 & \text{if } 5 < x \leqslant 6 \\ \$1.67 & \text{if } 6 < x \leqslant 7 \\ \$1.90 & \text{if } 7 < x \leqslant 8 \\ \$2.13 & \text{if } 8 < x \leqslant 9 \\ \$2.36 & \text{if } 9 < x \leqslant 10 \\ \$2.59 & \text{if } 10 < x \leqslant 11 \\ \$2.82 & \text{if } 11 < x \leqslant 12 \end{cases}$

50. $f(x) = \begin{cases} 3 + x & \text{for } x \leq 0 \\ \sqrt{x} & \text{for } 0 < x < 4 \\ x^2 - 4x - 1 & \text{for } x \geq 4 \end{cases}$

51. f(x) = INT(x - 2)

We can define this function by a piecewise
function with an infinite number of statements.

$$f(x) = INT(x - 2) = \begin{cases} \cdot \\ \cdot \\ \cdot \\ -4 & \text{if } -2 \leqslant x < -1 \\ -3 & \text{if } -1 \leqslant x < 0 \\ -2 & \text{if } 0 \leqslant x < 1 \\ -1 & \text{if } 1 \leqslant x < 2 \\ 0 & \text{if } 2 \leqslant x < 3 \\ 1 & \text{if } 3 \leqslant x < 4 \\ \cdot \\ \cdot \\ \cdot \end{cases}$$

We graph the function.

$f(x) = INT(x - 2)$

52.

$f(x) = INT(x) - 1$

53. f(x) = INT(x) + 2

We can define the function by a piecewise
function with an infinite number of statements.

$$f(x) = INT(x) + 2 = \begin{cases} \cdot \\ \cdot \\ \cdot \\ -1 & \text{if } -3 \leqslant x < -2 \\ 0 & \text{if } -2 \leqslant x < -1 \\ 1 & \text{if } -1 \leqslant x < 0 \\ 2 & \text{if } 0 \leqslant x < 1 \\ \cdot \\ \cdot \\ \cdot \end{cases}$$

$f(x) = INT(x) + 2$

54.

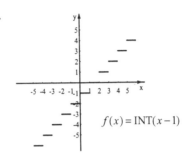

$f(x) = INT(x - 1)$

55. P(y) = 0.1522y - 298.592

a) P(1993) = 0.1522(1993) - 298.592 =
       303.3346 - 298.592 ≈ 4.74

The average price of a ticket in 1993 will
be $4.74.

P(1995) = 0.1522(1995) - 298.592 =
       303.639 - 298.592 ≈ 5.05

The average price of a ticket in 1995 will
be $5.05.

P(2000) = 0.1522(2000) - 298.592 =
       304.4 - 298.592 ≈ 5.81

The average price of a ticket in 2000 will
be $5.81.

b)   8.00 = 0.1522y - 298.592   [Substituting
                                  8.00 for P(y)]

306.592 = 0.1522y

2014 ≈ y

The average price of a ticket will be $8.00
in 2014.

56. a) N(6) = 6(6 - 1) = 30

b) N(10) = 10(10 - 1) = 90

57. E(T) = 1000(100 - T) + 580(100 - T)²

a) E(99.5) = 1000(100 - 99.5) + 580(100 - 99.5)²
          = 1000(0.5) + 580(0.5)²
          = 500 + 580(0.25) = 500 + 145
          = 645 m above sea level

b) E(100) = 1000(100 - 100) + 580(100 - 100)²
          = 1000·0 + 580(0)² = 0 + 0
          = 0 m above sea level, or at sea level

58. $T(0.5) = 0.5^{1.31} \approx 0.4$ acres

$T(10) = 10^{1.31} \approx 20.4$ acres

$T(20) = 20^{1.31} \approx 50.6$ acres

$T(40) = 40^{1.31} \approx 125.5$ acres

$T(100) = 100^{1.31} \approx 416.9$ acres

$T(200) = 200^{1.31} \approx 1033.6$ acres

59. a) $L = W + 4$, so $W = L - 4$.

Area = length × width, so

$A(L) = L(L - 4)$, or $L^2 - 4L$.

b) $L = W + 4$, and area = length × width, so

$A(W) = (W + 4)W$, or $W^2 + 4W$.

60. a) $b = 2h - 3$, so

$A(h) = \frac{1}{2}(2h - 3)h$, or $\frac{1}{2}h(2h - 3)$.

b) $b = 2h - 3$, so $h = \frac{b + 3}{2}$.

$A(b) = \frac{1}{2}b\left[\frac{b + 3}{2}\right]$

61. First express y in terms of x.

$2x + 2y = 34$

$2y = 34 - 2x$

$y = \frac{1}{2}(34 - 2x)$

$y = 17 - x$

The area is given by $A = xy$, so

$A(x) = x(17 - x)$, or $17x - x^2$.

62. $2x + 2y = 48$, so $y = 24 - x$ and

$A(x) = x(24 - x)$, or $24x - x^2$.

63. The diameter of the circle is $2 \cdot 8$, or 16 ft.
We can use the Pythagorean theorem to express y in terms of x.

$x^2 + y^2 = 16^2$

$x^2 + y^2 = 256$

$y^2 = 256 - x^2$

$y = \sqrt{256 - x^2}$ Taking the positive square root

The area is given by $A = xy$, so

$A(x) = x\sqrt{256 - x^2}$.

64. $x^2 + y^2 = 20^2$, so $y = \sqrt{400 - x^2}$, and

$A(x) = x\sqrt{400 - x^2}$.

65. We make a drawing.

The volume is given by V = length × width × height, so we have

$$V(x) = x \cdot x \cdot \frac{10 - x}{2}$$

$$V(x) = \frac{10x^2 - x^3}{2}$$

$$V(x) = 5x^2 - \frac{x^3}{2}.$$

66.

$A(x) = x(30 - x)$, or $30x - x^2$

67. First we use the volume to express y in terms of x.

$x \cdot x \cdot y = 108$

$y = \frac{108}{x^2}$

Then we write an expression for the surface area.

$SA(x) = x^2 + 4 \cdot x \cdot \frac{108}{x^2}$

$SA(x) = x^2 + \frac{432}{x}$

68. $x^2 y = 320$, so $y = \frac{320}{x^2}$.

$C(x) = 1.5x^2 + 1 \cdot x^2 + 2.5(4)x \cdot \frac{320}{x^2}$

$C(x) = 2.5x^2 + \frac{3200}{x}$

69. We will use similar triangles, expressing all distances in feet. $\left(6 \text{ in.} = \frac{1}{2} \text{ ft, s in.} = \frac{s}{12} \text{ ft,}\right.$ and d yd $= 3d$ ft$\left.\right)$ We have

$$\frac{3d}{7} = \frac{\frac{1}{2}}{\frac{s}{12}}$$

$$\frac{s}{12} \cdot 3d = 7 \cdot \frac{1}{2}$$

$$\frac{sd}{4} = \frac{7}{2}$$

$$d = \frac{4}{s} \cdot \frac{7}{2}, \text{ so}$$

$$d(s) = \frac{14}{s}.$$

70. We will use the Pythagorean theorem.

$$h^2 + 3700^2 = d^2$$

$$h^2 = d^2 - 3700^2$$

$$h^2 = d^2 - 13,690,000$$

$$h(d) = \sqrt{d^2 - 13,690,000} \quad \text{Taking the positive square root}$$

71. a) The volume of the tank is the sum of the volume of a sphere with radius r and a right circular cylinder with radius r and height 6 ft.

$$V(r) = \frac{4}{3}\pi r^3 + 6\pi r^2$$

  b) The surface area of the tank is the sum of the surface area of a sphere with radius r and the lateral surface area of a right circular cylinder with radius r and height 6 ft.

$$S(r) = 4\pi r^2 + 12\pi r$$

72. We make a drawing.

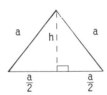

We first use the Pythagorean theorem to express the height h in terms of a.

$$h^2 + \left[\frac{a}{2}\right]^2 = a^2$$

$$h^2 + \frac{a^2}{4} = a^2$$

$$h^2 = \frac{3a^2}{4}$$

$$h = \frac{a\sqrt{3}}{2}$$

Then we write an expression for the area in terms of a.

$$A(a) = \frac{1}{2} \cdot a \cdot \frac{a\sqrt{3}}{2}$$

$$A(a) = \frac{a^2\sqrt{3}}{4}$$

73. The distance from A to S is $4 - x$. Using the Pythagorean theorem, we find that the distance from S to C is $\sqrt{1 + x^2}$. Then $C(x) = 3000(4 - x) + 5000\sqrt{1 + x^2}$.

74. a) We position a coordinate system as shown below.

The equation of the line containing $(6,0)$ and $(0,10)$ is given by

$$y - 10 = \frac{10 - 0}{0 - 6}(x - 0), \text{ or } y = -\frac{5}{3}x + 10.$$

Now (r,h) is a point on the line so,

$$h = -\frac{5}{3}r + 10, \text{ or}$$

$$h(r) = \frac{30 - 5r}{3}.$$

  b) $V = \pi r^2 h$

$$V(r) = \pi r^2 \left[\frac{30 - 5r}{3}\right] \quad \text{Substituting for h}$$

  c) We first express h in terms of r.

$$h = \frac{30 - 5r}{3}$$

$$3h = 30 - 5r$$

$$5r = 30 - 3h$$

$$r = \frac{30 - 3h}{5}$$

$$V = \pi r^2 h$$

$$V(h) = \pi \left[\frac{30 - 3h}{5}\right]^2 h \quad \text{Substituting for r}$$

75. $f(x) = \frac{|x|}{x}$

We compute some function values, plot these points, look for a pattern, and sketch the graph. Note that x cannot be zero.

x	f(x)
-3	-1
-2	-1
-1	-1
1	1
2	1
3	1

76.

$$g(x) = \frac{x}{|x|}$$

77. INT(x) = 4 for 4 ⩽ x < 5, so the possible inputs are {x|4 ⩽ x < 5}.

78. {x|-3 ⩽ x < -2}

79. a) $\text{INT}\left[\frac{547}{3}\right] = \text{INT}\left[182\frac{1}{3}\right] = 182$

The bowling average is 182.

b) $\text{INT}\left[\frac{4621}{27}\right] = \text{INT}\left[171\frac{4}{27}\right] = 171$

The bowling average is 171.

80. a) $f_4(7/8) = f_4(0.875000...) = 0$
$f_4(17/23) = f_4(0.739130...) = 1$
$f_4(-49/37) = f_4(-1.324324...) = 3$
$f_4(\sqrt{11}) = f_4(3.316624...) = 6$

b) Domain: The set of all real numbers
Range: {0,1,2,3,4,5,6,7,8,9}

c) $\pi \approx 3.141592654...$
$f_4(\pi) + f_5(\pi) + f_6(\pi) + f_7(\pi) =$
$5 + 9 + 2 + 6 = 22$

81.

INT(y) = INT(x)

This is not the graph of a function, because it fails the vertical line test.

82.

$$f(x) = \begin{cases} 4x^2 - 5x + 3, & x \le -1 \\ 4.4x^3, & -1 < x < 4 \\ |-3x^2 - 4x|, & x \ge 4 \end{cases}$$

DOT MODE

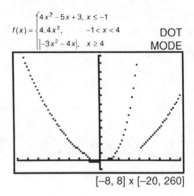

[−8, 8] x [−20, 260]

83.

$$f(x) = \begin{cases} x|x - x^2|, & x < 0 \\ \dfrac{x^3}{1 + x}, & x \ge 0 \end{cases}$$

DOT MODE

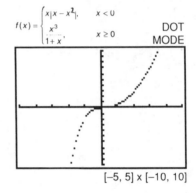

[−5, 5] x [−10, 10]

84. About 71.6 lb

Exercise Set 3.6

1. Test for symmetry with respect to the x-axis.

    3y = x² + 4   (Original equation)
    3(-y) = x² + 4   (Replacing y by -y)
    -3y = x² + 4   (Simplifying)

Since the resulting equation is not equivalent to the original, the graph is not symmetric with respect to the x-axis.

Test for symmetry with respect to the y-axis.

    3y = x² + 4   (Original equation)
    3y = (-x)² + 4   (Replacing x by -x)
    3y = x² + 4   (Simplifying)

Since the resulting equation is equivalent to the original, the graph is symmetric with respect to the y-axis.

Test for symmetry with respect to the origin.

    3y = x² + 4   (Original equation)
    3(-y) = (-x)² + 4   (Replacing x by -x and y by -y)
    -3y = x² + 4   (Simplifying)

Since the resulting equation is not equivalent to the original, the graph is not symmetric with respect to the origin.

2. $5y = 2x^2 - 3$

    x-axis: $5(-y) = 2x^2 - 3$

                 $-5y = 2x^2 - 3$ Not equivalent to the original equation

The graph is not symmetric with respect to the x-axis.

    y-axis: $5y = 2(-x)^2 - 3$

                 $5y = 2x^2 - 3$ Equivalent to the original equation

The graph is symmetric with respect to the y-axis.

    Origin: $5(-y) = 2(-x)^2 - 3$

                 $-5y = 2x^2 - 3$ Not equivalent to the original equation

The graph is not symmetric with respect to the origin.

3. Test for symmetry with respect to the x-axis.

     $y^3 = 2x^2$ (Original equation)

   $(-y)^3 = 2x^2$ (Replacing y by -y)

    $-y^3 = 2x^2$ (Simplifying)

Since the resulting equation is not equivalent to the original, the graph is not symmetric with respect to the x-axis.

Test for symmetry with respect to the y-axis.

$y^3 = 2x^2$ (Original equation)

$y^3 = 2(-x)^2$ (Replacing x by -x)

$y^3 = 2x^2$ (Simplifying)

Since the resulting equation is equivalent to the original, the graph is symmetric with respect to the y-axis.

Test for symmetry with respect to the origin.

     $y^3 = 2x^2$ (Original equation)

  $(-y)^3 = 2(-x)^2$ (Replacing x by -x and y by -y)

   $-y^3 = 2x^2$ (Simplifying)

Since the resulting equation is not equivalent to the original, the graph is not symmetric with respect to the origin.

4. $3y^3 = 4x^2$

    x-axis: $3(-y)^3 = 4x^2$

              $-3y^3 = 4x^2$ Not equivalent to the original equation

The graph is not symmetric with respect to the x-axis.

    y-axis: $3y^3 = 4(-x)^2$

              $3y^3 = 4x^2$ Equivalent to the original equation

The graph is symmetric with respect to the y-axis.

    Origin: $3(-y)^3 = 4(-x)^2$

              $-3y^3 = 4x^2$ Not equivalent to the original equation

The graph is not symmetric with respect to the origin.

5. Test for symmetry with respect to the x-axis.

$2x^4 + 3 = y^2$ (Original equation)

$2x^4 + 3 = (-y)^2$ (Replacing y by -y)

$2x^4 + 3 = y^2$ (Simplifying)

Since the resulting equation is equivalent to the original, the graph is symmetric with respect to the x-axis.

Test for symmetry with respect to the y-axis.

  $2x^4 + 3 = y^2$ (Original equation)

$2(-x)^4 + 3 = y^2$ (Replacing x by -x)

   $2x^4 + 3 = y^2$ (Simplifying)

Since the resulting equation is equivalent to the original, the graph is symmetric with respect to the y-axis.

Test for symmetry with respect to the origin.

  $2x^4 + 3 = y^2$ (Original equation)

$2(-x)^4 + 3 = (-y)^2$ (Replacing x by -x and y by -y)

   $2x^4 + 3 = y^2$ (Simplifying)

Since the resulting equation is equivalent to the original, the graph is symmetric with respect to the origin.

6. $3y^2 = 2x^4 - 5$

    x-axis: $3(-y)^2 = 2x^4 - 5$

              $3y^2 = 2x^4 - 5$ Equivalent to the original equation

The graph is symmetric with respect to the x-axis.

    y-axis: $3y^2 = 2(-x)^4 - 5$

              $3y^2 = 2x^4 - 5$ Equivalent to the original equation

The graph is symmetric with respect to the y-axis.

    Origin: $3(-y)^2 = 2(-x)^4 - 5$

              $3y^2 = 2x^4 - 5$ Equivalent to the original equation

The graph is symmetric with respect to the origin.

7. Test for symmetry with respect to the x-axis.

  $2y^2 = 5x^2 + 12$ (Original equation)

$2(-y)^2 = 5x^2 + 12$ (Replacing y by -y)

  $2y^2 = 5x^2 + 12$ (Simplifying)

Since the resulting equation is equivalent to the original, the graph is symmetric with respect to the x-axis.

Test for symmetry with respect to the y-axis.

$2y^2 = 5x^2 + 12$ (Original equation)

$2y^2 = 5(-x)^2 + 12$ (Replacing x by -x)

$2y^2 = 5x^2 + 12$ (Simplifying)

Since the resulting equation is equivalent to the original, the graph is symmetric with respect to the y-axis.

Test for symmetry with respect to the origin.

$2y^2 = 5x^2 + 12$ (Original equation)

$2(-y)^2 = 5(-x)^2 + 12$ (Replacing x by -x and y by -y)

$2y^2 = 5x^2 + 12$ (Simplifying)

Since the resulting equation is equivalent to the original, the graph <u>is symmetric</u> with respect to the origin.

8. $3x^2 - 2y^2 = 7$

x-axis: $3x^2 - 2(-y)^2 = 7$

$3x^2 - 2y^2 = 7$ Equivalent to the original equation

The graph is symmetric with respect to the x-axis.

y-axis: $3(-x)^2 - 2y^2 = 7$

$3x^2 - 2y^2 = 7$ Equivalent to the original equation

The graph is symmetric with respect to the y-axis.

Origin: $3(-x)^2 - 2(-y)^2 = 7$

$3x^2 - 2y^2 = 7$ Equivalent to the original equation

The graph is symmetric with respect to the origin.

9. Test for symmetry with respect to the x-axis.

$2x - 5 = 3y$ (Original equation)

$2x - 5 = 3(-y)$ (Replacing y by -y)

$2x - 5 = -3y$ (Simplifying)

Since the resulting equation is not equivalent to the original, the graph <u>is not symmetric</u> with respect to the x-axis.

Test for symmetry with respect to the y-axis.

$2x - 5 = 3y$ (Original equation)

$2(-x) - 5 = 3y$ (Replacing x by -x)

$-2x - 5 = 3y$ (Simplifying)

Since the resulting equation is not equivalent to the original, the graph <u>is not symmetric</u> with respect to the y-axis.

Test for symmetry with respect to the origin.

$2x - 5 = 3y$ (Original equation)

$2(-x) - 5 = 3(-y)$ (Replacing x by -x and y by -y)

$-2x - 5 = -3y$ (Simplifying)

or

$2x + 5 = 3y$ (Multiplying by -1)

Since the resulting equation is not equivalent to the original, the graph <u>is not symmetric</u> with respect to the origin.

10. $5y = 4x + 5$

x-axis: $5(-y) = 4x + 5$

$-5y = 4x + 5$ Not equivalent to the original equation

The graph is not symmetric with respect to the x-axis.

y-axis: $5y = 4(-x) + 5$

$5y = -4x + 5$ Not equivalent to the original equation

The graph is not symmetric with respect to the y-axis.

Origin: $5(-y) = 4(-x) + 5$

$-5y = -4x + 5$ Not equivalent to the original equation

The graph is not symmetric with respect to the origin.

11. Test for symmetry with respect to the a-axis.

$3b^3 = 4a^3 + 2$ (Original equation)

$3(-b)^3 = 4a^3 + 2$ (Replacing b by -b)

$-3b^3 = 4a^3 + 2$ (Simplifying)

Since the resulting equation is not equivalent to the original, the graph <u>is not symmetric</u> with respect to the a-axis.

Test for symmetry with respect to the b-axis.

$3b^3 = 4a^3 + 2$ (Original equation)

$3b^3 = 4(-a)^3 + 2$ (Replacing a by -a)

$3b^3 = -4a^3 + 2$ (Simplifying)

Since the resulting equation is not equivalent to the original, the graph <u>is not symmetric</u> with respect to the b-axis.

Test for symmetry with respect to the origin.

$3b^3 = 4a^3 + 2$ (Original equation)

$3(-b)^3 = 4(-a)^3 + 2$ (Replacing a by -a and b by -b)

$-3b^3 = -4a^3 + 2$ (Simplifying)

or

$3b^3 = 4a^3 - 2$ (Multiplying by -1)

Since the resulting equation is not equivalent to the original, the graph <u>is not symmetric</u> with respect to the origin.

12. $p^3 - 4q^3 = 12$

p-axis: $p^3 - (-q)^3 = 12$

$p^3 + 4q^3 = 12$ Not equivalent to the original equation

The graph is not symmetric with respect to the p-axis.

q-axis: $(-p)^3 - 4q^3 = 12$

$-p^3 - 4q^3 = 12$ Not equivalent to the original equation

The graph is not symmetric with respect to the q-axis.

Origin: $(-p)^3 - 4(-q)^3 = 12$

$-p^3 + 4q^3 = 12$ Not equivalent to the original equation

The graph is not symmetric with respect to the origin.

13. $3x^2 - 2y^2 = 3$ (Original equation)

     $3(-x)^2 - 2(-y)^2 = 3$ (Replacing x by -x
                                       and y by -y)

         $3x^2 - 2y^2 = 3$ (Simplifying)

Since the resulting equation is equivalent to the original equation, the graph <u>is symmetric</u> with respect to the origin.

14. $5y^2 = -7x^2 + 4$ (Original equation)

   $5(-y)^2 = -7(-x)^2 + 4$

      $5y^2 = -7x^2 + 4$ Equivalent to the original
                                   equation

The graph is symmetric with respect to the origin.

15. $5x - 5y = 0$ (Original equation)

    $5(-x) - 5(-y) = 0$ (Replacing x by -x
                                   and y by -y)

      $-5x + 5y = 0$ (Simplifying)

        $5x - 5y = 0$ (Multiplying by -1)

Since the resulting equation is equivalent to the original equation, the graph <u>is symmetric</u> with respect to the origin.

16. $3x = 3y$ (Original equation)

  $3(-x) = 3(-y)$

    $-3x = -3y$

      $3x = 3y$ Equivalent to the original equation

The graph is symmetric with respect to the origin.

17. $3x + 3y = 0$ (Original equation)

    $3(-x) + 3(-y) = 0$ (Replacing x by -x
                                   and y by -y)

      $-3x - 3y = 0$ (Simplifying)

        $3x + 3y = 0$ (Multiplying by -1)

Since the resulting equation is equivalent to the original equation, the graph <u>is symmetric</u> with respect to the origin.

18. $7x = -7y$ (Original equation)

  $7(-x) = -7(-y)$

    $-7x = 7y$

      $7x = -7y$ Equivalent to the original equation

The graph is symmetric with respect to the origin.

19. $3x = \dfrac{5}{y}$ (Original equation)

  $3(-x) = \dfrac{5}{-y}$ (Replacing x by -x and y by -y)

    $-3x = -\dfrac{5}{y}$ (Simplifying)

      $3x = \dfrac{5}{y}$ (Multiplying by -1)

Since the resulting equation is equivalent to the original, the graph <u>is symmetric</u> with respect to the origin.

20. $3y = \dfrac{7}{x}$ (Original equation)

  $3(-y) = \dfrac{7}{-x}$

    $-3y = -\dfrac{7}{x}$

      $3y = \dfrac{7}{x}$ Equivalent to the original equation

The graph is symmetric with respect to the origin.

21. $y = |2x|$ (Original equation)

  $-y = |2(-x)|$ (Replacing x by -x and y by -y)

  $-y = |-2x|$

  $-y = |2x|$

Since the resulting equation is not equivalent to the original, the graph <u>is not symmetric</u> with respect to the origin.

22. $3x = |y|$ (Original equation)

  $3(-x) = |-y|$

   $-3x = |y|$ Not equivalent to the original equation

The graph is not symmetric with respect to the origin.

23. $3a^2 + 4a = 2b$ (Original equation)

  $3(-a)^2 + 4(-a) = 2(-b)$ (Replacing a by -a
                                     and b by -b)

       $3a^2 - 4a = -2b$

or

    $-3a^2 + 4a = 2b$

Since the resulting equation is not equivalent to the original, the graph <u>is not symmetric</u> with respect to the origin.

24. $5v = 7u^2 - 2u$ (Original equation)

  $5(-v) = 7(-u)^2 - 2(-u)$

    $-5v = 7u^2 + 2u$

      $5v = -7u^2 - 2u$ Not equivalent to the original equation

The graph is not symmetric with respect to the origin.

25. $3x = 4y$ (Original equation)

  $3(-x) = 4(-y)$ (Replacing x by -x and y by -y)

   $-3x = -4y$ (Simplifying)

    $3x = 4y$ (Multiplying by -1)

Since the resulting equation is equivalent to the original, the graph <u>is symmetric</u> with respect to the origin.

26. $6x + 7y = 0$ (Original equation)

  $6(-x) + 7(-y) = 0$

    $-6x - 7y = 0$

      $6x + 7y = 0$ Equivalent to the original
                                   equation

The graph is symmetric with respect to the origin.

27. $xy = 12$ (Original equation)

  $(-x)(-y) = 12$ (Replacing x by -x and y by -y)

     $xy = 12$ (Simplifying)

Since the resulting equation is equivalent to the original, the graph is symmetric with respect to the origin.

28. $y = -\dfrac{4}{x}$ (Original equation)

  $-y = -\dfrac{4}{-x}$

  $-y = \dfrac{4}{x}$

  $y = -\dfrac{4}{x}$ Equivalent to the original equation

The graph is symmetric with respect to the origin.

29. a) The graph is symmetric with respect to the y-axis. Thus the function is even.

  Reflect the graph across the origin. Are the graphs the same? No.

  The graph is not symmetric with respect to the origin. Thus the function is not odd.

  b) The graph is symmetric with respect to the y-axis. Thus the function is even.

  Reflect the graph across the origin. Are the graphs the same? No.

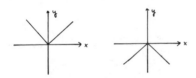

  The graph is not symmetric with respect to the origin. Thus the function is not odd.

  c) Reflect the graph across the y-axis. Are the graphs the same? No.

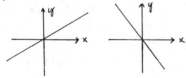

  The graph is not symmetric with respect to the y-axis. Thus the function is not even.

Reflect the graph across the origin. Are the graphs the same? Yes.

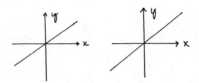

The graph is symmetric with respect to the origin. Thus the function is odd.

  d) Reflect the graph across the y-axis. Are the graphs the same? No.

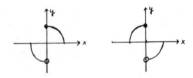

The graph is not symmetric with respect to the y-axis. Thus the function is not even.

Reflect the graph across the origin. Are the graphs the same? No.

The graph is not symmetric with respect to the origin. Thus the function is not odd.

Therefore the function is neither even nor odd.

30. a) The graph is not symmetric with respect to the y-axis, so the function is not even.

  The graph is symmetric with respect to the origin, so the function is odd.

  b) The graph is symmetric with respect to the y-axis, so the function is even.

  The graph is not symmetric with respect to the origin, so the function is not odd.

  c) The graph is not symmetric with respect to the y-axis, so the function is not even.

  The graph is not symmetric with respect to the origin, so the function is not odd.

  d) The graph is not symmetric with respect to the y-axis, so the function is not even.

  The graph is not symmetric with respect to the origin, so the function is not odd.

31. $f(x) = 2x^2 + 4x$

$f(-x) = 2(-x)^2 + 4(-x) = 2x^2 - 4x$

$-f(x) = -(2x^2 + 4x) = -2x^2 - 4x$

Since $f(x)$ and $f(-x)$ are not the same for all x in the domain, <u>f is not an even function.</u>

Since $f(-x)$ and $-f(x)$ are not the same for all x in the domain, f <u>is not an odd function.</u>

Thus, $f(x) = 2x^2 + 4x$ is <u>neither</u> even nor odd.

32. $f(x) = -3x^3 + 2x$

$f(-x) = -3(-x)^3 + 2(-x) = 3x^3 - 2x$

$-f(x) = 3x^3 - 2x$

$f(x) \neq f(-x)$ for all x in the domain, so f is not even.

$f(-x) = -f(x)$ for all x in the domain, so f is odd.

33. $f(x) = 3x^4 - 4x^2$

$f(-x) = 3(-x)^4 - 4(-x)^2 = 3x^4 - 4x^2$

$-f(x) = -(3x^4 - 4x^2) = -3x^4 + 4x^2$

Since $f(x)$ and $f(-x)$ are the same for all x in the domain, <u>f is an even function.</u>

Since $f(-x)$ and $-f(x)$ are not the same for all x in the domain, <u>f is not an odd function.</u>

34. $f(x) = 5x^2 + 2x^4 - 1$

$f(-x) = 5(-x)^2 + 2(-x)^4 - 1 = 5x^2 + 2x^4 - 1$

$-f(x) = -5x^2 - 2x^4 + 1$

$f(x) = f(-x)$ for all x in the domain, so f is even.

$f(-x) \neq -f(x)$ for all x in the domain, so f is not odd.

35. $f(x) = 7x^3 + 4x - 2$

$f(-x) = 7(-x)^3 + 4(-x) - 2 = -7x^3 - 4x - 2$

$-f(x) = -(7x^3 + 4x - 2) = -7x^3 - 4x + 2$

Since $f(x)$ and $f(-x)$ are not the same for all x in the domain, <u>f is not an even function.</u>

Since $f(-x)$ and $-f(x)$ are not the same for all x in the domain, <u>f is not an odd function.</u>

Thus, $f(x) = 7x^3 + 4x - 2$ is <u>neither</u> even nor odd.

36. $f(x) = 4x$

$f(-x) = 4(-x) = -4x$

$-f(x) = -4x$

$f(x) \neq f(-x)$ for all x in the domain, so f is not even.

$f(-x) = -f(x)$ for all x in the domain, so f is odd.

37. $f(x) = |3x|$

$f(-x) = |3(-x)| = |-3x| = |3x|$

$-f(x) = -|3x|$

Since $f(x)$ and $f(-x)$ are the same for all x in the domain, <u>f is an even function.</u>

Since $f(-x)$ and $-f(x)$ are not the same for all x in the domain, <u>f is not an odd function.</u>

38. $f(x) = x^{24}$

$f(-x) = (-x)^{24} = x^{24}$

$-f(x) = -x^{24}$

$f(x) = f(-x)$ for all x in the domain, so f is even.

$f(-x) \neq -f(x)$ for all x in the domain, so f is not odd.

39. $f(x) = x^{17}$

$f(-x) = (-x)^{17} = -x^{17}$

$-f(x) = -(x^{17}) = -x^{17}$

Since $f(x)$ and $f(-x)$ are not the same for all x in the domain, <u>f is not an even function.</u>

Since $f(-x)$ and $-f(x)$ are the same for all x in the domain, <u>f is an odd function.</u>

40. $f(x) = x + \dfrac{1}{x}$

$f(-x) = -x + \dfrac{1}{-x} = -x - \dfrac{1}{x}$

$-f(x) = -x - \dfrac{1}{x}$

$f(x) \neq f(-x)$ for all x in the domain, so f is not even.

$f(-x) = -f(x)$ for all x in the domain, so f is odd.

41. $f(x) = x - |x|$

$f(-x) = (-x) - |(-x)| = -x - |x|$

$-f(x) = -(x - |x|) = -x + |x|$

Since $f(x)$ and $f(-x)$ are not the same for all x in the domain, <u>f is not an even function.</u>

Since $f(-x)$ and $-f(x)$ are not the same for all x in the domain, <u>f is not an odd function.</u>

Therefore, $f(x) = x - |x|$ is <u>neither</u> even nor odd.

42. $f(x) = \sqrt{x}$

$f(-x) = \sqrt{-x}$

$-f(x) = -\sqrt{x}$

$f(x) \neq f(-x)$ for all x in the domain, so f is not even.

$f(-x) \neq -f(x)$ for all x in the domain, so f is not odd.

43. $f(x) = \sqrt[3]{x}$

$f(-x) = \sqrt[3]{-x} = -\sqrt[3]{x}$

$-f(x) = -(\sqrt[3]{x}) = -\sqrt[3]{x}$

Since f(x) and f(-x) are not the same for all x in the domain, <u>f is not an even function.</u>

Since f(-x) and -f(x) are the same for all x in the domain, <u>f is an odd function.</u>

44. $f(x) = 7$

$f(-x) = 7$

$-f(x) = -7$

f(x) = f(-x) for all x in the domain, so f is even.

f(-x) ≠ -f(x) for all x in the domain, so f is not odd.

45. $f(x) = 0$

$f(-x) = 0$

$-f(x) = -(0) = 0$

Since f(x) and f(-x) are the same for all x in the domain, <u>f is an even function.</u>

Since f(-x) and -f(x) are the same for all x in the domain, <u>f is an odd function.</u>

46. $f(x) = -\dfrac{1}{x}$

$f(-x) = -\dfrac{1}{-x} = \dfrac{1}{x}$

$-f(x) = \dfrac{1}{x}$

f(x) ≠ f(-x) for all x in the domain, so f is not even.

f(-x) = -f(x) for all x in the domain, so f is odd.

47.   The vertices of the original polygon are (0, 4), (4, 4), (-2, -2), and (1, -2).

When the graph is reflected across the x-axis the vertices will be (0, -4), (4, -4), (-2, 2), and (1, 2).

48.

49.   The vertices of the original polygon are (0, 4), (4, 4), (1, -2), and (-2, -2).

When the graph is reflected across the line y = x, the vertices will be (4, 0), (4, 4), (-2, 1), and (-2, -2).

50.

51.   See the answer section in the text.

52.   Neither

53.   Odd

54.   Even

55.   Neither

56.   Odd

57.   Even

Exercise Set 3.7

1. $f(x) = x - 3$, $g(x) = x + 4$

    a) $(f + g)(x) = f(x) + g(x) = (x - 3) + (x + 4) = 2x + 1$

    $(f - g)(x) = f(x) - g(x) = (x - 3) - (x + 4) = -7$

    $fg(x) = f(x)g(x) = (x - 3)(x + 4) = x^2 + x - 12$

    $ff(x) = [f(x)]^2 = (x - 3)^2 = x^2 - 6x + 9$

    $(f/g)(x) = \dfrac{f(x)}{g(x)} = \dfrac{x - 3}{x + 4}$

    $(g/f)(x) = \dfrac{g(x)}{f(x)} = \dfrac{x + 4}{x - 3}$

    $f \circ g(x) = f(g(x)) = f(x + 4) = (x + 4) - 3 = x + 1$

    $g \circ f(x) = g(f(x)) = g(x - 3) = (x - 3) + 4 = x + 1$

    b) The domain of f is the set of all real numbers. The domain of g is the set of all real numbers. Then the domain of f + g, f - g, fg, and ff is the set of all real numbers. Since $g(-4) = 0$, the domain of f/g is {x∣x is a real number and $x \neq -4$}. Since $f(3) = 0$, the domain of g/f is {x∣x is a real number and $x \neq 3$}. The domain of f ∘ g and of g ∘ f is the set of all real numbers.

2. a) $(f + g)(x) = x^2 + 2x + 4$

    $(f - g)(x) = x^2 - 2x - 6$

    $fg(x) = 2x^3 + 5x^2 - 2x - 5$

    $ff(x) = x^4 - 2x^2 + 1$

    $(f/g)(x) = \dfrac{x^2 - 1}{2x + 5}$

    $(g/f)(x) = \dfrac{2x + 5}{x^2 - 1}$

    $f \circ g(x) = (2x + 5)^2 - 1 = 4x^2 + 20x + 24$

    $g \circ f(x) = 2(x^2 - 1) + 5 = 2x^2 + 3$

    b) The domain of f and of g is the set of all real numbers. Then the domain of f + g, f - g, fg and ff is the set of all real numbers. Since $g\left(-\dfrac{5}{2}\right) = 0$, the domain of f/g is $\left\{x \middle| x \text{ is a real number and } x \neq -\dfrac{5}{2}\right\}$. Since $f(1) = 0$ and $f(-1) = 0$, the domain of g/f is {x∣x is a real number and $x \neq 1$ and $x \neq -1$}. The domain of f ∘ g and of g ∘ f is the set of all real numbers.

3. $f(x) = x^3$, $g(x) = 2x^2 + 9x - 3$

    a) $(f + g)(x) = f(x) + g(x) = x^3 + 2x^2 + 9x - 3$

    $(f - g)(x) = f(x) - g(x) = x^3 - 2x^2 - 9x + 3$

    $fg(x) = f(x)g(x) = x^3(2x^2 + 9x - 3) = 2x^5 + 9x^4 - 3x^3$

    $ff(x) = [f(x)]^2 = (x^3)^2 = x^6$

    $(f/g)(x) = \dfrac{f(x)}{g(x)} = \dfrac{x^3}{2x^2 + 9x - 3}$

    $(g/f)(x) = \dfrac{2x^2 + 9x - 3}{x^3}$

    $f \circ g(x) = f(g(x)) = f(2x^2 + 9x - 3) = (2x^2 + 9x - 3)^3$

    $g \circ f(x) = g(f(x)) = g(x^3) = 2x^6 + 9x^3 - 3$

    b) The domain of f is the set of all real numbers. The domain of g is the set of all real numbers. Then the domain of f + g, f - g, fg, and ff is the set of all real numbers. Since $g(x) = 0$ when $x = \dfrac{-9 \pm \sqrt{105}}{4}$, the domain of f/g is {x∣x is a real number and $x \neq \dfrac{-9 \pm \sqrt{105}}{4}$}. Since $f(0) = 0$, the domain of g/f is {x∣x is a real number and $x \neq 0$}. The domain of f ∘ g and of g ∘ f is the set of all real numbers.

4. a) $(f + g)(x) = x^2 + \sqrt{x}$, $(f - g)(x) = x^2 - \sqrt{x}$, $fg(x) = x^2\sqrt{x}$, $ff(x) = x^4$, $(f/g)(x) = x^2/\sqrt{x} = x\sqrt{x}$, $(g/f)(x) = \dfrac{\sqrt{x}}{x^2}$, $f \circ g(x) = (\sqrt{x})^2 = x$, $g \circ f(x) = \sqrt{x^2} = |x|$

    b) The domain of f is the set of all real numbers, and the domain of g is {x∣x is a real number and $x \geq 0$}. Then the domain of f + g, f - g, and fg is {x∣x is a real number and $x \geq 0$}. The domain of ff is the set of all real numbers. The domain of f/g and of g/f is {x∣x is a real number and $x > 0$}. The domain of f ∘ g is {x∣x is a real number and $x \geq 0$}, and the domain of g ∘ f is the set of all real numbers.

In Exercises 5 - 20, $f(x) = x^2 - 4$ and $g(x) = 2x + 5$.

5. $(f - g)(3) = f(3) - g(3) = (3^2 - 4) - (2 \cdot 3 + 5) = 5 - 11 = -6$

6. $(f + g)(-1) = [(-1^2) - 4] + [2(-1) + 5] = 0$

7. $(f - g)(x) = f(x) - g(x) = (x^2 - 4) - (2x + 5) = x^2 - 2x - 9$

8. $(f + g)(x) = (x^2 - 4) + (2x + 5) = x^2 + 2x + 1$

9. $fg(3) = f(3)g(3) = (3^2 - 4)(2 \cdot 3 + 5) = 5 \cdot 11 = 55$

10. $(f/g)(-1) = \dfrac{(-1)^2 - 4}{2(-1) + 5} = -1$

11. $(g/f)(-2) = \dfrac{g(-2)}{f(-2)} = \dfrac{2(-2) + 5}{(-2)^2 - 4} = \dfrac{-4 + 5}{4 - 4} = \dfrac{1}{0}$, which does not exist

12. $(f/g)(-2.5) = \dfrac{(-2.5)^2 - 4}{2(-2.5) + 5} = \dfrac{2.25}{0}$

    Does not exist

13. $fg(x) = f(x)g(x) = (x^2 - 4)(2x + 5) =$
    $2x^3 + 5x^2 - 8x - 20$

14. $(f/g)(x) = \dfrac{x^2 - 4}{2x + 5}$

15. $(g/f)(x) = \dfrac{g(x)}{f(x)} = \dfrac{2x + 5}{x^2 - 4}$

16. $ff(x) = (x^2 - 4)(x^2 - 4) = x^4 - 8x^2 + 16$

17. $f \circ g(x) = f(g(x)) = f(2x + 5) = (2x + 5)^2 - 4 =$
    $4x^2 + 20x + 25 - 4 = 4x^2 + 20x + 21$

18. $f \circ f(x) = (x^2 - 4)^2 - 4 = x^4 - 8x^2 + 12$

19. $g \circ g(x) = g(g(x)) = g(2x + 5) = 2(2x + 5) + 5 =$
    $4x + 10 + 5 = 4x + 15$

20. $g \circ f(x) = 2(x^2 - 4) + 5 = 2x^2 - 3$

21. $R(x) = 60x - 0.4x^2$, $C(x) = 3x + 13$

    a) $P(x) = R(x) - C(x)$
    $= (60x - 0.4x^2) - (3x + 13)$
    $= -0.4x^2 + 57x - 13$

    b) $R(20) = 60(20) - 0.4(20)^2$
    $= 1200 - 0.4(400) = 1200 - 160$
    $= 1040$

    $C(20) = 3(20) + 13 = 60 + 13$
    $= 73$

    $P(20) = R(20) - C(20)$
    $= 1040 - 73$
    $= 967$

22. a) $P(x) = -0.001x^2 + 13.8x - 60$
    b) $R(100) = 1500$, $C(100) = 190$, $P(100) = 1310$

23. $f \circ g(x) = f(g(x)) = f\left[\dfrac{5}{4}x\right] = \dfrac{4}{5} \cdot \dfrac{5}{4}x = x$

    $g \circ f(x) = g(f(x)) = g\left[\dfrac{4}{5}x\right] = \dfrac{5}{4} \cdot \dfrac{4}{5}x = x$

24. $f \circ g(x) = (x - 3) + 3 = x$
    $g \circ f(x) = (x + 3) - 3 = x$

25. $f \circ g(x) = f(g(x)) = f\left[\dfrac{x + 7}{3}\right] = 3\left[\dfrac{x + 7}{3}\right] - 7 =$
    $x + 7 - 7 = x$

    $g \circ f(x) = g(f(x)) = g(3x - 7) = \dfrac{(3x - 7) + 7}{3} =$
    $\dfrac{3x}{3} = x$

26. $f \circ g(x) = \dfrac{2}{3}(1.5x + 1.2) - \dfrac{4}{5} = x + 0.8 - \dfrac{4}{5} = x$

    $g \circ f(x) = 1.5\left[\dfrac{2}{3}x - \dfrac{4}{5}\right] + 1.2 = x - 1.2 + 1.2 = x$

27. $f \circ g(x) = f(g(x)) = f(\sqrt[3]{x + 1}) = (\sqrt[3]{x + 1})^3 - 1 =$
    $x + 1 - 1 = x$

    $g \circ f(x) = g(f(x)) = g(x^3 - 1) = \sqrt[3]{(x^3 - 1) + 1} =$
    $\sqrt[3]{x^3} = x$

28. $f \circ g(x) = \sqrt[5]{x^5 - 2 + 2} = x$
    $g \circ f(x) = (\sqrt[5]{x + 2})^5 - 2 = x + 2 - 2 = x$

29. $f \circ g(x) = f(g(x)) = f(x^2 - 5) = \sqrt{x^2 - 5 + 5} =$
    $\sqrt{x^2} = |x|$

    $g \circ f(x) = g(f(x)) = g(\sqrt{x + 5}) = (\sqrt{x + 5})^2 - 5 =$
    $x + 5 - 5 = x$

30. $f \circ g(x) = (\sqrt[4]{x})^4 = x$
    $g \circ f(x) = \sqrt[4]{x^4} = |x|$

31. $f \circ g(x) = f(g(x)) = f\left[\dfrac{1}{1 + x}\right] = \dfrac{1 - \left[\dfrac{1}{1 + x}\right]}{\dfrac{1}{1 + x}} =$

    $\dfrac{\dfrac{1 + x - 1}{1 + x}}{\dfrac{1}{1 + x}} = \dfrac{x}{1 + x} \cdot \dfrac{1 + x}{1} = x$

    $g \circ f(x) = g(f(x)) = g\left[\dfrac{1 - x}{x}\right] = \dfrac{1}{1 + \left[\dfrac{1 - x}{x}\right]} =$

    $\dfrac{1}{\dfrac{x + 1 - x}{x}} = \dfrac{1}{\dfrac{1}{x}} = 1 \cdot \dfrac{x}{1} = x$

32. $f \circ g(x) = \dfrac{\left[\dfrac{3x - 4}{5x - 2}\right]^2 - 1}{\left[\dfrac{3x - 4}{5x - 2}\right]^2 + 1} = \dfrac{-8x^2 - 2x + 6}{17x^2 - 22x + 10}$

    $g \circ f(x) = \dfrac{3\left[\dfrac{x^2 - 1}{x^2 + 1}\right] - 4}{5\left[\dfrac{x^2 - 1}{x^2 + 1}\right] - 2} = \dfrac{-x^2 - 7}{3x^2 - 7}$

33. $f \circ g(x) = f(g(x)) = f(12) = -6$
    $g \circ f(x) = g(f(x)) = g(-6) = 12$

34. $f \circ g(x) = 20$, $g \circ f(x) = 0.2(20) + 1 = 5$

35. h(x) = (4 - 3x)⁵

This is 4 - 3x to the 5th power. The most obvious answer is f(x) = x⁵ and g(x) = 4 - 3x.

36. $f(x) = \sqrt[3]{x}$, g(x) = x² - 8

37. $h(x) = \dfrac{1}{(x - 1)^4}$

This is 1 divided by (x - 1) to the 4th power. One obvious answer is $f(x) = \dfrac{1}{x^4}$ and g(x) = (x - 1).

38. $f(x) = \dfrac{1}{\sqrt{x}}$, g(x) = 3x + 7

39. $f(x) = \dfrac{x - 1}{x + 1}$, g(x) = x³

40. f(x) = |x|, g(x) = 9x² - 4

41. $f(x) = x^6$, $g(x) = \dfrac{2 + x^3}{2 - x^3}$

42. f(x) = x⁴, $g(x) = \sqrt{x} - 3$

43. $f(x) = \sqrt{x}$, $g(x) = \dfrac{x - 5}{x + 2}$

44. $f(x) = \sqrt{1 + x}$, $g(x) = \sqrt{1 + x}$

45. f(x) = x⁵ + x⁴ + x³ - x² + 4x, g(x) = x + 3

46. h(x) = 4(x - 1)²ᐟ³ + 5

f(x) = 4x²ᐟ³ + 5, g(x) = x - 1

47. a) Recall that distance = rate × time. Then
$$a(t) = 250t.$$

b) The plane's distance from the control tower is the sum of 300 ft and the distance a the plane has traveled down the runway. Thus,
$$P(a) = 300 + a.$$

c) (P ∘ a)(t) = P(a(t)) = 300 + 250t

This function gives the plane's distance from the control tower in terms of the time t the plane travels.

48. a) r(t) = 3t

b) A(r) = πr²

c) (A ∘ r)(t) = π(3t)², or 9πt²

This function gives the area of the ripple in terms of the time, t.

49. First we graph both functions on the same axes.

Then we graph y = (f + g)(x) by adding second coordinates. The following table shows some examples.

First coordinate	Second coordinates		
x	f(x)	g(x)	(f + g)(x)
-1	1	5	6
0	0	3	3
1	1	1	2
2	4	-1	3
3	9	-3	6

We sketch the graph of y = (f + g)(x).

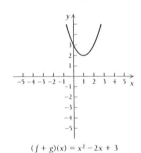

$(f + g)(x) = x^2 - 2x + 3$

50.

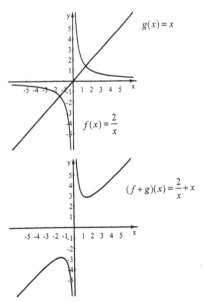

$g(x) = x$

$f(x) = \dfrac{2}{x}$

$(f + g)(x) = \dfrac{2}{x} + x$

51. First we graph both functions on the same axes.

Then we graph y = (f + g)(x) by adding second coordinates. The following table shows some examples. Note that we can only add second coordinates for first coordinates x such that x ⩾ 0.

First coordinate	Second coordinates		
x	f(x)	g(x)	(f + g)(x)
0	0	1	1
0.5	0.707	0.75	1.457
1	1	0	1
1.5	1.225	-1.25	-0.025
2	1.414	-3	-1.586
3	1.732	-8	-6.268

We sketch the graph of y = (f + g)(x).

$(f + g)(x) = 1 - x^2 + \sqrt{x}$

52.

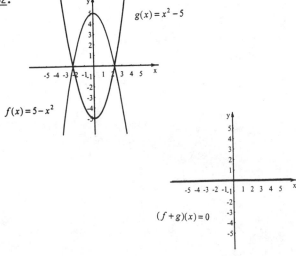

$(f + g)(x) = 0$

53. $f \circ g(x) = f(g(x)) = f(2x - 1) = 3(2x - 1) + b =$
    $6x - 3 + b$

   $g \circ f(x) = g(f(x)) = g(3x + b) = 2(3x + b) - 1 =$
    $6x + 2b - 1$

   Now $f \circ g(x) = g \circ f(x)$ means
    $6x - 3 + b = 6x + 2b - 1$, or
    $-2 = b$

54. $f \circ g(x) = 3(mx + b) - 4 = 3mx + 3b - 4 = x$, so
    $f \circ g(0) = 3b - 4 = 0$, so $b = \frac{4}{3}$.

   $g \circ f(x) = m(3x - 4) + b = 3mx - 4m + \frac{4}{3} = x$, so
    $g \circ f(0) = -4m + \frac{4}{3} = 0$, so $m = \frac{1}{3}$.

55. $f \circ f(x) = f(f(x)) = \dfrac{1}{1 - \dfrac{1}{1 - x}} = \dfrac{1}{\dfrac{1 - x - 1}{1 - x}} =$

   $\dfrac{1}{\dfrac{-x}{1 - x}} = \dfrac{1 - x}{-x}$, or $\dfrac{x - 1}{x}$

   $f \circ f \circ f(x) = f[f(f(x))] = \dfrac{1}{1 - \dfrac{x - 1}{x}} =$

   $\dfrac{1}{\dfrac{x - (x - 1)}{x}} = \dfrac{1}{\dfrac{1}{x}} = x$

56. Let f(x) and g(x) be even functions. Then by definition f(x) = f(-x) and g(x) = g(-x). Now f ∘ g(x) = f(g(x)) = f(g(-x)) = f ∘ g(-x) and g ∘ f(x) = g(f(x)) = g(f(-x)) = g ∘ f(-x). Thus the composition of two even functions is even.

57. See the answer section in the text.

58. Let f(x) and g(x) be odd functions. By definition f(-x) = -f(x), or f(x) = -f(-x), and g(-x) = -g(x), or g(x) = -g(-x). Then fg(x) = f(x)·g(x) = [-f(-x)]·[-g(-x)] = f(-x)·g(-x) = fg(-x), so fg is even.

59. See the answer section in the text.

60. Let f(x) be an even function, and let g(x) be an odd function. By definition f(x) = f(-x) and g(-x) = -g(x), or g(x) = -g(-x). Then fg(x) = f(x)·g(x) = f(-x)·[-g(-x)] = -f(-x)·g(-x) = -fg(-x), and fg is odd.

61. See the answer section in the text.

62. $E(-x) = \dfrac{f(-x) + f(-(-x))}{2} = \dfrac{f(-x) + f(x)}{2} = E(x)$.

   Thus E(x) is even.

63. See the answer section in the text.

64. $E(x) + O(x) = \dfrac{f(x) + f(-x)}{2} + \dfrac{f(x) - f(-x)}{2} =$

   $\dfrac{2f(x)}{2} = f(x)$

65. f(x) = |x| + INT(x)

This function can also be expressed as a piecewise function with an infinite number of statements:

$$f(x) = |x| + INT(x) = \begin{cases} \vdots \\ -x - 3 & \text{if } -3 \leqslant x < -2 \\ -x - 2 & \text{if } -2 \leqslant x < -1 \\ -x - 1 & \text{if } -1 \leqslant x < 0 \\ x & \text{if } 0 \leqslant x < 1 \\ x + 1 & \text{if } 1 \leqslant x < 2 \\ x + 2 & \text{if } 2 \leqslant x < 3 \\ \vdots \end{cases}$$

We sketch a graph of the function.

$f(x) = |x| + INT(x)$

Exercise Set 3.8

1. f(x) = |x| - 3

By Theorem 5, the graph of f(x) = |x| - 3 is a shift of the graph of f(x) = |x| downward 3 units.

- - - - -   f(x) = |x|
_____   f(x) = |x| - 3

2. f(x) = 2 + |x|

3. f(x) = |x - 1|

The equation f(x) = |x - 1| is obtained from the equation f(x) = |x| is obtained by replacing x by x - 1. By Theorem 6, the graph of f(x) = |x - 1| is a shift of the graph of f(x) = |x| one unit to the right.

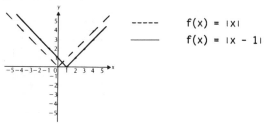

- - - - -   f(x) = |x|
_____   f(x) = |x - 1|

4. f(x) = |x + 2|

5. f(x) = -4|x|

By Theorem 7, the graph of f(x) = -4|x| can be obtained from the graph of f(x) = |x| by stretching vertically and reflecting across the x-axis. The y-coordinate of each ordered-pair solution of f(x) = |x| is multiplied by -4.

- - - - -   f(x) = |x|
_____   f(x) = -4|x|

6. f(x) = 3|x|

7. $f(x) = \frac{1}{3}|x|$

By Theorem 7, the graph of $f(x) = \frac{1}{3}|x|$ can be obtained from the graph of $f(x) = |x|$ by shrinking vertically. The y-coordinate of each ordered-pair solution of $f(x) = |x|$ is multiplied by $\frac{1}{3}$.

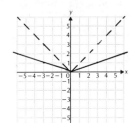

```
-----     f(x) = |x|
_____     f(x) = 1/3 |x|
```

8. $f(x) = -\frac{1}{4}|x|$

9. $f(x) = |2x|$, or $f(x) = 2|x|$

By Theorem 7, the graph of $f(x) = |2x|$ can be obtained from the graph of $f(x) = |x|$ by stretching vertically. The y-coordinate of each ordered-pair solution of $f(x) = |x|$ is multiplied by 2. (Equivalently, we could use Theorem 4 and shrink the graph of $f(x) = |x|$ horizontally. The result is the same in either case.)

```
-----     f(x) = |x|
_____     f(x) = |2x|
```

10. $f(x) = \left|\frac{x}{3}\right|$

11. $f(x) = |x - 2| + 3$

We translate the graph of $f(x) = |x|$ two units to the right (Theorem 6) and upward 3 units (Theorem 5).

```
-----     f(x) = |x|
_____     f(x) = |x - 2| + 3
```

12. $f(x) = 2|x + 1| - 3$

13. $f(x) = -3|x - 2|$

We translate the graph of $f(x) = |x|$ to the right 2 units (Theorem 6), stretch it vertically, and reflect it across the x-axis (Theorem 7).

```
-----     f(x) = |x|
_____     f(x) = -3|x - 2|
```

14. $f(x) = \frac{1}{3}|x + 2| + 1$

15. $y = 2 + f(x)$

We translate the graph of $y = f(x)$ upward 2 units (Theorem 5).

```
-----     y = f(x)
_____     y = 2 + f(x)
```

<u>16.</u>   y = f(x) - 1

<u>17.</u>   y = f(x - 1)

We translate the graph of y = f(x) one unit to the right (Theorem 6).

-----   y = f(x)

———   y = f(x - 1)

<u>18.</u>   y = f(x + 2)

<u>19.</u>   y = -2f(x)

We stretch the graph of y = f(x) vertically and reflect it across the x-axis (Theorem 7). The y-coordinate of each ordered-pair solution of y = f(x) is multiplied by -2.

-----   y = f(x)

——— $\frac{y}{-2}$ = f(x)

<u>20.</u>   y = 3f(x)

<u>21.</u>   y = $\frac{1}{3}$f(x)

We shrink the graph of y = f(x) vertically (Theorem 7). The y-coordinate of each ordered-pair solution of y = f(x) is multiplied by $\frac{1}{3}$.

-----   y = f(x)

———   y = $\frac{1}{3}$f(x)

<u>22.</u>   y = $-\frac{1}{2}$f(x)

<u>23.</u>   y = f(2x)

We shrink the graph of y = f(x) horizontally (Theorem 8). The x-coordinate of each ordered-pair solution of y = f(x) is divided by 2.

-----   y = f(x)

———   y = f(2x)

24.   y = f(3x)

25.   y = f(-2x)

We shrink the graph of y = f(x) horizontally and reflect it across the y-axis (Theorem 8). The x-coordinate of each ordered-pair solution of y = f(x) is divided by -2.

```
----- 	 y = f(x)
_____ 	 y = f(-2x)
```

26.   y = f(-3x)

27. $y = f\left[\frac{x}{-2}\right]$, or $y = f\left[-\frac{1}{2}x\right]$

We stretch the graph of y = f(x) horizontally and reflect it across the y-axis (Theorem 8). The x-coordinate of each ordered-pair solution of y = f(x) is divided by $-\frac{1}{2}$.

```
----- 	 y = f(x)
_____ 	 y = f[x/-2]
```

(8,0)

28. $y = f\left[\frac{1}{3}x\right]$

(-12,0)   (9,0)

29.   y = f(x - 2) + 3

We translate the graph of y = f(x) two units to the right (Theorem 6) and upward 3 units (Theorem 5).

(2,7)

```
----- 	 y = f(x)
_____ 	 y = f(x - 2) + 3
```

30.   y = -3f(x - 2)

(4,12)

(2,-12)

31.   y = 2·f(x + 1) - 2

We translate the graph of y = f(x) one unit to the left to obtain the graph of y = f(x + 1). (Theorem 6)

Then we stretch the graph of y = f(x + 1) vertically, multiplying each y-coordinate by 2, to obtain the graph of y = 2·f(x + 1). (Theorem 7) Finally we translate the graph of y = 2·f(x + 1) downward 2 units to obtain the graph of y = 2·f(x + 1) - 2. (Theorem 5)

```
----- 	 y = f(x)
_____ 	 y = 2·f(x + 1) - 2
```

(1,-10)

32. $y = \frac{1}{2}f(x + 2) - 1$

33. $y = -\frac{1}{2}f(x - 3) + 2$

We translate the graph of $y = f(x)$ three units to the right to obtain the graph of $y = f(x - 3)$. (Theorem 6)

Then we shrink the graph of $y = f(x - 3)$ vertically and reflect it across the x-axis, multiplying each y-coordinate by $-\frac{1}{2}$, to obtain the graph of $y = -\frac{1}{2}f(x - 3)$. (Theorem 7)

Finally we translate the graph of $y = -\frac{1}{2}f(x - 3)$ upward 2 units to obtain the graph of $y = -\frac{1}{2}f(x - 3) + 2$. (Theorem 5)

----- $y = f(x)$

——— $y = -\frac{1}{2}f(x - 3) + 2$

34. $y = -3f(x - 1) + 4$

35. $y = -2f(x + 1) - 1$

We translate the graph of $y = f(x)$ one unit to the left to obtain the graph of $y = f(x + 1)$. (Theorem 6)

Then we stretch the graph of $y = f(x + 1)$ vertically and reflect it across the x-axis, multiplying each y-coordinate by -2, to obtain the graph of $y = -2f(x + 1)$. (Theorem 7)
Finally we translate the graph of $y = -2f(x + 1)$ downward 1 unit to obtain the graph of $y = -2f(x + 1) - 1$. (Theorem 5)

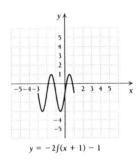

$y = -2f(x + 1) - 1$

36.

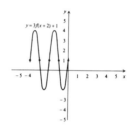

37. $y = \frac{5}{2}f(x - 3) - 2$

We translate the graph of $y = f(x)$ three units to the right to obtain the graph of $y = f(x - 3)$. (Theorem 6)

Then we stretch the graph of $y = f(x - 3)$ vertically, multiplying each y-coordinate by $\frac{5}{2}$, to obtain the graph of $y = \frac{5}{2}f(x - 3)$.

(Theorem 7)

Finally we translate the graph of $y = \frac{5}{2}f(x - 3)$ downward 2 units to obtain the graph of $y = \frac{5}{2}f(x - 3) - 2$. (Theorem 5)

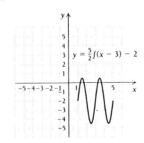

38. $y = -\frac{2}{3}f(x - 4) + 3$

39. $y = -\sqrt{2}\, f(x + 1.8)$

The graph of $y = f(x)$ is translated 1.8 units to the left to obtain the graph of $y = f(x + 1.8)$. Then the graph of $y = f(x + 1.8)$ is stretched vertically and reflected across the x-axis, multiplying each y-coordinate by $-\sqrt{2}$.

40. $y = \frac{\sqrt{3}}{2} \cdot f(x - 2.5) - 5.3$

Translate 2.5 units to the right, then shrink vertically by a factor of $\frac{\sqrt{3}}{2}$; finally translate 5.3 units downward.

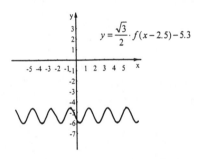

41. The original graph is shifted upward two units. A formula for the transformed function is $g(x) = f(x) + 2$, or $g(x) = x^3 - 3x^2 + 2$.

42. The original graph is shrunk vertically by a factor of $\frac{1}{2}$. We have $h(x) = \frac{1}{2}f(x)$, or $h(x) = \frac{1}{2}(x^3 - 3x^2)$.

43. The original graph is shifted to the left one unit. A formula for the transformed function is $k(x) = f(x + 1)$, or $k(x) = (x + 1)^3 - 3(x + 1)^2$.

44. The original graph is shifted to the right two units and upward one unit. A formula for the transformed function is $t(x) = (x - 2)^3 - 3(x - 2)^2 + 1$.

45. - - - - - - - - - (1) $y = f(x)$ is the given function

—— —— (2) $y = 3f(2x)$ is the result of shrinking (1) horizontally by a factor of $\frac{1}{2}$ and stretching vertically by a factor of 3

———— (3) $y = 3f\left[2\left(x + \frac{1}{4}\right)\right]$, the required graph, is a shift of (2) to the left $\frac{1}{4}$ unit.

46. (1) $y = f(x)$ is the given graph.

(2) $y = -f(5x)$ is the result of reflecting (1) across the x-axis and then shrinking horizontally by a factor of $\frac{1}{5}$.

(3) $y = -4 \cdot f[5(x + 2)]$, the required graph, is a stretching of (2) vertically by a factor of 4 followed by a shift to the left 2 units.

47. $f(x) = x^2|x|$

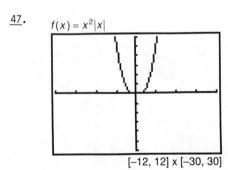

$[-12, 12] \times [-30, 30]$

$f(x) = (4.7x)^2 |4.7x|$

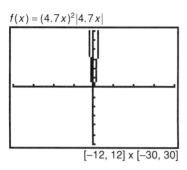

[−12, 12] x [−30, 30]

$f(x) = -2.5x^2 |x|$

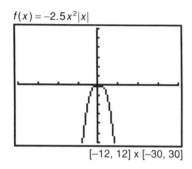

[−12, 12] x [−30, 30]

$f(x) = x^2 |x| - 11.5$

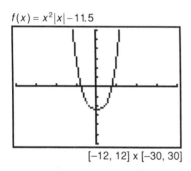

[−12, 12] x [−30, 30]

$f(x) = (x + 9.9)^2 |x + 9.9|$

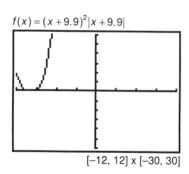

[−12, 12] x [−30, 30]

48. $f(x) = \dfrac{1 - 4x^3}{x^2}$

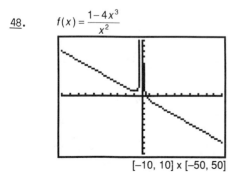

[−10, 10] x [−50, 50]

$f(x) = \dfrac{1 - 4x^3}{x^2} + 34.1$

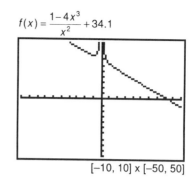

[−10, 10] x [−50, 50]

$f(x) = \dfrac{1 - 4x^3}{3x^2}$

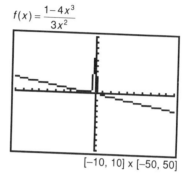

[−10, 10] x [−50, 50]

$f(x) = \dfrac{1 - 4(0.35x)^3}{(0.35x)^2}$

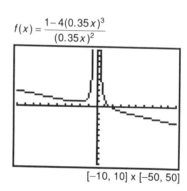

[−10, 10] x [−50, 50]

$f(x) = \dfrac{1 - 4(x - 8.1)^3}{(x - 8.1)^2}$

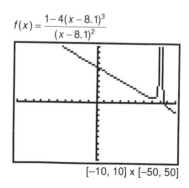

[−10, 10] x [−50, 50]

Exercise Set 4.1

<u>1.</u> $f(x) = x^2$

$f(x) = (x - 0)^2 + 0$ [In the form
$f(x) = a(x - h)^2 + k$]

a) The vertex is $(0, 0)$.

b) The line of symmetry goes through the vertex;
it is the line $x = 0$.

c) Since the coefficient of x^2 is positive
$(1 > 0)$, the parabola opens upward. Thus we
have a <u>minimum</u> value which is 0.

<u>2.</u> $f(x) = -5x^2$

$f(x) = -5(x - 0)^2 + 0$

a) $(0, 0)$,   b) $x = 0$,   c) 0 is a maximum,
because the coefficient of x^2 is negative.

<u>3.</u> $f(x) = -2(x - 9)^2$

$f(x) = -2(x - 9)^2 + 0$ [In the form
$f(x) = a(x - h)^2 + k$]

a) The vertex is $(9, 0)$.

b) The line of symmetry goes through the vertex;
it is the line $x = 9$.

c) Since the coefficient of x^2 is negative
$(-2 < 0)$, the parabola opens downward. Thus
we have a <u>maximum</u> value which is 0.

<u>4.</u> $f(x) = 5(x - 7)^2$

$f(x) = 5(x - 7)^2 + 0$

a) $(7, 0)$,   b) $x = 7$,   c) 0 is a minimum,
because the coefficient of x^2 is positive.

<u>5.</u> $f(x) = 2(x - 1)^2 - 4$

$f(x) = 2(x - 1)^2 + (-4)$ [In the form
$f(x) = a(x - h)^2 + k$]

a) The vertex is $(1, -4)$

b) The line of symmetry goes through the vertex;
it is the line $x = 1$.

c) Since the coefficient of x^2 is positive
$(2 > 0)$, the parabola opens upward. Thus we
have a <u>minimum</u> value which is -4.

<u>6.</u> $f(x) = -(x + 4)^2 - 3$

$f(x) = -[x - (-4)]^2 + (-3)$

a) $(-4, -3)$,   b) $x = -4$,   c) -3 is a maximum,
because the coefficient of x^2 is negative.

<u>7.</u> a) $f(x) = -x^2 + 2x + 3$

$= -(x^2 - 2x) + 3$

$= -(x^2 - 2x + 1 - 1) + 3$

(Adding 1 - 1 inside parentheses)

$= -(x^2 - 2x + 1) + 1 + 3$

$= -(x - 1)^2 + 4$ [In the form
$f(x) = a(x - h)^2 + k$]

b) The vertex is $(1, 4)$.

c) Since the coefficient of x^2 is negative
$(-1 < 0)$, the parabola opens downward. Thus
we have a <u>maximum</u> value which is 4.

<u>8.</u> a) $f(x) = -x^2 + 8x - 7$

$f(x) = -(x^2 - 8x + 16 - 16) - 7$

$f(x) = -(x - 4)^2 + 9$

b) $(4, 9)$

c) 9 is a maximum, because the coefficient of
x^2 is negative.

<u>9.</u> a) $f(x) = x^2 + 3x$

$= x^2 + 3x + \frac{9}{4} - \frac{9}{4}$ $\left(\text{Adding } \frac{9}{4} - \frac{9}{4}\right)$

$= \left(x + \frac{3}{2}\right)^2 - \frac{9}{4}$

$= \left[x - \left(-\frac{3}{2}\right)\right]^2 + \left(-\frac{9}{4}\right)$

[In the form $f(x) = a(x - h)^2 + k$]

b) The vertex is $\left(-\frac{3}{2}, -\frac{9}{4}\right)$.

c) Since the coefficient of x^2 is positive
$(1 > 0)$, the parabola opens upward. Thus we
have a <u>minimum</u> value which is $-\frac{9}{4}$.

<u>10.</u> a) $f(x) = x^2 - 9x$

$f(x) = x^2 - 9x + \frac{81}{4} - \frac{81}{4}$

$f(x) = \left(x - \frac{9}{2}\right)^2 + \left(-\frac{81}{4}\right)$

b) $\left(\frac{9}{2}, -\frac{81}{4}\right)$

c) $-\frac{81}{4}$ is a minimum, because the coefficient
of x^2 is positive.

<u>11.</u> a) $f(x) = -\frac{3}{4}x^2 + 6x$

$= -\frac{3}{4}(x^2 - 8x)$

$= -\frac{3}{4}(x^2 - 8x + 16 - 16)$

(Adding 16 - 16 inside
parentheses)

$= -\frac{3}{4}(x^2 - 8x + 16) + 12$

$= -\frac{3}{4}(x - 4)^2 + 12$

[In the form $f(x) = a(x - h)^2 + k$]

b) The vertex is $(4, 12)$.

c) Since the coefficient of x^2 is negative
$\left(-\frac{3}{4} < 0\right)$, the parabola opens downward. Thus
we have a <u>maximum</u> value which is 12.

12. a) $f(x) = \frac{3}{2}x^2 + 3x$

$f(x) = \frac{3}{2}(x^2 + 2x + 1 - 1)$

$f(x) = \frac{3}{2}(x + 1)^2 - \frac{3}{2}$

$f(x) = \frac{3}{2}[x - (-1)]^2 + \left[-\frac{3}{2}\right]$

b) $\left[-1, -\frac{3}{2}\right]$

c) $-\frac{3}{2}$ is a minimum, because the coefficient of of x^2 is positive.

13. a) $f(x) = 3x^2 + x - 4$

$= 3\left[x^2 + \frac{1}{3}x\right] - 4$

$= 3\left[x^2 + \frac{1}{3}x + \frac{1}{36} - \frac{1}{36}\right] - 4$

$\left[\text{Adding } \frac{1}{36} - \frac{1}{36} \text{ inside parentheses}\right]$

$= 3\left[x^2 + \frac{1}{3}x + \frac{1}{36}\right] - \frac{1}{12} - 4$

$= 3\left[x + \frac{1}{6}\right]^2 - \frac{49}{12}$

$= 3\left[x - \left[-\frac{1}{6}\right]\right]^2 + \left[-\frac{49}{12}\right]$

[In the form $f(x) = a(x - h)^2 + k$]

b) The vertex is $\left[-\frac{1}{6}, -\frac{49}{12}\right]$.

c) Since the coefficient of x^2 is positive $(3 > 0)$, the parabola opens upward. Thus we have a _minimum_ value which is $-\frac{49}{12}$.

14. a) $f(x) = -2x^2 + x - 1$

$f(x) = -2\left[x^2 - \frac{1}{2}x + \frac{1}{16} - \frac{1}{16}\right] - 1$

$f(x) = -2\left[x - \frac{1}{4}\right]^2 + \left[-\frac{7}{8}\right]$

b) $\left[\frac{1}{4}, -\frac{7}{8}\right]$

c) $-\frac{7}{8}$ is a maximum, because the coefficient of x^2 is negative.

15. $f(x) = -5(x + 2)^2$

$f(x) = -5[x - (-2)]^2 + 0$

The value 0 is a maximum since the coefficient -5 is negative.

16. $f(x) = 0.4(x - 3)^2 + 0$

Minimum: 0

17. $f(x) = 8(x - 1)^2 + 5$

The value 5 is a minimum since the coefficient 8 is positive.

18. $f(x) = -6(x - 4)^2 + (-11)$

Maximum: -11

19. $f(x) = -4x^2 + x - 13$

$a = -4, b = 1, c = -13$

Since we want only the maximum or minimum value of the function, we find the second coordinate of the vertex:

$-\frac{b^2 - 4ac}{4a} = -\frac{1^2 - 4(-4)(-13)}{4(-4)}$

$= -\frac{207}{16}$

The value $-\frac{207}{16}$ is a maximum since the coefficient of x^2 is negative.

20. $f(x) = \frac{2}{3}x^2 + 0.1x + 3.9$

$-\frac{b^2 - 4ac}{4a} = -\frac{(0.1)^2 - 4\left[\frac{2}{3}\right](3.9)}{4\left[\frac{2}{3}\right]} = 3.89625$

Minimum: 3.89625

21. $f(x) = \frac{1}{2}x^2 - \frac{2}{5}x - \frac{67}{100}$

$a = \frac{1}{2}, b = -\frac{2}{5}, c = -\frac{67}{100}$

The second coordinate of the vertex is

$-\frac{b^2 - 4ac}{4a} = -\frac{\left[-\frac{2}{5}\right]^2 - 4\left[\frac{1}{2}\right]\left[-\frac{67}{100}\right]}{4\left[\frac{1}{2}\right]}$

$= -\frac{3}{4}.$

The value $-\frac{3}{4}$ is a minimum since the coefficient of x^2 is positive.

22. $f(x) = -31.8x^2 + 12.3x - 17.2$

$-\frac{b^2 - 4ac}{4a} = -\frac{(12.3)^2 - 4(-31.8)(-17.2)}{4(-31.8)} \approx 16.0106$

Maximum: -16.0106

23. $q(x) = -\$120{,}000x^2 + \$430{,}000x - \$240{,}000$

$a = -\$120{,}000, b = \$430{,}000, c = -\$240{,}000$

The second coordinate of the vertex is

$-\frac{b^2 - 4ac}{4a} =$

$-\frac{(\$430{,}000)^2 - 4(-\$120{,}000)(-\$240{,}000)}{4(-\$120{,}000)} =$

$\$\frac{435{,}625}{3}$

The value $\$\frac{435{,}625}{3}$ is a maximum since the coefficient of x^2 is negative.

24. $g(x) = \sqrt{8}x^2 - \pi x + \sqrt{5}$

$-\dfrac{b^2 - 4ac}{4a} = -\dfrac{(-\pi)^2 - 4\sqrt{8}\sqrt{5}}{4\sqrt{8}} =$

$-\dfrac{\pi^2 - 8\sqrt{10}}{8\sqrt{2}} \approx 1.3637$

Minimum: $-\dfrac{\pi^2 - 8\sqrt{10}}{8\sqrt{2}} \approx 1.3637$

x	f(x)
4	3
3	4
5	4
2	7
6	7

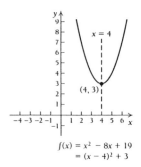

$f(x) = x^2 - 8x + 19$
$= (x - 4)^2 + 3$

25. $f(x) = -x^2 + 2x + 3$

$= -(x^2 - 2x) + 3$

$= -(x^2 - 2x + 1 - 1) + 3$ (Adding 1 - 1)

$= -(x^2 - 2x + 1) + 1 + 3$

$= -(x - 1)^2 + 4$

It is not necessary to rewrite the function in the form $f(x) = a(x - h)^2 + k$, but it can be helpful. Since the coefficient of x^2 is negative, the parabola opens downward. The vertex is (1, 4). The line of symmetry is x = 1. We calculate several input-output pairs and plot these points.

x	f(x)
1	4
0	3
2	3
-1	0
3	0

$f(x) = -x^2 + 2x + 3$
$= -(x - 1)^2 + 4$

28. $f(x) = -x^2 - 8x - 17$

$= -(x + 4)^2 - 1$

x	f(x)
-6	-5
-5	-2
-4	-1
-3	-2
-2	-5

$f(x) = -x^2 - 8x - 17$

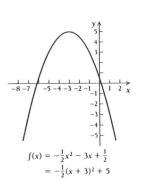

29. $f(x) = -\dfrac{1}{2}x^2 - 3x + \dfrac{1}{2}$

$= -\dfrac{1}{2}(x^2 + 6x) + \dfrac{1}{2}$

$= -\dfrac{1}{2}(x^2 + 6x + 9 - 9) + \dfrac{1}{2}$ (Adding 9 - 9)

$= -\dfrac{1}{2}(x^2 + 6x + 9) + \dfrac{9}{2} + \dfrac{1}{2}$

$= -\dfrac{1}{2}(x + 3)^2 + 5$

$= -\dfrac{1}{2}[x - (-3)]^2 + 5$

Since the coefficient of x^2 is negative, the parabola opens downward. The vertex is (-3, 5). The line of symmetry is x = -3. We calculate several input-output pairs and plot these points.

26. $f(x) = x^2 - 3x - 4$

$= \left(x - \dfrac{3}{2}\right)^2 - \dfrac{25}{4}$

x	f(x)
-2	6
-1	0
0	-4
1	-6
$\frac{3}{2}$	$-\frac{25}{4}$
2	-6
4	0
5	6

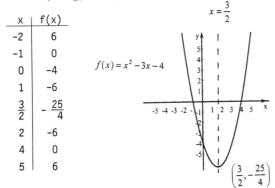

$f(x) = x^2 - 3x - 4$

$\left(\dfrac{3}{2}, -\dfrac{25}{4}\right)$

x	f(x)
-3	5
-4	$\frac{9}{2}$
-2	$\frac{9}{2}$
-5	3
-1	3

$f(x) = -\dfrac{1}{2}x^2 - 3x + \dfrac{1}{2}$
$= -\dfrac{1}{2}(x + 3)^2 + 5$

27. $f(x) = x^2 - 8x + 19$

$= (x^2 - 8x + 16 - 16) + 19$ (Adding 16 - 16)

$= (x^2 - 8x + 16) - 16 + 19$

$= (x - 4)^2 + 3$

Since the coefficient of x^2 is positive, the parabola opens upward. The vertex is (4, 3). The line of symmetry is x = 4. We calculate several input-output pairs and plot these points.

30. $f(x) = 2x^2 - 4x - 2$
$= 2(x - 1)^2 - 4$

x	f(x)
-1	4
0	-2
1	-4
2	-2
3	4

$x = 1$

$f(x) = 2x^2 - 4x - 2$

$(1, -4)$

31. $f(x) = 3x^2 - 24x + 50$
$= 3(x^2 - 8x) + 50$
$= 3(x^2 - 8x + 16 - 16) + 50$ (Adding $16 - 16$)
$= 3(x^2 - 8x + 16) - 48 + 50$
$= 3(x - 4)^2 + 2$

Since the coefficient of x^2 is positive, the parabola opens upward. The vertex is $(4, 2)$. The line of symmetry is $x = 4$. We calculate several input-output pairs and plot these points.

x	f(x)
4	2
3	5
5	5
2	14
6	14

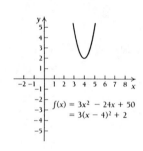

$f(x) = 3x^2 - 24x + 50$
$= 3(x - 4)^2 + 2$

32. $f(x) = -2x^2 + 2x + 1$
$= -2\left(x - \frac{1}{2}\right)^2 + \frac{3}{2}$

x	f(x)
-1	-3
0	1
$\frac{1}{2}$	$\frac{3}{2}$
1	1
2	-3

$x = \frac{1}{2}$

$f(x) = -2x^2 + 2x + 1$

$\left(\frac{1}{2}, \frac{3}{2}\right)$

33. $f(x) = -x^2 + 2x + 3$

We solve the equation $-x^2 + 2x + 3 = 0$.
$x^2 - 2x - 3 = 0$ (Multiplying by -1)
$(x + 1)(x - 3) = 0$

$x + 1 = 0$ or $x - 3 = 0$
$x = -1$ or $x = 3$

Thus the x-intercepts are $(-1, 0)$ and $(3, 0)$.

34. $f(x) = x^2 - 3x - 4$

$x^2 - 3x - 4 = 0$
$(x + 1)(x - 4) = 0$

$x = -1$ or $x = 4$
$(-1, 0), (4, 0)$

35. $f(x) = x^2 - 8x + 5$

We solve the equation $x^2 - 8x + 5 = 0$.

$a = 1, \quad b = -8, \quad c = 5$

$x = \dfrac{-(-8) \pm \sqrt{(-8)^2 - 4 \cdot 1 \cdot 5}}{2 \cdot 1} = \dfrac{8 \pm \sqrt{64 - 20}}{2}$

$= \dfrac{8 \pm \sqrt{44}}{2} = \dfrac{8 \pm 2\sqrt{11}}{2} = 4 \pm \sqrt{11}$

Thus the x-intercepts are $(4 - \sqrt{11}, 0)$ and $(4 + \sqrt{11}, 0)$.

36. $f(x) = -x^2 - 3x - 3$

$x^2 + 3x + 3 = 0$
$b^2 - 4ac = 3^2 - 4 \cdot 1 \cdot 3 = -3$, so there are no x-intercepts.

37. $f(x) = -5x^2 + 6x - 5$

We solve the equation
$-5x^2 + 6x - 5 = 0$.
$5x^2 - 6x + 5 = 0$

$a = 5, \quad b = -6, \quad c = 5$

$b^2 - 4ac$ (the discriminant) $= -64 < 0$

Thus, there are no x-intercepts.

38. $f(x) = 2x^2 + x - 5$

$2x^2 + x - 5 = 0$

$x = \dfrac{-1 \pm \sqrt{1^2 - 4(2)(-5)}}{2 \cdot 2} = \dfrac{-1 \pm \sqrt{41}}{4}$

$\left[\dfrac{-1 - \sqrt{41}}{4}, 0\right], \quad \left[\dfrac{-1 + \sqrt{41}}{4}, 0\right]$

39. Familiarize and Translate: Let x and y represent the numbers, and let Q = the product. We have $x + y = 50$, so $y = 50 - x$. Then Q is given by
$$Q = xy$$
$$Q(x) = x(50 - x) = 50x - x^2. \quad \text{(Substituting } 50 - x \text{ for } y\text{)}$$

Carry out: We want to maximize this function. We find the first coordinate of the vertex of the function:

$$-\frac{b}{2a} = -\frac{50}{2(-1)} = 25$$

Since the leading coefficient of $Q(x) = 50x - x^2$, -1, is negative, we know that the function has a maximum value. Note that $y = 50 - 25$, or 25, when $x = 25$.

Check: We go over our work. We could also examine the graph of the function and estimate the maximum value.

State: The two numbers that have the maximum product are 25 and 25.

<u>40</u>. x - y = 16, so x = y + 16.

Maximize P(y) = y(y + 16).

y = -8, and x = 8

<u>41</u>. Familiarize and Translate: We first draw a picture. Let h = the height and b = the base.

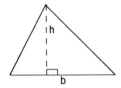

Since the sum of the base and height is 20 cm, we have

b + h = 20 and b = 20 - h.

Then the area is given by

$$A = \frac{1}{2} bh$$

$$A(h) = \frac{1}{2} (20 - h)h = 10h - \frac{1}{2} h^2.$$

Carry out: We find the first coordinate of the vertex:

$$- \frac{b}{2a} = - \frac{10}{2\left[- \frac{1}{2}\right]} = 10$$

Since the leading coefficient of the function, $- \frac{1}{2}$, is negative, we know that the function has a maximum value. The maximum value occurs when h = 10. Note that b = 20 - 10, or 10, when h = 10.

Check: We go over our work. We could also examine the graph of the function and estimate the maximum value.

State: The area is a maximum when the base is 10 cm and the height is 10 cm.

<u>42</u>. b + h = 138, so b = 138 - h.

Maximize A(h) = (138 - h)h.

h = 69 yd, and b = 69 yd.

<u>43</u>. Familiarize and Translate: Using the drawing in the text, we see that the area is given by A(x) = (120 - 2x)x, or A(x) = 120x - 2x².

Carry out: We find the vertex of the function. The first coordinate of the vertex is

$$- \frac{b}{2a} = - \frac{120}{2(-2)} = 30.$$

We find the second coordinate by substituting:

A(30) = 120(30) - 2(30)² = 3600 - 1800 = 1800

The vertex is (30, 1800). Since the leading coefficient of A(x), -2, is negative, we know that the function has a maximum value. The maximum value is 1800 when x = 30. Note that 120 - 2x = 120 - 2(30) = 60 when x = 30.

Check: We go over our work. We could also examine the graph of the function and estimate the maximum value.

State: Dimensions of 30 yd by 60 yd will maximize the area. The maximum area is 1800 yd².

<u>44</u>. Maximize A(x) = (240 - 3x)x.

x = 40 yd and 240 - 3x = 120 yd, so the largest area is 40·120 = 4800 yd².

<u>45</u>. Familiarize and Translate: We make a drawing. Let ℓ = the length and w = the width of the room.

Since the perimeter is 54 ft, we have

2ℓ + 2w = 54 and ℓ = 27 - w.

Then the area is given by

A = ℓw

A(w) = (27 - w)w = 27w - w².

Carry out: We find the vertex of the function. The first coordinate of the vertex is given by

$$- \frac{b}{2a} = - \frac{27}{2(-1)} = 13.5.$$

We find the second coordinate by substituting:

A(13.5) = 27(13.5) - (13.5)² = 364.5 - 182.25 = 182.25

The vertex is (13.5, 182.25). Since the leading coefficient of A(w), -1, is negative, we know the function has a maximum value. The maximum value is 182.25 when w = 13.5. Note that ℓ = 27 - 13.5 = 13.5 when w = 13.5.

Check: We go over our work. We could also examine the graph of the function and estimate the maximum value.

State: The dimensions are 13.5 ft by 13.5 ft. The area is 182.25 ft².

<u>46</u>. 2ℓ + 2w = 34, so ℓ = 17 - w.

Maximize A(w) = (17 - w)w.

w = 8.5 ft and ℓ = 8.5 ft and the maximum area is (8.5)(8.5), or 72.25 ft².

47. P(x) = R(x) - C(x)

    P(x) = (50x - 0.5x²) - (4x + 10)

    P(x) = -0.5x² + 46x - 10

    We find the vertex of P(x). The first coordinate is

    $$-\frac{b}{2a} = -\frac{46}{2(-0.5)} = 46.$$

    We substitute to find the second coordinate:

    P(46) = -0.5(46)² + 46(46) - 10

          = -1058 + 2116 - 10

          = 1048

    The vertex is (46, 1048). Since the leading coefficient of P(x), -0.5, is negative, we know that the function has a maximum value. Thus, the maximum profit is $1048, and it occurs when 46 units are produced and sold.

48. Maximize P(x) = (50x - 0.5x²) - (10x + 3) = -0.5x² + 40x - 3. The maximum profit is $797 when x = 40 units.

49. P(x) = R(x) - C(x)

    P(x) = 2x - (0.01x² + 0.6x + 30)

    P(x) = -0.01x² + 1.4x - 30

    We find the vertex of P(x). The first coordinate is

    $$-\frac{b}{2a} = -\frac{1.4}{2(-0.01)} = 70.$$

    We find the second coordinate by substituting:

    P(70) = -0.01(70)² + 1.4(70) - 30

          = -49 + 98 - 30

          = 19

    The vertex is (70, 19). Since the leading coefficient of P(x), -0.01, is negative, we know the function has a maximum value. Thus, the maximum profit is $19, and it occurs when 70 units are produced and sold.

50. Maximize P(x) = 5x - (0.001x² + 1.2x + 60) = -0.001x² + 3.8x - 60. The maximum profit is $3550 when x = 1900 units.

51. s(t) = -4.9t² + v₀t + h

    s(t) = -4.9t² + 147t + 560   (Substituting)

    a) We find the vertex of s(t). The first coordinate is

    $$-\frac{b}{2a} = -\frac{147}{2(-4.9)} = 15.$$

    We find the second coordinate by substituting:

    s(15) = -4.9(15)² + 147(15) + 560 = 1662.5

    The vertex is (15, 1662.5). Since the leading coefficient of s(t), -4.9, is negative, we know the function has a maximum value. Thus, the rocket has a maximum height of 1662.5 m, and it is attained 15 sec after the end of the burn.

b) We set s(t) = 0 and solve for t. We use the quadratic formula.

   -4.9t² + 147t + 560 = 0

   a = -4.9, b = 147, c = 560

   $$t = \frac{-b \pm \sqrt{b^2 - 4ac}}{2a}$$

   $$t = \frac{-147 - \sqrt{147^2 - 4(-4.9)(560)}}{2(-4.9)}$$ Taking the negative square root (t > 0)

   t ≈ 33.420

The rocket will reach the ground about 33.420 sec after the end of the burn.

52. $\frac{1}{2} \cdot 2\pi x + 2x + 2y = 24$, so $y = 12 - \frac{\pi x}{2} - x$.

    $A(x) = \frac{1}{2} \cdot \pi x^2 + 2x\left[12 - \frac{\pi x}{2} - x\right]$

    $A(x) = \frac{\pi x^2}{2} + 24x - \pi x^2 - 2x^2$

    $A(x) = 24x - \frac{\pi x^2}{2} - 2x^2$, or $24x - \left[\frac{\pi}{2} + 2\right]x^2$

    The first coordinate of the vertex of A(x) is $\frac{24}{\pi + 4}$, and $y = \frac{24}{\pi + 4}$ when $x = \frac{24}{\pi + 4}$. The coefficient of x² is negative, so the maximum amount of light will enter when the dimensions of the rectangular part of the window are $\frac{24}{\pi + 4}$ ft by $\frac{24}{\pi + 4}$ ft.

53. f(x) = |x² - 1|

    First graph f(x) = x² - 1.

x	f(x)
0	-1
-1	0
1	0
2	3
-2	3

    Then reflect the negative values across the x-axis. The point (0, -1) is now (0, 1).

54. $f(x) = |3 - 2x - x^2|$

$= |-(x + 1)^2 + 4|$

x	f(x)
-4	5
-3	0
-2	3
-1	4
0	3
1	0
2	5

55. $f(x) = 2.31x^2 - 3.135x - 5.89$

$-\dfrac{b^2 - 4ac}{4a} = -\dfrac{(-3.135)^2 - 4(2.31)(-5.89)}{4(2.31)} \approx$

-6.9537

The value of -6.9537 is a minimum since the coefficient of x^2 is positive.

56. $f(x) = -18.8x^2 + 7.92x + 6.18$

$-\dfrac{b^2 - 4ac}{4a} = -\dfrac{(7.92)^2 - 4(-18.8)(6.18)}{4(-18.8)} \approx$

7.0141

Maximum: 7.0141

57. $f(x) = ax^2 + 3x - 8$

The first coordinate of the vertex, $-\dfrac{b}{2a}$, is -2:

$-\dfrac{3}{2a} = -2$

$\dfrac{3}{4} = a$

58. $-\dfrac{b^2 - 4(-4)(3)}{4(-4)} = 50$, and $b = \pm 4\sqrt{47}$.

59. $f(x) = -0.2x^2 - 3x + c$

The second coordinate of the vertex, $-\dfrac{b^2 - 4ac}{4a}$, is -225:

$-\dfrac{(-3)^2 - 4(-0.2)(c)}{4(-0.2)} = -225$

$\dfrac{9 + 0.8c}{0.8} = -225$

$9 + 0.8c = -180$

$0.8c = -189$

$c = -236.25$, or $-\dfrac{945}{4}$

60. $f(x) = a(x - h)^2 + k$

$1 = a(-3 - 4)^2 - 5$, so $a = \dfrac{6}{49}$. Then

$f(x) = \dfrac{6}{49}(x - 4)^2 - 5$, or

$f(x) = \dfrac{6}{49}x^2 - \dfrac{48}{49}x - \dfrac{149}{49}$.

61. $f(x) = qx^2 - 2x + q$

The first coordinate of the vertex is

$-\dfrac{b}{2a} = -\dfrac{-2}{2q} = \dfrac{1}{q}$.

We substitute to find the second coordinate of the vertex:

$f\left(\dfrac{1}{q}\right) = q\left(\dfrac{1}{q^2}\right) - 2\left(\dfrac{1}{q}\right) + q$

$= \dfrac{1}{q} - \dfrac{2}{q} + q$

$= \dfrac{-1 + q^2}{q}$, or $\dfrac{q^2 - 1}{q}$

The vertex is $\left(\dfrac{1}{q}, \dfrac{q^2 - 1}{q}\right)$.

62. $-\dfrac{b}{2a} = -\dfrac{p}{2(-3)} = \dfrac{p}{6}$

Line of symmetry: $x = \dfrac{p}{6}$

63. $f(x) = x^2 - 6x + c$

The second coordinate of the vertex, $-\dfrac{b^2 - 4ac}{4a}$, is 0.

$-\dfrac{(-6)^2 - 4 \cdot 1 \cdot c}{4 \cdot 1} = 0$

$36 - 4c = 0$

$36 = 4c$

$9 = c$

64. $-\dfrac{b}{2(-0.1)} = 0$, so $b = 0$.

65. Familiarize: Let x = the number of $1 increases in the ticket price. When the ticket price is 6 + x, then the average attendance will be 70,000 - 10,000x.

Translate:

Revenue =

$\begin{bmatrix} \text{Price per} \\ \text{ticket} \end{bmatrix} \cdot \begin{bmatrix} \text{Average} \\ \text{attendance} \end{bmatrix} + \$1.50 \cdot \begin{bmatrix} \text{Average} \\ \text{attendance} \end{bmatrix}$

$R(x) =$

$(6 + x) \cdot (70{,}000 - 10{,}000x) + 1.5(70{,}000 - 10{,}000x)$

$R(x) =$

$420{,}000 + 10{,}000x - 10{,}000x^2 + 105{,}000 - 15{,}000x$

$R(x) = -10{,}000x^2 - 5000x + 525{,}000$

Carry out: We find the value of x for which R(x) is a maximum. The first coordinate of the vertex is

$-\dfrac{b}{2a} = -\dfrac{-5000}{2(-10{,}000)} = -0.25$.

Since the coefficient of x^2 is negative, R(x) has a maximum value. It occurs when x = -0.25. When x = -0.25, the price per ticket is $6 + x = $6 + (-$0.25), or $5.75. The number of people that will attend is 70,000 - 10,000(-0.25), or 72,500.

Check: We go over our work. We could also examine the graph of the function and estimate the first coordinate of the vertex.

State: $5.75 per ticket should be charged to maximize revenue. At that price, 72,500 people will attend.

66. Maximize $P(x) = (20 + x)(30 - x) - 2(30 - x)$.

The maximum value occurs when $x = 6$. Thus the charge per unit should be $20 + $6, or $26.

67. Familiarize: Let x = the number of additional trees that are planted per acre. Then the total number of trees per acre will be $20 + x$, and the yield per tree will be $30 - x$ bushels.

Translate:

$$\text{Yield} = \begin{bmatrix} \text{Number of trees} \\ \text{per acre} \end{bmatrix} \cdot \begin{bmatrix} \text{Yield} \\ \text{per tree} \end{bmatrix}$$

$$Y(x) = (20 + x) \cdot (30 - x)$$

$$Y(x) = 600 + 10x - x^2$$

Carry out: We find the value of x for which $Y(x)$ is a maximum. The first coordinate of the vertex of $Y(x)$ is

$$-\frac{b}{2a} = -\frac{10}{2(-1)} = 5.$$

Since the coefficient of x^2 is negative, the function has a maximum value. It occurs when $x = 5$. When $x = 5$, the number of trees per acre is $20 + 5$, or 25 trees.

Check: We go over our work. We could also examine the graph of the function and estimate the first coordinate of the vertex.

State: In order to get the highest yield, 25 trees per acre should be planted.

68. Let x = the number of $0.10 increases in the admission price. Maximize $R(x) = (3 + 0.1x)(100 - x)$. The maximum occurs when $x = 35$, so the admission charge should be $3 + $0.10(35), or $6.50.

69. Familiarize: First we find the radius r of a circle with circumference x:

$$2\pi r = x$$

$$r = \frac{x}{2\pi}$$

Then we find the length s of a side of a square with perimeter $24 - x$:

$$4s = 24 - x$$

$$s = \frac{24 - x}{4}$$

Translate:

$$S = \text{area of circle} + \text{area of square}$$

$$S = \pi r^2 + s^2$$

$$S(x) = \pi \left[\frac{x}{2\pi}\right]^2 + \left[\frac{24 - x}{4}\right]^2$$

$$S(x) = \frac{x^2}{4\pi} + \left[\frac{24 - x}{4}\right]^2$$

$$S(x) = \left[\frac{1}{4\pi} + \frac{1}{16}\right]x^2 - 3x + 36$$

Carry out: We find the value of x for which $S(x)$ is a minimum. The first coordinate of the vertex of $S(x)$ is

$$-\frac{b}{2a} = -\frac{-3}{2\left[\frac{1}{4\pi} + \frac{1}{16}\right]} = \frac{3}{\frac{1}{2\pi} + \frac{1}{8}} = \frac{24\pi}{4 + \pi}.$$

Since the coefficient of x^2 is positive, the function has a minimum value. It occurs when $x = \frac{24\pi}{4 + \pi}$. Thus one piece will be $\frac{24\pi}{4 + \pi}$ in., and then the other piece will be $24 - \frac{24\pi}{4 + \pi}$, or $\frac{96}{4 + \pi}$ in.

Check: We go over our work.

State: One piece of string should be $\frac{24\pi}{4 + \pi}$ in. and then the other piece would be $\frac{96}{4 + \pi}$ in.

70.

Using similar triangles, we have

$$\frac{9}{12} = \frac{y}{12 - x}, \text{ or } y = 9 - \frac{3}{4}x.$$

$$A = xy = x\left[9 - \frac{3}{4}x\right] = 9x - \frac{3}{4}x^2$$

The maximum value of A occurs when $x = 6$. Hence the dimensions are 6 cm and $9 - \frac{3}{4} \cdot 6$, or $\frac{9}{2}$ cm, and the maximum area is $6 \cdot \frac{9}{2}$, or 27 cm².

71. Vertex: $(0.9, -10.0)$
     x-intercepts: $(-0.8, 0)$, $(2.6, 0)$

72. Vertex: $(-9.1, 50.0)$
     x-intercepts: none

73. a) 12.9 sec

     b) 920.6 m

     c) 26.6 sec

Exercise Set 4.2

---

1. The intersection of two sets consists of those element <u>common</u> to the sets.

$$\{3, 4, 5, 8, 10\} \cap \{1, 2, 3, 4, 5, 6, 7\}$$
$$= \{3, 4, 5\}$$

Only the elements 3, 4, and 5 are in <u>both</u> sets.

2. $\{1, 2, 3, 4, 5, 6, 7, 8, 10\}$

3. The union of two sets consists of the elements that are in <u>one or both</u> of the sets.

   {0, 2, 4, 6, 8} ∪ {4, 6, 9} = {0, 2, 4, 6, 8, 9}

   Note that the elements 4 and 6 are in both sets, but each is listed only once in the union.

4. {4, 6}

5. {a, b, c} ∩ {c, d} = {c}

   Since the element c is the only element which is in <u>both</u> sets, the intersection only contains c.

6. {a, b, c, d}

7. Graph: {x│7 ⩽ x} ∪ {x│x < 9}

   Graph the solution sets separately, and then find the union.

   Graph: {x│7 ⩽ x}   (7 ⩽ x means x ⩾ 7)

   The solid circle at 7 indicates that 7 is in the solution set.

   Graph: {x│x < 9}

   The open circle at 9 indicates that 9 is not in the solution set.

   Now graph the union:

   {x│7 ⩽ x} ∪ {x│x < 9} = The set of all real numbers, or (−∞, ∞).

8. $\left\{x\middle|-\frac{1}{2} \leqslant x\right\} \cup \left\{x\middle|x < \frac{1}{2}\right\}$ = The set of all real numbers, or (−∞, ∞).

9. Graph: $\left\{x\middle|-\frac{1}{2} \leqslant x\right\} \cap \left\{x\middle|x < \frac{1}{2}\right\}$

   Graph the solution sets separately, and then find the intersection.

   Graph: $\left\{x\middle|-\frac{1}{2} \leqslant x\right\}$ $\left(-\frac{1}{2} \leqslant x \text{ means } x \geqslant -\frac{1}{2}\right)$

   The solid circle indicates that $-\frac{1}{2}$ is in the solution set.

Graph: $\left\{x\middle|x < \frac{1}{2}\right\}$

The open circle at $\frac{1}{2}$ indicates that $\frac{1}{2}$ is not in the solution set.

Now graph the intersection:

$\left\{x\middle|-\frac{1}{2} \leqslant x\right\} \cap \left\{x\middle|x < \frac{1}{2}\right\} = \left\{x\middle|-\frac{1}{2} \leqslant x < \frac{1}{2}\right\}$, or

$\left[-\frac{1}{2}, \frac{1}{2}\right)$

10. $\left\{x\middle|x > \frac{1}{4}\right\} \cap \left\{x\middle|1 \geqslant x\right\} = \left\{x\middle|\frac{1}{4} < x \leqslant 1\right\}$, or $\left(\frac{1}{4}, 1\right]$

11. Graph: {x│x < −π} ∪ {x│x > π}

    Graph the solution sets separately, and then find the union.

    Graph: {x│x < −π}

    The open circle at −π indicates that −π is not in the solution set.

    Graph: {x│x > π}

    The open circle at π indicates that π is not in the solution set.

    Now graph the union:

    {x│x < −π} ∪ {x│x > π} = {x│x < −π or x > π}, or

    (−∞, −π) ∪ (π, ∞)

12. {x│−π ⩽ x} ∩ {x│x < π} = {x│−π ⩽ x < π}, or

    [−π, π)

13. Graph: {x|x < -7} ∪ {x|x = -7}

    Graph the solution sets separately, and then find the union.

    Graph: {x|x < -7}

    The open circle at -7 indicates that -7 is not in the solution set.

    Graph: {x|x = -7}

    The solid circle at -7 indicates that -7 is in the solution set.

    Now graph the union:

    {x|x < -7} ∪ {x|x = -7} = {x|x ≤ -7}, or (-∞, -7]

14. $\left\{x \middle| x > \frac{1}{2}\right\}$ ∪ $\left\{x \middle| x = \frac{1}{2}\right\}$ = $\left\{x \middle| x \geq \frac{1}{2}\right\}$, or $\left[\frac{1}{2}, \infty\right]$

15. Graph: {x|x ≥ 5} ∩ {x|x ≤ -3}

    Graph the solution sets separately, and then find the intersection.

    Graph: {x|x ≥ 5}

    The solid circle at 5 indicates that 5 is in the solution set.

    Graph: {x|x ≤ -3}

    The solid circle at -3 indicates that -3 is in the solution set.

    There are no elements in the intersection.

    {x|x ≥ 5} ∩ {x|x ≤ -3} = Ø

16. {x|x ≥ -3} ∪ {x|x ≤ 0} = The set of all real numbers, or (-∞, ∞)

17. -2 ≤ x + 1 < 4

    -3 ≤ x < 3   (Adding -1)

    The solution set is {x|-3 ≤ x < 3}, or [-3, 3).

18. -3 < x + 2 ≤ 5

    -5 < x ≤ 3

    {x|-5 < x ≤ 3}, or (-5, 3]

19. 5 ≤ x - 3 ≤ 7

    8 ≤ x ≤ 10   (Adding 3)

    The solution set is {x|8 ≤ x ≤ 10}, or [8, 10].

20. -1 < x - 4 < 7

    3 < x < 11

    {x|3 < x < 11}, or (3, 11)

21. -3 ≤ x + 4 ≤ -3

    -7 ≤ x ≤ -7

    The solution set is {-7}.

22. -5 < x + 2 < -5

    -7 < x < -7

    Ø

23. -2 < 2x + 1 < 5

    -3 < 2x < 4   (Adding -1)

    $-\frac{3}{2} < x < 2$ (Multiplying by $\frac{1}{2}$)

    The solution set is $\left\{x \middle| -\frac{3}{2} < x < 2\right\}$, or $\left[-\frac{3}{2}, 2\right]$.

24. -3 ≤ 5x + 1 ≤ 3

    -4 ≤ 5x ≤ 2

    $-\frac{4}{5} ≤ x ≤ \frac{2}{5}$

    $\left\{x \middle| -\frac{4}{5} ≤ x ≤ \frac{2}{5}\right\}$, or $\left[-\frac{4}{5}, \frac{2}{5}\right]$

25. -4 ≤ 6 - 2x < 4

    -10 ≤ -2x < -2   (Adding -6)

    5 ≥ x > 1   (Multiplying by $-\frac{1}{2}$)

    or 1 < x ≤ 5

    The solution set is {x|1 < x ≤ 5}, or (1, 5].

26. -3 < 1 - 2x ≤ 3

    -4 < -2x ≤ 2

    2 > x ≥ -1

    {x|-1 ≤ x < 2}, or [-1, 2)

27. $-5 < \frac{1}{2}(3x + 1) \leqslant 7$

    $-10 < 3x + 1 \leqslant 14$ (Multiplying by 2)

    $-11 < 3x \leqslant 13$ (Adding -1)

    $-\frac{11}{3} < x \leqslant \frac{13}{3}$ $\left[\text{Multiplying by } \frac{1}{3}\right]$

The solution set is $\left\{x \middle| -\frac{11}{3} < x \leqslant \frac{13}{3}\right\}$, or $\left[-\frac{11}{3}, \frac{13}{3}\right]$.

28. $\frac{2}{3} \leqslant -\frac{4}{5}(x - 3) < 1$

    $-\frac{5}{6} \geqslant x - 3 > -\frac{5}{4}$

    $\frac{13}{6} \geqslant x > \frac{7}{4}$

    $\left\{x \middle| \frac{7}{4} < x \leqslant \frac{13}{6}\right\}$, or $\left[\frac{7}{4}, \frac{13}{6}\right]$

29. $3x \leqslant -6$ or $x - 1 > 0$

    $x \leqslant -2$ or $x > 1$

The solution set is $\{x | x \leqslant -2 \text{ or } x > 1\}$, or $(-\infty, -2] \cup (1, \infty)$.

30. $2x < 8$ or $x + 3 \geqslant 1$

    $x < 4$ or $x \geqslant -2$

The set of all real numbers, or $(-\infty, \infty)$.

31. $2x + 3 \leqslant -4$ or $2x + 3 \geqslant 4$

    $2x \leqslant -7$ or $2x \geqslant 1$

    $x \leqslant -\frac{7}{2}$ or $x \geqslant \frac{1}{2}$

The solution set is $\left\{x \middle| x \leqslant -\frac{7}{2} \text{ or } x \geqslant \frac{1}{2}\right\}$, or $\left[-\infty, -\frac{7}{2}\right] \cup \left[\frac{1}{2}, \infty\right)$.

32. $3x - 1 < -5$ or $3x - 1 > 5$

    $3x < -4$ or $3x > 6$

    $x < -\frac{4}{3}$ or $x > 2$

    $\left\{x \middle| x < -\frac{4}{3} \text{ or } x > 2\right\}$, or

    $\left[-\infty, -\frac{4}{3}\right] \cup (2, \infty)$.

33. $2x - 20 < -0.8$ or $2x - 20 > 0.8$

    $2x < 19.2$ or $2x > 20.8$

    $x < 9.6$ or $x > 10.4$

The solution set is $\{x | x < 9.6 \text{ or } x > 10.4\}$, or $(-\infty, 9.6) \cup (10.4, \infty)$.

34. $5x + 11 \leqslant -4$ or $5x + 11 \geqslant 4$

    $5x \leqslant -15$ or $5x \geqslant -7$

    $x \leqslant -3$ or $x \geqslant -\frac{7}{5}$

$\left\{x \middle| x \leqslant -3 \text{ or } x \geqslant -\frac{7}{5}\right\}$, or

$(-\infty, -3] \cup \left[-\frac{7}{5}, \infty\right]$

35. $x + 14 \leqslant -\frac{1}{4}$ or $x + 14 \geqslant \frac{1}{4}$

    $x \leqslant -\frac{57}{4}$ or $x \geqslant -\frac{55}{4}$

The solution set is $\left\{x \middle| x \leqslant -\frac{57}{4} \text{ or } x \geqslant -\frac{55}{4}\right\}$, or

$\left[-\infty, -\frac{57}{4}\right] \cup \left[-\frac{55}{4}, \infty\right]$.

36. $x - 9 < -\frac{1}{2}$ or $x - 9 > \frac{1}{2}$

    $x < \frac{17}{2}$ or $x > \frac{19}{2}$

$\left\{x \middle| x < \frac{17}{2} \text{ or } x > \frac{19}{2}\right\}$, or

$\left[-\infty, \frac{17}{2}\right) \cup \left[\frac{19}{2}, \infty\right]$

37. We first make a drawing.

Let x represent the width. Then $2x + 2(15.23)$, or $2x + 30.46$, represents the perimeter. The perimeter is greater than 40.23 cm and less than 137.8 cm. We now have the following inequality.

$40.23 < 2x + 30.46 < 137.8$

$\phantom{40.23 < }9.77 < 2x < 107.34$ (Adding -30.46)

$4.885 < x < 53.67$ $\left[\text{Multiplying by } \frac{1}{2}\right]$

Widths greater than 4.885 cm and less than 53.67 cm will give a perimeter greater than 40.23 cm and less than 137.8 cm. We can express this as $\{x | 4.885 \text{ cm} < x < 53.67 \text{ cm}\}$.

38. Solve: $0 < \frac{1}{2}(b)(15) \leqslant 305.4$

$\{b | 0 \text{ m} < b \leqslant 40.72 \text{ m}\}$

<u>39.</u> Let x represent the score on the fourth test. The average of the four scores is $\frac{83 + 87 + 93 + x}{4}$. This average must be greater than or equal to 90. We solve the following inequality.

$$\frac{83 + 87 + 93 + x}{4} \geqslant 90$$

$$83 + 87 + 93 + x \geqslant 360$$

$$263 + x \geqslant 360$$

$$x \geqslant 97$$

The score on the fourth test must be greater than or equal to 97. It will of course be less than or equal to 100%. We can express this as $\{x | 97\% \leqslant x \leqslant 100\%\}$. Yes, an A is possible.

<u>40.</u> Solve: $90 \leqslant \frac{75 + 70 + 83 + x}{4} \leqslant 100$

$\{x | 132\% \leqslant x \leqslant 172\%\}$. No.

<u>41.</u> We substitute $\frac{5}{9}$ (F - 32) for C in the inequality.

$$1083° \leqslant \frac{5}{9}(F - 32) \leqslant 2580°$$

$$1949.4° \leqslant F - 32 \leqslant 4644° \quad \left[\text{Multiplying by } \frac{9}{5}\right]$$

$$1981.4° \leqslant F \leqslant 4676°$$

<u>42.</u> Solve: $2 \leqslant 1 + \frac{1}{33} d \leqslant 10$

33 ft $\leqslant$ d $\leqslant$ 297 ft

<u>43.</u> $2 < 0.027d + 0.32 < 4$

$2000 < 27d + 320 < 4000$ (Clearing decimals)

$$1680 < 27d < 3680$$

$$\frac{1680}{27} < d < \frac{3680}{27}$$

$$62\frac{2}{9} < d < 136\frac{8}{27}$$

The solution set is $\left\{d \middle| 62\frac{2}{9} \text{ mi} < d < 136\frac{8}{27} \text{ mi}\right\}$.

<u>44.</u> Solve: $2000 < 5200 - 512.50t < 4000$

$\left\{t \middle| 2\frac{14}{41} \text{ yr} < t < 6\frac{10}{41} \text{ yr}\right\}$

<u>45.</u> $x \leqslant 3x - 2 \leqslant 2 - x$

$x \leqslant 3x - 2$ and $3x - 2 \leqslant 2 - x$

$-2x \leqslant -2$ and $4x \leqslant 4$

$x \geqslant 1$ and $x \leqslant 1$

The word "and" corresponds to set intersection.

The solution set is

$\{x | x \geqslant 1\} \cap \{x | x \leqslant 1\}$, or $\{1\}$.

<u>46.</u> $2x \leqslant 5 - 7x < 7 + x$

$2x \leqslant 5 - 7x$ and $5 - 7x < 7 + x$

$9x \leqslant 5$ and $-8x < 2$

$x \leqslant \frac{5}{9}$ and $x > -\frac{1}{4}$

$\left\{x \middle| -\frac{1}{4} < x \leqslant \frac{5}{9}\right\}$, or $\left[-\frac{1}{4}, \frac{5}{9}\right]$

<u>47.</u> $(x + 1)^2 > x(x - 3)$

$x^2 + 2x + 1 > x^2 - 3x$

$2x + 1 > -3x$

$5x > -1$

$x > -\frac{1}{5}$

The solution set is $\left\{x \middle| x > -\frac{1}{5}\right\}$, or $\left[-\frac{1}{5}, \infty\right)$.

<u>48.</u> $(x + 4)(x - 5) > (x + 1)(x - 7)$

$x^2 - x - 20 > x^2 - 6x - 7$

$5x > 13$

$x > \frac{13}{5}$

$\left\{x \middle| x > \frac{13}{5}\right\}$, or $\left[\frac{13}{5}, \infty\right)$

<u>49.</u> $(x + 1)^2 \leqslant (x + 2)^2 \leqslant (x + 3)^2$

$x^2 + 2x + 1 \leqslant x^2 + 4x + 4 \leqslant x^2 + 6x + 9$

$2x + 1 \leqslant 4x + 4 \leqslant 6x + 9$

$2x + 1 \leqslant 4x + 4$ and $4x + 4 \leqslant 6x + 9$

$-2x \leqslant 3$ and $-2x \leqslant 5$

$x \geqslant -\frac{3}{2}$ and $x \geqslant -\frac{5}{2}$

The word "and" corresponds to set intersection.

The solution set is

$\left\{x \middle| x \geqslant -\frac{3}{2}\right\} \cap \left\{x \middle| x \geqslant -\frac{5}{2}\right\}$, or $\left\{x \middle| x \geqslant -\frac{3}{2}\right\}$, or $\left[-\frac{3}{2}, \infty\right)$.

<u>50.</u> $(x - 1)(x + 1) < (x + 1)^2 \leqslant (x - 3)^2$

$(x-1)(x+1) < (x+1)^2$ and $(x+1)^2 \leqslant (x-3)^2$

$x^2-1 < x^2+2x+1$ and $x^2+2x+1 \leqslant x^2-6x+9$

$-2 < 2x$ and $8x \leqslant 8$

$-1 < x$ and $x \leqslant 1$

$\{x | -1 < x \leqslant 1\}$, or $(-1, 1]$

51. $f(x) = \dfrac{\sqrt{x + 2}}{\sqrt{x - 2}}$

The radicand in the denominator must be greater than 0. Thus, x - 2 > 0, or x > 2. Also the radicand in the numerator must be greater than or equal to 0. Thus, x + 2 ⩾ 0, or x ⩾ -2. The domain of f(x) is the intersection of the two solution sets.

{x⎮x > 2} ∩ {x⎮x ⩾ -2} = {x⎮x > 2}.

The domain of f(x) is {x⎮x > 2}, or (2, ∞).

52. $f(x) = \dfrac{\sqrt{3 - x}}{\sqrt{x + 5}}$

3 - x ⩾ 0 and x + 5 > 0

3 ⩾ x and   x > -5

{x⎮-5 < x ⩽ 3}, or (-5, 3]

53. {x⎮-5.2 < x ⩽ 9}, or (-5.2, 9]

54. {x⎮0.5 ⩽ x < 4.1}, or [0.5, 4.1)

55. {x⎮x < -0.2 or x ⩾ 6.2}, or (-∞, -0.2) ∪ [6.2, ∞)

56. {x⎮x ⩽ -2.2 or x > -1.2}, or (-∞, 2.2] ∪ (-1.2, ∞)

Exercise Set 4.3

1. ⎮x⎮ = 7

To solve we look for all numbers x whose distance from 0 is 7. There are two of them, so there are two solutions, -7 and 7. The graph is as follows.

{-7, 7}

2. {-4.5, 4.5}

3. ⎮x⎮ < 7

To solve we look for all numbers x whose distance from 0 is less than 7. These are the numbers between -7 and 7. The solution set and its graph are as follows.

{x⎮-7 < x < 7}, or (-7, 7)

4. {x⎮-4.5 ⩽ x ⩽ 4.5}, or [-4.5, 4.5]

5. ⎮x⎮ ⩾ 4.5

To solve we look for all numbers x whose distance from 0 is greater than or equal to 4.5. The solution set and its graph are as follows.

{x⎮x ⩽ -4.5 or x ⩾ 4.5}, or (-∞, -4.5] ∪ [4.5, ∞)

6. {x⎮x < -7 or x > 7}, or (-∞, -7) ∪ (7, ∞)

7. ⎮x - 1⎮ = 4

Method 1:

The solutions are those numbers x whose distance from 1 is 4. Thus to find the solutions graphically we locate 1. Then we locate those numbers 4 units to the left and 4 units to the right.

The solution set is {-3, 5}.

Method 2:

⎮x - 1⎮ = 4

x - 1 = -4 or x - 1 = 4   (Property A1)
    x = -3 or   x = 5   (Adding 1)

The solution set is {-3, 5}.

8. ⎮x - 7⎮ = 5

I.

{2, 12}

II. x - 7 = -5   or   x - 7 = 5
       x = 2   or   x = 12

{2, 12}

9. ⎮x + 8⎮ < 9, or ⎮x - (-8)⎮ < 9

Method 1:

The solutions are those numbers x whose distance from -8 is less than 9. Thus to find the solutions graphically we locate -8. Then we locate those numbers that are less than 9 units to the left and less than 9 units to the right.

The solution set is {x⎮-17 < x < 1}, or (-17, 1).

Method 2:

⎮x + 8⎮ < 9

-9 < x + 8 < 9   (Property A2)
-17 < x < 1   (Adding -8)

The solution set is {x⎮-17 < x < 1}, or (-17, 1).

10. $|x + 6| \leqslant 10$, or $|x - (-6)| \leqslant 10$

   I.

       $\{x | -16 \leqslant x \leqslant 4\}$, or $[-16, 4]$

   II. $-10 \leqslant x + 6 \leqslant 10$

       $\{x | -16 \leqslant x \leqslant 4\}$, or $[-16, 4]$

11. $|x + 8| \geqslant 9$, or $|x - (-8)| \geqslant 9$

   Method 1:

   The solutions are those numbers x whose distance from -8 is greater than or equal to 9. Thus to find the solutions graphically we locate -8. Then we locate those numbers that are greater than or equal to 9 units to the left and greater than or equal to 9 units to the right.

   The solution set is $\{x | x \leqslant -17 \text{ or } x \geqslant 1\}$, or $(-\infty, -17] \cup [1, \infty)$.

   Method 2:

   $|x + 8| \geqslant 9$

   $x + 8 \leqslant -9$ or $x + 8 \geqslant 9$ (Property A3)

     $x \leqslant -17$ or $x \geqslant 1$ (Adding -8)

   The solution set is $\{x | x \leqslant -17 \text{ or } x \geqslant 1\}$, or $(-\infty, -17] \cup [1, \infty)$.

12. $|x + 6| > 10$, or $|x - (-6)| > 10$

   I.

       $\{x | x < -16 \text{ or } x > 4\}$, or $(-\infty, -16) \cup (4, \infty)$

   II. $x + 6 < -10$ or $x + 6 > 10$

        $x < -16$ or $x > 4$

       $\{x | x < -16 \text{ or } x > 4\}$, or $(-\infty, -16) \cup (4, \infty)$

13. $\left|x - \dfrac{1}{4}\right| < \dfrac{1}{2}$

   Method 1:

   The solutions are those numbers x whose distance from $\dfrac{1}{4}$ is less than $\dfrac{1}{2}$. Thus to find the solutions graphically we locate $\dfrac{1}{4}$. Then we locate those numbers that are less than $\dfrac{1}{2}$ unit to the left and less than $\dfrac{1}{2}$ unit to the right.

   The solution set is $\left\{x \middle| -\dfrac{1}{4} < x < \dfrac{3}{4}\right\}$, or $\left[-\dfrac{1}{4}, \dfrac{3}{4}\right]$.

Method 2:

$\left|x - \dfrac{1}{4}\right| < \dfrac{1}{2}$

$-\dfrac{1}{2} < x - \dfrac{1}{4} < \dfrac{1}{2}$ (Property A2)

$-\dfrac{1}{4} < x < \dfrac{3}{4}$ $\left[\text{Adding } \dfrac{1}{4}\right]$

The solution set is $\left\{x \middle| -\dfrac{1}{4} < x < \dfrac{3}{4}\right\}$, or $\left[-\dfrac{1}{4}, \dfrac{3}{4}\right]$.

14. $|x - 0.5| \leqslant 0.2$

   I.

       $\{x | 0.3 \leqslant x \leqslant 0.7\}$, or $[0.3, 0.7]$

   II. $-0.2 \leqslant x - 0.5 \leqslant 0.2$

       $0.3 \leqslant x \leqslant 0.7$

       $\{x | 0.3 \leqslant x \leqslant 0.7\}$, or $[0.3, 0.7]$

15. $|3x| = 1$

   $3x = -1$ or $3x = 1$ (Property A1)

   $x = -\dfrac{1}{3}$ or $x = \dfrac{1}{3}$ $\left[\text{Multiplying by } \dfrac{1}{3}\right]$

   The solution set is $\left\{-\dfrac{1}{3}, \dfrac{1}{3}\right\}$.

16. $|5x| = 4$

   $5x = -4$ or $5x = 4$

   $x = -\dfrac{4}{5}$ or $x = \dfrac{4}{5}$

   $\left\{-\dfrac{4}{5}, \dfrac{4}{5}\right\}$

17. $|3x + 2| = 1$

   $3x + 2 = -1$ or $3x + 2 = 1$ (Property A1)

     $3x = -3$ or $3x = -1$ (Adding -2)

      $x = -1$ or $x = -\dfrac{1}{3}$ $\left[\text{Multiplying by } \dfrac{1}{3}\right]$

   The solution set is $\left\{-1, -\dfrac{1}{3}\right\}$.

18. $|7x - 4| = 8$

   $7x - 4 = -8$ or $7x - 4 = 8$

     $7x = -4$ or $7x = 12$

     $x = -\dfrac{4}{7}$ or $x = \dfrac{12}{7}$

   $\left\{-\dfrac{4}{7}, \dfrac{12}{7}\right\}$

19. $|3x| < 1$

$-1 < 3x < 1$ (Property A2)

$-\frac{1}{3} < x < \frac{1}{3}$ $\left[\text{Multiplying by } \frac{1}{3}\right]$

The solution set is $\left\{x \middle| -\frac{1}{3} < x < \frac{1}{3}\right\}$, or $\left(-\frac{1}{3}, \frac{1}{3}\right)$.

20. $|5x| \leqslant 4$

$-4 \leqslant 5x \leqslant 4$

$-\frac{4}{5} \leqslant x \leqslant \frac{4}{5}$

$\left\{x \middle| -\frac{4}{5} \leqslant x \leqslant \frac{4}{5}\right\}$, or $\left[-\frac{4}{5}, \frac{4}{5}\right]$

21. $|2x + 3| \leqslant 9$

$-9 \leqslant 2x + 3 \leqslant 9$ (Property A2)

$-12 \leqslant 2x \leqslant 6$ (Adding -3)

$-6 \leqslant x \leqslant 3$ $\left[\text{Multiplying by } \frac{1}{2}\right]$

The solution set is $\{x | -6 \leqslant x \leqslant 3\}$, or $[-6, 3]$.

22. $|2x + 3| < 13$

$-13 < 2x + 3 < 13$

$-16 < 2x < 10$

$-8 < x < 5$

$\{x | -8 < x < 5\}$, or $(-8, 5)$

23. $|x - 5| > 0.1$

$x - 5 < -0.1 \text{ or } x - 5 > 0.1$ (Property A3)

$x < 4.9 \quad \text{ or } \quad x > 5.1$ (Adding 5)

The solution set is $\{x | x < 4.9 \text{ or } x > 5.1\}$, or $(-\infty, 4.9) \cup (5.1, \infty)$.

24. $|x - 7| \geqslant 0.4$

$x - 7 \leqslant -0.4 \text{ or } x - 7 \geqslant 0.4$

$x \leqslant 6.6 \quad \text{ or } \quad x \geqslant 7.4$

$\{x | x \leqslant 6.6 \text{ or } x \geqslant 7.4\}$, or $(-\infty, 6.6] \cup [7.4, \infty)$

25. $\left|x + \frac{2}{3}\right| \leqslant \frac{5}{3}$

$-\frac{5}{3} \leqslant x + \frac{2}{3} \leqslant \frac{5}{3}$ (Property A2)

$-\frac{7}{3} \leqslant x \leqslant \frac{3}{3}$ $\left[\text{Adding } -\frac{2}{3}\right]$

The solution set is $\left\{x \middle| -\frac{7}{3} \leqslant x \leqslant 1\right\}$, or $\left[-\frac{7}{3}, 1\right]$.

26. $\left|x + \frac{3}{4}\right| < \frac{1}{4}$

$-\frac{1}{4} < x + \frac{3}{4} < \frac{1}{4}$

$-1 < x < -\frac{1}{2}$

$\left\{x \middle| -1 < x < -\frac{1}{2}\right\}$, or $\left(-1, -\frac{1}{2}\right)$

27. $|6 - 4x| \leqslant 8$

$-8 \leqslant 6 - 4x \leqslant 8$ (Property A2)

$-14 \leqslant -4x \leqslant 2$ (Adding -6)

$\frac{14}{4} \geqslant x \geqslant -\frac{2}{4}$ $\left[\text{Multiplying by } -\frac{1}{4}\right]$

$\frac{7}{2} \geqslant x \geqslant -\frac{1}{2}$

The solution set is $\left\{x \middle| -\frac{1}{2} \leqslant x \leqslant \frac{7}{2}\right\}$, or $\left[-\frac{1}{2}, \frac{7}{2}\right]$.

28. $|5 - 2x| > 10$

$5 - 2x < -10 \text{ or } 5 - 2x > 10$

$-2x < -15 \text{ or } \quad -2x > 5$

$x > \frac{15}{2} \text{ or } \quad x < -\frac{5}{2}$

$\left\{x \middle| x > \frac{15}{2} \text{ or } x < -\frac{5}{2}\right\}$, or $\left(-\infty, -\frac{5}{2}\right) \cup \left(\frac{15}{2}, \infty\right)$

29. $\left|\frac{2x + 1}{3}\right| > 5$

$\frac{2x + 1}{3} < -5 \text{ or } \frac{2x + 1}{3} > 5$ (Property A3)

$2x + 1 < -15 \text{ or } 2x + 1 > 15$ (Multiplying by 3)

$2x < -16 \text{ or } \quad 2x > 14$ (Adding -1)

$x < -8 \quad \text{ or } \quad x > 7$ $\left[\text{Multiplying by } \frac{1}{2}\right]$

The solution set is $\{x | x < -8 \text{ or } x > 7\}$, or $(-\infty, -8) \cup (7, \infty)$.

30. $\left|\frac{3x + 2}{4}\right| \leqslant 5$

$-5 \leqslant \frac{3x + 2}{4} \leqslant 5$

$-20 \leqslant 3x + 2 \leqslant 20$

$-22 \leqslant 3x \leqslant 18$

$-\frac{22}{3} \leqslant x \leqslant 6$

$\left\{x \middle| -\frac{22}{3} \leqslant x \leqslant 6\right\}$, or $\left[-\frac{22}{3}, 6\right]$

31. $\left|\frac{13}{4} + 2x\right| > \frac{1}{4}$

$\frac{13}{4} + 2x < -\frac{1}{4} \text{ or } \frac{13}{4} + 2x > \frac{1}{4}$ (Property A3)

$2x < -\frac{14}{4} \text{ or } \quad 2x > -\frac{12}{4}$

$2x < -\frac{7}{2} \text{ or } \quad 2x > -3$

$x < -\frac{7}{4} \text{ or } \quad x > -\frac{3}{2}$

The solution set is $\left\{x \middle| x < -\frac{7}{4} \text{ or } x > -\frac{3}{2}\right\}$, or $\left(-\infty, -\frac{7}{4}\right) \cup \left(-\frac{3}{2}, \infty\right)$.

32. $\left|\frac{5}{6} + 3x\right| < \frac{7}{6}$

$-\frac{7}{6} < \frac{5}{6} + 3x < \frac{7}{6}$

$-2 < 3x < \frac{1}{3}$

$-\frac{2}{3} < x < \frac{1}{9}$

$\left\{x \middle| -\frac{2}{3} < x < \frac{1}{9}\right\}$, or $\left(-\frac{2}{3}, \frac{1}{9}\right)$

33. $\left|\frac{3 - 4x}{2}\right| \leqslant \frac{3}{4}$

$-\frac{3}{4} \leqslant \frac{3 - 4x}{2} \leqslant \frac{3}{4}$ (Property A2)

$-3 \leqslant 6 - 8x \leqslant 3$ (Multiplying by 4)

$-9 \leqslant -8x \leqslant -3$ (Adding -6)

$\frac{9}{8} \geqslant x \geqslant \frac{3}{8}$ $\left[\text{Multiplying by } -\frac{1}{8}\right]$

The solution set is $\left\{x \middle| \frac{3}{8} \leqslant x \leqslant \frac{9}{8}\right\}$, or $\left[\frac{3}{8}, \frac{9}{8}\right]$.

34. $\left|\frac{2x - 1}{3}\right| \geqslant \frac{5}{6}$

$\frac{2x - 1}{3} \leqslant -\frac{5}{6}$ or $\frac{2x - 1}{3} \geqslant \frac{5}{6}$

$2x - 1 \leqslant -\frac{5}{2}$ or $2x - 1 \geqslant \frac{5}{2}$

$2x \leqslant -\frac{3}{2}$ or $2x \geqslant \frac{7}{2}$

$x \leqslant -\frac{3}{4}$ or $x \geqslant \frac{7}{4}$

$\left\{x \middle| x \leqslant -\frac{3}{4} \text{ or } x \geqslant \frac{7}{4}\right\}$, or $\left[-\infty, -\frac{3}{4}\right] \cup \left[\frac{7}{4}, \infty\right]$

35. $|x| = -3$

Since $|x| \geqslant 0$ for all x, there is no x such that $|x|$ would be negative. There is no solution. The solution set is $\varnothing$.

36. $|x| < -3$

$|x| \geqslant 0$ for all x, so there is no solution. The solution set is $\varnothing$.

37. $|2x - 4| < -5$

Since $|2x - 4| \geqslant 0$ for all x, there is no x such that $|2x - 4|$ would be less than -5. There is no solution. The solution set is $\varnothing$.

38. $|3x + 5| < 0$

$|3x + 5| \geqslant 0$ for all x, so there is no solution. The solution set is $\varnothing$.

39. $|x + 17.217| > 5.0012$

$x + 17.217 < -5.0012$ or $x + 17.217 > 5.0012$

                              (Property A3)

$x < -22.2182$ or $x > -12.2158$

                         (Adding -17.217)

The solution set is $\{x | x < -22.2182$ or $x > -12.2158\}$, or $(-\infty, -22.2182) \cup (-12.2158, \infty)$.

40. $|x - 2.0245| < 0.1011$

$-0.1011 < x - 2.0245 < 0.1011$

$1.9234 < x < 2.1256$

$\{x | 1.9234 < x < 2.1256\}$, or $(1.9234, 2.1256)$

41. $|-2.1437x + 7.8814| \geqslant 9.1132$

$-2.1437x + 7.8814 \leqslant -9.1132$

$-2.1437x \leqslant -16.9946$

$x \geqslant 7.9277$

or

$-2.1437x + 7.8814 \geqslant 9.1132$

$-2.1437x \geqslant 1.2318$

$x \leqslant -0.5746$

The solution set is $\{x | x \leqslant -0.5746$ or $x \geqslant 7.9277\}$, or $(-\infty, -0.5746] \cup [7.9277, \infty)$.

42. $|3.0147x - 8.9912| \leqslant 6.0243$

$-6.0243 \leqslant 3.0147x - 8.9912 \leqslant 6.0243$

$2.9669 \leqslant 3.0147x \leqslant 15.0155$

$0.9841 \leqslant x \leqslant 4.9808$

$\{x | 0.9841 \leqslant x \leqslant 4.9808\}$, or $[0.9841, 4.9808]$

43. $|2x - 8| = |x + 3|$

$2x - 8 = x + 3$ or $2x - 8 = -(x + 3)$

$x = 11$ or $2x - 8 = -x - 3$

$x = 11$ or $3x = 5$

$x = 11$ or $x = \frac{5}{3}$

The solution set is $\left\{\frac{5}{3}, 11\right\}$.

44. $|x - 7| = |3x + 4|$

$x - 7 = 3x + 4$ or $x - 7 = -(3x + 4)$

$-\frac{11}{2} = x$ or $x = \frac{3}{4}$

$\left\{-\frac{11}{2}, \frac{3}{4}\right\}$

45. $\left|\dfrac{2x + 3}{6}\right| = \left|\dfrac{4 - 5x}{8}\right|$

$\dfrac{2x + 3}{6} = \dfrac{4 - 5x}{8}$ or $\dfrac{2x + 3}{6} = -\left(\dfrac{4 - 5x}{8}\right)$

$4(2x + 3) = 3(4 - 5x)$ or $\dfrac{2x + 3}{6} = \dfrac{5x - 4}{8}$

$8x + 12 = 12 - 15x$ or $4(2x + 3) = 3(5x - 4)$

$23x = 0$ or $8x + 12 = 15x - 12$

$x = 0$ or $24 = 7x$

$x = 0$ or $\dfrac{24}{7} = x$

The solution set is $\left\{0, \dfrac{24}{7}\right\}$.

46. $\left|\dfrac{2}{3} - \dfrac{5}{6}x\right| = \left|\dfrac{3}{4} + \dfrac{3}{5}x\right|$

$\dfrac{2}{3} - \dfrac{5}{6}x = \dfrac{3}{4} + \dfrac{3}{5}x$ or $\dfrac{2}{3} - \dfrac{5}{6}x = -\left(\dfrac{3}{4} + \dfrac{3}{5}x\right)$

$-\dfrac{5}{86} = x$ or $\dfrac{85}{14} = x$

$\left\{-\dfrac{5}{86}, \dfrac{85}{14}\right\}$

47. $|x - 2| = x - 2$

By the definition of absolute value,

$|x - 2| = x - 2$ for $x - 2 \geqslant 0$, or $x \geqslant 2$.

The solution set is $\{x | x \geqslant 2\}$, or $[2, \infty)$.

48. $|4x - 5| = x + 1$

$4x - 5 = x + 1$ or $4x - 5 = -(x + 1)$

$x = 2$ or $x = \dfrac{4}{5}$

$\left\{\dfrac{4}{5}, 2\right\}$

49. $|7x - 2| = x + 5$

$7x - 2 = x + 5$ or $7x - 2 = -(x + 5)$

$6x = 7$ or $7x - 2 = -x - 5$

$x = \dfrac{7}{6}$ or $8x = -3$

$x = \dfrac{7}{6}$ or $x = -\dfrac{3}{8}$

The solution set is $\left\{-\dfrac{3}{8}, \dfrac{7}{6}\right\}$.

50. $|x - 3| = 3x - 8$

$x - 3 = 3x - 8$ or $x - 3 = -(3x - 8)$

$\dfrac{5}{2} = x$ or $x = \dfrac{11}{4}$

$\left\{\dfrac{5}{2}, \dfrac{11}{4}\right\}$

51. $|3x - 4| \leqslant 2x + 1$

$-(2x + 1) \leqslant 3x - 4 \leqslant 2x + 1$

$-2x - 1 \leqslant 3x - 4 \leqslant 2x + 1$

$-1 \leqslant 5x - 4 \leqslant 4x + 1$ (Adding 2x)

We write the conjunction, solve each inequality separately, and then find the intersection of the solution sets.

$-1 \leqslant 5x - 4$ and $5x - 4 \leqslant 4x + 1$

$3 \leqslant 5x$ and $x \leqslant 5$

$\dfrac{3}{5} \leqslant x$ and $x \leqslant 5$

The solution set is $\left[\dfrac{3}{5}, \infty\right] \cap [-\infty, 5] = \left[\dfrac{3}{5}, 5\right]$, or $\left\{x \Big| \dfrac{3}{5} \leqslant x \leqslant 5\right\}$.

52. $|5x + 8| \leqslant 4 - 3x$

$-(4 - 3x) \leqslant 5x + 8 \leqslant 4 - 3x$

$-4 + 3x \leqslant 5x + 8 \leqslant 4 - 3x$

$-4 \leqslant 2x + 8 \leqslant 4 - 6x$

$-4 \leqslant 2x + 8$ and $2x + 8 \leqslant 4 - 6x$

$-6 \leqslant x$ and $x \leqslant -\dfrac{1}{2}$

$\left\{x \Big| -6 \leqslant x \leqslant -\dfrac{1}{2}\right\}$, or $\left[-6, -\dfrac{1}{2}\right]$

53. $|3x - 4| \geqslant 2x + 1$

$3x - 4 \leqslant -(2x + 1)$ or $3x - 4 \geqslant 2x + 1$

$3x - 4 \leqslant -2x - 1$ or $x \geqslant 5$

$5x \leqslant 3$ or $x \geqslant 5$

$x \leqslant \dfrac{3}{5}$ or $x \geqslant 5$

The solution set is $\left\{x \Big| x \leqslant \dfrac{3}{5} \text{ or } x \geqslant 5\right\}$, or $\left[-\infty, \dfrac{3}{5}\right] \cup [5, \infty)$.

54. $|5x + 8| \geqslant 4 - 3x$

$5x + 8 \leqslant -(4 - 3x)$ or $5x + 8 \geqslant 4 - 3x$

$x \leqslant -6$ or $x \geqslant -\dfrac{1}{2}$

$\left\{x \Big| x \leqslant -6 \text{ or } x \geqslant -\dfrac{1}{2}\right\}$, or $\left[-\infty, -6\right] \cup \left[-\dfrac{1}{2}, \infty\right]$

55. $|4x - 5| = |x| + 1$

If $x \geqslant 0$, then $|x| = x$ and we solve:

$4x - 5 = x + 1$ or $4x - 5 = -(x + 1)$

$3x = 6$ or $4x - 5 = -x - 1$

$x = 2$ or $5x = 4$

$x = 2$ or $x = \dfrac{4}{5}$

If $x < 0$, then $|x| = -x$ and we solve:

$4x - 5 = -x + 1$ or $4x - 5 = -(-x + 1)$

$\quad 5x = 6 \qquad$ or $\quad 4x - 5 = x - 1$

$\qquad x = \dfrac{6}{5} \qquad$ or $\qquad 3x = 4$

$\qquad x = \dfrac{6}{5} \qquad$ or $\qquad x = \dfrac{4}{3}$

Since $\dfrac{6}{5} > 0$ and $\dfrac{4}{3} > 0$, this case yields no solution.

The solution set is $\left\{\dfrac{4}{5},\ 2\right\}$.

56. $|2x + 3| = |x| + 8$.

If $x \geqslant 0$, then $|x| = x$ and we have:

$2x + 3 = x + 8$ or $2x + 3 = -(x + 8)$

$\qquad x = 5 \qquad$ or $\qquad x = -\dfrac{11}{3}$

Only 5 is greater than or equal to 0.

If $x < 0$, then $|x| = -x$ and we have:

$2x + 3 = -x + 8$ or $2x + 3 = -(-x + 8)$

$\qquad x = \dfrac{5}{3} \qquad$ or $\qquad x = -11$

Only -11 is less than 0.

$\{5,\ -11\}$

57. $\big|\,|x| - 1\,\big| = 3$

$\quad |x| - 1 = -3$ or $|x| - 1 = 3 \qquad$ (Property A1)

$\qquad |x| = -2$ or $\qquad |x| = 4$

The solution set of $|x| = -2$ is $\emptyset$.

The solution set of $|x| = 4$ is $\{-4,\ 4\}$.

$\quad \emptyset \cup \{-4,\ 4\} = \{-4,\ 4\}$

The solution set of $\big|\,|x| - 1\,\big| = 3$ is $\{-4,\ 4\}$.

58. $|x + 2| > x$ clearly holds when $x \leqslant 0$ and when $x > 0$. The solution set is the set of all real numbers, or $(-\infty,\ \infty)$.

59. $|x + 2| \leqslant |x - 5|$

Divide the set of reals into three intervals:

$\quad x \geqslant 5$

$-2 \leqslant x < 5$

$\quad x < -2$

Find the solution set of $|x + 2| \leqslant |x - 5|$ for each interval. Then take the union of the three solution sets.

If $x \geqslant 5$, then $|x + 2| = x + 2$ and $|x - 5| = x - 5$.

Solve: $\quad x \geqslant 5$ and $x + 2 \leqslant x - 5$

$\qquad\qquad x \geqslant 5$ and $\quad 2 \leqslant -5 \qquad$ (False)

The solution set for this interval is $\emptyset$.

If $-2 \leqslant x < 5$, $|x + 2| = x + 2$ and $|x - 5| = -(x - 5)$.

Solve: $\quad -2 \leqslant x < 5$ and $x + 2 \leqslant -(x - 5)$

$\qquad\qquad -2 \leqslant x < 5$ and $x + 2 \leqslant -x + 5$

$\qquad\qquad -2 \leqslant x < 5$ and $\quad 2x \leqslant 3$

$\qquad\qquad -2 \leqslant x < 5$ and $\qquad x \leqslant \dfrac{3}{2}$

The solution set for this interval is $\left\{x \,\middle|\, -2 \leqslant x \leqslant \dfrac{3}{2}\right\}$.

If $x < -2$, then $|x + 2| = -(x + 2)$ and $|x - 5| = -(x - 5)$.

Solve: $x < -2$ and $-(x + 2) \leqslant -(x - 5)$

$\qquad\quad x < -2$ and $\quad -x - 2 \leqslant -x + 5$

$\qquad\quad x < -2$ and $\qquad\quad -2 \leqslant 5$

The solution set for this interval is $\{x \mid x < -2\}$.

The <u>union</u> of the above three solution sets is $\left\{x \,\middle|\, x \leqslant \dfrac{3}{2}\right\}$, or $\left[-\infty,\ \dfrac{3}{2}\right]$. This set is the solution of $|x + 2| \leqslant |x - 5|$.

60. $3x - 1 < -(5x - 2)$ or $3x - 1 > 5x - 2$. These give $x < \dfrac{3}{8}$ or $x < \dfrac{1}{2}$. Hence the solution set is $\left\{x \,\middle|\, x < \dfrac{1}{2}\right\}$, or $\left(-\infty,\ \dfrac{1}{2}\right)$.

61. $|x| + |x - 1| < 10$

If $x < 0$, then $|x| = -x$ and $|x - 1| = -(x - 1)$.

Solve: $x < 0$ and $-x + [-(x - 1)] < 10$

$\qquad\quad x < 0$ and $\qquad -x - x + 1 < 10$

$\qquad\quad x < 0$ and $\qquad\quad -2x + 1 < 10$

$\qquad\quad x < 0$ and $\qquad\qquad -2x < 9$

$\qquad\quad x < 0$ and $\qquad\qquad\quad x > -\dfrac{9}{2}$

The solution set for this interval is $\left\{x \,\middle|\, -\dfrac{9}{2} < x < 0\right\}$.

If $x \geqslant 0$, then $|x| = x$ and we have:

$x \geqslant 0$ and $\qquad x + |x - 1| < 10$

$x \geqslant 0$ and $\qquad\quad |x - 1| < 10 - x$

$x \geqslant 0$ and $-(10 - x) < x - 1 < 10 - x$

$x \geqslant 0$ and $x - 10 < x - 1$ and $x - 1 < 10 - x$

$x \geqslant 0$ and $\quad -10 < -1$ and $\quad x < \dfrac{11}{2}$

The solution set for this interval is $\left\{x \,\middle|\, 0 \leqslant x < \dfrac{11}{2}\right\}$.

The <u>union</u> of the two solution sets above is $\left\{x \,\middle|\, -\dfrac{9}{2} < x < \dfrac{11}{2}\right\}$, or $\left(-\dfrac{9}{2},\ \dfrac{11}{2}\right)$. This set is the solution set of $|x| + |x - 1| < 10$.

62. $|x| - |x - 3| < 7$ (1)

If $x \leqslant 0$, then $|x| = -x$ and $|x - 3| = -(x - 3)$, so we have $-x + (x - 3) < 7$ or $0 < 10$ which holds for all $x \leqslant 0$.

If $x > 0$, then $|x| = x$ and we have $x - |x - 3| < 7$ or $|x - 3| > x - 7$. Thus $x - 3 < -(x - 7)$ or $x - 3 > x - 7$ which give $x < 5$ or $0x > -4$. Thus (1) holds for all $x > 0$. Hence the solution set is the set of all real numbers, or $(-\infty, \infty)$.

63. $|x - 3| + |2x + 5| > 6$

Divide the set of real numbers into three intervals:

$x \geqslant 3$

$-\frac{5}{2} \leqslant x < 3$

$x < -\frac{5}{2}$

Find the solution set of $|x - 3| + |2x + 5| > 6$ for each interval. Then take the union of the three solution sets.

If $x \geqslant 3$, then $|x - 3| = x - 3$ and $|2x + 5| = 2x + 5$.

Solve: $x \geqslant 3$ and $x - 3 + 2x + 5 > 6$

          $x \geqslant 3$ and $3x > 4$

          $x \geqslant 3$ and $x > \frac{4}{3}$

The solution set for this interval is $[3, \infty)$.

If $-\frac{5}{2} \leqslant x < 3$, then $|x - 3| = -(x - 3)$ and $|2x + 5| = 2x + 5$.

Solve: $-\frac{5}{2} \leqslant x < 3$ and $-(x - 3) + 2x + 5 > 6$

      $-\frac{5}{2} \leqslant x < 3$ and $-x + 3 + 2x + 5 > 6$

      $-\frac{5}{2} \leqslant x < 3$ and $x > -2$

The solution set for this interval is $(-2, 3)$.

If $x < -\frac{5}{2}$, then $|x - 3| = -(x - 3)$ and $|2x + 5| = -(2x + 5)$.

Solve: $x < -\frac{5}{2}$ and $-(x - 3) + [-(2x + 5)] > 6$

          $x < -\frac{5}{2}$ and $-x + 3 - 2x - 5 > 6$

          $x < -\frac{5}{2}$ and $-3x > 8$

          $x < -\frac{5}{2}$ and $x < -\frac{8}{3}$

The solution set for this interval is $\left(-\infty, -\frac{8}{3}\right]$.

The union of the above solution sets is $\left(-\infty, -\frac{8}{3}\right] \cup (-2, \infty)$. This is the solution set of $|x - 3| + |2x + 5| > 6$.

64. $|p - 4| + |p + 4| < 8$

If $p \geqslant 4$, we have $p - 4 + p + 4 < 8$, or $p < 4$. This yields no solution.

If $-4 \leqslant p < 4$, we have $-(p - 4) + p + 4 < 8$, or $8 < 8$. This yields no solution.

If $p < -4$, we have $-(p - 4) - (p + 4) < 8$, or $p > -4$. This yields no solution.

The solution set is $\emptyset$.

65. $|x - 3| + |2x + 5| + |3x - 1| = 12$ (1)

If $x < -\frac{5}{2}$, we have $-(x - 3) - (2x + 5) - (3x - 1) = 12$, and $x = -\frac{13}{6}$. Since $-\frac{13}{6} < -\frac{5}{2}$, this case yields no solution.

If $x \leqslant 0$, we have $-(x - 3) + |2x + 5| - (3x - 1) = 12$ or $|2x + 5| = 4x + 8$; then $x = -\frac{3}{2}$. We now notice that x must be less than, say, 3; otherwise the left member of Eq. (1) would be greater than 12.

If $x > 0$ (and $x < 3$), we have from (1), $-(x - 3) + (2x + 5) + |3x - 1| = 12$ or $|3x - 1| = 4 - x$; then $x = \frac{5}{4}$ or $x = -\frac{3}{2}$. $\left[\text{Only } \frac{5}{4} \text{ is in the interval } (0, 3).\right]$ The solution set is $\left\{-\frac{3}{2}, \frac{5}{4}\right\}$.

66. $|x - x_0| < \delta$

    $-\delta < x - x_0 < \delta$

  $x_0 - \delta < x < x_0 + \delta$

$\{x | x_0 - \delta < x < x_0 + \delta\}$, or $(x_0 - \delta, x_0 + \delta)$

67. See the answer section in the text.

68. PROVE: $|a + b| \leqslant |a| + |b|$

From Exercise 67 we have $-|a| \leqslant a \leqslant |a|$ and $-|b| \leqslant b \leqslant |b|$.

Adding, we have $-\big[|a| + |b|\big] \leqslant (a + b) \leqslant |a| + |b|$ or $|a + b| \leqslant |a| + |b|$.

69. See the answer section in the text.

70. a) $-\frac{b - a}{2} < x - \frac{a + b}{2} < \frac{b - a}{2}$

     $-\frac{b - a}{2} + \frac{a + b}{2} < x < \frac{b - a}{2} + \frac{a + b}{2}$

                              $\left[\text{Adding } \frac{a + b}{2}\right]$

          $\frac{2a}{2} < x < \frac{2b}{2}$

           $a < x < b$

b) Using the result of part (a) with a = -5 and b = 5, we have $|x| < 5$.

c) Using the result of part (a) with a = -6 and b = 6, we have $|x| < 6$.

d) Using the result of part (a) with a = -1 and b = 7, we have $|x - 3| < 4$.

e) Using the result of part (a) with a = -5 and b = 1, we have $|x + 2| < 3$.

71. See the answer section in the text.

72. $|f(x) - L| < \varepsilon$

$-\varepsilon < f(x) - L < \varepsilon$

$L - \varepsilon < f(x) < L + \varepsilon$

$\{x | L - \varepsilon < f(x) < L + \varepsilon\}$, or $(L - \varepsilon, L + \varepsilon)$

73.-82. See Exercises 55-64.

Exercise Set 4.4

1. $(x + 5)(x - 3) > 0$

The solutions of $f(x) = (x + 5)(x - 3) = 0$ are -5 and 3. They divide the real-number line into three intervals as shown:

We try a test number in each interval.
A: Test -6, $f(-6) = (-6 + 5)(-6 - 3) = 9$
B: Test 0, $f(0) = (0 + 5)(0 - 3) = -15$
C: Test 4, $f(4) = (4 + 5)(4 - 1) = 9$

Function values are positive in intervals A and C. The solution set is $(-\infty, -5) \cup (3, \infty)$.

2. $(x + 4)(x - 1) > 0$

A: Test -5, $f(-5) = (-5 + 4)(-5 - 1) = 6$
B: Test 0, $f(0) = (0 + 4)(0 - 1) = -4$
C: Test 2, $f(2) = (2 + 4)(2 - 1) = 6$
$(-\infty, -4) \cup (1, \infty)$

3. $(x - 1)(x + 2) \leqslant 0$

The solutions of $f(x) = (x - 1)(x + 2) = 0$ are 1 and -2. They divide the real-number line into three intervals as shown:

We try a test number in each interval.
A: Test -3, $f(-3) = (-3 - 1)(-3 + 2) = 4$;
B: Test 0, $f(0) = (0 - 1)(0 + 2) = -2$;
C: Test 3, $f(3) = (3 - 1)(3 + 2) = 10$

Function values are negative in interval B. The inequality symbol is $\leqslant$, so we need to include the intercepts. The solution set is $[-2,1]$.

4. $(x + 5)(x - 3) \leqslant 0$

See Exercise 1.

$[-5, 3]$

5. $x^2 + x - 2 < 0$

$(x - 1)(x + 2) < 0$ Factoring

See the diagram and test numbers in Exercise 3. The solution set is $\{x | -2 < x < 1\}$, or $(-2,1)$.

6. $x^2 - x - 2 < 0$

$(x - 2)(x + 1) < 0$

A: Test -3, $f(-3) = (-3)^2 - (-3) - 2 = 10$
B: Test 0, $f(0) = 0^2 - 0 - 2 = -2$
C: Test 3, $f(3) = 3^2 - 3 - 2 = 4$
$\{x | -1 < x < 2\}$, or $(-1,2)$

7. $x^2 \geqslant 1$, or $x^2 - 1 \geqslant 0$

$(x + 1)(x - 1) \geqslant 0$ Factoring

The solutions of $f(x) = (x + 1)(x - 1) = 0$ are -1 and 1. They divide the real-number line into three intervals as shown:

We try a test number in each interval.
A: Test -2, $f(-2) = (-2 + 1)(-2 - 1) = 3$
B: Test 0, $f(0) = (0 + 1)(0 - 1) = -1$
C: Test 2, $f(2) = (2 + 1)(2 - 1) = 3$

Function values are positive in intervals A and C. The inequality symbol is $\geqslant$, so we need to include the intercepts. The solution set is $(-\infty, -1] \cup [1, \infty)$.

<u>8.</u> $x^2 < 25$, or $x^2 - 25 < 0$

$(x + 5)(x - 5) < 0$

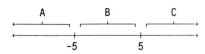

A: Test -6, $f(-6) = (-6 + 5)(-6 - 5) = 11$

B: Test 0, $f(0) = (0 + 5)(0 - 5) = -25$

C: Test 6, $f(6) = (6 + 5)(6 - 5) = 11$

$(-5, 5)$

<u>9.</u> $9 - x^2 \leqslant 0$

$(3 + x)(3 - x) \leqslant 0$ Factoring

The solutions of $f(x) = (3 + x)(3 - x) = 0$ are -3 and 3. They divide the real-number line into three intervals as shown:

We try a test number in each interval.

A: Test -4, $f(-4) = [3 + (-4)][3 - (-4)] = -7$

B: Test 0, $f(0) = (3 + 0)(3 - 0) = 9$

C: Test 4, $f(4) = (3 + 4)(3 - 4) = -7$

Function values are negative in intervals A and C. The inequality symbol is $\leqslant$, so we need to include the intercepts. The solution set is $(-\infty, -3] \cup [3, \infty)$.

<u>10.</u> $4 - x^2 \geqslant 0$

$(2 + x)(2 - x) \geqslant 0$

A: Test -3, $f(-3) = [2 + (-3)][2 - (-3)] = -5$

B: Test 0, $f(0) = (2 + 0)(2 - 0) = 4$

C: Test 3, $f(3) = (2 + 3)(2 - 3) = -5$

$[-2, 2]$

<u>11.</u> $x^2 - 2x + 1 \geqslant 0$

$(x - 1)^2 \geqslant 0$

The solution of $(x - 1)^2 = 0$ is 1. For all real-number values of x except 1, $(x - 1)^2$ will be positive. Thus the solution set is $\{x | x$ is a real number$\}$, or $(-\infty, \infty)$.

<u>12.</u> $x^2 + 6x + 9 < 0$

$(x + 3)^2 < 0$

Since $(x + 3)^2 \geqslant 0$ for all real-number values of x, the solution set is $\emptyset$.

<u>13.</u> $x^2 + 8 < 6x$

$x^2 - 6x + 8 < 0$

$(x - 4)(x - 2) < 0$

The solutions of $f(x) = (x - 4)(x - 2) = 0$ are 4 and 2. They divide the real-number line into three intervals as shown:

We try a test number in each interval.

A: Test 0, $f(0) = (0 - 4)(0 - 2) = 8$

B: Test 3, $f(3) = (3 - 4)(3 - 2) = -1$

C: Test 5, $f(5) = (5 - 4)(5 - 2) = 3$

Function values are negative in interval B. The solution set is $(2, 4)$.

<u>14.</u> $x^2 - 12 > 4x$

$x^2 - 4x - 12 > 0$

$(x + 2)(x - 6) > 0$

A: Test -3, $f(-3) = (-3 + 2)(-3 - 6) = 9$

B: Test 0, $f(0) = (0 + 2)(0 - 6) = -12$

C: Test 7, $f(7) = (7 + 2)(7 - 6) = 9$

$(-\infty, -2) \cup (6, \infty)$

<u>15.</u> $4x^2 + 7x < 15$

$4x^2 + 7x - 15 < 0$

$(4x - 5)(x + 3) < 0$

The solutions of $f(x) = (4x - 5)(x + 3) = 0$ are $\frac{5}{4}$ and -3. They divide the real-number line into three intervals as shown:

We try a test number in each interval.

A: Test -4, $f(-4) = [4(-4) - 5][-4 + 3] = 21$

B: Test 0, $f(0) = (4 \cdot 0 - 5)(0 + 3) = -15$

C: Test 2, $f(2) = (4 \cdot 2 - 5)(2 + 3) = 15$

Function values are negative in interval B. The solution set is $\left[-3, \frac{5}{4}\right]$.

<u>16.</u> $4x^2 + 7x \geqslant 15$

$4x^2 + 7x - 15 \geqslant 0$

See Exercise 15.

$(-\infty, -3] \cup \left[\frac{5}{4}, \infty\right]$

17. $2x^2 + x > 5$

$2x^2 + x - 5 > 0$

The solutions of $f(x) = 2x^2 + x - 5 = 0$ are

$\dfrac{-1 \pm \sqrt{41}}{4}$. They divide the real-number line

into three intervals as shown:

$$\dfrac{-1 - \sqrt{41}}{4} \qquad \dfrac{-1 + \sqrt{41}}{4}$$

We try a test number in each interval. Note that

$\dfrac{-1 - \sqrt{41}}{4} \approx -1.9$ and $\dfrac{-1 + \sqrt{41}}{4} \approx 1.4$.

A: Test -4, $f(-4) = 2(-4)^2 + (-4) - 5 = 23$

B: Test 0, $f(0) = 2(0)^2 + 0 - 5 = -5$

C: Test 3, $f(3) = 2(3)^2 + 3 - 5 = 16$

Function values are positive in intervals A and
C. The solution set is
$\left\{ x \mid x < \dfrac{-1 - \sqrt{41}}{4} \text{ or } x > \dfrac{-1 + \sqrt{41}}{4} \right\}$, or

$\left(-\infty, \dfrac{-1 - \sqrt{41}}{4} \right] \cup \left[\dfrac{-1 + \sqrt{41}}{4}, \infty \right]$.

18. $2x^2 + x \leqslant 2$

$2x^2 + x - 2 \leqslant 0$

$$\dfrac{-1 - \sqrt{17}}{4} \qquad \dfrac{-1 + \sqrt{17}}{4}$$

A: Test -2, $f(-2) = 2(-2)^2 + (-2) - 2 = 4$

B: Test 0, $f(0) = 2(0)^2 + 0 - 2 = -2$

C: Test 1, $f(1) = 2(1)^2 + 1 - 2 = 1$

$\left[\dfrac{-1 - \sqrt{17}}{4}, \dfrac{-1 + \sqrt{17}}{4} \right]$

19. $3x(x + 2)(x - 2) < 0$

The solutions of $f(x) = 3x(x + 2)(x - 2) = 0$ are
0, -2, and 2. They divide the real-number line
into four intervals as shown:

We try a test number in each interval.

A: Test -3, $f(-3) = 3(-3)(-3 + 2)(-3 - 2) = -45$

B: Test -1, $f(-1) = 3(-1)(-1 + 2)(-1 - 2) = 9$

C: Test 1, $f(1) = 3(1)(1 + 2)(1 - 2) = -9$

D: Test 3, $f(3) = 3(3)(3 + 2)(3 - 2) = 45$

Function values are negative in intervals A and
C. The solution set is $(-\infty, -2) \cup (0, 2)$.

20. $5x(x + 1)(x - 1) > 0$

A: Test -2, $f(-2) = 5(-2)(-2 + 1)(-2 - 1) = -30$

B: Test $-\dfrac{1}{2}$, $f\left(-\dfrac{1}{2} \right) = 5\left(-\dfrac{1}{2} \right)\left(-\dfrac{1}{2} + 1 \right)\left(-\dfrac{1}{2} - 1 \right) = \dfrac{15}{8}$

C: Test $\dfrac{1}{2}$, $f\left(\dfrac{1}{2} \right) = 5\left(\dfrac{1}{2} \right)\left(\dfrac{1}{2} + 1 \right)\left(\dfrac{1}{2} - 1 \right) = -\dfrac{15}{8}$

D: Test 2, $f(2) = 5(2)(2 + 1)(2 - 1) = 30$

$(-1, 0) \cup (1, \infty)$

21. $(x + 3)(x - 2)(x + 1) > 0$

The solutions of $f(x) = (x + 3)(x - 2)(x + 1) = 0$
are -3, 2, and -1. They divide the real-number
line as shown:

We try a test number in each interval.

A: Test -4, $f(-4) = (-4 + 3)(-4 - 2)(-4 + 1) = -18$

B: Test -2, $f(-2) = (-2 + 3)(-2 - 2)(-2 + 1) = 4$

C: Test 0, $f(0) = (0 + 3)(0 - 2)(0 + 1) = -6$

D: Test 3, $f(3) = (3 + 3)(3 - 2)(3 + 1) = 24$

Function values are positive in intervals B and D.
The solution set is $(-3, -1) \cup (2, \infty)$.

22. $(x - 1)(x + 2)(x - 4) < 0$

A: Test -3, $f(-3) = (-3 - 1)(-3 + 2)(-3 - 4) = -28$

B: Test 0, $f(0) = (0 - 1)(0 + 2)(0 - 4) = 8$

C: Test 2, $f(2) = (2 - 1)(2 + 2)(2 - 4) = -8$

D: Test 5, $f(5) = (5 - 1)(5 + 2)(5 - 4) = 28$

$(-\infty, -2) \cup (1, 4)$

23. $(x + 3)(x + 2)(x - 1) < 0$

The solutions of $f(x) = (x + 3)(x + 2)(x - 1) = 0$
are -3, -2, and 1. They divide the real-number
line into four intervals as shown:

We try a test number in each interval.

A: Test -4, $f(-4) = (-4 + 3)(-4 + 2)(-4 - 1) = -10$

B: Test $-\frac{5}{2}$, $f\left(-\frac{5}{2}\right) =$

$$\left(-\frac{5}{2} + 3\right)\left(-\frac{5}{2} + 2\right)\left(-\frac{5}{2} - 1\right) = \frac{7}{8}$$

C: Test 0, $f(0) = (0 + 3)(0 + 2)(0 - 1) = -6$

D: Test 2, $f(2) = (2 + 3)(2 + 2)(2 - 1) = 20$

Function values are negative in intervals A and C. The solution set is $\{x \mid x < -3$ or $-2 < x < 1\}$, or $(-\infty, -3) \cup (-2, 1)$.

24. $(x - 2)(x - 3)(x + 1) < 0$

A: Test -2, $f(-2) = (-2 - 2)(-2 - 3)(-2 + 1) = -20$

B: Test 0, $f(0) = (0 - 2)(0 - 3)(0 + 1) = 6$

C: Test $\frac{5}{2}$, $f\left(\frac{5}{2}\right) = \left(\frac{5}{2} - 2\right)\left(\frac{5}{2} - 3\right)\left(\frac{5}{2} + 1\right) = -\frac{7}{8}$

D: Test 4, $f(4) = (4 - 2)(4 - 3)(4 + 1) = 10$

$\{x \mid x < -1$ or $2 < x < 3\}$, or $(-\infty, -1) \cup (2, 3)$

25. $\frac{1}{4 - x} < 0$

We write the related equation by changing the < symbol to =:

$$\frac{1}{4 - x} = 0$$

Then we solve the related equation:

$$(4 - x) \cdot \frac{1}{4 - x} = (4 - x) \cdot 0$$

$$1 = 0 \quad \text{False equation}$$

The related equation has no solution. Next we find the replacements that make the denominator 0:

$$4 - x = 0$$
$$4 = x$$

The number 4 divides the number line as shown:

Try test numbers in each interval:

A: Test 0, $\quad \dfrac{1}{4 - x} < 0$

$$\dfrac{1}{4 - 0} \;\Big|\; 0$$
$$\dfrac{1}{4} \;\Big|\; \text{FALSE}$$

The number 0 is not a solution of the inequality, so the interval A is not part of the solution set.

B: Test 5, $\quad \dfrac{1}{4 - x} < 0$

$$\dfrac{1}{4 - 5} \;\Big|\; 0$$
$$-1 \;\Big|\; \text{TRUE}$$

The number 5 is a solution of the inequality, so the interval B is part of the solution set.

The solution set is $(4, \infty)$.

26. $\dfrac{-4}{2x + 5} > 0$

The related equation $\dfrac{-4}{2x + 5} = 0$ has no solution. Also $2x + 5 = 0$ when $x = -\frac{5}{2}$, so $-\frac{5}{2}$ is not a meaningful replacement.

A: Test -3, $\quad \dfrac{-4}{2x + 5} > 0$

$$\dfrac{-4}{2(-3) + 5} \;\Big|\; 0$$
$$4 \;\Big|\; \text{TRUE}$$

B: Test 0, $\quad \dfrac{-4}{2x + 5} > 0$

$$\dfrac{-4}{2 \cdot 0 + 5} \;\Big|\; 0$$
$$-\dfrac{4}{5} \;\Big|\; \text{FALSE}$$

$\left(-\infty, -\dfrac{5}{2}\right)$

27. $3 < \dfrac{1}{x}$

Solve the related equation.

$$3 = \dfrac{1}{x}$$
$$x = \dfrac{1}{3}$$

Find the replacements that are not meaningful.

$$x = 0$$

Use the numbers $\frac{1}{3}$ and 0 to divide the number line into intervals as shown.

Try test numbers in each interval.

A: Test -1, $\quad 3 < \dfrac{1}{x}$

$$3 \;\Big|\; \dfrac{1}{-1}$$
$$\;\Big|\; -1 \quad \text{FALSE}$$

The number -1 is not a solution of the inequality, so the interval A is not in the solution set.

B: Test $\frac{1}{4}$, $\qquad 3 < \frac{1}{x}$

$$3 \;\Bigg|\; \dfrac{1}{\frac{1}{4}}$$

$\qquad\qquad$ 4 $\quad$ TRUE

The number $\frac{1}{4}$ is a solution of the inequality, so the interval B is in the solution set.

C: Test 1, $\qquad 3 < \frac{1}{x}$

$$3 \;\Bigg|\; \dfrac{1}{1}$$

$\qquad\qquad$ 1 $\quad$ FALSE

The number 1 is not a solution of the inequality, so the interval C is not in the solution set.

The solution set is $\left[0, \frac{1}{3}\right]$.

28. $\frac{1}{x} \leqslant 5$

Solve the related equation.

$$\frac{1}{x} = 5$$

$$\frac{1}{5} = x$$

Also, 0 is not a meaningful replacement.

```
      A         B         C
  <---------|---------|--------->
            |         |
            0        1/5
```

A: Test -1, $\qquad \frac{1}{x} \leqslant 5$

$$\dfrac{1}{-1} \;\Bigg|\; 5$$

$\qquad\quad$ -1 $\Big|\quad$ TRUE

B: Test $\frac{1}{10}$, $\qquad \frac{1}{x} \leqslant 5$

$$\dfrac{1}{\frac{1}{10}} \;\Bigg|\; 5$$

$\qquad\qquad$ 10 $\Big|\quad$ FALSE

C: Test 1, $\qquad \frac{1}{x} \leqslant 5$

$$\dfrac{1}{1} \;\Bigg|\; 5$$

$\qquad\qquad$ 1 $\Big|\quad$ TRUE

$(-\infty, 0) \cup \left[\frac{1}{5}, \infty\right)$

29. $\frac{3x + 2}{x - 3} > 0$

Solve the related equation.

$$\frac{3x + 2}{x - 3} = 0$$

$$3x + 2 = 0$$

$$3x = -2$$

$$x = -\frac{2}{3}$$

Find replacements that are not meaningful.

$$x - 3 = 0$$

$$x = 3$$

Use the numbers $-\frac{2}{3}$ and 3 to divide the number line into intervals as shown.

```
      A         B         C
  <--------|---------|-------->
           |         |
          -2/3        3
```

Try test numbers in each interval.

A: Test -1, $\qquad \dfrac{3x + 2}{x - 3} > 0$

$$\dfrac{3(-1) + 2}{-1 - 3} \;\Bigg|\; 0$$

$$\dfrac{-1}{-4}$$

$\qquad\quad \dfrac{1}{4} \;\Big|\quad$ TRUE

The number -1 is a solution of the inequality, so the interval A is part of the solution set.

B: Test 0, $\qquad \dfrac{3x + 2}{x - 3} > 0$

$$\dfrac{3 \cdot 0 + 2}{0 - 3} \;\Bigg|\; 0$$

$$\dfrac{2}{-3}$$

$\qquad\quad -\dfrac{2}{3} \;\Big|\quad$ FALSE

The number 0 is not a solution of the inequality, so the interval B is not part of the solution set.

C: Test 4, $\qquad \dfrac{3x + 2}{x - 3} > 0$

$$\dfrac{3 \cdot 4 + 2}{4 - 3} \;\Bigg|\; 0$$

$\qquad\qquad$ 14 $\;\Big|\quad$ TRUE

The number 4 is a solution of the inequality, so the interval C is part of the solution set.

The solution set is $\left[-\infty, -\frac{2}{3}\right] \cup (3, \infty)$.

30. $\frac{5 - 2x}{4x + 3} < 0$

Solve the related equation.

$$\frac{5 - 2x}{4x + 3} = 0$$

$$5 - 2x = 0$$

$$\frac{5}{2} = x$$

Find replacements that are not meaningful.

$$4x + 3 = 0$$

$$x = -\frac{3}{4}$$

$$-\frac{3}{4} \qquad \frac{5}{2}$$

A: Test -1, $\qquad \dfrac{5 - 2x}{4x + 3} < 0$

$$\dfrac{5 - 2(-1)}{4(-1) + 3} \bigg| 0$$

$$-7 \bigg| \text{TRUE}$$

B: Test 0, $\qquad \dfrac{5 - 2x}{4x + 3} < 0$

$$\dfrac{5 - 2 \cdot 0}{4 \cdot 0 + 3} \bigg| 0$$

$$\frac{5}{3} \bigg| \text{FALSE}$$

C: Test 3, $\qquad \dfrac{5 - 2x}{4x + 3} < 0$

$$\dfrac{5 - 2 \cdot 3}{4 \cdot 3 + 3} \bigg| 0$$

$$-\frac{1}{15} \bigg| \text{TRUE}$$

$$\left(-\infty, -\frac{3}{4}\right) \cup \left[\frac{5}{2}, \infty\right)$$

31. $\dfrac{x + 2}{x} \leqslant 0$

Solve the related equation.

$$\frac{x + 2}{x} = 0$$

$$x + 2 = 0$$

$$x = -2$$

Find the replacements that are not meaningful.

$$x = 0$$

The numbers -2 and 0 divide the number line into intervals as shown.

$$-2 \qquad 0$$

Try test numbers in each interval.

A: Test -3, $\qquad \dfrac{x + 2}{x} \leqslant 0$

$$\dfrac{-3 + 2}{-3} \bigg| 0$$

$$\frac{1}{3} \bigg| \text{FALSE}$$

The number -3 is not a solution of the inequality, so the interval A is not in the solution set.

B: Test -1, $\qquad \dfrac{x + 2}{x} \leqslant 0$

$$\dfrac{-1 + 2}{-1} \bigg| 0$$

$$-1 \bigg| \text{TRUE}$$

The number -1 is a solution of the inequality, so the interval B is in the solution set.

C: Test 1, $\qquad \dfrac{x + 2}{x} \leqslant 0$

$$\dfrac{1 + 2}{1} \bigg| 0$$

$$3 \bigg| \text{FALSE}$$

The number 1 is not a solution of the inequality, so the interval C is not in the solution set.

The solution set includes the interval B. The number -2 is also included since the inequality symbol is $\leqslant$ and -2 is a solution of the related equation. The number 0 is not included, since it is not a meaningful replacement. The solution set is [-2, 0).

32. $\dfrac{x}{x - 3} \geqslant 0$

Solve the related equation.

$$\frac{x}{x - 3} = 0$$

$$x = 0$$

Find the replacements that are not meaningful.

$$x - 3 = 0$$

$$x = 3$$

$$0 \qquad 3$$

A: Test -1, $\qquad \dfrac{x}{x - 3} \geqslant 0$

$$\dfrac{-1}{-1 - 3} \bigg| 0$$

$$\frac{1}{4} \bigg| \text{TRUE}$$

B: Test 1, $\qquad \dfrac{x}{x - 3} \geqslant 0$

$$\dfrac{1}{1 - 3} \bigg| 0$$

$$-\frac{1}{2} \bigg| \text{FALSE}$$

C: Test 4, $\qquad \dfrac{x}{x - 3} \geqslant 0$

$$\dfrac{4}{4 - 3} \bigg| 0$$

$$4 \bigg| \text{TRUE}$$

$$(-\infty, 0] \cup (3, \infty)$$

33. $\dfrac{x + 1}{2x - 3} \geqslant 1$

Solve the related equation.

$$\dfrac{x + 1}{2x - 3} = 1$$
$$x + 1 = 2x - 3$$
$$4 = x$$

Find replacements that are not meaningful.

$$2x - 3 = 0$$
$$x = \dfrac{3}{2}$$

Use the numbers 4 and $\dfrac{3}{2}$ to divide the number line as shown.

Try test numbers in each interval.

A: Test 0,
$$\begin{array}{c|c} \dfrac{x + 1}{2x - 3} \geqslant 1 & \\ \hline \dfrac{0 + 1}{2 \cdot 0 - 3} & 1 \\ \\ -\dfrac{1}{3} & \text{FALSE} \end{array}$$

The interval A is not in the solution set.

B: Test 2,
$$\begin{array}{c|c} \dfrac{x + 1}{2x - 3} \geqslant 1 & \\ \hline \dfrac{2 + 1}{2 \cdot 2 - 3} & 1 \\ \\ 3 & \text{TRUE} \end{array}$$

The interval B is in the solution set.

C: Test 5,
$$\begin{array}{c|c} \dfrac{x + 1}{2x - 3} \geqslant 1 & \\ \hline \dfrac{5 + 1}{2 \cdot 5 - 3} & 1 \\ \\ \dfrac{6}{7} & \text{FALSE} \end{array}$$

The interval C is not in the solution set. The solution set includes the interval B. The number 4 is also included, since the inequality is $\geqslant$ and 4 is a solution of the related equation. The number $\dfrac{3}{2}$ is not included, since it is not a meaningful replacement. The solution set is $\left[\dfrac{3}{2},\ 4\right]$.

34. $\dfrac{x - 1}{x - 2} \geqslant 3$

Solve the related equation.

$$\dfrac{x - 1}{x - 2} = 3$$
$$x - 1 = 3(x - 2)$$
$$x - 1 = 3x - 6$$
$$5 = 2x$$
$$\dfrac{5}{2} = x$$

Find replacements that are not meaningful.

$$x - 2 = 0$$
$$x = 2$$

A: Test 0,
$$\begin{array}{c|c} \dfrac{x - 1}{x - 2} \geqslant 3 & \\ \hline \dfrac{0 - 1}{0 - 2} & 3 \\ \\ \dfrac{1}{2} & \text{FALSE} \end{array}$$

B: Test $\dfrac{9}{4}$,
$$\begin{array}{c|c} \dfrac{x - 1}{x - 2} \geqslant 3 & \\ \hline \dfrac{\frac{9}{4} - 1}{\frac{9}{4} - 2} & 3 \\ \\ \dfrac{\frac{5}{4}}{\frac{1}{4}} & \\ \\ 5 & \text{TRUE} \end{array}$$

C: Test 3,
$$\begin{array}{c|c} \dfrac{x - 1}{x - 2} \geqslant 3 & \\ \hline \dfrac{3 - 1}{3 - 2} & 3 \\ \\ 2 & \text{FALSE} \end{array}$$

$\left[2,\ \dfrac{5}{2}\right]$

35. $\dfrac{x + 1}{x + 2} \leqslant 3$

Solve the related equation.

$$\dfrac{x + 1}{x + 2} = 3$$
$$x + 1 = 3(x + 2)$$
$$x + 1 = 3x + 6$$
$$-5 = 2x$$
$$-\dfrac{5}{2} = x$$

Find the replacements that are not meaningful.

$$x + 2 = 0$$
$$x = -2$$

Use the numbers $-\frac{5}{2}$ and -2 to divide the number line as shown.

Try test numbers in each interval.

A: Test -3, $\dfrac{x + 1}{x + 2} \leqslant 3$

$$\dfrac{-3 + 1}{-3 + 2} \;\Big|\; 3$$

$$2 \;\Big|\; \text{TRUE}$$

The interval A is in the solution set.

B: Test $-\frac{9}{4}$, $\dfrac{x + 1}{x + 2} \leqslant 3$

$$\dfrac{-\frac{9}{4} + 1}{-\frac{9}{4} + 2} \;\Big|\; 3$$

$$\dfrac{-\frac{5}{4}}{-\frac{1}{4}} \;\Big|\;$$

$$5 \;\Big|\; \text{FALSE}$$

The interval B is not in the solution set.

C: Test 0, $\dfrac{x + 1}{x + 2} \leqslant 3$

$$\dfrac{0 + 1}{0 + 2} \;\Big|\; 3$$

$$\dfrac{1}{2} \;\Big|\; \text{TRUE}$$

The interval C is in the solution set.

The number $-\frac{5}{2}$ is in the solution set since the inequality is $\leqslant$, but -2 is not included since it is not a meaningful replacement. The solution set is $\left[-\infty, -\frac{5}{2}\right] \cup (-2, \infty)$.

36. $\dfrac{x + 1}{2x - 3} \leqslant 1$

See Exercise 33.

$\left[-\infty, \frac{3}{2}\right) \cup [4, \infty)$

37. $\dfrac{x - 6}{x} > 1$

Solve the related equation.

$$\dfrac{x - 6}{x} = 1$$

$$x - 6 = x$$

$$-6 = 0$$

The related equation has no solution. We see that 0 is not a meaningful replacement. Use the number 0 to divide the number line as shown.

Try test numbers in each interval.

A: Test -1, $\dfrac{x - 6}{x} > 1$

$$\dfrac{-1 - 6}{-1} \;\Big|\; 1$$

$$7 \;\Big|\; \text{TRUE}$$

The interval A is in the solution set.

B: Test 1, $\dfrac{x - 6}{x} > 1$

$$\dfrac{1 - 6}{1} \;\Big|\; 1$$

$$-5 \;\Big|\; \text{FALSE}$$

The interval B is not in the solution set. The solution set is $(-\infty, 0)$.

38. $\dfrac{x}{x + 3} > -1$

The solution of the related equation is $-\frac{3}{2}$, and -3 is not a meaningful replacement.

A: Test -4, $\dfrac{x}{x + 3} > -1$

$$\dfrac{-4}{-4 + 3} \;\Big|\; -1$$

$$4 \;\Big|\; \text{TRUE}$$

B: Test -2, $\dfrac{x}{x + 3} > -1$

$$\dfrac{-2}{-2 + 3} \;\Big|\; -1$$

$$-2 \;\Big|\; \text{FALSE}$$

C: Test 0, $\dfrac{x}{x + 3} > -1$

$$\dfrac{0}{0 + 3} \;\Big|\; -1$$

$$0 \;\Big|\; \text{TRUE}$$

$(-\infty, -3) \cup \left[-\frac{3}{2}, \infty\right]$

39. $(x + 1)(x - 2) > (x + 3)^2$
Solve the related equation.
$$(x + 1)(x - 2) = (x + 3)^2$$
$$x^2 - x - 2 = x^2 + 6x + 9$$
$$-11 = 7x$$
$$-\dfrac{11}{7} = x$$

All real numbers are meaningful replacements.

Use the number $-\frac{11}{7}$ to divide the number line as shown.

Try test numbers in each interval.

A: Test -2,
$$\frac{(x + 1)(x - 2) > (x + 3)^2}{(-2 + 1)(-2 - 2) \mid (-2 + 3)^2}$$
$$4 \mid 1 \qquad \text{TRUE}$$

The interval A is in the solution set.

B: Test 0,
$$\frac{(x + 1)(x - 2) > (x + 3)^2}{(0 + 1)(0 - 2) \mid (0 + 3)^2}$$
$$-2 \mid 9 \qquad \text{FALSE}$$

The interval B is not in the solution set.
The solution set is $\left[-\infty, -\frac{11}{7}\right]$.

40. $(x - 4)(x + 3) > (x - 1)^2$

The solution of the related equation is 13.
All real numbers are meaningful replacements.

```
        A         B
    ←——————+——————————→
    ←——————+——————————→
            13
```

A: Test 0,
$$\frac{(x - 4)(x + 3) > (x - 1)^2}{(0 - 4)(0 + 3) \mid (0 - 1)^2}$$
$$-12 \mid 1 \qquad \text{FALSE}$$

B: Test 14,
$$\frac{(x - 4)(x + 3) > (x - 1)^2}{(14 - 4)(14 + 3) \mid (14 - 1)^2}$$
$$170 \mid 169 \qquad \text{TRUE}$$

$(13, \infty)$

41. $x^3 - x^2 > 0$
$x^2(x - 1) > 0$

The solutions of $f(x) = x^2(x - 1) = 0$ are 0 and 1.
They divide the number line into intervals as shown.

```
        A      B      C
    ←——————+——————+——————→
    ←——————+——————+——————→
            0      1
```

Try a test number in each interval.

A: Test -1, $f(-1) = (-1)^3 - (-1)^2 = -2$

B: Test $\frac{1}{2}$, $f\left(\frac{1}{2}\right) = \left(\frac{1}{2}\right)^3 - \left(\frac{1}{2}\right)^2 = -\frac{1}{8}$

C: Test 2, $f(2) = 2^3 - 2^2 = 4$

Function values are positive in interval C.
The solution set is $(1, \infty)$.

42. $x^3 - 4x > 0$
$x(x + 2)(x - 2) > 0$

```
        A       B       C       D
    ←————+———————+———————+———————+————→
    ←————+———————+———————+———————+————→
        -2       0       2
```

A: Test -3, $f(-3) = (-3)^3 - 4(-3) = -15$
B: Test -1, $f(-1) = (-1)^3 - 4(-1) = 3$
C: Test 1, $f(1) = 1^3 - 4 \cdot 1 = -3$
D: Test 3, $f(3) = 3^3 - 4 \cdot 3 = 15$

$(-2, 0) \cup (2, \infty)$

43. $x + \frac{4}{x} > 4$

Solve the related equation.

$$x + \frac{4}{x} = 4$$
$$x^2 + 4 = 4x$$
$$x^2 - 4x + 4 = 0$$
$$(x - 2)(x - 2) = 0$$
$$x = 2$$

We see that 0 is not a meaningful replacement.
Use the numbers 2 and 0 to divide the number line as shown.

```
        A       B       C
    ←——————+———————+——————→
    ←——————+———————+——————→
            0       2
```

Try test numbers in each interval.

A: Test -1,
$$\frac{x + \frac{4}{x} > 4}{-1 + \frac{4}{-1} \mid 4}$$
$$-5 \mid \qquad \text{FALSE}$$

The interval A is not in the solution set.

B: Test 1,
$$\frac{x + \frac{4}{x} > 4}{1 + \frac{4}{1} \mid 4}$$
$$5 \mid \qquad \text{TRUE}$$

The interval B is in the solution set.

C: Test 4,
$$\frac{x + \frac{4}{x} > 4}{4 + \frac{4}{4} \mid 4}$$
$$5 \mid \qquad \text{TRUE}$$

The interval C is in the solution set. The solution set is $(0, 2) \cup (2, \infty)$.

44. $\frac{1}{x^2} \leqslant \frac{1}{x^3}$

See Exercise 45 below.

$(0, 1]$

45. $\frac{1}{x^3} \leqslant \frac{1}{x^2}$

Solve the related equation.

$$\frac{1}{x^3} = \frac{1}{x^2}$$

$$x^3 \cdot \frac{1}{x^3} = x^3 \cdot \frac{1}{x^2}$$

$$1 = x$$

We see that 0 is not a meaningful replacement. Use the numbers 1 and 0 to divide the number line as shown.

Try test numbers in each interval.

A: Test -1,

$$\begin{array}{c|c} \frac{1}{x^3} \leqslant \frac{1}{x^2} & \\ \hline \frac{1}{(-1)^3} & \frac{1}{(-1)^2} \\ -1 & 1 \quad \text{TRUE} \end{array}$$

The interval A is in the solution set.

B: Test $\frac{1}{2}$,

$$\begin{array}{c|c} \frac{1}{x^3} \leqslant \frac{1}{x^2} & \\ \hline \frac{1}{\left(\frac{1}{2}\right)^3} & \frac{1}{\left(\frac{1}{2}\right)^2} \\ 8 & 4 \quad \text{FALSE} \end{array}$$

The interval B is not in the solution set.

C: Test 2,

$$\begin{array}{c|c} \frac{1}{x^3} \leqslant \frac{1}{x^2} & \\ \hline \frac{1}{2^3} & \frac{1}{2^2} \\ \frac{1}{8} & \frac{1}{4} \quad \text{TRUE} \end{array}$$

The interval C is in the solution set. The number 1 is also in the solution set since the inequality is $\leqslant$, but 0 is not included since it is not a meaningful replacement. The solution set is $(-\infty, 0) \cup [1, \infty)$.

46. $x + \frac{1}{x} > 2$

The solution of the related equation is 1, and 0 is not a meaningful replacement.

Try test numbers in each interval.

A: Test -1,

$$\begin{array}{c|c} x + \frac{1}{x} > 2 & \\ \hline -1 + \frac{1}{-1} & 2 \\ -2 & \text{FALSE} \end{array}$$

B: Test $\frac{1}{2}$,

$$\begin{array}{c|c} x + \frac{1}{x} > 2 & \\ \hline \frac{1}{2} + \frac{1}{\frac{1}{2}} & 2 \\ 2\frac{1}{2} & \text{TRUE} \end{array}$$

C: Test 2,

$$\begin{array}{c|c} x + \frac{1}{x} > 2 & \\ \hline 2 + \frac{1}{2} & 2 \\ 2\frac{1}{2} & \text{TRUE} \end{array}$$

$(0, 1) \cup (1, \infty)$

47. $\frac{2 + x - x^2}{x^2 + 5x + 6} < 0$

Solve the related equation.

$$\frac{2 + x - x^2}{x^2 + 5x + 6} = 0$$

$$2 + x - x^2 = 0$$

$$(2 - x)(1 + x) = 0$$

$$x = 2 \quad \text{or} \quad x = -1$$

Find the replacements that are not meaningful.

$$x^2 + 5x + 6 = 0$$

$$(x + 3)(x + 2) = 0$$

$$x = -3 \quad \text{or} \quad x = -2$$

Use the numbers -3, -2, -1, and 2 to divide the number line into intervals as shown.

Try test numbers in each interval.

A: Test -4,

$$\begin{array}{c|c} \frac{2 + x - x^2}{x^2 + 5x + 6} < 0 & \\ \hline \frac{2 + (-4) - (-4)^2}{(-4)^2 + 5(-4) + 6} & 0 \\ \frac{-18}{2} & \\ -9 & \text{TRUE} \end{array}$$

The interval A is in the solution set.

B: Test $-\frac{5}{2}$,

$$\begin{array}{c|c} \frac{2 + x - x^2}{x^2 + 5x + 6} < 0 & \\ \hline \frac{2 + \left(-\frac{5}{2}\right) - \left(-\frac{5}{2}\right)^2}{\left(-\frac{5}{2}\right)^2 + 5\left(-\frac{5}{2}\right) + 6} & 0 \\ \frac{-\frac{27}{4}}{-\frac{1}{4}} & \\ 27 & \text{FALSE} \end{array}$$

The interval B is not in the solution set.

C: Test $-\frac{3}{2}$,

$$\frac{2 + x - x^2}{x^2 + 5x + 6} < 0$$

$$\frac{2 + \left(-\frac{3}{2}\right) - \left(-\frac{3}{2}\right)^2}{\left(-\frac{3}{2}\right)^2 + 5\left(-\frac{3}{2}\right) + 6} \;\middle|\; 0$$

$$\frac{-\frac{7}{4}}{\frac{3}{4}} \;\middle|$$

$$-\frac{7}{3} \;\middle|\; \text{TRUE}$$

The interval C is in the solution set.

D: Test 0,

$$\frac{2 + x - x^2}{x^2 + 5x + 6} < 0$$

$$\frac{2 + 0 - 0^2}{0^2 + 5 \cdot 0 + 6} \;\middle|\; 0$$

$$\frac{2}{6} \;\middle|$$

$$\frac{1}{3} \;\middle|\; \text{FALSE}$$

The interval D is not in the solution set.

E: Test 3,

$$\frac{2 + x - x^2}{x^2 + 5x + 6} < 0$$

$$\frac{2 + 3 - 3^2}{3^2 + 5 \cdot 3 + 6} \;\middle|\; 0$$

$$-\frac{4}{30} \;\middle|$$

$$-\frac{2}{15} \;\middle|\; \text{TRUE}$$

The interval E is in the solution set.

The solution set is $(-\infty, -3) \cup (-2, -1) \cup (2, \infty)$.

48. $\frac{4}{x^2} - 1 > 0$

The solutions of the related equation are -2 and 2, and 0 is not a meaningful replacement.

A: Test -3,

$$\frac{4}{x^2} - 1 > 0$$

$$\frac{4}{(-3)^2} - 1 \;\middle|\; 0$$

$$-\frac{5}{9} \;\middle|\; \text{FALSE}$$

B: Test -1,

$$\frac{4}{x^2} - 1 > 0$$

$$\frac{4}{(-1)^2} - 1 \;\middle|\; 0$$

$$3 \;\middle|\; \text{TRUE}$$

C: Test 1,

$$\frac{4}{x^2} - 1 > 0$$

$$\frac{4}{1^2} - 1 \;\middle|\; 0$$

$$3 \;\middle|\; \text{TRUE}$$

D: Test 3

$$\frac{4}{x^2} - 1 > 0$$

$$\frac{4}{3^2} - 1 \;\middle|\; 0$$

$$-\frac{5}{9} \;\middle|\; \text{FALSE}$$

$(-2, 0) \cup (0, 2)$

49. $x^4 - 2x^2 \leqslant 0$

$x^2(x^2 - 2) \leqslant 0$

The solutions of $f(x) = x^2(x^2 - 2) = 0$ are 0, $-\sqrt{2}$, and $\sqrt{2}$. They divide the number line as shown.

Try a test number in each interval. Note that $-\sqrt{2} \approx -1.4$ and $\sqrt{2} \approx 1.4$.

A: Test -2, $f(-2) = (-2)^4 - 2(-2)^2 = 8$

B: Test -1, $f(-1) = (-1)^4 - 2(-1)^2 = -1$

C: Test 1, $f(1) = 1^4 - 2(1)^2 = -1$

D: Test 2, $f(2) = 2^4 - 2(2)^2 = 8$

The solution set is $[-\sqrt{2}, \sqrt{2}]$.

50. $x^4 - 3x^2 > 0$

$x^2(x^2 - 3) > 0$

A: Test -2, $f(-2) = (-2)^4 - 3(-2)^2 = 4$

B: Test -1, $f(-1) = (-1)^4 - 3(-1)^2 = -2$

C: Test 1, $f(1) = 1^4 - 3(1)^2 = -2$

D: Test 2, $f(2) = 2^4 - 3(2)^2 = 4$

$(-\infty, -\sqrt{3}) \cup (\sqrt{3}, \infty)$

51. $\left|\dfrac{x + 3}{x - 4}\right| < 2$

$-2 < \dfrac{x + 3}{x - 4} < 2$

$-2 < \dfrac{x + 3}{x - 4}$ and $\dfrac{x + 3}{x - 4} < 2$

First solve $-2 < \dfrac{x + 3}{x - 4}$.

We solve the related equation.

$$-2 = \frac{x + 3}{x - 4}$$

$$-2(x - 4) = x + 3$$

$$-2x + 8 = x + 3$$

$$5 = 3x$$

$$\frac{5}{3} = x$$

Find the replacements that are not meaningful.

$$x - 4 = 0$$
$$x = 4$$

Use the number $\frac{5}{3}$ and 4 to divide the number line as shown.

Try test numbers in each interval.

A: Test 0, $-2 < \dfrac{x + 3}{x - 4}$

$$-2 \; \Big| \; \dfrac{0 + 3}{0 - 4}$$
$$- \dfrac{3}{4} \quad \text{TRUE}$$

The interval A is in the solution set.

B: Test 3, $-2 < \dfrac{x + 3}{x - 4}$

$$-2 \; \Big| \; \dfrac{3 + 3}{3 - 4}$$
$$-6 \quad \text{FALSE}$$

The interval B is not in the solution set.

C: Test 5, $-2 < \dfrac{x + 3}{x - 4}$

$$-2 \; \Big| \; \dfrac{5 + 3}{5 - 4}$$
$$8 \quad \text{TRUE}$$

The interval C is in the solution set.
The solution set for this portion of the conjunction is $\left[-\infty, \dfrac{5}{3}\right] \cup (4, \infty)$.

Next solve $\dfrac{x + 3}{x - 4} < 2$.

We solve the related equation.

$$\frac{x + 3}{x - 4} = 2$$
$$x + 3 = 2(x - 4)$$
$$x + 3 = 2x - 8$$
$$11 = x$$

As before, 4 is not a meaningful replacement. Use the numbers 4 and 11 to divide the number line as shown.

Try test numbers in each interval.

A: Test 0, $\dfrac{x + 3}{x - 4} < 2$

$$\dfrac{0 + 3}{0 - 4} \; \Big| \; 2$$
$$- \dfrac{3}{4} \quad \text{TRUE}$$

The interval A is in the solution set.

B: Test 5, $\dfrac{x + 3}{x - 4} < 2$

$$\dfrac{5 + 3}{5 - 4} \; \Big| \; 2$$
$$8 \quad \text{FALSE}$$

The interval B is not in the solution set.

C: Test 12, $\dfrac{x + 3}{x - 4} < 2$

$$\dfrac{12 + 3}{12 - 4} \; \Big| \; 2$$
$$\dfrac{15}{8} \quad \text{TRUE}$$

The interval C is in the solution set. The solution set for this portion of the conjunction is $(-\infty, 4) \cup (11, \infty)$.

The solution set of the original inequality is the intersection of the solution sets for the two portions of the conjunction.

$$\left[\left[-\infty, \frac{5}{3}\right] \cup (4, \infty)\right] \cap [(-\infty, 4) \cup (11, \infty)] =$$

$$\left[-\infty, \frac{5}{3}\right] \cup (11, \infty)$$

52. $|x^2 - 5| = |5 - x^2| = 5 - x^2$ when $5 - x^2 \geqslant 0$ by the definition of absolute value.

A: Test -3, $f(-3) = 5 - (-3)^2 = -4$
B: Test 0, $f(0) = 5 - 0^2 = 5$
C: Test 3, $f(3) = 5 - 3^2 = -4$

$[-\sqrt{5}, \sqrt{5}]$

53. $(7 - x)^{-2} < 0$

$$\frac{1}{(7 - x)^2} < 0$$

Since $(7 - x)^2 \geqslant 0$ for all values of x, $\dfrac{1}{(7 - x)^2} > 0$ for all meaningful replacements. The solution set is $\emptyset$.

54. $(1 - x)^3 > 0$ when $1 - x > 0$, or $1 > x$
$(-\infty, 1)$

55. $\left|1 + \frac{1}{x}\right| < 3$

$-3 < 1 + \frac{1}{x} < 3$

$-3 < 1 + \frac{1}{x}$ and $1 + \frac{1}{x} < 3$

First solve $-3 < 1 + \frac{1}{x}$

We solve the related equation.

$-3 = 1 + \frac{1}{x}$

$-4 = \frac{1}{x}$

$-4x = 1$

$x = -\frac{1}{4}$

We see that 0 is not a meaningful replacement. Use the numbers $-\frac{1}{4}$ and 0 to divide the number line as shown.

Try test numbers in each interval.

A: Test -1, $\dfrac{-3 < 1 + \frac{1}{x}}{-3 \left|\begin{array}{l} 1 + \frac{1}{-1} \\ \\ 0 \end{array}\right.}$ TRUE

The interval A is in the solution set.

B: Test $-\frac{1}{8}$, $\dfrac{-3 < 1 + \frac{1}{x}}{-3 \left|\begin{array}{l} 1 + \frac{1}{-\frac{1}{8}} \\ 1 - 8 \\ -7 \end{array}\right.}$ FALSE

The interval B is not in the solution set.

C: Test 1, $\dfrac{-3 < 1 + \frac{1}{x}}{-3 \left|\begin{array}{l} 1 + \frac{1}{1} \\ 2 \end{array}\right.}$ TRUE

The interval C is in the solution set.

The solution set for this portion of the conjunction is $\left[-\infty, -\frac{1}{4}\right] \cup (0, \infty)$.

Next we solve $1 + \frac{1}{x} < 3$.
We solve the related equation.

$1 + \frac{1}{x} = 3$

$\frac{1}{x} = 2$

$1 = 2x$

$\frac{1}{2} = x$

Again, 0 is not a meaningful replacement. We use the numbers $\frac{1}{2}$ and 0 to divide the number line as shown.

Try test numbers in each interval.

A: Test -1, $\dfrac{1 + \frac{1}{x} < 3}{1 + \frac{1}{-1} \left|\begin{array}{l} 3 \\ \\ 0 \end{array}\right.}$ TRUE

The interval A is in the solution set.

B: Test $\frac{1}{4}$, $\dfrac{1 + \frac{1}{x} < 3}{1 + \frac{1}{\frac{1}{4}} \left|\begin{array}{l} 3 \\ \\ 1 + 4 \\ 5 \end{array}\right.}$ FALSE

The interval B is not in the solution set.

C: Test 1, $\dfrac{1 + \frac{1}{x} < 3}{1 + \frac{1}{1} \left|\begin{array}{l} 3 \\ 2 \end{array}\right.}$ TRUE

The interval C is in the solution set.
The solution set for this portion of the conjunction is $(-\infty, 0) \cup \left[\frac{1}{2}, \infty\right)$.

The solution set of the original inequality is the intersection of the solution sets for the two portions of the conjunction.

$\left[\left[-\infty, -\frac{1}{4}\right] \cup (0, \infty)\right] \cap \left[(-\infty, 0) \cup \left[\frac{1}{2}, \infty\right)\right] =$
$\left[-\infty, -\frac{1}{4}\right] \cup \left[\frac{1}{2}, \infty\right)$

56. $(x + 5)^{-2} > 0$

$\frac{1}{(x + 5)^2} > 0$

$(x + 5)^2 > 0$ for all values of x except -5. The solution set is $(-\infty, -5) \cup (-5, \infty)$.

57.
$$|x|^2 - 4|x| + 4 \geqslant 9$$
$$|x|^2 - 4|x| - 5 \geqslant 0$$
$$(|x| - 5)(|x| + 1) \geqslant 0$$

The solutions of $f(x) = (|x| - 5)(|x| + 1) = 0$ are -5 and 5. They divide the number line as shown.

Try a test number in each interval.

A: Test -6, $f(-6) = |-6|^2 - 4|-6| - 5 = 7$

B: Test 0, $f(0) = |0|^2 - 4|0| - 5 = -5$

C: Test 6, $f(6) = |6|^2 - 4|6| - 5 = 7$

The solution set is $(-\infty, -5] \cup [5, \infty)$.

58.
$$2|x|^2 - |x| + 2 \leqslant 5$$
$$2|x|^2 - |x| - 3 \leqslant 0$$
$$(2|x| - 3)(|x| + 1) \leqslant 0$$

A: Test -2, $f(-2) = 2|-2|^2 - |-2| - 3 = 3$

B: Test 0, $f(0) = 2|0|^2 - |0| - 3 = -3$

C: Test 2, $f(2) = 2|2|^2 - |2| - 3 = 3$

$$\left[-\frac{3}{2}, \frac{3}{2}\right]$$

59. $\left|2 - \frac{1}{x}\right| \leqslant 2 + \left|\frac{1}{x}\right|$

Note that $\frac{1}{x}$ is not defined when $x = 0$. Thus $x \neq 0$.

Divide the set of real numbers into three intervals:

$x < 0$

$0 < x < \frac{1}{2}$

$x \geqslant \frac{1}{2}$

Find the solution set of $\left|2 - \frac{1}{x}\right| \leqslant 2 + \left|\frac{1}{x}\right|$ for each interval. Then take the union of the three solution sets.

If $x < 0$, then $\left|2 - \frac{1}{x}\right| = 2 - \frac{1}{x}$ and $\left|\frac{1}{x}\right| = -\frac{1}{x}$.

Solve: $x < 0$ and $2 - \frac{1}{x} \leqslant 2 - \frac{1}{x}$

$\qquad x < 0$ and $\qquad 2 \leqslant 2$

The solution set for this interval is $\{x | x < 0\}$.

If $0 < x < \frac{1}{2}$, then $\left|2 - \frac{1}{x}\right| = -\left(2 - \frac{1}{x}\right)$ and $\left|\frac{1}{x}\right| = \frac{1}{x}$.

Solve: $0 < x < \frac{1}{2}$ and $-\left(2 - \frac{1}{x}\right) \leqslant 2 + \frac{1}{x}$

$\qquad 0 < x < \frac{1}{2}$ and $\quad -2 + \frac{1}{x} \leqslant 2 + \frac{1}{x}$

$\qquad 0 < x < \frac{1}{2}$ and $\qquad -2 \leqslant 2$

The solution set for this interval is $\left\{x | 0 < x < \frac{1}{2}\right\}$.

If $x \geqslant \frac{1}{2}$, then $\left|2 - \frac{1}{x}\right| = 2 - \frac{1}{x}$ and $\left|\frac{1}{x}\right| = \frac{1}{x}$.

Solve: $x \geqslant \frac{1}{2}$ and $2 - \frac{1}{x} \leqslant 2 + \frac{1}{x}$

$\qquad x \geqslant \frac{1}{2}$ and $\quad -\frac{1}{x} \leqslant \frac{1}{x}$

$\qquad x \geqslant \frac{1}{2}$ and $\qquad -1 \leqslant 1$

True for all x such that $x \geqslant \frac{1}{2}$. The solution set for this interval is $\left\{x | x \geqslant \frac{1}{2}\right\}$.

The <u>union</u> of the above three solution sets is the set of all real numbers except 0, or $(-\infty, 0) \cup (0, \infty)$.

60. $\dfrac{(x - 2)^2(x - 3)^3(x + 1)}{(x + 2)(4 - x)} \geqslant 0$

A: $f(-3) < 0$

B: $f\left[-\frac{3}{2}\right] > 0$

C: $f(0) < 0$

D: $f\left[\frac{5}{2}\right] < 0$

E: $f\left[\frac{7}{2}\right] > 0$

F: $f(5) < 0$

$(-2, -1] \cup [3, 4) \cup [2, 2]$

61.
$$|x^2 + 3x - 1| < 3$$
$$-3 < x^2 + 3x - 1 < 3$$

$-3 < x^2 + 3x - 1$ and $x^2 + 3x - 1 < 3$, or

$0 < x^2 + 3x + 2$ and $x^2 + 3x - 4 < 0$

First we solve $0 < x^2 + 3x + 2$. We solve the related equation.

$$0 = x^2 + 3x + 2$$
$$0 = (x + 2)(x + 1)$$
$$x = -2 \text{ or } x = -1$$

Use the numbers -2 and -1 to divide the number line as shown.

Try test numbers in each interval.

A: Test -3, $f(-3) = (-3)^2 + 3(-3) + 2 = 2$

B: Test $-\frac{3}{2}$, $f\left[-\frac{3}{2}\right] = \left[-\frac{3}{2}\right]^2 + 3\left[-\frac{3}{2}\right] + 2 = -\frac{1}{4}$

C: Test 0, $f(0) = 0^2 + 3\cdot0 + 2 = 2$

The solution set for this portion of the conjunction is $(-\infty, -2) \cup (-1, \infty)$.

Next we solve $x^2 + 3x - 4 < 0$.

Solve the related equation.

$$x^2 + 3x - 4 = 0$$
$$(x + 4)(x - 1) = 0$$
$$x = -4 \quad \text{or} \quad x = 1$$

Use the numbers -4 and 1 to divide the number line as shown.

Try test numbers in each interval.

A: Test -5, $f(-5) = (-5)^2 + 3(-5) - 4 = 6$

B: Test 0, $f(0) = 0^2 + 3\cdot0 - 4 = -4$

C: Test 2, $f(2) = 2^2 + 3\cdot2 - 4 = 6$

The solution set for this portion of the conjunction is $(-4, 1)$.

The solution set for the original inequality is the intersection of the solution sets for the two portions of the disjunction.

$[(-\infty, -2) \cup (-1, \infty)] \cap (-4, 1) =$
$(-4, -2) \cup (-1, 1)$

62. $|1 + 5x - x^2| \geqslant 5$

$1 + 5x - x^2 \leqslant -5 \quad \text{or} \quad 1 + 5x - x^2 \geqslant 5$

First solve $1 + 5x - x^2 \leqslant -5$.

$$6 + 5x - x^2 \leqslant 0$$
$$(6 - x)(1 + x) \leqslant 0$$

A: $f(-2) = -8$

B: $f(0) = 6$

C: $f(7) = -8$

$(-\infty, -1] \cup [6, \infty)$

Next solve $1 + 5x - x^2 \geqslant 5$.

$$-4 + 5x - x^2 \geqslant 0$$
$$(-4 + x)(1 - x) \geqslant 0$$

A: $f(0) = -4$

B: $f(2) = 2$

C: $f(5) = -4$

$[1, 4]$

The solution set of the original inequality is the union of the solution sets for the two portions of the disjunction.

$(-\infty, -1] \cup [1, 4] \cup [6, \infty)$

63. Familiarize: We first make a drawing.

We let h represent the height and h + 4 the base.

Translate: The area is $\frac{1}{2}(h + 4)h$. We now have an inequality:

$$\frac{1}{2}h(h + 4) > 10$$
$$h(h + 4) > 20$$
$$h^2 + 4h > 20$$
$$h^2 + 4h - 20 > 0$$

Carry out: Using the quadratic formula, we find that the solutions of $f(x) = h^2 + 4h - 20$ are $-2 \pm 2\sqrt{6}$. Since h must be positive we use $-2 + 2\sqrt{6}$ to divide the interval $(0, \infty)$ as shown.

Try a test number in each interval.   Note that $-2 + 2\sqrt{6} \approx 2.9$.

A: Test 1, $f(1) = 1^2 + 4\cdot1 - 20 = -15$

B: Test 3, $f(3) = 3^2 + 4\cdot3 - 20 = 1$

Function values are positive in interval B.

Check: We go over our work.

State: The area of the triangle will be greater than 10 cm² for $\{h | h > -2 + 2\sqrt{6} \text{ cm}\}$.

64. Solve: $A = w(w + 3) > 15 (w > 0)$

$\left\{w \left| w > \dfrac{-3 + \sqrt{69}}{2} \text{ m}\right.\right\}$

65. a) $-3x^2 + 630x - 6000 > 0$

 $x^2 - 210x + 2000 < 0$ [Multiplying by $-\frac{1}{3}$]

 $(x - 200)(x - 10) < 0$

The solutions of $f(x) = (x - 200)(x - 10) = 0$ are 200 and 10. Since x must be positive, we use 10 and 200 to divide the interval $(0, \infty)$ as shown.

A: Test 1, $f(1) = (1 - 200)(1 - 10) = 1791$

B: Test 100, $f(100) = (100 - 200)(100 - 10) = -9000$

C: Test 201, $f(201) = (201 - 200)(201 - 10) = 191$

Note that $P(x) > 0$ is equivalent to $f(x) < 0$. Then the solution set is $\{x | 10 < x < 200\}$.

 b) Note that $P(x) < 0$ for $f(x) > 0$. Then the solution set is $\{x | 0 < x < 10 \text{ or } x > 200\}$.

66. a) Solve: $-16t^2 + 32t + 1920 > 1920$ $(t > 0)$

 $\{t | 0 \text{ sec} < t < 2 \text{ sec}\}$

 b) Solve: $-16t^2 + 32t + 1920 < 640$ $(t > 0)$

 $\{t | t > 10 \text{ sec}\}$

67. a) Solve $R(x) = C(x)$.

 $50x - x^2 = 5x + 350$

 $0 = x^2 - 45x + 350$

 $0 = (x - 35)(x - 10)$

 $x = 35$ or $x = 10$

The break even values are 10 units and 35 units.

 b) $R(x) > C(x)$

 $50x - x^2 > 5x + 350$

 $0 > x^2 - 45x + 350$

 $0 > (x - 35)(x - 10)$

The solutions of $f(x) = (x - 35)(x - 10) = 0$ are 35 and 10. We will restrict x to positive values.

A
B
C

0   10   35

A: Test 1, $f(1) = 1^2 - 45 \cdot 1 + 350 = 306$

B: Test 11, $f(11) = 11^2 - 45 \cdot 11 + 350 = -24$

C: Test 36, $f(36) = 36^2 - 45 \cdot 36 + 350 = 26$

Note that $R(x) > C(x)$ corresponds to $f(x) < 0$. There is a profit for $\{x | 10 < x < 35\}$.

 c) $R(x) < C(x)$

 $50x - x^2 < 5x + 350$

 $0 < x^2 - 45x + 350$

 $0 < (x - 35)(x - 10)$

From part (b) we see that the function values of $f(x) = (x - 35)(x - 10)$ are greater than zero for $\{x | 0 < x < 10 \text{ or } x > 35\}$.

68. a) Solve: $R(x) = C(x)$

 $80x - x^2 = 10x + 600$

 $x = 10$ or $x = 60$

 b) Solve: $R(x) > C(x)$

 $80x - x^2 > 10x + 60$

 $\{x | 10 < x < 60\}$

 c) Solve: $R(x) < C(x)$

 $80x - x^2 < 10x + 60$

 $\{x | x < 10 \text{ or } x > 60\}$ (Of course, we would expect x to be positive as well.)

69. The discriminant of $x^2 + kx + 1 = 0$ is $k^2 - 4$.

 a) There are two real-number solutions when the discriminant is positive, so we solve $k^2 - 4 > 0$, or $(k + 2)(k - 2) > 0$.

The solutions of $f(k) = (k + 2)(k - 2) = 0$ are -2 and 2. They divide the real-number line as shown.

A
B
C

-2   2

A: Test -3, $f(-3) = (-3 + 2)(-3 - 2) = 5$

B: Test 0, $f(0) = (0 + 2)(0 - 2) = -4$

C: Test 3, $f(3) = (3 + 2)(3 - 2) = 5$

The solution set is $\{k | k < -2 \text{ or } k > 2\}$, or $(-\infty, -2) \cup (2, \infty)$.

 b) There is no real-number solution when the discriminant is negative, so we solve $k^2 - 4 < 0$. Using the test points in part (a), we see that the solution set is $\{k | -2 < k < 2\}$, or $(-2, 2)$.

70. $2x^2 - kx + 1 = 0$ has the discriminant $k^2 - 8$.

 a) $k^2 - 8 > 0$ gives $\left\{ k \middle| k < -2\sqrt{2} \text{ or } k > 2\sqrt{2} \right\}$.

 b) $k^2 - 8 < 0$ gives $\left\{ k \middle| -2\sqrt{2} < k < 2\sqrt{2} \right\}$.

71. $f(x) = \sqrt{1 - x^2}$

The radicand must be nonnegative, so we solve $1 - x^2 \geq 0$, or $x^2 - 1 \leq 0$ (multiplying by -1). Using the test points in Exercise 7, we see that the domain is $\{x | -1 \leq x \leq 1\}$, or $[-1, 1]$.

72. Solve $1 - x^2 > 0$, or $x^2 - 1 < 0$. Using the test points in Exercise 7, we see that the domain is $\{x | -1 < x < 1\}$, or $(-1, 1)$.

73. $g(x) = \sqrt{x^2 + 2x - 3}$

    The radicand must be nonnegative, so we solve $x^2 + 2x - 3 \geqslant 0$, or $(x + 3)(x - 1) \geqslant 0$. The solutions of $f(x) = (x + 3)(x - 1) = 0$ are -3 and 1. They divide the real-number line as shown.

    A: Test -4, $f(-4) = (-4)^2 + 2(-4) - 3 = 5$
    B: Test 0, $f(0) = 0^2 + 2 \cdot 0 - 3 = -3$
    C: Test 2, $f(2) = 2^2 + 2 \cdot 2 - 3 = 5$

    The domain is $\{x | x \leqslant -3 \text{ or } x \geqslant 1\}$, or $(-\infty, -3] \cup [1, \infty)$.

74. Solve $4 - x^2 \geqslant 0$. We did this in Exercise 10. The domain is $\{x | -2 \leqslant x \leqslant 2\}$, or $[-2, 2]$.

75. From the graph we determine the following:
    The solutions of $f(x) = 0$ are -2, 1, and 3.
    The solution of $f(x) < 0$ is $\{x | x < -2 \text{ or } 1 < x < 3\}$, or $(-\infty, -2) \cup (1,3)$.
    The solution of $f(x) > 0$ is $\{x | -2 < x < 1 \text{ or } x > 3\}$, or $(-2,1) \cup (3,\infty)$.

76. $f(x) = 0$ for $x = -2$ and $x = 1$;
    $f(x) < 0$ for $\{x | x < -2\}$, or $(-\infty,-2)$;
    $f(x) > 0$ for $\{x | -2 < x < 1 \text{ or } x > 1\}$, or $(-2,1) \cup (1,\infty)$

77. From the graph we determine the following:
    $f(x)$ has no zeros.
    The solutions $f(x) < 0$ are $\{x | x < 0\}$, or $(-\infty,0)$.
    The solutions of $f(x) > 0$ are $\{x | x > 0\}$, or $(0,\infty)$.

78. $f(x) = 0$ for $x = 0$ and $x = 1$;
    $f(x) < 0$ for $\{x | 0 < x < 1\}$, or $(0,1)$;
    $f(x) > 0$ for $\{x | x > 1\}$, or $(1,\infty)$

79. From the graph we determine the following:
    The solutions of $f(x) = 0$ are -2, 1, 2, and 3.
    The solutions of $f(x) < 0$ are $\{x | -2 < x < 1 \text{ or } 2 < x < 3\}$, or $(-2,1) \cup (2,3)$.
    The solutions of $f(x) > 0$ are $\{x | x < -2 \text{ or } 1 < x < 2 \text{ or } x > 3\}$, or $(-\infty,-2) \cup (1,2) \cup (3,\infty)$.

80. $f(x) = 0$ for $x = -2$, $x = 0$, and $x = 1$;
    $f(x) < 0$ for $\{x | x < -3 \text{ or } -2 < x < 0 \text{ or } 1 < x < 2\}$, or $(-\infty,-3) \cup (-2,0) \cup (1,2)$;
    $f(x) > 0$ for $\{x | -3 < x < -2 \text{ or } 0 < x < 1 \text{ or } x > 2\}$, or $(-3,-2) \cup (0,1) \cup (2,\infty)$

Exercise Set 4.5

1. $f(x) = \frac{1}{3}x^6$

   The graph of $f(x) = \frac{1}{3}x^6$ has the same general shape as $f(x) = x^2$. This is an even function, so it is symmetric with respect to the y-axis. We can compute some function values and use symmetry to find others.

x	0	1	2	3	-1	-2	-3
f(x)	0	$\frac{1}{3}$	$\frac{64}{3}$	243	$\frac{1}{3}$	$\frac{64}{3}$	243

   Found using symmetry

2.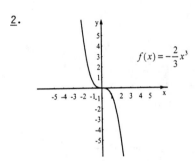

   $f(x) = -\frac{2}{3}x^3$

3. $f(x) = -0.6x^5$

   The graph of $f(x) = -0.6x^5$ has the same general shape as $f(x) = x^3$ reflected across the x-axis (since $-0.6 < 0$). It is an odd function, so it is symmetric with respect to the origin. We can compute some function values and use symmetry to find others.

x	0	1	2	-1	-2
f(x)	0	-0.6	-19.2	0.6	19.2

   Found using symmetry

4.

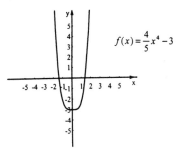

$f(x) = \frac{4}{5}x^4 - 3$

5. $f(x) = (x + 1)^5 - 4$

The graph of $f(x) = (x + 1)^5 - 4$ is a transformation of $f(x) = x^5$, so its graph will have the same general shape as $f(x) = x^3$. We compute some function values.

x	-3	-2	-1	0	1	2
f(x)	-36	-5	-4	-3	28	239

$f(x) = (x + 1)^5 - 4$

6.

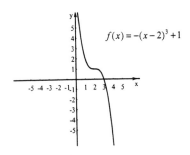

$f(x) = -(x - 2)^3 + 1$

7. $f(x) = \frac{1}{4}(x + 1)^4$

This function is a transformation of $f(x) = x^4$, so its graph will have the same general shape as $f(x) = x^2$. We compute some function values.

x	-4	-3	-2	-1	0	1	2
f(x)	$\frac{81}{4}$	4	$\frac{1}{4}$	0	$\frac{1}{4}$	4	$\frac{81}{4}$

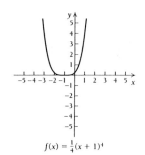

$f(x) = \frac{1}{4}(x + 1)^4$

8.

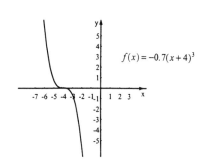

$f(x) = -0.7(x+4)^3$

9. $f(x) = (x + 3)(x - 2)(x + 1)$

The zeros of this function are -3, 2, and -1. They divide the real-number line into 4 open intervals as indicated in the table below. We try a test value in each interval and determine the sign of the function for values of x in the interval.

Interval	$(-\infty, -3)$	$(-3, -1)$	$(-1, 2)$	$(2, \infty)$
Test value	$f(-4) = -18$	$f(-2) = 4$	$f(0) = -6$	$f(3) = 24$
Sign of f(x)	-	+	-	+
Location of points on graph	Below x-axis	Above x-axis	Below x-axis	Above x-axis

We use the information in the table, calculate some additional function values if needed, plot points, and sketch the graph.

$f(x) = (x + 3)(x - 2)(x + 1)$

10.

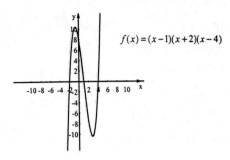

$$f(x) = (x-1)(x+2)(x-4)$$

11. $f(x) = 9x^2 - x^4$
        $= x^2(9 - x^2)$
        $= x^2(3 + x)(3 - x)$

The zeros of the function are 0, -3, and 3.

Interval	$(-\infty, -3)$	$(-3, 0)$	$(0, 3)$	$(3, \infty)$
Test value	$f(-4) = -112$	$f(-1) = 8$	$f(1) = 8$	$f(4) = -112$
Sign of $f(x)$	−	+	+	−
Location of points on graph	Below x-axis	Above x-axis	Above x-axis	Below x-axis

$$f(x) = 9x^2 - x^4$$

12.

$$f(x) = 4x^2 - x^4$$

13. $f(x) = x^4 - x^3$
        $= x^3(x - 1)$

The zeros of the function are 0 and 1.

Interval	$(-\infty, 0)$	$(0, 1)$	$(1, \infty)$
Test value	$f(-1) = 2$	$f\left(\frac{1}{2}\right) = -\frac{1}{16}$	$f(2) = 8$
Sign of $f(x)$	+	−	+
Location of points on graph	Above x-axis	Below x-axis	Above x-axis

$$f(x) = x^4 - x^3$$

14.

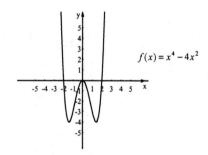

$$f(x) = x^4 - 4x^2$$

15. $f(x) = x^3 - 4x$
        $= x(x^2 - 4)$
        $= x(x + 2)(x - 2)$

The zeros of the function are 0, -2, and 2.

Interval	$(-\infty, -2)$	$(-2, 0)$	$(0, 2)$	$(2, \infty)$
Test value	$f(-3) = -15$	$f(-1) = 3$	$f(1) = -3$	$f(3) = 15$
Sign of $f(x)$	−	+	−	+
Location of points on graph	Below x-axis	Above x-axis	Below x-axis	Above x-axis

$$f(x) = x^3 - 4x$$

16.

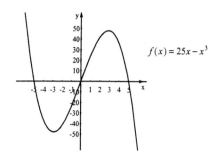

$f(x) = 25x - x^3$

Interval	$(-\infty, -\sqrt{5})$	$(-\sqrt{5}, -2)$	$(-2, 2)$	$(2, \sqrt{5})$	$(\sqrt{5}, \infty)$
Test value	$f(-3) = 20$	$f(-2.1) = -0.2419$	$f(0) = 20$	$f(2.1) = -0.2419$	$f(3) = 20$
Sign of $f(x)$	+	–	+	–	+
Location of points on graph	Above x-axis	Below x-axis	Above x-axis	Below x-axis	Above x-axis

17. $f(x) = x^3 + x^2 - 2x$

   $= x(x^2 + x - 2)$

   $= x(x + 2)(x - 1)$

The zeros of the function are 0, -2, and 1.

Interval	$(-\infty, -2)$	$(-2, 0)$	$(0, 1)$	$(1, \infty)$
Test value	$f(-3) = -12$	$f(-1) = 2$	$f\left(\frac{1}{2}\right) = -\frac{5}{8}$	$f(2) = 8$
Sign of $f(x)$	–	+	–	+
Location of points on graph	Below x-axis	Above x-axis	Below x-axis	Above x-axis

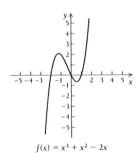

$f(x) = x^3 + x^2 - 2x$

18.

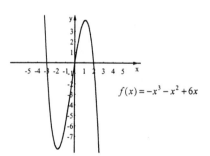

$f(x) = -x^3 - x^2 + 6x$

19. $f(x) = x^4 - 9x^2 + 20$

   $= (x^2 - 4)(x^2 - 5)$

   $= (x + 2)(x - 2)(x + \sqrt{5})(x - \sqrt{5})$

The zeros of the function are -2, 2, $-\sqrt{5}$, and $\sqrt{5}$.

$f(x) = x^4 - 9x^2 + 20$

20.

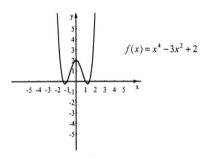

$f(x) = x^4 - 3x^2 + 2$

21. $f(x) = x^3 - 3x^2 - 4x + 12$

   $= x^2(x - 3) - 4(x - 3)$

   $= (x^2 - 4)(x - 3)$

   $= (x + 2)(x - 2)(x - 3)$

The zeros of the function are -2, 2, and 3.

Interval	$(-\infty, -2)$	$(-2, 2)$	$(2, 3)$	$(3, \infty)$
Test value	$f(-3) = -30$	$f(0) = 12$	$f\left(\frac{5}{2}\right) = -\frac{9}{8}$	$f(4) = 12$
Sign of $f(x)$	–	+	–	+
Location of points on graph	Below x-axis	Above x-axis	Below x-axis	Above x-axis

$f(x) = x^3 - 3x^2 - 4x + 12$

22.

$$f(x) = x^3 - 2x^2 - 9x + 18$$

23. $f(x) = -x^4 - 3x^3 - 3x^2$

$\qquad = -x^2(x^2 + 3x + 3)$

The discriminant of $x^2 + 3x + 3 = 0$ is negative, so the only zero of the function is 0.

Interval	$(-\infty, 0)$	$(0, \infty)$
Test value	$f(-1) = -1$	$f(1) = -7$
Sign of $f(x)$	–	–
Location of points on graph	Below x-axis	Below x-axis

$f(x) = -x^4 - 3x^3 - 3x^2$

24.

$f(x) = -3x^4 - x^3 + 2x^2$

25. $f(x) = x(x - 2)(x + 1)(x + 3)$

The zeros of the function are 0, 2, -1, and -3.

Interval	$(-\infty,-3)$	$(-3,-1)$	$(-1,0)$	$(0,2)$	$(2,\infty)$
Test value	$f(-4) =$ 72	$f(-2) =$ –8	$f\left(-\frac{1}{2}\right) =$ $\frac{25}{16}$	$f(1) =$ –8	$f(3) =$ 72
Sign of $f(x)$	+	–	+	–	+
Location of points on graph	Above x-axis	Below x-axis	Above x-axis	Below x-axis	Above x-axis

$f(x) = x(x - 2)(x + 1)(x + 3)$

26.

$f(x) = x(x - 1)(x - 2)(x - 3)$

27. a) 1 unit: $y = \frac{1}{13}(1)^3 - \frac{1}{14}(1) \approx 0.0055$

2 units: $y = \frac{1}{13}(2)^3 - \frac{1}{14}(2) \approx 0.4725$

3 units: $y = \frac{1}{13}(3)^3 - \frac{1}{14}(3) \approx 1.8626$

6 units: $y = \frac{1}{13}(6)^3 - \frac{1}{14}(6) \approx 16.1868$

8 units: $y = \frac{1}{13}(8)^3 - \frac{1}{14}(8) \approx 38.8132$

9 units: $y = \frac{1}{13}(9)^3 - \frac{1}{14}(9) \approx 55.4341$

10 units: $y = \frac{1}{13}(10)^3 - \frac{1}{14}(10) \approx 76.2088$

b)

$y = \frac{1}{13}x^3 - \frac{1}{14}x$

28. a) 4.03, 5.79, 7.00, 7.38, 6.65, 4.54, 0.78

b) $N(t) = -0.046t^3 + 2.08t + 2$

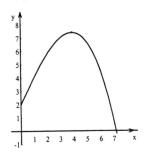

29. a) 5 ft 7 in. = 67 in.

$W(67) = \left(\dfrac{67}{12.3}\right)^3 \approx 161.6$ lb

5 ft 10 in. = 70 in.

$W(70) = \left(\dfrac{70}{12.3}\right)^3 \approx 184.3$ lb

b) 6 ft 1 in. = 73 in.

$W(73) = \left(\dfrac{73}{12.3}\right)^3 \approx 209.1$ lb

He should watch his weight.

30. a) 7.68 watts, 15 watts, 50.625 watts

b) Solve: $120 = 0.015V^3$
   $V = 20$ mph

31. a) We make a drawing.

The length of the box is x, the width is x, the height is $\dfrac{10 - x}{2}$. Thus, the volume is given by

$V(x) = x \cdot x \cdot \left[\dfrac{10 - x}{2}\right] = x^2\left[\dfrac{10 - x}{2}\right]$, or

$V(x) = 5x^2 - \dfrac{x^3}{2}$.

b) The zeros of V(x) are 0 and 10.

Interval	$(-\infty, 0)$	$(0, 10)$	$(10, \infty)$
Test value	$V(-1) = \dfrac{11}{2}$	$V(1) = \dfrac{9}{2}$	$V(11) = -\dfrac{121}{2}$
Sign of f(x)	+	+	−
Location of points on graph	Above x-axis	Above x-axis	Below x-axis

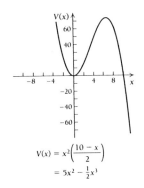

$$V(x) = x^2\left(\dfrac{10 - x}{2}\right)$$
$$= 5x^2 - \dfrac{1}{2}x^3$$

c) Using the table in part b), we see that the function is positive over $(-\infty, 0)$, and $(0, 10)$.

32. a) $V(x) = x^2\left[\dfrac{8 - x}{2}\right]$, or $V(x) = 4x^2 - \dfrac{x^3}{2}$

b)

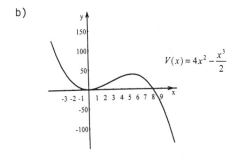

$$V(x) = 4x^2 - \dfrac{x^3}{2}$$

c) $(-\infty, 0) \cup (0, 8)$

33. The functions for which $f(-x) = f(x)$ are those in Exercises 1, 4, 11, 12, 14, 19, and 20.

34. Exercise 2, 3, 15 and 16

35. Every exponent of the polynomial function must be even or $f(x) = c$.

36. Every exponent of the polynomial function must be odd and the constant term must be 0.

37. The zeros of the function are -3, -2, and 1.

38. The function has a zero at about -3.337.

39. The function has zeros at -1 and 2 and at about -1.41421 and 1.41421.

40. The function has zeros at -2, 0, 3, and at about -1.73215 and 1.73215.

41. a) $f(x) = -0.046x^3 + 2.08x + 2$

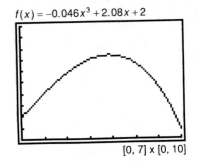

[0, 7] x [0, 10]

b) The zeros of the function are approximately -6.17908, -0.98251, and 7.16159.

c) The concentration will be 0 after about 7.2 hr.

Exercise Set 4.6

1. $P(x) = x^3 - 9x^2 + 14x + 24$

   $P(4) = 4^3 - 9 \cdot 4^2 + 14 \cdot 4 + 24 = 0$
   Since $P(4) = 0$, 4 is a root of $P(x)$.

   $P(5) = 5^3 - 9 \cdot 5^2 + 14 \cdot 5 + 24 = -6$
   Since $P(5) \neq 0$, 5 is not a root of $P(x)$.

   $P(-2) = (-2)^3 - 9(-2)^2 + 14(-2) + 24 = -48$
   Since $P(-2) \neq 0$, -2 is not a root of $P(x)$.

2. $P(x) = 2x^3 - 3x^2 + x - 1$

   $P(2) = 2 \cdot 2^3 - 3 \cdot 2^2 + 2 - 1 = 5$
   $P(2) \neq 0$, so 2 is not a root of $P(x)$.

   $P(3) = 2 \cdot 3^3 - 3 \cdot 3^2 + 3 - 1 = 29$
   $P(3) \neq 0$, so 3 is not a root of $P(x)$.

   $P(-1) = 2(-1)^3 - 3(-1)^2 + (-1) - 1 = -7$
   $P(-1) \neq 0$, so -1 is not a root of $P(x)$.

3. Using the techniques in subsection [b], we divide to determine whether each binomial is a factor of $P(x)$.

   a)
   $$\begin{array}{r} x^2 - 5x - 6 \\ x - 4\overline{)x^3 - 9x^2 + 14x + 24} \\ \underline{x^3 - 4x^2} \\ -5x^2 + 14x \\ \underline{-5x^2 + 20x} \\ -6x + 24 \\ \underline{-6x + 24} \\ 0 \end{array}$$

   Since the remainder is 0, $x - 4$ is a factor of $P(x)$.

   b)
   $$\begin{array}{r} x^2 - 4x - 6 \\ x - 5\overline{)x^3 - 9x^2 + 14x + 24} \\ \underline{x^3 - 5x} \\ -4x^2 + 14x \\ \underline{-4x^2 + 20x} \\ -6x + 24 \\ \underline{-6x + 30} \\ -6 \end{array}$$

   Since the remainder is not 0, $x - 5$ is not a factor of $P(x)$.

   c)
   $$\begin{array}{r} x^2 - 11x + 36 \\ x + 2\overline{)x^3 - 9x^2 + 14x + 24} \\ \underline{x^3 + 2x^2} \\ -11x^2 + 14x \\ \underline{-11x^2 - 22x} \\ 36x + 24 \\ \underline{36x + 72} \\ -48 \end{array}$$

   Since the remainder is not 0, $x + 2$ is not a factor of $P(x)$.

4. Using the technique in subsection [b], we divide to determine whether each binomial is a factor of $P(x)$.

   a)
   $$\begin{array}{r} 2x^2 + x + 3 \\ x - 2\overline{)2x^3 - 3x^2 + x - 1} \\ \underline{2x^3 - 4x^2} \\ x^2 + x \\ \underline{x^2 - 2x} \\ 3x - 1 \\ \underline{3x - 6} \\ 5 \end{array}$$

   Since the remainder is not 0, $x - 2$ is not a factor of $P(x)$.

b)
$$x - 3 \overline{\smash{\big)}\, \begin{array}{l} 2x^2 + 3x + 10 \\ 2x^3 - 3x^2 + x - 1 \end{array}}$$
$$\underline{2x^3 - 6x^2}$$
$$3x^2 + x$$
$$\underline{3x^2 - 9x}$$
$$10x - 1$$
$$\underline{10x - 30}$$
$$29$$

Since the remainder is not 0, $x - 3$ is not a factor of $P(x)$.

c)
$$x + 1 \overline{\smash{\big)}\, \begin{array}{l} 2x^2 - 5x + 6 \\ 2x^3 - 3x^2 + x - 1 \end{array}}$$
$$\underline{2x^3 + 2x^2}$$
$$-5x^2 + x$$
$$\underline{-5x^2 - 5x}$$
$$6x - 1$$
$$\underline{6x + 6}$$
$$-7$$

Since the remainder is not 0, $x + 1$ is not a factor of $P(x)$.

5.
$$x - 2 \overline{\smash{\big)}\, \begin{array}{l} x^2 + 8x + 15 \\ x^3 + 6x^2 - x - 30 \end{array}}$$
$$\underline{x^3 - 2x^2}$$
$$8x^2 - x$$
$$\underline{8x^2 - 16x}$$
$$15x - 30$$
$$\underline{15x - 30}$$
$$0$$

$$x^3 + 6x^2 - x - 30 = (x - 2)(x^2 + 8x + 15) + 0$$

6. See the work in Exercise 4(a).
$$2x^3 - 3x^2 + x - 1 = (x - 2)(2x^2 + x + 3) + 5$$

7.
$$x - 3 \overline{\smash{\big)}\, \begin{array}{l} x^2 + 9x + 26 \\ x^3 + 6x^2 - x - 30 \end{array}}$$
$$\underline{x^3 - 3x^2}$$
$$9x^2 - x$$
$$\underline{9x^2 - 27x}$$
$$26x - 30$$
$$\underline{26x - 78}$$
$$48$$

$$x^3 + 6x^2 - x - 30 = (x - 3)(x^2 + 9x + 26) + 48$$

8. See the work in Exercise 4(b).
$$2x^3 - 3x^2 + x - 1 = (x - 3)(2x^2 + 3x + 10) + 29$$

9.
$$x + 2 \overline{\smash{\big)}\, \begin{array}{l} x^2 - 2x + 4 \\ x^3 + 0x^2 + 0x - 8 \end{array}}$$
$$\underline{x^3 + 2x^2}$$
$$-2x^2 + 0x$$
$$\underline{-2x^2 - 4x}$$
$$4x - 8$$
$$\underline{4x + 8}$$
$$-16$$

$$x^3 - 8 = (x + 2)(x^2 - 2x + 4) - 16$$

10.
$$x + 1 \overline{\smash{\big)}\, \begin{array}{l} x^2 - x + 1 \\ x^3 + 0x^2 + 0x + 27 \end{array}}$$
$$\underline{x^3 + x^2}$$
$$-x^2 + 0x$$
$$\underline{-x^2 - x}$$
$$x + 27$$
$$\underline{x + 1}$$
$$26$$

$$x^3 + 27 = (x + 1)(x^2 - x + 1) + 26$$

11.
$$x^2 + 4 \overline{\smash{\big)}\, \begin{array}{l} x^2 + 5 \\ x^4 + 9x^2 + 20 \end{array}}$$
$$\underline{x^4 + 4x^2}$$
$$5x^2 + 20$$
$$\underline{5x^2 + 20}$$
$$0$$

$$x^4 + 9x^2 + 20 = (x^2 + 4)(x^2 + 5) + 0$$

12.
$$x^2 + x + 1 \overline{\smash{\big)}\, \begin{array}{l} x^2 - x + 1 \\ x^4 + 0x^3 + x^2 + 0x + 2 \end{array}}$$
$$\underline{x^4 + x^3 + x^2}$$
$$-x^3 + 0x$$
$$\underline{-x^3 - x^2 - x}$$
$$x^2 + x + 2$$
$$\underline{x^2 + x + 1}$$
$$1$$

$$x^4 + x^2 + 2 = (x^2 + x + 1)(x^2 - x + 1) + 1$$

13. $2x^2-x+1 \overline{\smash{\big)}\,5x^7 + 0x^6 + 0x^5 - 3x^4 + 0x^3 + 2x^2 + 0x - 3}$

quotient: $\dfrac{5}{2} x^5 + \dfrac{5}{4} x^4 - \dfrac{5}{8} x^3 - \dfrac{39}{16} x^2 - \dfrac{29}{32} x + \dfrac{113}{64}$

$5x^7 - \dfrac{5}{2} x^6 + \dfrac{5}{2} x^5$

$\dfrac{5}{2} x^6 - \dfrac{5}{2} x^5 - 3x^4$

$\dfrac{5}{2} x^6 - \dfrac{5}{4} x^5 + \dfrac{5}{4} x^4$

$-\dfrac{5}{4} x^5 - \dfrac{17}{4} x^4 + 0x^3$

$-\dfrac{5}{4} x^5 + \dfrac{5}{8} x^4 - \dfrac{5}{8} x^3$

$-\dfrac{39}{8} x^4 + \dfrac{5}{8} x^3 + 2x^2$

$-\dfrac{39}{8} x^4 + \dfrac{39}{16} x^3 - \dfrac{39}{16} x^2$

$-\dfrac{29}{16} x^3 + \dfrac{71}{16} x^2 + 0x$

$-\dfrac{29}{16} x^3 + \dfrac{29}{32} x^2 - \dfrac{29}{32} x$

$\dfrac{113}{32} x^2 + \dfrac{29}{32} x - 3$

$\dfrac{113}{32} x^2 - \dfrac{113}{64} x + \dfrac{113}{64}$

$\dfrac{171}{64} x - \dfrac{305}{64}$

$5x^7 - 3x^4 + 2x^2 - 3$

$= (2x^2 - x + 1)\left(\dfrac{5}{2} x^5 + \dfrac{5}{4} x^4 - \dfrac{5}{8} x^3 - \dfrac{39}{16} x^2 - \dfrac{29}{32} x + \dfrac{113}{64}\right) + \left(\dfrac{171}{64} x - \dfrac{305}{64}\right)$

14. $3x^2 + 2x - 1 \overline{\smash{\big)}\,6x^5 + 4x^4 + 0x^3 - 3x^2 + x - 2}$

quotient: $2x^3 + \dfrac{2}{3} x - \dfrac{13}{9}$

$6x^5 + 4x^4 - 2x^3$

$2x^3 - 3x^2 + x$

$2x^3 + \dfrac{4}{3} x^2 - \dfrac{2}{3} x$

$-\dfrac{13}{3} x^2 + \dfrac{5}{3} x - 2$

$-\dfrac{13}{3} x^2 - \dfrac{26}{9} x + \dfrac{13}{9}$

$\dfrac{41}{9} x - \dfrac{31}{9}$

$6x^5 + 4x^4 - 3x^2 + x - 2 =$

$(3x^2 + 2x - 1)\left(2x^3 + \dfrac{2}{3} x - \dfrac{13}{9}\right) + \left(\dfrac{41}{9} x - \dfrac{31}{9}\right)$

15. $(2x^4 + 7x^3 + x - 12) \div (x + 3)$

$= (2x^4 + 7x^3 + 0x^2 + x - 12) \div [x - (-3)]$

$-3 \;\underline{|\; \begin{array}{rrrrr} 2 & 7 & 0 & 1 & -12 \\ & -6 & -3 & 9 & -30 \end{array}}$
$ \begin{array}{rrrr|r} 2 & 1 & -3 & 10 & -42 \end{array}$

The quotient is $2x^3 + x^2 - 3x + 10$.
The remainder is -42.

16. $2 \;\underline{|\; \begin{array}{rrr} 1 & -7 & 13 & 3 \\ & 2 & -10 & 6 \end{array}}$
$ \begin{array}{rrr|r} 1 & -5 & 3 & 9 \end{array}$

$Q(x) = x^2 - 5x + 3$, $R(x) = 9$

17. $(x^3 - 2x^2 - 8) \div (x + 2)$

$= (x^3 - 2x^2 + 0x - 8) \div [x - (-2)]$

$-2 \;\underline{|\; \begin{array}{rrrr} 1 & -2 & 0 & -8 \\ & -2 & 8 & -16 \end{array}}$
$ \begin{array}{rrr|r} 1 & -4 & 8 & -24 \end{array}$

The quotient is $x^2 - 4x + 8$.
The remainder is -24.

18. $2 \;\underline{|\; \begin{array}{rrrr} 1 & 0 & -3 & 10 \\ & 2 & 4 & 2 \end{array}}$
$ \begin{array}{rrr|r} 1 & 2 & 1 & 12 \end{array}$

$Q(x) = x^2 + 2x + 1$, $R(x) = 12$

19. $(x^4 - 1) \div (x - 1)$

$= (x^4 + 0x^3 + 0x^2 + 0x - 1) \div (x - 1)$

$1 \;\underline{|\; \begin{array}{rrrrr} 1 & 0 & 0 & 0 & -1 \\ & 1 & 1 & 1 & 1 \end{array}}$
$ \begin{array}{rrrr|r} 1 & 1 & 1 & 1 & 0 \end{array}$

The quotient is $x^3 + x^2 + x + 1$.
The remainder is 0.

20. $-2 \;\underline{|\; \begin{array}{rrrrrr} 1 & 0 & 0 & 0 & 0 & 32 \\ & -2 & 4 & -8 & 16 & -32 \end{array}}$
$ \begin{array}{rrrrr|r} 1 & -2 & 4 & -8 & 16 & 0 \end{array}$

$Q(x) = x^4 - 2x^3 + 4x^2 - 8x + 16$, $R(x) = 0$

21. $(2x^4 + 3x^2 - 1) \div \left(x - \dfrac{1}{2}\right)$

$= (2x^4 + 0x^3 + 3x^2 + 0x - 1) \div \left(x - \dfrac{1}{2}\right)$

$\dfrac{1}{2} \;\underline{|\; \begin{array}{rrrrr} 2 & 0 & 3 & 0 & -1 \\ & 1 & \dfrac{1}{2} & \dfrac{7}{4} & \dfrac{7}{8} \end{array}}$
$\phantom{\frac{1}{2}\;|\;} \begin{array}{rrrr|r} 2 & 1 & \dfrac{7}{2} & \dfrac{7}{4} & -\dfrac{1}{8} \end{array}$

The quotient is $2x^3 + x^2 + \dfrac{7}{2} x + \dfrac{7}{4}$.

The remainder is $-\dfrac{1}{8}$.

22. $\dfrac{1}{4} \;\underline{|\; \begin{array}{rrrrr} 3 & 0 & -2 & 0 & 2 \\ & \dfrac{3}{4} & \dfrac{3}{16} & -\dfrac{29}{64} & -\dfrac{29}{256} \end{array}}$
$\phantom{\frac{1}{4}\;|\;} \begin{array}{rrrr|r} 3 & \dfrac{3}{4} & -\dfrac{29}{16} & -\dfrac{29}{64} & \dfrac{483}{256} \end{array}$

$Q(x) = 3x^3 + \dfrac{3}{4} x^2 - \dfrac{29}{16} x - \dfrac{29}{64}$, $R(x) = \dfrac{483}{256}$

<u>23.</u> $(x^4 - y^4) \div (x - y)$

$= (x^4 + 0x^3 + 0x^2 + 0x - y^4) \div (x - y)$

```
y | 1    0    0    0    -y⁴
  |      y   y²   y³    y⁴
    1    y   y²   y³ |  0
```

The quotient is $x^3 + x^2y + xy^2 + y^3$.
The remainder is 0.

<u>24.</u>
```
-i | 1   3i    -4i      -2
   |     -i     2    -4 - 2i
     1   2i   2 - 4i | -6 - 2i
```

$Q(x) = x^2 + 2ix + (2 - 4i)$, $R(x) = -6 - 2i$

<u>25.</u> $P(x) = x^3 - 6x^2 + 11x - 6$

Find $P(1)$.
```
1 | 1   -6   11   -6
  |      1   -5    6
    1   -5    6 |  0
```

$P(1) = 0$

Find $P(-2)$.
```
-2 | 1   -6   11    -6
   |      -2   16   -54
     1   -8   27 |  -60
```

$P(-2) = -60$

Find $P(3)$.
```
3 | 1   -6   11   -6
  |      3   -9    6
    1   -3    2 |  0
```

$P(3) = 0$

<u>26.</u>
```
-3 | 1    7   -12   -3
   |      -3   -12   72
     1    4   -24 |  69
```

$P(-3) = 69$

```
-2 | 1    7   -12   -3
   |      -2   -10   44
     1    5   -22 |  41
```

$P(-2) = 41$

```
1 | 1    7   -12   -3
  |      1    8   -4
    1    8   -4 |  -7
```

$P(1) = -7$

<u>27.</u> $P(x) = 2x^5 - 3x^4 + 2x^3 - x + 8$

Find $P(20)$.
```
20 | 2   -3     2       0       -1         8
   |     40   740   14,840   296,800   5,935,980
     2   37   742   14,840   296,799 | 5,935,988
```

$P(20) = 5,935,988$

Find $P(-3)$.
```
-3 | 2   -3    2    0    -1      8
   |     -6   27   -87   261   -780
     2   -9   29   -87   260 | -772
```

$P(-3) = -772$

<u>28.</u>
```
-10 | 1   -10    20      0       -5        -100
    |     -10   200   -2200   22,000   -219,950
      1   -20   220   -2200   21,995 | -220,050
```

$P(-10) = -220,050$

```
5 | 1   -10   20     0     -5     -100
  |       5   -25   -25   -125   -650
    1    -5   -5    -25   -130 | -750
```

$P(5) = -750$

<u>29.</u> $P(x) = x^4 - 16$

Find $P(2)$.
```
2 | 1   0   0   0   -16
  |     2   4   8    16
    1   2   4   8 |   0
```

$P(2) = 0$

Find $P(-2)$.
```
-2 | 1    0   0    0   -16
   |      -2   4   -8    16
     1   -2   4   -8 |   0
```

$P(-2) = 0$.

Find $P(3)$.
```
3 | 1   0   0    0   -16
  |     3   9   27    81
    1   3   9   27 |  65
```

$P(3) = 65$.

<u>30.</u>
```
2 | 1   0   0    0    0    32
  |     2   4    8   16    32
    1   2   4    8   16 |  64
```

$P(2) = 64$
$P(-2) = 0$ (See Exercise 20.)

```
3 | 1   0   0    0    0    32
  |     3   9   27   81   243
    1   3   9   27   81 | 275
```

$P(3) = 275$

31. $P(x) = 3x^3 + 5x^2 - 6x + 18$

    If -3 is a root of $P(x)$, then $P(-3) = 0$.
    Find $P(-3)$ using synthetic division.

    $$\begin{array}{r|rrrr} -3 & 3 & 5 & -6 & 18 \\ & & -9 & 12 & -18 \\ \hline & 3 & -4 & 6 & \,|\, 0 \end{array}$$

    Since $P(-3) = 0$, -3 is a root of $P(x)$.

    If 2 is a root of $P(x)$, then $P(2) = 0$.
    Find $P(2)$ using synthetic division.

    $$\begin{array}{r|rrrr} 2 & 3 & 5 & -6 & 18 \\ & & 6 & 22 & 32 \\ \hline & 3 & 11 & 16 & \,|\, 50 \end{array}$$

    Since $P(2) \neq 0$, 2 is not a root of $P(x)$.

32. $$\begin{array}{r|rrrr} -4 & 3 & 11 & -2 & 8 \\ & & -12 & 4 & -8 \\ \hline & 3 & -1 & 2 & \,|\, 0 \end{array}$$

    $P(-4) = 0$, so -4 is a root of $P(x)$.

    $$\begin{array}{r|rrrr} 2 & 3 & 11 & -2 & 8 \\ & & 6 & 34 & 64 \\ \hline & 3 & 17 & 32 & \,|\, 72 \end{array}$$

    $P(2) \neq 0$, so 2 is not a root of $P(x)$.

33. $P(x) = x^3 - \frac{7}{2}x^2 + x - \frac{3}{2}$

    If -3 is a root of $P(x)$, then $P(-3) = 0$.
    Find $P(-3)$ using synthetic division.

    $$\begin{array}{r|rrrr} -3 & 1 & -\frac{7}{2} & 1 & -\frac{3}{2} \\ & & -3 & \frac{39}{2} & -\frac{123}{2} \\ \hline & 1 & -\frac{13}{2} & \frac{41}{2} & \,|\, -63 \end{array}$$

    Since $P(-3) \neq 0$, -3 is not a root of $P(x)$.

    If $\frac{1}{2}$ is a root of $P(x)$, then $P\left(\frac{1}{2}\right) = 0$.
    Find $P\left(\frac{1}{2}\right)$ using synthetic division.

    $$\begin{array}{r|rrrr} \frac{1}{2} & 1 & -\frac{7}{2} & 1 & -\frac{3}{2} \\ & & \frac{1}{2} & -\frac{3}{2} & -\frac{1}{4} \\ \hline & 1 & -3 & -\frac{1}{2} & \,|\, -\frac{7}{4} \end{array}$$

    Since $P\left(\frac{1}{2}\right) \neq 0$, $\frac{1}{2}$ is not a root of $P(x)$.

34. $$\begin{array}{r|rrrr} i & 1 & 2 & 1 & 2 \\ & & i & -1 + 2i & -2 \\ \hline & 1 & 2 + i & 2i & \,|\, 0 \end{array}$$

    $P(i) = 0$, so i is a root of $P(x)$.

    $$\begin{array}{r|rrrr} -i & 1 & 2 & 1 & 2 \\ & & -i & -1 - 2i & -2 \\ \hline & 1 & 2 - i & -2i & \,|\, 0 \end{array}$$

    $P(-i) = 0$, so $-i$ is a root of $P(x)$.

    $$\begin{array}{r|rrr} -2 & 1 & 2 & 1 & 2 \\ & & -2 & 0 & -2 \\ \hline & 1 & 0 & 1 & \,|\, 0 \end{array}$$

    $P(-2) = 0$, so -2 is a root of $P(x)$.

35. $P(x) = x^3 + 4x^2 + x - 6$

    Try $x - 1$. Use synthetic division to see whether $P(1) = 0$.

    $$\begin{array}{r|rrrr} 1 & 1 & 4 & 1 & -6 \\ & & 1 & 5 & 6 \\ \hline & 1 & 5 & 6 & \,|\, 0 \end{array}$$

    Since $P(1) = 0$, $x - 1$ is a factor of $P(x)$.
    Thus $P(x) = (x - 1)(x^2 + 5x + 6)$.

    Factoring the trinomial we get
    $P(x) = (x - 1)(x + 2)(x + 3)$.

    To solve the equation $P(x) = 0$, use the principle of zero products.
    $(x - 1)(x + 2)(x + 3) = 0$

    $x - 1 = 0$ or $x + 2 = 0$ or $x + 3 = 0$
    $\quad x = 1$ or $\quad x = -2$ or $\quad x = -3$

    The solutions are 1, -2, and -3.

36. $$\begin{array}{r|rrrr} 2 & 1 & 5 & -2 & -24 \\ & & 2 & 14 & 24 \\ \hline & 1 & 7 & 12 & \,|\, 0 \end{array}$$

    $P(x) = (x - 2)(x^2 + 7x + 12)$
    $\quad\quad = (x - 2)(x + 3)(x + 4)$
    The roots are 2, -3, and -4.

37. $P(x) = x^3 - 6x^2 + 3x + 10$

    Try $x - 1$. Use synthetic division to see whether $P(1) = 0$.

    $$\begin{array}{r|rrrr} 1 & 1 & -6 & 3 & 10 \\ & & 1 & -5 & -2 \\ \hline & 1 & -5 & -2 & \,|\, 8 \end{array}$$

    Since $P(1) \neq 0$, $x - 1$ is not a factor of $P(x)$.

    Try $x + 1$. Use synthetic division to see whether $P(-1) = 0$.

```
-1 | 1   -6    3    10
   |     -1    7   -10
     1   -7   10 |   0
```

Since P(-1) = 0, x + 1 is a factor of P(x).
Thus P(x) = (x + 1)(x² - 7x + 10).

Factoring the trinomial we get
P(x) = (x + 1)(x - 2)(x - 5).

To solve the equation P(x) = 0, use the principle of zero products.

(x + 1)(x - 2)(x - 5) = 0

x + 1 = 0 or x - 2 = 0 or x - 5 = 0
   x = -1 or   x = 2 or   x = 5

The solutions are -1, 2, and 5.

38.
```
1 | 1    2   -13   10
  |      1    3   -10
    1    3   -10 |  0
```

P(x) = (x - 1)(x² + 3x - 10)
     = (x - 1)(x - 2)(x + 5)
The roots are 1, 2, and -5.

39. P(x) = x³ - x² - 14x + 24

Try x + 1, x - 1, and x + 2. Using synthetic division we find that P(-1) ≠ 0, P(1) ≠ 0, and P(-2) ≠ 0. Thus x + 1, x - 2, and x + 2 are not factors of P(x).

Try x - 2. Use synthetic division to see whether P(2) = 0.
```
2 | 1   -1   -14   24
  |      2    2   -24
    1    1   -12 |  0
```

Since P(2) = 0, x - 2 is a factor of P(x).
Thus P(x) = (x - 2)(x² + x - 12).

Factoring the trinomial we get
P(x) = (x - 2)(x + 4)(x - 3).

To solve the equation P(x) = 0, use the principle of zero products.

(x - 2)(x + 4)(x - 3) = 0

x - 2 = 0 or x + 4 = 0 or x - 3 = 0
   x = 2 or   x = -4 or   x = 3

The solutions are 2, -4, and 3.

40.
```
2 | 1   -3   -10   24
  |      2   -2   -24
    1   -1   -12 |  0
```

P(x) = (x - 2)(x² - x - 12)
     = (x - 2)(x - 4)(x + 3)
The roots are 2, 4, and -3.

41. P(x) = x⁴ - x³ - 19x² + 49x - 30

Try x - 1. Use synthetic division to see whether P(1) = 0.
```
1 | 1   -1   -19    49   -30
  |      1    0   -19    30
    1    0   -19    30 |   0
```

Since P(1) = 0, x - 1 is a factor of P(x).
Thus P(x) = (x - 1)(x³ - 19x + 30).

We continue to use synthetic division to factor Q(x) = x³ - 19x + 30. Trying x - 1, x + 1, and x + 2 we find that Q(1) ≠ 0, Q(-1) ≠ 0, and Q(-2) ≠ 0. Thus x - 1, x + 1, and x + 2 are not factors of x³ - 19x + 30. Try x - 2.
```
2 | 1    0   -19    30
  |      2    4   -30
    1    2   -15 |   0
```

Since Q(2) = 0, x - 2 is a factor of x³ - 19x + 30.

Thus P(x) = (x - 1)(x - 2)(x² + 2x - 15).

Factoring the trinomial we get
P(x) = (x - 1)(x - 2)(x - 3)(x + 5).

To solve the equation P(x) = 0, use the principle of zero products.

(x - 1)(x - 2)(x - 3)(x + 5) = 0

x - 1 = 0 or x - 2 = 0 or x - 3 = 0 or x + 5 = 0
   x = 1 or   x = 2 or   x = 3 or   x = -5

The solutions are 1, 2, 3, and -5.

42.
```
-1 | 1   11   41    61    30
   |     -1  -10   -31   -30
     1   10   31    30 |   0
```
```
-2 | 1   10   31    30
   |     -2  -16   -30
     1    8   15 |   0
```

P(x) = (x + 1)(x + 2)(x² + 8x + 15)
     = (x + 1)(x + 2)(x + 3)(x + 5)
The roots are -1, -2, -3, and -5.

43. We solve f(n) = 0.

$\frac{1}{2}(n^2 - n) = 0$

n² - n = 0   (Multiplying by 2)

n(n - 1) = 0

n = 0 or n = 1

The zeros of the function are 0 and 1.

44. N(t) = -0.046t³ + 2.08t + 2

Using the intermediate value theorem (Section 4.5) we determine that there is a real root at approximately 7.16.

45. We solve $W(h) = 0$, $0 \leqslant h < \infty$.

$$\left(\frac{h}{12.3}\right)^3 = 0$$

$$\frac{h^3}{(12.3)^3} = 0$$

$$h^3 = 0 \quad \text{[Multiplying by } (12.3)^3\text{]}$$

$$h = 0$$

The root of the polynomial is 0.

46. $y = \frac{1}{13}x^3 - \frac{1}{14}x$

Solve: $\frac{1}{13}x^3 - \frac{1}{14}x = 0$

$$x\left(\frac{1}{13}x^2 - \frac{1}{14}\right) = 0$$

$x = 0$ or $x = \pm\sqrt{\frac{13}{14}}$

$x = 0$ or $x \approx \pm 0.9636$

Only 0 and 0.9636 are in [0, 2].

47. $\frac{6x^2}{x^2 + 11} + \frac{60}{x^3 - 7x^2 + 11x - 77} = \frac{1}{x - 7}$

LCM is $(x^2 + 11)(x - 7)$.

$$(x^2+11)(x-7)\left[\frac{6x^2}{x^2+11} + \frac{60}{(x^2+11)(x-7)}\right] = (x^2+11)(x-7)\cdot\frac{1}{x-7}$$

$$6x^2(x - 7) + 60 = x^2 + 11$$

$$6x^3 - 42x^2 + 60 = x^2 + 11$$

$$6x^3 - 43x^2 + 49 = 0$$

Use synthetic division to find factors of $P(x) = 6x^3 - 43x^2 + 49$. Try $x + 1$. Use synthetic division to see whether $P(-1) = 0$.

```
-1 | 6   -43    0    49
   |      -6   49   -49
     6   -49   49  |  0
```

Since $P(-1) = 0$, $x + 1$ is a factor of $P(x)$. Thus $P(x) = (x + 1)(6x^2 - 49x + 49)$. Factoring the trinomial we get $P(x) = (x + 1)(6x - 7)(x - 7)$.

To solve $P(x) = 0$, use the principle of zero products.

$(x + 1)(6x - 7)(x - 7) = 0$

$x + 1 = 0$ or $6x - 7 = 0$ or $x - 7 = 0$

$x = -1$ or $6x = 7$ or $x = 7$

$x = -1$ or $x = \frac{7}{6}$ or $x = 7$

The value $x = 7$ does not check, but $x = -1$ and $x = \frac{7}{6}$ do. The solutions are -1 and $\frac{7}{6}$.

48. $\frac{2x^2}{x^2 - 1} + \frac{4}{x + 3} = \frac{32}{x^3 + 3x^2 - x - 3}$

LCM is $(x + 1)(x - 1)(x + 3)$

$2x^2(x + 3) + 4(x + 1)(x - 1) = 32$

$2x^3 + 6x^2 + 4x^2 - 4 = 32$

$2x^3 + 10x^2 - 36 = 0$

$x^3 + 5x^2 - 18 = 0$

```
-3 | 1    5    0   -18
   |     -3   -6    18
     1    2   -6  |   0
```

$(x + 3)(x^2 + 2x - 6) = 0$

$x = -3$ or $x = -1 \pm \sqrt{7}$

Only $-1 \pm \sqrt{7}$ check.

49. To solve $x^3 + 2x^2 - 13x + 10 > 0$ we first find the solutions of $f(x) = x^3 + 2x^2 - 13x + 10 = 0$. Using synthetic division we find the solutions to be -5, 1, and 2. They divide the real-number line as shown.

Try a test number in each interval.

A: $f(-6) = (-6)^3 + 2(-6)^2 - 13(-6) + 10 = -56$

B: $f(0) = 0^3 + 2\cdot0^2 - 13\cdot0 + 10 = 10$

C: $f\left(\frac{3}{2}\right) = \left(\frac{3}{2}\right)^3 + 2\left(\frac{3}{2}\right)^2 - 13\left(\frac{3}{2}\right) + 10 = -\frac{13}{8}$

D: $f(3) = 3^3 + 2\cdot3^2 - 13\cdot3 + 10 = 16$

The solution set is $\{x \mid -5 < x < 1 \text{ or } x > 2\}$.

50. $x^4 - x^3 - 19x^2 + 49x - 30 < 0$

```
1 | 1   -1   -19    49   -30
  |      1    0    -19    30
    1    0   -19    30  |  0
```

```
2 | 1    0   -19    30
  |      2    4    -30
    1    2   -15  |  0
```

$f(x) = (x - 1)(x - 2)(x^2 + 2x - 15)$

$= (x - 1)(x - 2)(x + 5)(x - 3)$

The solutions of $f(x) = 0$ are 1, 2, -5, and 3.

A: Test -6, $f(-6) > 0$

B: Test 0, $f(0) < 0$

C: Test $\frac{3}{2}$, $f\left(\frac{3}{2}\right) > 0$

D: Test $\frac{5}{2}$, $f\left(\frac{5}{2}\right) < 0$

E: Test 4, $f(4) > 0$

$\{x \mid -5 < x < 1 \text{ or } 2 < x < 3\}$

51. $P(x) = x^3 - kx^2 + 3x + 7k$

Think of $x + 2$ as $x - (-2)$.

Find $P(-2)$.

```
-2 | 1    -k       3        7k
   |      -2     2k + 4    -4k - 14
   ----------------------------------
     1   -k - 2   2k + 7  | 3k - 14
```

Thus $P(-2) = 3k - 14$.

We know that if $x + 2$ is a factor of $P(x)$, then $P(-2) = 0$.

We solve $0 = 3k - 14$ for k.

$0 = 3k - 14$

$14 = 3k$

$\dfrac{14}{3} = k$

52. a) -485.1587,   b) -485.1587

53. Divide $x^2 + kx + 4$ by $x - 1$.

```
1 | 1    k       4
  |      1      k + 1
  ------------------------
    1   k + 1 | k + 5
```

The remainder is $k + 5$.

Divide $x^2 + kx + 4$ by $x + 1$.

```
-1 | 1    k       4
   |      -1     -k + 1
   -------------------------
     1   k - 1 | -k + 5
```

The remainder is $-k + 5$.

Set $k + 5 = -k + 5$ and solve for k.

$k + 5 = -k + 5$

$2k = 0$

$k = 0$

54.
```
-2 | 1    -3       2k
   |       -2      10
   -----------------------
     1    -5 | 10 + 2k
```

$10 + 2k = 7$

$k = -\dfrac{3}{2}$

55. See the answer section in the text.

56. Let $f(x) = x^n - a^n$. Then $f(a) = 0$ so that $x - a$ is a factor.

1. $P(x) = (x + 3)^2(x - 1) = (x + 3)(x + 3)(x - 1)$

The factor $x + 3$ occurs twice. Thus the root -3 has a multiplicity of two.

The factor $x - 1$ occurs only one time. Thus the root 1 has a mulitplicity of one.

2. 3, Multiplicity 2; -4, Multiplicity 3; 0, Multiplicity 4

3. $x^3(x - 1)^2(x + 4) = 0$

$x \cdot x \cdot x (x - 1)(x - 1)(x + 4) = 0$

The factor x occurs three times. Thus the root 0 has a multiplicity of three.

The factor $x - 1$ occurs twice. Thus the root 1 has a multiplicity of two.

The factor $x + 4$ occurs only one time. Thus the root -4 has a multiplicity of one.

4. $P(x) = (x^2 - 5x + 6)^2$

$\qquad = [(x - 3)(x - 2)]^2$

$\qquad = (x - 3)^2(x - 2)^2$

3, Multiplicity 2; 2, Multiplicity 2

5. $P(x) = x^4 - 4x^2 + 3$

We factor as follows:

$P(x) = (x^2 - 3)(x^2 - 1)$

$\qquad = (x - \sqrt{3})(x + \sqrt{3})(x - 1)(x + 1)$

The roots of the polynomial are $\sqrt{3}$, $-\sqrt{3}$, 1, and -1. Each has multiplicity of one.

6. $P(x) = x^4 - 10x^2 + 9$

$\qquad = (x^2 - 9)(x^2 - 1)$

$\qquad = (x + 3)(x - 3)(x + 1)(x - 1)$

± 3, ± 1; each has multiplicity of 1

7. $P(x) = x^3 + 3x^2 - x - 3$

We factor by grouping:

$P(x) = x^2(x + 3) - (x + 3)$

$\qquad = (x^2 - 1)(x + 3)$

$\qquad = (x - 1)(x + 1)(x + 3)$

The roots of the polynomial are 1, -1, and -3. Each has multiplicity of one.

8. $P(x) = x^3 - x^2 - 2x + 2$

$\qquad = x^2(x - 1) - 2(x - 1)$

$\qquad = (x^2 - 2)(x - 1)$

$\qquad = (x - \sqrt{2})(x + \sqrt{2})(x - 1)$

$\sqrt{2}$, $-\sqrt{2}$, 1; each has multiplicity of 1.

9. Find a polynomial of degree 3 with -2, 3, and 5 as roots.

By Theorem 6 such a polynomial has factors $x + 2$, $x - 3$, and $x - 5$, so we have

$$P(x) = a_n(x + 2)(x - 3)(x - 5).$$

The number a_n can be any nonzero number. The simplest polynomial will be obtained if we let it be 1. Multiplying the factors, we obtain

$$P(x) = (x + 2)(x - 3)(x - 5)$$
$$= (x^2 - x - 6)(x - 5)$$
$$= x^3 - 6x^2 - x + 30$$

10. $P(x) = (x - 2)(x - i)(x + i)$
$$= (x - 2)(x^2 + 1)$$
$$= x^3 - 2x^2 + x - 2$$

11. Find a polynomial of degree 3 with -3, 2i, and -2i as roots.

By Theorem 6 such a polynomial has factors $x + 3$, $x - 2i$, and $x + 2i$, so we have

$$P(x) = a_n(x + 3)(x - 2i)(x + 2i).$$

The number a_n can be any nonzero number. The simplest polynomial will be obtained if we let it be 1. Multiplying the factors, we obtain

$$P(x) = (x + 3)(x - 2i)(x + 2i)$$
$$= (x + 3)(x^2 + 4)$$
$$= x^3 + 3x^2 + 4x + 12$$

12. $P(x) = [x - (1 + 4i)][x - (1 - 4i)](x + 1)$
$$= (x^2 - 2x + 17)(x + 1)$$
$$= x^3 - x^2 + 15x + 17$$

13. Find a polynomial of degree 3 with $\sqrt{2}$, $-\sqrt{2}$, and $\sqrt{3}$ as roots.

By Theorem 6 such a polynomial has factors $x - \sqrt{2}$, $x + \sqrt{2}$, and $x - \sqrt{3}$, so we have

$$P(x) = a_n(x - \sqrt{2})(x + \sqrt{2})(x - \sqrt{3}).$$

The number a_n can be any nonzero number. The simplest polynomial will be obtained if we let it be 1. Multiplying the factors, we obtain

$$P(x) = (x - \sqrt{2})(x + \sqrt{2})(x - \sqrt{3})$$
$$= (x^2 - 2)(x - \sqrt{3})$$
$$= x^3 - \sqrt{3}\,x^2 - 2x + 2\sqrt{3}$$

14. $P(x) = (x + 2)(x - 3)^2(x + 1)$
$$= x^4 - 3x^3 - 7x^2 + 15x + 18$$

15. A polynomial or polynomial equation of degree 5 has at most 5 roots. Three of the roots are 6, $-3 + 4i$, and $4 - \sqrt{5}$. Using Theorems 10 and 11 we know that $-3 - 4i$ and $4 + \sqrt{5}$ are also roots.

16. $1 + i$

17. Find a polynomial of lowest degree with rational coefficients that has $1 + i$ and 2 as some of its roots.

$1 - i$ is also a root.   (Theorem 10)

Thus the polynomial is

$$a_n(x - 2)[x - (1 + i)][x - (1 - i)].$$

If we let $a_n = 1$, we obtain

$$(x - 2)[(x - 1) - i][(x - 1) + i]$$
$$= (x - 2)[(x - 1)^2 - i^2]$$
$$= (x - 2)(x^2 - 2x + 1 + 1)$$
$$= (x - 2)(x^2 - 2x + 2)$$
$$= x^3 - 4x^2 + 6x - 4$$

18. $P(x) = [x - (2 - i)][x - (2 + i)](x + 1)$
$$= x^3 - 3x^2 + x + 5$$

19. Find a polynomial of lowest degree with rational coefficients that has -4i and 5 as some of its roots.

4i is also a root.   (Theorem 10)

Thus the polynomial is

$$a_n(x - 5)(x + 4i)(x - 4i).$$

If we let $a_n = 1$, we obtain

$$(x - 5)[x^2 - (4i)^2]$$
$$= (x - 5)(x^2 + 16)$$
$$= x^3 - 5x^2 + 16x - 80$$

20. $P(x) =$
$$[x-(2-\sqrt{3})][x-(2+\sqrt{3})][x-(1+i)][x-(1-i)] =$$
$$x^4 - 6x^3 + 11x^2 - 10x + 2$$

21. Find a polynomial of lowest degree with rational coefficients that has $\sqrt{5}$ and -3i as some of its roots.

$-\sqrt{5}$ is also a root.   (Theorem 11)
3i is also a root.   (Theorem 10)

Thus the polynomial is

$$a_n(x - \sqrt{5})(x + \sqrt{5})(x + 3i)(x - 3i).$$

If we let $a_n = 1$, we obtain

$$(x^2 - 5)(x^2 + 9)$$
$$= x^4 + 4x^2 - 45$$

22. $P(x) = (x + \sqrt{2})(x - \sqrt{2})(x - 4i)(x + 4i)$
$$= x^4 + 14x^2 - 32$$

23. If $-i$ is a root of $x^4 - 5x^3 + 7x^2 - 5x + 6$, i is also a root (Theorem 10). Thus $x + i$ and $x - i$ or $(x + i)(x - i)$ which is $x^2 + 1$ are factors of the polynomial. Divide $x^4 - 5x^3 + 7x^2 - 5x + 6$ by $x^2 + 1$.

$$
\begin{array}{r}
x^2 - 5x + 6 \\
x^2 + 1 \overline{\smash{)}\, x^4 - 5x^3 + 7x^2 - 5x + 6} \\
\underline{x^4 \qquad\quad + x^2} \\
-5x^3 + 6x^2 - 5x \\
\underline{-5x^3 \qquad\quad - 5x} \\
6x^2 \qquad + 6 \\
\underline{6x^2 \qquad + 6} \\
0
\end{array}
$$

Thus

$x^4 - 5x^3 + 7x^2 - 5x + 6 = (x + i)(x - i)(x^2 - 5x + 6)$

$\qquad\qquad\qquad = (x + i)(x - i)(x - 2)(x - 3)$

Using the principle of zero products we find the other roots to be i, 2, and 3.

24. $(x - 2i)$ and $(x + 2i)$ are both factors of $P(x) = x^4 - 16$.

$(x - 2i)(x + 2i) = x^2 + 4$

$$
\begin{array}{r}
x^2 - 4 \\
x^2 + 4 \overline{\smash{)}\, x^4 + 0x^2 - 16} \\
\underline{x^4 + 4x^2} \\
-4x^2 - 16 \\
\underline{-4x^2 - 16} \\
0
\end{array}
$$

$(x - 2i)(x + 2i)(x^2 - 4) = 0$

$(x - 2i)(x + 2i)(x + 2)(x - 2) = 0$

The other roots are $-2i$, -2, and 2.

25. $x^3 - 6x^2 + 13x - 20 = 0$

If 4 is a root, then $x - 4$ is a factor. Use synthetic division to find another factor.

$$
\begin{array}{r|rrrr}
4 & 1 & -6 & 13 & -20 \\
  &   & 4 & -8 & 20 \\
\hline
  & 1 & -2 & 5 & 0
\end{array}
$$

$(x - 4)(x^2 - 2x + 5) = 0$

$x - 4 = 0$ or $x^2 - 2x + 5 = 0$ (Principle of zero products)

$x = 4$ or $x = \dfrac{2 \pm \sqrt{4 - 20}}{2}$ (Quadratic formula)

$x = 4$ or $x = \dfrac{2 \pm 4i}{2} = 1 \pm 2i$

The other roots are $1 + 2i$ and $1 - 2i$.

26.
$$
\begin{array}{r|rrrr}
2 & 1 & 0 & 0 & -8 \\
  &   & 2 & 4 & 8 \\
\hline
  & 1 & 2 & 4 & 0
\end{array}
$$

$(x - 2)(x^2 + 2x + 4) = 0$

$x = 2$ or $x = -1 \pm i\sqrt{3}$

The other roots are $-1 + i\sqrt{3}$ and $-1 - i\sqrt{3}$.

27. $P(x) = x^5 - 3x^2 + 1$

Since the leading coefficient is 1, the only possibilities for rational roots (Theorem 12) are the factors of the last coefficient 1: 1 and -1.

28. $P(x) = x^7 + 37x^5 - 6x^2 + 12$

c: ± 1, ± 2, ± 3, ± 4, ± 6, ± 12

d: ± 1

$\dfrac{c}{d}$: $\pm (1, 2, 3, 4, 6, 12)$

29. $P(x) = 15x^6 + 47x^2 + 2$

By Theorem 12, if c/d, a rational number in lowest terms, is a root of $P(x)$, then c must be a factor of 2 and d must be a factor of 15.

The possibilities for c and d are

c: 1, -1, 2, -2   d: 1, -1, 3, -3, 5, -5, 15, -15

The resulting possibilities for c/d are

$\dfrac{c}{d}$: $1, -1, \dfrac{1}{3}, -\dfrac{1}{3}, \dfrac{1}{5}, -\dfrac{1}{5}, \dfrac{1}{15}, -\dfrac{1}{15}$

$\qquad 2, -2, \dfrac{2}{3}, -\dfrac{2}{3}, \dfrac{2}{5}, -\dfrac{2}{5}, \dfrac{2}{15}, -\dfrac{2}{15}$

30. $P(x) = 10x^{25} + 3x^{17} - 35x + 6$

c: ± 1, ± 2, ± 3, ± 6

d: ± 1, ± 2, ± 5, ± 10

$\dfrac{c}{d}$: $\pm \left[1, 2, 3, 6, \dfrac{1}{2}, \dfrac{3}{2}, \dfrac{1}{5}, \dfrac{2}{5}, \dfrac{3}{5}, \dfrac{6}{5}, \dfrac{1}{10}, \dfrac{3}{10}\right]$

31. $P(x) = x^3 + 3x^2 - 2x - 6$

Using Theorem 12, the only possible rational roots are 1, -1, 2, -2, 3, -3, 6 and -6. Of these eight possibilities we know that at most three of them can be roots because $P(x)$ is of degree 3. Use synthetic division to determine which are roots.

$$
\begin{array}{r|rrrr}
1 & 1 & 3 & -2 & -6 \\
  &   & 1 & 4 & 2 \\
\hline
  & 1 & 4 & 2 & -4
\end{array}
$$
$P(1) \neq 0$, so 1 is not a root.

$$
\begin{array}{r|rrrr}
-1 & 1 & 3 & -2 & -6 \\
   &   & -1 & -2 & 4 \\
\hline
   & 1 & 2 & -4 & -2
\end{array}
$$
$P(-1) \neq 0$, so -1 is not a root.

$$
\begin{array}{r|rrrr}
2 & 1 & 3 & -2 & -6 \\
  &   & 2 & 10 & 16 \\
\hline
  & 1 & 5 & 8 & 10
\end{array}
$$
$P(2) \neq 0$, so 2 is not a root.

$$
\begin{array}{r|rrrr}
-2 & 1 & 3 & -2 & -6 \\
   &   & -2 & -2 & 8 \\
\hline
   & 1 & 1 & -4 & 2
\end{array}
$$

$P(-2) \neq 0$, so -2 is not a root.

$$
\begin{array}{r|rrrr}
3 & 1 & 3 & -2 & -6 \\
  &   & 3 & 18 & 48 \\
\hline
  & 1 & 6 & 16 & 42
\end{array}
$$

$P(3) \neq 0$, so 3 is not a root.

$$
\begin{array}{r|rrrr}
-3 & 1 & 3 & -2 & -6 \\
   &   & -3 & 0 & 6 \\
\hline
   & 1 & 0 & -2 & 0
\end{array}
$$

$P(-3) = 0$, so -3 <u>is</u> a root.

We can now express $P(x)$ as follows:

$P(x) = (x + 3)(x^2 - 2)$.

To find the other roots we solve the quadratic equation $x^2 - 2 = 0$. The other roots are $\sqrt{2}$ and $-\sqrt{2}$. These are irrational numbers. Thus the only rational root is -3.

We write the polynomial in factored form:

$P(x) = (x + 3)(x - \sqrt{2})(x + \sqrt{2})$

(Note that we could have also used factoring by grouping in this exercise.)

32.

$$
\begin{array}{r|rrrr}
1 & 1 & -1 & -3 & 3 \\
  &   & 1 & 0 & -3 \\
\hline
  & 1 & 0 & -3 & 0
\end{array}
$$

$(x - 1)(x^2 - 3) = 0$

The roots are 1, $\sqrt{3}$, and $-\sqrt{3}$. The only rational root is 1.

$(x - 1)(x - \sqrt{3})(x + \sqrt{3}) = 0$

(Note that we could also have used factoring by grouping.)

33. $x^3 - 3x + 2 = 0$

Using Theorem 12, the only possible rational roots are 1, -1, 2, and -2. At most three of these can be roots because the polynomial is of degree 3. Use synthetic division to determine which are roots.

$$
\begin{array}{r|rrrr}
1 & 1 & 0 & -3 & 2 \\
  &   & 1 & 1 & -2 \\
\hline
  & 1 & 1 & -2 & 0
\end{array}
$$

1 <u>is</u> a root

We can now express the equation as follows:
$(x - 1)(x^2 + x - 2) = 0$

To find the other roots we solve the following quadratic equation:

$x^2 + x - 2 = 0$

$(x + 2)(x - 1) = 0$

$x = -2 \quad \text{or} \quad x = 1$

The rational roots are 1 and -2. (One is a root with multiplicity of 2.)

We write the polynomial in factored form:

$(x - 1)^2(x + 2) = 0$

34. $P(x) = x^3 - 3x + 4$

The possible rational roots are ± 1, ± 2, ± 4. Synthetic division shows that none of these is a root. Thus there are no rational roots.

35. $P(x) = x^3 - 5x^2 + 11x - 19$

Using Theorem 12, the only possible rational roots are 1, -1, 19, and -19. At most three of these can be roots because $P(x)$ is of degree 3. Use synthetic division to determine which are roots.

$$
\begin{array}{r|rrrr}
1 & 1 & -5 & 11 & -19 \\
  &   & 1 & -4 & 7 \\
\hline
  & 1 & -4 & 7 & -12
\end{array}
$$

$P(1) \neq 0$, so 1 is not a root.

$$
\begin{array}{r|rrrr}
-1 & 1 & -5 & 11 & -19 \\
   &   & -1 & 6 & -17 \\
\hline
   & 1 & -6 & 17 & -36
\end{array}
$$

$P(-1) \neq 0$, so -1 is not a root.

$$
\begin{array}{r|rrrr}
19 & 1 & -5 & 11 & -19 \\
   &   & 19 & 266 & 5263 \\
\hline
   & 1 & 14 & 277 & 5244
\end{array}
$$

$P(19) \neq 0$, so 19 is not a root.

$$
\begin{array}{r|rrrr}
-19 & 1 & -5 & 11 & -19 \\
    &   & -19 & 456 & -8873 \\
\hline
    & 1 & -24 & 467 & -8892
\end{array}
$$

$P(19) \neq 0$, so -19 is not a root.

There are no rational roots.

36. $P(x) = x^3 - 7x^2 - 2x + 23$

The possible rational roots are ± 1 and ± 23. Synthetic division shows that none of these is a root. Thus there are no rational roots.

37. $P(x) = 5x^4 - 4x^3 + 19x^2 - 16x - 4$

Using Theorem 12, the only possible rational roots are $\pm \left[1, 2, 4, \dfrac{1}{5}, \dfrac{2}{5}, \dfrac{4}{5} \right]$. Of these twelve possibilities we know that at most four of them can be roots because $P(x)$ is of degree 4. Using synthetic division we determine that the only rational roots are 1 and $-\dfrac{1}{5}$.

$$
\begin{array}{r|rrrrr}
1 & 5 & -4 & 19 & -16 & -4 \\
  &   & 5 & 1 & 20 & 4 \\
\hline
  & 5 & 1 & 20 & 4 & 0
\end{array}
$$

$P(1) = 0$, so 1 is a root.

We can now express $P(x)$ as follows:
$P(x) = (x - 1)(5x^3 + x^2 + 20x + 4)$.

We now use $Q(x) = 5x^3 + x^2 + 20x + 4$ and check to see if 1 is a double root and check for other possible rational roots. The only other rational root is $-\dfrac{1}{5}$.

$$
\begin{array}{r|rrrr}
-\dfrac{1}{5} & 5 & 1 & 20 & 4 \\
  &   & -1 & 0 & -4 \\
\hline
  & 5 & 0 & 20 & 0
\end{array}
$$

$Q\left(-\frac{1}{5}\right) = 0$, so $-\frac{1}{5}$ is a root.

We can now express $P(x)$ as follows:

$P(x) = (x - 1)\left[x + \frac{1}{5}\right](5x^2 + 20)$

To find the other roots we solve the quadratic equation $5x^2 + 20 = 0$.

$5x^2 + 20 = 0$

$\qquad 5x^2 = -20$

$\qquad\ x^2 = -4$

$\qquad\ \ x = \pm\, 2i$

The other roots are $2i$ and $-2i$, neither of which is rational. The only rational roots are 1 and $-\frac{1}{5}$.

We write the polynomial in factored form:

$P(x) = (x - 1)\left[x + \frac{1}{5}\right](x - 2i)(x + 2i)$

38. $P(x) = 3x^4 - 4x^3 + x^2 + 6x - 2$

The possible rational roots are $\pm\left[1, 2, \frac{1}{3}, \frac{2}{3}\right]$.

```
-1 |  3   -4    1    6   -2
   |      -3    7   -8    2      -1 is a root
   _____
      3   -7    8   -2 |  0
```

```
 1/3 | 3   -7    8   -2
     |     1   -2    2            1/3 is a root
   _____
       3   -6    6 |  0
```

$P(x) = (x + 1)\left[x - \frac{1}{3}\right](3x^2 - 6x + 6)$

$\qquad = 3(x + 1)\left[x - \frac{1}{3}\right](x^2 - 2x + 2)$

The roots are -1, $\frac{1}{3}$, and $1 \pm i$. The rational roots are -1 and $\frac{1}{3}$.

$P(x) = 3(x + 1)\left[x - \frac{1}{3}\right](x - 1 - i)(x - 1 + i)$

39. $P(x) = x^4 - 3x^3 - 20x^2 - 24x - 8$

Using Theorem 12, the only possible rational roots are 1, -1, 2, -2, 4, -4, 8, and -8. Of these eight possibilities, we know that at most four of them can be roots because $P(x)$ is of degree 4. Using synthetic division we determine that the only rational roots are -1 and -2.

```
-1 | 1   -3   -20   -24   -8
   |     -1     4    16    8
   _____
     1   -4   -16    -8 |  0
```

$P(-1) = 0$, so -1 is a root.

We can now express $P(x)$ as follows:

$P(x) = (x + 1)(x^3 - 4x^2 - 16x - 8)$.

We now use $Q(x) = x^3 - 4x^2 - 16x - 8$ and check to see if -1 is a double root and check for other possible rational roots. The only other rational root is -2.

```
-2 | 1   -4   -16   -8
   |     -2    12    8
   _____
     1   -6    -4 |  0
```

$Q(-2) = 0$, so -2 is a root.

We can now express $P(x)$ as follows:

$P(x) = (x + 1)(x + 2)(x^2 - 6x - 4)$.

Since the factor $x^2 - 6x - 4$ is quadratic, use the quadratic formula to find the other roots, $3 + \sqrt{13}$ and $3 - \sqrt{13}$. These are irrational numbers. The only rational roots are -1 and -2.

We write the polynomial in factored form:

$P(x) = (x + 1)(x + 2)(x - 3 - \sqrt{13})(x - 3 + \sqrt{13})$

40. $P(x) = x^4 + 5x^3 - 27x^2 + 31x - 10$

The possible rational roots are $\pm$ (1, 2, 5, 10).

```
1 | 1    5   -27    31   -10
  |      1     6   -21    10       1 is a root
  _____
    1    6   -21    10 |  0
```

```
2 | 1    6   -21    10
  |      2    16   -10              2 is a root
  _____
    1    8    -5 |  0
```

$P(x) = (x - 1)(x - 2)(x^2 + 8x - 5)$

The roots are 1, 2, and $-4 \pm \sqrt{21}$. The rational roots are 1 and 2.

$P(x) = (x - 1)(x - 2)(x + 4 - \sqrt{21})(x + 4 + \sqrt{21})$

41. $P(x) = x^3 - 4x^2 + 2x + 4$

Using Theorem 12, the only possible rational roots are 1, -1, 2, -2, 4, and -4. Of these six possibilities, we know that at most three of them can be roots, because $P(x)$ is of degree 3. Use synthetic division to determine which are roots.

```
 1 | 1   -4    2    4          P(1) ≠ 0, so 1 is
   |      1   -3   -1          not a root.
   _____
     1   -3   -1 |  3
```

```
-1 | 1   -4    2    4          P(-1) ≠ 0, so -1 is
   |     -1    5   -7          not a root.
   _____
     1   -5    7 | -3
```

```
 2 | 1   -4    2    4          P(2) = 0, so 2 is
   |      2   -4   -4          a root.
   _____
     1   -2   -2 |  0
```

We can now express $P(x)$ as

$P(x) = (x - 2)(x^2 - 2x - 2)$.

To find the other roots we use the quadratic formula to solve the equation $x^2 - 2x - 2 = 0$. The other roots are $1 + \sqrt{3}$ and $1 - \sqrt{3}$. These are irrational roots.

The only rational root is 2.

We write the polynomial in factored form:
$P(x) = (x - 2)(x - 1 - \sqrt{3})(x - 1 + \sqrt{3})$

42. $P(x) = x^3 - 8x^2 + 17x - 4$

The possible rational roots are $\pm (1, 2, 4)$.

$$\begin{array}{r|rrrr} 4 & 1 & -8 & 17 & -4 \\ & & 4 & -16 & 4 \\ \hline & 1 & -4 & 1 & 0 \end{array}$$ 4 is a root

$P(x) = (x - 4)(x^2 - 4x + 1)$

The roots are 4 and $2 \pm \sqrt{3}$. The only rational root is 4.

$P(x) = (x - 4)(x - 2 - \sqrt{3})(x - 2 + \sqrt{3})$

43. $P(x) = x^3 + 8$

Using Theorem 12, the only possible rational roots are 1, -1, 2, -2, 4, -4, 8, and -8. Of these eight possibilities we know that at most three of them can be roots because $P(x)$ is of degree 3. Using synthetic division we determine that -2 is the only rational root.

$$\begin{array}{r|rrrr} -2 & 1 & 0 & 0 & 8 \\ & & -2 & 4 & -8 \\ \hline & 1 & -2 & 4 & 0 \end{array}$$

$P(-2) = 0$, so -2 is a root.

We can now express $P(x)$ as follows:
$P(x) = (x + 2)(x^2 - 2x + 4)$

Since the factor $x^2 - 2x + 4$ is quadratic, use the quadratic formula to find the other roots, $1 + i\sqrt{3}$ and $1 - i\sqrt{3}$. These are irrational numbers. Thus the only rational root is -2.

We write the polynomial in factored form:
$P(x) = (x + 2)(x - 1 - i\sqrt{3})(x - 1 + i\sqrt{3})$

44. $x^3 - 8 = 0$

The possible rational roots are $\pm (1, 2, 4, 8)$.

$$\begin{array}{r|rrrr} 2 & 1 & 0 & 0 & -8 \\ & & 2 & 4 & 8 \\ \hline & 1 & 2 & 4 & 0 \end{array}$$

$(x - 2)(x^2 + 2x + 4) = 0$

The roots are 2 and $-1 \pm i\sqrt{3}$. The only rational root is 2.

$(x - 2)(x + 1 - i\sqrt{3})(x + 1 + i\sqrt{3}) = 0$

45. $P(x) = \frac{1}{3}x^3 - \frac{1}{2}x^2 - \frac{1}{6}x + \frac{1}{6}$

$6P(x) = 2x^3 - 3x^2 - x + 1$

We multiplied by 6, the LCM of the denominators. This equation is equivalent to the first, and all coefficients on the right are integers. Thus any root of $6P(x)$ is a root of $P(x)$.

The possible rational roots of $2x^3 - 3x^2 - x + 1$ are 1, -1, $\frac{1}{2}$, and $-\frac{1}{2}$. Of these four possibilities we know that at most three of them can be roots because the degree of $6P(x)$ is 3. Using synthetic division we determine that $\frac{1}{2}$ is a root.

$$\begin{array}{r|rrrr} \frac{1}{2} & 2 & -3 & -1 & 1 \\ & & 1 & -1 & -1 \\ \hline & 2 & -2 & -2 & 0 \end{array}$$

We can now express $6P(x)$ as follows:
$6P(x) = \left(x - \frac{1}{2}\right)(2x^2 - 2x - 2)$

$\qquad = 2\left(x - \frac{1}{2}\right)(x^2 - x - 1)$

Use the quadratic formula to find the other roots, $\frac{1 + \sqrt{5}}{2}$ and $\frac{1 - \sqrt{5}}{2}$. These are irrational numbers. Thus the only rational root is $\frac{1}{2}$.

We write the polynomial in factored form:
$6P(x) = 2\left(x - \frac{1}{2}\right)\left(x - \frac{1 + \sqrt{5}}{2}\right)\left(x - \frac{1 - \sqrt{5}}{2}\right)$, so

$P(x) = \frac{1}{3}\left(x - \frac{1}{2}\right)\left(x - \frac{1 + \sqrt{5}}{2}\right)\left(x - \frac{1 - \sqrt{5}}{2}\right)$

46. $P(x) = \frac{2}{3}x^3 - \frac{1}{2}x^2 + \frac{2}{3}x - \frac{1}{2}$

$6P(x) = 4x^3 - 3x^2 + 4x - 3$

The possible rational roots of $6P(x)$, and hence of $P(x)$, are $\pm \left(1, 3, \frac{1}{2}, \frac{3}{2}, \frac{1}{4}, \frac{3}{4}\right)$.

$$\begin{array}{r|rrrr} \frac{3}{4} & 4 & -3 & 4 & -3 \\ & & 3 & 0 & 3 \\ \hline & 4 & 0 & 4 & 0 \end{array}$$ $\frac{3}{4}$ is a root

$6P(x) = \left(x - \frac{3}{4}\right)(4x^2 + 4)$

$\qquad = 4\left(x - \frac{3}{4}\right)(x^2 + 1)$

The roots are $\frac{3}{4}$ and $\pm i$. The only rational root is $\frac{3}{4}$.

$P(x) = \frac{1}{6} \cdot 4\left(x - \frac{3}{4}\right)(x - i)(x + i)$

$\qquad = \frac{2}{3}\left(x - \frac{3}{4}\right)(x - i)(x + i)$

(Note that we could also have used factoring by grouping.)

47. $P(x) = x^4 + 32$

Using Theorem 12, the only possible rational roots are ± (1, 2, 4, 8, 16, 32). Of these twelve possibilities we know that at most four of them can be roots because $P(x)$ is of degree 4. Use synthetic division to check each possibility.

```
1 | 1   0   0   0   32        -1 | 1   0   0   0   32
  |     1   1   1    1           |    -1   1  -1    1
  ─────────────────────         ──────────────────────
    1   1   1   1 | 33            1  -1   1  -1 | 33

2 | 1   0   0   0   32        -2 | 1   0   0   0   32
  |     2   4   8   16           |    -2   4  -8   16
  ─────────────────────         ──────────────────────
    1   2   4   8 | 48            1  -2   4  -8 | 48
```

$P(1) \neq 0$, $P(-1) \neq 0$, $P(2) \neq 0$, $P(-2) \neq 0$; therefore 1, -1, 2, and -2 are not roots. Similarly we can show that ± (4, 8, 16, 32) are not roots. Thus there are <u>no</u> rational roots.

48. $x^6 + 8 = 0$

The possible rational roots are ± (1, 2, 4, 8). Synthetic division shows that none of these is a root. Thus there are no rational roots.

49. $x^3 - x^2 - 4x + 3 = 0$

The possible rational roots are 1, -1, 3, and -3. Of these four possibilities, at most three of them can be roots because the polynomial equation is of degree 3. Use synthetic division to check each possibility.

```
1 | 1  -1  -4   3        -1 | 1  -1  -4   3
  |     1   0  -4           |    -1   2   2
  ──────────────────        ──────────────────
    1   0  -4 | -1           1  -2  -2 | 5

3 | 1  -1  -4   3        -3 | 1  -1  -4    3
  |     3   6   6           |    -3  12  -24
  ──────────────────        ───────────────────
    1   2   2 | 9            1  -4   8 | -21
```

$P(1) \neq 0$, $P(-1) \neq 0$, $P(3) \neq 0$, $P(-3) \neq 0$; therefore 1, -1, 3, and -3 are not roots. Thus there are <u>no</u> rational roots.

50. $P(x) = 2x^3 + 3x^2 + 2x + 3$

The possible rational roots are $\pm \left[1, 3, \frac{1}{2}, \frac{3}{2}\right]$.

```
-3/2 | 2   3   2   3
     |    -3   0  -3                -3/2 is a root
     ──────────────────
       2   0   2 | 0
```

$P(x) = \left[x + \frac{3}{2}\right](2x^2 + 2) = 2\left[x + \frac{3}{2}\right](x^2 + 1)$.

Since $x^2 + 1$ has only complex roots, $-\frac{3}{2}$ is the only rational root. (Note that we could have used factoring by grouping.)

51. $x^4 + 2x^3 + 2x^2 - 4x - 8 = 0$

The possible rational roots are ± (1, 2, 4, 8). Of these eight possibilities, at most four of them can be roots because the polynomial equation is of degree 4. Use synthetic division to check each possibility.

```
1 | 1   2   2  -4  -8
  |     1   3   5   1
  ──────────────────────
    1   3   5   1 | -7

-1 | 1   2   2  -4  -8
   |    -1  -1  -1   5
  ──────────────────────
     1   1   1  -5 | -3

2 | 1   2   2  -4  -8
  |     2   8  20  32
  ──────────────────────
    1   4  10  16 | 24

-2 | 1   2   2  -4  -8
   |    -2   0  -4  16
  ──────────────────────
     1   0   2  -8 | 8
```

$P(1) \neq 0$, $P(-1) \neq 0$, $P(2) \neq 0$, $P(-2) \neq 0$; therefore 1, -1, 2, and -2 are not roots. Similarly we can show that 4, -4, 8, and -8 are not roots. Thus there are <u>no</u> rational roots.

52. $x^4 + 6x^3 + 17x^2 + 36x + 66 = 0$

The possible rational roots are ± (1, 2, 3, 6, 11, 22, 33, 66). Synthetic division shows that none of these is a root. Thus there are no rational roots.

53. $P(x) = x^5 - 5x^4 + 5x^3 + 15x^2 - 36x + 20$

The possible rational roots are ± (1, 2, 4, 5, 10, 20). Of these twelve possibilities at most five of them can be roots because $P(x)$ is of degree 5. Using synthetic division we determine the only rational roots are -2, 1, and 2.

```
-2 | 1  -5   5   15  -36   20
   |    -2  14  -38   46  -20
  ─────────────────────────────
     1  -7  19  -23   10 | 0
```

$P(-2) = 0$, so -2 is a root.

We now use $x^4 - 7x^3 + 19x^2 - 23x + 10$ and check other possible roots. Synthetic division shows that -2 is not a double root. We try 1.

```
1 | 1  -7  19  -23   10
  |     1  -6   13  -10        1 is a root
  ────────────────────────
    1  -6  13  -10 | 0
```

We now use $x^3 - 6x^2 + 13x - 10$ and check other possible roots. Synthetic division shows that 1 is not a double root. We try 2.

```
2 | 1  -6  13  -10
  |     2  -8   10            2 is a root
  ──────────────────
    1  -4   5 | 0
```

$P(x) = (x + 2)(x - 1)(x - 2)(x^2 - 4x + 5)$

Using the discriminant, we determine that $x^2 - 4x + 5$ has two nonreal roots. Thus the rational roots are -2, 1, and 2.

54. $P(x) = x^5 - 3x^4 - 3x^3 + 9x^2 - 4x + 12$

The possible rational roots are
± (1, 2, 3, 4, 6, 12).

```
2 | 1  -3  -3   9  -4  12
  |     2  -2 -10  -2 -12      2 is a root
    1  -1  -5  -1  -6 | 0
```

```
3 | 1  -1  -5  -1  -6
  |     3   6   3   6          3 is a root
    1   2   1   2 | 0
```

```
-2 | 1   2   1   2
   |    -2   0  -2             -2 is a root
     1   0   1 | 0
```

$P(x) = (x - 2)(x - 3)(x + 2)(x^2 + 1)$

The roots of $x^2 + 1$ are not rational. Thus the rational roots are 2, 3, and -2.

55. $x^3 - 4x^2 + x - 4 = 0$

$x^2(x - 4) + (x - 4) = 0$ Factoring by grouping

$(x^2 + 1)(x - 4) = 0$

$x - 4 = 0$ or $x^2 + 1 = 0$

$x = 4$ or $x^2 = -1$

$x = 4$ or $x = \pm i$

The solutions are 4, i, and -i.

56. $x^3 - x^2 - 7x + 15 = 0$

The possible rational roots are ± (1, 3, 5, 15).

```
-3 | 1  -1  -7  15
   |    -3  12 -15            -3 is a root
     1  -4   5 | 0
```

$(x + 3)(x^2 - 4x + 5) = 0$

$x = -3$ or $x = 2 \pm i$

57. $x^4 - 2x^3 - 2x - 1 = 0$

The possible rational roots are ± 1. Synthetic division shows that neither of these is a root.

Using synthetic division we find that i is a root.

```
i | 1  -2      0      -2      -1
  |     i   -2i - 1   2 - i    1
    1 -2 + i -2i - 1   -i  | 0
```

Using Theorem 10 we know that if i is a root then -i is also a root. Thus $(x - i)(x + i)$, or $x^2 + 1$, is a factor of $x^4 - 2x^3 - 2x - 1$. Using division we find that $x^2 - 2x - 1$ is also a factor.

$$x^2 + 1 \overline{)\begin{array}{l} x^2 - 2x - 1 \\ x^4 - 2x^3 + 0x^2 - 2x - 1 \end{array}}$$

```
                x^2 - 2x - 1
x^2 + 1 ) x^4 - 2x^3 + 0x^2 - 2x - 1
          x^4         + x^2
          ──────────────────
               -2x^3 -  x^2 - 2x
               -2x^3        - 2x
               ──────────────────
                       -x^2      - 1
                       -x^2      - 1
                       ──────────────
                                    0
```

Therefore, $(x - i)(x + i)(x^2 - 2x - 1) = 0$. Using the principle of zero products and the quadratic formula, we find that the roots are i, -i, $1 + \sqrt{2}$, and $1 - \sqrt{2}$.

58. $x^4 + 9x^2 - 112 = 0$

Let $u = x^2$.

$u^2 + 9u - 112 = 0$

$(u + 16)(u - 7) = 0$

$u = -16$ or $u = 7$

$x^2 = -16$ or $x^2 = 7$

$x = \pm 4i$ or $x = \pm \sqrt{7}$

59. If the equation has a double root, the discriminant must be 0.

$(2a)^2 - 4 \cdot 1 \cdot b = 0$ gives $b = a^2$.

Then $x^2 + 2ax + a^2 = 0$ has the double root -a.

60. For $P(x) = a_n x^n + a_{n-1} x^{n-1} + \ldots + a_0$ with a_i positive, consider any positive x. Every term will be positive, hence $P(x) > 0$.

61. Solve $x^3 - 64 = 0$

One root is 4. We use synthetic division and express the polynomial in factored form.

```
4 | 1   0   0  -64
  |     4  16   64
    1   4  16 |  0
```

$x^3 - 64 = (x - 4)(x^2 + 4x + 16) = 0$

The discriminant of $x^2 + 4x + 16$ is -48, so the other roots of the polynomial are not real numbers. Thus, the length of a side is 4 cm.

62. Solve: $x^3 = 125$, or $x^3 - 125 = 0$

The only real root is 5, so the length of a side is 5 cm.

63.

$V = \ell w h$ (Volume formula for rectangular solid)

$48 = (10 - 2x)(10 - 2x)(x)$

(Substituting 10 - 2x for ℓ and w, x for h, and 48 for V)

$48 = 100x - 40x^2 + 4x^3$

$12 = 25x - 10x^2 + x^3$

$0 = x^3 - 10x^2 + 25x - 12$

The possible rational roots of this equation are $\pm$ (1, 2, 3, 4, 6, 12). Using synthetic division we find that 3 is the only rational root.

$$3 \begin{array}{|rrrr} 1 & -10 & 25 & -12 \\ & 3 & -21 & 12 \\ \hline 1 & -7 & 4 & 0 \end{array}$$

We can now express the polynomial equation as follows:

$0 = (x - 3)(x^2 - 7x + 4)$

Since the factor $x^2 - 7x + 4$ is quadratic, we use the quadratic formula to find the other roots, $\frac{7 + \sqrt{33}}{2}$ and $\frac{7 - \sqrt{33}}{2}$. Since the length, x, must be positive and less then 5, $\frac{7 + \sqrt{33}}{2}$ is not a possible solution. The length of a side of the square can be 3 cm or $\frac{7 - \sqrt{33}}{2}$ cm.

64. Solve: $x(20 - 2x)^2 = 500$ or
$x^3 - 20x^2 + 100x - 125 = 0$
$x = 5$ cm or $\frac{15 - 5\sqrt{5}}{2}$ cm

65. See the answer section in the text.

66. Each pair of nonreal roots, $a \pm bi$, gives a quadratic factor $x^2 - 2ax + a^2 + b^2$ with real coefficients. Each real root c gives a linear factor $(x - c)$. Hence $P(x)$ is composed of linear and quadratic factors with real coefficients.

67. See the answer section in the text.

68. Generalization: $\sqrt{N}$ is rational if and only if $x^2 - N = 0$ has rational roots, where N is a positive integer.

Proof: If $x^2 - N = 0$ has a rational root r, then r is an integer factor of N such that $r^2 - N = 0$. That is, $N = r^2$, so that N has the rational (integer) square roots, $\pm r$. If $x^2 - N = 0$ has no rational roots, then its roots, $\pm\sqrt{N}$, are irrational.

69. $x^3 + 7 = 0$
The possible rational roots are 1, -1, 7, and -7. Synthetic division shows that none of these is a root. Since $x^3 + 7 = 0$, we know $x^3 = -7$ and one root is $x = -\sqrt[3]{7}$. We use synthetic division.

$$-\sqrt[3]{7} \begin{array}{|rrrr} 1 & 0 & 0 & 7 \\ & -\sqrt[3]{7} & \sqrt[3]{7^2} & -7 \\ \hline 1 & -\sqrt[3]{7} & \sqrt[3]{7^2} & 0 \end{array}$$

We can write the equation in factored form.

$(x + \sqrt[3]{7})(x^2 - \sqrt[3]{7}x + \sqrt[3]{7^2}) = 0$

Solve $x^2 - \sqrt[3]{7}x + \sqrt[3]{7^2}$ using the quadratic formula.

$x = \dfrac{\sqrt[3]{7} \pm \sqrt{\sqrt[3]{7^2} - 4\sqrt[3]{7^2}}}{2}$

$x = \dfrac{\sqrt[3]{7} \pm \sqrt{-3\sqrt[3]{7^2}}}{2} = \dfrac{\sqrt[3]{7} \pm \sqrt{-3 \cdot 7^{2/3}}}{2}$

$x = \dfrac{\sqrt[3]{7} \pm \sqrt[3]{7}\sqrt{-3}}{2}$ $\quad (\sqrt{7^{2/3}} = (7^{2/3})^{1/2} = 7^{1/3})$

$x = \sqrt[3]{7}\left[\dfrac{1 \pm i\sqrt{3}}{2}\right]$

The roots are $-\sqrt[3]{7}$, $\sqrt[3]{7}\left[\dfrac{1}{2} + \dfrac{\sqrt{3}}{2}i\right]$, and $\sqrt[3]{7}\left[\dfrac{1}{2} - \dfrac{\sqrt{3}}{2}i\right]$.

70. $x^3 - 5 = 0$
The possible rational roots are ± 1 and ± 5. Synthetic division shows that none of these is a root. We know $x^3 = 5$, so $\sqrt[3]{5}$ is a root.

$$\sqrt[3]{5} \begin{array}{|rrrr} 1 & 0 & 0 & -5 \\ & \sqrt[3]{5} & \sqrt[3]{5^2} & 5 \\ \hline 1 & \sqrt[3]{5} & \sqrt[3]{5^2} & 0 \end{array}$$

$(x + \sqrt[3]{5})(x^2 + \sqrt[3]{5}x + \sqrt[3]{5^2}) = 0$
Using the quadratic formula, we find that the other roots are $\sqrt[3]{5}\left[-\dfrac{1}{2} \pm \dfrac{\sqrt{3}}{2}i\right]$.

71. $P(x) = x^3 - 31x^2 + 230x - 200$

a) Solve $x^3 - 31x^2 + 230x - 200 = 0$
The possible rational roots are ± 1, ± 2, ± 4, ± 5, ± 8, ± 10, ± 20, ± 25, ± 40, ± 50, ± 100, ± 200.

$$1 \begin{array}{|rrrr} 1 & -31 & 230 & -200 \\ & 1 & -30 & 200 \\ \hline 1 & -30 & 200 & 0 \end{array}$$

We see that 1 is a root.
Then $(x - 1)(x^2 - 30x + 200) = 0$.

Solve $x^2 - 30x + 200 = 0$.
$(x - 10)(x - 20) = 0$
$x = 10$ or $x = 20$

The break-even values are 1, 10, and 20.

b) Solve $x^3 - 31x^2 + 230x - 200 > 0$, $x \geqslant 0$.
The numbers 1, 10, and 20 divide the nonnegative portion of the real number line as shown.

Try a test number in each interval.

A: $P\left(\frac{1}{2}\right) = \left(\frac{1}{2}\right)^3 - 31\left(\frac{1}{2}\right)^2 + 230\left(\frac{1}{2}\right) - 200 =$
$-\frac{741}{8}$

B: $P(2) = 2^3 - 31(2)^2 + 230 \cdot 2 - 200 = 144$

C: $P(11) = 11^3 - 31(11)^2 + 230 \cdot 11 - 200 = -90$

D: $P(21) = 21^3 - 31(21)^2 + 230 \cdot 21 - 200 = 220$

The nonnegative values of x for which the company makes a profit are {x|1 < x < 10 or x > 20}.

c) Using the results of part (b) we see that the nonnegative values of x for which the company has a loss are {x|0 ≤ x < 1 or 10 < x < 20}.

72. Solve: $(w + 3)(w)(w - 1) = 3\frac{3}{8}$

The dimensions are $\frac{9}{2}$ m × $\frac{3}{2}$ m × $\frac{1}{2}$ m.

Exercise Set 4.8

1. $P(x) = 3x^5 - 2x^2 + x - 1$

a) From positive to negative: a variation
b) From negative to positive: a variation
c) From positive to negative: a variation

The number of variations of sign is three. Therefore, the number of positive real roots is either 3 or 1.

$P(-x) = 3(-x)^5 - 2(-x)^2 + (-x) - 1$
$= -3x^5 - 2x^2 - x - 1$

a) From negative to negative: no variation
b) From negative to negative: no variation
c) From negative to negative: no variation

There are no variations of sign. Thus, there are no negative real roots of P(x).

2. $P(x) = 5x^6 - 3x^3 + x^2 - x$

There are 3 variations of sign. Thus the number of positive real roots is 3 or 1.

$P(-x) = 5x^6 + 3x^3 + x^2 + x$

There are no variations of sign, so there are no negative real roots.

3. $P(x) = 6x^7 + 2x^2 + 5x + 4$

a) From positive to positive: no variation
b) From positive to positive: no variation
c) From positive to positive: no variation

There are no variations of sign. Thus, there are no positive real roots.

$P(-x) = 6(-x)^7 + 2(-x)^2 + 5(-x) + 4$
$= -6x^7 + 2x^2 - 5x + 4$

a) From negative to positive: a variation
b) From positive to negative: a variation
c) From negative to positive: a variation

The number of variations of sign is three. Therefore, the number of negative real roots is 3 or 1.

4. $P(x) = -3x^5 - 7x^3 - 4x - 5$

There are no variations of sign, so there are no positive real roots.

$P(-x) = 3x^5 + 7x^3 + 4x - 5$

There is one variation of sign. Thus the number of negative real roots is 1.

5. $P(p) = 3p^{18} + 2p^4 - 5p^2 + p + 3$

a) From positive to positive: no variation
b) From positive to negative: a variation
c) From negative to positive: a variation
d) From positive to positive: no variation

The number of variations of sign is two. Therefore, the number of positive real roots is either 2 or 0.

$P(-p) = 3(-p)^{18} + 2(-p)^4 - 5(-p)^2 + (-p) + 3$
$= 3p^{18} + 2p^4 - 5p^2 - p + 3$

a) From positive to positive: no variation
b) From positive to negative: a variation
c) From negative to negative: no variation
d) From negative to positive: a variation

The number of variations of sign is two. Therefore, the number of negative real roots of P(p) is 2 or 0.

6. $P(t) = 5t^{12} - 7t^4 + 3t^2 + t + 1$

There are two variations of sign. Thus the number of positive real roots is 2 or 0.

$P(-t) = 5t^{12} - 7t^4 + 3t^2 - t + 1$

There are four variations of sign. Thus the number of negative real roots is 4, 2, or 0.

7. $P(x) = 7x^6 + 3x^4 - x - 10$

The number of variations of sign is 1. Therefore, the number of positive real roots is 1.

$P(-x) = 7(-x)^6 + 3(-x)^4 - (-x) - 10$
$= 7x^6 + 3x^4 + x - 10$

The number of variations of sign is 1. Therefore, the number of negative real roots is 1.

8. $P(z) = -z^{10} + 8z^7 + z^3 + 6z - 1$

   There are two variations of sign. Thus the number of positive real roots is 2 or 0.

   $P(-z) = -z^{10} - 8z^7 - z^3 - 6z - 1$

   There are no variations of sign, so there are no negative real roots.

9. $P(t) = -4t^5 - t^3 + 2t^2 + 1$

   The number of variations of sign is 1. Therefore, the number of positive real roots is 1.

   $P(-t) = -4(-t)^5 - (-t)^3 + 2(-t)^2 + 1$

   $\qquad = 4t^5 + t^3 + 2t^2 + 1$

   There are no variations of sign. Therefore, there are no negative real roots.

10. $P(x) = x^6 + 2x^4 - 9x^3 - 4$

    There is one variation of sign. Thus the number of positive real roots is 1.

    $P(-x) = x^6 + 2x^4 + 9x^3 - 4$

    There is one variation of sign. Thus the number of negative real roots is 1.

11. $P(y) = y^4 + 13y^3 - y + 5$

    The number of variations of sign is two. Therefore, the number of positive real roots is 2 or 0.

    $P(-y) = (-y)^4 + 13(-y)^3 - (-y) + 5$

    $\qquad = y^4 - 13y^3 + y + 5$

    The number of variations of sign is two. Therefore, the number of negative real roots is 2 or 0.

12. $P(y) = 7y^9 - 6y^6 + 5y^3 + 3y^2 - 2$

    There are three variations of sign. Thus the number of positive real roots is 3 or 1.

    $P(-y) = -7y^9 - 6y^6 - 5y^3 + 3y^2 - 2$

    There are two variations of sign. Thus the number of negative real roots is 2 or 0.

13. $P(x) = 3x^4 - 15x^2 + 2x - 3$

    Try 1:

    ```
    1 | 3   0   -15    2    -3
      |     3    3   -12   -10
      ------------------------
        3   3   -12   -10 | -13
    ```

    Since some of the coefficients of the quotient and the remainder are negative, there is no guarantee that 1 is an upper bound.

    Try 2:

    ```
    2 | 3   0   -15    2    -3
      |     6    12   -6    -8
      ------------------------
        3   6    -3   -4 | -11
    ```

    Again there is no guarantee that 2 is an upper bound.

Try 3:

```
3 | 3   0   -15    2    -3
  |     9    27   36   114
  -------------------------
    3   9    12   38 | 111
```

Since all of the numbers in the bottom row are nonnegative, 3 is an upper bound. Thus, 3 is the smallest positive integer that is guaranteed by Theorem 15 to be an upper bound to the roots of $P(x)$.

Next we choose a negative number. Try -1:

```
-1 | 3    0   -15    2    -3
   |     -3     3    12   -14
   --------------------------
     3   -3   -12    14 | -17
```

Since the numbers in the bottom row are not alternately positive and negative, -1 is not guaranteed to be a lower bound.

Try -2:

```
-2 | 3    0   -15    2    -3
   |     -6    12     6   -16
   --------------------------
     3   -6    -3     8 | -19
```

By Theorem 15, -2 is not guaranteed to be a lower bound.

Try -3:

```
-3 | 3    0   -15     2    -3
   |     -9    27   -36   102
   ---------------------------
     3   -9    12   -34 | 99
```

Since the numbers in the bottom row are alternately positive and negative, -3 is a lower bound. Thus, -3 is the largest negative integer that is guaranteed by Theorem 15 to be a lower bound to the roots of $P(x)$.

14. $P(x) = 4x^4 - 14x^2 + 4x - 2$

    ```
    1 | 4    0   -14    4    -2
      |      4     4   -10   -6
      ------------------------
        4    4   -10   -6 | -8
    ```

    1 is not guaranteed to be an upper bound.

    ```
    2 | 4    0   -14    4    -2
      |      8    16     4   16
      ------------------------
        4    8     2    8 | 14
    ```

    2 is the smallest positive integer that is guaranteed by Theorem 15 to be an upper bound to the roots of $P(x)$.

    ```
    -2 | 4    0   -14    4    -2
       |     -8    16   -4     0
       ----------------------
         4   -8     2    0 | -2
    ```

    -2 is not guaranteed to be a lower bound.

    ```
    -3 | 4     0   -14     4     -2
       |     -12    36   -66    186
       -----------------------------
         4   -12    22   -62 | 184
    ```

    -3 is the largest negative integer guaranteed by Theorem 15 to be a lower bound to the roots of $P(x)$.

15. $P(x) = 6x^3 - 17x^2 - 3x - 1$

Try 2:

```
2 | 6   -17    -3    -1
  |      12   -10   -26
    6    -5   -13 | -27
```

Since some of the coefficients of the quotient and the remainder are negative, there is no guarantee that 2 is an upper bound.

Try 3:

```
3 | 6   -17    -3    -1
  |      18     3     0
    6     1     0 |  -1
```

Since the remainder is negative, there is no guarantee that 3 is an upper bound.

Try 4:

```
4 | 6   -17    -3    -1
  |      24    28   100
    6     7    25 |  99
```

Since all of the numbers in the bottom row are nonnegative, 4 is an upper bound. Thus, 4 is the smallest positive integer that is guaranteed by Theorem 15 to be an upper bound to the roots of $P(x)$.

Next we choose a negative number. Try -1:

```
-1 | 6   -17    -3    -1
   |      -6    23   -20
     6   -23    20 | -21
```

Since the numbers in the bottom row are alternately positive and negative, -1 is a lower bound. Since -1 is the largest negative integer, then -1 is the largest negative integer that is guaranteed by Theorem 15 to be a lower bound to the roots of $P(x)$.

16. $P(x) = 5x^3 - 15x^2 + 15x - 4$

```
2 | 5   -15    15    -4
  |      10   -10    10
    5    -5     5 |   6
```

2 is not guaranteed to be an upper bound.

```
3 | 5   -15    15    -4
  |      15     0    45
    5     0    15 |  41
```

3 is the smallest positive integer that is guaranteed by Theorem 15 to be an upper bound of the roots of $P(x)$.

```
-1 | 5   -15    15    -4
   |      -5    20   -35
     5   -20    35 | -39
```

-1 is the largest negative integer that is guaranteed by Theorem 15 to be a lower bound to the roots of $P(x)$.

17. $P(x) = -3x^4 + 15x^3 - 2x + 3$

$-P(x) = -(-3x^4 + 15x^3 - 2x + 3)$

$\quad\quad = 3x^4 - 15x^3 + 2x - 3$

Since $P(x) = 0$ and $-P(x) = 0$ are equivalent equations, we will consider $-P(x)$.

Try 4:

```
4 | 3   -15     0     2     -3
  |      12   -12   -48   -184
    3    -3   -12   -46 | -187
```

Since some of the numbers in the bottom row are negative, 4 is not guaranteed to be an upper bound.

Try 5:

```
5 | 3   -15     0     2    -3
  |      15     0     0    10
    3     0     0     2 |   7
```

Since all of the numbers in the bottom row are nonnegative, 5 is an upper bound. Thus, 5 is the smallest positive integer that is guaranteed by Theorem 15 to be an upper bound to the roots of $P(x)$.

Next we choose a negative number. Try -1:

```
-1 | 3   -15     0     2    -3
   |      -3    18   -18    16
     3   -18    18   -16 |  13
```

Since the numbers in the bottom row are alternately positive and negative, -1 is a lower bound. Since -1 is the largest negative integer, -1 is the largest negative integer guaranteed by Theorem 15 to be a lower bound to the roots of $P(x)$.

18. $P(x) = -4x^4 + 17x^3 - 3x + 2$

Consider $-P(x) = 4x^4 - 17x^3 + 3x - 2$.

```
4 | 4   -17     0     3    -2
  |      16    -4   -16   -52
    4    -1    -4   -13 | -54
```

4 is not an upper bound.

```
5 | 4   -17     0     3    -2
  |      20    15    75   390
    4     3    15    78 | 388
```

5 is the smallest positive integer that is guaranteed by Theorem 15 to be an upper bound to the roots of $P(x)$.

```
-1 | 4   -17     0     3    -2
   |      -4    21   -21    18
     4   -21    21   -18 |  16
```

-1 is the largest negative integer that is guaranteed by Theorem 15 to be a lower bound to the roots of $P(x)$.

19. $P(x) = 6x^3 + 15x^2 + 3x - 1$

Try 1:

```
1 | 6   15    3   -1
  |      6   21   24
    6   21   24 | 23
```

Since all of the numbers in the bottom row are nonnegative, 1 is an upper bound. Since 1 is the smallest positive integer, then 1 is the smallest positive integer guaranteed by Theorem 15 to be an upper bound to the roots of $P(x)$.

Next we choose a negative number. Try -2:

```
-2 | 6   15    3   -1
   |     -12   -6    6
     6    3   -3 |  5
```

-2 is not guaranteed by Theorem 15 to be a lower bound.

Try -3:

```
-3 | 6   15    3    -1
   |     -18    9   -36
     6   -3   12 | -37
```

Since the numbers in the bottom row are alternately positive and negative, -3 is a lower bound. Thus, -3 is the largest negative integer guaranteed by Theorem 15 to be a lower bound to the roots of $P(x)$.

20. $P(x) = 6x^3 + 12x^2 + 5x - 3$

```
1 | 6   12    5   -3
  |      6   18   23
    6   18   23 | 20
```

1 is the smallest positive integer that is guaranteed by Theorem 15 to be an upper bound to the roots of $P(x)$.

```
-1 | 6   12    5   -3
   |     -6   -6    1
     6    6   -1 | -2
```

-1 is not guaranteed by Theorem 15 to be a lower bound.

```
-2 | 6   12    5    -3
   |    -12    0   -10
     6    0    5 | -13
```

-2 is the largest positive integer guaranteed by Theorem 15 to be a lower bound to the roots of $P(x)$.

21. $P(x) = x^4 - 2x^2 + 12x - 8$

There are three variations of sign, so the number of positive real roots is 3 or 1.

$P(-x) = (-x)^4 - 2(-x)^2 + 12(-x) - 8$
$\qquad = x^4 - 2x^2 - 12x - 8$

There is one variation of sign, so the number of negative real roots of $P(x)$ is 1.

Look for an upper bound. Use Theorem 15.

Try 1:

```
1 | 1    0   -2   12   -8
  |      1    1   -1   11
    1    1   -1   11 |  3
```

Since one of the coefficients of the quotient is negative, 1 is not guaranteed to be a lower bound.

Try 2:

```
2 | 1    0   -2   12   -8
  |      2    4    4   32
    1    2    2   16 | 24
```

Since all of the numbers in the bottom row are nonnegative, 2 is an upper bound.

Look for a lower bound. Use Theorem 15.

Try -2:

```
-2 | 1    0   -2   12    -8
   |     -2    4   -4   -16
     1   -2    2    8 | -24
```

-2 is not guaranteed to be a lower bound.

Try -3:

```
-3 | 1    0   -2   12    -8
   |     -3    9  -21    27
     1   -3    7   -9 |  19
```

Since the numbers in the bottom row are alternately positive and negative, -3 is a lower bound.

22. $P(x) = x^4 - 6x^2 + 20x - 24$

There are 3 variations of sign, so the number of positive real roots is 3 or 1.

$P(-x) = x^4 - 6x^2 - 20x - 24$

There is 1 variation of sign, so there is 1 negative real root.

Look for an upper bound. Use Theorem 15.

```
2 | 1    0   -6   20   -24
  |      2    4   -4    32
    1    2   -2   16 |   8
```

2 is not guaranteed to be an upper bound.

```
3 | 1    0   -6   20   -24
  |      3    9    9    87
    1    3    3   29 |  63
```

3 is an upper bound.

Look for a lower bound. Use Theorem 15.

```
-3 | 1    0   -6   20   -24
   |     -3    9   -9   -33
     1   -3    3   11 | -57
```

-3 is not guaranteed to be a lower bound.

```
-4 | 1    0    -6    20    -24
           -4   16   -40    80
     1   -4    10   -20 | 56
```

-4 is a lower bound.

23. $P(x) = x^4 - 2x^2 - 8$

There is one variation of sign, so the number of positive real roots is 1.

$P(-x) = (-x)^4 - 2(-x)^2 - 8$
$= x^4 - 2x^2 - 8$

There is one variation of sign, so the number of negative real roots is 1. Since the degree of the equation is 4 and there is only one positive real root and one negative real root, there must be two nonreal roots.

Look for an upper bound. Use Theorem 15.
Try 1:

```
1 | 1    0    -2    0    -8
          1    1   -1   -1
     1    1   -1   -1 | -9
```

Since some of the coefficients of the quotient and the remainder are negative, 1 is not guaranteed to be an upper bound.

Try 2:

```
2 | 1    0    -2    0    -8
          2    4    4    8
     1    2    2    4 | 0
```

Since all of the numbers in the bottom row are nonnegative, 2 is an upper bound. Also note that 2 is a root, $P(2) = 0$.

Look for a lower bound. Use Theorem 15.
Try -1:

```
-1 | 1    0    -2    0    -8
          -1    1    1   -1
      1   -1   -1    1 | -9
```

-1 is not guaranteed to be a lower bound.

Try -2:

```
-2 | 1    0    -2    0    -8
          -2    4   -4    8
      1   -2    2   -4 | 0
```

Since the numbers in the bottom row are alternately positive and negative, -2 is a lower bound.

24. $P(x) = 3x^4 - 5x^2 - 4$

There is one variation of sign, so there is 1 positive real root.

$P(-x) = 3x^4 - 5x^2 - 4$

There is one variation of sign, so there is 1 negative real root. Since the degree of the equation is 4 and there are only 2 real roots, there must be two nonreal roots.

Look for an upper bound. Use Theorem 15.

```
1 | 3    0    -5    0    -4
          3    3   -2   -2
     3    3   -2   -2 | -6
```

1 is not guaranteed to be an upper bound.

```
2 | 3    0    -5    0    -4
          6   12   14   28
     3    6    7   14 | 24
```

2 is an upper bound.
Look for a lower bound. Use Theorem 15.

```
-1 | 3    0    -5    0    -4
          -3    3    2   -2
      3   -3   -2    2 | -6
```

-1 is not guaranteed to be a lower bound.

```
-2 | 3    0    -5    0    -4
          -6   12  -14   28
      3   -6    7  -14 | 24
```

-2 is a lower bound.

25. $P(x) = x^4 - 9x^2 - 6x + 4$

There are two variations of sign, so the number of positive real roots is 2 or 0.

$P(-x) = (-x)^4 - 9(-x)^2 - 6(-x) + 4$
$= x^4 - 9x^2 + 6x + 4$

There are two variations of sign, so the number of negative real roots of $P(x)$ is 2 or 0.

Look for an upper bound. Use Theorem 15.
Try 3:

```
3 | 1    0    -9    -6     4
          3    9    0   -18
     1    3    0   -6 | -14
```

Since one of the coefficients of the quotient and the remainder are negative, 3 is not guaranteed to be an upper bound.

Try 4:

```
4 | 1    0    -9    -6     4
          4   16   28    88
     1    4    7   22 | 92
```

Since all of the numbers in the bottom row are nonnegative, 4 is an upper bound.

Look for a lower bound. Use Theorem 15.
Try -2:

```
-2 | 1    0    -9    -6     4
          -2    4   10   -8
      1   -2   -5    4 | -4
```

-2 is not guaranteed to be a lower bound.

Try -3:

```
-3 | 1    0   -9   -6    4
   |     -3    9    0   18
     1   -3    0   -6 | 22
```

Since the numbers in the bottom row are alternately positive and negative, -3 is a lower bound.

26. $P(x) = x^4 - 21x^2 + 4x + 6$

There are two variations of sign, so the number of positive real roots is 2 or 0.

$P(-x) = x^4 - 21x^2 - 4x + 6$

There are two variations of sign, so the number of negative real roots is 2 or 0.

Look for an upper bound. Use Theorem 15.

```
4 | 1    0   -21    4     6
  |      4   16   -20   -64
    1    4   -5   -16 | -58
```

4 is not guaranteed to be an upper bound.

```
5 | 1    0   -21    4     6
  |      5   25    20   120
    1    5    4    24 | 126
```

5 is an upper bound.

Look for a lower bound. Use Theorem 15.

```
-4 | 1    0   -21    4     6
   |     -4   16    20   -96
     1   -4   -5    24 | -90
```

-4 is not guaranteed to be a lower bound.

```
-5 | 1    0   -21    4     6
   |     -5   25   -20    80
     1   -5    4   -16 | 86
```

-5 is a lower bound.

27. $P(x) = x^4 + 3x^2 + 2$

There are no variations of sign. Thus there are no positive real roots.

$P(-x) = (-x)^4 + 3(-x)^2 + 2$

$= x^4 + 3x^2 + 2$

There are no variations of sign. Thus there are no negative real roots. Since the degree of the equation is 4, there are 4 nonreal roots.

Since there are no real roots, there is no upper bound and no lower bound.

28. $P(x) = x^4 + 5x^2 + 6$

There are no variations of sign, so there are no positive real roots.

$P(-x) = x^4 + 5x^2 + 6$

There are no variations of sign, so there are no negative real roots. Since the degree of the equation is 4, there are 4 nonreal roots.

Since there are no real roots, there is no upper bound and no lower bound.

29. $P(x) = x^3 - 3x - 2$

The possible rational roots are 1, -1, 2, and -2. Synthetic division shows that -1 is a root with multiplicity of 2 and 2 is also a root. Thus all the roots are rational.

30. $x^3 - 3x^2 + 3 = 0$

31. $x^3 - 3x - 4 = 0$

The possible rational roots are 1, -1, 2, -2, 4, and -4. Synthetic division shows that none of these is a root. Sketch a graph of the polynomial $P(x) = x^3 - 3x - 4$.

We see from the graph that there seems to be a root between 2 and 3. Checking function values confirms this: $P(2) = -2$ and $P(3) = 14$. To find a better approximation we compute additional function values.

x	P(x)
2	-2
2.1	-1.039
2.2	0.048

Since $P(2.1) < 0$, there is no root between 2 and 2.1.

Since $P(2.1) < 0$ and $P(2.2) > 0$, there is a root between 2.1 and 2.2.

We have the accuracy desired, so we stop. Since 0.048 is closer to 0 than -1.039, we accept 2.2 as a better approximation to the nearest tenth.

32. $x^3 - 3x^2 + 5 = 0$

The method of bisection gives -1.1.

33. $x^4 + x^2 + 1 = 0$

$P(x) = x^4 + x^2 + 1$ has no variations in sign and hence no positive real roots. $P(-x) = (-x)^4 + (-x)^2 + 1 = x^4 + x^2 + 1$ also has no variations in sign and hence $P(x)$ has no negative real roots. Thus the equation has no real roots.

34. Neither $P(x)$ nor $P(-x)$ has a variation of sign, so there are no real roots.

35. $x^4 - 6x^2 + 8 = 0$

The possible rational roots are ± 1, ± 2, ± 4, and ± 8. Using synthetic division we find that 2 and -2 are roots and we can factor the polynomial as follows: $(x - 2)(x + 2)(x^2 - 2)$. Solving $x^2 - 2 = 0$, we find that the irrational roots are $\sqrt{2}$ and $-\sqrt{2}$, or 1.4 and -1.4 to the nearest tenth.

36. $x^4 - 4x^2 + 2 = 0$

The method of bisection gives -1.8, -0.8, 0.8, 1.8.

37. $x^5 + x^4 - x^3 - x^2 - 2x - 2 = 0$

The possible rational roots are ± 1 and ± 2. Using synthetic division we find that -1 is a root and we can factor the polynomial as follows: $(x + 1)(x^4 - x^2 - 2)$. We can solve $x^4 - x^2 - 2 = 0$ by substituting u for x^2, factoring, and solving for u and then for x. We get $x = \pm \sqrt{2}$ or $x = \pm i$. The irrational roots are $\sqrt{2}$ and $-\sqrt{2}$, or 1.4 and -1.4 to the nearest tenth.

38. $x^5 - 2x^4 - 2x^3 + 4x^2 - 3x + 6 = 0$

The possible rational roots are ± 1, ± 2, ± 3, and ± 6. Synthetic division shows that 2 is the only rational root and we can factor the polynomial as follows: $(x - 2)(x^4 - 2x^2 - 3)$. The real solutions of $x^4 - 2x^2 - 3 = 0$ are $x = \pm \sqrt{3} \approx \pm 1.7$.

39. $P(x) = 2x^5 + 2x^3 - x^2 - 1$

x	P(x)	
0	-1	
1	2	
0.5	-0.9375	Since $P(0.5) < 0$, there is a root between 0.5 and 1.
0.7	-0.46786	Since $P(0.7) < 0$, there is a root between 0.7 and 1.
0.8	0.03936	Since $P(0.8) > 0$, there is a root between 0.7 and 0.8.
0.75	-0.24414	Since $P(0.75) < 0$, there is a root between 0.75 and 0.8.
0.79	-0.02261	Since $P(0.79) < 0$, there is a root between 0.79 and 0.8.

We have the accuracy we desire, so we stop. Since -0.02261 is closer to 0 than 0.03936, we accept 0.79 as a better approximation to the nearest hundredth.

40. $P(x) = x^4 - 2x^3 - 3x^2 + 4x + 2$

x	P(x)	
1	2	
2	-2	
1.5	-0.4375	There is a root between 1 and 1.5.
1.4	0.0736	There is a root between 1.4 and 1.5.
1.41	0.0217	There is a root between 1.41 and 1.5.
1.42	-0.0299	There is a root between 1.41 and 1.42.

Since 0.0217 is closer to 0 than -0.0299, we accept 1.41 as the better approximation to the nearest hundredth.

41. $P(x) = x^3 - 2x^2 - x + 4$

The possible rational roots are ± 1, ± 2, and ± 4. Synthetic division shows that none of these is a root. Sketch a graph of the polynomial.

The graph shows that there seems to be a root between -2 and -1. We check function values to confirm this: $P(-2) = -10$, $P(-1) = 2$. We do further computations to find a better approximation.

x	P(x)
-1	2
-1.1	1.349
-1.2	0.592
-1.3	-0.277
-1.25	0.1719
-1.27	-0.0042
-1.26	0.0844

Since P(-1.1) > 0, there is no root between -1.1 and -1.

Since P(-1.2) > 0, there is no root between -1.2 and -1.1.

Since P(-1.3) < 0, there is a root between -1.3 and -1.2.

Since P(-1.25) > 0, there is a root between -1.3 and -1.25.

Since P(-1.27) < 0, there is a root between -1.27 and -1.25.

Since P(-1.26) > 0, there is a root between -1.27 and -1.26.

We have the desired accuracy, so we stop. Since -0.0042 is closer to 0 than 0.0844, we accept -1.27 as the better approximation to the nearest hundredth.

<u>42.</u> $P(x) = x^3 - 4x^2 + x + 3$

P(-1) = -3 and P(0) = 3, so there is a root between -1 and 0. P(1) = 1 and P(2) = -3, so there is a root between 1 and 2. P(3) = -3 and P(4) = 7, so there is a root between 3 and 4. The method of bisection gives the roots as -0.70, 1.24, and 3.46, approximated to the nearest hundredth.

<u>43.</u> See the answer section in the text.

<u>44.</u> f(x) has one variation in sign; hence one positive root. f(-x) has no variation in sign; hence no negative roots. Zero is not a root. Hence there is exactly one real root.

<u>45.</u> -1.3

<u>46.</u> -1.88, 0.35, 1.53

<u>47.</u> 1.5, 5.7

<u>48.</u> -7, -5, -2, 1, 3, 6

<u>49.</u> 7.16 hr

<u>50.</u> 0.08, or 8%

Exercise Set 4.9

<u>1.</u> $f(x) = \dfrac{1}{x - 3}$

a) The function is neither even nor odd and no symmetries are apparent.

b) The degree of the numerator is less than the degree of the denominator, so the x-axis is an asymptote.

c) The zero of the denominator is 3, so x = 3 is a vertical asymptote. The function has no zeros.

d) The vertical asymptote divides the x-axis into intervals. To find where the function is positive or negative, we try a test point in each interval.

Interval	(-∞, 3)	(3, ∞)
Test value	$f(0) = -\dfrac{1}{3}$	$f(4) = 1$
Sign of f(x)	-	+
Location of points on graph	Below x-axis	Above x-axis

e) We make a table of function values.

x	$3\frac{1}{8}$	$3\frac{1}{2}$	4	5	8	$2\frac{3}{4}$	2	1	0	-2
f(x)	8	2	1	$\frac{1}{2}$	$\frac{1}{5}$	-4	-1	$-\frac{1}{2}$	$-\frac{1}{3}$	$-\frac{1}{5}$

f) Using all available information, we draw the graph.

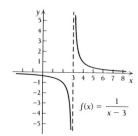

$$f(x) = \frac{1}{x - 3}$$

<u>2.</u> $f(x) = \dfrac{1}{x - 5}$

a) Neither even nor odd; no apparent symmetries

b) Horizontal asymptote: x-axis

c) Vertical asymptote: x = 5
Function has no zeros

d)

Interval	(-∞, 5)	(5, ∞)
Test value	$f(0) = -\dfrac{1}{5}$	$f(6) = 1$
Sign of f(x)	-	+
Location of points on graph	Below x-axis	Above x-axis

e), f)

x	f(x)
0	$-\frac{1}{5}$
3	$-\frac{1}{2}$
4	-1
$4\frac{1}{2}$	-2
$5\frac{1}{2}$	2
6	1
7	$\frac{1}{2}$

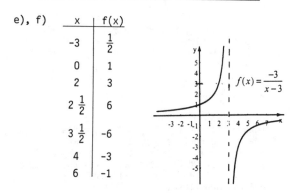

$$f(x) = \frac{1}{x-5}$$

3. $f(x) = \dfrac{-2}{x-5}$

a) The function is neither even nor odd and no symmetries are apparent.

b) The degree of the numerator is less than the degree of the denominator, so the x-axis is an asymptote.

c) The zero of the denominator is 5, so x = 5 is a vertical asymptote. The function has no zeros.

d) The vertical asymptote divides the x-axis into intervals. To find where the function is positive or negative, we try a test point in each interval.

Interval	$(-\infty, 5)$	$(5, \infty)$
Test value	$f(0) = \frac{2}{5}$	$f(6) = -2$
Sign of f(x)	+	−
Location of points on graph	Above x-axis	Below x-axis

e) We make a table of function values.

x	-3	0	2	4	$4\frac{2}{3}$	$5\frac{1}{3}$	6	8	11
f(x)	$\frac{1}{4}$	$\frac{2}{5}$	$\frac{2}{3}$	2	6	-6	-2	$-\frac{2}{3}$	$-\frac{1}{3}$

f) Using all available information, we draw the graph.

$$f(x) = \frac{-2}{x-5}$$

4. $f(x) = \dfrac{-3}{x-3}$

a) Neither even nor odd; no apparent symmetries

b) Horizontal asymptote: x-axis

c) Vertical asymptote: x = 3
Function has no zeros

d)

Interval	$(-\infty, 3)$	$(3, \infty)$
Test value	f(0) = 1	f(4) = -3
Sign of f(x)	+	−
Location of points on graph	Above x-axis	Below x-axis

e), f)

x	f(x)
-3	$\frac{1}{2}$
0	1
2	3
$2\frac{1}{2}$	6
$3\frac{1}{2}$	-6
4	-3
6	-1

$$f(x) = \frac{-3}{x-3}$$

5. $f(x) = \dfrac{2x+1}{x}$

a) The function is neither even nor odd and no symmetries are apparent.

b) Since the numerator and denominator have the same degree, the horizontal asymptote can be determined by dividing the leading coefficients of the two polynomials. Thus $2 \div 1 = 2$, and we know that y = 2 is a horizontal asymptote.

c) The zero of the denominator is 0, so x = 0 (the y-axis) is a vertical asymptote. The zero of the function is $-\frac{1}{2}$.

d) The vertical asymptote and the zero of the function divide the x-axis into intervals. To find where the function is positive or negative, we try a test number in each interval.

Interval	$\left(-\infty, -\frac{1}{2}\right]$	$\left(-\frac{1}{2}, 0\right)$	$(0, \infty)$
Test value	f(-1) = 1	$f\left(-\frac{1}{4}\right) = -8$	f(1) = 3
Sign of f(x)	+	−	+
Location of points on graph	Above x-axis	Below x-axis	Above x-axis

e) We make a table of function values.

x	-100	-10	-3	$-\frac{1}{2}$	$-\frac{1}{10}$	1	4	10	100
f(x)	$1\frac{99}{100}$	$1\frac{9}{10}$	$1\frac{2}{3}$	0	-8	3	$2\frac{1}{4}$	$2\frac{1}{10}$	$2\frac{1}{100}$

f) Using all available information, we draw the graph.

$$f(x) = \frac{2x + 1}{x}$$

6. $f(x) = \dfrac{3x - 1}{x}$

a) Neither even nor odd; no apparent symmetries

b) Horizontal asymptote: y = 3

c) Vertical asymptote: x = 0   (y-axis)

   Zero of function: $\frac{1}{3}$

d)

Interval	$(-\infty, 0)$	$\left[0, \frac{1}{3}\right]$	$\left[\frac{1}{3}, \infty\right]$
Test value	f(-1) = 4	$f\left[\frac{1}{4}\right]$ = -1	f(1) = 2
Sign of f(x)	+	-	+
Location of points on graph	Above x-axis	Below x-axis	Above x-axis

e), f)

x	f(x)
-2	$3\frac{1}{2}$
-1	4
$-\frac{1}{2}$	5
$\frac{1}{6}$	-3
$\frac{1}{3}$	0
$\frac{1}{2}$	1
1	2
2	$2\frac{1}{2}$

$$f(x) = \frac{3x - 1}{x}$$

7. $f(x) = \dfrac{1}{(x - 2)^2}$

a) The function is neither even nor odd and no symmetries are apparent.

b) The degree of the numerator is less than the degree of the denominator, so the x-axis is an asymptote.

c) The zero of the denominator is 2, so x = 2 is a vertical asymptote. The function has no zeros.

d) $(x - 2)^2 > 0$ for all $x \neq 2$, so f(x) is positive at each point in the domain.

e) We make a table of function values.

x	$2\frac{1}{2}$	3	4	5	$1\frac{1}{2}$	1	0	-1
f(x)	4	1	$\frac{1}{4}$	$\frac{1}{9}$	4	1	$\frac{1}{4}$	$\frac{1}{9}$

f) Using all available information, we draw the graph.

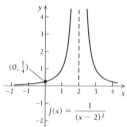

$$f(x) = \frac{1}{(x - 2)^2}$$

8. $f(x) = \dfrac{-2}{(x - 3)^2}$

a) Neither even nor odd; no apparent symmetries

b) Horizontal asymptote: x-axis

c) Vertical asymptote: x = 3

   Function has no zeros

d)

Interval	$(-\infty, 3)$	$(3, \infty)$
Test value	$f(0) = -\frac{2}{9}$	f(4) = -2
Sign of f(x)	-	-
Location of points on graph	Below x-axis	Below x-axis

e), f)

x	f(x)
-1	$-\frac{1}{8}$
0	$-\frac{2}{9}$
2	-2
$2\frac{1}{2}$	-8
$3\frac{1}{2}$	-8
4	-2
6	$-\frac{2}{9}$

$f(x) = \dfrac{-2}{(x-3)^2}$

<u>9</u>. $f(x) = \dfrac{2}{x^2}$

a) The function is even, so it is symmetric with respect to the y-axis.

b) The degree of the numerator is less than the degree of the denominator, so the x-axis is an asymptote.

c) The zero of the denominator is 0, so x = 0 (the y-axis) is a vertical asymptote. The function has no zeros.

d) $x^2 > 0$ for all $x \neq 0$, so f(x) is positive at each point in the domain.

e) We make a table of function values.

x	$\pm\frac{1}{2}$	± 1	± 2	± 3	± 4
f(x)	8	2	$\frac{1}{2}$	$\frac{2}{9}$	$\frac{1}{8}$

f) Using all available information, we draw the graph.

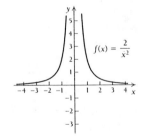

$f(x) = \dfrac{2}{x^2}$

<u>10</u>. $f(x) = \dfrac{1}{3x^2}$

a) Even function – symmetric with respect to the y-axis

b) Horizontal asymptote: x-axis

c) Vertical asymptote: x = 0   (y-axis)

Function has no zeros

d) $3x^2 > 0$ for all $x \neq 0$, so f(x) is positive at each point in the domain.

e), f)

x	f(x)
± 2	$\frac{1}{12}$
± 1	$\frac{1}{3}$
$\pm\frac{1}{2}$	$\frac{4}{3}$
$\pm\frac{1}{3}$	3

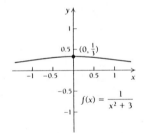

$f(x) = \dfrac{1}{3x^2}$

<u>11</u>. $f(x) = \dfrac{1}{x^2 + 3}$

a) The function is even, so the graph is symmetric with respect to the y-axis.

b) The degree of the numerator is less than the degree of the denominator, so the x-axis is an asymptote.

c) The denominator has no zeros, so there are no vertical asymptotes. The function has no zeros.

d) $x^2 + 3 > 0$ for all real numbers x, so f(x) is positive for all real numbers x.

e) We make a table of function values.

x	0	± 1	± 2	± 3
f(x)	$\frac{1}{3}$	$\frac{1}{4}$	$\frac{1}{7}$	$\frac{1}{12}$

f) Using all available information, we draw the graph.

$f(x) = \dfrac{1}{x^2 + 3}$

$\left(0, \frac{1}{3}\right)$

<u>12</u>. $f(x) = \dfrac{-1}{x^2 + 2}$

a) Even function – symmetric with respect to the y-axis

b) Horizontal asymptote: x-axis

c) No vertical asymptotes

Function has no zeros

d) $x^2 + 2 > 0$ for all real values of x, so f(x) < 0 for all real values of x.

e), f)

x	f(x)
± 2	$-\frac{1}{6}$
± 1	$-\frac{1}{3}$
0	$-\frac{1}{2}$

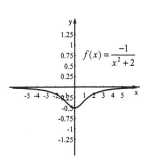

$f(x) = \dfrac{-1}{x^2 + 2}$

---

13. $f(x) = \dfrac{x - 1}{x + 2}$

a) The function is neither even nor odd and no symmetries are apparent.

b) Since the numerator and denominator have the same degree, the horizontal asymptote can be determined by dividing the leading coefficients of the two polynomials. Thus $1 \div 1 = 1$, and we know that $y = 1$ is a horizontal asymptote.

c) The zero of the denominator is -2, so $x = -2$ is a vertical asymptote. The zero of the function is 1.

d) The vertical asymptote and the zero of the function divide the x-axis into intervals. To find where the function is positive or negative, we try a test point in each interval.

Interval	$(-\infty, -2)$	$(-2, 1)$	$(1, \infty)$
Test value	$f(-3) = 4$	$f(0) = -\frac{1}{2}$	$f(2) = \frac{1}{4}$
Sign of f(x)	+	−	+
Location of points on graph	Above x-axis	Below x-axis	Above x-axis

e) We make a table of function values.

x	-6	-4	-3	$-2\frac{1}{2}$	$-1\frac{1}{2}$	-1	0	1	2	4	6	20
f(x)	$\frac{7}{4}$	$\frac{5}{2}$	4	7	-5	-2	$-\frac{1}{2}$	0	$\frac{1}{4}$	$\frac{1}{2}$	$\frac{5}{8}$	$\frac{19}{22}$

f) Using all available information, we draw the graph.

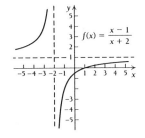

$f(x) = \dfrac{x - 1}{x + 2}$

---

14. $f(x) = \dfrac{x - 2}{x + 1}$

a) Neither even nor odd; no apparent symmetries

b) Horizontal asymptote: $y = 1$

c) Vertical asymptote: $x = -1$
Zero of function: 2

d)

Interval	$(-\infty, -1)$	$(-1, 2)$	$(2, \infty)$
Test value	$f(-2) = 4$	$f(0) = -2$	$f(3) = \frac{1}{4}$
Sign of f(x)	+	−	+
Location of points on graph	Above x-axis	Below x-axis	Above x-axis

e), f)

x	f(x)
-4	2
-2	4
$-1\frac{1}{2}$	7
$-\frac{1}{2}$	-5
0	-2
1	$-\frac{1}{2}$
2	0
5	$\frac{1}{2}$

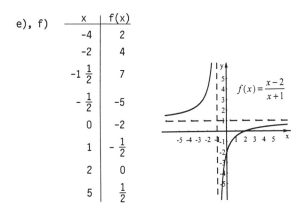

$f(x) = \dfrac{x - 2}{x + 1}$

---

15. $f(x) = \dfrac{3x}{x^2 + 5x + 4} = \dfrac{3x}{(x + 4)(x + 1)}$

a) The function is neither even nor odd and no symmetries are apparent.

b) The degree of the denominator is greater than that of the numerator. Thus the x-axis is an asymptote.

c) The zeros of the denominator are -4 and -1, so $x = -4$ and $x = -1$ are vertical asymptotes. The zero of the function is 0.

d) The vertical asymptotes and the zero of the function divide the x-axis into intervals. To find where the function is positive or negative, we try a test point in each interval.

Interval	Test value	Sign of $f(x)$	Location of points on graph
$(-\infty, -4)$	$f(-5) = -\frac{15}{4}$	$-$	Below x-axis
$(-4, -1)$	$f(-2) = 3$	$+$	Above x-axis
$(-1, 0)$	$f\left(-\frac{1}{2}\right) = -\frac{6}{7}$	$-$	Below x-axis
$(0, \infty)$	$f(1) = \frac{3}{10}$	$+$	Above x-axis

e) We make a table of function values.

x	-6	-5	$-\frac{9}{2}$	$-\frac{7}{2}$	-3	-2	$-\frac{3}{2}$
$f(x)$	$-\frac{9}{5}$	$-\frac{15}{4}$	$-\frac{54}{7}$	$\frac{42}{5}$	$\frac{9}{2}$	3	$\frac{18}{5}$

x	$-\frac{3}{4}$	$-\frac{1}{2}$	0	1	2	3
$f(x)$	$-\frac{36}{13}$	$-\frac{6}{7}$	0	$\frac{3}{10}$	$\frac{1}{3}$	$\frac{9}{28}$

f) Using all the information, we draw the graph.

$$f(x) = \frac{3x}{x^2 + 5x + 4}$$

16. $f(x) = \dfrac{x + 3}{2x^2 - 5x - 3} = \dfrac{x + 3}{(2x + 1)(x - 3)}$

   a) Neither even nor odd; no apparent symmetries

   b) Horizontal asymptote: x-axis

   c) Vertical asymptotes: $x = -\frac{1}{2}$, $x = 3$
       Zero of function: $x = -3$

   d)

Interval	$(-\infty, -3)$	$\left[-3, -\frac{1}{2}\right]$	$\left[-\frac{1}{2}, 3\right]$	$(3, \infty)$
Test value	$f(-4) = -\frac{1}{49}$	$f(-1) = \frac{1}{2}$	$f(0) = -1$	$f(4) = \frac{7}{9}$
Sign of $f(x)$	$-$	$+$	$-$	$+$
Location of points on graph	Below x-axis	Above x-axis	Below x-axis	Above x-axis

e), f)

x	$f(x)$
-8	-0.0303
-7	-0.0308
-6	-0.0303
-5	-0.0277
-4	-0.0204
-3	0
-2	$\frac{1}{15}$
-1	$\frac{1}{2}$
$-\frac{3}{4}$	$1\frac{1}{5}$

x	$f(x)$
$-\frac{1}{4}$	$-1\frac{9}{13}$
0	-1
1	$-\frac{2}{3}$
2	-1
$2\frac{1}{2}$	$-1\frac{5}{6}$
$3\frac{1}{2}$	$1\frac{5}{8}$
4	$\frac{7}{9}$

$$f(x) = \frac{x + 3}{2x^2 - 5x - 3}$$

17. $f(x) = \dfrac{x^2 - 4}{x - 1} = \dfrac{(x + 2)(x - 2)}{x - 1}$

   a) The function is neither even nor odd and no symmetries are apparent.

   b) The degree of the numerator is one greater than that of the denominator. Dividing numerator by denominator will show that $y = x + 1$ is an oblique asymptote.

   c) The zero of the denominator is 1, so $x = 1$ is a vertical asymptote. The zeros of the function are -2 and 2.

   d) The vertical asymptote and the zeros of the function divide the x-axis into intervals. To find where the function is positive or negative, we try a test point in each interval.

Interval	Test value	Sign of $f(x)$	Location of points on graph
$(-\infty, -2)$	$f(-3) = -\frac{5}{4}$	$-$	Below x-axis
$(-2, 1)$	$f(0) = 4$	$+$	Above x-axis
$(1, 2)$	$f\left(\frac{3}{2}\right) = -\frac{7}{2}$	$-$	Below x-axis
$(2, \infty)$	$f(3) = \frac{5}{2}$	$+$	Above x-axis

e) We make a table of function values.

x	-3	-2	-1	0	$\frac{1}{2}$	$\frac{3}{2}$	2	3
f(x)	$-1\frac{1}{4}$	0	$1\frac{1}{2}$	4	$7\frac{1}{2}$	$-3\frac{1}{2}$	0	$2\frac{1}{2}$

f) Using all available information, we draw the graph.

$$f(x) = \frac{x^2 - 4}{x - 1}$$

18. $f(x) = \frac{x^2 - 9}{x + 1} = \frac{(x + 3)(x - 3)}{x + 1}$

a) Neither even nor odd; no apparent symmetries

b) Oblique asymptote: y = x - 1

c) Vertical asymptote: x = -1
    Zeros of function: -3, 3

d)

Interval	$(-\infty, -3)$	$(-3, -1)$	$(-1, 3)$	$(3, \infty)$
Test value	$f(-4) = -\frac{7}{3}$	$f(-2) = 5$	$f(0) = -9$	$f(4) = \frac{7}{5}$
Sign of f(x)	-	+	-	+
Location of points on graph	Below x-axis	Above x-axis	Below x-axis	Above x-axis

e), f)

x	f(x)
-4	$-2\frac{1}{3}$
-3	0
-2	5
$-1\frac{1}{2}$	$13\frac{1}{2}$
0	-9

x	f(x)
1	-4
2	$-1\frac{2}{3}$
3	0
4	$1\frac{2}{5}$
5	$2\frac{2}{3}$

$$f(x) = \frac{x^2 - 9}{x + 1}$$

19. $f(x) = \frac{x^2 + x - 2}{2x^2 + 1} = \frac{(x + 2)(x - 1)}{2x^2 + 1}$

a) The function is neither even nor odd and no symmetries are apparent.

b) Since the numerator and denominator have the same degree, the horizontal asymptote can be determined by dividing the leading coefficients of the two polynomials. Thus 1 ÷ 2 = 1/2, and we know that y = 1/2 is a horizontal asymptote.

c) The denominator has no zeros, so there are no vertical asymptotes. The zeros of the function are -2 and 1.

d) The zeros of the function divide the x-axis into intervals. To find where the function is positive or negative, we try a test point in each interval.

Interval	$(-\infty, -2)$	$(-2, 1)$	$(1, \infty)$
Test value	$f(-3) = \frac{4}{19}$	$f(0) = -2$	$f(2) = \frac{4}{9}$
Sign of f(x)	+	-	+
Location of points on graph	Above x-axis	Below x-axis	Above x-axis

e) We make a table of function values.

x	-5	-3	-2	-1	0	1	2	3
f(x)	$\frac{6}{17}$	$\frac{4}{19}$	0	$-\frac{2}{3}$	-2	0	$\frac{4}{9}$	$\frac{10}{19}$

f) Using all the information, we draw the graph.

$$f(x) = \frac{x^2 + x - 2}{2x^2 + 1}$$

20. $f(x) = \frac{x^2 - 2x - 3}{3x^2 + 2} = \frac{(x - 3)(x + 1)}{3x^2 + 2}$

a) Neither even nor odd; no apparent symmetries

b) Horizontal asymptote: $y = \frac{1}{3}$

c) No vertical asymptote
    Zeros of function: -1, 3

d)

Interval	$(-\infty, -1)$	$(-1, 3)$	$(3, \infty)$
Test value	$f(-2) = \frac{5}{14}$	$f(0) = -\frac{3}{2}$	$f(4) = \frac{1}{10}$
Sign of $f(x)$	+	-	+
Location of points on graph	Above x-axis	Below x-axis	Above x-axis

e), f)

x	f(x)
-2	$\frac{5}{14}$
-1	0
$-\frac{1}{2}$	$-\frac{7}{11}$
0	$-1\frac{1}{2}$
$\frac{1}{2}$	$-1\frac{4}{11}$

x	f(x)
1	$-\frac{4}{5}$
2	$-\frac{3}{14}$
3	0
4	$\frac{1}{10}$

$$f(x) = \frac{x^2 - 2x - 3}{3x^2 + 2}$$

21. $f(x) = \dfrac{x - 1}{x^2 - 2x - 3} = \dfrac{x - 1}{(x - 3)(x + 1)}$

a) The function is neither even nor odd and no symmetries are apparent.

b) The degree of the denominator is greater than the degree of the numerator. Thus the x-axis is an asymptote.

c) The zeros of the denominator are 3 and -1, so x = 3 and x = -1 are vertical asymptotes. The zero of the function is 1.

d) The vertical asymptotes and the zeros of the function divide the x-axis into intervals. To find where the function is positive or negative, we try a test point in each interval.

Interval	Test value	Sign of $f(x)$	Location of points on graph
$(-\infty, -1)$	$f(-2) = -\frac{3}{5}$	-	Below x-axis
$(-1, 1)$	$f(0) = \frac{1}{3}$	+	Above x-axis
$(1, 3)$	$f(2) = -\frac{1}{3}$	-	Below x-axis
$(3, \infty)$	$f(4) = \frac{3}{5}$	+	Above x-axis

e) We make a table of function values.

x	-5	-3	-2	$-\frac{3}{2}$	$-\frac{1}{2}$	0	1
f(x)	$-\frac{3}{16}$	$-\frac{1}{3}$	$-\frac{3}{5}$	$-\frac{10}{9}$	$\frac{6}{7}$	$\frac{1}{3}$	0

x	2	$\frac{5}{2}$	4	5
f(x)	$-\frac{1}{3}$	$-\frac{6}{7}$	$\frac{3}{5}$	$\frac{1}{3}$

f) Using all available information, we draw the graph.

$$f(x) = \frac{x - 1}{x^2 - 2x - 3}$$

22. $f(x) = \dfrac{x + 2}{x^2 + 2x - 15} = \dfrac{x + 2}{(x + 5)(x - 3)}$

a) Neither even nor odd; no apparent symmetries

b) Horizontal asymptote: x -axis

c) Vertical asymptotes: x = -5, x = 3

Zero of function: -2

d)

Interval	$(-\infty, -5)$	$(-5, -2)$	$(-2, 3)$	$(3, \infty)$
Test value	$f(-6) = -\frac{4}{9}$	$f(-3) = \frac{1}{12}$	$f(0) = -\frac{2}{15}$	$f(4) = \frac{2}{3}$
Sign of $f(x)$	-	+	-	+
Location of points on graph	Below x-axis	Above x-axis	Below x-axis	Above x-axis

e), f)

x	f(x)
-6	$-\frac{4}{9}$
$-5\frac{1}{2}$	$-\frac{14}{17}$
$-4\frac{1}{2}$	$\frac{2}{3}$
-4	$\frac{2}{7}$
-2	0
0	$-\frac{2}{15}$

x	f(x)
1	$-\frac{1}{4}$
2	$-\frac{4}{7}$
$2\frac{1}{2}$	$-1\frac{1}{5}$
$3\frac{1}{2}$	$1\frac{5}{17}$
4	$\frac{2}{3}$

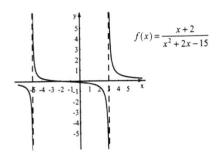

$$f(x) = \frac{x+2}{x^2+2x-15}$$

23. $f(x) = \dfrac{x+2}{(x-1)^3}$

a) The function is neither even nor odd and no symmetries are apparent.

b) The degree of the denominator is greater than the degree of the numerator. Thus the x-axis is an asymptote.

c) The zero of the denominator is 1, so x = 1 is a vertical asymptote. The zero of the function is -2.

d) The vertical asymptote and the zero of the function divide the x-axis into intervals. To find where the function is positive or negative, we try a test point in each interval.

Interval	$(-\infty, -2)$	$(-2, 1)$	$(1, \infty)$
Test value	$f(-3) = \frac{1}{64}$	$f(0) = -2$	$f(2) = 4$
Sign of f(x)	+	-	+
Location of points on graph	Above x-axis	Below x-axis	Above x-axis

e) Make a table of function values.

x	-5	-4	-3	-2	-1	0	$\frac{1}{2}$
f(x)	$\frac{1}{72}$	$\frac{2}{125}$	$\frac{1}{64}$	0	$-\frac{1}{8}$	-2	-20

x	$\frac{3}{2}$	2	3
f(x)	28	4	$\frac{5}{8}$

f) Using all available information, we draw the graph.

$$f(x) = \frac{x+2}{(x-1)^3}$$

24. $f(x) = \dfrac{x-3}{(x+1)^3}$

a) Neither even nor odd; no apparent symmetries

b) Horizontal asymptote: x-axis

c) Vertical asymptote: x = -1
    Zero of function: 3

d)

Interval	$(-\infty, -1)$	$(-1, 3)$	$(3, \infty)$
Test value	$f(-2) = 5$	$f(0) = -3$	$f(4) = \frac{1}{125}$
Sign of f(x)	+	-	+
Location of points on graph	Above x-axis	Below x-axis	Above x-axis

e), f)

x	f(x)
-3	$\frac{3}{4}$
-2	5
$-\frac{1}{2}$	-28
0	-3
$\frac{1}{2}$	$-\frac{20}{27}$

x	f(x)
1	$-\frac{1}{4}$
2	$-\frac{1}{27}$
3	0
4	0.00800
5	0.00926
6	0.00875

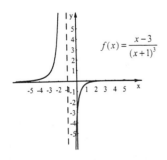

$$f(x) = \frac{x-3}{(x+1)^3}$$

213

25. $f(x) = \dfrac{x^3 + 1}{x} = \dfrac{(x + 1)(x^2 - x + 1)}{x}$

a) The function is neither even nor odd and no symmetries are apparent.

b) The degree of the numerator is two greater than the denominator. There are no horizontal or oblique asymptotes.

c) The zero of the denominator is 0, so x = 0 (the y-axis) is a vertical asymptote. The only real-number zero of the function is -1.

d) The vertical asymptote and the real zero of the function divide the x-axis into intervals. To find where the function is positive or negative, we try a test point in each interval.

Interval	$(-\infty, -1)$	$(-1, 0)$	$(0, \infty)$
Test value	$f(-2) = \frac{7}{2}$	$f\left(-\frac{1}{2}\right) = -\frac{7}{4}$	$f(1) = 2$
Sign of f(x)	+	-	+
Location of points on graph	Above x-axis	Below x-axis	Above x-axis

e) Make a table of function values.

x	-3	-2	-1	$-\frac{1}{2}$	$\frac{1}{2}$	1	2	3
f(x)	$\frac{26}{3}$	$\frac{7}{2}$	0	$-\frac{7}{4}$	$\frac{9}{4}$	2	$\frac{9}{2}$	$\frac{28}{3}$

f) Draw the graph using all the known information.

$f(x) = \dfrac{x^3 + 1}{x}$

26. $f(x) = \dfrac{x^3 - 1}{x} = \dfrac{(x - 1)(x^2 + x + 1)}{x}$

a) Neither even nor odd; no apparent symmetries

b) No horizontal or oblique asymptotes.

c) Vertical asymptote: y-axis (x = 0)
    Zero of function: 1

d)

Interval	$(-\infty, 0)$	$(0, 1)$	$(1, \infty)$
Test value	$f(-1) = 2$	$f(0.5) = -1.75$	$f(2) = 3.5$
Sign of f(x)	+	-	+
Location of points on graph	Above x-axis	Below x-axis	Above x-axis

e), f)

x	f(x)
-3	≈ 9.3
-2	4.5
-1	2
-0.5	2.25
-0.2	5.04

x	f(x)
0.2	-4.96
0.5	-1.75
1	0
2	3.5
3	≈ 8.7

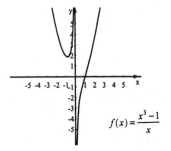

$f(x) = \dfrac{x^3 - 1}{x}$

27. $f(x) = \dfrac{x^3 + 2x^2 - 15x}{x^2 - 5x - 14} = \dfrac{x(x + 5)(x - 3)}{(x + 2)(x - 7)}$

a) The function is neither even nor odd and no symmetries are apparent.

b) The degree of the numerator is one greater than that of the denominator. Dividing numerator by denominator will show that y = x + 7 is an oblique asymptote.

c) The zeros of the denominator are -2 and 7, so x = -2 and x = 7 are vertical asymptotes. The zeros of the function are 0, -5, and 3.

d) The vertical asymptotes and the zeros of the function divide the x-axis into intervals. To find where the function is positive or negative, we try a test value in each interval.

Interval	Test value	Sign of f(x)	Location of points on graph
$(-\infty, -5)$	$f(-6) = -\frac{27}{26}$	-	Below x-axis
$(-5, -2)$	$f(-3) = \frac{18}{5}$	+	Above x-axis
$(-2, 0)$	$f(-1) = -2$	-	Below x-axis

Interval	Test value	Sign of f(x)	Location of points on graph
(0, 3)	$f(1) = \frac{2}{3}$	+	Above x-axis
(3, 7)	$f(4) = -2$	−	Below x-axis
(7, ∞)	$f(8) = 52$	+	Above x-axis

e) Make a table of function values.

x	−100	−10	−8	−7	−6	−5	−4	−3	−2.5
f(x)	−93.3	−4.8	−2.9	−2	−1.0	0	1.3	3.6	7.2

x	−2.1	−1.9	−1.5	−1	0	1	2	3	4	5
f(x)	34.1	−32.4	−5.6	−2	0	0.7	0.7	0	−2	−7.1

x	6	7.1	7.5	8	10	20	100
f(x)	−24.8	387	88.8	52	29.2	29.7	107

f) Draw the graph using all available information.

$$f(x) = \frac{x^3 + 2x^2 - 15x}{x^2 - 5x - 14}$$

28. $f(x) = \dfrac{x^3 + 2x^2 - 3x}{x^2 - 25} = \dfrac{x(x + 3)(x - 1)}{(x + 5)(x - 5)}$

a) Neither even nor odd; no apparent symmetries

b) Oblique asymptote: $y = x + 2$

c) Vertical asymptotes: $x = -5$, $x = 5$
    Zeros of function: -3, 0, 1

d)

Interval	Test value	Sign of f(x)	Location of points on graph
(−∞, −5)	$f(-6) = -\frac{126}{11}$	−	Below x-axis
(−5, −3)	$f(-4) = \frac{20}{9}$	+	Above x-axis

Interval	Test value	Sign of f(x)	Location of points on graph
(−3, 0)	$f(-1) = -\frac{1}{6}$	−	Below x-axis
(0, 1)	$f\left(\frac{1}{2}\right) = \frac{7}{198}$	+	Above x-axis
(1, 5)	$f(2) = -\frac{10}{21}$	−	Below x-axis
(5, ∞)	$f(6) = \frac{270}{11}$	+	Above x-axis

e), f)

x	f(x)		x	f(x)
−6	$-\frac{126}{11} \approx -11.5$		$\frac{1}{2}$	$\frac{7}{198} \approx 0.035$
−4	$2\frac{2}{9}$		1	0
−3	0		2	$-\frac{10}{21}$
−2	$-\frac{2}{7}$		3	$-2\frac{1}{4}$
−1	$-\frac{1}{6}$		4	$-9\frac{1}{3}$
0	0		6	$\frac{270}{11} \approx 24.5$

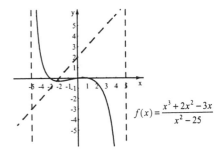

$$f(x) = \frac{x^3 + 2x^2 - 3x}{x^2 - 25}$$

29. $f(x) = \dfrac{5x^4}{x^4 + 1}$

a) The function is even, so the graph is symmetric about the y-axis.

b) The degree of the numerator equals the degree of the denominator, so $y = \frac{5}{1}$, or $y = 5$, is a horizontal asymptote.

c) The denominator has no zeros, so there are no vertical asymptotes. The zero of the function is 0.

d) $5x^4 \geq 0$ for all real x and $x^4 + 1 > 0$ for all real x, so $f(x) \geq 0$ for all real values of x.

e) We make a table of function values.

x	± 5	± 3	± 1	0
f(x)	4.99	4.94	2.5	0

215

f) Using all available information, we draw the graph.

$$f(x) = \frac{5x^4}{x^4 + 1}$$

30. $f(x) = \dfrac{x + 1}{x^2 + x - 6} = \dfrac{x + 1}{(x + 3)(x - 2)}$

a) Neither even nor odd; no apparent symmetries

b) Horizontal asymptote: x-axis

c) Vertical asymptotes: x = -3, x = 2
    Zero of function: -1

d)

Interval	$(-\infty, -3)$	$(-3,-1)$	$(-1,2)$	$(2,\infty)$
Test value	$f(-4) = -\frac{1}{2}$	$f(-2) = \frac{1}{4}$	$f(0) = -\frac{1}{6}$	$f(3) = \frac{2}{3}$
Sign of f(x)	−	+	−	+
Location of points on graph	Below x-axis	Above x-axis	Below x-axis	Above x-axis

e), f)

x	-5	-4	-2	-1	0	1	3	4	5
f(x)	$-\frac{2}{7}$	$-\frac{1}{2}$	$\frac{1}{4}$	0	$-\frac{1}{6}$	$-\frac{1}{2}$	$\frac{2}{3}$	$\frac{5}{14}$	$\frac{1}{4}$

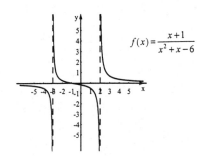

$$f(x) = \frac{x+1}{x^2+x-6}$$

31. $f(x) = \dfrac{x^2 - x - 2}{x + 2} = \dfrac{(x - 2)(x + 1)}{x + 2}$

a) The function is neither even nor odd, and no symmetries are apparent.

b) The degree of the numerator is one more than the degree of the denominator. Dividing the numerator by the denominator will show that the line y = x - 3 is an oblique asymptote.

c) The zero of the denominator is -2, so x = -2 is a vertical asymptote. The zeros of the function are 2 and -1.

d) The vertical asymptote and the zeros of the function divide the x-axis into intervals. To find where the function is positive or negative, we try a test point in each interval.

Interval	Test value	Sign of f(x)	Location of points on graph
$(-\infty, -2)$	$f(-3) = -10$	−	Below x-axis
$(-2, -1)$	$f\left(-\frac{3}{2}\right) = \frac{7}{2}$	+	Above x-axis
$(-1, 2)$	$f(0) = -1$	−	Below x-axis
$(2, \infty)$	$f(3) = \frac{4}{5}$	+	Above x-axis

e) Make a table of function values.

x	-5	-3	$-\frac{3}{2}$	-1	0	1	2
f(x)	$-\frac{28}{3}$	-10	$\frac{7}{2}$	0	-1	$-\frac{2}{3}$	0

x	3	5
f(x)	$\frac{4}{5}$	$\frac{18}{7}$

f) Using all available information, we draw the graph.

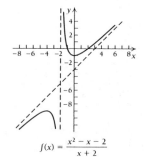

$$f(x) = \frac{x^2 - x - 2}{x + 2}$$

32. $f(x) = \dfrac{x^2}{x^2 - x - 2} = \dfrac{x^2}{(x - 2)(x + 1)}$

a) Neither even nor odd; no apparent symmetries

b) Horizontal asymptote: y = 1

c) Vertical asymptotes: x = -1, x = 2
    Zero of function: 0

d)

Interval	$(-\infty, -1)$	$(-1,0)$	$(0,2)$	$(2,\infty)$
Test value	$f(-2) = 1$	$f\left(-\frac{1}{2}\right) =$ $-\frac{1}{5}$	$f(1) =$ $-\frac{1}{2}$	$f(3) =$ $\frac{9}{4}$
Sign of $f(x)$	+	−	−	+
Location of points on graph	Above x-axis	Below x-axis	Below x-axis	Above x-axis

e), f)

x	−5	−3	−2	$-\frac{3}{2}$	$-\frac{6}{5}$	$-\frac{1}{2}$	0
$f(x)$	$\frac{25}{28}$	$\frac{9}{10}$	1	$\frac{9}{7}$	$\frac{9}{4}$	$-\frac{1}{5}$	0

x	$\frac{1}{2}$	1	$\frac{3}{2}$	3	4
$f(x)$	$-\frac{1}{9}$	$-\frac{1}{2}$	$-\frac{9}{5}$	$\frac{9}{4}$	$\frac{8}{5}$

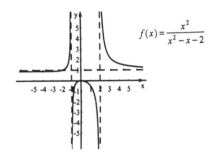

$$f(x) = \frac{x^2}{x^2 - x - 2}$$

33.   a)   We use the formula $d = rt$:

$$d = rt$$

$$t = \frac{d}{r} \quad \text{(Solving for } t\text{)}$$

$$t = \frac{500}{r} \quad \text{(Substituting 500 for } d\text{)}$$

b)   The graph over $(0, \infty)$ is one branch of a hyperbola.

$$t = \frac{500}{r}$$

Time, in hours

Speed, in miles per hour

34.   a) $R = \dfrac{10r}{10 + r}$

b)

$$R = \frac{10r}{10+r}$$

c)   Domain: $(0, \infty)$, range: $(0, 10)$

d) $R = \dfrac{10}{\dfrac{10}{r} + 1}$

The total resistance approaches 10.

35. $f(x) = \dfrac{x^3 + 4x^2 + x - 6}{x^2 - x - 2} = \dfrac{(x + 3)(x + 2)(x - 1)}{(x - 2)(x + 1)}$

(We can use the rational roots theorem and synthetic division to factor the numerator.)

a)   The function is neither even nor odd, and no symmetries are apparent.

b)   The degree of the numerator is one more than the degree of the denominator. Dividing the numerator by the denominator will show that the line $y = x + 5$ is an oblique asymptote.

c)   The zeros of the denominator are 2 and −1, so $x = 2$ and $x = -1$ are vertical asymptotes. The zeros of the function are −3, −2, and 1.

d)   We find where the function is positive or negative.

Interval	Test value	Sign of $f(x)$	Location of points on graph
$(-\infty, -3)$	$f(-4) = -\frac{5}{9}$	−	Below x-axis
$(-3, -2)$	$f\left(-\frac{5}{2}\right) = \frac{7}{54}$	+	Above x-axis
$(-2, -1)$	$f\left(-\frac{3}{2}\right) = -\frac{15}{14}$	−	Below x-axis
$(-1, 1)$	$f(0) = 3$	+	Above x-axis
$(1, 2)$	$f\left(\frac{3}{2}\right) = -\frac{63}{10}$	−	Below x-axis
$(2, \infty)$	$f(3) = 15$	+	Above x-axis

e) We make a table of function values.

x	-5	-4	-3	$-\frac{5}{2}$	-2	$-\frac{3}{2}$	0
f(x)	$-\frac{9}{7}$	$-\frac{5}{9}$	0	$\frac{7}{54}$	0	$-\frac{15}{14}$	3

x	1	$\frac{3}{2}$	3	5	7	9
f(x)	0	$-\frac{63}{10}$	15	$\frac{112}{9}$	$\frac{27}{2}$	$\frac{528}{35}$

f) Using all available information, we draw the graph.

$$f(x) = \frac{x^3 + 4x^2 + x - 6}{x^2 - x - 2}$$

36. $f(x) = \dfrac{2x^3 + x^2 - 8x - 4}{x^3 + x^2 - 9x - 9} = \dfrac{(2x + 1)(x - 2)(x + 2)}{(x + 1)(x + 3)(x - 3)}$

a) Neither even nor odd; no apparent symmetries

b) Horizontal asymptote: y = 2

c) Vertical asymptotes: x = -3, x = -1, x = 3
    Zeros of function: -2, $-\frac{1}{2}$, 2

d)

Interval	Test value	Sign of f(x)	Location of points on graph
$(-\infty, -3)$	$f(-4) = 4$	+	Above x-axis
$(-3, -2)$	$f\left(-\frac{5}{2}\right) = -\frac{24}{11}$	−	Below x-axis
$(-2, -1)$	$f\left(-\frac{3}{2}\right) = \frac{28}{27}$	+	Above x-axis
$\left[-1, -\frac{1}{2}\right]$	$f\left(-\frac{3}{4}\right) = -\frac{22}{27}$	−	Below x-axis
$\left[-\frac{1}{2}, 2\right]$	$f(0) = \frac{4}{9}$	+	Above x-axis
$(2, 3)$	$f\left(\frac{5}{2}\right) = -\frac{108}{77}$	−	Below x-axis
$(3, \infty)$	$f(4) = \frac{108}{35}$	+	Above x-axis

e), f)

x	-4	$-\frac{5}{2}$	-2	$-\frac{3}{2}$	$-\frac{3}{4}$	$-\frac{1}{2}$	0
f(x)	4	$-\frac{24}{11}$	0	$\frac{28}{27}$	$-\frac{22}{27}$	0	$\frac{4}{9}$

x	1	2	$\frac{5}{2}$	4	5
f(x)	$\frac{9}{16}$	0	$-\frac{108}{77}$	$\frac{108}{35}$	$\frac{77}{32}$

$$f(x) = \frac{2x^3 + x^2 - 8x - 4}{x^3 + x^2 - 9x - 9}$$

37. a) The distance of the round trip is 2·300, or 600 km, so $t_0 = \dfrac{600 \text{ km}}{200 \text{ km/h}} = 3$ hr.

We substitute:

$$T = \frac{(200)^2(3)}{(200)^2 - w^2} = \frac{120{,}000}{40{,}000 - w^2}$$

b) For w = 5 km/h:

$$T = \frac{120{,}000}{40{,}000 - 5^2} \approx 3.001876 \text{ hr}$$

For w = 10 km/h:

$$T = \frac{120{,}000}{40{,}000 - 10^2} \approx 3.007519 \text{ hr}$$

For w = 20 km/h:

$$T = \frac{120{,}000}{40{,}000 - 20^2} \approx 3.030303 \text{ hr}$$

c) The wind speed must be nonnegative, and it must also be less than the speed of the plane in still air. Thus the domain is $\{w | 0 \le w < 200\}$.

For w = 0, T = 3; for other values of w in the domain, T > 3. Thus the range is $\{T | T \ge 3\}$.

d)

38. a) S = area of base + 4·area of a side

= x² + 4xy

Now we express y in terms of x:

Volume = 108 = x²y

$$\frac{108}{x^2} = y$$

Thus, S = x² + 4x$\left[\frac{108}{x^2}\right]$, or

$$S = x^2 + \frac{432}{x}.$$

b)

$S = x^2 + \dfrac{432}{x}$

c) Using the graph, we estimate that the minimum surface area is 108 cm². This occurs when x = 6 cm.

39. $f(x) = \dfrac{x^4 + 3x^3 + 21x^2 - 50x + 80}{x^4 + 8x^3 - x^2 + 20x - 10}$

[−20, 10] x [−20, 20]

40. $f(x) = \dfrac{x^3 + x^2 + x}{x^2 - 1}$

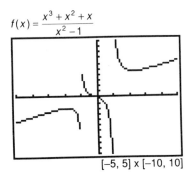

[−5, 5] x [−10, 10]

41. $f(x) = \dfrac{x^3}{x^2 - 1}$

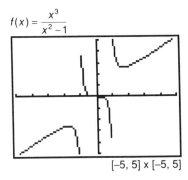

[−5, 5] x [−5, 5]

42. $f(x) = \dfrac{x^3 + 4}{x}$

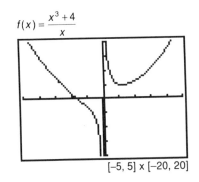

[−5, 5] x [−20, 20]

Exercise Set 5.1

1. We interchange the first and second coordinates of each ordered pair to find the inverse of the relation. It is

    {(1, 0), (6, 5), (-4, -2)}.

2. {(3, -1), (5, 2), (5, -3), (0, 2)}

3. We interchange the first and second coordinates of each ordered pair to find the inverse of the relation. It is

    {(8, 7), (8, -2), (-4, 3), (-8, 8)}.

4. {(-1, -1), (4, -3)}

5. Interchange x and y.
    y = 4x - 5
    ↓   ↓
    x = 4y - 5   (Equation of the inverse relation)

6. x = 3y + 5

7. Interchange x and y.
    $x^2 - 3y^2 = 3$
    ↓   ↓
    $y^2 - 3x^2 = 3$ (Equation of the inverse relation)

8. $2y^2 + 5x^2 = 4$

9. Interchange x and y.
    $y = 3x^2 + 2$
    ↓   ↓
    $x = 3y^2 + 2$ (Equation of the inverse relation)

10. $x = 5y^2 - 4$

11. Interchange x and y.
    xy = 7
    ↓↓
    yx = 7   (Equation of the inverse relation)

12. yx = -5

13. Graph $y = x^2 + 1$. A few solutions of the equation are (0, 1), (1, 2), (-1, 2), (2, 5), and (-2, 5). Plot these points and draw the curve. Then reflect the graph of $y = x^2 + 1$ across the line y = x (----). A few solutions of the inverse relation, $x = y^2 + 1$, are (1, 0), (2, 1), (2, -1), (5, 2), and (5, -2). Both graphs are shown below.

14.

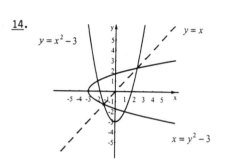

15. Graph x = |y|. A few solutions of the equation are (0, 0), (2, 2), (2, -2), (5, 5), and (5, -5). Plot these points and draw the graph. Then reflect the graph across the line y = x (----). A few solutions of the inverse relation, y = |x|, are (0, 0), (2, 2), (-2, 2), (5, 5), and (-5, 5). Both graphs are shown below.

16.

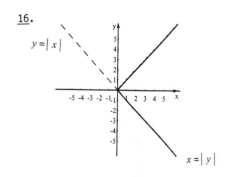

17. The graph of f(x) = 5x - 8 is shown below.

Since there is no horizontal line that crosses the graph more than once, the function is one-to-one.

18.

The function is one-to-one.

19. The graph of f(x) = x² - 7 is shown below.

There are many horizontal lines that cross the graph more than once. In particular, the line y = 4 crosses the graph more than once. The function is not one-to-one.

20.

The function is not one-to-one.

21. The graph of g(x) = 3 is shown below.

Since the horizontal line y = 3 crosses the graph more than once, the function is not one-to-one.

22.

The function is not one-to-one.

23. The graph of g(x) = |x| is shown below.

There are many horizontal lines that cross the graph more than once. In particular, the line y = 3 crosses the graph more than once. The function is not one-to-one.

24.

The function is not one-to-one.

25. The graph of f(x) = |x + 1| is shown below.

The line y = 2 is one of many lines that cross the graph more than once. The function is not one-to-one.

26.

The function is not one-to-one.

27. The graph of g(x) = $\frac{-4}{x}$ is shown below.

Since there is no horizontal line that crosses the graph more than once, the function is one-to-one.

28.

The function is one-to-one.

29. a) The graph of f(x) = x + 4 is shown below. It passes the horizontal line test, so it is one-to-one.

b) Replace f(x) by y: y = x + 4

Interchange x and y: x = y + 4

Solve for y: x − 4 = y

Replace y by $f^{-1}(x)$: $f^{-1}(x)$ = x − 4

30. a)

The function is one-to-one.

b) y = x + 5   Replace f(x).

x = y + 5   Interchange variables.

x − 5 = y   Solve for y.

$f^{-1}(x)$ = x − 5   Replace y.

31. a) The graph of f(x) = 5 − x is shown below. It passes the horizontal line test, so the function is one-to-one.

b) Replace f(x) by y: y = 5 − x

Interchange x and y: x = 5 − y

Solve for y: y = 5 − x

Replace y by $f^{-1}(x)$: $f^{-1}(x)$ = 5 − x

32. a)

The function is one-to-one.

b)   y = 7 - x   Replace f(x).

       x = 7 - y   Interchange variables.

       y = 7 - x   Solve for y.

       $f^{-1}(x) = 7 - x$ Replace y.

<u>33.</u>   a)   The graph of g(x) = x - 3 is shown below. It passes the horizontal line test, so the function is one-to-one.

    b)   Replace g(x) by y: y = x - 3

        Interchange x and y: x = y - 3

        Solve for y: x + 3 = y

        Replace y by $g^{-1}(x)$: $g^{-1}(x) = x + 3$

<u>34.</u>   a)   The function is one-to-one.

    b)   y = x - 10   Replace g(x).

        x = y - 10   Interchange variables.

        x + 10 = y   Solve for y.

        $g^{-1}(x) = x + 10$ Replace y.

<u>35.</u>   a)   The graph of f(x) = 2x is shown below. It passes the horizontal line test, so the function is one-to-one.

    b)   Replace f(x) by y: y = 2x

        Interchange x and y: x = 2y

        Solve for y: $\frac{x}{2} = y$

        Replace y by $f^{-1}(x)$: $f^{-1}(x) = \frac{x}{2}$

<u>36.</u>   a)   The function is one-to-one.

    b)   y = 5x   Replace f(x).

        x = 5y   Interchange variables.

        $\frac{x}{5} = y$ Solve for y.

        $f^{-1}(x) = \frac{x}{5}$ Replace y.

<u>37.</u>   a)   The graph of g(x) = 2x + 5 is shown below. It passes the horizontal line test, so the function is one-to-one.

    b)   Replace g(x) by y: y = 2x + 5

        Interchange variables: x = 2y + 5

        Solve for y: x - 5 = 2y

                 $\frac{x - 5}{2} = y$

        Replace y by $g^{-1}(x)$: $g^{-1}(x) = \frac{x - 5}{2}$

<u>38.</u>   a)   The function is one-to-one.

    b)   y = 5x + 8   Replace g(x).

        x = 5y + 8   Interchange variables.

        $\frac{x - 8}{5} = y$ Solve for y.

        $g^{-1}(x) = \frac{x - 8}{5}$ Replace y.

39. a) The graph of $h(x) = \dfrac{4}{x + 7}$ is shown below. It passes the horizontal line test, so the function is one-to-one.

b) Replace h(x) by y: $y = \dfrac{4}{x + 7}$

Interchange x and y: $x = \dfrac{4}{y + 7}$

Solve for y: $x(y + 7) = 4$

$y + 7 = \dfrac{4}{x}$

$y = \dfrac{4}{x} - 7$

Replace y by $h^{-1}(x)$: $h^{-1}(x) = \dfrac{4}{x} - 7$

40. a)

The function is one-to-one.

b) $y = \dfrac{1}{x - 6}$ Replace h(x).

$x = \dfrac{1}{y - 6}$ Interchange variables.

$y - 6 = \dfrac{1}{x}$ Solve for y.

$y = \dfrac{1}{x} + 6$

$h^{-1}(x) = \dfrac{1}{x} + 6$ Replace y.

41. a) The graph of $f(x) = \dfrac{1}{x}$ is shown below. It passes the horizontal line test, so the function is one-to-one.

b) Replace f(x) by y: $y = \dfrac{1}{x}$

Interchange x and y: $x = \dfrac{1}{y}$

Solve for y: $xy = 1$

$y = \dfrac{1}{x}$

Replace y by $f^{-1}(x)$: $f^{-1}(x) = \dfrac{1}{x}$

42. a) The function is one-to-one. (See Exercise 27.)

b) $y = -\dfrac{4}{x}$ Replace f(x).

$x = -\dfrac{4}{y}$ Interchange variables.

$y = -\dfrac{4}{x}$ Solve for y.

$f^{-1}(x) = -\dfrac{4}{x}$ Replace y.

43. a) The graph of $f(x) = \dfrac{2x + 3}{4}$ is shown below. It passes the horizontal line test, so the function is one-to-one.

b) Replace f(x) by y: $y = \dfrac{2x + 3}{4}$

Interchange x and y: $x = \dfrac{2y + 3}{4}$

Solve for y: $4x = 2y + 3$

$4x - 3 = 2y$

$\dfrac{4x - 3}{2} = y$

Replace y by $f^{-1}(x)$: $f^{-1}(x) = \dfrac{4x - 3}{2}$

44. a)

The function is one-to-one.

b) $y = \dfrac{3x - 5}{4}$ Replace f(x).

$x = \dfrac{3y - 5}{4}$ Interchange variables.

$\dfrac{4x + 5}{3} = y$ Solve for y.

$f^{-1}(x) = \dfrac{4x + 5}{3}$ Replace y.

45. a) The graph of $g(x) = \dfrac{x + 4}{x - 3}$ is shown below. It passes the horizontal line test, so the function is one-to-one.

b) Replace g(x) by y: $y = \dfrac{x + 4}{x - 3}$

Interchange x and y: $x = \dfrac{y + 4}{y - 3}$

Solve for y: $(y - 3)x = y + 4$

$xy - 3x = y + 4$

$xy - y = 3x + 4$

$y(x - 1) = 3x + 4$

$y = \dfrac{3x + 4}{x - 1}$

Replace y by $g^{-1}(x)$: $g^{-1}(x) = \dfrac{3x + 4}{x - 1}$

46. a)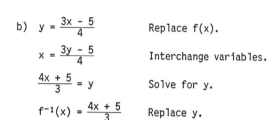

The function is one-to-one.

b) $y = \dfrac{5x - 3}{2x + 1}$ Replace g(x).

$x = \dfrac{5y - 3}{2y + 1}$ Interchange variables.

$\dfrac{x + 3}{5 - 2x} = y$ Solve for y.

$g^{-1}(x) = \dfrac{x + 3}{5 - 2x}$ Replace y.

47. a) The graph of $f(x) = x^3 - 1$ is shown below. It passes the horizontal line test, so the function is one-to-one.

b) Replace f(x) by y: $y = x^3 - 1$
Interchange x and y: $x = y^3 - 1$
Solve for y: $x + 1 = y^3$

$\sqrt[3]{x + 1} = y$

Replace y by $f^{-1}(x)$: $f^{-1}(x) = \sqrt[3]{x + 1}$

48. a)

The function is one-to-one.

b) $y = x^3 + 7$ Replace f(x).
$x = y^3 + 7$ Interchange variables.
$\sqrt[3]{x - 7} = y$ Solve for y.
$f^{-1}(x) = \sqrt[3]{x - 7}$ Replace y.

49. a) The graph of $G(x) = (x - 4)^3$ is shown below. It passes the horizontal line test, so the function is one-to-one.

b) Replace $G(x)$ by y: $y = (x - 4)^3$

Interchange x and y: $x = (y - 4)^3$

Solve for y: $\sqrt[3]{x} = y - 4$

$\sqrt[3]{x} + 4 = y$

Replace y by $G^{-1}(x)$: $G^{-1}(x) = \sqrt[3]{x} + 4$

50. a)

The function is one-to-one.

b) $y = (x + 5)^3$ Replace $G(x)$.

$x = (y + 5)^3$ Interchange variables.

$\sqrt[3]{x} - 5 = y$ Solve for y.

$G^{-1}(x) = \sqrt[3]{x} - 5$ Replace y.

51. a) The graph of $f(x) = \sqrt[3]{x}$ is shown below. It passes the horizontal line test, so the function is one-to-one.

b) Replace $f(x)$ by y: $y = \sqrt[3]{x}$

Interchange x and y: $x = \sqrt[3]{y}$

Solve for y: $x^3 = y$

Replace y by $f^{-1}(x)$: $f^{-1}(x) = x^3$

52. a)

The function is one-to-one.

b) $y = \sqrt[3]{x - 8}$ Replace $f(x)$.

$x = \sqrt[3]{y - 8}$ Interchange variables.

$x^3 + 8 = y$ Solve for y.

$f^{-1}(x) = x^3 + 8$ Replace y.

53. a) The graph of $f(x) = 4x^2 + 3$, $x > 3$, is shown below. It passes the horizontal line test, so the function is one-to-one.

b) Replace $f(x)$ by y: $y = 4x^2 + 3$

Interchange x and y: $x = 4y^2 + 3$

Solve for y: $x - 3 = 4y^2$

$\dfrac{x - 3}{4} = y^2$

$\dfrac{\sqrt{x - 3}}{2} = y$

(We take the principal square root since $x > 3$ in the original function.)

Replace y by $f^{-1}(x)$: $f^{-1}(x) = \dfrac{\sqrt{x - 3}}{2}$
for all x in the range of $f(x)$, or

$f^{-1}(x) = \dfrac{\sqrt{x - 3}}{2}$, $x > 39$

54. a)

The function is one-to-one.

b) $y = 5x^2 - 2$ Replace $f(x)$.

$x = 5y^2 - 2$ Interchange variables

$\sqrt{\dfrac{x + 2}{5}} = y$ Solve for y, taking the principal square root since $x > 2$ in the original function.

$f^{-1}(x) = \sqrt{\dfrac{x + 2}{5}}$, $x > 18$ Replace y. Restrict the domain of $f^{-1}(x)$ to the range of $f(x)$.

55. a) The graph of $f(x) = \sqrt{x + 1}$ is shown below. It passes the horizontal line test, so the function is one-to-one.

b) Replace $f(x)$ by y: $y = \sqrt{x + 1}$

Interchange x and y: $x = \sqrt{y + 1}$

Solve for y: $x^2 = y + 1$

$x^2 - 1 = y$

Replace y by $f^{-1}(x)$: $f^{-1}(x) = x^2 - 1$ for all x in the range of $f(x)$, or $f^{-1}(x) = x^2 - 1$, $x \geqslant 0$.

56. a)

The function is one-to-one.

b) $y = \sqrt{2x - 3}$ Replace $g(x)$.

$x = \sqrt{2y - 3}$ Interchange variables.

$\dfrac{x^2 + 3}{2} = y$ Solve for y.

$g^{-1}(x) = \dfrac{x^2 + 3}{2}$, $x \geqslant 0$ Replace y, restricting the domain of $g^{-1}(x)$ to the range of $g(x)$.

57. Only c) passes the horizontal line test, and thus has an inverse that is a function.

58. Only d) passes the horizontal line test.

59. First graph $f(x) = \frac{1}{2}x - 4$. Then graph the inverse by flipping the graph of $f(x) = \frac{1}{2}x - 4$ over the line $y = x$. The graph of the inverse function can also be found by first finding a formula for the inverse and then substituting to find function values.

60.

61. Use the procedure described in Exercise 59 to graph the function and its inverse.

62.

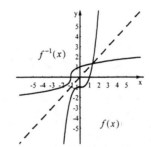

63. Use the procedure described in Exercise 59 to graph the function and its inverse.

64.

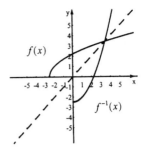

65. Use the procedure described in Exercise 59 to graph the function and its inverse.

66.

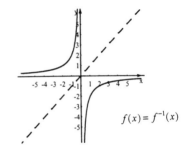

67. Use the procedure described in Exercise 59 to graph the function and its inverse.

68.

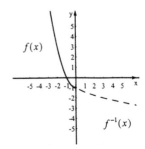

69. We find $f^{-1} \circ f(x)$ and $f \circ f^{-1}(x)$ and check to see that each is x.

   a) $f^{-1} \circ f(x) = f^{-1}(f(x)) = f^{-1}\left[\frac{7}{8}x\right] = \frac{8}{7}\left[\frac{7}{8}x\right] = x$

   b) $f \circ f^{-1}(x) = f(f^{-1}(x)) = f\left[\frac{8}{7}x\right] = \frac{7}{8}\left[\frac{8}{7}x\right] = x$

70. a) $f^{-1} \circ f(x) = 4\left[\frac{x+5}{4}\right] - 5 = x + 5 - 5 = x$

   b) $f \circ f^{-1}(x) = \frac{4x - 5 + 5}{4} = \frac{4x}{4} = x$

71. We find $f^{-1} \circ f(x)$ and $f \circ f^{-1}(x)$ and check to see that each is x.

   a) $f^{-1} \circ f(x) = f^{-1}(f(x)) = f^{-1}\left[\frac{1-x}{x}\right] =$

   $\dfrac{1}{\dfrac{1-x}{x} + 1} = \dfrac{1}{\dfrac{1-x+x}{x}} = \dfrac{1}{\dfrac{1}{x}} = x$

   b) $f \circ f^{-1}(x) = f(f^{-1}(x)) = f\left[\frac{1}{x+1}\right] =$

   $\dfrac{1 - \dfrac{1}{x+1}}{\dfrac{1}{x+1}} = \dfrac{\dfrac{x+1-1}{x+1}}{\dfrac{1}{x+1}} = \dfrac{\dfrac{x}{x+1}}{\dfrac{1}{x+1}} = x$

72. a) $f^{-1} \circ f(x) = \sqrt[3]{x^3 - 4 + 4} = \sqrt[3]{x^3} = x$

   b) $f \circ f^{-1}(x) = \left(\sqrt[3]{x+4}\right)^3 - 4 = x + 4 - 4 = x$

73. Using Theorem 1 we have
   $f^{-1}(f(3)) = 3$ and $f(f^{-1}(-125)) = -125$.

74. 5; -12 (Using Theorem 1)

75. Using Theorem 1, we have
   $f^{-1}(f(12,053)) = 12,053$ and $f(f^{-1}(-17,243)) = -17,243$.

76. 489; -17,422 (Using Theorem 1)

77. a) $f(8) = 8 + 32 = 40$

   Size 40 in France corresponds to size 8 in the U.S.

   $f(10) = 10 + 32 = 42$

   Size 42 in France corresponds to size 10 in the U.S.

   $f(14) = 14 + 32 = 46$

   Size 46 in France corresponds to size 14 in the U.S.

   $f(18) = 18 + 32 = 50$

   Size 50 in France corresponds to size 18 in the U.S.

b) The graph of f(x) = x + 32 is shown below.

f(x) = x + 32

It passes the horizontal line test, so the function is one-to-one and, hence, has an inverse that is a function. We now find a formula for the inverse.

Replace f(x) by y: y = x + 32

Interchange x and y: x = y + 32

Solve for y: x - 32 = y

Replace y by f⁻¹(x): f⁻¹(x) = x - 32

c) f⁻¹(40) = 40 - 32 = 8

Size 8 in the U.S. corresponds to size 40 in France.

f⁻¹(42) = 42 - 32 = 10
Size 10 in the U.S. corresponds to size 42 in France.

f⁻¹(46) = 46 - 32 = 14

Size 14 in the U.S. corresponds to size 46 in France.

f⁻¹(50) = 50 - 32 = 18

Size 18 in the U.S. corresponds to size 50 in France.

78. a) g(8) = 2(8 + 12) = 2·20 = 40

g(10) = 2(10 + 12) = 2·22 = 44

g(14) = 2(14 + 12) = 2·26 = 52

g(18) = 2(18 + 12) = 2·30 = 60

b) The graph of g(x) = 2(x + 12) is a straight line with intercepts (0,24) and (-12,0). Therefore, it passes the horizontal line test and has an inverse that is a function.

y = 2(x + 12)   Replace g(x).

x = 2(y + 12)   Interchange variables.

$\frac{x - 24}{2}$ = y   Solve for y.

g⁻¹(x) = $\frac{x - 24}{2}$, or $\frac{x}{2}$ - 12   Replace y.

c) g⁻¹(40) = $\frac{40 - 24}{2}$ = $\frac{16}{2}$ = 8

g⁻¹(44) = $\frac{44 - 24}{2}$ = $\frac{20}{2}$ = 10

g⁻¹(52) = $\frac{52 - 24}{2}$ = $\frac{28}{2}$ = 14

g⁻¹(60) = $\frac{60 - 24}{2}$ = $\frac{36}{2}$ = 18

79. The graph of f(x) = 5 is shown below. Since the horizontal line y = 5 crosses the graph in more than one place, the function does not have an inverse that is a function.

80. C(x) = $\frac{100 + 5x}{x}$

y = $\frac{100 + 5x}{x}$ Replace C(x).

x = $\frac{100 + 5y}{y}$ Interchange variables.

y = $\frac{100}{x - 5}$ Solve for y.

C⁻¹(x) = $\frac{100}{x - 5}$

C⁻¹(x) gives the number of people in the group, where x is the cost per person, in dollars.

81. Check to see if g ∘ f(x) = x and f ∘ g(x) = x.

a) g ∘ f(x) = g(f(x)) = g$\left(\frac{2}{3}\right)$ = $\frac{3}{2}$

Since g ∘ f(x) ≠ x, the functions are not inverses of each other.

82. a) g ∘ f(x) = (⁵√x)⁵ = x

b) f ∘ g(x) = ⁵√x⁵ = x

The functions are inverses of each other.

83. Check to see if g ∘ f(x) = x and f ∘ g(x) = x.

a) g ∘ f(x) = g(f(x)) = g(⁴√x) = (⁴√x)⁴ = x

b) f ∘ g(x) = f(g(x)) = f(x⁴) = ⁴√x⁴ = |x|

For x < 0, |x| = -x and f ∘ g(x) ≠ x.

The functions are not inverses of each other.

84. a) g ∘ f(x) = $\frac{7\left[\frac{2x - 5}{4x + 7}\right] - 4}{5\left[\frac{2x - 3}{4x + 7}\right] + 2}$

= $\frac{14x - 35 - 16x - 28}{10x - 15 + 8x + 14}$ = $\frac{-2x - 63}{18x - 1}$ ≠ x

The functions are not inverses of each other.

85. Answers may vary. f(x) = $\frac{3}{x}$, f(x) = 1 - x, f(x) = x

86. Consider any two inputs a and b, a < b, of an increasing function f(x). Then f(a) < f(b). Thus, if a ≠ b, f(a) ≠ f(b) and the function is one-to-one.

87. Graph $y = \frac{1}{x^2}$.

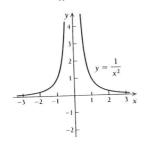

Test $y = \frac{1}{x^2}$ for symmetry with respect to the x-axis.

Replace y by $-y$: $-y = \frac{1}{x^2}$

Since $y = \frac{1}{x^2}$ is not equivalent to $-y = \frac{1}{x^2}$, $y = \frac{1}{x^2}$ is not symmetric with respect to the x-axis.

Test $y = \frac{1}{x^2}$ for symmetry with respect to the y-axis.

Replace x by $-x$: $y = \frac{1}{(-x)^2} = \frac{1}{x^2}$

Since the equations are equivalent, $y = \frac{1}{x^2}$ is symmetric with respect to the y-axis.

Test $y = \frac{1}{x^2}$ for symmetry with respect to the origin.

Replace x by $-x$ and y by $-y$: $-y = \frac{1}{(-x)^2} = \frac{1}{x^2}$

Since $y = \frac{1}{x^2}$ is not equivalent to $-y = \frac{1}{x^2}$, $y = \frac{1}{x^2}$ is not symmetric with respect to the origin.

88. C and F are inverses.

89.

 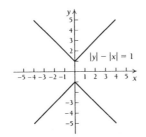

Test $|x| - |y| = 1$ for symmetry with respect to the x-axis.

Replace y by $-y$: $|x| - |-y| = 1$
$$|x| - |y| = 1$$

Since the equations are equivalent, $|x| - |y| = 1$ is symmetric with respect to the x-axis.

Test $|x| - |y| = 1$ for symmetry with respect to the y-axis.

Replace x by $-x$: $|-x| - |y| = 1$
$$|x| - |y| = 1$$

Since the equations are equivalent, $|x| - |y| = 1$ is symmetric with respect to the y-axis.

Test $|x| - |y| = 1$ for symmetry with respect to the origin:

Replace x by $-x$ and y by $-y$: $|-x| - |-y| = 1$
$$|x| - |y| = 1$$

Since the equations are equivalent, $|x| - |y| = 1$ is symmetric with respect to the origin.

90. a) The inverse of the given function $y = \frac{|x|}{x}$ is $x = \frac{|y|}{y}$.

The graphs are as shown:

$y = \frac{|x|}{x}$

b) Each of the two graphs is symmetric with respect to the origin. Neither is symmetric with respect to the x-axis or the y-axis.

91. The function fails the horizontal line test. Thus it is not one-to-one and does not have an inverse that is a function.

92.
$$f(x) = (3x - 9)^3$$
$$f^{-1}(x) = \frac{\sqrt[3]{x} + 9}{3}$$

[-9, 9] x [-6, 6]

The function passes the horizontal line test, so it is one-to-one. We find the inverse function.

$y = (3x - 9)^3$

$x = (3y - 9)^3$ Interchange variables.

$y = \frac{\sqrt[3]{x} + 9}{3}$ Solve for y.

93. $f(x) = \sqrt{2x - 1}$

   $f^{-1}(x) = \dfrac{x^2 + 1}{2}$

[0, 6] x [0, 4]

The function passes the horizontal line test, so it is one-to-one. We find the inverse function.

$y = \sqrt{2x - 1}$

$x = \sqrt{2y - 1}$ Interchange x and y.

$x^2 = 2y - 1$ Solve for y.

$x^2 + 1 = 2y$

$\dfrac{x^2 + 1}{2} = y,\ x \geqslant 0$ Restrict the domain of the inverse function to the range of the original function.

94. The function passes the horizontal line test, so it is one-to-one. We find the inverse function.

$y = \sqrt[4]{90x}$

$x = \sqrt[4]{90y}$ Interchange variables.

$y = \dfrac{x^4}{90},\ x \geqslant 0$ Solve for y. Restrict the domain of the inverse function to the range of the original function.

Exercise Set 5.2

---

1. Graph: $y = 2^x$

   We compute some function values, thinking of y as f(x), and keep the results in a table.

   $f(0) = 2^0 = 1$

   $f(1) = 2^1 = 2$

   $f(2) = 2^2 = 4$

   $f(-1) = 2^{-1} = \dfrac{1}{2^1} = \dfrac{1}{2}$

   $f(-2) = 2^{-2} = \dfrac{1}{2^2} = \dfrac{1}{4}$

x	y, or f(x)
0	1
1	2
2	4
-1	$\dfrac{1}{2}$
-2	$\dfrac{1}{4}$

   Next we plot these points and connect them with a smooth curve.

$y = f(x) = 2^x$

2.

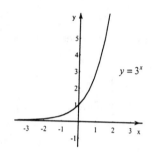

$y = 3^x$

3. Graph: $y = 5^x$

   We compute some function values, thinking of y as f(x), and keep the results in a table.

   $f(0) = 5^0 = 1$

   $f(1) = 5^1 = 5$

   $f(2) = 5^2 = 25$

   $f(-1) = 5^{-1} = \dfrac{1}{5^1} = \dfrac{1}{5}$

   $f(-2) = 5^{-2} = \dfrac{1}{5^2} = \dfrac{1}{25}$

x	y, or f(x)
0	1
1	5
2	25
-1	$\dfrac{1}{5}$
-2	$\dfrac{1}{25}$

   Next we plot these points and connect them with a smooth curve.

$y = 5^x$

4.

$y = 6^x$

5. Graph: $y = 2^{x+1}$

We compute some function values, thinking of y as f(x), and keep the results in a table.

$f(0) = 2^{0+1} = 2^1 = 2$

$f(-1) = 2^{-1+1} = 2^0 = 1$

$f(-2) = 2^{-2+1} = 2^{-1} = \frac{1}{2^1} = \frac{1}{2}$

$f(-3) = 2^{-3+1} = 2^{-2} = \frac{1}{2^2} = \frac{1}{4}$

$f(1) = 2^{1+1} = 2^2 = 4$

$f(2) = 2^{2+1} = 2^3 = 8$

x	y, or f(x)
0	2
-1	1
-2	$\frac{1}{2}$
-3	$\frac{1}{4}$
1	4
2	8

Next we plot these points and connect them with a smooth curve.

6.

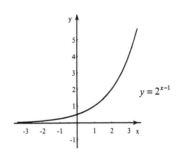

7. Graph: $y = 3^{x-2}$

We compute some function values, thinking of y as f(x), and keep the results in a table.

$f(0) = 3^{0-2} = 3^{-2} = \frac{1}{3^2} = \frac{1}{9}$

$f(1) = 3^{1-2} = 3^{-1} = \frac{1}{3^1} = \frac{1}{3}$

$f(2) = 3^{2-2} = 3^0 = 1$

$f(3) = 3^{3-2} = 3^1 = 3$

$f(4) = 3^{4-2} = 3^2 = 9$

$f(-1) = 3^{-1-2} = 3^{-3} = \frac{1}{3^3} = \frac{1}{27}$

$f(-2) = 3^{-2-2} = 3^{-4} = \frac{1}{3^4} = \frac{1}{81}$

x	y, or f(x)
0	$\frac{1}{9}$
1	$\frac{1}{3}$
2	1
3	3
4	9
-1	$\frac{1}{27}$
-2	$\frac{1}{81}$

Next we plot these points and connect them with a smooth curve.

8.

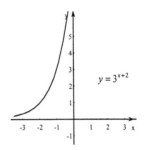

9. Graph: $y = 2^x - 3$

We construct a table of values, thinking of y as f(x). Then we plot the points and connect them with a smooth curve.

$f(0) = 2^0 - 3 = 1 - 3 = -2$

$f(1) = 2^1 - 3 = 2 - 3 = -1$

$f(2) = 2^2 - 3 = 4 - 3 = 1$

$f(3) = 2^3 - 3 = 8 - 3 = 5$

$f(-1) = 2^{-1} - 3 = \frac{1}{2} - 3 = -\frac{5}{2}$

$f(-2) = 2^{-2} - 3 = \frac{1}{4} - 3 = -\frac{11}{4}$

x	y, or f(x)
0	-2
1	-1
2	1
3	5
-1	$-\frac{5}{2}$
-2	$-\frac{11}{4}$

10.

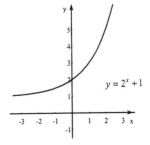

11. Graph: $y = 5^{x+3}$

We construct a table of values, thinking of y as f(x). Then we plot the points and connect them with a smooth curve.

$f(0) = 5^{0+3} = 5^3 = 125$
$f(-1) = 5^{-1+3} = 5^2 = 25$
$f(-2) = 5^{-2+3} = 5^1 = 5$
$f(-3) = 5^{-3+3} = 5^0 = 1$
$f(-4) = 5^{-4+3} = 5^{-1} = \frac{1}{5}$
$f(-5) = 5^{-5+3} = 5^{-2} = \frac{1}{25}$

x	y, or f(x)
0	125
-1	25
-2	5
-3	1
-4	$\frac{1}{5}$
-5	$\frac{1}{25}$

12.

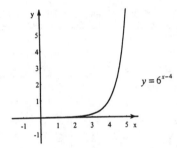

$y = 6^{x-4}$

13. Graph: $y = \left(\frac{1}{2}\right)^{x}$

We construct a table of values, thinking of y as f(x). Then we plot the points and connect them with a smooth curve.

$f(0) = \left(\frac{1}{2}\right)^0 = 1$

$f(1) = \left(\frac{1}{2}\right)^1 = \frac{1}{2}$

$f(2) = \left(\frac{1}{2}\right)^2 = \frac{1}{4}$

$f(3) = \left(\frac{1}{2}\right)^3 = \frac{1}{8}$

$f(-1) = \left(\frac{1}{2}\right)^{-1} = \frac{1}{\left(\frac{1}{2}\right)^1} = \frac{1}{\frac{1}{2}} = 2$

$f(-2) = \left(\frac{1}{2}\right)^{-2} = \frac{1}{\left(\frac{1}{2}\right)^2} = \frac{1}{\frac{1}{4}} = 4$

$f(-3) = \left(\frac{1}{2}\right)^{-3} = \frac{1}{\left(\frac{1}{2}\right)^3} = \frac{1}{\frac{1}{8}} = 8$

x	y, or f(x)
0	1
1	$\frac{1}{2}$
2	$\frac{1}{4}$
3	$\frac{1}{8}$
-1	2
-2	4
-3	8

$y = \left(\frac{1}{2}\right)^x$

$y = \left(\frac{1}{3}\right)^x$

14.

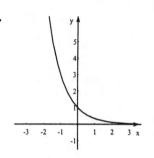

15. Graph: $y = \left(\frac{1}{5}\right)^{x}$

We construct a table of values, thinking of y as f(x). Then we plot the points and connect them with a smooth curve.

$f(0) = \left(\frac{1}{5}\right)^0 = 1$

$f(1) = \left(\frac{1}{5}\right)^1 = \frac{1}{5}$

$f(2) = \left(\frac{1}{5}\right)^2 = \frac{1}{25}$

$f(-1) = \left(\frac{1}{5}\right)^{-1} = \frac{1}{\frac{1}{5}} = 5$

$f(-2) = \left(\frac{1}{5}\right)^{-2} = \frac{1}{\frac{1}{25}} = 25$

x	y, or f(x)
0	1
1	$\frac{1}{5}$
2	$\frac{1}{25}$
-1	5
-2	25

$y = \left(\frac{1}{5}\right)^x$

16.

$y = \left(\frac{1}{4}\right)^x$

17. Graph: $y = 2^{2x-1}$

We construct a table of values, thinking of y as f(x). Then we plot the points and connect them with a smooth curve.

$f(0) = 2^{2 \cdot 0 - 1} = 2^{-1} = \frac{1}{2}$

$f(1) = 2^{2 \cdot 1 - 1} = 2^1 = 2$

$f(2) = 2^{2 \cdot 2 - 1} = 2^3 = 8$

$f(-1) = 2^{2(-1)-1} = 2^{-3} = \frac{1}{8}$

$f(-2) = 2^{2(-2)-1} = 2^{-5} = \frac{1}{32}$

x	y, or f(x)
0	$\frac{1}{2}$
1	2
2	8
-1	$\frac{1}{8}$
-2	$\frac{1}{32}$

x	y, or f(x)
0	$-\frac{5}{2}$
1	-2
2	-1
3	1
4	5
-1	$-\frac{11}{4}$
-2	$-\frac{23}{8}$

18.

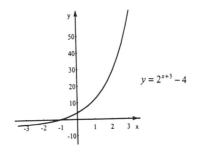

19. Graph: $y = 2^{x-1} - 3$

We construct a table of values, thinking of y as f(x). Then we plot the points and connect them with a smooth curve.

$f(0) = 2^{0-1} - 3 = 2^{-1} - 3 = \frac{1}{2} - 3 = -\frac{5}{2}$

$f(1) = 2^{1-1} - 3 = 2^0 - 3 = 1 - 3 = -2$

$f(2) = 2^{2-1} - 3 = 2^1 - 3 = 2 - 3 = -1$

$f(3) = 2^{3-1} - 3 = 2^2 - 3 = 4 - 3 = 1$

$f(4) = 2^{4-1} - 3 = 2^3 - 3 = 8 - 3 = 5$

$f(-1) = 2^{-1-1} - 3 = 2^{-2} - 3 = \frac{1}{4} - 3 = -\frac{11}{4}$

$f(-2) = 2^{-2-1} - 3 = 2^{-3} - 3 = \frac{1}{8} - 3 = -\frac{23}{8}$

20.

21. Graph: $x = 2^y$

We can find ordered pairs by choosing values for y and then computing values for x.

For $y = 0$, $x = 2^0 = 1$.

For $y = 1$, $x = 2^1 = 2$.

For $y = 2$, $x = 2^2 = 4$.

For $y = 3$, $x = 2^3 = 8$.

For $y = -1$, $x = 2^{-1} = \frac{1}{2^1} = \frac{1}{2}$.

For $y = -2$, $x = 2^{-2} = \frac{1}{2^2} = \frac{1}{4}$.

For $y = -3$, $x = 2^{-3} = \frac{1}{2^3} = \frac{1}{8}$.

x	y
1	0
2	1
4	2
8	3
$\frac{1}{2}$	-1
$\frac{1}{4}$	-2
$\frac{1}{8}$	-3

(1) Choose values for y.

(2) Compute values for x.

22.

$x = 6^y$

23. Graph: $x = \left(\frac{1}{2}\right)^y$

We can find ordered pairs by choosing values for
y and then computing values for x. Then we plot
these points and connect them with a smooth curve.

For y = 0, $x = \left(\frac{1}{2}\right)^0 = 1.$

For y = 1, $x = \left(\frac{1}{2}\right)^1 = \frac{1}{2}.$

For y = 2, $x = \left(\frac{1}{2}\right)^2 = \frac{1}{4}.$

For y = 3, $x = \left(\frac{1}{2}\right)^3 = \frac{1}{8}.$

For y = -1, $x = \left(\frac{1}{2}\right)^{-1} = \frac{1}{\frac{1}{2}} = 2.$

For y = -2, $x = \left(\frac{1}{2}\right)^{-2} = \frac{1}{\frac{1}{4}} = 4.$

For y = -3, $x = \left(\frac{1}{2}\right)^{-3} = \frac{1}{\frac{1}{8}} = 8.$

x	y
1	0
$\frac{1}{2}$	1
$\frac{1}{4}$	2
$\frac{1}{8}$	3
2	-1
4	-2
8	-3

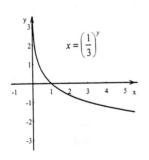

$x = \left(\frac{1}{2}\right)^y$

24.

$x = \left(\frac{1}{3}\right)^y$

25. Graph: $x = 5^y$

We can find ordered pairs by choosing values for
y and then computing values for x. Then we plot
these points and connect them with a smooth curve.

For y = 0, $x = 5^0 = 1.$

For y = 1, $x = 5^1 = 5.$

For y = 2, $x = 5^2 = 25.$

For y = -1, $x = 5^{-1} = \frac{1}{5}.$

For y = -2, $x = 5^{-2} = \frac{1}{25}.$

x	y
1	0
5	1
25	2
$\frac{1}{5}$	-1
$\frac{1}{25}$	-2

$x = 5^y$

26.

$x = 3^y$

27. Graph: $x = \left(\frac{2}{3}\right)^y$

We can find ordered pairs by choosing values for
y and then computing values for x. Then we plot
these points and connect them with a smooth curve.

For y = 0, $x = \left(\frac{2}{3}\right)^0 = 1.$

For y = 1, $x = \left(\frac{2}{3}\right)^1 = \frac{2}{3}.$

For y = 2, $x = \left(\frac{2}{3}\right)^2 = \frac{4}{9}.$

For y = 3, $x = \left(\frac{2}{3}\right)^3 = \frac{8}{27}.$

For y = -1, $x = \left(\frac{2}{3}\right)^{-1} = \frac{1}{\frac{2}{3}} = \frac{3}{2}.$

For y = -2, $x = \left(\frac{2}{3}\right)^{-2} = \frac{1}{\frac{4}{9}} = \frac{9}{4}.$

For y = -3, $x = \left(\frac{2}{3}\right)^{-3} = \frac{1}{\frac{8}{27}} = \frac{27}{8}.$

x	y
1	0
$\frac{2}{3}$	1
$\frac{4}{9}$	2
$\frac{8}{27}$	3
$\frac{3}{2}$	-1
$\frac{9}{4}$	-2
$\frac{27}{8}$	-3

$x = \left(\frac{2}{3}\right)^y$

28.

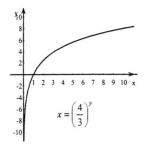

$$x = \left(\frac{4}{3}\right)^y$$

29. Graph $y = 2^x$ (see Exercise 1) and $x = 2^y$ (see Exercise 21) using the same set of axes.

30.

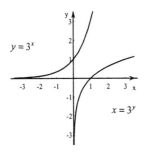

31. Graph $y = \left[\frac{1}{2}\right]^x$ (see Exercise 13) and $x = \left[\frac{1}{2}\right]^y$ (see Exercise 23) using the same set of axes.

32.

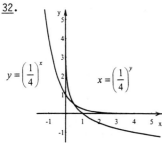

33. a) Keep in mind that t represents the number of years after 1985 and that N is given in millions.

For 1986, t = 1:
$$N(1) = 7.5(6)^{0.5(1)} = 7.5(6)^{0.5} \approx 18.4 \text{ million};$$

For 1987, t = 1987 - 1985, or 2:
$$N(2) = 7.5(6)^{0.5(2)} = 7.5(6) = 45 \text{ million};$$

For 1990, t = 1990 - 1985, or 5:
$$N(5) = 7.5(6)^{0.5(5)} = 7.5(6)^{2.5} \approx 661.4 \text{ million};$$

For 1995, t = 1995 - 1985, or 10:
$$N(10) = 7.5(6)^{0.5(10)} = 7.5(6)^5 = 58,320 \text{ million};$$

For 2000, t = 2000 - 1985, or 15:
$$N(15) = 7.5(6)^{0.5(15)} = 7.5(6)^{7.5} \approx 5,142,752.7 \text{ million}$$

b) Use the function values computed in part (a) to draw the graph of the function.

34. a) $N(10) = 3000(2)^{10/20} \approx 4243$;
$N(20) = 3000(2)^{20/20} = 6000$;
$N(30) = 3000(2)^{30/20} \approx 8485$;
$N(40) = 3000(2)^{40/20} = 12,000$;
$N(60) = 3000(2)^{60/20} = 24,000$

b)

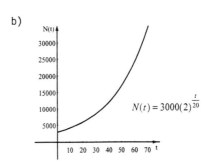

35. a) Substitute $50,000 for P and 9%, or 0.09, for
         i in the formula $A = P(1 + i)^t$:
         $A(t) = \$50,000(1 + 0.09)^t = \$50,000(1.09)^t$

     b) Substitute for t.
         $A(0) = \$50,000(1.09)^0 = \$50,000$;
         $A(4) = \$50,000(1.09)^4 \approx \$70,579.08$;
         $A(8) = \$50,000(1.09)^8 \approx \$99,628.13$;
         $A(10) = \$50,000(1.09)^{10} \approx \$118,368.18$

     c) We use the function values computed in part
         (b) to draw the graph. Note that the axes
         are scaled differently because of the large
         numbers.

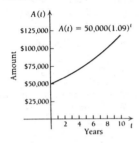

36. a) $N(0) = 250,000\left(\frac{1}{4}\right)^0 = 250,000$;

         $N(1) = 250,000\left(\frac{1}{4}\right)^1 = 62,500$;

         $N(4) = 250,000\left(\frac{1}{4}\right)^4 \approx 977$;

         $N(10) = 250,000\left(\frac{1}{4}\right)^{10} \approx 0$

     b)

37. a) Substitute for t.

         $V(0) = \$5200(0.75)^0 = \$5200$;
         $V(1) = \$5200(0.75)^1 = \$3900$;
         $V(2) = \$5200(0.75)^2 = \$2925$;
         $V(5) = \$5200(0.75)^5 \approx \$1233.98$;
         $V(10) = \$5200(0.75)^{10} \approx \$292.83$

     b) Use the function values computed in part (a)
         to draw the graph of the function.

38. a) $N(3) = 2.3(3)^{0.033(3)} \approx 2.6$ lb;
         $N(13) = 2.3(3)^{0.033(13)} \approx 3.7$ lb;
         $N(59) = 2.3(3)^{0.033(59)} \approx 19.5$ lb;
         $N(70) = 2.3(3)^{0.033(70)} \approx 29.1$ lb

     b)

39. Use a calculator.

     a) $7^3 = 343$

     b) $7^{3.1} \approx 416.681217$

     c) $7^{3.14} \approx 450.409815$

     d) $7^{3.141} \approx 451.287125$

     e) $7^{3.1415} \approx 451.726421$

     f) $7^{3.14159} \approx 451.805540$

40. $7^\pi \approx 451.807873$ and $\pi^7 \approx 3020.293228$, so π^7 is
     larger.

41. Since the bases are the same, the one with the
     larger exponent is the larger number. Thus
     $\pi^{3.2}$ is larger.

42.

43. Graph: $f(x) = (2.7)^x$

     Use a calculator with a power key to construct
     a table of values. (We will round values to the
     nearest hundredth.) Then plot these points and
     connect them with a smooth curve.

x	f(x)
0	1
1	2.7
2	7.29
3	19.68
-1	0.37
-2	0.14

44.

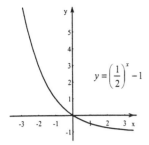

$$y = \left(\frac{1}{2}\right)^x - 1$$

x	y, or f(x)
0	2
1	$3\frac{1}{3}$
2	$9\frac{1}{9}$
-1	$3\frac{1}{3}$
-2	$9\frac{1}{9}$

$y = 3^x + 3^{-x}$

45. Graph: $y = 2^x + 2^{-x}$

Construct a table of values, thinking of y as f(x). Then plot these points and connect them with a curve.

$f(0) = 2^0 + 2^{-0} = 1 + 1 = 2$

$f(1) = 2^1 + 2^{-1} = 2 + \frac{1}{2} = 2\frac{1}{2}$

$f(2) = 2^2 + 2^{-2} = 4 + \frac{1}{4} = 4\frac{1}{4}$

$f(3) = 2^3 + 2^{-3} = 8 + \frac{1}{8} = 8\frac{1}{8}$

$f(-1) = 2^{-1} + 2^{-(-1)} = \frac{1}{2} + 2 = 2\frac{1}{2}$

$f(-2) = 2^{-2} + 2^{-(-2)} = \frac{1}{4} + 4 = 4\frac{1}{4}$

$f(-3) = 2^{-3} + 2^{-(-3)} = \frac{1}{8} + 8 = 8\frac{1}{8}$

x	y, or f(x)
0	2
1	$2\frac{1}{2}$
2	$4\frac{1}{4}$
3	$8\frac{1}{8}$
-1	$2\frac{1}{2}$
-2	$4\frac{1}{4}$
-3	$8\frac{1}{8}$

$y = 2^x + 2^{-x}$

46.

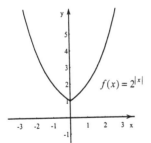

$f(x) = 2^{|x|}$

47. Graph: $y = 3^x + 3^{-x}$

We construct a table of values, thinking of y as f(x). Then plot these points and connect them with a curve.

$f(0) = 3^0 + 3^{-0} = 1 + 1 = 2$

$f(1) = 3^1 + 3^{-1} = 3 + \frac{1}{3} = 3\frac{1}{3}$

$f(2) = 3^2 + 3^{-2} = 9 + \frac{1}{9} = 9\frac{1}{9}$

$f(-1) = 3^{-1} + 3^{-(-1)} = \frac{1}{3} + 3 = 3\frac{1}{3}$

$f(-2) = 3^{-2} + 3^{-(-2)} = \frac{1}{9} + 9 = 9\frac{1}{9}$

48.

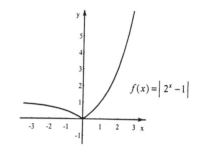

$f(x) = \left| 2^x - 1 \right|$

49. Graph: $y = 2^{-(x-1)}$

We construct a table of values, thinking of y as f(x). Then plot these points and connect them with a curve.

$f(0) = 2^{-(0-1)} = 2^1 = 2$

$f(1) = 2^{-(1-1)} = 2^0 = 1$

$f(2) = 2^{-(2-1)} = 2^{-1} = \frac{1}{2}$

$f(4) = 2^{-(4-1)} = 2^{-3} = \frac{1}{8}$

$f(-1) = 2^{-(-1-1)} = 2^2 = 4$

$f(-2) = 2^{-(-2-1)} = 2^3 = 8$

x	y, or f(x)
0	2
1	1
2	$\frac{1}{2}$
4	$\frac{1}{8}$
-1	4
-2	8

$y = 2^{-(x-1)}$

50.

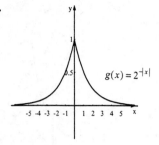

$g(x) = 2^{-|x|}$

51. Graph $y = |2^x - 2|$

We construct a table of values, thinking of y as f(x). Then plot these points and connect them with a curve.

$f(0) = |2^0 - 2| = |1 - 2| = 1$

$f(1) = |2^1 - 2| = |2 - 2| = 0$

$f(2) = |2^2 - 2| = |4 - 2| = 2$

$f(3) = |2^3 - 2| = |8 - 2| = 6$

$f(-1) = |2^{-1} - 2| = \left|\frac{1}{2} - 2\right| = \frac{3}{2}$

$f(-2) = |2^{-2} - 2| = \left|\frac{1}{4} - 2\right| = \frac{7}{4}$

$f(-4) = |2^{-4} - 2| = \left|\frac{1}{16} - 2\right| = \frac{31}{16}$

x	y, or f(x)
0	1
1	0
2	2
3	6
-1	$\frac{3}{2}$
-2	$\frac{7}{4}$
-4	$\frac{31}{16}$

$y = |2^x - 2|$

52.

$y = 1^x$

$x = 1^y$

53. $y = 3^{-(x-1)}$ $x = 3^{-(y-1)}$

x	y
0	3
1	1
2	$\frac{1}{3}$
3	$\frac{1}{9}$
-1	9

x	y
3	0
1	1
$\frac{1}{3}$	2
$\frac{1}{9}$	3
9	-1

$x = 3^{-(y-1)}$

$y = 3^{-(x-1)}$

54.

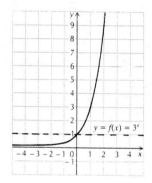

$y = f(x) = 3^x$

$\{x | x \leqslant 0\}$

55. First we graph $y = 2^x$.

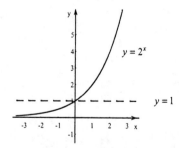

$y = 2^x$

$y = 1$

Then we study the graph to see which inputs give outputs greater than 1. (These are the inputs whose outputs are above the dashed line y = 1.) We see that all inputs greater than 0 give outputs greater than 1. The solution set is {x|x > 0}.

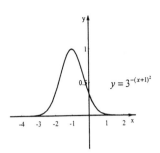

56. a) We substitute for t.

$S(10) = 200[1 - (0.86)^{10}] \approx 155.7$ words per minute;

$S(20) = 200[1 - (0.86)^{20}] \approx 190.2$ words per minute;

$S(40) = 200[1 - (0.86)^{40}] \approx 199.5$ words per minute;

$S(100) = 200[1 - (0.86)^{100}] \approx 199.9999$ words per minute

b) Use the function values computed in part (a) to draw the graph of the function.

x	y
0	$\frac{1}{3}$
1	$\frac{1}{81}$
-1	1
-2	$\frac{1}{3}$
-3	$\frac{1}{81}$

59. Graph: $y = |2^{x^2} - 8|$

$f(-3) = |2^{(-3)^2} - 8| = |2^9 - 8| = 504$

$f(-2) = |2^{(-2)^2} - 8| = |2^4 - 8| = 8$

$f(-1) = |2^{(-1)^2} - 8| = |2^1 - 8| = 6$

$f(0) = |2^{0^2} - 8| = |2^0 - 8| = 7$

$f(1) = |2^{1^2} - 8| = |2^1 - 8| = 6$

$f(2) = |2^{2^2} - 8| = |2^4 - 8| = 8$

$f(3) = |2^{3^2} - 8| = |2^9 - 8| = 504$

57. Graph: $y = 2^{-x^2}$

$f(-3) = 2^{-3^2} = 2^{-9} = \frac{1}{512}$

$f(-2) = 2^{-2^2} = 2^{-4} = \frac{1}{16}$

$f(-1) = 2^{-1^2} = 2^{-1} = \frac{1}{2}$

$f(0) = 2^{-0^2} = 2^0 = 1$

$f(1) = 2^{-1^2} = 2^{-1} = \frac{1}{2}$

$f(2) = 2^{-2^2} = 2^{-4} = \frac{1}{16}$

x	y, or f(x)
-3	$\frac{1}{512}$
-2	$\frac{1}{16}$
-1	$\frac{1}{2}$
0	1
1	$\frac{1}{2}$
2	$\frac{1}{16}$

x	y, or f(x)
-3	504
-2	8
-1	6
0	7
1	6
2	8
3	504

60. a) $A(t) = \$1,000,000(1.0885)^t$

b) 10.1 yr

c) 13.0 yr

d) $2,440,000

58. Graph: $y = f(x) = 3^{-(x+1)^2}$

$f(0) = 3^{-(0+1)^2} = 3^{-1} = \frac{1}{3}$

$f(1) = 3^{-(1+1)^2} = 3^{-4} = \frac{1}{81}$

$f(-1) = 3^{-(-1+1)^2} = 3^0 = 1$

$f(-2) = 3^{-(-2+1)^2} = 3^{-1} = \frac{1}{3}$

$f(-3) = 3^{-(-3+1)^2} = 3^{-4} = \frac{1}{81}$

Exercise Set 5.3

1. Graph: $y = \log_7 x$

The equation $y = \log_7 x$ is equivalent to $7^y = x$. We can find ordered pairs by choosing values for y and computing the corresponding x-values.

For $y = 0$, $x = 7^0 = 1$.

For $y = 1$, $x = 7^1 = 7$.

For $y = 2$, $x = 7^2 = 49$.

For $y = -1$, $x = 7^{-1} = \frac{1}{7}$.

For $y = -2$, $x = 7^{-2} = \frac{1}{49}$.

241

x, or 7^y	y
1	0
7	1
49	2
$\frac{1}{7}$	-1
$\frac{1}{49}$	-2

└── (1) Select y.
└── (2) Compute x.

We plot the set of ordered pairs and connect the points with a smooth curve.

$y = \log_7 x$

2.

$y = \log_6 x$

3. Graph: $y = \log_{10} x$

The equation $y = \log_{10} x$ is equivalent to $10^y = x$. We can find ordered pairs by choosing values for y and computing the corresponding x-values.

For $y = 0$, $x = 10^0 = 1$.
For $y = 1$, $x = 10^1 = 10$.
For $y = 2$, $x = 10^2 = 100$.
For $y = -1$, $x = 10^{-1} = \frac{1}{10}$.
For $y = -2$, $x = 10^{-2} = \frac{1}{100}$.

x, or 10^y	y
1	0
10	1
100	2
$\frac{1}{10}$	-1
$\frac{1}{100}$	-2

We plot the set of ordered pairs and connect the points with a smooth curve.

$y = \log_{10} x$

4.

$y = \log_2 x$

5. Graph: $f(x) = \log_4 x$

Think of $f(x)$ as y. Then $y = \log_4 x$ is equivalent to $4^y = x$. We find ordered pairs by choosing values for y and computing the corresponding x-values. Then we plot the points and connect them with a smooth curve.

For $y = 0$, $x = 4^0 = 1$.
For $y = 1$, $x = 4^1 = 4$.
For $y = 2$, $x = 4^2 = 16$.
For $y = -1$, $x = 4^{-1} = \frac{1}{4}$.
For $y = -2$, $x = 4^{-2} = \frac{1}{16}$.

x, or 4^y	y
1	0
4	1
16	2
$\frac{1}{4}$	-1
$\frac{1}{16}$	-2

$f(x) = \log_4 x$

6.

$f(x) = \log_5 x$

7. Graph: $f(x) = \log_{1/2} x$

   Think of $f(x)$ as y. Then $y = \log_{1/2} x$ is equivalent to $\left(\frac{1}{2}\right)^y = x$. We construct a table of values, plot these points, and connect them with a smooth curve.

   For $y = 0$, $x = \left(\frac{1}{2}\right)^0 = 1$.

   For $y = 1$, $x = \left(\frac{1}{2}\right)^1 = \frac{1}{2}$.

   For $y = 2$, $x = \left(\frac{1}{2}\right)^2 = \frac{1}{4}$.

   For $y = -1$, $x = \left(\frac{1}{2}\right)^{-1} = 2$.

   For $y = -2$, $x = \left(\frac{1}{2}\right)^{-2} = 4$.

   For $y = -3$, $x = \left(\frac{1}{2}\right)^{-3} = 8$.

x, or $\left(\frac{1}{2}\right)^y$	y
1	0
$\frac{1}{2}$	1
$\frac{1}{4}$	2
2	-1
4	-2
8	-3

8.

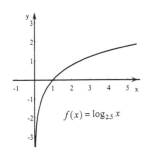

9. Graph: $f(x) = \log_2 (x + 3)$

   Think of $f(x)$ as y. Then $y = \log_2 (x + 3)$ is equivalent to $2^y = x + 3$, or $2^y - 3 = x$. We construct a table of values, plot these points, and connect them with a smooth curve.

   For $y = 0$, $x = 2^0 - 3 = 1 - 3 = -2$

   For $y = 1$, $x = 2^1 - 3 = 2 - 3 = -1$

   For $y = 2$, $x = 2^2 - 3 = 4 - 3 = 1$

   For $y = 3$, $x = 2^3 - 3 = 8 - 3 = 5$

   For $y = -1$, $x = 2^{-1} - 3 = \frac{1}{2} - 3 = -\frac{5}{2}$

   For $y = -2$, $x = 2^{-2} - 3 = \frac{1}{4} - 3 = -\frac{11}{4}$

x, or $2^y - 3$	y
-2	0
-1	1
1	2
5	3
$-\frac{5}{2}$	-1
$-\frac{11}{4}$	-2

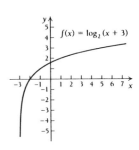

Note that this is the graph of $f(x) = \log_2 x$ (see Exercise 4) shifted 3 units to the left.

10. $y = \log_3 (x - 2)$

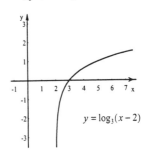

11. Graph: $f(x) = \log_2 x + 3$

    Think of $f(x)$ as y. Then $y = \log_2 x + 3$ is equivalent to $y - 3 = \log_2 x$ or $2^{y-3} = x$. We construct a table of values, plot these points, and connect them with a smooth curve.

    For $y = 0$, $x = 2^{0-3} = 2^{-3} = \frac{1}{8}$.

    For $y = 1$, $x = 2^{1-3} = 2^{-2} = \frac{1}{4}$.

    For $y = 2$, $x = 2^{2-3} = 2^{-1} = \frac{1}{2}$.

    For $y = 3$, $x = 2^{3-3} = 2^0 = 1$.

    For $y = 5$, $x = 2^{5-3} = 2^2 = 4$.

    For $y = -1$, $x = 2^{-1-3} = 2^{-4} = \frac{1}{16}$.

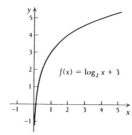

    Note that this is the graph of $f(x) = \log_2 x$ (see Exercise 4) shifted upward 3 units.

12.

$f(x) = \log_3 x - 1$

13. Graph $f(x) = 3^x$ (see Exercise Set 5.2, Exercise 2) and $f^{-1}(x) = \log_3 x$ (see Margin Exercise 1 in this section) on the same set of axes.

$f(x) = 3^x$

$f^{-1}(x) = \log_3 x$

14.

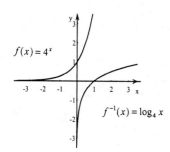

$f(x) = 4^x$

$f^{-1}(x) = \log_4 x$

15. $10^3 = 1000 \longrightarrow 3 = \log_{10} 1000$ The exponent is the logarithm.

The base remains the same.

16. $2 = \log_{10} 100$

17. $5^{-3} = \dfrac{1}{125} \longrightarrow -3 = \log_5 \dfrac{1}{125}$ The exponent is the logarithm.

The base remains the same.

18. $-5 = \log_4 \dfrac{1}{1024}$

19. $8^{1/3} = 2 \longrightarrow \dfrac{1}{3} = \log_8 2$

20. $\dfrac{1}{4} = \log_{16} 2$

21. $10^{0.3010} = 2 \longrightarrow 0.3010 = \log_{10} 2$

22. $0.4771 = \log_{10} 3$

23. $e^3 = t \longrightarrow 3 = \log_e t$

24. $k = \log_p 3$

25. $Q^t = x \longrightarrow t = \log_Q x$

26. $m = \log_p V$

27. $e^3 = 20.0855 \longrightarrow 3 = \log_e 20.0855$

28. $2 = \log_e 7.3891$

29. $e^{-1} = 0.3679 \longrightarrow -1 = \log_e 0.3679$

30. $-6 = \log_e 0.00247$

31. $t = \log_4 7 \longrightarrow 4^t = 7$ The logarithm is the exponent.

The base remains the same.

32. $6^h = 29$

33. $\log_2 32 = 5 \longrightarrow 2^5 = 32$ The logarithm is the exponent.

The base remains the same.

34. $5^1 = 5$

35. $\log_{10} 0.1 = -1 \longrightarrow 10^{-1} = 0.1$

36. $10^{-2} = 0.01$

37. $\log_{10} 7 = 0.845 \longrightarrow 10^{0.845} = 7$

38. $10^{0.4771} = 3$

39. $\log_e 30 = 3.4012 \longrightarrow e^{3.4012} = 30$

40. $e^{2.3026} = 10$

41. $\log_t Q = k \longrightarrow t^k = Q$

42. $m^a = P$

43. $\log_e 0.38 = -0.9676 \longrightarrow e^{-0.9676} = 0.38$

44. $e^{-0.0987} = 0.906$

45. $\log_r M = -x \longrightarrow r^{-x} = M$

46. $c^{-w} = W$

47. $\log_{10} x = 3$

$10^3 = x$ Converting to an exponential equation

$1000 = x$ Computing 10^3

48. $\log_2 16 = x$
     $2^x = 2^4$
     $x = 4$

49. $\log_3 3 = x$
     $3^x = 3$ Converting to an exponential equation
     $3^x = 3^1$
     $x = 1$ The exponents are the same.

50. $\log_5 \frac{1}{25} = x$
     $5^x = 5^{-2}$
     $x = -2$

51. $\log_3 x = 2$
     $3^2 = x$ Converting to an exponential equation
     $9 = x$ Computing 3^2

52. $\log_4 x = 3$
     $4^3 = x$
     $64 = x$

53. $\log_x 16 = 2$
     $x^2 = 16$ Converting to an exponential equation
     $x = 4$ or $x = -4$ Taking square roots
     $\log_4 16 = 2$ because $4^2 = 16$. Thus, 4 is a solution. Since all logarithm bases must be positive, $\log_{-4} 16$ is not defined and −4 is not a solution.

54. $\log_x 64 = 3$
     $x^3 = 64$
     $x = 4$

55. $\log_2 x = -1$
     $2^{-1} = x$ Converting to an exponential equation
     $\frac{1}{2} = x$ Simplifying

56. $\log_3 x = -2$
     $3^{-2} = x$
     $\frac{1}{9} = x$

57. $\log_8 x = \frac{1}{3}$
     $8^{1/3} = x$
     $2 = x$

58. $\log_{32} x = \frac{1}{5}$
     $32^{1/5} = x$
     $2 = x$

59. Let $\log_{10} 1000 = x$.
     Then $10^x = 1000$
     $10^x = 10^3$
     $x = 3.$
     Thus, $\log_{10} 1000 = 3$.

60. The exponent to which 10 is raised to get 10,000,000 is 7.

61. Let $\log_{10} 0.1 = x$.
     Then $10^x = 0.1 = \frac{1}{10}$
     $10^x = 10^{-1}$
     $x = -1.$
     Thus, $\log_{10} 0.1 = -1$.

62. The exponent to which 10 is raised to get 0.001 is −3.

63. Let $\log_{10} 1 = x$.
     Then $10^x = 1$
     $10^x = 10^0$ $(10^0 = 1)$
     $x = 0.$
     Thus, $\log_{10} 1 = 0$.

64. The exponent to which 10 is raised to get 10 is 1.

65. Let $\log_5 625 = x$.
     Then $5^x = 625$
     $5^x = 5^4$
     $x = 4.$
     Thus, $\log_5 625 = 4$.

66. The exponent to which 2 is raised to get 64 is 6.

67. Let $\log_5 \frac{1}{25} = x$.
     Then $5^x = \frac{1}{25}$
     $5^x = 5^{-2}$
     $x = -2.$
     Thus, $\log_5 \frac{1}{25} = -2$.

68. The exponent to which 2 is raised to get $\frac{1}{16}$ is −4.

69. Let $\log_3 1 = x$.
     Then $3^x = 1$
     $3^x = 3^0$ $(3^0 = 1)$
     $x = 0.$
     Thus, $\log_3 1 = 0$.

70. The exponent to which 8 is raised to get 8 is 1.

71. Find $\log_e 1$.

    We know that $\log_e 1$ is the exponent to which e is raised to get 1. That exponent is 0. Therefore, $\log_e 1 = 0$.

72. The exponent to which e is raised to get e is 1.

73. Find $\log_{81} 9$.

    We know that $\log_{81} 9$ is the exponent to which 81 is raised to get 9. Since $9 = \sqrt{81} = 81^{1/2}$, it follows that the exponent is $\frac{1}{2}$. Therefore, $\log_{81} 9 = \frac{1}{2}$.

74. The exponent to which 8 is raised to get 2 is $\frac{1}{3}$.

75. Find $\log_e e^5$.

    We know that $\log_e e^5$ is the exponent to which e is raised to get e^5. That exponent is 5. Therefore, $\log_e e^5 = 5$.

76. The exponent to which e is raised to get e^{-2} is -2.

77. Graph: $y = \left(\frac{2}{3}\right)^x$ Graph: $y = \log_{2/3} x$, or $x = \left(\frac{2}{3}\right)^y$

x	y, or $\left(\frac{2}{3}\right)^x$
0	1
1	$\frac{2}{3}$
2	$\frac{4}{9}$
3	$\frac{8}{27}$
-1	$\frac{3}{2}$
-2	$\frac{9}{4}$
-3	$\frac{27}{8}$

x, or $\left(\frac{2}{3}\right)^y$	y
1	0
$\frac{2}{3}$	1
$\frac{4}{9}$	2
$\frac{8}{27}$	3
$\frac{3}{2}$	-1
$\frac{9}{4}$	-2
$\frac{27}{8}$	-3

78.

$y = |\log_2 x|$

79. Graph: $y = \log_2 |x|$

x	$\pm\frac{1}{4}$	$\pm\frac{1}{2}$	± 1	± 2	± 4
y	-2	-1	0	1	2

$y = \log_2 |x|$

80. $|\log_3 x| = 3$

    $\log_3 x = 3$ or $\log_3 x = -3$

    $3^3 = x$ or $3^{-3} = x$

    $27 = x$ or $\frac{1}{27} = x$

81. $\log_{125} x = \frac{2}{3}$

    $125^{2/3} = x$

    $(5^3)^{2/3} = x$

    $5^2 = x$

    $25 = x$

82. $\log_\pi \pi^4 = x$

    $\pi^x = \pi^4$

    $x = 4$

83. $\log_{\sqrt{5}} x = -3$

    $(\sqrt{5})^{-3} = x$, or $5^{-3/2} = x$

84. $\log_b b^{2x^2} = x$

    $b^x = b^{2x^2}$

    $x = 2x^2$

    $0 = 2x^2 - x$

    $0 = x(2x - 1)$

    $x = 0$ or $x = \frac{1}{2}$

85. $\log_4 (3x - 2) = 2$

$$4^2 = 3x - 2$$
$$16 = 3x - 2$$
$$18 = 3x$$
$$6 = x$$

86. $\log_8 (2x - 3) = -1$

$$8^{-1} = 2x - 3$$
$$\frac{1}{8} = 2x - 3$$
$$1 = 16x - 24$$
$$25 = 16x$$
$$\frac{25}{16} = x$$

87. $\log_x \sqrt[5]{36} = \frac{1}{10}$

$$x^{1/10} = \sqrt[5]{36}$$
$$x^{1/10} = 36^{1/5}$$
$$(x^{1/10})^{10} = (36^{1/5})^{10}$$
$$x = 36^2$$
$$x = 1296$$

88. $\log_{10} (x^2 + 21x) = 2$

$$10^2 = x^2 + 21x$$
$$0 = x^2 + 21x - 100$$
$$0 = (x + 25)(x - 4)$$
$$x = -25 \quad \text{or} \quad x = 4$$

89. Let $\log_{1/4} \frac{1}{64} = x.$

Then $\left[\frac{1}{4}\right]^X = \frac{1}{64}$

$$\left[\frac{1}{4}\right]^X = \left[\frac{1}{4}\right]^3$$
$$x = 3.$$

Thus, $\log_{1/4} \frac{1}{64} = 3.$

90. $\log_{81} 3 \cdot \log_3 81 = \frac{1}{4} \cdot 4 = 1$

91. $\log_{10} (\log_4 (\log_3 81))$

$= \log_{10} (\log_4 4) \qquad (\log_3 81 = 4)$
$= \log_{10} 1 \qquad\qquad (\log_4 4 = 1)$
$= 0$

92. $\log_2 (\log_2 (\log_4 256)) = \log_2 (\log_2 4)$

$$= \log_2 2 = 1$$

93. Let $\log_{\sqrt{3}} \frac{1}{81} = x.$

Then $(\sqrt{3})^X = \frac{1}{81}$

$$(3^{1/2})^X = \frac{1}{3^4}$$
$$3^{X/2} = 3^{-4}$$
$$\frac{x}{2} = -4$$
$$x = -8$$

Thus, $\log_{\sqrt{3}} \frac{1}{81} = -8.$

94. Let $\log_{1/5} 25 = x.$

Then $\left[\frac{1}{5}\right]^X = 25$

$$5^{-X} = 5^2$$
$$-x = 2$$
$$x = -2$$

95. $f(x) = 3^X$

3^X is defined for all real numbers. Thus the domain is the set of all real numbers.

96. $\{x \mid x > 0\}$

97. $f(x) = \log_a x^2$

The domain of a logarithmic function is the set of all positive real numbers. Since $x^2 > 0$ for all real numbers, except 0, the domain is $\{x \mid x \neq 0\}.$

98. $\{x \mid x > 0\}$

99. $f(x) = \log_{10} (3x - 4)$

The domain of a logarithmic function is the set of all positive real numbers. Thus, we solve
$$3x - 4 > 0$$
$$3x > 4$$
$$x > \frac{4}{3}$$

The domain is $\left\{x \mid x > \frac{4}{3}\right\}.$

100. $\{x \mid x \neq 0\}$

101. Let $y = \log_2 x.$ The graph shows y is negative for $\{x \mid 0 < x < 1\}.$

x	y
$\frac{1}{4}$	-2
$\frac{1}{2}$	-1
1	0
2	1
4	2
8	3

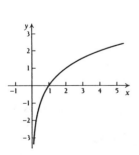

102. Solve $\log_2 (x - 3) \geqslant 4$ by graphing. To do this we first graph $y = \log_2 (x - 3)$ (or $2^y = x - 3$, or $2^y + 3 = x$).

Next we study the graph to see for which inputs the outputs are greater than or equal to 4. We see that $\log_2 (x - 3) \geqslant 4$ for those values of x for which $x \geqslant 19$. Thus the solution set of $\log_2 (x - 3) \geqslant 4$ is $\{x \mid x \geqslant 19\}$.

Exercise Set 5.4

1. $\log_2 (64 \cdot 8) = \log_2 64 + \log_2 8$ Property 1

2. $\log_3 81 + \log_3 27$

3. $\log_4 (32 \cdot 64) = \log_4 32 + \log_4 64$ Property 1

4. $\log_5 125 + \log_5 25$

5. $\log_c QP = \log_c Q + \log_c P$ Property 1

6. $\log_t 9 + \log_t Y$

7. $\log_b 8 + \log_b 90 = \log_b (8 \cdot 90)$ Property 1
   $= \log_b 720$

8. $\log_a (75 \cdot 2) = \log_a 150$

9. $\log_c P + \log_c Q = \log_c PQ$ Property 1

10. $\log_e MT$

11. $\log_a x^4 = 4 \log_a x$ Property 2

12. $3 \log_b t$

13. $\log_c y^5 = 5 \log_c y$ Property 2

14. $8 \log_{10} y$

15. $\log_b Q^{-6} = -6 \log_b Q$ Property 2

16. $-6 \log_c K$

17. $\log_a \frac{76}{13} = \log_a 76 - \log_a 13$ Property 3

18. $\log_t M - \log_t 8$

19. $\log_b \frac{5}{4} = \log_b 5 - \log_b 4$ Property 3

20. $\log_a x - \log_a y$

21. $\log_a 18 - \log_a 5 = \log_a \frac{18}{5}$ Property 3

22. $\log_b \frac{54}{6}$, or $\log_b 9$

23. $\log_a x^3 y^2 z = \log_a x^3 + \log_a y^2 + \log_a z$
       Property 1
   $= 3 \log_a x + 2 \log_a y + \log_a z$
       Property 2

24. $\log_a 6 + \log_a x + \log_a y^5 + \log_a z^4 =$
    $\log_a 6 + \log_a x + 5 \log_a y + 4 \log_a z$

25. $\log_b \frac{x^2 y}{b^3} = \log_b x^2 y - \log_b b^3$ Property 3
    $= \log_b x^2 + \log_b y - \log_b b^3$ Property 1
    $= \log_b x^2 + \log_b y - 3$ Property 4
    $= 2 \log_b x + \log_b y - 3$ Property 2

26. $\log_b (p^2 q^5) - \log_b (m^4 b^9)$
    $= \log_b p^2 + \log_b q^5 - \log_b m^4 - \log_b b^9$
    $= 2 \log_b p + 5 \log_b q - 4 \log_b m - 9$

27. $\log_c \sqrt[3]{\frac{x^4}{y^3 z^2}}$
    $= \log_c \left[\frac{x^4}{y^3 z^2} \right]^{1/3}$
    $= \frac{1}{3} \log_c \frac{x^4}{y^3 z^2}$ Property 2
    $= \frac{1}{3} (\log_c x^4 - \log_c y^3 z^2)$ Property 3
    $= \frac{1}{3} [\log_c x^4 - (\log_c y^3 + \log_c z^2)]$ Property 1
    $= \frac{1}{3} (\log_c x^4 - \log_c y^3 - \log_c z^2)$ Removing parentheses
    $= \frac{1}{3} (4 \log_c x - 3 \log_c y - 2 \log_c z)$ Property 2

28. $\frac{1}{2} \log_a \frac{x^6}{p^5 q^8}$
    $= \frac{1}{2} [\log_a x^6 - \log_a (p^5 q^8)]$
    $= \frac{1}{2} (6 \log_a x - \log_a p^5 - \log_a q^8)$
    $= \frac{1}{2} (6 \log_a x - 5 \log_a p - 8 \log_a q)$

29. $\log_a \sqrt[4]{\dfrac{m^8 n^{12}}{a^3 b^5}}$

$= \dfrac{1}{4} \log_a \dfrac{m^8 n^{12}}{a^3 b^5}$ Property 2

$= \dfrac{1}{4} (\log_a m^8 n^{12} - \log_a a^3 b^5)$ Property 3

$= \dfrac{1}{4} [\log_a m^8 + \log_a n^{12} - (\log_a a^3 + \log_a b^5)]$
$\hphantom{= \dfrac{1}{4} [\log_a m^8 + \log_a n^{12}}$ Property 1

$= \dfrac{1}{4} (\log_a m^8 + \log_a n^{12} - \log_a a^3 - \log_a b^5)$
$\hphantom{= \dfrac{1}{4} (\log_a m^8}$ Removing
$\hphantom{= \dfrac{1}{4} (\log_a m^8 + \log}$ parentheses

$= \dfrac{1}{4} (\log_a m^8 + \log_a n^{12} - 3 - \log_a b^5)$ Property 4

$= \dfrac{1}{4} (8 \log_a m + 12 \log_a n - 3 - 5 \log_a b)$
$\hphantom{= \dfrac{1}{4} (8 \log_a m + 12 \log_a n}$ Property 2

30. $\log_a \sqrt{\dfrac{a^6 b^8}{a^2 b^5}} = \log_a \sqrt{a^4 b^3}$

$= \dfrac{1}{2} (\log_a a^4 + \log_a b^3)$

$= \dfrac{1}{2} (4 + 3 \log_a b)$

$= 2 + \dfrac{3}{2} \log_a b$

31. $\dfrac{2}{5} \log_a x - \dfrac{1}{3} \log_a y = \log_a x^{\frac{2}{5}} - \log_a y^{\frac{1}{3}}$
$\hphantom{\dfrac{2}{5} \log_a x - \dfrac{1}{3} \log_a y =}$ Property 2

$\hphantom{\dfrac{2}{5} \log_a x} = \log_a \dfrac{x^{\frac{2}{5}}}{y^{\frac{1}{3}}}$ Property 3

32. $\log_a x^{1/2} + \log_a y^4 - \log_a x^3$
$= \log_a (x^{1/2} y^4) - \log_a x^3$

$= \log_a \dfrac{x^{\frac{1}{2}} y^4}{x^3}, \text{ or } \log_a x^{-\frac{5}{2}} y^4$

33. $\log_a 2x + 3(\log_a x - \log_a y)$
$= \log_a 2x + 3 \log_a x - 3 \log_a y$
$= \log_a 2x + \log_a x^3 - \log_a y^3$ Property 2
$= \log_a 2x^4 - \log_a y^3$ Property 1
$= \log_a \dfrac{2x^4}{y^3}$ Property 3

34. $\log_a x^2 - \log_a (\sqrt{x})^2$
$= \log_a \dfrac{x^2}{x}$
$= \log_a x$

35. $\log_a \dfrac{a}{\sqrt{x}} - \log_a \sqrt{ax}$

$= \log_a ax^{-1/2} - \log_a a^{1/2} x^{1/2}$

$= \log_a \dfrac{ax^{-1/2}}{a^{1/2} x^{1/2}}$ Property 3

$= \log_a \dfrac{a^{1/2}}{x}$

$= \log_a \dfrac{\sqrt{a}}{x}$

We can simplify this further as follows:

$\log_a \dfrac{\sqrt{a}}{x} = \log_a \sqrt{a} - \log_a x$ Property 3

$\hphantom{\log_a \dfrac{\sqrt{a}}{x}} = \log_a a^{1/2} - \log_a x$ Writing
$\hphantom{\log_a \dfrac{\sqrt{a}}{x} = \log_a a^{1/2}}$ exponential
$\hphantom{\log_a \dfrac{\sqrt{a}}{x} = \log_a a^{1/2}}$ notation

$\hphantom{\log_a \dfrac{\sqrt{a}}{x}} = \dfrac{1}{2} - \log_a x$ Property 4

36. $\log_a \dfrac{x^2 - 4}{x - 2} = \log_a \dfrac{(x + 2)(x - 2)}{x - 2}$
$\hphantom{\log_a \dfrac{x^2 - 4}{x - 2}} = \log_a (x + 2)$

37. $\log_b 15 = \log_b (3 \cdot 5)$
$\hphantom{\log_b 15} = \log_b 3 + \log_b 5$ Property 1
$\hphantom{\log_b 15} = 0.5283 + 0.7740$
$\hphantom{\log_b 15} = 1.3023$

38. $\log_b \dfrac{5}{3} = \log_b 5 - \log_b 3$
$\hphantom{\log_b \dfrac{5}{3}} = 0.7740 - 0.5283$
$\hphantom{\log_b \dfrac{5}{3}} = 0.2457$

39. $\log_b \dfrac{3}{5} = \log_b 3 - \log_b 5$ Property 3
$\hphantom{\log_b \dfrac{3}{5}} = 0.5283 - 0.7740$
$\hphantom{\log_b \dfrac{3}{5}} = -0.2457$

40. $\log_b \dfrac{1}{5} = \log_b 1 - \log_b 5 = 0 - 0.7740 = -0.7740$

41. $\log_b \dfrac{1}{3} = \log_b 1 - \log_b 3$ Property 3
$\hphantom{\log_b \dfrac{1}{3}} = 0 - 0.5283$ ($\log_b 1 = 0$)
$\hphantom{\log_b \dfrac{1}{3}} = -0.5283$

42. $\log_b \sqrt{b} = \log_b b^{1/2} = \dfrac{1}{2}$

43. $\log_b \sqrt{b^3} = \log_b b^{3/2}$ Writing exponential
$\hphantom{\log_b \sqrt{b^3} = \log_b b^{3/2}}$ notation
$\hphantom{\log_b \sqrt{b^3}} = \dfrac{3}{2}$ Property 4

44. $\log_b 5b = \log_b 5 + \log_b b = 0.7740 + 1 = 1.7740$

45. $\log_b 3b = \log_b 3 + \log_b b$ Property 1
$\hphantom{\log_b 3b} = 0.5283 + 1$ ($\log_b b = 1$)
$\hphantom{\log_b 3b} = 1.5283$

46. $\log_b 9 = \log_b 3^2 = 2 \log_b 3 = 2(0.5283) = 1.0566$

47. $\log_b 25 = \log_b 5^2$

    $= 2 \log_b 5$ Property 2

    $= 2(0.7740) = 1.548$

48. $\log_b 75 = \log_b (3 \cdot 5^2) = \log_b 3 + 2 \log_b 5 = 0.5283 + 2(0.7740) = 2.0763$

49. $\log_t t^{11} = 11$ Property 4

50. 3

51. $\log_e e^{|x-4|} = |x - 4|$ Property 4

52. $\sqrt{5}$

53. $3^{\log_3 4x} = 4x$ Property 5

54. $4x - 3$

55. $a^{\log_a Q} = Q$ Property 5

56. e^5

57. $a^{\log_a x} = 15$

    $x = 15$ Property 5

58. $5^{\log_5 8} = 2x$

    $8 = 2x$

    $4 = x$

59. $\log_e e^x = -7$

    $x = -7$ Property 4

60. $x = 2.7$

61. $\dfrac{\log_a M}{\log_a N} = \log_a M - \log_a N$

    Let $M = a^2$ and $N = a$. Then $\dfrac{\log_a a^2}{\log_a a} = \dfrac{2}{1} = 2$, but $\log_a a^2 - \log_a a = 2 - 1 = 1$. Thus the statement is false.

62. $\dfrac{\log_a M}{\log_a N} = \log_a \dfrac{M}{N}$

    Let $M = a^2$ and $N = a$. Then $\dfrac{\log_a a^2}{\log_a a} = \dfrac{2}{1} = 2$, but $\log_a \dfrac{a^2}{a} = \log_a a = 1$. Thus the statement is false.

63. $\dfrac{\log_a M}{c} = \dfrac{1}{c} \log_a M = \log_a M^{1/c}$

    The statement is true by Property 2.

64. $\log_N (M \cdot N)^x = x \log_N (M \cdot N)$

    $= x(\log_N M + \log_N N)$

    $= x(\log_N M + 1)$

    $= x \log_N M + x$

    The statement is true.

65. $\log_a 2x = 2 \log_a x$

    Let $x = a$. Then $\log_a 2a = \log_a 2 + \log_a a = \log_a 2 + 1$, but $2 \log_a a = 2 \cdot 1 = 2$. Thus the statement is false in general.

66. $\log_a 2x = \log_a 2 + \log_a x$ is true by Property 1.

67. $\log_a (M + N) = \log_a M + \log_a N$

    Let $M = N = a$. Then $\log_a (a + a) = \log_a 2a = \log_a 2 + 1$ (see Exercise 65), but $\log_a a + \log_a a = 1 + 1 = 2$. Thus the statement is false in general.

68. $\log_a x^3 = 3 \log_a x$ is true by Property 2.

69. $\log_c a - \log_c b = \log_c \left[\dfrac{a}{b}\right]$ is true by Property 3.

70. The statement is false. See Exercise 61.

71. $\log_a (x^8 - y^8) - \log_a (x^2 + y^2)$

    $= \log_a \dfrac{x^8 - y^8}{x^2 + y^2}$ Property 3

    $= \log_a \dfrac{(x^4 + y^4)(x^2 + y^2)(x + y)(x - y)}{x^2 + y^2}$ Factoring

    $= \log_a [(x^4 + y^4)(x^2 - y^2)]$ Simplifying

    $= \log_a (x^6 - x^4y^2 + x^2y^4 - y^6)$ Multiplying

72. $\log_a (x + y) + \log_a (x^2 - xy + y^2) = \log_a(x + y)(x^2 - xy + y^2) = \log_a (x^3 + y^3)$

73. $\log_a \sqrt{4 - x^2}$

    $= \log_a (4 - x^2)^{1/2}$

    $= \dfrac{1}{2} \log_a (4 - x^2)$

    $= \dfrac{1}{2} \log_a [(2 + x)(2 - x)]$

    $= \dfrac{1}{2} [\log_a (2 + x) + \log_a (2 - x)]$

74. $\log_a \dfrac{x - y}{\sqrt{x^2 - y^2}}$

    $= \log_a (x - y) - \dfrac{1}{2} \log_a (x + y)(x - y)$

    $= \log_a (x - y) - \dfrac{1}{2} \log_a (x + y) - \dfrac{1}{2} \log_a (x - y)$

    $= \dfrac{1}{2} \log_a (x - y) - \dfrac{1}{2} \log_a (x + y)$

75. $\log_a \dfrac{\sqrt[3]{x^2 z}}{\sqrt[3]{y^2 z^{-2}}}$

$= \log_a \left[\dfrac{x^2 z^3}{y^2}\right]^{1/3}$

$= \dfrac{1}{3}(\log_a x^2 z^3 - \log_a y^2)$

$= \dfrac{1}{3}(2\log_a x + 3\log_a z - 2\log_a y)$

$= \dfrac{1}{3}[2\cdot 2 + 3\cdot 4 - 2\cdot 3]$ Substituting

$= \dfrac{1}{3}(10)$

$= \dfrac{10}{3}$

76. $(x-4)\cdot\log_a a^x = x$

$\quad (x-4)x = x$

$\quad x^2 - 5x = 0$

$\quad x(x-5) = 0$

$x = 0 \ \text{ or } \ x = 5$

77. $\log_a 3x = \log_a 3 + \log_a x$

$\log_a 3x = \log_a 3x$ Property 1

We get an equation that is true for all values of x for which the logarithm function is defined. Thus, the solution is $\{x \mid x > 0\}$, or $(0, \infty)$.

78. $\log_\pi \pi^{2x+3} = 4$

$\quad 2x + 3 = 4$

$\quad\quad x = \dfrac{1}{2}$

79. $3^{\log_3 (8x-4)} = 5$

$\quad\quad 8x - 4 = 5$ Property 5

$\quad\quad\quad 8x = 9$

$\quad\quad\quad x = \dfrac{9}{8}$

80. $4^{2\log_4 x} = 7$

$\quad 4^{\log_4 x^2} = 7$

$\quad\quad x^2 = 7$

$\quad\quad x = \pm\sqrt{7}$

Only $\sqrt{7}$ checks.

81. $8^{2\log_8 x + \log_8 x} = 27$

$\quad\quad 8^{3\log_8 x} = 27$

$\quad\quad 8^{\log_8 x^3} = 27$

$\quad\quad\quad x^3 = 27$ Property 5

$\quad\quad\quad x = 3$

82. $\log_a x^2 = 2\log_a x$ or $2\log_a x = 2\log_a x$ is true for $\{x \mid x > 0\}$.

83. $\log_b \dfrac{5}{x+2} = \log_b 5 - \log_b (x+2)$

$\log_b \dfrac{5}{x+2} = \log_b \dfrac{5}{x+2}$ Property 3

The equation is true for all values of x for which the logarithm function is defined. That is, for all x for which $\dfrac{5}{x+2} > 0$, or

$\quad x + 2 > 0$

$\quad\quad x > -2.$

The solution set is $\{x \mid x > -2\}$, or $(-2, \infty)$.

84. $\log_a \left(\dfrac{1}{x}\right) = \log_a x^{-1} = -1\cdot\log_a x = -1\cdot 2 = -2$

85. $\log_a x = 2$

$\quad a^2 = x$

Let $\log_{1/a} x = n$ and solve for n.

$\log_{1/a} a^2 = n$ Substituting a^2 for x

$\left(\dfrac{1}{a}\right)^n = a^2$

$(a^{-1})^n = a^2$

$a^{-n} = a^2$

$-n = 2$

$n = -2$

Thus, $\log_{1/a} x = -2$ when $\log_a x = 2$.

86. $\log_a \dfrac{1}{x} = \log_a 1 - \log_a x = -\log_a x$

87. $\log_a \dfrac{x + \sqrt{x^2 - 5}}{5} \cdot \dfrac{x - \sqrt{x^2 - 5}}{x - \sqrt{x^2 - 5}}$

$= \log_a \dfrac{5}{5(x - \sqrt{x^2 - 5})} = \log_a \dfrac{1}{x - \sqrt{x^2 - 5}}$

$= \log_a 1 - \log_a (x - \sqrt{x^2 - 5})$

$= -\log_a (x - \sqrt{x^2 - 5}).$

88. Let $M = \log_a \left(\dfrac{1}{x}\right)$ or $\dfrac{1}{x} = a^M$ or $x = \left(\dfrac{1}{a}\right)^M$

or $\log_{\frac{1}{a}} x = M.$

89. See the answer section in the text.

Exercise Set 5.5

---

1. 0.4771

2. 0.8451

3. 0.9031

4. 1.1139

5. 0.3692

6. 0.4871

7. 1.8129

8. 1.9243

9. 1.7952

10. 1.0334

11. 2.7259

12. 2.2923

13. 4.1271

14. 4.9689

15. -0.2441

16. -0.1612

17. -1.2840

18. -0.4123

19. -2.0084

20. -3.2905

21. 0.0011

22. 79,104.2833

23. Does not exist

24. Does not exist

25. 1.0986

26. 0.6931

27. 2.0794

28. 2.5649

29. 4.4067

30. 3.9120

31. 9.0318

32. 6.6962

33. -5.1328

34. -7.9020

35. 2.8044

36. 0.0017

37. 0.0000027

38. 54,515,738.62

39. Find $\log_4 100$. We will use common logarithms in the change-of-base formula:

$$\log_b M = \frac{\log_a M}{\log_a b}$$

Substitute 10 for a, 4 for b, and 100 for M.

$$\log_4 100 = \frac{\log_{10} 100}{\log_{10} 4}$$

$$\approx \frac{2.0000}{0.6021} \quad \text{(Using a calculator)}$$

$$\approx 3.3219$$

40. $\dfrac{\log 20}{\log 3} \approx 2.7268$

41. Find $\log_2 12$. We will use common logarithms in the change-of-base formula:

$$\log_b M = \frac{\log_a M}{\log_a b}$$

Substitute 10 for a, 2 for b, and 12 for M.

$$\log_2 12 = \frac{\log_{10} 12}{\log_{10} 2}$$

$$\approx \frac{1.0792}{0.3010} \quad \text{(Using a calculator)}$$

$$\approx 3.5850$$

42. $\dfrac{\log 40}{\log 5} \approx 2.2920$

43. Find $\log_{100} 0.3$. We will use common logarithms in the change-of-base formula:

$$\log_b M = \frac{\log_a M}{\log_a b}$$

Substitute 10 for a, 100 for b, and 0.3 for M.

$$\log_{100} 0.3 = \frac{\log_{10} 0.3}{\log_{10} 100}$$

$$\approx \frac{-0.52288}{2} \quad \text{(Using a calculator)}$$

$$= -0.26144$$

44. $\dfrac{\log 50}{\log 200} \approx 0.7384$

45. Find $\log_{0.5} 7$. We will use common logarithms in the change-of-base formula:

$$\log_b M = \frac{\log_a M}{\log_a b}$$

Substitute 10 for a, 0.5 for b and 7 for M.

$$\log_{0.5} 7 = \frac{\log_{10} 7}{\log_{10} 0.5}$$

$$\approx \frac{0.8451}{-0.3010} \quad \text{(Using a calculator)}$$

$$\approx -2.8074$$

46. $\dfrac{\log 2}{\log 0.1} \approx -0.3010$

47. Find $\log_3 0.3$. We will use common logarithms in the change-of-base formula:

$$\log_b M = \frac{\log_a M}{\log_b b}$$

Substitute 10 for a, 3 for b, and 0.3 for M.

$$\log_3 0.3 = \frac{\log_{10} 0.3}{\log_{10} 3}$$
$$\approx \frac{-0.5229}{0.4771} \qquad \text{(Using a calculator)}$$
$$\approx -1.0959$$

48. $\dfrac{\log 0.06}{\log 2} \approx -4.0589$

49. Find $\log_\pi 100$. We will use common logarithms in the change-of-base formula:

$$\log_b M = \frac{\log_a M}{\log_a b}$$

Substitute 10 for a, π for b, and 100 for M.

$$\log_\pi 100 = \frac{\log_{10} 100}{\log_{10} \pi}$$
$$\approx \frac{2.0000}{0.4971} \qquad \text{(Using a calculator)}$$
$$\approx 4.0229$$

50. $\dfrac{\log 25}{\log \pi} \approx 2.8119$

51. See the answer section in the text.

52. $\log x = \dfrac{\ln x}{\ln 10} = \dfrac{1}{\ln 10} \cdot \ln x = 0.4343 \ln x$

53. Graph $y = f(x) = 10^x$

We use a calculator to find function values.

x	y, or f(x)
-1	0.1
0	1
0.5	3.1623
1	10
1.5	31.6228
2	100
2.5	316.2278
3	1000
3.1	1258.9254

54.

55. Graph $y = f^{-1}(x) = \log x$.

We can interchange the first and second coordinates in each pair found in Exercise 53 to obtain ordered pairs on the graph of $y = \log x$.

56.

57. $\dfrac{\log_5 8}{\log_5 2} = \dfrac{\log_5 2^3}{\log_5 2} = \dfrac{3 \log_5 2}{\log_5 2} = 3$

58. $\dfrac{\log_3 64}{\log_3 16} = \dfrac{\log_3 2^6}{\log_3 2^4} = \dfrac{6 \log_3 2}{4 \log_3 2} = \dfrac{3}{2}$

59.
$$\log 872x = 5.3442$$
$$\log 872 + \log x = 5.3442$$
$$2.940516485 + \log x \approx 5.3442$$
$$\log x \approx 2.403683515$$
$$x = 253.3282 \qquad \text{Finding the inverse}$$

60.
$$\log 43x^2 = 8.0166$$
$$\log 43 + \log x^2 = 8.0166$$
$$\log x^2 = 8.0166 - \log 43 \approx 6.383131544$$
$$x^2 \approx 10^{6.383131544}$$
$$x \approx \pm 1554.4107$$

61.
$$\log 784 + \log x = \log 2322$$
$$2.894316063 + \log x \approx 3.365862215$$
$$\log x \approx 0.471546152$$
$$x \approx 2.9617 \qquad \text{Finding the inverse}$$

62. $\dfrac{2.34}{\ln x} = \dfrac{57}{4.03}$

    $\ln x = \dfrac{2.34(4.03)}{57} \approx 0.165442105$

    $x \approx 1.1799$

63. Let $a = e$, $b = 10$, $M = e$. Substitute in the change-of-base formula.

    $\log e = \dfrac{\ln e}{\ln 10} = \dfrac{1}{\ln 10}$

64. Let $a = e$, $b = 10$, $M = M$. Substitute in the change-of-base formula.

    $\log M = \dfrac{\ln M}{\ln 10}$

65. Let $a = M$, $b = b$, $M = M$. Substitute in the change-of-base formula.

    $\log_b M = \dfrac{\log_M M}{\log_M b} = \dfrac{1}{\log_M b}$

66. Let $a = 10$, $b = e$, $M = M$. Substitute in the change-of-base formula.

    $\ln M = \dfrac{\log M}{\log e}$

67. See the answer section in the text.

68. 2, 2.25, 2.48832, 2.593742, 2.704814, 2.716924

69. $f(t) = t^{\frac{1}{t-1}}$

    $f(0.5) = 0.5^{\frac{1}{0.5-1}} = 0.5^{-\frac{1}{0.5}} = 0.5^{-2} = 4$

    $f(0.9) = 0.9^{\frac{1}{0.9-1}} = 0.9^{-\frac{1}{0.1}} = 0.9^{-10} \approx 2.867972$

    $f(0.99) = 0.99^{\frac{1}{0.99-1}} = 0.99^{-\frac{1}{0.01}} = 0.99^{-100} \approx$ 2.731999

    $f(0.999) = 0.999^{\frac{1}{0.999-1}} = 0.999^{-\frac{1}{0.001}} =$ $0.999^{-1000} \approx 2.719642$

    $f(0.9999) = 0.9999^{\frac{1}{0.9999-1}} = 0.9999^{-\frac{1}{0.0001}} =$ $0.9999^{-10,000} \approx 2.718418$

70. $e^\pi \approx 23.1407$, $\pi^e \approx 22.4592$
    e^π is larger.

71. $e^{\sqrt{\pi}} \approx 5.8853$, $\sqrt{e^\pi} \approx 4.8105$

    $e^{\sqrt{\pi}}$ is larger.

72. Use a calculator to find the inverse function in both base 10 and base e and compare with the value of x. Study graphs if possible.

73. $y = 4.5^x$
    $y = \log_{4.5} x$

[−6, 6] x [−4, 4]

74. $y = 6.7^x$
    $y = \log_{6.7} x$

[−6, 6] x [−4, 4]

75. $y = 0.15^x$
    $y = \log_{0.15} x$

[−3, 3] x [−2, 2]

76. $y = 0.95^x$
    $y = \log_{0.95} x$

[−6, 6] x [−4, 4]

Exercise Set 5.6

1. Graph f(x) = 2e^X.

   Use a calculator to find approximate values of 2e^X, and use these values to draw the graph.

x	2e^X
-2	0.3
-1	0.7
0	2
1	5.4
2	14.8

2.

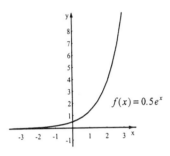

3. Graph f(x) = e^((1/2)X).

   Use a calculator to find approximate values of e^((1/2)X), and use these values to draw the graph.

x	e^((1/2)X)
-2	0.4
-1	0.6
0	1
1	1.6
2	2.7

4.

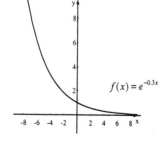

5. Graph f(x) = e^(X+1).

   Use a calculator to find approximate values of e^(X+1), and use these values to draw the graph.

x	e^(X+1)
-2	0.4
-1	1
0	2.7
1	7.4
2	20.1

6.

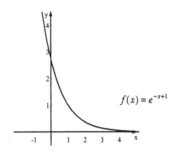

7. Graph f(x) = e^(2X) + 1.

   Use a calculator to find approximate values of e^(2X) + 1, and use these values to draw the graph.

x	e^(2X) + 1
-2	1.02
-1	1.1
0	2
1	8.4
2	55.6

8.

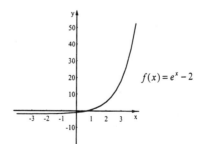

9. Graph $f(x) = 1 - e^{-0.01X}$, for nonnegative values of x. Use a calculator to find approximate values of $1 - e^{-0.01X}$ for nonnegative values of x, and use these values to draw the graph.

x	$1 - e^{-0.01X}$
0	0
100	0.63
200	0.86
300	0.95
400	0.98

10.

11. Graph $f(x) = 2(1 - e^{-X})$, for nonnegative values of x. Use a calculator to find approximate values of $2(1 - e^{-X})$ for nonnegative values of x, and use these values to draw the grpah.

x	$2(1 - e^{-X})$
0	0
1	1.26
2	1.73
3	1.90
4	1.96

12.

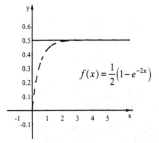

13. Graph $f(x) = 4 \ln x$.

Find some solutions with a calculator, plot them, and draw the graph.

x	0.25	0.5	1	1.5	2	3
$4 \ln x$	-5.55	-2.77	0	1.62	2.77	4.39

14.

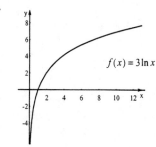

15. Graph $f(x) = \frac{1}{2} \ln x$.

Find some solutions with a calculator, plot them, and draw the graph.

x	0.5	1	2	4	7	8
$\frac{1}{2} \ln x$	-0.35	0	0.35	0.69	0.97	1.04

16.

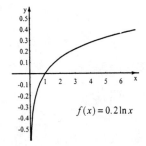

17. Graph f(x) = ln (x - 2).

Find some solutions using a calculator, plot them, and draw the graph. When x = 3,
f(x) = ln (3 - 2) = ln 1 = 0, and so on.

x	2.5	3	4	6	8	10
ln (x-2)	-0.69	0	0.69	1.39	1.79	2.08

18.

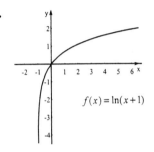

19. Graph f(x) = 2 - ln x.

Find some solutions using a calculator, plot them, and draw the graph.

x	0.25	0.5	1	2	4
2 - ln x	3.39	2.69	2	1.31	0.61

x	7	8	10
2 - ln x	0.05	-0.08	-0.30

20.

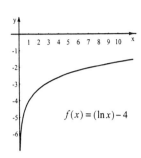

21. P(t) = 1 - e^{-0.2t}

a) $P(1) = 1 - e^{-0.2(1)} = 1 - e^{-0.2} \approx 0.181$, or 18.1%

$P(4) = 1 - e^{-0.2(4)} = 1 - e^{-0.8} \approx 0.551$, or 55.1%

$P(6) = 1 - e^{-0.2(6)} = 1 - e^{-1.2} \approx 0.699$, or 69.9%

$P(12) = 1 - e^{-0.2(12)} = 1 - e^{-2.4} \approx 0.909$, or 90.9%

b) Plot the points (0, 0%), (1, 18.1%), (4, 55.1%), (6, 69.9%), and (12, 90.9%) and draw the graph.

22. a) $w(1) = 100(1 - e^{-0.3(1)}) \approx 26$
$w(5) = 100(1 - e^{-0.3(5)}) \approx 78$
$w(8) = 100(1 - e^{-0.3(8)}) \approx 91$
$w(10) = 100(1 - e^{-0.3(10)}) \approx 95$

b)

23. $V(t) = \$58(1 - e^{-1.1t}) + \$20$

    a) $V(1) = \$58(1 - e^{-1.1(1)}) + \$20$

            $= \$58(1 - e^{-1.1}) + \$20$

            $\approx \$58.69$

      $V(2) = \$58(1 - e^{-1.1(2)}) + \$20$

            $= \$58(1 - e^{-2.2}) + \$20$

            $\approx \$71.57$

      $V(4) = \$58(1 - e^{-1.1(4)}) + \$20$

            $= \$58(1 - e^{-4.4}) + \$20$

            $\approx \$77.29$

      $V(6) = \$58(1 - e^{-1.1(6)}) + \$20$

            $= \$58(1 - e^{-6.6}) + \$20$

            $\approx \$77.92$

     $V(12) = \$58(1 - e^{-1.1(12)}) + \$20$

            $= \$58(1 - e^{-13.2}) + \$20$

            $\approx \$77.99 +$

    b)   Plot the points (0, \$20), (1, \$58.69), (2, \$71.57), (4, \$77.29), (6, \$77.92), and (12, \$77.99 +) and draw the graph.

24.   a) $P(10) = 1 - e^{-0.03(10)} \approx 0.259$, or 25.9%

        $P(30) = 1 - e^{-0.03(30)} \approx 0.593$, or 59.3%

        $P(60) = 1 - e^{-0.03(60)} \approx 0.835$, or 83.5%

        $P(120) = 1 - e^{-0.03(120)} \approx 0.973$, 97.3%

    b)

25.   Graph $g(x) = e^{|x|}$.

Use a calculator to find some values of $e^{|x|}$, and use these values to draw the graph.

x	$e^{|x|}$
-3	20.09
-2	7.39
-1	2.72
0	1
1	2.72
2	7.39

26.

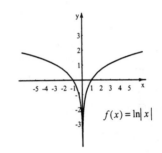

$$f(x) = \ln|x|$$

27.   Graph $f(x) = |\ln x|$.

Find some solutions using a calculator, plot them, and draw the graph.

x	0.25	0.5	1	3	6	10
$|\ln x|$	1.39	0.69	0	1.10	1.79	2.30

28.

$$g(x) = |\ln(x-1)|$$

29. Graph $f(x) = \dfrac{e^x + e^{-x}}{2}$

Use a calculator to find some values of $\dfrac{e^x + e^{-x}}{2}$, and use these values to draw the graph.

x	$\dfrac{e^x + e^{-x}}{2}$
-3	13.76
-2	3.76
-1	1.54
0	1
1	1.54
2	3.76

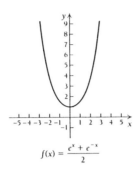

$$f(x) = \frac{e^x + e^{-x}}{2}$$

30.

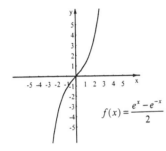

$$f(x) = \frac{e^x - e^{-x}}{2}$$

31. $N(t) = \dfrac{4800}{6 + 794e^{-0.4t}}$

   a) $N(3) = \dfrac{4800}{6 + 794e^{-0.4(3)}} = \dfrac{4800}{6 + 794e^{-1.2}} \approx 20$

   $N(5) = \dfrac{4800}{6 + 794e^{-0.4(5)}} = \dfrac{4800}{6 + 794e^{-2}} \approx 42$

   $N(10) = \dfrac{4800}{6 + 794e^{-0.4(10)}} = \dfrac{4800}{6 + 794e^{-4}} \approx 234$

   $N(15) = \dfrac{4800}{6 + 794e^{-0.4(15)}} = \dfrac{4800}{6 + 794e^{-6}} \approx 602$

   b) Plot the points (0, 6), (3, 20), (5, 42), (10, 234), and (15, 602) and draw the graph.

$$N(t) = \frac{4800}{6 + 794e^{-0.4t}}$$

32. a) $P(0.2) = \dfrac{20{,}000}{10 + 1990e^{-6(0.2)}} \approx 33$

   $P(0.5) = \dfrac{20{,}000}{10 + 1990e^{-6(0.5)}} \approx 183$

   $P(0.8) = \dfrac{20{,}000}{10 + 1990e^{-6(0.8)}} \approx 758$

   $P(1) = \dfrac{20{,}000}{10 + 1990e^{-6\cdot1}} \approx 1339$

   $P(1.5) = \dfrac{20{,}000}{10 + 1990e^{-6(1.5)}} \approx 1952$

   $P(2) = \dfrac{20{,}000}{10 + 1990e^{-6\cdot2}} \approx 1998$

   b)

$$P(t) = \frac{20{,}000}{10 + 1990e^{-6t}}$$

33. a) $f(x) = x^2 e^{-x}$

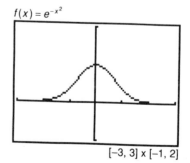

$[-5, 5] \times [-5, 5]$

   b) From the graph we see that 0 is the only zero of the function.

   c) The function has no maximum value. The minimum value is 0.

34. a) $f(x) = e^{-x^2}$

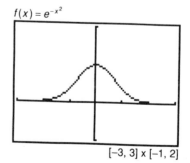

$[-3, 3] \times [-1, 2]$

   b) None

   c) Maximum: 1; no minimum

35. a) $f(x) = x^2 \ln x$

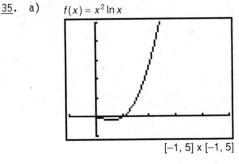

$[-1, 5] \times [-1, 5]$

b) From the graph we see that 1 is the only zero of the function.

c) The function has no maximum value. The minimum value is about -0.2.

36. a) $f(x) = \dfrac{\ln x}{x^2}$

$[-1, 5] \times [-2, 1]$

b) 1

c) Maximum: about 0.18; no minimum

37.-42. See Exercises 25 - 30.

Exercise Set 5.7

1. $2^x = 32$
    $2^x = 2^5$
    $x = 5$ The exponents are the same.

2. $4^x = 256$
    $4^x = 4^4$
    $x = 4$

3. $3^x = 81$
    $3^x = 3^4$
    $x = 4$ The exponents are the same.

4. $5^x = 625$
    $5^x = 5^4$
    $x = 4$

5. $2^{2x} = 8$
    $2^{2x} = 2^3$
    $2x = 3$ The exponents are the same.
    $x = \dfrac{3}{2}$

6. $4^{5x} = 32$
    $(2^2)^{5x} = 2^5$
    $10x = 5$
    $x = \dfrac{1}{2}$

7. $3^{7x} = 27$
    $3^{7x} = 3^3$
    $7x = 3$
    $x = \dfrac{3}{7}$

8. $5^{3x} = 125$
    $5^{3x} = 5^3$
    $3x = 3$
    $x = 1$

9. $2^x = 33$
    $\log 2^x = \log 33$ Taking the common logarithm on both sides
    $x \log 2 = \log 33$ Property 2
    $x = \dfrac{\log 33}{\log 2}$
    $x \approx \dfrac{1.5185}{0.3010}$
    $x \approx 5.0444$

10. $2^x = 20$
     $x \log 2 = \log 20$
     $x = \dfrac{\log 20}{\log 2} \approx 4.3219$

11. $2^x = 40$
     $\log 2^x = \log 40$
     $x \log 2 = \log 40$
     $x = \dfrac{\log 40}{\log 2}$
     $x \approx \dfrac{1.6021}{0.3010}$
     $x \approx 5.3219$

12. $2^x = 19$
     $x \log 2 = \log 19$
     $x = \dfrac{\log 19}{\log 2} \approx 4.2479$

13. $5^{4x-7} = 125$
    $5^{4x-7} = 5^3$
    $4x - 7 = 3$
    $4x = 10$
    $x = \dfrac{10}{4} = \dfrac{5}{2}$

14. $4^{3x+5} = 16$
    $4^{3x+5} = 4^2$
    $3x + 5 = 2$
    $x = -1$

15. $3^{x^2+4x} = \dfrac{1}{27}$
    $3^{x^2+4x} = 3^{-3}$
    $x^2 + 4x = -3$
    $x^2 + 4x + 3 = 0$
    $(x + 3)(x + 1) = 0$
    $x = -3 \quad \text{or} \quad x = -1$

16. $27 = 3^{5x} \cdot 9^{x^2}$
    $3^3 = 3^{5x} \cdot 3^{2x^2}$
    $3^3 = 3^{5x+2x^2}$
    $3 = 5x + 2x^2$
    $0 = 2x^2 + 5x - 3$
    $0 = (2x - 1)(x + 3)$
    $x = \dfrac{1}{2} \quad \text{or} \quad x = -3$

17. $84^x = 70$
    $\log 84^x = \log 70$
    $x \log 84 = \log 70$
    $x = \dfrac{\log 70}{\log 84}$
    $x \approx \dfrac{1.8451}{1.9243}$
    $x \approx 0.9589$

18. $28^x = 10$
    $x \log 28 = \log 10$
    $x = \dfrac{\log 10}{\log 28} \approx 0.6910$

19. $e^t = 1000$
    $\ln e^t = \ln 1000$
    $t = \ln 1000 \quad$ Property 4
    $t \approx 6.9078$

20. $e^t = 100$
    $t = \ln 100 \approx 4.6052$

21. $e^{-t} = 0.3$
    $\ln e^{-t} = \ln 0.3$
    $-t = \ln 0.3$
    $t = -\ln 0.3$
    $t \approx 1.2040$

22. $e^{-t} = 0.04$
    $-t = \ln 0.04$
    $t = -\ln 0.04 \approx 3.2189$

23. $e^{-0.03t} = 0.08$
    $\ln e^{-0.03t} = \ln 0.08$
    $-0.03t = \ln 0.08$
    $t = \dfrac{\ln 0.08}{-0.03}$
    $t \approx \dfrac{-2.5257}{-0.03}$
    $t \approx 84.1910$

24. $e^{0.09t} = 4$
    $0.09t = \ln 4$
    $t = \dfrac{\ln 4}{0.09} \approx 15.4033$

25. $3^x = 2^{x-1}$
    $\ln 3^x = \ln 2^{x-1}$
    $x \ln 3 = (x - 1) \ln 2$
    $x \ln 3 = x \ln 2 - \ln 2$
    $\ln 2 = x \ln 2 - x \ln 3$
    $\ln 2 = x(\ln 2 - \ln 3)$
    $\dfrac{\ln 2}{\ln 2 - \ln 3} = x$
    $\dfrac{0.6931}{0.6931 - 1.0986} \approx x$
    $-1.7095 \approx x$

26. $5^{x+2} = 4^{x-1}$
    $(x + 2) \log 5 = (x - 1) \log 4$
    $2 \log 5 + \log 4 = x \log 4 - x \log 5$
    $\dfrac{2 \log 5 + \log 4}{\log 4 - \log 5} = x$
    $-20.6377 \approx x$

27. $(3.9)^x = 48$
    $\log (3.9)^x = \log 48$
    $x \log 3.9 = \log 48$
    $x = \dfrac{\log 48}{\log 3.9}$
    $x \approx \dfrac{1.6812}{0.5911}$
    $x \approx 2.8444$

28. $(5.6)^x = 100$
    $x \log 5.6 = 2$
    $x = \dfrac{2}{\log 5.6} \approx 2.6731$

29. $250 - (1.87)^x = 0$

$250 = (1.87)^x$

$\log 250 = \log (1.87)^x$

$\log 250 = x \log 1.87$

$\dfrac{\log 250}{\log 1.87} = x$

$\dfrac{2.3979}{0.2718} \approx x$

$8.8211 \approx x$

30. $4805 - (21.3)^t = 0$

$4805 = (21.3)^t$

$\log 4805 = t \log 21.3$

$t = \dfrac{\log 4805}{\log 21.3} \approx 2.7716$

31. $4^{2x} = 8^{3x-4}$

$(2^2)^{2x} = (2^3)^{3x-4}$

$2^{4x} = 2^{9x-12}$ Multiplying exponents

$4x = 9x - 12$

$-5x = -12$

$x = \dfrac{12}{5}$

32. $25^{3x-2} = 625^{2x+7}$

$(5^2)^{3x-2} = (5^4)^{2x+7}$

$6x - 4 = 8x + 28$

$-32 = 2x$

$-16 = x$

33. $\dfrac{e^x - e^{-x}}{t} = 5$

$e^x - e^{-x} = 5t$ Multiplying by t

$e^{2x} - 1 = 5te^x$ Multiplying by e^x

$(e^x)^2 - 5t \cdot e^x - 1 = 0$

This equation is reducible to quadratic with $u = e^x$. We use the quadratic formula with $a = 1$, $b = -5t$ and $c = -1$.

$e^x = \dfrac{-(-5t) \pm \sqrt{(-5t)^2 - 4 \cdot 1 \cdot (-1)}}{2 \cdot 1}$

$= \dfrac{5t \pm \sqrt{25t^2 + 4}}{2}$

$\ln e^x = \ln \left(\dfrac{5t \pm \sqrt{25t^2 + 4}}{2} \right)$ Taking the natural logarithm on both sides

$x = \ln \left(\dfrac{5t \pm \sqrt{25t^2 + 4}}{2} \right)$ Property 4

34. $e^x + e^{-x} = 5$

$e^{2x} + 1 = 5e^x$

$e^{2x} - 5e^x + 1 = 0$

$e^x = \dfrac{5 \pm \sqrt{21}}{2}$

$x = \ln \left(\dfrac{5 \pm \sqrt{21}}{2} \right) \approx \pm 1.5668$

35. $\dfrac{e^x + e^{-x}}{e^x - e^{-x}} = t$

$e^x + e^{-x} = te^x - te^{-x}$ Multiplying by $e^x - e^{-x}$

$e^{2x} + 1 = te^{2x} - t$ Multiplying by e^x

$t + 1 = te^{2x} - e^{2x}$

$t + 1 = e^{2x}(t - 1)$

$\dfrac{t + 1}{t - 1} = e^{2x}$

$\ln \left[\dfrac{t + 1}{t - 1} \right] = \ln e^{2x}$

$\ln \left[\dfrac{t + 1}{t - 1} \right] = 2x$

$\dfrac{1}{2} \ln \left[\dfrac{t + 1}{t - 1} \right] = x$

36. $\dfrac{5^x - 5^{-x}}{5^x + 5^{-x}} = t$

$5^x - 5^{-x} = 5^x t + 5^{-x} t$

$5^{2x} - 1 = 5^{2x} t + t$

$5^{2x}(1 - t) = t + 1$

$5^{2x} = \dfrac{t + 1}{1 - t}$

$2x = \log_5 \left[\dfrac{t + 1}{1 - t} \right]$

$x = \dfrac{1}{2} \log_5 \left[\dfrac{t + 1}{1 - t} \right]$

37. $\log_5 x = 4$

$x = 5^4$ Writing an equivalent exponential equation

$x = 625$

38. $\log_2 x = 2$

$x = 2^2 = 4$

39. $\log_5 x = -3$

$x = 5^{-3}$ Writing an equivalent exponential equation

$x = \dfrac{1}{125}$

40. $\log_{25} x = \dfrac{1}{2}$

$x = 25^{1/2} = 5$

41. $\log x = 2$ The base is 10.

$x = 10^2$

$x = 100$

42. $\log x = 1$

$x = 10^1 = 10$

43. $\log x = -3$ The base is 10.

$x = 10^{-3}$

$x = \dfrac{1}{1000}$, or 0.001

44. $\log x = -4$

    $x = 10^{-4}$, or 0.0001

45. $\ln x = 1$

    $x = e^1 = e$

46. $\ln x = 3$

    $x = e^3$

47. $\ln x = -2$

    $x = e^{-2}$

48. $\ln x = -1$

    $x = e^{-1}$

49. $\log_5 (8 - 7x) = 3$

    $5^3 = 8 - 7x$ Writing an equivalent exponential equation

    $125 = 8 - 7x$

    $117 = -7x$

    $-\dfrac{117}{7} = x$

The answer checks. The solution is $-\dfrac{117}{7}$.

50. $\log_2 (10 + 3x) = 5$

    $2^5 = 10 + 3x$

    $\dfrac{22}{3} = x$

51. $\log x + \log (x - 9) = 1$ The base is 10.

    $\log_{10} [x(x - 9)] = 1$ Property 1

    $x(x - 9) = 10^1$

    $x^2 - 9x = 10$

    $x^2 - 9x - 10 = 0$

    $(x - 10)(x + 1) = 0$

$x = 10$ or $x = -1$

Check: For 10:

$$\frac{\log x + \log (x - 9) = 1}{\log 10 + \log (10 - 9) \; | \; 1}$$
$$\log 10 + \log 1 \;|$$
$$1 + 0 \;|$$
$$1 \;|$$

    For -1:

$$\frac{\log x + \log (x - 9) = 1}{\log (-1) + \log (-1 - 9) \; | \; 1}$$

The number -1 does not check, because negative numbers do not have logarithms. The solution is 10.

52. $\log x + \log (x + 9) = 1$

    $\log [x(x + 9)] = 1$

    $x^2 + 9x = 10$

    $x^2 + 9x - 10 = 0$

    $(x + 10)(x - 1) = 0$

$x = -10$ or $x = 1$

Only 1 checks.

53. $\log x - \log (x + 3) = -1$ The base is 10.

    $\log_{10} \dfrac{x}{x + 3} = -1$ Property 3

    $\dfrac{x}{x + 3} = 10^{-1}$

    $\dfrac{x}{x + 3} = \dfrac{1}{10}$

    $10x = x + 3$

    $9x = 3$

    $x = \dfrac{1}{3}$

The answer checks. The solution is $\dfrac{1}{3}$.

54. $\log (x + 9) - \log x = 1$

    $\log \dfrac{x + 9}{x} = 1$

    $\dfrac{x + 9}{x} = 10$

    $x + 9 = 10x$

    $1 = x$

55. $\log_2 (x + 1) + \log_2 (x - 1) = 3$

    $\log_2 [(x + 1)(x - 1)] = 3$ Property 1

    $(x + 1)(x - 1) = 2^3$

    $x^2 - 1 = 8$

    $x^2 = 9$

    $x = \pm 3$

The number 3 checks, but -3 does not. The solution is 3.

56. $\log_8 (x + 1) - \log_8 x = 2$

    $\log_8 \left[\dfrac{x + 1}{x} \right] = 2$

    $\dfrac{x + 1}{x} = 64$

    $x + 1 = 64x$

    $\dfrac{1}{63} = x$

57. $\log_8 (x + 1) - \log_8 x = \log_8 4$

$\log_8 \left[\dfrac{x + 1}{x}\right] = \log_8 4$ Property 3

$\dfrac{x + 1}{x} = 4$ Taking antilogarithms

$x + 1 = 4x$

$1 = 3x$

$\dfrac{1}{3} = x$

The answer checks. The solution is $\dfrac{1}{3}$.

58. $\log (2x + 1) - \log (x - 2) = 1$

$\log \left[\dfrac{2x + 1}{x - 2}\right] = 1$

$\dfrac{2x + 1}{x - 2} = 10$

$2x + 1 = 10x - 20$

$\dfrac{21}{8} = x$

59. $\log_4 (x + 3) + \log_4 (x - 3) = 2$

$\log_4 [(x + 3)(x - 3)] = 2$ Property 1

$(x + 3)(x - 3) = 4^2$

$x^2 - 9 = 16$

$x^2 = 25$

$x = \pm 5$

The number 5 checks, but -5 does not. The solution is 5.

60. $\log_5 (x + 4) + \log_5 (x - 4) = 2$

$\log_5 [(x + 4)(x - 4)] = 2$

$x^2 - 16 = 25$

$x^2 = 41$

$x = \pm\sqrt{41}$

Only $\sqrt{41}$ checks.

61. $\log \sqrt[4]{x} = \sqrt{\log x}$

$\log x^{1/4} = \sqrt{\log x}$ Writing exponential notation

$\dfrac{1}{4} \log x = \sqrt{\log x}$ Property 2

$\dfrac{1}{16} (\log x)^2 = \log x$ Squaring both sides

$\dfrac{1}{16} (\log x)^2 - \log x = 0$

Let $u = \log x$, substitute and solve for u.

$\dfrac{1}{16}u^2 - u = 0$

$u\left[\dfrac{1}{16}u - 1\right] = 0$

$u = 0$ or $u = 16$

$\log x = 0$ or $\log x = 16$

$x = 1$ or $x = 10^{16}$

Both numbers check. The solutions are 1 and 10^{16}.

62. $\log \sqrt[3]{x} = \sqrt{\log x}$

$\log x^{1/3} = \sqrt{\log x}$

$\dfrac{1}{3} \log x = \sqrt{\log x}$

$\dfrac{1}{9} (\log x)^2 = \log x$

$\dfrac{1}{9} (\log x)^2 - \log x = 0$

Let $u = \log x$, substitute, and solve for u. We obtain:

$u = 0$ or $u = 9$

$\log x = 0$ or $\log x = 9$

$x = 1$ or $x = 10^9$

63. $\log_5 \sqrt{x^2 + 1} = 1$

$\sqrt{x^2 + 1} = 5^1$

$x^2 + 1 = 25$ Squaring both sides

$x^2 = 24$

$x = \pm\sqrt{24}$,   or $\pm 2\sqrt{6}$

Both numbers check. The solutions are $\pm 2\sqrt{6}$.

64. $\log \sqrt{x} = \sqrt{\log x}$

$\dfrac{1}{2} \log x = \sqrt{\log x}$

$\dfrac{1}{4} (\log x)^2 = \log x$

$\dfrac{1}{4} (\log x)^2 - \log x = 0$

Let $u = \log x$, substitute, and solve for u. We obtain:

$u = 0$ or $u = 4$

$\log x = 0$ or $\log x = 4$

$x = 1$ or $x = 10{,}000$

65. $\log x^2 = (\log x)^2$

$2 \log x = (\log x)^2$

$0 = (\log x)^2 - 2 \log x$

Let $u = \log x$.

$0 = u^2 - 2u$

$0 = u(u - 2)$

$u = 0$ or $u = 2$

$\log x = 0$ or $\log x = 2$

$x = 10^0$ or $x = 10^2$

$x = 1$ or $x = 100$

Both numbers check. The solutions are 1 and 100.

66. $(\log_3 x)^2 - \log_3 x^2 = 3$

        $(\log_3 x)^2 - 2 \log_3 x - 3 = 0$

Let $u = \log_3 x$, substitute, and solve for u. We obtain:

     $u = 3$ or $u = -1$

   $\log_3 x = 3$ or $\log_3 x = -1$

      $x = 27$ or $x = \frac{1}{3}$

67. $\log_3 (\log_4 x) = 0$

         $\log_4 x = 3^0$ Writing an equivalent exponential equation

         $\log_4 x = 1$

             $x = 4^1$

             $x = 4$

The answer checks. The solution is 4.

68. $\log (\log x) = 2$

        $\log x = 100$

           $x = 10^{100}$

69. $(\log_a x)^{-1} = \log_a x^{-1}$

    $\dfrac{1}{\log_a x} = \log_a x^{-1}$ Writing $(\log_a x)^{-1}$ with a positive exponent

    $\dfrac{1}{\log_a x} = -\log_a x$ Property 2

        $1 = -(\log_a x)^2$ Multiplying by $\log_a x$

     $-1 = (\log_a x)^2$

Since $(\log_a x)^2 \geqslant 0$ for all values of x, the equation has no real-number solution. The solution set is $\emptyset$.

70. $|\log_5 x| = 2$

   $\log_5 x = 2$ or $\log_5 x = -2$

      $x = 25$ or $x = \frac{1}{25}$

71. $\log_7 \sqrt{x^2 - 9} = 1$

      $\sqrt{x^2 - 9} = 7^1$

        $x^2 - 9 = 49$ Squaring both sides

           $x^2 = 58$

            $x = \pm\sqrt{58}$

Both numbers check. The solutions are $\pm\sqrt{58}$.

72. $x \log \frac{1}{6} = \log 6$

     $x = \dfrac{\log 6}{\log \frac{1}{6}} = \dfrac{\log 6}{-\log 6} = -1$

73. $\log (\log x) = 3$ The base is 10.

        $\log x = 10^3 = 1000$

           $x = 10^{1000}$

74. $2^{x^2+4x} = \frac{1}{8}$

        $2^{x^2+4x} = 2^{-3}$

       $x^2 + 4x = -3$

    $x^2 + 4x + 3 = 0$

   $(x + 3)(x + 1) = 0$

   $x = -3$ or $x = -1$

75. $\log_3 |x| = 2$

        $|x| = 3^2 = 9$

   $x = 9$ or $x = -9$

76. $\log_5 |x| = 3$

        $|x| = 5^3 = 125$

   $x = 125$ or $x = -125$

77. $\log x^{\log x} = 4$

   $\log x (\log x) = 4$ Property 2

     $(\log x)^2 = 4$

  $\log x = 2$ or $\log x = -2$

     $x = 10^2$ or $x = 10^{-2}$

     $x = 100$ or $x = \frac{1}{100}$

Both answers check. The solutions are 100 and $\frac{1}{100}$.

78. $\log \sqrt{2x} = \sqrt{\log 2x}$

      $\frac{1}{2} \log 2x = \sqrt{\log 2x}$

      $\frac{1}{4} (\log 2x)^2 = \log 2x$

  $\frac{1}{4}(\log 2x)^2 - \log 2x = 0$

Let $u = \log 2x$, substitute, and solve for u. We obtain:

     $u = 0$ or $u = 4$

  $\log 2x = 0$ or $\log 2x = 4$

     $2x = 10^0$ or $2x = 10^4$

      $x = \frac{1}{2}$ or $x = 5000$

79. $\log_a a^{x^2} + 5x = 24$

        $x^2 + 5x = 24$ Property 4

    $x^2 + 5x - 24 = 0$

   $(x + 8)(x - 3) = 0$

   $x = -8$ or $x = 3$

80.

$$x^{\log x} = \frac{x^3}{100}$$

$$\log x^{\log x} = \log \frac{x^3}{100}$$

$$(\log x)^2 - 3 \log x + 2 = 0$$

Let $u = \log x$.

$$(u - 2)(u - 1) = 0$$

$$u = 2 \quad \text{or} \quad u = 1$$

$$\log x = 2 \quad \text{or} \quad \log x = 1$$

$$x = 100 \quad \text{or} \quad x = 10$$

81.

$$x^{\log_{10} x} = \frac{x^{-4}}{1000}$$

$$x^{\log_{10} x} \cdot x^4 = \frac{1}{1000} \qquad \text{Multiplying by } x^4$$

$$x^{\log_{10} x + 4} = \frac{1}{1000} \qquad \text{Adding exponents}$$

$$\log_{10} x^{\log_{10} x + 4} = \log_{10} \frac{1}{1000}$$

$$(\log_{10} x + 4)\log_{10} x = -3$$

$$(\log_{10} x)^2 + 4 \log_{10} x + 3 = 0$$

Let $u = \log_{10} x$.

$$u^2 + 4u + 3 = 0$$

$$(u + 3)(u + 1) = 0$$

$$u = -3 \quad \text{or} \quad u = -1$$

$$\log_{10} x = -3 \quad \text{or} \quad \log_{10} x = -1$$

$$x = 10^{-3} \quad \text{or} \quad x = 10^{-1}$$

$$x = \frac{1}{1000} \quad \text{or} \quad x = \frac{1}{10}$$

Both numbers check. The solutions are $\frac{1}{1000}$ and $\frac{1}{10}$.

82. $5^{2x} - 9 \cdot 5^x + 14 = 0$

Let $u = 5^x$.

$$(u - 7)(u - 2) = 0$$

$$u = 7 \quad \text{or} \quad u = 2$$

$$5^x = 7 \quad \text{or} \quad 5^x = 2$$

$$x \log 5 = \log 7 \quad \text{or} \quad x \log 5 = \log 2$$

$$x = \frac{\log 7}{\log 5} \quad \text{or} \quad x = \frac{\log 2}{\log 5}$$

$$x \approx 1.2091 \quad \text{or} \quad x \approx 0.4307$$

83. $(32^{x-2})(64^{x+1}) = 16^{2x-3}$

$$(2^5)^{x-2}(2^6)^{x+1} = (2^4)^{2x-3}$$

$$(2^{5x-10})(2^{6x+6}) = 2^{8x-12} \qquad \text{Multiplying exponents}$$

$$2^{11x-4} = 2^{8x-12} \qquad \text{Simplifying}$$

$$11x - 4 = 8x - 12$$

$$3x = -8$$

$$x = -\frac{8}{3}$$

84. $49^{x+2} = 5140 + 49^x$

$$49^{x+2} - 49^x = 5140$$

$$49^x(49^2 - 1) = 5140$$

$$49^x = \frac{5140}{2400}$$

$$x \log 49 = \log \left(\frac{5140}{2400}\right)$$

$$x = \frac{\log \left(\frac{5140}{2400}\right)}{\log 49} \approx 0.1957$$

85. $4^{3x} - 4^{3x-1} = 48$

$$4^{3x-1}(4 - 1) = 48 \qquad \text{Factoring}$$

$$(3)4^{3x-1} = 48$$

$$4^{3x-1} = 16$$

$$4^{3x-1} = 4^2$$

$$3x - 1 = 2$$

$$3x = 3$$

$$x = 1$$

86.

$$x^{\log x} = 100x$$

$$\log x^{\log x} = \log 100x$$

$$(\log x)^2 = 2 + \log x$$

$$(\log x)^2 - \log x - 2 = 0$$

Let $u = \log x$.

$$(u - 2)(u + 1) = 0$$

$$u = 2 \quad \text{or} \quad u = -1$$

$$\log x = 2 \quad \text{or} \quad \log x = -1$$

$$x = 100 \quad \text{or} \quad x = \frac{1}{10}$$

87.

$$\frac{(e^{3x+1})^2}{e^4} = e^{10x}$$

$$\frac{e^{6x+2}}{e^4} = e^{10x}$$

$$e^{6x-2} = e^{10x}$$

$$6x - 2 = 10x$$

$$-2 = 4x$$

$$-\frac{1}{2} = x$$

88.

$$\frac{\sqrt{(e^{2x} \cdot e^{-5x})^{-4}}}{e^x \div e^{-x}} = e^7$$

$$\frac{e^{6x}}{e^{2x}} = e^7$$

$$e^{4x} = e^7$$

$$4x = 7$$

$$x = \frac{7}{4}$$

89.
$$P = P_0 e^{kt}$$
$$\ln P = \ln (P_0 e^{kt})$$
$$\ln P = \ln P_0 + \ln e^{kt}$$
$$\ln P = \ln P_0 + kt \qquad \text{Property 4}$$
$$\ln P - \ln P_0 = kt$$
$$\frac{\ln P - \ln P_0}{k} = t$$

90.
$$P = P_0 e^{-kt}$$
$$\ln P = \ln (P_0 e^{-kt})$$
$$\ln P = \ln P_0 + \ln e^{-kt}$$
$$\ln P = \ln P_0 - kt$$
$$t = \frac{\ln P_0 - \ln P}{k}$$

91.
$$T = T_0 + (T_1 - T_0) e^{-kt}$$
$$T - T_0 = (T_1 - T_0) e^{-kt}$$
$$\frac{T - T_0}{T_1 - T_0} = e^{-kt}$$
$$\ln \left(\frac{T - T_0}{T_1 - T_0}\right) = \ln e^{-kt}$$
$$\ln \left(\frac{T - T_0}{T_1 - T_0}\right) = -kt \qquad \text{Property 4}$$
$$-\frac{1}{k} \ln \left(\frac{T - T_0}{T_1 - T_0}\right) = t$$

92.
$$\log_a Q = \frac{1}{3} \log_a y + b$$
$$\log_a Q = \log_a y^{\frac{1}{3}} + b \qquad \text{Property 2}$$
$$\log_a Q - \log_a y^{\frac{1}{3}} = b$$
$$\log_a \frac{Q}{y^{\frac{1}{3}}} = b \qquad \text{Property 3}$$
$$\frac{Q}{y^{\frac{1}{3}}} = a^b$$
$$Q = a^b y^{\frac{1}{3}}, \text{ or } a^b \sqrt[3]{y}$$

93. $\log_5 125 = 3$ and $\log_{125} 5 = \frac{1}{3}$, so

$x = (\log_{125} 5)^{\log_5 125}$ is equivalent to
$x = \left[\frac{1}{3}\right]^3 = \frac{1}{27}$. Then $\log_3 x = \log_3 \frac{1}{27} = -3$.

94. $2^y = 16^{x-3}$ and $3^{y+2} = 27^x$
$2^y = (2^4)^{x-3}$ and $3^{y+2} = (3^3)^x$
$y = 4x - 12$ and $y + 2 = 3x$
$12 = 4x - y$ and $2 = 3x - y$

Solving this system of equations we get $x = 10$ and $y = 28$. Then $x + y = 10 + 28 = 38$.

95. $|\log_a x| = \log_a |x|$

Case I: Assume $0 < a < 1$.

  A. Assume $0 < x \leqslant 1$. Then $|\log_a x| = \log_a x$ and $|x| = x$. We have:
$$\log_a x = \log_a x$$
  This is true for all values of x in the interval under consideration, $0 < x \leqslant 1$.

  B. Assume $x > 1$. Then $|\log_a x| = -\log_a x$ and $|x| = x$. We have:
$$-\log_a x = \log_a x$$
$$0 = 2 \log_a x$$
$$0 = \log_a x^2$$
$$a^0 = x^2$$
$$1 = x^2$$
$$\pm 1 = x$$

  This yields no solution, since we have assumed $x > 1$.

Case II. Assume $a > 1$.

  A. Assume $0 < x < 1$. Then $|\log_a x| = -\log_a x$ and $|x| = x$. We have:
$$-\log_a x = \log_a x$$
$$0 = 2 \log_a x$$
$$\pm 1 = x \quad \text{(See Case IB above)}$$

  This yields no solution, since we have assumed $0 < x < 1$.

  B. Assume $x \geqslant 1$. Then $|\log_a x| = \log_a x$ and $|x| = x$. We have:
$$\log_a x = \log_a x$$
  This is true for all values of x in the interval under consideration, $x \geqslant 1$.

The solution is as follows:

If $0 < a < 1$, $0 < x \leqslant 1$, and if $a > 1$, $x \geqslant 1$.

96. Case I: $0 < x < 1$
$$-\log_5 x + 3 \log_5 x = 4$$
$$2 \log_5 x = 4$$
$$\log_5 x = 2$$
$$x = 25$$

This case yields no solution, since we have assumed $0 < x < 1$.

Case II: $x \geqslant 1$
$$\log_5 x + 3 \log_5 x = 4$$
$$4 \log_5 x = 4$$
$$\log_5 x = 1$$
$$x = 5$$

97. $(0.5)^x < \frac{4}{5}$

$\log (0.5)^x < \log \frac{4}{5}$

$x \log 0.5 < \log 0.8$ Property 2; writing $\frac{4}{5}$ as 0.8

$x > \dfrac{\log 0.8}{\log 0.5}$ Reversing the inequality symbol ($\log 0.5 < 0$)

or $x > 0.3219$

98. $8x^{0.3} - 8x^{-0.3} = 63$

$8x^{0.6} - 8 = 63x^{0.3}$

$8x^{0.6} - 63x^{0.3} - 8 = 0$

Let $u = x^{0.3}$

$(8u + 1)(u - 8) = 0$

$u = -\frac{1}{8}$ or $u = 8$

$x^{0.3} = -2^{-3}$ or $x^{0.3} = 2^3$

$x = 2^{-10}$ or $x = 2^{10}$

Only 2^{10} checks.

99. $2 \log_3 (x - 2y) = \log_3 x + \log_3 y$

$\log_3 (x - 2y)^2 = \log_3 (xy)$ Properties 2 and 1

$(x - 2y)^2 = xy$

$x^2 - 4xy + 4y^2 = xy$

$x^2 - 5xy + 4y^2 = 0$

$(x - 4y)(x - y) = 0$

$x - 4y = 0$ or $x - y = 0$

$x = 4y$ or $x = y$

$\dfrac{x}{y} = 4$ $\dfrac{x}{y} = 1$

100. $\log_2 [\log_3 (\log_4 x)] = 0$ yields $x = 64$.

$\log_3 [\log_2 (\log_4 y)] = 0$ yields $y = 16$.

$\log_4 [\log_3 (\log_2 z)] = 0$ yields $z = 8$.

Then $x + y + z = 64 + 16 + 8 = 88$.

101. $a = \log_8 225$, so $8^a = 225 = 15^2$.

$b = \log_2 15$, so $2^b = 15$.

Then $8^a = (2^b)^2$

$(2^3)^a = 2^{2b}$

$2^{3a} = 2^{2b}$

$3a = 2b$

$a = \frac{2}{3}b.$

102. $4^{\log_{16} 27} = 2^x 3^y$

Let $\log_{16} 27 = z$. Then

$27 = 16^z = 4^{2z}$, so

$4^z = \sqrt{27} = 3^{\frac{3}{2}}.$

$3^{\frac{3}{2}} = 2^x 3^y$

$0 = 2^x 3^y - 3^{\frac{3}{2}}$

$0 = 3^{\frac{3}{2}}\left(2^x 3^{y - \frac{3}{2}} - 1\right)$

$2^x 3^{y - \frac{3}{2}} = 1$

$3^{y - \frac{3}{2}} = 2^{-x}$

$\left(y - \frac{3}{2}\right) \log 3 = -x \log 2$

$y \log 3 - \frac{3}{2} \log 3 = -x \log 2$

$y = \dfrac{\frac{3}{2} \log 3 - x \log 2}{\log 3}$

The general solution is $\left(x,\ \dfrac{\frac{3}{2} \log 3 - x \log 2}{\log 3}\right).$

When $x = 0$, we have $\left(0, \frac{3}{2}\right).$

103.–122. See <u>69</u>.–<u>88</u>.

Exercise Set 5.8

1. a) One billion is 1000 million, so we set $N(t) = 1000$ and solve for t:

$1000 = 7.5(6)^{0.5t}$

$\dfrac{1000}{7.5} = (6)^{0.5t}$

$\log \dfrac{1000}{7.5} = \log(6)^{0.5t}$

$\log 1000 - \log 7.5 = 0.5t \log 6$

$t = \dfrac{\log 1000 - \log 7.5}{0.5 \log 6}$

$t \approx 5.5$

After about 5.5 years, one billion compact discs will be sold in a year.

b) When $t = 0$, $N(t) = 7.5(6)^{0.5(0)} = 7.5(6)^0 = 7.5(1) = 7.5$. Twice this initial number is 15, so we set $N(t) = 15$ and solve for t:

$15 = 7.5(6)^{0.5t}$

$2 = (6)^{0.5t}$

$\log 2 = \log(6)^{0.5t}$

$\log 2 = 0.5t \log 6$

$t = \dfrac{\log 2}{0.5 \log 6} \approx 0.8$

The doubling time is about 0.8 year.

2. a) $60,000 = 3000(2)^{t/20}$

$20 = (2)^{t/20}$

$\log 20 = \dfrac{t}{20} \log 2$

$t = \dfrac{20 \log 20}{\log 2} \approx 86.4$ minutes

b) $100,000,000 = 3000(2)^{t/20}$

$\dfrac{100,000}{3} = (2)^{t/20}$

$\log \dfrac{100,000}{3} = \dfrac{t}{20} \log 2$

$t = \dfrac{20 \log\left(\dfrac{100,000}{3}\right)}{\log 2} \approx 300.5$ minutes

c) $6000 = 3000(2)^{t/20}$

$2 = (2)^{t/20}$

$1 = \dfrac{t}{20}$

$t = 20$ minutes

3. a) We have

$A(t) = \$50,000(1.09)^{t}.$

b) We set $A(t) = \$450,000$ and solve for t:

$450,000 = 50,000(1.09)^{t}$

$\dfrac{450,000}{50,000} = (1.09)^{t}$

$9 = (1.09)^{t}$

$\log 9 = \log (1.09)^{t}$ Taking the common logarithm on both sides

$\log 9 = t \log 1.09$ Property 2

$t = \dfrac{\log 9}{\log 1.09} \approx 25.5$

It will take about 25.5 years for the $50,000 to grow to $450,000.

c) We set $A(t) = \$100,000$ and solve for t:

$100,000 = 50,000(1.09)^{t}$

$2 = (1.09)^{t}$

$\log 2 = \log (1.09)^{t}$

Taking the common logarithm on both sides

$\log 2 = t \log 1.09$ Property 2

$t = \dfrac{\log 2}{\log 1.09} \approx 8.04$

The doubling time is about 8.04 years.

4. a) $60,000 = 250,000\left(\dfrac{1}{4}\right)^{t}$

$\dfrac{60,000}{250,000} = \left(\dfrac{1}{4}\right)^{t}$

$0.24 = (0.25)^{t}$

$\log 0.24 = t \log 0.25$

$t = \dfrac{\log 0.24}{\log 0.25} \approx 1.0$ year

b) $10 = 250,000\left(\dfrac{1}{4}\right)^{t}$

$\dfrac{10}{250,000} = \left(\dfrac{1}{4}\right)^{t}$

$0.00004 = (0.25)^{t}$

$\log 0.00004 = t \log 0.25$

$t = \dfrac{\log 0.00004}{\log 0.25} \approx 7.3$ years

5. a) We set $V(t) = \$1200$ and solve for t.

$1200 = 5200(0.8)^{t}$

$\dfrac{3}{13} = (0.8)^{t}$

$\log \dfrac{3}{13} = \log (0.8)^{t}$

$\log \dfrac{3}{13} = t \log 0.8$

$t = \dfrac{\log \left(\dfrac{3}{13}\right)}{\log 0.8} \approx 6.6$

After about 6.6 years the salvage value will be $1200.

b) We set $V(t) = \dfrac{1}{2}(\$5200)$, or $2600, and solve for t.

$2600 = 5200(0.8)^{t}$

$0.5 = (0.8)^{t}$

$\log 0.5 = \log (0.8)^{t}$

$\log 0.5 = t \log 0.8$

$t = \dfrac{\log 0.5}{\log 0.8} \approx 3.1$

After about 3.1 years the salvage value will be half of its original value.

6. a) $20 = 2.3(3)^{0.033t}$

$\dfrac{20}{2.3} = 3^{0.033t}$

$\log \left(\dfrac{20}{2.3}\right) = 0.033t \log 3$

$t = \dfrac{\log \left(\dfrac{20}{2.3}\right)}{0.033 \log 3} \approx 59.7$ years

b) $4.6 = 2.3(3)^{0.033t}$

$2 = (3)^{0.033t}$

$\log 2 = 0.033t \log 3$

$t = \dfrac{\log 2}{0.033 \log 3} \approx 19.1$ years

7. a) $S(0) = 68 - 20 \log (0 + 1) = 68 - 20 \log 1 = 68 - 20(0) = 68\%$

b) $S(4) = 68 - 20 \log (4 + 1) = 68 - 20 \log 5 \approx 54\%$

$S(24) = 68 - 20 \log (24 + 1) = 68 - 20 \log 25 \approx 40\%$

c) Using the values we computed in parts (a) and
(b) and any others we wish to calculate, we
sketch the graph:

$S(t) = 68 - 20 \log (t + 1)$

d) We set $S(t) = 50$ and solve for t:

$$50 = 68 - 20 \log (t + 1)$$
$$-18 = -20 \log (t + 1)$$
$$0.9 = \log (t + 1)$$
$$10^{0.9} = t + 1 \qquad \text{Using the definintion of logarithms}$$
$$7.9 \approx t + 1$$
$$6.9 \approx t$$

After about 6.9 months, the average score was
50.

8. a) $S(0) = 78 - 15 \log (0 + 1) = 78 - 15(0) = 78\%$

    b) $S(4) = 78 - 15 \log (4 + 1) \approx 68\%$
        $S(24) = 78 - 15 \log (24 + 1) \approx 57\%$

    c)

$S(t) = 78 - 15 \log(t + 1)$

    d) $$30 = 78 - 15 \log (t + 1)$$
        $$-48 = -15 \log (t + 1)$$
        $$3.2 = \log (t + 1)$$
        $$10^{3.2} = t + 1$$
        $$1585 \approx t + 1$$
        $$t \approx 1584 \text{ months}$$

9. a) $N(1) = 1000 + 200 \log 1 = 1000 + 200(0) = 1000$ units

    b) $N(5) = 1000 + 200 \log 5 \approx 1140$ units

    c) Using the values computed in parts (a) and (b)
and any others we wish to calculate, we can
sketch the graph:

$N(a) = 1000 + 200 \log a$

d) Set $N(a) = 1276$ and solve for a.

$$1276 = 1000 + 200 \log a$$
$$276 = 200 \log a$$
$$1.38 = \log a$$
$$10^{1.38} = a \qquad \text{Using the definition of logarithms}$$
$$23.98833 \approx a$$

About \$23,988.33 would have to be spent.

10. a) $N(1) = 2000 + 500 \log 1 = 2000$ units

    b) $N(8) = 2000 + 500 \log 8 \approx 2452$ units

    c)

$N(a) = 2000 + 500 \log a$

    d) $$5000 = 2000 + 500 \log a$$
        $$6 = \log a$$
        $$1,000,000 = a$$

\$1,000,000 thousand, or \$1,000,000,000 would
have to be spent.

11. We substitute 1.6×10^{-4} for H^+ in the formula for
pH.

$pH = -\log [H^+] = -\log [1.6 \times 10^{-4}] =$
$-[\log 1.6 + \log 10^{-4}] \approx -[0.2041 - 4] =$
$-[-3.7959] = 3.7959 \approx 3.8$

The pH of pineapple juice is about 3.8.

12. $pH = -\log [H^+] = -\log [4.0 \times 10^{-8}] =$
$-[\log 4.0 + \log -8] \approx -[-7.3979] \approx 7.4$

13. We substitute 6.3×10^{-5} for H^+ in the formula
for pH.

$pH = -\log [H^+] = -\log [6.3 \times 10^{-5}] =$
$-[\log 6.3 + \log 10^{-5}] \approx -[0.7993 - 5] =$
$-[-4.2007] = 4.2007 \approx 4.2$

The pH of a tomato is about 4.2.

14. pH = $-\log$ [H$^+$] = $-\log$ [1.6×10^{-8}] =
$-[\log 1.6 + \log 10^{-8}] \approx 7.8$

15. We substitute 5.4 for pH in the formula and solve for H$^+$.

$$5.4 = -\log \text{ [H}^+\text{]}$$
$$-5.4 = \log \text{ [H}^+\text{]}$$
$$10^{-5.4} = \text{H}^+ \qquad \text{Using the definition of logarithm}$$
$$0.0000040 \approx \text{H}^+$$
$$4.0 \times 10^{-6} \approx \text{H}^+$$

The hydrogen ion concentration of rainwater is about 4.0×10^{-6} moles/liter.

16.
$$7 = -\log \text{ [H}^+\text{]}$$
$$-7 = \log \text{ [H}^+\text{]}$$
$$10^{-7} \text{moles/liter} = \text{H}^+$$

17. We substitute 4.8 for pH in the formula and solve for H$^+$.

$$4.8 = -\log \text{ [H}^+\text{]}$$
$$-4.8 = \log \text{ [H}^+\text{]}$$
$$10^{-4.8} = \text{H}^+ \qquad \text{Using the definition of logarithm}$$
$$0.000016 \approx \text{H}^+$$
$$1.6 \times 10^{-5} \approx \text{H}^+$$

The hydrogen ion concentration of wine is about 1.6×10^{-5} moles/liter.

18.
$$3.2 = -\log \text{ [H}^+\text{]}$$
$$-3.2 = \log \text{ [H}^+\text{]}$$
$$10^{-3.2} = \text{H}^+$$
$$0.00063 \approx \text{H}^+$$
$$\text{H}^+ \approx 6.3 \times 10^{-4} \text{ moles/liter}$$

19. We substitute into the formula.

$$R = \log \frac{10^{8.25} I_0}{I_0} = \log 10^{8.25} = 8.25$$

20. $R = \log \dfrac{10^5 I_0}{I_0} = \log 10^5 = 5$

21. We substitute into the formula.

$$R = \log \frac{10^{9.6} \cdot I_0}{I_0} = \log 10^{9.6} = 9.6$$

22.
$$7.2 = \log \frac{I}{I_0}$$
$$10^{7.2} = \frac{I}{I_0}$$
$$10^{7.2} \cdot I_0 = I$$

23. We substitute into the formula.

$$L = 10 \log \frac{2510\ I_0}{I_0} = 10 \log 2510 \approx 10(3.399674) \approx$$
34 decibels

24. $L = 10 \log \dfrac{2,500,000\ I_0}{I_0} = 10 \log 2,500,000 \approx$
64 decibels

25. We substitute into the formula.

$$L = 10 \log \frac{10^6\ I_0}{I_0} = 10 \log 10^6 = 10(6) =$$
60 decibels

26. $L = 10 \log \dfrac{10^9\ I_0}{I_0} = 10 \log 10^9 = 90$ decibels

27. a) Substitute 100 for S(t) and solve for t.
$$100 = 200[1 - (0.86)^t]$$
$$0.5 = 1 - (0.86)^t$$
$$(0.86)^t = 0.5$$
$$\log(0.86)^t = \log 0.5$$
$$t \log 0.86 = \log 0.5$$
$$t = \frac{\log 0.5}{\log 0.86} \approx 4.6$$

The typist's speed will be 100 words per minute after she has studied typing for about 4.6 hours.

b) Substitute 150 for S(t) and solve for t.
$$150 = 200[1 - (0.86)^t]$$
$$0.75 = 1 - (0.86)^t$$
$$(0.86)^t = 0.25$$
$$\log(0.86)^t = \log 0.25$$
$$t \log 0.86 = \log 0.25$$
$$t = \frac{\log 0.25}{\log 0.86} \approx 9.2$$

About 9.2 hours of studying occurred in the course.

28. a) $A = \$100,000(1.02)^{4t}$

b)
$$1,000,000 = 100,000(1.02)^{4t}$$
$$10 = (1.02)^{4t}$$
$$\log 10 = 4t \log 1.02$$
$$\frac{\log 10}{4 \log 1.02} = t$$
$$t \approx 29.1 \text{ years}$$

c)
$$200,000 = 100,000(1.02)^{4t}$$
$$2 = (1.02)^{4t}$$
$$\log 2 = 4t \log 1.02$$
$$\frac{\log 2}{4 \log 1.02} = t$$
$$t \approx 8.8 \text{ years}$$

29. $R = \log \dfrac{I}{I_0}$
$$\frac{I}{I_0} = 10^R$$
$$I = 10^R\ I_0$$

30. $L = 10 \log \frac{I}{I_0}$

$0.1L = \log \frac{I}{I_0}$

$\frac{I}{I_0} = 10^{0.1L}$

$I = 10^{0.1L} I_0$

31. $pH = -\log [H^+]$

$-pH = \log [H^+]$

$[H^+] = 10^{-pH}$

32. a) $L_1 = 10 \log \frac{I_1}{I_0}, \quad L_2 = 10 \log \frac{I_2}{I_0}$

$L_2 - L_1 = 10 \log \frac{I_2}{I_0} - 10 \log \frac{I_1}{I_0}$

$= 10 \log \frac{\frac{I_2}{I_0}}{\frac{I_1}{I_0}}$

$= 10 \log \frac{I_2}{I_1}$

b) $L_1 + L_2 = 10 \log \frac{I_1}{I_0} + 10 \log \frac{I_2}{I_0} =$

$10 \log \left[\frac{I_1 I_2}{I_0^2}\right]$

33. a)   We substitute -1.5 for M_1 and -0.3 for M_2.

$-0.3 - (-1.5) = 2.5 \log \frac{I_1}{I_2}$

$1.2 = 2.5 \log \frac{I_1}{I_2}$

$0.48 = \log \frac{I_1}{I_2}$

$10^{0.48} = \frac{I_1}{I_2}$

$3 \approx \frac{I_1}{I_2}$

b)   We substitute -1.5 for M_1 and 12.6 for M_2.

$12.6 - (-1.5) = 2.5 \log \frac{I_1}{I_2}$

$14.1 = 2.5 \log \frac{I_1}{I_2}$

$5.64 = \log \frac{I_1}{I_2}$

$10^{5.64} = \frac{I_1}{I_2}$

$436,515.8 \approx \frac{I_1}{I_2}$

c)   We substitute 5 for $M_2 - M_1$.

$5 = 2.5 \log \frac{I_1}{I_2}$

$2 = \log \frac{I_1}{I_2}$

$10^2 = \frac{I_1}{I_2}$

$100 = \frac{I_1}{I_2}$

$100 I_2 = I_1$

One star is 100 times brighter than the other.

34. a)   Solve $14.9 = 4.75 - 2.5 \log \left[\frac{L}{3.9 \times 10^{26}}\right]$.

$L \approx 3.4 \times 10^{22}$ watts

b)   Solve $1.4 = 4.75 - 2.5 \log \left[\frac{L}{3.9 \times 10^{26}}\right]$.

$L \approx 8.5 \times 10^{27}$ watts

c) $M = 4.75 - 2.5 \log \left[\frac{L}{3.9 \times 10^{26}}\right]$

$\frac{4.75 - M}{2.5} = \log \left[\frac{L}{3.9 \times 10^{26}}\right]$

$10^{\frac{4.75-M}{2.5}} = \frac{L}{3.9 \times 10^{26}}$

$3.9 \times 10^{26} \times 10^{\frac{4.75-M}{2.5}} = L$

$3.9 \times 10^{26 + \frac{4.75-M}{2.5}} = L$, or

$3.9 \times 10^{\frac{69.75-M}{2.5}} = L$

Exercise Set 5.9

---

1. We substitute 7900 for P, since P is in thousands.

$R(P) = 0.37 \ln P + 0.05$

$R(7900) = 0.37 \ln 7900 + 0.05$

≈ 3.4 ft/sec   Finding ln 7900 on a calculator

2. $R(853) = 0.37 \ln 853 + 0.05 \approx 2.5$ ft/sec

3. We substitute 50.4 for P in the function, since P is in thousands.

$R(50.4) = 0.37 \ln 50.4 + 0.05$

≈ 1.5 ft/sec

4. $R(106) = 0.37 \ln 106 + 0.05 \approx 1.8$ ft/sec

5. a)   We can use the function $C(t) = C_0 e^{kt}$ as a model. At $t = 0$ (1962), the cost was 5¢, or $0.05. We substitute 0.05 for C_0 and 9.7%, or 0.097, for k:

$C(t) = 0.05 e^{0.097t}$

b)   In 1990, $t = 1990 - 1962$, or 28. We substitute 28 for t:

$C(28) = 0.05 e^{0.097(28)}$

$= 0.05 e^{2.716}$

≈ 0.76

In 1993 a Hershey bar will cost about $0.76.

In 2000, $t = 2000 - 1962$, or 38. We substitute 38 for t:

$C(38) = 0.05 e^{0.097(38)}$

$= 0.05 e^{3.686}$

≈ 1.99

In 2000 a Hershey bar will cost about $1.99.

c) We set C(t) = 5 and solve for t:

$$5 = 0.05\,e^{0.097t}$$
$$100 = e^{0.097t}$$
$$\ln 100 = \ln e^{0.097t}$$
$$\ln 100 = 0.097t$$
$$\frac{\ln 100}{0.097} = t$$
$$47.5 \approx t$$

A Hershey bar will cost $5 about 47.5 years after 1962.

d) Using the ordered pairs found in parts (b) and (c) and any others we wish to compute, we draw the graph:

e) To find the doubling time, we set C(t) = 2($0.05), or $0.10 and solve for t:

$$0.1 = 0.05\,e^{0.097t}$$
$$2 = e^{0.097t}$$
$$\ln 2 = \ln e^{0.097t}$$
$$\ln 2 = 0.097t$$
$$\frac{\ln 2}{0.097} = t$$

(Note: We could also have used the expression relating the growth rate k and doubling time T: $T = \frac{\ln 2}{k}$.)

$$7.1 \approx t$$

The doubling time is about 7.1 years.

6. a) $P(t) = 5e^{0.028t}$, where t is the number of years after 1987 and P is in billions.

b) $P(9) = 5e^{0.028(9)} \approx 6.4$ billion
    $P(13) = 5e^{0.028(13)} \approx 7.2$ billion

c) $6 = 5e^{0.028t}$
        $1.2 = e^{0.028t}$
        $\ln 1.2 = 0.028t$ Property 4
        $\frac{\ln 1.2}{0.028} = t$
        $6.5 \approx t$

The population will be 6.0 billion about 6.5 years after 1987.

d)

7. a) We can use the function $P(t) = P_0\,e^{kt}$ as a model. We substitute 6%, or 0.06, for k.
        $$P(t) = P_0\,e^{0.06t}$$

b) In 1995, t = 1995 - 1967, or 28. We substitute 28 for t and $100 for P_0.
        $$C(28) = \$100\,e^{0.06(28)}$$
        $$= \$100\,e^{1.68}$$
        $$\approx \$536.56$$

Goods and services that cost $100 in 1967 will cost about $536.56 in 1995.

c) In 2000, t = 2000 - 1967, or 33. We substitute 33 for t and $100 for P_0.
        $$C(33) = \$100\,e^{0.06(33)}$$
        $$= \$100\,e^{1.98}$$
        $$\approx \$724.27$$

Goods and services that cost $100 in 1967 will cost about $724.27 in 2000.

d) Using the ordered pairs found in parts (b) and (c) and any others we wish to compute, we draw the graph:

8. a) $P(t) = 100\,e^{0.117t}$

b) $P(7) = 100\,e^{0.117(7)} \approx 227$

c)

d) $t = \dfrac{\ln 2}{0.117} \approx 5.9$ days

9. a) We plot the ordered pairs given in the table and sketch the following graph. We draw a curve as close to the data points as possible. It is very close to the graph of an exponential function.

b) The exponential growth function is $C(t) = C_0\, e^{kt}$. Substituting 80 for C_0, we have

$$C(t) = 80\, e^{kt},$$

where t is the number of years after 1967.

To find k using the data point $C(21) = \$1350$ thousand, we substitute \$1350 for $C(t)$ and 21 for t and solve for k:

$$1350 = 80\, e^{k(21)}$$
$$16.875 = e^{21k}$$
$$\ln 16.875 = \ln e^{21k}$$
$$\ln 16.875 = 21k$$
$$\frac{\ln 16.875}{21} = k$$
$$0.135 \approx k$$

The exponential growth function for the cost of a Super Bowl commercial is

$$C(t) = 80\, e^{0.135t}.$$

c) The year 1995 is 28 years from 1967. We let $t = 28$ and find $C(28)$:

$$C(28) = 80\, e^{0.135(28)} \approx 3505$$

The cost of a 60-second commercial will be about \$3505 thousand, or \$3,505,000 in 1995.

d) We set $C(t) = 3000$ (\$3000 thousand is \$3,000,000) and solve for t:

$$3000 = 80\, e^{0.135t}$$
$$37.5 = e^{0.135t}$$
$$\ln 37.5 = \ln e^{0.135t}$$
$$\ln 37.5 = 0.135t$$
$$\frac{\ln 37.5}{0.135} = t$$
$$26.8 \approx t$$

The cost of a commercial will be \$3,000,000 about 26.8 years after 1967.

e) We can set $C(t) = 160$ and solve for t, or we can use the expression relating growth rate k and doubling time T, $T = \dfrac{\ln 2}{k}$. We will use the latter.

$$T = \frac{\ln 2}{0.135} \approx 5.1 \text{ years}$$

10. a) $P(t) = 52\, e^{kt}$, where t is the number of years after 1970.

$$66 = 52\, e^{k(8)}$$
$$\frac{33}{26} = e^{8k}$$
$$\ln \frac{33}{26} = \ln e^{8k}$$
$$\frac{\ln \frac{33}{26}}{8} = k$$
$$0.03 \approx k$$
$$P(t) = 52\, e^{0.03t}$$

b) $P(24) = 52\, e^{0.03(24)} \approx 107\cent$, or \$1.07

c) $T = \dfrac{\ln 2}{0.03} \approx 23$ years

d)
$$300 = 52\, e^{0.03t}$$
$$\frac{75}{13} = e^{0.03t}$$
$$\ln \frac{75}{13} = \ln e^{0.03t}$$
$$\frac{\ln \frac{75}{13}}{0.03} = t$$
$$58 \approx t$$

In about 58 years from 1970

11. a) Substitute 0.09 for k:
$$P(t) = P_0\, e^{0.09t}$$

b) To find the balance after one year, set $P_0 = 5000$ and $t = 1$. We find $P(1)$:

$$P(1) = 5000\, e^{0.09(1)} = 5000\, e^{0.09} \approx \$5470.87$$

To find the balance after 2 years, set $P_0 = 5000$ and $t = 2$. We find $P(2)$:

$$P(2) = 5000\, e^{0.09(2)} = 5000\, e^{0.18} \approx \$5986.09$$

c) We will use the expression relating growth rate k and doubling time T. (We could also set $P(t) = 10,000$ and solve for t.)

$$T = \frac{\ln 2}{0.09} \approx 7.7 \text{ years}$$

12. a) $P(t) = P_0\, e^{0.1t}$

b) $P(1) = 35{,}000\, e^{0.1(1)} \approx \$38{,}680.98$
$P(2) = 35{,}000\, e^{0.1(2)} \approx \$42{,}749.10$

c) $T = \dfrac{\ln 2}{0.1} \approx 6.9$ years

13. We will use the expression relating growth rate k and doubling time T:
$$T = \frac{\ln 2}{k}.$$

Substitute 3.5%, or 0.035, for k:
$$T = \frac{\ln 2}{0.035} \approx 19.8 \text{ years}$$

14. $T = \frac{\ln 2}{0.01} \approx 69.3 \text{ years}$

15. We will use the expression relating growth rate k and doubling time T:
$$k = \frac{\ln 2}{T}$$

$$k = \frac{\ln 2}{7} \approx 0.099$$

The annual interest rate is about 9.9%.

16. $k = \frac{\ln 2}{5.4} \approx 0.128$, or 12.8%

17. a) The exponential growth function is $V(t) = V_0 e^{kt}$, where t is the number of years after 1947. Since $V_0 = 84,000$ we have
$$V(t) = 84,000 e^{kt}.$$

In 1987 (t = 40), we know that $V(t) = 53,900,000$. We substitute and solve for k.
$$53,900,000 = 84,000 e^{k(40)}$$

$$\frac{1925}{3} = e^{40k}$$

$$\ln \frac{1925}{3} = \ln e^{40k}$$

$$\ln \frac{1925}{3} = 40k$$

$$\frac{\ln \frac{1925}{3}}{40} = k$$

$$0.16 \approx k$$

The exponential growth rate is about 0.16, or 16%. The exponential growth function is $V(t) = 84,000 e^{0.16t}$, where t is the number of years after 1947.

b) In 2007, t = 60. We find V(60).
$$V(60) = 84,000 e^{0.16(60)} = 84,000 e^{9.6} \approx \$1,240,241,652$$

c) We will use the expression relating growth rate k and doubling time T. (We could also set V(t) = 168,000 and solve for t.)
$$T = \frac{\ln 2}{k} = \frac{\ln 2}{0.16} \approx 4.3 \text{ years}$$

d) We set V(t) = 1,000,000,000 and solve for t.
$$1,000,000,000 = 84,000 e^{0.16t}$$

$$\frac{250,000}{21} = e^{0.16t}$$

$$\ln \frac{250,000}{21} = \ln e^{0.16t}$$

$$\ln \frac{250,000}{21} = 0.16t$$

$$\frac{\ln \frac{250,000}{21}}{0.16} = t$$

$$58.7 \approx t$$

The value of the painting will be $1 billion about 58.7 years after 1947.

18. a)
$$27 = 7.75 e^{k(4)}$$

$$\frac{27}{7.75} = e^{4k}$$

$$\ln \frac{27}{7.75} = 4k$$

$$\frac{\ln \frac{27}{7.75}}{4} = k$$

$$0.31 \approx k$$

$V(t) = 7.75 e^{0.31t}$, where t is the number of years after 1983.

b) $V(12) = 7.75 e^{0.31(12)} \approx \$319.80$
$V(17) = 7.75 e^{0.31(17)} \approx \$1506.72$

c) $T = \frac{\ln 2}{0.31} \approx 2.2 \text{ years}$

d)
$$2000 = 7.75 e^{0.31t}$$

$$\frac{2000}{7.75} = e^{0.31t}$$

$$\ln \frac{2000}{7.75} = 0.31t$$

$$\frac{\ln \frac{2000}{7.75}}{0.31} = t$$

$$t \approx 17.9 \text{ years}$$

19. Using the expression relating growth rate k and doubling time T, we substitute 4%, or 0.04, for k:
$$T = \frac{\ln 2}{0.04} \approx 17.3 \text{ years from 1990}$$

20. $T = \frac{\ln 2}{0.1} \approx 6.9 \text{ years from 1990}$

21. a) The exponential growth function with $P_0 = 2,812,000$ is $P(t) = 2,812,000\ e^{kt}$, where t is the number of years after 1970. To find k we substitue 14 for t and 3,097,000 for P and solve for k.

$$3,097,000 = 2,812,000\ e^{k(14)}$$

$$\frac{3,097,000}{2,812,000} = e^{14k}$$

$$\ln \frac{3,097,000}{2,812,000} = \ln e^{14k}$$

$$\ln \frac{3,097,000}{2,812,000} = 14k$$

$$\frac{\ln \frac{3,097,000}{2,812,000}}{14} = k$$

$$0.007 \approx k$$

The value of k is about 0.007, or 0.7%. The exponential growth function is

$$P(t) = 2,812,000\ e^{0.007t},$$

where t is the number of years after 1970.

b) In 1996, $t = 1996 - 1970$, or 26. We find $P(26)$.

$$P(26) = 2,812,000\ e^{0.007(26)} =$$
$$2,812,000\ e^{0.182} \approx 3,373,315$$

In 1996 the population of Los Angeles will be about 3,373,315.

22. a)
$$843,000 = 786,000\ e^{k(4)}$$

$$\frac{843,000}{786,000} = e^{4k}$$

$$\ln \frac{843,000}{786,000} = 4k$$

$$\frac{\ln \frac{843,000}{786,000}}{4} = k$$

$$k \approx 0.018, \text{ or } 1.8\%$$

$P(t) = 786,000\ e^{0.018t}$, where t is the number of years after 1980.

b) $P(20) = 786,000\ e^{0.018(20)} \approx 1,126,597$

23. We will use the function derived in Example 7:
$$P(t) = P_0\ e^{-0.00012t}$$

If the mummy has lost 46% of its carbon-14, then 54% (P_0) is the amount present. To find the age of the mummy, we substitute 54% (P_0), or 0.54 P_0, for $P(t)$ and solve for t.

$$0.54\ P_0 = P_0\ e^{-0.00012t}$$

$$0.54 = e^{-0.00012t}$$

$$\ln 0.54 = \ln e^{-0.00012t}$$

$$\ln 0.54 \approx -0.00012t$$

$$t \approx \frac{\ln 0.54}{-0.00012} \approx 5135 \text{ years}$$

24.
$$P(t) = P_0\ e^{-0.00012t}$$
$$0.65\ P_0 = P_0\ e^{-0.00012t}$$
$$0.65 = e^{-0.00012t}$$
$$\ln 0.65 = -0.00012t$$
$$t = \frac{\ln 0.65}{-0.00012} \approx 3590 \text{ years}$$

25. We use the function $P(t) = P_0\ e^{-kt}$, $k > 0$. When $t = 3$, $P(t) = \frac{1}{2}\ P_0$. We substitute and solve for k.

$$\frac{1}{2}\ P_0 = P_0\ e^{-k(3)}, \text{ or } \frac{1}{2} = e^{-3k}$$

$$\ln \frac{1}{2} = \ln e^{-3k} = -3k$$

$$k = \frac{\ln 0.5}{-3} \approx 0.231$$

The decay rate is 0.231, or 23.1% per minute.

26.
$$P(t) = P_0\ e^{-kt}, \ k > 0$$
$$\frac{1}{2}\ P_0 = P_0\ e^{-k(22)}$$
$$\frac{1}{2} = e^{-22k}$$
$$\ln 0.5 = -22k$$
$$k = \frac{\ln 0.5}{-22} \approx 0.032, \text{ or } 3.2\% \text{ per year}$$

27. We use the function $P(t) = P_0\ e^{-kt}$, $k > 0$. For iodine-131, $k = 9.6\%$, or 0.096. To find the half-life we substitute 0.096 for k and $\frac{1}{2}\ P_0$ for $P(t)$, and solve for t.

$$\frac{1}{2}\ P_0 = P_0\ e^{-0.096t}, \text{ or } \frac{1}{2} = e^{-0.096t}$$

$$\ln \frac{1}{2} = \ln e^{-0.096t} = -0.096t$$

$$t = \frac{\ln 0.5}{-0.096} \approx 7.2 \text{ days}$$

28.
$$P(t) = P_0\ e^{-kt}, \ k > 0$$
$$\frac{1}{2}\ P_0 = P_0\ e^{-0.063t}$$
$$\frac{1}{2} = e^{-0.063t}$$
$$\ln 0.5 = -0.063t$$
$$t = \frac{\ln 0.5}{-0.063} \approx 11 \text{ years}$$

29. a) The value of k in the function is 0.007, so the animal loses 0.7% of its weight each day.

b) Find $W(30)$.
$$W(30) = W_0\ e^{-0.007(30)} = W_0\ e^{-0.21} \approx 0.811\ W_0$$
After 30 days, about 0.811, or 81.1%, of its initial weight W_0 remains.

30. a) $P(365) = 60\ e^{-0.006(365)} \approx 6.7$ watts

    b) $30 = 60\ e^{-0.006t}$

    $0.5 = e^{-0.006t}$

    $\ln 0.5 = -0.006t$

    $t = \dfrac{\ln 0.5}{-0.006} \approx 115.5$ days

    c) $10 = 60\ e^{-0.006t}$

    $\dfrac{1}{6} = e^{-0.006t}$

    $\ln \dfrac{1}{6} = -0.006t$

    $t = \dfrac{\ln \dfrac{1}{6}}{-0.006} \approx 298.6$ days

    d) $P(0) = 60$ watts

31. a) Substitute 14.7 for P_0 and 2000 for a.
    $P = 14.7\ e^{-0.00005(2000)} = 14.7\ e^{-0.1} \approx$
    13.3 lb/in²

    b) Substitute 14.7 for P_0 and 14,162 for a.
    $P = 14.7\ e^{-0.00005(14,162)} = 14.7\ e^{-0.7081} \approx$
    7.24 lb/in²

    c) Substitute 1.47 for P and 14.7 for P_0, and solve for a.

    $1.47 = 14.7\ e^{-0.00005a}$

    $0.1 = e^{-0.00005a}$

    $\ln 0.1 = \ln e^{-0.00005a}$

    $\ln 0.1 = -0.00005a$

    $a = \dfrac{\ln 0.1}{-0.00005} \approx 46,052$ ft

    d) Substitute 14.7 for P_0 and 0.39 for P and solve for a.

    $0.39 = 14.7\ e^{-0.00005a}$

    $\dfrac{0.39}{14.7} = e^{-0.00005a}$

    $\ln \dfrac{0.39}{14.7} = \ln e^{-0.00005a}$

    $\ln \dfrac{0.39}{14.7} = -0.00005a$

    $\dfrac{\ln \dfrac{0.39}{14.7}}{-0.00005} = a$

    $a \approx 72,589$ ft

32. a) $V(0) = \$46,000$

    b) $V(2) = \$46,000\ e^{-2} \approx \$6225.42$

33. a) At 1 m: $I = I_0\ e^{-1.4(1)} \approx 0.247\ I_0$
    24.7% of I_0 remains.

    At 3 m: $I = I_0\ e^{-1.4(3)} \approx 0.015\ I_0$
    1.5% of I_0 remains.

At 5 m: $I = I_0\ e^{-1.4(5)} \approx 0.0009\ I_0$
0.09% of I_0 remains.

At 50 m: $I = I_0\ e^{-1.4(50)} \approx (3.98 \times 10^{-31})\ I_0$
$3.98 \times 10^{-31} = (3.98 \times 10^{-29}) \times 10^{-2}$, so
(3.98×10^{-29})% remains.

b) $I = I_0\ e^{-1.4(10)} \approx 0.0000008\ I_0$
0.00008% remains

34. $50,000 = P_0\ e^{0.08(18)}$
    $P_0 \approx \$11,846.39$

35. $v = c\ \ln R$

    $\dfrac{v}{c} = \ln R$

    $R = e^{\frac{v}{c}}$

36. $i = \dfrac{V}{R}\left[1 - e^{-(R/L)t}\right]$

    $\dfrac{iR}{V} = 1 - e^{-(R/L)t}$

    $e^{-(R/L)t} = 1 - \dfrac{iR}{V}$

    $-\dfrac{R}{L}t = \ln\left(1 - \dfrac{iR}{V}\right)$

    $t = -\dfrac{L}{R}\left[\ln\left(1 - \dfrac{iR}{V}\right)\right]$

37. Measure the atmospheric pressure P at the top of building. Substitute that value in the equation $P = 14.7\ e^{-0.00005a}$, and solve for the height, or altitude, a, of the top of the building. Also measure the atmospheric pressure at the base of the building and solve for the altitude of the base. Then subtract to find the height of the building.

38. To find k we substitute 105 for T_1, 32 for T_0, 5 for t, and 70 for $T(t)$ and solve for k.

    $70 = 32 + |105 - 32|\ e^{-k(5)}$

    $38 = 73\ e^{-5k}$

    $\dfrac{38}{73} = e^{-5k}$

    $\ln \dfrac{38}{73} = \ln e^{-5k}$

    $\ln \dfrac{38}{73} = -5k$

    $k = \dfrac{\ln \dfrac{38}{73}}{-5} \approx 0.13$

The function is
    $T(t) = 32 + 73\ e^{-0.13t}.$

We find $T(10)$.
    $T(10) = 32 + 73\ e^{-0.13(10)} \approx 51.9°$ F

39. To find k we substitute 94.6 for T_1, 70 for T_0, 60 for t (1 hr = 60 min), and 93.4 for T(t).

$$93.4 = 70 + |94.6 - 70| e^{-k(60)}$$

$$23.4 = 24.6\, e^{-60k}$$

$$\frac{23.4}{24.6} = e^{-60k}$$

$$\ln \frac{23.4}{24.6} = \ln e^{-60k}$$

$$\ln \frac{23.4}{24.6} = -60k$$

$$k = \frac{\ln \dfrac{23.4}{24.6}}{-60} \approx 0.0008$$

The function is

$$T(t) = 70 + 24.6\, e^{-0.0008t}.$$

We substitute 98.6 for T(t) and solve for t.

$$98.6 = 70 + 24.6\, e^{-0.0008t}$$

$$28.6 = 24.6\, e^{-0.0008t}$$

$$\frac{28.6}{24.6} = e^{-0.0008t}$$

$$\ln \frac{28.6}{24.6} = \ln e^{-0.0008t}$$

$$\ln \frac{28.6}{24.6} = -0.0008t$$

$$t = \frac{\ln \dfrac{28.6}{24.6}}{-0.0008} \approx -188$$

The murder was committed at approximately 188 minutes, or about 3 hours, before 12:00 PM, or at about 9:00 AM.

Exercise Set 6.1

1. See the answer section in the text.

2.

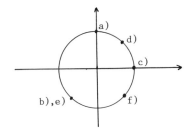

3. See the answer section in the text.

4.

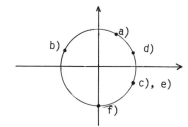

5. See the answer section in the text.

6.

7.

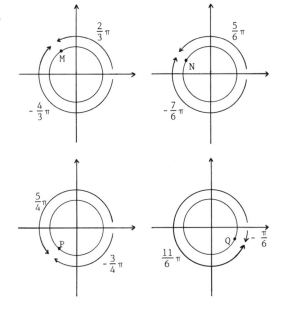

8. M: $\frac{\pi}{3}$, $-\frac{5\pi}{3}$;   N: $\frac{7\pi}{4}$, $-\frac{\pi}{4}$

   P: $\frac{4\pi}{3}$, $-\frac{2\pi}{3}$;   Q: $\frac{7\pi}{6}$, $-\frac{5\pi}{6}$

9.

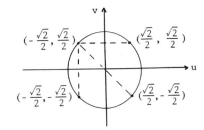

a) $\left(-\frac{\sqrt{2}}{2}, -\frac{\sqrt{2}}{2}\right)$,   b) $\left(\frac{\sqrt{2}}{2}, \frac{\sqrt{2}}{2}\right)$,

c) $\left(\frac{\sqrt{2}}{2}, -\frac{\sqrt{2}}{2}\right)$

10. a) $\left(-\frac{3}{4}, -\frac{\sqrt{7}}{4}\right)$,   b) $\left(\frac{3}{4}, \frac{\sqrt{7}}{4}\right)$,   c) $\left(\frac{3}{4}, -\frac{\sqrt{7}}{4}\right)$

11.

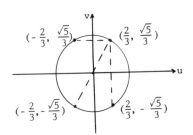

a) $\left(\frac{2}{3}, -\frac{\sqrt{5}}{3}\right)$,   b) $\left(-\frac{2}{3}, \frac{\sqrt{5}}{3}\right)$,   c) $\left(-\frac{2}{3}, -\frac{\sqrt{5}}{3}\right)$

12. a) $\left(-\frac{\sqrt{3}}{2}, \frac{1}{2}\right)$,   b) $\left(\frac{\sqrt{3}}{2}, -\frac{1}{2}\right)$,   c) $\left(\frac{\sqrt{3}}{2}, \frac{1}{2}\right)$

13.

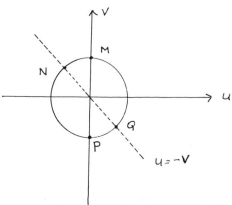

M and P are intercepts of the unit circle. The coordinates of M are (0, 1), and the coordinates of P are (0, -1). N is the intersection of the unit circle with the line u = -v. Then for N we know that u = -v, u < 0, and v > 0 (since N is in quadrant II). We substitute in the equation of the unit circle:

$$u^2 + v^2 = 1$$
$$(-v)^2 + v^2 = 1, \text{ or } 2v^2 = 1$$
$$v^2 = \frac{1}{2}$$
$$v = \sqrt{\frac{1}{2}}, \text{ or } \frac{\sqrt{2}}{2} \qquad (v > 0)$$

Then $u = -v = -\frac{\sqrt{2}}{2}$.

The coordinates of N are $\left[-\frac{\sqrt{2}}{2}, \frac{\sqrt{2}}{2}\right]$.

Q is the reflection of N across the origin. Hence its coordinates are $\left[\frac{\sqrt{2}}{2}, -\frac{\sqrt{2}}{2}\right]$.

14. M and P are intercepts of the unit circle. The coordinates of M are (1, 0), and the coordinates of P are (-1, 0). N is on the line $u = v$. Both coordinates of N are positive since N is in quadrant I. We substitute in the equation of the unit circle:

$$u^2 + u^2 = 1$$
$$2u^2 = 1$$
$$u^2 = \frac{1}{2}$$
$$u = \sqrt{\frac{1}{2}}, \text{ or } \frac{\sqrt{2}}{2}$$

Then $u = v = \frac{\sqrt{2}}{2}$, so the coordinates of N are $\left[\frac{\sqrt{2}}{2}, \frac{\sqrt{2}}{2}\right]$. Q is the reflection of N across the origin. Hence the coordinates of Q are $\left[-\frac{\sqrt{2}}{2}, -\frac{\sqrt{2}}{2}\right]$.

15. The point determined by $-\frac{\pi}{6}$ is a reflection across the u-axis of the point determined by $\frac{\pi}{6}$, $\left[\frac{\sqrt{3}}{2}, \frac{1}{2}\right]$. The first coordinates are the same, and the second coordinates are opposites of each other. The coordinates of the point determined by $-\frac{\pi}{6}$ are $\left[\frac{\sqrt{3}}{2}, -\frac{1}{2}\right]$.

16. The point determined by $-\frac{\pi}{3}$ is a reflection across the u-axis of the point determined by $\frac{\pi}{3}$. Its coordinates are $\left[\frac{1}{2}, -\frac{\sqrt{3}}{2}\right]$.

17. The point determined by $-\alpha$ is a reflection across the u-axis of the point determined by α, $\left[\frac{3}{4}, -\frac{\sqrt{7}}{4}\right]$. The first coordinates are the same, and the second coordinates are opposites of each other. The coordinates of the point determined by $-\alpha$ are $\left[\frac{3}{4}, \frac{\sqrt{7}}{4}\right]$.

18. The point determined by $-\beta$ is a reflection across the u-axis of the point determined by β. Its coordinates are $\left[-\frac{2}{3}, -\frac{\sqrt{5}}{3}\right]$.

19. We use the results of Exercise 7 to find the numbers.

M: $\frac{2\pi}{3} + 2\pi$, or $\frac{8\pi}{3}$

N: $\frac{5\pi}{6} + 2\pi$, or $\frac{17\pi}{6}$

P: $\frac{5\pi}{4} + 2\pi$, or $\frac{13\pi}{4}$

Q: $\frac{11\pi}{6} + 2\pi$, or $\frac{23\pi}{6}$

20. M: $-\frac{5\pi}{3} - 2\pi$, or $-\frac{11\pi}{3}$;

N: $-\frac{\pi}{4} - 2\pi$, or $-\frac{9\pi}{4}$;

P: $-\frac{2\pi}{3} - 2\pi$, or $-\frac{8\pi}{3}$;

Q: $-\frac{5\pi}{6} - 2\pi$, or $-\frac{17\pi}{6}$

21. We substitute in the equation of the unit circle.

$$u^2 + v^2 = 1$$
$$\left[-\frac{1}{3}\right]^2 + v^2 = 1$$
$$\frac{1}{9} + v^2 = 1$$
$$v^2 = \frac{8}{9}$$
$$v = \pm\frac{\sqrt{8}}{3} = \pm\frac{2\sqrt{2}}{3}$$

The v-coordinate of the point is $\frac{2\sqrt{2}}{3}$ or $-\frac{2\sqrt{2}}{3}$.

22. $u^2 + \left[-\frac{\sqrt{21}}{5}\right]^2 = 1$

$$u^2 = \frac{4}{25}$$
$$u = \pm\frac{2}{5}$$

Exercise Set 6.2

1. The point $\frac{\pi}{4}$ has coordinates $\left[\frac{\sqrt{2}}{2}, \frac{\sqrt{2}}{2}\right]$ on the unit circle. The value of the sine function is the second coordinate.

$$\sin\frac{\pi}{4} = \frac{\sqrt{2}}{2}$$

2. 0

3. The point $\frac{\pi}{6}$ has coordinates $\left[\frac{\sqrt{3}}{2}, \frac{1}{2}\right]$ on the unit circle. The value of the sine function is the second coordinate.

$$\sin\frac{\pi}{6} = \frac{1}{2}$$

4. $-\frac{\sqrt{2}}{2}$

5. The point $\frac{3\pi}{2}$ has coordinates $(0, -1)$ on the unit circle.

$$\sin \frac{3\pi}{2} = -1$$

6. 1

7. The point $\frac{\pi}{3}$ has coordinates $\left[\frac{1}{2}, \frac{\sqrt{3}}{2}\right]$ on the unit circle.

$$\sin \frac{\pi}{3} = \frac{\sqrt{3}}{2}$$

8. $\frac{\sqrt{2}}{2}$

9. The point $\frac{7\pi}{4}$ has coordinates $\left[\frac{\sqrt{2}}{2}, -\frac{\sqrt{2}}{2}\right]$ on the unit circle.

$$\sin \frac{7\pi}{4} = -\frac{\sqrt{2}}{2}$$

10. 0

11. The point $\frac{5\pi}{6}$ has coordinates $\left[-\frac{\sqrt{3}}{2}, \frac{1}{2}\right]$ on the unit circle.

$$\sin \frac{5\pi}{6} = \frac{1}{2}$$

12. $-\frac{\sqrt{2}}{2}$

13. The point $-\pi$ has coordinates $(-1, 0)$ on the unit circle.

$$\sin (-\pi) = 0$$

14. -1

15. The point $-\frac{3\pi}{4}$ has coordinates $\left[-\frac{\sqrt{2}}{2}, -\frac{\sqrt{2}}{2}\right]$ on the unit circle.

$$\sin \left[-\frac{3\pi}{4}\right] = -\frac{\sqrt{2}}{2}$$

16. $\frac{\sqrt{2}}{2}$

17. The point $-\frac{5\pi}{4}$ has coordinates $\left[-\frac{\sqrt{2}}{2}, \frac{\sqrt{2}}{2}\right]$ on the unit circle.

$$\sin \left[-\frac{5\pi}{4}\right] = \frac{\sqrt{2}}{2}$$

18. 1

19. The point $-\frac{\pi}{3}$ has coordinates $\left[\frac{1}{2}, -\frac{\sqrt{3}}{2}\right]$ on the unit circle.

$$\sin \left[-\frac{\pi}{3}\right] = -\frac{\sqrt{3}}{2}$$

20. 0

21. The point $-\frac{2\pi}{3}$ has coordinates $\left[-\frac{1}{2}, -\frac{\sqrt{3}}{2}\right]$ on the unit circle.

$$\sin \left[-\frac{2\pi}{3}\right] = -\frac{\sqrt{3}}{2}$$

22. $-\frac{1}{2}$

23. The value of the cosine function of a number is the first coordinate of the point on the unit circle determined by the number. See Exercise 1 for the coordinates of the point $\frac{\pi}{4}$ on the unit circle.

$$\cos \frac{\pi}{4} = \frac{\sqrt{2}}{2}$$

24. -1

25. The point $\frac{5\pi}{4}$ has coordinates $\left[-\frac{\sqrt{2}}{2}, -\frac{\sqrt{2}}{2}\right]$ on the unit circle.

$$\cos \frac{5\pi}{4} = -\frac{\sqrt{2}}{2}$$

26. $\frac{\sqrt{3}}{2}$

27. The point $\frac{\pi}{2}$ has coordinates $(0, 1)$ on the unit circle.

$$\cos \frac{\pi}{2} = 0$$

28. $\frac{1}{2}$

29. The point $\frac{3\pi}{4}$ has coordinates $\left[-\frac{\sqrt{2}}{2}, \frac{\sqrt{2}}{2}\right]$ on the unit circle.

$$\cos \frac{3\pi}{4} = -\frac{\sqrt{2}}{2}$$

30. $\frac{\sqrt{2}}{2}$

31. $\cos \frac{3\pi}{2} = 0$ (See Exercise 5.)

32. $-\frac{\sqrt{3}}{2}$

33. The point $-\frac{\pi}{4}$ has coordinates $\left[\frac{\sqrt{2}}{2}, -\frac{\sqrt{2}}{2}\right]$ on the unit circle.

$$\cos \left[-\frac{\pi}{4}\right] = \frac{\sqrt{2}}{2}$$

34. -1

35. The point 2π has coordinates $(1, 0)$ on the unit circle.

$$\cos 2\pi = 1$$

36. 0

37. $\cos\left(-\frac{3\pi}{4}\right) = -\frac{\sqrt{2}}{2}$ (See Exercise 15.)

38. $-\frac{\sqrt{2}}{2}$

39. The point $-\frac{3\pi}{2}$ has coordinates (0, 1) on the unit circle.

$$\cos\left(-\frac{3\pi}{2}\right) = 0$$

40. $\frac{1}{2}$

41. The point $-\frac{\pi}{6}$ has coordinates $\left(\frac{\sqrt{3}}{2}, -\frac{1}{2}\right)$ on the unit circle.

$$\cos\left(-\frac{\pi}{6}\right) = \frac{\sqrt{3}}{2}$$

42. $\frac{\sqrt{2}}{2}$

43. $\cos\left(-\frac{2\pi}{3}\right) = -\frac{1}{2}$ (See Exercise 21.)

44. 1

45. $\cos(-x) = \cos x$

46. $\sin(-x) = -\sin x$

47. $\sin(x + \pi) = -\sin x$

48. $\sin(x - \pi) = -\sin x$

49. $\cos(\pi - x) = -\cos x$

50. $\sin(\pi - x) = \sin x$

51. $\cos(x + 2k\pi) = \cos x$

52. $\sin(x + 2k\pi) = \sin x$

53. $\cos(x - \pi) = -\cos x$

54. $\cos(x + \pi) = -\cos x$

55. See the answer section in the text.

56. a) See Margin Exercise 8.

     b) Same as a).

c)

d) Same

57. See the answer section in the text.

58. a) See Margin Exercise 3.

     b)

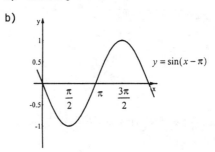

     c) Same as b).

     d) Same

59. See the answer section in the text.

60. a) See Margin Exercise 8.

     b)

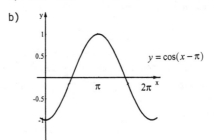

     c) Same as b).

     d) Same

61. a) $\sin\frac{\pi}{2} = 1$

$\sin\left(\frac{\pi}{2} + 2\pi\right) = 1$ $\sin\left(\frac{\pi}{2} - 2\pi\right) = 1$

$\sin\left(\frac{\pi}{2} + 2\cdot 2\pi\right) = 1$ $\sin\left(\frac{\pi}{2} - 2\cdot 2\pi\right) = 1$

$\sin\left(\frac{\pi}{2} + 3\cdot 2\pi\right) = 1$ $\sin\left(\frac{\pi}{2} - 3\cdot 2\pi\right) = 1$

$\sin\left(\frac{\pi}{2} + k\cdot 2\pi\right) = 1$, k any integer

Thus

$x = \frac{\pi}{2} + 2k\pi$, k any integer

b) $\sin \frac{3\pi}{2} = -1$

$\sin \left[\frac{3\pi}{2} + 2\pi\right] = -1$ $\sin \left[\frac{3\pi}{2} - 2\pi\right] = -1$

$\sin \left[\frac{3\pi}{2} + 2\cdot2\pi\right] = -1$ $\sin \left[\frac{3\pi}{2} - 2\cdot2\pi\right] = -1$

$\sin \left[\frac{3\pi}{2} + 3\cdot2\pi\right] = -1$ $\sin \left[\frac{3\pi}{2} - 3\cdot2\pi\right] = -1$

$\sin \left[\frac{3\pi}{2} + k\cdot2\pi\right] = -1$, k any integer

Thus

$x = \frac{3\pi}{2} + 2k\pi$, k any integer

62. a) $\cos (0 + k\cdot2\pi) = 1$, so $x = 2k\pi$, k any integer

b) $\cos (\pi + k\cdot2\pi) = -1$, so $x = \pi + 2k\pi$, or $(2k + 1)\pi$, k any integer

63. For which numbers, x, is $\sin x = 0$?

$\sin 0 = 0$
$\sin \pi = 0$ $\sin (-\pi) = 0$
$\sin 2\pi = 0$ $\sin (-2\pi) = 0$
$\sin 3\pi = 0$ $\sin (-3\pi) = 0$
$\sin 4\pi = 0$ $\sin (-4\pi) = 0$
In general, $\sin k\pi = 0$, k any integer.
Thus $x = k\pi$, k any integer.

64. $\cos \frac{\pi}{2} = 0$ $\cos \left[-\frac{\pi}{2}\right] = 0$

$\cos \frac{3\pi}{2} = 0$ $\cos \left[-\frac{3\pi}{2}\right] = 0$

$\cos \frac{5\pi}{2} = 0$ $\cos \left[-\frac{5\pi}{2}\right] = 0$

In general, $\cos \left[\frac{\pi}{2} + k\pi\right] = 0$, k any integer.

Thus $x = \frac{\pi}{2} + k\pi$, k any integer

65. $f(x) = x^2 + 2x$ $g(x) = \cos x$

$f \circ g(x) = f(g(x)) = f(\cos x)$
$\qquad = (\cos x)^2 + 2 \cos x$
$\qquad = \cos^2 x + 2 \cos x$

$g \circ f(x) = g(f(x)) = g(x^2 + 2x)$
$\qquad = \cos (x^2 + 2x)$

66. For example,

$\sin \left[\frac{\pi}{4} + \frac{\pi}{4}\right] = \sin \frac{\pi}{2} = 1$, but

$\sin \frac{\pi}{4} + \sin \frac{\pi}{4} = \frac{\sqrt{2}}{2} + \frac{\sqrt{2}}{2} = \sqrt{2}$

67. See the answer section in the text.

68.

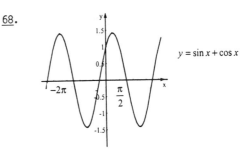

69. $y = \sin^2 x = \sin x \cdot \sin x$

It is helpful to graph the function.

Domain: Set of all real numbers

Range: Set of all real numbers from 0 to 1 inclusive.

Period: π [$\sin^2 x = \sin^2(x + k\pi)$, k any integer]

Amplitude: $\frac{1}{2}$ $\left[\frac{1}{2}$ of $(1 - 0)$ is $\frac{1}{2}.\right]$

70.

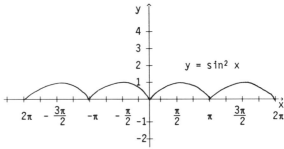

Domain: Set of all real numbers

Range: Set of all real numbers from 1 to 2 inclusive.

Period: π

Amplitude: $\frac{1}{2}$

71. $f(x) = \sqrt{\cos x}$
Solve $\cos x \geq 0$.

Since $\cos x \geq 0$ when x is in the intervals $\left[-\frac{\pi}{2} + 2k\pi, \frac{\pi}{2} + 2k\pi\right]$, k any integer, the domain consists of the intervals $\left[-\frac{\pi}{2} + 2k\pi, \frac{\pi}{2} + 2k\pi\right]$, k any integer.

72. $\sin x = 0$ for $x = k\pi$, k any integer. (See Exercise 63.) Thus the domain is the set of all real numbers except $k\pi$ for any integer k.

73. $f(x) = \dfrac{\sin x}{\cos x}$

Note that $\cos x = 0$ when $x = \dfrac{\pi}{2} + k\pi$ for any integer k. Thus the domain is the set of all real numbers except $\dfrac{\pi}{2} + k\pi$ for any integer k.

74. $\sin x > 0$ when x is in the intervals $(2k\pi, (2k + 1)\pi)$. Thus the domain consists of the intervals $(2k\pi, (2k + 1)\pi)$, k any integer.

75. $f(x) = \dfrac{\sin x}{x}$, when $0 < x < \dfrac{\pi}{2}$

$\dfrac{\sin \pi/2}{\pi/2} \approx 0.6369$

$\dfrac{\sin 3\pi/8}{3\pi/8} \approx 0.7846$

$\dfrac{\sin \pi/4}{\pi/4} \approx 0.9008$

$\dfrac{\sin \pi/8}{\pi/8} \approx 0.9750$

The limit of $\dfrac{\sin x}{x}$ as x approaches 0 is 1.

76.

For $-\pi \leqslant x \leqslant \pi$ we see that $\sin x < \cos x$ when $-\dfrac{3\pi}{4} < x < \dfrac{\pi}{4}$.

Exercise Set 6.3

1. $\dfrac{\pi}{4}$ determines a point on the unit circle with coordinates $\left[\dfrac{\sqrt{2}}{2}, \dfrac{\sqrt{2}}{2}\right]$. Then

$$\cot \dfrac{\pi}{4} = \dfrac{\cos \frac{\pi}{4}}{\sin \frac{\pi}{4}} = \dfrac{\frac{\sqrt{2}}{2}}{\frac{\sqrt{2}}{2}} = 1.$$

2. $\dfrac{-\frac{\sqrt{2}}{2}}{\frac{\sqrt{2}}{2}} = -1$

3. $\dfrac{\pi}{6}$ determines a point on the unit circle with coordinates $\left[\dfrac{\sqrt{3}}{2}, \dfrac{1}{2}\right]$. Then

$$\tan \dfrac{\pi}{6} = \dfrac{\sin \frac{\pi}{6}}{\cos \frac{\pi}{6}} = \dfrac{\frac{1}{2}}{\frac{\sqrt{3}}{2}} = \dfrac{1}{\sqrt{3}} = \dfrac{\sqrt{3}}{3}.$$

4. $\dfrac{-\frac{\sqrt{3}}{2}}{\frac{1}{2}} = -\sqrt{3}$

5. See Exercise 1.

$\sec \dfrac{\pi}{4} = \dfrac{1}{\cos \frac{\pi}{4}} = \dfrac{1}{\frac{\sqrt{2}}{2}} = \dfrac{2}{\sqrt{2}} = \sqrt{2}$

6. $\dfrac{1}{\frac{\sqrt{2}}{2}} = \dfrac{2}{\sqrt{2}} = \sqrt{2}$

7. $\dfrac{3\pi}{2}$ determines a point on the unit circle with coordinates $(0, -1)$. Then

$$\tan \dfrac{3\pi}{2} = \dfrac{\sin \frac{3\pi}{2}}{\cos \frac{3\pi}{2}} = \dfrac{-1}{0}, \text{ which is undefined.}$$

8. $\dfrac{-1}{0}$; undefined

9. $\dfrac{2\pi}{3}$ determines a point on the unit circle with coordinates $\left[-\dfrac{1}{2}, \dfrac{\sqrt{3}}{2}\right]$.

$$\tan \dfrac{2\pi}{3} = \dfrac{\sin \frac{2\pi}{3}}{\cos \frac{2\pi}{3}} = \dfrac{\frac{\sqrt{3}}{2}}{-\frac{1}{2}} = -\sqrt{3}$$

10. $\dfrac{-\frac{1}{2}}{-\frac{\sqrt{3}}{2}} = \dfrac{1}{\sqrt{3}} = \dfrac{\sqrt{3}}{3}$

11. $-\dfrac{7\pi}{4}$ determines a point on the unit circle with coordinates $\left[\dfrac{\sqrt{2}}{2}, \dfrac{\sqrt{2}}{2}\right]$.

$$\sec \left[-\dfrac{7\pi}{4}\right] = \dfrac{1}{\cos \left[-\frac{7\pi}{4}\right]} = \dfrac{1}{\frac{\sqrt{2}}{2}} = \dfrac{2}{\sqrt{2}} = \sqrt{2}$$

12. $\dfrac{1}{\frac{\sqrt{3}}{2}} = \dfrac{2}{\sqrt{3}} = \dfrac{2\sqrt{3}}{3}$

13. $\frac{5\pi}{6}$ determines a point on the unit circle with coordinates $\left[-\frac{\sqrt{3}}{2}, \frac{1}{2}\right]$.

$$\tan \frac{5\pi}{6} = \frac{\sin \frac{5\pi}{6}}{\cos \frac{5\pi}{6}} = \frac{\frac{1}{2}}{-\frac{\sqrt{3}}{2}} = -\frac{1}{\sqrt{3}} = -\frac{\sqrt{3}}{3}$$

14. $\dfrac{-\frac{\sqrt{3}}{2}}{-\frac{1}{2}} = \sqrt{3}$

15. $\sin(-x) = -\sin x$

The sine function is an odd function.

$\cos(-x) = \cos x$

The cosine function is an even function.

$$\tan(-x) = \frac{\sin(-x)}{\cos(-x)} = \frac{-\sin x}{\cos x}$$

$$= -\frac{\sin x}{\cos x} = -\tan x$$

The tangent function is an odd function.

$$\cot(-x) = \frac{\cos(-x)}{\sin(-x)} = \frac{\cos x}{-\sin x}$$

$$= -\frac{\cos x}{\sin x} = -\cot x$$

The cotangent function is an odd function.

$$\sec(-x) = \frac{1}{\cos(-x)} = \frac{1}{\cos x} = \sec x$$

The secant function is an even function.

$$\csc(-x) = \frac{1}{\sin(-x)} = \frac{1}{-\sin x} = -\frac{1}{\sin x} = -\csc x$$

The cosecant function is an odd function.

16. See Exercise 15.

17. See the graph and the list of properties for each function in Sections 6.2 and 6.3 in the text. The sin, cos, sec, and csc functions are periodic, with period 2π.

18. tangent, cotangent (See Exercise 17 and Section 6.3.)

19.

Function	I	II	III	IV
sin x	+	+	−	−
cos x	+	−	−	+
tan x = $\frac{\sin x}{\cos x}$	+	−	+	−

The tangent function is positive in the first and third quadrants and negative in the second and fourth quadrants.

20. Since $\cot x = \frac{1}{\tan x}$, the cotangent function is positive in the same quadrants in which the tangent function is positive and negative in the same quadrant in which the tangent function is negative. See Exercise 19.

Positive: I and III

Negative: II and IV

21.

	I	II	III	IV
cos x	+	−	−	+
sec x = $\frac{1}{\cos x}$	+	−	−	+

The secant function is positive in the first and fourth quadrants and negative in the second and third quadrants.

22. The cosecant function is positive in the same quadrants in which the sine function is positive and negative in the same quadrants in which the sine function is negative.

Positive: I and II

Negative: III and IV

23. See table in text.

$\frac{\pi}{16}$:　$\tan \frac{\pi}{16} = \frac{\sin(\pi/16)}{\cos(\pi/16)} \approx \frac{0.19509}{0.98079} \approx 0.19891$

$\cot \frac{\pi}{16} = \frac{\cos(\pi/16)}{\sin(\pi/16)} \approx \frac{0.98079}{0.19509} \approx 5.02737$

$\sec \frac{\pi}{16} = \frac{1}{\cos(\pi/16)} \approx \frac{1}{0.98079} \approx 1.01959$

$\csc \frac{\pi}{16} = \frac{1}{\sin(\pi/16)} \approx \frac{1}{0.19509} = 5.12584$

$\frac{\pi}{8}$:　$\tan \frac{\pi}{8} = \frac{\sin(\pi/8)}{\cos(\pi/8)} \approx \frac{0.38268}{0.92388} \approx 0.41421$

$\cot \frac{\pi}{8} = \frac{\cos(\pi/8)}{\sin(\pi/8)} \approx \frac{0.92388}{0.38268} \approx 2.41424$

$\sec \frac{\pi}{8} = \frac{1}{\cos(\pi/8)} \approx \frac{1}{0.92388} \approx 1.08239$

$\csc \frac{\pi}{8} = \frac{1}{\sin(\pi/8)} \approx \frac{1}{0.38268} \approx 2.61315$

$\frac{\pi}{6}$:　$\sin \frac{\pi}{6} = \frac{1}{2} = 0.50000$

$\cos \frac{\pi}{6} = \frac{\sqrt{3}}{2} \approx \frac{1.73205}{2} \approx 0.86603$

$\tan \frac{\pi}{6} = \frac{\sin(\pi/6)}{\cos(\pi/6)} \approx \frac{0.50000}{0.86603} \approx 0.57735$

$\cot \frac{\pi}{6} = \frac{\cos(\pi/6)}{\sin(\pi/6)} \approx \frac{0.86603}{0.50000} \approx 1.73206$

$\sec \frac{\pi}{6} = \frac{1}{\cos(\pi/6)} \approx \frac{1}{0.86603} \approx 1.15469$

$\csc \frac{\pi}{6} = \frac{1}{\sin(\pi/6)} = \frac{1}{0.50000} = 2.00000$

$\frac{\pi}{4}$: $\sin \frac{\pi}{4} = \frac{\sqrt{2}}{2} \approx \frac{1.41421}{2} \approx 0.70711$

$\cos \frac{\pi}{4} = \frac{\sqrt{2}}{2} \approx 0.70711$

$\tan \frac{\pi}{4} = \frac{\sin (\pi/4)}{\cos (\pi/4)} \approx \frac{0.70711}{0.70711} = 1.00000$

$\cot \frac{\pi}{4} = \frac{\cos (\pi/4)}{\sin (\pi/4)} \approx \frac{0.70711}{0.70711} = 1.00000$

$\sec \frac{\pi}{4} = \frac{1}{\cos (\pi/4)} \approx \frac{1}{0.70711} \approx 1.41421$

$\csc \frac{\pi}{4} = \frac{1}{\sin (\pi/4)} \approx \frac{1}{0.70711} \approx 1.41421$

$\frac{3\pi}{8}$: $\tan \frac{3\pi}{8} = \frac{\sin (3\pi/8)}{\cos (3\pi/8)} \approx \frac{0.92388}{0.38268} \approx 2.41424$

$\cot \frac{3\pi}{8} = \frac{1}{\tan (3\pi/8)} \approx \frac{1}{2.41424} \approx 0.41421$

$\sec \frac{3\pi}{8} = \frac{1}{\cos (3\pi/8)} \approx \frac{1}{0.38268} \approx 2.61315$

$\csc \frac{3\pi}{8} = \frac{1}{\sin (3\pi/8)} \approx \frac{1}{0.92388} \approx 1.08239$

$\frac{7\pi}{16}$: $\tan \frac{7\pi}{16} = \frac{\sin (7\pi/16)}{\cos (7\pi/16)} \approx \frac{0.98079}{0.19509} \approx 5.02737$

$\cot \frac{7\pi}{16} = \frac{1}{\tan (7\pi/16)} \approx \frac{1}{5.02737} \approx 0.19891$

$\sec \frac{7\pi}{16} = \frac{1}{\cos (7\pi/16)} \approx \frac{1}{0.19509} \approx 5.12584$

$\csc \frac{7\pi}{16} = \frac{1}{\sin (7\pi/16)} \approx \frac{1}{0.98079} \approx 1.01959$

24.

	$-\frac{\pi}{16}$	$-\frac{\pi}{8}$	$-\frac{\pi}{6}$	$-\frac{\pi}{4}$	$-\frac{\pi}{3}$
sin	-0.19509	-0.38268	-0.50000	-0.70711	-0.86603
cos	0.98079	0.92388	0.86603	0.70711	0.50000
tan	-0.19891	-0.41421	-0.57735	-1.00000	-1.73206
cot	-5.02737	-2.41424	-1.73206	-1.00000	-0.57735
sec	1.01959	1.08239	1.15469	1.41421	2.00000
csc	-5.12584	-2.61315	-2.00000	-1.41421	-1.15469

25. From Example 7, we know that

$\sin s = \pm \sqrt{1 - \cos^2 s}$,

where the sign of the radical depends on the quadrant in which s lies. Since s is in the first quadrant, the sine function is positive.

$\sin s = \sqrt{1 - \cos^2 s} = \sqrt{1 - \left(\frac{1}{3}\right)^2} = \sqrt{1 - \frac{1}{9}} =$

$\sqrt{\frac{8}{9}} = \frac{\sqrt{8}}{3} = \frac{2\sqrt{2}}{3}$

Now that we know sin s and cos s, we can find the other function values.

$\tan s = \frac{\sin s}{\cos s} = \frac{\frac{2\sqrt{2}}{3}}{\frac{1}{3}} = 2\sqrt{2}$

$\cot s = \frac{1}{\tan s} = \frac{1}{2\sqrt{2}} = \frac{\sqrt{2}}{4}$

$\sec s = \frac{1}{\cos s} = \frac{1}{\frac{1}{3}} = 3$

$\csc s = \frac{1}{\sin s} = \frac{1}{\frac{2\sqrt{2}}{3}} = \frac{3}{2\sqrt{2}} = \frac{3\sqrt{2}}{4}$

26. $\cos s = \pm \sqrt{1 - \sin^2 s}$ (See Example 6.)
Since s is in quadrant I, cos s is positive.

$\cos s = \sqrt{1 - \left(\frac{2}{3}\right)^2} = \sqrt{\frac{5}{9}} = \frac{\sqrt{5}}{3}$

$\tan s = \frac{\frac{2}{3}}{\frac{\sqrt{5}}{3}} = \frac{2}{\sqrt{5}} = \frac{2\sqrt{5}}{5}$

$\cot s = \frac{1}{\frac{2}{\sqrt{5}}} = \frac{\sqrt{5}}{2}$

$\sec s = \frac{1}{\frac{\sqrt{5}}{3}} = \frac{3}{\sqrt{5}} = \frac{3\sqrt{5}}{5}$

$\csc s = \frac{1}{\frac{2}{3}} = \frac{3}{2}$

27. Solving the identity $1 + \tan^2 s = \sec^2 s$ for sec s we get

$\sec s = \pm \sqrt{1 + \tan^2 s}$,

where the sign of the radical depends on the quadrant in which s lies. We know s is in the third quadrant, $\sec s = \frac{1}{\cos s}$, and the cosine function is negative in the third quadrant, so the secant function is also negative in the third quadrant. Thus,

$\sec s = -\sqrt{1 + \tan^2 s} = -\sqrt{1 + 3^2} = -\sqrt{10}$.

Next we find cos s:

$\cos s = \frac{1}{\sec s} = \frac{1}{-\sqrt{10}} = -\frac{\sqrt{10}}{10}$

Since the sine function is negative in the third quadrant, we have

$\sin s = -\sqrt{1 - \cos^2 s} = -\sqrt{1 - \left(-\frac{\sqrt{10}}{10}\right)^2} =$

$-\sqrt{1 - \frac{10}{100}} = -\sqrt{\frac{9}{10}} = -\frac{3}{\sqrt{10}} = -\frac{3\sqrt{10}}{10}$.

Next we find csc s:

$$\csc s = \frac{1}{\sin s} = \frac{1}{-\frac{3\sqrt{10}}{10}} = -\frac{\sqrt{10}}{3}$$

Finally we find cot s:

$$\cot s = \frac{1}{\tan s} = \frac{1}{3}$$

28. $1 + \cot^2 s = \csc^2 s$, so $\csc s = \pm\sqrt{1 + \cot^2 s}$. Since s is in quadrant III, csc s is negative.

$$\csc s = -\sqrt{1 + 4^2} = -\sqrt{17}$$

$$\sin s = \frac{1}{-\sqrt{17}} = -\frac{\sqrt{17}}{17}$$

cos s is negative in quadrant III, so we have

$$\cos s = -\sqrt{1 - \sin^2 s} = -\sqrt{1 - \left(-\frac{\sqrt{17}}{17}\right)^2} =$$

$$-\sqrt{\frac{16}{17}} = -\frac{4}{\sqrt{17}} = -\frac{4\sqrt{17}}{17}.$$

$$\sec s = \frac{1}{-\frac{4}{\sqrt{17}}} = -\frac{\sqrt{17}}{4}$$

$$\tan s = \frac{-\frac{\sqrt{17}}{17}}{-\frac{4\sqrt{17}}{17}} = \frac{1}{4}$$

29. First we find cos s:

$$\cos s = \frac{1}{\sec s} = \frac{1}{-\frac{5}{3}} = -\frac{3}{5}$$

Since the sine function is positive in the second quadrant, we have

$$\sin s = \sqrt{1 - \cos^2 s} = \sqrt{1 - \left(-\frac{3}{5}\right)^2} = \sqrt{1 - \frac{9}{25}} =$$

$$\sqrt{\frac{16}{25}} = \frac{4}{5}.$$

Now that we have sin s and cos s, we can find the remaining function values.

$$\tan s = \frac{\sin s}{\cos s} = \frac{\frac{4}{5}}{-\frac{3}{5}} = -\frac{4}{3}$$

$$\cot s = \frac{1}{\tan s} = \frac{1}{-\frac{4}{3}} = -\frac{3}{4}$$

$$\csc s = \frac{1}{\sin s} = \frac{1}{\frac{4}{5}} = \frac{5}{4}$$

30. $\sin s = \frac{1}{-\frac{5}{4}} = -\frac{4}{5}$

cos s is positive in quadrant IV, so we have

$$\cos s = \sqrt{1 - \sin^2 s} = \sqrt{1 - \left(-\frac{4}{5}\right)^2} = \sqrt{\frac{9}{25}} = \frac{3}{5}.$$

$$\tan s = \frac{-\frac{4}{5}}{\frac{3}{5}} = -\frac{4}{3}$$

$$\cot s = \frac{1}{-\frac{4}{3}} = -\frac{3}{4}$$

$$\sec s = \frac{1}{\frac{3}{5}} = \frac{5}{3}$$

31. Since the cosine function is negative in the third quadrant, we have

$$\cos s = -\sqrt{1 - \sin^2 s} = -\sqrt{1 - \left(-\frac{2}{5}\right)^2} =$$

$$-\sqrt{\frac{21}{25}} = -\frac{\sqrt{21}}{5}.$$

Now that we have sin s and cos s, we can find the other function values:

$$\tan s = \frac{\sin s}{\cos s} = \frac{-\frac{2}{5}}{-\frac{\sqrt{21}}{5}} = \frac{2}{\sqrt{21}} = \frac{2\sqrt{21}}{21}$$

$$\cot s = \frac{1}{\tan s} = \frac{1}{\frac{2\sqrt{21}}{21}} = \frac{\sqrt{21}}{2}$$

$$\sec s = \frac{1}{\cos s} = \frac{1}{-\frac{\sqrt{21}}{5}} = -\frac{5}{\sqrt{21}} = -\frac{5\sqrt{21}}{21}$$

$$\csc s = \frac{1}{\sin s} = \frac{1}{-\frac{2}{5}} = -\frac{5}{2}$$

32. sin s is negative in quadrant III, so we have

$$\sin s = -\sqrt{1 - \cos^2 s} = -\sqrt{1 - \left(-\frac{1}{6}\right)^2} = -\sqrt{\frac{35}{36}} = -\frac{\sqrt{35}}{6}.$$

$$\tan s = \frac{-\frac{\sqrt{35}}{6}}{-\frac{1}{6}} = \sqrt{35}$$

$$\cot s = \frac{1}{\sqrt{35}} = \frac{\sqrt{35}}{35}$$

$$\sec s = \frac{1}{-\frac{1}{6}} = -6$$

$$\csc s = \frac{1}{-\frac{\sqrt{35}}{6}} = -\frac{6}{\sqrt{35}} = -\frac{6\sqrt{35}}{35}$$

33. See the answer section in the text.

34. The graph of tan (x + π) is like that of tan x, but moved π units to the left. This graph is identical to that of tan x.

35. See the answer section in the text.

36. If the graph of sec x were translated to the right $\frac{\pi}{2}$ units, the graph of csc x would be obtained. There are other descriptions.

37. Studying the graphs of the six circular functions we see that

sin x = 0 when x = 0, ± π, ± 2π, ± 3π, ...

cos x = 0 when x = ± $\frac{\pi}{2}$, ± $\frac{3}{2}$ π, ± $\frac{5}{2}$ π, ...

tan x = 0 when x = 0, ± π, ± 2π, ± 3π, ...

cot x = 0 when x = ± $\frac{\pi}{2}$, ± $\frac{3}{2}$ π, ± $\frac{5}{2}$ π, ...

sec x is never 0.

$\left[\text{Think: } \sec x = \frac{1}{\cos x}; \frac{1}{\cos x} \text{ is never } 0\right]$

csc x is never 0.

$\left[\text{Think: } \csc x = \frac{1}{\sin x}; \frac{1}{\sin x} \text{ is never } 0\right]$

In the sine and tangent functions, the same inputs give outputs of 0. Also in the cosine and cotangent functions, the same inputs give outputs of 0.

38. The tangent and secant functions have the same asymptotes. The cotangent and cosecant functions have the same asymptotes. The inputs producing zero outputs of the first two occur where the asymptotes of the latter occur, and conversely.

39. See the answer section in the text.

40.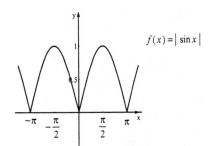

41. See the answer section in the text.

42.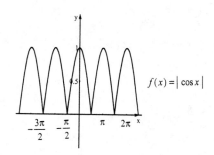

43. See the answer section in the text.

44.

It is true that sin x > csc x for all x in the intervals $\left[\pi + 2k\pi, \frac{3\pi}{2} + 2k\pi\right]$ and $\left(\frac{3\pi}{2} + 2k\pi, 2\pi + 2k\pi\right)$.

45. See the answer section in the text.

Exercise Set 6.4

1.

The terminal side lies in the <u>first</u> quadrant.

2. IV

3.

The terminal side lies in the <u>third</u> quadrant.

4. II

5.

The terminal side lies in the <u>first</u> quadrant.

6. III

7.

$\frac{11\pi}{4}$

The terminal side lies in the <u>second</u> quadrant.

8. II

9. To get two positive angles coterminal with 58° we add 360° and 720°:

58° + 360° = 418° and 58° + 720° = 778°

To get two negative angles coterminal with 58° we add -360° and -720°:

58° + (-360°) = -302° and 58° + (-720°) = -662°

Answers may vary.

10. Positive: 320° + 360° = 680°
                    320° + 720° = 1040°

Negative: 320° - 360° = -40°
                    320° - 720° = -400°

Answers may vary.

11. To get two positive angles coterminal with -120° we add 360° and 720°:

-120° + 360° = 240° and -120° + 720° = 600°

To get two negative angles coterminal with -120° we add -360° and -720°:

-120° + (-360°) = -480° and -120° + (-720°) = -840°

Answers may vary.

12. Positive: -215° + 360° = 145°
                    -215° + 720° = 505°

Negative: -215° - 360° = -575°
                    -215° - 720° = -935°

Answers may vary.

13. 90° = 89°60'   180° = 179°60'
          -57°23'   -57°23'
          32°37'   122°37'

The complement of 57°23' is 32°37' and the supplement is 122°37'.

14. 90° = 89°60'   180° = 179°60'
          -47°38'   -47°38'
          42°22'   132°22'

15. 90° = 89°59'60"
          -73°45'11"
          16°14'49"

180° = 179°59'60"
          -73°45'11"
          106°14'49"

The complement of 73°45'11" is 16°14'49" and the supplement is 106°14'49".

16. 90° = 89°59'60"
          -12°03'14"
          77°56'46"

180° = 179°59'60"
          -12°03'14"
          167°56'46"

17. 90° - 67.31° = 22.69°,
     180° - 67.31° = 112.69°

The complement of 67.31° is 22.69° and the supplement is 112.69°.

18. 90° - 13.68° = 76.32°,
     180° - 13.68° = 166.32°

19. 90° - 11.2344° = 78.7656°,
     180° - 11.2344° = 168.7656°

The complement of 11.2344° is 78.7656° and the supplement is 168.7656°.

20. 90° - 85.06312° = 4.93688°,
     180° - 85.06312° = 94.93688°

21. 8.6° = 8° + 0.6 × 1°

Now substituting 60' for 1°,
0.6 × 1° = 0.6 × 60' = 36'.

So 8.6° = 8° 36'.

22. 47.8° = 47° + 0.8 × 60' = 47°48'

23. 72.25° = 72° + 0.25 × 1°

Substituting 60' for 1°,
0.25 × 1° = 0.25 × 60' = 15'.

So 72.25° = 72° 15'.

24. 11.75° = 11° + 0.75 × 60' = 11°45'

25. 46.38° = 46° + 0.38 × 1°
           = 46° + 0.38 × 60'   (1° = 60')
           = 46° + 22.8'
           ≈ 46° 23'

26. $85.21° = 85° + 0.21 \times 60' \approx 85° \, 13'$

27. $67.84° = 67° + 0.84 \times 1°$
$= 67° + 0.84 \times 60'$ $(1° = 60')$
$= 67° + 50.4'$
$\approx 67° \, 50'$

28. $38.48° = 38° + 0.48 \times 60' \approx 38° \, 29'$

29. $87.3456° = 87° + 0.3456 \times 1°$
$= 87° + 0.3456 \times 60'$ $(1° = 60')$
$= 87° + 20.736'$
$= 87° \, 20' + 0.736 \times 1'$
$= 87° \, 20' + 0.736 \times 60''$ $(1' = 60'')$
$= 87° \, 20' + 44.16''$
$\approx 87° \, 20' \, 44''$

30. $11.0256° = 11° + 0.0256 \times 60'$
$= 11° + 1.536'$
$= 11° + 1' + 0.536 \times 60''$
$\approx 11° \, 1' \, 32''$

31. $48.02498° = 48° + 0.02498 \times 1°$
$= 48° + 0.02498 \times 60'$ $(1° = 60')$
$= 48° + 1.4988'$
$= 48° \, 1' + 0.4988 \times 1'$
$= 48° \, 1' + 0.4988 \times 60''$ $(1' = 60'')$
$= 48° \, 1' + 29.928''$
$\approx 48° \, 1' \, 30''$

32. $27.899461° = 27° + 0.899461 \times 60'$
$= 27° + 53.96766'$
$= 27° + 53' + 0.96766 \times 60''$
$\approx 27° \, 53' \, 58''$

33. $9° \, 45' = 9° + \left(\frac{45}{60}\right)°$ $\left(1' = \frac{1}{60}°\right)$
$= 9° + 0.75°$
$= 9.75°$

34. $52°15' = 52° + \left(\frac{15}{60}\right)° = 52.25°$

35. $35° \, 50' = 35° + \left(\frac{50}{60}\right)°$ $\left(1' = \frac{1}{60}°\right)$
$\approx 35° + 0.83°$
$= 35.83°$

36. $64°40' = 64° + \left(\frac{40}{60}\right)° \approx 64.67°$

37. $80° \, 33' = 80° + \left(\frac{33}{60}\right)°$ $\left(1' = \frac{1}{60}°\right)$
$= 80° + 0.55°$
$= 80.55°$

38. $27°19' = 27° + \left(\frac{19}{60}\right)° \approx 27.32°$

39. $3° \, 2' = 3° + \left(\frac{2}{60}\right)°$ $\left(1' = \frac{1}{60}°\right)$
$\approx 3° + 0.03°$
$= 3.03°$

40. $10°08' = 10° + \left(\frac{8}{60}\right)° \approx 10.13°$

41. $19° \, 47' \, 23'' = 19° + \left(\frac{47}{60}\right)° + \left(\frac{23}{3600}\right)°$
$\left(1' = \frac{1}{60}° \text{ and } 1'' = \frac{1}{3600}°\right)$
$\approx 19° + 0.7833° + 0.0064°$
$= 19.7897°$

42. $49°38'46'' = 49° + \left(\frac{38}{60}\right)° + \left(\frac{46}{3600}\right)° \approx 49.6461°$

43. $31° \, 57' \, 55'' = 31° + \left(\frac{57}{60}\right)° + \left(\frac{55}{3600}\right)°$
$\left(1' = \frac{1}{60}° \text{ and } 1'' = \frac{1}{3600}°\right)$
$\approx 31° + 0.95° + 0.0153°$
$= 31.9653°$

44. $76°11'34'' = 76° + \left(\frac{11}{60}\right)° + \left(\frac{34}{3600}\right)° \approx 76.1928°$

45. $30° = 30° \cdot \frac{\pi \text{ radians}}{180°} = \frac{\pi}{6} \text{ radians, or } \frac{\pi}{6}.$

46. $15° \cdot \frac{\pi \text{ radians}}{180°} = \frac{\pi}{12}$

47. $60° = 60° \cdot \frac{\pi \text{ radians}}{180°} = \frac{\pi}{3} \text{ radians, or } \frac{\pi}{3}.$

48. $200° \cdot \frac{\pi \text{ radians}}{180°} = \frac{10\pi}{9}$

49. $75° = 75° \cdot \frac{\pi \text{ radians}}{180°} = \frac{5\pi}{12} \text{ radians, or } \frac{5\pi}{12}.$

50. $300° \cdot \frac{\pi \text{ radians}}{180°} = \frac{5\pi}{3}$

51. $37.71° = 37.71° \cdot \frac{\pi \text{ radians}}{180°}$
$= 0.2095\pi \text{ radians, or } 0.2095\pi$

52. $12.73° \cdot \frac{\pi \text{ radians}}{180°} \approx 0.0707\pi$

53. $214.6° = 214.6° \cdot \frac{\pi \text{ radians}}{180°}$
$\approx 1.1922\pi \text{ radians, or } 1.1922\pi$

54. $73.87° \cdot \frac{\pi \text{ radians}}{180°} \approx 0.4104\pi$

55. $120° = 120° \cdot \frac{\pi \text{ radians}}{180°} \approx 2.094$

56. $240° \cdot \frac{\pi \text{ radians}}{180°} \approx 4.189$

57. $320° = 320° \cdot \frac{\pi \text{ radians}}{180°} \approx 5.585$

58. $75° \cdot \frac{\pi \text{ radians}}{180°} \approx 1.309$

59. $200° = 200° \cdot \dfrac{\pi \text{ radians}}{180°} \approx 3.491$

60. $300° \cdot \dfrac{\pi \text{ radians}}{180°} \approx 5.236$

61. $117.8° = 117.8° \cdot \dfrac{\pi \text{ radians}}{180°} \approx 2.056$

62. $231.2° \cdot \dfrac{\pi \text{ radians}}{180°} \approx 4.035$

63. $1.354° = 1.354° \cdot \dfrac{\pi \text{ radians}}{180°} \approx 0.024$

64. $327.9° \cdot \dfrac{\pi \text{ radians}}{180°} \approx 5.723$

65. $1 \text{ radian} = 1 \text{ radian} \cdot \dfrac{180°}{\pi \text{ radians}}$

   $\approx \left(\dfrac{180}{\pi}\right)° \approx 57.30°$

66. $2 \text{ radians} \cdot \dfrac{180°}{\pi \text{ radians}} \approx 114.59°$

67. $8\pi = 8\pi \text{ radians} \cdot \dfrac{180°}{\pi \text{ radians}}$

   $= 8 \cdot 180° = 1440°$

68. $-12\pi \text{ radians} \cdot \dfrac{180°}{\pi \text{ radians}} = -2160°$

69. $\dfrac{3\pi}{4} = \dfrac{3\pi}{4} \text{ radians} \cdot \dfrac{180°}{\pi \text{ radians}}$

   $= \dfrac{3}{4} \cdot 180° = 135°$

70. $\dfrac{5\pi}{4} \text{ radians} \cdot \dfrac{180°}{\pi \text{ radians}} = 225°$

71. $1.303 = 1.303 \text{ radians} \cdot \dfrac{180°}{\pi \text{ radians}}$

   $\approx \dfrac{1.303 \cdot 180°}{\pi} \approx 74.66°$

72. $2.347 \text{ radians} \cdot \dfrac{180°}{\pi \text{ radians}} \approx 134.47°$

73. $0.7532\pi = 0.7532\pi \text{ radians} \cdot \dfrac{180°}{\pi \text{ radians}}$

   $= 0.7532 \cdot 180° = 135.576°$

74. $-1.205\pi \text{ radians} \cdot \dfrac{180°}{\pi \text{ radians}} = -216.9°$

75.
$0° = 0$ radians	$180° = \pi$
$30° = \dfrac{\pi}{6}$	$225° = \dfrac{5\pi}{4}$
$60° = \dfrac{\pi}{3}$	$270° = \dfrac{3\pi}{2}$
$135° = \dfrac{3\pi}{4}$	$315° = \dfrac{7\pi}{4}$

76. $-30° = -\dfrac{\pi}{6}$, $-60° = -\dfrac{\pi}{3}$, $-90° = -\dfrac{\pi}{2}$,

   $-135° = -\dfrac{3\pi}{4}$, $-225° = -\dfrac{5\pi}{4}$, $-270° = -\dfrac{3\pi}{2}$,

   $-315° = -\dfrac{7\pi}{4}$

77. $\theta = \dfrac{s}{r}$

   θ is radian measure of central angle, s is arc length, and r is radius length.

   $\theta = \dfrac{132 \text{ cm}}{120 \text{ cm}}$ (Substituting 132 cm for s and 120 cm for r)

   $\theta = \dfrac{11}{10}$, or 1.1 (The unit is understood to be radians)

   $1.1 \text{ radians} = 1.1 \text{ radians} \cdot \dfrac{180°}{\pi \text{ radians}} \approx 63°$.

78. $\theta = \dfrac{65 \text{ cm}}{200 \text{ cm}} = 0.325$

   $0.325 \text{ radians} \cdot \dfrac{180°}{\pi \text{ radians}} \approx 19°$

79. In 60 minutes the minute hand rotates 2π radians. In 50 minutes it rotates

   $\dfrac{50}{60} \cdot 2\pi$, or about 5.236 radians.

80. $r = 14 \text{ in.} \cdot \dfrac{1 \text{ ft}}{12 \text{ in.}} \cdot \dfrac{1 \text{ mi}}{5280 \text{ ft}} = \dfrac{7}{31,680} \text{ mi}$

   $\theta = \dfrac{1 \text{ mi}}{\frac{7}{31,680} \text{ mi}} \approx 4526$

81. $\theta = \dfrac{s}{r}$, or $s = r\theta$

   $s = 10m(1.6)$ (Substituting 10m for r and 1.6 for θ)

   $s = 16 \text{ m}$

82. $s = r\theta = 5m(2.1) = 10.5 \text{ m}$

83. Since the linear speed must be in cm/min, the given angular speed, 7 radians/sec, must be changed to radians/min.

   $\omega = \dfrac{7 \text{ radians}}{1 \text{ sec}} \cdot \dfrac{60 \text{ sec}}{1 \text{ min}} = \dfrac{420 \text{ radians}}{1 \text{ min}}$

   $r = \dfrac{d}{2} = \dfrac{15 \text{ cm}}{2} = 7.5 \text{ cm}$

   Using $v = r\omega$, we have

   $v = 7.5 \text{ cm} \cdot \dfrac{420}{1 \text{ min}}$ (Substituting and omitting the word radians)

   $= 3150 \dfrac{\text{cm}}{\text{min}}$

84. $r = 30 \text{ cm} \cdot \dfrac{1 \text{ m}}{100 \text{ cm}} = 0.3 \text{ m}$

   $\omega = \dfrac{3 \text{ radians}}{1 \text{ sec}} \cdot \dfrac{60 \text{ sec}}{1 \text{ min}} = \dfrac{180 \text{ radians}}{1 \text{ min}}$

   $v = r\omega = 0.3 \text{ m} \cdot \dfrac{180}{1 \text{ min}} = 54 \text{ m/min}$

85. First change ω to radians per second.

$$\omega = 33\tfrac{1}{3}\ \frac{\text{rev}}{\text{min}} \cdot \frac{2\pi}{1\ \text{rev}} \cdot \frac{1\ \text{min}}{60\ \text{sec}}$$

$$= \frac{10\pi}{9}\ \frac{\text{radians}}{\text{sec}}$$

Using $v = r\omega$, we have

$$v = 15\ \text{cm} \cdot \frac{\frac{10\pi}{9}}{1\ \text{sec}} \approx 52.36\ \frac{\text{cm}}{\text{sec}}$$

86. $\omega = 45\ \dfrac{\text{rev}}{\text{min}} \cdot \dfrac{2\pi}{1\ \text{rev}} \cdot \dfrac{1\ \text{min}}{60\ \text{sec}} = \dfrac{3\pi}{2}\ \dfrac{\text{radians}}{\text{sec}}$

$$v = r\omega = 8.7\ \text{cm} \cdot \frac{\frac{3\pi}{2}}{\text{sec}} \approx 41.0\ \text{cm/sec}$$

87. First find ω in radians per hour.

$$\omega = \frac{1\ \text{rev}}{24\ \text{hr}} \cdot \frac{2\pi}{1\ \text{rev}} = \frac{\pi}{12}\ \frac{\text{radians}}{\text{hr}}$$

Using $v = r\omega$, we have

$$v = 4000\ \text{mi} \cdot \frac{\pi}{12\ \text{hr}} \approx 1047\ \text{mph}$$

88. $\omega = \dfrac{1\ \text{rev}}{365.25\ \text{days}} \cdot \dfrac{2\pi}{1\ \text{rev}} \cdot \dfrac{1\ \text{day}}{24\ \text{hr}} = \dfrac{\pi}{4383}\ \dfrac{\text{radians}}{\text{hr}}$

$$v = r\omega = 93{,}000{,}000\ \text{mi} \cdot \frac{\frac{\pi}{4383}}{\text{hr}} \approx 66{,}659\ \text{mph}$$

89. The units of distance for v and r must be the same. Thus,

$$v = 11\ \frac{\text{m}}{\text{s}} \cdot \frac{100\ \text{cm}}{1\ \text{m}} = 1100\ \frac{\text{cm}}{\text{s}}$$

$$r = \frac{d}{2} = \frac{32\ \text{cm}}{2} = 16\ \text{cm}$$

Using $v = r\omega$ in the form $\omega = \dfrac{v}{r}$, we have

$$\omega = \frac{1100\ \text{cm/s}}{16\ \text{cm}} = 68.75\ \text{radians/s}$$

90. $v = \dfrac{10\ \text{km}}{1\ \text{hr}} \cdot \dfrac{1000\ \text{m}}{1\ \text{km}} = 10{,}000\ \text{m/h}$

$$\omega = \frac{v}{r} = \frac{10{,}000\ \text{m/h}}{7\ \text{m}}$$

$$\approx 1429\ \text{radians/hr}$$

91. First change ω to radians per hour.

$$\omega = 14\ \frac{\text{rev}}{\text{min}} \cdot \frac{2\pi}{1\ \text{rev}} \cdot \frac{60\ \text{min}}{1\ \text{hr}} = 1680\pi\ \frac{\text{radians}}{\text{hr}}$$

Next change 10 ft to miles.

$$r = 10\ \text{ft} \cdot \frac{1\ \text{mi}}{5280\ \text{ft}} = \frac{1}{528}\ \text{mi}$$

Using $v = r\omega$, we have

$$v = \frac{1}{528}\ \text{mi} \cdot \frac{1680\pi}{1\ \text{hr}} \approx 10.0\ \text{mph}$$

92. $\omega = \dfrac{16\ \text{rev}}{1\ \text{min}} \cdot \dfrac{2\pi}{1\ \text{rev}} \cdot \dfrac{60\ \text{min}}{1\ \text{hr}} = 1920\pi\ \text{radians/hr}$

$$r = \frac{1}{528}\ \text{mi} \quad (\text{See Exercise 91.})$$

$$v = r\omega = \frac{1}{528}\ \text{mi} \cdot \frac{1920\pi}{\text{hr}} \approx 11.4\ \text{mph}$$

93. $\omega = 12\ \dfrac{\text{rev}}{\text{min}} \cdot \dfrac{2\pi}{1\ \text{rev}} = 24\pi\ \dfrac{\text{radians}}{\text{min}}$

$$r = \frac{d}{2} = \frac{24\ \text{in.}}{2} = 12\ \text{in.} = 1\ \text{ft}$$

Using $v = r\omega$, we have

$$v = 1\ \text{ft} \cdot \frac{24\pi}{\text{min}} \approx 75.40\ \frac{\text{ft}}{\text{min}}$$

The bike will travel 75.40 ft in 1 min.

94. $\omega = 10\ \dfrac{\text{rev}}{\text{sec}} \cdot \dfrac{2\pi}{1\ \text{rev}} \cdot \dfrac{60\ \text{sec}}{1\ \text{min}} = 1200\pi\ \dfrac{\text{radians}}{\text{min}}$

$$r = 15\ \text{in.} \cdot \frac{1\ \text{ft}}{12\ \text{in.}} = 1.25\ \text{ft}$$

$$s = r\theta = r(\omega t) =$$

$$1.25\ \text{ft} \cdot 1200\pi\ \frac{\text{radians}}{\text{min}} \cdot 1\ \text{min} \approx$$

$$4712\ \text{ft}$$

95. First find v in ft/sec.

$$v = 30\ \frac{\text{mi}}{\text{hr}} \cdot \frac{5280\ \text{ft}}{1\ \text{mi}} \cdot \frac{1\ \text{hr}}{60\ \text{min}} \cdot \frac{1\ \text{min}}{60\ \text{sec}} = 44\ \frac{\text{ft}}{\text{sec}}$$

Next find r in ft.

$$r = 14\ \text{in.} = 14\ \text{in.} \cdot \frac{1\ \text{ft}}{12\ \text{in.}} = \frac{7}{6}\ \text{ft.}$$

Using $v = r\omega$, we have

$$44\ \frac{\text{ft}}{\text{sec}} = \frac{7}{6}\ \text{ft} \cdot \omega$$

$$\frac{6}{7} \cdot 44\ \frac{\text{radians}}{\text{sec}} = \omega$$

$$37.7\ \frac{\text{radians}}{\text{sec}} \approx \omega$$

If $\omega = 37.7\ \dfrac{\text{radians}}{\text{sec}}$, then the angle through which a wheel rotates is $37.7\ \dfrac{\text{radians}}{\text{sec}} \cdot 10\ \text{sec}$, or 377 radians.

96. $v = 40\ \dfrac{\text{mi}}{\text{hr}} \cdot \dfrac{5280\ \text{ft}}{1\ \text{mi}} \cdot \dfrac{1\ \text{hr}}{3600\ \text{sec}} = \dfrac{176}{3}\ \text{ft/sec}$

$$r = 15\ \text{in.} \cdot \frac{1\ \text{ft}}{12\ \text{in.}} = \frac{5}{4}\ \text{ft}$$

$$v = r\omega$$

$$\frac{176}{3}\ \frac{\text{ft}}{\text{sec}} = \frac{5}{4}\ \text{ft} \cdot \omega$$

$$46.93\ \frac{\text{radians}}{\text{sec}} \approx \omega$$

In 12 sec the wheel rotates through $46.93\ \dfrac{\text{radians}}{\text{sec}} \cdot 12\ \text{sec} \approx 563$ radians.

97. $90° = \frac{\pi}{2}$ radians = 100 grads

Note the following:

$1 = \frac{90°}{100 \text{ grads}}$; also $\frac{100 \text{ grads}}{90°} = 1$

$1 = \frac{\frac{\pi}{2} \text{ radians}}{100 \text{ grads}} = \frac{\pi \text{ radians}}{200 \text{ grads}}$; also $\frac{200 \text{ grads}}{\pi \text{ radians}} = 1$

a) $48° = 48° \cdot \frac{100 \text{ grads}}{90°}$

$= \frac{48}{90} \cdot 100 \text{ grads} \approx 53.33 \text{ grads}$

b) $153° = 153° \cdot \frac{100 \text{ grads}}{90°}$

$= \frac{153}{90} \cdot 100 \text{ grads} = 170 \text{ grads}$

c) $\frac{\pi}{8}$ radians $= \frac{\pi}{8}$ radians $\cdot \frac{200 \text{ grads}}{\pi \text{ radians}}$

$= \frac{200}{8} \text{ grads} = 25 \text{ grads}$

d) $\frac{5\pi}{7}$ radians $= \frac{5\pi}{7}$ radians $\cdot \frac{200 \text{ grads}}{\pi \text{ radians}}$

$= \frac{5}{7} \cdot 200 \text{ grads} \approx 142.86 \text{ grads}$

98. a) $100 \text{ mils} = 100 \text{ mils} \cdot \frac{90}{1600 \text{ mils}} = 5.625°$

$= 5° + 0.625 \times 60'$

$= 5° + 37.5'$

$= 5° + 37' + 0.5 \times 60''$

$= 5° \; 37' \; 30''$

b) $350 \text{ mils} = 350 \text{ mils} \cdot \frac{90}{1600 \text{ mils}} = 19.6875°$

$= 19° + 0.6875 \times 60'$

$= 19° + 41.25'$

$= 19° + 41' + 0.25 \times 60''$

$= 19° \; 41' \; 15''$

99. One degree of latitude is $\frac{1}{360}$ of the circumference of the earth.

$C = \pi d$, or $2\pi r$

When $r = 6400$ km, $C = 2\pi \cdot 6400 = 12{,}800\pi$ km.
Thus 1° of latitude is $\frac{1}{360} \cdot 12{,}800\pi \approx 111.7$ km.

When $r = 4000$ mi, $C = 2\pi \cdot 4000 = 8000\pi$ mi.
Thus 1° of latitude is $\frac{1}{360} \cdot 8000\pi \approx 69.8$ mi.

100. $C = 360 \text{ degrees} \cdot \frac{60 \text{ minutes}}{1 \text{ degree}} \cdot \frac{1 \text{ nautical mile}}{1 \text{ minute}} =$
21,600 nautical miles

$2\pi r = C$

$2\pi r = 21{,}600$ nautical miles

$r = \frac{21{,}600}{2\pi} \approx 3438$ nautical miles

101.

Use $\alpha = \frac{s}{r}$.

The arc, s, is approximately 8000 miles, the approximate length of the earth's diameter. The radius, r, is approximately the sum of the earth's distance away from the astronaut, 240,000 miles, and the earth's radius, 4000 miles. Thus r is approximately 244,000 miles.

$\alpha = \frac{s}{r}$

$\alpha = \frac{8{,}000}{240{,}000}$ (Substituting 8000 for s and 240,000 for r)

$\alpha = \frac{1}{30}$ radian

102.

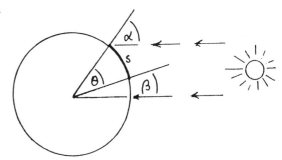

$s \approx 500$ mi; $\theta = \alpha - \beta \approx 7.2°$.

$7.2° \cdot \frac{\pi \text{ radians}}{180°} = 0.04\pi$ radians

$r = \frac{s}{\theta} = \frac{500 \text{ mi}}{0.04\pi} = \frac{12{,}500}{\pi}$ mi

$C = 2\pi r = 2\pi \left(\frac{12{,}500}{\pi} \text{ mi} \right) = 25{,}000$ mi

103.

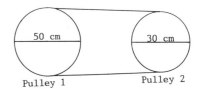

Since the pulleys are connected by the same belt, their linear speed v, will be the same.

$v = r_1\omega_1 = r_2\omega_2$

Then $\frac{r_1}{r_2} = \frac{\omega_2}{\omega_1}$

Find ω_1, the angular speed of the larger pulley, in radians/sec. The larger pulley makes 12 revolutions per minute (each revolution is 2π radians).

$$\omega_1 = \frac{12 \text{ rev}}{1 \text{ min}} \cdot \frac{2\pi}{1 \text{ rev}} \cdot \frac{1 \text{ min}}{60 \text{ sec}} = 0.4\pi \text{ radians/sec}$$

$$\frac{r_1}{r_2} = \frac{\omega_2}{\omega_1}$$

$$\frac{25}{15} = \frac{\omega_2}{0.4\pi} \qquad \text{(Substituting)}$$

$$0.4\pi \cdot \frac{25}{15} = \omega_2$$

$$2.094 \approx \omega_2$$

The smaller pulley has an angular speed of about 2.094 radians/sec.

104.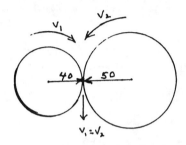

$$\omega_1 = 20 \frac{\text{rev}}{\text{min}} \cdot \frac{2\pi}{1 \text{ rev}} \cdot \frac{1 \text{ min}}{60 \text{ sec}} = \frac{2\pi}{3} \text{ radians/sec}$$

$$v_1 = v_2, \text{ or}$$

$$r_1\omega_1 = r_2\omega_2, \text{ or}$$

$$(40)\left[\frac{2\pi}{3}\right] = (50)(\omega_2); \text{ then}$$

$$\omega_2 = \frac{8\pi}{15} \approx 1.676 \text{ radians/sec}$$

105. a) Angular acceleration $\approx \dfrac{(2500 - 800) \text{ rpm}}{4.3 \text{ sec}}$

$$\approx 395.35 \text{ rpm/sec}$$

b) $395.35 \dfrac{\text{rpm}}{\text{sec}} = 395.35 \dfrac{\text{rev}}{\text{min}} \cdot \dfrac{1}{\text{sec}}$

$$= 395.35 \frac{\text{rev}}{\text{min}} \cdot \frac{1}{\text{sec}} \cdot \frac{2\pi \text{ radians}}{1 \text{ rev}} \cdot$$

$$\frac{1 \text{ min}}{60 \text{ sec}}$$

$$\approx 41.40 \text{ radians/sec}^2, \text{ or } 41.40$$
$$\text{radians/sec/sec}$$

106. a) Acceleration =

$$\frac{v_2 - v_1}{t} = \frac{325 - 175}{12} = 12.5 \text{ knots/sec}$$

b) Abbreviate "nautical mile(s)" as NM.

$$1 \text{ knot} = 1 \frac{\text{NM}}{\text{hr}} \cdot \frac{1'}{1 \text{ Nm}} \cdot \frac{1 \text{ hr}}{3600 \text{ sec}} \cdot \frac{\pi}{180°} \cdot \frac{1°}{60'}$$

$$= \frac{\pi}{38,880,000} \text{ radians/sec}$$

Then 12.5 knots/sec

$$= 12.5 \frac{\text{knots}}{\text{sec}} \cdot \frac{\frac{\pi}{38,880,000} \frac{\text{radians}}{\text{sec}}}{1 \text{ knot}}$$

$$\approx 1.01 \times 10^{-6} \text{ radians/sec}^2$$

107.

In going from 7:00 to 7:45, the hour hand moves $\frac{3}{4}(30°) = 22.5° = \phi$. Then $\theta = 60° - \phi = 37.5°$.

108.

The minute hand moves through $\frac{1}{60} \cdot 360°$, or $6°$ in 1 minute; therefore it moves $(6x)°$ in x minutes. From the figure we see that

$$\phi + 90° = \theta \text{ or } \frac{6x°}{12} + 90° = 6x°, \text{ so that}$$

$$x = \frac{180}{11} \approx 16.3636 \text{ minutes after 12:00. Thus}$$

the time is 12:16:22 (to the nearest second).

109. From Exercise 100, the earth's diameter = 2(3438) = 6876 nautical miles.

Then $\dfrac{7926.4 \text{ statute mi}}{6876 \text{ nautical miles}} \approx$

1.15 statute mi/nautical mile.

110.

a = 38° 28' 45" − 38° 27' 30" = 1' 15" = 1.25' = 1.25 nautical miles.

b = 82° 57' 15" − 82° 56' 30" = 45" = 0.75' = 0.75 nautical miles.

c = $\sqrt{(1.25)^2 + (0.75)^2} \approx 1.46$ nautical miles

Exercise Set 6.5

<u>1.</u> $\cos 180° = \cos \pi = -1$

<u>2.</u> $\cot 0° = \cot 0$; undefined

<u>3.</u> $\sin 45° = \sin \frac{\pi}{4} = \frac{\sqrt{2}}{2}$

<u>4.</u> $\tan 45° = \tan \frac{\pi}{4} = 1$

<u>5.</u> $\cos (-135°) = \cos \left[-\frac{3\pi}{4}\right] = -\frac{\sqrt{2}}{2}$

<u>6.</u> $\sin 150° = \sin \frac{5\pi}{6} = \frac{1}{2}$

<u>7.</u> $\cot (-60°) = \cot \left[-\frac{\pi}{3}\right] = -\frac{1}{\sqrt{3}}$, or $-\frac{\sqrt{3}}{3}$

<u>8.</u> $\tan (-120°) = \tan \left[-\frac{2\pi}{3}\right] = \sqrt{3}$

<u>9.</u>

We first determine r.

$r = \sqrt{x^2 + y^2}$

$r = \sqrt{(-12)^2 + 5^2}$

$\quad = \sqrt{144 + 25}$

$\quad = \sqrt{169}$

$\quad = 13$

Substituting -12 for x, 5 for y, and 13 for r, the trigonometric function values of θ are

$\sin \theta = \frac{y}{r} = \frac{5}{13}$

$\cos \theta = \frac{x}{r} = \frac{-12}{13} = -\frac{12}{13}$

$\tan \theta = \frac{y}{x} = \frac{5}{-12} = -\frac{5}{12}$

$\cot \theta = \frac{x}{y} = \frac{-12}{5} = -\frac{12}{5}$

$\sec \theta = \frac{r}{x} = \frac{13}{-12} = -\frac{13}{12}$

$\csc \theta = \frac{r}{y} = \frac{13}{5}$

<u>10.</u> $r = \sqrt{(-12)^2 + (-5)^2} = \sqrt{169} = 13$

$\sin \theta = -\frac{5}{13}$

$\cos \theta = -\frac{12}{13}$

$\tan \theta = \frac{5}{12}$

$\cot \theta = \frac{12}{5}$

$\sec \theta = -\frac{13}{12}$

$\csc \theta = -\frac{13}{5}$

<u>11.</u>

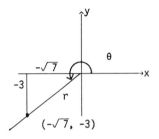

$r = \sqrt{x^2 + y^2}$

$\quad = \sqrt{(-\sqrt{7})^2 + (-3)^2}$

$\quad = \sqrt{7 + 9}$

$\quad = \sqrt{16}$

$\quad = 4$

$\sin \theta = \frac{y}{r} = \frac{-3}{4} = -\frac{3}{4}$

$\cos \theta = \frac{x}{r} = \frac{-\sqrt{7}}{4} = -\frac{\sqrt{7}}{4}$

$\tan \theta = \frac{y}{x} = \frac{-3}{-\sqrt{7}} = \frac{3}{\sqrt{7}}$, or $\frac{3\sqrt{7}}{7}$

$\cot \theta = \frac{x}{y} = \frac{-\sqrt{7}}{-3} = \frac{\sqrt{7}}{3}$

$\sec \theta = \frac{r}{x} = \frac{4}{-\sqrt{7}} = -\frac{4}{\sqrt{7}}$, or $-\frac{4\sqrt{7}}{7}$

$\csc \theta = \frac{r}{y} = \frac{4}{-3} = -\frac{4}{3}$

<u>12.</u> $r = \sqrt{(\sqrt{7})^2 + (-3)^2} = \sqrt{16} = 4$

$\sin \theta = -\frac{3}{4}$

$\cos \theta = \frac{\sqrt{7}}{4}$

$\tan \theta = -\frac{3}{\sqrt{7}}$, or $-\frac{3\sqrt{7}}{7}$

$\cot \theta = -\frac{\sqrt{7}}{3}$

$\sec \theta = \frac{4}{\sqrt{7}}$, or $\frac{4\sqrt{7}}{7}$

$\csc \theta = -\frac{4}{3}$

<u>13</u>. First we draw the graph of 2x + 3y = 0 and
determine a quadrant IV solution of the equation.

Using (3, -2), we determine r:

$$r = \sqrt{3^2 + (-2)^2} = \sqrt{13}$$

Then using x = 3, y = -2, and r = $\sqrt{13}$, we
find

$$\sin \theta = \frac{-2}{\sqrt{13}} = -\frac{2\sqrt{13}}{13},$$

$$\cos \theta = \frac{3}{\sqrt{13}} = \frac{3\sqrt{13}}{13},$$

$$\tan \theta = \frac{-2}{3} = -\frac{2}{3}.$$

<u>14</u>. A quadrant II solution of 4x + y = 0 is (-1, 4).
Then

$$r = \sqrt{(-1)^2 + 4^2} = \sqrt{17}.$$

$$\sin \theta = \frac{4}{\sqrt{17}} = \frac{4\sqrt{17}}{17}$$

$$\cos \theta = \frac{-1}{\sqrt{17}} = -\frac{\sqrt{17}}{17}$$

$$\tan \theta = \frac{4}{-1} = -4$$

<u>15</u>. First we draw the graph of 5x - 4y = 0 and
determine a quadrant I solution of the equation.

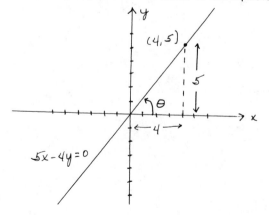

Using (4, 5), we determine r:

$$r = \sqrt{4^2 + 5^2} = \sqrt{41}$$

Then using x = 4, y = 5, and r = $\sqrt{41}$, we find

$$\sin \theta = \frac{5}{\sqrt{41}} = \frac{5\sqrt{41}}{41},$$

$$\cos \theta = \frac{4}{\sqrt{41}} = \frac{4\sqrt{41}}{41},$$

$$\tan \theta = \frac{5}{4}.$$

<u>16</u>. A quadrant III solution of y = 0.8x is (-10, -8).
Then

$$r = \sqrt{(-10)^2 + (-8)^2} = \sqrt{164} = 2\sqrt{41}.$$

$$\sin \theta = \frac{-8}{2\sqrt{41}} = -\frac{4\sqrt{41}}{41}$$

$$\cos \theta = \frac{-10}{2\sqrt{41}} = -\frac{5\sqrt{41}}{41}$$

$$\tan \theta = \frac{-8}{-10} = \frac{4}{5}$$

<u>17</u>. 270° < 319° < 360°, so P(x, y) is in the fourth
quadrant. The cosine and secant are positive,
and the other four function values are negative.

<u>18</u>. -57° is in quadrant IV. The cosine and secant are
positive, and the other four function values are
negative.

<u>19</u>.

-620° has the same terminal side as 100°.

90° < 100° < 180°, so P(x, y) is in the second
quadrant. The sine and cosecant are positive and
the other four function values are negative.

<u>20</u>. 194° is in quadrant III. The tangent and
cotangent are positive, and the other four
function values are negative.

21.

-215° has the same terminal side as 145°.

90° < 145° < 180°, so P(x, y) is in the second quadrant. The sine and cosecant are positive and the other four function values are negative.

22. 290° is in quadrant IV. The cosine and secant are positive and the other four function values are negative.

23. 90° < 91° < 180°, so P(x, y) is in the second quadrant. The sine and cosecant are positive and the other four function values are negative.

24. -272° is in quadrant I. All six function values are positive.

25.

Let (0, y) represent any point, other than the vertex, on the terminal side of a 90° angle in standard position. We note that the first coordinate is 0, the second coordinate is positive, and r = y.

$\sin 90° = \frac{y}{r} = 1$ (Since r = y)

$\cos 90° = \frac{0}{r} = 0$

$\tan 90° = \frac{y}{0}$, tan 90° is undefined

$\cot 90° = \frac{0}{y} = 0$

$\sec 90° = \frac{r}{0}$, sec 90° is undefined

$\csc 90° = \frac{y}{r} = 1$ (Since r = y)

26. Let (x, 0) represent any point, other than the vertex, on the terminal side of a 360° angle in standard position. The first coordinate is positive, the second coordinate is 0, and r = x.

$\sin 360° = \frac{0}{r} = 0$, $\cos 360° = \frac{x}{r} = 1$, $\tan 360° = \frac{0}{x} = 0$, $\cot 360° \left(\frac{x}{0}\right)$ is undefined, $\sec 360° = \frac{r}{x} = 1$, $\csc 360° \left(\frac{r}{0}\right)$ is undefined

27.

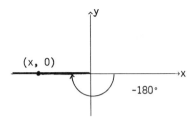

Let (x, 0) represent any point, other than the vertex, on the terminal side of a -180° angle in standard position. We note that the first coordinate is negative, the second coordinate is 0, and that x and r have the same absolute value.

$\sin (-180°) = \frac{0}{r} = 0$

$\cos (-180°) = \frac{x}{r} = -1$ (Since |x| = |r|, but x and r have opposite signs)

$\tan (-180°) = \frac{0}{x} = 0$

$\cot (-180°) = \frac{x}{0}$, cot (-180°) is undefined

$\sec (-180°) = \frac{r}{x} = -1$ (The reciprocal of cos (-180°))

$\csc (-180°) = \frac{r}{0}$, csc (-180°) is undefined

28. -270° is coterminal with 90°. See the discussion in Exercise 25.

sin (-270°) = 1, cos (-270°) = 0, tan (-270°) is undefined, cot (-270°) = 0, sec (-270°) is undefined, csc (-270°) = 1.

29. $\sin \theta = \frac{\text{opposite}}{\text{hypotenuse}} = \frac{8}{17}$ $\csc \theta = \frac{\text{hypotenuse}}{\text{opposite}} = \frac{17}{8}$

$\cos \theta = \frac{\text{adjacent}}{\text{hypotenuse}} = \frac{15}{17}$ $\sec \theta = \frac{\text{hypotenuse}}{\text{adjacent}} = \frac{17}{15}$

$\tan \theta = \frac{\text{opposite}}{\text{adjacent}} = \frac{8}{15}$ $\cot \theta = \frac{\text{adjacent}}{\text{opposite}} = \frac{15}{8}$

30. $\sin \phi = \frac{15}{17}$, $\cos \phi = \frac{8}{17}$, $\tan \phi = \frac{15}{8}$

$\csc \phi = \frac{17}{15}$, $\sec \phi = \frac{17}{8}$, $\cot \phi = \frac{8}{15}$

31. $\sin \theta = \frac{\text{opposite}}{\text{hypotenuse}} = \frac{3}{h}$ $\csc \theta = \frac{\text{hypotenuse}}{\text{opposite}} = \frac{h}{3}$

$\cos \theta = \frac{\text{adjacent}}{\text{hypotenuse}} = \frac{7}{h}$ $\sec \theta = \frac{\text{hypotenuse}}{\text{adjacent}} = \frac{h}{7}$

$\tan \theta = \frac{\text{opposite}}{\text{adjacent}} = \frac{3}{7}$ $\cot \theta = \frac{\text{adjacent}}{\text{opposite}} = \frac{7}{3}$

32. $\sin \phi = \frac{7}{h}$ $\cos \phi = \frac{4}{h}$, $\tan \phi = \frac{7}{4}$

$\csc \phi = \frac{h}{7}$, $\sec \phi = \frac{h}{4}$, $\cot \phi = \frac{4}{7}$

33. $\sin \theta = \dfrac{7.8023}{8.8781} \approx 0.8788$

    $\cos \theta = \dfrac{4.2361}{8.8781} \approx 0.4771$

    $\tan \theta = \dfrac{7.8023}{4.2361} \approx 1.8419$

    $\cot \theta = \dfrac{4.2361}{7.8023} \approx 0.5429$

    $\sec \theta = \dfrac{8.8781}{4.2361} \approx 2.0958$

    $\csc \theta = \dfrac{8.8781}{7.8023} \approx 1.1379$

34. $\sin \phi = \dfrac{4.2361}{8.8781} \approx 0.4771$, $\cos \phi = \dfrac{7.8023}{8.8781} \approx 0.8788$,

    $\tan \theta = \dfrac{4.2361}{7.8023} \approx 0.5429$, $\csc \theta = \dfrac{8.8781}{4.2361} \approx 2.0958$,

    $\sec \phi = \dfrac{8.8781}{7.8023} \approx 1.1379$, $\cot \theta = \dfrac{7.8023}{4.2361} \approx 1.8419$

35.

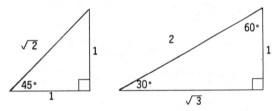

We use the triangles above to complete the table.

θ	sin	cos	tan	cot	sec	csc
45°	$\dfrac{\sqrt{2}}{2}$	$\dfrac{\sqrt{2}}{2}$	1	1	$\sqrt{2}$	$\sqrt{2}$
30°	$\dfrac{1}{2}$	$\dfrac{\sqrt{3}}{2}$	$\dfrac{\sqrt{3}}{3}$	$\sqrt{3}$	$\dfrac{2\sqrt{3}}{3}$	2
60°	$\dfrac{\sqrt{3}}{2}$	$\dfrac{1}{2}$	$\sqrt{3}$	$\dfrac{\sqrt{3}}{3}$	2	$\dfrac{2\sqrt{3}}{3}$

36.

θ	sin	cos	tan	cot	sec	csc
-45°	$-\dfrac{\sqrt{2}}{2}$	$\dfrac{\sqrt{2}}{2}$	-1	-1	$\sqrt{2}$	$-\sqrt{2}$
-30°	$-\dfrac{1}{2}$	$\dfrac{\sqrt{3}}{2}$	$-\dfrac{\sqrt{3}}{3}$	$-\sqrt{3}$	$\dfrac{2\sqrt{3}}{3}$	-2
-60°	$-\dfrac{\sqrt{3}}{2}$	$\dfrac{1}{2}$	$-\sqrt{3}$	$-\dfrac{\sqrt{3}}{3}$	2	$-\dfrac{2\sqrt{3}}{3}$

37. We know the length of the side opposite ∠B, and we want to find the length of the adjacent side. We can use the tangent ratio or the cotangent ratio. Here we use the cotangent:

    $\cot 30° = \dfrac{a}{36}$

    $\sqrt{3} = \dfrac{a}{36}$

    $36\sqrt{3} = a$

    $62.4 \text{ m} \approx a$

38. $\csc 60° = \dfrac{L}{28}$

    $L \approx 32.3 \text{ ft}$

39. First we sketch a third quadrant triangle. Since $\sin \theta = -\frac{1}{3}$, we have a leg of length 1 and the hypotenuse of length 3. The other leg must then have length $\sqrt{8}$, or $2\sqrt{2}$. Now we can read off the appropriate ratios:

$\cos \theta = \dfrac{-2\sqrt{2}}{3} = -\dfrac{2\sqrt{2}}{3}$

$\tan \theta = \dfrac{-1}{-2\sqrt{2}} = \dfrac{\sqrt{2}}{4}$

$\cot \theta = \dfrac{-2\sqrt{2}}{-1} = 2\sqrt{2}$

$\sec \theta = \dfrac{3}{-2\sqrt{2}} = -\dfrac{3\sqrt{2}}{4}$

$\csc \theta = \dfrac{3}{-1} = -3$

40.

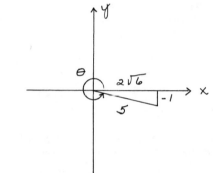

$\cos \theta = \dfrac{2\sqrt{6}}{5}$, $\tan \theta = \dfrac{-1}{2\sqrt{6}} = -\dfrac{\sqrt{6}}{12}$,

$\cot \theta = \dfrac{2\sqrt{6}}{-1} = -2\sqrt{6}$, $\sec \theta = \dfrac{5}{2\sqrt{6}} = \dfrac{5\sqrt{6}}{12}$,

$\csc \theta = \dfrac{5}{-1} = -5$

41.

$\sin \theta = -\dfrac{4}{5}$

$\tan \theta = -\dfrac{4}{3}$

$\cot \theta = -\dfrac{3}{4}$

$\sec \theta = \dfrac{5}{3}$

$\csc \theta = -\dfrac{5}{4}$

42.

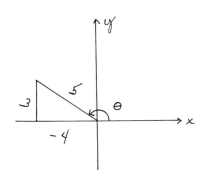

$\sin \theta = \frac{3}{5}$, $\tan \theta = -\frac{3}{4}$, $\cot \theta = -\frac{4}{3}$, $\sec \theta = -\frac{5}{4}$,

$\csc \theta = \frac{5}{3}$

43.

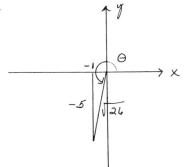

$\sin \theta = \frac{-1}{\sqrt{5}} = -\frac{\sqrt{5}}{5}$

$\cos \theta = \frac{2}{\sqrt{5}} = \frac{2\sqrt{5}}{5}$

$\tan \theta = \frac{-1}{2} = -\frac{1}{2}$

$\sec \theta = \frac{\sqrt{5}}{2}$

$\csc \theta = \frac{\sqrt{5}}{-1} = -\sqrt{5}$

44.

$\sin \theta = \frac{-5}{\sqrt{26}} = -\frac{5\sqrt{26}}{26}$, $\cos \theta = \frac{-1}{\sqrt{26}} = -\frac{\sqrt{26}}{26}$,

$\cot \theta = \frac{-1}{-5} = \frac{1}{5}$, $\sec \theta = \frac{\sqrt{26}}{-1} = -\sqrt{26}$,

$\csc \theta = \frac{\sqrt{26}}{-5} = -\frac{\sqrt{26}}{5}$

45.

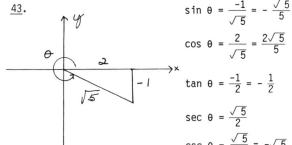

$\cos \theta = \frac{-2\sqrt{2}}{3} = -\frac{2\sqrt{2}}{3}$

$\tan \theta = \frac{1}{-2\sqrt{2}} = -\frac{\sqrt{2}}{4}$

$\cot \theta = \frac{-2\sqrt{2}}{1} = -2\sqrt{2}$

$\sec \theta = \frac{3}{-2\sqrt{2}} = -\frac{3\sqrt{2}}{4}$

$\csc \theta = \frac{3}{1} = 3$

46.

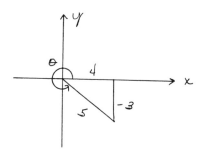

$\sin \theta = -\frac{3}{5}$, $\tan \theta = -\frac{3}{4}$, $\cot \theta = -\frac{4}{3}$, $\sec \theta = \frac{5}{4}$,

$\csc \theta = -\frac{5}{3}$

47. Since θ is an acute angle, we sketch a first quadrant triangle.

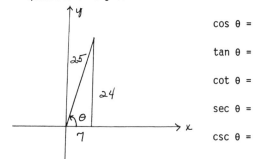

$\cos \theta = \frac{7}{25}$

$\tan \theta = \frac{24}{7}$

$\cot \theta = \frac{7}{24}$

$\sec \theta = \frac{25}{7}$

$\csc \theta = \frac{25}{24}$

48. $\cos \theta = 0.7 = \frac{7}{10}$

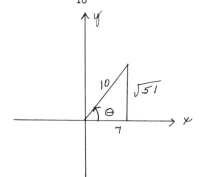

$\sin \theta = \frac{\sqrt{51}}{10}$, $\tan \theta = \frac{\sqrt{51}}{7}$, $\cot \theta = \frac{7}{\sqrt{51}} = \frac{7\sqrt{51}}{51}$,

$\sec \theta = \frac{10}{7}$, $\csc \theta = \frac{10}{\sqrt{51}} = \frac{10\sqrt{51}}{51}$

49. Since θ is an acute angle, we sketch a first quadrant triangle.

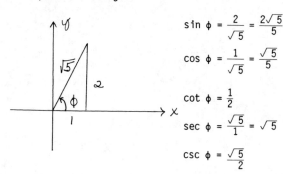

$\sin \phi = \dfrac{2}{\sqrt{5}} = \dfrac{2\sqrt{5}}{5}$

$\cos \phi = \dfrac{1}{\sqrt{5}} = \dfrac{\sqrt{5}}{5}$

$\cot \phi = \dfrac{1}{2}$

$\sec \phi = \dfrac{\sqrt{5}}{1} = \sqrt{5}$

$\csc \phi = \dfrac{\sqrt{5}}{2}$

50.

$\sin \phi = \dfrac{4}{\sqrt{17}} = \dfrac{4\sqrt{17}}{17}, \cos \phi = \dfrac{1}{\sqrt{17}} = \dfrac{\sqrt{17}}{17}$

$\tan \theta = 4, \cot \theta = \dfrac{1}{4}, \csc \phi = \dfrac{\sqrt{17}}{4}$

51. See the answer section in the text.

Exercise Set 6.6

1.

The terminal side makes a 45° angle with the x-axis. The reference angle is 45°. Find sec 45° and prefix the appropriate sign.

$\sec 45° = \dfrac{2}{\sqrt{2}}$, or $\sqrt{2}$

Since the secant function is also positive in the fourth quadrant,

$\sec 315° = \dfrac{2}{\sqrt{2}}$, or $\sqrt{2}$.

2. $\csc 315° = -\dfrac{2}{\sqrt{2}}$, or $-\sqrt{2}$ (See Exercise 1.)

3.

The terminal side makes a 30° angle with the x-axis. The reference angle is 30°. Find sin 30° and prefix the appropriate sign.

$\sin 30° = \dfrac{1}{2}$

Since the sine function is also positive in the second quadrant,

$\sin 150° = \dfrac{1}{2}$.

4. $\cos 150° = -\dfrac{\sqrt{3}}{2}$ (See Exercise 3.)

5.

The terminal side makes a 30° angle with the x-axis. The reference angle is 30°. Find cot 30° and prefix the appropriate sign.

$\cot 30° = \dfrac{3}{\sqrt{3}}$, or $\sqrt{3}$

Since the cotangent function is also positive in the third quadrant,

$\cot 570° = \dfrac{3}{\sqrt{3}}$, or $\sqrt{3}$.

6. $\tan 570° = \dfrac{1}{\sqrt{3}}$, or $\dfrac{\sqrt{3}}{3}$ (See Exercise 5.)

7.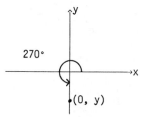

Note that the first coordinate is 0, the second coordinate is negative, and that |y| = r (r is always positive).

$\csc \theta = \dfrac{r}{y}$

$\csc 270° = \dfrac{r}{y} = -1$ (|y| = r, y is negative)

8. -450° is coterminal with 270°.

   sin (-450°) = -1   (See Exercise 7.)

9.

   The terminal side makes a 45° angle with the x-axis. The reference angle is 45°. Find cot 45° and prefix the appropriate sign.

   cot 45° = 1

   Since the cotangent function is negative in the second quadrant,

   cot (-225°) = -1.

10. sec (-225°) = -√2   (See Exercise 9.)

11.

   The terminal side makes a 30° angle with the x-axis. The reference angle is 30°. Find sin 30° and prefix the appropriate sign.

   sin 30° = $\frac{1}{2}$

   Since the sine function is negative in the fourth quadrant,

   sin 1050° = $-\frac{1}{2}$.

12. Reference angle: 45°

    675° is in quadrant IV, so cos 675° > 0.

    cos 675° = $\frac{\sqrt{2}}{2}$

13.

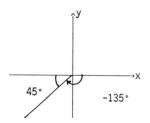

    The terminal side makes a 45° angle with the x-axis. The reference angle is 45°. Find tan 45° and prefix the appropriate sign.

    tan 45° = 1

    Since the tangent function is also positive in the third quadrant,

    tan (-135°) = 1.

14. sin (-135°) = $-\frac{\sqrt{2}}{2}$ (See Exercise 13.)

15.

    The terminal side makes a 45° angle with the x-axis. The reference angle is 45°. Find sec 45° and prefix the appropriate sign.

    sec 45° = $\frac{2}{\sqrt{2}}$, or √2

    Note that the terminal side of 1125° also lies in the first quadrant. Thus,

    sec 1125° = $\frac{2}{\sqrt{2}}$, or √2.

16. csc 1125° = √2   (See Exercise 15.)

17.

    The terminal side makes a 45° angle with the x-axis. The reference angle is 45°. Find sin 45° and prefix the appropriate sign.

    sin 45° = $\frac{\sqrt{2}}{2}$

    Since the sine function is also positive in the second quadrant,

    sin 495° = $\frac{\sqrt{2}}{2}$.

18. Reference angle: 30°
    330° is in quadrant IV, so cot 330° < 0.
    cot 330° = $-\sqrt{3}$

19. cos 5220° = cos (5040° + 180°)

The first coordinate is negative, the second coordinate is 0, and $|x| = r$ (r is always positive).

$\cos \theta = \dfrac{x}{r}$

$\cos 5220° = \dfrac{x}{r} = -1$ ($|x| = r$, r is negative)

20. -7560° is coterminal with 0°.
    sin (-7560°) = 0.

21. $\dfrac{13\pi}{4} = \dfrac{12\pi}{4} + \dfrac{\pi}{4}$

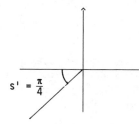

$\dfrac{13\pi}{4}$ is in the third quadrant, and the reference number is $\dfrac{\pi}{4}$. We find $\sin \dfrac{\pi}{4}$ and prefix the appropriate sign.

$\sin \dfrac{\pi}{4} = \dfrac{\sqrt{2}}{2}$

Since the sine function is negative in the third quadrant,

$\sin \dfrac{13\pi}{4} = -\dfrac{\sqrt{2}}{2}$.

22. Reference number: $\dfrac{\pi}{4}$
    $\dfrac{19\pi}{4}$ is in quadrant II, so $\cos \dfrac{19\pi}{4} < 0$.
    $\cos \dfrac{19\pi}{4} = -\dfrac{\sqrt{2}}{2}$

23. $\dfrac{11\pi}{3} = \dfrac{9\pi}{3} + \dfrac{2\pi}{3}$

$\dfrac{11\pi}{3}$ is in the fourth quadrant, and the reference number is $\dfrac{\pi}{3}$. We find $\tan \dfrac{\pi}{3}$ and prefix the appropriate sign.

$\tan \dfrac{\pi}{3} = \sqrt{3}$

Since the tangent function is negative in the fourth quadrant,

$\tan \dfrac{\pi}{3} = -\sqrt{3}$.

24. $\sec \dfrac{11\pi}{3} = 2$ (See Exercise 23.)

25. $\dfrac{23\pi}{6} = \dfrac{18\pi}{6} + \dfrac{5\pi}{6}$

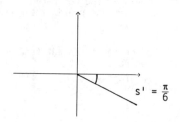

$\dfrac{23\pi}{6}$ is in the fourth quadrant, and the reference number is $\dfrac{\pi}{6}$. We know that in the fourth quadrant the cosine is positive and the sine and tangent are negative.

$\sin \dfrac{23\pi}{6} = -\dfrac{1}{2}$ $\csc \dfrac{23\pi}{6} = -2$

$\cos \dfrac{23\pi}{6} = \dfrac{\sqrt{3}}{2}$ $\sec \dfrac{23\pi}{6} = \dfrac{2}{\sqrt{3}}$, or $\dfrac{2\sqrt{3}}{3}$

$\tan \dfrac{23\pi}{6} = -\dfrac{1}{\sqrt{3}}$, or $-\dfrac{\sqrt{3}}{3}$ $\cot \dfrac{23\pi}{6} = -\sqrt{3}$

26. $-\dfrac{29\pi}{3}$ is in the first quadrant, and the reference number is $\dfrac{\pi}{3}$.

$\sin \left(-\dfrac{29\pi}{3}\right) = \dfrac{\sqrt{3}}{2}$, $\cos \left(-\dfrac{29\pi}{3}\right) = \dfrac{1}{2}$,

$\tan \left(-\dfrac{29\pi}{3}\right) = \sqrt{3}$, $\cot \left(-\dfrac{29\pi}{3}\right) = \dfrac{\sqrt{3}}{3}$

$\sec \left(-\dfrac{29\pi}{3}\right) = 2$, $\csc \left(-\dfrac{29\pi}{3}\right) = \dfrac{2\sqrt{3}}{3}$

27. $-\dfrac{19\pi}{3} = -\left(\dfrac{18\pi}{3} + \dfrac{\pi}{3}\right)$

$-\dfrac{19\pi}{3}$ is in the fourth quadrant, and the reference number is $\dfrac{\pi}{3}$. We know that in the fourth quadrant, the cosine is positive and the sine and tangent are negative.

$$\sin\left(-\frac{19\pi}{3}\right) = -\frac{\sqrt{3}}{2}$$

$$\cos\left(-\frac{19\pi}{3}\right) = \frac{1}{2}$$

$$\tan\left(-\frac{19\pi}{3}\right) = -\sqrt{3}$$

$$\csc\left(-\frac{19\pi}{3}\right) = -\frac{2}{\sqrt{3}}, \text{ or } -\frac{2\sqrt{3}}{3}$$

$$\sec\left(-\frac{19\pi}{3}\right) = 2$$

$$\cot\left(-\frac{19\pi}{3}\right) = -\frac{1}{\sqrt{3}}, \text{ or } -\frac{\sqrt{3}}{3}$$

28. $\frac{37\pi}{6}$ is in the first quadrant, and the reference number is $\frac{\pi}{6}$.

$$\sin\frac{37\pi}{6} = \frac{1}{2}, \cos\frac{37\pi}{6} = \frac{\sqrt{3}}{2}, \tan\frac{37\pi}{6} = \frac{\sqrt{3}}{3},$$

$$\cot\frac{37\pi}{6} = \sqrt{3}, \sec\frac{37\pi}{6} = \frac{2\sqrt{3}}{3}, \csc\frac{37\pi}{6} = 2$$

29. $\frac{31\pi}{3} = \frac{30\pi}{3} + \frac{\pi}{3}$

We see that $\frac{31\pi}{3}$ is in the first quadrant, and the reference number is $\frac{\pi}{3}$. In the first quadrant, all the function values are positive.

$$\sin\frac{31\pi}{3} = \frac{\sqrt{3}}{2}$$

$$\cos\frac{31\pi}{3} = \frac{1}{2}$$

$$\tan\frac{31\pi}{3} = \sqrt{3}$$

$$\csc\frac{31\pi}{3} = \frac{2}{\sqrt{3}}, \text{ or } \frac{2\sqrt{3}}{3}$$

$$\sec\frac{31\pi}{3} = 2$$

$$\cot\frac{31\pi}{3} = \frac{1}{\sqrt{3}}, \text{ or } \frac{\sqrt{3}}{3}$$

30. $-\frac{25\pi}{6}$ is in the fourth quadrant, and the reference number is $\frac{\pi}{6}$.

$$\sin\left(-\frac{25\pi}{6}\right) = -\frac{1}{2}, \cos\left(-\frac{25\pi}{6}\right) = \frac{\sqrt{3}}{2},$$

$$\tan\left(-\frac{25\pi}{6}\right) = -\frac{\sqrt{3}}{3}, \cot\left(-\frac{25\pi}{6}\right) = -\sqrt{3},$$

$$\sec\left(-\frac{25\pi}{6}\right) = \frac{2\sqrt{3}}{3}, \csc\left(-\frac{25\pi}{6}\right) = -2$$

31. We see that -750° is in the fourth quadrant and the reference angle is 30°. In the fourth quadrant the cosine is positive and the sine and tangent are negative.

$$\sin(-750°) = -\frac{1}{2}$$

$$\cos(-750°) = \frac{\sqrt{3}}{2}$$

$$\tan(-750°) = -\frac{1}{\sqrt{3}}, \text{ or } -\frac{\sqrt{3}}{3}$$

$$\csc(-750°) = -2$$

$$\sec(-750°) = \frac{2}{\sqrt{3}}, \text{ or } \frac{2\sqrt{3}}{3}$$

$$\cot(-750°) = -\sqrt{3}$$

32. 1590° is in the second quadrant, and the reference angle is 30°.

$$\sin 1590° = \frac{1}{2}, \cos 1590° = -\frac{\sqrt{3}}{2},$$

$$\tan 1590° = -\frac{\sqrt{3}}{3}, \cot 1590° = -\sqrt{3},$$

$$\sec 1590° = -\frac{2\sqrt{3}}{3}, \csc 1590° = 2$$

33. Use a calculator to find cos 18°.

Enter 18 and then press the $\boxed{\cos}$ key.
cos 18° ≈ 0.951057

34. 0.601815

35. Use a calculator to find tan 2.6°.

Enter 2.6 and then press the $\boxed{\tan}$ key.
tan 2.6° ≈ 0.045410

36. 0.821149

37. Use a calculator to find sin 62° 20'.

We first convert to degrees and decimal parts of degrees on a calculator.

$$62° \ 20' = 62° + \left(\frac{20}{60}\right)° ≈ 62.33333333°$$

Then press the $\boxed{\sin}$ key.

sin 62° 20' ≈ 0.885664

38. 55° 30' = 55.5°
tan 55° 30' ≈ 1.455009

39. Use a calculator to find cos 15° 35'.

We first convert to degrees and decimal parts of degrees on a calculator.

$$15° \ 35' = 15° + \left(\frac{35}{60}\right)° ≈ 15.58333333°$$

Then press the $\boxed{\cos}$ key.
cos 15° 35' ≈ 0.963241

40. $40° 55' \approx 40.91666666°$

$\tan (40° 55') \approx 0.654961$

41. Use a calculator to find csc 29° 11' 36". We first convert to degrees and decimal parts of degrees on a calculator.

$29° 11' 36" = 29° + \left(\frac{11}{60}\right)° + \left(\frac{36}{3600}\right)°$

$= 29° + 0.18333333° + 0.01°$

$\approx 29.19333333°$

Now press the $\boxed{\sin}$ key, and then press the reciprocal key.

$\csc 29° 11' 36" = \frac{1}{\sin 29° 11' 36"}$

≈ 2.050197

42. $54° 44' 53" \approx 54.74805556$

$\cot (54° 44' 53") \approx 0.706781$

43. Use a calculator to find sec 10° 31' 42".

We first convert to degrees and decimal parts of degrees.

$10° 31' 42" = 10° + \left(\frac{31}{60}\right)° + \left(\frac{42}{3600}\right)°$

$\approx 10° + 0.51666667° + 0.01166667°$

$\approx 10.52833333°$

Now press the $\boxed{\cos}$ key, and then press the reciprocal key.

$\sec 10° 31' 42" = \frac{1}{\cos 10° 31' 42"}$

≈ 1.017124

44. $45° 15' 23" \approx 45.25638889°$

$\csc 45° 15' 23" \approx 1.407927$

45. Use a calculator to find sin 561.2344°. Enter 561.2344 and then press the $\boxed{\sin}$ key.

$\sin 561.2344° \approx -0.362184$

46. -1.405422

47. Use a calculator to find cot (-900.23°). Enter -900.23, press the $\boxed{\tan}$ key, and then press the reciprocal key.

$\cot (-900.23°) = \frac{1}{\tan (-900.23°)} \approx -249.1107$

48. 1.000006

49. Use a calculator to find tan 295° 14'.

We first convert to degrees and decimal parts of degrees on a calculator.

$295° 14' = 295° + \left(\frac{14}{60}\right)° \approx 295.23333333°$

Then press the $\boxed{\tan}$ key.

$\tan 295° 14' \approx -2.121903$

50. $230° 53' \approx 230.8833333$

$\cos (230° 53') \approx -0.630902$

51. Use a calculator to find sec 146.9°.

Enter 146.9, press the $\boxed{\cos}$ key, and then press the reciprocal key.

$\sec 146.9° = \frac{1}{\cos 146.9°} \approx -1.193718$

52. 0.989272

53. Use a calculator to find sin 756° 25'. We first convert to degrees and decimal parts of degrees on a calculator.

$756° 25' = 756° + \left(\frac{25}{60}\right)° \approx 756.4166667°$

Then press the $\boxed{\sin}$ key.

$\sin 756° 25' \approx 0.593653$

54. $820° 40' \approx 820.6666667°$

$\cot (820° 40') \approx -0.188349$

55. Use a calculator to find cos (-1000.85°).

Enter -1000.85 and press the $\boxed{\cos}$ key.

$\cos (-1000.85°) \approx 0.188238$

56. -0.107752

57. Find sin 37 using a calculator.

With the calculator in radian mode, enter 37 and then press the $\boxed{\sin}$ key.

$\sin 37 \approx -0.643538$

58. 0.862349

59. Find cos (-10) using a calculator.

With the calculator in radian mode, enter -10 and then press the $\boxed{\cos}$ key.

$\cos (-10) \approx -0.839072$

60. 0.756802

61. Find tan 5π using a calculator.

Using the $\boxed{\pi}$ key, we find $5\pi \approx 15.70796327$. Then, with the calculator in radian mode, press the $\boxed{\tan}$ key.

$\tan 5\pi = 0$

62. Undefined

63. Find cot 1000 using a calculator.

With the calculator in radian mode, enter 1000, press the $\boxed{\tan}$ key, and then press the reciprocal key.

$\cot 1000 = \frac{1}{\tan 1000} \approx 0.680122$

64. 0.463021

65. Find sec $\left[-\frac{\pi}{5}\right]$ using a calculator.

Using the $\boxed{\pi}$ key we find $-\frac{\pi}{5} \approx -0.62831853$.

Using radian mode, press the $\boxed{\cos}$ key and then press the reciprocal key.

$$\sec\left[-\frac{\pi}{5}\right] = \frac{1}{\cos\left[-\frac{\pi}{5}\right]} \approx 1.236068$$

66. -0.324920

67. Find sec $\frac{10\pi}{7}$ using a calculator.

Using the $\boxed{\pi}$ key, we find $\frac{10\pi}{7} \approx 4.487989505$. With the calculator in radian mode, press the $\boxed{\cos}$ key and then press the reciprocal key.

$$\sec\frac{10\pi}{7} = \frac{1}{\cos\frac{10\pi}{7}} \approx -4.493959$$

68. 0.797473

69. Find cos (-13π) using a calculator.

Using the $\boxed{\pi}$ key, we find $-13\pi \approx -40.8407045$. Then, with the calculator in radian mode, press the $\boxed{\cos}$ key.

cos (-13π) = -1

70. 0

71. Find tan 2.5 using a calculator.

With the calculator in radian mode, enter 2.5 and then press the $\boxed{\tan}$ key.
tan 2.5 ≈ -0.747022

72. -0.530323

73. With the calculator in degree mode, enter 0.5125 and press the $\boxed{\sin^{-1}}$ key.

θ = sin⁻¹ 0.5125 ≈ 30.83°.
With the calculator in radian mode, enter 0.5125 and press the $\boxed{\sin^{-1}}$ key.

θ = sin⁻¹ 0.5125 ≈ 0.5381

74. 34.50°, 0.6022

75. With the calculator in degree mode, enter 0.6512 and press the $\boxed{\cos^{-1}}$ key.

θ = cos⁻¹ 0.6512 ≈ 49.37°
With the calculator in radian mode, repeat this process.

θ = cos⁻¹ 0.6512 ≈ 0.8616

76. 55.29°, 0.9649

77. With the calculator in degree mode, enter 7.425 and press the $\boxed{\tan^{-1}}$ key.

θ = tan⁻¹ 7.425 ≈ 82.33°
With the calculator in radian mode, repeat this process.

θ = tan⁻¹ 7.425 ≈ 1.4369

78. 72.46°, 1.2646

79. csc θ = $\frac{1}{\sin\theta}$ = 6.277

sin θ = $\frac{1}{6.277}$ ≈ 0.1593

With the calculator in degree mode, enter 0.1593 and press the $\boxed{\sin^{-1}}$ key.

θ = sin⁻¹ 0.1593 ≈ 9.17°
With the calculator in radian mode, repeat this process.

θ = sin⁻¹ 0.1593 ≈ 0.1600

80. 31.67°, 0.5528

81. sin θ = -0.9956, 270° < θ < 360°

We find the reference angle, ignoring the fact that sin θ is negative. Enter 0.9956 and press the $\boxed{\sin^{-1}}$ key. The reference angle is approximately 84.62°.

θ = 360° - 84.62° = 275.38°

82. Reference angle: 25.55°
θ = 180° - 25.55° = 154.45°

83. cos θ = -0.9388, 180° < θ < 270°

We find the reference angle, ignoring the fact that cos θ is negative. Enter 0.9388 and press the $\boxed{\cos^{-1}}$ key. The reference angle is approximately 20.15°.

θ = 180° + 20.15° = 200.15°

84. Reference angle: 84.32°

θ = 180° - 84.32° = 95.68°

85. tan θ = 0.2460,   180° < θ < 270°

Enter 0.2460 and press the $\boxed{\tan^{-1}}$ key. The reference angle is approximately 13.82°.

θ = 180° + 13.82° = 193.82°

86. Reference angle: 71.87°

θ = 360° - 71.87° = 288.13°

87. sec θ = -1.0485,   90° < θ < 180°

Find the reference angle, ignoring the fact that sec θ is negative. Enter 1.0485, press the reciprocal key, and then press the $\boxed{\cos^{-1}}$ key. The reference angle is approximately 17.49°.

θ = 180° - 17.49° = 162.51°

88. Reference angle = θ = 72.59°

89. sin θ = 0.5766, $\frac{\pi}{2} < \theta < \pi$

With the calculator in radian mode, enter 0.5766, and press the $\boxed{\sin^{-1}}$ key. The reference number is 0.6146

θ = π - 0.6146 ≈ 3.1416 - 0.6146 = 2.5270

90. Reference number: 1.0915

θ = 2π - 1.0915 ≈ 5.1917

91. cos θ = -0.211499, $\frac{\pi}{2} < \theta < \pi$

We find the reference number, ignoring the fact that cos θ is negative. With the calculator in radian mode, enter 0.211499 and press the $\boxed{\cos^{-1}}$ key. The reference angle is 1.3577.

θ = π - 1.3577 ≈ 3.1416 - 1.3577 = 1.7839

92. Reference number: 0.3517

θ = π + 0.3517 ≈ 3.4933

93. tan θ = -19.0541, $\frac{3\pi}{2} < \theta < 2\pi$

We find the reference number, ignoring the fact that tan θ is negative. With the calculator in radian mode, enter 19.0541 and press the $\boxed{\tan^{-1}}$ key. The reference angle is 1.5184.

θ = 2π - 1.5184 ≈ 6.2832 - 1.5184 = 4.7648

94. Reference number: 1.5398

θ = π + 1.5398 ≈ 4.6814

95. $\csc \theta = \dfrac{1}{\sin \theta} = 11.21048, \; 0 < \theta < \dfrac{\pi}{2}.$

$\sin \theta = \dfrac{1}{11.21048} \approx 0.08920$

With the calculator in radian mode, enter 0.08920 and press the $\boxed{\sin^{-1}}$ key.

$\theta = 0.0893$

96. Reference number: 1.3326

$\theta = \pi - 1.3326 \approx 1.8090$

97. We draw the terminal side of an angle of 390°.

The reference angle is 30°.

Let d be the vertical distance of the valve cap above the center of the wheel.

$\dfrac{d}{24.5} = \sin 30°$

$d = 24.5 \sin 30°$

$\quad = 24.5 \times \dfrac{1}{2}$

$\quad = 12.25$

The distance above the ground is then 12.25 in. + 26 in. = 38.25 in.

98.

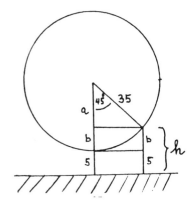

765° is in the first quadrant, and the reference angle is 45°.

$a = 35 \cos 45° = \dfrac{35}{\sqrt{2}}$

$h = 5 + b$

$\quad = 5 + (35 - a)$

$\quad = 40 - \dfrac{35}{\sqrt{2}}$

$\quad \approx 15.3 \text{ ft}$

99. Using a calculator, we see that an angle must be 0.0670 radians.

100. 0.0669   (Using Table 3)

101. $\sin 0.5 = 0.5 - \dfrac{(0.5)^3}{6} + \dfrac{(0.5)^5}{120}$

$\quad \approx 0.5 - 0.02083 + 0.00026$

$\quad = 0.47943$

The values are the same, rounded to four decimal places.

102.

Domain: Set of all real numbers except odd multiples of 90°.

103. $\sin \theta \approx \theta$ when θ is small and when θ is in radian measure.

We convert 31' 59" to radian measure:

$31' \; 59" = \left(\dfrac{31}{60}\right)° + \left(\dfrac{59}{3600}\right)° \approx 0.5331°$

$0.5331° \cdot \dfrac{\pi}{180°} \approx 0.0093$

We make a drawing. Let d represent the diameter of the sun.

Earth   d

$\qquad$ 93,000,000 mi

$\sin 0.0093 = \dfrac{d}{93,000,000}$

$\quad 0.0093 \approx \dfrac{d}{93,000,000}$ $(\sin 0.0093 \approx 0.0093)$

$\quad 865,000 \approx d$

The diameter of the sun is about 865,000 miles.

104. Solve $\dfrac{\sin 27°}{\sin r} = 1.52$ for r.

$r = 17.38°$

105. a) When $y = 0$, the quadratic equation

$0 = -\dfrac{1}{2}gt^2 + (V \sin \theta)t + h$ has the positive root $t_1 = \dfrac{V \sin \theta + \sqrt{V^2 \sin^2 \theta + 2gh}}{g}.$

b) In $x = (V \cos \theta)t$, substitute the value for t_1 to obtain

$x = (V \cos \theta) \dfrac{V \sin \theta + \sqrt{V^2 \sin^2 \theta + 2gh}}{g}.$

c) Write the answer in part b) as follows:

$gx - V^2 \sin \theta \cos \theta$

$= V \cos \theta \sqrt{V^2 \sin^2 \theta + 2gh}.$

Squaring both sides we obtain, after simplifying,

$V^2 = \dfrac{x^2 g}{2 \cos\theta \, (x \sin\theta + h \cos\theta)}$. Using the

given data: x = 21.6, h = 1.6, θ = 44°,

g = 9.8, we find V ≈ 14.026 m/sec.

d) The answer to b) shows that x increases as
   h increases; thus a taller shotputter can put
   the shot a greater distance than a shorter
   shotputter.

e) In the given equations for x and y, solve the

   first equation for V: $V = \dfrac{x}{t \cos\theta}$.

   Substitute in the second equation to obtain

   $y = -\dfrac{1}{2} g t^2 + x \tan\theta + h$. Using the given

   data, $8 = -\dfrac{1}{2}(32)t^2 + 300 \tan 20° + 4.5$, or

   $16t^2 = 300 \tan 20° - 3.5$ so that

   t ≈ 2.57 sec; then

   $V = \dfrac{300}{2.57 \cos 20°} ≈ 124$ ft/sec.

Exercise Set 6.7

1. y = sin x + 2   (A = 1, B = 2, C = 1, D = 0)
   Amplitude: 1, period: 2π, phase shift: 0

   The graph of y = sin x + 2 is a translation of
   y = sin x upward 2 units.

2. Amplitude: 1, period: 2π, phase shift: 0

3. $y = \dfrac{1}{2} \sin x$ $\left[A = \dfrac{1}{2}, B = 0, C = 1, D = 0\right]$

   Amplitude: $\dfrac{1}{2}$, period: 2π, phase shift: 0

   The graph of $y = \dfrac{1}{2} \sin x$ is a vertical shrinking
   of the graph of y = sin x.

4. Amplitude: $\dfrac{1}{3}$, period: 2π, phase shift: 0

5. y = 2 cos x   (A = 2, B = 0, C = 1, D = 0)
   Amplitude: 2, period: 2π, phase shift: 0

   The graph of y = 2 cos x is a vertical stretching
   of the graph of y = cos x.

6. Amplitude: 3, period: 2π, phase shift: 0

7. $y = -\dfrac{1}{2} \cos x$ $\left[A = -\dfrac{1}{2}, B = 0, C = 1, D = 0\right]$

   Amplitude: $\left|-\dfrac{1}{2}\right| = \dfrac{1}{2}$, period: 2π, phase shift: 0

   The graph of $y = -\dfrac{1}{2} \cos x$ is a vertical shrinking
   of the graph of y = cos x. There is also a
   reflection across the x-axis since A < 0.

8. Amplitude: 2, period: 2π, phase shift: 0

<u>9.</u> y = cos 2x   (A = 1, B = 0, C = 2, D = 0)

Amplitude: 1, period: $\frac{2\pi}{2} = \pi$, phase shift: 0

The graph of y = cos 2x is a horizontal shrinking of the graph of y = cos x.

<u>10.</u> Amplitude: 1, period: $\frac{2\pi}{3}$, phase shift: 0

<u>11.</u> y = cos (-2x)   (A = 1, B = 0, C = -2, D = 0)

Amplitude: 1, period: $\left|\frac{2\pi}{-2}\right| = \pi$,

phase shift: 0

The graph of y = cos (-2x) is a horizontal shrinking of the graph of y = cos x. There is also a reflection across the y-axis since C < 0. Note that the graphs of y = cos 2x and y = cos (-2x) are identical. The cosine function is an even function, cos (-2x) = cos 2x.

<u>12.</u> The graph of y = cos (-3x) is the same as the graph of y = cos 3x. See the graph in Exercise 10 above.

<u>13.</u> y = sin $\frac{1}{2}$ x $\left[A = 1, B = 0, C = \frac{1}{2}, D = 0\right]$

Amplitude: 1, period: $\frac{2\pi}{\frac{1}{2}} = 4\pi$, phase shift: 0

The graph of y = sin $\frac{1}{2}$ x is a horizontal stretching of the graph of y = sin x.

<u>14.</u> Amplitude: 1, period: 6π, phase shift: 0

<u>15.</u> y = sin $\left[-\frac{1}{2} x\right]$ $\left[A = 1, B = 0, C = -\frac{1}{2}, D = 0\right]$

Amplitude: 1, period: $\left|\frac{2\pi}{-\frac{1}{2}}\right| = 4\pi$,

phase shift: 0

The graph of y = sin $\left[-\frac{1}{2} x\right]$ is a horizontal stretching of the graph of y = sin x. There is also a reflection across the y-axis since C < 0.

<u>16.</u> The graph of y = cos $\left[-\frac{1}{3} x\right]$ is the same as the graph of y = cos $\frac{1}{3}$ x. See the graph in Exercise 14 above.

<u>17.</u> y = cos (2x - π) = cos $\left[2\left[x - \frac{\pi}{2}\right]\right]$

          (A = 1, B = 0, C = 2, D = π)

Amplitude: 1, period: $\frac{2\pi}{2} = \pi$, phase shift: $\frac{\pi}{2}$

The $\frac{\pi}{2}$ translates the graph of y = cos 2x (see Exercise 9) a distance of $\frac{\pi}{2}$ to the right.

<u>18.</u> y = sin (2x + π) = sin $\left[2\left[x - \left[-\frac{\pi}{2}\right]\right]\right]$

Amplitude: 1, period: π, phase shift: $-\frac{\pi}{2}$

<u>19.</u> y = 2 cos $\left[\frac{1}{2} x - \frac{\pi}{2}\right]$ = 2 cos $\left[\frac{1}{2} (x - \pi)\right]$

          $\left[A = 2, B = 0, C = \frac{1}{2}, D = \frac{\pi}{2}\right]$

The graph of y = 2 cos $\left[\frac{1}{2} (x - \pi)\right]$ has an amplitude of 2, a period of 4π $\left[2\pi \div \frac{1}{2} = 4\pi\right]$, and a phase shift of π.

First graph y = cos x.

The graph of $y = \cos \frac{1}{2} x$ is a horizontal stretching of the graph of $y = \cos x$. The period of $y = \cos x$ is 2π. The period of $y = \cos \frac{1}{2} x$ is 4π.

The graph of $y = 2 \cos \frac{1}{2} x$ is a vertical stretching of the graph of $y = \cos \frac{1}{2} x$. The amplitude of $y = \cos \frac{1}{2} x$ is 1. The amplitude of $y = 2 \cos \frac{1}{2} x$ is 2.

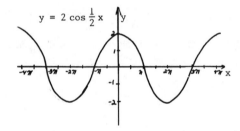

The graph of $y = 2 \cos \frac{1}{2} (x - \pi)$ is a translation of the graph of $y = 2 \cos \frac{1}{2} x$ a distance of π to the right.

20. $y = 4 \sin \left[\frac{1}{4}x + \frac{\pi}{8} \right] = 4 \sin \left[\frac{1}{4} \left[x - \left[-\frac{\pi}{2} \right] \right] \right]$

(1) $y = \sin x$ is the starting graph.

(2) $y = \sin \frac{1}{4} x$ results from stretching (1) horizontally by a factor of 4.

(3) $y = \sin \left[\frac{1}{4} \left[x - \left[-\frac{\pi}{2} \right] \right] \right]$ results from translating (2) to the left through $\frac{\pi}{2}$ units.

(4) $y = 4 \sin \left[\frac{1}{4} \left[x - \left[-\frac{\pi}{2} \right] \right] \right] = 4 \sin \left[\frac{x}{4} + \frac{\pi}{8} \right]$ results from stretching (3) vertically by a factor of 4.

Amplitude: 4, period: 8π, phase shift: $-\frac{\pi}{2}$

21. $y = -3 \cos (4x - \pi) = -3 \cos \left[4 \left[x - \frac{\pi}{4} \right] \right]$

$(A = -3, B = 0, C = 4, D = \pi)$

The graph of $y = -3 \cos \left[4 \left[x - \frac{\pi}{4} \right] \right]$ has an amplitude of 3, a period of $\frac{\pi}{2}$ $\left[2\pi \div 4 = \frac{\pi}{2} \right]$, and a phase shift of $\frac{\pi}{4}$.

First graph $y = \cos x$.

The graph of $y = \cos 4x$ is a horizontal shrinking of the graph of $y = \cos x$. The period of $y = \cos x$ is 2π. The period of $y = \cos 4x$ is $\frac{\pi}{2}$.

The graph of $y = -3 \cos 4x$ is a vertical stretching of the graph of $y = \cos 4x$. The amplitude of $y = \cos 4x$ is 1. The amplitude of $y = -3 \cos 4x$ is 3. The graph is also a reflection across the x-axis since B is negative.

The graph of $y = -3 \cos 4\left(x - \frac{\pi}{4}\right)$ is a translation of the graph of $y = -3 \cos 4x$ a distance of $\frac{\pi}{4}$ to the right.

$y = -3 \cos 4\left(x - \frac{\pi}{4}\right)$

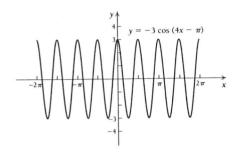
$y = -3 \cos (4x - \pi)$

22. $y = -3 \sin \left(2x + \frac{\pi}{2}\right) = -3 \sin \left[2\left(x - \left(-\frac{\pi}{4}\right)\right)\right]$

(1) $y = \sin x$ is the starting graph.

(2) $y = \sin 2x$ results from shrinking (1) horizontally by a factor of $\frac{1}{2}$.

(3) $y = \sin \left[2\left(x - \left(-\frac{\pi}{4}\right)\right)\right]$ results from translating (2) to the left through $\frac{\pi}{4}$ units.

(4) $y = 3 \sin \left[2\left(x - \left(-\frac{\pi}{4}\right)\right)\right]$ results from stretching (3) vertically by a factor of 3.

(5) $y = -3 \sin \left[2\left(x - \left(-\frac{\pi}{4}\right)\right)\right]$ results from reflecting (4) across the x-axis.

Amplitude: 3, period: π, phase shift: $-\frac{\pi}{4}$

$y = -3 \sin \left(2x + \frac{\pi}{2}\right)$

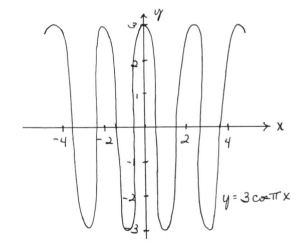

23. $y = 2 + 3 \cos (\pi x - 3)$, or

$y = 2 + 3 \cos \left[\pi \left(x - \frac{3}{\pi}\right)\right]$

$(A = 3, B = 2, C = \pi, D = 3)$

The graph of $y = 2 + 3 \cos \pi \left(x - \frac{3}{\pi}\right)$ has an amplitude of 3, a period of $2(2\pi \div \pi = 2)$, and a phase shift of $\frac{3}{\pi}$.

First graph $y = \cos x$.

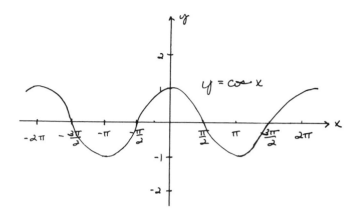
$y = \cos x$

The graph of $y = \cos \pi x$ is a horizontal shrinking of the graph of $y = \cos x$. The period of $y = \cos x$ is 2π. The period of $y = \cos \pi x$ is 2.

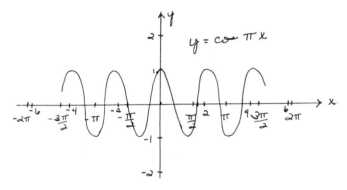
$y = \cos \pi x$

The graph of $y = 3 \cos \pi x$ is a vertical stretching of the graph of $y = \cos \pi x$. The amplitude of $y = \cos \pi x$ is 1. The amplitude of $y = 3 \cos \pi x$ is 3.

$y = 3 \cos \pi x$

The graph of $y = 3 \cos \left[\pi \left(x - \frac{3}{\pi}\right)\right]$ is a translation of the graph of $y = 3 \cos \pi x$ a distance of $\frac{3}{\pi}$ to the right.

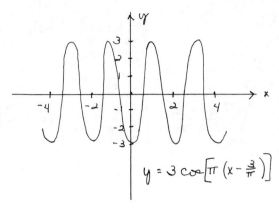

$$y = 3 \cos\left[\pi\left(x - \tfrac{3}{\pi}\right)\right]$$

The graph of $y = 2 + 3 \cos\left[\pi\left(x - \tfrac{3}{\pi}\right)\right]$ is a translation of the graph of $y = 3 \cos\left[\pi\left(x - \tfrac{3}{\pi}\right)\right]$ up 2 units.

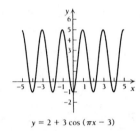

$$y = 2 + 3 \cos(\pi x - 3)$$

24. $y = 5 - 2 \cos\left[\tfrac{\pi}{2}x + \tfrac{\pi}{2}\right] = 5 - 2 \cos\left[\tfrac{\pi}{2}(x - (-1))\right]$

(1) $y = \cos x$ is the starting graph.

(2) $y = \cos \tfrac{\pi}{2}x$ results from shrinking (1) horizontally by a factor of $\tfrac{2}{\pi}$.

(3) $y = -2 \cos \tfrac{\pi}{2}x$ results from stretching (2) vertically by a factor of 2 and reflecting it across the x-axis.

(4) $y = -2 \cos\left[\tfrac{\pi}{2}(x - (-1))\right]$ results from translating (3) 1 unit to the left.

(5) $y = 5 - 2 \cos\left[\tfrac{\pi}{2}(x - (-1))\right]$ results from translating (4) up 5 units.

Amplitude: 2, period: 4, phase shift: -1

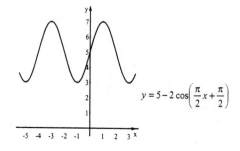

$$y = 5 - 2 \cos\left(\tfrac{\pi}{2}x + \tfrac{\pi}{2}\right)$$

25. $y = 3 \cos\left[3x - \tfrac{\pi}{2}\right]$ $\left[A = 3,\ B = 0,\ C = 3,\ D = \tfrac{\pi}{2}\right]$

$y = 3 \cos 3\left[x - \tfrac{\pi}{6}\right]$

The amplitude is 3.

The period is $2\pi \div 3$, or $\tfrac{2\pi}{3}$.

The phase shift is $\tfrac{\pi}{6}$.

26. $y = 4 \sin\left[4x - \tfrac{\pi}{3}\right] = 4 \sin\left[4\left(x - \tfrac{\pi}{12}\right)\right]$

Amplitude: 4,   Period: $\tfrac{2\pi}{4} = \tfrac{\pi}{2}$,   Phase shift: $\overline{1}$

27. $y = -5 \cos\left[4x + \tfrac{\pi}{3}\right]$

$y = -5 \cos\left[4x - \left(-\tfrac{\pi}{3}\right)\right]$ $\left[\begin{array}{l}A = -5,\ B = 0,\ C = 4 \\ D = -\tfrac{\pi}{3}\end{array}\right]$

$y = -5 \cos 4\left[x - \left(-\tfrac{\pi}{12}\right)\right]$

The amplitude is $|-5|$, or 5.

The period is $2\pi \div 4$, or $\tfrac{\pi}{2}$.

The phase shift is $-\tfrac{\pi}{12}$.

28. $y = -4 \sin\left[5x + \tfrac{\pi}{2}\right] = -4 \sin\left[5\left(x - \left(-\tfrac{\pi}{10}\right)\right)\right]$

Amplitude: $|-4| = 4$,   Period: $\tfrac{2\pi}{5}$,

Phase shift: $-\tfrac{\pi}{10}$

29. $y = \tfrac{1}{2} \sin(2\pi x + \pi)$

$y = \tfrac{1}{2} \sin\left[2\pi x - (-\pi)\right]$

$\left[A = \tfrac{1}{2},\ B = 0,\ C = 2\pi,\ D = -\pi\right]$

$y = \tfrac{1}{2} \sin 2\pi\left[x - \left(-\tfrac{1}{2}\right)\right]$

The amplitude is $\tfrac{1}{2}$.

The period is $2\pi \div 2\pi$, or 1.

The phase shift is $-\tfrac{1}{2}$.

30. $y = -\tfrac{1}{4} \cos(\pi x - 4) = -\tfrac{1}{4} \cos\left[\pi\left[x - \tfrac{4}{\pi}\right]\right]$

Amplitude: $\left|-\tfrac{1}{4}\right| = \tfrac{1}{4}$,   Period: $\tfrac{2\pi}{\pi} = 2$,

Phase shift: $\tfrac{4}{\pi}$

31. $y = 2 \cos x + \cos 2x$

Graph $y = 2 \cos x$ and $y = \cos 2x$ on the same set of axes. Then graphically add some ordinates to obtain points on the graph of $y = 2 \cos x + \cos 2x$.

32.

37. y = 3 cos x + sin 2x

Graph y = 3 cos x and y = sin 2x on the same
set of axes. Then graphically add some ordinates
to obtain points on the graph of y = 3 cos x +
sin 2x.

33. y = sin x + cos 2x

Graph y = sin x and y = cos 2x on the same set of
axes. Then graphically add some ordinates to
obtain points on the graph of y = sin x + cos 2x.

38. To graph y = 3 sin x - cos 2x, graph y = 3 sin x
and y = -cos 2x on the same set of axes. Then
graphically add some ordinates to obtain points
on the graph of y = 3 sin x - cos 2x.

34.   , graph y = 2 sin x

39. T(t) = 101.6° + 3° sin $\left(\frac{\pi}{8}t\right)$

a) Start with the graph of y = sin t.

Then graph y = sin $\left(\frac{\pi}{8}t\right)$. The period is
2π ÷ $\frac{\pi}{8}$, or 16. The graph is stretched
horizontally.

Then graph y = 3 sin $\left(\frac{\pi}{8}t\right)$. The amplitude is
3. The graph is stretched vertically.

Then graph y = 101.6° + 3° sin $\left(\frac{\pi}{8}t\right)$. The
graph is translated up 101.6 units.

35. y = sin x - cos x

Graph y = sin x and y = -cos x on the same set
of axes. Then graphically add some ordinates to
obtain points on the graph of y = sin x - cos x.

36. To graph y = 3 cos x - sin x, graph y = 3 cos x
and y = -sin x on the same set of axes. Then
graphically add some ordinates to obtain points
on the graph of y = 3 cos x - sin x.

$$T(t) = 101.6° + 3° \sin\left(\tfrac{\pi}{8}t\right)$$

b) The maximum value occurs on day 4 when the sine function takes its maximum value, 1. It is 101.6° + 3°·1, or 104.6°.

The minimum value occurs on day 12 when the sine function takes its minimum value, -1. It is 101.6° + 3°(-1), or 98.6°.

40. a)

$$S(t) = 10\left(1 - \cos\tfrac{\pi}{6}t\right)$$

b) $\dfrac{2\pi}{\frac{\pi}{6}} = 12$

c) $0 in July (at t = 0 and t = 12)

d) $20,000 in January (at t = 6)

41. $y = 3000\left[\cos\tfrac{\pi}{45}(t - 10)\right]$

a) Start with the graph of y = cos t.

Then graph $y = \cos\left[\tfrac{\pi}{45}t\right]$. The period is $2\pi \div \tfrac{\pi}{45}$, or 90. The graph is stretched horizontally.

Then graph $y = 3000\left[\cos\left[\tfrac{\pi}{4}t\right]\right]$. The amplitude is 3000. The graph is stretched vertically.

Then graph $y = 3000\left[\cos\tfrac{\pi}{45}(t - 10)\right]$. The phase shift is 10. The graph is translated 10 units to the right.

$$y = 3000[\cos\tfrac{\pi}{45}(t - 10)]$$

b) Amplitude: 3000, period: 90, phase shift: 10

42. $y = 3 \sin\left[\tfrac{\pi}{4}x + \tfrac{\pi}{4}\right] = 3 \sin\left[\tfrac{\pi}{4}(x - (-1))\right]$

a)

$$y = 3 \sin\left(\tfrac{\pi}{4}x + \tfrac{\pi}{4}\right)$$

b) Amplitude: 3, period: $\dfrac{2\pi}{\frac{\pi}{4}} = 8$, phase shift: -1

43. We use $y = A \sin\left[C\left(x - \tfrac{D}{C}\right)\right] + B$.

|A| = 8.6. Choose A = 8.6; $\tfrac{2\pi}{C} = 5$, or $C = \tfrac{2\pi}{5}$; $\tfrac{D}{C} = -11$; B = any real number. We choose B = 0.

We have $y = 8.6 \sin\left[\tfrac{2\pi}{5}(x - (-11))\right]$, or

$y = 8.6 \sin\left[\tfrac{2\pi}{5}(x + 11)\right]$. Answers may vary.

44. Use $y = A \sin\left[C\left(x - \tfrac{D}{C}\right)\right] + B$.

|A| = 6.7. Choose A = 6.7; $\tfrac{2\pi}{C} = \pi$, or C = 2, and $\tfrac{D}{C} = \tfrac{4}{7}$. We choose B = 0.

$y = 6.7 \cos\left[2\left(x - \tfrac{4}{7}\right)\right]$. Answers may vary.

45. We use $y = \cos\left[C\left(x - \tfrac{D}{C}\right)\right] + B$.

|A| = 16. Choose A = 16; $\tfrac{2\pi}{C} = \tfrac{\pi}{3}$, or C = 6; $\tfrac{D}{C} = -\tfrac{2}{\pi}$, B = any real number. We choose B = 0.

We have $y = 16 \cos\left[6\left(x - \left[-\tfrac{2}{\pi}\right]\right)\right]$, or

$y = 16 \cos\left[6\left(x + \tfrac{2}{\pi}\right)\right]$. Answers may vary.

46. Use $y = A \sin\left[C\left(x - \tfrac{D}{C}\right)\right] + B$.

|A| = 34. Choose A = 34; $\tfrac{2\pi}{C} = \tfrac{\pi}{5}$, or C = 10; $\tfrac{D}{C} = -\tfrac{8}{\pi}$. We choose B = 0.

$y = 34 \sin\left[10\left(x - \left[-\tfrac{8}{\pi}\right]\right)\right]$, or $34 \sin\left[10\left(x + \tfrac{8}{\pi}\right)\right]$. Answers may vary.

47. $y = |4 \sin x|$

Start with y = sin x. Then graph y = 4 sin x. The graph is stretched vertically by a factor of 4. Then the portions of the graph that lie below the x-axis are reflected across the x-axis since y = |4 sin x| = -4 sin x for sin x < 0.

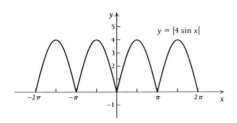

$y = |4 \sin x|$

48.

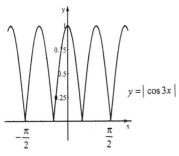

$y = |\cos 3x|$

49. y = x + sin x

Graph y = x and y = sin x on the same set of
axes. Then graphically add some ordinates to
obtain points on the graph of y = x + sin x.

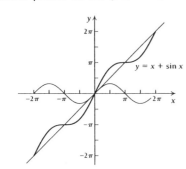

$y = x + \sin x$

50.

$y = \cos x - x$

51. $y = \cos 2x + 2x$

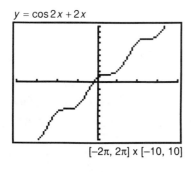

$[-2\pi, 2\pi] \times [-10, 10]$

52. $y = \cos 3x + \sin 3x$

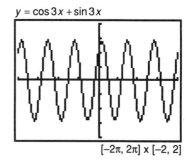

$[-2\pi, 2\pi] \times [-2, 2]$

53. $y = 4\cos 2x - 2\sin x$

$[-2\pi, 2\pi] \times [-8, 8]$

54. $y = 7.5 \cos x + \sin 2x$

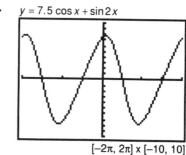

$[-2\pi, 2\pi] \times [-10, 10]$

Exercise Set 6.8

1. y = -tan x

Reflect the graph of y = tan x across the x-axis.

$y = -\tan x$

2.

$y = -\cot x$

3. y = -csc x

Reflect the graph of y = csc x across the x-axis.

$y = -\csc x$

4.

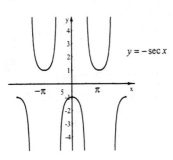

$y = -\sec x$

5. y = sec (-x)

sec (-x) = sec x, so we graph y = sec x.

$y = \sec (-x)$

6.

$y = \csc (-x)$

7. y = cot (-x)

cot (-x) = -cot x, so we graph y = -cot x. This is the reflection of the graph of y = cot x across the x-axis.

$y = \cot (-x)$

8.

$y = \tan (-x)$

9. y = -2 + cot x

This is the graph of y = cot x translated down 2 units.

$y = -2 + \cot x$

10.

$y = -3 + \sec x$

11. $y = -\dfrac{3}{2}$ csc x

The graph of y = csc x is stretched vertically by a factor of $\dfrac{3}{2}$ and is also reflected across the x-axis.

$$y = -\frac{3}{2}\csc x$$

$$y = \sec\left(-\frac{1}{2}x\right)$$

12.

$$y = 0.25\cot x + 3$$

16.

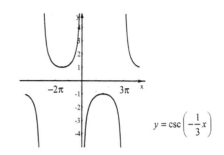

$$y = \csc\left(-\frac{1}{3}x\right)$$

13. y = cot 2x

Start with the graph of y = cot x. The period of
the cotangent function is π, so the period of
y = cot 2x is $\frac{\pi}{2}$.

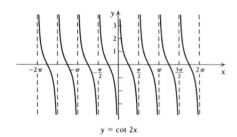

$$y = \cot 2x$$

17. y = 2 sec (x − π)

Start with the graph of y = sec x.

Then graph y = 2 sec x. The graph of y = sec x
is stretched vertically by a factor of 2.

Then graph y = 2 sec (x − π). The graph of
y = 2 sec x is translated π units to the right.

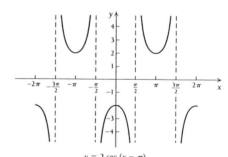

$$y = 2\sec(x - \pi)$$

14.

$$y = 2\tan\frac{1}{2}x$$

18.

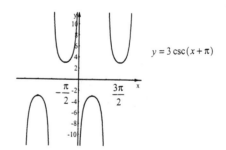

$$y = 3\csc(x + \pi)$$

15. y = sec $\left(-\frac{1}{2}x\right)$

sec $\left(-\frac{1}{2}x\right)$ = sec $\left(\frac{1}{2}x\right)$, so we graph y = sec $\left(\frac{1}{2}x\right)$.
Start with the graph of y = sec x. The period of
the secant function is 2π, so the period of
y = sec $\left(\frac{1}{2}x\right)$ is 2π ÷ $\frac{1}{2}$, or 4π.

19. $y = 4 \tan \left[\frac{1}{4}x + \frac{\pi}{8}\right] = 4 \tan \left[\frac{1}{4}\left[x + \frac{\pi}{2}\right]\right]$

Start with the graph of $y = \tan x$.

Then graph $y = \tan \frac{1}{4}x$. The period is $\pi \div \frac{1}{4} = 4\pi$.

Then graph $y = 4 \tan \frac{1}{4}x$. The previous graph is stretched vertically by a factor of 4.

Then graph $y = 4 \tan \left[\frac{1}{4}\left[x + \frac{\pi}{2}\right]\right]$. The previous graph is translated $\frac{\pi}{2}$ units to the left.

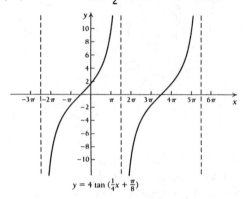

$y = 4 \tan \left(\frac{1}{4}x + \frac{\pi}{8}\right)$

20.

$y = 2 \sec \left(\frac{1}{2}x - \frac{\pi}{2}\right)$

21. $y = -3 \cot \left[2x + \frac{\pi}{2}\right] = -3 \cot \left[2\left[x + \frac{\pi}{4}\right]\right]$

Start with the graph of $y = \cot x$.

Then graph $y = \cot 2x$. The period is $\frac{\pi}{2}$.

Then graph $y = -3 \cot 2x$. The previous graph is stretched vertically by a factor of 3 and is reflected across the x-axis.

Then graph $y = -3 \cot \left[2\left[x + \frac{\pi}{4}\right]\right]$. The previous graph is translated $\frac{\pi}{4}$ units to the left.

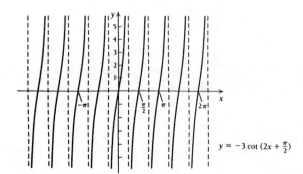

$y = -3 \cot \left(2x + \frac{\pi}{2}\right)$

22.

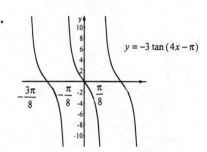

$y = -3 \tan (4x - \pi)$

23. $y = 4 \sec (2x - \pi) = 4 \sec \left[2\left[x - \frac{\pi}{2}\right]\right]$

Start with the graph of $y = \sec x$.

Then graph $y = \sec 2x$. The period is $2\pi \div 2$, or π.

Then graph $y = 4 \sec 2x$. The previous graph is stretched vertically by a factor of 4.

Then graph $y = 4 \sec \left[2\left[x - \frac{\pi}{2}\right]\right]$. The previous graph is translated $\frac{\pi}{2}$ units to the right.

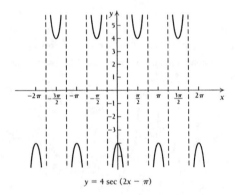

$y = 4 \sec (2x - \pi)$

24.

$y = 2 \csc \left(\frac{1}{2}x - \frac{3\pi}{4}\right)$

25. $f(x) = e^{-x/2} \cos x$

This function is the product of $g(x) = e^{-x/2}$ and $h(x) = \cos x$. Thus, we can multiply ordinates to find function values. Note that $-1 \le \cos x \le 1$ and $e^{-x/2} > 0$ for all real numbers x. Thus,

$-e^{-x/2} \le e^{-x/2} \cos x \le e^{-x/2}$.

The graph of f is constrained between the graphs of $y = -e^{-x/2}$ and $y = e^{-x/2}$. Also, $f(x) = 0$ when $x = \frac{\pi}{2} + k\pi$, k an integer.

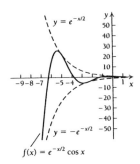

$y = e^{-x/2}$

$y = -e^{-x/2}$

$f(x) = e^{-x/2} \cos x$

26.

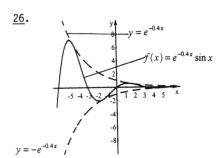

$y = e^{-0.4x}$

$f(x) = e^{-0.4x} \sin x$

$y = -e^{-0.4x}$

27. $f(x) = 0.6x^2 \cos x$

This function is the product of $g(x) = 0.6x^2$ and $h(x) = \cos x$. Thus, we can multiply ordinates to find function values. Note that $-1 \leqslant \cos x \leqslant 1$ and $0.6x^2 \geqslant 0$ for all real numbers x. Thus,

$$-0.6x^2 \leqslant 0.6x^2 \cos x \leqslant 0.6x^2.$$

The graph of f is constrained between the graphs of $y = -0.6x^2$ and $y = 0.6x^2$. Also, $f(x) = 0$ when $x = \frac{\pi}{2} + k\pi$, k an integer, and when $x = 0$.

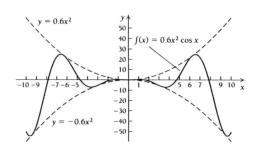

$y = 0.6x^2$

$f(x) = 0.6x^2 \cos x$

$y = -0.6x^2$

28.

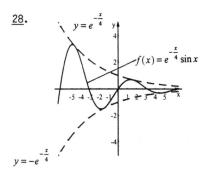

$y = e^{-\frac{x}{4}}$

$f(x) = e^{-\frac{x}{4}} \sin x$

$y = -e^{-\frac{x}{4}}$

29. $f(x) = x \sin x$

This function is the product of $g(x) = x$ and $h(x) = \sin x$. Thus, we can multiply ordinates to find function values. Note that $-1 \leqslant \sin x \leqslant 1$. Thus, for $x \geqslant 0$, $-x \leqslant x \sin x \leqslant x$ and, for $x < 0$, $-x \geqslant x \sin x \geqslant x$. That is $-|x| \leqslant x \sin x \leqslant |x|$. The graph of f is constrained between the graphs of $y = -|x|$ and $y = |x|$. Also, $f(x) = 0$ when $x = k\pi$, k an integer.

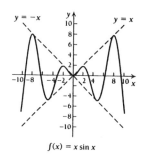

$y = -x$

$y = x$

$f(x) = x \sin x$

30.

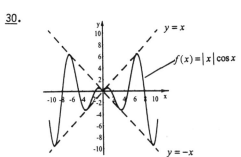

$y = x$

$f(x) = |x| \cos x$

$y = -x$

31. $f(x) = 2^{-x} \sin x$

This function is the product of $g(x) = 2^{-x}$ and $h(x) = \sin x$. Thus, we can multiply ordinates to find function values. Note that $-1 \leqslant \sin x \leqslant 1$ and $2^{-x} > 0$ for all real numbers x. Thus,

$$-2^{-x} \leqslant 2^{-x} \sin x \leqslant 2^{-x}.$$

The graph of f is constrained between the graphs of $y = -2^{-x}$ and $y = 2^{-x}$. Also, $f(x) = 0$ when $x = \frac{\pi}{2} + k\pi$, k an integer.

$y = 2^{-x}$

$y = -2^{-x}$

$f(x) = 2^{-x} \sin x$

32.

33. f(x) = |tan x|

Start with the graph of f(x) = tan x. Then reflect across the x-axis all points that lie below the x-axis, since |tan x| = -tan x when tan x < 0.

34.

35.

36.

37.

38.

39. $d(t) = 6e^{-0.8t} \cos(6\pi t) + 4$

a)

b) As t increases, $e^{-0.8t}$ decreases, and hence $6e^{-0.8t} \cos(6\pi t)$ decreases in the long run and approaches 0. Then the spring would be 4 inches from the ceiling when it stops bobbing.

40. a)

b) 98.6°

41. a) The period is $\frac{1}{2}$. The graph of d(t) = 10 tan (2πt) is a vertical stretching of the graph of d(t) = tan (2πt) by a factor of 10.

$d(t) = 10 \tan (2\pi t)$

   b) The values of t for which the function is undefined are those values for which the beam is parallel to the wall.

42. Zeros occur at -9.43, -6.28, -3.14, 3.14, 6.28, and 9.43.

43. In the interval [-4, 4], the function has zeros at x = -3.14 and at x = 3.14.

44. Zeros occur at -9.43, -6.28, -3.14, 0, 3.14, 6.28, and 9.43.

45. In the interval [-12, 12], the function has zeros at x = -6.28 and at x = 6.28.

46. In the interval [-5, 5], the function has zeros at -3.14, 0, and 3.14.

47. In the interval [-2, 2], the function has zeros at x = -0.84 and x = -0.41.

Exercise Set 7.1

<u>1.</u> $(\sin x - \cos x)(\sin x + \cos x)$

$= \sin^2 x - \cos^2 x$

<u>2.</u> $(\tan y - \cot y)(\tan y + \cot y) = \tan^2 y - \cot^2 y$

<u>3.</u> $\tan x (\cos x - \csc x)$

$= \dfrac{\sin x}{\cos x} \left[\cos x - \dfrac{1}{\sin x} \right]$

$= \sin x - \dfrac{1}{\cos x}$

$= \sin x - \sec x$

<u>4.</u> $\cot x (\sin x + \sec x)$

$= \dfrac{\cos x}{\sin x} \left[\sin x + \dfrac{1}{\cos x} \right]$

$= \cos x + \dfrac{1}{\sin x}$

$= \cos x + \csc x$

<u>5.</u> $\cos y \sin y (\sec y + \csc y)$

$= \cos y \sin y \left[\dfrac{1}{\cos y} + \dfrac{1}{\sin y} \right]$

$= \sin y + \cos y$

<u>6.</u> $\tan y \sin y (\cot y - \csc y)$

$= \tan y \sin y \left[\dfrac{1}{\tan y} - \dfrac{1}{\sin y} \right]$

$= \sin y - \tan y$

<u>7.</u> $(\sin x + \cos x)(\csc x - \sec x)$

$= \sin x \csc x - \sin x \sec x + \cos x \csc x -$
$\qquad\qquad\qquad\qquad\qquad \cos x \sec x$

$= \sin x \cdot \dfrac{1}{\sin x} - \sin x \cdot \dfrac{1}{\cos x} + \cos x \cdot \dfrac{1}{\sin x} -$
$\qquad\qquad\qquad\qquad\qquad \cos x \cdot \dfrac{1}{\cos x}$

$= 1 - \dfrac{\sin x}{\cos x} + \dfrac{\cos x}{\sin x} - 1$

$= \cot x - \tan x$

<u>8.</u> $(\sin x + \cos x)(\sec x + \csc x)$

$= \sin x \sec x + \sin x \csc x + \cos x \sec x +$
$\quad \cos x \csc x$

$= \sin x \cdot \dfrac{1}{\cos x} + \sin x \cdot \dfrac{1}{\sin x} + \cos x \cdot \dfrac{1}{\cos x} +$
$\quad \cos x \cdot \dfrac{1}{\sin x}$

$= \tan x + 1 + 1 + \cot x$

$= 2 + \tan x + \cot x$

<u>9.</u> $(\sin y - \cos y)^2$

$= \sin^2 y - 2 \sin y \cos y + \cos^2 y$

$= 1 - 2 \sin y \cos y \qquad (\sin^2 y + \cos^2 y = 1)$

<u>10.</u> $(\sin y + \cos y)^2$

$= \sin^2 y + 2 \sin y \cos y + \cos^2 y$

$= 1 + 2 \sin y \cos y$

<u>11.</u> $(1 + \tan x)^2$

$= 1 + 2 \tan x + \tan^2 x$

$= \sec^2 x + 2 \tan x \qquad (1 + \tan^2 x = \sec^2 x)$

<u>12.</u> $(1 + \cot x)^2$

$= 1 + 2 \cot x + \cot^2 x$

$= 2 \cot x + \csc^2 x$

<u>13.</u> $(\sin y - \csc y)^2$

$= \sin^2 y - 2 \sin y \csc y + \csc^2 y$

$= \sin^2 y - 2 \sin y \cdot \dfrac{1}{\sin y} + \csc^2 y$

$= \sin^2 y + \csc^2 y - 2$

<u>14.</u> $(\cos y + \sec y)^2$

$= \cos^2 y + 2 \cos y \sec y + \sec^2 y$

$= \cos^2 y + 2 \cos y \cdot \dfrac{1}{\cos y} + \sec^2 y$

$= \cos^2 y + \sec^2 y + 2$

<u>15.</u> $(\cos x - \sec x)(\cos^2 x + \sec^2 x + 1)$

$= \cos^3 x + \cos x \sec^2 x + \cos x - \sec x \cos^2 x -$
$\quad \sec^3 x - \sec x$

$= \cos^3 x + \cos x \cdot \dfrac{1}{\cos^2 x} + \cos x - \dfrac{1}{\cos x} \cdot \cos^2 x -$
$\quad \sec^3 x - \dfrac{1}{\cos x}$

$= \cos^3 x + \dfrac{1}{\cos x} + \cos x - \cos x - \sec^3 x - \dfrac{1}{\cos x}$

$= \cos^3 x - \sec^3 x$

<u>16.</u> $(\sin x + \csc x)(\sin^2 x + \csc^2 x - 1)$

$= \sin^3 x + \sin x \csc^2 x - \sin x + \csc x \sin^2 x +$
$\quad \csc^3 x - \csc x$

$= \sin^3 x + \sin x \cdot \dfrac{1}{\sin^2 x} - \sin x +$
$\quad \dfrac{1}{\sin x} \cdot \sin^2 x + \csc^3 x - \dfrac{1}{\sin x}$

$= \sin^3 x + \dfrac{1}{\sin x} - \sin x + \sin x + \csc^3 x - \dfrac{1}{\sin x}$

$= \sin^3 x + \csc^3 x$

<u>17.</u> $(\cot x - \tan x)(\cot^2 x + 1 + \tan^2 x)$

$= \cot^3 x + \cot x + \cot x \tan^2 x - \tan x \cot^2 x -$
$\quad \tan x - \tan^3 x$

$= \cot^3 x + \cot x + \cot x \cdot \dfrac{1}{\cot^2 x} - \dfrac{1}{\cot x} \cdot \cot^2 x -$
$\quad \dfrac{1}{\cot x} - \tan^3 x$

$= \cot^3 x + \cot x + \dfrac{1}{\cot x} - \cot x - \dfrac{1}{\cot x} - \tan^3 x$

$= \cot^3 x - \tan^3 x$

18. $(\cot y + \tan y)(\cot^2 y - 1 + \tan^2 y)$

    $= \cot^3 y - \cot y + \cot y \tan^2 y + \tan y \cot^2 y -$
    $\quad \tan y + \tan^3 y$

    $= \cot^3 y - \cot y + \dfrac{1}{\tan y} \cdot \tan^2 y +$

    $\quad \dfrac{1}{\cot y} \cdot \cot^2 y - \tan y + \tan^3 y$

    $= \cot^3 y - \cot y + \tan y + \cot y - \tan y + \tan^3 y$

    $= \cot^3 y + \tan^3 y$

19. $(1 - \sin x)(1 + \sin x)$

    $= 1 - \sin^2 x$

    $= \cos^2 x$

20. $(1 + \cos x)(1 - \cos x)$

    $= 1 - \cos^2 x$

    $= \sin^2 x$

21. $\sin x \cos x + \cos^2 x$

    $= \cos x (\sin x + \cos x)$

22. $\sec x \csc x - \csc^2 x$

    $= \csc x (\sec x - \csc x)$

23. $\sin^2 \theta - \cos^2 \theta$

    $= (\sin \theta + \cos \theta)(\sin \theta - \cos \theta)$

24. $\tan^2 \theta - \cot^2 \theta$

    $= (\tan \theta - \cot \theta)(\tan \theta + \cot \theta)$

25. $\tan x + \sin (\pi - x)$

    $= \dfrac{\sin x}{\cos x} + \sin x \qquad [\sin (\pi - x) = \sin x]$

    $= \sin x \left[\dfrac{1}{\cos x} + 1 \right]$

    $= \sin x (\sec x + 1)$

26. $\cot x - \cos (\pi - x)$

    $= \dfrac{\cos x}{\sin x} + \cos x \quad [\cos (\pi - x) = -\cos x]$

    $= \cos x \left[\dfrac{1}{\sin x} + 1 \right]$

    $= \cos x (\csc x + 1)$

27. $\sin^4 x - \cos^4 x$

    $= (\sin^2 x + \cos^2 x)(\sin^2 x - \cos^2 x)$

    $= \sin^2 x - \cos^2 x$

    $= (\sin x + \cos x)(\sin x - \cos x)$

28. $\tan^4 x - \sec^4 x$

    $= (\tan^2 x - \sec^2 x)(\tan^2 x + \sec^2 x)$

    $= -1(\tan^2 x + \sec^2 x)$

    $= -\tan^2 x - \sec^2 x$

29. $3 \cot^2 y + 6 \cot y + 3$

    $= 3(\cot^2 y + 2 \cot y + 1)$

    $= 3(\cot y + 1)^2$

30. $4 \sin^2 y + 8 \sin y + 4$

    $= 4(\sin^2 y + 2 \sin y + 1)$

    $= 4(\sin y + 1)^2$

31. $\csc^4 x + 4 \csc^2 x - 5$

    $= (\csc^2 x + 5)(\csc^2 x - 1)$

    $= (\csc^2 x + 5)(\csc x + 1)(\csc x - 1)$

32. $-8 + \tan^4 x - 2 \tan^2 x$

    $= (\tan^2 x + 2)(\tan^2 x - 4)$

    $= (\tan^2 x + 2)(\tan x - 2)(\tan x + 2)$

33. $\sin^3 y + 27$

    $= (\sin y)^3 + 3^3$

    $= (\sin y + 3)(\sin^2 y - 3 \sin y + 9)$

34. $1 - 125 \tan^3 y$

    $= (1 - 5 \tan y)(1 + 5 \tan y + 25 \tan^2 y)$

35. $\sin^3 v - \csc^3 v$

    $= (\sin v - \csc v)(\sin^2 v + \sin v \csc v + \csc^2 v)$

    $= (\sin v - \csc v)(\sin^2 v + 1 + \csc^2 v)$

    $\qquad \left[\sin v \csc v = \sin v \cdot \dfrac{1}{\sin v} = 1 \right]$

36. $\cos^3 u - \sec^3 u$

    $= (\cos u - \sec u)(\cos^2 u + \cos u \sec u + \sec^2 u)$

    $= (\cos u - \sec u) \left[\cos^2 u + \cos u \cdot \dfrac{1}{\cos u} + \sec^2 u \right]$

    $= (\cos u - \sec u)(\cos^2 u + 1 + \sec^2 u)$

37. $\dfrac{\sin^2 x \cos x}{\cos^2 x \sin x}$

    $= \dfrac{\sin x}{\cos x} \cdot \dfrac{\sin x \cos x}{\sin x \cos x}$

    $= \dfrac{\sin x}{\cos x}$

    $= \tan x$

38. $\dfrac{\cos^2 x \sin x}{\sin^2 x \cos x}$

    $= \dfrac{\cos x}{\sin x}$

    $= \cot x$

39. $\dfrac{4 \sin x \cos^3 x}{18 \sin^2 x \cos x}$

    $= \dfrac{2}{9} \cdot \dfrac{\cos^2 x}{\sin x} \cdot \dfrac{\sin x \cos x}{\sin x \cos x}$

    $= \dfrac{2 \cos^2 x}{9 \sin x}$

40. $\dfrac{30 \sin^3 x \cos x}{6 \cos^2 x \sin x}$

 $= \dfrac{5 \sin^2 x}{\cos x}$

41. $\dfrac{\cos^2 x - 2 \cos x + 1}{\cos x - 1}$

 $= \dfrac{(\cos x - 1)^2}{\cos x - 1}$

 $= \cos x - 1$

42. $\dfrac{\sin^2 x + 2 \sin x + 1}{\sin x + 1}$

 $= \dfrac{(\sin x + 1)^2}{\sin x + 1}$

 $= \sin x + 1$

43. $\dfrac{\cos^2 \alpha - 1}{\cos \alpha - 1}$

 $= \dfrac{(\cos \alpha + 1)(\cos \alpha - 1)}{\cos \alpha - 1}$

 $= \cos \alpha + 1$

44. $\dfrac{\sin^2 \alpha - 1}{\sin \alpha + 1}$

 $= \dfrac{(\sin \alpha + 1)(\sin \alpha - 1)}{\sin \alpha + 1}$

 $= \sin \alpha - 1$

45. $\dfrac{4 \tan x \sec x + 2 \sec x}{6 \sin x \sec x + 2 \sec x}$

 $= \dfrac{2 \sec x \,(2 \tan x + 1)}{2 \sec x \,(3 \sin x + 1)}$

 $= \dfrac{2 \tan x + 1}{3 \sin x + 1}$

46. $\dfrac{6 \tan x \sin x - 3 \sin x}{9 \sin^2 x + 3 \sin x}$

 $= \dfrac{3 \sin x \,(2 \tan x - 1)}{3 \sin x \,(3 \sin x + 1)}$

 $= \dfrac{2 \tan x - 1}{3 \sin x + 1}$

47. $\dfrac{\csc(-\theta)}{\cot(-\theta)} = \dfrac{-\csc \theta}{-\cot \theta}$

 $= \dfrac{\dfrac{1}{\sin \theta}}{\dfrac{\cos \theta}{\sin \theta}}$

 $= \dfrac{1}{\sin \theta} \cdot \dfrac{\sin \theta}{\cos \theta}$

 $= \dfrac{1}{\cos \theta}$

 $= \sec \theta$

48. $\tan(-\beta) + \cot(-\beta)$

 $= -\tan \beta - \cot \beta$

 $= -\dfrac{\sin \beta}{\cos \beta} - \dfrac{\cos \beta}{\sin \beta}$

 $= \dfrac{-\sin^2 \beta - \cos^2 \beta}{\sin \beta \cos \beta}$

 $= -\dfrac{1}{\sin \beta \cos \beta}$, or $-\csc \beta \sec \beta$

49. $\dfrac{\sin^4 x - \cos^4 x}{\sin^2 x - \cos^2 x}$

 $= \dfrac{(\sin^2 x + \cos^2 x)(\sin^2 x - \cos^2 x)}{\sin^2 x - \cos^2 x}$

 $= 1 \qquad\qquad (\sin^2 x + \cos^2 x = 1)$

50. $\dfrac{\sec^4 x - \tan^4 x}{\sec^2 x + \tan^2 x}$

 $= \dfrac{(\sec^2 x + \tan^2 x)(\sec^2 x - \tan^2 x)}{\sec^2 x + \tan^2 x}$

 $= 1 \qquad\qquad (\sec^2 x - \tan^2 x = 1)$

51. $\dfrac{2 \sin^2 x}{\cos^3 x} \cdot \left[\dfrac{\cos x}{2 \sin x}\right]^2$

 $= \dfrac{2 \sin^2 x}{\cos^3 x} \cdot \dfrac{\cos^2 x}{4 \sin^2 x}$

 $= \dfrac{1}{2} \cdot \dfrac{1}{\cos x} \cdot \dfrac{\cos^2 x \sin^2 x}{\cos^2 x \sin^2 x}$

 $= \dfrac{1}{2 \cos x}$, or $\dfrac{1}{2} \sec x$

52. $\dfrac{4 \cos^3 x}{\sin^2 x} \cdot \left[\dfrac{\sin x}{4 \cos x}\right]^2$

 $= \dfrac{4 \cos^3 x \sin^2 x}{16 \sin^2 x \cos^2 x}$

 $= \dfrac{\cos x}{4}$

53. $\dfrac{3 \sin x}{\cos^2 x} \cdot \dfrac{\cos^2 x + \cos x \sin x}{\cos^2 x - \sin^2 x}$

 $= \dfrac{3 \sin x}{\cos^2 x} \cdot \dfrac{\cos x \,(\cos x + \sin x)}{(\cos x - \sin x)(\cos x + \sin x)}$

 $= 3 \cdot \dfrac{\sin x}{\cos x} \cdot \dfrac{1}{\cos x - \sin x} \cdot \dfrac{\cos x(\cos x + \sin x)}{\cos x(\cos x + \sin x)}$

 $= \dfrac{3 \tan x}{\cos x - \sin x}$

54. $\dfrac{5 \cos x}{\sin^2 x} \cdot \dfrac{\sin^2 x - \sin x \cos x}{\sin^2 x - \cos^2 x}$

 $= \dfrac{5 \cos x \sin x \,(\sin x - \cos x)}{\sin^2 x(\sin x + \cos x)(\sin x - \cos x)}$

 $= \dfrac{5 \cos x}{\sin x(\sin x + \cos x)}$

 $= \dfrac{5 \cot x}{\sin x + \cos x}$

55. $\dfrac{\tan^2 \gamma}{\sec \gamma} \div \dfrac{3 \tan^3 \gamma}{\sec \gamma}$

 $= \dfrac{\tan^2 \gamma}{\sec \gamma} \cdot \dfrac{\sec \gamma}{3 \tan^3 \gamma}$

 $= \dfrac{1}{3 \tan \gamma} \cdot \dfrac{\sec \gamma \tan^2 \gamma}{\sec \gamma \tan^2 \gamma}$

 $= \dfrac{1}{3} \cot \gamma$

56. $\dfrac{\cot^3\phi}{\csc\phi} \div \dfrac{4\cot^2\phi}{\csc\phi}$

$= \dfrac{\cot^3\phi}{\csc\phi} \cdot \dfrac{\csc\phi}{4\cot^2\phi}$

$= \dfrac{1}{4}\cot\phi$

57. $\dfrac{1}{\sin^2 y - \cos^2 y} - \dfrac{2}{\cos y + \sin y}$

$= \dfrac{1}{\sin^2 y - \cos^2 y} - \dfrac{2}{\sin y + \cos y} \cdot \dfrac{\sin y - \cos y}{\sin y - \cos y}$

$= \dfrac{1 - 2\sin y + 2\cos y}{\sin^2 y - \cos^2 y}$

58. $\dfrac{3}{\cos y - \sin y} - \dfrac{2}{\sin^2 y - \cos^2 y}$

$= \dfrac{3(\cos y + \sin y) + 2}{(\cos y - \sin y)(\cos y + \sin y)}$

$= \dfrac{3\cos y + 3\sin y + 2}{\cos^2 y - \sin^2 y}$, or

$\dfrac{-3\cos y - 3\sin y - 2}{\sin^2 y - \cos^2 y}$

59. $\left(\dfrac{\sin x}{\cos x}\right)^2 - \dfrac{1}{\cos^2 x}$

$= \tan^2 x - \sec^2 x$

$= -1 \qquad\qquad (1 + \tan^2 x = \sec^2 x)$

60. $\left(\dfrac{\cot x}{\csc x}\right)^2 + \dfrac{1}{\csc^2 x}$

$= \dfrac{\cot^2 x + 1}{\csc^2 x}$

$= \dfrac{\csc^2 x}{\csc^2 x}$

$= 1$

61. $\dfrac{\sin^2 x - 9}{2\cos x + 1} \cdot \dfrac{10\cos x + 5}{3\sin x + 9}$

$= \dfrac{(\sin x + 3)(\sin x - 3)}{2\cos x + 1} \cdot \dfrac{5(2\cos x + 1)}{3(\sin x + 3)}$

$= \dfrac{5(\sin x - 3)}{3}$

62. $\dfrac{9\cos^2 x - 25}{2\cos x - 2} \cdot \dfrac{\cos^2 x - 1}{6\cos x - 10}$

$= \dfrac{(3\cos x + 5)(3\cos x - 5)(\cos x + 1)(\cos x - 1)}{2(\cos x - 1)(2)(3\cos x - 5)}$

$= \dfrac{(3\cos x + 5)(\cos x + 1)}{4}$

63. $\sqrt{\sin^2 x \cos x} \cdot \sqrt{\cos x}$

$= \sqrt{\sin^2 x \cos^2 x}$

$= \sin x \cos x$

64. $\sqrt{\cos^2 x \sin x} \cdot \sqrt{\sin x}$

$= \sqrt{\cos^2 x \sin^2 x}$

$= \cos x \sin x$

65. $\sqrt{\sin^3 y} + \sqrt{\sin y \cos^2 y}$

$= \sin y \sqrt{\sin y} + \cos y \sqrt{\sin y}$

$= \sqrt{\sin y}\,(\sin y + \cos y)$

66. $\sqrt{\cos y \sin^2 y} - \sqrt{\cos^3 y}$

$= \sin y \sqrt{\cos y} - \cos y \sqrt{\cos y}$

$= \sqrt{\cos y}\,(\sin y - \cos y)$

67. $\sqrt{\sin^2 x + 2\cos x \sin x + \cos^2 x}$

$= \sqrt{(\sin x + \cos x)^2}$

$= \sin x + \cos x$

68. $\sqrt{\tan^2 x - 2\tan x \sin x + \sin^2 x}$

$= \sqrt{(\tan x - \sin x)^2}$

$= \tan x - \sin x$

69. $(1 - \sqrt{\sin y})(\sqrt{\sin y} + 1)$

$= (1 - \sqrt{\sin y})(1 + \sqrt{\sin y})$

$= 1 - \sin y \qquad\qquad \left[(\sqrt{\sin y})^2 = \sin y\right]$

70. $(2 - \sqrt{\tan y})(\sqrt{\tan y} + 2)$

$= 4 - \tan y$

71. $\sqrt{\sin x}\,(\sqrt{2\sin x} + \sqrt{\sin x \cos x})$

$= \sqrt{2\sin^2 x} + \sqrt{\sin^2 x \cos x}$

$= \sin x \cdot \sqrt{2} + \sin x \cdot \sqrt{\cos x}$

$= \sin x\,(\sqrt{2} + \sqrt{\cos x})$

72. $\sqrt{\cos x}\,(\sqrt{2\cos x} + \sqrt{\sin x \cos x})$

$= \sqrt{2\cos^2 x} + \sqrt{\sin x \cos^2 x}$

$= \cos x \sqrt{2} + \cos x \sqrt{\sin x}$

$= \cos x\,(\sqrt{2} + \sqrt{\sin x})$

73. $\sqrt{\dfrac{\sin x}{\cos x}}$

$= \sqrt{\dfrac{\sin x}{\cos x} \cdot \dfrac{\cos x}{\cos x}}$

$= \sqrt{\dfrac{\sin x \cos x}{\cos^2 x}}$

$= \dfrac{\sqrt{\sin x \cos x}}{\cos x}$

$\left[\text{Note that } \sqrt{\dfrac{\sin x}{\cos x}} \text{ could also be expressed as } \sqrt{\tan x}.\right]$

74. $\sqrt{\dfrac{\cos x}{\sin x}}$

$= \sqrt{\dfrac{\cos x \sin x}{\sin^2 x}}$

$= \dfrac{\sqrt{\sin x \cos x}}{\sin x}$

$\left[\text{Note that } \sqrt{\dfrac{\cos x}{\sin x}} \text{ could also be expressed as } \sqrt{\cot x}.\right]$

75. $\sqrt{\dfrac{\sin x}{\cot x}}$

$= \sqrt{\dfrac{\sin x}{\cot x} \cdot \dfrac{\cot x}{\cot x}}$

$= \sqrt{\dfrac{\sin x \cot x}{\cot^2 x}}$

$= \dfrac{\sqrt{\cos x}}{\cot x} \quad \left[\sqrt{\sin x \cot x} = \sqrt{\sin x \cdot \dfrac{\cos x}{\sin x}} = \sqrt{\cos x}\right]$

76. $\sqrt{\dfrac{\cos x}{\tan x}}$

$= \sqrt{\dfrac{\cos x \tan x}{\tan^2 x}}$

$= \dfrac{\sqrt{\cos x \cdot \dfrac{\sin x}{\cos x}}}{\tan x}$

$= \dfrac{\sqrt{\sin x}}{\tan x}$

77. $\sqrt{\dfrac{\cos^2 x}{2 \sin^2 x}}$

$= \sqrt{\dfrac{\cot^2 x}{2} \cdot \dfrac{2}{2}}$

$= \dfrac{\sqrt{2} \cot x}{2}$

78. $\sqrt{\dfrac{\sin^2 x}{3 \cos^2 x}}$

$= \sqrt{\dfrac{3 \sin^2 x}{9 \cos^2 x}}$

$= \dfrac{\sqrt{3} \sin x}{3 \cos x}$

$= \dfrac{\sqrt{3} \tan x}{3}$

79. $\sqrt{\dfrac{1 + \sin x}{1 - \sin x}}$

$= \sqrt{\dfrac{1 + \sin x}{1 - \sin x} \cdot \dfrac{1 - \sin x}{1 - \sin x}}$

$= \sqrt{\dfrac{1 - \sin^2 x}{(1 - \sin x)^2}}$

$= \dfrac{\sqrt{\cos^2 x}}{1 - \sin x} \qquad (1 - \sin^2 x = \cos^2 x)$

$= \dfrac{\cos x}{1 - \sin x}$

80. $\sqrt{\dfrac{1 - \cos x}{1 + \cos x}}$

$= \sqrt{\dfrac{1 - \cos^2 x}{(1 + \cos x)^2}}$

$= \dfrac{\sqrt{\sin^2 x}}{1 + \cos x}$

$= \dfrac{\sin x}{1 + \cos x}$

81. $\sqrt{\dfrac{\sin x}{\cos x}} = \sqrt{\dfrac{\sin x}{\cos x} \cdot \dfrac{\sin x}{\sin x}}$

$\phantom{\sqrt{\dfrac{\sin x}{\cos x}}} = \sqrt{\dfrac{\sin^2 x}{\cos x \sin x}}$

$\phantom{\sqrt{\dfrac{\sin x}{\cos x}}} = \dfrac{\sin x}{\sqrt{\cos x \sin x}}$

82. $\sqrt{\dfrac{\cos x}{\sin x}} = \sqrt{\dfrac{\cos^2 x}{\sin x \cos x}}$

$\phantom{\sqrt{\dfrac{\cos x}{\sin x}}} = \dfrac{\cos x}{\sqrt{\sin x \cos x}}$

83. $\sqrt{\dfrac{\sin x}{\cot x}} = \sqrt{\dfrac{\sin x}{\cot x} \cdot \dfrac{\sin x}{\sin x}}$

$\phantom{\sqrt{\dfrac{\sin x}{\cot x}}} = \sqrt{\dfrac{\sin^2 x}{\cos x}} \quad \left[\cot x \cdot \sin x = \dfrac{\cos x}{\sin x} \cdot \sin x = \cos x\right]$

$\phantom{\sqrt{\dfrac{\sin x}{\cot x}}} = \dfrac{\sin x}{\sqrt{\cos x}}$

84. $\sqrt{\dfrac{\cos x}{\tan x}} = \sqrt{\dfrac{\cos^2 x}{\cos x \tan x}}$

$\phantom{\sqrt{\dfrac{\cos x}{\tan x}}} = \dfrac{\cos x}{\sqrt{\cos x \cdot \dfrac{\sin x}{\cos x}}}$

$\phantom{\sqrt{\dfrac{\cos x}{\tan x}}} = \dfrac{\cos x}{\sqrt{\sin x}}$

85. $\sqrt{\dfrac{\cos^2 x}{2 \sin^2 x}} = \sqrt{\dfrac{\cot^2 x}{2}} = \dfrac{\cot x}{\sqrt{2}}$

86. $\sqrt{\dfrac{\sin^2 x}{3 \cos^2 x}} = \dfrac{\sin x}{\sqrt{3} \cos x}$

$\phantom{\sqrt{\dfrac{\sin^2 x}{3 \cos^2 x}}} = \dfrac{\tan x}{\sqrt{3}}$

87. $\sqrt{\dfrac{1 + \sin x}{1 - \sin x}} = \sqrt{\dfrac{1 + \sin x}{1 - \sin x} \cdot \dfrac{1 + \sin x}{1 + \sin x}}$

$\qquad = \sqrt{\dfrac{(1 + \sin x)^2}{1 - \sin^2 x}}$

$\qquad = \dfrac{1 + \sin x}{\sqrt{\cos^2 x}}$

$\qquad = \dfrac{1 + \sin x}{\cos x}$

88. $\sqrt{\dfrac{1 - \cos x}{1 + \cos x}} = \sqrt{\dfrac{(1 - \cos x)^2}{1 - \cos^2 x}}$

$\qquad = \dfrac{1 - \cos x}{\sqrt{\sin^2 x}}$

$\qquad = \dfrac{1 - \cos x}{\sin x}$

89. $\sqrt{a^2 - x^2} = \sqrt{a^2 - (a \sin \theta)^2}$ (Substituting)

$\qquad = \sqrt{a^2 - a^2 \sin^2 \theta}$

$\qquad = \sqrt{a^2(1 - \sin^2 \theta)}$

$\qquad = \sqrt{a^2 \cos^2 \theta}$

$\qquad = a \cos \theta$ $\left[\begin{array}{l} a > 0 \text{ and } \cos \theta > 0 \\ \text{for } 0 < \theta < \dfrac{\pi}{2} \end{array}\right]$

Then $\cos \theta = \dfrac{\sqrt{a^2 - x^2}}{a}$.

Also $x = a \sin \theta$, so $\sin \theta = \dfrac{x}{a}$.   Then

$\tan \theta = \dfrac{\sin \theta}{\cos \theta} = \dfrac{\dfrac{x}{a}}{\dfrac{\sqrt{a^2 - x^2}}{a}} = \dfrac{x}{a} \cdot \dfrac{a}{\sqrt{a^2 - x^2}}$

$\qquad\qquad = \dfrac{x}{\sqrt{a^2 - x^2}}$.

90. $\sqrt{4 + x^2} = \sqrt{4 + 4 \tan^2 \theta} = \sqrt{4(1 + \tan^2 \theta)} =$

$2\sqrt{\sec^2 \theta} = 2 \sec \theta$

$\sin \theta = \dfrac{x}{\sqrt{4 + x^2}}$

$\cos \theta = \dfrac{2}{\sqrt{4 + x^2}}$

91. $x = 3 \sec \theta$

$\quad x = \dfrac{3}{\cos \theta}$ $\left[\sec \theta = \dfrac{1}{\cos \theta}\right]$

$\cos \theta = \dfrac{3}{x}$

$\sqrt{x^2 - 9} = \sqrt{(3 \sec \theta)^2 - 9}$ (Substituting)

$\qquad = \sqrt{9 \sec^2 \theta - 9}$

$\qquad = \sqrt{9(\sec^2 \theta - 1)}$

$\qquad = \sqrt{9 \tan^2 \theta}$

$\qquad = 3 \tan \theta$ $\left[\tan \theta > 0 \text{ for } 0 < \theta < \dfrac{\pi}{2}\right]$

Then $\tan \theta = \dfrac{\sqrt{x^2 - 9}}{3}$

$\dfrac{\sin \theta}{\cos \theta} = \dfrac{\sqrt{x^2 - 9}}{3}$

$\dfrac{\sin \theta}{\dfrac{3}{x}} = \dfrac{\sqrt{x^2 - 9}}{3}$ $\left[\cos \theta = \dfrac{3}{x}\right]$

$\sin \theta = \dfrac{3}{x} \cdot \dfrac{\sqrt{x^2 - 9}}{3}$

$\sin \theta = \dfrac{\sqrt{x^2 - 9}}{x}$.

92. $\sqrt{x^2 - a^2} = \sqrt{a^2 \sec^2 \theta - a^2} = \sqrt{a^2 (\sec^2 \theta - 1)} =$

$a\sqrt{\tan^2 \theta} = a \tan \theta$

$\sin \theta = \dfrac{\sqrt{x^2 - a^2}}{x}$

$\cos \theta = \dfrac{a}{x}$

93. $\dfrac{x^2}{\sqrt{1 - x^2}} = \dfrac{\sin^2 \theta}{\sqrt{1 - \sin^2 \theta}}$ (Substituting)

$\qquad = \dfrac{\sin^2 \theta}{\sqrt{\cos^2 \theta}}$

$\qquad = \dfrac{\sin^2 \theta}{\cos \theta} = \sin \theta \cdot \dfrac{\sin \theta}{\cos \theta}$

$\qquad = \sin \theta \tan \theta$

94. $\dfrac{\sqrt{x^2 - 16}}{x^2} = \dfrac{\sqrt{16 \sec^2 \theta - 16}}{16 \sec^2 \theta} = \dfrac{\sqrt{16(\sec^2 \theta - 1)}}{16 \sec^2 \theta} =$

$\dfrac{4\sqrt{\tan^2 \theta}}{16 \sec^2 \theta} = \dfrac{\tan \theta}{4 \sec^2 \theta} = \dfrac{1}{4} \cdot \dfrac{\sin \theta}{\cos \theta} \cdot \cos^2 \theta =$

$\dfrac{\sin \theta \cos \theta}{4}$

95.   See the answer section in the text.

96.   Let $\theta = \dfrac{3\pi}{2}$.

97.   See the answer section in the text.

98.   Let $x = \dfrac{3\pi}{4}$.

99.   See the answer section in the text.

100.   Let $\theta = \dfrac{\pi}{2}$.

101.   See the answer section in the text.

102.   Let $\theta = \dfrac{\pi}{4}$.

103.   See the answer section in the text.

Exercise Set 7.2

1. $\sin 75° = \sin (45° + 30°)$
$= \sin 45° \cos 30° + \cos 45° \sin 30°$
$= \dfrac{\sqrt{2}}{2} \cdot \dfrac{\sqrt{3}}{2} + \dfrac{\sqrt{2}}{2} \cdot \dfrac{1}{2}$
$= \dfrac{\sqrt{6}}{4} + \dfrac{\sqrt{2}}{4} = \dfrac{\sqrt{6} + \sqrt{2}}{4}$

2. $\cos 75° = \cos (30° + 45°)$
$= \cos 30° \cos 45° - \sin 30° \sin 45°$
$= \dfrac{\sqrt{3}}{2} \cdot \dfrac{\sqrt{2}}{2} - \dfrac{1}{2} \cdot \dfrac{\sqrt{2}}{2}$
$= \dfrac{\sqrt{6} - \sqrt{2}}{4}$

3. $\sin 15° = \sin (45° - 30°)$
$= \sin 45° \cos 30° - \cos 45° \sin 30°$
$= \dfrac{\sqrt{2}}{2} \cdot \dfrac{\sqrt{3}}{2} - \dfrac{\sqrt{2}}{2} \cdot \dfrac{1}{2}$
$= \dfrac{\sqrt{6}}{4} - \dfrac{\sqrt{2}}{4} = \dfrac{\sqrt{6} - \sqrt{2}}{4}$

4. $\cos 15° = \cos (45° - 30°)$
$= \cos 45° \cos 30° + \sin 45° \sin 30°$
$= \dfrac{\sqrt{2}}{2} \cdot \dfrac{\sqrt{3}}{2} + \dfrac{\sqrt{2}}{2} \cdot \dfrac{1}{2}$
$= \dfrac{\sqrt{6} + \sqrt{2}}{4}$

5. $\sin 105° = \sin (60° + 45°)$
$= \sin 60° \cos 45° + \cos 60° \sin 45°$
$= \dfrac{\sqrt{3}}{2} \cdot \dfrac{\sqrt{2}}{2} + \dfrac{1}{2} \cdot \dfrac{\sqrt{2}}{2}$
$= \dfrac{\sqrt{6} + \sqrt{2}}{4}$

6. $\cos 105° = \cos (45° + 60°)$
$= \cos 45° \cos 60° - \sin 45° \sin 60°$
$= \dfrac{\sqrt{2}}{2} \cdot \dfrac{1}{2} - \dfrac{\sqrt{2}}{2} \cdot \dfrac{\sqrt{3}}{2}$
$= \dfrac{\sqrt{2} - \sqrt{6}}{4}$

7. $\tan 75° = \tan (45° + 30°)$
$= \dfrac{\tan 45° + \tan 30°}{1 - \tan 45° \tan 30°}$
$= \dfrac{1 + \dfrac{\sqrt{3}}{3}}{1 - 1 \cdot \dfrac{\sqrt{3}}{3}} = \dfrac{3 + \sqrt{3}}{3 - \sqrt{3}}$

8. $\cot 15° = \cot (45° - 30°) = \dfrac{1}{\tan (45° - 30°)}$
$= \dfrac{1 + \tan 45° \tan 30°}{\tan 45° - \tan 30°}$
$= \dfrac{1 + 1 \cdot \dfrac{\sqrt{3}}{3}}{1 - \dfrac{\sqrt{3}}{3}}$
$= \dfrac{3 + \sqrt{3}}{3 - \sqrt{3}}$

9. $\sin 37° \cos 22° + \cos 37° \sin 22° = \sin(37° + 22°)$
$= \sin 59°$, or
0.8572

10. $\cos 37° \cos 22° - \sin 22° \sin 37°$
$= \cos (37° + 22°)$
$= \cos 59°$, or 0.5150

11. $\dfrac{\tan 20° + \tan 32°}{1 - \tan 20° \tan 32°} = \tan (20° + 32°)$
$= \tan 52°$, or 1.2799

12. $\dfrac{\tan 35° - \tan 12°}{1 + \tan 35° \tan 12°} = \tan (35° - 12°)$
$= \tan 23°$, or 0.4245

Use the figures and function values below for Exercises 13 - 18.

$\sin u = \dfrac{3}{5}$ $\sin v = \dfrac{4}{5}$

$\cos u = \dfrac{4}{5}$ $\cos v = \dfrac{3}{5}$

$\tan u = \dfrac{3}{4}$ $\tan v = \dfrac{4}{3}$

13. $\sin (u + v) = \sin u \cos v + \cos u \sin v$
$= \dfrac{3}{5} \cdot \dfrac{3}{5} + \dfrac{4}{5} \cdot \dfrac{4}{5}$
$= \dfrac{9}{25} + \dfrac{16}{25} = \dfrac{25}{25} = 1$

14. $\sin (u - v) = \sin u \cos v - \cos u \sin v$
$= \dfrac{3}{5} \cdot \dfrac{3}{5} - \dfrac{4}{5} \cdot \dfrac{4}{5}$
$= - \dfrac{7}{25}$

15. Use drawings above Exercise 13.

$\cos (u + v) = \cos u \cos v - \sin u \sin v$

$$= \frac{4}{5} \cdot \frac{3}{5} - \frac{3}{5} \cdot \frac{4}{5}$$

$$= \frac{12}{25} - \frac{12}{25} = 0$$

16. $\cos (u - v) = \cos u \cos v + \sin u \sin v$

$$= \frac{4}{5} \cdot \frac{3}{5} + \frac{3}{5} \cdot \frac{4}{5}$$

$$= \frac{24}{25}$$

17. Use drawings above Exercise 13.

$\tan (u + v) = \dfrac{\tan u + \tan v}{1 - \tan u \tan v}$

$$= \frac{\frac{3}{4} + \frac{4}{3}}{1 - \frac{3}{4} \cdot \frac{4}{3}} = \frac{\frac{3}{4} + \frac{4}{3}}{0}$$

Division by 0 is undefined. Thus tan (u + v) is undefined.

18. $\tan (u - v) = \dfrac{\tan u - \tan v}{1 + \tan u \tan v}$

$$= \frac{\frac{3}{4} - \frac{4}{3}}{1 + \frac{3}{4} \cdot \frac{4}{3}}$$

$$= -\frac{7}{24}$$

19. Given: $\sin \theta = 0.6249$ and $\cos \phi = 0.1102$.

Find $\cos \theta$ and $\sin \phi$ using the following identity:
$\sin^2 x + \cos^2 x = 1$

If $\sin \theta = 0.6249$, then
$(0.6249)^2 + \cos^2 \theta = 1$

$\cos^2 \theta = 1 - 0.3905 = 0.6095$

$\cos \theta = 0.7807$

If $\cos \phi = 0.1102$, then
$\sin^2 \phi + (0.1102)^2 = 1$

$\sin^2 \phi = 1 - 0.0121 = 0.9879$

$\sin \phi = 0.9939$

$\sin (\theta + \phi) = \sin \theta \cos \phi + \cos \theta \sin \phi$

$$= (0.6249)(0.1102) + (0.7807)(0.9939)$$

$$= 0.0689 + 0.7759$$

$$= 0.8448$$

20. From Exercise 19 we know that $\cos \theta = 0.7807$ and $\sin \phi = 0.9939$.

$\cos (\theta + \phi) = \cos \theta \cos \phi - \sin \theta \sin \phi$

$$= -0.5350$$

21. $\sin (\alpha + \beta) + \sin (\alpha - \beta)$
$= (\sin \alpha \cos \beta + \cos \alpha \sin \beta) +$
$\qquad\qquad (\sin \alpha \cos \beta - \cos \alpha \sin \beta)$
$= 2 \sin \alpha \cos \beta$

22. $\sin (\alpha + \beta) - \sin (\alpha - \beta)$
$= \sin \alpha \cos \beta + \cos \alpha \sin \beta -$
$\qquad (\sin \alpha \cos \beta - \cos \alpha \sin \beta)$
$= 2 \cos \alpha \sin \beta$

23. $\cos (\alpha + \beta) + \cos (\alpha - \beta)$
$= (\cos \alpha \cos \beta - \sin \alpha \sin \beta) +$
$\qquad\qquad (\cos \alpha \cos \beta + \sin \alpha \sin \beta)$
$= 2 \cos \alpha \cos \beta$

24. $\cos (\alpha + \beta) - \cos (\alpha - \beta)$
$= \cos \alpha \cos \beta - \sin \alpha \sin \beta -$
$\qquad (\cos \alpha \cos \beta + \sin \alpha \sin \beta)$
$= -2 \sin \alpha \cos \beta$

25. $\cos (u + v) \cos v + \sin (u + v) \sin v$
$= (\cos u \cos v - \sin u \sin v) \cos v +$
$\qquad (\sin u \cos v + \cos u \sin v) \sin v$
$= \cos u \cos^2 v - \sin u \sin v \cos v +$
$\qquad\qquad \sin u \cos v \sin v + \cos u \sin^2 v$
$= \cos u (\cos^2 v + \sin^2 v)$
$= \cos u$

26. $\sin (u - v) \cos v + \cos (u - v) \sin v$
$= (\sin u \cos v - \cos u \sin v) \cos v +$
$\qquad (\cos u \cos v + \sin u \sin v) \sin v$
$= \sin u \cos^2 v + \sin u \sin^2 v$
$= \sin u (\cos^2 v + \sin^2 v)$
$= \sin u$

27. Solve each equation for y; then determine the slope of each line.

$\ell_1: 2x = 3 - 2y \qquad \ell_2: x + y = 5$

$\qquad y = -x + \frac{3}{2} \qquad\qquad y = -x + 5$

Thus $m_1 = -1$ and the   Thus $m_2 = -1$ and the
y-intercept is $\frac{3}{2}$.   y-intercept is 5.

The lines do not form an angle. The lines are parallel. When the formula is used, the result is 0°.

28. ℓ_1 has $m_1 = \frac{\sqrt{3}}{3}$; ℓ_2 has $m_2 = \sqrt{3}$.

Then $\tan \phi = \dfrac{\sqrt{3} - \frac{\sqrt{3}}{3}}{1 + \sqrt{3} \cdot \frac{\sqrt{3}}{3}} = \dfrac{\sqrt{3}}{3}$,

and $\phi = \frac{\pi}{6}$.

29. Find the slope of each line.

    ℓ_1: $y = 3$ ($y = 0x + 3$)

    Thus $m = 0$.

    ℓ_2: $x + y = 5$

            $y = -x + 5$

    Thus $m = -1$.

    Let ϕ be the smallest angle from ℓ_1 to ℓ_2.

    $\tan \phi = \dfrac{-1 - 0}{1 + (-1)(0)}$ $\left[\tan \phi = \dfrac{m_2 - m_1}{1 + m_2 m_1}\right]$

    $\qquad = \dfrac{-1}{1} = -1$

    Since $\tan \phi$ is negative, we know that ϕ is obtuse. Thus $\phi = \dfrac{3\pi}{4}$, or $135°$.

30. ℓ_1 has $m_1 = -2$; ℓ_2 has $m_2 = 2$.

    Then $\tan \phi = \dfrac{2 - (-2)}{1 + 2(-2)} = -\dfrac{4}{3}$,

    and $\phi = 126.87°$.

31.

    Position a set of coordinate axes as shown above. Let ℓ_1 be the line containing the points $(0, 0)$ and $(40, 10)$. Find its slope.

    $m_1 = \tan \alpha = \dfrac{10}{40} = \dfrac{1}{4}$

    Let ℓ_2 be the line containing the points $(0, 0)$ and $(40, 30)$. Find its slope.

    $m_2 = \tan \beta = \dfrac{30}{40} = \dfrac{3}{4}$

    Now ϕ is the smallest positive angle from ℓ_1 to ℓ_2.

    $\tan \phi = \dfrac{\dfrac{3}{4} - \dfrac{1}{4}}{1 + \dfrac{3}{4} \cdot \dfrac{1}{4}} = \dfrac{\dfrac{1}{2}}{\dfrac{19}{16}} = \dfrac{8}{19} \approx 0.4211$

    $\phi \approx 22.83°$

32. $\dfrac{\sin (x + h) - \sin x}{h}$

    $= \dfrac{\sin x \cos h + \cos x \sin h - \sin x}{h}$

    $= \dfrac{\sin x \cos h - \sin x}{h} + \dfrac{\cos x \sin h}{h}$

    $= \sin x \left[\dfrac{\cos h - 1}{h}\right] + \cos x \left[\dfrac{\sin h}{h}\right]$

33. See the answer section in the text.

34. $\dfrac{\tan (x + h) - \tan x}{h}$

    $= \dfrac{\dfrac{\tan x + \tan h}{1 - \tan x \tan h} - \tan x}{h}$

    $= \dfrac{\tan x + \tan h - \tan x + \tan^2 x \tan h}{(1 - \tan x \tan h)h}$

    $= \dfrac{\tan h (1 + \tan^2 x)}{(1 - \tan x \tan h)h} = \dfrac{\sec^2 x}{1 - \tan x \tan h}\left[\dfrac{\tan h}{h}\right]$

35. $\tan \phi = \dfrac{m_2 - m_1}{1 + m_2 m_1}$

    $\tan 45° = \dfrac{\dfrac{4}{3} - m_1}{1 + \dfrac{4}{3} \cdot m_1}$

    $1 = \dfrac{4 - 3m_1}{3 + 4m_1}$

    $3 + 4m_1 = 4 - 3m_1$

    $7m_1 = 1$

    $m_1 = \dfrac{1}{7}$

36. $\tan 30° = \dfrac{\dfrac{2}{3} - m_1}{1 + \dfrac{2}{3} m_1}$

    $m_1 = \dfrac{2\sqrt{3} - 3}{2 + 3\sqrt{3}} \approx 0.0645$

37. Find the slope of ℓ_1.

    $m_1 = \dfrac{-1 - 4}{5 - (-2)} = \dfrac{-5}{7} = -\dfrac{5}{7}$

    Use the following formula to determine the slope of ℓ_2.

    $\tan \phi = \dfrac{m_2 - m_1}{1 + m_2 m_1}$

    $\tan 45° = \dfrac{m_2 - \left(-\dfrac{5}{7}\right)}{1 + m_2 \left(-\dfrac{5}{7}\right)}$

    $1 = \dfrac{7m_2 + 5}{7 - 5m_2}$

    $7 - 5m_2 = 7m_2 + 5$

    $2 = 12m_2$

    $\dfrac{1}{6} = m_2$

38.

ℓ_1 is vertical; ℓ_2 has $m_2 = \dfrac{-4 - 6}{0 - 2} = 5,$

and $m_2 = \tan \theta_2 = 5$ so that $\theta_2 = 78.7°.$
Then $\phi = 90° + \theta_2 = 168.7°,$ the
smallest <u>positive</u> angle from ℓ_1 to $\ell_2.$

39. $\sin 2\theta = \sin (\theta + \theta)$
$= \sin \theta \cos \theta + \cos \theta \sin \theta$
$= 2 \sin \theta \cos \theta$

40. $\cos 2\theta = \cos (\theta + \theta)$
$= \cos \theta \cos \theta - \sin \theta \sin \theta$
$= \cos^2 - \sin^2 \theta,$
or $1 - 2 \sin^2 \theta,$ $(\cos^2\theta = 1 - \sin^2\theta)$
or $2 \cos^2 \theta - 1$ $(\sin^2\theta = 1 - \cos^2\theta)$

41. See the answer section in the text.

42. $\cot (\alpha - \beta)$

$= \dfrac{\cos (\alpha - \beta)}{\sin (\alpha - \beta)}$

$= \dfrac{\cos \alpha \cos \beta + \sin \alpha \sin \beta}{\sin \alpha \cos \beta - \cos \alpha \sin \beta} \cdot \dfrac{\frac{1}{\sin \alpha \sin \beta}}{\frac{1}{\sin \alpha \sin \beta}}$

$= \dfrac{\cot \alpha \cot \beta + 1}{\cot \beta - \cot \alpha}$

43. See the answer section in the text.

44. $\cos \left[x - \dfrac{3\pi}{2}\right] = \cos x \cos \dfrac{3\pi}{2} + \sin x \sin \dfrac{3\pi}{2}$
$= (\cos x)(0) + (\sin x)(-1)$
$= -\sin x$

45. See the answer section in the text.

46. $\sin \left[x - \dfrac{3\pi}{2}\right] = \sin x \cos \dfrac{3\pi}{2} - \cos x \sin \dfrac{3\pi}{2}$
$= (\sin x)(0) - (\cos x)(-1)$
$= \cos x$

47. See the answer section in the text.

48. $\tan \left[x - \dfrac{\pi}{4}\right] = \dfrac{\tan x - \tan \frac{\pi}{4}}{1 + \tan x \tan \frac{\pi}{4}}$

$= \dfrac{\tan x - 1}{\tan x + 1}$

49. See the answer section in the text.

50. $\dfrac{\sin (\alpha + \beta)}{\sin (\alpha - \beta)} = \dfrac{\sin \alpha \cos \beta + \cos \alpha \sin \beta}{\sin \alpha \cos \beta - \cos \alpha \sin \beta}$

$= \dfrac{\frac{\sin \alpha \cos \beta + \cos \alpha \sin \beta}{\cos \alpha \cos \beta}}{\frac{\sin \alpha \cos \beta - \cos \alpha \sin \beta}{\cos \alpha \cos \beta}}$

$= \dfrac{\frac{\sin \alpha}{\cos \alpha} + \frac{\sin \beta}{\cos \beta}}{\frac{\sin \alpha}{\cos \alpha} - \frac{\sin \beta}{\cos \beta}} = \dfrac{\tan \alpha + \tan \beta}{\tan \alpha - \tan \beta}$

51. See the answer section in the text.

52. $\cos (\alpha + \beta) \cdot \cos (\alpha - \beta)$
$= (\cos \alpha \cos \beta - \sin \alpha \sin \beta)(\cos \alpha \cos \beta + \sin \alpha \sin \beta)$
$= \cos^2\alpha \cos^2\beta - \sin^2\alpha \sin^2\beta$
$= (1 - \sin^2\alpha)(1 - \sin^2\beta) - \sin^2\alpha \sin^2\beta$
$= 1 - \sin^2\beta - \sin^2\alpha + \sin^2\alpha \sin^2\beta - \sin^2\alpha \sin^2\beta$
$= 1 - \sin^2\beta - \sin^2\alpha$
$= \cos^2\alpha - \sin^2\beta$

53. See the answer section in the text.

54. $\sin [(\alpha + \beta) + \gamma]$
$= \sin (\alpha + \beta) \cos \gamma + \cos (\alpha + \beta) \sin \gamma$
$= (\sin \alpha \cos \beta + \cos \alpha \sin \beta) \cos \gamma +$
$\quad (\cos \alpha \cos \beta - \sin \alpha \sin \beta) \sin \gamma$
$= \sin \alpha \cos \beta \cos \gamma + \cos \alpha \sin \beta \cos \gamma +$
$\quad \cos \alpha \cos \beta \sin \gamma - \sin \alpha \sin \beta \sin \gamma$

Exercise Set 7.3

1. Since 25° and 65° are complements, we have
$\sin 25° = \cos 65° = 0.4226$
$\cos 25° = \sin 65° = 0.9063$
$\tan 25° = \cot 65° = 0.4663$
$\cot 25° = \tan 65° = 2.145$
$\sec 25° = \csc 65° = 1.103$
$\csc 25° = \sec 65° = 2.366$

2. Since 32° and 58° are complements, we have

sin 58° = 0.8480   csc 58° = 1.179

cos 58° = 0.5299   sec 58° = 1.887

tan 58° = 1.600   cot 58° = 0.6249

3. a) $\tan 22.5° = \dfrac{\sin 22.5°}{\cos 22.5°} = \dfrac{\frac{\sqrt{2 - \sqrt{2}}}{2}}{\frac{\sqrt{2 + \sqrt{2}}}{2}}$

$= \dfrac{\sqrt{2 - \sqrt{2}}}{\sqrt{2 + \sqrt{2}}}$

$\cot 22.5° = \dfrac{1}{\tan 22.5°} = \dfrac{\sqrt{2 + \sqrt{2}}}{\sqrt{2 - \sqrt{2}}}$

$\sec 22.5° = \dfrac{1}{\cos 22.5°} = \dfrac{2}{\sqrt{2 + \sqrt{2}}}$

$\csc 22.5° = \dfrac{1}{\sin 22.5°} = \dfrac{2}{\sqrt{2 - \sqrt{2}}}$

b) Since 67.5° and 22.5° are complements, we have

$\sin 67.5° = \cos 22.5° = \dfrac{\sqrt{2 + \sqrt{2}}}{2}$

$\cos 67.5° = \sin 22.5° = \dfrac{\sqrt{2 - \sqrt{2}}}{2}$

$\tan 67.5° = \cot 22.5° = \dfrac{\sqrt{2 + \sqrt{2}}}{\sqrt{2 - \sqrt{2}}}$

$\cot 67.5° = \tan 22.5° = \dfrac{\sqrt{2 - \sqrt{2}}}{\sqrt{2 + \sqrt{2}}}$

$\sec 67.5° = \csc 22.5° = \dfrac{2}{\sqrt{2 - \sqrt{2}}}$

$\csc 67.5° = \sec 22.5° = \dfrac{2}{\sqrt{2 + \sqrt{2}}}$

4. a) $\tan \dfrac{\pi}{12} = \dfrac{\sin \frac{\pi}{12}}{\cos \frac{\pi}{12}} = \dfrac{\sqrt{2 - \sqrt{3}}}{\sqrt{2 + \sqrt{3}}}$,

$\cot \dfrac{\pi}{12} = \dfrac{1}{\tan \frac{\pi}{12}} \dfrac{\sqrt{2 + \sqrt{3}}}{\sqrt{2 - \sqrt{3}}}$,

$\csc \dfrac{\pi}{12} = \dfrac{1}{\sin \frac{\pi}{12}} \dfrac{2}{\sqrt{2 - \sqrt{3}}}$,

$\sec \dfrac{\pi}{12} = \dfrac{1}{\cos \frac{\pi}{12}} \dfrac{2}{\sqrt{2 + \sqrt{3}}}$

b) Since $\dfrac{\pi}{12}$ and $\dfrac{5\pi}{12}$ are complements, we have

$\sin \dfrac{5\pi}{12} = \dfrac{\sqrt{2 + \sqrt{3}}}{2}$, $\cos \dfrac{5\pi}{12} = \dfrac{\sqrt{2 - \sqrt{3}}}{2}$,

$\tan \dfrac{5\pi}{12} = \dfrac{\sqrt{2 + \sqrt{3}}}{\sqrt{2 - \sqrt{3}}}$, $\cot \dfrac{5\pi}{12} = \dfrac{\sqrt{2 - \sqrt{3}}}{\sqrt{2 + \sqrt{3}}}$,

$\csc \dfrac{5\pi}{12} = \dfrac{2}{\sqrt{2 + \sqrt{3}}}$, $\sec \dfrac{5\pi}{12} = \dfrac{2}{\sqrt{2 - \sqrt{3}}}$

5. See the answer section in the text.

6. $\cot \left(x - \dfrac{\pi}{2}\right) = \dfrac{\cos \left(x - \frac{\pi}{2}\right)}{\sin \left(x - \frac{\pi}{2}\right)} = \dfrac{\sin x}{-\cos x} = -\tan x$

7. See the answer section in the text.

8. $\sec \left(x + \dfrac{\pi}{2}\right) = \dfrac{1}{\cos \left(x + \frac{\pi}{2}\right)} = \dfrac{1}{-\sin x} = -\csc x$

9. See the answer section in the text.

10. $\cos (\theta - 270°) = \cos \theta \cos 270° + \sin \theta \sin 270°$

$= \cos \theta \cdot 0 + \sin \theta \cdot (-1)$

$= -\sin \theta$

11. $\tan (\theta + 270°) = \dfrac{\sin (\theta + 270°)}{\cos (\theta + 270°)}$

$= \dfrac{\sin \theta \cos 270° + \cos \theta \sin 270°}{\cos \theta \cos 270° - \sin \theta \sin 270°}$

$= \dfrac{\sin \theta \cdot 0 + \cos \theta \cdot (-1)}{\cos \theta \cdot 0 - \sin \theta \cdot (-1)}$

$= -\dfrac{\cos \theta}{\sin \theta}$

$= -\cot \theta$

12. $\sin (\theta - 270°) = \sin \theta \cos 270° - \cos \theta \sin 270°$

$= \sin \theta \cdot 0 - \cos \theta \cdot (-1)$

$= \cos \theta$

13. $\sin (\theta + 450°) = \sin \theta \cos 450° + \cos \theta \sin 450°$

$= \sin \theta \cdot 0 + \cos \theta \cdot 1$

$= \cos \theta$

14. $\cos (\theta - 450°) = \cos \theta \cos 450° + \sin \theta \sin 450°$

$= \cos \theta \cdot 0 + \sin \theta \cdot 1$

$= \sin \theta$

15. $\sec (\pi - \theta) = \dfrac{1}{\cos (\pi - \theta)}$

$= \dfrac{1}{\cos \pi \cos \theta + \sin \pi \sin \theta}$

$= \dfrac{1}{-1 \cdot \cos \theta + 0 \cdot \sin \theta}$

$= -\sec \theta$

<u>16.</u> $\csc (\pi + \theta) = \dfrac{1}{\sin (\pi + \theta)}$

$= \dfrac{1}{\sin \pi \cos \theta + \cos \pi \sin \theta}$

$= \dfrac{1}{0 \cdot \cos \theta + (-1) \cdot \sin \theta}$

$= -\csc \theta$

<u>17.</u> $\tan (x - 4\pi) = \dfrac{\sin (x - 4\pi)}{\cos (x - 4\pi)}$

$= \dfrac{\sin x \cos 4\pi - \cos x \sin 4\pi}{\cos x \cos 4\pi + \sin x \sin 4\pi}$

$= \dfrac{\sin x \cdot 1 - \cos x \cdot 0}{\cos x \cdot 1 + \sin x \cdot 0}$

$= \tan x$

<u>18.</u> $\sec (x - 10\pi) = \dfrac{1}{\cos (x - 10\pi)}$

$= \dfrac{1}{\cos x \cos 10\pi + \sin x \sin 10\pi}$

$= \dfrac{1}{\cos x \cdot 1 + \sin x \cdot 0}$

$= \sec x$

<u>19.</u> $\cos \left[\dfrac{9\pi}{2} + x\right] = \cos \dfrac{9\pi}{2} \cos x - \sin \dfrac{9\pi}{2} \sin x$

$= 0 \cdot \cos x - 1 \cdot \sin x$

$= -\sin x$

<u>20.</u> $\cot \left[\dfrac{9\pi}{2} - x\right] = \dfrac{\cos \left[\dfrac{9\pi}{2} - x\right]}{\sin \left[\dfrac{9\pi}{2} - x\right]}$

$= \dfrac{\cos \dfrac{9\pi}{2} \cos x + \sin \dfrac{9\pi}{2} \sin x}{\sin \dfrac{9\pi}{2} \cos x + \cos \dfrac{9\pi}{2} \sin x}$

$= \dfrac{0 \cdot \cos x + 1 \cdot \sin x}{1 \cdot \cos x + 0 \cdot \sin x}$

$= \tan x$

<u>21.</u> $\csc (540° - \theta) = \dfrac{1}{\sin (540° - \theta)}$

$= \dfrac{1}{\sin 540° \cos \theta - \cos 540° \sin \theta}$

$= \dfrac{1}{0 \cdot \cos \theta - (-1) \sin \theta}$

$= \csc \theta$

<u>22.</u> $\tan (540° + \theta) = \dfrac{\sin (540° + \theta)}{\cos (540° + \theta)}$

$= \dfrac{\sin 540° \cos \theta + \cos 540° \sin \theta}{\cos 540° \cos \theta - \sin 540° \sin \theta}$

$= \dfrac{0 \cdot \cos \theta + (-1) \sin \theta}{-1 \cdot \cos \theta - 0 \cdot \sin \theta}$

$= \tan \theta$

<u>23.</u> $\cot \left[x - \dfrac{3\pi}{2}\right] = \dfrac{\cos \left[x - \dfrac{3\pi}{2}\right]}{\sin \left[x - \dfrac{3\pi}{2}\right]}$

$= \dfrac{\cos x \cos \dfrac{3\pi}{2} + \sin x \sin \dfrac{3\pi}{2}}{\sin x \cos \dfrac{3\pi}{2} - \cos x \sin \dfrac{3\pi}{2}}$

$= \dfrac{\cos x \cdot 0 + \sin x (-1)}{\sin x \cdot 0 - \cos x (-1)}$

$= -\tan x$

<u>24.</u> $\sin \left[x + \dfrac{11\pi}{2}\right] = \sin x \cos \dfrac{11\pi}{2} + \cos x \sin \dfrac{11\pi}{2}$

$= \sin x \cdot 0 + \cos x \cdot (-1)$

$= -\cos x$

<u>25.</u> We sketch a second quadrant triangle.

a) $\cos \theta = \dfrac{-2\sqrt{2}}{3} = -\dfrac{2\sqrt{2}}{3}$

$\tan \theta = \dfrac{1}{-2\sqrt{2}} = -\dfrac{\sqrt{2}}{4}$

$\cot \theta = \dfrac{-2\sqrt{2}}{1} = -2\sqrt{2}$

$\sec \theta = \dfrac{3}{-2\sqrt{2}} = -\dfrac{3\sqrt{2}}{4}$

$\csc \theta = \dfrac{3}{1} = 3$

b) Since θ and $\dfrac{\pi}{2} - \theta$ are complements, we have

$\sin \left[\dfrac{\pi}{2} - \theta\right] = \cos \theta = -\dfrac{2\sqrt{2}}{3}$

$\cos \left[\dfrac{\pi}{2} - \theta\right] = \sin \theta = \dfrac{1}{3}$

$\tan \left[\dfrac{\pi}{2} - \theta\right] = \cot \theta = -2\sqrt{2}$

$\cot \left[\dfrac{\pi}{2} - \theta\right] = \tan \theta = -\dfrac{\sqrt{2}}{4}$

$\sec \left[\dfrac{\pi}{2} - \theta\right] = \csc \theta = 3$

$\csc \left[\dfrac{\pi}{2} - \theta\right] = \sec \theta = -\dfrac{3\sqrt{2}}{4}$

c) $\sin (\pi + \theta) = \sin \pi \cos \theta + \cos \pi \sin \theta$

$= 0 \cdot \cos \theta + (-1) \sin \theta$

$= -\sin \theta$

$\cos (\pi + \theta) = \cos \pi \cos \theta - \sin \pi \sin \theta$

$= -1 \cdot \cos \theta - 0 \cdot \sin \theta$

$= -\cos \theta$

$\sin (\pi + \theta) = -\sin \theta = -\frac{1}{3}$

$\cos (\pi + \theta) = -\cos \theta = \frac{2\sqrt{2}}{3}$

$\tan (\pi + \theta) = \frac{\sin (\pi + \theta)}{\cos (\pi + \theta)} = -\frac{\sqrt{2}}{4}$

$\cot (\pi + \theta) = \frac{1}{\tan (\pi + \theta)} = -2\sqrt{2}$

$\sec (\pi + \theta) = \frac{1}{\cos (\pi + \theta)} = \frac{3\sqrt{2}}{4}$

$\csc (\pi + \theta) = \frac{1}{\sin (\pi + \theta)} = -3$

d) $\sin (\pi - \theta) = \sin \pi \cos \theta - \cos \pi \sin \theta$
   $= 0 \cdot \cos \theta - (-1) \sin \theta$
   $= \sin \theta$

$\cos (\pi - \theta) = \cos \pi \cos \theta + \sin \pi \sin \theta$
   $= -1 \cdot \cos \theta + 0 \cdot \sin \theta$
   $= -\cos \theta$

$\sin (\pi - \theta) = \sin \theta = \frac{1}{3}$

$\cos (\pi - \theta) = -\cos \theta = \frac{2\sqrt{2}}{3}$

$\tan (\pi - \theta) = \frac{\sin (\pi - \theta)}{\cos (\pi - \theta)} = \frac{\sqrt{2}}{4}$

$\cot (\pi - \theta) = \frac{1}{\tan (\pi - \theta)} = 2\sqrt{2}$

$\sec (\pi - \theta) = \frac{1}{\cos (\pi - \theta)} = \frac{3\sqrt{2}}{4}$

$\csc (\pi - \theta) = \frac{1}{\sin (\pi - \theta)} = 3$

e) $\sin (2\pi - \theta) = \sin 2\pi \cos \theta - \cos 2\pi \sin \theta$
   $= 0 \cdot \cos \theta - 1 \cdot \sin \theta$
   $= -\sin \theta$

$\cos (2\pi - \theta) = \cos 2\pi \cos \theta + \sin 2\pi \sin \theta$
   $= 1 \cdot \cos \theta + 0 \cdot \sin \theta$
   $= \cos \theta$

$\sin (2\pi - \theta) = -\sin \theta = -\frac{1}{3}$

$\cos (2\pi - \theta) = \cos \theta = -\frac{2\sqrt{2}}{3}$

$\tan (2\pi - \theta) = \frac{\sin (2\pi - \theta)}{\cos (2\pi - \theta)} = \frac{\sqrt{2}}{4}$

$\cot (2\pi - \theta) = \frac{1}{\tan (2\pi - \theta)} = 2\sqrt{2}$

$\sec (2\pi - \theta) = \frac{1}{\cos (2\pi - \theta)} = -\frac{3\sqrt{2}}{4}$

$\csc (2\pi - \theta) = \frac{1}{\sin (2\pi - \theta)} = -3$

26.

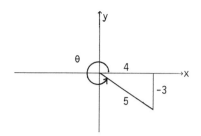

a) $\sin \theta = -\frac{3}{5}$, $\tan \theta = -\frac{3}{4}$, $\cot \theta = -\frac{4}{3}$,

$\sec \theta = \frac{5}{4}$, $\csc \theta = -\frac{5}{3}$

b) Since $\sin \left[\frac{\pi}{2} + \theta\right] = \cos \theta$, $\cos \left[\frac{\pi}{2} + \theta\right] = -\sin \theta$, we have

$\sin \left[\frac{\pi}{2} + \theta\right] = \frac{4}{5}$, $\cos \left[\frac{\pi}{2} + \theta\right] = \frac{3}{5}$,

$\tan \left[\frac{\pi}{2} + \theta\right] = \frac{4}{3}$, $\cot \left[\frac{\pi}{2} + \theta\right] = \frac{3}{4}$,

$\sec \left[\frac{\pi}{2} + \theta\right] = \frac{5}{3}$, $\csc \left[\frac{\pi}{2} + \theta\right] = \frac{5}{4}$

c) From Exercise 25(c), we know $\sin (\pi + \theta) = -\sin \theta$ and $\cos (\pi + \theta) = -\cos \theta$. Then we have

$\sin (\pi + \theta) = \frac{3}{5}$, $\cos (\pi + \theta) = -\frac{4}{5}$

$\tan (\pi + \theta) = -\frac{3}{4}$, $\cot (\pi + \theta) = -\frac{4}{3}$,

$\sec (\pi + \theta) = -\frac{5}{4}$, $\csc (\pi + \theta) = \frac{5}{3}$

d) From Exercise 25(d), we know $\sin (\pi - \theta) = \sin \theta$ and $\cos (\pi - \theta) = -\cos \theta$. Then we have

$\sin (\pi - \theta) = -\frac{3}{5}$, $\cos (\pi - \theta) = -\frac{4}{5}$,

$\tan (\pi - \theta) = \frac{3}{4}$, $\cot (\pi - \theta) = \frac{4}{3}$,

$\sec (\pi - \theta) = -\frac{5}{4}$, $\csc (\pi - \theta) = -\frac{5}{3}$

e) From Exercise 25(e), we know $\sin (2\pi - \theta) = -\sin \theta$ and $\cos (2\pi - \theta) = \cos \theta$. Then we have

$\sin (2\pi - \theta) = \frac{3}{5}$, $\cos (2\pi - \theta) = \frac{4}{5}$,

$\tan (2\pi - \theta) = \frac{3}{4}$, $\cot (2\pi - \theta) = \frac{4}{3}$,

$\sec (2\pi - \theta) = \frac{5}{4}$, $\csc (2\pi - \theta) = \frac{5}{3}$

27. a) We sketch a first quadrant triangle. Note that $0.45399 = \frac{0.45399}{1}$. We can use the Pythagorean theorem to find the length of the other leg.

$$\cos 27° = \frac{0.89101}{1} = 0.89101$$

$$\tan 27° = \frac{0.45399}{0.89101} \approx 0.50952$$

$$\cot 27° = \frac{0.89101}{0.45399} \approx 1.9626$$

$$\sec 27° = \frac{1}{0.89101} \approx 1.1223$$

$$\csc 27° = \frac{1}{0.45399} \approx 2.2027$$

b) Since 63° and 27° are complements, we have

sin 63° = cos 27° = 0.89101
cos 63° = sin 27° = 0.45399
tan 63° = cot 27° = 1.9626
cot 63° = tan 27° = 0.50952
sec 63° = csc 27° = 2.2027
csc 63° = sec 27° = 1.1223

28.

a) sin 54° = 0.80902, cos 54° = 0.58779,
    tan 54° = 1.3764, sec 54° = 1.7013,
    csc 54° = 1.2361

b) Since 54° and 36° are complements, we have
    sin 36° = 0.58779, cos 36° = 0.80902,
    tan 36° = 0.72654, cot 36° = 1.3764,
    sec 36° = 1.2361,   csc 36° = 1.7013

29.

We know $\sin\left(x + \frac{\pi}{2}\right) = \cos x$, so sin 128° = sin (38° + 90°) = cos 38° = 0.78801.

Using $\cos^2\theta + \sin^2\theta = 1$, find cos 128°.
$(\cos 128°)^2 + (\sin 128°)^2 = 1$
$(\cos 128°)^2 + (0.78801)^2 = 1$
$\qquad (\cos 128°)^2 \approx 1 - 0.62096$
$\qquad\qquad \cos 128° \approx -0.61566$

$\qquad\qquad$ (cosine is negative
$\qquad\qquad$ in quadrant II)

$$\tan 128° = \frac{0.78801}{-0.61566} \approx -1.27994$$

$$\cot 128° = \frac{1}{-1.27994} \approx -0.78129$$

$$\sec 128° = \frac{1}{-0.61566} \approx -1.62427$$

$$\csc 128° = \frac{1}{0.78801} \approx 1.26902$$

30. From Exercise 11, we know tan (θ + 270°) = -cot θ. Then tan (73° + 270°) = tan (343°) = $-\frac{1}{\tan 73°}$ = $-\frac{1}{3.27085} \approx -0.30573$.

Also cot 343° = $\frac{1}{\tan 343°}$ = -3.27085.

Using $1 + \tan^2\theta = \sec^2\theta$ and noting that 343° is in quadrant IV, we find sec 343° = $\sqrt{1 + (-0.30573)^2} \approx 1.04569$. Then cos 343° = $\frac{1}{\sec 343°} = \frac{1}{1.04569} \approx 0.95631$. Using $\sin^2\theta + \cos^2\theta = 1$ and recalling that 343° is in quadrant IV, we find sin 343° = $-\sqrt{1 - (0.95631)^2} \approx -0.29237$. Then csc 343° = $\frac{1}{\sin 343°} = \frac{1}{-0.29237} \approx -3.42032$. (Answers may vary slightly due to rounding differences.)

31. $\sin\left(\frac{\pi}{2} - x\right)\left[\sec x - \cos x\right]$

$= -\sin\left(x - \frac{\pi}{2}\right)\left[\frac{1}{\cos x} - \cos x\right]$

$\qquad\left[\sin\left(\frac{\pi}{2} - x\right) = \sin\left[-\left(x - \frac{\pi}{2}\right)\right] = -\sin\left(x - \frac{\pi}{2}\right)\right]$

$= -(-\cos x)\left(\frac{1 - \cos^2 x}{\cos x}\right)$ $\qquad\left[\sin\left(x - \frac{\pi}{2}\right) = -\cos x\right]$

$= 1 - \cos^2 x$

$= \sin^2 x$

32. $\cos\left(\frac{\pi}{2} - x\right)[\csc x - \sin x]$

$= \cos\left[-\left(x - \frac{\pi}{2}\right)\right]\left[\frac{1}{\sin x} - \sin x\right]$

$= \cos\left(x - \frac{\pi}{2}\right)\left[\frac{1 - \sin^2 x}{\sin x}\right]$

$= \sin x\left[\frac{\cos^2 x}{\sin x}\right]$

$= \cos^2 x$

33. $\sin x \cos y - \cos \left[x + \frac{\pi}{2}\right] \tan y$

= $\sin x \cos y - (- \sin x) \tan y$

$$\left[\cos \left[x + \frac{\pi}{2}\right] = - \sin x\right]$$

= $\sin x \cos y + \sin x \tan y$

= $\sin x (\cos y + \tan y)$

34. $\cos \left[x - \frac{\pi}{2}\right] \tan y + \sin x \cot y$

= $\sin x \tan y + \sin x \cot y$

= $\sin x (\tan y + \cot y)$ [We could stop here.]

= $\sin x \left[\frac{\sin y}{\cos y} + \frac{\cos y}{\sin y}\right]$

= $\sin x \left[\frac{\sin^2 y + \cos^2 y}{\cos y \sin y}\right]$

= $\sin x \left[\frac{1}{\cos y \sin y}\right]$

= $\sin x \sec y \csc y$

35. $\cos (\pi - x) + \cot x \sin \left[x - \frac{\pi}{2}\right]$

= $\cos \pi \cos x + \sin \pi \sin x +$
  $\cot x (-\cos x)$ $\left[\sin \left[x - \frac{\pi}{2}\right] = -\cos x\right]$

= $-\cos x + 0 - \cot x \cos x$

= $-\cos x (1 + \cot x)$

36. $\sin (\pi - x) - \tan x \cos \left[\frac{\pi}{2} - x\right]$

= $\sin \pi \cos x - \cos \pi \sin x -$
  $\tan x \cos \left[-\left[x - \frac{\pi}{2}\right]\right]$

= $-(-1 \cdot \sin x) - \tan x \cos \left[x - \frac{\pi}{2}\right]$

= $\sin x - \tan x \sin x$

= $\sin x (1 - \tan x)$

37. $\dfrac{\cos^2 x - 1}{\sin \left[\frac{\pi}{2} - x\right] - 1}$

= $\dfrac{(\cos x + 1)(\cos x - 1)}{\cos x - 1}$

$$\left[\sin \left[\frac{\pi}{2} - x\right] = -\sin \left[x - \frac{\pi}{2}\right] = \cos x\right]$$

= $\cos x + 1$

38. $\dfrac{\sin^2 x - 1}{\cos \left[\frac{\pi}{2} - x\right] + 1} = \dfrac{(\sin x + 1)(\sin x - 1)}{\cos \left[-\left[x - \frac{\pi}{2}\right]\right] + 1}$

= $\dfrac{(\sin x + 1)(\sin x - 1)}{\cos \left[x - \frac{\pi}{2}\right] + 1}$

= $\dfrac{(\sin x + 1)(\sin x - 1)}{\sin x + 1}$

= $\sin x - 1$

39. $\dfrac{\sin x - \cos \left[x - \frac{\pi}{2}\right] \cos x}{-\sin x - \cos \left[x - \frac{\pi}{2}\right] \tan x}$

= $\dfrac{\sin x - \sin x \cos x}{-\sin x - \sin x \tan x}$ $\left[\cos \left[x - \frac{\pi}{2}\right] = \sin x\right]$

= $\dfrac{\sin x (1 - \cos x)}{-\sin x (1 + \tan x)}$

= $\dfrac{\cos x - 1}{1 + \tan x}$ $[-1(1 - \cos x) = \cos x - 1]$

40. $\dfrac{\cos x - \sin \left[\frac{\pi}{2} - x\right] \sin x}{\cos x - \cos(\pi - x) \tan x}$

= $\dfrac{\cos x - \sin \left[-\left[x - \frac{\pi}{2}\right]\right] \sin x}{\cos x - (\cos \pi \cos x + \sin \pi \sin x) \tan x}$

= $\dfrac{\cos x + \sin \left[x - \frac{\pi}{2}\right] \sin x}{\cos x - (-1) \cos x \tan x}$

= $\dfrac{\cos x - \cos x \sin x}{\cos x + \cos x \tan x}$

= $\dfrac{\cos x(1 - \sin x)}{\cos x(1 + \tan x)}$

= $\dfrac{1 - \sin x}{1 + \tan x}$

41. $\dfrac{\cos^2 x + 2 \sin \left[x - \frac{\pi}{2}\right] + 1}{\sin \left[\frac{\pi}{2} - x\right] - 1}$

= $\dfrac{\cos^2 x + 2(-\cos x) + 1}{-\sin \left[x - \frac{\pi}{2}\right] - 1}$ $\left[\sin \left[x - \frac{\pi}{2}\right] = -\cos x\right]$

= $\dfrac{\cos^2 x - 2 \cos x + 1}{\cos x - 1}$

= $\dfrac{(\cos x - 1)^2}{\cos x - 1}$

= $\cos x - 1$

42. $\dfrac{\sin^2 x - 2 \cos \left[x - \frac{\pi}{2}\right] + 1}{\cos \left[\frac{\pi}{2} - x\right] - 1}$

= $\dfrac{\sin^2 x - 2 \sin x + 1}{\cos \left[-\left[x - \frac{\pi}{2}\right]\right] - 1}$

= $\dfrac{(\sin x - 1)^2}{\cos \left[x - \frac{\pi}{2}\right] - 1}$

= $\dfrac{(\sin x - 1)^2}{\sin x - 1}$

= $\sin x - 1$

43. $\dfrac{\sin^2 y \cos \left[y + \frac{\pi}{2}\right]}{\cos^2 y \cos \left[\frac{\pi}{2} - y\right]}$

= $\dfrac{\sin^2 y (-\sin y)}{\cos^2 y (\sin y)}$ $\left[\cos \left[\frac{\pi}{2} - y\right] = \cos \left[y - \frac{\pi}{2}\right] = \sin y\right]$

= $-\tan^2 y$

44. $\dfrac{\cos^2 y \, \sin\left(y + \frac{\pi}{2}\right)}{\sin^2 y \, \sin\left(\frac{\pi}{2} - y\right)}$

$= \dfrac{\cos^2 y \, \cos y}{\sin^2 y \, \sin\left[-\left(y - \frac{\pi}{2}\right)\right]}$

$= \dfrac{\cos^3 y}{\sin^2 y\left[-\sin\left(y - \frac{\pi}{2}\right)\right]}$

$= \dfrac{\cos^3 y}{\sin^2 y[-(-\cos y)]}$

$= \dfrac{\cos^2 y}{\sin^2 y}$

$= \cot^2 y$

Exercise Set 7.4

1. Sketch a first quadrant triangle. Since $\sin \theta = \frac{4}{5}$, label the leg parallel to the y-axis 4 and the hypotenuse 5. Using the Pythagorean theorem we know the other leg has length 3.

From this diagram we find that $\cos \theta = \frac{3}{5}$ and $\tan \theta = \frac{4}{3}$.

$\sin 2\theta = 2 \sin \theta \cos \theta = 2 \cdot \frac{4}{5} \cdot \frac{3}{5} = \frac{24}{25}$

$\cos 2\theta = \cos^2\theta - \sin^2\theta = \left(\frac{3}{5}\right)^2 - \left(\frac{4}{5}\right)^2 = \frac{9}{25} - \frac{16}{25}$

$\qquad\qquad = -\frac{7}{25}$

$\tan 2\theta = \dfrac{2 \tan \theta}{1 - \tan^2\theta} = \dfrac{2 \cdot \frac{4}{3}}{1 - \left(\frac{4}{3}\right)^2} = \dfrac{\frac{8}{3}}{-\frac{7}{9}} = -\frac{24}{7}$

Since $\sin 2\theta$ is positive and $\cos 2\theta$ is negative, we know that 2θ is in quadrant II.

2.

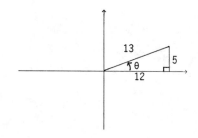

$\sin 2\theta = 2 \sin \theta \cos \theta$

$\qquad = 2 \cdot \frac{5}{13} \cdot \frac{12}{13} = \frac{120}{169}.$

$\cos 2\theta = \cos^2 \theta - \sin^2 \theta$

$\qquad = \left(\frac{12}{13}\right)^2 - \left(\frac{5}{13}\right)^2 = \frac{119}{169}.$

$\tan 2\theta = \dfrac{\sin 2\theta}{\cos 2\theta} = \dfrac{120}{119}$

2θ is in quadrant I since $\sin 2\theta > 0$ and $\cos 2\theta > 0$.

3. Sketch a third quadrant triangle. Since $\cos \theta = -\frac{4}{5}$, label the leg on the x-axis -4 and the hypotenuse 5. Using the Pythagorean theorem we know the other leg has length 3.

From this diagram we find that $\sin \theta = -\frac{3}{5}$ and $\tan \theta = \frac{3}{4}$.

$\sin 2\theta = 2 \sin \theta \cos \theta = 2\left(-\frac{3}{5}\right)\left(-\frac{4}{5}\right) = \frac{24}{25}$

$\cos 2\theta = \cos^2\theta - \sin^2\theta$

$\qquad = \left(-\frac{4}{5}\right)^2 - \left(-\frac{3}{5}\right)^2 = \frac{16}{25} - \frac{9}{25} = \frac{7}{25}$

$\tan 2\theta = \dfrac{2 \tan \theta}{1 - \tan^2\theta}$

$\qquad = \dfrac{2 \cdot \frac{3}{4}}{1 - \left(\frac{3}{4}\right)^2} = \dfrac{\frac{3}{2}}{\frac{7}{16}} = \frac{24}{7}$

Since both $\sin 2\theta$ and $\cos 2\theta$ are positive, we know that 2θ is in quadrant I.

4.

$\sin 2\theta = 2 \sin \theta \cos \theta = 2 \cdot \frac{-4}{5} \cdot \frac{-3}{5} = \frac{24}{25}$

$\cos 2\theta = \cos^2 \theta - \sin^2 \theta = \left(-\frac{3}{5}\right)^2 - \left(-\frac{4}{5}\right)^2 = -\frac{7}{25}$

$\tan 2\theta = \dfrac{\sin 2\theta}{\cos 2\theta} = -\dfrac{24}{7}$

2θ is in quadrant II since $\sin 2\theta > 0$ and $\cos 2\theta < 0$.

5. Sketch a third quadrant triangle. Since $\tan \theta = \dfrac{4}{3}$, label the leg on the x-axis –3 and the leg parallel to the y-axis –4. Using the Pythagorean theorem we know the hypotenuse has length 5.

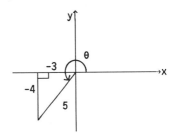

From this diagram we find that $\sin \theta = -\dfrac{4}{5}$ and $\cos \theta = -\dfrac{3}{5}$.

$\sin 2\theta = 2 \sin \theta \cos \theta$

$\qquad = 2\left(-\dfrac{4}{5}\right)\left(-\dfrac{3}{5}\right) = \dfrac{24}{25}$

$\cos 2\theta = \cos^2\theta - \sin^2\theta$

$\qquad = \left(-\dfrac{3}{5}\right)^2 - \left(-\dfrac{4}{5}\right)^2 = \dfrac{9}{25} - \dfrac{16}{25} = -\dfrac{7}{25}$

$\tan 2\theta = \dfrac{2 \tan \theta}{1 - \tan^2\theta}$

$\qquad = \dfrac{2 \cdot \dfrac{4}{3}}{1 - \left(\dfrac{4}{3}\right)^2} = \dfrac{\dfrac{8}{3}}{-\dfrac{7}{9}} = -\dfrac{24}{7}$

Since $\sin 2\theta$ is positive and $\cos 2\theta$ is negative, 2θ is in quadrant II.

6. Same as Exercise 3.

7. $\sin 4\theta = \sin 2(2\theta)$

$\qquad = 2 \sin 2\theta \cos 2\theta$

$\qquad = 2(2 \sin \theta \cos \theta)(\cos^2\theta - \sin^2\theta)$

$\qquad = 4 \sin \theta \cos^3\theta - 4 \sin^3\theta \cos \theta$

or

$\sin 4\theta = \sin 2(2\theta)$

$\qquad = 2 \sin 2\theta \cos 2\theta$

$\qquad = 2(2 \sin \theta \cos \theta)(2 \cos^2\theta - 1)$

$\qquad = 8 \sin \theta \cos^3\theta - 4 \sin \theta \cos \theta$

or

$\sin 4\theta = \sin 2(2\theta)$

$\qquad = 2 \sin 2\theta \cos 2\theta$

$\qquad = 2(2 \sin \theta \cos \theta)(1 - 2 \sin^2\theta)$

$\qquad = 4 \sin \theta \cos \theta - 8 \sin^3\theta \cos \theta$

8. $\cos 4\theta$

$= \cos 2(2\theta)$

$= 1 - 2 \sin^2 2\theta$

$= 1 - 2(2 \sin \theta \cos \theta)^2$

$= 1 - 8 \sin^2 \theta \cos^2 \theta$

or

$\cos 4\theta$

$= \cos 2(2\theta)$

$= \cos^2 2\theta - \sin^2 2\theta$

$= (\cos^2 \theta - \sin^2 \theta)^2 - (2 \sin \theta \cos \theta)^2$

$= \cos^4 \theta - 6 \sin^2 \theta \cos^2 \theta + \sin^4 \theta$

or

$\cos 4\theta$

$= \cos 2(2\theta)$

$= 2 \cos^2 2\theta - 1$

$= 2(2 \cos^2 \theta - 1)^2 - 1$

$= 8 \cos^4 \theta - 8 \cos^2 \theta + 1$

9. $\sin^4\theta = \sin^2\theta \cdot \sin^2\theta$

$\qquad = \dfrac{1 - \cos 2\theta}{2} \cdot \dfrac{1 - \cos 2\theta}{2}$

$\qquad = \dfrac{1 - 2 \cos 2\theta + \cos^2 2\theta}{4}$

$\qquad = \dfrac{1 - 2 \cos 2\theta + \dfrac{1 + \cos 4\theta}{2}}{4}$

$\qquad = \dfrac{2 - 4 \cos 2\theta + 1 + \cos 4\theta}{8}$

$\qquad = \dfrac{3 - 4 \cos 2\theta + \cos 4\theta}{8}$

10. $\cos^4 \theta = (\cos^2 \theta)^2$

$\qquad = \left(\dfrac{1 + \cos 2\theta}{2}\right)^2$

$\qquad = \dfrac{1}{4}(1 + 2 \cos 2\theta + \cos^2 2\theta)$

$\qquad = \dfrac{1}{4}\left(1 + 2 \cos 2\theta + \dfrac{1 + \cos 4\theta}{2}\right)$

$\qquad = \dfrac{3 + 4 \cos 2\theta + \cos 4\theta}{8}$

11. $\sin 75° = \sin \dfrac{150°}{2}$

$\qquad = \sqrt{\dfrac{1 - \cos 150°}{2}} = \sqrt{\dfrac{1 - (-\sqrt{3}/2)}{2}}$

$\qquad = \sqrt{\dfrac{2 + \sqrt{3}}{4}} = \dfrac{\sqrt{2 + \sqrt{3}}}{2}$

The expression is positive because 75° is in the first quadrant.

12. $\cos 75° = \cos \dfrac{150°}{2} = \sqrt{\dfrac{1 + \cos 150°}{2}} = \dfrac{\sqrt{2 - \sqrt{3}}}{2}$

13. $\tan 75° = \tan \dfrac{150°}{2}$

$$= \frac{\sin 150°}{1 + \cos 150°} = \frac{\dfrac{1}{2}}{1 + \left(-\dfrac{\sqrt{3}}{2}\right)}$$

$$= \frac{1}{2 - \sqrt{3}}, \text{ or } 2 + \sqrt{3}$$

14. $\tan \dfrac{\phi}{2} = \sqrt{\dfrac{1 - \cos \phi}{1 + \cos \phi}}$ where $\phi = 135°$.

Then $\tan 67.5° = \sqrt{\dfrac{1 - \left(-\dfrac{\sqrt{2}}{2}\right)}{1 + \left(-\dfrac{\sqrt{2}}{2}\right)}} = 1 + \sqrt{2}$.

15. $\sin \dfrac{5\pi}{8} = \sin \dfrac{\dfrac{5\pi}{4}}{2}$

$$= \sqrt{\frac{1 - \cos (5\pi/4)}{2}} = \sqrt{\frac{1 - (-\sqrt{2}/2)}{2}}$$

$$= \sqrt{\frac{2 + \sqrt{2}}{4}} = \frac{\sqrt{2 + \sqrt{2}}}{2}$$

The expression is positive because $\dfrac{5\pi}{8}$ is in the second quadrant.

16. $\cos \dfrac{\phi}{2} = -\sqrt{\dfrac{1 + \cos \phi}{2}}$ where $\phi = \dfrac{5\pi}{4}$.

Then $\cos \dfrac{5\pi}{8} = -\sqrt{\dfrac{1 + \cos \dfrac{5\pi}{4}}{2}} = -\sqrt{\dfrac{1 - \dfrac{\sqrt{2}}{2}}{2}}$

$$= -\frac{\sqrt{2 - \sqrt{2}}}{2}.$$

17. $112.5° = \dfrac{5\pi}{8}$. This is the same as Exercise 15.

18. $\cos \dfrac{\phi}{2} = \sqrt{\dfrac{1 + \cos \phi}{2}}$, where $\phi = 45°$.

Then $\cos 22.5° = \sqrt{\dfrac{1 + \cos 45°}{2}} = \sqrt{\dfrac{1 + (\sqrt{2}/2)}{2}}$

$$= \frac{\sqrt{2 + \sqrt{2}}}{2}.$$

19. $\cos \dfrac{\pi}{8} = \cos \dfrac{\dfrac{\pi}{4}}{2}$

$$= \sqrt{\frac{1 + \cos (\pi/4)}{2}} = \sqrt{\frac{1 + (\sqrt{2}/2)}{2}}$$

$$= \sqrt{\frac{2 + \sqrt{2}}{4}} = \frac{\sqrt{2 + \sqrt{2}}}{2}$$

The expression is positive because $\dfrac{\pi}{8}$ is in the first quadrant.

20. $\tan \dfrac{\phi}{2} = \sqrt{\dfrac{1 - \cos \phi}{1 + \cos \phi}}$, where $\phi = 30°$.

Then $\tan 15° = \sqrt{\dfrac{1 - (\sqrt{3}/2)}{1 + (\sqrt{3}/2)}} = \sqrt{\dfrac{2 - \sqrt{3}}{2 + \sqrt{3}}}$.

21. $\sin 22.5° = \sin \dfrac{45°}{2}$

$$= \sqrt{\frac{1 - \cos 45°}{2}} = \sqrt{\frac{1 - (\sqrt{2}/2)}{2}}$$

$$= \sqrt{\frac{2 - \sqrt{2}}{4}} = \frac{\sqrt{2 - \sqrt{2}}}{2}$$

The expression is positive because $22.5°$ is in the first quadrant.

22. $\tan \dfrac{\phi}{2} = -\sqrt{\dfrac{1 - \cos \phi}{1 + \cos \phi}}$, where $\phi = 225°$.

Then $\tan 112.5° = -\sqrt{\dfrac{1 - (-\sqrt{2}/2)}{1 + (-\sqrt{2}/2)}}$

$$= -\sqrt{\frac{2 + \sqrt{2}}{2 - \sqrt{2}}}$$

23. First find $\cos \theta$ using the following identity:
$$\sin^2\theta + \cos^2\theta = 1$$
$$(0.3416)^2 + \cos^2\theta = 1$$
$$\cos^2\theta = 1 - 0.11669056,$$
$$\cos \theta = 0.9398 \quad (\theta \text{ is in quadrant I})$$

$\sin 2\theta = 2 \sin \theta \cos \theta$
$$= 2(0.3416)(0.9398)$$
$$= 0.6421$$

24. $\cos 2\theta = 1 - 2 \sin^2 \theta = 1 - 2(0.3416)^2 = 0.7666$

25. $\sin 4\theta = 4 \sin \theta \cos^3\theta - 4 \sin^3\theta \cos \theta$
(See Exercise 7)
$$= 4(0.3416)(0.9398)^3 - 4(0.3416)^3(0.9398)$$
$$= 0.9844$$

26. $\cos 4\theta = 2(\cos 2\theta)^2 - 1$ where $\cos 2\theta = 0.7666$
from Exercise 24.

Then $\cos 4\theta = 0.1754$.

27. $\sin \dfrac{\theta}{2} = \sqrt{\dfrac{1 - \cos \theta}{2}} \quad \left(\dfrac{\theta}{2} \text{ is in quadrant I}\right)$

$$= \sqrt{\frac{1 - 0.9398}{2}} \quad \text{(See Exercise 23.)}$$

$$= 0.1735$$

28. $\cos \dfrac{\theta}{2} = \sqrt{\dfrac{1 + \cos \theta}{2}}$ where $\cos \theta = 0.9398$ from
from Exercise 23.

Then $\cos \dfrac{\theta}{2} = 0.9848$.

29. $\dfrac{\sin 2x}{2 \sin x} = \dfrac{2 \sin x \cos x}{2 \sin x} = \cos x$

30. $\dfrac{\sin 2x}{2 \cos x} = \dfrac{2 \sin x \cos x}{2 \cos x} = \sin x$

31. $1 - 2 \sin^2 \dfrac{x}{2} = 1 - 2\left[\dfrac{1 - \cos x}{2}\right]$

     $= 1 - 1 + \cos x$

     $= \cos x$

32. $2 \cos^2 \dfrac{x}{2} - 1 = \cos 2\left[\dfrac{x}{2}\right] = \cos x$

33. $2 \sin \dfrac{x}{2} \cos \dfrac{x}{2} = \sin 2\left[\dfrac{x}{2}\right] = \sin x$

34. $2 \sin 2x \cos 2x = \sin 2(2x) = \sin 4x$

35. $\cos^2 \dfrac{x}{2} - \sin^2 \dfrac{x}{2} = \cos 2\left[\dfrac{x}{2}\right] = \cos x$

36. $\cos^4 x - \sin^4 x$

     $= (\cos^2 x + \sin^2 x)(\cos^2 x - \sin^2 x)$

     $= (1) \cdot (\cos 2x)$

     $= \cos 2x$

37. $(\sin x + \cos x)^2 - \sin 2x$

     $= \sin^2 x + 2 \sin x \cos x + \cos^2 x - \sin 2x$

     $= \sin^2 x + \sin 2x + \cos^2 x - \sin 2x$

     $= 1$

38. $(\sin x - \cos x)^2 + (\sin 2x)$

     $= (\sin^2 x - 2 \sin x \cos x + \cos^2 x)$
     $\qquad + (2 \sin x \cos x)$

     $= \sin^2 x + \cos^2 x$

     $= 1$

39. $2 \sin^2 \dfrac{x}{2} + \cos x$

     $= 2\left[\dfrac{1 - \cos x}{2}\right] + \cos x$

     $= 1 - \cos x + \cos x$

     $= 1$

40. $2 \cos^2 \dfrac{x}{2} - \cos x = 2\left[\dfrac{1 + \cos 2 \cdot \frac{x}{2}}{2}\right] - \cos x = 1$

41. $(-4 \cos x \sin x + 2 \cos 2x)^2 +$
    $\qquad\qquad (2 \cos 2x + 4 \sin x \cos x)^2$

    $= (16\cos^2 x \sin^2 x - 16 \sin x \cos x \cos 2x + 4 \cos^2 2x) +$
    $\quad (4 \cos^2 2x + 16 \sin x \cos x \cos 2x + 16 \sin^2 x \cos^2 x)$

    $= 8 \cos^2 2x + 32 \cos^2 x \sin^2 x$

    $= 8(\cos^2 x - \sin^2 x)^2 + 32 \cos^2 x \sin^2 x$

    $= 8(\cos^4 x - 2 \cos^2 x \sin^2 x + \sin^4 x) + 32 \cos^2 x \sin^2 x$

    $= 8 \cos^4 x + 16 \cos^2 x \sin^2 x + 8 \sin^4 x$

    $= 8(\cos^4 x + 2 \cos^2 x \sin^2 x + \sin^4 x)$

    $= 8(\cos^2 x + \sin^2 x)^2$

    $= 8$

42. $(-4 \cos 2x + 8 \cos x \sin x)^2 +$
    $\qquad\qquad (8 \sin x \cos x + 4 \cos 2x)^2$

    $= (-4 \cos 2x + 4 \sin 2x)^2 + (4 \sin 2x + 4 \cos 2x)^2$

    $= 16(\sin 2x - \cos 2x)^2 + 16(\sin 2x + \cos 2x)^2$

    $= 16[2(\sin^2 2x + \cos^2 2x)]$

    $= 32$

43. $2 \sin x \cos^3 x + 2 \sin^3 x \cos x$

    $= 2 \sin x \cos x(\cos^2 x + \sin^2 x)$

    $= 2 \sin x \cos x$

    $= \sin 2x$

44. $2 \sin x \cos^3 x - 2 \sin^3 x \cos x$

    $= (2 \sin x \cos x)(\cos^2 x - \sin^2 x)$

    $= (\sin 2x)(\cos 2x)$

    $= \dfrac{1}{2} \sin 4x$

45. $(\sin x + \cos x)^2$

    $= \sin^2 x + 2 \sin x \cos x + \cos^2 x$

    $= 1 + \sin 2x$

    Thus $(\sin x + \cos x)^2 = 1 + \sin 2x$.

46. $\cos^4 x - \sin^4 x$

    $= (\cos^2 x + \sin^2 x)(\cos^2 x - \sin^2 x)$

    $= (1)(\cos 2x)$

    $= \cos 2x$

47. $\dfrac{2 \cot x}{\cot^2 x - 1} = \dfrac{2 \dfrac{\cos x}{\sin x}}{\dfrac{\cos^2 x}{\sin^2 x} - 1}$

    $= \dfrac{2 \cos x}{\sin x} \cdot \dfrac{\sin^2 x}{\cos^2 x - \sin^2 x}$

    $= \dfrac{2 \cos x}{\sin x} \cdot \dfrac{\sin^2 x}{\cos 2x}$

    $= \dfrac{2 \cos x \sin x}{\cos 2x}$

    $= \dfrac{\sin 2x}{\cos 2x}$

    $= \tan 2x$

    Thus $\dfrac{2 \cot x}{\cot^2 x - 1} = \tan 2x$.

48. $\dfrac{2 - \sec^2 x}{\sec^2 x} \cdot \dfrac{\cos^2 x}{\cos^2 x} = \dfrac{2\cos^2 x - 1}{1} = \cos 2x$

49. $2\sin^2 2x + \cos 4x$

     $= 2\sin^2 2x + \cos 2(2x)$

     $= 2\sin^2 2x + (\cos^2 2x - \sin^2 2x)$

     $= \sin^2 2x + \cos^2 2x$

     $= 1$

     Thus $2\sin^2 2x + \cos 4x = 1$.

50. $\dfrac{1 + \sin 2x + \cos 2x}{1 + \sin 2x - \cos 2x}$

     $= \dfrac{1 + (2\sin x \cos x) + (2\cos^2 x - 1)}{1 + (2\sin x \cos x) - (1 - 2\sin^2 x)}$

     $= \dfrac{2\cos x (\sin x + \cos x)}{2\sin x (\cos x + \sin x)}$

     $= \cot x$

51. $\dfrac{\pi}{2} \leqslant 2\theta \leqslant \pi$, so $\dfrac{\pi}{4} \leqslant \theta \leqslant \dfrac{\pi}{2}$ and all the function values for θ are positive.

     We sketch a second quadrant triangle.

     We see that $\cos 2\theta = -\dfrac{2\sqrt{6}}{5}$.

     $\cos 2\theta = 1 - 2\sin^2\theta$

     $-\dfrac{2\sqrt{6}}{5} = 1 - 2\sin^2\theta$

     $2\sin^2\theta = 1 + \dfrac{2\sqrt{6}}{5} = \dfrac{5 + 2\sqrt{6}}{5}$

     $\sin^2\theta = \dfrac{5 + 2\sqrt{6}}{10}$

     $\sin\theta = \sqrt{\dfrac{5 + 2\sqrt{6}}{10}}$, or $\sqrt{\dfrac{1}{2} + \dfrac{\sqrt{6}}{5}}$

     $\cos 2\theta = 2\cos^2\theta - 1$

     $-\dfrac{2\sqrt{6}}{5} = 2\cos^2\theta - 1$

     $1 - \dfrac{2\sqrt{6}}{5} = 2\cos^2\theta$

     $\dfrac{5 - 2\sqrt{6}}{10} = \cos^2\theta$

     $\sqrt{\dfrac{5 - 2\sqrt{6}}{10}} = \cos\theta$, or

     $\sqrt{\dfrac{1}{2} - \dfrac{\sqrt{6}}{5}} = \cos\theta$

$\tan\theta = \dfrac{\sin\theta}{\cos\theta} = \dfrac{\sqrt{\dfrac{5 + 2\sqrt{6}}{10}}}{\sqrt{\dfrac{5 - 2\sqrt{6}}{10}}} = \sqrt{\dfrac{5 + 2\sqrt{6}}{5 - 2\sqrt{6}}}$

52. $\dfrac{3\pi}{2} \leqslant 2\theta \leqslant 2\pi$, so $\dfrac{3\pi}{4} \leqslant \theta \leqslant \pi$; $\sin\theta$ is positive; $\cos\theta$ and $\tan\theta$ are negative.

     $\cos 2\theta = 1 - 2\sin^2\theta$

     $\dfrac{7}{12} = 1 - 2\sin^2\theta$

     $2\sin^2\theta = \dfrac{5}{12}$

     $\sin^2\theta = \dfrac{5}{24}$

     $\sin\theta = \sqrt{\dfrac{5}{24}} = \dfrac{\sqrt{30}}{12}$

     $\cos 2\theta = 2\cos^2\theta - 1$

     $\dfrac{7}{12} = 2\cos^2\theta - 1$

     $\dfrac{19}{12} = 2\cos^2\theta$

     $\dfrac{19}{24} = \cos^2\theta$

     $-\sqrt{\dfrac{19}{24}} = \cos\theta$, or

     $-\dfrac{\sqrt{114}}{12} = \cos\theta$

     $\tan\theta = \dfrac{\sin\theta}{\cos\theta} = \dfrac{\dfrac{\sqrt{30}}{12}}{-\dfrac{\sqrt{114}}{12}} = -\sqrt{\dfrac{5}{19}} = -\dfrac{\sqrt{95}}{19}$

53.   Since $\dfrac{3\pi}{2} \leqslant \theta \leqslant 2\pi$, $\cos\theta$ is positive and $\sin\theta$ and $\tan\theta$ are negative.

     $\tan\dfrac{\theta}{2} = -\sqrt{\dfrac{1 - \cos\theta}{1 + \cos\theta}}$

     $-\dfrac{1}{4} = -\sqrt{\dfrac{1 - \cos\theta}{1 + \cos\theta}}$

     $\dfrac{1}{16} = \dfrac{1 - \cos\theta}{1 + \cos\theta}$

     $1 + \cos\theta = 16 - 16\cos\theta$

     $17\cos\theta = 15$

     $\cos\theta = \dfrac{15}{17}$

     $\sin^2\theta + \cos^2\theta = 1$

     $\sin^2\theta + \left(\dfrac{15}{17}\right)^2 = 1$

     $\sin^2\theta = \dfrac{64}{289}$

     $\sin\theta = -\dfrac{8}{17}$

     $\tan\theta = \dfrac{\sin\theta}{\cos\theta} = \dfrac{-\dfrac{8}{17}}{\dfrac{15}{17}} = -\dfrac{8}{15}$

·54. Since $\pi < \theta \leqslant \frac{3\pi}{2}$, tan θ is positive and sin θ and cos θ are negative.

$$\tan \frac{\theta}{2} = -\sqrt{\frac{1-\cos\theta}{1+\cos\theta}}$$

$$-\frac{5}{3} = -\sqrt{\frac{1-\cos\theta}{1+\cos\theta}}$$

$$\frac{25}{9} = \frac{1-\cos\theta}{1+\cos\theta}$$

$$25 + 25\cos\theta = 9 - 9\cos\theta$$

$$34\cos\theta = -16$$

$$\cos\theta = -\frac{16}{34} = -\frac{8}{17}$$

$$\sin\theta = -\sqrt{1-\cos^2\theta} = -\sqrt{1-\left(-\frac{8}{17}\right)^2} = -\frac{15}{17}$$

$$\tan\theta = \frac{\sin\theta}{\cos\theta} = \frac{-\frac{15}{17}}{-\frac{8}{17}} = \frac{15}{8}$$

55. a) We substitute 42° for φ.

$$N(42°) = 6066 - 31\cos(2 \cdot 42°)$$
$$= 6066 - 31\cos 84°$$
$$\approx 6062.76 \text{ ft}$$

b) We substitute 90° for φ.

$$N(90°) = 6066 - 31\cos(2 \cdot 90°)$$
$$= 6066 - 31\cos 180°$$
$$= 6066 - 31(-1) = 6066 + 31$$
$$= 6097 \text{ ft}$$

c) We substitute $2\cos^2\phi - 1$ for cos 2φ.

$$N(\phi) = 6066 - 31(2\cos^2\phi - 1), \text{ or}$$
$$N(\phi) = 6097 - 62\cos^2\phi$$

56. a) g = 9.78049(1 + 0.005288 sin² 42° −
                          0.000006 sin² 84°)
      ≈ 9.80359 m/sec²

b) g = 9.78049(1 + 0.005288 sin² 40° −
                          0.000006 sin² 80°)
      ≈ 9.80180 m/sec²

c) g = 9.78049[1 + 0.005288 sin²φ −
                    0.000006(2 sin φ cos φ)²]
   g = 9.78049(1 + 0.005288 sin²φ −
                    0.000024 sin²φ cos² φ)
   g = 9.78049[1 + 0.005288 sin²φ −
                    0.000024 sin²φ(1 − sin²φ)]
   g = 9.78049(1 + 0.005264 sin²φ +
                    0.000024 sin⁴φ)

d) g is greatest at 90° N and 90° S (that is, at the poles).

   g is least at 0° (that is, at the equator).

57. Since $\cos^2 x - \sin^2 x = \cos 2x$, we graph the equivalent function, $f(x) = \cos 2x$.

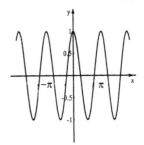

58. Since $|\sin x \cos x| = \frac{1}{2}|\sin 2x|$, we graph the equivalent function $y = \frac{1}{2}|\sin 2x|$.

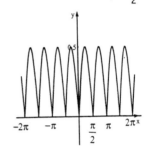

Exercise Set 7.5

Note: Answers for the odd-numbered exercises 1 − 81 are in the answer section in the text.

2.

sec x − sin x tan x	cos x
$\frac{1}{\cos x} - \sin x \cdot \frac{\sin x}{\cos x}$	
$\frac{1 - \sin^2 x}{\cos x}$	
$\frac{\cos^2 x}{\cos x}$	
cos x	

4.

$\frac{1}{\sin\theta\cos\theta} - \frac{\cos\theta}{\sin\theta}$	$\frac{\sin\theta\cos\theta}{1-\sin^2\theta}$
$\frac{1-\cos^2\theta}{\sin\theta\cos\theta}$	$\frac{\sin\theta\cos\theta}{\cos^2\theta}$
$\frac{\sin^2\theta}{\sin\theta\cos\theta}$	$\frac{\sin\theta}{\cos\theta}$
$\frac{\sin\theta}{\cos\theta}$	

6.

$\dfrac{1-\cos x}{\sin x}$	$\dfrac{\sin x}{1+\cos x}$
	$\dfrac{\sin x}{1+\cos x}\cdot\dfrac{1-\cos x}{1-\cos x}$
	$\dfrac{\sin x\,(1-\cos x)}{1-\cos^2 x}$
	$\dfrac{\sin x\,(1-\cos x)}{\sin^2 x}$
	$\dfrac{1-\cos x}{\sin x}$

8.

$\dfrac{\cot\theta-1}{1-\tan\theta}$	$\dfrac{\csc\theta}{\sec\theta}$
$\dfrac{\dfrac{\cos\theta}{\sin\theta}-1}{1-\dfrac{\sin\theta}{\cos\theta}}$	$\dfrac{\dfrac{1}{\sin\theta}}{\dfrac{1}{\cos\theta}}$
$\dfrac{\dfrac{\cos\theta-\sin\theta}{\sin\theta}}{\dfrac{\cos\theta-\sin\theta}{\cos\theta}}$	$\dfrac{\cos\theta}{\sin\theta}$
$\dfrac{\cos\theta}{\sin\theta}$	

10.

$\dfrac{\sin x-\cos x}{\sec x-\csc x}$	$\dfrac{\cos x}{\csc x}$
$\dfrac{\sin x-\cos x}{\dfrac{1}{\cos x}-\dfrac{1}{\sin x}}$	$\sin x\cos x$
$\dfrac{\sin x-\cos x}{\dfrac{\sin x-\cos x}{\sin x\cos x}}$	
$\sin x\cos x$	

12.

$\dfrac{\cos^2\theta+\cot\theta}{\cos^2\theta-\cot\theta}$	$\dfrac{\cos^2\theta\,\tan\theta+1}{\cos^2\theta\,\tan\theta-1}$
$\dfrac{\cos^2\theta+\dfrac{\cos\theta}{\sin\theta}}{\cos^2\theta-\dfrac{\cos\theta}{\sin\theta}}$	$\dfrac{\cos^2\theta\,\dfrac{\sin\theta}{\cos\theta}+1}{\cos^2\theta\,\dfrac{\sin\theta}{\cos\theta}-1}$
$\dfrac{\cos\theta\left(\cos\theta+\dfrac{1}{\sin\theta}\right)}{\cos\theta\left(\cos\theta-\dfrac{1}{\sin\theta}\right)}$	$\dfrac{\sin\theta\cos\theta+1}{\sin\theta\cos\theta-1}$
$\dfrac{\cos\theta+\dfrac{1}{\sin\theta}}{\cos\theta-\dfrac{1}{\sin\theta}}$	
$\dfrac{\dfrac{\sin\theta\cos\theta+1}{\sin\theta}}{\dfrac{\sin\theta\cos\theta-1}{\sin\theta}}$	
$\dfrac{\sin\theta\cos\theta+1}{\sin\theta\cos\theta-1}$	

14.

$\dfrac{2\tan\theta}{1+\tan^2\theta}$	$\sin 2\theta$
$\dfrac{2\tan\theta}{\sec^2\theta}$	$2\sin\theta\cos\theta$
$\dfrac{2\sin\theta}{\cos\theta}\cdot\dfrac{\cos^2\theta}{1}$	
$2\sin\theta\cos\theta$	

16.

$\cot 2\theta$	$\dfrac{\cot^2\theta-1}{2\cot\theta}$
$\dfrac{\cos 2\theta}{\sin 2\theta}$	$\dfrac{\dfrac{\cos^2\theta}{\sin^2\theta}-1}{2\,\dfrac{\cos\theta}{\sin\theta}}$
$\dfrac{\cos^2\theta-\sin^2\theta}{2\sin\theta\cos\theta}$	$\dfrac{1}{2}\left[\dfrac{\cos^2\theta-\sin^2\theta}{\sin^2\theta}\cdot\dfrac{\sin\theta}{\cos\theta}\right]$
	$\dfrac{\cos^2\theta-\sin^2\theta}{2\sin\theta\cos\theta}$

18.

$\dfrac{\cos(\alpha-\beta)}{\cos\alpha\sin\beta}$	$\tan\alpha+\cot\beta$
$\dfrac{\cos\alpha\cos\beta+\sin\alpha\sin\beta}{\cos\alpha\sin\beta}$	
$\dfrac{\cos\alpha\cos\beta}{\cos\alpha\sin\beta}+\dfrac{\sin\alpha\sin\beta}{\cos\alpha\sin\beta}$	
$\dfrac{\cos\beta}{\sin\beta}+\dfrac{\sin\alpha}{\cos\alpha}$	
$\cot\beta+\tan\alpha$	

20.

$2\sin\theta\cos^3\theta+2\sin^3\theta\cos\theta$	$\sin 2\theta$
$2\sin\theta\cos\theta(\cos^2\theta+\sin^2\theta)$	$2\sin\theta\cos\theta$
$2\sin\theta\cos\theta$	

22.

$\dfrac{\tan\theta-\sin\theta}{2\tan\theta}$	$\sin^2\dfrac{\theta}{2}$
$\dfrac{1}{2}\left[\dfrac{\dfrac{\sin\theta}{\cos\theta}-\sin\theta}{\dfrac{\sin\theta}{\cos\theta}}\right]$	$\dfrac{1-\cos\theta}{2}$
$\dfrac{1}{2}\dfrac{\sin\theta-\sin\theta\cos\theta}{\cos\theta}\cdot\dfrac{\cos\theta}{\sin\theta}$	
$\dfrac{1-\cos\theta}{2}$	

24.

$\dfrac{\cos^4 x-\sin^4 x}{1-\tan^4 x}$	$\cos^4 x$
$\dfrac{\cos^4 x-\sin^4 x}{1-\dfrac{\sin^4 x}{\cos^4 x}}$	
$\dfrac{\cos^4 x-\sin^4 x}{\dfrac{\cos^4 x-\sin^4 x}{\cos^4 x}}$	
$\cos^4 x$	

26.

$$\left(\frac{1 + \tan\,\theta}{1 - \tan\,\theta}\right)^2 \quad \bigg| \quad \frac{1 + \sin\,2\theta}{1 - \sin\,2\theta}$$

$$\left[\frac{\dfrac{\cos\,\theta + \sin\,\theta}{\cos\,\theta}}{\dfrac{\cos\,\theta - \sin\,\theta}{\cos\,\theta}}\right]^2 \quad \bigg| \quad \frac{1 + 2\,\sin\,\theta\,\cos\,\theta}{1 - 2\,\sin\,\theta\,\cos\,\theta}$$

$$\frac{\cos^2\theta + 2\,\sin\,\theta\,\cos\,\theta + \sin^2\theta}{\cos^2\theta - 2\,\sin\,\theta\,\cos\,\theta + \sin^2\theta}$$

$$\frac{1 + 2\,\sin\,\theta\,\cos\,\theta}{1 - 2\,\sin\,\theta\,\cos\,\theta}\,\bigg|$$

28.

$$\frac{\sin^3 t + \cos^3 t}{\sin\,t + \cos\,t} \quad \bigg| \quad \frac{2 - \sin\,2t}{2}$$

$$\frac{(\sin\,t + \cos\,t)(\sin^2 t - \sin\,t\,\cos\,t + \cos^2 t)}{\sin\,t + \cos\,t} \quad \bigg| \quad \frac{2 - 2\,\sin\,t\,\cos\,t}{2}$$

$$1 - \sin\,t\,\cos\,t \,\bigg|\, 1 - \sin\,t\,\cos\,t$$

30.

$$\cos\,(\alpha + \beta)\,\cos\,(\alpha - \beta) \quad \bigg| \quad \cos^2\alpha - \sin^2\beta$$

$$(\cos\,\alpha\,\cos\,\beta - \sin\,\alpha\,\sin\,\beta)(\cos\,\alpha\,\cos\,\beta + \sin\,\alpha\,\sin\,\beta)$$

$$\cos^2\alpha\,\cos^2\beta - \sin^2\alpha\,\sin^2\beta$$

$$(1 - \sin^2\alpha)(1 - \sin^2\beta) - \sin^2\alpha\,\sin^2\beta$$

$$1 - \sin^2\alpha - \sin^2\beta + \sin^2\alpha\,\sin^2\beta - \sin^2\alpha\,\sin^2\beta$$

$$1 - \sin^2\alpha - \sin^2\beta$$

$$\cos^2\alpha - \sin^2\beta\,\bigg|$$

32.

$$\sin\,(\alpha + \beta) + \sin\,(\alpha - \beta) \quad \bigg| \quad 2\,\sin\,\alpha\,\cos\,\beta$$

$$\sin\,\alpha\,\cos\,\beta + \cos\,\alpha\,\sin\,\beta + \sin\,\alpha\,\cos\,\beta - \cos\,\alpha\,\sin\,\beta$$

$$2\,\sin\,\alpha\,\cos\,\beta\,\bigg|$$

34.

$$\cos^2 x\,(1 - \sec^2 x) \quad \bigg| \quad -\sin^2 x$$

$$\cos^2 x\,(-\tan^2 x)$$

$$\cos^2 x\,\left(-\frac{\sin^2 x}{\cos^2 x}\right)$$

$$-\sin^2 x\,\bigg|$$

36.

$$\tan\,\theta\,(\tan\,\theta + \cot\,\theta) \quad \bigg| \quad \sec^2\theta$$

$$\tan^2\theta + \tan\,\theta\,\cot\,\theta$$

$$\tan^2\theta + 1$$

$$\sec^2\theta\,\bigg|$$

38.

$$\frac{\tan x + \sin x}{1 + \sec x} \quad \bigg| \quad \sin x$$

$$\frac{\dfrac{\sin x}{\cos x} + \dfrac{\sin x}{1}}{1 + \dfrac{1}{\cos x}}$$

$$\frac{\dfrac{\sin x + \sin x \cos x}{\cos x}}{\dfrac{\cos x + 1}{\cos x}}$$

$$\frac{\sin x\,(1 + \cos x)}{\cos x} \cdot \frac{\cos x}{\cos x + 1}$$

$$\sin x$$

40.

$$\frac{1 + \tan^2\theta}{\csc^2\theta} \quad \bigg| \quad \tan^2\theta$$

$$\frac{\sec^2\theta}{\csc^2\theta} \quad \bigg| \quad \frac{\sin^2\theta}{\cos^2\theta}$$

$$\frac{1}{\cos^2\theta} \cdot \frac{\sin^2\theta}{1}$$

$$\frac{\sin^2\theta}{\cos^2\theta}$$

42.

$$\frac{1 + \cos^2 x}{\sin^2 x} \quad \bigg| \quad 2\csc^2 x - 1$$

$$\frac{1}{\sin^2 x} + \frac{\cos^2 x}{\sin^2 x}$$

$$\csc^2 x + \cot^2 x$$

$$\csc^2 x + \csc^2 x - 1$$

$$2\csc^2 x - 1$$

44.

$$\frac{\csc x - \sin x}{\cot x} \quad \bigg| \quad \cos x$$

$$\frac{\dfrac{1}{\sin x} - \sin x}{\dfrac{\cos x}{\sin x}}$$

$$\frac{1 - \sin^2 x}{\sin x} \cdot \frac{\sin x}{\cos x}$$

$$\frac{1 - \sin^2 x}{\cos x}$$

$$\frac{\cos^2 x}{\cos x}$$

$$\cos x$$

46.

$$\frac{\csc\theta - \sin\theta}{\cos^2\theta} \quad \bigg| \quad \csc\theta$$

$$\frac{\dfrac{1}{\sin\theta} - \sin\theta}{\cos^2\theta} \quad \bigg| \quad \frac{1}{\sin\theta}$$

$$\frac{1 - \sin^2\theta}{\sin\theta} \cdot \frac{1}{\cos^2\theta}$$

$$\frac{\cos^2\theta}{\sin\theta} \cdot \frac{1}{\cos^2\theta}$$

$$\frac{1}{\sin\theta}$$

48.

$$\frac{1 + \sin x}{1 - \sin x} + \frac{\sin x - 1}{1 + \sin x} \quad \bigg| \quad 4\sec x \tan x$$

$$\frac{(1 + \sin x)^2 - (1 - \sin x)^2}{1 - \sin^2 x} \quad \bigg| \quad 4 \cdot \frac{1}{\cos x} \cdot \frac{\sin x}{\cos x}$$

$$\frac{(1 + 2\sin x + \sin^2 x) - (1 - 2\sin x + \sin^2 x)}{\cos^2 x} \quad \bigg| \quad \frac{4\sin x}{\cos^2 x}$$

$$\frac{4\sin x}{\cos^2 x}$$

50.

$$\cos^2\theta \cot^2\theta \quad \bigg| \quad \cot^2\theta - \cos^2\theta$$

$$(1 - \sin^2\theta)\cot^2\theta$$

$$\cot^2\theta - \sin^2\theta \cdot \frac{\cos^2\theta}{\sin^2\theta}$$

$$\cot^2\theta - \cos^2\theta$$

52.

$$\frac{\cos^2 x - 1}{1 - \sec^2 x} \quad \bigg| \quad \frac{1}{\tan^2 x + 1}$$

$$\frac{-\sin^2 x}{-\tan^2 x} \quad \bigg| \quad \frac{1}{\sec^2 x}$$

$$\sin^2 x \cdot \frac{\cos^2 x}{\sin^2 x} \quad \bigg| \quad \cos^2 x$$

$$\cos^2 x$$

54.

$$\tan\theta - \cot\theta \quad \bigg| \quad (\sec\theta - \csc\theta)(\sin\theta + \cos\theta)$$

$$\frac{\sin\theta}{\cos\theta} - \frac{\cos\theta}{\sin\theta} \quad \bigg| \quad \left(\frac{1}{\cos\theta} - \frac{1}{\sin\theta}\right)(\sin\theta + \cos\theta)$$

$$\frac{\sin^2\theta - \cos^2\theta}{\cos\theta\sin\theta} \quad \bigg| \quad \left(\frac{\sin\theta - \cos\theta}{\sin\theta\cos\theta}\right)\left(\frac{\sin\theta + \cos\theta}{1}\right)$$

$$\frac{\sin^2\theta - \cos^2\theta}{\sin\theta\cos\theta}$$

56.

$$\csc x - \cot x \quad \bigg| \quad \frac{1}{\csc x + \cot x}$$

$$\frac{1}{\sin x} - \frac{\cos x}{\sin x} \quad \bigg| \quad \frac{1}{\dfrac{1}{\sin x} + \dfrac{\cos x}{\sin x}}$$

$$\frac{1 - \cos x}{\sin x} \cdot \frac{1 + \cos x}{1 + \cos x} \quad \bigg| \quad \frac{1}{\dfrac{1 + \cos x}{\sin x}}$$

$$\frac{1 - \cos^2 x}{\sin x\,(1 + \cos x)} \quad \bigg| \quad \frac{\sin x}{1 + \cos x}$$

$$\frac{\sin^2 x}{\sin x\,(1 + \cos x)}$$

$$\frac{\sin x}{1 + \cos x}$$

58.

$$2\sin^2\theta \cos^2\theta + \cos^4\theta \quad \bigg| \quad 1 - \sin^4\theta$$

$$\cos^2\theta(2\sin^2\theta + \cos^2\theta) \quad \bigg| \quad (1 + \sin^2\theta)(1 - \sin^2\theta)$$

$$\cos^2\theta(\sin^2\theta + \sin^2\theta + \cos^2\theta) \quad \bigg| \quad (1 + \sin^2\theta)(\cos^2\theta)$$

$$\cos^2\theta(\sin^2\theta + 1)$$

60.

$$\dfrac{\cot \theta}{\csc \theta - 1} \quad \bigg| \quad \dfrac{\csc \theta + 1}{\cot \theta}$$

$$\dfrac{\cot \theta}{\csc \theta - 1} \cdot \dfrac{\csc \theta + 1}{\csc \theta + 1}$$

$$\dfrac{\cot \theta(\csc \theta + 1)}{\csc^2\theta - 1}$$

$$\dfrac{\cot \theta(\csc \theta + 1)}{\cot^2\theta}$$

$$\dfrac{\csc \theta + 1}{\cot \theta}$$

62.

$$\dfrac{1 + \sin x}{1 - \sin x} \quad \bigg| \quad (\sec x + \tan x)^2$$

$$\dfrac{1 + \sin x}{1 - \sin x} \cdot \dfrac{1 + \sin x}{1 + \sin x} \quad \bigg| \quad \left(\dfrac{1}{\cos x} + \dfrac{\sin x}{\cos x}\right)^2$$

$$\dfrac{(1 + \sin x)^2}{1 - \sin^2 x} \quad \bigg| \quad \dfrac{(1 + \sin x)^2}{\cos^2 x}$$

$$\dfrac{(1 + \sin x)^2}{\cos^2 x}$$

64.

$$\sec^4\theta - \tan^2\theta \quad \bigg| \quad \tan^4\theta + \sec^2\theta$$

$$\sec^4\theta - (\sec^2\theta - 1) \quad \bigg| \quad (\tan^2\theta)^2 + \sec^2\theta$$

$$\sec^4\theta - \sec^2\theta + 1 \quad \bigg| \quad (\sec^2\theta - 1)^2 + \sec^2\theta$$

$$\quad \bigg| \quad \sec^4\theta - 2\sec^2\theta + 1 + \sec^2\theta$$

$$\quad \bigg| \quad \sec^4\theta - \sec^2\theta + 1$$

66.

$$1 + \sec x \quad \bigg| \quad \csc x(\sin x + \tan x)$$

$$1 + \dfrac{1}{\cos x} \quad \bigg| \quad \dfrac{1}{\sin x}\left(\dfrac{\sin x}{1} + \dfrac{\sin x}{\cos x}\right)$$

$$\quad \bigg| \quad 1 + \dfrac{1}{\cos x}$$

68.

$$\dfrac{\sin^3\theta - \cos^3\theta}{\sin \theta - \cos \theta} \quad \bigg| \quad \sin \theta \cos \theta + 1$$

$$\dfrac{(\sin\theta-\cos\theta)(\sin^2\theta+\sin\theta \cos\theta+\cos^2\theta)}{\sin \theta - \cos \theta}$$

$$\sin^2\theta + \sin \theta \cos \theta + \cos^2\theta$$

$$\sin \theta \cos \theta + 1$$

70.

$$2\sec^2 x + \dfrac{\csc x}{1 - \csc x} \quad \bigg| \quad \dfrac{\csc x}{\csc x + 1}$$

$$2 \cdot \dfrac{1}{\cos^2 x} + \dfrac{\dfrac{1}{\sin x}}{1 - \dfrac{1}{\sin x}} \quad \bigg| \quad \dfrac{\dfrac{1}{\sin x}}{\dfrac{1}{\sin x} + 1}$$

$$\dfrac{2}{\cos^2 x} + \dfrac{\dfrac{1}{\sin x}}{\dfrac{\sin x - 1}{\sin x}} \quad \bigg| \quad \dfrac{\dfrac{1}{\sin x}}{\dfrac{1 + \sin x}{\sin x}}$$

$$\dfrac{2}{\cos^2 x} + \dfrac{1}{\sin x - 1} \quad \bigg| \quad \dfrac{1}{1+\sin x} \cdot \dfrac{1-\sin x}{1-\sin x}$$

$$\dfrac{2}{\cos^2 x} + \dfrac{1}{\sin x - 1} \cdot \dfrac{\sin x + 1}{\sin x + 1} \quad \bigg| \quad \dfrac{1 - \sin x}{1 - \sin^2 x}$$

$$\dfrac{2}{\cos^2 x} + \dfrac{\sin x + 1}{\sin^2 x - 1} \quad \bigg| \quad \dfrac{1 - \sin x}{\cos^2 x}$$

$$\dfrac{2}{\cos^2 x} + \dfrac{\sin x + 1}{-\cos^2 x}$$

$$\dfrac{1 - \sin x}{\cos^2 x}$$

72.

$$\cos \theta + \dfrac{\sin \theta}{\cot \theta - 1} \quad \bigg| \quad \dfrac{\cos \theta}{1 - \tan \theta} - \sin \theta$$

$$\cos \theta + \dfrac{\sin \theta}{\dfrac{\cos \theta}{\sin \theta} - 1} \quad \bigg| \quad \dfrac{\cos \theta}{1 - \dfrac{\sin \theta}{\cos \theta}} - \sin \theta$$

$$\cos \theta + \dfrac{\sin \theta}{1} \cdot \dfrac{\sin \theta}{\cos \theta - \sin \theta} \quad \bigg| \quad \dfrac{\cos \theta}{1} \cdot \dfrac{\cos \theta}{\cos \theta - \sin \theta}$$

$$\quad \bigg| \quad - \sin \theta$$

$$\cos \theta + \dfrac{\sin^2\theta}{\cos \theta - \sin \theta} \quad \bigg| \quad \dfrac{\cos^2\theta}{\cos \theta - \sin \theta} - \sin \theta$$

$$\dfrac{\cos^2\theta-\cos \theta \sin\theta+\sin^2\theta}{\cos \theta - \sin \theta} \quad \bigg| \quad \dfrac{\cos^2\theta-\sin \theta \cos \theta+\sin^2\theta}{\cos \theta - \sin \theta}$$

74.

$$\dfrac{\cos x + \cot x}{1 + \csc x} \quad \bigg| \quad \cos x$$

$$\dfrac{\dfrac{\cos x}{1} + \dfrac{\cos x}{\sin x}}{1 + \dfrac{1}{\sin x}}$$

$$\dfrac{\sin x \cos x + \cos x}{\sin x} \cdot \dfrac{\sin x}{\sin x + 1}$$

$$\dfrac{\cos x(\sin x + 1)}{\sin x + 1}$$

$$\cos x$$

76.

$$\sec^2\theta - \csc^2\theta \quad \bigg| \quad \dfrac{\tan \theta - \cot \theta}{\sin \theta \cos \theta}$$

$$\dfrac{1}{\cos^2\theta} - \dfrac{1}{\sin^2\theta} \quad \bigg| \quad \dfrac{\dfrac{\sin \theta}{\cos \theta} - \dfrac{\cos \theta}{\sin \theta}}{\sin \theta \cos \theta}$$

$$\dfrac{\sin^2\theta - \cos^2\theta}{\cos^2\theta \sin^2\theta} \quad \bigg| \quad \dfrac{\sin^2\theta - \cos^2\theta}{\sin \theta \cos \theta} \cdot \dfrac{1}{\sin \theta \cos \theta}$$

$$\quad \bigg| \quad \dfrac{\sin^2\theta - \cos^2\theta}{\sin^2\theta \cos^2\theta}$$

78.

$\sec^4 x - 4\tan^2 x$	$(1 - \tan^2 x)^2$
$(\sec^2 x)^2 - 4\tan^2 x$	$1 - 2\tan^2 x + \tan^4 x$
$(1 + \tan^2 x)^2 - 4\tan^2 x$	
$1 + 2\tan^2 x + \tan^4 x - 4\tan^2 x$	
$1 - 2\tan^2 x + \tan^4 x$	

80.

$\dfrac{\tan^2 x + \sec^2 x}{\sec^4 x}$	$1 - \sin^4 x$
$\dfrac{\dfrac{\sin^2 x}{\cos^2 x} + \dfrac{1}{\cos^2 x}}{\dfrac{1}{\cos^4 x}}$	$(1 - \sin^2 x)(1 + \sin^2 x)$
$\dfrac{\dfrac{\sin^2 x + 1}{\cos^2 x}}{\dfrac{1}{\cos^4 x}}$	$\cos^2 x\,(\sin^2 x + 1)$
$\cos^2 x(\sin^2 x + 1)$	

82. Using the first sum-product identity proved in Margin Exercise 8, we have

$$2\sin\frac{x+y}{2}\cos\frac{x-y}{2}$$

$$= 2 \cdot \frac{1}{2}\left[\sin\left(\frac{x+y}{2} + \frac{x-y}{2}\right) + \sin\left(\frac{x+y}{2} - \frac{x-y}{2}\right)\right]$$

$$= \sin x + \sin y$$

The other formulas follow similarly.

83. We will use the identity

$$\sin x - \sin y = 2\cos\frac{x+y}{2}\sin\frac{x-y}{2},$$

where $x = 3\theta$ and $y = 5\theta$.

$$\sin 3\theta - \sin 5\theta = 2\cos\left(\frac{3\theta + 5\theta}{2}\right) \cdot \sin\left(\frac{3\theta - 5\theta}{2}\right)$$

$$= 2\cos 4\theta \sin(-\theta)$$

$$= -2\cos 4\theta \sin\theta \qquad (\sin(-\theta) = -\sin\theta)$$

84. Use the identity

$$\sin x - \sin y = 2\cos\frac{x+y}{2}\sin\frac{x-y}{2}.$$

$$\sin 7x - \sin 4x = 2\cos\frac{11x}{2}\sin\frac{3x}{2}$$

85. We will use the identity

$$\sin x + \sin y = 2\sin\frac{x+y}{2}\cos\frac{x-y}{2},$$

where $x = 8\theta$ and $y = 5\theta$.

$$\sin 8\theta + \sin 5\theta = 2\sin\left(\frac{8\theta + 5\theta}{2}\right) \cdot \cos\left(\frac{8\theta - 5\theta}{2}\right)$$

$$= 2\sin\frac{13\theta}{2}\cos\frac{3\theta}{2}$$

86. Use the identity

$$\cos y - \cos x = 2\sin\frac{x+y}{2}\sin\frac{x-y}{2}.$$

$$\cos\theta - \cos 7\theta = 2\sin\frac{8\theta}{2}\sin\frac{6\theta}{2}$$

$$= 2\sin 4\theta \sin 3\theta$$

87. We will use the identity
$$\sin u \cdot \sin v = \frac{1}{2}\left[\cos(u-v) - \cos(u+v)\right],$$
where u is 7u and v is 5u.
$$\sin 7u \sin 5u = \frac{1}{2}\left[\cos(7u-5u) - \cos(7u+5u)\right]$$
$$= \frac{1}{2}(\cos 2u - \cos 12u)$$

88. Use the identity
$$\sin u \cdot \cos v = \frac{1}{2}[\sin(u+v) + \sin(u-v)].$$
$$2\sin 7\theta \cos 3\theta = \sin 10\theta + \sin 4\theta$$

89. We will use the identity
$$\cos u \cdot \sin v = \frac{1}{2}\left[\sin(u+v) - \sin(u-v)\right],$$
where u is θ and v is 7θ.
$$7\cos\theta\sin 7\theta = 7\cdot\frac{1}{2}\left[\sin(\theta+7\theta) - \sin(\theta-7\theta)\right]$$
$$= \frac{7}{2}\left[\sin 8\theta - \sin(-6\theta)\right]$$
$$= \frac{7}{2}(\sin 8\theta + \sin 6\theta) \qquad (\sin(-6\theta) = -\sin 6\theta)$$

90. Use the identity
$$\cos u \cdot \sin v = \frac{1}{2}[\sin(u+v) - \sin(u-v)].$$
$$\cos 2t \sin t = \frac{1}{2}(\sin 3t - \sin t)$$

91. We will use the identity
$$\cos u \cdot \sin v = \frac{1}{2}\left[\sin(u+v) - \sin(u-v)\right],$$
where u is 55° and v is 25°.
$$\cos 55° \sin 25° = \frac{1}{2}\left[\sin(55°+25°) - \sin(55°-25°)\right]$$
$$= \frac{1}{2}(\sin 80° - \sin 30°), \text{ or}$$
$$\frac{1}{2}\left(\sin 80° - \frac{1}{2}\right), \text{ or} \qquad\qquad \left(\sin 30° = \frac{1}{2}\right)$$
$$\frac{1}{2}\sin 80° - \frac{1}{4}$$

92. Use the identity
$$\cos u \cdot \cos v = \frac{1}{2}[\cos(u-v) + \cos(u+v)].$$
$$7\cos 5\theta \cos 7\theta = \frac{7}{2}[\cos(-2\theta) + \cos 12\theta]$$
$$= \frac{7}{2}(\cos 2\theta + \cos 12\theta)$$

Answers for the odd-numbered exercises 93 - 111 are in the answer section in the text.

94.

$\tan 2x(\cos x + \cos 3x)$	$\sin x + \sin 3x$
$\dfrac{\sin 2x}{\cos 2x}\left[2\cos\dfrac{4x}{2}\cos\dfrac{-2x}{2}\right]$	$2\sin\dfrac{4x}{2}\cos\dfrac{-2x}{2}$
$\dfrac{\sin 2x}{\cos 2x}(2\cos 2x\cos x)$	$2\sin 2x\cos x$
$2\sin 2x\cos x$	

96.

$\tan\dfrac{x+y}{2}$	$\dfrac{\sin x + \sin y}{\cos x + \cos y}$
$\dfrac{\sin\dfrac{x+y}{2}}{\cos\dfrac{x+y}{2}}$	$\dfrac{2\sin\dfrac{x+y}{2}\cos\dfrac{x-y}{2}}{2\cos\dfrac{x+y}{2}\cos\dfrac{x-y}{2}}$
	$\dfrac{\sin\dfrac{x+y}{2}}{\cos\dfrac{x+y}{2}}$

98.

$\tan\dfrac{\theta+\phi}{2}\tan\dfrac{\phi-\theta}{2}$	$\dfrac{\cos\theta-\cos\phi}{\cos\theta+\cos\phi}$
	$\dfrac{2\sin\dfrac{\phi+\theta}{2}\sin\dfrac{\phi-\theta}{2}}{2\cos\dfrac{\phi+\theta}{2}\cos\dfrac{\phi-\theta}{2}}$
	$\tan\dfrac{\theta+\phi}{2}\tan\dfrac{\phi-\theta}{2}$

100.

$\sin 2\theta + \sin 4\theta + \sin 6\theta$	$4\cos\theta\cos 2\theta\sin 3\theta$
$2\sin\dfrac{6\theta}{2}\cos\dfrac{-2\theta}{2}+\sin 6\theta$	
$2\sin 3\theta\cos\theta + 2\sin 3\theta\cos 3\theta$	
$2\sin 3\theta(\cos\theta+\cos 3\theta)$	
$2\sin 3\theta\left[2\cos\dfrac{4\theta}{2}\cos\dfrac{2\theta}{2}\right]$	
$2\sin 3\theta(2\cos 2\theta\cos\theta)$	
$4\cos\theta\cos 2\theta\sin 3\theta$	

102.

$\ln |\tan x|$	$-\ln |\cot x|$
$\ln\left|\dfrac{1}{\cot x}\right|$	
$\ln |1| - \ln |\cot x|$	
$0 - \ln |\cot x|$	
$-\ln |\cot x|$	

104.

$\ln |\csc x|$	$-\ln |\sin x|$
$\ln\left|\dfrac{1}{\sin x}\right|$	
$\ln |1| - \ln |\sin x|$	
$-\ln |\sin x|$	

106.

$e^{\ln |\cos t|}$	$|\cos t|$
$|\cos t|$	

108.

$\ln \, \mid\sec \theta + \tan \theta\mid$	$-\ln \, \mid\sec \theta - \tan \theta\mid$
$\ln \, \left\lvert\sec \theta + \tan \theta \cdot \dfrac{\sec \theta - \tan \theta}{\sec \theta - \tan \theta}\right\rvert$	
$\ln \, \left\lvert\dfrac{\sec^2\theta - \tan^2\theta}{\sec \theta - \tan \theta}\right\rvert$	
$\ln \, \left\lvert\dfrac{1}{\sec \theta - \tan \theta}\right\rvert$	
$\ln \, \mid 1\mid - \ln \, \mid\sec \theta - \tan \theta\mid$	
$0 - \ln \, \mid\sec \theta - \tan \theta\mid$	
$- \ln \, \mid\sec \theta - \tan \theta\mid$	

110. If $I_1 = I_2$, then $\sin \theta = \dfrac{I_1 \cos \phi}{\sqrt{(I_1 \cos \phi)^2 + (I_2 \sin \phi)^2}}$

   becomes $\sin \theta = \dfrac{I_1 \cos \phi}{\sqrt{I_1{}^2 (\cos^2 \phi + \sin^2 \phi)}}$ or

   $\sin \theta = \cos \phi$.

112. Using the given equations for E_1 and E_2 we have

   (a) $\dfrac{E_1 + E_2}{2} = \dfrac{\sqrt{2} \, E_t \cos \left[\theta + \frac{\pi}{P}\right] + \sqrt{2} \, E_t \cos \left[\theta - \frac{\pi}{P}\right]}{2}$

   $= \dfrac{\sqrt{2} \, E_t \left[\left[\cos \theta \cos \frac{\pi}{P} - \sin \theta \sin \frac{\pi}{P}\right] + \left[\cos \theta \cos \frac{\pi}{P} + \sin \theta \sin \frac{\pi}{P}\right]\right]}{2}$

   $= \dfrac{\sqrt{2} \, E_t \left[2 \cos \theta \cos \frac{\pi}{P}\right]}{2}$

   $= \sqrt{2} \, E_t \cos \theta \cos \frac{\pi}{P}$

   (b) $\dfrac{E_1 - E_2}{2} = \dfrac{\sqrt{2} \, E_t \cos \left[\theta + \frac{\pi}{P}\right] - \sqrt{2} \, E_t \cos \left[\theta - \frac{\pi}{P}\right]}{2}$

   $= \dfrac{\sqrt{2} \, E_t \left[\left[\cos \theta \cos \frac{\pi}{P} - \sin \theta \sin \frac{\pi}{P}\right] - \left[\cos \theta \cos \frac{\pi}{P} + \sin \theta \sin \frac{\pi}{P}\right]\right]}{2}$

   $= \dfrac{\sqrt{2} \, E_t \left[-2 \sin \theta \sin \frac{\pi}{P}\right]}{2}$

   $= -\sqrt{2} \, E_t \sin \theta \sin \frac{\pi}{P}$

Exercise Set 7.6

---

1. Find $\arcsin \dfrac{\sqrt{2}}{2}$.

   The only number in the restricted range $\left[-\frac{\pi}{2}, \frac{\pi}{2}\right]$ whose sine is $\frac{\sqrt{2}}{2}$ is $\frac{\pi}{4}$, or 45°.

2. $\frac{\pi}{3}$, or 60°

3. Find $\cos^{-1} \dfrac{\sqrt{2}}{2}$.

   The only number in the restricted range $[0, \pi]$ whose cosine is $\frac{\sqrt{2}}{2}$ is $\frac{\pi}{4}$, or 45°.

4. $\frac{\pi}{6}$, or 30°

5. Find $\sin^{-1} \left[-\dfrac{\sqrt{2}}{2}\right]$.

   The only number in the restricted range $\left[-\frac{\pi}{2}, \frac{\pi}{2}\right]$ whose sine is $-\frac{\sqrt{2}}{2}$ is $-\frac{\pi}{4}$, or -45°.

6. $-\frac{\pi}{3}$, or -60°

7. Find arccos $\left[-\frac{\sqrt{2}}{2}\right]$.

   The only number in the restricted range $[0, \pi]$ whose cosine is $-\frac{\sqrt{2}}{2}$ is $\frac{3\pi}{4}$, or $135°$.

8. $\frac{5\pi}{6}$, or $150°$

9. Find arctan $\sqrt{3}$.

   The only number in the restricted range $\left[-\frac{\pi}{2}, \frac{\pi}{2}\right]$ whose tangent is $\sqrt{3}$ is $\frac{\pi}{3}$, or $60°$.

10. $\frac{\pi}{6}$, or $30°$

11. Find $\cot^{-1} 1$.

    The only number in the restricted range $(0, \pi)$ whose cotangent is 1 is $\frac{\pi}{4}$, or $45°$.

12. $\frac{\pi}{6}$, or $30°$

13. Find arctan $\left[-\frac{\sqrt{3}}{3}\right]$.

    The only number in the restricted range $\left[-\frac{\pi}{2}, \frac{\pi}{2}\right]$ whose tangent is $-\frac{\sqrt{3}}{3}$ is $-\frac{\pi}{6}$, or $-30°$.

14. $-\frac{\pi}{3}$, or $-60°$

15. Find arccot (-1).

    The only number in the restricted range $(0, \pi)$ whose cotangent is -1 is $\frac{3\pi}{4}$, or $135°$.

16. $\frac{5\pi}{6}$, or $150°$

17. Find arcsec 1.

    The only number in the restricted range $\left[0, \frac{\pi}{2}\right] \cup \left[\pi, \frac{3\pi}{2}\right]$ whose secant is 1 is 0, or $0°$.

18. $\frac{\pi}{3}$, or $60°$

19. Find $\csc^{-1} 1$.

    The only number in the restricted range $\left[0, \frac{\pi}{2}\right] \cup \left[-\pi, -\frac{\pi}{2}\right]$ whose cosecant is 1 is $\frac{\pi}{2}$, or $90°$.

20. $\frac{\pi}{6}$, or $30°$

21. Find arcsin $\left[-\frac{\sqrt{2}}{2}\right]$.

    The only number in the restricted range $\left[-\frac{\pi}{2}, \frac{\pi}{2}\right]$ whose sine is $-\frac{\sqrt{2}}{2}$ is $-\frac{\pi}{4}$, or $-45°$.

22. $\frac{\pi}{6}$, or $30°$

23. Find $\cos^{-1} \frac{1}{2}$.

    The only number in the restricted range $[0, \pi]$ whose cosine is $\frac{1}{2}$ is $\frac{\pi}{3}$, or $60°$.

24. $\frac{\pi}{4}$, or $45°$

25. Find arcsin $\left[-\frac{\sqrt{3}}{2}\right]$.

    The only number in the restricted range $\left[-\frac{\pi}{2}, \frac{\pi}{2}\right]$ whose sine is $-\frac{\sqrt{3}}{2}$ is $-\frac{\pi}{3}$, or $-60°$.

26. $-\frac{\pi}{6}$, or $-30°$

27. Find $\cos^{-1} \left[-\frac{1}{2}\right]$.

    The only number in the restricted range $[0, \pi]$ whose cosine is $-\frac{1}{2}$ is $\frac{2\pi}{3}$, or $120°$.

28. $\frac{\pi}{2}$, or $90°$

29. Find $\tan^{-1} 1$.

    The only number in the restricted range $\left[-\frac{\pi}{2}, \frac{\pi}{2}\right]$ whose tangent is 1 is $\frac{\pi}{4}$, or $45°$.

30. 0, or $0°$

31. Find arccot $\left[-\frac{\sqrt{3}}{3}\right]$.

    The only number in the restricted range $(0, \pi)$ whose cotangent is $-\frac{\sqrt{3}}{3}$ is $\frac{2\pi}{3}$, or $120°$.

32. $\frac{5\pi}{6}$, or $150°$

33. $23.00°$

34. $74.01°$

35. $-38.31°$

36. $-60.15°$

37. $36.97°$

38. $22.10°$

39. 168.82°

40. 105.76°

41. 20.17°

42. 47.49°

43. 38.33°

44. 64.50°

45. 31.09°

46. 226.02°

47. -170.83°

    Some calculators may give
    arccsc (-6.2774) = -9.17°. To find the
    inverse function value in the restricted
    range $\left[0, \frac{\pi}{2}\right] \cup \left[-\pi, -\frac{\pi}{2}\right]$, we compute
    -180° + 9.17° = -170.83°.

48. 64.15°

49. 13.50°

50. 26.83°

51. -39.50°

52. -55.00°

53. -62.70°

54. 107.07°

55. -22.23°

56. -13.55°

57. 170.44°
    (180° - 9.56°, or 170.44°, is in the restricted
    range.)

58. 142.83°

59. 177.51°
    (180° - 2.49°, or 177.51°, is in the restricted
    range.)

60. 89.64°

61.

    $y = \sec^{-1} x$

62.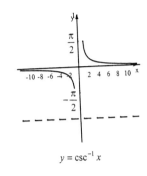

    $y = \csc^{-1} x$

63. See the answer section in the text.

64. Let x = 1. Then $\cos^{-1} 1 = 0$, but
    $(\cos 1)^{-1} \approx (0.5403)^{-1} \approx 1.8508$.

65. See the answer section in the text.

66. Let x = 1. Then $\cot^{-1} 1 = \frac{\pi}{4} \approx 0.7854$, but
    $(\cot 1)^{-1} \approx (0.6421)^{-1} \approx 1.5574$.

67. See the answer section in the text.

68. Let x = 0. Then $(\cos^{-1} 0)^2 + (\sin^{-1} 0)^2 = \left(\frac{\pi}{2}\right)^2 + 0^2 \approx 2.4674 \ne 1$.

69. We see from the triangle in the text that
    $\tan \theta = \dfrac{\text{opposite side}}{\text{adjacent side}} = \dfrac{50}{b}$. That is, θ is the
    number whose tangent is $\frac{50}{b}$, and $-\frac{\pi}{2} < \theta < \frac{\pi}{2}$, so
    $\theta = \tan^{-1} \frac{50}{b}$.

70. $\sin \theta = \dfrac{2000}{h}$, $-\frac{\pi}{2} \le \theta \le \frac{\pi}{2}$, so $\theta = \sin^{-1} \left(\dfrac{2000}{h}\right)$.

71. a) Using a calculator, we find
    $16 \tan^{-1} \frac{1}{5} - 4 \tan^{-1} \frac{1}{239} \approx 3.141592654$.

    b) This expression seems to approximate π.

Exercise Set 7.7

1. Since 0.3 is in the interval [-1, 1],
   sin (arcsin 0.3) = 0.3.

2. 0.2

3. The domain of the inverse tangent function is
   $(-\infty, \infty)$, so tan [tan^{-1} (-4.2)] = -4.2

4. -1.5

5. $\arcsin \left[\sin \frac{2\pi}{3}\right]$

   $= \arcsin \frac{\sqrt{3}}{2}$ $\qquad \left[\sin \frac{2\pi}{3} = \frac{\sqrt{3}}{2}\right]$

   $= \frac{\pi}{3}$ $\qquad \left[\text{The restricted range of the arcsin function is } \left[-\frac{\pi}{2}, \frac{\pi}{2}\right]\right.$

   Note: $\arcsin \left[\sin \frac{2\pi}{3}\right] \neq \frac{2\pi}{3}$ because $\frac{2\pi}{3}$ is not in the range of the arcsine function.

6. $\arccos \left[\cos \frac{3\pi}{2}\right] = \arccos (0) = \frac{\pi}{2}$

7. $\sin^{-1} \left[\sin \left(-\frac{3\pi}{4}\right)\right]$

   $= \sin^{-1} \left[-\frac{\sqrt{2}}{2}\right]$ $\qquad \left[\sin \left(-\frac{3\pi}{4}\right) = -\frac{\sqrt{2}}{2}\right]$

   $= -\frac{\pi}{4}$ $\qquad \left[\text{The restricted range of the arcsin function is } \left[-\frac{\pi}{2}, \frac{\pi}{2}\right]\right.$

   Note: $\sin^{-1} \left[\sin \left(-\frac{3\pi}{4}\right)\right] \neq -\frac{3\pi}{4}$ because $-\frac{3\pi}{4}$ is not in the range of the arcsine function.

8. $\cos^{-1} \left[\cos \left(-\frac{\pi}{4}\right)\right] = \cos^{-1} \left[\frac{\sqrt{2}}{2}\right] = \frac{\pi}{4}$

9. $\sin^{-1} \left[\sin \frac{\pi}{5}\right] = \frac{\pi}{5}$ because $\frac{\pi}{5}$ is in the range of the arcsine function.

10. $\frac{\pi}{7}$ $\qquad \left[\frac{\pi}{7} \text{ is in the range of } \cos^{-1}.\right]$

11. $\tan^{-1} \left[\tan \frac{2\pi}{3}\right]$

    $= \tan^{-1} (-\sqrt{3})$ $\qquad \left[\tan \frac{2\pi}{3} = -\sqrt{3}\right]$

    $= -\frac{\pi}{3}$ $\qquad \left[\text{The restricted range of the arctangent function is } \left(-\frac{\pi}{2}, \frac{\pi}{2}\right).\right]$

    Note: $\tan^{-1} \left[\tan \frac{2\pi}{3}\right] \neq \frac{2\pi}{3}$ because $\frac{2\pi}{3}$ is not in the range of the arctangent function.

12. $\frac{2\pi}{3}$ $\qquad \left[\frac{2\pi}{3} \text{ is in the range of } \cot^{-1}.\right]$

13. $\sin (\arctan \sqrt{3})$

    $= \sin \frac{\pi}{3}$

    $= \frac{\sqrt{3}}{2}$

14. $\sin \left[\arctan \frac{\sqrt{3}}{3}\right] = \sin \left[\frac{\pi}{6}\right] = \frac{1}{2}$

15. $\cos \left[\arcsin \frac{\sqrt{3}}{2}\right]$

    $= \cos \frac{\pi}{3}$

    $= \frac{1}{2}$

16. $\cos \left[\arcsin \frac{\sqrt{2}}{2}\right] = \cos \left[\frac{\pi}{4}\right] = \frac{\sqrt{2}}{2}$

17. $\tan \left[\cos^{-1} \frac{\sqrt{2}}{2}\right]$

    $= \tan \frac{\pi}{4}$

    $= 1$

18. $\tan \left[\cos^{-1} \frac{\sqrt{3}}{2}\right] = \tan \left[\frac{\pi}{6}\right] = \frac{\sqrt{3}}{3}$

19. $\cos^{-1} \left[\sin \frac{\pi}{3}\right]$

    $= \cos^{-1} \frac{\sqrt{3}}{2}$

    $= \frac{\pi}{6}$

20. $\cos^{-1} (\sin \pi) = \cos^{-1} (0) = \frac{\pi}{2}$

21. $\arcsin \left[\cos \frac{\pi}{6}\right]$

    $= \arcsin \frac{\sqrt{3}}{2}$

    $= \frac{\pi}{3}$

22. $\arcsin \left[\cos \frac{\pi}{4}\right] = \arcsin \left[\frac{\sqrt{2}}{2}\right] = \frac{\pi}{4}$

23. $\sin^{-1} \left[\tan \frac{\pi}{4}\right]$

    $= \sin^{-1} 1$

    $= \frac{\pi}{2}$

24. $\sin^{-1} \left[\tan \left(-\frac{\pi}{4}\right)\right] = \sin^{-1} (-1) = -\frac{\pi}{2}$

<u>25.</u> Find $\sin\left[\arctan\frac{x}{2}\right]$.

We draw two right triangles with legs x and 2 so that $\tan\theta = \frac{x}{2}$.

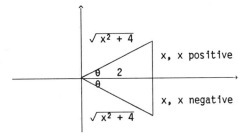

We find the length of the hypotenuse and then read off the sine ratio. In either case, we get

$$\sin\left[\arctan\frac{x}{2}\right] = \frac{x}{\sqrt{x^2 + 4}}.$$

<u>26.</u>

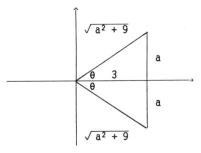

$$\sin\left[\arctan\frac{a}{3}\right] = \frac{a}{\sqrt{a^2 + 9}}$$

<u>27.</u> Find $\tan\left[\cos^{-1}\frac{3}{x}\right]$.

Since the restricted range of the inverse cosine function is $[0, \pi]$, we draw a first quadrant right triangle with one leg 3 and hypotenuse x (x > 0) so that $\cos\theta = \frac{3}{x}$.

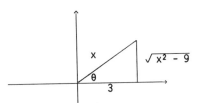

We find the length of the other leg and read off the tangent ratio.

$$\tan\left[\cos^{-1}\frac{3}{x}\right] = \frac{\sqrt{x^2 - 9}}{3}$$

<u>28.</u> Since the range of $\sin^{-1}$ is $[-\pi/2, \pi/2]$, we draw a first quadrant triangle with one leg 5 and hypotenuse y(y > 0) so that $\sin\theta = \frac{5}{y}$.

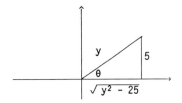

$$\cot\left[\sin^{-1}\frac{5}{y}\right] = \frac{\sqrt{y^2 - 25}}{5}.$$

<u>29.</u> Find $\cot\left[\sin^{-1}\frac{a}{b}\right]$.

We draw two right triangles with one leg a and hypotenuse of length b (b > 0) so that $\sin\theta = \frac{a}{b}$.

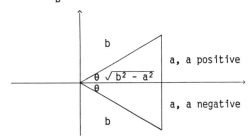

We find the length of the other leg and then read off the cotangent ratio. In either case, we get

$$\cot\left[\sin^{-1}\frac{a}{b}\right] = \frac{\sqrt{b^2 - a^2}}{a}.$$

<u>30.</u>

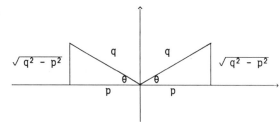

$$\tan\left[\cos^{-1}\frac{p}{q}\right] = \frac{\sqrt{q^2 - p^2}}{p}$$

<u>31.</u> Find $\cos\left[\tan^{-1}\frac{\sqrt{2}}{3}\right]$.

We wish to find the cosine of an angle whose tangent is $\frac{\sqrt{2}}{3}$.

The length of the hypotenuse is $\sqrt{11}$.

Thus, $\cos\left[\tan^{-1}\frac{\sqrt{2}}{3}\right] = \frac{3}{\sqrt{11}}$.

32.

$$\cos\left[\tan^{-1}\frac{\sqrt{3}}{4}\right] = \frac{4}{\sqrt{19}}.$$

33. Find tan (arcsin 0.1)

We wish to find the tangent of an angle whose sine is 0.1, or $\frac{1}{10}$.

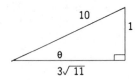

The length of the other leg is $3\sqrt{11}$.

Thus, tan (arcsin 0.1) $= \frac{1}{3\sqrt{11}}$.

34.

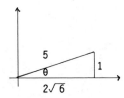

$$\tan (\arcsin 0.2) = \frac{1}{2\sqrt{6}}$$

35. Find cot [cos^{-1} (-0.2)].

We wish to find the cotangent of an angle whose cosine is -0.2, or $\frac{-2}{10}$.

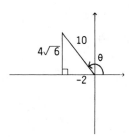

The length of the other leg is $4\sqrt{6}$.

Thus, cot $\left[\cos^{-1} (-0.2)\right] = \frac{-2}{4\sqrt{6}} = -\frac{1}{2\sqrt{6}}$.

36.

$$\cot [\cos^{-1} (-0.3)] = \frac{-3}{\sqrt{91}}, \text{ or } -\frac{3}{\sqrt{91}}$$

37. Find sin (arccot y).

We draw two right triangles with legs y and 1 so that cot $\theta = \frac{y}{1}$.

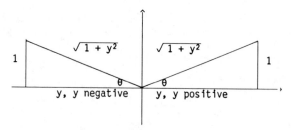

We find the length of the hypotenuse and then read off the sine ratio. In either case we get

$$\sin (\text{arccot } y) = \frac{1}{\sqrt{1 + y^2}}.$$

38. See Exercise 37. Replace y with x. Then cos (arccot x) $= \frac{x}{\sqrt{1 + x^2}}$.

39. Find cos (arctan t).

We draw two right triangles with legs t and 1 so that tan $\theta = \frac{t}{1}$.

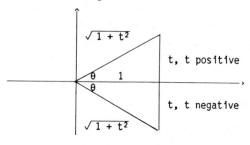

We find the length of the hypotenuse and then read off the cosine ratio. In either case we get

$$\cos (\arctan t) = \frac{1}{\sqrt{1 + t^2}}$$

40. See the drawing in Exercise 39.

$$\sin (\arctan t) = \frac{t}{\sqrt{1 + t^2}}$$

41. Find cot (sin^{-1} y).

We draw two right triangles with one leg y and hypotenuse 1 so that sin $\theta = \frac{y}{1}$.

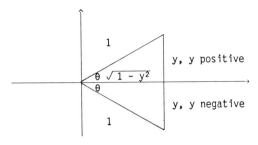

We find the length of the other leg and then read off the cotangent ratio. In either case we get

$$\cot(\sin^{-1} y) = \frac{\sqrt{1 - y^2}}{y}.$$

42.

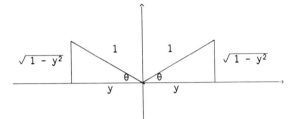

$$\tan(\cos^{-1} y) = \frac{\sqrt{1 - y^2}}{y}$$

43. Find $\sin(\cos^{-1} x)$.

We draw two right triangles with one leg x and hypotenuse 1 so that $\cos\theta = \frac{x}{1}$.

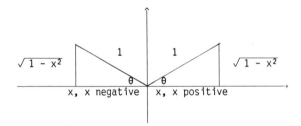

We find the length of the other leg and then read off the sine ratio. In either case we get

$$\sin(\cos^{-1} x) = \frac{\sqrt{1 - x^2}}{1}, \text{ or } \sqrt{1 - x^2}.$$

44.

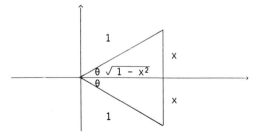

$$\cos(\sin^{-1} x) = \sqrt{1 - x^2}$$

45.

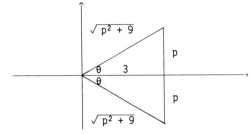

$$\tan\left(\arcsin\frac{p}{\sqrt{p^2 + 9}}\right) = \frac{p}{3}$$

46.

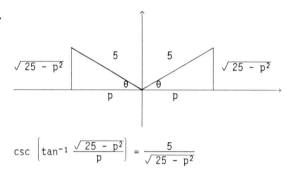

$$\csc\left(\tan^{-1}\frac{\sqrt{25 - p^2}}{p}\right) = \frac{5}{\sqrt{25 - p^2}}$$

47. $\tan\left(\frac{1}{2}\arcsin\frac{4}{5}\right)$

$= \tan\frac{\theta}{2}$ $\left(\text{Letting } \theta = \arcsin\frac{4}{5}\right)$

$= \dfrac{\sin\theta}{1 + \cos\theta}$ (Half-angle identity)

$= \dfrac{\frac{4}{5}}{1 + \frac{3}{5}}$

$= \dfrac{\frac{4}{5}}{\frac{8}{5}}$

$= \dfrac{1}{2}$

48. $\tan\left(\frac{1}{2}\arcsin\frac{1}{2}\right)$

$= \tan\frac{\theta}{2}$ $\left(\text{Letting } \theta = \arcsin\frac{1}{2}\right)$

$= \dfrac{\sin\theta}{1 + \cos\theta}$

$= \dfrac{\frac{1}{2}}{1 + \frac{\sqrt{3}}{2}}$

$= \dfrac{1}{2 + \sqrt{3}} = \dfrac{2 - \sqrt{3}}{1} = 2 - \sqrt{3}$

49. $\cos \left[\frac{1}{2} \arcsin \frac{1}{2}\right]$

$= \cos \frac{\theta}{2}$ $\left[\text{Letting } \theta = \arcsin \frac{1}{2}\right]$

$= \sqrt{\dfrac{1 + \cos \theta}{2}}$ (Half-angle identity)
(θ is a 1st quadrant angle)

$= \sqrt{\dfrac{1 + \frac{\sqrt{3}}{2}}{2}}$

$= \sqrt{\dfrac{2 + \sqrt{3}}{4}}$

$= \dfrac{\sqrt{2 + \sqrt{3}}}{2}$

50. $\cos \left[\frac{1}{2} \arcsin \frac{\sqrt{3}}{2}\right] = \cos \left[\frac{1}{2} \cdot 60°\right] = \frac{\sqrt{3}}{2}$

51. $\sin \left[2 \cos^{-1} \frac{3}{5}\right]$

$= \sin 2\theta$ $\left[\text{Letting } \theta = \cos^{-1} \frac{3}{5}\right]$

$= 2 \sin \theta \cos \theta$ (Double-angle identity)

$= 2 \cdot \frac{4}{5} \cdot \frac{3}{5}$

$= \frac{24}{25}$

52. $\sin \left[2 \cos^{-1} \frac{1}{2}\right] = \sin (2 \cdot 60°) = \frac{\sqrt{3}}{2}$

53. $\cos \left[2 \sin^{-1} \frac{5}{13}\right]$

$= \cos 2\theta$ $\left[\text{Letting } \theta = \sin^{-1} \frac{5}{13}\right]$

$= 1 - 2 \sin^2\theta$ (Double-angle identity)

$= 1 - 2 \cdot \left[\frac{5}{13}\right]^2$

$= 1 - \frac{50}{169}$

$= \frac{119}{169}$

54. $\cos \left[2 \cos^{-1} \frac{4}{5}\right] = \cos (2\theta)$, where $\cos \theta = \frac{4}{5}$;

then $\cos 2\theta = 2 \cos^2 \theta - 1 = 2\left(\frac{4}{5}\right)^2 - 1 = \frac{7}{25}$.

55. $\sin \left[\sin^{-1} \frac{1}{2} + \cos^{-1} \frac{3}{5}\right]$

$= \sin (u + v)$ $\left[\begin{array}{l}\text{Letting } u = \sin^{-1} \frac{1}{2} \text{ and} \\ v = \cos^{-1} \frac{3}{5}\end{array}\right]$

$= \sin u \cos v + \cos u \sin v$ (Sum identity)

$= \sin \left[\sin^{-1} \frac{1}{2}\right] \cdot \cos \left[\cos^{-1} \frac{3}{5}\right] +$
$\quad\quad \cos \left[\sin^{-1} \frac{1}{2}\right] \cdot \sin \left[\cos^{-1} \frac{3}{5}\right]$

$= \frac{1}{2} \cdot \frac{3}{5} + \frac{\sqrt{3}}{2} \cdot \frac{4}{5}$

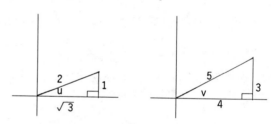

$= \frac{3 + 4\sqrt{3}}{10}$

56. $\sin \left[\sin^{-1} \frac{1}{2} - \cos^{-1} \frac{4}{5}\right] = \sin (u - v)$, where

$u = \sin^{-1} \frac{1}{2}$ and $v = \cos^{-1} \frac{4}{5}$.

$\sin (u - v) = \sin u \cos v - \cos u \sin v$

$= \frac{1}{2} \cdot \frac{4}{5} - \frac{\sqrt{3}}{2} \cdot \frac{3}{5}$

$= \frac{4 - 3\sqrt{3}}{10}$.

57. $\cos \left[\sin^{-1} \frac{\sqrt{2}}{2} + \cos^{-1} \frac{3}{5}\right]$

$= \cos (u + v)$ $\left[\begin{array}{l}\text{Letting } u = \sin^{-1} \frac{\sqrt{2}}{2} \text{ and} \\ v = \cos^{-1} \frac{3}{5}\end{array}\right]$

$= \cos u \cos v - \sin u \sin v$ (Sum identity)

$= \cos \left[\sin^{-1} \frac{\sqrt{2}}{2}\right] \cdot \cos \left[\cos^{-1} \frac{3}{5}\right] -$
$\quad\quad \sin \left[\sin^{-1} \frac{\sqrt{2}}{2}\right] \cdot \sin \left[\cos^{-1} \frac{3}{5}\right]$

$= \frac{\sqrt{2}}{2} \cdot \frac{3}{5} - \frac{\sqrt{2}}{2} \cdot \frac{4}{5}$

$= -\frac{\sqrt{2}}{10}$

58. $\cos\left[\sin^{-1}\frac{4}{5} - \cos^{-1}\frac{1}{2}\right] = \cos(u - v)$, where
    $u = \sin^{-1}\frac{4}{5}$ and $v = \cos^{-1}\frac{1}{2}$.

$\cos(u - v) = \cos u \cos v + \sin u \sin v$

$\qquad = \frac{3}{5} \cdot \frac{1}{2} + \frac{4}{5} \cdot \frac{\sqrt{3}}{2}$

$\qquad = \frac{3 + 4\sqrt{3}}{10}$.

59.

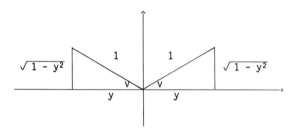

$\sin(\sin^{-1} x + \cos^{-1} y)$
$= \sin(u + v) \qquad$ (Letting $u = \sin^{-1} x$ and
$\qquad\qquad\qquad\qquad v = \cos^{-1} y$)
$= \sin u \cos v + \cos u \sin v \qquad$ (Sum identity)
$= \sin(\sin^{-1} x) \cdot \cos(\cos^{-1} y) +$
$\qquad\qquad \cos(\sin^{-1} x) \cdot \sin(\cos^{-1} y)$
$= x \cdot y + \sqrt{1 - x^2} \cdot \sqrt{1 - y^2}$
$= xy + \sqrt{(1 - x^2)(1 - y^2)}$

60. See the drawings in Exercise 59.

$\sin(\sin^{-1} x - \cos^{-1} y) = \sin(u - v)$, where
$u = \sin^{-1} x$ and $v = \cos^{-1} y$.

$\sin(u - v) = \sin u \cos v - \cos u \sin v$

$\qquad = \frac{x}{1} \cdot \frac{y}{1} - \frac{\sqrt{1 - x^2}}{1} \cdot \frac{\sqrt{1 - y^2}}{1}$

$\qquad = xy - \sqrt{(1 - x^2)(1 - y^2)}$.

61. See the drawings in Exercise 59.

$\cos(\sin^{-1} x + \cos^{-1} y)$
$= \cos(u + v) \qquad$ (Letting $u = \sin^{-1} x$ and
$\qquad\qquad\qquad\qquad v = \cos^{-1} y$)
$= \cos u \cos v - \sin u \sin v \qquad$ (Sum identity)
$= \cos(\sin^{-1} x) \cdot \cos(\cos^{-1} y) -$
$\qquad\qquad \sin(\sin^{-1} x) \cdot \sin(\cos^{-1} y)$
$= \sqrt{1 - x^2} \cdot y - x \cdot \sqrt{1 - y^2}$
$= y\sqrt{1 - x^2} - x\sqrt{1 - y^2}$

62. See the drawings in Exercise 59.

$\cos(\sin^{-1} x - \cos^{-1} y) = \cos(u - v)$, where
$u = \sin^{-1} x$ and $v = \cos^{-1} y$.

$\cos(u - v) = \cos u \cos v + \sin u \sin v$

$\qquad = y\sqrt{1 - x^2} + x\sqrt{1 - y^2}$.

63.

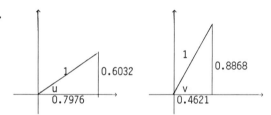

$\sin(\sin^{-1} 0.6032 + \cos^{-1} 0.4621)$
$= \sin(u + v) \qquad$ (Letting $u = \sin^{-1} 0.6032$ and
$\qquad\qquad\qquad\qquad v = \cos^{-1} 0.4621$)
$= \sin u \cos v + \cos u \sin v$
$= \sin(\sin^{-1} 0.6032) \cdot \cos(\cos^{-1} 0.4621) +$
$\qquad \cos(\sin^{-1} 0.6032) \cdot \sin(\cos^{-1} 0.4621)$
$\approx 0.6032 \cdot 0.4621 + 0.7976 \cdot 0.8868$
≈ 0.9861

64.

$\cos(\sin^{-1} 0.7325 - \cos^{-1} 0.4838) = \cos(u - v)$,
where $u = \sin^{-1} 0.7325$ and $v = \cos^{-1} 0.4838$.

$\cos(u - v) = \cos u \cos v + \sin u \sin v$
$\qquad\qquad \approx 0.6808 \cdot 0.4838 + 0.7325 \cdot 0.8752$
$\qquad\qquad \approx 0.9705$

65. See the first drawing in Exercise 59.

$\sin\theta = x$, $\cos\theta = \sqrt{1 - x^2}$, $\tan\theta = \frac{x}{\sqrt{1 - x^2}}$,

$\cot\theta = \frac{\sqrt{1 - x^2}}{x}$, $\sec\theta = \frac{1}{\sqrt{1 - x^2}}$, $\csc\theta = \frac{1}{x}$

66. See the drawing in Exercise 43.

$\sin \theta = \sqrt{1 - x^2}$, $\cos \theta = x$, $\tan \theta = \dfrac{\sqrt{1 - x^2}}{x}$,

$\cot \theta = \dfrac{x}{\sqrt{1 - x^2}}$, $\sec \theta = \dfrac{1}{x}$, $\csc \theta = \dfrac{1}{\sqrt{1 - x^2}}$

67.

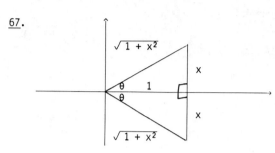

$\sin \theta = \dfrac{x}{\sqrt{1 + x^2}}$, $\cos \theta = \dfrac{1}{\sqrt{1 + x^2}}$, $\tan \theta = x$,

$\cot \theta = \dfrac{1}{x}$, $\sec \theta = \sqrt{1 + x^2}$, $\csc \theta = \dfrac{\sqrt{1 + x^2}}{x}$

68. See the drawing in Exercise 37. Replace y with x.

$\sin \theta = \dfrac{1}{\sqrt{1 + x^2}}$, $\cos \theta = \dfrac{x}{\sqrt{1 + x^2}}$, $\tan \theta = \dfrac{1}{x}$,

$\cot \theta = x$, $\sec \theta = \dfrac{\sqrt{1 + x^2}}{x}$, $\csc \theta = \sqrt{1 + x^2}$

69. See the answer section in the text.

70.

$\tan^{-1} x + \cot^{-1} x$	$\dfrac{\pi}{2}$
$\sin (\tan^{-1} x + \cot^{-1} x)$	$\sin \dfrac{\pi}{2}$
$\sin (\tan^{-1} x) \cos (\cot^{-1} x) +$ $\cos (\tan^{-1} x) \sin (\cot^{-1} x)$	1
$\dfrac{x}{\sqrt{1 + x^2}} \cdot \dfrac{x}{\sqrt{1 + x^2}} + \dfrac{1}{\sqrt{1 + x^2}} \cdot \dfrac{1}{\sqrt{1 + x^2}}$	
$\dfrac{x^2 + 1}{x^2 + 1}$	
1	

71. See the answer section in the text.

72.

$\tan^{-1} x$	$\sin^{-1} \dfrac{x}{\sqrt{x^2 + 1}}$
$\sin (\tan^{-1} x)$	$\sin \left[\sin^{-1} \dfrac{x}{\sqrt{x^2 + 1}} \right]$
$\dfrac{x}{\sqrt{x^2 + 1}}$	$\dfrac{x}{\sqrt{x^2 + 1}}$

73. See the answer section in the text.

74.

$\arccos x$	$\arctan \dfrac{\sqrt{1 - x^2}}{x}$
$\cos (\arccos x)$	$\cos \left[\arctan \dfrac{\sqrt{1 - x^2}}{x} \right]$
x	x

75.

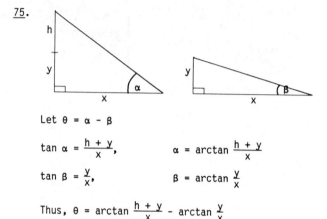

Let $\theta = \alpha - \beta$

$\tan \alpha = \dfrac{h + y}{x}$, $\alpha = \arctan \dfrac{h + y}{x}$

$\tan \beta = \dfrac{y}{x}$, $\beta = \arctan \dfrac{y}{x}$

Thus, $\theta = \arctan \dfrac{h + y}{x} - \arctan \dfrac{y}{x}$

76. From Exercise 75 we have

$\theta = \tan^{-1} \dfrac{h + y}{x} - \tan^{-1} \dfrac{y}{x}$; then

$\theta = \tan^{-1} \dfrac{25 + 7}{20} - \tan^{-1} \dfrac{7}{20}$

$\approx 57.99° - 19.29°$

$= 38.7°$.

Exercise Set 7.8

---

1. $\sin x = \dfrac{\sqrt{3}}{2}$

   Since $\sin x$ is positive, the solutions are to be found in the first and second quadrants.

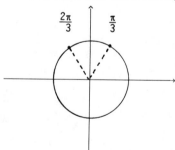

   The solutions are $\dfrac{\pi}{3} + 2k\pi$ or $\dfrac{2\pi}{3} + 2k\pi$, where k is any integer.

2. The solutions are in the first and fourth quadrants. They are $\dfrac{\pi}{6} + 2k\pi$ or $\dfrac{11\pi}{6} + 2k\pi$, where k is any integer.

3. $\cos x = \dfrac{1}{\sqrt{2}}$, or $\dfrac{\sqrt{2}}{2}$

Since cos x is positive, the solutions are to be found in the first and fourth quadrants.

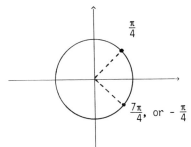

The solutions are $\dfrac{\pi}{4} + 2k\pi$ or $\dfrac{7\pi}{4} + 2k\pi$, where k is any integer; this can also be expressed as $\dfrac{\pi}{4} + 2k\pi$ or $-\dfrac{\pi}{4} + 2k\pi$ where k is any integer.

4. The solutions are in the first and third quadrants. They are $\dfrac{\pi}{3} + k\pi$, where k is any integer.

5. $\sin x = 0.3448$

Using a calculator, we find the reference angle is 20.17°, or 20° 10'. Since sin x is positive, the solutions are to be found in the first and second quadrants.

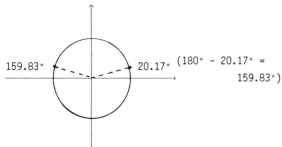

$(180° - 20.17° = 159.83°)$

The solutions are 20.17° + k·360° or 159.83° + k·360°, where k is any integer.

6. Using a calculator, we find the reference angle is 50.16°. The solutions are in the first and fourth quadrants. They are 50.16° + k·360° or 309.84° + k·360°, where k is any integer.

7. $\cos x = -0.5495$

Using a calculator, we find the reference angle is 56.67°. Since cos x is negative, the solutions are in the second and third quadrants.

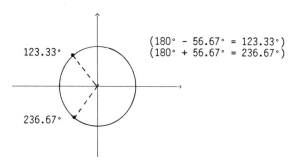

$(180° - 56.67° = 123.33°)$
$(180° + 56.67° = 236.67°)$

The solutions in [0°, 360°) are 123.33° and 236.67°.

8. Using a calculator, we find the reference angle is 25.33°. The solutions are in the third and fourth quadrants. They are 180° + 25.33°, or 205.33° and 360° - 25.33°, or 334.67°.

9. $2 \sin x + \sqrt{3} = 0$

$2 \sin x = -\sqrt{3}$

$\sin x = -\dfrac{\sqrt{3}}{2}$

There are two points on the unit circle for which the sine is $-\dfrac{\sqrt{3}}{2}$.

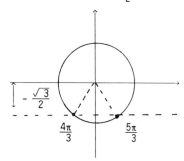

The solutions in [0, 2π) are $\dfrac{4\pi}{3}$ and $\dfrac{5\pi}{3}$.

10. $\sqrt{3} \tan x + 1 = 0$

$\tan x = -\dfrac{1}{\sqrt{3}}$

$x = \dfrac{5\pi}{6}, \dfrac{11\pi}{6}$

11. $2 \tan x + 3 = 0$

$2 \tan x = -3$

$\tan x = -1.5$

Using a calculator, we find the reference angle is 56.31°. Since tan x is negative, the solutions are in the second and fourth quadrants.

$(180° - 56.31° = 123.69°)$
$(360° - 56.31° = 303.69°)$

The solutions in $[0°, 360°)$ are 123.69° and 303.69°.

12. $4 \sin x - 1 = 0$

$\sin x = \frac{1}{4}$

$x = 14.48°, 165.52°$

13. $4 \sin^2 x - 1 = 0$

$4 \sin^2 x = 1$

$\sin^2 x = \frac{1}{4}$

$\sin x = \pm \frac{1}{2}$

Use the unit circle to find those numbers having a sine of $\frac{1}{2}$ or $-\frac{1}{2}$.

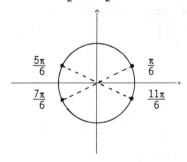

The solutions in $[0, 2\pi)$ are $\frac{\pi}{6}$, $\frac{5\pi}{6}$, $\frac{7\pi}{6}$, and $\frac{11\pi}{6}$.

14. $2 \cos^2 x = 1$

$\cos x = \pm \frac{\sqrt{2}}{2}$

$x = \frac{\pi}{4}, \frac{3\pi}{4}, \frac{5\pi}{4}, \frac{7\pi}{4}$.

15. $\cot^2 x - 3 = 0$

$\cot^2 x = 3$

$\cot x = \pm \sqrt{3}$

Use the unit circle to find those numbers having a cotangent of $\sqrt{3}$ or $-\sqrt{3}$.

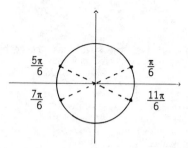

The solutions in $[0, 2\pi)$ are $\frac{\pi}{6}$, $\frac{5\pi}{6}$, $\frac{7\pi}{6}$, and $\frac{11\pi}{6}$.

16. $\csc^2 x - 4 = 0$

$\frac{1}{\sin^2 x} - 4 = 0$

$\sin^2 x = \frac{1}{4}$

$\sin x = \pm \frac{1}{2}$

$x = \frac{\pi}{6}, \frac{5\pi}{6}, \frac{7\pi}{6}, \frac{11\pi}{6}$

17. $2 \sin^2 x + \sin x = 1$

$2 \sin^2 x + \sin x - 1 = 0$

$(2 \sin x - 1)(\sin x + 1) = 0$

$2 \sin x - 1 = 0$ or $\sin x + 1 = 0$

$2 \sin x = 1$ or $\sin x = -1$

$\sin x = \frac{1}{2}$ or $\sin x = -1$

Use a unit circle to find those numbers having a sine of $\frac{1}{2}$ or -1.

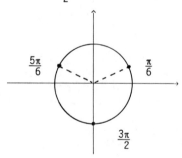

The solutions in $[0, 2\pi)$ are $\frac{\pi}{6}$, $\frac{5\pi}{6}$, and $\frac{3\pi}{2}$.

18. $(2 \cos x + 1)(\cos x + 1) = 0$ gives

$\cos x = -\frac{1}{2}$ with $x = \frac{2\pi}{3}, \frac{4\pi}{3}$ and

$\cos x = -1$ with $x = \pi$.

19.
$$\cos^2 x + 2 \cos x = 3$$
$$\cos^2 x + 2 \cos x - 3 = 0$$
$$(\cos x + 3)(\cos x - 1) = 0$$

$\cos x + 3 = 0$ or $\cos x - 1 = 0$

$\cos x = -3$ or $\cos x = 1$

Since cosines are never less than -1, cos x = -3 has no solution. There is one point on the unit circle for which the cosine is 1. Thus the solution in [0, 2π) is 0.

20. $(2 \sin x - 3)(\sin x + 1) = 0$ gives

$\sin x = \dfrac{3}{2}$ with no solution and

$\sin x = -1$ with $x = \dfrac{3\pi}{2}$.

21.
$$4 \sin^3 x - \sin x = 0$$
$$\sin x(4 \sin^2 x - 1) = 0$$
$$\sin x(2 \sin x + 1)(2 \sin x - 1) = 0$$

$\sin x = 0$ or $2 \sin x + 1 = 0$

$\sin x = 0$ or $\sin x = -\dfrac{1}{2}$

$x = 0, \pi$ or $x = \dfrac{7\pi}{6}, \dfrac{11\pi}{6}$

or $2 \sin x - 1 = 0$

or $\sin x = \dfrac{1}{2}$

or $x = \dfrac{\pi}{6}, \dfrac{5\pi}{6}$

The solutions in [0, 2π) are $0, \dfrac{\pi}{6}, \dfrac{5\pi}{6}, \pi, \dfrac{7\pi}{6},$ and $\dfrac{11\pi}{6}$.

22. $(\cos x)(2 \cos x - \sqrt{3}) = 0$ gives

$\cos x = 0$ with $x = \dfrac{\pi}{2}, \dfrac{3\pi}{2}$ and

$\cos x = \dfrac{\sqrt{3}}{2}$ with $x = \dfrac{\pi}{6}, \dfrac{11\pi}{6}$.

23.
$$2 \sin^2 \theta + 7 \sin \theta = 4$$
$$2 \sin^2 \theta + 7 \sin \theta - 4 = 0$$
$$(2 \sin \theta - 1)(\sin \theta + 4) = 0$$

$2 \sin \theta - 1 = 0$ or $\sin \theta + 4 = 0$

$\sin \theta = \dfrac{1}{2}$ or $\sin \theta = -4$

$\theta = \dfrac{\pi}{6}, \dfrac{5\pi}{6}$ Since sines are never less than -1, sin θ = -4 has no solution.

The solutions in [0, 2π) are $\dfrac{\pi}{6}$ and $\dfrac{5\pi}{6}$.

24. $(2 \sin \theta - 1)(\sin \theta - 2) = 0$ gives

$\sin \theta = \dfrac{1}{2}$ with $\theta = \dfrac{\pi}{6}, \dfrac{5\pi}{6}$ and

$\sin \theta = 2$ with no solution.

25.
$$6 \cos^2 \phi + 5 \cos \phi + 1 = 0$$
$$(3 \cos \phi + 1)(2 \cos \phi + 1) = 0$$

$3 \cos \phi + 1 = 0$ or $2 \cos \phi + 1 = 0$

$\cos \phi = -\dfrac{1}{3}$ or $\cos \phi = -\dfrac{1}{2}$

$\phi = 109.47°, 250.53°,$ or $\phi = 120°, 240°$

The solutions in [0, 360°) are 109.47°, 120°, 240°, 250.53°.

26. $(2 \sin \phi - 1)(\sin \phi + 1) = 0$ gives

$\sin \phi = \dfrac{1}{2}$ with $\phi = \dfrac{\pi}{6}, \dfrac{5\pi}{6}$ and

$\sin \phi = -1$ with $\phi = \dfrac{3\pi}{2}$.

27.
$$2 \sin t \cos t + 2 \sin t - \cos t - 1 = 0$$
$$2 \sin t(\cos t + 1) - (\cot t + 1) = 0$$
$$(2 \sin t - 1)(\cos t + 1) = 0$$

$2 \sin t - 1 = 0$ or $\cos t + 1 = 0$

$\sin t = \dfrac{1}{2}$ or $\cos t = -1$

$t = \dfrac{\pi}{6}, \dfrac{5\pi}{6}$ or $t = \pi$

The solutions in [0, 2π) are $\dfrac{\pi}{6}, \dfrac{5\pi}{6},$ and π.

28. $(2 \sin t + 1)(\tan t - 1) = 0$ gives

$\sin t = -\dfrac{1}{2}$ with $t = \dfrac{7\pi}{6}, \dfrac{11\pi}{6}$ and

$\tan t = 1$ with $t = \dfrac{\pi}{4}, \dfrac{5\pi}{4}$.

29.
$$\cos 2x \sin x + \sin x = 0$$
$$(1 - 2 \sin^2 x)\sin x + \sin x = 0$$
$$\sin x - 2 \sin^3 x + \sin x = 0$$
$$-2 \sin^3 x + 2 \sin x = 0$$
$$2 \sin x(1 - \sin^2 x) = 0$$

$2 \sin x = 0$ or $1 - \sin^2 x = 0$

$\sin x = 0$ or $\sin^2 x = 1$

$x = 0, \pi$ or $\sin x = \pm 1$

$x = 0, \pi$ or $x = \dfrac{\pi}{2}, \dfrac{3\pi}{2}$

The solutions in [0, 2π) are $0, \dfrac{\pi}{2}, \pi,$ and $\dfrac{3\pi}{2}$.

30. $2 \sin x \cos^2 x - \sin x = 0$ or
$\sin x(2 \cos^2 x - 1) = 0$ gives

$\sin x = 0$ with $x = 0, \pi$ and

$\cos x = \pm \dfrac{\sqrt{2}}{2}$ with $x = \dfrac{\pi}{4}, \dfrac{3\pi}{4}, \dfrac{5\pi}{4}, \dfrac{7\pi}{4}$.

31. $5 \sin^2 x - 8 \sin x = 3$

$5 \sin^2 x - 8 \sin x - 3 = 0$

$\sin x = \dfrac{8 \pm \sqrt{64 + 60}}{10}$ (Using the quadratic formula)

$\sin x = \dfrac{8 \pm \sqrt{124}}{10}$

$\sin x \approx -0.31355$ or $\sin x \approx 1.91355$

Since sines are never greater than 1, the second equation has no solution. Using the first equation, we find the reference angle is 18.27°. Since sin x is negative, the solutions are to be found in the third and fourth quadrants. The solutions are 198.27° and 341.73°.

32. $\cos^2 x + 6 \cos x + 4 = 0$

$\cos x = \dfrac{-6 \pm \sqrt{20}}{2}$

$\cos x \approx -0.7639$ or $\cos x \approx -5.2361$

$\cos x = -5.2361$ gives no solution.

$\cos x = -0.7639$ gives $x = 139.81°$ or

$\quad x = 220.19°.$

33. $2 \tan^2 x = 3 \tan x + 7$

$2 \tan^2 x - 3 \tan x - 7 = 0$

$\tan x = \dfrac{3 \pm \sqrt{9 + 56}}{4}$ (Using the quadratic formula)

$\tan x = \dfrac{3 \pm \sqrt{65}}{4}$

$\tan x \approx -1.2656$ or $\tan x \approx 2.7656$

Using the first equation, we find the reference angle is 51.69°. Since tan x is negative, the solutions will be found in the second and fourth quadrants. The solutions of tan x = -1.2656 are 128.31° and 308.31°.

Using the second equation, we find the reference angle is 70.12°. Since tan x is positive, the solutions will be found in the first and third quadrants. The solutions of tan x = 2.7656 are 70.12° and 250.12°.

34. $3 \sin^2 x = 3 \sin x + 2$

$3 \sin^2 x - 3 \sin x - 2 = 0$

$\sin x = \dfrac{3 \pm \sqrt{33}}{6}$

$\sin x \approx 1.4574$ or $\sin x \approx -0.4574$

$\sin x = 1.4574$ gives no solution.

$\sin x = -0.4574$ gives $x = 207.22°$

$\quad$ or $x = 332.78°$

35. $7 = \cot^2 x + 4 \cot x$

$0 = \cot^2 x + 4 \cot x - 7$

$\cot x = \dfrac{-4 \pm \sqrt{16 + 28}}{2}$ (Using the quadratic formula)

$\cot x = \dfrac{-4 \pm \sqrt{44}}{2}$

$\cot x \approx 1.3166$ or $\cot x \approx -5.3166$

Using the first equation, we find the reference angle is 37.22°. Since cot x is positive, the solutions will be found in the first and third quadrants. The solutions of cot x = 1.3166 are 37.22° and 217.22°.

Using the second equation, we find the reference angle is 10.65°. Since cot x is negative, the solutions will be found in the second and fourth quadrants. The solutions of cot x = -5.3166 are 169.35° and 349.35°.

36. $3 \tan^2 x + 2 \tan x = 7$

$3 \tan^2 x + 2 \tan x - 7 = 0$

$\tan x = \dfrac{-2 \pm \sqrt{88}}{6}$

$\tan x \approx 1.2301$ or $\tan x \approx -1.8968$

$\tan x = 1.2301$ gives $x = 50.89°$

$\quad$ and $x = 230.89°.$

$\tan x = -1.8968$ gives $x = 117.80°$

$\quad$ and $x = 297.80°.$

37. $|\sin x| = \dfrac{\sqrt{3}}{2}$

$\sin x = \dfrac{\sqrt{3}}{2}$ or $\sin x = -\dfrac{\sqrt{3}}{2}$

$x = \dfrac{\pi}{3}, \dfrac{2\pi}{3}$ or $x = \dfrac{4\pi}{3}, \dfrac{5\pi}{3}$

or 60°, 120°, 240°, 300°

38. $|\cos x| = \dfrac{1}{2}$ or $\cos x = \pm \dfrac{1}{2}$; then

$x = \dfrac{\pi}{3}, \dfrac{5\pi}{3}, \dfrac{2\pi}{3}, \dfrac{4\pi}{3}.$

39. $\sqrt{\tan x} = \sqrt[4]{3}$

$(\tan x)^{1/2} = 3^{1/4}$

$\quad \tan^2 x = 3$ (Raising both sides to the fourth power)

$\quad \tan x = \pm \sqrt{3}$

$\quad x = \dfrac{\pi}{3}, \dfrac{2\pi}{3}, \dfrac{4\pi}{3}, \dfrac{5\pi}{3}$

When tan x is negative $\sqrt{\tan x}$ is undefined. Thus the only solutions are $\dfrac{\pi}{3}$ and $\dfrac{4\pi}{3}$ (or 60° and 240°).

40. $(3\sqrt{\sin x} - 1)(4\sqrt{\sin x} - 1) = 0$ gives

$\sin x = \dfrac{1}{9}$ with $x = 6.38°$, 173.62° and

$\sin x = \dfrac{1}{16}$ with $x = 3.58°$, 176.42°.

41. $16 \cos^4 x - 16 \cos^2 x + 3 = 0$

$(4 \cos^2 x - 1)(4 \cos^2 x - 3) = 0$

$4 \cos^2 x - 1 = 0$ or $4 \cos^2 x - 3 = 0$

$\cos^2 x = \dfrac{1}{4}$ or $\cos^2 x = \dfrac{3}{4}$

$\cos x = \pm \dfrac{1}{2}$ or $\cos x = \pm \dfrac{\sqrt{3}}{2}$

$x = \dfrac{\pi}{3}, \dfrac{2\pi}{3},$ or $x = \dfrac{\pi}{6}, \dfrac{5\pi}{6},$

  $\dfrac{4\pi}{3}, \dfrac{5\pi}{3}$ $\dfrac{7\pi}{6}, \dfrac{11\pi}{6}$

The solutions are

$\dfrac{\pi}{6}, \dfrac{\pi}{3}, \dfrac{2\pi}{3}, \dfrac{5\pi}{6}, \dfrac{7\pi}{6}, \dfrac{4\pi}{3}, \dfrac{5\pi}{3},$ and $\dfrac{11\pi}{6}$.

or $30°, 60°, 120°, 150°, 210°, 240°, 300°,$ and $330°$.

42. $\ln (\cos x) = 0$

$\cos x = 1$

$x = 0$

43. $e^{\sin x} = 1$

$\ln e^{\sin x} = \ln 1$

$\sin x = 0$

$x = 0, \pi$

44. $\sin (\ln x) = -1$

$\ln x = \dfrac{3\pi}{2}$

$x = e^{3\pi/2}$

45. $e^{\ln \sin x} = 1$

$\sin x = 1$

$x = \dfrac{\pi}{2}$

46. a) See Exercise 69, Exercise Set 7.6.

  b) $\theta = \tan^{-1} \dfrac{50}{40} = \tan^{-1} 1.25 \approx 51.34°$

47. a) We make a drawing.

  $\sin \theta = \dfrac{\text{opposite side}}{\text{hypotenuse}} = \dfrac{2000}{h}$

  b) $\sin \theta = \dfrac{2000}{3000}$ (Substituting)

    $\theta = \sin^{-1} \dfrac{2000}{3000} \approx 41.81°$

48.

x	$\sin x$	$\tan \dfrac{x}{2}$
0	0	0
$\dfrac{\pi}{4}$	0.7	0.4
$\dfrac{\pi}{2}$	1	1
$\dfrac{3\pi}{4}$	0.7	2.4
$\dfrac{5\pi}{4}$	-0.7	-2.4
$\dfrac{3\pi}{2}$	-1	-1
$\dfrac{7\pi}{4}$	-0.7	-0.4
2π	0	0
$\vdots$	$\vdots$	$\vdots$

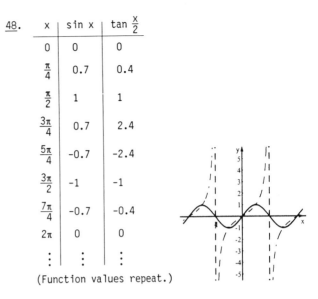

(Function values repeat.)

From the graph it is clear that $\sin x$ and $\tan \dfrac{x}{2}$ have equal values at $x = k \cdot 2\pi$ and $x = \dfrac{\pi}{2} + k \cdot \pi$ where k is any integer.

Exercise Set 7.9

1. $\tan x \sin x - \tan x = 0$

  $\tan x(\sin x - 1) = 0$

$\tan x = 0$ or $\sin x - 1 = 0$

  $x = 0, \pi$ or $\sin x = 1$

              $x = \dfrac{\pi}{2}$

The value $\dfrac{\pi}{2}$ does not check, but the other values do. Thus the solutions in $[0, 2\pi)$ are 0 and π.

2. $\sin x (2 \cos x + 1) = 0$ gives

$\sin x = 0$ with $x = 0, \pi$ and

$\cos x = -\dfrac{1}{2}$ with $x = \dfrac{2\pi}{3}, \dfrac{4\pi}{3}$.

All values check.

3. $2 \sec x \tan x + 2 \sec x + \tan x + 1 = 0$

  $2 \sec x(\tan x + 1) + (\tan x + 1) = 0$

    $(2 \sec x + 1)(\tan x + 1) = 0$

$2 \sec x + 1 = 0$ or $\tan x + 1 = 0$

  $\sec x = -\dfrac{1}{2}$ or $\tan x = -1$

  $\cos x = -2$ $x = \dfrac{3\pi}{4}, \dfrac{7\pi}{4}$

  No solution

Both values check. The solutions in $[0, 2\pi)$ are $\dfrac{3\pi}{4}$ and $\dfrac{7\pi}{4}$.

4. $(2 \cos x - 1)(\csc x - 2) = 0$ gives

$\cos x = \frac{1}{2}$ with $x = \frac{\pi}{3}, \frac{5\pi}{3}$ and

$\sin x = \frac{1}{2}$ with $x = \frac{\pi}{6}, \frac{5\pi}{6}$.

All values check.

5. $\sin 2x - \cos x = 0$

$2 \sin x \cos x - \cos x = 0$

$\cos x(2 \sin x - 1) = 0$

$\cos x = 0$ or $2 \sin x - 1 = 0$

$x = \frac{\pi}{2}, \frac{3\pi}{2}$ or $\sin x = \frac{1}{2}$

$x = \frac{\pi}{6}, \frac{5\pi}{6}$

All values check. The solutions in $[0, 2\pi)$ are $\frac{\pi}{6}, \frac{\pi}{2}, \frac{5\pi}{6}$, and $\frac{3\pi}{2}$.

6. $(1 - 2 \sin^2 x) - \sin x - 1 = 0$ or

$(\sin x)(2 \sin x + 1) = 0$ gives

$\sin x = 0$ with $x = 0, \pi$ and

$\sin x = -\frac{1}{2}$ with $x = \frac{7\pi}{6}, \frac{11\pi}{6}$.

All values check.

7. $\sin 2x \sin x - \cos x = 0$

$2 \sin x \cos x \cdot \sin x - \cos x = 0$

$\cos x(2 \sin^2 x - 1) = 0$

$\cos x = 0$ or $2 \sin^2 x - 1 = 0$

$x = \frac{\pi}{2}, \frac{3\pi}{2}$ or $\sin^2 x = \frac{1}{2}$

$\sin x = \pm \frac{\sqrt{2}}{2}$

$x = \frac{\pi}{4}, \frac{3\pi}{4}, \frac{5\pi}{4}, \frac{7\pi}{4}$

All values check. The solutions in $[0, 2\pi)$ are $\frac{\pi}{4}, \frac{\pi}{2}, \frac{3\pi}{4}, \frac{5\pi}{4}, \frac{3\pi}{2}, \frac{7\pi}{4}$.

8. $(2 \sin x \cos x) \cos x - \sin x = 0$ or

$\sin x (2 \cos^2 x - 1) = 0$ gives

$\sin x = 0$ with $x = 0, \pi$ and

$\cos x = \pm \frac{\sqrt{2}}{2}$ with $x = \frac{\pi}{4}, \frac{7\pi}{4}, \frac{3\pi}{4}, \frac{5\pi}{4}$.

All values check.

9. $\sin 2x + 2 \sin x \cos x = 0$

$\sin 2x + \sin 2x = 0$

$2 \sin 2x = 0$

$\sin 2x = 0$

$2x = 0, \pi, 2\pi, 3\pi$

$x = 0, \frac{\pi}{2}, \pi, \frac{3\pi}{2}$

All values check. The solutions in $[0, 2\pi)$ are $0, \frac{\pi}{2}, \pi$, and $\frac{3\pi}{2}$.

10. $\sin x (\cos 2x + 1) = 0$ or $\sin x (2 \cos^2 x) = 0$

gives $\sin x = 0$ with $x = 0, \pi$ and

$\cos x = 0$ with $x = \frac{\pi}{2}, \frac{3\pi}{2}$.

All values check.

11. $\cos 2x \cos x + \sin 2x \sin x = 1$

$(1 - 2 \sin^2 x)\cos x + 2 \sin x \cos x \cdot \sin x = 1$

$\cos x - 2 \sin^2 x \cos x + 2 \sin^2 x \cos x = 1$

$\cos x = 1$

$x = 0$

The value 0 checks. The only solution in $[0, 2\pi)$ is 0.

12. $(2 \sin x \cos x) \sin x - (1 - 2 \sin^2 x)\cos x$

$= -\cos x$ or

$4 \sin^2 x \cos x = 0$ gives

$\sin x = 0$ with $x = 0, \pi$ and

$\cos x = 0$ with $x = \frac{\pi}{2}, \frac{3\pi}{2}$.

All values check.

13. $\sin 4x - 2 \sin 2x = 0$

$\sin 2(2x) - 2 \sin 2x = 0$

$2 \sin 2x \cos 2x - 2 \sin 2x = 0$

$\sin 2x(\cos 2x - 1) = 0$

$\sin 2x = 0$ or $\cos 2x - 1 = 0$

$\sin 2x = 0$ or $\cos 2x = 1$

$2x = 0, \pi, 2\pi, 3\pi$ or $2x = 0, 2\pi$

$x = 0, \frac{\pi}{2}, \pi, \frac{3\pi}{2}$ $x = 0, \pi$

All values check. The solutions in $[0, 2\pi)$ are $0, \frac{\pi}{2}, \pi$, and $\frac{3\pi}{2}$.

14. $(2 \sin 2x \cos 2x) + 2 \sin 2x = 0$ or

$\qquad 2 \sin 2x (\cos 2x + 1) = 0$ gives

$\sin 2x = 0$ with $2x = 0, \pi, 2\pi, 3\pi$

$\qquad\qquad$ or $x = 0, \frac{\pi}{2}, \pi, \frac{3\pi}{2}$ and

$\cos 2x = -1$ with $2x = \pi, 3\pi$

$\qquad\qquad$ or $x = \frac{\pi}{2}, \frac{3\pi}{2}$ (again).

All values check.

15. $\qquad\qquad \sin 2x + 2 \sin x - \cos x - 1 = 0$

$2 \sin x \cos x + 2 \sin x - \cos x - 1 = 0$

$\quad 2 \sin x(\cos x + 1) - (\cos x + 1) = 0$

$\qquad\qquad (2 \sin x - 1)(\cos x + 1) = 0$

$2 \sin x - 1 = 0$ or $\cos x + 1 = 0$

$\qquad \sin x = \frac{1}{2}$ or $\cos x = -1$

$\qquad x = \frac{\pi}{6}, \frac{5\pi}{6}$ or $\qquad\qquad x = \pi$

All values check. The solutions in $[0, 2\pi)$ are $\frac{\pi}{6}, \frac{5\pi}{6}$, and π.

16. $(2 \sin x \cos x) + \sin x + 2 \cos x + 1 = 0$ or

$\qquad\qquad (\sin x + 1)(2 \cos x + 1) = 0$ gives

$\sin x = -1$ with $x = \frac{3\pi}{2}$ and

$\cos x = -\frac{1}{2}$ with $x = \frac{2\pi}{3}, \frac{4\pi}{3}$.

All values check.

17. $\sec^2 x = 4 \tan^2 x$

$\sec^2 x = 4(\sec^2 x - 1)$

$\sec^2 x = 4 \sec^2 x - 4$

$\qquad 4 = 3 \sec^2 x$

$\qquad \frac{4}{3} = \sec^2 x$

$\pm \frac{2}{\sqrt{3}} = \sec x$

$\pm \frac{\sqrt{3}}{2} = \cos x$

$\qquad x = \frac{\pi}{6}, \frac{5\pi}{6}, \frac{7\pi}{6}, \frac{11\pi}{6}$

All values check. The solutions in $[0, 2\pi)$ are $\frac{\pi}{6}, \frac{5\pi}{6}, \frac{7\pi}{6}$, and $\frac{11\pi}{6}$.

18. $(1 + \tan^2 x) - 2 \tan^2 x = 0$ or

$\qquad\qquad 1 - \tan^2 x = 0$ gives

$\tan x = 1$ with $x = \frac{\pi}{4}, \frac{5\pi}{4}$ and

$\tan x = -1$ with $x = \frac{3\pi}{4}, \frac{7\pi}{4}$.

All values check.

19. $\qquad \sec^2 x + 3 \tan x - 11 = 0$

$(1 + \tan^2 x) + 3 \tan x - 11 = 0$

$\qquad \tan^2 x + 3 \tan x - 10 = 0$

$\qquad (\tan x + 5)(\tan x - 2) = 0$

$\tan x + 5 = 0$ or $\tan x - 2 = 0$

$\quad \tan x = -5$ or $\tan x = 2$

$\quad x = 101.31°$, or $\qquad x = 63.43°$,

$\qquad 281.31°$ $\qquad\qquad\qquad 243.43°$

All values check. The solutions in $[0, 360°)$ are $63.43°$, $101.31°$, $243.43°$, and $281.31°$.

20. $\qquad\quad \tan^2 x + 4 = 2(1 + \tan^2 x) + \tan x$ or

$(\tan x - 1)(\tan x + 2) = 0$ gives

$\tan x = 1$ with $x = 45°$, $225°$ and

$\tan x = -2$ with $x = 116.57°$, $296.57°$.

All values check.

21. $\qquad\qquad \cot x = \tan (2x - 3\pi)$

$\qquad\qquad \cot x = \dfrac{\tan 2x - \tan 3\pi}{1 + \tan 2x \tan 3\pi}$

$\qquad\qquad \cot x = \dfrac{\tan 2x - 0}{1 + \tan 2x \cdot 0}$

$\qquad\qquad \cot x = \tan 2x$

$\qquad\qquad \dfrac{1}{\tan x} = \dfrac{2 \tan x}{1 - \tan^2 x}$

$\qquad\qquad$ (In this form of the equation, x cannot be $\pi/2$ and $3\pi/2$. Therefore $\pi/2$ and $3\pi/2$ must also be checked in the original equation.)

$\quad 1 - \tan^2 x = 2 \tan^2 x$

$\qquad\qquad 1 = 3 \tan^2 x$

$\qquad\qquad \frac{1}{3} = \tan^2 x$

$\qquad \pm \frac{\sqrt{3}}{3} = \tan x$

$\frac{\pi}{6}, \frac{5\pi}{6}, \frac{7\pi}{6}, \frac{11\pi}{6} = x$

These values and also $\frac{\pi}{2}$ and $\frac{3\pi}{2}$ check. The solutions in $[0, 2\pi)$ are $\frac{\pi}{6}, \frac{\pi}{2}, \frac{5\pi}{6}, \frac{7\pi}{6}, \frac{3\pi}{2}$, and $\frac{11\pi}{6}$.

22. $\tan x = \cot 2x$ or $\tan x = \dfrac{1 - \tan^2 x}{2 \tan x}$ gives

$\tan x = \pm \dfrac{1}{\sqrt{3}}$ with $x = \frac{\pi}{6}, \frac{7\pi}{6}, \frac{5\pi}{6}, \frac{11\pi}{6}$.

All values check.

23. $\cos (\pi - x) + \sin \left(x - \frac{\pi}{2}\right) = 1$

$(-\cos x) + (-\cos x) = 1$

$-2 \cos x = 1$

$\cos x = -\frac{1}{2}$

$x = \frac{2\pi}{3}, \frac{4\pi}{3}$

Both values check. The solutions in $[0, 2\pi)$ are $\frac{2\pi}{3}$ and $\frac{4\pi}{3}$.

24. $\sin x + \sin x = 1$ gives

$\sin x = \frac{1}{2}$ with $x = \frac{\pi}{6}, \frac{5\pi}{6}$.

Both values check.

25. $\dfrac{\cos^2 x - 1}{\sin \left(\frac{\pi}{2} - x\right) - 1} = \dfrac{\sqrt{2}}{2} + 1$

$\dfrac{(\cos x + 1)(\cos x - 1)}{\cos x - 1} = \dfrac{\sqrt{2}}{2} + 1$

$\cos x + 1 = \dfrac{\sqrt{2}}{2} + 1$

$\cos x = \dfrac{\sqrt{2}}{2}$

$x = \frac{\pi}{4}, \frac{7\pi}{4}$

Both values check. The solutions in $[0, 2\pi)$ are $\frac{\pi}{4}$ and $\frac{7\pi}{4}$.

26. $\dfrac{\sin^2 x - 1}{\sin x + 1} = \dfrac{\sqrt{2}}{2} - 1$ or

$\sin x - 1 = \dfrac{\sqrt{2}}{2} - 1$ gives

$\sin x = \dfrac{\sqrt{2}}{2}$ with $x = \frac{\pi}{4}, \frac{3\pi}{4}$.

Both values check.

27. $2 \cos x + 2 \sin x = \sqrt{6}$

$\cos x + \sin x = \dfrac{\sqrt{6}}{2}$

$\cos^2 x + 2 \sin x \cos x + \sin^2 x = \dfrac{6}{4}$

$\sin 2x + 1 = \dfrac{3}{2}$

$\sin 2x = \dfrac{1}{2}$

$2x = \frac{\pi}{6}, \frac{5\pi}{6}, \frac{13\pi}{6}, \frac{17\pi}{6}$

$x = \frac{\pi}{12}, \frac{5\pi}{12}, \frac{13\pi}{12}, \frac{17\pi}{12}$

The values $\frac{13\pi}{12}$ and $\frac{17\pi}{12}$ do not check, but the other values do. The solutions in $[0, 2\pi)$ are $\frac{\pi}{12}$ and $\frac{5\pi}{12}$.

28. $\cos x + \sin x = \dfrac{\sqrt{2}}{2}$ or $(\cos x + \sin x)^2 = \dfrac{1}{2}$ or

$2 \sin x \cos x = -\dfrac{1}{2}$ or $\sin 2x = -\dfrac{1}{2}$ gives

$2x = \frac{7\pi}{6}, \frac{11\pi}{6}, \frac{19\pi}{6}, \frac{23\pi}{6}$

or $x = \frac{7\pi}{12}, \frac{11\pi}{12}, \frac{19\pi}{12}, \frac{23\pi}{12}$.

Only $\frac{7\pi}{12}$ and $\frac{23\pi}{12}$ check.

29. $\sqrt{3} \cos x - \sin x = 1$

$\sqrt{3} \cos x = 1 + \sin x$

$3 \cos^2 x = 1 + 2 \sin x + \sin^2 x$

$3(1 - \sin^2 x) = 1 + 2 \sin x + \sin^2 x$

$3 - 3 \sin^2 x = 1 + 2 \sin x + \sin^2 x$

$0 = 4 \sin^2 x + 2 \sin x - 2$

$0 = 2 \sin^2 x + \sin x - 1$

$0 = (2 \sin x - 1)(\sin x + 1)$

$2 \sin x - 1 = 0$ or $\sin x + 1 = 0$

$\sin x = \dfrac{1}{2}$ or $\sin x = -1$

$x = \frac{\pi}{6}, \frac{5\pi}{6}$ or $x = \frac{3\pi}{2}$

The value $\frac{5\pi}{6}$ does not check, but the other values do check. The solutions in $[0, 2\pi)$ are $\frac{\pi}{6}$ and $\frac{3\pi}{2}$.

30. $\cos x - \sin x = \dfrac{2}{\sqrt{2}}$ or $(\cos x - \sin x)^2 = 2$ or

$1 - 2 \sin x \cos x = 2$ gives

$\sin 2x = -1$ with $2x = \frac{3\pi}{2}, \frac{7\pi}{2}$

or $x = \frac{3\pi}{4}, \frac{7\pi}{4}$.

Only $\frac{7\pi}{4}$ checks.

31. $\sec^2 x + 2 \tan x = 6$

$1 + \tan^2 x + 2 \tan x = 6$

$\tan^2 x + 2 \tan x - 5 = 0$

$\tan x = \dfrac{-2 \pm \sqrt{4 + 20}}{2} = \dfrac{-2 \pm \sqrt{24}}{2}$

$\tan x \approx 1.4495$ or $\tan x \approx -3.4495$

Using the first equation, we find the reference angle is 0.9669 (radians). Thus the solutions of $\tan x = 1.4495$ are 0.9669 and $\pi + 0.9669$, or 4.1085.

Using the second equation, we find the reference angle is 1.2886. Thus the solutions of $\tan x = -3.4495$ are $\pi - 1.2886$, or 1.8530, and $2\pi - 1.2886$, or 4.9946.

All four values check.

32.

$$6 \tan^2 x = 5 \tan x + \sec^2 x$$
$$6 \tan^2 x = 5 \tan x + 1 + \tan^2 x$$
$$5 \tan^2 x - 5 \tan x - 1 = 0$$
$$\tan x = \frac{5 \pm \sqrt{45}}{10}$$

$\tan x \approx 1.1708$ or $\tan x \approx -0.1708$

$\tan x = 1.1708$ gives $x = 0.8639$ or $x = 4.0055$

$\tan x = -0.1708$ gives $x = 2.9724$ or $x = 6.1140$

All values check.

33.

$$3 \cos 2x + \sin x = 1$$
$$3(1 - 2 \sin^2 x) + \sin x = 1$$
$$3 - 6 \sin^2 x + \sin x = 1$$
$$0 = 6 \sin^2 x - \sin x - 2$$
$$0 = (3 \sin x - 2)(2 \sin x + 1)$$

$3 \sin x - 2 = 0$ or $2 \sin x + 1 = 0$

$\sin x = \frac{2}{3}$ or $\sin x = -\frac{1}{2}$

$x = 0.7297, 2.4119$ or $x = \frac{7\pi}{6}, \frac{11\pi}{6}$

(or 3.6652, 5.7596)

All four values check.

34.

$$5 \cos 2x + \sin x = 4$$
$$5(1 - 2 \sin^2 x) + \sin x = 4$$
$$0 = 10 \sin^2 x - \sin x - 1$$
$$\sin x = \frac{1 \pm \sqrt{41}}{20}$$

$\sin x \approx 0.3702$ or $\sin x \approx -0.2702$

$\sin x = 0.3702$ gives $x = 0.3792$ or $x = 2.7624$

$\sin x = -0.2702$ gives $x = 3.4152$ or $x = 6.0096$

All values check.

35. $T(t) = 101.6° + 3° \sin \left[\frac{\pi}{8} t \right], 0 \leqslant t \leqslant 12$

$103 = 101.6 + 3 \sin \left[\frac{\pi}{8} t \right]$ (Substituting)

$1.4 = 3 \sin \left[\frac{\pi}{8} t \right]$

$0.4667 \approx \sin \left[\frac{\pi}{8} t \right]$

$\frac{\pi}{8} t \approx 0.4855, 2.6561$ $\left[\begin{array}{l} 0 \leqslant t \leqslant 12, \text{ so} \\ 0 \leqslant \frac{\pi}{8} t \leqslant \frac{3\pi}{2} \end{array} \right]$

$t \approx 1.24, 6.76$

Both values check.

The patient's temperature was 103° at $t \approx 1.24$ days and $t \approx 6.76$ days.

36.   Note that $0 \leqslant t \leqslant 240$, so

$-10 \leqslant t - 10 \leqslant 230$ and

$\frac{\pi}{45} (-10) \leqslant \frac{\pi}{45} (t - 10) \leqslant \frac{\pi}{45} (230)$, or

$-\frac{2\pi}{9} \leqslant \frac{\pi}{45} (t - 10) \leqslant \frac{46\pi}{9}$.

$3000 = 5000 \left[\cos \frac{\pi}{45} (t - 10) \right]$

$0.6 = \cos \frac{\pi}{45} (t - 10)$

We will consider only first quadrant solutions. Solutions in the fourth quadrant represent positions south of the equator.

$\frac{\pi}{45} (t - 10) \approx 0.9273, 7.2105, 13.4937$

$t \approx 23.28$ min, 113.28 min, 203.28 min

37. $N(\phi) = 6066 - 31 \cos 2\phi$

We consider ϕ in the interval [0°, 90°] since we want latitude north.

$6040 = 6066 - 31 \cos 2\phi$ (Substituting)

$-26 = -31 \cos 2\phi$

$0.8387 \approx \cos 2\phi$ (0° $\leqslant 2\phi \leqslant$ 180°)

$2\phi \approx 33.0°$

$\phi \approx 16.5°$

The value checks.

At about 16.5° N the length of a British nautical mile is found to be 6040 ft.

38.   Using the result of Exercise 56, Exercise Set 7.4, we have $9.8 = 9.78049 (1 + 0.0005264 \sin^2 \phi + 0.000024 \sin^4 \phi)$.

We solve for 0° $\leqslant \phi \leqslant$ 90°.

$\phi \approx 37.95615°$ N

39.   Sketch a triangle having an angle θ whose cosine is $\frac{3}{5}$. Using the Pythagorean theorem we know the other leg has length 4. Then $\sin \theta = \frac{4}{5}$. Thus, $\arccos \frac{3}{5} = \arcsin \frac{4}{5}$.

$\arccos x = \arccos \frac{3}{5} - \arcsin \frac{4}{5}$

$\arccos x = 0$

$\cos 0 = x$

$1 = x$

40. $\sin^{-1} x = \tan^{-1} \frac{1}{3} + \tan^{-1} \frac{1}{2}$ or

$\sin^{-1} x = \alpha + \beta$ where $\alpha = \tan^{-1} \frac{1}{3}$, and $\beta = \tan^{-1} \frac{1}{2}$.

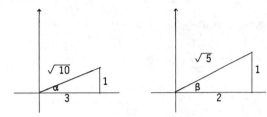

Then $x = \sin (\alpha + \beta)$

$= \sin \alpha \cos \beta + \cos \alpha \sin \beta$

$= \dfrac{1}{\sqrt{10}} \cdot \dfrac{2}{\sqrt{5}} + \dfrac{3}{\sqrt{10}} \cdot \dfrac{1}{\sqrt{5}}$

$= \dfrac{\sqrt{2}}{2}$.

41. First graph $y = \sin x - \cos x$. Then graph $y = \cot x$ on the same set of axes and find the points of intersection of the graphs. The solutions are 1.15, 5.65, -0.63, -0.513, etc.

42. $\pm 1.12, \pm 2.77, \pm 6.44, \pm 9.32$, etc.

43. $\sin x = 5 \cos x$

$\dfrac{\sin x}{\cos x} = 5$

$\tan x = 5$

$x \approx 1.3734$ (Finding x in quadrant I)

Then $\sin x \cos x = \sin (1.3734) \cos (1.3734)$

$\approx 0.1923.$

Exercise Set 8.1

1.

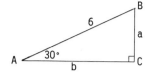

To solve this triangle find B, a, and b.

B = 90° − 30° = 60°

$\frac{a}{6}$ = sin 30°

a = 6 sin 30°

a = 3

$\frac{b}{6}$ = cos 30°

b = 6 cos 30°

b = $3\sqrt{3}$ = 5

2. A = 90° − 45° = 45°

$\frac{a}{10}$ = cos 45°

a = $5\sqrt{2}$ = 7.07

$\frac{b}{10}$ = sin 45°

b = $5\sqrt{2}$ = 7.07

3.

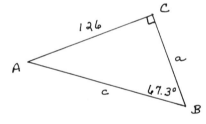

To solve this triangle, find A, a, and c.

A = 90° − 67.3° = 22.7°

cot 67.3° = $\frac{a}{126}$

a = 126 cot 67.3°

a = 53

csc 67.3° = $\frac{c}{126}$

c = 126 csc 67.3°

c = 137

4. A = 90° − 26.7° = 63.3°

cot 26.7° = $\frac{a}{0.17}$

a = 0.34

csc 26.7° = $\frac{c}{0.17}$

c = 0.38

5.

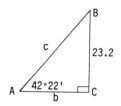

To solve this triangle find B, b, and c.

B = 90° − 42° 22' = 47° 38'

$\frac{b}{23.2}$ = cot 42° 22'

b = 23.2 cot 42° 22'

b = 25.4

$\frac{c}{23.2}$ = csc 42° 22'

c = 23.2 csc 42° 22'

c = 34.4

6. B = 90° − 28° 34' = 61° 26'

cot 28° 34' = $\frac{b}{17.3}$

b = 31.8

csc 28° 34' = $\frac{c}{17.3}$

c = 36.2

7.

To solve this triangle find B, b, and c.

B = 90° − 36° 12' = 53° 48'

$\frac{b}{27.2}$ = cot 36° 12'

b = 27.2 cot 36° 12'

b = 37.2

$\frac{c}{27.2}$ = csc 36° 12'

c = 27.2 csc 36° 12'

c = 46.1

8. B = 90° − 87° 43' = 2° 17'

cot 87° 43' = $\frac{b}{9.73}$

b = 0.39

csc 87° 43' = $\frac{c}{9.73}$

c = 9.74

9.

To solve this triangle find A, a, and c.

A = 90° - 12.65° = 77.35°

$\dfrac{a}{98.1}$ = cot 12.65°

a = 98.1 cot 12.65°

a = 437.1

$\dfrac{c}{98.1}$ = csc 12.65°

c = 98.1 csc 12.65°

c = 448.0

10. A = 90° - 69.88° = 20.12°

cot 69.88° = $\dfrac{a}{127}$

a = 46.5

csc 69.88° = $\dfrac{c}{127}$

c = 135

11.

To solve this triangle find B, a, and c.

B = 90° - 17.4° = 72.6°

$\dfrac{a}{13.6}$ = tan 17.4°

a = 13.6 tan 17.4°

a = 4.3

$\dfrac{c}{13.6}$ = sec 17.4°

c = 13.6 sec 17.4°

c = 14.3

12. B = 90° - 78.7° = 11.3°

tan 78.7° = $\dfrac{a}{1340}$

a = 6706

sec 78.7° = $\dfrac{c}{1340}$

c = 6839

13.

To solve this triangle find A, b, and c.

A = 90° - 23° 12' = 66° 48'

$\dfrac{b}{350}$ = tan 23° 12'

b = 350 tan 23° 12'

b = 150

$\dfrac{c}{350}$ = sec 23° 12'

c = 350 sec 23° 12'

c = 381

14. A = 90° - 69° 22' = 20° 38'

tan 69° 22' = $\dfrac{b}{240}$

b = 637

sec 69° 22' = $\dfrac{c}{240}$

c = 681

15.

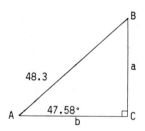

To solve this triangle find B, a, and b.

B = 90° - 47.58° = 42.42°

$\dfrac{a}{48.3}$ = sin 47.58°

a = 48.3 sin 47.58°

a = 35.7

$\dfrac{b}{48.3}$ = cos 47.58°

b = 48.3 cos 47.58°

b = 32.6

16. B = 90° - 88.92° = 1.08°

sin 88.92° = $\dfrac{a}{3950}$

a = 3949

cos 88.92° = $\dfrac{b}{3950}$

b = 74

17.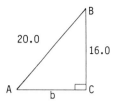

To solve this triangle find A, a, and b.

A = 90° - 82.3° = 7.7°

$\frac{a}{0.982}$ = cos 82.3°

a = 0.982 cos 82.3°

a = 0.132

$\frac{b}{0.982}$ = sin 82.3°

b = 0.982 sin 82.3°

b = 0.973

18. A = 90° - 56.5° = 33.5°

cos 56.5° = $\frac{a}{0.0447}$

a = 0.0247

sin 56.5° = $\frac{b}{0.0447}$

b = 0.0373

19.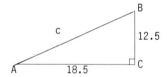

To solve this triangle find c, A, and B.

tan A = $\frac{12.5}{18.5}$ = 0.6757

A = 34.05°

B = 90° - 34.05° = 55.95°

csc A = $\frac{c}{12.5}$

csc 34.05° = $\frac{c}{12.5}$

c = 12.5 csc 34.05°

c = 22.3

20. tan A = $\frac{10.2}{20.4}$

A = 26.57°

B = 90° - 26.57° = 63.43°

csc A = $\frac{c}{10.2}$

csc 26.57° = $\frac{c}{10.2}$

c = 22.8

21.

To solve this triangle find b, A, and B.

sin A = $\frac{16.0}{20.0}$ = 0.8000

Thus A = 53.13°

B = 90° - 53.13° = 36.87°

cos A = $\frac{b}{20.0}$

cos 53.13° = $\frac{b}{20.0}$

b = 20.0 cos 53.13°

b = 12.0

22. sin A = $\frac{15.0}{45.0}$

A = 19.47°

B = 90° - 19.47° = 70.53°

cos A = $\frac{b}{45.0}$

cos 19.47° = $\frac{b}{45.0}$

b = 42.4

23.

To solve this triangle find a, A, and B.

cos A = $\frac{1.86}{4.02}$ = 0.4627

A = 62.44°

B = 90° - 62.44° = 27.56°

sin A = $\frac{a}{4.02}$

sin 62.44° = $\frac{a}{4.02}$

a = 4.02 sin 62.44°

a = 3.56

24. $\sin B = \dfrac{100}{450}$

     $B = 12.84°$

     $A = 90° - 12.84° = 77.16°$

     $\cos B = \dfrac{a}{450}$

     $\cos 12.84° = \dfrac{a}{450}$

     $a = 439$

25.

$\dfrac{h}{14.5} = \tan 73.2°$

$h = 14.5 \tan 73.2°$

$h = 48.0 \text{ ft}$

26.

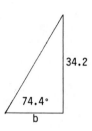

$\cot 74.4° = \dfrac{b}{34.2}$

$b = 9.55 \text{ ft}$

27.

$\dfrac{h}{455} = \sin 31.7°$

$h = 455 \sin 31.7°$

$h = 239 \text{ ft}$

28.

$\csc 41.3° = \dfrac{c}{114}$

$c = 171 \text{ ft}$

29.

$\tan \theta = \dfrac{3}{100} = 0.03$

$\theta = 1.72°$

30.

$\sin \theta = \dfrac{120}{670}$

$\theta = 10.32°$

31.

$\tan \theta = \dfrac{6}{10.3} = 0.5825$

$\theta = 30.22°$

32.

$\tan \theta = \dfrac{35}{20} = 1.75$

$\theta = 60.26°$

33.

$\dfrac{d}{2500} = \tan 82.3°$

$d = 2500 \tan 82.3°$

$d = 18,490 \text{ ft, or } 3.5 \text{ mi}$

34.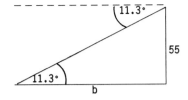

$$\cot 11.3° = \frac{b}{55}$$
$$b = 275 \text{ ft}$$

35.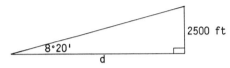

$$\frac{d}{2500} = \cot 8° 20'$$
$$d = 2500 \cot 8° 20'$$
$$d = 17,067 \text{ ft}$$

36.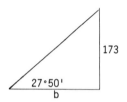

$$\cot 27° 50' = \frac{b}{173}$$
$$b = 328 \text{ ft}$$

37.

$$\frac{d}{12} = \tan 63° 20'$$
$$d = 12 \tan 63° 20'$$
$$d = 24 \text{ km}$$

38.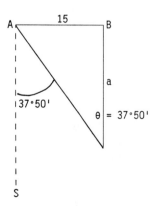

$$\frac{a}{15} = \cot 37° 50'$$
$$a = 19.3 \text{ km}$$

39.

$$\frac{r}{15.25} = \sec 54°$$
$$r = 15.25 \sec 54°$$
$$r = 25.9 \text{ cm}$$

40.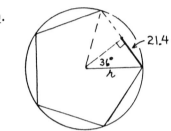

$$36° = \frac{1}{2} \cdot \frac{360°}{5}$$
$$\sin 36° = \frac{21.4}{r}$$
$$r = 36.4 \text{ cm}$$

41.

$$\frac{r}{\frac{25}{6}} = \sec 60°$$
$$r = \frac{25}{6} \sec 60°$$
$$r = \frac{25}{3}, \text{ or } 8.33 \text{ cm}$$

42.

$\theta = \frac{1}{2} \cdot \frac{360°}{8} = 22.5°$

$\sin 22.5 = \frac{x}{15.8}$

$x = 96.7$ cm

43.

$\tan \theta = \frac{50}{75} \approx 0.6667$

$\theta = 33.7°$

$\phi = \theta + 10.5° = 33.7° + 10.5° = 44.2°$

$\tan 44.2° = \frac{50 + \ell}{75}$

$75 \tan 44.2° = 50 + \ell$

$72.9 = 50 + \ell$

$23 = \ell$

The length of the antenna is 23 ft.

44.

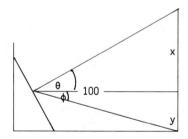

$\theta = 18° \ 40'$

$\phi = 6° \ 20'$

$\frac{x}{100} = \tan 18° \ 40'$

$\frac{y}{100} = \tan 6° \ 20'$

$x + y = 44.9$ ft

45.

The distance to find is d, which is $d_1 - d_2$.

$\frac{d_1}{2} = \cot \theta_1$ $\qquad$ $\frac{d_2}{2} = \cot \theta_2$

$d_1 = 2 \cot 13.5°$ $\qquad$ $d_2 = 2 \cot 81.2°$

$d = d_1 - d_2 = 2 \cot 13.5° - 2 \cot 81.2°$

$\qquad = 2(\cot 13.5° - \cot 81.2°)$

$\qquad = 8$ km

46.

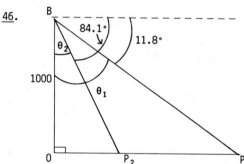

$\frac{OP_1}{1000} = \tan \theta_1$ and $\frac{OP_2}{1000} = \tan \theta_2$

where $\theta_1 = 90° - 11.8°$, $\theta_2 = 90° - 84.1°$.

Then $OP_1 = 1000 \tan 78.2° = 4787$

and $OP_2 = 1000 \tan 5.9° = 103$.

$P_1P_2 = 4787 - 103 = 4684$ m.

47.

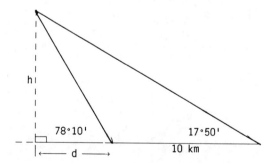

First find d. Then solve for h.

$\frac{h}{d} = \tan 78° \ 10'$ $\qquad$ $\frac{h}{d + 10} = \tan 17° \ 50'$

$h = d \tan 78° \ 10'$ $\qquad$ $h = (d + 10) \tan 17° \ 50'$

$d \tan 78° \ 10' = d \tan 17° \ 50' + 10 \tan 17° \ 50'$

$d(\tan 78° \ 10' - \tan 17° \ 50') = 10 \tan 17° \ 50'$

$$d = \frac{10 \tan 17° \ 50'}{\tan 78° \ 10' - \tan 17° \ 50'}$$

$$d = 0.7227$$

$\dfrac{h}{0.7227} = \tan 78° \ 10'$

$\quad h = 0.7227 \tan 78° \ 10'$

$\quad h = 3.4 \text{ km}$

<u>48.</u>

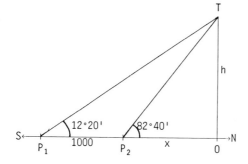

$\dfrac{h}{1000 + x} = \tan 12° \ 20'$ and $\dfrac{h}{x} = \tan 82° \ 40'$.

$(1000 + x) \tan 12° \ 20' = x \tan 82° \ 40'$.

Then $x = \dfrac{1000 \tan 12° \ 20'}{\tan 82° \ 40' - \tan 12° \ 20'} = 29$

and $h = x \tan 82° \ 40' = 225$ ft.

<u>49.</u>

At 120 km/h, in 2 hr the plane travels 120·2, or 240 km.

$\quad \theta = 243° - 180° = 63°$

$\dfrac{d}{240} = \cos 63°$

$\quad d = 240 \cos 63°$

$\quad d = 109 \text{ km}$

<u>50.</u>

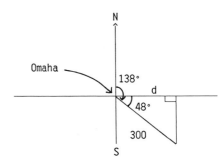

$\dfrac{d}{300} = \cos 48°$

$\quad d = 201 \text{ km}$

<u>51.</u>

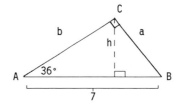

$\dfrac{b}{7} = \cos 36°$

$b = 7 \cos 36°$

$b = 5.66$

$\dfrac{h}{5.66} = \sin 36°$

$\quad h = 5.66 \sin 36°$

$\quad h = 3.3$

<u>52.</u> $\dfrac{\frac{a}{2}}{5} = \sin 36°$

$\quad a = 10 \sin 36°$

$\quad a = 5.9$

<u>53.</u> See the answer section in the text.

<u>54.</u>

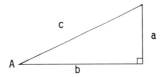

Area $= \dfrac{1}{2} b \cdot a$ where $a = c \sin A$, so

Area $= \dfrac{1}{2} bc \sin A$.

55.

The earth's radius is approximately 4000 miles.
Use the Pythagorean theorem to find d (in miles):

$d^2 + 4000^2 = (4000 + h)^2$

$d^2 + 4000^2 = 4000^2 + 8000h + h^2$

$d^2 = 8000h + h^2$

$d = \sqrt{8000h + h^2}$, where d and h are in miles

When h = 1000 ft:

$1000 \text{ ft} \cdot \dfrac{1 \text{ mi}}{5280 \text{ ft}} = \dfrac{1000}{5280} \text{ mi} = \dfrac{25}{132} \text{ mi}$

$d = \sqrt{8000\left[\dfrac{25}{132}\right] + \left[\dfrac{25}{132}\right]^2}$

$= 38.9 \text{ mi}$

56.

$C = L - H$

$d^2 = L^2 - H^2 = (L + H)(L - H) = C(L + H)$

$C = \dfrac{d^2}{L + H} \approx \dfrac{d^2}{2L}$

57. $\tan \theta = \dfrac{8}{1.5} \approx 5.3333$

$\theta = 79.38°$

58.

Let $x = \overline{VP}$ and $r = \dfrac{d}{2}$; then $\dfrac{r}{x} = \tan 27°$.

a) $\dfrac{1}{x} = \tan 27°$; $x = 1.96$

b) $\dfrac{r}{3.93} = \tan 27°$; $d = 2r = 4.00$

c) $\dfrac{d/2}{\overline{VP}} = \tan 27°$; $d = 1.02\ \overline{VP}$

d) $\overline{VP} = 0.98\ d$

59.

H is the perceived location of the plane;

A is the actual location of plane when heard.

Plane's speed, 200 mph ≈ 293 ft/sec.

$\csc 20° = \dfrac{c}{3000}$ $\cot 20° = \dfrac{b}{3000}$

$c = 3000 \csc 20°$ $b = 3000 \cot 20°$

$c = 8771 \text{ ft}$ $b = 8242$

The time it takes the plane to fly from P to A
is approximately the same time it takes the sound
to travel from P to V. We use the formula
distance = rate × time to find this time.

$d = rt$

$8771 = 1100t$

$8 \approx t$

Then the distance a from P to A is given by
a = 293·8 = 2344 ft.   Then d = b - a =
8242 - 2344 = 5898.

$\tan \theta = \dfrac{3000}{d} = \dfrac{3000}{5898} \approx 0.5086$

$\theta = 27°$

60. 87°53' = 14,162 ft ≈ 2.682197 mi

$\sin 87°53' = \dfrac{R}{R + 2.682197}$ gives

$R = \dfrac{2.682197 \sin 87° 53'}{1 - \sin 87° 53'} = 3928 \text{ mi}$

Exercise Set 8.2

1.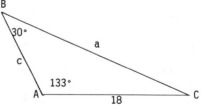

To solve this triangle find C, a, and c.

C = 180° - (133° + 30°) = 17°

Use the law of sines to find a and c.

Find a:

$$\frac{a}{\sin A} = \frac{b}{\sin B}$$

$$\frac{a}{\sin 133°} = \frac{18}{\sin 30°}$$

$$a = \frac{18 \sin 133°}{\sin 30°} = 26$$

Find c:

$$\frac{c}{\sin C} = \frac{b}{\sin B}$$

$$\frac{c}{\sin 17°} = \frac{18}{\sin 30°}$$

$$c = \frac{18 \sin 17°}{\sin 30°} = 11$$

2. $A = 180° - (120° + 30°) = 30°$

$$\frac{a}{\sin A} = \frac{b}{\sin B}, \text{ or } \frac{16}{\sin 30°} = \frac{b}{\sin 120°}$$

$$b = 28$$

$$\frac{a}{\sin A} = \frac{c}{\sin C}, \text{ or } \frac{16}{\sin 30°} = \frac{c}{\sin 30°}$$

$$c = 16$$

3.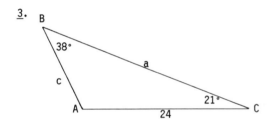

To solve this triangle find A, a, and c.
A = 180° - (38° + 21°) = 121°

Use the law of sines to find a and c.

Find a:

$$\frac{a}{\sin A} = \frac{b}{\sin B}$$

$$\frac{a}{\sin 121°} = \frac{24}{\sin 38°}$$

$$a = \frac{24 \sin 121°}{\sin 38°} = 33$$

Find c:

$$\frac{c}{\sin C} = \frac{b}{\sin B}$$

$$\frac{c}{\sin 21°} = \frac{24}{\sin 38°}$$

$$c = \frac{24 \sin 21°}{\sin 38°} = 14$$

4. $B = 180° - (131° + 23°) = 26°$

$$\frac{a}{\sin A} = \frac{b}{\sin B}, \text{ or } \frac{a}{\sin 131°} = \frac{10}{\sin 26°}$$

$$a = 17$$

$$\frac{c}{\sin C} = \frac{b}{\sin B}, \text{ or } \frac{c}{\sin 23°} = \frac{10}{\sin 26°}$$

$$c = 9$$

5.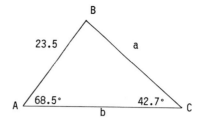

To solve this triangle find B, a, and b.
B = 180° - (68.5° + 42.7°) = 68.8°

Use the law of sines to find a and b.

$$\frac{a}{\sin A} = \frac{c}{\sin C}$$

$$\frac{a}{\sin 68.5°} = \frac{23.5}{\sin 42.7°}$$

$$a = \frac{23.5 \sin 68.5°}{\sin 42.7°} = 32.2 \text{ cm}$$

$$\frac{b}{\sin B} = \frac{c}{\sin C}$$

$$\frac{b}{\sin 68.8°} = \frac{23.5}{\sin 42.7°}$$

$$b = \frac{23.5 \sin 68.8°}{\sin 42.7°} = 32.3 \text{ cm}$$

6. $A = 180° - (118.3° + 45.6°) = 16.1°$

$$\frac{a}{\sin A} = \frac{b}{\sin B}, \text{ or } \frac{a}{\sin 16.1°} = \frac{42.1}{\sin 118.3°}$$

$$a = 13.3 \text{ ft}$$

$$\frac{c}{\sin C} = \frac{b}{\sin B}, \text{ or } \frac{c}{\sin 45.6°} = \frac{42.1}{\sin 118.3°}$$

$$c = 34.2 \text{ ft}$$

7. $A = 180° - (37.48° + 32.16°) = 110.36°$

$$\frac{a}{\sin A} = \frac{c}{\sin C}$$

$$\frac{a}{\sin 110.36°} = \frac{3}{\sin 32.16°}$$

$$a = \frac{3 \times \sin 110.36°}{\sin 32.16°} = 5 \text{ mi}$$

$$\frac{b}{\sin B} = \frac{c}{\sin C}$$

$$\frac{b}{\sin 37.48°} = \frac{3}{\sin 32.16°}$$

$$b = \frac{3 \times \sin 37.48°}{\sin 32.16°} = 3 \text{ mi}$$

8. $B = 180° - (32.76° + 21.97°) = 125.27°$

$$\frac{b}{\sin B} = \frac{a}{\sin A}, \text{ or } \frac{b}{\sin 125.27°} = \frac{200}{\sin 32.76°}$$

$$b = 302 \text{ m}$$

$$\frac{c}{\sin C} = \frac{a}{\sin A}, \text{ or } \frac{c}{\sin 21.97°} = \frac{200}{\sin 32.76°}$$

$$c = 138 \text{ m}$$

9. $C = 180° - (16° 56' + 59° 23') = 103° 41'$

$$\frac{a}{\sin A} = \frac{c}{\sin C}$$

$$\frac{a}{\sin 16° 56'} = \frac{6019}{\sin 103° 41'}$$

$$a = \frac{6019 \times \sin 16° 56'}{\sin 103° 41'} = 1804 \text{ km}$$

$$\frac{b}{\sin B} = \frac{c}{\sin C}$$

$$\frac{b}{\sin 59° 23'} = \frac{6019}{\sin 103° 41'}$$

$$b = \frac{6019 \times \sin 59° 23'}{\sin 103° 41'} = 5331 \text{ km}$$

10. $B = 180° - (120° 18' + 27° 46') = 31° 56'$

$$\frac{b}{\sin B} = \frac{a}{\sin A}, \text{ or } \frac{b}{\sin 31° 56'} = \frac{16,435}{\sin 120° 18'}$$

$$b = 10,068 \text{ mi}$$

$$\frac{c}{\sin C} = \frac{a}{\sin A}, \text{ or } \frac{c}{\sin 27° 46'} = \frac{16,435}{\sin 120° 18'}$$

$$c = 8868 \text{ mi}$$

11. $B = 180° - (129° 32' + 18° 28') = 32°$

$$\frac{a}{\sin A} = \frac{b}{\sin B}$$

$$\frac{a}{\sin 129° 32'} = \frac{1204}{\sin 32°}$$

$$a = \frac{1204 \times \sin 129° 32'}{\sin 32°} = 1752 \text{ in.}$$

$$\frac{c}{\sin C} = \frac{b}{\sin B}$$

$$\frac{c}{\sin 18° 28'} = \frac{1204}{\sin 32°}$$

$$c = \frac{1204 \times \sin 18° 28'}{\sin 32°} = 720 \text{ in.}$$

12. $A = 180° - (37° 51' + 19° 47') = 122° 22'$

$$\frac{a}{\sin A} = \frac{b}{\sin B}, \text{ or } \frac{a}{\sin 122° 22'} = \frac{240.123}{\sin 37° 51'}$$

$$a = 331 \text{ mm}$$

$$\frac{c}{\sin C} = \frac{b}{\sin B}, \text{ or } \frac{c}{\sin 19° 47'} = \frac{240.123}{\sin 37° 51'}$$

$$c = 132 \text{ mm}$$

13. Find B:

$$\frac{b}{\sin B} = \frac{a}{\sin A}$$

$$\frac{34}{\sin B} = \frac{24}{\sin 36.5°}$$

$$\sin B = \frac{34 \sin 36.5°}{24} = 0.8427$$

There are two angles less than 180° having a sine of 0.8427. They are 57.4° and 122.6°. This gives us two possible solutions.

Solution I

If $B = 57.4°$
then $C = 180° - (36.5° + 57.4°) = 86.1°$.

Find c:

$$\frac{c}{\sin C} = \frac{a}{\sin A}$$

$$\frac{c}{\sin 86.1°} = \frac{24}{\sin 36.5°}$$

$$c = \frac{24 \sin 86.1°}{\sin 36.5°} = 40$$

Solution II

If $B = 122.6°$,
then $C = 180° - (36.5° + 122.6°) = 20.9°$.

Find c:

$$\frac{c}{\sin C} = \frac{a}{\sin A}$$

$$\frac{c}{\sin 20.9°} = \frac{24}{\sin 36.5°}$$

$$c = \frac{24 \sin 20.9°}{\sin 36.5°} = 14$$

14. $\dfrac{b}{\sin B} = \dfrac{c}{\sin C}, \text{ or } \dfrac{27}{\sin B} = \dfrac{28}{\sin 43.2°}$

$B = 41.3°$
$A = 180° - (41.3° + 43.2°) = 95.5°$

$$\frac{a}{\sin A} = \frac{c}{\sin C}, \text{ or } \frac{a}{\sin 95.5°} = \frac{28}{\sin 43.2°}$$

$$a = 41$$

15. Find C:

$$\frac{c}{\sin C} = \frac{a}{\sin A}$$

$$\frac{13.5}{\sin C} = \frac{17.2}{\sin 116.3°}$$

$$\sin C = \frac{13.5 \sin 116.3°}{17.2} = 0.7036$$

Then $C = 44.7°$ or $C = 135.3°$. An angle of 135.3° cannot be an angle of this triangle because it already has an angle of 116.3° and these two would total more than 180°. Thus $C = 44.7°$.

Find B:
$B = 180° - (116.3° + 44.7°) = 19.0°$

Find b:

$$\frac{b}{\sin B} = \frac{a}{\sin A}$$

$$\frac{b}{\sin 19.0°} = \frac{17.2}{\sin 116.3°}$$

$$b = \frac{17.2 \sin 19.0°}{\sin 116.3°} = 6.2$$

16. $\dfrac{b}{\sin B} = \dfrac{a}{\sin A}, \text{ or } \dfrac{18.2}{\sin B} = \dfrac{28.3}{\sin 47.8°}$

$B = 28.5°$

$C = 180° - (28.5° + 47.8°) = 103.7°$

$\dfrac{c}{\sin C} = \dfrac{a}{\sin A}$, or $\dfrac{c}{\sin 103.7°} = \dfrac{28.3}{\sin 47.8°}$

$c = 37.1$

17. Find B:

$\dfrac{b}{\sin B} = \dfrac{c}{\sin C}$

$\dfrac{24.2}{\sin B} = \dfrac{30.3}{\sin 61° \ 10'}$

$\sin B = \dfrac{24.2 \sin 61° \ 10'}{30.3} = 0.6996$

Then B = 44° 24' or B = 135° 36'. An angle of 135° 36' cannot be an angle of this triangle because it already has an angle of 61° 10' and the two would total more than 180°. Thus B = 44° 24'.

Find A:

A = 180° - (61° 10' + 44° 24') = 74° 26'

Find a:

$\dfrac{a}{\sin A} = \dfrac{c}{\sin C}$

$\dfrac{a}{\sin 74° \ 26'} = \dfrac{30.3}{\sin 61° \ 10'}$

$a = \dfrac{30.3 \sin 74° \ 26'}{\sin 61° \ 10'} = 33.3$

18. $\dfrac{a}{\sin A} = \dfrac{b}{\sin B}$, or $\dfrac{25.1}{\sin A} = \dfrac{32.6}{\sin 58° \ 40'}$

$A = 41° \ 7'$

$C = 180° - (41° \ 7' + 58° \ 40') = 80° \ 13'$

$\dfrac{c}{\sin C} = \dfrac{b}{\sin B}$, or $\dfrac{c}{\sin 80° \ 13'} = \dfrac{32.6}{\sin 58° \ 40'}$

$c = 37.6$

19. $\dfrac{b}{\sin B} = \dfrac{a}{\sin A}$

$\dfrac{2345}{\sin B} = \dfrac{2345}{\sin 124.67°}$

$\sin B = \dfrac{2345 \times \sin 124.67°}{2345} = 0.8224$

Then B = 55.33° or B = 124.67°. An angle of 55.33° cannot be an angle of this triangle because it already has an angle of 124.67° and the two would total 180°. An angle of 124.67° cannot be an angle of this triangle either because the two 124.67° angles would total more than 180°.

There is no solution.

20. $\dfrac{b}{\sin B} = \dfrac{c}{\sin C}$, or $\dfrac{56.78}{\sin B} = \dfrac{56.78}{\sin 83.78°}$

$B = 83.78°$

$A = 180° - (83.78° + 83.78°) = 12.44°$

$\dfrac{a}{\sin A} = \dfrac{c}{\sin C}$, or $\dfrac{a}{\sin 12.44°} = \dfrac{56.78}{\sin 83.78°}$

$a = 12.30$ yd

21. $\dfrac{b}{\sin B} = \dfrac{a}{\sin A}$

$\dfrac{10.07}{\sin B} = \dfrac{20.01}{\sin 30.3°}$

$\sin B = \dfrac{10.07 \sin 30.3°}{20.01} = 0.2539$

$B = 14.7°$

$C = 180° - (30.3° + 14.7°) = 135.0°$

$\dfrac{c}{\sin C} = \dfrac{a}{\sin A}$

$\dfrac{c}{\sin 135.0°} = \dfrac{20.01}{\sin 30.3°}$

$c = \dfrac{20.01 \sin 135.0°}{\sin 30.3°} = 28.04$ cm

22. $\dfrac{c}{\sin C} = \dfrac{a}{\sin A}$, or $\dfrac{45.6}{\sin C} = \dfrac{23.8}{\sin 115°}$

Then sin C = 1.7365 and there is no solution.

23. $\dfrac{b}{\sin B} = \dfrac{a}{\sin A}$

$\dfrac{8000}{\sin B} = \dfrac{4000}{\sin 32° \ 52'}$

$\sin B = \dfrac{8000 \times \sin 32° \ 52'}{4000} = 1.0854$

Since there is no angle having a sine greater than 1, there is no solution.

24. $\dfrac{b}{\sin B} = \dfrac{a}{\sin A}$

$\dfrac{6}{\sin B} = \dfrac{2}{\sin 30°}$

$\sin B = \dfrac{6 \times \sin 30°}{2} = 1.5$

Since there is no angle having a sine greater than 1, there is no solution.

25. $\dfrac{b}{\sin B} = \dfrac{c}{\sin C}$

$\dfrac{4.157}{\sin B} = \dfrac{3.446}{\sin 51° \ 48'}$

$\sin B = \dfrac{4.157 \times \sin 51° \ 48'}{3.446} = 0.9480$

Then B = 71° 26' or B = 108° 34'

Solution I

If B = 71° 26', then
A = 180° - (71° 26' + 51° 48') = 56° 46'.

$\dfrac{a}{\sin A} = \dfrac{c}{\sin C}$

$\dfrac{a}{\sin 56° \ 46'} = \dfrac{3.446}{\sin 51° \ 48'}$

$a = \dfrac{3.446 \times \sin 56° \ 46'}{\sin 51° \ 48'} = 3.668$

Solution II
If B = 108° 34',
then A = 180° - (108° 34' + 51° 48') = 19° 38'.

$$\frac{a}{\sin A} = \frac{c}{\sin C}$$

$$\frac{a}{\sin 19° 38'} = \frac{3.446}{\sin 51° 48'}$$

$$a = \frac{3.446 \times \sin 19° 38'}{\sin 51° 48'} = 1.473 \text{ km}$$

26. $\frac{b}{\sin B} = \frac{c}{\sin C}$, or $\frac{43.67}{\sin B} = \frac{38.86}{\sin 48.76°}$

Then B = 57.68° or B = 122.32°.

Solution I
If B = 57.68°, then A = 180° - (57.68° + 48.76°) = 73.56°.

$$\frac{a}{\sin A} = \frac{c}{\sin C}, \text{ or } \frac{a}{\sin 73.56°} = \frac{38.86}{\sin 48.76°}$$

a = 49.57 mm

Solution II
If B = 122.32°, then
A = 180° - (122.32° + 48.76°) = 8.92°.

$$\frac{a}{\sin A} = \frac{c}{\sin C}, \text{ or } \frac{a}{\sin 8.92°} = \frac{38.86}{\sin 48.76°}$$

a = 8.01 mm

27. $\frac{b}{\sin B} = \frac{a}{\sin A}$

$$\frac{18.4}{\sin B} = \frac{15.6}{\sin 89°}$$

$$\sin B = \frac{18.4 \times \sin 89°}{15.6} = 1.1793$$

Since there is no angle having a sine greater than 1, there is no solution.

28. $\frac{c}{\sin C} = \frac{b}{\sin B}$, or $\frac{10.0}{\sin C} = \frac{8.0}{\sin 36°}$

Then C = 47° or C = 133°.

Solution I
If C = 47°, then A = 180° - (36° + 47°) = 97°.

$$\frac{a}{\sin A} = \frac{b}{\sin B}, \text{ or } \frac{a}{\sin 97°} = \frac{8.0}{\sin 36°},$$

and a = 13.5 ft.

Solution II
If C = 133°, then A = 180° - (36° + 133°) = 11°.

$$\frac{a}{\sin A} = \frac{b}{\sin B}, \text{ or } \frac{a}{\sin 11°} = \frac{8.0}{\sin 36°},$$

and a = 2.6 ft.

29. $\frac{c}{\sin C} = \frac{a}{\sin A}$

$$\frac{110.0}{\sin C} = \frac{90.0}{\sin 41° 50'}$$

$$\sin C = \frac{110.0 \times \sin 41° 50'}{90.0} = 0.8152$$

Then C = 54° 36' or C = 125° 24'.

Solution I
If C = 54° 36', then
B = 180° - (41° 50' + 54° 36') = 83° 34'.

$$\frac{b}{\sin B} = \frac{a}{\sin A}$$

$$\frac{b}{\sin 83° 34'} = \frac{90.0}{\sin 41° 50'}$$

$$b = \frac{90.0 \times \sin 83° 34'}{\sin 41° 50'} = 134.1 \text{ mi}$$

Solution II
If C = 125° 24', then
B = 180° - (41° 50' + 125° 24') = 12° 46'.

$$\frac{b}{\sin B} = \frac{a}{\sin A}$$

$$\frac{b}{\sin 12° 46'} = \frac{90.0}{\sin 41° 50'}$$

$$b = \frac{90.0 \times \sin 12° 46'}{\sin 41° 50'} = 29.8 \text{ mi}$$

30. $\frac{a}{\sin A} = \frac{c}{\sin C}$, or $\frac{56.2}{\sin A} = \frac{22.1}{\sin 46° 30'}$

Then sin A = 1.8446, and there is no solution.

31. $K = \frac{1}{2} ac \sin B$ (Theorem 2)

$K = \frac{1}{2}(7.2)(3.4) \sin 42°$ (Substituting)

K = 8.2 ft²

32. $K = \frac{1}{2} bc \sin A$

$K = \frac{1}{2}(10)(13) \sin 17° 12' = 19$ in²

33. $K = \frac{1}{2} ab \sin C$ (Theorem 2)

$K = \frac{1}{2} \cdot 4 \cdot 6 \cdot \sin 82° 54'$ (Substituting)

K = 12 yd²

34. $K = \frac{1}{2} ab \sin C$

$K = \frac{1}{2}(1.5)(2.1) \sin 75.16° = 1.5$ m²

35. $K = \frac{1}{2} ac \sin B$

$K = \frac{1}{2}(46.12)(36.74) \sin 135.2°$

K = 596.98 ft²

36. $K = \frac{1}{2} bc \sin A$

$K = \frac{1}{2}(18.2)(23.7) \sin 113° = 198.5$ cm²

37.

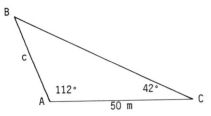

Find B:

B = 180° - (112° + 42°) = 26°

Find c:

$$\frac{c}{\sin C} = \frac{b}{\sin B}$$

$$\frac{c}{\sin 42°} = \frac{50}{\sin 26°}$$

$$c = \frac{50 \sin 42°}{\sin 26°} = 76$$

The width of the crater is 76 m.

38.

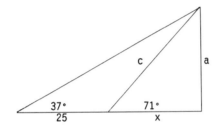

cot 71° = $\frac{x}{a}$, so x = a cot 71°.

cot 37° = $\frac{x + 25}{a}$, so x + 25 = a cot 37°.

Then x + 25 = a cot 71° + 25 = a cot 37°.

sin 71° = $\frac{a}{c}$, so a = c sin 71°.

Then c sin 71° cot 71° + 25 = c sin 71° cot 37°, so

$$c = \frac{25}{\sin 71° \cot 37° - \sin 71° \cot 71°} = 27 \text{ ft}$$

39.

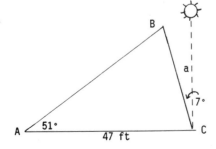

Find C: C = 90° - 7° = 83°

Find B: B = 180° - (51° + 83°) = 46°

Find a: (a is the length of the pole.)

$$\frac{a}{\sin A} = \frac{b}{\sin B}$$

$$\frac{a}{\sin 51°} = \frac{47}{\sin 46°}$$

$$a = \frac{47 \sin 51°}{\sin 46°} = 51$$

The pole is 51 ft long.

40.

x = 38 cos 10° and y = 38 sin 10°.

Also a + y = x tan 23° so that

a = x tan 23° - y

= 38 cos 10° tan 23° - 38 sin 10°

= 9 ft

41.

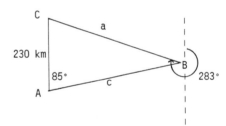

Find B: B = 283° - 180° - 85° = 18°

Find C: C = 180° - (85° + 18°) = 77°

Find a:

$$\frac{a}{\sin A} = \frac{b}{\sin B}$$

$$\frac{a}{\sin 85°} = \frac{230}{\sin 18°}$$

$$a = \frac{230 \sin 85°}{\sin 18°} = 742$$

Find c:

$$\frac{c}{\sin C} = \frac{b}{\sin B}$$

$$\frac{c}{\sin 77°} = \frac{230}{\sin 18°}$$

$$c = \frac{230 \sin 77°}{\sin 18°} = 725$$

The plane flew a total of 742 + 725, or 1467 km.

42.

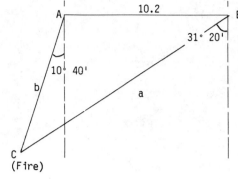

(Fire)

A = 90° + 10° 40' = 100° 40'

B = 90° - 31° 20' = 58° 40'

C = 180° - (100° 40' + 58° 40') = 20° 40'

$\frac{b}{\sin B} = \frac{c}{\sin C}$, or $\frac{b}{\sin 58° 40'} = \frac{10.2}{\sin 20° 40'}$

b = 24.7 km

$\frac{a}{\sin A} = \frac{c}{\sin C}$, or $\frac{a}{\sin 100° 40'} = \frac{10.2}{\sin 20° 40'}$

a = 28.4 km

43.

(Fire)

A = 45° + (360° - 295°) = 110°

B = 255° - 180° - 45° = 30°

C = 180° - (110° + 30°) = 40°

The distance from Tower A to the fire is b:

$\frac{b}{\sin B} = \frac{c}{\sin C}$

$\frac{b}{\sin 30°} = \frac{45}{\sin 40°}$

$b = \frac{45 \times \sin 30°}{\sin 40°} = 35$ mi

The distance from Tower B to the fire is a:

$\frac{a}{\sin A} = \frac{c}{\sin C}$

$\frac{a}{\sin 110°} = \frac{45}{\sin 40°}$

$a = \frac{45 \times \sin 110°}{\sin 40°} = 66$ mi

44.

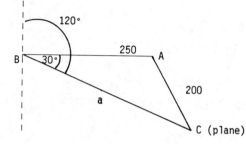

C (plane)

$\frac{c}{\sin C} = \frac{b}{\sin B}$, or $\frac{250}{\sin C} = \frac{200}{\sin 30°}$

C = 39°

A = 180° - (30° + 39°) = 111°

$\frac{a}{\sin A} = \frac{b}{\sin B}$, or $\frac{a}{\sin 111°} = \frac{200}{\sin 30°}$

a = 373 km

45.

Find B: B = 90° - 65° 10' = 24° 50'

Find C:

$\frac{c}{\sin C} = \frac{b}{\sin B}$

$\frac{7.2}{\sin C} = \frac{5.1}{\sin 24° 50'}$

$\sin C = \frac{7.2 \sin 24° 50'}{5.1} = 0.5929$

Then C = 36° 20' or C = 143° 40'.

If C = 143° 40',
then A = 180° - (24° 50' + 143° 40') = 11° 30'.

Find a:

$\frac{a}{\sin A} = \frac{b}{\sin B}$

$\frac{a}{\sin 11° 30'} = \frac{5.1}{\sin 24° 50'}$

$a = \frac{5.1 \sin 11° 30'}{\sin 24° 50'} = 2.4$

If C = 36° 20',
then A = 180° - (24° 50' + 36° 20') = 118° 50'.

Find a:

$\frac{a}{\sin A} = \frac{b}{\sin B}$

$\frac{a}{\sin 118° 50'} = \frac{5.1}{\sin 24° 50'}$

$a = \frac{5.1 \sin 118° 50'}{\sin 24° 50'} = 10.6$

The boat is either 2.4 km or 10.6 km from lighthouse B.

46.

C (Freighter)

25° 40'

b

B (Mackinac Island)   65° 20'   10° 10'

35 mi.

A (Cheboygan)

$A = 65° 20' - 10° 10' = 55° 10'$

$B = 180° - 25° 40' - 65° 20' = 89°$

$C = 180° - (55° 10' + 89°) = 35° 50'$

$\dfrac{b}{\sin B} = \dfrac{c}{\sin C}$, or $\dfrac{b}{\sin 89°} = \dfrac{35}{\sin 35° 50'}$

$b = 60$ mi

47. a) $\dfrac{a}{\sin A} = \dfrac{b}{\sin B}$, so $a = \dfrac{b \sin A}{\sin B}$.

$\dfrac{c}{\sin C} = \dfrac{b}{\sin B}$, so $c = \dfrac{b \sin C}{\sin B}$.

$\dfrac{a + b}{c} = \dfrac{\dfrac{b \sin A}{\sin B} + b}{\dfrac{b \sin C}{\sin B}}$ (Substituting)

$= \dfrac{\dfrac{b \sin A + b \sin B}{\sin B}}{\dfrac{b \sin C}{\sin B}}$

$= \dfrac{b(\sin A + \sin B)}{b \sin C}$

$= \dfrac{\sin A + \sin B}{\sin C}$

$= \dfrac{2 \sin \frac{1}{2} (A + B) \cos \frac{1}{2} (A - B)}{\sin C}$

(Using a sum-product identity)

$= \dfrac{2 \sin \frac{1}{2} (A + B) \cos \frac{1}{2} (A - B)}{2 \sin \frac{1}{2} C \cos \frac{1}{2} C}$

$= \dfrac{\sin \frac{1}{2} (A + B) \cos \frac{1}{2} (A - B)}{\sin \frac{1}{2} C \cos \frac{1}{2} [\pi - (A + B)]}$

$[C = \pi - (A + B)]$

$= \dfrac{\sin \frac{1}{2} (A + B) \cos \frac{1}{2} (A - B)}{\sin \frac{1}{2} C \cos \left[\frac{\pi}{2} - \frac{1}{2} (A + B)\right]}$

$= \dfrac{\sin \frac{1}{2} (A + B) \cos \frac{1}{2} (A - B)}{\sin \frac{1}{2} C \sin \frac{1}{2} (A + B)}$

$= \dfrac{\cos \frac{1}{2} (A - B)}{\sin \frac{1}{2} C}$

b) We substitute as in part (a).

$\dfrac{a - b}{c} = \dfrac{\dfrac{b \sin A}{\sin B} - b}{\dfrac{b \sin C}{\sin B}}$

$= \dfrac{\dfrac{b \sin A - b \sin B}{\sin B}}{\dfrac{b \sin C}{\sin B}}$

$= \dfrac{\sin A - \sin B}{\sin C}$

$= \dfrac{2 \cos \frac{1}{2} (A + B) \sin \frac{1}{2} (A - B)}{2 \sin \frac{1}{2} C \cos \frac{1}{2} C}$

$= \dfrac{\cos \frac{1}{2} (A + B) \sin \frac{1}{2} (A - B)}{\sin \frac{1}{2} [\pi - (A + B)] \cos \frac{1}{2} C}$

$= \dfrac{\cos \frac{1}{2} (A + B) \sin \frac{1}{2} (A - B)}{\cos \frac{1}{2} (A + B) \cos \frac{1}{2} C}$

$= \dfrac{\sin \frac{1}{2} (A - B)}{\cos \frac{1}{2} C}$

48. Use Theorem 2 and the law of sines.

$K = \frac{1}{2} bc \sin A$ and $b = \dfrac{c \sin B}{\sin C}$, so

$K = \dfrac{c^2 \sin A \sin B}{2 \sin C}$.

$K = \frac{1}{2} ab \sin C$ and $b = \dfrac{a \sin B}{\sin A}$, so

$K = \dfrac{a^2 \sin B \sin C}{2 \sin A}$

$K = \frac{1}{2} bc \sin A$ and $c = \dfrac{b \sin C}{\sin B}$, so

$K = \dfrac{b^2 \sin A \sin C}{2 \sin B}$.

49. See the answer section in the text.

50.

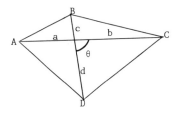

For the quadrilateral ABCD, we have:

Area $= \frac{1}{2} bd \sin \theta + \frac{1}{2} ac \sin \theta +$

$\quad \frac{1}{2} ad \sin (180° - \theta) + \frac{1}{2} bc \sin (180° - \theta)$

$= \frac{1}{2} (bd + ac + ad + bc) \sin \theta$

$= \frac{1}{2} (a + b)(c + d) \sin \theta$

51. See the answer section in the text.

52. Suppose that objects at A and B are moving as shown, with velocities v_a and v_b and paths intersecting at P. Let θ be the bearing from A to B, assumed constant.

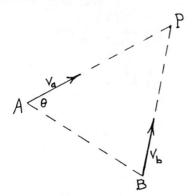

At a later time, t, A will have moved a distance of $v_a t$ and B a distance of $v_b t$. A'B' is parallel to AB because θ is constant. Let x = MN.

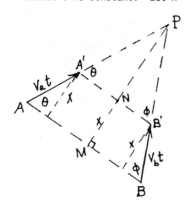

Let T be the time at which A arrives at P. Then AP = v_aT. Since $\frac{x}{AA'}$ = sin θ and $\frac{x}{BB'}$ = sin ϕ, we have AA' sin θ = BB' sin ϕ, then $v_a t$ sin θ = $v_b t$ sin ϕ. Therefore, $\frac{\sin \theta}{\sin \phi} = \frac{v_b t}{v_a t}$, and at time T, $\frac{\sin \theta}{\sin \phi} = \frac{v_b T}{v_a T}$. Note that sin $\theta = \frac{MP}{AP}$ and sin $\phi = \frac{MP}{BP}$, so that AP sin θ = BP sin ϕ and $\frac{\sin \theta}{\sin \phi} = \frac{BP}{AP}$. Therefore, $\frac{BP}{AP} = \frac{v_b T}{v_a T}$ so BP = AP $\cdot \frac{v_b T}{v_a T}$ = AP $\cdot \frac{v_b T}{AP} = v_b T$. Thus at time T, the object that was at B will be at point P.

Exercise Set 8.3

1.

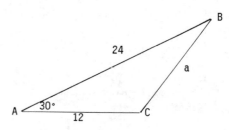

To solve this triangle find a, B, and C.

From the law of cosines,
$a^2 = b^2 + c^2 - 2bc \cos A$
$a^2 = 12^2 + 24^2 - 2 \cdot 12 \cdot 24 \cos 30°$
$a^2 = 144 + 576 - 576 \cos 30°$
$a^2 = 221$
 $a = 15$

Next we use the law of cosines again to find a second angle.
 $b^2 = a^2 + c^2 - 2ac \cos B$
 $12^2 = 15^2 + 24^2 - 2(15)(24) \cos B$
 $144 = 225 + 576 - 720 \cos B$
 $-657 = -720 \cos B$
cos B = 0.9125
 B = 24°

The third angle is easy to find.
C = 180° - (30° + 24°) = 126°

2. $c^2 = a^2 + b^2 - 2ab \cos C$ or
 $c^2 = 15^2 + 12^2 - 2 \cdot 15 \cdot 12 \cos 60°$, and c = 14.
 $a^2 = b^2 + c^2 - 2bc \cos A$ or
 $15^2 = 12^2 + (14)^2 - 2(12)(14) \cos A$,
 and A = 70°. Then B = 180° - (70° + 60°) = 50°.

3. B

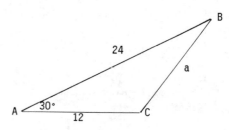

To solve this triangle find a, B, and C.

From the law of cosines,
$a^2 = b^2 + c^2 - 2bc \cos A$
$a^2 = 12^2 + 15^2 - 2 \cdot 12 \cdot 15 \cos 133°$
$a^2 = 144 + 225 - 360 \cos 133°$
$a^2 = 615$
 $a = 25$

Next we use the law of cosines again to find a second angle.

$b^2 = a^2 + c^2 - 2ac \cos B$

$12^2 = 25^2 + 15^2 - 2(25)(15) \cos B$

$144 = 625 + 225 - 750 \cos B$

$-706 = -750 \cos B$

$\cos B = 0.9413$

$B = 20°$

The third angle is easy to find.

$C = 180° - (133° + 20°) = 27°.$

4. $b^2 = a^2 + c^2 - 2ac \cos B$ or

$b^2 = 31^2 + 25^2 - 2 \cdot 31 \cdot 25 \cos 116°,$ and $b = 48.$

$a^2 = b^2 + c^2 - 2bc \cos A$ or

$31^2 = 48^2 + 25^2 - 2(48)(25) \cos A,$

and $A = 35°.$ Then $C = 180° - (35° + 116°) = 29°.$

5.

B$^{72° \ 40'}$

16

78

A

b

C

To solve this triangle find b, A, and C.

From the law of cosines,

$b^2 = a^2 + c^2 - 2ac \cos B$

$b^2 = 78^2 + 16^2 - 2 \cdot 78 \cdot 16 \cos 72° \ 40'$

$b^2 = 6084 + 256 - 2496 \cos 72° \ 40'$

$b^2 = 5596$

$b = 75 \ m$

Next we use the law of cosines again to find a second angle.

$a^2 = b^2 + c^2 - 2bc \cos A$

$78^2 = 75^2 + 16^2 - 2 \cdot 75 \cdot 16 \cos A$

$6084 = 5625 + 256 - 2400 \cos A$

$203 = -2400 \cos A$

$\cos A = -0.0846$

$A = 94° \ 51'$

Then $C = 180° - (94° \ 51' + 72° \ 40') = 12° \ 29'$

6. $a^2 = b^2 + c^2 - 2bc \cos A$ or

$a^2 = 68^2 + 14^2 - 2 \cdot 68 \cdot 14 \cos 24° \ 30',$

and $a = 56 \ ft.$

$b^2 = a^2 + c^2 - 2ac \cos B$ or

$68^2 = 56^2 + 14^2 - 2(56)(14) \cos B,$

and $B = 145° \ 29'.$ Then $C =$

$180° - (24° \ 30' + 145° \ 29') = 10° \ 1'.$

7. $c^2 = a^2 + b^2 - 2ab \cos C$

$c^2 = (25.4)^2 + (73.8)^2 - 2(25.4)(73.8) \cos 22.28°$

$c^2 = 645.16 + 5446.44 - 3749.04 \cos 22.28°$

$c^2 = 2622$

$c = 51.2 \ cm$

Next we use the law of cosines again to find a second angle.

$a^2 = b^2 + c^2 - 2bc \cos A$

$(25.4)^2 = (73.8)^2 + (51.2)^2 - 2(73.8)(51.2) \cos A$

$645.16 = 5446.44 + 2621.44 - 7557.12 \cos A$

$-7422.72 = -7557.12 \cos A$

$\cos A = 0.9822$

Then $A = 10.82°.$

And $B = 180° - (10.82° + 22.28°) = 146.90°.$

8. $b^2 = a^2 + c^2 - 2ac \cos B$ or

$b^2 = (23.78)^2 + (25.74)^2 -$

$\quad\quad\quad\quad 2(23.78)(25.74) \cos 72.66°,$

and $b = 29.38 \ km.$

$a^2 = b^2 + c^2 - 2bc \cos A$ or

$(23.78)^2 = (29.38)^2 + (25.74)^2 -$

$\quad\quad\quad\quad 2(29.38)(25.74) \cos A,$

and $A = 50.59°.$ Then $C =$

$180° - (50.59° + 72.66°) = 56.75°.$

9. $a^2 = b^2 + c^2 - 2bc \cos A$

$a^2 = (15.8)^2 + (18.4)^2 -$

$\quad\quad\quad\quad 2(15.8)(18.4) \cos 96° \ 13'$

$a^2 = 249.64 + 338.56 - 581.44 \cos 96° \ 13'$

$a^2 = 651$

$a = 25.5 \ yd$

Next we use the law of cosines again to find a second angle.

$b^2 = a^2 + c^2 - 2ac \cos B$

$(15.8)^2 = (25.5)^2 + (18.4)^2 - 2(25.5)(18.4) \cos B$

$249.64 = 650.25 + 338.56 - 938.4 \cos B$

$-739.17 = -938.4 \cos B$

$\cos B = 0.7877$

Then $B = 38° \ 2'.$

And $C = 180° - (96° \ 13' + 38° \ 2') = 45° \ 45'.$

10. $c^2 = a^2 + b^2 - 2ab \cos C$ or

$c^2 = 6^2 + 9^2 - 2 \cdot 6 \cdot 9 (\cos 28° \ 43'),$ and

$c = 5 \ mm$

$a^2 = b^2 + c^2 - 2bc \cos A$ or

$6^2 = 9^2 + 5^2 - 2 \cdot 9 \cdot 5 \cos A,$ and

$A = 38° \ 57'.$ Then $B =$

$180° - (38° \ 57' + 28° \ 43') = 112° \ 20'.$

11. $c^2 = a^2 + b^2 - 2ab \cos C$
$c^2 = (60.12)^2 + (40.23)^2 -$
$\qquad\qquad 2(60.12)(40.23) \cos 48.7°$
$c^2 = 3614.4144 + 1618.4529 - 4837.2552 \cos 48.7°$
$c^2 = 2040$
$c = 45.17$ mi

Next we use the law of cosines again to find a second angle.
$\qquad a^2 = b^2 + c^2 - 2bc \cos A$
$(60.12)^2 = (40.23)^2 + (45.17)^2 -$
$\qquad\qquad 2(40.23)(45.17) \cos A$
$3614.4144 = 1618.4529 + 2040.3289 -$
$\qquad\qquad\qquad 3634.3782 \cos A$
$-44.3674 = -3634.3782 \cos A$
$\quad \cos A = 0.0122$

Then $A = 89.3°$.
And $B = 180° - (89.3° + 48.7°) = 42.0°$.

12. $a^2 = b^2 + c^2 - 2bc \cos A$ or
$a^2 = (10.2)^2 + (17.3)^2 - 2(10.2)(17.3)\cos 53.456°$,
and $a = 13.9$ in.

$\qquad b^2 = a^2 + c^2 - 2ac \cos B$ or
$(10.2)^2 = (13.9)^2 + (17.3)^2 - 2(13.9)(17.3) \cos B$,
and $B = 36.127°$. Then $C =$
$180° - (53.456° + 36.127°) = 90.417°$.

13.

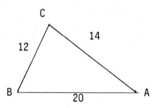

To solve this triangle find A, B, and C.

Find A:
$\qquad a^2 = b^2 + c^2 - 2bc \cos A$
$\quad 12^2 = 14^2 + 20^2 - 2 \cdot 14 \cdot 20 \cos A$
$\quad 144 = 196 + 400 - 560 \cos A$
$\quad -452 = -560 \cos A$
$\cos A = 0.8071$

Thus $A = 36.18°$.

Find B:
$\qquad b^2 = a^2 + c^2 - 2ac \cos B$
$\quad 14^2 = 12^2 + 20^2 - 2 \cdot 12 \cdot 20 \cos B$
$\quad 196 = 144 + 400 - 480 \cos B$
$\quad -348 = -480 \cos B$
$\cos B = 0.7250$

Thus $B = 43.53°$.

Then $C = 180° - (36.18° + 43.53°) = 100.29°$.

14. $a^2 = b^2 + c^2 - 2bc \cos A$ or
$22^2 = 22^2 + 35^2 - 2 \cdot 22 \cdot 35 \cos A$,
and $A = 37.30°$.

$B = A$ since $b = a$, so $B = 37.30°$.
Then $C = 180° - (37.30° + 37.30°) = 105.40°$.

15. Find A:
$\qquad a^2 = b^2 + c^2 - 2bc \cos A$
$\quad 16^2 = 20^2 + 32^2 - 2 \cdot 20 \cdot 32 \cos A$
$\quad 256 = 400 + 1024 - 1280 \cos A$
$\quad -1168 = -1280 \cos A$
$\cos A = 0.9125$

Thus $A = 24.15°$.

Find B:
$\qquad b^2 = a^2 + c^2 - 2ac \cos B$
$\quad 20^2 = 16^2 + 32^2 - 2 \cdot 16 \cdot 32 \cos B$
$\quad 400 = 256 + 1024 - 1024 \cos B$
$\quad -880 = -1024 \cos B$
$\cos B = 0.8594$

Thus $B = 30.75°$.
Then $C = 180° - (24.15° + 30.75°) = 125.10°$.

16. $\qquad a^2 = b^2 + c^2 - 2bc \cos A$
$(2.2)^2 = (4.1)^2 + (2.4)^2 - 2(4.1)(2.4) \cos A$

$\qquad A = 25.72°$

$\qquad c^2 = a^2 + b^2 - 2ab \cos C$
$(2.4)^2 = (2.2)^2 + (4.1)^2 - 2(2.2)(4.1) \cos C$
$\qquad C = 28.26°$

Then $B = 180° - (25.72° + 28.26°) = 125.99°$.

17. Find A:
$\qquad a^2 = b^2 + c^2 - 2bc \cos A$
$\quad 2^2 = 3^2 + 8^2 - 2 \cdot 3 \cdot 8 \cos A$
$\quad 4 = 9 + 64 - 48 \cos A$
$\quad -69 = -48 \cos A$
$\cos A = 1.4375$

Since there is no angle whose cosine is greater than 1, there is no solution.

18. $\qquad a^2 = b^2 + c^2 - 2bc \cos A$
$\quad 17^2 = (15.4)^2 + (1.5)^2 - 2(15.4)(1.5) \cos A$
$\cos A = -1.0734$

There is no solution.

19. Find A:
$$a^2 = b^2 + c^2 - 2bc \cos A$$
$$(11.2)^2 = (5.4)^2 + 7^2 - 2(5.4)(7) \cos A$$
$$125.44 = 29.16 + 49 - 75.6 \cos A$$
$$47.28 = -75.6 \cos A$$
$$\cos A = -0.6254$$

Thus $A = 128.71°$.

Find B:
$$b^2 = a^2 + c^2 - 2ac \cos B$$
$$(5.4)^2 = (11.2)^2 + 7^2 - 2(11.2)(7) \cos B$$
$$29.16 = 125.44 + 49 - 156.8 \cos B$$
$$-145.28 = -156.8 \cos B$$
$$\cos B = 0.9265$$

Thus $B = 22.10°$.
Then $C = 180° - (128.71° + 22.10°) = 29.19°$.

20.
$$a^2 = b^2 + c^2 - 2bc \cos A$$
$$(26.12)^2 = (21.34)^2 + (19.25)^2 -$$
$$2(21.34)(19.25) \cos A$$
$$A = 79.93°$$
$$b^2 = a^2 + c^2 - 2ac \cos B$$
$$(21.34)^2 = (26.12)^2 + (19.25)^2 -$$
$$2(26.12)(19.25) \cos B$$
$$B = 53.55°$$
Then $C = 180° - (79.93° + 53.55°) = 46.52°$.

21. We are given two sides and the angle opposite one of them. The law of sines applies.
$$C = 180° - (70° + 12°) = 98°$$
$$\frac{a}{\sin A} = \frac{b}{\sin B}$$
$$\frac{a}{\sin 70°} = \frac{21.4}{\sin 12°}$$
$$a = \frac{21.4 \times \sin 70°}{\sin 12°} = 96.7$$
$$\frac{c}{\sin C} = \frac{b}{\sin B}$$
$$\frac{c}{\sin 98°} = \frac{21.4}{\sin 12°}$$
$$c = \frac{21.4 \times \sin 98°}{\sin 12°} = 101.9$$

22. Law of cosines
$$b^2 = a^2 + c^2 - 2ac \cos B$$
$$b^2 = 15^2 + 7^2 - 2 \cdot 15 \cdot 7 \cos 62°$$
$$b = 13$$
$$a^2 = b^2 + c^2 - 2bc \cos A$$
$$15^2 = 13^2 + 7^2 - 2 \cdot 13 \cdot 7 \cos A$$
$$A = 92° \quad \text{and} \quad C = 180° - (92° + 62°) = 26°.$$

23. We are given all three sides of the triangle. The law of cosines applies.

Find A:
$$a^2 = b^2 + c^2 - 2bc \cos A$$
$$(3.3)^2 = (2.7)^2 + (2.8)^2 - 2(2.7)(2.8) \cos A$$
$$10.89 = 7.29 + 7.84 - 15.12 \cos A$$
$$-4.24 = -15.12 \cos A$$
$$\cos A = 0.2804$$

Thus $A = 73.71°$.

Find B:
$$b^2 = a^2 + c^2 - 2ac \cos B$$
$$(2.7)^2 = (3.3)^2 + (2.8)^2 - 2(3.3)(2.8) \cos B$$
$$7.29 = 10.89 + 7.84 - 18.48 \cos B$$
$$-11.44 = -18.48 \cos B$$
$$\cos B = 0.6190$$

Thus $B = 51.75°$.

Then $C = 180° - (73.71° + 51.75°) = 54.54°$.

24. Law of sines
$$\frac{a}{\sin A} = \frac{b}{\sin B}, \text{ or } \frac{1.5}{\sin 58°} = \frac{2.5}{\sin B}$$
$\sin B = 1.4134$, so there is no solution.

25. We are given two sides of the triangle and the included angle. The law of cosines applies.
$$c^2 = a^2 + b^2 - 2ab \cos C$$
$$c^2 = 60^2 + 40^2 - 2(60)(40) \cos 47°$$
$$c^2 = 3600 + 1600 - 4800 \cos 47°$$
$$c^2 = 1926$$
$$c = 44$$
Next we use the law of cosines again to find a second angle.
$$a^2 = b^2 + c^2 - 2bc \cos A$$
$$60^2 = 40^2 + 44^2 - 2(40)(44) \cos A$$
$$3600 = 1600 + 1936 - 3520 \cos A$$
$$64 = -3520 \cos A$$
$$\cos A = -0.0182$$

Then $A = 91°$ and $B = 180° - (47° + 91°) = 42°$.

26. Law of cosines
$$a^2 = b^2 + c^2 - 2bc \cos A$$
$$(3.6)^2 = (6.2)^2 + (4.1)^2 - 2(6.2)(4.1) \cos A$$
$$A = 33.71°$$
$$b^2 = a^2 + c^2 - 2ac \cos B$$
$$(6.2)^2 = (3.6)^2 + (4.1)^2 - 2(3.6)(4.1) \cos B$$
$$B = 107.08° \quad \text{and}$$
$$C = 180° - (33.71° + 107.08°) = 39.21°$$

27. We are given two angles and the side opposite one of them. The law of sines applies.

$A = 180° - (110° \ 30' + 8° \ 10') = 61° \ 20'$

$$\frac{a}{\sin A} = \frac{c}{\sin C}$$

$$\frac{a}{\sin 61° \ 20'} = \frac{0.912}{\sin 8° \ 10'}$$

$$a = \frac{0.912 \times \sin 61° \ 20'}{\sin 8° \ 10'}$$

$$a = 5.633$$

$$\frac{b}{\sin B} = \frac{c}{\sin C}$$

$$\frac{b}{\sin 110° \ 30'} = \frac{0.912}{\sin 8° \ 10'}$$

$$b = \frac{0.912 \times \sin 110° \ 30'}{\sin 8° \ 10'}$$

$$b = 6.014$$

28. Law of sines

$A = 180° - (52° + 15°) = 113°$

$$\frac{a}{\sin A} = \frac{b}{\sin B}, \quad \text{or} \quad \frac{a}{\sin 113°} = \frac{60.4}{\sin 52°}$$

$$a = 70.6$$

$$\frac{c}{\sin C} = \frac{b}{\sin B}, \quad \text{or} \quad \frac{c}{\sin 15°} = \frac{60.4}{\sin 52°}$$

$$c = 19.8$$

29.

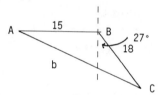

Find B: $B = 90° + 27° = 117°$

Find b:

$b^2 = a^2 + c^2 - 2ac \cos B$

$b^2 = 18^2 + 15^2 - 2 \cdot 18 \cdot 15 \cos 117°$

$b^2 = 324 + 225 - 540 \cos 117°$

$b^2 = 794.16$

$b = 28$

Find A:

$a^2 = b^2 + c^2 - 2bc \cos A$

$18^2 = 28^2 + 15^2 - 2(28)(15) \cos A$

$324 = 784 + 225 - 840 \cos A$

$-685 = -840 \cos A$

$\cos A = 0.8155$

Thus $A = 35° \ 22'$ and $90° - 35° \ 22' = 54° \ 38'$.

The ship is 28 nautical mi from the harbor in a direction of S54° 38'E.

30.

$B = 220° - 90° = 130°$

$b^2 = a^2 + c^2 - 2ac \cos 130°$

$b^2 = 200^2 + 147^2 - 2 \cdot 200 \cdot 147 \cos 130°$

$b = 315$ km

$a^2 = b^2 + c^2 - 2bc \cos A$

$200^2 = 315^2 + 147^2 - 2 \cdot 315 \cdot 147 \cos A$

$A = 29°$

The direction from the airport is $270° - 29° = 241°$.

31.

2 hr × 25 knots = 50 nautical mi
2 hr × 20 knots = 40 nautical mi

Find A: $A = 15° + 32° = 47°$

Find a:

$a^2 = b^2 + c^2 - 2bc \cos A$

$a^2 = 50^2 + 40^2 - 2 \cdot 50 \cdot 40 \cos 47°$

$a^2 = 2500 + 1600 - 4000 \cos 47°$

$a^2 = 1372$

$a = 37$

The ships are 37 nautical mi apart.

32.

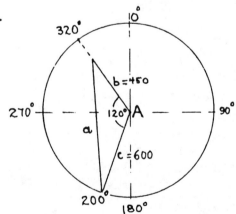

$A = 320° - 200° = 120°$

$b = (150)(3) = 450$ and $c = (200)(3) = 600$.

Then $a^2 = b^2 + c^2 - 2bc \cos A$.

$a^2 = 450^2 + 600^2 - 2 \cdot 450 \cdot 600 \cos 120°$

$a = 912$ km

33.

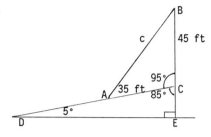

Since $D = 5°$ and $E = 90°$, $\angle DCE = 90° - 5° = 85°$
and $\angle ACB = 180° - 85° = 95°$.

Using the law of cosines,

$c^2 = 45^2 + 35^2 - 2 \cdot 45 \cdot 35 \cos 95°$

$c^2 = 2025 + 1225 - 3150 \cos 95°$

$c^2 = 3525$

$c = 59$

The length of the rope must be 59 ft.

34.

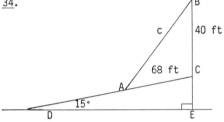

$\angle DCE = 90° - 15° = 75°$, so $\angle ACB = 180° - 75° = 105°$.

$c^2 = a^2 + b^2 - 2bc \cos C$

$c^2 = 40^2 + 68^2 - 2 \cdot 40 \cdot 68 \cos 105°$

$c = 87$ ft

35. The perimeter is 5.5 m. The length of the third side is 5.5 - (1.5 + 2), or 2 m.

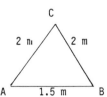

Find A:

$a^2 = b^2 + c^2 - 2bc \cos A$

$2^2 = (1.5)^2 + 2^2 - 2(1.5)(2) \cos A$

$4 = 2.25 + 4 - 6 \cos A$

$-2.25 = -6 \cos A$

$\cos A = 0.375$

Thus $A = 67.98°$. Since $\triangle ABC$ is isosceles B is also 67.98°.

Find C:

$C = 180° - (67.98° + 67.98°) = 44.04°$

The angles are 67.98°, 67.98°, and 44.04°.

36. $a = 120$ ft, $b = 150$ ft, $c = 100$ ft

$120^2 = 150^2 + 100^2 - 2 \cdot 150 \cdot 100 \cos A$

$A = 52.89°$

$150^2 = 120^2 + 100^2 - 2 \cdot 120 \cdot 100 \cos B$

$B = 85.46°$

$C = 180° - (52.89° + 85.46°) = 41.65°$

37.

Using the law of cosines,

$d^2 = 65^2 + 46^2 - 2 \cdot 65 \cdot 46 \cdot \cos 45°$

$d^2 = 4225 + 2116 - 5980 \cos 45°$

$d = 46$

The distance from the pitcher's mound to first base is 46 ft.

38.

$d^2 = 60.5^2 + 90^2 - 2(60.5)(90) \cos 45°$

$d = 63.7$ ft

39.

Let b represent the other base, d represent the diagonal, and h the height.

a) Find d:

Using the law of cosines,

$d^2 = 10^2 + 14^2 - 2 \cdot 10 \cdot 14 \cos 80°$

$d^2 = 100 + 196 - 280 \cos 80°$

$d = 16$

The length of the diagonal is 16 ft.

391

b) Find h:

$$\frac{h}{10} = \sin 80°$$

$$h = 10 \sin 80°$$

$$h = 9.85$$

Find ∠CBD:

Using the law of sines,

$$\frac{10}{\sin \angle CBD} = \frac{16}{\sin 100°}$$

$$\sin \angle CBD = \frac{10 \sin 100°}{16} = 0.6155$$

Thus ∠CBD = 38°.

Then ∠CDB = 180° - (100° + 38°) = 42°.

Find b:

Using the law of sines,

$$\frac{b}{\sin 42°} = \frac{16}{\sin 100°}$$

$$b = \frac{16 \sin 42°}{\sin 100°} = 10.87$$

Area $= \frac{1}{2} h(b_1 + b_2)$

Area $= \frac{1}{2} (9.85)(10.87 + 14)$

$= 122$ ft²   (Answers may vary slightly due to rounding.)

40.

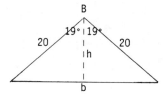

$b^2 = a^2 + c^2 - 2ac \cos B$, or

$b^2 = 20^2 + 20^2 - 2·20·20 \cos 38°$

$b = 13$

$\cos 19° = \frac{h}{20}$, so h = 19

Area $= \frac{1}{2} bh = \frac{1}{2} · 13 · 19 \approx 124$

41.

Let b = 70 yd; then find h.

$$\frac{h}{50} = \sin 78°$$

$$h = 50 \sin 78°$$

Area = b·h

Area = 70·50 sin 78°

$= 3424$ yd²

42.

$a = \sqrt{75^2 - 10^2} = 74$

$b = 180 - a = 106$

$\sin \alpha = \frac{10}{75}$; $\alpha = 8°$

$\tan \beta = \frac{10}{106}$; $\beta = 5°$

The correction is $\alpha + \beta = 8° + 5° = 13°$.

43.

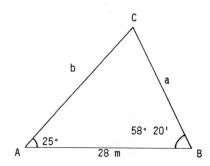

We are given two angles and a side of a triangle. The law of sines applies.

C = 180° - (25° + 58° 20') = 96° 40'

$$\frac{a}{\sin A} = \frac{c}{\sin C}$$

$$\frac{a}{\sin 25°} = \frac{28}{\sin 96° 40'}$$

$$a = \frac{28 \times \sin 25°}{\sin 96° 40'} = 12$$

$$\frac{b}{\sin B} = \frac{c}{\sin C}$$

$$\frac{b}{\sin 58° 20'} = \frac{28}{\sin 96° 40'}$$

$$b = \frac{28 \times \sin 58° 20'}{\sin 96° 40'} = 24$$

The lengths of the other two sides are 12 m and 24 m.

44.

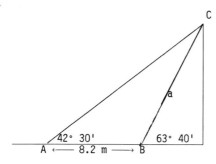

In △ ABC, B = 180° - 63° 40' = 116° 20' and
C = 180° - (42° 30' + 116° 20') = 21° 10'.

$$\frac{a}{\sin A} = \frac{c}{\sin C}, \text{ or } \frac{a}{\sin 42° 30'} = \frac{8.2}{\sin 21° 10'}$$
$$a = 15.3 \text{ m}$$

45.

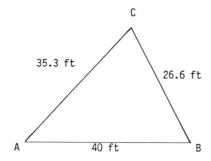

We are given all three sides of a triangle. The
law of cosines applies.

Find A:

$$a^2 = b^2 + c^2 - 2bc \cos A$$
$$(26.6)^2 = (35.3)^2 + 40^2 - 2(35.3)(40) \cos A$$
$$707.56 = 1246.09 + 1600 - 2824 \cos A$$
$$-2138.53 = -2824 \cos A$$
$$\cos A = 0.7573$$

Then A = 40.78°.

Find B:

$$b^2 = a^2 + c^2 - 2ac \cos B$$
$$(35.3)^2 = (26.6)^2 + 40^2 - 2(26.6)(40) \cos B$$
$$1246.09 = 707.56 + 1600 - 2128 \cos B$$
$$-1061.47 = -2128 \cos B$$
$$\cos B = 0.4988$$

Then B = 60.08° and
C = 180° - (40.78° + 60.08°) = 79.14°.

46.

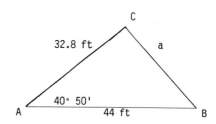

$$a^2 = b^2 + c^2 - 2bc \cos A$$
$$a^2 = (32.8)^2 + 44^2 - 2(32.8)(44) \cos 40.8°$$
$$a = 28.8 \text{ ft}$$

47.

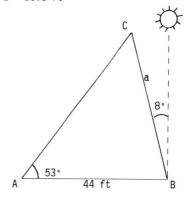

B = 90° - 8° = 82°

Now we have two angles and a side of a triangle.
The law of sines applies.

C = 180° - (53° + 82°) = 45°

$$\frac{a}{\sin A} = \frac{c}{\sin C}$$
$$\frac{a}{\sin 53°} = \frac{44}{\sin 45°}$$
$$a = \frac{44 \times \sin 53°}{\sin 45°} = 50 \text{ ft}$$

48.

Make a larger drawing of △ ABC.

B = 90° + 6° = 96°

$b^2 = a^2 + c^2 - 2ac \cos B$

$b^2 = 42^2 + 35^2 - 2 \cdot 42 \cdot 35 \cos 96°$

b = 57 ft

<u>49.</u> Place the figure on a coordinate system as shown.

Let (x, y) be the coordinates of point Q. The coordinates of point P are (1.4 + 1.1, 0), or (2.5, 0). The length of QR is 1.8 + 1.4, or 3.2.

We use the law of cosines to find d.

$d^2 = (2.5)^2 + (3.2)^2 - 2(2.5)(3.2) \cos 109°$

$d^2 = 6.25 + 10.24 - 16 \cos 109°$

d = 4.7 cm

<u>50.</u>

$\dfrac{58}{\sin C} = \dfrac{50}{\sin 41°}$, and C = 50°.

Then φ = 180° - (41° + 50°) = 89°.

<u>51.</u> $K = \frac{1}{2} bc \sin A$

$K^2 = \frac{1}{4} b^2c^2 \sin^2 A$ Squaring both sides

$K^2 = \frac{1}{4} b^2c^2 (1 - \cos^2 A)$

$K^2 = \frac{1}{4} b^2c^2 - \frac{1}{4} b^2c^2 \cos^2 A$

Now, the law of cosines gives us

$a^2 = b^2 + c^2 - 2bc \cos A$ so

$bc \cos A = \dfrac{-a^2 + b^2 + c^2}{2}$ and

$b^2c^2 \cos^2 A = \left[\dfrac{-a^2 + b^2 + c^2}{2}\right]^2.$

We substitute in the expression for K^2:

$K^2 = \frac{1}{4} b^2c^2 - \frac{1}{4} \left[\dfrac{-a^2 + b^2 + c^2}{2}\right]^2$

$= \frac{1}{4} b^2c^2 - \frac{1}{4} \cdot \frac{1}{4} (-a^2 + b^2 + c^2)^2$

$= \frac{1}{16} \left[4b^2c^2 - (-a^2 + b^2 + c^2)^2\right]$

$= \frac{1}{16} \left[2bc + (-a^2 + b^2 + c^2)\right]\left[2bc - (-a^2 + b^2 + c^2)\right]$

$= \frac{1}{16} \left[(b^2 + 2bc + c^2) - a^2\right]\left[a^2 - (b^2 - 2bc + c^2)\right]$

$= \frac{1}{16} \left[(b + c)^2 - a^2\right]\left[a^2 - (b - c)^2\right]$

$= \frac{1}{16}(b + c + a)(b + c - a)(a - b + c)(a + b - c)$

$= \frac{1}{2} (a + b + c) \cdot \left[\frac{1}{2} (a + b + c) - a\right] \cdot$

$\left[\frac{1}{2} (a + b + c) - b\right] \cdot \left[\frac{1}{2} (a + b + c) - c\right]$

Thus, $K^2 = s(s - a)(s - b)(s - c)$, where $s = \frac{1}{2} (a + b + c).$

Then $K = \sqrt{s(s - a)(s - b)(s - c)}$, where $s = \frac{1}{2} (a + b + c).$

<u>52.</u> a = 40, b = 35.3, c = 26.6

$s = \frac{1}{2} (40 + 35.3 + 26.6) = 50.95$

$K = \sqrt{50.95(50.95 - 40)(50.95 - 35.3)(50.95 - 26.6)}$

$K = 461.1$ ft^2

<u>53.</u>

First consider Δ ABC and find B:

$b^2 = a^2 + c^2 - 2ac \cos B$

$90^2 = 50^2 + 60^2 - 2 \cdot 50 \cdot 60 \cos B$

$8100 = 2500 + 3600 - 6000 \cos B$

$2000 = -6000 \cos B$

$\cos B = -0.3333$

B = 109.5°

Then in the parallelogram ABCD, the measure of angle A is 180° - 109.5°, or 70.5°.

Now consider ∆ ABD and find the length of the side opposite A (that is, the length of the other diagonal of the parallelogram.)

$a^2 = b^2 + d^2 - 2bd \cos A$

$a^2 = 50^2 + 60^2 - 2 \cdot 50 \cdot 60 \cos 70.5°$

$a^2 = 2500 + 3600 - 6000 \cos 70.5°$

$a = 64$ in.

54.

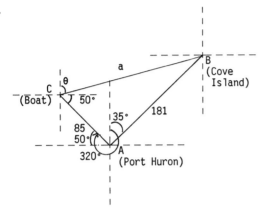

$A = 35° + (360° - 320°) = 75°$

$a^2 = b^2 + c^2 - 2bc \cos A$

$a^2 = 85^2 + 181^2 - 2 \cdot 85 \cdot 181 \cos 75°$

$a = 179$ mi

$c^2 = a^2 + b^2 - 2ab \cos C$

$181^2 = 179^2 + 85^2 - 2 \cdot 179 \cdot 85 \cos C$

$C = 78°$ so $\theta = 90° + 50° - 78° = 62°$

The new heading must be 62°.

55.

Find ∠ABC, ∠CAB, and ∠ACB:

The angle of incidence equals the angle of reflection. Thus ∠ABC = 180° - (14° + 14°), or 152°. Then ∠CAB = 180° - (25° + 152°), or 3°, ∠ACB = 11° + 14°, or 25°.

Find a:

$\dfrac{a}{20} = \csc 14°$

$a = 20 \csc 14° = 82.7$

Find c:

Using the law of sines,

$\dfrac{c}{\sin 25°} = \dfrac{82.7}{\sin 3°}$

$c = \dfrac{82.7 \sin 25°}{\sin 3°} = 668$

Find x:

$\dfrac{x}{668} = \sin 14°$

$x = 668 \sin 14° = 162$ ft

The height of the tree is 162 ft.

56.

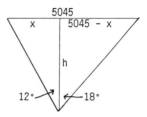

$\tan 12° = \dfrac{x}{h}$, or $x = h \tan 12°$

$\tan 18° = \dfrac{5045 - x}{h} = \dfrac{5045 - h \tan 12°}{h}$

Then $h = \dfrac{5045}{\tan 18° + \tan 12°} = 9386$ ft

57.

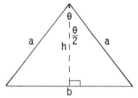

Let b represent the base, h the height, and θ the included angle.

Find h:

$\dfrac{h}{a} = \cos \dfrac{\theta}{2}$

$h = a \cos \dfrac{\theta}{2}$

Find b:

$b^2 = a^2 + a^2 - 2 \cdot a \cdot a \cos \theta$

$b^2 = 2a^2 - 2a^2 \cos \theta$

$b^2 = 2a^2(1 - \cos \theta)$

$b = \sqrt{2}\, a \sqrt{1 - \cos \theta}$

Find A (area):

$A = \dfrac{1}{2} bh$

$A = \dfrac{1}{2} \left[\sqrt{2}\, a \sqrt{1 - \cos \theta} \right] \left[a \cos \dfrac{\theta}{2} \right]$

$A = \left[a \sqrt{\dfrac{1 - \cos \theta}{2}} \right] \left[a \sqrt{\dfrac{1 + \cos \theta}{2}} \right]$

$A = \dfrac{1}{2} a^2 \sqrt{1 - \cos^2 \theta} = \dfrac{1}{2} a^2 \sqrt{\sin^2 \theta}$

$A = \dfrac{1}{2} a^2 \sin \theta$

The maximum area occurs when θ is 90°.

58.

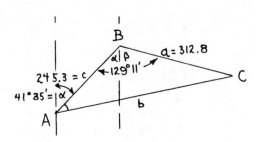

a) $\alpha + \beta = 129°\ 11'$; thus

   $\beta = 129°\ 11' - 41°\ 35' = 87°\ 36'$ and the bearing of BC is S 87° 36' E.

b) $b^2 = (312.8)^2 + (245.3)^2 -$
   $2(312.8)(245.3) \cos 129°\ 11'$

   $b = 504.9$ ft

   $$\frac{504.9}{\sin 129°\ 11'} = \frac{312.8}{\sin A}$$

   $A = 28°\ 42'$

   $\alpha + A = 41°\ 35' + 28°\ 42' = 70°\ 17'$, so the bearing of AC is N 70° 17' E.

59. See the answer section in the text.

60. From Exercise 59 we have

   $2bc \cos A + 2ac \cos B + 2ab \cos C = a^2 + b^2 + c^2$.

   Multiplying each term on both sides of the equation by $\frac{1}{2abc}$ we obtain

   $$\frac{\cos A}{a} + \frac{\cos B}{b} + \frac{\cos C}{c} = \frac{a^2 + b^2 + c^2}{2abc}.$$

61. We add labels to the drawing in the text.

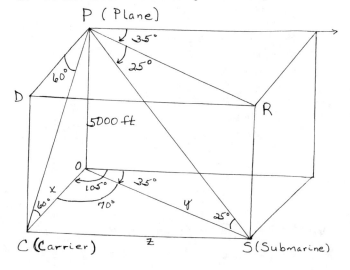

We find x using Δ PCO:

$$\cot 60° = \frac{x}{5000}$$

   $x = 5000 \cot 60°$

   $x = 2886.75$

We find y using Δ PSO:

$$\cot 25° = \frac{y}{5000}$$

   $y = 5000 \cot 25°$

   $y = 10,722.53$

Finally, we use Δ OCS and the law of cosines to find z, the distance from the submarine to the carrier.

$z^2 = x^2 + y^2 - 2xy \cos 70°$

$z^2 = (2886.75)^2 + (10,722.53)^2 -$
   $2(2886.75)(10,722.53) \cos 70°$

 $z = 10,106$ ft

62.

Consider Δ QEO:

$$\frac{\overline{QE}}{\sin 118°} = \frac{6380}{\sin 31°}$$

   $$\overline{QE} = \frac{6380 \times \sin 118°}{\sin 31°} = 10,937$$

Consider Δ QES:

$$\frac{\overline{QS}}{\sin 69°} = \frac{\overline{QE}}{\sin 47°}$$

   $$\overline{QS} = \frac{10,937 \times \sin 69°}{\sin 47°} = 13,961$$

Consider Δ OQS:

$\overline{OS}^2 = 6380^2 + \overline{QS}^2 - 2 \cdot \overline{QS} \cdot 6380 \cos 95°$

$\overline{OS}^2 = 6380^2 + (13,961)^2 - 2(6380)(13,961) \cos 95°$

$\overline{OS} = 15,847$

Then the distance of the satellite from the earth, $\overline{PS}$, is $15,847 - 6380 = 9467$ km.

Exercise Set 8.4

1.

Find the resultant, **s**, and the angle, α, it makes with vector **a**. Consider the following triangle:

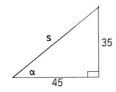

Find s:

Using the Pythagorean theorem, $s^2 = 35^2 + 45^2$.

Then $s = \sqrt{3250} = 57.0$, to the nearest tenth.

Find α:

$\tan \alpha = \frac{35}{45} = 0.7778$

Thus α = 38°, to the nearest degree.

2.

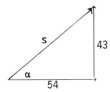

$s^2 = 54^2 + 43^2$; s = 69.0.

$\tan \alpha = \frac{43}{54}$; α = 39°.

3.

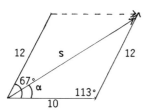

Find the resultant, **s**, and the angle, α, it makes with vector **a**. Consider the following triangle:

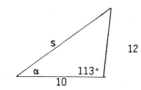

Find s:

Using the law of cosines,

$s^2 = 10^2 + 12^2 - 2 \cdot 10 \cdot 12 \cos 113°$

Then $s = \sqrt{338} = 18.4$.

Find α:

Using the law of sines,

$\frac{12}{\sin \alpha} = \frac{18.4}{\sin 113°}$

$\sin \alpha = \frac{12 \sin 113°}{18.4} = 0.6003$

Thus α = 37°.

4.

$s^2 = 25^2 + 30^2 - 2 \cdot 25 \cdot 30 \cos 105°$; s = 43.7.

$\frac{30}{\sin \alpha} = \frac{43.7}{\sin 105°}$; α = 42°.

5.

Find the resultant, **s**, and the angle, α, it makes with vector **a**. Consider the following triangle:

Find s:

Using the law of cosines,

$s^2 = 20^2 + 20^2 - 2 \cdot 20 \cdot 20 \cos 63°$

Then $s = \sqrt{437} = 20.9$.

Find α:

Since the triangle is isosceles and the angle between the congruent sides is 63°, we know that

$\alpha = \frac{1}{2}(180° - 63°) = \frac{1}{2}(117°) = 59°$; to the nearest degree.

6.

$s^2 = 30^2 + 30^2 - 2 \cdot 30 \cdot 30 \cos 57°$; s = 28.6.

$\frac{30}{\sin \alpha} = \frac{28.6}{\sin 57°}$; α = 62°.

7.

Find the resultant, **s**, and the angle, α, it makes with vector **a**. Consider the following triangle:

Find s:

Using the law of cosines,

$s^2 = 23^2 + 47^2 - 2 \cdot 23 \cdot 47 \cos 153°$

Then $s = \sqrt{4664} = 68.3$.

Find α:

Using the law of sines,

$\dfrac{47}{\sin \alpha} = \dfrac{68.3}{\sin 153°}$

$\sin \alpha = \dfrac{47 \sin 153°}{68.3} = 0.3124$

Thus α = 18°.

8.

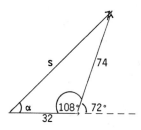

$s^2 = 32^2 + 74^2 - 2 \cdot 32 \cdot 74 \cos 108°; \quad s = 89.2.$

$\dfrac{74}{\sin \alpha} = \dfrac{89.2}{\sin 108°}; \quad \alpha = 52°.$

9.

Find |s|:

Using the Pythagorean theorem,

$|s|^2 = (12.3)^2 + (5.8)^2$

Then $|s| = \sqrt{184.93} = 13.6$ newtons.

Find α:

$\tan \alpha = \dfrac{12.3}{5.8}$

Then α = 65°.

10.

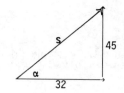

$|s|^2 = 32^2 + 45^2; \quad |s| = 55$ newtons.

$\tan \alpha = \dfrac{45}{32}; \quad \alpha = 55°.$

11.

Find |s|:

Using the law of cosines,

$|s|^2 = 420^2 + 300^2 - 2 \cdot 420 \cdot 300 \cos 130°$

Then $|s| = \sqrt{428,386} = 655$ newtons.

Find α:

Using the law of sines,

$\dfrac{300}{\sin \alpha} = \dfrac{655}{\sin 130°}$

$\sin \alpha = \dfrac{300 \sin 130°}{655} = 0.3508$

Thus α = 21°.

12.

$|s|^2 = 410^2 + 600^2 - 2 \cdot 410 \cdot 600 \cos 133°; \quad |s| = 929$ newtons.

$\dfrac{600}{\sin \alpha} = \dfrac{929}{\sin 133°}; \quad \alpha = 28°.$

<u>13.</u>

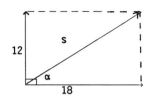

Find |s|, the speed of the balloon, and α, the angle it makes with the horizontal. Consider the following triangle:

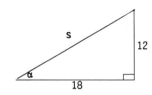

Find |s|:

$|s|^2 = 18^2 + 12^2$

Then $|s| = \sqrt{468} = 22$.

Find α:

$\tan \alpha = \frac{12}{18}$

Thus α = 34°.

The speed of the balloon is 22 ft/sec, and it makes a 34° angle with the horizontal.

<u>14.</u>

$|s|^2 = 10^2 + 5^2$; |s| = 11 ft/sec.

$\tan \alpha = \frac{10}{5}$; α = 63°.

<u>15.</u>

Find |s|:

Using the law of cosines,

$|s|^2 = 750^2 + 150^2 - 2 \cdot 750 \cdot 150 \cos 75°$

Then $|s| = \sqrt{526,770} = 726$.

Find α:

Using the law of sines,

$\frac{150}{\sin \alpha} = \frac{726}{\sin 75°}$

$\sin \alpha = \frac{150 \sin 75°}{726} = 0.1996$

Thus α = 12°.

The resultant force is 726 lb, and the boat is moving in the direction 35° + 12°, or 47°.

<u>16.</u>

θ = 10° + (180° − 50°) = 140°.

$|s|^2 = 650^2 + 100^2 - 2 \cdot 650 \cdot 100 \cos 140°$;
|s| = 729 lb.

$\frac{100}{\sin \alpha} = \frac{729}{\sin 140°}$; α = 5°.

Thus the resultant direction is 220° + 5° = 225°.

<u>17.</u>

Note:

180° − (20° + 90°) = 70°

180° − 70° = 110°

399

80°

90° − 80° = 10°

10°   110°   180° − (10° + 110°) = 60°

Find |**d**|:

Using the law of cosines,

|**d**|² = 120² + 200² − 2·120·200 cos 60°

Then |**d**| = √30,400 = 174.

Use the law of sines to find θ in this triangle.

120   60°
θ
174   200

$\dfrac{200}{\sin\theta} = \dfrac{174}{\sin 60°}$

$\sin\theta = \dfrac{200 \sin 60°}{174} = 0.9954$

Thus θ = 85°.

Now we can find α.

α = 180° − (80° + 85°) = 15°

The ship is 174 nautical miles from the starting point in the direction S 15° E.

18.

θ = 10° + 58° = 68°.

s² = 210² + 170² − 2·210·170 cos 68°; s = 215 km.

$\dfrac{170}{\sin\beta} = \dfrac{215}{\sin 68°}$; β = 47°.

Then ε = 47° − 32° = 15°.

Thus the direction of s is 360° − 15° = 345°.

19.

3
15   θ

Find θ:

$\sin\theta = \dfrac{3}{15} = 0.2000$

Thus θ = 12°.

The boat should be pointed at an angle of 12° upstream.

20.

$\sin\theta = \dfrac{25}{150}$; θ ≈ 10°.

Then the direction of vector **a** is

90° − (10° + 10°) = 70°.

21.

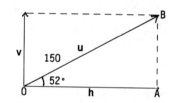

From △ OAB, we find

|**h**| = 150 cos 52° = 92

|**v**| = 150 sin 52° = 118

22.

h
63°
v   170

|**h**| = 170 cos 63° = 77

|**v**| = 170 sin 63° = 151

23.

From the drawing we find

$|s| = 250 \cos 40° = 192$ km/h

$|w| = 250 \sin 40° = 161$ km/h

24.

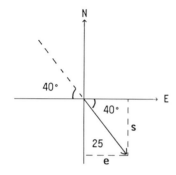

$s = 25 \sin 40° = 16$ mph

$e = 25 \cos 40° = 19$ mph

25.

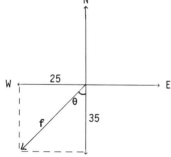

Find $|f|$:

$|f| = \sqrt{25^2 + 35^2} = 43$ newtons

Find θ:

$\tan \theta = \dfrac{25}{35}$

$\theta = 36°$

The vector **f** has a magnitude of 43 newtons and a direction of S 36° W.

26.

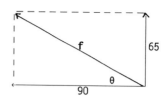

$|f| = \sqrt{90^2 + 65^2} = 111$ newtons

$\tan \theta = \dfrac{65}{90}$

$\theta = 36°$

27.

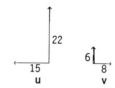

a) Adding the east-west components, we obtain 7 west. Adding the north-south components, we obtain 28 north. The components of **u + v** are 7 west and 28 north.

b)

Find θ:

$\tan \theta = \dfrac{28}{7} = 4$

$\theta = 76°$

Thus $90° - 76° = 14°$.

Find $|u + v|$:

$|u + v| = \sqrt{7^2 + 28^2} = 28.9$

The vector **u + v** has a magnitude of 28.9 and a direction of N 14° W.

28.

a) Adding right-left components, we obtain 23 right.

Adding upward-downward components, we obtain 13 upward.

b)

$|u + v| = \sqrt{23^2 + 13^2} = 26$

$\tan \theta = \dfrac{13}{23}$

$\theta = 29°$

Then $90° - 29° = 61°$.

u + v has magnitude 26 and direction N 61° E.

29. $<3, 7> + <2, 9>$
$= <3 + 2, 7 + 9>$
$= <5, 16>$

30. $<2, -5>$

31. $<17, 7.6> + <-12.2, 6.1>$
$= <17 + (-12.2), 7.6 + 6.1>$
$= <4.8, 13.7>$

32. $<-7.3, 19.3>$

33. $<-650, -750> + <-12, 324>$
$= <-650 + (-12), -750 + 324>$
$= <-662, -426>$

34. $<-429, -717>$

35.   Let **v** = $<3, 4>$.

$\tan \theta = \dfrac{4}{3}$

$\theta = 53°$

$|v| = \sqrt{3^2 + 4^2} = 5$

Thus polar notation for **v** is (5, 53°).

36.

$\tan \theta = \dfrac{3}{4}$

$\theta = 37°$

$|v| = \sqrt{4^2 + 3^2} = 5$

Polar notation: (5, 37°)

37.   Let **v** = $<10, -15>$.

The reference angle is ϕ.

$\tan \phi = \dfrac{-15}{10}$

$\phi = -56°$

$\theta = 360° - 56° = 304°$

$|v| = \sqrt{10^2 + (-15)^2} = 18$

Thus polar notation for **v** is (18, 304°) or (18, -56°).

38.

$\tan \phi = \dfrac{-10}{17}$

$\phi = -30°$

$\theta = 360° - 30° = 330°$

$|v| = \sqrt{17^2 + (-10)^2} = 20$

Polar notation: (20, 330°) or (20, -30°)

<u>39.</u> Let **v** = <-3, -4>.

The reference angle is φ.

tan φ = $\frac{-4}{-3}$

φ = 53°

θ = 180° + 53° = 233°

|**v**| = $\sqrt{(-3)^2 + (-4)^2}$ = 5

Thus polar notation for **v** is (5, 233°).

<u>40.</u>

tan φ = $\frac{-3}{-4}$

φ = 37°

θ = 180° + 37° = 217°

|**v**| = $\sqrt{(-4)^2 + (-3)^2}$ = 5

Polar notation: (5, 217°)

<u>41.</u> Let **v** = <-10, 15>.

The reference angle is φ.

tan φ = $\frac{15}{-10}$

φ = 56°

θ = 180° - 56° = 124°

|**v**| = $\sqrt{(-10)^2 + 15^2}$ = 18

Thus polar notation for **v** is (18, 124°).

<u>42.</u>

tan φ = $\frac{10}{-17}$

φ = 30°

θ = 180° - 30° = 150°

|**v**| = $\sqrt{(-17)^2 + 10^2}$ = 20

Polar notation: (20, 150°)

<u>43.</u> **v** = (4, 30°)

From the drawing we have

x = 4 cos 30° = 3.5

y = 4 sin 30° = 2

Thus rectangular notation for **v** is <3.5, 2>.

<u>44.</u>

x = 8 cos 60° = 4

y = 8 sin 60° = 6.9

Rectangular notation: <4, 6.9>

45. **v** = (10, 235°)

From the drawing we have

x = 10 cos 235° = -5.7
y = 10 sin 235° = -8.2

Thus rectangular notation for **v** is <-5.7, -8.2>.

46.

x = 15 cos 210° = -13.0
y = 15 sin 210° = -7.5

Rectangular notation: <-13.0, -7.5>

47. **v** = (20, 330°)

From the drawing we have

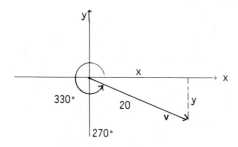

x = 20 cos 330° = 17.3
y = 20 sin 330° = -10

Thus rectangular notation for **v** is <17.3, -10>.

48.

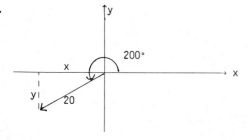

x = 20 cos 200° = -18.8
y = 20 sin 200° = -6.8

Rectangular notation: <-18.8, -6.8>

49. **v** = (100, -45°)

From the drawing we have

x = 100 cos (-45°) = 70.7
y = 100 sin (-45°) = -70.7

Thus rectangular notation for **v** is <70.7, -70.7>.

50.

x = 150 cos 60° = 75
y = 150 sin 60° = 130.0

Rectangular notation: <75, 130.0>

51. 3**u** + 2**v** = 3<3, 4> + 2< 5, 12>
    = <9, 12> + <10, 24>
    = <9 + 10, 12 + 24>
    = <19, 36>

52. 3**u** - 2**v** = <9, 12> - <10, 24>   (See Exercise 51.)
    = <-1, -12>

53. (**u** + **v**) - **w** = (<3, 4> + <5, 12>) - <-6, 8>
    = <8, 16> + <6, -8>
    = <14, 8>

54. **u** - (**v** + **w**) = <3, 4> - (<5, 12> + <-6, 8>)
    = <3, 4> - <-1, 20>
    = <4, -16>

55. |**u**| = |<3, 4>| = $\sqrt{3^2 + 4^2}$ = $\sqrt{25}$ = 5

    |**v**| = |<5, 12>| = $\sqrt{5^2 + 12^2}$ = $\sqrt{169}$ = 13

    |**u**| + |**v**| = 5 + 13 = 18

56. |**u**| - |**v**| = 5 - 13   (See Exercise 55.)

    = -8

57. |**u** + **v**| = |<3, 4> + <5, 12>|

    = |<8, 16>|

    = $\sqrt{8^2 + 16^2}$ = $\sqrt{64 + 256}$

    = $\sqrt{320}$

    = 17.9

58. |**u** - **v**| = |<3, 4> - <5, 12>| = |<-2, -8>|

    = $\sqrt{(-2)^2 + (-8)^2}$

    = 8.2

59. 2|**u** + **v**| = 2(17.9)   (See Exercise 57.)

    = 35.8

60. 2|**u**| + 2|**v**| = 2·5 + 2·13   (See Exercise 55.)

    = 36

61. Let PQ = <x, y>. Then QP = <-x, -y> and
    PQ + QP = <x, y> + <-x, -y> = <0, 0> = 0

62. (Assume neither |**u**| nor |**v**| is zero.)

    If **u·v** = |**u**||**v**| cos θ = 0, then cos θ = 0, or
    θ = 90° and the vectors are perpendicular.

    If **u** and **v** are perpendicular, then θ = 90° so
    u·v = |**u**||**v**| cos 90° = |**u**||**v**|·0 = 0.

63. See the answer section in the text.

64.

    Let **u** = <3, 4> have direction θ,

    where θ = $\tan^{-1} \frac{4}{3}$.

    Let **v** = $\frac{\mathbf{u}}{|\mathbf{u}|}$ = $< \frac{3}{5}, \frac{4}{5} >$ have direction φ,

    where φ = $\tan^{-1} \dfrac{\frac{4}{5}}{\frac{3}{5}}$ = $\tan^{-1} \frac{4}{3}$.

    Thus the two vectors have the same direction

    and the length of **v** is $\sqrt{\left(\frac{3}{5}\right)^2 + \left(\frac{4}{5}\right)^2}$ = 1.

65. See the answer section in the text.

See text answer section for odd exercise answers 1.-23.

Even exercises 2. - 24.

25.

    Find |**v**|:

    |**v**| = $\sqrt{4^2 + 4^2}$ = $\sqrt{32}$ = $4\sqrt{2}$

    Find θ:

    tan θ = $\frac{4}{4}$ = 1

    θ = 45°

    Polar coordinates of the point (4, 4) are
    ($4\sqrt{2}$, 45°).

26. |**v**| = $\sqrt{5^2 + 5^2}$ = $5\sqrt{2}$

    tan θ = $\frac{5}{5}$ = 1

    θ = 45°   (The point is in quadrant I)

    Polar coordinates: ($5\sqrt{2}$, 45°)

27.

    |**v**| = 5

    θ = 90°

    Polar coordinates of the point (0, 5) are (5, 90°).

28. $|\mathbf{v}| = \sqrt{0^2 + (-3)^2} = 3$

    The terminal side of θ is on the negative y-axis.

    θ = 270°

    Polar coordinates: (3, 270°)

29.

    $|\mathbf{v}| = 4$

    θ = 0°

    Polar coordinates of the point (4, 0) are (4, 0°)

30. $|\mathbf{v}| = \sqrt{(-5)^2 + 0^2} = 5$

    The terminal side of θ is on the negative x-axis.

    θ = 180°

    Polar coordinates: (5, 180°)

31.

    Find $|\mathbf{v}|$:

    $|\mathbf{v}| = \sqrt{3^2 + (3\sqrt{3})^2} = \sqrt{36} = 6$

    Find θ:

    $\tan \theta = \frac{3\sqrt{3}}{3} = \sqrt{3}$

    θ = 60°

    Polar coordinates of the point (3, 3√3) are (6, 60°)

32. $|\mathbf{v}| = \sqrt{(-3)^2 + (-3\sqrt{3})^2} = 6$

    $\tan \theta = \frac{-3\sqrt{3}}{-3} = \sqrt{3}$

    θ = 240°   (The point is in quadrant III.)

    Polar coordinates: (6, 240°)

33.

Find $|\mathbf{v}|$:

$|\mathbf{v}| = \sqrt{(\sqrt{3})^2 + 1^2} = \sqrt{4} = 2$

Find θ:

$\tan \theta = \frac{1}{\sqrt{3}}$

θ = 30°

Polar coordinates of the point (√3, 1) are (2, 30°).

34. $|\mathbf{v}| = \sqrt{(-\sqrt{3})^2 + 1} = 2$

    $\tan \theta = \frac{1}{-\sqrt{3}}$

    θ = 150°   (The point is in quadrant II.)

    Polar coordinates: (2, 150°)

35.

Find $|\mathbf{v}|$:

$|\mathbf{v}| = \sqrt{(3\sqrt{3})^2 + 3^2} = \sqrt{36} = 6$

Find θ:

$\tan \theta = \frac{3}{3\sqrt{3}} = \frac{1}{\sqrt{3}}$

θ = 30°

Polar coordinates of the point (3√3, 3) are (6, 30°).

36. $|\mathbf{v}| = \sqrt{(4\sqrt{3})^2 + (-4)^2} = 8$

    $\tan \theta = \frac{-4}{4\sqrt{3}} = -\frac{1}{\sqrt{3}}$

    θ = 330°   (The point is in quadrant IV.)

    Polar coordinates: (8, 330°)

37.

$x = 4 \cos 45° = 4 \cdot \frac{1}{\sqrt{2}} = \frac{4}{\sqrt{2}}$, or $2\sqrt{2}$

$y = 4 \sin 45° = 4 \cdot \frac{1}{\sqrt{2}} = \frac{4}{\sqrt{2}}$, or $2\sqrt{2}$

Cartesian coordinates of the point (4, 45°) are $\left[\dfrac{4}{\sqrt{2}}, \dfrac{4}{\sqrt{2}}\right]$, or $(2\sqrt{2}, 2\sqrt{2})$.

<u>38.</u> $x = 5 \cos 60° = \dfrac{5}{2}$

$y = 5 \sin 60° = \dfrac{5\sqrt{3}}{2}$

Cartesian coordinates: $\left[\dfrac{5}{2}, \dfrac{5\sqrt{3}}{2}\right]$

<u>39.</u>

$x = 0 \cos 23° = 0$
$y = 0 \sin 23° = 0$

Cartesian coordinates of the point (0, 23°) are (0, 0).

<u>40.</u> $x = 0 \cos (-34°) = 0$
$y = 0 \sin (-34°) = 0$
Cartesian coordinates: (0, 0)

<u>41.</u>

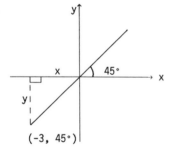

$x = -3 \cos 45° = -3 \cdot \dfrac{1}{\sqrt{2}} = -\dfrac{3}{\sqrt{2}}$, or $-\dfrac{3\sqrt{2}}{2}$

$y = -3 \cos 45° = -3 \cdot \dfrac{1}{\sqrt{2}} = -\dfrac{3}{\sqrt{2}}$, or $-\dfrac{3\sqrt{2}}{2}$

Cartesian coordinates of the point (-3, 45°) are $\left[-\dfrac{3}{\sqrt{2}}, -\dfrac{3}{\sqrt{2}}\right]$, or $\left[-\dfrac{3\sqrt{2}}{2}, -\dfrac{3\sqrt{2}}{2}\right]$.

<u>42.</u> $x = -5 \cos 30° = -\dfrac{5\sqrt{3}}{2}$

$y = -5 \sin 30° = -\dfrac{5}{2}$

Cartesian coordinates: $\left[-\dfrac{5\sqrt{3}}{2}, -\dfrac{5}{2}\right]$

<u>43.</u>

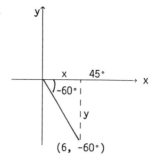

$x = 6 \cos (-60°) = 6 \cdot \dfrac{1}{2} = 3$

$y = 6 \sin (-60°) = 6\left[-\dfrac{\sqrt{3}}{2}\right] = -3\sqrt{3}$

Cartesian coordinates of the point (6, -60°) are $(3, -3\sqrt{3})$.

<u>44.</u> $x = 3 \cos (-120°) = -\dfrac{3}{2}$

$y = 3 \sin (-120°) = -\dfrac{3\sqrt{3}}{2}$

Cartesian coordinates: $\left[-\dfrac{3}{2}, -\dfrac{3\sqrt{3}}{2}\right]$

<u>45.</u>

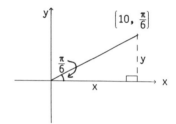

$x = 10 \cos \dfrac{\pi}{6} = 10 \cdot \dfrac{\sqrt{3}}{2} = 5\sqrt{3}$

$y = 10 \sin \dfrac{\pi}{6} = 10 \cdot \dfrac{1}{2} = 5$

Cartesian coordinates of the point $\left[10, \dfrac{\pi}{6}\right]$ are $(5\sqrt{3}, 5)$.

<u>46.</u> $x = 12 \cos \dfrac{3\pi}{4} = -6\sqrt{2}$

$y = 12 \sin \dfrac{3\pi}{4} = 6\sqrt{2}$

Cartesian coordinates: $(-6\sqrt{2}, 6\sqrt{2})$

47.

$$x = -5 \cos \frac{5\pi}{6} = -5\left(-\frac{\sqrt{3}}{2}\right) = \frac{5\sqrt{3}}{2}$$

$$y = -5 \sin \frac{5\pi}{6} = -5 \cdot \frac{1}{2} = -\frac{5}{2}$$

Cartesian coordinates of the point $\left(-5, \frac{5\pi}{6}\right)$ are $\left(\frac{5\sqrt{3}}{2}, -\frac{5}{2}\right)$.

48. $x = -6 \cos \frac{3\pi}{4} = 3\sqrt{2}$

$y = -6 \sin \frac{3\pi}{4} = -3\sqrt{2}$

Cartesian coordinates: $(3\sqrt{2}, -3\sqrt{2})$

49.
$$3x + 4y = 5$$
$$3r \cos \theta + 4r \sin \theta = 5 \qquad (x = r \cos \theta,$$
$$y = r \sin \theta)$$
$$r(3 \cos \theta + 4 \sin \theta) = 5$$

50.
$$5x + 3y = 4$$
$$5r \cos \theta + 3r \sin \theta = 4$$
$$r(5 \cos \theta + 3 \sin \theta) = 4$$

51.
$$x = 5$$
$$r \cos \theta = 5 \qquad (x = r \cos \theta)$$

52.
$$y = 4$$
$$r \sin \theta = 4$$

53.
$$x^2 + y^2 = 36$$
$$(r \cos \theta)^2 + (r \sin \theta)^2 = 36 \qquad (x = r \cos \theta,$$
$$y = r \sin \theta)$$
$$r^2 \cos^2\theta + r^2 \sin^2\theta = 36$$
$$r^2(\cos^2\theta + \sin^2\theta) = 36$$
$$r^2 = 36 \qquad (\cos^2\theta + \sin^2\theta = 1)$$

54.
$$x^2 + y^2 = 16$$
$$(r \cos \theta)^2 + (r \sin \theta)^2 = 16$$
$$r^2 = 16$$

55.
$$x^2 - 4y^2 = 4$$
$$(r \cos \theta)^2 - 4(r \sin \theta)^2 = 4$$
$$r^2 \cos^2\theta - 4r^2 \sin^2\theta = 4$$
$$r^2(\cos^2\theta - 4 \sin^2\theta) = 4$$

56.
$$x^2 - 5y^2 = 5$$
$$(r \cos \theta)^2 - 5(r \sin \theta)^2 = 5$$
$$r^2(\cos^2 \theta - 5 \sin^2 \theta) = 5$$

57.
$$r = 5$$
$$+ \sqrt{x^2 + y^2} = 5 \qquad \text{(Substituting for } r\text{)}$$
$$x^2 + y^2 = 25 \qquad \text{(Squaring)}$$

58.
$$r = 8$$
$$+ \sqrt{x^2 + y^2} = 8$$
$$x^2 + y^2 = 64$$

59. $\tan \theta = \frac{y}{x}$

$\tan \frac{\pi}{4} = \frac{y}{x} \qquad \left(\theta = \frac{\pi}{4}\right)$

$1 = \frac{y}{x}$

$x = y$

60. $\tan \theta = \frac{y}{x}$

$\tan \frac{3\pi}{4} = \frac{y}{x} \qquad \left(\theta = \frac{3\pi}{4}\right)$

$-1 = \frac{y}{x}$

$y = -x$

61. $r \sin \theta = 2$

$\quad y = 2 \qquad (y = r \sin \theta)$

62. $r \cos \theta = 5$

$\quad x = 5$

63.
$$r = 4 \cos \theta$$
$$r^2 = 4r \cos \theta \qquad \text{(Multiplying by } r\text{)}$$
$$x^2 + y^2 = 4x \qquad (x^2 + y^2 = r^2, \; x = r \cos \theta)$$

64.
$$r = -3 \sin \theta$$
$$r^2 = -3(r \sin \theta)$$
$$x^2 + y^2 = -3y$$

65.
$$r - r \sin \theta = 2$$
$$r - y = 2 \qquad (y = r \sin \theta)$$
$$r = 2 + y$$
$$r^2 = 4 + 4y + y^2 \qquad \text{(Squaring)}$$
$$x^2 + y^2 = 4 + 4y + y^2 \qquad (x^2 + y^2 = r^2)$$
$$x^2 - 4y = 4$$

66.
$$r + r \cos \theta = 3$$
$$\pm \sqrt{x^2 + y^2} + x = 3$$
$$x^2 + y^2 = (3 - x)^2$$
$$y^2 = -6x + 9$$

67. $r - 2 \cos \theta = 3 \sin \theta$
$r^2 - 2r \cos \theta = 3r \sin \theta$ (Multiplying by r)
$x^2 + y^2 - 2x = 3y$ ($x^2 + y^2 = r^2$,
                              $x = r \cos \theta, y = r \sin \theta$)
$x^2 - 2x + y^2 - 3y = 0$

68. $r + 5 \sin \theta = 7 \cos \theta$
$r^2 + 5(r \sin \theta) = 7(r \cos \theta)$
$(x^2 + y^2) + 5y = 7x$
$x^2 - 7x + y^2 + 5y = 0$

69. Graph: $r = 4 \cos \theta$

First make a table of values.

θ	$\cos \theta$	$r = 4 \cos \theta$
0°	1	4
30°	0.866	3.46
45°	0.707	2.83
60°	0.5	2
90°	0	0
120°	-0.5	-2
135°	-0.707	-2.83
150°	-0.866	-3.46
180°	-1	-4
210°	-0.866	-3.46
225°	-0.707	-2.83

Note that points are beginning to repeat. Plot these points and draw the graph.

70.

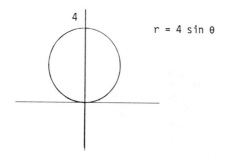

$r = 4 \sin \theta$

71. Graph: $r = 1 - \cos \theta$

First make a table of values.

θ	$\cos \theta$	$r = 1 - \cos \theta$
0°	1	0
30°	0.866	0.134
45°	0.707	0.293
60°	0.5	0.5
90°	0	1
120°	-0.5	1.5
135°	-0.707	1.707
150°	-0.866	1.866
180°	-1	2
210°	-0.866	1.866
225°	-0.707	1.707
240°	-0.5	1.5
270°	0	1
300°	0.5	0.5
315°	0.707	0.293
330°	0.866	0.134
360°	1	0
390°	0.866	0.134

Note that points are beginning to repeat. Plot these points and draw the graph.

$r = 1 - \cos \theta$

72. $r = 1 - \sin \theta$

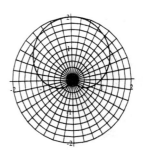

<u>73</u>. Graph: r = sin 2θ

First make a table of values.

θ	2θ	r = sin 2θ
0°	0°	0
30°	60°	0.866
45°	90°	1
60°	120°	0.866
90°	180°	0
120°	240°	-0.866
135°	270°	-1
150°	300°	-0.866
180°	360°	0
210°	420°	0.866
225°	450°	1
240°	480°	0.866
270°	540°	0
300°	600°	-0.866
315°	630°	-1
330°	660°	-0.866
360°	720°	0
390°	780°	0.866

Note that points are beginning to repeat. Plot these points and draw the graph.

$r = \sin 2\theta$

<u>74</u>. r = 3 cos 2θ

<u>75</u>. Graph: r = 2 cos 3θ

First make a table of values.

θ	3θ	r = 2 cos 3θ
0°	0°	2
30°	90°	0
45°	135°	-1.414
60°	180°	-2
90°	270°	0
120°	360°	2
135°	405°	1.414
150°	450°	0
180°	540°	-2
210°	630°	0
225°	675°	1.414
240°	720°	2
270°	810°	0
300°	900°	-2
315°	945°	-1.414
330°	990°	0
360°	1080°	2
390°	1170°	0

Note that points are beginning to repeat. Plot these points and draw the graph.

$r = 2 \cos 3\theta$

<u>76</u>. r = sin 3θ

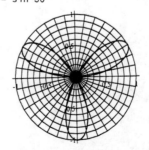

77. Graph: r cos θ = 4

Express the function as $r = \dfrac{4}{\cos \theta}$. Then make a table of values.

θ	cos θ	$r = \dfrac{4}{\cos \theta}$
0°	1	4
30°	0.866	4.62
45°	0.707	5.66
60°	0.5	8
90°	0	Undefined
120°	-0.5	-8
135°	-0.707	-5.66
150°	-0.866	-4.62
180°	-1	-4
210°	-0.866	-4.62
225°	-0.707	-5.66

Note that points are begining to repeat. Plot these points and draw the graph.

r cos θ = 4

78. r sin θ = 6

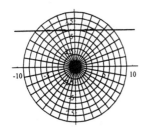

79. Graph: $r = \dfrac{5}{1 + \cos \theta}$

Make a table of values.

θ	cos θ	$r = \dfrac{5}{1 + \cos \theta}$
0°	1	2.5
30°	0.866	2.68
45°	0.707	2.93
60°	0.5	3.33
90°	0	5
120°	-0.5	10
135°	-0.707	17.07
150°	-0.866	37.32
180°	-1	Undefined
210°	-0.866	37.32
225°	-0.707	17.07
240°	-0.5	10
270°	0	5
300°	0.5	3.33
315°	0.707	2.93
330°	0.866	2.68
360°	1	2.5
390°	0.866	2.68

Note that points are beginning to repeat. Plot these points and draw the graph.

$r = \dfrac{5}{1 + \cos \theta}$

80. $r = \dfrac{3}{1 + \sin \theta}$

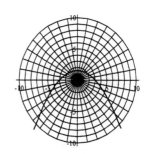

81. Graph: r = θ

    We make a table of values.

θ	r
0	0
$\frac{\pi}{4}$	$\frac{\pi}{4}$, or 0.785
$\frac{\pi}{2}$	$\frac{\pi}{2}$, or 1.571
$\frac{3\pi}{4}$	$\frac{3\pi}{4}$, or 2.356
π	π, or 3.142
$\frac{3\pi}{2}$	$\frac{3\pi}{2}$, or 4.712
2π	2π, or 6.283
$\frac{5\pi}{2}$	$\frac{5\pi}{2}$, or 7.854

    Plot these points; take note of the fact that, as θ increases, r also increases; draw the graph.

$r = \theta$

82. r = 3θ

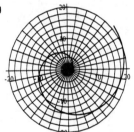

83. Graph: $r^2 = \sin 2\theta$

    We make a table of values. Note that we cannot choose values of θ for which sin 2θ is negative since r^2 is nonnegative.

θ	0	$\frac{\pi}{8}$	$\frac{\pi}{4}$	$\frac{3\pi}{8}$	$\frac{\pi}{2}$
r	0	± 0.841	± 1	± 0.841	0

θ	π	$\frac{9\pi}{8}$	$\frac{5\pi}{4}$	$\frac{11\pi}{8}$	$\frac{3\pi}{2}$
r	0	± 0.841	± 1	± 0.841	0

    We only need to plot the points for $0 \leqslant \theta \leqslant \frac{\pi}{2}$.

    The repetition has already begun for $\pi \leqslant \theta \leqslant \frac{3\pi}{2}$.

$r^2 = \sin 2\theta$

84. $r^2 = \sin 2\theta$

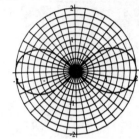

85. Graph: $r = e^{\theta/10}$ or $\ln r = \frac{\theta}{10}$

    We make a table of values.

θ	−π	$-\frac{3\pi}{4}$	$-\frac{\pi}{2}$	$-\frac{\pi}{4}$
r	0.730	0.790	0.855	0.924

θ	0	$\frac{\pi}{4}$	$\frac{\pi}{2}$	$\frac{3\pi}{4}$	π
r	1	1.082	1.170	1.266	1.369

θ	$\frac{5\pi}{4}$	$\frac{3\pi}{2}$	$\frac{7\pi}{4}$	2π	$\frac{9\pi}{4}$
r	1.481	1.602	1.732	1.874	2.028

    Plot these points; take note of the fact that, as θ increases, r also increases; draw the graph.

$r = e^{\theta/10}$

<u>86</u>. $r = 10^{2\theta}$, or

   $\log r = 2\theta$

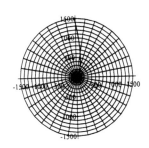

<u>87</u>. $r = \sec^2 \dfrac{\theta}{2}$ or $r = \dfrac{1}{\cos^2 \dfrac{\theta}{2}}$ or $r = \dfrac{1}{\dfrac{1 + \cos \theta}{2}}$

   or

   $r = \dfrac{2}{1 + \cos \theta}$

   $r + r \cos \theta = 2$

   $\pm \sqrt{x^2 + y^2} + x = 2$

   $x^2 + y^2 = (2 - x)^2$

   $x^2 + y^2 = 4 - 4x + x^2$

   $y^2 = -4x + 4$

<u>88</u>.

<u>89</u>. $r = \sin\theta \tan\theta$

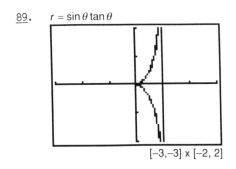

$[-3,-3] \times [-2, 2]$

<u>90</u>. $r = \cos 2\theta \sec\theta$

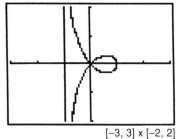

$[-3, 3] \times [-2, 2]$

<u>91</u>. $r = 2\cos 2\theta - 1$

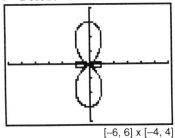

$[-6, 6] \times [-4, 4]$

<u>92</u>.

   $r = \cos 2\theta - 2$

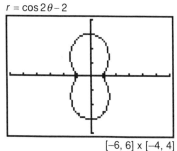

$[-6, 6] \times [-4, 4]$

<u>93</u>. $r = \frac{1}{4}\tan^2 \theta \sec\theta$

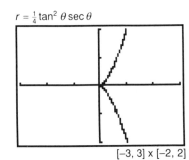

$[-3, 3] \times [-2, 2]$

<u>94</u>.

   $r = \sin 2\theta + \cos\theta$

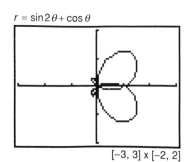

$[-3, 3] \times [-2, 2]$

Exercise Set 8.6

1.   Imaginary

$(3 + 2i) + (2 - 5i)$
$= (3 + 2) + (2 - 5)i$
$= 5 - 3i$

2.   Imaginary

3.   Imaginary

$(-5 + 3i) + (-2 - 3i)$
$= (-5 - 2) + (3 - 3)i$
$= -7 + 0i = -7$

4.   Imaginary

5.   Imaginary

$(2 - 3i) + (-5 + 4i)$
$= (2 - 5) + (-3 + 4)i$
$= -3 + i$

6.   Imaginary

7.   Imaginary

$(-2 - 5i) + (5 + 3i)$
$= (-2 + 5) + (-5 + 3)i$
$= 3 - 2i$

8.   Imaginary

9. $3(\cos 30° + i \sin 30°)$

$a = 3 \cos 30° = 3 \cdot \dfrac{\sqrt{3}}{2} = \dfrac{3\sqrt{3}}{2}$

$b = 3 \sin 30° = 3 \cdot \dfrac{1}{2} = \dfrac{3}{2}$

Thus $3(\cos 30° + i \sin 30°) = \dfrac{3\sqrt{3}}{2} + \dfrac{3}{2}\, i.$

10. $a = 6 \cos 150° = -3\sqrt{3}$
$b = 6 \sin 150° = 3$

Rectangular notation: $-3\sqrt{3} + 3i$

11. $10 \operatorname{cis} 270° = 10(\cos 270° + i \sin 270°)$

$a = 10 \cos 270° = 10 \cdot 0 = 0$
$b = 10 \sin 270° = 10(-1) = -10$

Thus $10 \operatorname{cis} 270° = 0 + (-10)i = -10i.$

12. $a = 5 \cos(-60°) = \dfrac{5}{2}$

$b = 5 \sin(-60°) = -\dfrac{5\sqrt{3}}{2}$

Rectangular notation: $\dfrac{5}{2} - \dfrac{5\sqrt{3}}{2}\, i$

13. $\sqrt{8}\left[\cos\frac{\pi}{4} + i\sin\frac{\pi}{4}\right]$

    $a = \sqrt{8}\cos\frac{\pi}{4} = \sqrt{8}\cdot\frac{\sqrt{2}}{2} = 2$

    $b = \sqrt{8}\sin\frac{\pi}{4} = \sqrt{8}\cdot\frac{\sqrt{2}}{2} = 2$

    Thus $\sqrt{8}\left[\cos\frac{\pi}{4} + i\sin\frac{\pi}{4}\right] = 2 + 2i$

14. $a = 5\cos\frac{\pi}{3} = \frac{5}{2}$

    $b = 5\sin\frac{\pi}{3} = \frac{5\sqrt{3}}{2}$

    Rectangular notation: $\frac{5}{2} + \frac{5\sqrt{3}}{2}i$

15. $\sqrt{8}\text{ cis }\frac{5\pi}{4} = \sqrt{8}\left[\cos\frac{5\pi}{4} + i\sin\frac{5\pi}{4}\right]$

    $a = \sqrt{8}\cos\frac{5\pi}{4} = \sqrt{8}\left[-\frac{\sqrt{2}}{2}\right] = -2$

    $b = \sqrt{8}\sin\frac{5\pi}{4} = \sqrt{8}\left[-\frac{\sqrt{2}}{2}\right] = -2$

    Thus $\sqrt{8}\text{ cis }\frac{5\pi}{4} = -2 - 2i$.

16. $a = \sqrt{8}\cos\left[-\frac{\pi}{4}\right] = 2$

    $b = \sqrt{8}\sin\left[-\frac{\pi}{4}\right] = -2$

    Rectangular notation: $2 - 2i$

17. $1 - i$

    $a = 1$ and $b = -1$

    $r = \sqrt{a^2 + b^2} = \sqrt{1^2 + (-1)^2} = \sqrt{2}$

    $\sin\theta = \frac{b}{r} = \frac{-1}{\sqrt{2}} = -\frac{\sqrt{2}}{2}$

    $\cos\theta = \frac{a}{r} = \frac{1}{\sqrt{2}} = \frac{\sqrt{2}}{2}$

    Thus $\theta = \frac{7\pi}{4}$, or 315°, and we have

    $1 - i = \sqrt{2}\text{ cis }\frac{7\pi}{4}$, or $\sqrt{2}\text{ cis }315°$.

18. $r = \sqrt{(\sqrt{3})^2 + 1^2} = 2$

    $\sin\theta = \frac{1}{2}$ and $\cos\theta = \frac{\sqrt{3}}{2}$, so $\theta = \frac{\pi}{6}$, or 30°.

    $\sqrt{3} + i = 2\text{ cis }\frac{\pi}{6}$, or $2\text{ cis }30°$.

19. $10\sqrt{3} - 10i$

    $a = 10\sqrt{3}$ and $b = -10$

    $r = \sqrt{a^2 + b^2} = \sqrt{(10\sqrt{3})^2 + (-10)^2} = \sqrt{400} = 20$

    $\sin\theta = \frac{b}{r} = \frac{-10}{20} = -\frac{1}{2}$

$\cos\theta = \frac{a}{r} = \frac{10\sqrt{3}}{20} = \frac{\sqrt{3}}{2}$

Thus $\theta = \frac{11\pi}{6}$, or 330°, and we have

$10\sqrt{3} - 10i = 20\text{ cis }\frac{11\pi}{6}$, or $20\text{ cis }330°$.

20. $r = \sqrt{(-10\sqrt{3})^2 + 10^2} = 20$

    $\sin\theta = \frac{1}{2}$ and $\cos\theta = -\frac{\sqrt{3}}{2}$, so $\theta = \frac{5\pi}{6}$, or 150°.

    $-10\sqrt{3} + 10i = 20\text{ cis }\frac{5\pi}{6}$, or $20\text{ cis }150°$.

21. -5 (Think $-5 + 0i$)

    $a = -5$ and $b = 0$

    $r = \sqrt{a^2 + b^2} = \sqrt{(-5)^2 + 0^2} = \sqrt{25} = 5$

    $\sin\theta = \frac{b}{r} = \frac{0}{5} = 0$

    $\cos\theta = \frac{-5}{5} = -1$

    Thus $\theta = \pi$, or 180°, and we have

    $-5 = 5\text{ cis }\pi$, or $5\text{ cis }180°$.

22. $r = \sqrt{0^2 + (-5)^2} = 5$

    $\sin\theta = -1$ and $\cos\theta = 0$, so $\theta = \frac{3\pi}{2}$, or 270°.

    $-5i = 5\text{ cis }\frac{3\pi}{2}$, or $5\text{ cis }270°$.

23. $(1 - i)(2 + 2i)$

    Find polar notation for $1 - i$.

    $a = 1$, $b = -1$, and $r = \sqrt{1^2 + (-1)^2} = \sqrt{2}$

    $\sin\theta = \frac{-1}{\sqrt{2}} = -\frac{\sqrt{2}}{2}$, $\cos\theta = \frac{1}{\sqrt{2}} = \frac{\sqrt{2}}{2}$

    Thus $\theta = \frac{7\pi}{4}$, or 315°, and $1 - i = \sqrt{2}\text{ cis }315°$.

    Find polar notation for $2 + 2i$.

    $a = 2$, $b = 2$, and $r = \sqrt{2^2 + 2^2} = \sqrt{8} = 2\sqrt{2}$

    $\sin\theta = \frac{2}{2\sqrt{2}} = \frac{\sqrt{2}}{2}$, $\cos\theta = \frac{2}{2\sqrt{2}} = \frac{\sqrt{2}}{2}$

    Thus $\theta = \frac{\pi}{4}$, or 45°, and $2 + 2i = 2\sqrt{2}\text{ cis }45°$

    $(1 - i)(2 + 2i)$

    $= \sqrt{2}\text{ cis }315° \cdot 2\sqrt{2}\text{ cis }45°$

    $= \sqrt{2}\cdot 2\sqrt{2}\text{ cis }(315° + 45°)$ (Theorem 4)

    $= 4\text{ cis }360°$

    $= 4\text{ cis }0°$, or 4

24. For $1 + i\sqrt{3}$: $r = \sqrt{1^2 + (\sqrt{3})^2} = 2$

    $\sin \theta = \frac{\sqrt{3}}{2}$ and $\cos \theta = \frac{1}{2}$, so $\theta = 60°$.

    $1 + i\sqrt{3} = 2 \text{ cis } 60°$

    For $1 + i$: $r = \sqrt{1^2 + 1^2} = \sqrt{2}$

    $\sin \theta = \frac{1}{\sqrt{2}}$ and $\cos \theta = \frac{1}{\sqrt{2}}$, so $\theta = 45°$.

    $1 + i = \sqrt{2} \text{ cis } 45°$

    $(2 \text{ cis } 60°)(\sqrt{2} \text{ cis } 45°) = 2\sqrt{2} \text{ cis } 105°$

25. $(2\sqrt{3} + 2i)(2i)$

    Find polar notation for $2\sqrt{3} + 2i$.

    $a = 2\sqrt{3}$, $b = 2$, and $r = \sqrt{(2\sqrt{3})^2 + 2^2}$

    $\qquad\qquad\qquad\qquad = \sqrt{16} = 4$

    $\sin \theta = \frac{2}{4} = \frac{1}{2}$, $\qquad \cos \theta = \frac{2\sqrt{3}}{4} = \frac{\sqrt{3}}{2}$

    Thus $\theta = \frac{\pi}{6}$, or $30°$, and $2\sqrt{3} + 2i = 4 \text{ cis } 30°$.

    Find polar notation for $2i$.

    $a = 0$, $b = 2$, and $r = \sqrt{0^2 + 2^2} = 2$

    $\sin \theta = \frac{2}{2} = 1$, $\qquad \cos \theta = \frac{0}{2} = 0$

    Thus $\theta = \frac{\pi}{2}$, or $90°$, and $2i = 2 \text{ cis } 90°$.

    $\quad (2\sqrt{3} + 2i)(2i)$

    $= 4 \text{ cis } 30° \cdot 2 \text{ cis } 90°$

    $= 4 \cdot 2 \text{ cis } (30° + 90°)$ (Theorem 4)

    $= 8 \text{ cis } 120°$

26. For $3\sqrt{3} - 3i$: $r = \sqrt{(3\sqrt{3})^2 + (-3)^2} = 6$

    $\sin \theta = -\frac{1}{2}$ and $\cos \theta = \frac{\sqrt{3}}{2}$, so $\theta = 330°$.

    $3\sqrt{3} - 3i = 6 \text{ cis } 330°$

    $2i = 2 \text{ cis } 90°$ (See Exercise 25.)

    $(6 \text{ cis } 330°)(2 \text{ cis } 90°) = 12 \text{ cis } 420° = 12 \text{ cis } 60°$

27. $\frac{1 - i}{1 + i}$

    Find polar notation for $1 - i$.

    $a = 1$, $b = -1$, and $r = \sqrt{2}$

    $\sin \theta = \frac{-1}{\sqrt{2}} = -\frac{\sqrt{2}}{2}$, $\qquad \cos \theta = \frac{1}{\sqrt{2}} = \frac{\sqrt{2}}{2}$

    Thus $\theta = \frac{7\pi}{4}$, or $315°$, and $1 - i = \sqrt{2} \text{ cis } 315°$.

    Find polar notation for $1 + i$.

    $a = 1$, $b = 1$, and $r = \sqrt{2}$

    $\sin \theta = \frac{1}{\sqrt{2}} = \frac{\sqrt{2}}{2}$, $\qquad \cos \theta = \frac{1}{\sqrt{2}} = \frac{\sqrt{2}}{2}$

Thus $\theta = \frac{\pi}{4}$, or $45°$, and $1 + i = \sqrt{2} \text{ cis } 45°$.

$\frac{1 - i}{1 + i} = \frac{\sqrt{2} \text{ cis } 315°}{\sqrt{2} \text{ cis } 45°}$

$\qquad = \frac{\sqrt{2}}{\sqrt{2}} \text{ cis } (315° - 45°)$ (Theorem 5)

$\qquad = \text{cis } 270°$, or $-i$

28. $1 - i = \sqrt{2} \text{ cis } 315°$ (See Exercise 27.)

    For $\sqrt{3} - i$: $r = \sqrt{(\sqrt{3})^2 + (-1)^2} = 2$

    $\sin \theta = -\frac{1}{2}$ and $\cos \theta = \frac{\sqrt{3}}{2}$, so $\theta = 330°$.

    $\sqrt{3} - i = 2 \text{ cis } 330°$

    $\frac{\sqrt{2} \text{ cis } 315°}{2 \text{ cis } 330°} = \frac{\sqrt{2}}{2} \text{ cis } (-15°) = \frac{\sqrt{2}}{2} \text{ cis } 345°$

29. $\frac{2\sqrt{3} - 2i}{1 + \sqrt{3} i}$

    Find polar notation for $2\sqrt{3} - 2i$.

    $a = 2\sqrt{3}$, $b = -2$, and $r = \sqrt{(2\sqrt{3})^2 + (-2)^2}$

    $\qquad\qquad\qquad\qquad = \sqrt{16} = 4$

    $\sin \theta = \frac{-2}{4} = -\frac{1}{2}$, $\qquad \cos \theta = \frac{2\sqrt{3}}{4} = \frac{\sqrt{3}}{2}$

    Thus $\theta = \frac{11\pi}{6}$, or $330°$, and $2\sqrt{3} - 2i = 4 \text{ cis } 330°$.

    Find polar notation for $1 + \sqrt{3} i$.

    $a = 1$, $b = \sqrt{3}$, and $r = \sqrt{1^2 + (\sqrt{3})^2} = \sqrt{4} = 2$

    $\sin \theta = \frac{\sqrt{3}}{2}$, $\qquad \cos \theta = \frac{1}{2}$

    Thus $\theta = \frac{\pi}{3}$, or $60°$, and $1 + \sqrt{3} i = 2 \text{ cis } 60°$.

    $\frac{2\sqrt{3} - 2i}{1 + \sqrt{3} i} = \frac{4 \text{ cis } 330°}{2 \text{ cis } 60°}$

    $\qquad = \frac{4}{2} \text{ cis } (330° - 60°)$

    $\qquad = 2 \text{ cis } 270°$, or $-2i$

30. For $3 - 3\sqrt{3}i$: $r = \sqrt{3^2 + (-3\sqrt{3})^2} = 6$

    $\sin \theta: -\frac{\sqrt{3}}{2}$ and $\cos \theta = \frac{1}{2}$, so $\theta = 300°$

    $3 - 3\sqrt{3}i = 6 \text{ cis } 300°$

    $\sqrt{3} - i = 2 \text{ cis } 330°$ (See Exercise 28.)

    $\frac{6 \text{ cis } 300°}{2 \text{ cis } 330°} = 3 \text{ cis } (-30°) = 3 \text{ cis } 330°$

31. See the answer section in the text.

32. $z = a + bi$, $|z| = \sqrt{a^2 + b^2}$

    $\bar{z} = a - bi$, $|\bar{z}| = \sqrt{a^2 + (-b)^2} = \sqrt{a^2 + b^2}$

    $\quad |z| = |\bar{z}|$

33. See the answer section in the text.

34. $|(a + bi)^2| = |a^2 - b^2 + 2abi|$

$$= \sqrt{(a^2 - b^2)^2 + 4a^2b^2}$$

$$= \sqrt{a^4 + 2a^2b^2 + b^4}$$

$$= a^2 + b^2$$

$|a + bi|^2 = (\sqrt{a^2 + b^2})^2 = a^2 + b^2$

35. See the answer section in the text.

36. $\dfrac{z}{w} = \dfrac{r_1 \text{cis } \theta_1}{r_2 \text{cis } \theta_2} = \dfrac{r_1}{r_2} \text{cis } (\theta_1 - \theta_2)$

$$\left|\frac{z}{w}\right| = \sqrt{\left[\frac{r_1}{r_2} \cos (\theta_1 - \theta_2)\right]^2 + \left[\frac{r_1}{r_2} \sin (\theta_1 - \theta_2)\right]^2}$$

$$= \sqrt{\frac{r_1{}^2}{r_2{}^2}} = \frac{|r_1|}{|r_2|}$$

$|z| = \sqrt{(r_1 \cos \theta_1)^2 + (r_1 \sin \theta_1)^2}$

$$= \sqrt{r_1{}^2} = |r_1|$$

$|w| = \sqrt{(r_2 \cos \theta_2)^2 + (r_2 \sin \theta_2)^2}$

$$= \sqrt{r_2{}^2} = |r_2|$$

Then $\left|\dfrac{z}{w}\right| = \dfrac{|r_1|}{|r_2|} = \dfrac{|z|}{|w|}$.

37. Graph: $|z| = 1$

Let $z = a + bi$

Then $|a + bi| = 1$

$\sqrt{a^2 + b^2} = 1$ (Definition)

$a^2 + b^2 = 1$

The graph of $a^2 + b^2 = 1$ is a circle whose radius is 1 and whose center is (0, 0).

The graph is in the answer section in the text.

38.
$$z + \bar{z} = 3$$
$$(a + bi) + (a - bi) = 3$$
$$2a = 3$$
$$a = \frac{3}{2}$$

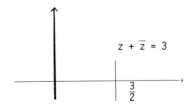

39. $(\cos \theta + i \sin \theta)^{-1}$

$$= \frac{1}{\cos \theta + i \sin \theta} \cdot \frac{\cos \theta - i \sin \theta}{\cos \theta - i \sin \theta}$$

$$= \frac{\cos \theta - i \sin \theta}{\cos^2 \theta + \sin^2 \theta}$$

$$= \cos \theta - i \sin \theta$$

40. $(5 \text{ cis } 20°)^3 = [(5 \text{ cis } 20°)(5 \text{ cis } 20°)](5 \text{ cis } 20°)$

$$= [25 \text{ cis } 40°](5 \text{ cis } 20°)$$

$$= 125 \text{ cis } 60°$$

Exercise Set 8.7

1. $\left(2 \text{ cis } \dfrac{\pi}{3}\right)^3 = 2^3 \text{ cis } \left(3 \cdot \dfrac{\pi}{3}\right)$ (Theorem 6)

$$= 8 \text{ cis } \pi$$

2. $\left(3 \text{ cis } \dfrac{\pi}{2}\right)^4 = 3^4 \text{ cis } \left(4 \cdot \dfrac{\pi}{2}\right) = 81 \text{ cis } 2\pi$

3. $\left(2 \text{ cis } \dfrac{\pi}{6}\right)^6 = 2^6 \text{ cis } \left(6 \cdot \dfrac{\pi}{6}\right)$ (Theorem 6)

$$= 64 \text{ cis } \pi$$

4. $\left(2 \text{ cis } \dfrac{\pi}{5}\right)^5 = 2^5 \text{ cis } 5 \cdot \dfrac{\pi}{5} = 32 \text{ cis } \pi$

5. $(1 + i)^6$

We first find polar notation for $1 + i$. See Exercise 27 in Exercise Set 8.6.

$1 + i = \sqrt{2} \text{ cis } 45°$

$(1 + i)^6 = (\sqrt{2} \text{ cis } 45°)^6$

$$= (\sqrt{2})^6 \text{ cis } (6 \cdot 45°) \quad \text{(Theorem 6)}$$

$$= 8 \text{ cis } 270°$$

6. $(1 - i)^6 = (\sqrt{2} \text{ cis } 315°)^6$

$$= (\sqrt{2})^6 \text{ cis } (6 \cdot 315°)$$

$$= 8 \text{ cis } 1890°$$

$$= 8 \text{ cis } 90°$$

7. $(2 \text{ cis } 240°)^4 = 2^4 \text{ cis } (4 \cdot 240°)$ (Theorem 6)

$$= 16 \text{ cis } 960°$$

$$= 16 \text{ cis } 240°$$

$$= 16(\cos 240° + i \sin 240°)$$

$$= 16\left(-\frac{1}{2} - \frac{\sqrt{3}}{2} i\right)$$

$$= -8 - 8\sqrt{3} i$$

8. $(2 \text{ cis } 120°)^4 = 2^4 \text{ cis } (4 \cdot 120°)$

$\qquad = 16 \text{ cis } 120°$

$\qquad = 16(\cos 120° + i \sin 120°)$

$\qquad = -8 + 8\sqrt{3}\, i$

9. $(1 + \sqrt{3}\, i)^4$

We first find polar notation for $1 + \sqrt{3}\, i$. See Exercise 29 in Exercise Set 8.6.

$\qquad 1 + \sqrt{3}\, i = 2 \text{ cis } 60°$

$(1 + \sqrt{3}\, i)^4 = (2 \text{ cis } 60°)^4$

$\qquad = 2^4 \text{ cis } (4 \cdot 60°) \qquad \text{(Theorem 6)}$

$\qquad = 16 \text{ cis } 240°$

$\qquad = 16(\cos 240° + i \sin 240°)$

$\qquad = 16\left[-\frac{1}{2} - \frac{\sqrt{3}}{2}\, i\right]$

$\qquad = -8 - 8\sqrt{3}\, i$

10. $(-\sqrt{3} + i)^6 = (2 \text{ cis } 150°)^6$

$\qquad = 2^6 \text{ cis } (6 \cdot 150°)$

$\qquad = 64 \text{ cis } 900°$

$\qquad = 64 \text{ cis } 180°$

$\qquad = 64(\cos 180° + i \sin 180°)$

$\qquad = -64$

11. $\left[\frac{1}{\sqrt{2}} + \frac{1}{\sqrt{2}}\, i\right]^{10}$

First find polar notation for $\frac{1}{\sqrt{2}} + \frac{1}{\sqrt{2}}\, i$.

$a = \frac{1}{\sqrt{2}}, \; b = \frac{1}{\sqrt{2}}, \text{ and } r = \sqrt{\left[\frac{1}{\sqrt{2}}\right]^2 + \left[\frac{1}{\sqrt{2}}\right]^2}$

$\qquad\qquad = \sqrt{1} = 1$

$\sin \theta = \dfrac{\frac{1}{\sqrt{2}}}{1} = \frac{1}{\sqrt{2}}, \text{ or } \frac{\sqrt{2}}{2}$

$\cos \theta = \dfrac{\frac{1}{\sqrt{2}}}{1} = \frac{1}{\sqrt{2}}, \text{ or } \frac{\sqrt{2}}{2}$

Thus $\theta = \frac{\pi}{4}$, or $45°$ and $\frac{1}{\sqrt{2}} + \frac{1}{\sqrt{2}}\, i = 1 \cdot \text{cis } 45°$, or cis $45°$.

$\left[\frac{1}{\sqrt{2}} + \frac{1}{\sqrt{2}}\, i\right]^{10} = (\text{cis } 45°)^{10}$

$\qquad = \text{cis } 450° \qquad \text{(Theorem 6)}$

$\qquad = \text{cis } 90°$

$\qquad = \cos 90° + i \sin 90°$

$\qquad = 0 + i, \text{ or } i$

12. $\left[\frac{1}{\sqrt{2}} - \frac{1}{\sqrt{2}}\, i\right]^{12} = (1 \text{ cis } 315°)^{12}$

$\qquad = 1^{12} \cdot \text{cis } (12 \cdot 315°)$

$\qquad = \text{cis } 3780°$

$\qquad = \text{cis } 180°$

$\qquad = \cos 180° + i \sin 180°$

$\qquad = -1$

13. $\left[\frac{\sqrt{3}}{2} + \frac{1}{2}\, i\right]^{12}$

First find polar notation for $\frac{\sqrt{3}}{2} + \frac{1}{2}\, i$.

$a = \frac{\sqrt{3}}{2}, \; b = \frac{1}{2}, \text{ and } r = \sqrt{\left[\frac{\sqrt{3}}{2}\right]^2 + \left[\frac{1}{2}\right]^2} = \sqrt{1} = 1$

$\sin \theta = \dfrac{\frac{1}{2}}{1} = \frac{1}{2}, \qquad \cos \theta = \dfrac{\frac{\sqrt{3}}{2}}{1} = \frac{\sqrt{3}}{2}$

Thus $\theta = \frac{\pi}{6}$, or $30°$, and $\frac{\sqrt{3}}{2} + \frac{1}{2}\, i = \text{cis } 30°$.

$\left[\frac{\sqrt{3}}{2} + \frac{1}{2}\, i\right]^{12} = (\text{cis } 30°)^{12}$

$\qquad = \text{cis } (12 \cdot 30°) \qquad \text{(Theorem 6)}$

$\qquad = \text{cis } 360°, \text{ or cis } 0°$

$\qquad = \cos 0° + i \sin 0°$

$\qquad = 1 + 0i, \text{ or } 1$

14. $\left[\frac{\sqrt{3}}{2} - \frac{1}{2}\, i\right]^{14} = (1 \text{ cis } 330°)^{14}$

$\qquad = 1^{14} \text{ cis } (14 \cdot 330°)$

$\qquad = \text{cis } 4620°$

$\qquad = \text{cis } 300°$

$\qquad = \cos 300° + i \sin 300°$

$\qquad = \frac{1}{2} - \frac{\sqrt{3}}{2}\, i$

15. $x^2 = i$

Find the square roots of i.

Polar notation for i is cis $90°$.

Using Theorem 7, we know

$(\text{cis } 90°)^{1/2} = \text{cis } \left[\frac{90°}{2} + k \cdot \frac{360°}{2}\right], \quad k = 0, 1$

$\qquad = \text{cis } (45° + k \cdot 180°), \quad k = 0, 1$

Thus the roots are

cis $45°$ when $k = 0$ and cis $225°$ when $k = 1$.

Rectangular notation for these roots is as follows:

cis $45° = \cos 45° + i \sin 45°$

$\qquad = \frac{\sqrt{2}}{2} + \frac{\sqrt{2}}{2}\, i$

cis $225° = \cos 225° + i \sin 225°$

$\qquad = -\frac{\sqrt{2}}{2} - \frac{\sqrt{2}}{2}\, i$

The roots are $\frac{\sqrt{2}}{2} + \frac{\sqrt{2}}{2}$ i and $-\frac{\sqrt{2}}{2} - \frac{\sqrt{2}}{2}$ i.

16. $-i = 1 \text{ cis } 270°$

$(1 \text{ cis } 270°)^{1/2} = 1^{1/2} \text{ cis } \left[\frac{270°}{2} + k \cdot \frac{360°}{2}\right],$
$$k = 0, 1$$
$$= \text{cis } (135° + k \cdot 180°), k = 0, 1$$

For k = 0: cis 135° = cos 135° + i sin 135° =
$$-\frac{\sqrt{2}}{2} + \frac{\sqrt{2}}{2} i$$

and

For k = 1: cis 315° = cos 315° + i sin 315° =
$$= \frac{\sqrt{2}}{2} - \frac{\sqrt{2}}{2} i$$

17. $x^2 = 2\sqrt{2} - 2\sqrt{2}$ i

Find the square roots of $2\sqrt{2} - 2\sqrt{2}$ i.
Polar notation for $2\sqrt{2} - 2\sqrt{2}$ i is 4 cis 315°.

Using Theorem 7, we know

$(4 \text{ cis } 315°)^{1/2} = 4^{1/2} \text{ cis } \left[\frac{315°}{2} + \frac{k \cdot 360°}{2}\right],$
$$k = 0, 1$$
$$= 2 \text{ cis } (157.5° + k \cdot 180°),$$
$$k = 0, 1$$

Thus the roots are
2 cis 157.5° when k = 0 and 2 cis 337.5°
when k = 1.

18. $1 + i = \sqrt{2} \text{ cis } 45°$

$(\sqrt{2} \text{ cis } 45°)^{1/2} = (\sqrt{2})^{1/2} \text{ cis } \left[\frac{45°}{2} + k \cdot \frac{360°}{2}\right],$
$$k = 0, 1$$
$$= \sqrt[4]{2} \text{ cis } (22.5° + k \cdot 180°),$$
$$k = 0, 1$$

The roots are $\sqrt[4]{2}$ cis 22.5° when k = 0 and
$\sqrt[4]{2}$ cis 202.5° when k = 1.

19. $x^2 = -1 + \sqrt{3}$ i

Find the square roots of $-1 + \sqrt{3}$ i.

Polar notation for $-1 + \sqrt{3}$ i is 2 cis 120°.

Using Theorem 7, we know

$(2 \text{ cis } 120°)^{1/2} = 2^{1/2} \text{ cis } \left[\frac{120°}{2} + k \cdot \frac{360°}{2}\right],$
$$k = 0, 1$$
$$= \sqrt{2} \text{ cis } (60° + k \cdot 180°), k = 0, 1$$

Thus the roots are

$\sqrt{2}$ cis 60° when k = 0 and $\sqrt{2}$ cis 240°
when k = 1.

Rectangular notation for these roots is as
follows:

$\sqrt{2} \text{ cis } 60° = \sqrt{2} \ (\cos 60° + i \sin 60°)$

$$= \sqrt{2} \left[\frac{1}{2} + \frac{\sqrt{3}}{2} i\right] = \frac{\sqrt{2}}{2} + \frac{\sqrt{6}}{2} i$$

$\sqrt{2} \text{ cis } 240° = \sqrt{2} \ (\cos 240° + i \sin 240°)$

$$= \sqrt{2} \left[-\frac{1}{2} - \frac{\sqrt{3}}{2} i\right] = -\frac{\sqrt{2}}{2} - \frac{\sqrt{6}}{2} i$$

The roots are $\frac{\sqrt{2}}{2} + \frac{\sqrt{6}}{2}$ i and $-\frac{\sqrt{2}}{2} - \frac{\sqrt{6}}{2}$ i.

20. $-\sqrt{3} - i = 2 \text{ cis } 210°$

$(2 \text{ cis } 210°)^{1/2} = 2^{1/2} \text{ cis } \left[\frac{210°}{2} + k \cdot \frac{360°}{2}\right],$
$$k = 0, 1$$
$$= \sqrt{2} \text{ cis } (105° + k \cdot 180°),$$
$$k = 0, 1$$

The roots are $\sqrt{2}$ cis 105° when k = 0 and
$\sqrt{2}$ cis 285° when k = 1.

21. $x^3 = i$

Find the cube roots of i.

Polar notation for i is cis 90°.

Using Theorem 7, we know

$(\text{cis } 90°)^{1/3} = 1^{1/3} \text{ cis } \left[\frac{90°}{3} + k \cdot \frac{360°}{3}\right],$
$$k = 0, 1, 2$$
$$= \text{cis } (30° + k \cdot 120°), k = 0, 1, 2$$

Thus the roots are

cis 30° when k = 0, cis 150° when k = 1, and
cis 270° when k = 2.

Rectangular notation for these roots is as
follows:

cis 30° = cos 30° + i sin 30° = $\frac{\sqrt{3}}{2} + \frac{1}{2}$ i

cis 150° = cos 150° + i sin 150° = $-\frac{\sqrt{3}}{2} + \frac{1}{2}$ i

cis 270° = cos 270° + i sin 270° = $-i$

22.   68.4321 = 68.4321 cis 0°

[68.4321 cis 0°]$^{1/3}$ =

$(68.4321)^{1/3}$ cis $\left[\dfrac{0°}{3} + k \cdot \dfrac{360°}{3}\right]$, k = 0, 1, 2

= 4.09 cis (0° + k·120°),

k = 0, 1, 2

The roots are 4.09 when k = 0,

4.09 cis 120° = 4.09$\left[-\dfrac{1}{2} + \dfrac{\sqrt{3}}{2}i\right]$

= -2.045 + 3.542i when k = 1, and

4.09 cis 240° = 4.09$\left[-\dfrac{1}{2} - \dfrac{\sqrt{3}}{2}i\right]$

= -2.045 - 3.542i when k = 2.

23.   Solve x^4 = 16.

Find the fourth roots of 16.

Polar notation for 16 is 16 cis 0°.

Using Theorem 7, we know

$(16 \text{ cis } 0°)^{1/4} = 16^{1/4}$ cis $\left[\dfrac{0°}{4} + k \cdot \dfrac{360°}{4}\right]$,

k = 0, 1, 2, 3

= 2 cis k·90°, k = 0, 1, 2, 3

Thus the roots are

2 cis 0° = 2(cos 0° + i sin 0°)   when k = 0

= 2(1 + 0i) = 2

2 cis 90° = 2(cos 90° + i sin 90°)   when k = 1

= 2(0 + i) = 2i

2 cis 180° = 2(cos 180° + i sin 180°) when k = 2

= 2(-1 + 0i) = -2

2 cis 270° = 2(cos 270° + i sin 270°) when k = 3

= 2(0 - i) = -2i

The graph of ± 2 and ± 2i is as follows:

24.   i = 1 · cis 90°

$i^{1/4} = 1^{1/4}$ cis $\left[\dfrac{90°}{4} + k \cdot \dfrac{360°}{4}\right]$, k = 0, 1, 2, 3

= cis (22.5 + k·90°), k = 0, 1, 2, 3.

The roots are cis 22.5° when k = 0,

cis 112.5° when k = 1,

cis 202.5° when k = 2,

and cis 292.5° when k = 3.

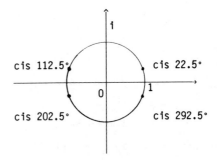

25.   -1 = 1 cis 180°

$(1 \text{ cis } 180°)^{1/5} = 1^{1/5}$ cis $\left[\dfrac{180°}{5} + k \cdot \dfrac{360°}{5}\right]$,

k = 0, 1, 2, 3, 4

The roots are 1 cis 36°, 1 cis 108°, 1 cis 180°, 1 cis 252° and 1 cis 324°, or cis 36°, cis 108°, cis 180°, cis 252°, cis 324°.

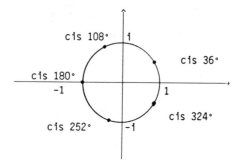

26.   1 = 1 cis 0°

$(1 \text{ cis } 0°)^{1/6} = 1^{1/6}$ cis $\left[\dfrac{0°}{6} + k \cdot \dfrac{360°}{6}\right]$,

k = 0, 1, 2, 3, 4, 5

= cis 0°, cis 60°, cis 120°,

cis 180°, cis 240°, cis 300°, or

1, $\dfrac{1}{2} + \dfrac{\sqrt{3}}{2}i$, $-\dfrac{1}{2} + \dfrac{\sqrt{3}}{2}i$, -1, $-\dfrac{1}{2} - \dfrac{\sqrt{3}}{2}i$,

$\dfrac{1}{2} - \dfrac{\sqrt{3}}{2}i$

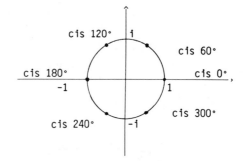

27. $-8 + i8\sqrt{3} = 16 \text{ cis } 120°$

$(16 \text{ cis } 120°)^{1/4} = 16^{1/4} \text{ cis } \left[\frac{120°}{4} + k \cdot \frac{360°}{4}\right],$
$$k = 0, 1, 2, 3$$

The roots are 2 cis 30°, 2 cis 120°, 2 cis 210°, 2 cis 300°, or $\sqrt{3} + i$, $-1 + \sqrt{3} i$, $-\sqrt{3} - i$, $1 - \sqrt{3} i$.

28. $-64i = 64 \text{ cis } 270°$

$(64 \text{ cis } 270°)^{1/3} = 64^{1/3} \text{ cis } \left[\frac{270°}{3} + k \cdot \frac{360°}{3}\right],$
$$k = 0, 1, 2$$
$$= 4 \text{ cis } 90°, 4 \text{ cis } 210°,$$
$$4 \text{ cis } 330°, \text{ or } 4i, -2\sqrt{3} - 2i,$$
$$2\sqrt{3} - 2i$$

29. $2\sqrt{3} - 2i = 4 \text{ cis } 330°$

$(4 \text{ cis } 330°)^{1/3} = 4^{1/3} \text{ cis } \left[\frac{330°}{3} + k \cdot \frac{360°}{3}\right],$
$$k = 0, 1, 2$$

The roots are $\sqrt[3]{4} \text{ cis } 110°$, $\sqrt[3]{4} \text{ cis } 230°$, $\sqrt[3]{4} \text{ cis } 350°$.

30. $1 - i\sqrt{3} = 2 \text{ cis } 300°$

$(2 \text{ cis } 300°)^{1/3} = 2^{1/3} \text{ cis } \left[\frac{300°}{3} + k \cdot \frac{360°}{3}\right],$
$$k = 0, 1, 2$$
$$= \sqrt[3]{2} \text{ cis } 100°, \sqrt[3]{2} \text{ cis } 220°,$$
$$\sqrt[3]{2} \text{ cis } 340°$$

31. $x^3 = 1$

The solutions of this equation are the cube roots of 1. These were found in Example 4 in the text.

32. $x^5 - 1 = 0$
$$x^5 = 1$$

Find the fifth roots of 1.
$$1 = 1 \text{ cis } 0°$$
$1^{1/5} = 1^{1/5} \text{ cis } \left[\frac{0°}{5} + k \cdot \frac{360°}{5}\right], k = 0, 1, 2, 3, 4$
$$= \text{ cis } 0°, \text{ cis } 72°, \text{ cis } 144°, \text{ cis } 216°,$$
$$\text{ cis } 288°$$

33. $x^5 + 1 = 0$
$$x^5 = -1$$

The solutions of this equation are the fifth roots of -1. These were found in Exercise 25 above.

34. $x^4 + i = 0$
$$x^4 = -i$$

Find the fourth roots of -i.
$$-i = 1 \text{ cis } 270°$$
$(1 \text{ cis } 270°)^{1/4} = 1^{1/4} \text{ cis } \left[\frac{270°}{4} + k \cdot \frac{360°}{4}\right],$
$$k = 0, 1, 2, 3$$
$$= \text{ cis } 67.5°, \text{ cis } 157.5°,$$
$$\text{ cis } 247.5°, \text{ cis } 337.5°$$

35. $x^5 + \sqrt{3} + i = 0$
$$x^5 = -\sqrt{3} - i$$

The solutions of this equation are the fifth roots of $-\sqrt{3} - i$.
$$-\sqrt{3} - i = 2 \text{ cis } 210°$$
$(2 \text{ cis } 210°)^{1/5} = 2^{1/5} \text{ cis } \left[\frac{210°}{5} + k \cdot \frac{360°}{5}\right],$
$$k = 0, 1, 2, 3, 4$$

The solutions are $\sqrt[5]{2} \text{ cis } 42°$, $\sqrt[5]{2} \text{ cis } 114°$, $\sqrt[5]{2} \text{ cis } 186°$, $\sqrt[5]{2} \text{ cis } 258°$, $\sqrt[5]{2} \text{ cis } 330°$

36. $x^3 + (4 - 4\sqrt{3} i) = 0$
$$x^3 = -4 + 4\sqrt{3} i$$

Find the cube roots of $-4 + 4\sqrt{3} i$.
$$-4 + 4\sqrt{3} i = 8 \text{ cis } 120°$$
$(8 \text{ cis } 120°)^{1/3} = 8^{1/3} \text{ cis } \left[\frac{120°}{3} + k \cdot \frac{360°}{3}\right],$
$$k = 0, 1, 2$$
$$= 2 \text{ cis } 40°, 2 \text{ cis } 160°,$$
$$2 \text{ cis } 280°$$

37. $x^4 + 81 = 0$
$$x^4 = -81$$

The solutions of this equation are the fourth roots of -81.
$$-81 = 81 \text{ cis } 180°$$
$(81 \text{ cis } 180°)^{1/4} = 81^{1/4} \text{ cis } \left[\frac{180°}{4} + k \cdot \frac{360°}{4}\right],$
$$k = 0, 1, 2, 3$$

The solutions are 3 cis 45°, 3 cis 135°, 3 cis 225°, 3 cis 315°, or $\frac{3\sqrt{2}}{2} + \frac{3\sqrt{2}}{2} i$, $-\frac{3\sqrt{2}}{2} + \frac{3\sqrt{2}}{2} i$, $-\frac{3\sqrt{2}}{2} - \frac{3\sqrt{2}}{2} i$, and $\frac{3\sqrt{2}}{2} - \frac{3\sqrt{2}}{2} i$.

38. $x^6 + 1 = 0$

$\qquad x^6 = -1$

Find the sixth roots of -1.

$-1 = 1 \text{ cis } 180°$

$(1 \text{ cis } 180°)^{1/6} = 1^{1/6} \text{ cis } \left[\dfrac{180°}{6} + k \cdot \dfrac{360°}{6}\right],$

$\qquad\qquad\qquad\qquad k = 0, 1, 2, 3, 4, 5$

$\qquad\qquad = \text{cis } 30°, \text{ cis } 90°, \text{ cis } 150°,$

$\qquad\qquad\quad \text{cis } 210°, \text{ cis } 270°, \text{ cis } 330°,$

$\qquad\qquad\quad \text{or } \dfrac{\sqrt{3}}{2} + \dfrac{1}{2} i, \ i, \ -\dfrac{\sqrt{3}}{2} + \dfrac{1}{2} i,$

$\qquad\qquad\quad -\dfrac{\sqrt{3}}{2} - \dfrac{1}{2} i, \ -i, \ \dfrac{\sqrt{3}}{2} - \dfrac{1}{2} i$

39. $x^2 + (1 - i)x + i = 0$

$a = 1, \quad b = 1 - i, \quad c = i$

$x = \dfrac{-(1 - i) \pm \sqrt{(1 - i)^2 - 4 \cdot 1 \cdot i}}{2 \cdot 1}$

$\quad = \dfrac{-1 + i \pm \sqrt{1 - 2i + i^2 - 4i}}{2}$

$\quad = \dfrac{-1 + i \pm \sqrt{-6i}}{2}$

Let $z = \sqrt{-6i} = [6 \text{ cis } 270°]^{1/2}$

$\qquad\quad = 6^{1/2} \text{ cis } \left[\dfrac{270°}{2} + k \cdot \dfrac{360°}{2}\right], k = 0, 1.$

Hence $z_1 = \sqrt{6} \text{ cis } 135° = -\sqrt{3} + \sqrt{3}\, i$

$\qquad\ \ z_2 = \sqrt{6} \text{ cis } 315° = \sqrt{3} - \sqrt{3}\, i.$

Thus, substituting for $\sqrt{-6i}$, we get

$x_1 = \dfrac{-1 + i - \sqrt{3} + \sqrt{3}\, i}{2} = -1.366 + 1.366i$

$x_2 = \dfrac{-1 + i + \sqrt{3} - \sqrt{3}\, i}{2} = 0.366 - 0.366i$

40. $3x^2 + (1 + 2i)x + (1 - i) = 0$

$x = \dfrac{-(1 + 2i) \pm \sqrt{(1 + 2i)^2 - 4 \cdot 3 \cdot (1 - i)}}{2 \cdot 3}$

$\ = \dfrac{-1 - 2i \pm \sqrt{-15 + 16i}}{6}$

Let $z = \sqrt{-15 + 16i}$

$\qquad = [21.93 \text{ cis } 136.85°]^{1/2}$

$\qquad = 4.68 \text{ cis } \left[\dfrac{136.85°}{2} + k \cdot \dfrac{360°}{2}\right], k = 0, 1.$

Let $z_1 = 4.68(\cos 68.42° + i \sin 68.42°)$ for $k = 0$

$\qquad = 1.72 + 4.35i;$ and

$\quad z_2 = 4.68(\cos 248.42° + i \sin 248.42°)$

$\qquad\qquad\qquad\qquad\qquad\qquad$ for $k = 1$

$\qquad = -1.72 - 4.35i.$

Then $x_1 = \dfrac{-1 - 2i + z_1}{6} = 0.12 + 0.39i,$ and

$\qquad x_2 = \dfrac{-1 - 2i + z_2}{6} = -0.45 - 1.06i$

41. $\pm 1.8612097, \pm 1.86120971$

42. No solution

43. $\pm 1.2311444, \pm 0.99601675 \pm 0.723648531,$
$\pm 0.38044455 \pm 1.170887911$

44. $-1.166529, -0.8936131 \pm 0.74983041i,$
$-0.2025656 \pm 1.1488071i, 0.58326452 \pm 1.0102441i,$
$1.0961787 \pm 0.39897641i$

Exercise Set 9.1

__1.__ We replace x by $\frac{1}{2}$ and y by 1.

$3x + y = \frac{5}{2}$	
$3 \cdot \frac{1}{2} + 1$	$\frac{5}{2}$
$\frac{3}{2} + \frac{2}{2}$	
$\frac{5}{2}$	

$2x - y = \frac{1}{4}$	
$2 \cdot \frac{1}{2} - 1$	$\frac{1}{4}$
$1 - 1$	
0	

The ordered pair $\left(\frac{1}{2}, 1\right)$ is not a solution of $2x - y = \frac{1}{4}$. Therefore it is not a solution of the system of equations.

__2.__

$x + 4y = -1$	
$-2 + 4 \cdot \frac{1}{4}$	-1
$-2 + 1$	
-1	

$2x + 8y = -2$	
$2(-2) + 8 \cdot \frac{1}{4}$	-2
$-4 + 2$	
-2	

$\left(-2, \frac{1}{4}\right)$ is a solution of the system of equations.

__3.__ Graph both lines on the same set of axes. The x and y-intercepts of the line x + y = 2 are (2, 0) and (0, 2). Plot these points and draw the line they determine. Next graph the line 3x + y = 0. Three of the points on the line are (0, 0), (-1, 3), and (2, -6). Plot these points and draw the line they determine.

The solution (point of intersection) seems to be the point (-1, 3).

Check:

x + y = 2	
-1 + 3	2
2	

3x + y = 0	
3(-1) + 3	0
-3 + 3	
0	

The solution is (-1, 3).

__4.__

__5.__ Graph both lines on the same set of axes. The intercepts of y + 1 = 2x are $\left(\frac{1}{2}, 0\right)$ and (0, -1). The intercepts of y - 1 = 2x are $\left(-\frac{1}{2}, 0\right)$ and (0, 1).

The lines have no point in common. The system has no solution.

__6.__

Infinitely many solutions

__7.__ x - 5y = 4,   (1)
y = 7 - 2x   (2)

Substitute 7 - 2x for y in Equation (1) and solve for x.

$$x - 5(7 - 2x) = 4$$
$$x - 35 + 10x = 4$$
$$11x = 39$$
$$x = \frac{39}{11}$$

Now substitute $\frac{39}{11}$ for x in either Equation (1) or or (2) and solve for y. We use Equation (2).

$$y = 7 - 2 \cdot \frac{39}{11}$$
$$y = 7 - \frac{78}{11}$$
$$y = -\frac{1}{11}$$

Check:

x - 5y = 4	
$\frac{39}{11} - 5\left(-\frac{1}{11}\right)$	4
$\frac{39}{11} + \frac{5}{11}$	
$\frac{44}{11}$	
4	

y = 7 - 2x	
$-\frac{1}{11}$	$7 - 2 \cdot \frac{39}{11}$
$-\frac{1}{11}$	$7 - \frac{78}{11}$
	$-\frac{1}{11}$

The solution is $\left(\frac{39}{11}, -\frac{1}{11}\right)$.

8. $3x - y = 5$,   (1)

   $x + y = \frac{1}{2}$ (2)

   Solve (1) for y and substitute in (2).

   $y = 3x - 5$

   $x + 3x - 5 = \frac{1}{2}$

   $4x = \frac{11}{2}$

   $x = \frac{11}{8}$

   Substitute in (2) and solve for y.

   $\frac{11}{8} + y = \frac{1}{2}$

   $y = -\frac{7}{8}$

   The solution is $\left(\frac{11}{8}, -\frac{7}{8}\right)$.

9. $x - 3y = 2$,   (1)

   $6x + 5y = -34$ (2)

   We multiply equation (1) by -6 and add the result to equation (2).

   $x - 3y = 2$, $\begin{array}{r} -6x + 18y = -12 \\ \underline{6x + 5y = -34} \\ 23y = -46 \end{array}$

   $23y = -46$ ⟵

   Now we solve the second equation for y. Then we substitute the result in the first equation to find x.

   $23y = -46$ $x - 3(-2) = 2$

   $y = -2$ $x + 6 = 2$

                      $x = -4$

   The solution is (-4, -2).

10. $x + 3y = 0$,   (1)

    $20x - 15y = 75$ (2)

    Multiply (1) by -20 and add:

    $x + 3y = 0$,

    $-75y = 75$

    $y = -1$; $x + 3(-1) = 0$, so $x = 3$.

    The solution is (3, -1).

11. $0.3x + 0.2y = -0.9$,

    $0.2x - 0.3y = -0.6$

    Multiply each equation by 10 to eliminate decimals.

    $3x + 2y = -9$,   (1)

    $2x - 3y = -6$ (2)

    Multiply equation (2) by 3 to make the x-coefficient a multiple of 3.

    $3x + 2y = -9$,

    $6x - 9y = -18$

    Then multiply equation (1) by -2 and add the result to equation (2).

    $3x + 2y = -9$ $\begin{array}{r} -6x - 4y = 18 \\ \underline{6x - 9y = -18} \\ -13y = 0 \end{array}$

    $-13y = 0$ ⟵

    Now solve the second equation for y and substitute in the first equation to find x.

    $-13y = 0$ $3x + 2\cdot 0 = -9$

    $y = 0$ $3x = -9$

                      $x = -3$

    The solution is (-3, 0).

12. $0.2x - 0.3y = 0.3$,

    $0.4x + 0.6y = -0.2$

    $2x - 3y = 3$ (1)

    $4x + 6y = -2$ (2)   (Clearing decimals)

    Multiply (1) by -2 and add:

    $2x - 3y = 3$,

    $12y = -8$

    $y = -\frac{2}{3}$; $2x - 3\left(-\frac{2}{3}\right) = 3$, so $x = \frac{1}{2}$.

    The solution is $\left(\frac{1}{2}, -\frac{2}{3}\right)$.

13. $\frac{1}{5}x + \frac{1}{2}y = 6$,

    $\frac{3}{5}x - \frac{1}{2}y = 2$

    Multiply each equation by 10 to clear of fractions.

    $2x + 5y = 60$,   (1)

    $6x - 5y = 20$ (2)

    Multiply equation (1) by -3 and add the result to equation (2).

    $2x + 5y = 60$, $\begin{array}{r} -6x - 15y = -180 \\ \underline{6x - 5y = 20} \\ -20y = -160 \end{array}$

    $-20y = -160$ ⟵

    Solve the second equation for y and substitute in the first equation to find x.

    $-20y = -160$ $2x + 5\cdot 8 = 60$

    $y = 8$ $2x + 40 = 60$

                         $2x = 20$

                         $x = 10$

    The solution is (10, 8).

14. $\frac{2}{3}x + \frac{3}{5}y = -17,$

$\frac{1}{2}x - \frac{1}{3}y = -1$

$10x + 9y = -255,$
$3x - 2y = -6$ (Clearing fractions)

Multiply the second equation by 10.

$10x + 9y = -255$ (1)
$30x - 20y = -60$ (2)

Multiply (1) by -3 and add:

$10x + 9y = -255$
$-47y = 705$

$y = -15;$ $10x + 9(-15) = -255,$ so $x = -12.$

The solution is $(-12, -15).$

15. $2a = 5 - 3b,$
$4a = 11 - 7b$

First write each equation in the form $Ax + By = C.$
$2a + 3b = 5,$ (1)
$4a + 7b = 11$ (2)

Multiply equation (1) by -2 and add the result to equation (2).

$2a + 3b = 5,$ $\begin{array}{r} -4a - 6b = -10 \\ 4a + 7b = 11 \\ \hline b = 1 \end{array}$
$b = 1$ ←

Substitute in the first equation to find $a.$

$2a + 3 \cdot 1 = 5$
$2a + 3 = 5$
$2a = 2$
$a = 1$

The solution is $(1, 1).$

16. $7(a - b) = 14,$
$2a = b + 5$

Multiply the first equation by $\frac{1}{7}$ and rewrite the second equation.

$a - b = 2,$ (1)
$2a - b = 5$ (2)

Multiply (1) by -2 and add.

$a - b = 2$
$b = 1$

Then $a - 1 = 2,$ so $a = 3.$
The solution is $(3, 1).$

17. Familiarize and Translate:

Let x and y represent the numbers. A system of equations results directly from the statements in the problem.

$x + y = -10,$ (The sum is -10.)
$x - y = 1$ (The difference is 1.)

Carry out: We solve the system.

Multiply the first equation by -1 and add the result to the second equation.

$x + y = -10,$
$-2y = 11$

Solve the second equation for y and then substitute into the first equation to find $x.$

$-2y = 11$ $x + \left(-\frac{11}{2}\right) = -10$

$y = -\frac{11}{2}$ $x = -\frac{20}{2} + \frac{11}{2} = -\frac{9}{2}$

Check:

The sum of $-\frac{9}{2}$ and $-\frac{11}{2}$ is $-\frac{20}{2},$ or -10. The difference is $-\frac{9}{2} - \left(-\frac{11}{2}\right),$ or $\frac{2}{2}$ which is 1.

State:

The numbers are $-\frac{9}{2}$ and $-\frac{11}{2}.$

18. Solve: $x + y = -1,$
        $x - y = 10$

$x = \frac{9}{2}$ and $y = -\frac{11}{2}$

19. Familiarize:

It helps to make a drawing. Then organize the information in a table. Let b = the speed of the boat and s = the speed of the stream. The speed upstream is $b - s.$ The speed downstream is $b + s.$

$d_1 = 46$ $t_1 = 2$ $r_1 = b + s$

Downstream

$d_2 = 51$ $t_2 = 3$ $r_2 = b - s$

Upstream

	Distance	Speed	Time
Downstream	46	$b + s$	2
Upstream	51	$b - s$	3

Translate:

Using $d = rt$ in each row of the table, we get a system of equations.

$46 = (b + s)2 = 2b + 2s,$ or $b + s = 23,$
$51 = (b - s)3 = 3b - 3s$ $b - s = 17$

Carry out:

Multiply the first equation by -1 and add the result to the second equation.

$$b + s = 23,$$
$$-2s = -6$$

Solve the second equation for s and then substitute in the first equation to find b.

$$-2s = -6 \qquad b + 3 = 23$$
$$s = 3 \qquad\quad b = 20$$

Check:

The speed downstream is 20 + 3, or 23 km/h. The distance downstream is 23·2, or 46 km. The speed upstream is 20 - 3, or 17 km/h. The distance upstream is 17·3, or 51 km. The values check.

State:

The speed of the boat is 20 km/h. The speed of the stream is 3 km/h.

20.

	Speed	Time	Distance
Downwind	p + w	3	3000
Upwind	p - w	4	3000

$$(p + w)3 = 3000,$$
$$(p - w)4 = 3000$$

Then p = 875 km/h,
     w = 125 km/h.

21. Familiarize:

We organize the information in a table. We let x = the number of liters of antifreeze A and y = the number of liters of antifreeze B.

	A	B	Mixture
Amount of antifreeze	x	y	20 liters
Percent of alcohol	18%	10%	15%
Amount of alcohol in antifreeze	18%x	10%y	0.15 × 20, or 3 liters

Translate:

If we add x and y in the first row, we get 20.

x + y = 20

If we add the amounts of alcohol in the third row, we get 3.

18%x + 10%y = 3

After changing percents to decimals and clearing, we have the following system:

$$x + \quad y = 20,$$
$$18x + 10y = 300$$

Carry out:

Multiply -18 times the first equation and add the result to the second equation.

$$x + y = 20,$$
$$-8y = -60$$

Solve the second equation for y and substitute in the first equation to find x.

$$-8y = -60 \qquad x + 7.5 = 20$$
$$y = 7.5 \qquad\quad x = 12.5$$

Check:

We add the amounts of antifreeze: 12.5 L + 7.5 L = 20 L. Thus the amount of antifreeze checks. Next, we check the amount of alcohol: 18%(12.5) + 10%(7.5) = 2.25 + 0.75, or 3 L. The amount of alcohol also checks.

State:

The solution of the problem is 12.5 L of A and 7.5 L of B.

22.

	A	B	Mixture
Amount of beer	a	b	50 L
Percent of alcohol	6%	2%	3.2%
Amount of alcohol in solution	6%a	2%b	0.032 × 50, or 1.6 L

$$a + b = 50,$$
$$0.06a + 0.02b = 1.6$$

Then a = 15 L and b = 35 L.

23. Familiarize:

We first make a drawing and organize the information in a table. Each car travels the same amount of time. Let t = the time and d = the distance traveled by the slower car. Then 528 - d = the distance traveled by the faster car.

	Distance	Speed	Time
Slow car	d	80	t
Fast car	528 - d	96	t

Translate:

Using d = rt in each row of the table, we get

$$d = 80t, \qquad\qquad d - 80t = 0,$$
$$\qquad\qquad\qquad\text{or}$$
$$528 - d = 96t \qquad d + 96t = 528.$$

Carry out:

Multiply the first equation by -1 and add the result to the second equation.

$$d - 80t = 0,$$
$$176t = 528$$

Solve the second equation for t. (We do not need to find d.)

$$176t = 528$$
$$t = 3$$

Check:

In 3 hours, one car travels 80·3, or 240 km, and the other car travels 96·3, or 288 km. The sum of the distances is 240 + 288, or 528 km. The value checks.

State:

In 3 hours the cars will be 528 km apart.

24.

	Distance	Speed	Time
First train	d	75	t
Second train	d	125	t - 2

$$d = 75t,$$
$$d = 125(t - 2)$$

Then d = 375 km. (We do not need to find t.)

25. Familiarize:

We first make a drawing and then organize the information in a table. The time is the same for each plane. Let t = the time and d = the distance traveled by the slower plane. Then 780 - d = the distance traveled by the faster plane.

t hours   190 km/h   200 km/h   t hours

d kilometers   780 - d kilometers

├─────────── 780 km ───────────┤

	Distance	Speed	Time
Slow plane	d	190	t
Fast plane	780 - d	200	t

Translate:

Using d = rt in each row of the table, we get

$$d = 190t,$$ $$d - 190t = 0,$$
                or
$$780 - d = 200t$$ $$d + 200t = 780.$$

Carry out:

Multiply the first equation by -1 and add the result to the second equation.

$$d - 190t = 0,$$
$$390t = 780$$

Solve the second equation for t. (We do not need to find d.)

$$390t = 780$$
$$t = 2$$

Check:

In 2 hours, one plane travels 2·190, or 380 km, and the other plane travels 2·200, or 400 km. The total distance is 380 + 400, or 780 km. The value checks.

State:

The planes will meet in 2 hours.

26.

	Distance	Speed	Time
Faster motorcycle	d	110	t
Slower motorcycle	350 - d	90	t

$$d = 110t,$$
$$350 - d = 90t$$

Then $t = 1\frac{3}{4}$ hr. (We do not need to find d.)

27. Familiarize and Translate:

Let x = the number of white scarves and y = the number of printed scarves. Thus, $4.95x worth of white ones and $7.95y worth of printed ones were sold. The total number of scarves was 40.

x + y = 40

The total sales were $282.

4.95x + 7.95y = 282, or 495x + 795y = 28,200

We solve the following system of equations:

$$x + y = 40,$$
$$495x + 795y = 28,200$$

Carry out:

Multiply -495 times the first equation and add the result to the second equation.

$$x + y = 40,$$
$$300y = 8400$$

Solve the second equation for y and then substitute in the first equation to find x.

$$300y = 8400 \qquad x + 28 = 40$$
$$y = 28 \qquad\qquad x = 12$$

Check:

The total number of scarves was 12 + 28, or 40. Total sales were 4.95(12) + 7.95(28), or 59.40 + 222.60, or $282. The values check.

State:

12 white scarves and 28 printed ones were sold.

28. w + y = 30,
     9.95w + 10.50y = 310.60

     Then w = 8 and y = 22.

29. Familiarize and Translate:

     Let x = Paula's age now and y = Bob's age now. It
     helps to organize the information in a table.

	Age now	Age four years from now
Paula	x	x + 4
Bob	y	y + 4

     Paula is 12 years older than Bob.

     x = y + 12,   or   x - y = 12

     Four years from now, Bob will be $\frac{2}{3}$ as old as
     Paula.

     $$y + 4 = \frac{2}{3}(x + 4)$$

     or

     $$3(y + 4) = 2(x + 4)$$
     $$3y + 12 = 2x + 8$$
     $$4 = 2x - 3y$$

     We now have a system of equations.

     x - y = 12,
     2x - 3y = 4

     Carry out:

     Multiply the first equation by -2 and add the
     result to the second equation.

     x - y = 12,
          -y = -20

     Complete the solution.

     -y = -20   x - 20 = 12
      y = 20   x = 32

     Check:

     If Paula is 32 and Bob 20, Paula is 12 years older
     than Bob. In four years, Paula will be 36 and
     Bob 24. Thus Bob will be $\frac{2}{3}$ as old as Paula
     $\left(24 = \frac{2}{3} \cdot 36\right)$. The ages check.

     State:

     Paula is 32, and Bob is 20.

30. Let m = Maria's age now and c = Carlos' age now.

	Age now	Age 4 years ago
Maria	m	m - 4
Carlos	c	c - 4

     c = m + 8

     $m - 4 = \frac{2}{3}(c - 4)$

     Then m = 20 and c = 28.

31. Familiarize:

     If helps to make a drawing. We let ℓ = the length
     and w = the width.

     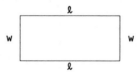

     The formula for the perimeter is P = 2ℓ + 2w.

     Translate:

     The perimeter is 190 m.

     2ℓ + 2w = 190,   or ℓ + w = 95

     The width is one-fourth the length.

     $w = \frac{1}{4}\ell$

     The resulting system is

     ℓ + w = 95,

     $w = \frac{1}{4}\ell$.

     Carry out:

     Substitute $\frac{1}{4}\ell$ for w in the first equation and
     solve for ℓ.

     ℓ + w = 95

     $\ell + \frac{1}{4}\ell = 95$

     $\frac{5}{4}\ell = 95$

     $\frac{4}{5} \cdot \frac{5}{4}\ell = \frac{4}{5} \cdot 95$

     $\ell = 76$

     Then substitute 76 for ℓ in one of the equations
     of the system and solve for w.

     ℓ + w = 95

     76 + w = 95

        w = 19

     Check:

     If ℓ = 76 m and w = 19 m, then the width is
     one-fourth the length. The perimeter is
     2·76 + 2·19, or 190 m. The values check.

     State:

     The length is 76 m; the width is 19 m.

32. $2\ell + 2w = 628$,

$w = \ell - 6$

Then $\ell = 160$ m and $w = 154$ m.

33. Familiarize:

We first make a drawing.

We let ℓ = the length and w = the width. The formula for the perimeter is $P = 2\ell + 2w$.

Translate:

The perimeter is 384 m.

$2\ell + 2w = 384$,   or $\ell + w = 192$

The length is 82 m greater than the width.

$\ell = w + 82$

The resulting system is

$\ell + w = 192$,

$\ell = w + 82$.

Carry out:

Substitute $w + 82$ for ℓ in the first equation and solve for w.

$\ell + w = 192$

$w + 82 + w = 192$

$2w + 82 = 192$

$2w = 110$

$w = 55$

Then substitute 55 for w in one of the original equations and solve for ℓ.

$\ell = w + 82$

$\ell = 55 + 82$

$\ell = 137$

Check:

The length is 82 greater than the width ($137 = 55 + 82$). The perimeter is $2 \cdot 137 + 2 \cdot 55$, or 384 m. The values check.

State:

The length is 137 m; the width is 55 m.

34. $2\ell + 2w = 86$

$\ell = w + 19$

Then $\ell = 31$, $w = 12$; and $A = 372$ cm^2.

35. Familiarize:

Let x = the amount invested at 9%, and let y = the amount invested at 10%. The interest earned by these investments is 9%x, or $0.09x$, and 10%y, or $0.1y$, respectively.

Translate:

The total investment is $15,000.

$x + y = 15,000$

The total interest is $1432.

$0.09x + 0.1y = 1432$, or $9x + 10y = 143,200$

The resulting system is

$x + y = 15,000$,

$9x + 10y = 143,200$.

Carry out:

Multiply the first equation by -9 and add.

$x + y = 15,000$,

$y = 8200$

Complete the solution.

$x + 8200 = 15,000$

$x = 6800$

Check:

The total investment is $8200 + $6800, or $15,000.

The total interest is $0.09(\$6800) + 0.1(\$8200)$, or $612 + $820, or $1432.

State:

$6800 is invested at 9%, and $8200 is invested at 10%.

36. Let x and y represent the amounts invested at 5% and 6%, respectively.

$y = x + 10,000$,

$0.05x + 0.06y = \$3900$

Then $x = \$30,000$ and $y = \$40,000$.

37. Familiarize:

Let d = the number of dimes and n = the number of nickels. The value of the dimes is $0.10d$, and the value of the nickels is $0.05n$.

Translate:

The total number of coins is 34.

$d + n = 34$

The total value is $1.90.

$0.10d + 0.05n = 1.90$, or $10d + 5n = 190$

The resulting system is

$d + n = 34$,

$10d + 5n = 190$.

Carry out:

Multiply the first equation by -10 and add.

$d + n = 34$,

$-5n = -150$

Complete the solution.

$-5n = -150$ $d + 30 = 34$

$n = 30$ $d = 4$

Check:

The total number of coins is $4 + 30$, or 34.
The total value is $0.10(4) + 0.05(30)$, or $0.40 + $1.50, or $1.90.

State:

There are 4 dimes and 30 nickels.

38. $d + q = 43$,

$0.10d + 0.25q = 7.60$

Then $d = 21$ and $q = 22$.

39. Familiarize:

We organize the information in a table. Let x = the number of pounds of $4.05 tobacco and y = the number of pounds of $2.70 tobacco.

	$4.05 tobacco	$2.70 tobacco	Mixture
Amount of tobacco	x	y	15 lb
Price per pound	$4.05	$2.70	$3.15
Total cost	$4.05x	$2.70y	$3.15 × 15, or $47.25

Translate:

If we add x and y in the first row, we get 15.

$x + y = 15$

If we add the amounts in the third row, we get $47.25.

$4.05x + 2.70y = 47.25$, or $405x + 270y = 4725$

The resulting system is

$x + y = 15$,

$405x + 270y = 4725$.

Carry out:

Multiply the first equation by −405 and add.

$x + y = 15$,

$-135y = -1350$

Complete the solution.

$-135y = -1350$	$x + 10 = 15$
$y = 10$	$x = 5$

Check:

The total amount of tobacco is 5 + 10, or 15 lb.

The total value of the mixture is $4.05(5) + $2.70(10), or $20.25 + $27.00, or $47.25.

State:

The dealer should use 5 lb of the $4.05 tobacco and 10 lb of the $2.70 tobacco.

40.

	Candy	Nuts	Mixture
Amount of ingredient	c	n	20 lb
Price per pound	$0.80	$0.70	$0.77
Total cost	$0.80c	$0.70n	$0.77 × 20, or $15.40

$c + n = 20$,

$0.80c + 0.70n = 15.40$, or $8c + 7n = 154$

Then $c = 14$ lb and $n = 6$ lb.

41. $\dfrac{x + y}{4} - \dfrac{x - y}{3} = 1$

$\dfrac{x - y}{2} + \dfrac{x + y}{4} = -9$

First multiply each equation by the LCM to clear fractions.

$3(x + y) - 4(x - y) = 12$ (Multiplying by 12)

$2(x - y) + (x + y) = -36$ (Multiplying by 4)

After simplifying, the resulting system is

$-x + 7y = 12$,

$3x - y = -36$.

Multiply the first equation by 3 and add the result to the second equation.

$-x + 7y = 12$

$20y = 0$

Complete the solution.

$20y = 0$	$-x + 7 \cdot 0 = 12$
$y = 0$	$-x = 12$
	$x = -12$

The solution is $(-12, 0)$.

42. Multiply the first equation by 6 and the second equation by 12 to clear fractions and simplify.

$5x + y = 0$,

$x + y = 0$

Interchange the equations.

$x + y = 0$,

$5x + y = 0$

Multiply the first equation by −5 and add

$x + y = 0$,

$-4y = 0$

$y = 0$

$x + 0 = 0$

$x = 0$

The solution is $(0, 0)$.

43. Familiarize:

We first make a drawing and then organize the information in a table. Using $d = rt$, we let $8t_1$ = the distance jogging and $4t_2$ = the distance walking.

Jogging 8 km/h t_1 hr   Walking 4 km/h t_2 hr

Home   University

├───────────── 6 km ─────────────┤

	Distance	Speed	Time
Jogging	$8t_1$	8	t_1
Walking	$4t_2$	4	t_2
Total	6		1

Translate:

The total distance is 6 km. The total time is 1 hour. A system of equations results from the columns in the table.

$$t_1 + t_2 = 1,$$
$$8t_1 + 4t_2 = 6$$

Carry out:

Multiply the first equation by -8 and add the result to the second equation.

$$t_1 + t_2 = 1$$
$$-4t_2 = -2$$

Complete the solution.

$$-4t_2 = -2 \qquad t_1 + t_2 = 1$$
$$t_2 = \frac{1}{2} \qquad t_1 = \frac{1}{2}$$

The jogging distance, $8t_1$, is $8 \cdot \frac{1}{2}$, or 4 km.

The walking distance, $4t_2$, is $4 \cdot \frac{1}{2}$, or 2 km.

Check:

The total distance is 4 + 2, or 6 km. The total time is $\frac{1}{2} + \frac{1}{2}$, or 1 hour. The values check.

State:

She jogs 4 km on each trip.

44. Let x = the number of years James has taught and
      y = the number of years Joan has taught.

$$x + y = 46,$$
$$x - 2 = 2.5(y - 2)$$

Then x = 32 yr and y = 14 yr.

45. Familiarize:

Let x = the number of one-book orders and y = the number of two-book orders. Then 12x = the amount taken in from the one-book orders and 20y = the amount taken in from the two-book orders. It helps to organize the information in a table.

	One-book orders	Two-book orders	Total
Number of orders	x	y	
Number of books	x	2y	880
Amount taken in	$12x	$20y	$9840

Translate:

The total number of books sold was 880.

x + 2y = 880   (See Row 2 of the table.)

The total amount of money taken in was $9840.

12x + 20y = 9840, or 3x + 5y = 2460   (See Row 3 of the table)

The resulting system of equations is

$$x + 2y = 880,$$
$$3x + 5y = 2460.$$

Carry out:

Multiply the first equation by -3 and add the result to the second equation.

$$x + 2y = 880,$$
$$-y = -180$$

Complete the solution.

$$-y = -180 \qquad x + 2 \cdot 180 = 880$$
$$y = 180 \qquad x + 360 = 880$$
$$x = 520$$

Check:

The total number of books sold was $520 + 2 \cdot 180$, or 880. The total amount taken in was $12 \cdot 520 + 20 \cdot 180$, or $9840. The values check.

State:

180 members ordered two books.

46. Let x = ten's digit and
      y = unit's digit.

Then x = 2 + 3y
and $10y + x = \frac{1}{2}(10x + y) - 13$.

Thus x = 8, y = 2; and the positive integer is 10x + y, or 82.

47. Familiarize and Translate:

Let x = the numerator and y = the denominator.
The numerator is 12 more than the denominator.

x = y + 12,   or   x - y = 12

The sum of the numerator and the denominator is 5 more than three times the denominator.

x + y = 3y + 5,   or   x - 2y = 5

The resulting system is

$$x - y = 12,$$
$$x - 2y = 5.$$

Carry out:

Multiply the first equation by -1 and add the result to the second equation.

$$x - y = 12,$$
$$-y = -7$$

Complete the solution.

$$-y = -7 \qquad x - 7 = 12$$
$$y = 7 \qquad x = 19$$

Check:

If $x = 19$ and $y = 7$, the fraction is $\frac{19}{7}$. The numerator is 12 more than the denominator. The sum of the numerator and the denominator, $19 + 7$ (or 26), is 5 more than three times the denominator ($26 = 5 + 3 \cdot 7$). The numbers check.

State:

The reciprocal of $\frac{19}{7}$ is $\frac{7}{19}$.

48. $A + B = 180°$,
    $A = 8° + 3B$

    Then $A = 137°$.   (We do not need to find B.)

49. Familiarize and Translate:

We let r_1 and r_2 represent the speeds of the trains. Organize the information in a table. Using $d = rt$, we let $3r_1$, $2r_2$, $1.5r_1$, and $3r_2$ represent the distances the trains travel.

First situation:

3 hours r_1 km/h r_2 km/h   2 hours

Union   Central

|—————————————— 216 km ——————————————|

Second situation:

1.5 hours r_1 km/h r_2 km/h   3 hours

Union   Central

|—————————————— 216 km ——————————————|

	Distance traveled in first situation	Distance traveled in second situation
Train$_1$ (from Union to Central)	$3r_1$	$1.5r_1$
Train$_2$ (from Central to Union)	$2r_2$	$3r_2$
Total	216	216

The total distance in each situation is 216 km. Thus, we have a system of equations.

$$3r_1 + 2r_2 = 216,$$
$$1.5r_1 + 3r_2 = 216.$$

Carry out:

Multiply the second equation by 2 to make the x-coefficient a multiple of 3.

$$3r_1 + 2r_2 = 216,$$
$$3r_1 + 6r_2 = 432$$

Now multiply the first equation by –1 and add.

$$3r_1 + 2r_2 = 216,$$
$$4r_2 = 216$$

Complete the solution.

$$4r_2 = 216 \qquad 3r_1 + 2 \cdot 54 = 216$$
$$r_2 = 54 \qquad 3r_1 + 108 = 216$$
$$3r_1 = 108$$
$$r_1 = 36$$

Check:

If $r_1 = 36$ and $r_2 = 54$, the total distance the trains travel in the first situation is $3 \cdot 36 + 2 \cdot 54$, or 216 km. The total distance they travel in the second situation is $1.5 \cdot 36 + 3 \cdot 54$, or 216 km. The values check.

State:

The speed of the first train is 36 km/h.
The speed of the second train is 54 km/h.

50. Let x = the amount of mixture replaced by 100% antifreeze and y = the amount of 30% mixture retained.

	Replaced	Retained	Total
Amount	x	y	16 L
Percent of antifreeze	100%	30%	50%
Amount of antifreeze	100%x	30%y	50% × 16, or 8 L

$$x + y = 16$$
$$x + 0.3y = 8$$

Then $x = 4\frac{4}{7}$ L.   (We do not need to find y.)

51. Familiarize:

Let x = the value of the horse.

Let y = the value of the compensation the stablehand was to receive after one year.

Translate:

If the stablehand had worked for one year, he would have received $240 and one horse.

$$y = 240 + x$$

$100 and one horse is $\frac{7}{12}$ of one year's compensation.

$$100 + x = \frac{7}{12}y$$

We have a system of equations:

$$y = 240 + x,$$
$$100 + x = \frac{7}{12}y$$

Carry out:

We substitute 240 + x for y in the second equation.

$$100 + x = \frac{7}{12}(240 + x)$$

$$100 + x = 140 + \frac{7}{12}x$$

$$\frac{5}{12}x = 40$$

$$x = 96$$

Check:

If the value of the horse is $96, the compensation after one year would have been $240 + $96, or $336. Since $\frac{7}{12} \cdot$ $336 = $196, or $100 + $96, the value checks.

State:

The value of the horse is $96.

52. Let x = the number of people ahead of you and y = the number of people behind you.

x = 2 + y,

x + 1 + y = 3y

Then x = 5.   (We do not need to find y).

53. Familiarize and Translate:

Let x = the number of girls in the family and y = the number of boys. Then Phil has x sisters and y - 1 brothers, and Phyllis has x - 1 sisters and y brothers.

	Brothers	Sisters
Phil	y - 1	x
Phyllis	y	x - 1

Phil has the same number of brothers and sisters.

y - 1 = x,   or   x - y = -1

Phyllis has twice as many brothers as sisters.

y = 2(x - 1),   or   2x - y = 2

We now have a system of equations.

  x - y = -1,

2x - y = 2

Carry out:

Multiply the first equation by -2 and add the result to the second equation.

    x - y = -1,

          y = 4

Complete the solution.

    x - 4 = -1

        x = 3

Check:

If there are 3 girls and 4 boys in the family, Phil has 3 brothers and 3 sisters and Phyllis has 2 sisters and 4 brothers. Thus, Phil has the same number of brothers and sisters, and Phyllis has twice as many brothers as sisters.

State:

There are 3 girls and 4 boys in the family.

54. Let c = city miles driven and h = highway miles driven.

Then   c + h = 465,

$$\frac{c}{18} + \frac{h}{24} = 23.$$

Hence c = 261 mi and h = 204 mi.

55. Substituting the given solutions in the equation y = mx + b, we get a system of equations.

    3 = -2m + b,   -2m + b = 3,
                      or
   -5 = 4m + b   4m + b = -5

Multiply the first equation by 2 and add.

   -2m + b = 3,

       3b = 1

Complete the solution.

    3b = 1 $-2m + \frac{1}{3} = 3$

     $b = \frac{1}{3}$ $-2m = \frac{8}{3}$

                        $m = -\frac{4}{3}$

56. Solve   3A - B = 1,

            -4A - 2B = 1.

$A = \frac{1}{10}$, $B = -\frac{7}{10}$

57. $\frac{1}{x} - \frac{3}{y} = 2$

$\frac{6}{x} + \frac{5}{y} = -34$

Substitute u for $\frac{1}{x}$ and v for $\frac{1}{y}$ to obtain a linear system.

  u - 3v =   2,

6u + 5v = -34

Multiply the first equation by -6 and add the result to the second equation.

    u - 3v = 2,

       23v = -46

Complete the solution for u and v.

    23v = -46   u - 3(-2) = 2

      v = -2   u + 6 = 2

                            u = -4

If $v = -2$, then $\frac{1}{y} = -2$, or $y = -\frac{1}{2}$.

If $u = -4$, then $\frac{1}{x} = -4$, or $x = -\frac{1}{4}$.

The values check. The solution of the original system is $\left(-\frac{1}{4}, -\frac{1}{2}\right)$.

58. Let $\sqrt[3]{x} = u$ and $\sqrt{y} = v$.

Then $2u + v = 0$
$5u + 2v = -5$.

Hence $u = -5$ and $x = u^3 = -125$;
$v = 10$ and $y = v^2 = 100$.
The solution is $(-125, 100)$.

59. $3|x| + 5|y| = 30$
$5|x| + 3|y| = 34$

Substitute u for $|x|$ and v for $|y|$ to obtain a linear system.

$3u + 5v = 30$,
$5u + 3v = 34$

Multiply the second equation by 3 to make the x-coefficient a multiple of 3.

$3u + 5v = 30$,
$15u + 9v = 102$

Now multiply the first equation by -5 and add.

$3u + 5v = 30$,
$-16v = -48$

Complete the solution for u and v.

$\begin{array}{ll} -16v = -48 & 3u + 5\cdot 3 = 30 \\ v = 3 & 3u + 15 = 30 \\ & 3u = 15 \\ & u = 5 \end{array}$

If $v = 3$, then $|y| = 3$ and $y = 3$ or -3.
If $u = 5$, then $|x| = 5$ and $x = 5$ or -5.

Thus, the solution set for the original system is $\{(5, 3), (5, -3), (-5, 3), (-5, -3)\}$.

60. Let $x^2 = u$ and $y^3 = v$. Solve

$15u + 2v = 6$,
$25u - 2v = -6$.

Then $u = 0$ and $x = 0$; $v = 3$ and $y = \sqrt[3]{3}$.

The solution is $(0, \sqrt[3]{3})$.

61. Familiarize:

First we convert the given distances to miles:

$300 \text{ ft} = \frac{300}{5280} \text{ mi} = \frac{5}{88} \text{ mi}$,

$500 \text{ ft} = \frac{500}{5280} \text{ mi} = \frac{25}{264} \text{ mi}$

Then at 10 mph, the student can run to point P in $\frac{\frac{5}{88}}{10}$, or $\frac{1}{176}$ hr, and she can run to point Q in $\frac{\frac{25}{264}}{10}$, or $\frac{5}{528}$ hr $\left[\text{using } d = rt, \text{ or } \frac{d}{r} = t\right]$.

Let d represent the distance, in miles, from the train to point P in the drawing in the text, and let r represent the speed of the train, in miles per hour.

We organize the information in a table.

	Distance	Speed	Time
Going to P	d	r	$\frac{1}{176}$
Going to Q	$d + \frac{5}{88} + \frac{25}{264}$	r	$\frac{5}{528}$

Translate:

Using $d = rt$ in each row of the table, we get a system of equations.

$d = r\left(\frac{1}{176}\right)$,

$d + \frac{5}{88} + \frac{25}{264} = r\left(\frac{5}{528}\right)$

Carry out:

We substitute $\frac{r}{176}$ for d in the second equation.

$\frac{r}{176} + \frac{5}{88} + \frac{25}{264} = \frac{5r}{528}$

$3r + 30 + 50 = 5r$ (Multiplying by 528)

$80 = 2r$

$40 = r$

Check:

The check is left to the student.

State:

The train is traveling 40 mph.

62. $(-0.187, 2.493)$

63. $(-4.699, 5.071)$

64. $(2.309, -2.457)$

65. $(-0.210, 0.505)$

Exercise Set 9.2

1. We substitute $(-1, 1, 0)$ in each of the three equations.

$\begin{array}{c|c} 2x + 3y - 5z = 1 \\ \hline 2(-1) + 3\cdot 1 - 5\cdot 0 & 1 \\ -2 + 3 - 0 & \\ 1 & \end{array}$ $\begin{array}{c|c} 6x - 6y + 10z = 3 \\ \hline 6(-1) - 6\cdot 1 + 10\cdot 0 & 3 \\ -6 - 6 + 0 & \\ -12 & \end{array}$

We do not need to proceed. Since (-1, 1, 0) is not a solution of one of the equations, it is not a solution of the system.

2.

$$2x + 3y - 5z = 1$$

$$\begin{array}{c|c} 2 \cdot \frac{1}{2} + 3 \cdot \frac{1}{3} - 5 \cdot \frac{1}{5} & 1 \\ 1 + 1 - 1 & \\ 1 & \end{array}$$

$$6x - 6y + 10z = 3$$

$$\begin{array}{c|c} 6 \cdot \frac{1}{2} - 6 \cdot \frac{1}{3} + 10 \cdot \frac{1}{5} & 3 \\ 3 - 2 + 2 & \\ 3 & \end{array}$$

$$4x - 9y + 5z = 0$$

$$\begin{array}{c|c} 4 \cdot \frac{1}{2} - 9 \cdot \frac{1}{3} + 5 \cdot \frac{1}{5} & 0 \\ 2 - 3 + 1 & \\ 0 & \end{array}$$

$\left(\frac{1}{2}, \frac{1}{3}, \frac{1}{5}\right)$ is a solution of the system.

3. $x + y + z = 2,$ (P1)
    $6x - 4y + 5z = 31,$ (P2)
    $5x + 2y + 2z = 13$ (P3)

Multiply (P1) by -6 and add the result to (P2). We also multiply (P1) by -5 and add the result to (P3).

$x + y + z = 2$ (P1)
$ -10y - z = 19$ (P2)
$ -3y - 3z = 3$ (P3)

Multiply (P3) by 10 to make the y-coefficient a multiple of the y-coefficient in (P2).

$x + y + z = 2$ (P1)
$ -10y - z = 19$ (P2)
$ -30y - 30z = 30$ (P3)

Multiply (P2) by -3 and add the result to (P3).

$x + y + z = 2$ (P1)
$ -10y - z = 19$ (P2)
$ -27z = -27$ (P3)

Solve (P3) for z.

$-27z = -27$
$z = 1$

Back-substitute 1 for z in (P2) and solve for y.

$-10y - z = 19$
$-10y - 1 = 19$
$-10y = 20$
$y = -2$

Back-substitute 1 for z and -2 for y in (P1) and solve for x.

$x + y + z = 2$
$x + (-2) + 1 = 2$
$x - 1 = 2$
$x = 3$

The solution is (3, -2, 1).

4. $x + 6y + 3z = 4,$ (P1)
    $2x + y + 2z = 3,$ (P2)
    $3x - 2y + z = 0$ (P3)

Multiply (P1) by -2 and add it to (P2). Also, multiply (P1) by -3 and add it to (P3).

$x + 6y + 3z = 4,$ (P1)
$ -11y - 4z = -5,$ (P2)
$ -20y - 8z = -12$ (P3)

Multiply (P3) by 11.

$x + 6y + 3z = 4,$ (P1)
$ -11y - 4z = -5,$ (P2)
$ -220y - 88z = -132$ (P3)

Multiply (P2) by -20 and add it to (P3).

$x + 6y + 3z = 4,$ (P1)
$ -11y - 4z = -5,$ (P2)
$ -8z = -32$ (P3)

Complete the solution.

$-8z = -32$
$z = 4$

$-11y - 4 \cdot 4 = -5$
$-11y = 11$
$y = -1$

$x + 6(-1) + 3 \cdot 4 = 4$
$x = -2$

The solution is (-2, -1, 4).

5. $x - y + 2z = -3$ (P1)
    $x + 2y + 3z = 4$ (P2)
    $2x + y + z = -3$ (P3)

Multiply (P1) by -1 and add the result to (P2). Also multiply (P1) by -2 and add the result to (P3).

$x - y + 2z = -3$ (P1)
$ 3y + z = 7$ (P2)
$ 3y - 3z = 3$ (P3)

Multiply (P2) by -1 and add the result to (P3).

$x - y + 2z = -3$ (P1)
$ 3y + z = 7$ (P2)
$ -4z = -4$ (P3)

Solve (P3) for z.

$$-4z = -4$$
$$z = 1$$

Back-substitute 1 for z in (P2) and solve for y.

$$3y + z = 7$$
$$3y + 1 = 7$$
$$3y = 6$$
$$y = 2$$

Back-substitute 1 for z and 2 for y in (P1) and solve for x.

$$x - y + 2z = -3$$
$$x - 2 + 2 \cdot 1 = -3$$
$$x = -3$$

The solution is (-3, 2, 1).

6. $x + y + z = 6,$ (P1)
    $2x - y - z = -3,$ (P2)
    $x - 2y + 3z = 6$ (P3)

Multiply (P1) by -2 and add it to (P2). Also, multiply (P1) by -1 and add it to (P3).

$x + y + z = 6,$ (P1)
$-3y - 3z = -15,$ (P2)
$-3y + 2z = 0$ (P3)

Multiply (P2) by -1 and add it to (P3).

$x + y + z = 6,$ (P1)
$-3y - 3z = -15,$ (P2)
$5z = 15$ (P3)

Complete the solution.

$$5z = 15$$
$$z = 3$$

$$-3y - 3 \cdot 3 = -15$$
$$-3y = -6$$
$$y = 2$$

$$x + 2 + 3 = 6$$
$$x = 1$$

The solution is (1, 2, 3).

7. $4a + 9b = 8$ (P1)
    $8a + 6c = -1$ (P2)
    $6b + 6c = -1$ (P3)

Multiply (P1) by -2 and add the result to (P2).

$4a + 9b = 8$ (P1)
$-18b + 6c = -17$ (P2)
$6b + 6c = -1$ (P3)

Multiply (P3) by 3 to make the b-coefficient a multiple of the b-coefficient in (P2).

$4a + 9b = 8$ (P1)
$-18b + 6c = -17$ (P2)
$18b + 18c = -3$ (P3)

Add (P2) to (P3).

$4a + 9b = 8$ (P1)
$-18b + 6c = -17$ (P2)
$24c = -20$ (P3)

Solve (P3) for c.

$$24c = -20$$
$$c = -\frac{20}{24} = -\frac{5}{6}$$

Back-substitute $-\frac{5}{6}$ for c in (P2) and solve for b.

$$-18b + 6c = -17$$
$$-18b + 6\left(-\frac{5}{6}\right) = -17$$
$$-18b - 5 = -17$$
$$-18b = -12$$
$$b = \frac{12}{18} = \frac{2}{3}$$

Back-substitute $\frac{2}{3}$ for b in (P1) and solve for a.

$$4a + 9b = 8$$
$$4a + 9 \cdot \frac{2}{3} = 8$$
$$4a + 6 = 8$$
$$4a = 2$$
$$a = \frac{1}{2}$$

The solution is $\left(\frac{1}{2}, \frac{2}{3}, -\frac{5}{6}\right)$.

8. $3p + 2r = 11,$ (P1)
    $q - 7r = 4,$ (P2)
    $p - 6q = 1$ (P3)

Interchange (P1) and (P3).

$p - 6q = 1,$ (P1)
$q - 7r = 4,$ (P2)
$3p + 2r = 11$ (P3)

Multiply (P1) by -3 and add it to (P3).

$p - 6q = 1,$ (P1)
$q - 7r = 4,$ (P2)
$18q + 2r = 8$ (P3)

Multiply (P2) by -18 and add it to (P3).

$p - 6q = 1,$ (P1)
$q - 7r = 4,$ (P2)
$128r = -64$ (P3)

Complete the solution.

$$128r = -64$$
$$r = -\frac{1}{2}$$

$$q - 7\left(-\frac{1}{2}\right) = 4$$
$$q = \frac{1}{2}$$

$$p - 6 \cdot \frac{1}{2} = 1$$
$$p = 4$$

The solution is $\left(4, \frac{1}{2}, -\frac{1}{2}\right)$.

9. $w + x + y + z = 2$ (P1)
    $w + 2x + 2y + 4z = 1$ (P2)
    $-w + x - y - z = -6$ (P3)
    $-w + 3x + y - z = -2$ (P4)

Multiply (P1) by – 1 and add to (P2). Add (P1) to (P3) and to (P4).

    $w + x + y + z = 2$ (P1)
    $x + y + 3z = -1$ (P2)
    $2x = -4$ (P3)
    $4x + 2y = 0$ (P4)

Solve (P3) for x.

$$2x = -4$$
$$x = -2$$

Back-substitute –2 for x in (P4) and solve for y.

$$4(-2) + 2y = 0$$
$$-8 + 2y = 0$$
$$2y = 8$$
$$y = 4$$

Back-substitute –2 for x and 4 for y in (P2) and solve for z.

$$-2 + 4 + 3z = -1$$
$$3z = -3$$
$$z = -1$$

Back-substitute –2 for x, 4 for y, and –1 for z in (P1) and solve for w.

$$w - 2 + 4 - 1 = 2$$
$$w = 1$$

The solution is $(1, -2, 4, -1)$.

10. $w + x - y + z = 0,$ (P1)
     $-w + 2x + 2y + z = 5,$ (P2)
     $-w + 3x + y - z = -4,$ (P3)
     $-2w + x + y - 3z = -7$ (P4)

Add (P1) to (P2) and (P3). Also, multiply (P1) by 2 and add it to (P4).

     $w + x - y + z = 0,$ (P1)
     $3x + y + 2z = 5,$ (P2)
     $4x = -4,$ (P3)
     $3x - y - z = -7$ (P4)

Multiply (P3) by 3.

     $w + x - y + z = 0,$ (P1)
     $3x + y + 2z = 5,$ (P2)
     $12x = -12,$ (P3)
     $3x - y - z = -7$ (P4)

Multiply (P2) by –4 and add it to (P3). Also, multiply (P2) by –1 and add it to (P4).

    $w + x - y + z = 0,$ (P1)
    $3x + y + 2z = 5,$ (P2)
    $-4y - 8z = -32,$ (P3)
    $-2y - 3z = -12$ (P4)

Multiply (P4) by 2.

    $w + x - y + z = 0,$ (P1)
    $3x + y + 2z = 5,$ (P2)
    $-4y - 8z = -32,$ (P3)
    $-4y - 6z = -24$ (P4)

Multiply (P3) by –1 and add it to (P4).

    $w + x - y + z = 0$ (P1)
    $3x + y + 2z = 5$ (P2)
    $-4y - 8z = -32$ (P3)
    $2z = 8$ (P4)

Complete the solution.

$$2z = 8$$
$$z = 4$$

$$-4y - 8 \cdot 4 = -32$$
$$-4y = 0$$
$$y = 0$$

$$3x + 0 + 2 \cdot 4 = 5$$
$$3x = -3$$
$$x = -1$$

$$w - 1 - 0 + 4 = 0$$
$$w = -3$$

The solution is $(-3, -1, 0, 4)$.

11. Familiarize and Translate:

    We let x, y, and z represent the first, second, and third numbers, respectively.

    The sum of the three numbers is 26.

    $x + y + z = 26$

    Twice the first minus the second is 2 less than the third.

    $2x - y = z - 2,$ or $2x - y - z = -2$

    The third is the second minus three times the first.

    $z = y - 3x,$ or $3x - y + z = 0$

    We now have a system of three equations.

    $x + y + z = 26,$
    $2x - y - z = -2,$
    $3x - y + z = 0$

    Carry out:

    We solve the system. The solution is $(8, 21, -3)$.

Check:

The sum of the numbers is 8 + 21 + (-3), or 26. Twice the first minus the second (2·8 - 21 = -5) is two less than the third (-3 - 2 = -5). The third (-3) is the second minus three times the first (21 - 3·8 = -3). The numbers check.

State:

The numbers are 8, 21, and -3.

12. $x + y + z = 5,$
$x - y + z = 1,$
$x \quad - z = 3 + y$

Then $x = 4$, $y = 2$, and $z = -1$.

13. Familiarize:

We make a drawing and use A, B, and C for the measures of the angles.

We must use the fact that the measures of the angles of a triangle add up to 180°.

Translate:

The sum of the angle measures is 180°.

$A + B + C = 180$

The measure of angle B is three times the measure of angle A.

$B = 3A$

The measure of angle C is 30° greater than the measure of angle A.

$C = A + 30$

We now have a system of equations.

$A + B + C = 180,$
$B = 3A,$
$C = A + 30$

Carry out:

We solve the system. The solution is (30, 90, 60).

Check:

The sum of the angle measures is 30 + 90 + 60, or 180°. The measure of angle B, 90°, is three times 30°, the measure of angle A. The measure of angle C, 60°, is 30° greater than the measure of angle A, 30°. The values check.

State:

The measures of angles A, B, and C are 30°, 90°, and 60°, respectively.

14. $B = 2 + 3A,$
$C = 8 + A,$
$A + B + C = 180$

Then $A = 34°$, $B = 104°$, and $C = 42°$.

15. Familiarize and Translate:

Let x, y, and z represent the number of quarts picked on Monday, Tuesday, and Wednesday, respectively.

She picked a total of 87 quarts.

$x + y + z = 87$

On Tuesday she picked 15 quarts more than on Monday.

$y = x + 15,$ or $x - y = -15$

On Wednesday she picked 3 quarts fewer than on Tuesday.

$z = y - 3,$ or $y - z = 3$

We now have a system of equations.

$x + y + z = 87,$
$x - y \quad = -15,$
$\quad y - z = 3$

Carry out:

We solve the system. The solution is (20, 35, 32).

Check:

The total quarts picked in three days was 20 + 35 + 32, or 87 quarts. On Tuesday she picked 35 quarts which is 15 more quarts than on Monday (20 + 15 = 35). On Wednesday she picked 32 quarts which is 3 quarts less than on Tuesday (35 - 3 = 32). The amounts check.

State:

The farmer picked 20 quarts on Monday, 35 quarts on Tuesday, and 32 quarts on Wednesday.

16. $T + F + S = 66,$
$T = 3 + F,$
$S = 6 + T$

Then $T = \$21$, $F = \$18$, and $S = \$27$.

17. Familiarize and Translate:

Let A, B, and C represent the number of board-feet of lumber produced per day by sawmills A, B, and C, respectively.

All three together can produce 7400 board-feet in a day.

$A + B + C = 7400$

A and B together can produce 4700 board-feet in a day.

$A + B = 4700$

B and C together can produce 5200 board-feet in a day.

$B + C = 5200$

We now have a system of equations.

A + B + C = 7400

A + B   = 4700

    B + C = 5200

Carry out:

We solve the system. The solution is (2200, 2500, 2700).

Check:

All three can produce 2200 + 2500 + 2700, or 7400 board-feet per day. A and B together can produce 2200 + 2500, or 4700 board-feet. B and C together can produce 2500 + 2700, or 5200 board-feet. All values check.

State:

In a day, sawmill A can produce 2200 board-feet, sawmill B can produce 2500 board-feet, and sawmill C can produce 2700 board-feet.

18. A + B + C = 5700,

    A + B   = 3400,

        B + C = 4200

    Then A = 1500, B = 1900, and C = 2300.

19. Familiarize and Translate:

    Let A, B, and C represent the number of linear feet per hour welders A, B, and C can weld, respectively.

    Together A, B, and C can weld 37 linear feet.

    A + B + C = 37

    A and B together can weld 22 linear feet.

    A + B = 22

    A and C together can weld 25 linear feet.

    A + C = 25

    We now have a system of equations.

    A + B + C = 37,

    A + B   = 22,

    A   + C = 25

    Carry out:

    We solve the system. The solution is (10, 12, 15).

    Check:

    Together all three can weld 10 + 12 + 15, or 37 linear feet per hour. A and B together can weld 10 + 12, or 22 linear feet. A and C together can weld 10 + 15, or 25 linear feet. The values check.

    State:

    Welder A can weld 10 linear feet per hour.
    Welder B can weld 12 linear feet per hour.
    Welder C can weld 15 linear feet per hour.

20. A + B + C = 3700,

    A + B   = 2200,

    A   + C = 2400

    Then A = 900 gal/hr,

         B = 1300 gal/hr, and

         C = 1500 gal/hr.

21. Familiarize:

    Let x, y, and z represent the number of par-3, par-4, and par-5 holes, respectively. A golfer who shoots par on every hole has 3x from the par-3 holes, 4y from the par-4 holes, and 5z from the par-5 holes.

    Translate:

    The total number of holes is 18.

    x + y + z = 18

    A golfer who shoots par on every hole has a total of 72.

    3x + 4y + 5z = 72

    The sum of the number of par-3 holes and the number of par-5 holes is 8.

    x + z = 8

    We have a system of equations.

     x + y + z = 18,
    3x + 4y + 5z = 72,
     x   + z = 8

    Carry out:

    We solve the system. The solution is (4, 10, 4).

    Check:

    The total number of holes is 4 + 10 + 4, or 18. A golfer who shoots par on every hole has 3·4 + 4·10 + 5·4, or 72. The sum of the number of par-3 holes and the number of par-5 holes is 4 + 4, or 8. The values check.

    State:

    There are 4 par-3 holes, 10 par-4 holes, and 4 par-5 holes.

22. x + y + z = 18,

    3x + 4y + 5z = 70,

    y = 2z

    Then x = 6, y = 8, z = 4.

23. Familiarize:

    Let x, y, and z represent the amounts invested at 7%, 8%, and 9%, respectively. Then the interest from each investment is 7%x or 0.07x, 8%y or 0.08y, and 9%z or 0.09z.

    Translate:

    The total investment is $2500.

    x + y + z = 2500

    The total interest is $212.

    0.07x + 0.08y + 0.09z = 212, or

    7x + 8y + 9z = 21,200

The amount invested at 9% is $1100 more than the amount invested at 8%.

z = y + 1100

We have a system of equations.

x + y + z = 2500,

7x + 8y + 9z = 21,200,

-y + z = 1100

Carry out:

We solve the system. The solution is (400, 500, 1600).

Check:

The total investment is $400 + $500 + $1600, or $2500. The total interest is 0.07($400) + 0.08($500) + 0.09($1600), or $28 + $40 + $144, or $212. The amount invested at 9%, $1600, is $1100 more than $500, the amount invested at 8%. The values check.

State:

$400 is invested at 7%, $500 is invested at 8%, and $1600 is invested at 9%.

24. x + y + z = 3500,

8x + 9y + 10z = 34,100,

z = y + 2600

Then x = $300, y = $300, z = $2900.

25. We wish to find a quadratic function

$f(x) = ax^2 + bx + c$

containing the three given points.

When we substitute, we get

for (1, 4) $4 = a \cdot 1^2 + b \cdot 1 + c$

for (-1, -2) $-2 = a \cdot (-1)^2 + b \cdot (-1) + c$

for (2, 13) $13 = a \cdot 2^2 + b \cdot 2 + c$

We now have a system of equations in three unknowns, a, b, and c:

a + b + c = 4,

a - b + c = -2,

4a + 2b + c = 13

We solve this system, obtaining (2, 3, -1). Thus the function we are looking for is

$f(x) = 2x^2 + 3x - 1$.

26. $f(x) = ax^2 + bx + c$

4 = a + b + c,

6 = a - b + c,

16 = 4a - 2b + c

The solution is (3, -1, 2), so $f(x) = 3x^2 - x + 2$.

27. a) We wish to find a quadratic function

$E(t) = at^2 + bt + c$

containing the three given points.

When we substitute, we get

for (1, 38) $38 = a \cdot 1^2 + b \cdot 1 + c$

for (2, 66) $66 = a \cdot 2^2 + b \cdot 2 + c$

for (3, 86) $86 = a \cdot 3^2 + b \cdot 3 + c$

We now have a system of equations in three unknowns, a, b, and c.

a + b + c = 38,

4a + 2b + c = 66,

9a + 3b + c = 86

We solve the system, obtaining (-4, 40, 2). Thus, the function we are looking for is $E(t) = -4t^2 + 40t + 2$.

b) $E(t) = -4t^2 + 40t + 2$

$E(4) = -4 \cdot 4^2 + 40 \cdot 4 + 2$

$= -64 + 160 + 2$

$= \$98$

28. a) $E(t) = at^2 + bt + c$

1000 = a + b + c,

2000 = 4a + 2b + c,

8000 = 9a + 3b + c

The solution is (2500, -6500, 5000), so $E(t) = 2500t^2 - 6500t + 5000$.

b) $E(4) = 2500 \cdot 4^2 - 6500 \cdot 4 + 5000 = \$19,000$

29. a) We wish to find a quadratic function

$f(x) = ax^2 + bx + c$

containing the points (5, 1121), (7, 626), and (9, 967).

When we substitute, we get

1121 = 25a + 5b + c,

626 = 49a + 7b + c,

967 = 81a + 9b + c.

We solve this system of equations, obtaining (104.5, -1501.5, 6016). Thus,

$f(x) = 104.5x^2 - 1501.5x + 6016$.

b) $f(4) = 104.5(4)^2 - 1501.5(4) + 6016 = 1682$

$f(6) = 104.5(6)^2 - 1501.5(6) + 6016 = 769$

$f(10) = 104.5(10)^2 - 1501.5(10) + 6016 = 1451$

30. a) Find a quadratic function $f(x) = ax^2 + bx + c$ containing (0, 0), (300, 1), and (500, 2).

0 = c,

1 = 90,000a + 300b

2 = 250,000a + 500b

Then $(a, b, c) = \left[\frac{1}{300,000}, \frac{7}{3000}, 0\right]$ and

$f(x) = \frac{1}{300,000}x^2 + \frac{7}{3000}x$

b) $f(650) = \frac{1}{300,000}(650)^2 + \frac{7}{3000}(650) = 2.925$ hr

c) $\frac{3}{2} = \frac{1}{300,000}x^2 + \frac{7}{3000}x$

$x \approx 407$

31. $\frac{2}{x} - \frac{1}{y} - \frac{3}{z} = -1,$

$\frac{2}{x} - \frac{1}{y} + \frac{1}{z} = -9,$

$\frac{1}{x} + \frac{2}{y} - \frac{4}{z} = 17$

First substitute u for $\frac{1}{x}$, v for $\frac{1}{y}$, and w for $\frac{1}{z}$ and solve for u, v, and w.

$2u - v - 3w = -1,$

$2u - v + w = -9,$

$u + 2v - 4w = 17$

Solving this system we get $(-1, 5, -2)$.

If $u = -1$ and $u = \frac{1}{x}$, then $\frac{1}{x} = -1$, or $x = -1$.

If $v = 5$ and $v = \frac{1}{y}$, then $\frac{1}{y} = 5$, or $y = \frac{1}{5}$.

If $w = -2$ and $w = \frac{1}{z}$, then $\frac{1}{z} = -2$, or $z = -\frac{1}{2}$.

The solution of the original system is $\left[-1, \frac{1}{5}, -\frac{1}{2}\right]$.

32. $\frac{2}{x} + \frac{2}{y} - \frac{3}{z} = 3,$

$\frac{1}{x} - \frac{2}{y} - \frac{3}{z} = 9,$

$\frac{7}{x} - \frac{2}{y} + \frac{9}{z} = -39$

Substitute u for $\frac{1}{x}$, v for $\frac{1}{y}$, and w for $\frac{1}{z}$ and then solve for u, v, and w.

$2u + 2v - 3w = 3,$

$u - 2v - 3w = 9,$

$7u - 2v + 9w = -39$

Solving this system we get $(-2, -1, -3)$.

Then $\frac{1}{x} = -2$, or $x = -\frac{1}{2}$; $\frac{1}{y} = -1$, or $y = -1$; and $\frac{1}{z} = -3$, or $z = -\frac{1}{3}$. The solution of the original system is $\left[-\frac{1}{2}, -1, -\frac{1}{3}\right]$.

33. Familiarize:

Let a, b, and c represent the time it would take A, B, and C, working alone, to do the job, respectively. Then A can do $\frac{1}{a}$ of the job in 1 hr, $\frac{2}{a}$ of the job in 2 hr and so on.

Translate:

Working together, A, B, and C can do a job in 2 hr.

$\frac{2}{a} + \frac{2}{b} + \frac{2}{c} = 1$

Working together, B and C can do the job in 4 hr.

$\frac{4}{b} + \frac{4}{c} = 1$

Working together, A and B can do the job in $\frac{12}{5}$ hr.

$\frac{\frac{12}{5}}{a} + \frac{\frac{12}{5}}{b} = 1$, or $\frac{12}{a} + \frac{12}{b} = 5$

We have a system of equations.

$\frac{2}{a} + \frac{2}{b} + \frac{2}{c} = 1,$

$\frac{4}{b} + \frac{4}{c} = 1,$

$\frac{12}{a} + \frac{12}{b} = 5$

Carry out:

Substitute x for $\frac{1}{a}$, y for $\frac{1}{b}$, and z for $\frac{1}{c}$ and solve for x, y, and z.

$2x + 2y + 2z = 1,$

$4y + 4z = 1,$

$12x + 12y = 5$

Solving this system we get $\left[\frac{1}{4}, \frac{1}{6}, \frac{1}{12}\right]$.

If $x = \frac{1}{4}$ and $x = \frac{1}{a}$, then $\frac{1}{a} = \frac{1}{4}$ or $a = 4$.

If $y = \frac{1}{6}$ and $y = \frac{1}{b}$, then $\frac{1}{b} = \frac{1}{6}$ or $b = 6$.

If $z = \frac{1}{12}$ and $z = \frac{1}{c}$, then $\frac{1}{c} = \frac{1}{12}$ or $c = 12$.

The solution of the original system is $(4, 6, 12)$.

Check:

The check is left to the student.

State:

Working alone, A can do the job in 4 hr, B can do the job in 6 hr, and C can do the job in 12 hr.

34. Let a, b, and c represent the time it would take A, B, and C, running alone, to fill the tank, respectively.

$$\frac{3}{a} + \frac{3}{b} + \frac{3}{c} = 1,$$

$$\frac{4}{a} \qquad + \frac{4}{c} = 1,$$

$$\frac{8}{a} + \frac{8}{b} \qquad = 1$$

Then $a = 24$ hr, $b = 12$ hr, $c = 4\frac{4}{5}$ hr.

35. Label the angle measures at the tips of the stars a, b, c, d, and e. Also label the angles of the pentagon p, q, r, s, and t.

Using the geometric fact that the sum of the angle measures of a triangle is 180°, we get 5 equations.

$p + b + d = 180$

$q + c + e = 180$

$r + a + d = 180$

$s + b + e = 180$

$t + a + c = 180$

Adding these equations, we get

$$(p + q + r + s + t) + 2a + 2b + 2c + 2d + 2e = 5(180)$$

The sum of the angle measures of any convex polygon with n sides is given by the formula $S = (n - 2)180$. Thus $p + q + r + s + t = (5 - 2)180$, or 540. We substitute and solve for $a + b + c + d + e$.

$540 + 2(a + b + c + d + e) = 900$

$2(a + b + c + d + e) = 360$

$a + b + c + d + e = 180$

The sum of the angle measures at the tips of the star is 180°.

36. Let h, t, and u represent the hundred's, ten's, and unit's digit of the year, respectively. (We know the thousand's digit is 1.) Using the given information we know the following:

$1 + h + t + u = 24,$

$u = 1 + h,$

$t = k \cdot 3$ and $u = m \cdot 3$

where k, m are positive integers.

We know $h > 5$ (there was no transcontinental railroad before 1600); and, since $u = 1 + h = m \cdot 3$, $h \neq 6$, $h \neq 7$, $h \neq 9$.

Thus $h = 8$ and $u = 9$. Then $1 + 8 + t + 9 = 24$, or $t = 6$.

The year is 1869.

37. Substituting, we get

$$A + \frac{3}{4}B + 3C = 12,$$

$$\frac{4}{3}A + B + 2C = 12,$$

$$2A + B + C = 12, \text{ or}$$

$4A + 3B + 12C = 48,$

$4A + 3B + 6C = 36,$ (Clearing fractions)

$2A + B + C = 12.$

Solving the system, we get $A = 3$, $B = 4$, and $C = 2$. The equation is $3x + 4y + 2z = 12$.

38. $1 = B - M - 2N,$

$2 = B - 3M + 6N,$

$1 = B - \frac{3}{2}M - N$

$B = 2$, $M = \frac{1}{2}$, $N = \frac{1}{4}$ and $y = 2 - \frac{1}{2}x - \frac{1}{4}z$

39. Familiarize and Translate:

Let a, s, and c represent the number of adults, students, and children in attendance, respectively.

The total attendance was 100.

$a + s + c = 100$

The total amount of money taken in was $100. $\left[\text{Express 50 cents as } \frac{1}{2} \text{ dollar.}\right]$

$$10a + 3s + \frac{1}{2}c = 100$$

The resulting system is

$a + s + c = 100,$

$10a + 3s + \frac{1}{2}c = 100.$

Carry out:

Multiply the first equation by 3 and then subtract it from the second equation to obtain $7a - \frac{5}{2}c = -200$ or

$a = \frac{5}{14}(c - 80)$ where $(c - 80)$ is a positive multiple of 14 (because a must be a positive integer). That is $(c - 80) = k \cdot 14$ or $c = 80 + k \cdot 14$, where k is a positive integer. If $k > 1$, then $c > 100$. This is impossible since the total attendance is 100. Thus $k = 1$, so $c = 80 + 1 \cdot 14 = 94$. Then $a = \frac{5}{14}(94 - 80) = \frac{5}{14} \cdot 14 = 5$, and $5 + s + 94 = 10$, or $s = 1$.

Check:

The total attendance is 5 + 1 + 94, or 100.

The total amount of money taken in was

$10·5 + $3·1 + $\frac{1}{2}$ · 94 = $100. The result checks.

State:

There were 5 adults, 1 student, and 94 children in attendance.

40. Let k, m denote positive integers; and denote the scores by a, b, c, d, e.

GIVEN: (1) a is prime; e is 3rd

(2) Each score ⩽ 200

(3) a − c = 23; d = k·10

(4) a + b + c + d + e = 885; b = m·8

(5) a − b < 10; d − b = 14.

The diagram below follows easily.

The greatest score d must be at least $\frac{1}{5}$ of the total 885.

Thus d ⩾ $\frac{885}{5}$ = 177;   d = 180 or 190 or 200, and k = 18 or 19 or 20, since d = 10·k.

Now   d − b = 14   or

(10k) − (8m) = 14   so that

m = $\frac{5k - 7}{4}$ which requires an odd k = 19;

then m = 22.

Thus b = 8m = 176; and d = 10·k = 190.

From a − b < 10 we have a < 186. Thus a is a prime such that 176 = b < a < 186. There are only two primes between 176 and 186: 179 and 181.

If a = 179, then it follows incorrectly that e is in second place. Thus a = 181 and we have b = 176, c = 158, d = 190, e = 180.

Exercise Set 9.3

Note: The answers to Exercises 19 and 20 are included in the answers to Exercises 1 − 18.

1. 9x − 3y = 15,   (1)

   6x − 2y = 10   (2)

Multiply equation (2) by 3 to make the x-coefficient a multiple of 9.

   9x − 3y = 15,

   18x − 6y = 30

Multiply equation (1) by −2 and add the result to equation (2).

Now we have

9x − 3y = 15,

   0 = 0.

which illustrates that the original system of equations is a <u>dependent</u> system of equations. For this particular system, there is an infinite solution set. The system is <u>consistent</u>.

These solutions can be described by expressing one variable in terms of the other. Since 0 = 0 contributes nothing, we solve 9x − 3y = 15 for x and obtain

x = $\frac{3y + 15}{9}$,   or $\frac{y + 5}{3}$

The ordered pairs in the solution set can be described in terms of y only.

$\left[\frac{y + 5}{3}, y\right]$

Any value chosen for y gives a value for x, and thus an ordered pair in the solution set.

We could have solved 9x − 3y = 15 for y obtaining y = $\frac{9x - 15}{3}$ or 3x − 5 and described the solution set in terms of x only.

(x, 3x − 5)

Then any value chosen for x would give a value for y, and thus an ordered pair in the solution set.

A few of the solutions are (0, −5), (1, −2), and (−1, −8).

2. 2s − 3t = 9,   (1)

   4s − 6t = 9   (2)

Multiply (1) by −2 and add.

2s − 3t = 9,

   0 = −9

The solution set is ∅. The system is <u>inconsistent</u> and <u>independent</u>.

3. 5c + 2d = 24,   (1)

   30c + 12d = 10   (2)

Multiply equation (1) by −6 and add the result to equation (2).

This gives us

5c + 2d = 24,

   0 = −134.

The second equation says that 0·x + 0·y = −134. There are no numbers x and y for which this is true. Thus, the system has no solutions. The solution set is ∅. The system is <u>inconsistent</u>. This system is not equivalent to a system of fewer than 2 linear equations. The system is <u>independent</u>.

4. $3x + 2y = 18,$ (1)
   $9x + 6y = 5$ (2)

Multiply (1) by -3 and add.

$3x + 2y = 18,$
$\qquad\ 0 = -49$

The solution set is ∅. The system is <u>inconsistent</u> and <u>independent</u>.

5. $3x + 2y = 5,$
   $4y = 10 - 6x$

Rewrite each equation in the form Ax + By = C.

$3x + 2y = 5,$ (1)
$6x + 4y = 10$ (2)

Multiply equation (1) by -2 and add.

$3x + 2y = 5,$
$\qquad 0 = 0$

The system is <u>dependent</u>. The equation $3x + 2y = 5$ has infinitely many solutions, so the system is <u>consistent</u>.

If we solve $3x + 2y = 5$ for x obtaining

$x = \dfrac{5 - 2y}{3},$

the ordered pairs in the solution set can be described in terms of y only.

$\left(\dfrac{5 - 2y}{3},\ y\right)$

If we solve $3x + 2y = 5$ for y obtaining

$y = \dfrac{5 - 3x}{2},$

the ordered pairs in the solution set can be described in terms of x only.

$\left(x,\ \dfrac{5 - 3x}{2}\right)$

A few of the solutions are $\left(0,\ \dfrac{5}{2}\right)$, (3, -2), and (-1, 4).

6. $5x + 2 = 7y,$
   $-14y + 4 = -10x$

$5x - 7y = -2,$ (1)   (Rewriting the equations)
$10x - 14y = -4$ (2)

Multiply (1) by -2 and add.

$5x - 7y = -2$
$\qquad\ 0 = 0$

The system is <u>dependent</u> and <u>consistent</u>. The solutions are of the form $\left(\dfrac{7y - 2}{5},\ y\right)$ or $\left(x,\ \dfrac{5x + 2}{7}\right)$. A few of the solutions are (1, 1), $\left(0,\ \dfrac{2}{7}\right)$, and (8, 6).

7. $12y - 8x = 6,$
   $4x + 3 = 6y$

Rewrite each equation in the form Ax + By = C.
$-8x + 12y = 6,$ (1)
$\ 4x - \ \ 6y = -3$ (2)

Multiply equation (2) by 2 to make the x-coefficient a multiple of -8.
$-8x + 12y = 6,$
$\ 8x - 12y = -6$

Now add equation (1) to equation (2).
$-8x + 12y = 6,$
$\qquad\quad 0 = 0$

The system is <u>dependent</u>. The equation $-8x + 12y = 6$ has infinitely many solutions, so the system is <u>consistent</u>.

If we solve $-8x + 12y = 6$ for x obtaining

$x = \dfrac{6y - 3}{4},$

the ordered pairs in the solution set can be described in terms of y only.

$\left(\dfrac{6y - 3}{4},\ y\right)$

If we solve $-8x + 12y = 6$ for y obtaining

$y = \dfrac{4x + 3}{6},$

the ordered pairs in the solution set can be described in terms of x only.

$\left(x,\ \dfrac{4x + 3}{6}\right)$

A few of the solutions are $\left(-\dfrac{3}{4},\ 0\right)$, $\left(\dfrac{9}{4},\ 2\right)$ and $\left(-\dfrac{9}{4},\ -1\right)$.

8. $16x - 12y = 10,$
   $6y + 5 = 8x$

$16x - 12y = 10,$ (1)   (Rewriting the equations)
$-8x + \ \ 6y = -5$ (2)

Multiply (2) by 2.
$\ 16x - 12y = 10,$
$-16x + 12y = -10$

Add.
$16x - 12y = 10,$
$\qquad\ 0 = 0$

The system is <u>dependent</u> and <u>consistent</u>. The solutions are of the form $\left(\dfrac{6y + 5}{8},\ y\right)$ or $\left(x,\ \dfrac{8x - 5}{6}\right)$. A few of the solutions are $\left(0,\ -\dfrac{5}{6}\right)$, $\left(1,\ \dfrac{1}{2}\right)$, and $\left(-1,\ -\dfrac{13}{6}\right)$.

9. $x + 2y - z = -8$, (P1)

$2x - y + z = 4$, (P2)

$8x + y + z = 2$ (P3)

Multiply (P1) by -2 and add the result to (P2).
Multiply (P1) by -8 and add the result to (P3).

$x + 2y - z = -8$, (P1)

$-5y + 3z = 20$, (P2)

$-15y + 9z = 66$ (P3)

Multiply (P2) by -3 and add the result to (P3).

$x + 2y - z = -8$, (P1)

$-5y + 3z = 20$, (P2)

$0 = 6$ (P3)

Since in (P3) we obtain a false equation $0 = 6$, the system has no solution. The solution set is Ø. The system is inconsistent. This system is not equivalent to a system of fewer than 3 equations. The system is independent.

10. $x + 2y - z = 4$, (P1)

$4x - 3y + z = 8$, (P2)

$5x - y = 12$ (P3)

Multiply (P1) by -4 and add the result to (P2).
Multiply (P1) by -5 and add the result to (P3).

$x + 2y - z = 4$, (P1)

$-11y + 5z = -8$, (P2)

$-11y + 5z = -8$ (P3)

Multiply (P2) by -1 and add the result to (P3).

$x + 2y - z = 4$, (P1)

$-11y + 5z = -8$, (P2)

$0 = 0$ (P3)

The system is dependent.

Solve (P2) for y.

$$y = \frac{5z + 8}{11}$$

Use (P1) to find x.

$$x + 2\left[\frac{5z + 8}{11}\right] - z = 4$$

$$11x + 10z + 16 - 11z = 44$$

$$x = \frac{z + 28}{11}$$

The solutions are of the form $\left[\frac{z + 28}{11}, \frac{5z + 8}{11}, z\right]$.

The system is consistent. A few of the solutions are $\left[\frac{28}{11}, \frac{8}{11}, 0\right]$, $\left[\frac{29}{11}, \frac{13}{11}, 1\right]$, and $\left[\frac{27}{11}, \frac{3}{11}, -1\right]$.

11. $2x + y - 3z = 1$,

$x - 4y + z = 6$,

$4x - 16y + 4z = 24$

First interchange the first two equations so all the x-coefficients are multiples of the first.

$x - 4y + z = 6$, (P1)

$2x + y - 3z = 1$, (P2)

$4x - 16y + 4z = 24$ (P3)

Multiply (P1) by -2 and add the result to (P2).
Multiply (P1) by -4 and add the result to (P3).

$x - 4y + z = 6$, (P1)

$9y - 5z = -11$, (P2)

$0 = 0$ (P3)

Now we know the system is dependent.

Solve (P2) for y.

$$9y - 5z = -11$$

$$9y = 5z - 11$$

$$y = \frac{5z - 11}{9}$$

Substitute $\frac{5z - 11}{9}$ for y in (P1) and solve for x.

$$x - 4y + z = 6$$

$$x - 4\left[\frac{5z - 11}{9}\right] + z = 6$$

$$9x - 4(5z - 11) + 9z = 54$$

$$9x - 20z + 44 + 9z = 54$$

$$9x = 11z + 10$$

$$x = \frac{11z + 10}{9}$$

The ordered triples in the solution set can be described as follows:

$$\left[\frac{11z + 10}{9}, \frac{5z - 11}{9}, z\right]$$

There is an infinite number of solutions. The system is consistent.

A few of the solutions are $\left[\frac{10}{9}, -\frac{11}{9}, 0\right]$, $\left[\frac{7}{3}, -\frac{2}{3}, 1\right]$, and $\left[\frac{32}{9}, -\frac{1}{9}, 2\right]$.

12. $4x + 12y + 16z = 4$, (P1)

$3x + 4y + 5z = 3$, (P2)

$x + 8y + 11z = 1$ (P3)

Interchange (P1) and (P3).

$x + 8y + 11z = 1$, (P1)

$3x + 4y + 5z = 3$, (P2)

$4x + 12y + 16z = 4$ (P3)

Multiply (P1) by -3 and add the result to (P2).
Multiply (P1) by -4 and add the result to (P3).

$x + 8y + 11z = 1$, (P1)

$-20y - 28z = 0$, (P2)

$-20y - 28z = 0$ (P3)

Multiply (P2) by -1 and add the result to (P3).

$$x + 8y + 11z = 1, \quad (P1)$$
$$-20y - 28z = 0, \quad (P2)$$
$$0 = 0 \quad (P3)$$

The system is <u>dependent</u>.

Solve (P2) for y.

$$-20y - 28z = 0$$
$$y = -\frac{7}{5}z$$

We use (P1) to find x.

$$x + 8\left(-\frac{7}{5}z\right) + 11z = 1$$
$$x = \frac{1}{5}z + 1, \text{ or } \frac{z + 5}{5}$$

The solutions are of the form $\left[\frac{z + 5}{5}, -\frac{7}{5}z, z\right]$.

The system is <u>consistent</u>. A few of the solutions are $(1,0,0)$, $(2,-7,5)$, and $\left(\frac{6}{5}, -\frac{7}{5}, 1\right)$.

13. $2x + y - 3z = 0,$
$x - 4y + z = 0,$
$4x - 16y + 4z = 0$

Note that this is a system of homogeneous equations. The trivial solution is $(0, 0, 0)$. There may or may not be other solutions.

First we interchange the first two equations so all the x-coefficients are multiples of the first:

$$x - 4y + z = 0, \quad (P1)$$
$$2x + y - 3z = 0, \quad (P2)$$
$$4x - 16y + 4z = 0 \quad (P3)$$

Multiply (P1) by -2 and add to (P2).
Multiply (P1) by -4 and add to (P3).

$$x - 4y + z = 0, \quad (P1)$$
$$9y - 5z = 0, \quad (P2)$$
$$0 = 0 \quad (P3)$$

Now we know that the system is <u>dependent</u>.

Solve (P2) for y.

$$9y - 5z = 0$$
$$9y = 5z$$
$$y = \frac{5}{9}z$$

Substitute $\frac{5}{9}z$ for y in (P1) and solve for x.

$$x - 4y + z = 0$$
$$x - 4\left(\frac{5}{9}z\right) + z = 0$$
$$x - \frac{20}{9}z + \frac{9}{9}z = 0$$
$$x - \frac{11}{9}z = 0$$
$$x = \frac{11}{9}z$$

The ordered triples in the solution set can be described as follows:

$$\left[\frac{11}{9}z, \frac{5}{9}z, z\right]$$

There is an infinite number of solutions. The system is <u>consistent</u>.

A few of the solutions are $(0, 0, 0)$, $\left(\frac{11}{8}, \frac{5}{18}, \frac{1}{2}\right)$ and $\left(-\frac{11}{9}, -\frac{5}{9}, -1\right)$.

14. $4x + 12y + 16z = 0,$
$3x + 4y + 5z = 0,$
$x + 8y + 11z = 0$

Following the same steps as in Exercise 12 we get

$$x + 8y + 11z = 0, \quad (P1)$$
$$-20y - 28z = 0, \quad (P2)$$
$$0 = 0 \quad (P3)$$

The system is <u>dependent</u>.

$y = -\frac{7}{5}z$, as in Exercise 12.

Use (P1) to find x.

$$x + 8\left(-\frac{7}{5}z\right) + 11z = 0$$
$$x = \frac{1}{5}z$$

The solutions are of the form $\left[\frac{1}{5}z, -\frac{7}{5}z, z\right]$. The system is <u>consistent</u>. A few of the solutions are $(0,0,0)$, $(1,-7,5)$, and $\left(\frac{1}{5}, -\frac{7}{5}, 1\right)$.

15. $x + y - z = -3, \quad (P1)$
$x + 2y + 2z = -1 \quad (P2)$

Multiply (P1) by -1 and add to (P2).

$$x + y - z = -3,$$
$$y + 3z = 2$$

Solve (P2) for y.

$$y + 3z = 2$$
$$y = -3z + 2$$

Substitute $-3z + 2$ for y in (P1) and solve for x.

$$x + y - z = -3$$
$$x + (-3z + 2) - z = -3$$
$$x - 4z + 2 = -3$$
$$x = 4z - 5$$

The system has an infinite set of solutions. The system is <u>consistent</u>. The ordered triples in the solutions can be described as follows:

$$(4z - 5, -3z + 2, z)$$

A few of the solutions are $(-5, 2, 0)$, $(-9, 5, -1)$, and $(3, -4, 2)$.

The system is <u>dependent</u>.

16. $x + y + 13z = 0,$ (P1)

   $x - y - 6z = 0$ (P2)

   Multiply (P1) by -1 and add the result to (P2).

   $x + y + 13z = 0,$ (P1)

   $-2y - 19z = 0$ (P2)

   Solve (P2) for y.

   $-2y - 19z = 0$

   $y = -\dfrac{19}{2}z$

   Use (P1) to find x.

   $x - \dfrac{19}{2}z + 13z = 0$

   $x = -\dfrac{7}{2}z$

   The solutions are of the form $\left[-\dfrac{7}{2}z, -\dfrac{19}{2}z, z\right]$.
   The system is <u>consistent</u> and <u>dependent</u>. A few
   of the solutions are $(0,0,0)$, $(-7,-19,2)$, and
   $\left[-\dfrac{7}{2}, -\dfrac{19}{2}, 1\right]$.

17. $2x + y + z = 0,$

   $x + y - z = 0,$

   $x + 2y + 2z = 0$

   Any homogeneous system like this always has a
   solution, because $(0, 0, 0)$ is a solution.
   There may or may not be other solutions.

   Interchange the first two equations.

   $x + y - z = 0,$ (P1)

   $2x + y + z = 0,$ (P2)

   $x + 2y + 2z = 0$ (P3)

   Multiply (P1) by -2 and add to (P2). Multiply
   (P1) by -1 and add to (P3).

   $x + y - z = 0,$ (P1)

   $-y + 3z = 0,$ (P2)

   $y + 3z = 0$ (P3)

   Add (P2) to (P3).

   $x + y - z = 0,$ (P1)

   $-y + 3z = 0,$ (P2)

   $6z = 0$ (P3)

   Solve (P3) for z.

   $6z = 0$

   $z = 0$

   Substitute 0 for z in (P2) and solve for y.

   $-y + 3z = 0$

   $-y + 3 \cdot 0 = 0$

   $-y = 0$

   $y = 0$

Substitute 0 for z and 0 for y in (P1) and solve
for x.

$x + y - z = 0$

$x + 0 - 0 = 0$

$x = 0$

The only solution is $(0, 0, 0)$. The system is
<u>consistent</u>. The system is not equivalent to a
system of fewer than 3 equations. Thus, the
system is <u>independent</u>.

18. Interchange the first and third equations.

   $x - y - z = 0,$

   $10x + 8y - z = 0,$

   $5x + 4y + z = 0$

   $x - y - z = 0,$ (P1)

   $18y + 9z = 0,$ (P2) $(-10(P1) + (P2))$

   $9y + 6z = 0$ (P3) $(-5(P1) + (P3))$

   Multiply (P3) by 2.

   $x - y - z = 0,$ (P1)

   $18y + 9z = 0,$ (P2)

   $18y + 12z = 0$ (P3)

   $x - y - z = 0,$ (P1)

   $18y + 9z = 0,$ (P2)

   $3z = 0$ (P3) $(-1(P2) + (P3))$

   Then $z = 0$, $y = 0$, $x = 0$. The only solution is
   $(0, 0, 0)$. The system is <u>independent</u> and
   <u>consistent</u>.

19. - 20. Answers in Exercises 1 - 18.

21. $4.026x - 1.448y = 18.32,$

   $0.724y = -9.16 + 2.013x$

   Multiply each equation by 1000 and rewrite in
   the form $Ax + By = C$.

   $4026x - 1448y = 18,320,$

   $2013x - 724y = 9160$

   Interchange the equations.

   $2013x - 724y = 9160,$ (1)

   $4026x - 1448y = 18,320$ (2)

   Multiply equation (1) by -2 and add.

   $2013x - 724y = 9160,$

   $0 = 0$

   The system is dependent.

   If we solve $2013x - 724y = 9160$ for x obtaining

   $x = \dfrac{9160 + 724y}{2013},$

   the ordered pairs in the solution set can be
   described in terms of y only.

   $\left[\dfrac{9160 + 724y}{2013}, y\right]$

If we solve $2013x - 724y = 9160$ for y obtaining

$$y = \frac{2013x - 9160}{724},$$

the ordered pairs in the solution set can be described in terms of x only.

$$\left[x, \frac{2013x - 9160}{724}\right]$$

22. Write the equations in the form $Ax + By = C$, clear decimals, and then interchange the equations.

$$40{,}570x + 142y = 5260, \qquad (1)$$
$$81{,}140x + 284y = 10{,}520 \qquad (2)$$

Multiply (1) by -2 and add.

$$40{,}570x + 142y = 5260,$$
$$0 = 0$$

The system is dependent. The solutions are of the form $\left[\dfrac{5260 - 142y}{40{,}570}, y\right]$ or $\left[x, \dfrac{5260 - 40{,}570x}{142}\right]$.

23. a)
$$w + x + y + z = 4, \qquad (P1)$$
$$w + x + y + z = 3, \qquad (P2)$$
$$w + x + y + z = 3 \qquad (P3)$$

Multiply (P1) by -1 and add the result to (P2) and to (P3).

$$w + x + y + z = 4, \qquad (P1)$$
$$0 = -1, \qquad (P2)$$
$$0 = -1 \qquad (P3)$$

Since we obtain the false equation $0 = -1$, the solution set is $\emptyset$.

b) Since there is no solution, the system is inconsistent.

c) Since (P2) and (P3) are identical, the system is equivalent to a system of fewer than 3 equations. It is dependent.

24. a) Add (P1) to (P2): also add (P1) to (P3).

$$w - 8x + 3y + 2z = 0, \qquad (P1)$$
$$-3x + 4y + z = 0, \qquad (P2)$$
$$-6x + 8y + 2z = 0, \qquad (P3)$$
$$3x - 4y - z = 0 \qquad (P4)$$

Multiply (P2) by -2 and add to (P3); add (P2) to (P4).

$$w - 8x + 3y + 2z = 0,$$
$$-3x + 4y + z = 0,$$
$$0 = 0,$$
$$0 = 0$$

The system is equivalent to a system of 2 equations. We express w and z in terms of x and y:

$$z = 3x - 4y$$
$$w = 8x - 3y - 2z = 8x - 3y - 2(3x - 4y) =$$
$$2x + 5y$$

The solutions are of the form $(2x + 5y, x, y, 3x - 4y)$.

b) There are solutions, so the system is consistent.

c) Since the system is equivalent to a system of fewer than 4 equations, it is dependent.

25.
$$6x - 9y = -3, \qquad (1)$$
$$-4x + 6y = k \qquad (2)$$

Multiply equation (2) by 3 to make the x-coefficient a multiple of 6.

$$6x - 9y = -3, \qquad (1)$$
$$-12x + 18y = 3k \qquad (2)$$

Multiply equation (1) by 2 and add the result to Equation (2).

$$6x - 9y = -3,$$
$$0 = -6 + 3k$$

If the system is to be dependent, it must be true that

$$-6 + 3k = 0 \quad \text{or}$$
$$k = 2.$$

26. Multiply the second equation by 4.

$$8x - 16y = 20, \qquad (1)$$
$$40x - 80y = 4k \qquad (2)$$

Multiply equation (1) by -5 and add it to equation (2).

$$8x - 16y = 20,$$
$$0 = -100 + 4k$$

Then $-100 + 4k = 0$, or $k = 25$.

27. Let a = the number of par 3 holes,
    b = the number of par 4 holes, and
    c = the number of par 5 holes.

Then
$$a + b + c = 18,$$
$$3a + 4b + 5c = 72,$$
$$a = c$$
or, equivalently,
$$a + b + c = 18,$$
$$b + 2c = 18,$$
$$0 = 0$$

The solutions are of the form $\{(a, 18 - 2a, a)\}$ where $1 \leqslant a \leqslant 8$, and a is an integer.

All permissible solutions are: (1, 16, 1),
                              (2, 14, 2),
                              (3, 12, 3),
                              (4, 10, 4),
                              (5, 8, 5),
                              (6, 6, 6),
                              (7, 4, 7),
                              (8, 2, 8).

28. Let x represent the ten's digit and y represent the one's digit.

$$10x + y = 4(x + y)$$
$$6x = 3y$$
$$2x = y$$

The solutions are two-digit integers with ten's digit x and one's digit 2x. The possible solutions are 12, 24, 36, and 48.

Exercise Set 9.4

---

1. $4x + 2y = 11$,
   $3x - y = 2$

Write a matrix using only the constants.

$$\begin{bmatrix} 4 & 2 & 11 \\ 3 & -1 & 2 \end{bmatrix}$$

Multiply row 2 by 4 to make the first number in row 2 a multiple of 4.

$$\begin{bmatrix} 4 & 2 & 11 \\ 12 & -4 & 8 \end{bmatrix}$$

Multiply row 1 by -3 and add it to row 2.

$$\begin{bmatrix} 4 & 2 & 11 \\ 0 & -10 & -25 \end{bmatrix}$$

Putting the variables back in, we have
$4x + 2y = 11$,   (1)
      $-10y = -25$ (2)

Solve (2) for y.
$-10y = -25$
$y = \frac{5}{2}$

Substitute $\frac{5}{2}$ for y in (1) and solve for x.

$4x + 2y = 11$
$4x + 2 \cdot \frac{5}{2} = 11$
$4x + 5 = 11$
$4x = 6$
$x = \frac{3}{2}$

The solution is $\left(\frac{3}{2}, \frac{5}{2}\right)$.

2. $\begin{bmatrix} 3 & -3 & 11 \\ 9 & -2 & 5 \end{bmatrix}$

$\downarrow R_2' = -3R_1 + R_2$

$\begin{bmatrix} 3 & -3 & 11 \\ 0 & 7 & -28 \end{bmatrix}$

$\downarrow R_1' = \frac{1}{7}R_1$

$\begin{bmatrix} 3 & -3 & 11 \\ 0 & 1 & -4 \end{bmatrix}$

Then $3x - 3y = 11$,
          $y = -4$

and $y = -4$, $x = -\frac{1}{3}$.

The solution is $\left(-\frac{1}{3}, -4\right)$.

3. $x + 2y - 3z = 9$,
    $2x - y + 2z = -8$,
    $3x - y - 4z = 3$

Write a matrix using only the constants.

$\begin{bmatrix} 1 & 2 & -3 & 9 \\ 2 & -1 & 2 & -8 \\ 3 & -1 & -4 & 3 \end{bmatrix}$

Multiply row 1 by -2 and add it to row 2.
Multiply row 1 by -3 and add it to row 3.

$\begin{bmatrix} 1 & 2 & -3 & 9 \\ 0 & -5 & 8 & -26 \\ 0 & -7 & 5 & -24 \end{bmatrix}$

Multiply row 3 by 5.

$\begin{bmatrix} 1 & 2 & -3 & 9 \\ 0 & -5 & 8 & -26 \\ 0 & -35 & 25 & -120 \end{bmatrix}$

Multiply row 2 by -7 and add to row 3.

$\begin{bmatrix} 1 & 2 & -3 & 9 \\ 0 & -5 & 8 & -26 \\ 0 & 0 & -31 & 62 \end{bmatrix}$

Putting the variables back in, we have
$x + 2y - 3z = 9$,   (1)
    $-5y + 8z = -26$,   (2)
           $-31z = 62$ (3)

Solve (3) for z.
$-31z = 62$
    $z = -2$

Substitute -2 for z in (2) and solve for y.
    $-5y + 8z = -26$
$-5y + 8(-2) = -26$
    $-5y - 16 = -26$
         $-5y = -10$
             $y = 2$

Substitute -2 for z and 2 for y in (1) and solve for x.

    $x + 2y - 3z = 9$
$x + 2(2) - 3(-2) = 9$
        $x + 10 = 9$
              $x = -1$

The solution is (-1, 2, -2).

4. $\begin{bmatrix} 1 & -1 & 2 & 0 \\ 1 & -2 & 3 & -1 \\ 2 & -2 & 1 & -3 \end{bmatrix}$

$\begin{array}{l} R_2' = -1 \cdot R_1 + R_2 \\ R_3' = -2R_1 + R_3 \end{array}$

$\begin{bmatrix} 1 & -1 & 2 & 0 \\ 0 & -1 & 1 & -1 \\ 0 & 0 & -3 & -3 \end{bmatrix}$

Then $x - y + 2z = 0$,
          $-y + z = -1$,
               $-3z = -3$

and $z = 1$, $y = 2$, $x = 0$. The solution is (0, 2, 1).

5. $5x - 3y = -2$,
   $4x + 2y = 5$

Write a matrix using only the constants.

$\begin{bmatrix} 5 & -3 & -2 \\ 4 & 2 & 5 \end{bmatrix}$

Multiply row 2 by 5.

$\begin{bmatrix} 5 & -3 & -2 \\ 20 & 10 & 25 \end{bmatrix}$

Multiply row 1 by -4 and add it to row 2.

$\begin{bmatrix} 5 & -3 & -2 \\ 0 & 22 & 33 \end{bmatrix}$

Putting the variables back in, we have
$5x - 3y = -2$,   (1)
      $22y = 33$ (2)

Solve (2) for y.
$22y = 33$
   $y = \frac{3}{2}$

Substitute $\frac{3}{2}$ for y in (1) and solve for x.

$$5x - 3y = -2$$
$$5x - 3 \cdot \frac{3}{2} = -2$$
$$5x - \frac{9}{2} = -\frac{4}{2}$$
$$5x = \frac{5}{2}$$
$$x = \frac{1}{2}$$

The solution is $\left(\frac{1}{2}, \frac{3}{2}\right)$.

6. $\begin{bmatrix} 3 & 4 & 7 \\ -5 & 2 & 10 \end{bmatrix}$

$\downarrow \quad R_2' = 3R_2$

$\begin{bmatrix} 3 & 4 & 7 \\ -15 & 6 & 30 \end{bmatrix}$

$\downarrow \quad R_2' = 5R_1 + R_2$

$\begin{bmatrix} 3 & 4 & 7 \\ 0 & 26 & 65 \end{bmatrix}$

Then $3x + 4y = 7$,
$\qquad 26y = 65$

and $y = \frac{5}{2}$, $x = -1$. The solution is $\left(-1, \frac{5}{2}\right)$.

7. $4x - y - 3z = 1$,
$8x + y - z = 5$,
$2x + y + 2z = 5$

Write a matrix using only the constants.

$\begin{bmatrix} 4 & -1 & -3 & 1 \\ 8 & 1 & -1 & 5 \\ 2 & 1 & 2 & 5 \end{bmatrix}$

First interchange rows 1 and 3 so that each number below the first number in the first row is a multiple of that number.

$\begin{bmatrix} 2 & 1 & 2 & 5 \\ 8 & 1 & -1 & 5 \\ 4 & -1 & -3 & 1 \end{bmatrix}$

Multiply row 1 by −4 and add it to row 2.
Multiply row 1 by −2 and add it to row 3.

$\begin{bmatrix} 2 & 1 & 2 & 5 \\ 0 & -3 & -9 & -15 \\ 0 & -3 & -7 & -9 \end{bmatrix}$

Multiply row 2 by −1 and add it to row 3.

$\begin{bmatrix} 2 & 1 & 2 & 5 \\ 0 & -3 & -9 & -15 \\ 0 & 0 & 2 & 6 \end{bmatrix}$

Putting the variables back in, we have

$$2x + y + 2z = 5, \quad (1)$$
$$-3y - 9z = -15, \quad (2)$$
$$2z = 6 \quad (3)$$

Solve (3) for z.

$$2z = 6$$
$$z = 3$$

Substitute 3 for z in (2) and solve for y.

$$-3y - 9z = -15$$
$$-3y - 9(3) = -15$$
$$-3y - 27 = -15$$
$$-3y = 12$$
$$y = -4$$

Substitute 3 for z and -4 for y in (1) and solve for x.

$$2x + y + 2z = 5$$
$$2x + (-4) + 2(3) = 5$$
$$2x - 4 + 6 = 5$$
$$2x = 3$$
$$x = \frac{3}{2}$$

The solution is $\left[\frac{3}{2}, -4, 3\right]$.

8. $\begin{bmatrix} 3 & 2 & 2 & 3 \\ 1 & 2 & -1 & 5 \\ 2 & -4 & 1 & 0 \end{bmatrix}$

$$\downarrow \quad R_1' = R_2$$
$$R_2' = R_1$$

$\begin{bmatrix} 1 & 2 & -1 & 5 \\ 3 & 2 & 2 & 3 \\ 2 & -4 & 1 & 0 \end{bmatrix}$

$$\downarrow \quad R_2' = -3R_1 + R_2,$$
$$R_3' = -2R_1 + R_3$$

$\begin{bmatrix} 1 & 2 & -1 & 5 \\ 0 & -4 & 5 & -12 \\ 0 & -8 & 3 & -10 \end{bmatrix}$

$$\downarrow \quad R_3' = -2R_2 + R_3$$

$\begin{bmatrix} 1 & 2 & -1 & 5 \\ 0 & -4 & 5 & -12 \\ 0 & 0 & -7 & 14 \end{bmatrix}$

Then $x + 2y - z = 5$,
$$-4y + 5z = -12,$$
$$-7z = 14$$

and $z = -2$, $y = \frac{1}{2}$, $x = 2$. The solution is
$\left[2, \frac{1}{2}, -2\right]$.

<u>9</u>.   p + q + r = 1,
    p + 2q + 3r = 4,
    4p + 5q + 6r = 7

Write a matrix using only the constants.

$$\begin{bmatrix} 1 & 1 & 1 & 1 \\ 1 & 2 & 3 & 4 \\ 4 & 5 & 6 & 7 \end{bmatrix}$$

Multiply row 1 by -1 and add it to row 2.
Multiply row 1 by -4 and add it to row 3.

$$\begin{bmatrix} 1 & 1 & 1 & 1 \\ 0 & 1 & 2 & 3 \\ 0 & 1 & 2 & 3 \end{bmatrix}$$

Multiply row 2 by -1 and add it to row 3.

$$\begin{bmatrix} 1 & 1 & 1 & 1 \\ 0 & 1 & 2 & 3 \\ 0 & 0 & 0 & 0 \end{bmatrix}$$

Putting the variables back in, we have

p + q + r = 1,
    q + 2r = 3,
         0 = 0

This system is dependent. In this case it has an infinite set of solutions.

Solve q + 2r = 3 for q.

q = -2r + 3

Substitute -2r + 3 for q in the first equation and solve for p.

        p + q + r = 1
p + (-2r + 3) + r = 1
        p - r + 3 = 1
             p - r = -2
                  p = r - 2

The solutions can be described as follows:

(r - 2, -2r + 3, r)

<u>10</u>.
$$\begin{bmatrix} 1 & 1 & 1 & 9 \\ 1 & -1 & -1 & -15 \\ 1 & 1 & 1 & 3 \end{bmatrix}$$

$$R_2' = -1 \cdot R_1 + R_2$$
$$R_3' = -1 \cdot R_1 + R_3$$

$$\begin{bmatrix} 1 & 1 & 1 & 9 \\ 0 & -2 & -2 & -24 \\ 0 & 0 & 0 & -6 \end{bmatrix}$$

Then m + n + t =   9,
          -2n - 2t = -24,
                 0t = -6

Since 0t = -6 is not true for any t, the system has no solution.

11. $-2w + 2x + 2y - 2z = -10,$
     $\ \ w + x + \ \ y + \ \ z = \ -5,$
     $3w + x - \ \ y + 4z = \ -2,$
     $\ \ w + 3x - 2y + 2z = \ -6$

Write a matrix using only the constants.

$$\begin{bmatrix} -2 & 2 & 2 & -2 & -10 \\ 1 & 1 & 1 & 1 & -5 \\ 3 & 1 & -1 & 4 & -2 \\ 1 & 3 & -2 & 2 & -6 \end{bmatrix}$$

Interchange rows 1 and 2.

$$\begin{bmatrix} 1 & 1 & 1 & 1 & -5 \\ -2 & 2 & 2 & -2 & -10 \\ 3 & 1 & -1 & 4 & -2 \\ 1 & 3 & -2 & 2 & -6 \end{bmatrix}$$

Multiply row 1 by 2 and add it to row 2.
Multiply row 1 by -3 and add it to row 3.
Multiply row 1 by -1 and add it to row 4.

$$\begin{bmatrix} 1 & 1 & 1 & 1 & -5 \\ 0 & 4 & 4 & 0 & -20 \\ 0 & -2 & -4 & 1 & 13 \\ 0 & 2 & -3 & 1 & -1 \end{bmatrix}$$

Interchange rows 2 and 3.

$$\begin{bmatrix} 1 & 1 & 1 & 1 & -5 \\ 0 & -2 & -4 & 1 & 13 \\ 0 & 4 & 4 & 0 & -20 \\ 0 & 2 & -3 & 1 & -1 \end{bmatrix}$$

Multiply row 2 by 2 and add it to row 3.
Add row 2 to row 4.

$$\begin{bmatrix} 1 & 1 & 1 & 1 & -5 \\ 0 & -2 & -4 & 1 & 13 \\ 0 & 0 & -4 & 2 & 6 \\ 0 & 0 & -7 & 2 & 12 \end{bmatrix}$$

Multiply row 4 by 4.

$$\begin{bmatrix} 1 & 1 & 1 & 1 & -5 \\ 0 & -2 & -4 & 1 & 13 \\ 0 & 0 & -4 & 2 & 6 \\ 0 & 0 & -28 & 8 & 48 \end{bmatrix}$$

Multiply row 3 by -7 and add it to row 4.

$$\begin{bmatrix} 1 & 1 & 1 & 1 & -5 \\ 0 & -2 & -4 & 1 & 13 \\ 0 & 0 & -4 & 2 & 6 \\ 0 & 0 & 0 & -6 & 6 \end{bmatrix}$$

Putting the variables back in, we get

$$w + x + y + z = -5, \qquad (1)$$
$$-2x - 4y + z = 13, \qquad (2)$$
$$-4y + 2z = 6, \qquad (3)$$
$$-6z = 6 \qquad (4)$$

Solve (4) for z.

$$-6z = 6$$
$$z = -1$$

Substitute -1 for z in (3) and solve for y.

$$-4y + 2(-1) = 6$$
$$-4y = 8$$
$$y = -2$$

Substitute -2 for y and -1 for z in (2) and solve for x.

$$-2x - 4(-2) + (-1) = 13$$
$$-2x + 8 - 1 = 13$$
$$-2x = 6$$
$$x = -3$$

Substitute -3 for x, -2 for y, and -1 for z in (1) and solve for w.

$$w + (-3) + (-2) + (-1) = -5$$
$$w - 6 = -5$$
$$w = 1$$

The solution is (1, -3, -2, -1).

12.
$$\begin{bmatrix} -1 & 2 & -3 & 1 & -8 \\ -1 & 1 & 1 & -1 & -4 \\ 1 & 1 & 1 & 1 & 22 \\ -1 & 1 & -1 & -1 & -14 \end{bmatrix}$$

$$R_2' = -1 \cdot R_1 + R_2,$$
$$R_3' = R_1 + R_3,$$
$$R_4' = -1 \cdot R_1 + R_4$$

$$\begin{bmatrix} -1 & 2 & -3 & 1 & -8 \\ 0 & -1 & 4 & -2 & 4 \\ 0 & 3 & -2 & 2 & 14 \\ 0 & -1 & 2 & -2 & -6 \end{bmatrix}$$

$$R_3' = 3R_2 + R_3,$$
$$R_4' = -1 \cdot R_2 + R_4$$

$$\begin{bmatrix} -1 & 2 & -3 & 1 & -8 \\ 0 & -1 & 4 & -2 & 4 \\ 0 & 0 & 10 & -4 & 26 \\ 0 & 0 & -2 & 0 & -10 \end{bmatrix}$$

$$R_3' = \frac{1}{2} R_4$$
$$R_4' = \frac{1}{2} R_3$$

$$\begin{bmatrix} -1 & 2 & -3 & 1 & -8 \\ 0 & -1 & 4 & -2 & 4 \\ 0 & 0 & -1 & 0 & -5 \\ 0 & 0 & 5 & -2 & 13 \end{bmatrix}$$

$$\downarrow R_4' = 5R_3 + R_4$$

$$\begin{bmatrix} -1 & 2 & -3 & 1 & -8 \\ 0 & -1 & 4 & -2 & 4 \\ 0 & 0 & -1 & 0 & -5 \\ 0 & 0 & 0 & -2 & -12 \end{bmatrix}$$

Then $-w + 2x - 3y + z = -8,$
$\qquad -x + 4y - 2z = 4,$
$\qquad\qquad -y = -5,$
$\qquad\qquad\qquad -2z = -12$

and $z = 6$, $y = 5$, $x = 4$, $w = 7$. The solution is $(7, 4, 5, 6)$.

13. $A + B = \begin{bmatrix} 1 & 2 \\ 4 & 3 \end{bmatrix} + \begin{bmatrix} -3 & 5 \\ 2 & -1 \end{bmatrix} = \begin{bmatrix} 1 + (-3) & 2 + 5 \\ 4 + 2 & 3 + (-1) \end{bmatrix} = \begin{bmatrix} -2 & 7 \\ 6 & 2 \end{bmatrix}$

14. $B + A = A + B = \begin{bmatrix} -2 & 7 \\ 6 & 2 \end{bmatrix}$ (See Exercise 13.)

15. $E + 0 = \begin{bmatrix} 1 & 3 \\ 2 & 6 \end{bmatrix} + \begin{bmatrix} 0 & 0 \\ 0 & 0 \end{bmatrix} = \begin{bmatrix} 1 + 0 & 3 + 0 \\ 2 + 0 & 6 + 0 \end{bmatrix} = \begin{bmatrix} 1 & 3 \\ 2 & 6 \end{bmatrix}$

16. $2A = \begin{bmatrix} 2\cdot 1 & 2\cdot 2 \\ 2\cdot 4 & 2\cdot 3 \end{bmatrix} = \begin{bmatrix} 2 & 4 \\ 8 & 6 \end{bmatrix}$

17. $3F = 3\begin{bmatrix} 3 & 3 \\ -1 & -1 \end{bmatrix} = \begin{bmatrix} 3\cdot 3 & 3\cdot 3 \\ 3\cdot(-1) & 3\cdot(-1) \end{bmatrix} = \begin{bmatrix} 9 & 9 \\ -3 & -3 \end{bmatrix}$

18. $(-1)D = \begin{bmatrix} -1\cdot 1 & -1\cdot 1 \\ -1\cdot 1 & -1\cdot 1 \end{bmatrix} = \begin{bmatrix} -1 & -1 \\ -1 & -1 \end{bmatrix}$

19. $3F = 3\begin{bmatrix} 3 & 3 \\ -1 & -1 \end{bmatrix} = \begin{bmatrix} 9 & 9 \\ -3 & -3 \end{bmatrix}$, $2A = 2\begin{bmatrix} 1 & 2 \\ 4 & 3 \end{bmatrix} = \begin{bmatrix} 2 & 4 \\ 8 & 6 \end{bmatrix}$

Then
$3F + 2A = \begin{bmatrix} 9 & 9 \\ -3 & -3 \end{bmatrix} + \begin{bmatrix} 2 & 4 \\ 8 & 6 \end{bmatrix} = \begin{bmatrix} 9 + 2 & 9 + 4 \\ -3 + 8 & -3 + 6 \end{bmatrix} = \begin{bmatrix} 11 & 13 \\ 5 & 3 \end{bmatrix}$

20. $A - B = \begin{bmatrix} 1 & 2 \\ 4 & 3 \end{bmatrix} - \begin{bmatrix} -3 & 5 \\ 2 & -1 \end{bmatrix} = \begin{bmatrix} 4 & -3 \\ 2 & 4 \end{bmatrix}$

21. $B - A = \begin{bmatrix} -3 & 5 \\ 2 & -1 \end{bmatrix} - \begin{bmatrix} 1 & 2 \\ 4 & 3 \end{bmatrix} = \begin{bmatrix} -3 & 5 \\ 2 & -1 \end{bmatrix} + \begin{bmatrix} -1 & -2 \\ -4 & -3 \end{bmatrix}$ [B - A = B + (-A)]

$= \begin{bmatrix} -3 + (-1) & 5 + (-2) \\ 2 + (-4) & -1 + (-3) \end{bmatrix} = \begin{bmatrix} -4 & 3 \\ -2 & -4 \end{bmatrix}$

22. $AB = \begin{bmatrix} 1 & 2 \\ 4 & 3 \end{bmatrix}\begin{bmatrix} -3 & 5 \\ 2 & -1 \end{bmatrix} = \begin{bmatrix} 1(-3) + 2\cdot2 & 1\cdot5 + 2(-1) \\ 4(-3) + 3\cdot2 & 4\cdot5 + 3(-1) \end{bmatrix} = \begin{bmatrix} 1 & 3 \\ -6 & 17 \end{bmatrix}$

23. $BA = \begin{bmatrix} -3 & 5 \\ 2 & -1 \end{bmatrix}\begin{bmatrix} 1 & 2 \\ 4 & 3 \end{bmatrix} = \begin{bmatrix} -3\cdot1 + 5\cdot4 & -3\cdot2 + 5\cdot3 \\ 2\cdot1 + (-1)4 & 2\cdot2 + (-1)3 \end{bmatrix} = \begin{bmatrix} 17 & 9 \\ -2 & 1 \end{bmatrix}$

24. $0F = 0 = \begin{bmatrix} 0 & 0 \\ 0 & 0 \end{bmatrix}$

25. $CD = \begin{bmatrix} 1 & -1 \\ -1 & 1 \end{bmatrix}\begin{bmatrix} 1 & 1 \\ 1 & 1 \end{bmatrix} = \begin{bmatrix} 1\cdot1 + (-1)\cdot1 & 1\cdot1 + (-1)\cdot1 \\ -1\cdot1 + 1\cdot1 & -1\cdot1 + 1\cdot1 \end{bmatrix} = \begin{bmatrix} 0 & 0 \\ 0 & 0 \end{bmatrix}$

26. $EF = \begin{bmatrix} 1 & 3 \\ 2 & 6 \end{bmatrix}\begin{bmatrix} 3 & 3 \\ -1 & -1 \end{bmatrix} = \begin{bmatrix} 1\cdot3 + 3(-1) & 1\cdot3 + 3(-1) \\ 2\cdot3 + 6(-1) & 2\cdot3 + 6(-1) \end{bmatrix} = \begin{bmatrix} 0 & 0 \\ 0 & 0 \end{bmatrix}$

27. $AI = \begin{bmatrix} 1 & 2 \\ 4 & 3 \end{bmatrix}\begin{bmatrix} 1 & 0 \\ 0 & 1 \end{bmatrix} = \begin{bmatrix} 1\cdot1 + 2\cdot0 & 1\cdot0 + 2\cdot1 \\ 4\cdot1 + 3\cdot0 & 4\cdot0 + 3\cdot1 \end{bmatrix} = \begin{bmatrix} 1 & 2 \\ 4 & 3 \end{bmatrix}$ (Note: AI = A)

28. $IA = A = \begin{bmatrix} 1 & 2 \\ 4 & 3 \end{bmatrix}$

29. $AB = \begin{bmatrix} 1 & 0 & -2 \\ 0 & -1 & 3 \\ 3 & 2 & 4 \end{bmatrix}\begin{bmatrix} -1 & -2 & 5 \\ 1 & 0 & -1 \\ 2 & -3 & 1 \end{bmatrix}$

$= \begin{bmatrix} 1(-1) + 0\cdot1 + (-2)2 & 1(-2) + 0\cdot0 + (-2)(-3) & 1\cdot5 + 0(-1) + (-2)1 \\ 0(-1) + (-1)1 + 3\cdot2 & 0(-2) + (-1)0 + 3(-3) & 0\cdot5 + (-1)(-1) + 3\cdot1 \\ 3(-1) + 2\cdot1 + 4\cdot2 & 3(-2) + 2\cdot0 + 4(-3) & 3\cdot5 + 2(-1) + 4\cdot1 \end{bmatrix}$

$= \begin{bmatrix} -5 & 4 & 3 \\ 5 & -9 & 4 \\ 7 & -18 & 17 \end{bmatrix}$

30. $BA = \begin{bmatrix} -1 & -2 & 5 \\ 1 & 0 & -1 \\ 2 & -3 & 1 \end{bmatrix} \begin{bmatrix} 1 & 0 & -2 \\ 0 & -1 & 3 \\ 3 & 2 & 4 \end{bmatrix}$

$= \begin{bmatrix} -1\cdot1 + (-2)\cdot0 + 5\cdot3 & -1\cdot0 + (-2)(-1) + 5\cdot2 & -1(-2) + (-2)3 + 5\cdot4 \\ 1\cdot1 + 0\cdot0 + (-1)3 & 1\cdot0 + 0(-1) + (-1)2 & 1(-2) + 0\cdot3 + (-1)4 \\ 2\cdot1 + (-3)0 + 1\cdot3 & 2\cdot0 + (-3)(-1) + 1\cdot2 & 2(-2) + (-3)3 + 1\cdot4 \end{bmatrix}$

$= \begin{bmatrix} 14 & 12 & 16 \\ -2 & -2 & -6 \\ 5 & 5 & -9 \end{bmatrix}$

31. $CI = \begin{bmatrix} -2 & 9 & 6 \\ -3 & 3 & 4 \\ 2 & -2 & 1 \end{bmatrix} \begin{bmatrix} 1 & 0 & 0 \\ 0 & 1 & 0 \\ 0 & 0 & 1 \end{bmatrix}$

$= \begin{bmatrix} -2\cdot1 + 9\cdot0 + 6\cdot0 & -2\cdot0 + 9\cdot1 + 6\cdot0 & -2\cdot0 + 9\cdot0 + 6\cdot1 \\ -3\cdot1 + 3\cdot0 + 4\cdot0 & -3\cdot0 + 3\cdot1 + 4\cdot0 & -3\cdot0 + 3\cdot0 + 4\cdot1 \\ 2\cdot1 + (-2)0 + 1\cdot0 & 2\cdot0 + (-2)1 + 1\cdot0 & 2\cdot0 + (-2)0 + 1\cdot1 \end{bmatrix}$

$= \begin{bmatrix} -2 & 9 & 6 \\ -3 & 3 & 4 \\ 2 & -2 & 1 \end{bmatrix}$ (Note: CI = C)

32. $IC = C = \begin{bmatrix} -2 & 9 & 6 \\ -3 & 3 & 4 \\ 2 & -2 & 1 \end{bmatrix}$

33. $\begin{bmatrix} -3 & 2 \end{bmatrix} \begin{bmatrix} 4 \\ -2 \end{bmatrix} = \begin{bmatrix} -3\cdot4 + 2(-2) \end{bmatrix} = \begin{bmatrix} -16 \end{bmatrix}$

34. $\begin{bmatrix} -2 & 0 & 4 \end{bmatrix} \begin{bmatrix} 8 \\ -6 \\ \frac{1}{2} \end{bmatrix} = \begin{bmatrix} -2\cdot8 + 0(-6) + 4 \cdot \frac{1}{2} \end{bmatrix} = \begin{bmatrix} -14 \end{bmatrix}$

35. $\begin{bmatrix} -5 & 1 & 2 \end{bmatrix} \begin{bmatrix} 1 & 3 \\ -1 & 0 \\ 4 & -2 \end{bmatrix} = \begin{bmatrix} -5\cdot1 + 1(-1) + 2\cdot4 & -5\cdot3 + 1\cdot0 + 2(-2) \end{bmatrix} = \begin{bmatrix} 2 & -19 \end{bmatrix}$

36. $\begin{bmatrix} -3 & 2 \\ 0 & 1 \\ -4 & 5 \end{bmatrix} \begin{bmatrix} 4 \\ 2 \end{bmatrix} = \begin{bmatrix} -3\cdot4 + 2\cdot2 \\ 0\cdot4 + 1\cdot2 \\ -4\cdot4 + 5\cdot2 \end{bmatrix} = \begin{bmatrix} -8 \\ 2 \\ -6 \end{bmatrix}$

37. $\begin{bmatrix} 3 & -2 & 4 \\ 2 & 1 & -5 \end{bmatrix} \begin{bmatrix} x \\ y \\ z \end{bmatrix} = \begin{bmatrix} 17 \\ 13 \end{bmatrix}$

38. $\begin{bmatrix} 3 & 2 & 5 \\ 4 & -3 & 2 \end{bmatrix} \begin{bmatrix} x \\ y \\ z \end{bmatrix} = \begin{bmatrix} 9 \\ 10 \end{bmatrix}$

39. $\begin{bmatrix} 1 & -1 & 2 & -4 \\ 2 & -1 & -1 & 1 \\ 1 & 4 & -3 & -1 \\ 3 & 5 & -7 & 2 \end{bmatrix} \begin{bmatrix} x \\ y \\ z \\ w \end{bmatrix} = \begin{bmatrix} 12 \\ 0 \\ 1 \\ 9 \end{bmatrix}$

40. $\begin{bmatrix} 2 & 4 & -5 & 12 \\ 4 & -1 & 12 & -1 \\ -1 & 4 & 0 & 2 \\ 2 & 10 & 1 & 0 \end{bmatrix} \begin{bmatrix} x \\ y \\ z \\ w \end{bmatrix} = \begin{bmatrix} 2 \\ 5 \\ 13 \\ 5 \end{bmatrix}$

41. $A = \begin{bmatrix} -1 & 0 \\ 2 & 1 \end{bmatrix}, \qquad B = \begin{bmatrix} 1 & -1 \\ 0 & 2 \end{bmatrix}$

$(A + B)(A - B) = \begin{bmatrix} 0 & -1 \\ 2 & 3 \end{bmatrix} \begin{bmatrix} -2 & 1 \\ 2 & -1 \end{bmatrix} = \begin{bmatrix} -2 & 1 \\ 2 & -1 \end{bmatrix}$

$A^2 - B^2 = \begin{bmatrix} -1 & 0 \\ 2 & 1 \end{bmatrix} \begin{bmatrix} -1 & 0 \\ 2 & 1 \end{bmatrix} - \begin{bmatrix} 1 & -1 \\ 0 & 2 \end{bmatrix} \begin{bmatrix} 1 & -1 \\ 0 & 2 \end{bmatrix}$

$= \begin{bmatrix} 1 & 0 \\ 0 & 1 \end{bmatrix} - \begin{bmatrix} 1 & -3 \\ 0 & 4 \end{bmatrix} = \begin{bmatrix} 0 & 3 \\ 0 & -3 \end{bmatrix}$

Thus, $(A + B)(A - B) \neq A^2 - B^2$.

42. $(A + B)(A + B) = \begin{bmatrix} -2 & -3 \\ 6 & 7 \end{bmatrix}$, $A^2 + 2AB + B^2 = \begin{bmatrix} 0 & -1 \\ 4 & 5 \end{bmatrix}$

Thus, $(A + B)(A + B) \neq A^2 + 2AB + B^2$.

43. $(A + B)(A - B) = \begin{bmatrix} -2 & 1 \\ 2 & -1 \end{bmatrix}$ (See Exercise 41.)

$A^2 = \begin{bmatrix} 1 & 0 \\ 0 & 1 \end{bmatrix}$ (See Exercise 41.)

$BA = \begin{bmatrix} 1 & -1 \\ 0 & 2 \end{bmatrix} \begin{bmatrix} -1 & 0 \\ 2 & 1 \end{bmatrix} = \begin{bmatrix} -3 & -1 \\ 4 & 2 \end{bmatrix}$

$AB = \begin{bmatrix} -1 & 0 \\ 2 & 1 \end{bmatrix} \begin{bmatrix} 1 & -1 \\ 0 & 2 \end{bmatrix} = \begin{bmatrix} -1 & 1 \\ 2 & 0 \end{bmatrix}$

$B^2 = \begin{bmatrix} 1 & -3 \\ 0 & 4 \end{bmatrix}$ (See Exercise 41.)

$A^2 + BA - AB - B^2 = \begin{bmatrix} 1 & 0 \\ 0 & 1 \end{bmatrix} + \begin{bmatrix} -3 & -1 \\ 4 & 2 \end{bmatrix} - \begin{bmatrix} -1 & 1 \\ 2 & 0 \end{bmatrix} - \begin{bmatrix} 1 & -3 \\ 0 & 4 \end{bmatrix}$

$= \begin{bmatrix} -2 & 1 \\ 2 & -1 \end{bmatrix}$

Therefore, $(A + B)(A - B) = A^2 + BA - AB - B^2$.

<u>44.</u> $(A + B)(A + B) = \begin{bmatrix} -2 & -3 \\ 6 & 7 \end{bmatrix}$ (See Exercise 42.)

$A^2 + BA + AB + B^2$

$= \begin{bmatrix} 1 & 0 \\ 0 & 1 \end{bmatrix} + \begin{bmatrix} -3 & -1 \\ 4 & 2 \end{bmatrix} + \begin{bmatrix} -1 & 1 \\ 2 & 0 \end{bmatrix} + \begin{bmatrix} 1 & -3 \\ 0 & 4 \end{bmatrix}$ (See Exercise 43.)

$= \begin{bmatrix} -2 & -3 \\ 6 & 7 \end{bmatrix}$

Therefore, $(A + B)(A + B) = A^2 + BA + AB + B^2$.

<u>45.</u> $A + B = \begin{bmatrix} a_{11} + b_{11} & a_{12} + b_{12} \\ a_{21} + b_{21} & a_{22} + b_{22} \end{bmatrix}$

$= \begin{bmatrix} b_{11} + a_{11} & b_{12} + a_{12} \\ b_{21} + a_{21} & b_{22} + a_{22} \end{bmatrix}$ (By commutativity of addition of real numbers)

$= B + A$

<u>46.</u> $A + (B + C) = \begin{bmatrix} a_{11} + (b_{11} + c_{11}) & a_{12} + (b_{12} + c_{12}) \\ a_{21} + (b_{21} + c_{21}) & a_{22} + (b_{22} + c_{22}) \end{bmatrix}$

$= \begin{bmatrix} (a_{11} + b_{11}) + c_{11} & (a_{12} + b_{12}) + c_{12} \\ (a_{21} + b_{21}) + c_{21} & (a_{22} + b_{22}) + c_{22} \end{bmatrix}$ (By associativity of addition of real numbers)

$= (A + B) + C$

<u>47.</u> See the answer section in the text.

<u>48.</u> $k(A + B) = \begin{bmatrix} k(a_{11} + b_{11}) & k(a_{12} + b_{12}) \\ k(a_{21} + b_{21}) & k(a_{22} + b_{22}) \end{bmatrix}$

$= \begin{bmatrix} ka_{11} + kb_{11} & ka_{12} + kb_{12} \\ ka_{21} + kb_{21} & ka_{22} + kb_{22} \end{bmatrix}$ (By the distributive law of real numbers)

$= \begin{bmatrix} ka_{11} & ka_{12} \\ ka_{21} & ka_{22} \end{bmatrix} + \begin{bmatrix} kb_{11} & kb_{12} \\ kb_{21} & kb_{22} \end{bmatrix}$

$= kA + kB$

49. $AI = \begin{bmatrix} a_{11} & a_{12} \\ a_{21} & a_{22} \end{bmatrix} \begin{bmatrix} 1 & 0 \\ 0 & 1 \end{bmatrix} = \begin{bmatrix} a_{11} \cdot 1 + a_{12} \cdot 0 & a_{11} \cdot 0 + a_{12} \cdot 1 \\ a_{21} \cdot 1 + a_{22} \cdot 0 & a_{21} \cdot 0 + a_{22} \cdot 1 \end{bmatrix}$

$\qquad = \begin{bmatrix} a_{11} & a_{12} \\ a_{21} & a_{22} \end{bmatrix} = A$

$\quad IA = \begin{bmatrix} 1 & 0 \\ 0 & 1 \end{bmatrix} \begin{bmatrix} a_{11} & a_{12} \\ a_{21} & a_{22} \end{bmatrix} = \begin{bmatrix} 1 \cdot a_{11} + 0 \cdot a_{21} & 1 \cdot a_{12} + 0 \cdot a_{22} \\ 0 \cdot a_{11} + 1 \cdot a_{21} & 0 \cdot a_{12} + 1 \cdot a_{22} \end{bmatrix}$

$\qquad = \begin{bmatrix} a_{11} & a_{12} \\ a_{21} & a_{22} \end{bmatrix} = A$

Thus, $AI = IA = A$.

50. Find BC. Then A(BC). Find AB. Then (AB)C. Then compare A(BC) and (AB)C.

Exercise Set 9.5

1. $\begin{vmatrix} -2 & -\sqrt{5} \\ -\sqrt{5} & 3 \end{vmatrix} = -2 \cdot 3 - (-\sqrt{5})(-\sqrt{5}) = -6 - 5 = -11$

2. $\begin{vmatrix} \sqrt{5} & -3 \\ 4 & 2 \end{vmatrix} = \sqrt{5}(2) - 4(-3) = 2\sqrt{5} + 12$

3. $\begin{vmatrix} x & 4 \\ x & x^2 \end{vmatrix} = x \cdot x^2 - x \cdot 4 = x^3 - 4x$

4. $\begin{vmatrix} y^2 & -2 \\ y & 3 \end{vmatrix} = y^2 \cdot 3 - y(-2) = 3y^2 + 2y$

5. $\begin{vmatrix} 3 & 1 & 2 \\ -2 & 3 & 1 \\ 3 & 4 & -6 \end{vmatrix} = 3 \begin{vmatrix} 3 & 1 \\ 4 & -6 \end{vmatrix} - (-2) \begin{vmatrix} 1 & 2 \\ 4 & -6 \end{vmatrix} + 3 \begin{vmatrix} 1 & 2 \\ 3 & 1 \end{vmatrix}$

$\qquad = 3(-22) + 2(-14) + 3(-5) = -66 - 28 - 15 = -109$

6. $\begin{vmatrix} 3 & -2 & 1 \\ 2 & 4 & 3 \\ -1 & 5 & 1 \end{vmatrix} = 3 \begin{vmatrix} 4 & 3 \\ 5 & 1 \end{vmatrix} - (-2) \begin{vmatrix} 2 & 3 \\ -1 & 1 \end{vmatrix} + 1 \begin{vmatrix} 2 & 4 \\ -1 & 5 \end{vmatrix}$

$\qquad = 3(-11) + 2 \cdot 5 + 1 \cdot 14 = -9$

7. $\begin{vmatrix} x & 0 & -1 \\ 2 & x & x^2 \\ -3 & x & 1 \end{vmatrix} = x \begin{vmatrix} x & x^2 \\ x & 1 \end{vmatrix} - 2 \begin{vmatrix} 0 & -1 \\ x & 1 \end{vmatrix} + (-3) \begin{vmatrix} 0 & -1 \\ x & x^2 \end{vmatrix}$

$\qquad = x(x - x^3) - 2(x) - 3(x) = x^2 - x^4 - 2x - 3x$
$\qquad = -x^4 + x^2 - 5x$

8. $\begin{vmatrix} x & 1 & -1 \\ x^2 & x & x \\ 0 & x & 1 \end{vmatrix} = 0 \begin{vmatrix} 1 & -1 \\ x & x \end{vmatrix} - x \begin{vmatrix} x & -1 \\ x^2 & x \end{vmatrix} + 1 \begin{vmatrix} x & 1 \\ x^2 & x \end{vmatrix}$

$= 0 - x \cdot 2x^2 + 1 \cdot 0 = -2x^3$

9. a_{11} is the element in the 1st row and 1st column. $a_{11} = 7$

a_{32} is the element in the 3rd row and 2nd column. $a_{32} = 2$

a_{22} is the element in the 2nd row and 2nd column. $a_{22} = 0$

10. $a_{13} = -6$, $a_{31} = 1$, $a_{23} = -3$

11. To find M_{11} we delete the 1st row and the 1st column.

$A = \begin{bmatrix} 7 & -4 & -6 \\ 2 & 0 & -3 \\ 1 & 2 & -5 \end{bmatrix}$

We calculate the determinant of the matrix formed by the remaining elements.

$M_{11} = \begin{vmatrix} 0 & -3 \\ 2 & -5 \end{vmatrix} = 0(-5) - 2(-3) = 0 + 6 = 6$

To find M_{32} we delete the 3rd row and the 2nd column.

$A = \begin{bmatrix} 7 & -4 & -6 \\ 2 & 0 & -3 \\ 1 & 2 & -5 \end{bmatrix}$

We calculate the determinant of the matrix formed by the remaining elements.

$M_{32} = \begin{vmatrix} 7 & -6 \\ 2 & -3 \end{vmatrix} = 7(-3) - 2(-6) = -21 + 12 = -9$

To find M_{22} we delete the 2nd row and the 2nd column.

$A = \begin{bmatrix} 7 & -4 & -6 \\ 2 & 0 & -3 \\ 1 & 2 & -5 \end{bmatrix}$

We calculate the determinant of the matrix formed by the remaining elements.

$M_{22} = \begin{vmatrix} 7 & -6 \\ 1 & -5 \end{vmatrix} = 7(-5) - 1(-6) = -35 + 6 = -29.$

12. $M_{13} = \begin{vmatrix} 2 & 0 \\ 1 & 2 \end{vmatrix} = 4$, $M_{31} = \begin{vmatrix} -4 & -6 \\ 0 & -3 \end{vmatrix} = 12$,

$M_{23} = \begin{vmatrix} 7 & -4 \\ 1 & 2 \end{vmatrix} = 18$

13. From Exercise 11, we know that $M_{11} = 6$, $M_{32} = -9$, and $M_{22} = -29$. We use this information to find the desired cofactors.

$A_{11} = (-1)^{1+1} M_{11} = (-1)^2 \cdot 6 = 1 \cdot 6 = 6$

$A_{32} = (-1)^{3+2} M_{32} = (-1)^5 \cdot (-9) = -1 \cdot (-9) = 9$

$A_{22} = (-1)^{2+2} M_{22} = (-1)^4 \cdot (-29) = 1 \cdot 29 \ -29$

14. We use the results of Exercise 12.

$A_{13} = (-1)^{1+3} \cdot M_{13} = 1 \cdot 4 = 4$, $A_{31} = (-1)^{3+1} M_{31} = 1 \cdot 12 = 12$,

$A_{23} = (-1)^{2+3} \cdot 18 = -1 \cdot 18 = -18$

15.

$$A = \begin{bmatrix} 7 & -4 & -6 \\ \boxed{2 \qquad 0 \qquad -3} \\ 1 & 2 & -5 \end{bmatrix}$$

Find $|A|$ by expanding about the second row.

$$|A| = (2)(-1)^{2+1} \cdot \begin{vmatrix} -4 & -6 \\ 2 & -5 \end{vmatrix} + (0)(-1)^{2+2} \cdot \begin{vmatrix} 7 & -6 \\ 1 & -5 \end{vmatrix} + (-3)(-1)^{2+3} \cdot \begin{vmatrix} 7 & -4 \\ 1 & 2 \end{vmatrix}$$

$$= 2(-1)(32) + 0 + (-3)(-1)(18) = -64 + 54 = -10$$

16. $|A| = -(-4)(-10 + 3) + 0 - (2)(-21 + 12) = -10$

17.

$$A = \begin{bmatrix} 7 & -4 & \boxed{-6} \\ 2 & 0 & \boxed{-3} \\ 1 & 2 & \boxed{-5} \end{bmatrix}$$

Find $|A|$ by expanding about the third column.

$$|A| = (-6)(-1)^{1+3} \cdot \begin{vmatrix} 2 & 0 \\ 1 & 2 \end{vmatrix} + (-3)(-1)^{2+3} \cdot \begin{vmatrix} 7 & -4 \\ 1 & 2 \end{vmatrix} + (-5)(-1)^{3+3} \cdot \begin{vmatrix} 7 & -4 \\ 2 & 0 \end{vmatrix}$$

$$= -6(1)(4) + (-3)(-1)(18) + (-5)(1)(8) = -24 + 54 - 40 = -10$$

18. $|A| = 7(0 + 6) - (-4)(-10 + 3) + (-6)(4 - 0) = -10$

19. To find M_{41} we delete the 4th row and the 1st column.

$$A = \begin{bmatrix} 1 & 0 & 0 & -2 \\ 4 & 1 & 0 & 0 \\ 5 & 6 & 7 & 8 \\ -2 & -3 & -1 & 0 \end{bmatrix}$$

We calculate the determinant of the matrix formed by the remaining elements.

$$M_{41} = \begin{vmatrix} \boxed{0 \quad 0 \quad -2} \\ 1 & 0 & 0 \\ 6 & 7 & 8 \end{vmatrix} = 0 + 0 + (-2)(-1)^{1+3} \cdot \begin{vmatrix} 1 & 0 \\ 6 & 7 \end{vmatrix} = -2 \cdot 1 \cdot 7 = -14$$

To find M_{33} we delete the 3rd row and the 3rd column.

$$A = \begin{bmatrix} 1 & 0 & 0 & -2 \\ 4 & 1 & 0 & 0 \\ 5 & 6 & 7 & 8 \\ -2 & -3 & -1 & 0 \end{bmatrix}$$

We calculate the determinant of the matrix formed by the remaining elements.

$$M_{33} = \begin{vmatrix} 1 & 0 & \boxed{-2} \\ 4 & 1 & \boxed{0} \\ -2 & -3 & \boxed{0} \end{vmatrix} = -2(-1)^{1+3} \cdot \begin{vmatrix} 4 & 1 \\ -2 & -3 \end{vmatrix} + 0 + 0 = -2 \cdot 1 \cdot (-10) = 20$$

20. $M_{12} = \begin{vmatrix} 4 & 0 & 0 \\ 5 & 7 & 8 \\ -2 & -1 & 0 \end{vmatrix} = 4 \begin{vmatrix} 7 & 8 \\ -1 & 0 \end{vmatrix} + 0 + 0 = 4 \cdot 8 = 32$

$$M_{44} = \begin{vmatrix} 1 & 0 & 0 \\ 4 & 1 & 0 \\ 5 & 6 & 7 \end{vmatrix} = 1 \cdot \begin{vmatrix} 1 & 0 \\ 6 & 7 \end{vmatrix} = 1 \cdot 7 = 7$$

21.

$$A = \begin{bmatrix} 1 & 0 & 0 & -2 \\ 4 & 1 & 0 & 0 \\ 5 & 6 & 7 & 8 \\ -2 & -3 & -1 & 0 \end{bmatrix} \qquad (a_{24} \text{ is } 0; \quad a_{43} \text{ is } -1)$$

A_{24} is the cofactor of the element a_{24}.

$A_{24} = (-1)^{2+4} M_{24}$ \qquad (M_{24} is the minor of a_{24})

$$= (-1)^6 \begin{vmatrix} 1 & 0 & 0 \\ 5 & 6 & 7 \\ -2 & -3 & -1 \end{vmatrix} \qquad \text{Think:} \quad A = \begin{bmatrix} 1 & 0 & 0 & -2 \\ 4 & 1 & 0 & 0 \\ 5 & 6 & 7 & 8 \\ -2 & -3 & -1 & 0 \end{bmatrix}$$

$$= (1)\left[1(-1)^{1+1} \cdot \begin{vmatrix} 6 & 7 \\ -3 & -1 \end{vmatrix} + 0(-1)^{1+2} \cdot \begin{vmatrix} 5 & 7 \\ -2 & -1 \end{vmatrix} + 0(-1)^{1+3} \cdot \begin{vmatrix} 5 & 6 \\ -2 & -3 \end{vmatrix} \right]$$

(Here we expanded about the first row.)

$= 1(1)[6(-1) - (-3)7] + 0 + 0 = -6 + 21 = 15$

A_{43} is the cofactor of the element a_{43}.

$A_{43} = (-1)^{4+3} M_{43}$ \qquad (M_{43} is the minor of a_{43})

$$= (-1)^7 \begin{vmatrix} 1 & 0 & -2 \\ 4 & 1 & 0 \\ 5 & 6 & 8 \end{vmatrix} \qquad \text{Think:} \quad A = \begin{bmatrix} 1 & 0 & 0 & -2 \\ 4 & 1 & 0 & 0 \\ 5 & 6 & 7 & 8 \\ -2 & -3 & -1 & 0 \end{bmatrix}$$

$$= (-1)\left[4(-1)^{2+1} \cdot \begin{vmatrix} 0 & -2 \\ 6 & 8 \end{vmatrix} + 1(-1)^{2+2} \cdot \begin{vmatrix} 1 & -2 \\ 5 & 8 \end{vmatrix} + 0(-1)^{2+3} \cdot \begin{vmatrix} 1 & 0 \\ 5 & 6 \end{vmatrix} \right]$$

(Here we expanded about the second row.)

$= (-1)[4(-1)(0 \cdot 8 - 6(-2)) + 1(1 \cdot 8 - 5(-2)) + 0]$

$= (-1)[-4(12) + 18] = (-1)(-30) = 30$

<u>22</u>. $A_{22} = (-1)^{2+2} \begin{vmatrix} 1 & 0 & -2 \\ 5 & 7 & 8 \\ -2 & -1 & 0 \end{vmatrix} = 1 \cdot \left[1 \cdot \begin{vmatrix} 7 & 8 \\ -1 & 0 \end{vmatrix} + 0 + (-2) \cdot \begin{vmatrix} 5 & 7 \\ -2 & -1 \end{vmatrix} \right]$

$= 1 \cdot (1 \cdot 8 - 2 \cdot 9) = -10$

$A_{34} = (-1)^{3+4} \begin{vmatrix} 1 & 0 & 0 \\ 4 & 1 & 0 \\ -2 & -3 & -1 \end{vmatrix} = -1 \cdot \left[1 \cdot \begin{vmatrix} 1 & 0 \\ -3 & -1 \end{vmatrix} + 0 + 0 \right]$

$= -1 \cdot 1 \cdot (-1) = 1$

<u>23</u>.

$A = \begin{bmatrix} \boxed{1 \quad 0 \quad 0 \quad -2} \\ 4 & 1 & 0 & 0 \\ 5 & 6 & 7 & 8 \\ -2 & -3 & -1 & 0 \end{bmatrix}$

Find |A| by expanding about the first row.

$|A| = (1)(-1)^{1+1} \cdot \begin{vmatrix} \boxed{1 \quad 0 \quad 0} \\ 6 & 7 & 8 \\ -3 & -1 & 0 \end{vmatrix} + 0 + 0 + (-2)(-1)^{1+4} \begin{vmatrix} \boxed{4 \quad 1 \quad 0} \\ 5 & 6 & 7 \\ -2 & -3 & -1 \end{vmatrix}$

$= 1 \cdot \left[1(-1)^{1+1} \cdot \begin{vmatrix} 7 & 8 \\ -1 & 0 \end{vmatrix} + 0 + 0 \right] + 2 \cdot \left[4(-1)^{1+1} \cdot \begin{vmatrix} 6 & 7 \\ -3 & -1 \end{vmatrix} \right] +$

$1(-1)^{1+2} \cdot \begin{vmatrix} 5 & 7 \\ -2 & -1 \end{vmatrix} + 0]$

$= 1[1(0 - (-8))] + 2[4(-6 - (-21)) + (-1)(-5 - (-14))]$

$= 1 \cdot 8 + 2 \cdot (60 - 9) = 8 + 102 = 110$

<u>24</u>.

$|A| = 0 + 0 + 7 \begin{vmatrix} 1 & 0 & -2 \\ 4 & 1 & 0 \\ -2 & -3 & 0 \end{vmatrix} - (-1) \begin{vmatrix} 1 & 0 & -2 \\ 4 & 1 & 0 \\ 5 & 6 & 8 \end{vmatrix}$

$= 7 \left[-2 \begin{vmatrix} 4 & 1 \\ -2 & -3 \end{vmatrix} + 0 + 0 \right] + 1 \cdot \left[1 \cdot \begin{vmatrix} 1 & 0 \\ 6 & 8 \end{vmatrix} + 0 + (-2) \begin{vmatrix} 4 & 1 \\ 5 & 6 \end{vmatrix} \right]$

$= 7(-2)(-10) + 8 - 2 \cdot 19 = 110$

25.
$$\begin{vmatrix} 5 & -4 & 2 & -2 \\ 3 & -3 & -4 & 7 \\ -2 & 3 & 2 & 4 \\ -8 & 9 & 5 & -5 \end{vmatrix}$$ (Here we will expand about the first column.)

$$= 5(-1)^{1+1} \cdot \begin{vmatrix} -3 & -4 & 7 \\ 3 & 2 & 4 \\ 9 & 5 & -5 \end{vmatrix} + 3(-1)^{2+1} \cdot \begin{vmatrix} -4 & 2 & -2 \\ 3 & 2 & 4 \\ 9 & 5 & -5 \end{vmatrix} +$$

$$(-2)(-1)^{3+1} \cdot \begin{vmatrix} -4 & 2 & -2 \\ -3 & -4 & 7 \\ 9 & 5 & -5 \end{vmatrix} + (-8)(-1)^{4+1} \cdot \begin{vmatrix} -4 & 2 & -2 \\ -3 & -4 & 7 \\ 3 & 2 & 4 \end{vmatrix}$$

$$= 5\left[-3(-1)^{1+1} \cdot \begin{vmatrix} 2 & 4 \\ 5 & -5 \end{vmatrix} + 3(-1)^{2+1} \cdot \begin{vmatrix} -4 & 7 \\ 5 & -5 \end{vmatrix} + 9(-1)^{3+1} \cdot \begin{vmatrix} -4 & 7 \\ 2 & 4 \end{vmatrix} \right] +$$

$$(-3)\left[-4(-1)^{1+1} \cdot \begin{vmatrix} 2 & 4 \\ 5 & -5 \end{vmatrix} + 3(-1)^{2+1} \cdot \begin{vmatrix} 2 & -2 \\ 5 & -5 \end{vmatrix} + 9(-1)^{3+1} \cdot \begin{vmatrix} 2 & -2 \\ 2 & 4 \end{vmatrix} \right] +$$

$$(-2)\left[-4(-1)^{1+1} \cdot \begin{vmatrix} -4 & 7 \\ 5 & -5 \end{vmatrix} + (-3)(-1)^{2+1} \cdot \begin{vmatrix} 2 & -2 \\ 5 & -5 \end{vmatrix} + 9(-1)^{3+1} \cdot \begin{vmatrix} 2 & -2 \\ -4 & 7 \end{vmatrix} \right] +$$

$$8\left[-4(-1)^{1+1} \cdot \begin{vmatrix} -4 & 7 \\ 2 & 4 \end{vmatrix} + (-3)(-1)^{2+1} \cdot \begin{vmatrix} 2 & -2 \\ 2 & 4 \end{vmatrix} + 3(-1)^{3+1} \cdot \begin{vmatrix} 2 & -2 \\ -4 & 7 \end{vmatrix} \right]$$

$$= 5[-3(-30) + (-3)(-15) + 9(-30)] + (-3)[-4(-30) + (-3)(0) + 9(12)] +$$
$$(-2)[-4(-15) + 3(0) + 9(6)] + 8[-4(-30) + 3(12) + 3(6)]$$

$$= 5(90 + 45 - 270) + (-3)(120 + 0 + 108) + (-2)(60 + 0 + 54) +$$
$$8(120 + 36 + 18)$$

$$= 5(-135) + (-3)(228) + (-2)(114) + 8(174) = -675 - 684 - 228 + 1392 = -195$$

26. $x\begin{vmatrix} y & s & t \\ 0 & z & u \\ 0 & 0 & w \end{vmatrix} = x \cdot y \begin{vmatrix} z & u \\ 0 & w \end{vmatrix} = xyzw$

27. $\begin{vmatrix} -4 & 5 \\ 6 & 10 \end{vmatrix}$

$= 5\begin{vmatrix} -4 & 1 \\ 6 & 2 \end{vmatrix}$ (Theorem 7, factoring 5 out of the second column)

$= 5 \cdot 2\begin{vmatrix} -4 & 1 \\ 3 & 1 \end{vmatrix}$ (Theorem 7, factoring 2 out of the second row)

$= 5 \cdot 2\begin{vmatrix} -4 & 1 \\ 7 & 0 \end{vmatrix}$ (Theorem 8, multiplying each element of the first row by −1 and adding the products to the corresponding elements of the second row)

$= 5 \cdot 2(0 - 7)$

$= 10(-7) = -70$

28. $\begin{vmatrix} 3 & -9 \\ -2 & 4 \end{vmatrix} = 3 \cdot 2 \begin{vmatrix} 1 & -3 \\ -1 & 2 \end{vmatrix}$ (Factoring 3 out of row 1 and 2 out of row 2)

$= 3 \cdot 2 \begin{vmatrix} 1 & -3 \\ 0 & -1 \end{vmatrix}$ (Adding row 1 to row 2)

$= 3 \cdot 2 \cdot (-1) = -6$

29. $\begin{vmatrix} 2 & 1 & 1 \\ 2 & -3 & -1 \\ -4 & 5 & 2 \end{vmatrix}$

$= \begin{vmatrix} 2 & 1 & 1 \\ 4 & -2 & 0 \\ -8 & 3 & 0 \end{vmatrix}$ (Theorem 8, adding the first row to the second row; also multiplying each element of the first row by -2 and adding the products to the corresponding elements of the third row)

$= 1(-1)^{1+3} \begin{vmatrix} 4 & -2 \\ -8 & 3 \end{vmatrix} + 0 + 0$ (Expanding the determinant about the third column)

$= 1(12 - 16) = -4$

30. $\begin{vmatrix} 1 & 2 & 4 \\ 2 & 3 & 5 \\ 3 & 1 & 6 \end{vmatrix} = \begin{vmatrix} 1 & 2 & 4 \\ 0 & -1 & -3 \\ 0 & -5 & -6 \end{vmatrix}$ (Multiplying row 1 by -2 and adding the result to row 2; also multiplying row 1 by -3 and adding the result to row 3)

$= 1 \cdot \begin{vmatrix} -1 & -3 \\ -5 & -6 \end{vmatrix} = 1 \cdot (-9) = -9$

31. $\begin{vmatrix} 11 & -15 & 20 \\ 16 & 24 & -8 \\ 6 & 9 & 15 \end{vmatrix}$

$= 8 \cdot \begin{vmatrix} 11 & -15 & 20 \\ 2 & 3 & -1 \\ 6 & 9 & 15 \end{vmatrix} = 8 \cdot 3 \begin{vmatrix} 11 & -15 & 20 \\ 2 & 3 & -1 \\ 2 & 3 & 5 \end{vmatrix}$ (Theorem 7, factoring 8 out of the second row and 3 out of the third row)

$= 8 \cdot 3 \cdot 3 \begin{vmatrix} 11 & -5 & 20 \\ 2 & 1 & -1 \\ 2 & 1 & 5 \end{vmatrix}$ (Theorem 7, factoring 3 out of the second column)

$= 8 \cdot 3 \cdot 3 \begin{vmatrix} 11 & -5 & 20 \\ 2 & 1 & -1 \\ 0 & 0 & 6 \end{vmatrix}$ (Theorem 8, multiplying each element of the second row by -1 and adding the products to the corresponding elements of the third row)

$= 8 \cdot 3 \cdot 3 \cdot 6 \begin{vmatrix} 11 & -5 & 20 \\ 2 & 1 & -1 \\ 0 & 0 & 1 \end{vmatrix}$ (Theorem 7 factoring 6 out of the third row)

$= 8 \cdot 3 \cdot 3 \cdot 6 \left[0 + 0 + 1(-1)^{3+3} \begin{vmatrix} 11 & -5 \\ 2 & 1 \end{vmatrix} \right]$ (Expanding the determinant about the third row)

$= 8 \cdot 3 \cdot 3 \cdot 6 \cdot 21 = 9072$

32.
$$\begin{vmatrix} 4 & -24 & 15 \\ -3 & 18 & -6 \\ 5 & -4 & 3 \end{vmatrix}$$

$$= 3\begin{vmatrix} 4 & -24 & 15 \\ -1 & 6 & -2 \\ 5 & -4 & 3 \end{vmatrix} \qquad \text{(Factoring 3 out of row 2)}$$

$$= 3\begin{vmatrix} 0 & 0 & 7 \\ -1 & 6 & -2 \\ 5 & -4 & 3 \end{vmatrix} \qquad \begin{array}{l}\text{(Multiplying row 2 by 4 and adding the}\\ \text{result to row 1)}\end{array}$$

$$= 3 \cdot 7 \cdot \begin{vmatrix} -1 & 6 \\ 5 & -4 \end{vmatrix} = 3 \cdot 7 \cdot (-26) = -546$$

33.
$$\begin{vmatrix} -3 & 0 & 2 & 6 \\ 2 & 4 & 0 & -1 \\ -1 & 0 & -5 & 2 \\ 0 & -1 & -2 & -3 \end{vmatrix}$$

$$= \begin{vmatrix} 0 & 0 & 17 & 0 \\ 2 & 4 & 0 & -1 \\ -1 & 0 & -5 & 2 \\ 0 & -1 & -2 & -3 \end{vmatrix} \qquad \begin{array}{l}\text{(Theorem 8, multiplying each element of the}\\ \text{third row by -3 and adding the products to}\\ \text{the corresponding elements of the first row)}\end{array}$$

$$= 17\begin{vmatrix} 0 & 0 & 1 & 0 \\ 2 & 4 & 0 & -1 \\ -1 & 0 & -5 & 2 \\ 0 & -1 & -2 & -3 \end{vmatrix} \qquad \text{(Theorem 7, factoring 17 out of the first row)}$$

$$= 17\left[0 + 0 + 1(-1)^{1+3}\begin{vmatrix} 2 & 4 & -1 \\ -1 & 0 & 2 \\ 0 & -1 & -3 \end{vmatrix} + 0 \right] \qquad \begin{array}{l}\text{(Expanding the determinant}\\ \text{about the first row)}\end{array}$$

$$= -17\begin{vmatrix} 2 & 4 & -1 \\ 1 & 0 & -2 \\ 0 & -1 & -3 \end{vmatrix} \qquad \begin{array}{l}\text{(Theorem 7, factoring -1 out of the}\\ \text{second row)}\end{array}$$

$$= -17\begin{vmatrix} 0 & 4 & 3 \\ 1 & 0 & -2 \\ 0 & -1 & -3 \end{vmatrix} \qquad \begin{array}{l}\text{(Theorem 8, multiplying each element of the}\\ \text{second row by -2 and adding the products to}\\ \text{the corresponding elements in the first row)}\end{array}$$

$$= -17\left[0 + 1(-1)^{2+1}\begin{vmatrix} 4 & 3 \\ -1 & -3 \end{vmatrix} + 0 \right] \qquad \begin{array}{l}\text{(Expanding the determinant about the}\\ \text{first column)}\end{array}$$

$$= -17 \cdot (-1) \cdot (-12 + 3) = 17(-9) = -153$$

34.
$$\begin{vmatrix} -2 & 1 & 0 & 5 \\ 3 & 0 & -4 & -2 \\ 4 & -6 & -8 & -1 \\ 8 & 0 & -2 & -3 \end{vmatrix}$$

$$= \begin{vmatrix} -2 & 1 & 0 & 5 \\ 3 & 0 & -4 & -2 \\ -8 & 0 & -8 & 29 \\ 8 & 0 & -2 & -3 \end{vmatrix}$$
(Multiplying row 1 by 6 and adding the result to row 3)

$$= -1 \cdot \begin{vmatrix} 3 & -4 & -2 \\ -8 & -8 & 29 \\ 8 & -2 & -3 \end{vmatrix}$$

$$= -1 \cdot \left(3 \cdot \begin{vmatrix} -8 & 29 \\ -2 & -3 \end{vmatrix} - (-4) \cdot \begin{vmatrix} -8 & 29 \\ 8 & -3 \end{vmatrix} + (-2) \cdot \begin{vmatrix} -8 & -8 \\ 8 & -2 \end{vmatrix} \right)$$

$$= -[3 \cdot 82 + 4(-208) - 2 \cdot 80] = 746$$

35.
$$\begin{vmatrix} x & y & z \\ 0 & 0 & 0 \\ p & q & r \end{vmatrix} = 0$$
(Theorem 4)

36.
$$\begin{vmatrix} 5 & 5 & 5 \\ 3 & 3 & 3 \\ 2 & -7 & 8 \end{vmatrix} = 5 \cdot 3 \cdot \begin{vmatrix} 1 & 1 & 1 \\ 1 & 1 & 1 \\ 2 & -7 & 8 \end{vmatrix}$$
(Factoring 5 out of row 1 and 3 out of row 2)

$$= 0$$
(Theorem 6)

37.
$$\begin{vmatrix} 2a & t & -7a \\ 2b & u & -7b \\ 2c & v & -7c \end{vmatrix}$$

$$= 2(-7) \begin{vmatrix} a & t & a \\ b & u & b \\ c & v & c \end{vmatrix}$$
(Theorem 7, factoring 2 out of the first column and -7 out of the third column)

$$= 2 \cdot (-7) \cdot 0 = 0$$
(Theorem 6; columns 1 and 3 are the same)

38.
$$\begin{vmatrix} a & -1 & 4a \\ b & 2 & 4b \\ x & 3 & 4x \end{vmatrix} = 4 \begin{vmatrix} a & -1 & a \\ b & 2 & b \\ x & 3 & x \end{vmatrix}$$
(Factoring 4 out of column 3)

$$= 0$$
(Theorem 6)

39.
$$\begin{vmatrix} x^2 & x & 1 \\ y^2 & y & 1 \\ z^2 & z & 1 \end{vmatrix}$$

$$= \begin{vmatrix} x^2 - y^2 & x - y & 0 \\ y^2 & y & 1 \\ z^2 - y^2 & z - y & 0 \end{vmatrix}$$
(Theorem 8, multiplying each element of the second row by -1 and adding the products to the corresponding elements of the first and third rows)

$$= (x - y)(z - y)\begin{vmatrix} x + y & 1 & 0 \\ y^2 & y & 1 \\ z + y & 1 & 0 \end{vmatrix}$$
(Theorem 7, factoring $x - y$ out of the first row and $z - y$ out of the third row)

$$= (x - y)(z - y)\begin{vmatrix} x - z & 0 & 0 \\ y^2 & y & 1 \\ z + y & 1 & 0 \end{vmatrix}$$
(Theorem 8, multiplying each element of the third row by -1 and adding the products to the corresponding elements of the first row)

$$= (x - y)(z - y)(x - z)(-1)$$
(Expanding the determinant about the first row)

$$= (x - y)(z - y)(z - x), \text{ or } (x - y)(y - z)(x - z), \text{ or } (y - x)(z - y)(x - z)$$

40.
$$\begin{vmatrix} 1 & 1 & 1 \\ a & b & c \\ a^2 & b^2 & c^2 \end{vmatrix} = \begin{vmatrix} 0 & 0 & 1 \\ a - c & b - c & c \\ a^2 - c^2 & b^2 - c^2 & c^2 \end{vmatrix}$$
(Multiplying column 3 by -1 and adding the result to column 1; also, multiplying column 3 by -1 and adding the result to column 2)

$$= (a - c)(b - c)\begin{vmatrix} 0 & 0 & 1 \\ 1 & 1 & c \\ a+c & b+c & c^2 \end{vmatrix}$$
(Factoring $a - c$ out of column 1 and $b - c$ out of column 2)

$$= (a - c)(b - c)\begin{vmatrix} 0 & 0 & 1 \\ 0 & 1 & c \\ a-b & b+c & c^2 \end{vmatrix}$$
(Multiplying column 2 by -1 and adding the result to column 1)

$$= (a - c)(b - c)(a - b)\begin{vmatrix} 0 & 1 \\ 1 & c \end{vmatrix}$$

$$= (a - c)(b - c)(a - b)(-1)$$
$$= (c - a)(b - c)(a - b), \text{ or } (a - c)(c - b)(a - b), \text{ or } (a - c)(b - c)(b - a)$$

41.
$$\begin{vmatrix} x & x^2 & x^3 \\ y & y^2 & y^3 \\ z & z^2 & z^3 \end{vmatrix}$$

$$= xyz\cdot\begin{vmatrix} 1 & x & x^2 \\ 1 & y & y^2 \\ 1 & z & z^2 \end{vmatrix}$$
(Theorem 7, factoring x out of the first row, y out of the second row, and z out of the third row)

$$= xyz\cdot\begin{vmatrix} 0 & x - z & x^2 - z^2 \\ 0 & y - z & y^2 - z^2 \\ 1 & z & z^2 \end{vmatrix}$$
(Theorem 8, multiplying each element of the third row by -1 and adding the products to the corresponding elements of the first and second rows)

$$= xyz(x - z)(y - z) \cdot \begin{vmatrix} 0 & 1 & x + z \\ 0 & 1 & y + z \\ 1 & z & z^2 \end{vmatrix}$$

(Theorem 7, factoring x - z out of the first row and y - z out of the second row)

$$= xyz(x - z)(y - z) \cdot \begin{vmatrix} 0 & 0 & x - y \\ 0 & 1 & y + z \\ 1 & z & z^2 \end{vmatrix}$$

(Theorem 8, multiplying each element of the second row by -1 and adding the products to the corresponding elements of the first row)

$$= xyz(x - z)(y - z)(x - y) \cdot \begin{vmatrix} 0 & 0 & 1 \\ 0 & 1 & y + z \\ 1 & z & z^2 \end{vmatrix}$$

(Theorem 7, factoring x - y out of the first row)

$$= xyz(x - z)(y - z)(x - y) \cdot \left[0 + 0 + 1(-1)^{1+3} \begin{vmatrix} 0 & 1 \\ 1 & z \end{vmatrix} \right]$$

(Expanding the determinant about the first row)

$$= xyz(x - z)(y - z)(x - y)(-1) \qquad \left(\begin{vmatrix} 0 & 1 \\ 1 & z \end{vmatrix} = 0 - 1 = -1 \right)$$

$= -xyz(x - z)(y - z)(x - y)$, or $xyz(z - x)(y - z)(x - y)$,

or $xyz(x - z)(z - y)(x - y)$, or $xyz(x - z)(y - z)(y - x)$

42.
$$\begin{vmatrix} 1 & 1 & 1 \\ a & b & c \\ a^3 & b^3 & c^3 \end{vmatrix}$$

$$= \begin{vmatrix} 0 & 0 & 1 \\ a - c & b - c & c \\ a^3 - c^3 & b^3 - c^3 & c^3 \end{vmatrix}$$

(Multiplying column 3 by -1 and adding the result to column 1; also, multiplying column 3 by -1 and adding the result to column 2)

$$= (a - c)(b - c) \begin{vmatrix} 0 & 0 & 1 \\ 1 & 1 & c \\ a^2 + ac + c^2 & b^2 + bc + c^2 & c^3 \end{vmatrix}$$

(Factoring a - c out of column 1 and b - c out of column 2)

$$= (a - c)(b - c) \begin{vmatrix} 0 & 0 & 1 \\ 0 & 1 & c \\ a^2+ac-b^2-bc & b^2+bc+c^2 & c^3 \end{vmatrix}$$

(Multiplying column 2 by -1 and adding the result to column 1)

$$= (a - c)(b - c)(a^2 + ac - b^2 - bc) \begin{vmatrix} 0 & 1 \\ 1 & c \end{vmatrix}$$

$= (a - c)(b - c)(a^2 - b^2 + ac - bc)(-1)$

$= (a - c)(b - c)[(a + b)(a - b) + c(a - b)](-1)$

$= (a - c)(b - c)(a - b)(a + b + c)(-1)$

$= (c - a)(b - c)(a - b)(a + b + c)$, or $(a - c)(c - b)(a - b)(a + b + c)$, or

$(a - c)(b - c)(b - a)(a + b + c)$

43. $-2x + 4y = 3$
    $3x - 7y = 1$

$$x = \frac{\begin{vmatrix} 3 & 4 \\ 1 & -7 \end{vmatrix}}{\begin{vmatrix} -2 & 4 \\ 3 & -7 \end{vmatrix}} = \frac{3(-7) - 1(4)}{-2(-7) - 3(4)} = \frac{-25}{2}$$

$$y = \frac{\begin{vmatrix} -2 & 3 \\ 3 & 1 \end{vmatrix}}{\begin{vmatrix} -2 & 4 \\ 3 & -7 \end{vmatrix}} = \frac{-2(1) - 3(3)}{2} = \frac{-11}{2}$$

The solution is $\left[-\frac{25}{2}, -\frac{11}{2}\right]$.

44.
$$x = \frac{\begin{vmatrix} -3 & -4 \\ 6 & 2 \end{vmatrix}}{\begin{vmatrix} 5 & -4 \\ 7 & 2 \end{vmatrix}} = \frac{18}{38} = \frac{9}{19}$$

$$y = \frac{\begin{vmatrix} 5 & -3 \\ 7 & 6 \end{vmatrix}}{\begin{vmatrix} 5 & -4 \\ 7 & 2 \end{vmatrix}} = \frac{51}{38}$$

45. $\sqrt{3}x + \pi y = -5$
    $\pi x - \sqrt{3}y = 4$

$$x = \frac{\begin{vmatrix} -5 & \pi \\ 4 & -\sqrt{3} \end{vmatrix}}{\begin{vmatrix} \sqrt{3} & \pi \\ \pi & -\sqrt{3} \end{vmatrix}} = \frac{5\sqrt{3} - 4\pi}{-3 - \pi^2} = \frac{-5\sqrt{3} + 4\pi}{3 + \pi^2}$$

$$y = \frac{\begin{vmatrix} \sqrt{3} & -5 \\ \pi & 4 \end{vmatrix}}{\begin{vmatrix} \sqrt{3} & \pi \\ \pi & -\sqrt{3} \end{vmatrix}} = \frac{4\sqrt{3} + 5\pi}{-3 - \pi^2} = \frac{-4\sqrt{3} - 5\pi}{3 + \pi^2}$$

The solution is $\left[\frac{-5\sqrt{3} + 4\pi}{3 + \pi^2}, \frac{-4\sqrt{3} - 5\pi}{3 + \pi^2}\right]$, or

$\left[\frac{-5\sqrt{3} + 4\pi}{3 + \pi^2}, \frac{4\sqrt{3} + 5\pi}{-3 - \pi^2}\right]$.

46.
$$x = \frac{\begin{vmatrix} 2 & -\sqrt{5} \\ -3 & \pi \end{vmatrix}}{\begin{vmatrix} \pi & -\sqrt{5} \\ \sqrt{5} & \pi \end{vmatrix}} = \frac{2\pi - 3\sqrt{5}}{\pi^2 + 5}$$

$$y = \frac{\begin{vmatrix} \pi & 2 \\ \sqrt{5} & -3 \end{vmatrix}}{\begin{vmatrix} \pi & -\sqrt{5} \\ \sqrt{5} & \pi \end{vmatrix}} = \frac{-3\pi - 2\sqrt{5}}{\pi^2 + 5}$$

47. $3x + 2y - z = 4$
    $3x - 2y + z = 5$
    $4x - 5y - z = -1$

$$x = \frac{\begin{vmatrix} 4 & 2 & -1 \\ 5 & -2 & 1 \\ -1 & -5 & -1 \end{vmatrix}}{\begin{vmatrix} 3 & 2 & -1 \\ 3 & -2 & 1 \\ 4 & -5 & -1 \end{vmatrix}}$$

$$= \frac{4\begin{vmatrix} -2 & 1 \\ -5 & -1 \end{vmatrix} - 5\begin{vmatrix} 2 & -1 \\ -5 & -1 \end{vmatrix} + (-1)\begin{vmatrix} 2 & -1 \\ -2 & 1 \end{vmatrix}}{3\begin{vmatrix} -2 & 1 \\ -5 & -1 \end{vmatrix} - 3\begin{vmatrix} 2 & -1 \\ -5 & -1 \end{vmatrix} + 4\begin{vmatrix} 2 & -1 \\ -2 & 1 \end{vmatrix}}$$

$$= \frac{4(7) - 5(-7) - 1(0)}{3(7) - 3(-7) + 4(0)}$$

$$= \frac{28 + 35}{21 + 21} = \frac{63}{42} = \frac{3}{2}$$

$$y = \frac{\begin{vmatrix} 3 & 4 & -1 \\ 3 & 5 & 1 \\ 4 & -1 & -1 \end{vmatrix}}{42}$$

$$= \frac{3\begin{vmatrix} 5 & 1 \\ -1 & -1 \end{vmatrix} - 3\begin{vmatrix} 4 & -1 \\ -1 & -1 \end{vmatrix} + 4\begin{vmatrix} 4 & -1 \\ 5 & 1 \end{vmatrix}}{42}$$

$$= \frac{3(-4) - 3(-5) + 4(9)}{42}$$

$$= \frac{-12 + 15 + 36}{42} = \frac{39}{42} = \frac{13}{14}$$

$$z = \frac{\begin{vmatrix} 3 & 2 & 4 \\ 3 & -2 & 5 \\ 4 & -5 & -1 \end{vmatrix}}{42}$$

$$= \frac{3\begin{vmatrix} -2 & 5 \\ -5 & -1 \end{vmatrix} - 3\begin{vmatrix} 2 & 4 \\ -5 & -1 \end{vmatrix} + 4\begin{vmatrix} 2 & 4 \\ -2 & 5 \end{vmatrix}}{42}$$

$$= \frac{3(27) - 3(18) + 4(18)}{42}$$

$$= \frac{81 - 54 + 72}{42} = \frac{99}{42} = \frac{33}{14}$$

The solution is $\left[\frac{3}{2}, \frac{13}{14}, \frac{33}{14}\right]$.

48.

$$x = \frac{\begin{vmatrix} 1 & -1 & 2 \\ 3 & -1 & 2 \\ 1 & 3 & 1 \end{vmatrix}}{\begin{vmatrix} 3 & -1 & 2 \\ 1 & -1 & 2 \\ -2 & 3 & 1 \end{vmatrix}} = \frac{14}{-14} = -1$$

$$y = \frac{\begin{vmatrix} 3 & 1 & 2 \\ 1 & 3 & 2 \\ -2 & 1 & 1 \end{vmatrix}}{-14} = \frac{12}{-14} = -\frac{6}{7}$$

$$z = \frac{\begin{vmatrix} 3 & -1 & 1 \\ 1 & -1 & 3 \\ -2 & 3 & 1 \end{vmatrix}}{-14} = \frac{-22}{-14} = \frac{11}{7}$$

49. $0x + 6y + 6z = -1$
     $8x + 0y + 6z = -1$
     $4x + 9y + 0z = 8$

$$x = \frac{\begin{vmatrix} -1 & 6 & 6 \\ -1 & 0 & 6 \\ 8 & 9 & 0 \end{vmatrix}}{\begin{vmatrix} 0 & 6 & 6 \\ 8 & 0 & 6 \\ 4 & 9 & 0 \end{vmatrix}}$$

$$= \frac{-1\begin{vmatrix} 0 & 6 \\ 9 & 0 \end{vmatrix} - (-1)\begin{vmatrix} 6 & 6 \\ 9 & 0 \end{vmatrix} + 8\begin{vmatrix} 6 & 6 \\ 0 & 6 \end{vmatrix}}{0\begin{vmatrix} 0 & 6 \\ 9 & 0 \end{vmatrix} - 8\begin{vmatrix} 6 & 6 \\ 9 & 0 \end{vmatrix} + 4\begin{vmatrix} 6 & 6 \\ 0 & 6 \end{vmatrix}}$$

$$= \frac{-1(-54) + 1(-54) + 8(36)}{0(-54) - 8(-54) + 4(36)} = \frac{54 - 54 + 288}{0 + 432 + 144}$$

$$= \frac{288}{576} = \frac{1}{2}$$

$$y = \frac{\begin{vmatrix} 0 & -1 & 6 \\ 8 & -1 & 6 \\ 4 & 8 & 0 \end{vmatrix}}{576} = \frac{384}{576} = \frac{2}{3}$$

$$z = \frac{\begin{vmatrix} 0 & 6 & -1 \\ 8 & 0 & -1 \\ 4 & 9 & 8 \end{vmatrix}}{576} = \frac{-480}{576} = -\frac{5}{6}$$

The solution is $\left(\frac{1}{2}, \frac{2}{3}, -\frac{5}{6}\right)$.

50.

$$x = \frac{\begin{vmatrix} 2 & 5 & 0 \\ 7 & 0 & -3 \\ -1 & 4 & 2 \end{vmatrix}}{\begin{vmatrix} 3 & 5 & 0 \\ 2 & 0 & -3 \\ 0 & 4 & 2 \end{vmatrix}} = \frac{-31}{16} = -\frac{31}{16}$$

$$y = \frac{\begin{vmatrix} 3 & 2 & 0 \\ 2 & 7 & -3 \\ 0 & -1 & 2 \end{vmatrix}}{16} = \frac{25}{16}$$

$$z = \frac{\begin{vmatrix} 3 & 5 & 2 \\ 2 & 0 & 7 \\ 0 & 4 & -1 \end{vmatrix}}{16} = \frac{-58}{16} = -\frac{29}{8}$$

51. $\begin{vmatrix} x & 5 \\ -4 & x \end{vmatrix} = 24$

     $x^2 + 20 = 24$
     $x^2 = 4$
     $x = \pm 2$

52. $\begin{vmatrix} y & 2 \\ 3 & y \end{vmatrix} = y$

     $y^2 - 6 = y$
     $y^2 - y - 6 = 0$
     $(y - 3)(y + 2) = 0$
     $y = 3$ or $y = -2$

53. $\begin{vmatrix} x & -3 \\ -1 & x \end{vmatrix} \geqslant 0$

     $x^2 - 3 \geqslant 0$

The solutions of $f(x) = x^2 - 3 = 0$ are $-\sqrt{3}$ and $\sqrt{3}$. They divide the real-number line as shown.

We try test numbers in each interval.

$f(-2) = (-2)^2 - 3 = 4 - 3 = 1$
$f(0) = 0^2 - 3 = -3$
$f(2) = 2^2 - 3 = 4 - 3 = 1$

Since the inequality is $\geqslant$, we include $\pm\sqrt{3}$ in the solution set. The solution set is $\{x | x \leqslant -\sqrt{3} \text{ or } x \geqslant \sqrt{3}\}$.

<u>54.</u> $\begin{vmatrix} y & -5 \\ -2 & y \end{vmatrix} < 0$

$y^2 - 10 < 0$

$\qquad y^2 < 10$

Then $-\sqrt{10} < y < \sqrt{10}$.

<u>55.</u> $\begin{vmatrix} x+3 & 4 \\ x-3 & 5 \end{vmatrix} = -7$

$(x + 3)(5) - (x - 3)4 = -7$

$\qquad 5x + 15 - 4x + 12 = -7$

$\qquad\qquad\qquad x + 27 = -7$

$\qquad\qquad\qquad\qquad x = -34$

<u>56.</u> $\begin{vmatrix} m + 2 & -3 \\ m + 5 & -4 \end{vmatrix} = 3m - 5$

$(m + 2)(-4) - (m + 5)(-3) = 3m - 5$

$\qquad -4m - 8 + 3m + 15 = 3m - 5$

$\qquad\qquad\qquad\qquad 12 = 4m$

$\qquad\qquad\qquad\qquad\; 3 = m$

<u>57.</u> $\begin{vmatrix} 2 & x & 1 \\ 1 & 2 & -1 \\ 3 & 4 & -2 \end{vmatrix} = -6$

$2\begin{vmatrix} 2 & -1 \\ 4 & -2 \end{vmatrix} - 1\begin{vmatrix} x & 1 \\ 4 & -2 \end{vmatrix} + 3\begin{vmatrix} x & 1 \\ 2 & -1 \end{vmatrix} = -6$

$\qquad 2(-4 + 4) - 1(-2x - 4) + 3(-x - 2) = -6$

$\qquad\qquad\qquad\qquad 2x + 4 - 3x - 6 = -6$

$\qquad\qquad\qquad\qquad\qquad\qquad -x - 2 = -6$

$\qquad\qquad\qquad\qquad\qquad\qquad\qquad -x = -4$

$\qquad\qquad\qquad\qquad\qquad\qquad\qquad\; x = 4$

<u>58.</u> $\begin{vmatrix} x & 2 & x \\ 3 & -1 & 1 \\ 1 & -2 & 2 \end{vmatrix} = -10$

Add the second column of the determinant to the third column.

$\begin{vmatrix} x & 2 & x + 2 \\ 3 & -1 & 0 \\ 1 & -2 & 0 \end{vmatrix} = -10$

$(x + 2)\begin{vmatrix} 3 & -1 \\ 1 & -2 \end{vmatrix} = -10$

$\qquad (x + 2)(-5) = -10$

$\qquad\qquad x + 2 = 2$

$\qquad\qquad\qquad\; x = 0$

<u>59.</u> - <u>64.</u>   Answers may vary

59. $2L + 2W = \begin{vmatrix} L & -W \\ 2 & 2 \end{vmatrix}$

60. $\begin{vmatrix} \pi & -h \\ \pi & r \end{vmatrix}$

61. $a^2 + b^2 = \begin{vmatrix} a & b \\ -b & a \end{vmatrix}$

62. $\begin{vmatrix} \frac{1}{2}h & -b \\ \frac{1}{2}h & a \end{vmatrix}$

63. $2\pi r^2 + 2\pi rh = \begin{vmatrix} 2\pi r & 2\pi r \\ -h & r \end{vmatrix}$

64. $\begin{vmatrix} x^2 & 1 \\ Q^2 & y^2 \end{vmatrix}$

65. $\begin{vmatrix} x & y & 1 \\ x_1 & y_1 & 1 \\ x_2 & y_2 & 1 \end{vmatrix} = 0$

We first evaluate the determinant. Here we evaluate by expanding about the 1st row.

$$x(-1)^{1+1} \cdot \begin{vmatrix} y_1 & 1 \\ y_2 & 1 \end{vmatrix} + y(-1)^{1+2} \cdot \begin{vmatrix} x_1 & 1 \\ x_2 & 1 \end{vmatrix} + 1(-1)^{1+3} \cdot \begin{vmatrix} x_1 & y_1 \\ x_2 & y_2 \end{vmatrix} = 0$$

$$x(y_1 - y_2) - y(x_1 - x_2) + 1(x_1 y_2 - x_2 y_1) = 0$$
$$xy_1 - xy_2 - yx_1 + yx_2 + x_1 y_2 - x_2 y_1 = 0$$

The two-point equation of the line that contains the points (x_1, y_1) and (x_2, y_2) is

$$y - y_1 = \frac{y_2 - y_1}{x_2 - x_1}(x - x_1)$$

$$(y - y_1)(x_2 - x_1) = (y_2 - y_1)(x - x_1) \qquad \text{(Multiplying by } x_2 - x_1\text{)}$$

$$yx_2 - yx_1 - y_1 x_2 + y_1 x_1 = y_2 x - y_2 x_1 - y_1 x + y_1 x_1 \qquad \text{(Using FOIL)}$$

$$xy_1 - xy_2 - yx_1 + yx_2 + x_1 y_2 - x_2 y_1 = 0$$

Thus $\begin{vmatrix} x & y & 1 \\ x_1 & y_1 & 1 \\ x_2 & y_2 & 1 \end{vmatrix} = 0$ and $y - y_1 = \frac{y_2 - y_1}{x_2 - x_1}(x - x_1)$ are equivalent.

66. From Exercise 65, we know that the equation of line ℓ through
(x_2, y_2), (x_3, y_3) is $\begin{vmatrix} x & y & 1 \\ x_2 & y_2 & 1 \\ x_3 & y_3 & 1 \end{vmatrix} = 0.$

Then (x_1, y_1) also lies on ℓ if and only if
$\begin{vmatrix} x_1 & y_1 & 1 \\ x_2 & y_2 & 1 \\ x_3 & y_3 & 1 \end{vmatrix} = 0.$

<u>67.</u> See the answer section in the text.

<u>68.</u> NOTICE: Parallel lines, by definition, are not coincident;

E_1, E_2 are the given equations;

m_1, m_2 are slopes;

D, D_x, D_y are the given determinants.

(I) If D = 0, then $a_1b_2 - a_2b_1 = 0$. If b_1, $b_2 \neq 0$ then

$\dfrac{-a_1}{b_1} = \dfrac{-a_2}{b_2}$ and $m_1 = m_2$. Thus, ℓ_1 and ℓ_2 are either parallel

or coincident. If either of b_1, b_2 is 0, so is the other, since

$a_1b_2 - a_2b_1 = 0$; and both lines are vertical and either parallel or

coincident.

(II) If the lines coincide, $E_2 = k \cdot E_1$, $k \neq 0$; and

ℓ_1: $a_1x + b_1y = c_1$,

ℓ_2: $ka_1x + kb_1y = kc_1$.

Then $D_x = 0$ <u>and</u> $D_y = 0$. Thus a sufficient condition for

<u>distinct</u> lines is $D_x \neq 0$ or $D_y \neq 0$.

In conclusion, sufficient conditions for two lines to be parallel

are: D = 0 and $D_x \neq 0$ or $D_y \neq 0$.

Exercise Set 9.6

<u>1.</u>

$$A = \begin{bmatrix} 3 & 2 \\ 5 & 3 \end{bmatrix}$$

$$\begin{bmatrix} 3 & 2 & 1 & 0 \\ 5 & 3 & 0 & 1 \end{bmatrix} = \begin{bmatrix} 3 & 2 & 1 & 0 \\ 15 & 9 & 0 & 3 \end{bmatrix} \quad R_2' = 3R_2$$

$$= \begin{bmatrix} 3 & 2 & 1 & 0 \\ 0 & -1 & -5 & 3 \end{bmatrix} \quad R_2' = -5R_1 + R_2$$

$$= \begin{bmatrix} 3 & 2 & 1 & 0 \\ 0 & 1 & 5 & -3 \end{bmatrix} \quad R_2' = -1 \cdot R_2$$

$$= \begin{bmatrix} 3 & 0 & -9 & 6 \\ 0 & 1 & 5 & -3 \end{bmatrix} \quad R_1' = -2R_2 + R_1$$

$$= \begin{bmatrix} 1 & 0 & -3 & 2 \\ 0 & 1 & 5 & -3 \end{bmatrix} \quad R_1' = \frac{1}{3} R_1$$

$$A^{-1} = \begin{bmatrix} -3 & 2 \\ 5 & -3 \end{bmatrix}$$

$\underline{2}.$ $\begin{bmatrix} 3 & 5 & 1 & 0 \\ 1 & 2 & 0 & 1 \end{bmatrix} = \begin{bmatrix} 3 & 5 & 1 & 0 \\ 3 & 6 & 0 & 3 \end{bmatrix}$ $R_2' = 3R_2$

$= \begin{bmatrix} 3 & 5 & 1 & 0 \\ 0 & 1 & -1 & 3 \end{bmatrix}$ $R_2' = -1 \cdot R_1 + R_2$

$= \begin{bmatrix} 3 & 0 & 6 & -15 \\ 0 & 1 & -1 & 3 \end{bmatrix}$ $R_1' = -5R_2 + R_1$

$= \begin{bmatrix} 1 & 0 & 2 & -5 \\ 0 & 1 & -1 & 3 \end{bmatrix}$ $R_1' = \frac{1}{3} R_1$

$A^{-1} = \begin{bmatrix} 2 & -5 \\ -1 & 3 \end{bmatrix}$

$\underline{3}.$ $A = \begin{bmatrix} 11 & 3 \\ 7 & 2 \end{bmatrix}$

$\begin{bmatrix} 11 & 3 & 1 & 0 \\ 7 & 2 & 0 & 1 \end{bmatrix} = \begin{bmatrix} 11 & 3 & 1 & 0 \\ 77 & 22 & 0 & 11 \end{bmatrix}$ $R_2' = 11R_2$

$= \begin{bmatrix} 11 & 3 & 1 & 0 \\ 0 & 1 & -7 & 11 \end{bmatrix}$ $R_2' = -7R_1 + R_2$

$= \begin{bmatrix} 11 & 0 & 22 & -33 \\ 0 & 1 & -7 & 11 \end{bmatrix}$ $R_1' = -3R_2 + R_1$

$= \begin{bmatrix} 1 & 0 & 2 & -3 \\ 0 & 1 & -7 & 11 \end{bmatrix}$ $R_1' = \frac{1}{11} R_1$

$A^{-1} = \begin{bmatrix} 2 & -3 \\ -7 & 11 \end{bmatrix}$

$\underline{4}.$ $\begin{bmatrix} 8 & 5 & 1 & 0 \\ 5 & 3 & 0 & 1 \end{bmatrix} = \begin{bmatrix} 8 & 5 & 1 & 0 \\ 40 & 24 & 0 & 8 \end{bmatrix}$ $R_2' = 8R_2$

$= \begin{bmatrix} 8 & 5 & 1 & 0 \\ 0 & -1 & -5 & 8 \end{bmatrix}$ $R_2' = -5R_1 + R_2$

$= \begin{bmatrix} 8 & 0 & -24 & 40 \\ 0 & -1 & -5 & 8 \end{bmatrix}$ $R_1' = 5R_2 + R_1$

$= \begin{bmatrix} 1 & 0 & -3 & 5 \\ 0 & 1 & 5 & -8 \end{bmatrix}$ $R_1' = \frac{1}{8} R_1$
$R_2' = -1 \cdot R_2$

$A^{-1} = \begin{bmatrix} -3 & 5 \\ 5 & -8 \end{bmatrix}$

5.

$$A = \begin{bmatrix} 4 & -3 \\ 1 & 2 \end{bmatrix}$$

$$\begin{bmatrix} 4 & -3 & 1 & 0 \\ 1 & 2 & 0 & 1 \end{bmatrix} = \begin{bmatrix} 1 & 2 & 0 & 1 \\ 4 & -3 & 1 & 0 \end{bmatrix} \quad \begin{array}{l} R_1' = R_2 \\ R_2' = R_1 \end{array}$$

$$= \begin{bmatrix} 1 & 2 & 0 & 1 \\ 0 & -11 & 1 & -4 \end{bmatrix} \quad R_2' = -4R_1 + R_2$$

$$= \begin{bmatrix} 11 & 22 & 0 & 11 \\ 0 & -11 & 1 & -4 \end{bmatrix} \quad R_1' = 11R_1$$

$$= \begin{bmatrix} 11 & 0 & 2 & 3 \\ 0 & -11 & 1 & -4 \end{bmatrix} \quad R_1' = 2R_2 + R_1$$

$$= \begin{bmatrix} 1 & 0 & \frac{2}{11} & \frac{3}{11} \\ 0 & 1 & -\frac{1}{11} & \frac{4}{11} \end{bmatrix} \quad \begin{array}{l} R_1' = \frac{1}{11} R_1 \\ R_2' = -\frac{1}{11} R_2 \end{array}$$

$$A^{-1} = \begin{bmatrix} \frac{2}{11} & \frac{3}{11} \\ -\frac{1}{11} & \frac{4}{11} \end{bmatrix}$$

6.

$$\begin{bmatrix} 0 & -1 & 1 & 0 \\ 1 & 0 & 0 & 1 \end{bmatrix} = \begin{bmatrix} 1 & 0 & 0 & 1 \\ 0 & -1 & 1 & 0 \end{bmatrix} \quad \begin{array}{l} R_1' = R_2 \\ R_2' = R_1 \end{array}$$

$$= \begin{bmatrix} 1 & 0 & 0 & 1 \\ 0 & 1 & -1 & 0 \end{bmatrix} \quad R_2' = -1 \cdot R_2$$

$$A^{-1} = \begin{bmatrix} 0 & 1 \\ -1 & 0 \end{bmatrix}$$

7.

$$A = \begin{bmatrix} 3 & 1 & 0 \\ 1 & 1 & 1 \\ 1 & -1 & 2 \end{bmatrix}$$

$$\begin{bmatrix} 3 & 1 & 0 & 1 & 0 & 0 \\ 1 & 1 & 1 & 0 & 1 & 0 \\ 1 & -1 & 2 & 0 & 0 & 1 \end{bmatrix}$$

$$= \begin{bmatrix} 1 & 1 & 1 & 0 & 1 & 0 \\ 3 & 1 & 0 & 1 & 0 & 0 \\ 1 & -1 & 2 & 0 & 0 & 1 \end{bmatrix} \quad \begin{array}{l} R_1' = R_2 \\ R_2' = R_1 \end{array}$$

$$= \begin{bmatrix} 1 & 1 & 1 & 0 & 1 & 0 \\ 0 & -2 & -3 & 1 & -3 & 0 \\ 0 & -2 & 1 & 0 & -1 & 1 \end{bmatrix} \begin{array}{l} R_2' = -3R_1 + R_2 \\ R_3' = -1 \cdot R_1 + R_3 \end{array}$$

$$= \begin{bmatrix} 1 & 1 & 1 & 0 & 1 & 0 \\ 0 & -2 & -3 & 1 & -3 & 0 \\ 0 & 0 & 4 & -1 & 2 & 1 \end{bmatrix} \begin{array}{l} \\ R_3' = -1 \cdot R_2 + R_3 \end{array}$$

$$= \begin{bmatrix} 4 & 4 & 4 & 0 & 4 & 0 \\ 0 & -8 & -12 & 4 & -12 & 0 \\ 0 & 0 & 4 & -1 & 2 & 1 \end{bmatrix} \begin{array}{l} R_1' = 4R_1 \\ R_2' = 4R_2 \end{array}$$

$$= \begin{bmatrix} 4 & 4 & 0 & 1 & 2 & -1 \\ 0 & -8 & 0 & 1 & -6 & 3 \\ 0 & 0 & 4 & -1 & 2 & 1 \end{bmatrix} \begin{array}{l} R_1' = -1 \cdot R_3 + R_1 \\ R_2' = 3R_3 + R_2 \end{array}$$

$$= \begin{bmatrix} 8 & 8 & 0 & 2 & 4 & -2 \\ 0 & -8 & 0 & 1 & -6 & 3 \\ 0 & 0 & 4 & -1 & 2 & 1 \end{bmatrix} \begin{array}{l} R_1' = 2R_1 \end{array}$$

$$= \begin{bmatrix} 8 & 0 & 0 & 3 & -2 & 1 \\ 0 & -8 & 0 & 1 & -6 & 3 \\ 0 & 0 & 4 & -1 & 2 & 1 \end{bmatrix} \begin{array}{l} R_1' = R_2 + R_1 \end{array}$$

$$= \begin{bmatrix} 1 & 0 & 0 & \frac{3}{8} & -\frac{1}{4} & \frac{1}{8} \\ 0 & 1 & 0 & -\frac{1}{8} & \frac{3}{4} & -\frac{3}{8} \\ 0 & 0 & 1 & -\frac{1}{4} & \frac{1}{2} & \frac{1}{4} \end{bmatrix} \begin{array}{l} R_1' = \frac{1}{8} R_1 \\ R_2' = -\frac{1}{8} R_2 \\ R_3' = \frac{1}{4} R_3 \end{array}$$

$$A^{-1} = \begin{bmatrix} \frac{3}{8} & -\frac{1}{4} & \frac{1}{8} \\ -\frac{1}{8} & \frac{3}{4} & -\frac{3}{8} \\ -\frac{1}{4} & \frac{1}{2} & \frac{1}{4} \end{bmatrix}$$

8. $$\begin{bmatrix} 1 & 0 & 1 & 1 & 0 & 0 \\ 2 & 1 & 0 & 0 & 1 & 0 \\ 1 & -1 & 1 & 0 & 0 & 1 \end{bmatrix}$$

$$= \begin{bmatrix} 1 & 0 & 1 & 1 & 0 & 0 \\ 0 & 1 & -2 & -2 & 1 & 0 \\ 0 & -1 & 0 & -1 & 0 & 1 \end{bmatrix} \begin{array}{l} R_2' = -2R_1 + R_2 \\ R_3' = -1 \cdot R_1 + R_3 \end{array}$$

$$= \begin{bmatrix} 1 & 0 & 1 & 1 & 0 & 0 \\ 0 & 1 & -2 & -2 & 1 & 0 \\ 0 & 0 & -2 & -3 & 1 & 1 \end{bmatrix} \begin{array}{l} \\ R_3' = R_2 + R_1 \end{array}$$

$$= \begin{bmatrix} 2 & 0 & 2 & 2 & 0 & 0 \\ 0 & 1 & -2 & -2 & 1 & 0 \\ 0 & 0 & -2 & -3 & 1 & 1 \end{bmatrix} \quad R_1' = 2R_1$$

$$= \begin{bmatrix} 2 & 0 & 0 & -1 & 1 & 1 \\ 0 & 1 & 0 & 1 & 0 & -1 \\ 0 & 0 & -2 & -3 & 1 & 1 \end{bmatrix} \quad \begin{array}{l} R_1' = R_3 + R_1 \\ R_2' = -1 \cdot R_3 + R_2 \end{array}$$

$$= \begin{bmatrix} 1 & 0 & 0 & -\frac{1}{2} & \frac{1}{2} & \frac{1}{2} \\ 0 & 1 & 0 & 1 & 0 & -1 \\ 0 & 0 & 1 & \frac{3}{2} & -\frac{1}{2} & -\frac{1}{2} \end{bmatrix} \quad \begin{array}{l} R_1' = \frac{1}{2} R_1 \\ \\ R_3' = -\frac{1}{2} R_3 \end{array}$$

$$A^{-1} = \begin{bmatrix} -\frac{1}{2} & \frac{1}{2} & \frac{1}{2} \\ 1 & 0 & -1 \\ \frac{3}{2} & -\frac{1}{2} & -\frac{1}{2} \end{bmatrix}$$

9.

$$A = \begin{bmatrix} 1 & -1 & 2 \\ 0 & 1 & 3 \\ 2 & 1 & -2 \end{bmatrix}$$

$$\begin{bmatrix} 1 & -1 & 2 & 1 & 0 & 0 \\ 0 & 1 & 3 & 0 & 1 & 0 \\ 2 & 1 & -2 & 0 & 0 & 1 \end{bmatrix}$$

$$= \begin{bmatrix} 1 & -1 & 2 & 1 & 0 & 0 \\ 0 & 1 & 3 & 0 & 1 & 0 \\ 0 & 3 & -6 & -2 & 0 & 1 \end{bmatrix} \quad R_3' = -2R_1 + R_3$$

$$= \begin{bmatrix} 1 & -1 & 2 & 1 & 0 & 0 \\ 0 & 1 & 3 & 0 & 1 & 0 \\ 0 & 0 & -15 & -2 & -3 & 1 \end{bmatrix} \quad R_3' = -3R_2 + R_3$$

$$= \begin{bmatrix} 15 & -15 & 30 & 15 & 0 & 0 \\ 0 & 5 & 15 & 0 & 5 & 0 \\ 0 & 0 & -15 & -2 & -3 & 1 \end{bmatrix} \quad \begin{array}{l} R_1' = 15R_1 \\ R_2' = 5R_2 \end{array}$$

$$= \begin{bmatrix} 15 & -15 & 0 & 11 & -6 & 2 \\ 0 & 5 & 0 & -2 & 2 & 1 \\ 0 & 0 & -15 & -2 & -3 & -1 \end{bmatrix} \quad \begin{array}{l} R_1' = 2R_3 + R_1 \\ R_2' = R_3 + R_2 \end{array}$$

$$= \begin{bmatrix} 15 & 0 & 0 & 5 & 0 & 5 \\ 0 & 5 & 0 & -2 & 2 & 1 \\ 0 & 0 & -15 & -2 & -3 & -1 \end{bmatrix} \quad R_1' = 3R_2 + R_1$$

$$= \begin{bmatrix} 1 & 0 & 0 & \frac{1}{3} & 0 & \frac{1}{3} \\ 0 & 1 & 0 & -\frac{2}{5} & \frac{2}{5} & \frac{1}{5} \\ 0 & 0 & 1 & \frac{2}{15} & \frac{1}{5} & -\frac{1}{15} \end{bmatrix} \quad \begin{array}{l} R_1' = \frac{1}{15} R_1 \\ R_2' = \frac{1}{5} R_2 \\ R_3' = -\frac{1}{15} R_3 \end{array}$$

$$A^{-1} = \begin{bmatrix} \frac{1}{3} & 0 & \frac{1}{3} \\ -\frac{2}{5} & \frac{2}{5} & \frac{1}{5} \\ \frac{2}{15} & \frac{1}{5} & -\frac{1}{15} \end{bmatrix}$$

10.
$$\begin{bmatrix} 1 & -1 & 2 & 1 & 0 & 0 \\ 0 & 1 & 2 & 0 & 1 & 0 \\ 1 & -3 & -4 & 0 & 0 & 1 \end{bmatrix}$$

$$= \begin{bmatrix} 1 & -1 & 2 & 1 & 0 & 0 \\ 0 & 1 & 2 & 0 & 1 & 0 \\ 0 & -2 & -6 & -1 & 0 & 1 \end{bmatrix} \quad R_3' = -1 \cdot R_1 + R_3$$

$$= \begin{bmatrix} 1 & -1 & 2 & 1 & 0 & 0 \\ 0 & 1 & 2 & 0 & 1 & 0 \\ 0 & 0 & -2 & -1 & 2 & 1 \end{bmatrix} \quad R_3' = 2R_2 + R_3$$

$$= \begin{bmatrix} 1 & -1 & 0 & 0 & 2 & 1 \\ 0 & 1 & 0 & -1 & 3 & 1 \\ 0 & 0 & -2 & -1 & 2 & 1 \end{bmatrix} \quad \begin{array}{l} R_1' = R_3 + R_1 \\ R_2' = R_3 + R_2 \end{array}$$

$$= \begin{bmatrix} 1 & 0 & 0 & -1 & 5 & 2 \\ 0 & 1 & 0 & -1 & 3 & 1 \\ 0 & 0 & -2 & -1 & 2 & 1 \end{bmatrix} \quad R_1' = R_2 + R_1$$

$$= \begin{bmatrix} 1 & 0 & 0 & -1 & 5 & 2 \\ 0 & 1 & 0 & -1 & 3 & 1 \\ 0 & 0 & 1 & \frac{1}{2} & -1 & -\frac{1}{2} \end{bmatrix} \quad R_3' = -\frac{1}{2} R_3$$

$$A^{-1} = \begin{bmatrix} -1 & 5 & 2 \\ -1 & 3 & 1 \\ \frac{1}{2} & -1 & -\frac{1}{2} \end{bmatrix}$$

11. We cannot obtain the identity matrix on the left using the Gauss-Jordan reduction method. Thus, A^{-1} does not exist.

12.

$$[A|I] = \begin{bmatrix} -2 & 5 & 3 & 1 & 0 & 0 \\ 4 & -1 & 3 & 0 & 1 & 0 \\ 7 & -2 & 5 & 0 & 0 & 1 \end{bmatrix} \text{ is equivalent to } \begin{bmatrix} 1 & 0 & 1 & \cdots \\ 0 & 1 & 1 & \cdots \\ 0 & 0 & 0 & \cdots \end{bmatrix}$$

and it is clear that no further row-equivalent operations will bring

$$\begin{bmatrix} 1 & 0 & 1 \\ 0 & 1 & 1 \\ 0 & 0 & 0 \end{bmatrix} \text{ to the form } \begin{bmatrix} 1 & 0 & 0 \\ 0 & 1 & 0 \\ 0 & 0 & 1 \end{bmatrix}. \text{ Thus } A^{-1} \text{ does not exist.}$$

13.

$$A = \begin{bmatrix} 1 & 2 & 3 & 4 \\ 0 & 1 & 3 & -5 \\ 0 & 0 & 1 & -2 \\ 0 & 0 & 0 & -1 \end{bmatrix}$$

$$\begin{bmatrix} 1 & 2 & 3 & 4 & 1 & 0 & 0 & 0 \\ 0 & 1 & 3 & -5 & 0 & 1 & 0 & 0 \\ 0 & 0 & 1 & -2 & 0 & 0 & 1 & 0 \\ 0 & 0 & 0 & -1 & 0 & 0 & 0 & 1 \end{bmatrix}$$

$$= \begin{bmatrix} 1 & 2 & 3 & 0 & 1 & 0 & 0 & 4 \\ 0 & 1 & 3 & 0 & 0 & 1 & 0 & -5 \\ 0 & 0 & 1 & 0 & 0 & 0 & 1 & -2 \\ 0 & 0 & 0 & -1 & 0 & 0 & 0 & 1 \end{bmatrix} \begin{array}{l} R_1' = 4R_4 + R_1 \\ R_2' = -5R_4 + R_2 \\ R_3' = -2R_4 + R_3 \\ \\ \end{array}$$

$$= \begin{bmatrix} 1 & 2 & 0 & 0 & 1 & 0 & -3 & 10 \\ 0 & 1 & 0 & 0 & 0 & 1 & -3 & 1 \\ 0 & 0 & 1 & 0 & 0 & 0 & 1 & -2 \\ 0 & 0 & 0 & -1 & 0 & 0 & 0 & 1 \end{bmatrix} \begin{array}{l} R_1' = -3R_3 + R_1 \\ R_2' = -3R_3 + R_2 \\ \\ \\ \end{array}$$

$$= \begin{bmatrix} 1 & 0 & 0 & 0 & 1 & -2 & 3 & 8 \\ 0 & 1 & 0 & 0 & 0 & 1 & -3 & 1 \\ 0 & 0 & 1 & 0 & 0 & 0 & 1 & -2 \\ 0 & 0 & 0 & -1 & 0 & 0 & 0 & 1 \end{bmatrix} \begin{array}{l} R_1' = -2R_2 + R_1 \\ \\ \\ \\ \end{array}$$

$$= \begin{bmatrix} 1 & 0 & 0 & 0 & 1 & -2 & 3 & 8 \\ 0 & 1 & 0 & 0 & 0 & 1 & -3 & 1 \\ 0 & 0 & 1 & 0 & 0 & 0 & 1 & -2 \\ 0 & 0 & 0 & 1 & 0 & 0 & 0 & -1 \end{bmatrix} \begin{array}{l} \\ \\ \\ R_4' = -1 \cdot R_4 \end{array}$$

$$A^{-1} = \begin{bmatrix} 1 & -2 & 3 & 8 \\ 0 & 1 & -3 & 1 \\ 0 & 0 & 1 & -2 \\ 0 & 0 & 0 & -1 \end{bmatrix}$$

<u>14.</u>

$$[A \mid I] = \begin{bmatrix} -2 & -3 & 4 & 1 & 1 & 0 & 0 & 0 \\ 0 & 1 & 1 & 0 & 0 & 1 & 0 & 0 \\ 0 & 4 & -6 & 1 & 0 & 0 & 1 & 0 \\ -2 & -2 & 5 & 1 & 0 & 0 & 0 & 1 \end{bmatrix} \text{ is row-equivalent to}$$

$$\begin{bmatrix} 1 & 0 & 0 & -\frac{17}{20} & \cdot & \cdot & \cdot & \cdot \\ 0 & 1 & 0 & \frac{1}{10} & \cdot & \cdot & \cdot & \cdot \\ 0 & 0 & 1 & \frac{-1}{10} & \cdot & \cdot & \cdot & \cdot \\ 0 & 0 & 0 & 0 & \cdot & \cdot & \cdot & \cdot \end{bmatrix}$$

and it is clear that no further row-equivalent operations will bring

$$\begin{bmatrix} 1 & 0 & 0 & -\frac{17}{20} \\ 0 & 1 & 0 & \frac{1}{10} \\ 0 & 0 & 1 & -\frac{1}{10} \\ 0 & 0 & 0 & 0 \end{bmatrix} \text{ to the form } \begin{bmatrix} 1 & 0 & 0 & 0 \\ 0 & 1 & 0 & 0 \\ 0 & 0 & 1 & 0 \\ 0 & 0 & 0 & 1 \end{bmatrix}.$$

Hence A^{-1} does not exist.

<u>15.</u> We cannot obtain the identity matrix on the left using the Gauss-Jordan reduction method. Then, A^{-1} does not exist.

<u>16.</u> We cannot obtain the identity matrix on the left using the Gauss-Jordan reduction method. Then, A^{-1} does not exist.

<u>17.</u> $11x + 3y = -4,$
    $7x + 2y = 5$

We write a matrix equation equivalent to this system.

$$\begin{bmatrix} 11 & 3 \\ 7 & 2 \end{bmatrix} \begin{bmatrix} x \\ y \end{bmatrix} = \begin{bmatrix} -4 \\ 5 \end{bmatrix}$$

We solve the matrix equation by multiplying by A^{-1} on the left on each side.

$$\begin{bmatrix} 2 & -3 \\ -7 & 11 \end{bmatrix} \begin{bmatrix} 11 & 3 \\ 7 & 2 \end{bmatrix} \begin{bmatrix} x \\ y \end{bmatrix} = \begin{bmatrix} 2 & -3 \\ -7 & 11 \end{bmatrix} \begin{bmatrix} -4 \\ 5 \end{bmatrix}$$

$$\begin{bmatrix} 1 & 0 \\ 0 & 1 \end{bmatrix} \begin{bmatrix} x \\ y \end{bmatrix} = \begin{bmatrix} -23 \\ 83 \end{bmatrix}$$

$$\begin{bmatrix} x \\ y \end{bmatrix} = \begin{bmatrix} -23 \\ 83 \end{bmatrix}$$

The solution of the system of equations is (-23, 83).

18.
$$\begin{bmatrix} x \\ y \end{bmatrix} = \begin{bmatrix} -3 & 5 \\ 5 & -8 \end{bmatrix} \begin{bmatrix} -6 \\ 2 \end{bmatrix} = \begin{bmatrix} 28 \\ -46 \end{bmatrix}$$

The solution of the system of equations is (28, -46).

19. 3x + y   = 2,
     2x - y + 2z = -5,
      x + y + z = 5

We write a matrix equation equivalent to this system.

$$\begin{bmatrix} 3 & 1 & 0 \\ 2 & -1 & 2 \\ 1 & 1 & 1 \end{bmatrix} \begin{bmatrix} x \\ y \\ z \end{bmatrix} = \begin{bmatrix} 2 \\ -5 \\ 5 \end{bmatrix}$$

We solve the matrix equation by multiplying by A^{-1} on the left on each side.

$$\frac{1}{9}\begin{bmatrix} 3 & 1 & -2 \\ 0 & -3 & 6 \\ -3 & 2 & 5 \end{bmatrix} \begin{bmatrix} 3 & 1 & 0 \\ 2 & -1 & 2 \\ 1 & 1 & 1 \end{bmatrix} \begin{bmatrix} x \\ y \\ z \end{bmatrix} = \frac{1}{9}\begin{bmatrix} 3 & 1 & -2 \\ 0 & -3 & 6 \\ -3 & 2 & 5 \end{bmatrix} \begin{bmatrix} 2 \\ -5 \\ 5 \end{bmatrix}$$

$$\begin{bmatrix} 1 & 0 & 0 \\ 0 & 1 & 0 \\ 0 & 0 & 1 \end{bmatrix} \begin{bmatrix} x \\ y \\ z \end{bmatrix} = \frac{1}{9}\begin{bmatrix} -9 \\ 45 \\ 9 \end{bmatrix}$$

$$\begin{bmatrix} x \\ y \\ z \end{bmatrix} = \begin{bmatrix} -1 \\ 5 \\ 1 \end{bmatrix}$$

The solution of the system of equations is (-1, 5, 1).

20.
$$\begin{bmatrix} x \\ y \\ z \end{bmatrix} = -\frac{1}{2}\begin{bmatrix} 1 & -1 & -1 \\ -3 & 0 & 2 \\ -2 & 1 & 1 \end{bmatrix} \begin{bmatrix} -4 \\ -3 \\ 1 \end{bmatrix} = \begin{bmatrix} 1 \\ -7 \\ -3 \end{bmatrix}$$

The solution of the system of equations is (1, -7, -3).

21. 4x - 3y = 2, $\begin{bmatrix} 4 & -3 \\ 1 & 2 \end{bmatrix} \begin{bmatrix} x \\ y \end{bmatrix} = \begin{bmatrix} 2 \\ -1 \end{bmatrix}$
      x + 2y = -1

The coefficient matrix is the matrix in Exercise 5. Its inverse is

$$\begin{bmatrix} \frac{2}{11} & \frac{3}{11} \\ -\frac{1}{11} & \frac{4}{11} \end{bmatrix}, \text{ or } \frac{1}{11}\begin{bmatrix} 2 & 3 \\ -1 & 4 \end{bmatrix}.$$

$$\begin{bmatrix} x \\ y \end{bmatrix} = \begin{bmatrix} \frac{2}{11} & \frac{3}{11} \\ -\frac{1}{11} & \frac{4}{11} \end{bmatrix} \begin{bmatrix} 2 \\ -1 \end{bmatrix} = \begin{bmatrix} \frac{1}{11} \\ -\frac{6}{11} \end{bmatrix}$$

The solution of the system is $\left(\frac{1}{11}, -\frac{6}{11}\right)$.

22.
$$\begin{bmatrix} 3 & 5 \\ 2 & 4 \end{bmatrix}\begin{bmatrix} x \\ y \end{bmatrix} = \begin{bmatrix} -4 \\ -2 \end{bmatrix}, \; A^{-1} = \begin{bmatrix} 2 & -\frac{5}{2} \\ -1 & \frac{3}{2} \end{bmatrix}$$

$$\begin{bmatrix} x \\ y \end{bmatrix} = \begin{bmatrix} 2 & -\frac{5}{2} \\ -1 & \frac{3}{2} \end{bmatrix}\begin{bmatrix} -4 \\ -2 \end{bmatrix} = \begin{bmatrix} -3 \\ 1 \end{bmatrix}$$

The solution of the system of equations is (-3, 1).

23. $7x - 2y = -3,$
$9x + 3y = 4$
$$\begin{bmatrix} 7 & -2 \\ 9 & 3 \end{bmatrix}\begin{bmatrix} x \\ y \end{bmatrix} = \begin{bmatrix} -3 \\ 4 \end{bmatrix}$$

The inverse of the coefficient matrix is $\begin{bmatrix} \frac{1}{13} & \frac{2}{39} \\ -\frac{3}{13} & \frac{7}{39} \end{bmatrix}$, or $\frac{1}{39}\begin{bmatrix} 3 & 2 \\ -9 & 7 \end{bmatrix}$.

$$\begin{bmatrix} x \\ y \end{bmatrix} = \begin{bmatrix} \frac{1}{13} & \frac{2}{39} \\ -\frac{3}{13} & \frac{7}{39} \end{bmatrix}\begin{bmatrix} -3 \\ 4 \end{bmatrix} = \begin{bmatrix} -\frac{1}{39} \\ \frac{55}{39} \end{bmatrix}$$

The solution of the system of equations is $\left(-\frac{1}{39}, \frac{55}{39}\right)$.

24.
$$\begin{bmatrix} 5 & 3 \\ 4 & -1 \end{bmatrix}\begin{bmatrix} x \\ y \end{bmatrix} = \begin{bmatrix} -2 \\ 1 \end{bmatrix}, \; A^{-1} = \frac{1}{17}\begin{bmatrix} 1 & 3 \\ 4 & -5 \end{bmatrix}$$

$$\begin{bmatrix} x \\ y \end{bmatrix} = \frac{1}{17}\begin{bmatrix} 1 & 3 \\ 4 & -5 \end{bmatrix}\begin{bmatrix} -2 \\ 1 \end{bmatrix} = \begin{bmatrix} \frac{1}{17} \\ -\frac{13}{17} \end{bmatrix}$$

The solution of the system of equations is $\left(\frac{1}{17}, -\frac{13}{17}\right)$.

25. $x \quad + z = 1,$
$2x + y \quad = 3,$
$x - y + z = 4$
$$\begin{bmatrix} 1 & 0 & 1 \\ 2 & 1 & 0 \\ 1 & -1 & 1 \end{bmatrix}\begin{bmatrix} x \\ y \\ z \end{bmatrix} = \begin{bmatrix} 1 \\ 3 \\ 4 \end{bmatrix}$$

The inverse of the coefficient matrix is

$$\frac{1}{2}\begin{bmatrix} -1 & 1 & 1 \\ 2 & 0 & -2 \\ 3 & -1 & -1 \end{bmatrix}.$$

$$\begin{bmatrix} x \\ y \\ z \end{bmatrix} = \frac{1}{2}\begin{bmatrix} -1 & 1 & 1 \\ 2 & 0 & -2 \\ 3 & -1 & -1 \end{bmatrix}\begin{bmatrix} 1 \\ 3 \\ 4 \end{bmatrix} = \begin{bmatrix} 3 \\ -3 \\ -2 \end{bmatrix}$$

The solution of the system of equations is (3, -3, -2).

26.
$$\begin{bmatrix} 1 & 2 & 3 \\ 2 & -3 & 4 \\ -3 & 5 & -6 \end{bmatrix} \begin{bmatrix} x \\ y \\ z \end{bmatrix} = \begin{bmatrix} -1 \\ 2 \\ 4 \end{bmatrix}, \quad A^{-1} = \begin{bmatrix} -2 & 27 & 17 \\ 0 & 3 & 2 \\ 1 & -11 & -7 \end{bmatrix}$$

$$\begin{bmatrix} x \\ y \\ z \end{bmatrix} = \begin{bmatrix} -2 & 27 & 17 \\ 0 & 3 & 2 \\ 1 & -11 & -7 \end{bmatrix} \begin{bmatrix} -1 \\ 2 \\ 4 \end{bmatrix} = \begin{bmatrix} 124 \\ 14 \\ -51 \end{bmatrix}$$

The solution of the system of equations is (124, 14, -51).

27.
$$\begin{aligned} 2w - 3x + 4y - 5z &= 0, \\ 3w - 2x + 7y - 3z &= 2, \\ w + x - y + z &= 1, \\ -w - 3x - 6y + 4z &= 6 \end{aligned} \qquad \begin{bmatrix} 2 & -3 & 4 & -5 \\ 3 & -2 & 7 & -3 \\ 1 & 1 & -1 & 1 \\ -1 & -3 & -6 & 4 \end{bmatrix} \begin{bmatrix} w \\ x \\ y \\ z \end{bmatrix} = \begin{bmatrix} 0 \\ 2 \\ 1 \\ 6 \end{bmatrix}$$

The inverse of the coefficient matrix is

$$\frac{1}{11,165} \begin{bmatrix} 1430 & 605 & 6985 & 495 \\ 440 & -1045 & 2145 & -1870 \\ -2035 & 2145 & -2640 & -275 \\ -3025 & 2585 & -605 & 1100 \end{bmatrix} .$$

$$\begin{bmatrix} w \\ x \\ y \\ z \end{bmatrix} = \frac{1}{11,165} \begin{bmatrix} 1430 & 605 & 6985 & 495 \\ 440 & -1045 & 2145 & -1870 \\ -2035 & 2145 & -2640 & -275 \\ -3025 & 2585 & -605 & 1100 \end{bmatrix} \begin{bmatrix} 0 \\ 2 \\ 1 \\ 6 \end{bmatrix}$$

$$= \begin{bmatrix} 1 \\ -1 \\ 0 \\ 1 \end{bmatrix}$$

The solution of the system of equations is (1, -1, 0, 1).

28.
$$\begin{bmatrix} 5 & -4 & 3 & -2 \\ 1 & 4 & -2 & 3 \\ 2 & -3 & 6 & -9 \\ 3 & -5 & 2 & -4 \end{bmatrix} \begin{bmatrix} w \\ x \\ y \\ z \end{bmatrix} = \begin{bmatrix} -6 \\ -5 \\ 14 \\ -3 \end{bmatrix}$$

$$A^{-1} = \frac{1}{302} \begin{bmatrix} 18 & 75 & 1 & 45 \\ -10 & 59 & 33 & -25 \\ 112 & -87 & 23 & -173 \\ 82 & -61 & -29 & -97 \end{bmatrix}$$

$$\begin{bmatrix} w \\ x \\ y \\ z \end{bmatrix} = \frac{1}{302} \begin{bmatrix} 18 & 75 & 1 & 45 \\ -10 & 59 & 33 & -25 \\ 112 & -87 & 23 & -173 \\ 82 & -61 & -29 & -97 \end{bmatrix} \begin{bmatrix} -6 \\ -5 \\ 14 \\ -3 \end{bmatrix} = \begin{bmatrix} -2 \\ 1 \\ 2 \\ -1 \end{bmatrix}$$

The solution of the system of equations is (-2, 1, 2, -1).

29.
$$\begin{bmatrix} a & b & c \\ d & e & f \\ g & h & i \end{bmatrix} \begin{bmatrix} 1 & 0 & 0 \\ 0 & 1 & 0 \\ 0 & 0 & 1 \end{bmatrix} = \begin{bmatrix} a & b & c \\ d & e & f \\ g & h & i \end{bmatrix}, \qquad AI = A$$

$$\begin{bmatrix} 1 & 0 & 0 \\ 0 & 1 & 0 \\ 0 & 0 & 1 \end{bmatrix} \begin{bmatrix} a & b & c \\ d & e & f \\ g & h & i \end{bmatrix} = \begin{bmatrix} a & b & c \\ d & e & f \\ g & h & i \end{bmatrix} \qquad IA = A$$

30. A^{-1} exists if and only if $x \neq 0$.

$$\begin{bmatrix} x | 1 \end{bmatrix} = \begin{bmatrix} 1 | \frac{1}{x} \end{bmatrix} \quad R_1' = \frac{1}{x} R_1$$

$$A^{-1} = \begin{bmatrix} \frac{1}{x} \end{bmatrix}$$

31.
$$A = \begin{bmatrix} x & 0 \\ 0 & y \end{bmatrix}$$

A^{-1} exists if and only if $xy \neq 0$.

$$\begin{bmatrix} x & 0 & 1 & 0 \\ 0 & y & 0 & 1 \end{bmatrix} = \begin{bmatrix} 1 & 0 & \frac{1}{x} & 0 \\ 0 & 1 & 0 & \frac{1}{y} \end{bmatrix} \quad \begin{matrix} R_1' = \frac{1}{x} R_1 \\ R_2' = \frac{1}{y} R_2 \end{matrix}$$

$$A^{-1} = \begin{bmatrix} \frac{1}{x} & 0 \\ 0 & \frac{1}{y} \end{bmatrix}$$

32. A^{-1} exists if and only if $xyz \neq 0$.

$$\begin{bmatrix} 0 & 0 & x & 1 & 0 & 0 \\ 0 & y & 0 & 0 & 1 & 0 \\ z & 0 & 0 & 0 & 0 & 1 \end{bmatrix} = \begin{bmatrix} z & 0 & 0 & 0 & 0 & 1 \\ 0 & y & 0 & 0 & 1 & 0 \\ 0 & 0 & x & 1 & 0 & 0 \end{bmatrix} \quad \begin{matrix} R_1' = R_3 \\ \\ R_3' = R_1 \end{matrix}$$

$$= \begin{bmatrix} 1 & 0 & 0 & 0 & 0 & \frac{1}{z} \\ 0 & 1 & 0 & 0 & \frac{1}{y} & 0 \\ 0 & 0 & 1 & \frac{1}{x} & 0 & 0 \end{bmatrix} \quad \begin{matrix} R_1' = \frac{1}{z} R_1 \\ R_2' = \frac{1}{y} R_2 \\ R_3' = \frac{1}{x} R_3 \end{matrix}$$

$$A^{-1} = \begin{bmatrix} 0 & 0 & \frac{1}{z} \\ 0 & \frac{1}{y} & 0 \\ \frac{1}{x} & 0 & 0 \end{bmatrix}$$

33.
$$A = \begin{bmatrix} x & 1 & 1 & 1 \\ 0 & y & 0 & 0 \\ 0 & 0 & z & 0 \\ 0 & 0 & 0 & w \end{bmatrix}$$

A^{-1} exists if and only if $xyzw \neq 0$.

$$\begin{bmatrix} x & 1 & 1 & 1 & 1 & 0 & 0 & 0 \\ 0 & y & 0 & 0 & 0 & 1 & 0 & 0 \\ 0 & 0 & z & 0 & 0 & 0 & 1 & 0 \\ 0 & 0 & 0 & w & 0 & 0 & 0 & 1 \end{bmatrix}$$

$$= \begin{bmatrix} -xw & -w & -w & -w & -w & 0 & 0 & 0 \\ 0 & y & 0 & 0 & 0 & 1 & 0 & 0 \\ 0 & 0 & z & 0 & 0 & 0 & 1 & 0 \\ 0 & 0 & 0 & w & 0 & 0 & 0 & 1 \end{bmatrix} \quad R_1' = -wR_1$$

$$= \begin{bmatrix} -xw & -w & -w & 0 & -w & 0 & 0 & 1 \\ 0 & y & 0 & 0 & 0 & 1 & 0 & 0 \\ 0 & 0 & z & 0 & 0 & 0 & 1 & 0 \\ 0 & 0 & 0 & w & 0 & 0 & 0 & 1 \end{bmatrix} \quad R_1' = R_4 + R_1$$

$$= \begin{bmatrix} -xzw & -zw & -zw & 0 & -zw & 0 & 0 & z \\ 0 & y & 0 & 0 & 0 & 1 & 0 & 0 \\ 0 & 0 & z & 0 & 0 & 0 & 1 & 0 \\ 0 & 0 & 0 & w & 0 & 0 & 0 & 1 \end{bmatrix} \quad R_1' = zR_1$$

$$= \begin{bmatrix} -xzw & -zw & 0 & 0 & -zw & 0 & w & z \\ 0 & y & 0 & 0 & 0 & 1 & 0 & 0 \\ 0 & 0 & z & 0 & 0 & 0 & 1 & 0 \\ 0 & 0 & 0 & w & 0 & 0 & 0 & 1 \end{bmatrix} \quad R_1' = wR_3 + R_1$$

$$= \begin{bmatrix} -xzyw & -zyw & 0 & 0 & -zyw & 0 & wy & yz \\ 0 & y & 0 & 0 & 0 & 1 & 0 & 0 \\ 0 & 0 & z & 0 & 0 & 0 & 1 & 0 \\ 0 & 0 & 0 & w & 0 & 0 & 0 & 1 \end{bmatrix} \quad R_1' = yR_1$$

$$= \begin{bmatrix} -xzyw & 0 & 0 & 0 & -zyw & zw & wy & yz \\ 0 & y & 0 & 0 & 0 & 1 & 0 & 0 \\ 0 & 0 & z & 0 & 0 & 0 & 1 & 0 \\ 0 & 0 & 0 & w & 0 & 0 & 0 & 1 \end{bmatrix} \quad R_1' = zwR_2 + R_1$$

$$= \begin{bmatrix} 1 & 0 & 0 & 0 & \frac{1}{x} & -\frac{1}{xy} & -\frac{1}{xz} & -\frac{1}{xw} \\ 0 & 1 & 0 & 0 & 0 & \frac{1}{y} & 0 & 0 \\ 0 & 0 & 1 & 0 & 0 & 0 & \frac{1}{z} & 0 \\ 0 & 0 & 0 & 1 & 0 & 0 & 0 & \frac{1}{w} \end{bmatrix} \begin{array}{l} R_1{}' = -\frac{1}{xzyw} R_1 \\[6pt] R_2{}' = \frac{1}{y} R_2 \\[6pt] R_3{}' = \frac{1}{z} R_3 \\[6pt] R_4{}' = \frac{1}{w} R_4 \end{array}$$

$$A^{-1} = \begin{bmatrix} \frac{1}{x} & -\frac{1}{xy} & -\frac{1}{xz} & -\frac{1}{xw} \\ 0 & \frac{1}{y} & 0 & 0 \\ 0 & 0 & \frac{1}{z} & 0 \\ 0 & 0 & 0 & \frac{1}{w} \end{bmatrix}$$

34. $\begin{bmatrix} a_1 & b_1 \\ a_2 & b_2 \end{bmatrix} \begin{bmatrix} x \\ y \end{bmatrix} = \begin{bmatrix} c_1 \\ c_2 \end{bmatrix}$ or $A \cdot X = C$.

Then $X = A^{-1}C$ or

$$X = \begin{bmatrix} \dfrac{b_2}{a_1b_2 - b_1a_2} & -\dfrac{b_1}{a_1b_2 - b_1a_2} \\ -\dfrac{a_2}{a_1b_2 - b_1a_2} & \dfrac{a_1}{a_1b_2 - b_1a_2} \end{bmatrix} \begin{bmatrix} c_1 \\ c_2 \end{bmatrix}.$$

Now $a_1b_2 - b_1a_2 = |A|$, so

$$X = \begin{vmatrix} \dfrac{b_2c_1 - b_1c_2}{|A|} \\ \dfrac{-a_2c_1 + a_1c_2}{|A|} \end{vmatrix}$$

Thus $x = \dfrac{b_2c_1 - b_1c_2}{|A|} = \dfrac{\begin{vmatrix} c_1 & b_1 \\ c_2 & b_2 \end{vmatrix}}{|A|} = \dfrac{D_x}{D}$; and

$y = \dfrac{a_1c_1 - a_2c_1}{|A|} = \dfrac{\begin{vmatrix} a_1 & c_1 \\ a_2 & c_2 \end{vmatrix}}{|A|} = \dfrac{D_y}{D}$.

Exercise Set 9.7

---

1. We replace x by −4 and y by 2.

$$\begin{array}{c|c} 2x + y > -5 \\ \hline 2(-4) + 2 & -5 \\ -8 + 2 & \\ -6 & \text{FALSE} \end{array}$$

Since −6 > −5 is false, (−4,2) is not a solution.

2. $$\begin{array}{c|c} 4x + 2y \leqslant 0 \\ \hline 4 \cdot 3 + 2(-6) & 0 \\ 0 & \text{TRUE} \end{array}$$

(3,−6) is a solution.

3. We replace x by 8 and y by 14.

$$\begin{array}{c|c} 2y - 3x \geqslant 5 \\ \hline 2 \cdot 14 - 3 \cdot 8 & 5 \\ 28 - 24 & \\ 4 & \text{FALSE} \end{array}$$

Since 4 ⩾ 5 is false, (8,14) is not a solution.

4. $$\begin{array}{c|c} 3x - y < -1 \\ \hline 3 \cdot 7 - 20 & -1 \\ 1 & \text{FALSE} \end{array}$$

(7,20) is not a solution.

5. Graph: y > 2x

We first graph the line y = 2x. We draw the line dashed since the inequality symbol is >. To determine which half-plane to shade, test a point not on the line. We try (1,1) and substitute:

$$\frac{y > 2x}{1 \;\bigg|\; 2 \cdot 1}$$
$$\quad\;\; 2 \quad \text{FALSE}$$

Since 1 > 2 is false, (1,1) is not a solution, nor are any points in the half-plane containing (1,1). The points in the opposite half-plane are solutions, so we shade that half-plane and obtain the graph.

6. 2y < x

7. Graph: y + x ⩾ 0

First graph the equation y + x = 0. A few solutions of this equation are (-2, 2), (0, 0), and (3, -3). Plot these points and draw the line solid since the inequality is ⩾.

Next determine which half-plane to shade by trying some point off the line. Here we use (2, 2) as a check.

$$\frac{y + x \geqslant 0}{2 + 2 \;\bigg|\; 0}$$
$$\quad\;\; 4 \quad\bigg|\quad \text{TRUE}$$

Since 4 ⩾ 0 is true, (2, 2) is a solution. Thus shade the half-plane containing (2, 2).

8. y + x < 0

9. Graph: y > x - 3

First graph the equation y = x - 3. The intercepts are (0,-3) and (3,0). Draw the line dashed since the inequality is >. To determine which half-plane to shade, test a point not on the line. We try (0, 0).

$$\frac{y > x - 3}{0 \;\bigg|\; 0 - 3}$$
$$\quad\;\; -3 \quad \text{TRUE}$$

Since 0 > -3 is true, (0,0) is a solution. Thus we shade the half-plane containing (0,0).

10. y ⩽ x + 4

11. Graph: x + y < 4

First graph the equation x + y = 4. The intercepts are (0,4) and (4,0). Draw the line dashed since the inequality is <. To determine which half-plane to shade, test a point not on the line. We try (0,0).

$$\frac{x + y < 4}{0 + 0 \;\bigg|\; 4}$$
$$\quad\;\; 0 \quad\bigg|\quad \text{TRUE}$$

Since 0 < 4 is true, (0,0) is a solution. Thus we shade the half-plane containing (0,0).

12. $x - y \geqslant 5$

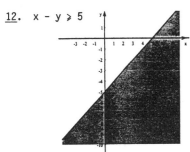

13. Graph: $3x - 2y \leqslant 6$

First graph the equation $3x - 2y = 6$. The y-intercept is $(0, -3)$, and the x-intercept is $(2, 0)$. Plot these points and draw the line solid since the inequality is $\leqslant$.

Next complete the graph by shading the correct half-plane. Since the line does not contain the origin, check the point $(0, 0)$ in the inequality to see if we get a true sentence.

$$\frac{3x - 2y \leqslant 6}{3(0) - 2(0) \mid 6}$$
$$0 \mid 6 \text{ TRUE}$$

Since $0 \leqslant 6$ is a true sentence, $(0, 0)$ is a solution. Thus shade the half-plane containing $(0, 0)$.

14. $2x - 5y < 10$

15. Graph: $3y + 2x \geqslant 6$

First graph the equation $3y + 2x = 6$. The y-intercept is $(0, 2)$, and the x-intercept is $(3, 0)$. Plot these points and draw the line solid since the inequality is $\geqslant$.

Next complete the graph by shading the correct half-plane. Since the line does not contain the origin, check the point $(0, 0)$ in the inequality to see if we get a true sentence.

$$\frac{3y + 2x \geqslant 6}{3 \cdot 0 + 2 \cdot 0 \mid 6}$$
$$0 \mid \text{FALSE}$$

Since $0 \geqslant 6$ is false, $(0, 0)$ is not a solution. We shade the half-plane which does not contain $(0, 0)$.

16. $2y + x \leqslant 4$

17. Graph: $3x - 2 \leqslant 5x + y$

$\qquad\qquad -2 \leqslant 2x + y \qquad$ (Adding $-3x$)

First graph $2x + y = -2$. The y-intercept is $(0, -2)$, and the x-intercept is $(-1, 0)$. Plot these points and draw the line solid since the inequality is $\leqslant$.

Next complete the graph by shading the correct half-plane. Since the line does not contain the origin, check the point $(0, 0)$.

$$\frac{2x + y \geqslant -2}{2(0) + 0 \mid -2}$$
$$0 \mid -2 \text{ TRUE}$$

Since $0 \geqslant -2$ is a true sentence, $(0, 0)$ is a solution. Thus shade the half-plane containing the origin.

$3x - 2 \leq 5x + y$

18. $2x - 6y \geq 8 + 4y$, or $2x - 10y \geq 8$

19. Graph: $x < -4$

We first graph the equation $x = -4$. The line is parallel to the y-axis with x-intercept $(-4, 0)$. We draw the line dashed since the inequality is $<$.

Next complete the graph by shading the correct half-plane. Since the line does not contain the origin, check the point $(0, 0)$.

$$\begin{array}{c|c} x < -4 \\ \hline 0 & -4 \quad \text{FALSE} \end{array}$$

Since $0 < -4$ is false, $(0, 0)$ is not a solution. Thus, we shade the half-plane which does not contain the origin.

20. $y \geq 5$

21. Graph: $y > -3$

First we graph the equation $y = -3$. We draw the line dashed since the inequality is $>$. To determine which half-plane to shade we test a point not on the line. We try $(0,0)$.

$$\begin{array}{c|c} y > -3 \\ \hline 0 & -3 \quad \text{TRUE} \end{array}$$

Since $0 > -3$ is true, $(0,0)$ is a solution. We shade the half-plane containing $(0,0)$.

$y > -3$

22. $x \leq 5$

23. Graph: $-4 < y < -1$

This is a conjunction of two inequalities

$-4 < y$ and $y < -1$.

We can graph $-4 < y$ and $y < -1$ separately and then graph the intersection.

$y < -1$

$-4 < y$

$-4 < y < -1$

24. -1 < y < 4

25. Graph: -4 ⩽ x ⩽ 4

This is a conjunction of inequalities

-4 ⩽ x and x ⩽ 4.

We can graph -4 ⩽ x and x ⩽ 4 separately and then graph the intersection.

-4 ≤ x ≤ 4

26. -3 ⩽ x ⩽ 3

27. Graph: y ⩾ |x|

First graph y = |x|. A few solutions of this equation are (0, 0), (1, 1), (-1, 1), (4, 4), and (-4, 4). Plot these points and draw the graph solid since the inequality is ⩾.

y = |x|

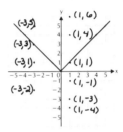

Note that in y ⩾ |x|, y is by itself. We interpret the graph of the inequality as the set of all ordered pairs (x, y) where the second coordinate y is greater than or equal to the absolute value of the first. Decide below which pairs satisfy the inequality and which do not.

We see that any pair above the graph of y = |x| is a solution as well as those in the graph of y = |x|. The graph is as follows.

28. y ⩽ |x|

29. Graph: $y \leqslant x$,

$y \geqslant 3 - x$

We graph the lines $y = x$ and $y = 3 - x$ using solid lines. The arrows at the ends of the lines indicate the region for each inequality. Note where the regions overlap and shade the region of solutions.

We find the vertex $\left(\frac{3}{2}, \frac{3}{2}\right)$ by solving the system

$y = x$,

$y = 3 - x$.

30. Graph: $y \geqslant x$,

$y \leqslant x - 5$

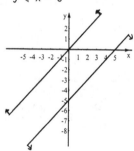

31. Graph $y \geqslant x$,

$y \leqslant x - 4$

We graph the lines $y = x$ and $y = x - 4$ using solid lines. The arrows at the ends of the lines indicate the region for each inequality. The regions do not overlap, so there are no vertices.

32. Graph: $y \geqslant x$,

$y \leqslant 2 - x$

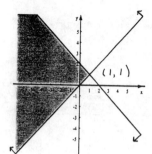

33. Graph: $y \geqslant -3$,

$x \geqslant 1$

We graph the lines $y = -3$ and $x = 1$ using solid lines. The arrows at the ends of the lines indicate the region for each inequality. Note where the regions overlap and shade the region of solutions.

We find the vertex $(1, -3)$ by solving the system

$y = -3$,

$x = 1$.

34. Graph: $y \leqslant -2$,

$x \geqslant 2$

35. Graph: $x \leqslant 3$,

$y \geqslant 2 - 3x$

We graph the lines $x = 3$ and $y = 2 - 3x$ using solid lines. The arrows at the ends of the lines indicate the region for each inequality. Note where the regions overlap and shade the region of solutions.

We find the vertex (3,-7) by solving the system

$$x = 3,$$
$$y = 2 - 3x.$$

36.   Graph: $x \geqslant -2,$

           $y \leqslant 3 - 2x$

37.   Graph: $x + y \leqslant 1,$

           $x - y \leqslant 2$

We graph the lines $x + y = 1$ and $x - y = 2$ using solid lines. The arrows at the ends of the lines indicate the region for each inequality. Note where the regions overlap and shade the region of solutions.

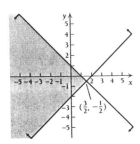

We find the vertex $\left[\frac{3}{2}, -\frac{1}{2}\right]$ by solving the system

$$x + y = 1,$$
$$x - y = 2.$$

38.   Graph: $y + 3x \geqslant 0,$

           $y + 3x \leqslant 2$

39.   Graph: $2y - x \leqslant 2,$

           $y + 3x \geqslant -1$

We graph the lines $2y - x = 2$ and $y + 3x = -1$ using solid lines. The arrows at the ends of the lines indicate the region for each inequality. Note where the regions overlap and shade the region of solutions.

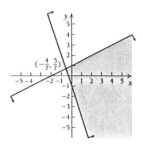

We find the vertex $\left[-\frac{4}{7}, \frac{5}{7}\right]$ by solving the system

$$2y - x = 2,$$
$$y + 3x = -1.$$

40.   Graph: $y \leqslant 2x + 1,$

           $y \geqslant -2x + 1,$

           $x \leqslant 2$

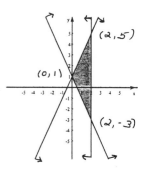

41.   Graph: $x - y \leqslant 2,$

           $x + 2y \geqslant 8,$

           $y \leqslant 4$

We graph the lines $x - y = 2$, $x + 2y = 8$, and $y = 4$ using solid lines. The arrows at the ends of the lines indicate the region for each inequality. Note where the regions overlap and shade the region of solutions.

We find the vertex (0,4) by solving the system
$$x + 2y = 8,$$
$$y = 4.$$

We find the vertex (6,4) by solving the system
$$x - y = 2,$$
$$y = 4.$$

We find the vertex (4,2) by solving the system
$$x - y = 2,$$
$$x + 2y = 8.$$

42. Graph: $x + 2y \leqslant 12,$
$$2x + y \leqslant 12,$$
$$x \geqslant 0,$$
$$y \geqslant 0$$

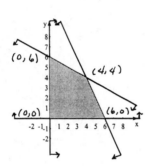

43. Graph: $4y - 3x \geqslant -12,$
$$4y + 3x \geqslant -36,$$
$$y \leqslant 0,$$
$$x \leqslant 0$$

Shade the intersection of the graphs of the four inequalities.

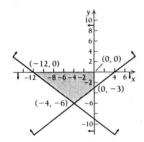

We find the vertex (-12, 0) by solving the system
$$4y + 3x = -36,$$
$$y = 0.$$

We find the vertex (0,0) by solving the system
$$y = 0,$$
$$x = 0.$$

We find the vertex (0,-3) by solving the system
$$4y - 3x = -12$$
$$x = 0.$$

We find the vertex (-4,-6) by solving the system
$$4y - 3x = -12,$$
$$4y + 3x = -36.$$

44. Graph: $8x + 5y \leqslant 40,$
$$x + 2y \leqslant 8,$$
$$x \geqslant 0,$$
$$y \geqslant 0$$

45. Graph: $3x + 4y \geqslant 12,$
$$5x + 6y \leqslant 30,$$
$$1 \leqslant x \leqslant 3$$

Shade the intersection of the graphs of the given inequalities.

We find the vertex $\left[1, \dfrac{25}{6}\right]$ by solving the system
$$5x + 6y = 30,$$
$$x = 1.$$

We find the vertex $\left[3, \dfrac{5}{2}\right]$ by solving the system
$$5x + 6y = 30,$$
$$x = 3.$$

We find the vertex $\left[3, \dfrac{3}{4}\right]$ by solving the system
$$3x + 4y = 12,$$
$$x = 3.$$

We find the vertex $\left[1, \dfrac{9}{4}\right]$ by solving the system
$$3x + 4y = 12,$$
$$x = 1.$$

46. Graph: $y - x \geqslant 1$,
    $y - x \leqslant 3$,
    $2 \leqslant x \leqslant 5$

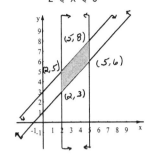

47. The graph of the domain is as follows:

Constraints:

$6x + 8y \leqslant 48$

$0 \leqslant y \leqslant 4$

$0 \leqslant x \leqslant 7$

We need to find the coordinate of each vertex.

Vertex A: (0, 0)

Vertex B:

   We solve the system $x = 0$ and $y = 4$.
   The coordinates of point B are (0, 4).

Vertex C:

   We solve the system $6x + 8y = 48$ and $y = 4$.
   The coordinates of point C are $\left(\frac{8}{3}, 4\right)$.

Vertex D:

   We solve the system $6x + 8y = 48$ and $x = 7$.
   The coordinates of point D are $\left(7, \frac{3}{4}\right)$.

Vertex E:

   We solve the system $x = 7$ and $y = 0$.
   The coordinates of point E are (7, 0).

We compute the value of P for each vertex.

Vertex	$P = 17x - 3y + 60$
A(0, 0)	$17 \cdot 0 - 3 \cdot 0 + 60 = 60$
B(0, 4)	$17 \cdot 0 - 3 \cdot 4 + 60 = 48$
$C\left(\frac{8}{3}, 4\right)$	$17 \cdot \frac{8}{3} - 3 \cdot 4 + 60 = 66\frac{2}{3}$
$D\left(7, \frac{3}{4}\right)$	$17 \cdot 7 - 3 \cdot \frac{3}{4} + 60 = 176\frac{3}{4}$
E(7, 0)	$17 \cdot 7 - 3 \cdot 0 + 60 = 179$

The maximum value of P is 179 when $x = 7$ and $y = 0$.

The minimum value of P is 48 when $x = 0$ and $y = 4$.

48. We graph the domain and find the vertices:

Vertex	$Q = 28x - 4y + 72$	
$\left(\frac{4}{5}, 4\right)$	$78\frac{2}{5}$	⟵ Minimum
(3, 4)	140	
$\left(3, \frac{5}{4}\right)$	151	⟵ Maximum

49. The graph of the domain is as follows:

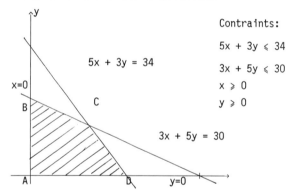

Contraints:

$5x + 3y \leqslant 34$

$3x + 5y \leqslant 30$

$x \geqslant 0$

$y \geqslant 0$

We need to find the coordinates of each vertex.

Vertex A: (0, 0)

Vertex B:

   We solve the system $3x + 5y = 30$ and $x = 0$.
   The coordinates of point B are (0, 6).

Vertex C:

   We solve the system $5x + 3y = 34$ and $3x + 5y = 30$. The coordinates of point C are (5, 3).

Vertex D:

   We solve the system $5x + 3y = 34$ and $y = 0$.
   The coordinates of point D are $\left(\frac{34}{5}, 0\right)$.

We compute the value of F for each vertex.

Vertex	F = 5x + 36y
A(0, 0)	$5 \cdot 0 + 36 \cdot 0 = 0$
B(0, 6)	$5 \cdot 0 + 36 \cdot 6 = 216$
C(5, 3)	$5 \cdot 5 + 36 \cdot 3 = 133$
D$\left(\frac{34}{5}, 0\right)$	$5 \cdot \frac{34}{5} + 36 \cdot 0 = 34$

The maximum value of F is 216 when x = 0 and y = 6.

The minimum value of F is 0 when x = 0 and y = 0.

50. We graph the domain and find the vertices:

Vertex	G = 16x + 14y
(0, 0)	0 ← Minimum
(0, 5.8)	81.2 ← Maximum
(2, 3)	74
(4, 0)	64

51. Let x = the number of Biscuit Jumbos and y = the number of Mitimite Biscuits to be made per day. The income I is given by

$$I = \$0.10x + \$0.08y$$

subject to the constraints

$$x + y \leqslant 200,$$
$$2x + y \leqslant 300$$
$$x \geqslant 0,$$
$$y \geqslant 0.$$

We graph the system of inequalities, determine the vertices, and find the value of I at each vertex.

Vertex	I = $0.10x + $0.08y
(0, 0)	$0.10(0) + $0.08(0) = $0
(0, 200)	$0.10(0) + $0.08(200) = $16
(100, 100)	$0.10(100) + $0.08(100) = $18
(150, 0)	$0.10(150) + $0.08(0) = $15

The company will have a maximum income of $18 when 100 of each type of biscuit is made.

52. Let x = the number of gallons the car uses and y = the number of gallons the moped uses. Find the maximum value of

$$M = 20x + 100y$$

subject to

$$x + y \leqslant 12,$$
$$0 \leqslant x \leqslant 10,$$
$$0 \leqslant y \leqslant 3.$$

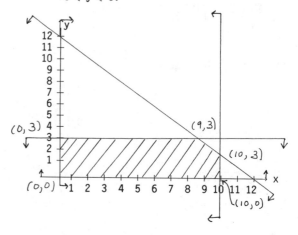

Vertex	M = 20x + 100y
(0, 0)	0
(0, 3)	300
(9, 3)	480
(10, 2)	400
(10, 0)	200

The maximum number of miles is 480 when the car uses 9 gal and the moped uses 3 gal.

53. Let x = the number of type A questions and y = the number of type B questions you answer. The score S is given by

$$S = 10x + 25y$$

subject to the constraints

$$3 \leqslant x \leqslant 12,$$
$$4 \leqslant y \leqslant 15,$$
$$x + y \leqslant 20.$$

We graph the system of inequalities, determine the vertices, and find the value of S at each vertex.

Vertex	S = 10x + 25y
(3, 4)	10·3 + 25·4 = 130
(3, 15)	10·3 + 25·15 = 405
(5, 15)	10·5 + 25·15 = 425
(12, 8)	10·12 + 25·8 = 320
(12, 4)	10·12 + 25·4 = 220

The maximum score is 425 points when 5 type A questions and 15 type B questions are answered.

54. Let x = the number of type A questions and y = the number of type B questions answered. Find the maximum value of

$$S = 4x + 7y$$

subject to

$$5 \leqslant x \leqslant 10,$$
$$3 \leqslant y \leqslant 10,$$
$$x + y \leqslant 18.$$

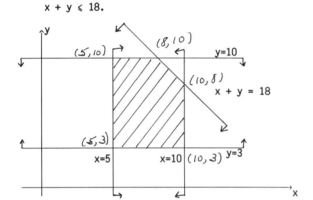

Vertex	S = 4x + 7y
(5, 3)	4·5 + 7·3 = 41
(5, 10)	4·5 + 7·10 = 90
(8, 10)	4·8 + 7·10 = 102
(10, 8)	4·10 + 7·8 = 96
(10, 3)	4·10 + 7·3 = 61

The maximum test score is 102 when 8 questions of type A and 10 questions of type B are answered.

55. Let x = the number of units of lumber and y = the number of units of plywood produced per week. The profit P is given by

$$P = \$20x + \$30y$$

subject to the constraints

$$x + y \leqslant 400,$$
$$x \geqslant 100,$$
$$y \geqslant 150.$$

We graph the system of inequalities, determine the vertices and find the value of P at each vertex.

Vertex	P = $20x + $30y
(100, 150)	$20·100 + $30·150 = $6500
(100, 300)	$20·100 + $30·300 = $11,000
(250, 150)	$20·250 + $30·150 = $9500

The maximum profit of $11,000 is achieved by producing 100 units of lumber and 300 units of plywood.

56. Let x = the corn acreage and y = the oats acreage. Find the maximum value of

$$P = \$40x + \$30y$$

subject to

$$x + y \leqslant 240,$$
$$2x + y \leqslant 320,$$
$$x \geqslant 0,$$
$$y \geqslant 0.$$

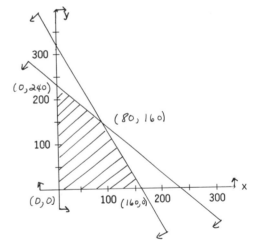

Vertex	P = $40x + $30y
(0, 0)	$0
(0, 240)	$7200
(80, 160)	$8000
(160, 0)	$6400

The maximum profit of $8000 occurs by planting 80 acres of corn and 160 acres of oats.

57. Let x = the amount invested in corporate bonds
and y = the amount invested in municipal bonds.
The income I is given by

$$I = 0.08x + 0.075y$$

subject to the constraints

$$x + y \leqslant \$40,000,$$
$$\$6000 \leqslant x \leqslant \$22,000,$$
$$y \leqslant \$30,000.$$

We graph the system of inequalities, determine
the vertices, and find the value of I at each
vertex.

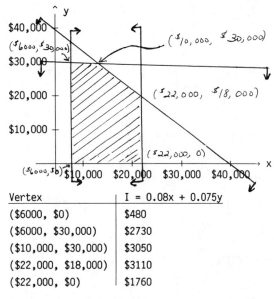

Vertex	I = 0.08x + 0.075y
($6000, $0)	$480
($6000, $30,000)	$2730
($10,000, $30,000)	$3050
($22,000, $18,000)	$3110
($22,000, $0)	$1760

The maximum income of $3110 occurs when $22,000
is invested in corporate bonds and $18,000 is
invested in municipal bonds.

58. Let x = the amount invested in bank X and y =
the amount invested in bank Y. Find the maximum
value of

$$I = 0.06x + 0.065y$$

subject to

$$x + y \leqslant \$22,000,$$
$$\$2000 \leqslant x \leqslant \$14,000$$
$$\$0 \leqslant y \leqslant \$15,000.$$

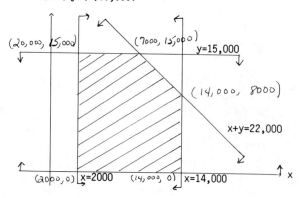

Vertex	I = 0.06x + 0.065y
($2000, $0)	$ 120
($2000, $15,000)	$1095
($7000, $15,000)	$1395
($14,000, $8000)	$1360
($14,000, $0)	$ 840

The maximum interest income is $1395 when $7000
is invested in bank X and $15,000 is invested
in bank Y.

59. Let x = the number of batches of Smello and y =
the number of batches of Roppo to be made. We
organize the information in a table.

	Composition		Number of lbs Available
	Smello	Roppo	
Number of Batches	x	y	
English tobacco	12	8	3000
Virginia tobacco	0	8	2000
Latakia tobacco	4	0	500
Profit per Batch	$10.56	$6.40	

The profit P is given by

$$P = \$10.56x + \$6.40y$$

subject to the constraints

$$12x + 8y \leqslant 3000,$$
$$8y \leqslant 2000,$$
$$4x \leqslant 500,$$
$$x \geqslant 0,$$
$$y \geqslant 0.$$

We graph the system of inequalities, determine
the vertices, and find the value of P at each
vertex.

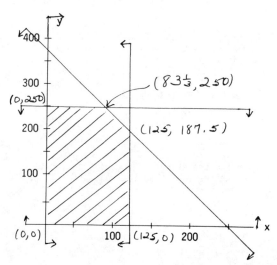

Vertex	$P = \$10.56x + \$6.40y$
$(0, 0)$	$0
$(125, 0)$	$1320
$(125, 187.5)$	$2520
$\left(83\frac{1}{3}, 250\right)$	$2480
$(0, 250)$	$1600

The maximum profit of $2520 occurs when 125 batches of Smello and 187.5 batches of Roppo are made.

60. Let x = the number of knit suits and y = the number of worsted suits made. Find the maximum value of

$$P = \$34x + \$31y$$

subject to

$$2x + 4y \leqslant 20,$$
$$4x + 2y \leqslant 16,$$
$$x \geqslant 0$$
$$y \geqslant 0.$$

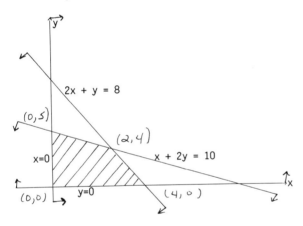

Vertex	$P = \$34x + \$31y$
$(0, 0)$	$\$34 \cdot 0 + \$31 \cdot 0 = \$0$
$(0, 5)$	$\$34 \cdot 0 + \$31 \cdot 5 = \$155$
$(2, 4)$	$\$34 \cdot 2 + \$31 \cdot 4 = \$192$
$(4, 0)$	$\$34 \cdot 4 + \$31 \cdot 0 = \$136$

The maximum profit per day is $192 when 2 knit suits and 4 worsted suits are made.

61. Graph: $y \geqslant x^2 - 2$
$\quad\quad\quad\quad y \leqslant 2 - x^2$

Graph the equation $y = x^2 - 2$. A few solutions are $(0, -2)$, $(1, -1)$, $(-1, -1)$, $(2, 2)$, and $(-2, 2)$. Plot these points and draw the graph solid since the inequality is $\geqslant$. Since for any point above the graph y is greater than $x^2 - 2$, we shade above $y = x^2 - 2$.

$y \geqslant x^2 - 2$

Graph the equation $y = 2 - x^2$. A few solutions are $(0, 2)$, $(1, 1)$, $(-1, 1)$, $(2, -2)$, and $(-2, -2)$. Plot these points and draw the graph solid since the inequality is $\leqslant$. Since for any point below the graph y is less than $2 - x^2$, we shade below $y = 2 - x^2$.

$y \leqslant 2 - x^2$

Now graph the intersection of the graphs.

62. $y < x + 1$
$\quad\;\; y \geqslant x^2$

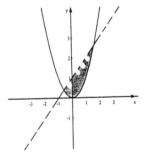

63. The team gets 2w points from w wins and t points from t ties. The number of wins and ties must each be nonnegative.

We have

$$2w + t \geqslant 60,$$
$$w \geqslant 0,$$
$$t \geqslant 0.$$

64. $75a + 35c > 1000,$
        $a \geqslant 0,$
        $c \geqslant 0$

65. Graph: $2L + 2W \leqslant 248,$
        $0 \leqslant L \leqslant 74,$
        $0 \leqslant W \leqslant 50$

66. $|x| + |y| \leqslant 1$

67.

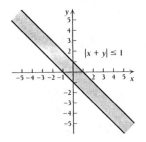

$|x + y| \leq 1$

68. $|x - y| > 0$

69.

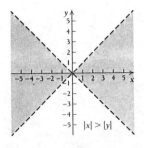

$|x| > |y|$

70. Let x = the number of chairs and y = the number of sofas produced. Find the maximum value of

$$I = \$20x + \$300y$$

subject to

$$20x + 100y \leqslant 1900,$$
$$x + 50y \leqslant 500,$$
$$2x + 20y \leqslant 240,$$
$$x \geqslant 0,$$
$$y \geqslant 0.$$

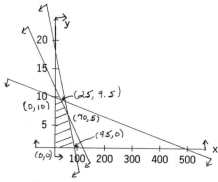

Vertex	$I = \$20x + \$300y$
(0, 0)	$0
(0, 10)	$3000
(25, 9.5)	$3350
(70, 5)	$2900
(95, 0)	$1900

The maximum income of $3350 occurs when 25 chairs and 9.5 sofas are made. (A more practical answer is that the maximum income of $3200 is achieved when 25 chairs and 9 sofas are made.)

71.　$3.5x + 5.8y \leq 10$
　　$2.1x - 12.3y \geq 9$
　　$x \geq -2.3$

[−10, 10] x [−10, 10]

Vertices:　(−2.30, 3.11), (−2.30, −1.12),
　　　　　　(3.17, −0.19)

72.　$20x - 45y > 105$
　　$12.5x + 13y < 10$
　　$0.7x - 7y > -35$

[−500, 500] x [−100, 100]

Vertices:　(21.29, 7.13), (−3.99, 4.60),
　　　　　　(2.21, 1.35)

Exercise Set 9.8

1.　$\dfrac{x + 7}{(x - 3)(x + 2)} = \dfrac{A}{x - 3} + \dfrac{B}{x + 2}$

　　$\dfrac{x + 7}{(x - 3)(x + 2)} = \dfrac{A(x + 2) + B(x - 3)}{(x - 3)(x + 2)}$　(Adding)

Equate the numerators:

$x + 7 = A(x + 2) + B(x - 3)$

Let $x + 2 = 0$, or $x = -2$.　Then we get

$-2 + 7 = 0 + B(-2 - 3)$

　　$5 = -5B$

　$-1 = B$

Next let $x - 3 = 0$, or $x = 3$.　Then we get

$3 + 7 = A(3 + 2) + 0$

　$10 = 5A$

　　$2 = A$

The decomposition is as follows:

$\dfrac{2}{x - 3} + \dfrac{-1}{x + 2}$

2.　$\dfrac{2x}{(x + 1)(x - 1)} = \dfrac{A}{x + 1} + \dfrac{B}{x - 1}$

　　$\dfrac{2x}{(x + 1)(x - 1)} = \dfrac{A(x - 1) + B(x + 1)}{(x + 1)(x - 1)}$

　　　　　　$2x = A(x - 1) + B(x + 1)$

Let $x = 1$:　$2 \cdot 1 = 0 + B(1 + 1)$

　　　　　　$2 = 2B$

　　　　　　$1 = B$

Let $x = -1$:　$2(-1) = A(-1 - 1) + 0$

　　　　　　　$-2 = -2A$

　　　　　　　$1 = A$

The decomposition is $\dfrac{1}{x + 1} + \dfrac{1}{x - 1}$.

3.　$\dfrac{7x - 1}{6x^2 - 5x + 1}$

　$= \dfrac{7x - 1}{(3x - 1)(2x - 1)}$　　(Factoring the denominator)

　$= \dfrac{A}{3x - 1} + \dfrac{B}{2x - 1}$

　$= \dfrac{A(2x - 1) + B(3x - 1)}{(3x - 1)(2x - 1)}$　　(Adding)

Equate the numerators:

$7x - 1 = A(2x - 1) + B(3x - 1)$

Let $2x - 1 = 0$, or $x = \frac{1}{2}$.　Then we get

$7\left(\frac{1}{2}\right) - 1 = 0 + B\left(3 \cdot \frac{1}{2} - 1\right)$

　　$\dfrac{5}{2} = \dfrac{1}{2} B$

　　$5 = B$

Next let $3x - 1 = 0$, or $x = \frac{1}{3}$.　We get

$7\left(\frac{1}{3}\right) - 1 = A\left(2 \cdot \frac{1}{3} - 1\right) + 0$

　　$\dfrac{7}{3} - 1 = A\left(\frac{2}{3} - 1\right)$

　　$\dfrac{4}{3} = -\dfrac{1}{3} A$

　　$-4 = A$

The decomposition is as follows:

$\dfrac{-4}{3x - 1} + \dfrac{5}{2x - 1}$

4.　$\dfrac{13x + 46}{12x^2 - 11x - 15} = \dfrac{13x + 46}{(4x + 3)(3x - 5)}$

　　　　　　$= \dfrac{A}{4x + 3} + \dfrac{B}{3x - 5}$

　　　　　　$= \dfrac{A(3x - 5) + B(4x + 3)}{(4x + 3)(3x - 5)}$

Let $x = \frac{5}{3}$:　$13 \cdot \frac{5}{3} + 46 = 0 + B\left(4 \cdot \frac{5}{3} + 3\right)$

　　　　　　$\dfrac{203}{3} = \dfrac{29}{3} B$

　　　　　　$7 = B$

Let $x = -\frac{3}{4}$: $13\left[-\frac{3}{4}\right] + 46 = A\left[3\left[-\frac{3}{4}\right] - 5\right] + 0$

$$\frac{145}{4} = -\frac{29}{4}A$$

$$-5 = A$$

The decomposition is $\frac{-5}{4x + 3} + \frac{7}{3x - 5}$.

5. $\frac{3x^2 - 11x - 26}{(x^2 - 4)(x + 1)}$

$= \frac{3x^2 - 11x - 26}{(x + 2)(x - 2)(x + 1)}$ (Factoring the denominator)

$= \frac{A}{x + 2} + \frac{B}{x - 2} + \frac{C}{x + 1}$

$= \frac{A(x-2)(x+1) + B(x+2)(x+1) + C(x+2)(x-2)}{(x + 2)(x - 2)(x + 1)}$

(Adding)

Equate the numerators:

$3x^2 - 11x - 26 = A(x - 2)(x + 1) +$
$\qquad\qquad B(x + 2)(x + 1) + C(x + 2)(x - 2)$

Let $x + 2 = 0$, or $x = -2$. Then, we get
$3(-2)^2 - 11(-2) - 26 = A(-2 - 2)(-2 + 1) + 0 + 0$
$\qquad 12 + 22 - 26 = A(-4)(-1)$
$\qquad\qquad 8 = 4A$
$\qquad\qquad 2 = A$

Next let $x - 2 = 0$, or $x = 2$. Then, we get
$3 \cdot 2^2 - 11 \cdot 2 - 26 = 0 + B(2 + 2)(2 + 1) + 0$
$\qquad 12 - 22 - 26 = B \cdot 4 \cdot 3$
$\qquad\qquad -36 = 12B$
$\qquad\qquad -3 = B$

Finally let $x + 1 = 0$, or $x = -1$. We get
$3(-1)^2 - 11(-1) - 26 = 0 + 0 + C(-1 + 2)(-1 - 2)$
$\qquad 3 + 11 - 26 = C(1)(-3)$
$\qquad\qquad -12 = -3C$
$\qquad\qquad 4 = C$

The decomposition is as follows:

$\frac{2}{x + 2} + \frac{-3}{x - 2} + \frac{4}{x + 1}$

6. $\frac{5x^2 + 9x - 56}{(x - 4)(x - 2)(x + 1)}$

$= \frac{A}{x - 4} + \frac{B}{x - 2} + \frac{C}{x + 1}$

$= \frac{A(x-2)(x+1) + B(x-4)(x+1) + C(x-4)(x-2)}{(x - 4)(x - 2)(x + 1)}$

$5x^2 + 9x - 56 = A(x - 2)(x + 1) +$
$\qquad\qquad B(x - 4)(x + 1) + C(x - 4)(x - 2)$

Let $x = 4$: $5 \cdot 4^2 + 9 \cdot 4 - 56 = A(4-2)(4+1) + 0 + 0$
$\qquad\qquad 60 = 10A$
$\qquad\qquad 6 = A$

Let $x = 2$: $5 \cdot 2^2 + 9 \cdot 2 - 56 = 0 + B(2-4)(2+1) + 0$
$\qquad\qquad -18 = -6B$
$\qquad\qquad 3 = B$

Let $x = -1$:
$5(-1)^2 + 9(-1) - 56 = 0 + 0 + C(-1 - 4)(-1 - 2)$
$\qquad\qquad -60 = 15C$
$\qquad\qquad -4 = C$

The decomposition is $\frac{6}{x - 4} + \frac{3}{x - 2} + \frac{-4}{x + 1}$.

7. $\frac{9}{(x + 2)^2(x - 1)}$

$= \frac{A}{x + 2} + \frac{B}{(x + 2)^2} + \frac{C}{x - 1}$

$= \frac{A(x + 2)(x - 1) + B(x - 1) + C(x + 2)^2}{(x + 2)^2(x - 1)}$ (Adding)

Equate the numerators:

$9 = A(x + 2)(x - 1) + B(x - 1) + C(x + 2)^2$ (1)

Let $x - 1 = 0$, or $x = 1$. Then, we get
$9 = 0 + 0 + C(1 + 2)^2$
$9 = 9C$
$1 = C$

Next let $x + 2 = 0$, or $x = -2$. Then, we get
$9 = 0 + B(-2 - 1) + 0$
$9 = -3B$
$-3 = B$

To find A we first simplify Eq. (1).

$9 = A(x^2 + x - 2) + B(x - 1) + C(x^2 + 4x + 4)$
$\quad = Ax^2 + Ax - 2A + Bx - B + Cx^2 + 4Cx + 4C$
$\quad = (A + C)x^2 + (A + B + 4C)x + (-2A - B + 4C)$

Then we equate the coefficients of x^2.
$0 = A + C$
$0 = A + 1$ (Substituting 1 for C)
$-1 = A$

The decomposition is as follows:

$\frac{-1}{x + 2} + \frac{-3}{(x + 2)^2} + \frac{1}{x - 1}$

8. $\frac{x^2 - x - 4}{(x - 2)^3}$

$= \frac{A}{x - 2} + \frac{B}{(x - 2)^2} + \frac{C}{(x - 2)^3}$

$= \frac{A(x - 2)^2 + B(x - 2) + C}{(x - 2)^3}$

$x^2 - x - 4 = A(x - 2)^2 + B(x - 2) + C$ (1)

Let $x = 2$: $2^2 - 2 - 4 = 0 + 0 + C$
$\qquad\qquad -2 = C$

Simplify Eq. (1).
$x^2 - x - 4 = Ax^2 - 4Ax + 4A + Bx - 2B + C$
$\qquad\qquad = Ax^2 + (-4A + B)x + (4A - 2B + C)$

Then $1 = A$ and

$-1 = -4A + B$, so $B = 3$.

The decomposition is $\dfrac{1}{x-2} + \dfrac{3}{(x-2)^2} + \dfrac{-2}{(x-2)^3}$.

9. $\quad \dfrac{2x^2 + 3x + 1}{(x^2 - 1)(2x - 1)}$

$= \dfrac{2x^2 + 3x + 1}{(x + 1)(x - 1)(2x - 1)}$ (Factoring the denominator)

$= \dfrac{A}{x + 1} + \dfrac{B}{x - 1} + \dfrac{C}{2x - 1}$

$= \dfrac{A(x-1)(2x-1) + B(x+1)(2x-1) + C(x+1)(x-1)}{(x + 1)(x - 1)(2x - 1)}$

    (Adding)

Equate the numerators:

$2x^2 + 3x + 1 = A(x - 1)(2x - 1) +$
$\qquad\qquad B(x + 1)(2x - 1) + C(x + 1)(x - 1)$

Let $x + 1 = 0$, or $x = -1$. Then, we get

$2(-1)^2 + 3(-1) + 1 = A(-1 - 1)[2(-1) - 1] + 0 + 0$

$\qquad 2 - 3 + 1 = A(-2)(-3)$

$\qquad\qquad 0 = 6A$

$\qquad\qquad 0 = A$

Next let $x - 1 = 0$, or $x = 1$. Then, we get

$2 \cdot 1^2 + 3 \cdot 1 + 1 = 0 + B(1 + 1)(2 \cdot 1 - 1) + 0$

$\qquad 2 + 3 + 1 = B \cdot 2 \cdot 1$

$\qquad\qquad 6 = 2B$

$\qquad\qquad 3 = B$

Finally we let $2x - 1 = 0$, or $x = \frac{1}{2}$. We get

$2\left(\frac{1}{2}\right)^2 + 3\left(\frac{1}{2}\right) + 1 = 0 + 0 + C\left(\frac{1}{2} + 1\right)\left(\frac{1}{2} - 1\right)$

$\qquad \frac{1}{2} + \frac{3}{2} + 1 = C \cdot \frac{3}{2} \cdot \left(-\frac{1}{2}\right)$

$\qquad\qquad 3 = -\frac{3}{4}C$

$\qquad\qquad -4 = C$

The decomposition is as follows:

$\dfrac{3}{x - 1} + \dfrac{-4}{2x - 1}$

10. $\quad \dfrac{x^2 - 10x + 13}{(x^2 - 5x + 6)(x - 1)}$

$= \dfrac{x^2 - 10x + 13}{(x - 3)(x - 2)(x - 1)}$

$= \dfrac{A}{x - 3} + \dfrac{B}{x - 2} + \dfrac{C}{x - 1}$

$= \dfrac{A(x-2)(x-1) + B(x-3)(x-1) + C(x-3)(x-2)}{(x - 3)(x - 2)(x - 1)}$

$x^2 - 10x + 13 = A(x - 2)(x - 1) +$
$\qquad\qquad B(x - 3)(x - 1) + C(x - 3)(x - 2)$

Let $x = 3$:

$3^2 - 10 \cdot 3 + 13 = A(3 - 2)(3 - 1) + 0 + 0$

$\qquad\qquad -8 = 2A$

$\qquad\qquad -4 = A$

Let $x = 2$:

$2^2 - 10 \cdot 2 + 13 = 0 + B(2 - 3)(2 - 1) + 0$

$\qquad\qquad -3 = -B$

$\qquad\qquad 3 = B$

Let $x = 1$:

$1^2 - 10 \cdot 1 + 13 = 0 + 0 + C(1 - 3)(1 - 2)$

$\qquad\qquad 4 = 2C$

$\qquad\qquad 2 = C$

The decomposition is $\dfrac{-4}{x - 3} + \dfrac{3}{x - 2} + \dfrac{2}{x - 1}$.

11. $\quad \dfrac{x^4 - 3x^3 - 3x^2 + 10}{(x + 1)^2(x - 3)}$

$= \dfrac{x^4 - 3x^3 - 3x^2 + 10}{x^3 - x^2 - 5x - 3}$ (Multiplying the denominator)

Since the degree of the numerator is greater than the degree of the denominator, we divide.

$$
\begin{array}{r}
x - 2 \\
x^3 - x^2 - 5x - 3 \overline{\smash{\big)}\, x^4 - 3x^3 - 3x^2 + 0x + 10} \\
\underline{x^4 - x^3 - 5x^2 - 3x } \\
-2x^3 + 2x^2 + 3x + 10 \\
\underline{-2x^3 + 2x^2 + 10x + 6} \\
-7x + 4
\end{array}
$$

The original expression is thus equivalent to the following:

$x - 2 + \dfrac{-7x + 4}{x^3 - x^2 - 5x - 3}$

We proceed to decompose the fraction.

$\dfrac{-7x + 4}{(x + 1)^2(x - 3)}$

$= \dfrac{A}{x + 1} + \dfrac{B}{(x + 1)^2} + \dfrac{C}{x - 3}$

$= \dfrac{A(x + 1)(x - 3) + B(x - 3) + C(x + 1)^2}{(x + 1)^2(x - 3)}$ (Adding)

Equate the numerators:

$-7x + 4 = A(x + 1)(x - 3) + B(x - 3) +$
$\qquad\qquad C(x + 1)^2$ (1)

Let $x - 3 = 0$, or $x = 3$. Then, we get

$-7 \cdot 3 + 4 = 0 + 0 + C(3 + 1)^2$

$\qquad -17 = 16C$

$\qquad -\dfrac{17}{16} = C$

Let $x + 1 = 0$, or $x = -1$. Then, we get

$-7(-1) + 4 = 0 + B(-1 - 3) + 0$

$\qquad 11 = -4B$

$\qquad -\dfrac{11}{4} = B$

To find A we first simplify Eq. (1).

$-7x + 4 = A(x^2-2x-3) + B(x-3) + C(x^2+2x+1)$

$\quad\quad = Ax^2 - 2Ax - 3A + Bx - 3B + Cx^2 - 2Cx + C$

$\quad\quad = (A + C)x^2 + (-2A + B - 2C)x +$

$\quad\quad\quad (-3A - 3B + C)$

Then equate the coefficients of x^2.

$\quad 0 = A + C$

Substituting $-\dfrac{17}{16}$ for C, we get $A = \dfrac{17}{16}$.

The decomposition is as follows:

$\dfrac{17/16}{x + 1} + \dfrac{-11/4}{(x + 1)^2} + \dfrac{-17/16}{x - 3}$

The original expression is equivalent to the following:

$x - 2 + \dfrac{17/16}{x + 1} + \dfrac{-11/4}{(x + 1)^2} + \dfrac{-17/16}{x - 3}$

12. $\dfrac{10x^3 - 15x^2 - 35x}{x^2 - x - 6} = 10x - 5 + \dfrac{20x - 30}{x^2 - x - 6}$

$\quad\quad\quad\quad\quad\quad\quad\quad\quad\quad \text{(Dividing)}$

$\dfrac{20x - 30}{x^2 - x - 6} = \dfrac{20x - 30}{(x - 3)(x + 2)}$

$\quad\quad\quad\quad = \dfrac{A}{x - 3} + \dfrac{B}{x + 2}$

$\quad\quad\quad\quad = \dfrac{A(x + 2) + B(x - 3)}{(x - 3)(x + 2)}$

$20x - 30 = A(x + 2) + B(x - 3)$

Let $x = 3$: $20 \cdot 3 - 30 = A(3 + 2) + 0$

$\quad\quad\quad\quad\quad\quad 30 = 5A$

$\quad\quad\quad\quad\quad\quad\; 6 = A$

Let $x = -2$: $20(-2) - 30 = 0 + B(-2 - 3)$

$\quad\quad\quad\quad\quad\quad\quad -70 = -5B$

$\quad\quad\quad\quad\quad\quad\quad\; 14 = B$

The decomposition is $10x - 5 + \dfrac{6}{x - 3} + \dfrac{14}{x + 2}$.

13. $\dfrac{-x^2 + 2x - 13}{(x^2 + 2)(x - 1)}$

$= \dfrac{Ax + B}{x^2 + 2} + \dfrac{C}{x - 1}$

$= \dfrac{(Ax + B)(x - 1) + C(x^2 + 2)}{(x^2 + 2)(x - 1)} \quad \text{(Adding)}$

Equate the numerators:

$-x^2 + 2x - 13 = (Ax + B)(x - 1) + C(x^2 + 2)$ (1)

Let $x - 1 = 0$, or $x = 1$. Then we get

$-1^2 + 2 \cdot 1 - 13 = 0 + C(1^2 + 2)$

$\quad -1 + 2 - 13 = C(1 + 2)$

$\quad\quad\quad\quad -12 = 3C$

$\quad\quad\quad\quad\; -4 = C$

To find A and B we first simplify Eq. (1).

$-x^2 + 2x - 13 = Ax^2 - Ax + Bx - B + Cx^2 + 2C$

$\quad\quad\quad\quad = (A+C)x^2 + (-A + B)x + (-B + 2C)$

Equate the coefficients of x^2:

$-1 = A + C$

Substituting -4 for C, we get $A = 3$.

Equate the constant terms:

$-13 = -B + 2C$

Substituting -4 for C, we get $B = 5$.

The decomposition is as follows:

$\dfrac{3x + 5}{x^2 + 2} + \dfrac{-4}{x - 1}$

14. $\dfrac{26x^2 + 208x}{(x^2 + 1)(x + 5)}$

$= \dfrac{Ax + B}{x^2 + 1} + \dfrac{C}{x + 5}$

$= \dfrac{(Ax + B)(x + 5) + C(x^2 + 1)}{(x^2 + 1)(x + 5)}$

$26x^2 + 208x = (Ax + B)(x + 5) + C(x^2 + 1)$ (1)

Let $x = -5$:

$26(-5)^2 + 208(-5) = 0 + C[(-5)^2 + 1]$

$\quad\quad\quad\quad -390 = 26C$

$\quad\quad\quad\quad\; -15 = C$

Simplify Eq. (1).

$26x^2 + 208x = Ax^2 + 5Ax + Bx + 5B + Cx^2 + C$

$\quad\quad\quad\quad = (A + C)x^2 + (5A + B)x + (5B + C)$

$26 = A + C$

$26 = A - 15$

$41 = A$

$0 = 5B + C$

$0 = 5B - 15$

$3 = B$

The decomposition is $\dfrac{41x + 3}{x^2 + 1} + \dfrac{-15}{x + 5}$.

15. $\dfrac{6 + 26x - x^2}{(2x - 1)(x + 2)^2}$

$= \dfrac{A}{2x - 1} + \dfrac{B}{x + 2} + \dfrac{C}{(x + 2)^2}$

$= \dfrac{A(x + 2)^2 + B(2x - 1)(x + 2) + C(2x - 1)}{(2x - 1)(x + 2)^2}$

$\quad\quad\quad\quad\quad\quad\quad\quad\quad \text{(Adding)}$

Equate the numerators:

$6 + 26x - x^2 = A(x + 2)^2 + B(2x - 1)(x + 2) +$

$\quad\quad\quad\quad\quad C(2x - 1)$ (1)

Let $2x - 1 = 0$, or $x = \dfrac{1}{2}$. Then, we get

$6 + 26 \cdot \dfrac{1}{2} - \left(\dfrac{1}{2}\right)^2 = A\left(\dfrac{1}{2} + 2\right)^2 + 0 + 0$

$\quad\quad 6 + 13 - \dfrac{1}{4} = A\left(\dfrac{5}{2}\right)^2$

$\quad\quad\quad\quad \dfrac{75}{4} = \dfrac{25}{4} A$

$\quad\quad\quad\quad\quad 3 = A$

Let $x + 2 = 0$, or $x = -2$. We get

$$6 + 26(-2) - (-2)^2 = 0 + 0 + C[2(-2) - 1]$$
$$6 - 52 - 4 = -5C$$
$$-50 = -5C$$
$$10 = C$$

To find B we first simplify Eq. (1).

$$6 + 26x - x^2 = A(x^2 + 4x + 4) + B(2x^2 + 3x - 2) + C(2x - 1)$$
$$= Ax^2 + 4Ax + 4A + 2Bx^2 + 3Bx - 2B + 2Cx - C$$
$$= (A + 2B)x^2 + (4A + 3B + 2C)x + (4A - 2B - C)$$

Equate the coefficients of x^2:

$$-1 = A + 2B$$

Substituting 3 for A, we obtain $B = -2$.

The decomposition is as follows:

$$\frac{3}{2x - 1} + \frac{-2}{x + 2} + \frac{10}{(x + 2)^2}$$

16. $\dfrac{5x^3 + 6x^2 + 5x}{(x^2 - 1)(x + 1)^3}$

$$= \frac{5x^3 + 6x^2 + 5x}{(x - 1)(x + 1)^4}$$

$$= \frac{A}{x - 1} + \frac{B}{x + 1} + \frac{C}{(x + 1)^2} + \frac{D}{(x + 1)^3} + \frac{E}{(x + 1)^4}$$

$$= \frac{A(x+1)^4 + B(x-1)(x+1)^3 + C(x-1)(x+1)^2 + D(x-1)(x+1) + E(x-1)}{(x - 1)(x + 1)^4}$$

$$5x^3 + 6x^2 + 5x =$$
$$A(x + 1)^4 + B(x - 1)(x + 1)^3 + C(x - 1)(x + 1)^2 + D(x - 1)(x + 1) + E(x - 1) \qquad (1)$$

Let $x = 1$: $5 \cdot 1^3 + 6 \cdot 1^2 + 5 \cdot 1 = A(1 + 1)^4$
$$16 = 16A$$
$$A = 1$$

Let $x = -1$: $5(-1)^3 + 6(-1)^2 + 5(-1) = E(-1 - 1)$
$$-4 = -2E$$
$$2 = E$$

Simplify Eq. (1).

$$5x^3 + 6x^2 + 5x = (A + B)x^4 + (4A + 2B + C)x^3 + (6A + C + D)x^2 + (4A - 2B - C + E)x + (A - B - C - D - E)$$

$$0 = A + B$$
$$0 = 1 + B$$
$$-1 = B$$

$$5 = 4A + 2B + C$$
$$5 = 4 \cdot 1 + 2(-1) + C$$
$$3 = C$$

$$0 = A - B - C - D - E$$
$$0 = 1 - (-1) - 3 - D - 2$$
$$D = -3$$

The decomposition is

$$\frac{1}{x - 1} + \frac{-1}{x + 1} + \frac{3}{(x + 1)^2} + \frac{-3}{(x + 1)^3} + \frac{2}{(x + 1)^4}.$$

17. $\dfrac{6x^3 + 5x^2 + 6x - 2}{2x^2 + x - 1}$

Since the degree of the numerator is greater than the degree of the denominator, we divide.

$$
\begin{array}{r}
3x + 1 \\
2x^2 + x - 1 \overline{\smash{\big)}\ 6x^3 + 5x^2 + 6x - 2} \\
\underline{6x^3 + 3x^2 - 3x } \\
2x^2 + 9x - 2 \\
\underline{2x^2 + x - 1} \\
8x - 1
\end{array}
$$

The original expression is equivalent to

$$3x + 1 + \frac{8x - 1}{2x^2 + x - 1}$$

We proceed to decompose the fraction.

$$\frac{8x - 1}{2x^2 + x - 1} = \frac{8x - 1}{(2x - 1)(x + 1)} \qquad \text{(Factoring the denominator)}$$

$$= \frac{A}{2x - 1} + \frac{B}{x + 1}$$

$$= \frac{A(x + 1) + B(2x - 1)}{(2x - 1)(x + 1)} \qquad \text{(Adding)}$$

Equate the numerators:

$$8x - 1 = A(x + 1) + B(2x - 1)$$

Let $x + 1 = 0$, or $x = -1$. Then we get

$$8(-1) - 1 = 0 + B[2(-1) - 1]$$
$$-8 - 1 = B(-2 - 1)$$
$$-9 = -3B$$
$$3 = B$$

Next let $2x - 1 = 0$, or $x = \frac{1}{2}$. We get

$$8\left(\frac{1}{2}\right) - 1 = A\left(\frac{1}{2} + 1\right) + 0$$
$$4 - 1 = A\left(\frac{3}{2}\right)$$
$$3 = \frac{3}{2}A$$
$$2 = A$$

The decomposition is

$$\frac{2}{2x - 1} + \frac{3}{x + 1}.$$

The original expression is equivalent to

$$3x + 1 + \frac{2}{2x - 1} + \frac{3}{x + 1}.$$

18. $\dfrac{2x^3 + 3x^2 - 11x - 10}{x^2 + 2x - 3} = 2x - 1 + \dfrac{-3x - 13}{x^2 + 2x - 3}$

    (Dividing)

    $\dfrac{-3x - 13}{x^2 + 2x - 3} = \dfrac{A}{x + 3} + \dfrac{B}{x - 1}$

    $= \dfrac{A(x - 1) + B(x + 3)}{(x + 3)(x - 1)}$

    $-3x - 13 = A(x - 1) + B(x + 3)$

    Let $x = -3$: $\;-3(-3) - 13 = A(-3 - 1) + 0$

    $-4 = -4A$

    $1 = A$

    Let $x = 1$: $\;-3\cdot1 - 13 = 0 + B(1 + 3)$

    $-16 = 4B$

    $-4 = B$

    The decomposition is $\;2x - 1 + \dfrac{1}{x + 3} + \dfrac{-4}{x - 1}$.

19. $\dfrac{2x^2 - 11x + 5}{(x - 3)(x^2 + 2x - 5)}$

    $= \dfrac{A}{x - 3} + \dfrac{Bx + C}{x^2 + 2x - 5}$

    $= \dfrac{A(x^2 + 2x - 5) + (Bx + C)(x - 3)}{(x - 3)(x^2 + 2x - 5)}$

    (Adding)

    Equate the numerators:

    $2x^2 - 11x + 5 = A(x^2 + 2x - 5) +$
    $\qquad\qquad\qquad (Bx + C)(x - 3)$ $\qquad$ (1)

    Let $x - 3 = 0$, or $x = 3$. Then, we get

    $2\cdot3^2 - 11\cdot3 + 5 = A(3^2 + 2\cdot3 - 5) + 0$

    $18 - 33 + 5 = A(9 + 6 - 5)$

    $-10 = 10A$

    $-1 = A$

    To find B and C, we first simplify Eq. (1).

    $2x^2 - 11x + 5 = Ax^2 + 2Ax - 5A + Bx^2 - 3Bx + Cx - 3C$

    $= (A + B)x^2 + (2A - 3B + C)x + (-5A - 3C)$

    Equate the coefficients of x^2:

    $2 = A + B$

    Substituting -1 for A, we get $B = 3$.

    Equate the constant terms:

    $5 = -5A - 3C$

    Substituting -1 for A, we get $C = 0$.

    The decomposition is as follows:

    $\dfrac{-1}{x - 3} + \dfrac{3x}{x^2 + 2x - 5}$

20. $\dfrac{3x^2 - 3x - 8}{(x - 5)(x^2 + x - 4)}$

    $= \dfrac{A}{x - 5} + \dfrac{Bx + C}{x^2 + x - 4}$

    $= \dfrac{A(x^2 + x - 4) + (Bx + C)(x - 5)}{(x - 5)(x^2 + x - 4)}$

    $3x^2 - 3x - 8 = A(x^2 + x - 4) +$
    $\qquad\qquad\qquad (Bx + C)(x - 5)$ $\qquad$ (1)

    Let $x = 5$: $\;3\cdot5^2 - 3\cdot5 - 8 = A(5^2 + 5 - 4) + 0$

    $52 = 26A$

    $2 = A$

    Simplify Eq. (1).

    $3x^2 - 3x - 8 = Ax^2 + Ax - 4A + Bx^2 - 5Bx + Cx - 5C$

    $= (A + B)x^2 + (A - 5B + C)x + (-4A - 5C)$

    $3 = A + B$

    $3 = 2 + B$

    $1 = B$

    $-8 = -4A - 5C$

    $-8 = -4\cdot2 - 5C$

    $0 = C$

    The decomposition is $\dfrac{2}{x - 5} + \dfrac{x}{x^2 + x - 4}$.

21. $\dfrac{-4x^2 - 2x + 10}{(3x + 5)(x + 1)^2}$

    The decomposition looks like

    $\dfrac{A}{3x + 5} + \dfrac{B}{x + 1} + \dfrac{C}{(x + 1)^2}$.

    Add and equate the numerators.

    $-4x^2 - 2x + 10 = A(x + 1)^2 + B(3x + 5)(x + 1) +$
    $\qquad\qquad\qquad\qquad\qquad C(3x + 5)$

    $= A(x^2 + 2x + 1) + B(3x^2 + 8x + 5)$
    $\qquad\qquad\qquad + C(3x + 5)$

    or

    $-4x^2 - 2x + 10 = (A + 3B)x^2 + (2A + 8B + 3C)x +$
    $\qquad\qquad\qquad\qquad\qquad (A + 5B + 5C)$

    Then equate corresponding coefficients.

    $-4 = A + 3B$ $\qquad$ (Coefficients of x^2-terms)

    $-2 = 2A + 8B + 3C$ $\qquad$ (Coefficients of x-terms)

    $10 = A + 5B + 5C$ $\qquad$ (Constant terms)

    We solve this system of three equations and find $A = 5$, $B = -3$, $C = 4$.

    The decomposition is

    $\dfrac{5}{3x + 5} + \dfrac{-3}{x + 1} + \dfrac{4}{(x + 1)^2}$.

22. $\dfrac{26x^2 - 36x + 22}{(x - 4)(2x - 1)^2} = \dfrac{A}{x - 4} + \dfrac{B}{2x - 1} + \dfrac{C}{(2x - 1)^2}$

Add and equate numerators.

$26x^2 - 36x + 22 = A(2x - 1)^2 + B(x - 4)(2x - 1) +$
$$C(x - 4)$$
$$= A(4x^2 - 4x + 1) +$$
$$B(2x^2 - 9x + 4) + C(x - 4)$$

or

$26x^2 - 36x + 22 = (4A + 2B)x^2 + (-4A - 9B + C)x +$
$$(A + 4B - 4C)$$

Solving the system of equations

$$26 = 4A + 2B,$$
$$-36 = -4A - 9B + C,$$
$$22 = A + 4B - 4C$$

we get $A = 6$, $B = 1$, and $C = -3$.

Then the decomposition is

$$\dfrac{6}{x - 4} + \dfrac{1}{2x - 1} + \dfrac{-3}{(2x - 1)^2}.$$

23. $\dfrac{36x + 1}{12x^2 - 7x - 10} = \dfrac{36x + 1}{(4x - 5)(3x + 2)}$

The decomposition looks like

$$\dfrac{A}{4x - 5} + \dfrac{B}{3x + 2}.$$

Add and equate the numerators.

$$36x + 1 = A(3x + 2) + B(4x - 5)$$
or $36x + 1 = (3A + 4B)x + (2A - 5B)$

Then equate corresponding coefficients.

$36 = 3A + 4B$ (Coefficients of x-terms)
$1 = 2A - 5B$ (Constant terms)

We solve this system of equations and find
$A = 8$ and $B = 3$.

The decomposition is

$$\dfrac{8}{4x - 5} + \dfrac{3}{3x + 2}.$$

24. $\dfrac{-17x + 61}{6x^2 + 39x - 21} = \dfrac{A}{6x - 3} + \dfrac{B}{x + 7}$

$$-17x + 61 = (A + 6B)x + (7A - 3B)$$
$$-17 = A + 6B,$$
$$61 = 7A - 3B$$

Then $A = 7$ and $B = -4$.

The decomposition is

$$\dfrac{7}{6x - 3} + \dfrac{-4}{x + 7}.$$

25. $\dfrac{-4x^2 - 9x + 8}{(3x^2 + 1)(x - 2)}$

The decomposition looks like

$$\dfrac{Ax + B}{3x^2 + 1} + \dfrac{C}{x - 2}.$$

Add and equate the numerators.

$$-4x^2 - 9x + 8 = (Ax + B)(x - 2) + C(3x^2 + 1)$$
$$= Ax^2 - 2Ax + Bx - 2B + 3Cx^2 + C$$
or $-4x^2 - 9x + 8 = (A + 3C)x^2 + (-2A + B)x +$
$$(-2B + C)$$

Then equate corresponding coefficients.

$-4 = A + 3C$ (Coefficients of x^2-terms)
$-9 = -2A + B$ (Coefficients of x-terms)
$8 = -2B + C$ (Constant terms)

We solve this system of equations and find
$A = 2$, $B = -5$, $C = -2$.

The decomposition is

$$\dfrac{2x - 5}{3x^2 + 1} + \dfrac{-2}{x - 2}.$$

26. $\dfrac{11x^2 - 39x + 16}{(x^2 + 4)(x - 8)} = \dfrac{Ax + B}{x^2 + 4} + \dfrac{C}{x - 8}$

$11x^2 - 39x + 16 = (A + C)x^2 + (-8A + B)x +$
$$(-8B + 4C)$$

$$11 = A + C,$$
$$-39 = -8A + B,$$
$$16 = -8B + 4C$$

Then $A = 5$, $B = 1$, and $C = 6$.

The decomposition is

$$\dfrac{5x + 1}{x^2 + 4} + \dfrac{6}{x - 8}.$$

27. $\dfrac{x}{x^4 - a^4}$

$$= \dfrac{x}{(x^2 + a^2)(x + a)(x - a)} \quad \text{(Factoring the denominator)}$$
$$= \dfrac{Ax + B}{x^2 + a^2} + \dfrac{C}{x + a} + \dfrac{D}{x - a}$$
$$= \dfrac{(Ax+B)(x+a)(x-a) + C(x^2+a^2)(x-a) + D(x^2+a^2)(x+a)}{(x^2 + a^2)(x + a)(x - a)}$$

Equate the numerators:

$x = (Ax + B)(x + a)(x - a) + C(x^2 + a^2)(x - a) +$
$$D(x^2 + a^2)(x + a)$$

Let $x - a = 0$, or $x = a$. Then, we get
$$a = 0 + 0 + D(a^2 + a^2)(a + a)$$
$$a = D(2a^2)(2a)$$
$$a = 4a^3D$$
$$\dfrac{1}{4a^2} = D$$

Let $x + a = 0$, or $x = -a$. We get
$$-a = 0 + C[(-a)^2 + a^2](-a - a) + 0$$
$$-a = C(2a^2)(-2a)$$
$$-a = -4a^3C$$
$$\dfrac{1}{4a^2} = C$$

Equate the coefficients of x^3:

$0 = A + C + D$

Substituting $\frac{1}{4a^2}$ for C and for D, we get

$A = -\frac{1}{2a^2}$.

Equate the constant terms:

$0 = -Ba^2 - Ca^3 + Da^3$

Substitute $\frac{1}{4a^2}$ for C and for D. Then solve for B.

$0 = -Ba^2 - \frac{1}{4a^2} \cdot a^3 + \frac{1}{4a^2} \cdot a^3$

$0 = -Ba^2$

$0 = B$

The decomposition is as follows:

$$\frac{-\frac{1}{2a^2}x}{x^2 + a^2} + \frac{\frac{1}{4a^2}}{x + a} + \frac{\frac{1}{4a^2}}{x - a}$$

28. $\dfrac{9x^3 - 24x^2 + 48x}{(x - 2)^4(x + 1)} = \dfrac{A}{x + 1} + \dfrac{P(x)}{(x - 2)^4}$

Add and equate numerators.

$9x^3 - 24x^2 + 48x = A(x - 2)^4 + P(x)(x + 1)$

Let $x = -1$:

$9(-1)^3 - 24(-1)^2 + 48(-1) = A(-1 - 2)^4 + 0$

$\qquad\qquad\qquad\qquad -81 = 81A$

$\qquad\qquad\qquad\qquad -1 = A$

Then $9x^3 - 24x^2 + 48x = -(x - 2)^4 + P(x)(x + 1)$

$\quad 9x^3 - 24x^2 + 48x = -x^4 + 8x^3 - 24x^2 + 32x -$

$\qquad\qquad\qquad\qquad 16 + P(x)(x + 1)$

$\quad x^4 + x^3 + 16x + 16 = P(x)(x + 1)$

$\qquad\qquad x^3 + 16 = P(x)$ (Dividing by $x + 1$)

Now decompose $\dfrac{x^3 + 16}{(x - 2)^4}$.

$\dfrac{x^3 + 16}{(x - 2)^4} = \dfrac{B}{x - 2} + \dfrac{C}{(x - 2)^2} + \dfrac{D}{(x - 2)^3} + \dfrac{E}{(x - 2)^4}$

Add and equate numerators.

$x^3 + 16 = B(x - 2)^3 + C(x - 2)^2 +$

$\qquad\qquad D(x - 2) + E$ $\qquad\qquad\qquad$ (1)

Let $x = 2$: $2^3 + 16 = 0 + 0 + 0 + E$

$\qquad\qquad\qquad\quad 24 = E$

Simplify Eq. (1).

$x^3 + 16 = Bx^3 + (-6B + C)x^2 + (12B - 4C + D)x +$

$\qquad\qquad (-8B + 4C - 2D + E)$

$1 = B$

$0 = -6B + C$

$0 = -6 \cdot 1 + C$

$6 = C$

$0 = 12B - 4C + D$

$0 = 12 \cdot 1 - 4 \cdot 6 + D$

$12 = D$

The decomposition is

$$\frac{-1}{x + 1} + \frac{1}{x - 2} + \frac{6}{(x - 2)^2} + \frac{12}{(x - 2)^3} + \frac{24}{(x - 2)^4}.$$

29. $f(x) = \dfrac{3x}{x^2 + 5x + 4} = \dfrac{3x}{(x + 4)(x + 1)}$

$\dfrac{3x}{(x + 4)(x + 1)} = \dfrac{A}{x + 4} + \dfrac{B}{x + 1}$

$\qquad\qquad\qquad = \dfrac{A(x + 1) + B(x + 4)}{(x + 4)(x + 1)}$

Equate the numerators:

$3x = A(x + 1) + B(x + 4)$

Let $x + 1 = 0$, or $x = -1$. We get

$3(-1) = 0 + B(-1 + 4)$

$\quad -3 = 3B$

$\quad -1 = B$

Next let $x + 4 = 0$, or $x = -4$. Then we get

$3(-4) = A(-4 + 1) + 0$

$\quad -12 = -3A$

$\qquad 4 = A$

The decomposition is $f(x) = \dfrac{4}{x + 4} + \dfrac{-1}{x + 1}$, or

$\dfrac{4}{x + 4} - \dfrac{1}{x + 1}$.

We graph by addition of ordinates (adding respective fraction values.)

If $x = 4$, $y = \dfrac{4}{4 + 4} - \dfrac{1}{4 + 1} = \dfrac{1}{2} - \dfrac{1}{5} = \dfrac{3}{10}$.

If $x = 2$, $y = \dfrac{4}{2 + 4} - \dfrac{1}{2 + 1} = \dfrac{2}{3} - \dfrac{1}{3} = \dfrac{1}{3}$.

If $x = 0$, $y = \dfrac{4}{0 + 4} - \dfrac{1}{0 + 1} = 1 - 1 = 0$.

If $x = -2$, $y = \dfrac{4}{-2 + 4} - \dfrac{1}{-2 + 1} = 2 + 1 = 3$.

Continue adding fraction values as above. Then plot these points and draw the graph. Note that $x = -4$ and $x = -1$ are vertical asymptotes.

$f(x) = \dfrac{3x}{x^2 + 5x + 4}$

30. $f(x) = \dfrac{x - 1}{x^2 - 2x - 3} = \dfrac{x - 1}{(x - 3)(x + 1)}$

$\dfrac{x - 1}{(x - 3)(x + 1)} = \dfrac{A}{x - 3} + \dfrac{B}{x + 1}$

Add and equate numerators.

$x - 1 = A(x + 1) + B(x - 3)$

Let $x = -1$: $-1 - 1 = 0 + B(-1 - 3)$

$\qquad\qquad\qquad -2 = -4B$

$\qquad\qquad\qquad \dfrac{1}{2} = B$

Let $x = 3$: $3 - 1 = A(3 + 1) + 0$

$\qquad\qquad\qquad 2 = 4A$

$\qquad\qquad\qquad \dfrac{1}{2} = A$

The decomposition is $f(x) = \dfrac{\frac{1}{2}}{x - 3} + \dfrac{\frac{1}{2}}{x + 1}$.

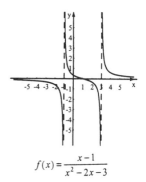

$f(x) = \dfrac{x - 1}{x^2 - 2x - 3}$

31. $\dfrac{1 + \ln x^2}{(\ln x + 2)(\ln x - 3)^2} = \dfrac{1 + 2 \ln x}{(\ln x + 2)(\ln x - 3)^2}$

Let $u = \ln x$. Then we have:

$\dfrac{1 + 2u}{(u + 2)(u - 3)^2} = \dfrac{A}{u + 2} + \dfrac{B}{(u - 3)} + \dfrac{C}{(u - 3)^2}$

$\qquad\qquad\qquad = \dfrac{A(u-3)^2 + B(u+2)(u-3) + C(u+2)}{(u + 2)(u - 3)^2}$

Equate the numerators:

$1 + 2u = A(u - 3)^2 + B(u + 2)(u - 3) + C(u + 2)$

Let $u - 3 = 0$, or $u = 3$.

$\qquad 1 + 2 \cdot 3 = 0 + 0 + C(5)$

$\qquad\qquad 7 = 5C$

$\qquad\qquad \dfrac{7}{5} = C$

Let $u + 2 = 0$, or $u = -2$.

$\qquad 1 + 2(-2) = A(-2 - 3)^2 + 0 + 0$

$\qquad\qquad -3 = 25A$

$\qquad\qquad -\dfrac{3}{25} = A$

To find B, we equate the coefficients of u^2:

$\qquad 0 = A + B$

Substituting $-\dfrac{3}{25}$ for A and solving for B, we get $B = \dfrac{3}{25}$.

The decomposition of $\dfrac{1 + 2u}{(u + 2)(u - 3)^2}$ is as follows:

$\qquad -\dfrac{3}{25(u + 2)} + \dfrac{3}{25(u - 3)} + \dfrac{7}{5(u - 3)^2}$

Substituting $\ln x$ for u we get

$-\dfrac{3}{25(\ln x + 2)} + \dfrac{3}{25(\ln x - 3)} + \dfrac{7}{5(\ln x - 3)^2}$.

32. $\dfrac{1}{e^{-x} + 3 + 2e^x} = \dfrac{e^x}{1 + 3e^x + 2e^{2x}}$

$\qquad\qquad\qquad$ (Multiplying by e^x/e^x)

Let $y = e^x$, decompose $\dfrac{y}{2y^2 + 3y + 1}$, and then substitute e^x for y. The result is $\dfrac{1}{e^x + 1} - \dfrac{1}{2e^x + 1}$.

1.
$$x^2 - y^2 = 0$$
$$(x + y)(x - y) = 0$$

$x + y = 0$ or $x - y = 0$
$y = -x$ or $y = x$

The graph consists of two intersecting lines.

2.
$$x^2 - 9y^2 = 0$$
$$(x + 3y)(x - 3y) = 0$$
$$y = -\frac{1}{3}x \text{ or } y = \frac{1}{3}x$$

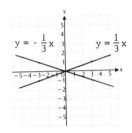

3.
$$3x^2 + xy - 2y^2 = 0$$
$$(3x - 2y)(x + y) = 0$$

$3x - 2y = 0$ or $x + y = 0$
$y = \frac{3}{2}x$ or $y = -x$

The graph consists of two intersecting lines.

4.

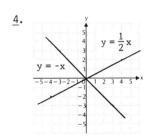

5. $2x^2 + y^2 = 0$

The expression $2x^2 + y^2$ is not factorable in the real-number system. The only real-number solution of the equation is (0, 0). The graph is the point (0, 0).

6. $5x^2 + y^2 = -3$

Since squares of numbers are never negative, the left side of the equation can never be negative. The equation has no real-number solution, hence has no graph.

7. $\dfrac{x^2}{4} + \dfrac{y^2}{1} = 1$

$$\frac{x^2}{2^2} + \frac{y^2}{1^2} = 1$$

The center of the ellipse is (0, 0); a = 2 and b = 1.

Two of the vertices are (-2, 0) and (2, 0). These are also the x-intercepts. The other two vertices are (0, -1) and (0, 1). These are also the y-intercepts.

Since a > b, we find c using $c^2 = a^2 - b^2$.

$$c^2 = a^2 - b^2 = 4 - 1 = 3$$

Thus $c = \sqrt{3}$.

The foci are on the x-axis. They are $(-\sqrt{3}, 0)$ and $(\sqrt{3}, 0)$.

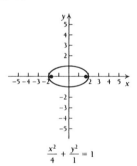

$$\frac{x^2}{4} + \frac{y^2}{1} = 1$$

8. V: (-1, 0),   (1, 0),
        (0, -2),   (0, 2)

$$c^2 = 4 - 1 = 3$$

F: $(0, -\sqrt{3})$, $(0, \sqrt{3})$

9. $16x^2 + 9y^2 = 144$

$$\frac{x^2}{9} + \frac{y^2}{16} = 1 \qquad \left[\text{Multiplying by } \tfrac{1}{144}\right]$$

$$\frac{x^2}{3^2} + \frac{y^2}{4^2} = 1$$

The center of the ellipse is (0, 0); a = 3 and b = 4.

Two of the vertices are (-3, 0) and (3, 0). These are also the x-intercepts. The other two vertices are (0, -4) and (0, 4). These are also the y-intercepts.

Since b > a, we find c using $c^2 = b^2 - a^2$.

$c^2 = b^2 - a^2 = 16 - 9 = 7$

Thus $c = \sqrt{7}$.

The foci are on the y-axis. They are $(0, -\sqrt{7})$ and $(0, \sqrt{7})$.

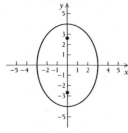

$16x^2 + 9y^2 = 144$

10. $9x^2 + 16y^2 = 144$

$$\frac{x^2}{16} + \frac{y^2}{9} = 1$$

V: (-4, 0),   (4, 0),

     (0, -3),   (0, 3)

$c^2 = 16 - 9 = 7$

F: $(-\sqrt{7}, 0)$, $(\sqrt{7}, 0)$

11. $2x^2 + 3y^2 = 6$

$$\frac{x^2}{3} + \frac{y^2}{2} = 1 \qquad \left[\text{Multiplying by } \tfrac{1}{6}\right]$$

$$\frac{x^2}{(\sqrt{3})^2} + \frac{y^2}{(\sqrt{2})^2} = 1$$

The center of the ellipse is (0, 0); a = $\sqrt{3}$ and b = $\sqrt{2}$.

Two of the vertices are $(-\sqrt{3}, 0)$ and $(\sqrt{3}, 0)$. These are also the x-intercepts. The other two vertices are $(0, -\sqrt{2})$ and $(0, \sqrt{2})$. These are also the y-intercepts.

Since a > b, we find c using $c^2 = a^2 - b^2$.

$c^2 = a^2 - b^2 = 3 - 2 = 1$

Thus c = 1.

The foci are on the x-axis. They are (-1, 0) and (1, 0).

$2x^2 + 3y^2 = 6$

12. $5x^2 + 7y^2 = 35$

$$\frac{x^2}{7} + \frac{y^2}{5} = 1$$

V: $(-\sqrt{7}, 0)$, $(\sqrt{7}, 0)$,

     $(0, -\sqrt{5})$, $(0, \sqrt{5})$

$c^2 = 7 - 5 = 2$

F: $(-\sqrt{2}, 0)$, $(\sqrt{2}, 0)$

13. $4x^2 + 9y^2 = 1$

$$\frac{x^2}{\frac{1}{4}} + \frac{y^2}{\frac{1}{9}} = 1$$

$$\frac{x^2}{\left(\frac{1}{2}\right)^2} + \frac{y^2}{\left(\frac{1}{3}\right)^2} = 1$$

The center of the ellipse is (0, 0); a = $\frac{1}{2}$ and b = $\frac{1}{3}$.

Two of the vertices are $\left(-\frac{1}{2}, 0\right)$ and $\left(\frac{1}{2}, 0\right)$. These are also the x-intercepts. The other two vertices are $\left(0, -\frac{1}{3}\right)$ and $\left(0, \frac{1}{3}\right)$. These are also the y-intercepts.

Since a > b, we find c using $c^2 = a^2 - b^2$.

$c^2 = a^2 - b^2 = \frac{1}{4} - \frac{1}{9} = \frac{5}{36}$

Thus $c = \frac{\sqrt{5}}{6}$.

The foci are on the x-axis. They are $\left(-\frac{\sqrt{5}}{6}, 0\right)$ and $\left(\frac{\sqrt{5}}{6}, 0\right)$.

$4x^2 + 9y^2 = 1$

14. $25x^2 + 16y^2 = 1$

$$\frac{x^2}{\frac{1}{25}} + \frac{y^2}{\frac{1}{16}} = 1$$

V: $\left[-\frac{1}{5}, 0\right]$, $\left[\frac{1}{5}, 0\right]$,

$\left[0, -\frac{1}{4}\right]$, $\left[0, \frac{1}{4}\right]$

$c^2 = \frac{1}{16} - \frac{1}{25} = \frac{9}{400}$

F: $\left[0, -\frac{3}{20}\right]$, $\left[0, \frac{3}{20}\right]$

15. $\frac{(x - 1)^2}{4} + \frac{(y - 2)^2}{1} = 1$

$$\frac{(x - 1)^2}{2^2} + \frac{(y - 2)^2}{1^2} = 1$$

The center is (1, 2); a = 2 and b = 1. Since a > b, we find c using $c^2 = a^2 - b^2$.

$c^2 = a^2 - b^2 = 4 - 1 = 3$

Thus $c = \sqrt{3}$.

Consider the ellipse $\frac{x^2}{2^2} + \frac{y^2}{1^2} = 1$.

The center is (0, 0); a = 2, b = 1, and $c = \sqrt{3}$.
The vertices are (-2, 0), (2, 0), (0, -1), and (0, 1).
The foci are $(-\sqrt{3}, 0)$ and $(\sqrt{3}, 0)$.

The vertices and foci of the translated ellipse are found by translation in the same way in which the center has been translated.

The vertices are

(-2 + 1, 0 + 2), (2 + 1, 0 + 2), (0 + 1, -1 + 2),
      and (0 + 1, 1 + 2).

or

(-1, 2), (3, 2), (1, 1), and (1, 3).

The foci are

$(-\sqrt{3} + 1, 0 + 2)$ and $(\sqrt{3} + 1, 0 + 2)$

or

$(1 - \sqrt{3}, 2)$ and $(1 + \sqrt{3}, 2)$.

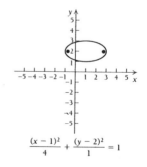

$$\frac{(x - 1)^2}{4} + \frac{(y - 2)^2}{1} = 1$$

16. C: (1, 2)

V: (0, 2), (2, 2),
    (1, 0), (1, 4)

$c^2 = 4 - 1 = 3$

F: $(1, 2 - \sqrt{3})$,
    $(1, 2 + \sqrt{3})$

17. $\frac{(x + 3)^2}{25} + \frac{(y - 2)^2}{16} = 1$

$$\frac{[x - (-3)]^2}{5^2} + \frac{(y - 2)^2}{4^2} = 1$$

The center is (-3, 2); a = 5 and b = 4. Since a > b, we find c using $c^2 = a^2 - b^2$.

$c^2 = a^2 - b^2 = 25 - 16 = 9$

Thus c = 3.

Consider the ellipse $\frac{x^2}{5^2} + \frac{y^2}{4^2} = 1$.

The center is (0, 0); a = 5, b = 4, and c = 3.
The vertices are (-5, 0), (5, 0), (0, -4) and (0, 4).
The foci are (-3, 0) and (3, 0).

The vertices and foci of the translated ellipse are found by translation in the same way in which the center has been translated.

The vertices are

(-5 - 3, 0 + 2), (5 - 3, 0 + 2), (0 - 3, -4 + 2),
and (0 - 3, 4 + 2)

or

(-8, 2), (2, 2), (-3, -2), and (-3, 6).

The foci are

(-3 - 3, 0 + 2) and (3 - 3, 0 + 2)

or

(-6, 2) and (0, 2).

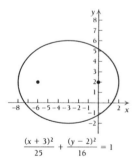

$$\frac{(x + 3)^2}{25} + \frac{(y - 2)^2}{16} = 1$$

18. C: (2, -3)

V: (-3, -3), (7, -3),
    (2, -7), (2, 1)

$c^2 = 25 - 16 = 9$

F: (-1, -3), (5, -3)

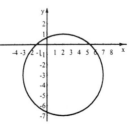

19. $3(x + 2)^2 + 4(y - 1)^2 = 192$

$$\frac{(x + 2)^2}{64} + \frac{(y - 1)^2}{48} = 1 \quad \left[\text{Multiplying by } \frac{1}{192}\right]$$

$$\frac{(x + 2)^2}{8^2} + \frac{(y - 1)^2}{(4\sqrt{3})^2} = 1$$

The center is (-2, 1); $a = 8$ and $b = 4\sqrt{3}$. Since $a > b$, we find c using $c^2 = a^2 - b^2$.

$c^2 = a^2 - b^2 = 64 - 48 = 16$

Thus $c = 4$.

Consider the ellipse $\frac{x^2}{8^2} + \frac{y^2}{(4\sqrt{3})^2} = 1$

The center is (0, 0); $a = 8$, $b = 4\sqrt{3}$, and $c = 4$.

The vertices are (-8, 0), (8, 0), (0, -4√3) and (0, 4√3).

The foci are (-4, 0) and (4, 0).

The vertices and foci of the translated ellipse are found by translation in the same way in which the center has been translated.

The vertices are

(-8 - 2, 0 + 1), (8 - 2, 0 + 1), (0 - 2, -4√3 + 1) and (0 - 2, 4√3 + 1)

or

(-10, 1), (6, 1), (-2, 1 - 4√3), and (-2, 1 + 4√3).

The foci are

(-4 - 2, 0 + 1) and (4 - 2, 0 + 1)

or

(-6, 1) and (2, 1).

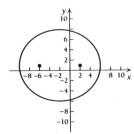

$3(x + 2)^2 + 4(y - 1)^2 = 192$

20. $4(x - 5)^2 + 3(y - 5)^2 = 192$

$$\frac{(x - 5)^2}{48} + \frac{(y - 5)^2}{64} = 1$$

C: (5, 5)

V: (5 - 4√3, 5), (5 + 4√3, 5),
   (5, -3), (5, 13)

$c^2 = 64 - 48 = 16$

F: (5, 1), (5, 9)

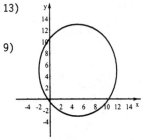

21. $4x^2 + 9y^2 - 16x + 18y - 11 = 0$

$(4x^2 - 16x) + (9y^2 + 18y) = 11$

$4(x^2 - 4x) + 9(y^2 + 2y) = 11$

$4(x^2 - 4x + 4) + 9(y^2 + 2y + 1) = 11 + 16 + 9$

$4(x - 2)^2 + 9(y + 1)^2 = 36$

$$\frac{(x - 2)^2}{9} + \frac{(y + 1)^2}{4} = 1$$

$$\frac{(x - 2)^2}{3^2} + \frac{[y - (-1)]^2}{2^2} = 1$$

The center is (2, -1); $a = 3$ and $b = 2$. Since $a > b$, we find c using $c^2 = a^2 - b^2$.

$c^2 = a^2 - b^2 = 9 - 4 = 5$

Thus $c = \sqrt{5}$.

Consider the ellipse $\frac{x^2}{3^2} + \frac{y^2}{2^2} = 1$.

The center is (0, 0); $a = 3$, $b = 2$, and $c = \sqrt{5}$.

The vertices are (-3, 0), (3, 0), (0, -2), and (0, 2).

The foci are (-√5, 0) and (√5, 0).

The vertices and foci of the translated ellipse are found by translation in the same way in which the center has been translated.

The vertices are

(-3 + 2, 0 - 1), (3 + 2, 0 - 1), (0 + 2, -2 - 1), and (0 + 2, 2 - 1)

or

(-1, -1), (5, -1), (2, -3), and (2, 1).

The foci are

(-√5 + 2, 0 - 1) and (√5 + 2, 0 - 1)

or

(2 - √5, -1) and (2 + √5, -1).

$4x^2 + 9y^2 - 16x + 18y - 11 = 0$

22. $x^2 + 2y^2 - 10x + 8y + 29 = 0$

$x^2 - 10x + 2(y^2 + 4y) = -29$

$x^2 - 10x + 25 + 2(y^2 + 4y + 4) = -29 + 25 + 8$

$(x - 5)^2 + 2(y + 2)^2 = 4$

$$\frac{(x - 5)^2}{4} + \frac{(y + 2)^2}{2} = 1$$

C: (5, -2)

V: (3, -2), (7, -2),
   (5, -2 - √2) (5, -2 + √2)

$c^2 = 4 - 2 = 2$

F: (5 - √2, -2), (5 + √2, -2)

23.
$$4x^2 + y^2 - 8x - 2y + 1 = 0$$
$$(4x^2 - 8x) + (y^2 - 2y) = -1$$
$$4(x^2 - 2x) + (y^2 - 2y) = -1$$
$$4(x^2 - 2x + 1) + (y^2 - 2y + 1) = -1 + 4 + 1$$
$$4(x - 1)^2 + (y - 1)^2 = 4$$
$$\frac{(x - 1)^2}{1^2} + \frac{(y - 1)^2}{2^2} = 1$$

The center is (1, 1); a = 1 and b = 2. Since b > a, we find c using $c^2 = b^2 - a^2$.

$$c^2 = b^2 - a^2 = 4 - 1 = 3$$

Thus c = $\sqrt{3}$.

Consider the ellipse $\frac{x^2}{1^2} + \frac{y^2}{2^2} = 1$.

The center is (0, 0); a = 1, b = 2, and c = $\sqrt{3}$.

The vertices are (-1, 0), (1, 0), (0, -2), and (0, 2).

The foci are (0, $-\sqrt{3}$) and (0, $\sqrt{3}$).

The vertices and foci of the translated ellipse are found by translation in the same way in which the center has been translated.

The vertices are

(-1 + 1, 0 + 1), (1 + 1, 0 + 1), (0 + 1, -2 + 1), and (0 + 1, 2 + 1)

or

(0, 1), (2, 1), (1, -1), and (1, 3).

The foci are

(0 + 1, $-\sqrt{3}$ + 1) and (0 + 1, $\sqrt{3}$ + 1)

or

(1, 1 - $\sqrt{3}$) and (1, 1 + $\sqrt{3}$).

$4x^2 + y^2 - 8x - 2y + 1 = 0$

24.
$$9x^2 + 4y^2 + 54x - 8y + 49 = 0$$
$$9(x^2 + 6x) + 4(y^2 - 2y) = -49$$
$$9(x^2 + 6x + 9) + 4(y^2 - 2y + 1) = -49 + 81 + 4$$
$$9(x + 3)^2 + 4(y - 1)^2 = 36$$
$$\frac{(x + 3)^2}{4} + \frac{(y - 1)^2}{9} = 1$$

C: (-3, 1)

V: (-5, 1),   (-1, 1)

     (-3, -2),   (-3, 4)

$c^2 = 9 - 4 = 5$

F: (-3, 1 - $\sqrt{5}$),

     (-3, 1 + $\sqrt{5}$)

25. Graph the vertices and sketch the axes of the ellipse.

The intersection of the axes, which is (0, 0), is the center of the ellipse. Note that a = 2 and b = 3. Now find an equation of the ellipse (in standard form).

$$\frac{(x - h)^2}{a^2} + \frac{(y - k)^2}{b^2} = 1$$
$$\frac{(x - 0)^2}{2^2} + \frac{(y - 0)^2}{3^2} = 1 \qquad \text{(Substituting)}$$
$$\frac{x^2}{4} + \frac{y^2}{9} = 1$$

26.

C: (0, 0), a = 1, b = 4

$$x^2 + \frac{y^2}{16} = 1$$

27. Graph the vertices and sketch the axes of the ellipse.

The intersection of the axes, which is (3, 1), is the center of the ellipse. Note that a = 2 and b = 5. Now find an equation of the ellipse (in standard form).

$$\frac{(x - h)^2}{a^2} + \frac{(y - k)^2}{b^2} = 1$$

$$\frac{(x - 3)^2}{2^2} + \frac{(y - 1)^2}{5^2} = 1 \qquad \text{(Substituting)}$$

$$\frac{(x - 3)^2}{4} + \frac{(y - 1)^2}{25} = 1$$

28.

29. Graph the center, (-2, 3), and sketch the axes of the ellipse. The major axis of length 4 is parallel to the y-axis. The minor axis of length 1 is parallel to the x-axis.

Note that $a = \frac{1}{2}$ and b = 2. Find an equation (in standard form) of the ellipse.

$$\frac{(x - h)^2}{a^2} + \frac{(y - k)^2}{b^2} = 1$$

$$\frac{[x - (-2)]^2}{\left(\frac{1}{2}\right)^2} + \frac{(y - 3)^2}{2^2} = 1 \qquad \text{(Substituting)}$$

$$\frac{(x + 2)^2}{\frac{1}{4}} + \frac{(y - 3)^2}{4} = 1$$

30. C: (0, 0), a = 3

$$\frac{x^2}{3^2} + \frac{y^2}{b^2} = 1$$

$$\frac{2^2}{3^2} + \frac{\left(\frac{22}{3}\right)^2}{b^2} = 1 \qquad \left[\text{Substituting}\left(2, \frac{22}{3}\right)\right]$$

$$\frac{4}{9} + \frac{484}{9b^2} = 1$$

$$\frac{484}{9b^2} = \frac{5}{9}$$

$$\frac{484}{5} = b^2$$

$$\frac{x^2}{9} + \frac{y^2}{\frac{484}{5}} = 1, \text{ or } \frac{x^2}{9} + \frac{5y^2}{484} = 1$$

31. a)

The relation is not a function. It does not pass the vertical line test.

b) $9x^2 + y^2 = 9$

$$y^2 = 9 - 9x^2$$

$$y = \pm\sqrt{9 - 9x^2}$$

$$y = \pm 3\sqrt{1 - x^2}$$

c)

The relation is a function. It does pass the vertical line test.

Domain: $\{x | -1 \leqslant x \leqslant 1\}$

Range: $\{y | 0 \leqslant y \leqslant 3\}$

d)

The relation is a function. It does pass the vertical line test.

Domain: $\{x | -1 \leqslant x \leqslant 1\}$

Range: $\{y | -3 \leqslant y \leqslant 0\}$

32. Circle with center (0, 0) and radius a.

33. Draw the graph as instructed.

34. 1 unit = 10^7 mi

From the diagram it is clear that
SF = $2[0.1 \times 10^7]$ or 2×10^6 mi.

35. The vertices are (-50, 0), (50, 0), (0, -12), and
(0, 12). The equation of the ellipse is
$\frac{x^2}{50^2} + \frac{y^2}{12^2} = 1$, or $\frac{x^2}{2500} + \frac{y^2}{144} = 1$.

36.

$\frac{x^2}{524^2} + \frac{y^2}{449^2} = 1$, or $\frac{x^2}{274,576} + \frac{y^2}{201,601} = 1$

37.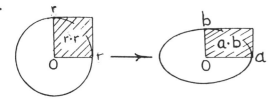

Stretching and shrinking, the area of the square,
r·r, becomes the area of the rectangle, a·b.
Hence, the area of the circle, π·r·r, becomes
the area of the ellipse, π·a·b.

b) a = 4, b = 5
    Area = π·4·5 = 20π

c) a = 524, b = 449
    Area = π·524·449 ≈ 739,141.4 ft²

38. C = C(x, y)

θ is the angle which BC makes with the positive
x-axis. Let AC = a, BC = b. Then, in all
quadrants, $\frac{x}{a}$ = cos θ and $\frac{y}{b}$ = sin θ.

Hence $\frac{x^2}{a^2} + \frac{y^2}{b^2} = 1$ which is the equation of an

ellipse.

39. C: (2.003125, -1.00515)

V: (-1.01718, -1.00515), (5.02343, -1.00515),
(2.003125, -3.018687), (2.003125, 1.008387).

40. C: (-3.0035, 1.002)

V: (-3.0035, -1.97008), (-3.0035, 3.97408)
(-1.02211, 1.002), (-4.98489, 1.002)

Exercise Set 10.2

1. $\frac{x^2}{9} - \frac{y^2}{1} = 1$

$\frac{(x - 0)^2}{3^2} - \frac{(y - 0)^2}{1^2} = 1$

The center is (0, 0); a = 3 and b = 1.
The vertices are (-3, 0) and (3, 0).

Since $c^2 = a^2 + b^2$, $c = \sqrt{a^2 + b^2} = \sqrt{9 + 1}$
                                        $= \sqrt{10}$.

The foci are $(-\sqrt{10}, 0)$ and $(\sqrt{10}, 0)$.

The asymptotes are y = $-\frac{1}{3}$ x and y = $\frac{1}{3}$ x.

$\frac{x^2}{9} - \frac{y^2}{1} = 1$

2. C: (0, 0)

 V: (-1, 0), (1, 0)

 $c = \sqrt{1 + 9} = \sqrt{10}$

 F: $(-\sqrt{10}, 0)$, $(\sqrt{10}, 0)$

 A: $y = 3x$, $y = -3x$

$$\frac{(x - 2)^2}{9} - \frac{(y + 5)^2}{1} = 1$$

3. $$\frac{(x - 2)^2}{9} - \frac{(y + 5)^2}{1} = 1$$

 $$\frac{(x - 2)^2}{3^2} - \frac{[y - (-5)]^2}{1^2} = 1$$

 The center is (2, -5); a = 3 and b = 1.

 The transverse axis is parallel to the x-axis.

 Since $c^2 = a^2 + b^2$, $c = \sqrt{a^2 + b^2} = \sqrt{9 + 1}$
 $= \sqrt{10}$.

 Consider the hyperbola $\frac{x^2}{3^2} - \frac{y^2}{1^2} = 1$.

 The center is (0, 0); a = 3, b = 1, and $c = \sqrt{10}$.
 The vertices are (-3, 0) and (3, 0).
 The foci are $(-\sqrt{10}, 0)$ and $(\sqrt{10}, 0)$.
 The asymptotes are $y = -\frac{1}{3}x$ and $y = \frac{1}{3}x$.

 The vertices, foci, and asymptotes of the translated hyperbola are found by translation in the same way in which the center has been translated.

 The vertices are (-3 + 2, 0 - 5) and
 (3 + 2, 0 - 5), or (-1, -5) and (5, -5).

 The foci are $(-\sqrt{10} + 2, 0 - 5)$ and
 $(\sqrt{10} + 2, 0 - 5)$, or $(2 - \sqrt{10}, -5)$ and
 $(2 + \sqrt{10}, -5)$.

 The asymptotes are

 $y - (-5) = -\frac{1}{3}(x - 2)$ and $y - (-5) = \frac{1}{3}(x - 2)$

 or $y = -\frac{1}{3}x - \frac{13}{3}$ and $y = \frac{1}{3}x - \frac{17}{3}$.

 Graph the hyperpola.

 First draw the rectangle which has
 (-3 + 2, 0 - 5), (3 + 2, 0 - 5), (0 + 2, -1 - 5),
 and (0 + 2, 1 - 5) or (-1, -5), (5, -5), (2, -6),
 and (2, -4) as midpoints of its four sides. Then
 draw the asymptotes and finally the branches of
 the hyperbola outward from the vertices toward the
 asymptotes.

4. C: (2, -5)

 V: (1, -5), (3, -5)

 $c = \sqrt{1 + 9} = \sqrt{10}$

 F: $(2 - \sqrt{10}, -5)$,
 $(2 + \sqrt{10}, -5)$

 A: $y + 5 = -3(x - 2)$, or
 $y = -3x + 1$ and
 $y + 5 = 3(x - 2)$, or
 $y = 3x - 11$

$$\frac{(x-2)^2}{1} - \frac{(y+5)^2}{9} = 1$$

5. $$\frac{(y + 3)^2}{4} - \frac{(x + 1)^2}{16} = 1$$

 $$\frac{[y - (-3)]^2}{2^2} - \frac{[x - (-1)]^2}{4^2} = 1$$

 The center is (-1, -3); a = 4 and b = 2.
 The transverse axis is parallel to the y-axis.

 Since $c^2 = a^2 + b^2$, $c = \sqrt{a^2 + b^2} = \sqrt{16 + 4}$
 $= 2\sqrt{5}$.

 Consider the hyperbola $\frac{y^2}{2^2} - \frac{x^2}{4^2} = 1$.

 The center is (0, 0); a = 4, b = 2, and $c = 2\sqrt{5}$.
 The vertices are (0, -2) and (0, 2).

 The foci are $(0, -2\sqrt{5})$ and $(0, 2\sqrt{5})$.

 The asymptotes are $y = -\frac{1}{2}x$ and $y = \frac{1}{2}x$.

 The vertices, foci, and asymptotes of the translated hyperbola are found by translation in the same way in which the center has been translated.

 The vertices are (0 - 1, -2 - 3) and
 (0 - 1, 2 - 3) or (-1, -5) and (-1, -1).

The foci are $(0 - 1, -2\sqrt{5} - 3)$ and
$(0 - 1, 2\sqrt{5} - 3)$ or $(-1, -3 - 2\sqrt{5})$ and
$(-1, -3 + 2\sqrt{5})$.

The asymptotes are

$y - (-3) = -\frac{1}{2}[x - (-1)]$ and

$y - (-3) = \frac{1}{2}[x - (-1)]$ or $y = -\frac{1}{2}x - \frac{7}{2}$

and $y = \frac{1}{2}x - \frac{5}{2}$.

Graph the hyperbola.

First draw the rectangle which has
$(0 - 1, -2 - 3)$, $(0 - 1, 2 - 3)$, $(4 - 1, 0 - 3)$,
and $(-4 - 1, 0 - 3)$ or $(-1, -5)$, $(-1, -1)$,
$(3, -3)$, and $(-5, -3)$ as midpoints of its four
sides. Then draw the asymptotes and finally the
branches of the hyperbola outward from the
vertices toward the asymptotes.

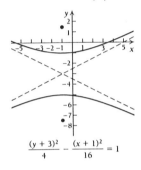

$$\frac{(y + 3)^2}{4} - \frac{(x + 1)^2}{16} = 1$$

6. C: $(-1, -3)$

V: $(-1, -8)$, $(-1, 2)$

$c = \sqrt{16 + 25} = \sqrt{41}$

F: $(-1, -3 - \sqrt{41})$,
   $(-1, -3 + \sqrt{41})$

A: $y + 3 = -\frac{5}{4}(x + 1)$, or $y = -\frac{5}{4}x - \frac{17}{4}$ and

   $y + 3 = \frac{5}{4}(x + 1)$, or $y = \frac{5}{4}x - \frac{7}{4}$

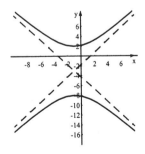

$$\frac{(y+3)^2}{25} - \frac{(x+1)^2}{16} = 1$$

7. $$x^2 - 4y^2 = 4$$
    $$\frac{x^2}{4} - \frac{y^2}{1} = 1$$
    $$\frac{(x - 0)^2}{2^2} - \frac{(y - 0)^2}{1^2} = 1$$

The center is $(0, 0)$; $a = 2$ and $b = 1$.
The vertices are $(-2, 0)$ and $(2, 0)$.
Since $c^2 = a^2 + b^2$, $c = \sqrt{a^2 + b^2} = \sqrt{4 + 1} = \sqrt{5}$.
The foci are $(-\sqrt{5}, 0)$ and $(\sqrt{5}, 0)$.
The asymptotes are $y = -\frac{1}{2}x$ and $y = \frac{1}{2}x$.

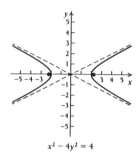

$x^2 - 4y^2 = 4$

8. $4x^2 - y^2 = 4$

   $x^2 - \frac{y^2}{4} = 1$

   C: $(0, 0)$

   V: $(-1, 0)$, $(1, 0)$

   $c = \sqrt{1 + 4} = \sqrt{5}$

   F: $(-\sqrt{5}, 0)$, $(\sqrt{5}, 0)$

   A: $y = -2x$, $y = 2x$

$4x^2 - y^2 = 4$

9. $$4y^2 - x^2 = 4$$
    $$y^2 - \frac{x^2}{4} = 1$$
    $$\frac{(y - 0)^2}{1^2} - \frac{(x - 0)^2}{2^2} = 1$$

The center is $(0, 0)$; $a = 2$ and $b = 1$.
The vertices are $(0, -1)$ and $(0, 1)$.
Since $c^2 = a^2 + b^2$, $c = \sqrt{a^2 + b^2} = \sqrt{4 + 1} = \sqrt{5}$.
The foci are $(0, -\sqrt{5})$ and $(0, \sqrt{5})$.
The asymptotes are $y = -\frac{1}{2}x$ and $y = \frac{1}{2}x$.

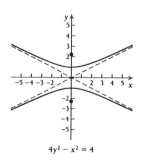

$4y^2 - x^2 = 4$

10. $y^2 - 4x^2 = 4$

$\dfrac{y^2}{4} - x^2 = 1$

C: $(0, 0)$

V: $(0, -2), (0, 2)$

$c = \sqrt{1 + 4} = \sqrt{5}$

F: $(0, -\sqrt{5}), (0, \sqrt{5})$

A: $y = -2x, \; y = 2x$

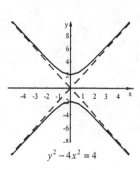

$y^2 - 4x^2 = 4$

11. $\qquad x^2 - y^2 = 2$

$\dfrac{x^2}{2} - \dfrac{y^2}{2} = 1$

$\dfrac{(x - 0)^2}{(\sqrt{2})^2} - \dfrac{(y - 0)^2}{(\sqrt{2})^2} = 1$

The center is $(0, 0)$; $a = \sqrt{2}$ and $b = \sqrt{2}$.

The vertices are $(-\sqrt{2}, 0)$ and $(\sqrt{2}, 0)$.

Since $c^2 = a^2 + b^2$, $c = \sqrt{a^2 + b^2} = \sqrt{2 + 2}$
$\qquad\qquad\qquad\qquad\qquad = \sqrt{4} = 2.$

The foci are $(-2, 0)$ and $(2, 0)$.

The asymptotes are $y = -x$ and $y = x$.

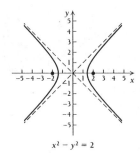

$x^2 - y^2 = 2$

12. $x^2 - y^2 = 3$

$\dfrac{x^2}{3} - \dfrac{y^2}{3} = 1$

C: $(0, 0)$

V: $(-\sqrt{3}, 0), (\sqrt{3}, 0)$

$c = \sqrt{3 + 3} = \sqrt{6}$

F: $(-\sqrt{6}, 0), (\sqrt{6}, 0)$

A: $y = -x, \; y = x$

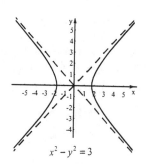

$x^2 - y^2 = 3$

13. $\qquad x^2 - y^2 = \dfrac{1}{4}$

$\dfrac{x^2}{\frac{1}{4}} - \dfrac{y^2}{\frac{1}{4}} = 1$

$\dfrac{(x - 0)^2}{\left(\frac{1}{2}\right)^2} - \dfrac{(y - 0)^2}{\left(\frac{1}{2}\right)^2} = 1$

The center is $(0, 0)$; $a = \dfrac{1}{2}$ and $b = \dfrac{1}{2}$.

The vertices are $\left[-\dfrac{1}{2}, 0\right]$ and $\left[\dfrac{1}{2}, 0\right]$.

Since $c^2 = a^2 + b^2$, $c = \sqrt{a^2 + b^2} = \sqrt{\dfrac{1}{4} + \dfrac{1}{4}}$
$\qquad\qquad\qquad\qquad\qquad = \sqrt{\dfrac{1}{2}} = \dfrac{\sqrt{2}}{2}.$

The foci are $\left[-\dfrac{\sqrt{2}}{2}, 0\right]$ and $\left[\dfrac{\sqrt{2}}{2}, 0\right]$.

The asymptotes are $y = -x$ and $y = x$.

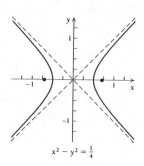

$x^2 - y^2 = \dfrac{1}{4}$

14. $x^2 - y^2 = \dfrac{1}{9}$

$\dfrac{x^2}{\frac{1}{9}} - \dfrac{y^2}{\frac{1}{9}} = 1$

C: $(0, 0)$

V: $\left[-\dfrac{1}{3}, 0\right], \left[\dfrac{1}{3}, 0\right]$

$c = \sqrt{\dfrac{1}{9} + \dfrac{1}{9}} = \dfrac{\sqrt{2}}{3}$

F: $\left[-\dfrac{\sqrt{2}}{3}, 0\right], \left[\dfrac{\sqrt{2}}{3}, 0\right]$

A: $y = -x, \; y = x$

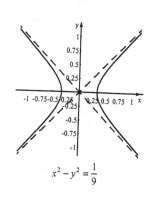

$x^2 - y^2 = \dfrac{1}{9}$

15. $\qquad x^2 - y^2 - 2x - 4y - 4 = 0$

$(x^2 - 2x) - (y^2 + 4y) = 4$

$(x^2 - 2x + 1) - (y^2 + 4y + 4) = 4 + 1 - 4$

$(x - 1)^2 - (y + 2)^2 = 1$

$\dfrac{(x - 1)^2}{1^2} - \dfrac{[y - (-2)]^2}{1^2} = 1$

The center of the hyperbola is $(1, -2)$; $a = 1$ and $b = 1$.

The transverse axis is parallel to the x-axis.

Since $c^2 = a^2 + b^2$, $c = \sqrt{a^2 + b^2} = \sqrt{1 + 1}$
$\qquad\qquad\qquad\qquad\qquad = \sqrt{2}.$

Consider the hyperbola $\dfrac{x^2}{1^2} - \dfrac{y^2}{1^2} = 1$

The center is $(0, 0)$; $a = 1$, $b = 1$, and $c = \sqrt{2}$.
The vertices are $(-1, 0)$ and $(1, 0)$.
The foci are $(-\sqrt{2}, 0)$ and $(\sqrt{2}, 0)$.
The asymptotes are $y = -x$ and $y = x$.

The vertices, foci, and asymptotes of the translated hyperbola are found in the same way in which the center has been translated.

The vertices are

(-1 + 1, 0 - 2) and (1 + 1, 0 - 2)

or

(0, -2) and (2, -2).

The foci are

$(-\sqrt{2} + 1, 0 - 2)$ and $(\sqrt{2} + 1, 0 - 2)$

or

$(1 - \sqrt{2}, -2)$ and $(1 + \sqrt{2}, -2)$.

The asymptotes are

y - (-2) = -(x - 1) and y - (-2) = x - 1

or

y = -x - 1 and y = x - 3.

$x^2 - y^2 - 2x - 4y - 4 = 0$

16. $4x^2 - y^2 + 8x - 4y - 4 = 0$

$4(x^2 + 2x + 1) - (y^2 + 4y + 4) = 4 + 4 - 4$

$(x + 1)^2 - \dfrac{(y + 2)^2}{4} = 1$

C: (-1, -2)

V: (-2, -2), (0, -2)

$c = \sqrt{1 + 4} = \sqrt{5}$

F: $(-1 - \sqrt{5}, -2),$
    $(-1 + \sqrt{5}, -2)$

A: y + 2 = -2(x + 1), or
    y = -2x - 4 and
    y + 2 = 2(x + 1), or
    y = 2x

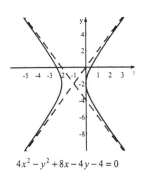

$4x^2 - y^2 + 8x - 4y - 4 = 0$

17. $36x^2 - y^2 - 24x + 6y - 41 = 0$

$(36x^2 - 24x) - (y^2 - 6y) = 41$

$36\left[x^2 - \dfrac{2}{3} x\right] - (y^2 - 6y) = 41$

$36\left[x^2 - \dfrac{2}{3} x + \dfrac{1}{9}\right] - (y^2 - 6y + 9) = 41 + 4 - 9$

$36\left[x - \dfrac{1}{3}\right]^2 - (y - 3)^2 = 36$

$\dfrac{\left[x - \dfrac{1}{3}\right]^2}{1} - \dfrac{(y - 3)^2}{36} = 1$

$\dfrac{\left[x - \dfrac{1}{3}\right]^2}{1^2} - \dfrac{(y - 3)^2}{6^2} = 1$

The center of the hyperbola is $\left[\dfrac{1}{3}, 3\right]$; a = 1 and b = 6.

The transverse axis is parallel to the x-axis.

Since $c^2 = a^2 + b^2$, $c = \sqrt{a^2 + b^2} = \sqrt{1 + 36}$
$= \sqrt{37}.$

Consider the hyperbola $\dfrac{x^2}{1^2} - \dfrac{y^2}{6^2} = 1$.

The center is (0, 0); a = 1, b = 6, and $c = \sqrt{37}$.
The vertices are (-1, 0) and (1, 0).
The foci are $(-\sqrt{37}, 0)$ and $(\sqrt{37}, 0)$.
The asymptotes are y = -6x and y = 6x.

The vertices, foci, and asymptotes of the translated hyperbola are found in the same way in which the center has been translated.

The vertices are

$\left[-1 + \dfrac{1}{3}, 0 + 3\right]$ and $\left[1 + \dfrac{1}{3}, 0 + 3\right]$

or

$\left[-\dfrac{2}{3}, 3\right]$ and $\left[\dfrac{4}{3}, 3\right]$.

The foci are

$\left[-\sqrt{37} + \dfrac{1}{3}, 0 + 3\right]$ and $\left[\sqrt{37} + \dfrac{1}{3}, 0 + 3\right]$

or

$\left[\dfrac{1}{3} - \sqrt{37}, 3\right]$ and $\left[\dfrac{1}{3} + \sqrt{37}, 3\right]$.

The asymptotes are

$y - 3 = -6\left[x - \dfrac{1}{3}\right]$ and $y - 3 = 6\left[x - \dfrac{1}{3}\right]$

or

y = -6x + 5 and y = 6x + 1.

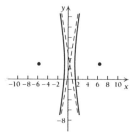

$36x^2 - y^2 - 24x + 6y - 41 = 0$

18. $9x^2 - 4y^2 + 54x + 8y + 45 = 0$

$9(x^2 + 6x + 9) - 4(y^2 - 2y + 1) = -45 + 81 - 4$

$\dfrac{(x + 3)^2}{\dfrac{32}{9}} - \dfrac{(y - 1)^2}{8} = 1$

C: (-3, 1)

V: $\left[-3 + \dfrac{4\sqrt{2}}{3}, 1\right]$

    $\left[-3 - \dfrac{4\sqrt{2}}{3}, 1\right]$

$c = \sqrt{\dfrac{32}{9} + 8} = \dfrac{2\sqrt{26}}{3}$

F: $\left(-3 + \dfrac{2\sqrt{26}}{3}, 1\right)$,

$\left(-3 - \dfrac{2\sqrt{26}}{3}, 1\right)$

A: $y - 1 = -\dfrac{2\sqrt{2}}{\dfrac{4\sqrt{2}}{3}}(x + 3)$, or

$y = -\dfrac{3}{2} - \dfrac{7}{2}$ and

$y - 1 = \dfrac{2\sqrt{2}}{\dfrac{4\sqrt{2}}{3}}(x + 3)$, or

$y = \dfrac{3}{2}x + \dfrac{11}{2}$

$9x^2 - 4y^2 + 54x + 8y + 45 = 0$

<u>19.</u> $9y^2 - 4x^2 - 18y + 24x - 63 = 0$

$9(y^2 - 2y) - 4(x^2 - 6x) = 63$

$9(y^2 - 2y + 1) - 4(x^2 - 6x + 9) = 63 + 9 - 36$

$9(y - 1)^2 - 4(x - 3)^2 = 36$

$\dfrac{(y - 1)^2}{4} - \dfrac{(x - 3)^2}{9} = 1$

The center of the hyperbola is (3, 1); a = 3 and b = 2.

The transverse axis is parallel to the y-axis. Since $c^2 = a^2 + b^2$, $c = \sqrt{a^2 + b^2} = \sqrt{9 + 4}$
$= \sqrt{13}$.

Consider the hyperbola $\dfrac{y^2}{4} - \dfrac{x^2}{9} = 1$.

The center is (0, 0); a = 3, b = 2, and $c = \sqrt{13}$. The vertices are (0, -2) and (0, 2). The foci are (0, $-\sqrt{13}$) and (0, $\sqrt{13}$). The asymptotes are $y = -\dfrac{2}{3}x$ and $y = \dfrac{2}{3}x$.

The vertices, foci, and asymptotes of the translated hyperbola are found in the same way in which the center has been translated.

The vertices are (0 + 3, -2 + 1) and (0 + 3, 2 + 1) or (3, -1) and (3, 3).

The foci are (0 + 3, $-\sqrt{13}$ + 1) and (0 + 3, $\sqrt{13}$ + 1) or (3, 1 $- \sqrt{13}$) and (3, 1 + $\sqrt{13}$).

The asymptotes are

$y - 1 = -\dfrac{2}{3}(x - 3)$ and $y - 1 = \dfrac{2}{3}(x - 3)$ or

$y = -\dfrac{2}{3}x + 3$ and $y = \dfrac{2}{3}x - 1$.

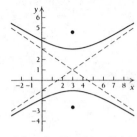

$9y^2 - 4x^2 - 18y + 24x - 63 = 0$

<u>20.</u> $x^2 - 25y^2 + 6x - 50y = 41$

$(x^2 + 6x + 9) - 25(y^2 + 2y + 1) = 41 + 9 - 25$

$\dfrac{(x + 3)^2}{25} - (y + 1)^2 = 1$

C: (-3, -1)

V: (2, -1), (-8, -1)

$c = \sqrt{25 + 1} = \sqrt{26}$

F: $(-3 + \sqrt{26}, -1)$, $(-3 - \sqrt{26}, -1)$

A: $y + 1 = -\dfrac{1}{5}(x + 3)$, or $y = -\dfrac{1}{5}x - \dfrac{8}{5}$ and

$y + 1 = \dfrac{1}{5}(x + 3)$, or $y = \dfrac{1}{5}x - \dfrac{2}{5}$

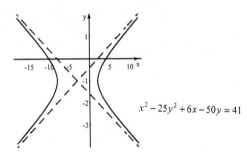

$x^2 - 25y^2 + 6x - 50y = 41$

<u>21.</u> $x^2 - y^2 - 2x - 4y = 4$

$(x^2 - 2x + 1) - (y^2 + 4y + 4) = 4 + 1 - 4$

$(x - 1)^2 - (y + 2)^2 = 1$, or

$\dfrac{(x - 1)^2}{1} - \dfrac{(y + 2)^2}{1} = 1$

The center of the hyperbola is (1, -2), a = 1 and b = 1.

The transverse axis is parallel to the x-axis. Since $c^2 = a^2 + b^2$, $c = \sqrt{a^2 + b^2} = \sqrt{1 + 1} = \sqrt{2}$.

Consider the hyperbola $\dfrac{x^2}{1} - \dfrac{y^2}{1} = 1$. The center is (0, 0); a = 1, b = 1, and $c = \sqrt{2}$. The vertices are (-1, 0) and (1, 0). The foci are $(-\sqrt{2}, 0)$ and $(\sqrt{2}, 0)$. The asymptotes are $y = -x$ and $y = x$.

The vertices, foci, and asymptotes of the translated hyperbola are found in the same way in which the center has been translated.

The vertices are (-1 + 1, 0 - 2) and (1 + 1, 0 - 2) or (0, -2) and (2, -2).

The foci are $(-\sqrt{2} + 1, 0 - 2)$ and $(\sqrt{2} + 1, 0 - 2)$ or $(1 - \sqrt{2}, -2)$ and $(1 + \sqrt{2}, -2)$.

The asymptotes are

y + 2 = -(x - 1) and y + 2 = x - 1, or
y = -x - 1 and y = x - 3.

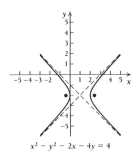

$x^2 - y^2 - 2x - 4y = 4$

22. $9y^2 - 4x^2 - 54y - 8x + 41 = 0$

$9(y^2 - 6y + 9) - 4(x^2 + 2x + 1) = -41 + 81 - 4$

$$\frac{(y - 3)^2}{4} - \frac{(x + 1)^2}{9} = 1$$

C: (-1, 3)

V: (-1, 5), (-1, 1)

$c = \sqrt{9 + 4} = \sqrt{13}$

F: $(-1, 3 + \sqrt{13})$, $(-1, 3 - \sqrt{13})$

A: $y - 3 = -\frac{2}{3}(x + 1)$, or $y = -\frac{2}{3}x + \frac{7}{3}$ and

$y - 3 = \frac{2}{3}(x + 1)$, or $y = \frac{2}{3}x + \frac{11}{3}$

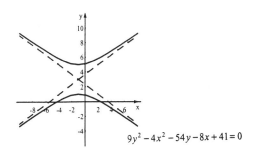

$9y^2 - 4x^2 - 54y - 8x + 41 = 0$

23. $y^2 - x^2 - 6x - 8y - 29 = 0$

$(y^2 - 8y) - (x^2 + 6x) = 29$

$(y^2 - 8y + 16) - (x^2 + 6x + 9) = 29 + 16 - 9$

$(y - 4)^2 - (x + 3)^2 = 36$

$$\frac{(y - 4)^2}{36} - \frac{(x + 3)^2}{36} = 1$$

The center of the hyperbola is (-3, 4); a = 6 and b = 6.

The transverse axis is parallel to the y-axis. Since $c^2 = a^2 + b^2$, $c = \sqrt{a^2 + b^2} = \sqrt{36 + 36}$
$= 6\sqrt{2}$.

Consider the hyperbola $\frac{y^2}{36} - \frac{x^2}{36} = 1$. The center is is (0, 0); a = 6, b = 6, and $c = 6\sqrt{2}$. The vertices are (0, -6) and (0, 6). The foci are $(0, -6\sqrt{2})$ and $(0, 6\sqrt{2})$. The asymptotes are y = -x and y = x.

The vertices, foci, and asymptotes of the translated hyperbola are found in the same way in which the center was translated.

The vertices are (0 - 3, 6 + 4) and (0 - 3, -6 + 4) or (-3, 10) and (-3, -2).

The foci are $(0 - 3, 6\sqrt{2} + 4)$ and $(0 - 3, -6\sqrt{2} + 4)$ or $(-3, 4 + 6\sqrt{2})$ and $(-3, 4 - 6\sqrt{2})$.

The asymptotes are

y - 4 = -(x + 3) and y - 4 = x + 3 or
  y = -x + 1 and y = x + 7.

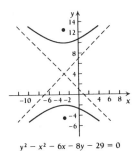

$y^2 - x^2 - 6x - 8y - 29 = 0$

24. $x^2 - y^2 = 8x - 2y - 13$

            $x^2 - 8x - y^2 + 2y = -13$

$(x^2 - 8x + 16) - (y^2 - 2y + 1) = -13 + 16 - 1$

$$\frac{(x - 4)^2}{2} - \frac{(y - 1)^2}{2} = 1$$

C: (4, 1)

V: $(4 + \sqrt{2}, 1)$, $(4 - \sqrt{2}, 1)$

$c = \sqrt{2 + 2} = 2$

F: (6, 1), (2, 1)

A: y - 1 = -(x - 4), or y = -x + 5 and
    y - 1 = x - 4, or y = x - 3

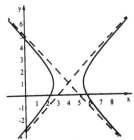

$x^2 - y^2 = 8x - 2y - 13$

25. $xy = 1$

Since $1 > 0$, the branches of the hyperbola lie in the first and third quadrants. The coordinate axes are its asymptotes.

x	y
$\frac{1}{4}$	4
$\frac{1}{2}$	2
1	1
$\frac{3}{2}$	$\frac{2}{3}$
3	$\frac{1}{3}$
4	$\frac{1}{4}$

x	y
$-\frac{1}{4}$	-4
$-\frac{1}{2}$	-2
-1	-1
$-\frac{3}{2}$	$-\frac{2}{3}$
-3	$-\frac{1}{3}$
-4	$-\frac{1}{4}$

26.

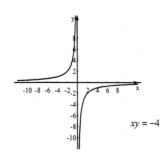

$xy = -4$

27. $xy = -8$

Since $-8 < 0$, the branches of the hyperbola lie in the second and fourth quadrants. The coordinates axes are its asymptotes.

x	y
1	-8
2	-4
4	-2
8	-1

x	y
-1	8
-2	4
-4	2
-8	1

$xy = -8$

28.

$xy = 3$

29.   If the asymptotes are $y = \pm \frac{3}{2} x$, then $a = 2$ and $b = 3$.

The center of the hyperbola is $(0, 0)$, the intersection of the asymptotes.

The vertices are $(-2, 0)$ and $(2, 0)$; thus the transverse axis is on the x-axis.

The standard form of the equation of the hyperbola must be in the form $\frac{x^2}{a^2} - \frac{y^2}{b^2} = 1$.

The equation is $\frac{x^2}{4} - \frac{y^2}{9} = 1$.

30. $c^2 = a^2 + b^2$, so $2^2 = 1^2 + b^2$ and $b^2 = 3$.
C: $(0, 0)$
$x^2 - \frac{y^2}{3} = 1$

31. $a = \frac{6}{2} = 3$; $b = \frac{11}{2}$

$\frac{[y - (-8)]^2}{\left(\frac{11}{2}\right)^2} - \frac{(x - 3)^2}{3^2} = 1$, or

$\frac{(y + 8)^2}{\frac{121}{4}} - \frac{(x - 3)^2}{9} = 1$

32.   The center of the hyperbola is the midpoint of the segment whose endpoints are the vertices: $\left[\frac{-9 - 5}{2}, \frac{4 + 4}{2}\right]$, or $(-7, 4)$. Since the line through the vertices is horizontal, the transverse axis is parallel to the x-axis. We have a parabola of the form $\frac{(x + 7)^2}{a^2} - \frac{(y - 4)^2}{b^2} = 1$.

Since the center is 2 units right of $(-9, 4)$ (and 2 units left of $(-5, 4)$), we know $a = 2$. The asymptotes are of the form $y - 4 = \pm \frac{b}{2} (x + 7) = \pm \frac{b}{2} x \pm \frac{7b}{2}$, with the positive alternative corresponding to $y = 3x + 25$ and the negative alternative corresponding to $y = -3x - 17$. Then $\frac{b}{2} = 3$, or $b = 6$.

We can now write the equation of the hyperbola:
$\frac{(x + 7)^2}{4} - \frac{(y - 4)^2}{36} = 1$

33.   The relation in Exercise 32 is
$\frac{(x + 7)^2}{4} - \frac{(y - 4)^2}{36} = 1$.

Interchange x and y to find the inverse of the relation:
$\frac{(y + 7)^2}{4} - \frac{(x - 4)^2}{36} = 1$

The center is $(4, -7)$.

The vertices are $(0 + 4, 2 - 7)$ and $(0 + 4, -2 - 7)$, or $(4, -5)$ and $(4, -9)$.

34. $\left[\dfrac{x - h}{a}\right]\left[\dfrac{x - h}{a}\right] - \left[\dfrac{y - k}{b}\right]\left[\dfrac{y - k}{b}\right] = 1$, so

$$\dfrac{(x - h)^2}{a^2} - \dfrac{(y - k)^2}{b^2} = 1$$

35. a) Graph: $x^2 - 4y^2 = 4$, or $\dfrac{x^2}{4} - \dfrac{y^2}{1} = 1$

The relation is not a function, because it fails the vertical line test.

b) $x^2 - 4y^2 = 4$

$x^2 - 4 = 4y^2$

$\dfrac{x^2 - 4}{4} = y^2$

$\pm \dfrac{1}{2}\sqrt{x^2 - 4} = y$

c) Graph: $y = \dfrac{1}{2}\sqrt{x^2 - 4}$

The relation is a function because it passes the vertical line test. The domain is $\{x \mid x \leqslant -2 \text{ or } x \geqslant 2\}$. The range is $\{y \mid y \geqslant 0\}$.

d) Graph: $y = -\dfrac{1}{2}\sqrt{x^2 - 4}$

The relation is a function, because it passes the vertical line test. The domain is $\{x \mid x \leqslant -2 \text{ or } x \geqslant 2\}$. The range is $\{y \mid y \leqslant 0\}$.

36.

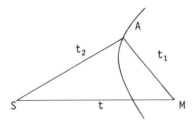

Let the constant v = the velocity of the pulses. Then, by hypothesis,

$(t + t_2) - t_1 = T_0$, a constant.

Now use: time = $\dfrac{\text{distance}}{\text{velocity}}$; then

$\dfrac{\overline{MS} + \overline{SA}}{v} - \dfrac{\overline{MA}}{v} = T_0$ or

$\overline{SA} - \overline{MA} = (T_0 v - \overline{MS})$, a constant.

Hence the (absolute value of the) difference of the distances from A to two fixed points M and S is a constant. By definition such a locus is a hyperbola.

37.

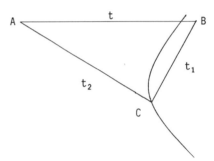

Let the constant b = the velocity of the bullet; let the constant s = the velocity of sound.

Then, by hypothesis,

$t_2 = t + t_1$. Now use: time = $\dfrac{\text{distance}}{\text{velocity}}$; then

$\dfrac{\overline{AC}}{s} = \dfrac{\overline{AB}}{b} + \dfrac{\overline{BC}}{s}$ or

$\overline{AC} - \overline{BC} = \dfrac{s}{b}\overline{AB}$, a constant.

Thus the (absolute value of the) difference of the distances from C to two fixed points A and B is a constant. By definition such a locus is a hyperbola.

38. C: $(-1.46, -0.96)$

V: $(-2.36, -0.96)$, $(-0.56, -0.96)$

F: $(y = -1.429x - 3.043,\ y = 1.429x + 1.129$

39. C: $(1.023, -2.044)$

V: $(-0.02418, -2.044)$ and $(2.07018, -2.044)$

A: $y = -x - 1.021$ and $y = x - 3.067$

Exercise Set 10.3

1. $x^2 = 20y$
   $x^2 = 4 \cdot 5 \cdot y$ (Writing $x^2 = 4py$)

   Vertex: (0, 0)
   Focus: (0, 5)   [(0, p)]
   Directrix: $y = -5$ ($y = -p$)

2. $x^2 = 16y$
   $x^2 = 4 \cdot 4 \cdot y$
   V: (0, 0)
   F: (0, 4)
   D: $y = -4$

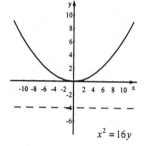

3. $y^2 = -6x$

   $y^2 = 4\left(-\frac{3}{2}\right)x$ (Writing $y^2 = 4px$)

   Vertex: (0, 0)

   Focus: $\left(-\frac{3}{2}, 0\right)$ [(p, 0)]

   Directrix: $x = -\left(-\frac{3}{2}\right) = \frac{3}{2}$ ($x = -p$)

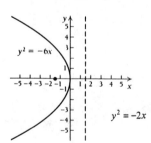

4. $y^2 = -2x$

   $y^2 = 4\left(-\frac{1}{2}\right)x$

   V: (0, 0)

   F: $\left(-\frac{1}{2}, 0\right)$

   D: $x = \frac{1}{2}$

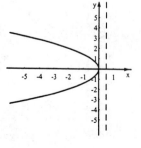

5. $x^2 - 4y = 0$
   $x^2 = 4y$
   $x^2 = 4 \cdot 1 \cdot y$ (Writing $x^2 = 4py$)

   Vertex: (0, 0)
   Focus: (0, 1)   [(0, p)]
   Directrix: $y = -1$ ($y = -p$)

6. $y^2 + 4x = 0$
   $y^2 = -4x$
   $y^2 = 4(-1)x$
   V: (0, 0)
   F: (-1, 0)
   D: $x = 1$

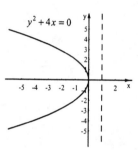

7. $y = 2x^2$

   $x^2 = \frac{1}{2}y$

   $x^2 = 4 \cdot \frac{1}{8} \cdot y$ (Writing $x^2 = 4py$)

   Vertex: (0, 0)

   Focus: $\left(0, \frac{1}{8}\right)$ [(0, p)]

   Directrix: $y = -\frac{1}{8}$ ($y = -p$)

8. V: (0, 0)

   F: $\left(0, \frac{1}{2}\right)$

   D: $y = -\frac{1}{2}$

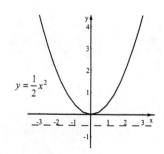

9. It helps to sketch a graph of the focus and the directrix.

The focus, (4, 0), is on the axis of symmetry, the x-axis. The vertex is (0, 0), and p is 4 - 0, or 4. The equation is of the type

$y^2 = 4px$

$y^2 = 4 \cdot 4 \cdot x$ (Substituting 4 for p)

$y^2 = 16x$

10. $x^2 = 4py$

$x^2 = 4\left(\frac{1}{4}\right)y$, or $x^2 = y$

11. It is helpful to sketch a graph of the focus and the directrix.

The focus, $(-\sqrt{2}, 0)$, is on the axis of symmetry, the x-axis. The vertex is (0, 0), and p = $-\sqrt{2}$ - 0, or $-\sqrt{2}$. The equation is of the type

$y^2 = 4px$

$y^2 = 4(-\sqrt{2})x$ (Substituting $-\sqrt{2}$ for p)

$y^2 = -4\sqrt{2}\,x$

12. $x^2 = 4py$

$x^2 = 4(-\pi)y$, or $x^2 = -4\pi y$

13. It is helpful to sketch a graph of the focus and the directrix.

The focus, (3, 2), is on the axis of symmetry, y = 2, which is parallel to the x-axis. The vertex is $\left[-\frac{1}{2}, 2\right]$, and p = 3 - $\left[-\frac{1}{2}\right]$, or $\frac{7}{2}$. The equation is of the type

$(y - k)^2 = 4p(x - h)$

$(y - 2)^2 = 4 \cdot \frac{7}{2}\left[x - \left[-\frac{1}{2}\right]\right]$ (Substituting)

$(y - 2)^2 = 14\left[x + \frac{1}{2}\right]$

14. $(x - h)^2 = 4p(y - k)$

$(x + 2)^2 = 4(3)(y - 0)$, or $(x + 2)^2 = 12y$

15. $(x + 2)^2 = -6(y - 1)$

$[x - (-2)]^2 = 4\left[-\frac{3}{2}\right](y - 1)$ $[(x - h)^2 = 4p(y-k)]$

Vertex: (-2, 1)   [(h, k)]

Focus: $\left[-2, 1 + \left[-\frac{3}{2}\right]\right]$, or $\left[-2, -\frac{1}{2}\right]$

                   [(h, k + p)]

Directrix: $y = 1 - \left[-\frac{3}{2}\right] = \frac{5}{2}$ (y = k - p)

$(x + 2)^2 = -6(y - 1)$

16. $(y - 3)^2 = -20(x + 2)$

$(y - 3)^2 = 4(-5)[x - (-2)]$

V: (-2, 3)

F: (-2 - 5, 3), or (-7, 3)

D: x = -2 - (-5) = 3

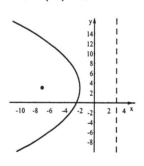

$(y - 3)^2 = -20(x + 2)$

17. $x^2 + 2x + 2y + 7 = 0$

$$x^2 + 2x = -2y - 7$$

$$(x^2 + 2x + 1) = -2y - 7 + 1 = -2y - 6$$

$$(x + 1)^2 = -2(y + 3)$$

$$[x - (-1)]^2 = 4\left[-\frac{1}{2}\right][y - (-3)]$$

$$[(x - h)^2 = 4p(y - k)]$$

Vertex: (-1, -3)   [(h, k)]

Focus: $\left[-1, -3 + \left[-\frac{1}{2}\right]\right]$, or $\left[-1, -\frac{7}{2}\right]$ [(h, k+p)]

Directrix: $y = -3 - \left[-\frac{1}{2}\right] = -\frac{5}{2}$ (y = k - p)

$x^2 + 2x + 2y + 7 = 0$

18. $y^2 + 6y - x + 16 = 0$

$$y^2 + 6y + 9 = x - 16 + 9$$

$$(y + 3)^2 = x - 7$$

$$[y - (-3)]^2 = 4\left[\frac{1}{4}\right](x - 7)$$

V: (7, -3)

F: $\left[7 + \frac{1}{4}, -3\right]$, or $\left[\frac{29}{4}, -3\right]$

D: $x = 7 - \frac{1}{4} = \frac{27}{4}$

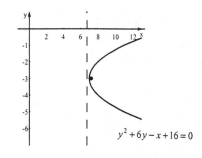

$y^2 + 6y - x + 16 = 0$

19. $x^2 - y - 2 = 0$

$$x^2 = y + 2$$

$$(x - 0)^2 = 4 \cdot \frac{1}{4} \cdot [y - (-2)]$$

$$[(x - h)^2 = 4p(y - k)]$$

Vertex: (0, -2)   [(h, k)]

Focus: $\left[0, -2 + \frac{1}{4}\right]$, or $\left[0, -\frac{7}{4}\right]$ [(h, k + p)]

Directrix: $y = -2 - \frac{1}{4} = -\frac{9}{4}$ (y = k - p)

$x^2 - y - 2 = 0$

20. $x^2 - 4x - 2y = 0$

$$x^2 - 4x + 4 = 2y + 4$$

$$(x - 2)^2 = 2(y + 2)$$

$$(x - 2)^2 = 4\left[\frac{1}{2}\right][y - (-2)]$$

V: (2, -2)

F: $\left[2, -2 + \frac{1}{2}\right]$, or $\left[2, -\frac{3}{2}\right]$

D: $y = -2 - \frac{1}{2} = -\frac{5}{2}$

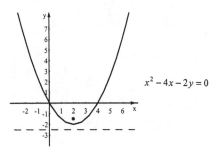

$x^2 - 4x - 2y = 0$

21. $$y = x^2 + 4x + 3$$

$$y - 3 = x^2 + 4x$$

$$y - 3 + 4 = x^2 + 4x + 4$$

$$y + 1 = (x + 2)^2$$

$$4 \cdot \frac{1}{4} \cdot [y - (-1)] = [x - (-2)]^2$$

$$[(x - h)^2 = 4p(y - k)]$$

Vertex: (-2, -1)   [(h, k)]

Focus: $\left[-2, -1 + \frac{1}{4}\right]$, or $\left[-2, -\frac{3}{4}\right]$

$$[(h, k + p)]$$

Directrix: $y = -1 - \frac{1}{4} = -\frac{5}{4}$ (y = k - p)

$y = x^2 + 4x + 3$

22.
$$y = x^2 + 6x + 10$$
$$y - 10 + 9 = x^2 + 6x + 9$$
$$y - 1 = (x + 3)^2$$
$$4\left[\frac{1}{4}\right](y - 1) = [x - (-3)]^2$$

V: $(-3, 1)$

F: $\left[-3, 1 + \frac{1}{4}\right]$, or $\left[-3, \frac{5}{4}\right]$

D: $y = 1 - \frac{1}{4} = \frac{3}{4}$

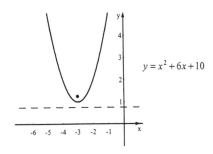

$y = x^2 + 6x + 10$

23. $4y^2 - 4y - 4x + 24 = 0$
$$y^2 - y - x + 6 = 0 \qquad \left[\text{Multiplying by } \frac{1}{4}\right]$$
$$y^2 - y = x - 6$$
$$y^2 - y + \frac{1}{4} = x - 6 + \frac{1}{4}$$
$$\left[y - \frac{1}{2}\right]^2 = x - \frac{23}{4}$$
$$\left[y - \frac{1}{2}\right]^2 = 4 \cdot \frac{1}{4}\left[x - \frac{23}{4}\right]$$
$$[(y - k)^2 = 4p(x - h)]$$

V: $\left[\frac{23}{4}, \frac{1}{2}\right]$ \qquad $[(h, k)]$

F: $\left[\frac{23}{4} + \frac{1}{4}, \frac{1}{2}\right]$, or $\left[6, \frac{1}{2}\right]$ \qquad $[(h + p, k)]$

D: $x = \frac{23}{4} - \frac{1}{4} = \frac{22}{4}$, or $\frac{11}{2}$ \qquad $(x = h - p)$

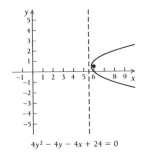

$4y^2 - 4y - 4x + 24 = 0$

24. $4y^2 + 4y - 4x - 16 = 0$
$$4\left[y^2 + y + \frac{1}{4}\right] = 4x + 16 + 1$$
$$4\left[y + \frac{1}{2}\right]^2 = 4x + 17$$
$$\left[y - \left[-\frac{1}{2}\right]\right]^2 = 4\left[\frac{1}{4}\right]\left[x - \left[-\frac{17}{4}\right]\right]$$

V: $\left[-\frac{17}{4}, -\frac{1}{2}\right]$

F: $\left[-\frac{17}{4} + \frac{1}{4}, -\frac{1}{2}\right]$, or $\left[-4, -\frac{1}{2}\right]$

D: $x = -\frac{17}{4} - \frac{1}{4} = -\frac{9}{2}$

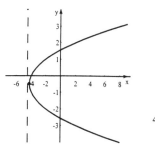

$4y^2 + 4y - 4x - 16 = 0$

25. $x + 1 = 2y^2$

Only one of the variables is squared, so the graph is not a circle, an ellipse, or a hyperbola. We find an equivalent equation:

$$(y - 0)^2 = 4\left[\frac{1}{8}\right](x + 1)$$

We have a parabola.

26.
$$10y + 40 = x^2 + y^2 + 8x$$
$$40 + 16 + 25 = (x^2 + 8x + 16) + (y^2 - 10y + 25)$$
$$81 = (x + 4)^2 + (y - 5)^2$$

Circle

27.
$$4y^2 + 25x^2 + 4 = 8y + 100x$$
$$25x^2 - 100x + 4y^2 - 8y = -4$$
$$25(x^2 - 4x + 4) + 4(y^2 - 2y + 1) = -4 + 100 + 4$$
$$25(x - 2)^2 + 4(y - 1)^2 = 100$$
$$\frac{(x - 2)^2}{4} + \frac{(y - 1)^2}{25} = 1$$

We have an ellipse.

28.
$$9x^2 + 24y = 4y^2 + 36x + 36$$
$$9(x^2 - 4x + 4) - 4(y^2 - 6y + 9) = 36 + 36 - 36$$
$$9(x - 2)^2 - 4(y - 3)^2 = 36$$
$$\frac{(x - 2)^2}{4} - \frac{(y - 3)^2}{9} = 1$$

Hyperbola

29.
$$2x + 13 + y^2 = 8y - x^2$$
$$(x^2 + 2x + 1) + (y^2 - 8y + 16) = -13 + 1 + 16$$
$$(x + 1)^2 + (y - 4)^2 = 4$$

We have a circle.

30. $x - \dfrac{5}{y} = 0$

$\qquad xy = 5$

Hyperbola

31.
$$x = -16y + y^2 + 7$$
$$x - 7 + 64 = y^2 - 16y + 64$$
$$x + 57 = (y - 8)^2$$
$$4\left[\frac{1}{4}\right](x + 57) = (y - 8)^2$$

We have a parabola.

32. $4x^2 - 3x + 13y^2 + 4y = 568$

We have an equation of the type
$Ax^2 + By^2 + Cx + Dy + E = 0$ with coefficients
of the squared terms not equal and both positive.
We have an ellipse.

33. $xy + 5x^2 = 9 + 7x^2 - 2x^2$

$\qquad xy = 9$

We have a hyperbola.

34. $69x^2 + 21y^2 = 234$

$$\dfrac{x^2}{\dfrac{78}{23}} + \dfrac{y^2}{\dfrac{78}{7}} = 1$$

Ellipse

35.

The graph of $x^2 - y^2 = 0$
is the union of the lines
$x = y$ and $x = -y$. The
others are respectively,
a hyperbola, a circle, and
a parabola.

36.

The graph of $x^2 - 4y^2 = 0$
is the union of the lines
$x = 2y$ and $x = -2y$. The
others are respectively,
a hyperbola, an ellipse,
and a parabola.

37. If the line of symmetry is parallel to the y-axis
and the vertex (h, k) is $(-1, 2)$, then the
equation is of the type
$(x - h)^2 = 4p(y - k)$.

Solve for p substituting $(-1, 2)$ for (h, k) and
$(-3, 1)$ for (x, y).
$$[-3 - (-1)]^2 = 4p(1 - 2)$$
$$4 = -4p$$
$$-1 = p$$

The equation of the parabola is
$$[x - (-1)]^2 = 4(-1)(y - 2)$$
or
$$(x + 1)^2 = -4(y - 2).$$

38.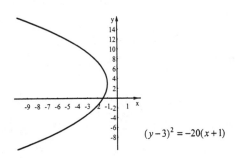

$(y - 3)^2 = -20(x + 1)$

a) Not a function

b) Not a function unless $p = 0$

39. If the line of symmetry is horizontal and the
vertex (h, k) is $(-2, 1)$, then the equation is
of the type $(y - k)^2 = 4p(x - h)$.

Find p by substituting $(-2, 1)$ for (h, k) and
$(-3, 5)$ for (x, y).
$$(5 - 1)^2 = 4p[-3 - (-2)]$$
$$16 = 4p(-1)$$
$$16 = -4p$$
$$-4 = p$$

The equation of the parabola is
$$(y - 1)^2 = 4(-4)[x - (-2)]$$
or $(y - 1)^2 = -16(x + 2).$

40.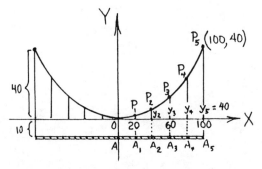

Since $P_5(100, 40)$ lies on the parabola $x^2 = 4py$,
we have $(100)^2 = 4p(40)$ so that $4p = 250$; thus
$x^2 = 250y$ is the equation of the cable. Then we

obtain

x	y		
0	0	$= y_0$ and $AO = 10 + y_0 = 10$ ft,
20	1.6	$= y_1$ and $A_1P_1 = 10 + y_1 = 11.6$ ft,
40	6.4	$= y_2$ and $A_2P_2 = 10 + y_2 = 16.4$ ft,
60	14.4	$= y_3$ and $A_3P_3 = 10 + y_3 = 24.4$ ft,
80	25.6	$= y_4$ and $A_4P_4 = 10 + y_4 = 35.6$ ft,
100	40	$= y_5$ and $A_5P_5 = 10 + y_5 = 50$ ft.

<u>41.</u> See the answer section in the text.

<u>42.</u>

If a load W is distributed uniformly <u>horizontally</u>, this means that W = kx; that is, if the horizontal dimension of the cable is doubled, then the load is doubled, etc. We think of the entire load W as being concentrated at point A $\left[\text{whose abscissa is } \frac{x}{2}\right]$, roughly the midpoint of arc OP.

If a load W is distributed uniformly <u>horizontally</u>, this means that W = kx; that is, if the horizontal dimension of the cable is doubled, then the load is doubled, etc. We think of the entire load W as being concentrated at point A $\left[\text{whose abscissa is } \frac{x}{2}\right]$, roughly the midpoint of arc OP.

A lever is in rotational equilibrium when the TORQUE(S) [or <u>moment of force</u> defined to be (FORCE) × (⊥ DISTANCE FROM FULCRUM)] tending to turn the lever clockwise about its fulcrum equals (in magnitude) the TORQUE(S) tending to turn the lever counter-clockwise.

Thinking of OP as a (rigid) lever with fulcrum at fixed point P, the torque due to F_1 (applied at O) tends to turn OP clockwise about P; the torque due to W (applied at A) tends to turn the lever counter-clockwise about P. These two torques are equal (in magnitude):

$$F_1 y = W \cdot \frac{x}{2} \quad \text{or}$$

$$F_1 y = (kx) \cdot \frac{x}{2}. \quad \text{Thus}$$

$$y = \frac{k}{2F_1} \cdot x^2, \text{ a parabola.}$$

[Since F_2 is applied at the fulcrum P, its torque is zero.]

<u>43.</u> V: (0.87, 0.35)

     F: (0.87, -0.19)

     D: y = 0.89

<u>44.</u> V: (6.90, 1.18)

     F: (6.82, 1.18)

     D: x = 6.98

Exercise Set 10.4

<u>1.</u> $x^2 + y^2 = 25,$ (1)

   $y - x = 1$ (2)

First solve Eq. (2) for y.

$y = x + 1$ (3)

Then substitute x + 1 for y in Eq. (1) and solve for x.

$$x^2 + y^2 = 25$$
$$x^2 + (x + 1)^2 = 25$$
$$x^2 + x^2 + 2x + 1 = 25$$
$$2x^2 + 2x - 24 = 0$$
$$x^2 + x - 12 = 0 \quad \text{Multiplying by } \frac{1}{2}$$
$$(x + 4)(x - 3) = 0 \quad \text{Factoring}$$

$x + 4 = 0$ or $x - 3 = 0$ Principle of zero products

     $x = -4$ or $x = 3$

Now substitute these numbers into Eq. (3) and solve for y.

$y = -4 + 1 = -3$

$y = 3 + 1 = 4$

The pairs (-4,-3) and (3,4) check, so they are the solutions.

<u>2.</u> $x^2 + y^2 = 100,$

   $y - x = 2$

   $y = x + 2$

$$x^2 + (x + 2)^2 = 100$$
$$x^2 + x^2 + 4x + 4 = 100$$
$$2x^2 + 4x - 96 = 0$$
$$x^2 + 2x - 48 = 0$$
$$(x + 8)(x - 6) = 0$$

$x = -8$ or $x = 6$

y = -8 + 2 = -6

y = 6 + 2 = 8

The pairs (-8,-6) and (6,8) check.

3. $4x^2 + 9y^2 = 36$,   (1)

$3y + 2x = 6$ (2)

First solve Eq. (2) for y.

$3y = -2x + 6$

$y = -\frac{2}{3}x + 2$ (3)

Then substitute $-\frac{2}{3}x + 2$ for y in Eq. (1) and solve for x.

$$4x^2 + 9y^2 = 36$$

$$4x^2 + 9\left(-\frac{2}{3}x + 2\right)^2 = 36$$

$$4x^2 + 9\left[\frac{4}{9}x^2 - \frac{8}{3}x + 4\right] = 36$$

$$4x^2 + 4x^2 - 24x + 36 = 36$$

$$8x^2 - 24x = 0$$

$$x^2 - 3x = 0$$

$$x(x - 3) = 0$$

x = 0 or x = 3

Now substitute these numbers in Eq. (3) and solve for y.

$y = -\frac{2}{3} \cdot 0 + 2 = 2$

$y = -\frac{2}{3} \cdot 3 + 2 = 0$

The pairs (0,2) and (3,0) check, so they are the solutions.

4. $9x^2 + 4y^2 = 36$,

$3x + 2y = 6$

$x = 2 - \frac{2}{3}y$

$$9\left[2 - \frac{2}{3}y\right]^2 + 4y^2 = 36$$

$$9\left[4 - \frac{8}{3}y + \frac{4}{9}y^2\right] + 4y^2 = 36$$

$$36 - 24y + 4y^2 + 4y^2 = 36$$

$$8y^2 - 24y = 0$$

$$y^2 - 3y = 0$$

$$y(y - 3) = 0$$

y = 0 or y = 3

$x = 2 - \frac{2}{3}(0) = 2$

$x = 2 - \frac{2}{3}(3) = 0$

The pairs (2,0) and (0,3) check.

5. $y^2 - x^2 = 9$ (1)

$2x - 3 = y$ (2)

Substitute 2x - 3 for y in Eq. (1) and solve for x.

$$y^2 - x^2 = 9$$

$$(2x - 3)^2 - x^2 = 9$$

$$4x^2 - 12x + 9 - x^2 = 9$$

$$3x^2 - 12x = 0$$

$$x^2 - 4x = 0$$

$$x(x - 4) = 0$$

x = 0 or   x = 4

Now substitute these numbers into the linear Eq. (2) and solve for y.

If x = 0, y = 2·0 - 3 = -3.

If x = 4, y = 2·4 - 3 = 5.

The pairs (0, -3) and (4, 5) check, hence are solutions.

6. x + y = -6,

xy = -7

y = -x - 6

x(-x - 6) = -7

$-x^2 - 6x = -7$

$0 = x^2 + 6x - 7$

$0 = (x + 7)(x - 1)$

x = -7 or x = 1

y = -(-7) - 6 = 1

y = -1 - 6 = -7

The pairs (-7, 1) and (1, -7) check.

7. $y^2 = x + 3$,   (1)

$2y = x + 4$ (2)

First solve Eq. (2) for x.

$2y - 4 = x$ (3)

Then substitute 2y - 4 for x in Eq. (1) and solve for y.

$$y^2 = x + 3$$

$$y^2 = (2y - 4) + 3$$

$$y^2 = 2y - 1$$

$$y^2 - 2y + 1 = 0$$

$$(y - 1)(y - 1) = 0$$

y = 1 or y = 1

Now substitute 1 for y in Eq. (3) and solve for x.

2·1 - 4 = x

-2 = x

The pair (-2,1) checks. It is the solution.

<u>8.</u> $y = x^2$,

$3x = y + 2$

$y = 3x - 2$

$3x - 2 = x^2$

$0 = x^2 - 3x + 2$

$0 = (x - 2)(x - 1)$

$x = 2$ or $x = 1$

$y = 3 \cdot 2 - 2 = 4$

$y = 3 \cdot 1 - 2 = 1$

The pairs $(2,4)$ and $(1,1)$ check.

<u>9.</u> $x^2 + 4y^2 = 25$, (1)

$x + 2y = 7$ (2)

First solve Eq. (2) for x.

$x = -2y + 7$ (3)

Then substitute $-2y + 7$ for x in Eq. (1) and solve for y.

$x^2 + 4y^2 = 25$

$(-2y + 7)^2 + 4y^2 = 25$

$4y^2 - 28y + 49 + 4y^2 = 25$

$8y^2 - 28y + 24 = 0$

$2y^2 - 7y + 6 = 0$

$(2y - 3)(y - 2) = 0$

$y = \frac{3}{2}$ or $y = 2$

Now substitute these numbers in Eq. (3) and solve for x.

$x = -2 \cdot \frac{3}{2} + 7 = 4$

$x = -2 \cdot 2 + 7 = 3$

The pairs $\left(4, \frac{3}{2}\right)$ and $(3,2)$ check, so they are the solutions.

<u>10.</u> $y^2 - x^2 = 16$,

$2x - y = 1$

$y = 2x - 1$

$(2x - 1)^2 - x^2 = 16$

$4x^2 - 4x + 1 - x^2 = 16$

$3x^2 - 4x - 15 = 0$

$(3x + 5)(x - 3) = 0$

$x = -\frac{5}{3}$ or $x = 3$

$y = 2\left(-\frac{5}{3}\right) - 1 = -\frac{13}{3}$

$y = 2(3) - 1 = 5$

The pairs $\left(-\frac{5}{3}, -\frac{13}{3}\right)$ and $(3,5)$ check.

<u>11.</u> $x^2 - xy + 3y^2 = 27$, (1)

$x - y = 2$ (2)

First solve Eq. (2) for y.

$x - 2 = y$ (3)

Then substitute $x - 2$ for y in Eq. (1) and solve for x.

$x^2 - xy + 3y^2 = 27$

$x^2 - x(x - 2) + 3(x - 2)^2 = 27$

$x^2 - x^2 + 2x + 3x^2 - 12x + 12 = 27$

$3x^2 - 10x - 15 = 0$

$x = \frac{-(-10) \pm \sqrt{(-10)^2 - 4(3)(-15)}}{2 \cdot 3}$

$= \frac{10 \pm \sqrt{100 + 180}}{6}$

$= \frac{10 \pm \sqrt{280}}{6}$

$= \frac{10 \pm 2\sqrt{70}}{6}$

$= \frac{5 \pm \sqrt{70}}{3}$

Now substitute these numbers in Eq. (3) and solve for y.

$y = \frac{5 + \sqrt{70}}{3} - 2 = \frac{-1 + \sqrt{70}}{3}$

$y = \frac{5 - \sqrt{70}}{3} - 2 = \frac{-1 - \sqrt{70}}{3}$

The pairs $\left(\frac{5 + \sqrt{70}}{3}, \frac{-1 + \sqrt{70}}{3}\right)$ and $\left(\frac{5 - \sqrt{70}}{3}, \frac{-1 - \sqrt{70}}{3}\right)$ check, so they are the solutions.

<u>12.</u> $2y^2 + xy + x^2 = 7$,

$x - 2y = 5$

$x = 2y + 5$

$2y^2 + (2y + 5)y + (2y + 5)^2 = 7$

$2y^2 + 2y^2 + 5y + 4y^2 + 20y + 25 = 7$

$8y^2 + 25y + 18 = 0$

$(8y + 9)(y + 2) = 0$

$y = -\frac{9}{8}$ or $y = -2$

$x = 2\left(-\frac{9}{8}\right) + 5 = \frac{11}{4}$

$x = 2(-2) + 5 = 1$

The pairs $\left(\frac{11}{4}, -\frac{9}{8}\right)$ and $(1, -2)$ check.

<u>13.</u> $3x + y = 7$ (1)

$4x^2 + 5y = 56$ (2)

First solve Eq. (1) for y.

$3x + y = 7$

$y = 7 - 3x$ (3)

Next substitute $7 - 3x$ for y in Eq. (2) and solve for x.

$$4x^2 + 5y = 56$$
$$4x^2 + 5(7 - 3x) = 56$$
$$4x^2 + 35 - 15x = 56$$
$$4x^2 - 15x - 21 = 0$$

Using the quadratic formula, we find that

$$x = \frac{15 - \sqrt{561}}{8} \text{ or } x = \frac{15 + \sqrt{561}}{8}.$$

Now substitute these numbers into Eq. (3) and solve for y.

If $x = \dfrac{15 - \sqrt{561}}{8}$, $y = 7 - 3\left[\dfrac{15 - \sqrt{561}}{8}\right]$, or

$\dfrac{11 + 3\sqrt{561}}{8}$.

If $x = \dfrac{15 + \sqrt{561}}{8}$, $y = 7 - 3\left[\dfrac{15 + \sqrt{561}}{8}\right]$, or

$\dfrac{11 - 3\sqrt{561}}{8}$.

The pairs $\left[\dfrac{15 - \sqrt{561}}{8}, \dfrac{11 + 3\sqrt{561}}{8}\right]$ and

$\left[\dfrac{15 + \sqrt{561}}{8}, \dfrac{11 - 3\sqrt{561}}{8}\right]$ check and are the

solutions.

14. $2y^2 + xy = 5$,
$4y + x = 7$
$x = -4y + 7$

$2y^2 + (-4y + 7)y = 5$
$2y^2 - 4y^2 + 7y = 5$
$0 = 2y^2 - 7y + 5$
$0 = (2y - 5)(y - 1)$

$y = \dfrac{5}{2}$ or $y = 1$

$x = -4\left[\dfrac{5}{2}\right] + 7 = -3$

$x = -4 \cdot 1 + 7 = 3$

The pairs $\left[-3, \dfrac{5}{2}\right]$ and $(3, 1)$ check.

15. $a + b = 7$,   (1)
$ab = 4$ (2)

First solve Eq. (1) for a.

$a = -b + 7$ (3)

Then substitute $-b + 7$ for a in Eq. (2) and solve for b.

$(-b + 7)b = 4$
$-b^2 + 7b = 4$
$0 = b^2 - 7b + 4$

$b = \dfrac{-(-7) \pm \sqrt{(-7)^2 - 4 \cdot 1 \cdot 4}}{2 \cdot 1}$

$b = \dfrac{7 \pm \sqrt{33}}{2}$

Now substitute these numbers in Eq. (3) and solve for a.

$a = -\left[\dfrac{7 + \sqrt{33}}{2}\right] + 7 = \dfrac{7 - \sqrt{33}}{2}$

$a = -\left[\dfrac{7 - \sqrt{33}}{2}\right] + 7 = \dfrac{7 + \sqrt{33}}{2}$

The pairs $\left[\dfrac{7 - \sqrt{33}}{2}, \dfrac{7 + \sqrt{33}}{2}\right]$ and

$\left[\dfrac{7 + \sqrt{33}}{2}, \dfrac{7 - \sqrt{33}}{2}\right]$ check, so they are the

solutions.

16. $p + q = -4$,
$pq = -5$
$p = -q - 4$

$(-q - 4)q = -5$
$-q^2 - 4q = -5$
$0 = q^2 + 4q - 5$
$0 = (q + 5)(q - 1)$

$q = -5$ or $q = 1$

$p = -(-5) - 4 = 1$
$p = -1 - 4 = -5$

The pairs $(1,-5)$ and $(-5,1)$ check.

17. $2a + b = 1$,   (1)
$b = 4 - a^2$ (2)

Eq. (2) is already solved for b. Substitute $4 - a^2$ for b in Eq. (1) and solve for a.

$2a + 4 - a^2 = 1$
$0 = a^2 - 2a - 3$
$0 = (a - 3)(a + 1)$

$a = 3$ or $a = -1$

Substitute these numbers in Eq. (2) and solve for b.

$b = 4 - 3^2 = -5$
$b = 4 - (-1)^2 = 3$

The pairs $(3,-5)$ and $(-1,3)$ check.

18. $4x^2 + 9y^2 = 36$,
$x + 3y = 3$
$x = -3y + 3$

$4(-3y + 3)^2 + 9y^2 = 36$
$4(9y^2 - 18y + 9) + 9y^2 = 36$
$36y^2 - 72y + 36 + 9y^2 = 36$
$45y^2 - 72y = 0$
$5y^2 - 8y = 0$
$y(5y - 8) = 0$

$y = 0$ or $y = \dfrac{8}{5}$

$x = -3 \cdot 0 + 3 = 3$

$x = -3\left[\dfrac{8}{5}\right] + 3 = -\dfrac{9}{5}$

The pairs $(3,0)$ and $\left[-\dfrac{9}{5}, \dfrac{8}{5}\right]$ check.

19. $a^2 + b^2 = 89$,   (1)

    $a - b = 3$ (2)

    First solve Eq. (2) for a.

    $a = b + 3$ (3)

    Then substitute $b + 3$ for a in Eq. (1) and solve for b.

    $(b + 3)^2 + b^2 = 89$

    $b^2 + 6b + 9 + b^2 = 89$

    $2b^2 + 6b - 80 = 0$

    $b^2 + 3b - 40 = 0$

    $(b + 8)(b - 5) = 0$

    $b = -8$ or $b = 5$

    Substitute these numbers in Eq. (3) and solve for a.

    $a = -8 + 3 = -5$

    $a = 5 + 3 = 8$

    The pairs $(-5,-8)$ and $(8,5)$ check.

20. $xy = 4$,

    $x + y = 5$

    $x = -y + 5$

    $(-y + 5)y = 4$

    $-y^2 + 5y = 4$

    $0 = y^2 - 5y + 4$

    $0 = (y - 4)(y - 1)$

    $y = 4$ or $y = 1$

    $x = -4 + 5 = 1$

    $x = -1 + 5 = 4$

    The pairs $(1,4)$ and $(4,1)$ check.

21. $x^2 + y^2 = 5$,   (1)

    $x - y = 8$ (2)

    First solve Eq. (2) for x.

    $x = y + 8$ (3)

    Then substitute $y + 8$ for x in Eq. (1) and solve for y.

    $(y + 8)^2 + y^2 = 5$

    $y^2 + 16y + 64 + y^2 = 5$

    $2y^2 + 16y + 59 = 0$

    $y = \dfrac{-16 \pm \sqrt{(16)^2 - 4(2)(59)}}{2 \cdot 2}$

    $y = \dfrac{-16 \pm \sqrt{-216}}{4}$

    $y = \dfrac{-16 \pm 6i\sqrt{6}}{4}$

    $y = -4 \pm \dfrac{3}{2}i\sqrt{6}$

    Now substitute these numbers in Eq. (3) and solve for x.

$x = -4 + \dfrac{3}{2}i\sqrt{6} + 8 = 4 + \dfrac{3}{2}i\sqrt{6}$

$x = -4 - \dfrac{3}{2}i\sqrt{6} + 8 = 4 - \dfrac{3}{2}i\sqrt{6}$

The pairs $\left(4 + \dfrac{3}{2}i\sqrt{6},\ -4 + \dfrac{3}{2}i\sqrt{6}\right)$ and $\left(4 - \dfrac{3}{2}i\sqrt{6},\ -4 - \dfrac{3}{2}i\sqrt{6}\right)$ check.

22. $4x^2 + 9y^2 = 36$,

    $y - x = 8$

    $y = x + 8$

    $4x^2 + 9(x + 8)^2 = 36$

    $4x^2 + 9(x^2 + 16x + 64) = 36$

    $4x^2 + 9x^2 + 144x + 576 = 36$

    $13x^2 + 144x + 540 = 0$

    $x = \dfrac{-144 \pm \sqrt{(144)^2 - 4(13)(540)}}{2 \cdot 13}$

    $x = \dfrac{-72 \pm 6\sqrt{51}}{13} = -\dfrac{72}{13} \pm \dfrac{6}{13}i\sqrt{51}$

    $y = -\dfrac{72}{13} + \dfrac{6}{13}i\sqrt{51} + 8 = \dfrac{32}{13} + \dfrac{6}{13}i\sqrt{51}$

    $y = -\dfrac{72}{13} - \dfrac{6}{13}i\sqrt{51} + 8 = \dfrac{32}{13} - \dfrac{6}{13}i\sqrt{51}$

    The pairs $\left(-\dfrac{72}{13} + \dfrac{6}{13}i\sqrt{51},\ \dfrac{32}{13} + \dfrac{6}{13}i\sqrt{51}\right)$ and $\left(-\dfrac{72}{13} - \dfrac{6}{13}i\sqrt{51},\ \dfrac{32}{13} - \dfrac{6}{13}i\sqrt{51}\right)$ check.

23. Familiarize: Let x = one number and y = the other number.

    Translate: We translate to a system of equations.

    The sum of two numbers is 12.

    $x + y = 12$

    The sum of their squares is 90.

    $x^2 + y^2 = 90$

    Carry out: We solve the system:

    $x + y = 12$,   (1)

    $x^2 + y^2 = 90$ (2)

    First solve Eq. (1) for y.

    $y = 12 - x$ (3)

    Then substitute $12 - x$ for y in Eq. (2) and solve for x.

    $x^2 + y^2 = 90$

    $x^2 + (12 - x)^2 = 90$

    $x^2 + 144 - 24x + x^2 = 90$

    $2x^2 - 24x + 54 = 0$

    $x^2 - 12x + 27 = 0$

    $(x - 9)(x - 3) = 0$

    $x = 9$ or $x = 3$

    Now substitute these numbers in Eq. (3) and solve for y.

y = 12 - 9 = 3

y = 12 - 3 = 9

Check: If the numbers are 9 and 3, the sum is 9 + 3, or 12. The sum of their squares is 81 + 9, or 90. The numbers check. The pair (3,9) does not give us another solution.

State: The numbers are 9 and 3.

24. Let x = one number and y = the other number. Solve the system:

x + y = 15,

$x^2 - y^2 = 15$

The solution is (8,7). The numbers are 8 and 7.

25. Familiarize: We first make a drawing. We let ℓ and w represent the length and width, respectively.

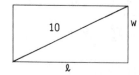

Translate: The perimeter is 28 cm.

2ℓ + 2w = 28, or ℓ + w = 14

Using the Pythagorean property we have another equation.

$ℓ^2 + w^2 = 10^2$, or $ℓ^2 + w^2 = 100$

Carry out: We solve the system:

ℓ + w = 14,   (1)

$ℓ^2 + w^2 = 100$ (2)

First solve Eq. (1) for w.

w = 14 - ℓ   (3)

Then substitute 14 - ℓ for w in Eq. (2) and solve for ℓ.

$$ℓ^2 + w^2 = 100$$
$$ℓ^2 + (14 - ℓ)^2 = 100$$
$$ℓ^2 + 196 - 28ℓ + ℓ^2 = 100$$
$$2ℓ^2 - 28ℓ + 96 = 0$$
$$ℓ^2 - 14ℓ + 48 = 0$$
$$(ℓ - 8)(ℓ - 6) = 0$$

ℓ = 8 or ℓ = 6

If ℓ = 8, then w = 14 - 8, or 6. If ℓ = 6, then w = 14 - 6, or 8. Since the length is usually considered to be longer than the width, we have the solution ℓ = 8 and w = 6, or (8,6).

Check: If ℓ = 8 and w = 6, then the perimeter is 2·8 + 2·6, or 28. The length of a diagonal is $\sqrt{8^2 + 6^2}$, or $\sqrt{100}$, or 10. The numbers check.

State: The length is 8 cm, and the width is 6 cm.

26. Let ℓ and w represent the length and width, respectively. Solve the system:

2ℓ + 2w = 6,

$ℓ^2 + w^2 = (\sqrt{5})^2$, or

ℓ + w = 3,

$ℓ^2 + w^2 = 5$

The solutions are (1,2) and (2,1). Choosing the larger number as the length, we have the solution. The length is 2 m, and the width is 1 m.

27. Familiarize: We first make a drawing. Let ℓ = the length and w = the width of the rectangle.

Translate:

Area: ℓw = 20

Perimeter: 2ℓ + 2w = 18, or ℓ + w = 9

Carry out: We solve the system:

Solve the second equation for ℓ: ℓ = 9 - w

Substitute 9 - w for ℓ in the first equation and solve for w.

$$(9 - w)w = 20$$
$$9w - w^2 = 20$$
$$0 = w^2 - 9w + 20$$
$$0 = (w - 5)(w - 4)$$

w = 5 or w = 4

If w = 5, then ℓ = 9 - w, or 4. If w = 4, then ℓ = 9 - 4, or 5. Since length is usually considered to be longer than width, we have the solution ℓ = 5 and w = 4, or (5,4).

Check: If ℓ = 5 and w = 4, the area is 5·4, or 20. The perimeter is 2·5 + 2·4, or 18. The numbers check.

State: The length is 5 in. and the width is 4 in.

28. Let ℓ and w represent the length and width, respectively. We solve the system:

ℓw = 2,

2ℓ + 2w = 6

The solutions are (1,2) and (2,1). We choose the larger number to be the length, so the length is 2 yd and the width is 1 yd.

29. Familiarize: We make a drawing of the field. Let ℓ = the length and w = the width.

Since it takes 210 yd of fencing to enclose the field, we know that the perimeter is 210 yd.

Translate:

Perimeter: 2ℓ + 2w = 210, or ℓ + w = 105

Area: ℓw = 2250

Carry out: We solve the system:

Solve the first equation for ℓ: $\ell = 105 - w$

Substitute $105 - w$ for ℓ in the second equation and solve for w.

$$(105 - w)w = 2250$$
$$105w - w^2 = 2250$$
$$0 = w^2 - 105w + 2250$$
$$0 = (w - 30)(w - 75)$$

$w = 30$ or $w = 75$

If $w = 30$, then $\ell = 105 - 30$, or 75. If $w = 75$, then $\ell = 105 - 75$, or 30. Since length is usually considered to be longer than width, we have the solution $\ell = 75$ and $w = 30$, or (75,30).

Check: If $\ell = 75$ and $w = 30$, the perimeter is $2 \cdot 75 + 2 \cdot 30$, or 210. The area is 75(30), or 2250. The numbers check.

State: The length is 75 yd and the width is 30 yd.

30. Let ℓ and w represent the length and width, respectively. Solve the system:

$$\sqrt{\ell^2 + w^2} = \ell + 1,$$

$$\sqrt{\ell^2 + w^2} = 2w + 3$$

The solutions are (12,5) and (-1,0). Only (12,5) has meaning in this problem. It checks. The length is 12 ft and the width is 5 ft.

31. Familiarize: Let x and y represent the numbers.

Translate: The product of the numbers is 2.

$$xy = 2$$

The sum of the reciprocals is $\frac{33}{8}$.

$$\frac{1}{x} + \frac{1}{y} = \frac{33}{8}$$

Carry out: We solve the system.

Solve the first equation for y: $y = \frac{2}{x}$

Substitute $\frac{2}{x}$ for y in the second equation and solve for x.

$$\frac{1}{x} + \frac{1}{\frac{2}{x}} = \frac{33}{8}$$

$$\frac{1}{x} + \frac{x}{2} = \frac{33}{8}$$

$$8 + 4x^2 = 33x \qquad \text{(Multiplying by } 8x\text{)}$$

$$4x^2 - 33x + 8 = 0$$

$$(4x - 1)(x - 8) = 0$$

$x = \frac{1}{4}$ or $x = 8$

If $x = \frac{1}{4}$, then $y = \frac{2}{\frac{1}{4}} = 8$. If $x = 8$, then $y = \frac{2}{8} = \frac{1}{4}$. In either case we get the pair of numbers $\frac{1}{4}$ and 8.

Check: $\frac{1}{4} \cdot 8 = 2$ and $\frac{1}{\frac{1}{4}} + \frac{1}{8} = 4\frac{1}{8} = \frac{33}{8}$. The numbers check.

State: The numbers are $\frac{1}{4}$ and 8.

32. Let (h,k) represent the point on the line $5x + 8y = -2$ which is the center of a circle that passes through the points $(-2,3)$ and $(-4,1)$. Then we have

$$\sqrt{[h - (-2)]^2 + (k - 3)^2} = \sqrt{[h - (-4)]^2 + (k - 1)^2},$$
$$\text{or } h + k = -1.$$

We get a second equation by substituting (h,k) in $5x + 8y = -2$.

$$5h + 8k = -2$$

The solution of the system, which is the center of the circle, is $(-2,1)$.

Next we find the length of the radius.

$$r = \sqrt{[-2 - (-2)]^2 + (1 - 3)^2} = 2$$

Then the equation of the circle is

$$(x + 2)^2 + (y - 1)^2 = 4.$$

33. Familiarize: Let x = the length of the longer piece and y = the length of the shorter piece. Then the lengths of the sides of the squares are $\frac{x}{4}$ and $\frac{y}{4}$.

Translate: The total length of the wire is 100 cm.

$$x + y = 100$$

The area of one square is 144 cm² greater than that of the other square.

$$\left(\frac{x}{4}\right)^2 = \left(\frac{y}{4}\right)^2 + 144$$

Carry out: We solve the system.

Solve the first equation for y: $y = 100 - x$

Substitute for y in the second equation and solve for x.

$$\left(\frac{x}{4}\right)^2 = \left(\frac{100 - x}{4}\right)^2 + 144$$

$$\frac{x^2}{16} = \frac{10,000 - 200x + x^2}{16} + 144$$

$$x^2 = 10,000 - 200x + x^2 + 2304$$

$$200x = 12,304$$

$$x = 61.52$$

If $x = 61.52$, $y = 100 - 61.52 = 38.48$.

Check: The total length of the wire is $61.52 + 38.48 = 100$ cm. The area of the larger square is $\left(\frac{61.52}{4}\right)^2$, or 236.5444 cm². This is 144 cm² greater than the area of the smaller square, $\left(\frac{38.48}{4}\right)^2$, or 92.5444 cm².

State: The wire should be cut into 61.52 cm and 38.48 cm lengths.

34. Factor: $x^3 + y^3 = (x + y)(x^2 - xy + y^2)$. We know that $x + y = 1$, so $(x + y)^2 = x^2 + 2xy + y^2 = 1$, or $x^2 + y^2 = 1 - 2xy$. We also know that $xy = 1$, so $x^2 + y^2 = 1 - 2 \cdot 1 = -1$. Then $x^3 + y^3 = 1 \cdot (-1 - 1) = -2$.

35. The equation of the ellipse is of the form

$$\frac{x^2}{a^2} + \frac{y^2}{b^2} = 1.$$

Substitute $\left[1, \frac{\sqrt{3}}{2}\right]$ and $\left[\sqrt{3}, \frac{1}{2}\right]$ for (x, y) to get two equations.

$$\frac{1^2}{a^2} + \frac{\left(\frac{\sqrt{3}}{2}\right)^2}{b^2} = 1, \text{ or } \frac{1}{a^2} + \frac{3}{4b^2} = 1$$

$$\frac{(\sqrt{3})^2}{a^2} + \frac{\left(\frac{1}{2}\right)^2}{b^2} = 1, \text{ or } \frac{3}{a^2} + \frac{1}{4b^2} = 1$$

Substitute u for $\frac{1}{a^2}$ and v for $\frac{1}{b^2}$.

$$u + \frac{3}{4}v = 1, \qquad\qquad 4u + 3v = 4,$$
$$\qquad\qquad\qquad \text{or}$$
$$3u + \frac{1}{4}v = 1 \qquad\qquad 12u + v = 4$$

Solving for u and v, we get $u = \frac{1}{4}$, $v = 1$.

Then $u = \frac{1}{a^2} = \frac{1}{4}$, so $a^2 = 4$; $v = \frac{1}{b^2} = 1$, so $b^2 = 1$.

Then the equation of the ellipse is

$$\frac{x^2}{4} + \frac{y^2}{1} = 1, \text{ or } \frac{x^2}{4} + y^2 = 1.$$

36. $\frac{x^2}{a^2} - \frac{y^2}{b^2} = 1$

Substitute each ordered pair for (x,y).

$$\frac{(-3)^2}{a^2} - \frac{\left(-\frac{3\sqrt{5}}{2}\right)^2}{b^2} = 1,$$

$$\frac{(-3)^2}{a^2} - \frac{\left(\frac{3\sqrt{5}}{2}\right)^2}{b^2} = 1,$$

$$\frac{\left(-\frac{3}{2}\right)^2}{a^2} - \frac{0^2}{b^2} = 1$$

$$\frac{9}{a^2} - \frac{45}{4b^2} = 1, \qquad (1)$$

$$\frac{9}{a^2} - \frac{45}{4b^2} = 1, \qquad (2)$$

$$\frac{9}{4a^2} = 1 \qquad (3)$$

Note that Eq. (1) and Eq. (2) are identical. Multiply both sides of Eq. (3) by 4:

$$\frac{9}{a^2} = 4$$

Substitute 4 for $\frac{9}{a^2}$ in Eq. (1) and solve for b^2.

$$4 - \frac{45}{4b^2} = 1$$

$$16b^2 - 45 = 4b^2$$

$$12b^2 = 45$$

$$b^2 = \frac{45}{12}, \text{ or } \frac{15}{4}$$

Solve Eq. (3) for a^2.

$$\frac{9}{4a^2} = 1$$

$$\frac{9}{4} = a^2$$

The equation of the hyperbola is $\frac{x^2}{\frac{9}{4}} - \frac{y^2}{\frac{15}{4}} = 1$.

37. $x - y = a + 2b$, $\qquad\qquad$ (1)
    $x^2 - y^2 = a^2 + 2ab + b^2$ $\qquad$ (2)

Solve Eq. (1) for x and substitute in Eq. (2). Then solve for y.

$$x = y + a + 2b \qquad\qquad (3)$$

$$(y + a + 2b)^2 - y^2 = a^2 + 2ab + b^2$$
$$y^2 + 2ay + 4by + a^2 + 4ab + 4b^2 - y^2 = a^2 + 2ab + b^2$$
$$2ay + 4by = -2ab - 3b^2$$
$$y(2a + 4b) = -2ab - 3b^2$$
$$y = \frac{-2ab - 3b^2}{2a + 4b}$$

Substitute for y in Eq. (3) and solve for x.

$$x = \frac{-2ab - 3b^2}{2a + 4b} + a + 2b$$

$$x = \frac{-2ab - 3b^2 + 2a^2 + 8ab + 8b^2}{2a + 4b}$$

$$x = \frac{2a^2 + 6ab + 5b^2}{2a + 4b}$$

The solution is $\left[\frac{2a^2 + 6ab + 5b^2}{2a + 4b}, \frac{-2ab - 3b^2}{2a + 4b}\right]$.

38. $\frac{x}{a - b} + \frac{y}{a + b} = 1$, $\qquad$ (1)
    $x^2 - y^2 = (a - b)^2$ $\qquad$ (2)

Solve Eq. (1) for x.
$$x(a + b) + y(a - b) = (a - b)(a + b)$$
$$x(a + b) + ay - by = a^2 - b^2$$
$$x(a + b) = a^2 - b^2 - ay + by$$
$$x = \frac{a^2 - b^2 - ay + by}{a + b} \qquad (3)$$

Substitute for x in Eq. (2) and solve for y.
$$\left[\frac{a^2 - b^2 - ay + by}{a + b}\right]^2 - y^2 = (a - b)^2$$
$$(a^2 - b^2 - ay + by)^2 - y^2(a + b)^2 = (a - b)^2(a + b)^2$$
$$a^4 - 2a^2b^2 + b^4 - 2a^3y + 2a^2by + 2ab^2y - 2b^3y + a^2y^2 - 2aby^2 + b^2y^2 - a^2y^2 - 2aby^2 - b^2y^2 = a^4 - 2a^2b^2 + b^4$$
$$-2a^3y + 2a^2by + 2ab^2y - 2b^3y - 4aby^2 = 0$$
$$\qquad\qquad\qquad\qquad\qquad\qquad \text{Simplifying}$$

$-a^3y + a^2by + ab^2y - b^3y - 2aby^2 = 0$

Multiplying by $\frac{1}{2}$

$y(-a^3 + a^2b + ab^2 - b^3 - 2aby) = 0$

$y = 0$ or $-a^3 + a^2b + ab^2 - b^3 - 2aby = 0$

$y = 0$ or $y = \dfrac{-a^3 + a^2b + ab^2 - b^3}{2ab} =$

$-\dfrac{(a^2 - b^2)(a - b)}{2ab}$

Substitute in Eq. (3) to find x.

When $y = 0$, $x = \dfrac{a^2 - b^2 - a(0) + b(0)}{a + b} = \dfrac{a^2 - b^2}{a + b} =$

$\dfrac{(a + b)(a - b)}{a + b} = a - b.$

When $y = -\dfrac{(a^2 - b^2)(a - b)}{2ab}$,

$x = \dfrac{a^2-b^2-a\left[-\dfrac{(a^2-b^2)(a-b)}{2ab}\right] + b\left[-\dfrac{(a^2-b^2)(a-b)}{2ab}\right]}{a + b} =$

$\dfrac{2ab(a^2 - b^2) + (a^2 - b^2)(a - b)(a - b)}{2ab(a + b)} =$

$\dfrac{2ab(a + b)(a - b) + (a + b)(a - b)^3}{2ab(a + b)} =$

$\dfrac{(a+b)[2ab(a-b) + (a-b)^3]}{2ab(a+b)} = \dfrac{2ab(a-b) + (a-b)^3}{2ab} =$

$\dfrac{2a^2b - 2ab^2 + a^3 - 3a^2b + 3ab^2 - b^3}{2ab} =$

$\dfrac{a^3 - a^2b + ab^2 - b^3}{2ab} = \dfrac{a^2(a - b) + b^2(a - b)}{2ab} =$

$\dfrac{(a - b)(a^2 + b^2)}{2ab}$

The solutions are $(a - b, 0)$ and

$\left[\dfrac{(a - b)(a^2 + b^2)}{2ab}, -\dfrac{(a^2 - b^2)(a - b)}{2ab}\right].$

39. Solve the system: $2L + 2W = P$,

$LW = A$

See the answer section in the text.

40. There is no number x such that

$\dfrac{x^2}{a^2} - \dfrac{\left[\dfrac{b}{a}x\right]^2}{b^2} = 1$, because the left side

simplifies to $\dfrac{x^2}{a^2} - \dfrac{x^2}{a^2}$ which is 0.

41. $(x - h)^2 + (y - k)^2 = r^2$

If $(2, 4)$ is a point on the circle, then
$(2 - h)^2 + (4 - k)^2 = r^2$.

If $(3, 3)$ is a point on the circle, then
$(3 - h)^2 + (3 - k)^2 = r^2$.

Thus

$$(2 - h)^2 + (4 - k)^2 = (3 - h)^2 + (3 - k)^2$$

$4 - 4h + h^2 + 16 - 8k + k^2 =$
$\qquad\qquad 9 - 6h + h^2 + 9 - 6k + k^2$

$\qquad -4h - 8k + 20 = -6h - 6k + 18$

$\qquad\qquad 2h - 2k = -2$

$\qquad\qquad h - k = -1$

If the center (h, k) is on the line $3x - y = 3$, then $3h - k = 3$.

Solving the system

$h - k = -1$,

$3h - k = 3$

we find that $(h, k) = (2, 3)$.

Find r, substituting $(2, 3)$ for (h, k) and $(2, 4)$ for (x, y). We could also use $(3, 3)$ for (x, y).

$(x - h)^2 + (y - k)^2 = r^2$
$(2 - 2)^2 + (4 - 3)^2 = r^2$
$\qquad\qquad 0 + 1 = r^2$
$\qquad\qquad\quad 1 = r^2$
$\qquad\qquad\quad 1 = r$

The equation of the circle whose center is $(2, 3)$ and whose radius is 1 is
$(x - 2)^2 + (y - 3)^2 = 1$.

42.

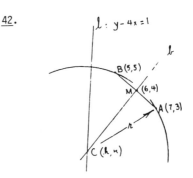

The center C lies on ℓ and b, the $\perp$ bisector of chord $\overline{AB}$. The equation of b is
$y - 4 = 1(x - 6)$ or $y - x = -2$.

Solving the system
$\ell: y - 4x = 1$,
$b: y - x = -2$,
we have $C(h, k) = (-1, -3)$.

The radius $r = \overline{CA} = \sqrt{8^2 + 6^2} = 10$.

Then an equation of the required circle is
$(x + 1)^2 + (y + 3)^2 = 10^2$.

43. $x^3 + y^3 = 72,$ (1)

$x + y = 6$ (2)

Solve Eq. (2) for y: $y = 6 - x$

Substitute for y in Eq. (1) and solve for x.

$x^3 + (6 - x)^3 = 72$

$x^3 + 216 - 108x + 18x^2 - x^3 = 72$

$18x^2 - 108x + 144 = 0$

$x^2 - 6x + 8 = 0$

$\left[\text{Multiplying by } \frac{1}{18}\right]$

$(x - 4)(x - 2) = 0$

$x = 4 \quad \text{or} \quad x = 2$

If $x = 4$, then $y = 6 - 4 = 2$.

If $x = 2$, then $y = 6 - 2 = 4$.

The pairs $(4, 2)$ and $(2, 4)$ check.

44. $1 - 20\lambda k^2 = 0,$ (1)

$2 - 10\lambda hk = 0,$ (2)

$hk^2 - 640,000 = 0$ (3)

From (2), $hk = \frac{2}{10\lambda} = \frac{1}{5\lambda}$.

Substitute in (3):

$\left[\frac{1}{5\lambda}\right]k - 640,000 = 0$

$k = 3,200,000\lambda$

Substitute in (1):

$1 - 20\lambda(3,200,000\lambda)^2 = 0$

$1 - 2.048 \times 10^{14}\lambda^3 = 0$

$\lambda \approx 0.000016956$

Then $k \approx 3,200,000(0.000016956) = 54.2592$.

Also $2 - 10(0.000016956)(h)(54.2592) = 0$, so $h \approx 217.386816$.

45. $(0.965, 4402.33), (-0.965, -4402.33)$

46. $(785, 45), (45, 785)$

47. $(2.11, -0.11), (-13.04, -13.34)$

48. $(7.37, -0.16), (0.19, -6.16)$

Exercise Set 10.5

1. $x^2 + y^2 = 25,$ (1)

$y^2 = x + 5$ (2)

We substitute $x + 5$ for y^2 in Eq. (1) and solve for x.

$x^2 + y^2 = 25$

$x^2 + (x + 5) = 25$

$x^2 + x - 20 = 0$

$(x + 5)(x - 4) = 0$

$x + 5 = 0 \quad \text{or} \quad x - 4 = 0$

$x = -5 \quad \text{or} \qquad x = 4$

Next we substitute these numbers for x in either Eq. (1) or Eq. (2) and solve for y. Here we use Eq. (2).

$y^2 = -5 + 5 = 0$ and $y = 0$.

$y^2 = 4 + 5 = 9$ and $y = \pm 3$.

The possible solutions are $(-5,0)$, $(4,3)$, and $(4,-3)$.

Check:

For $(-5,0)$:

$x^2 + y^2 = 25$		$y^2 = x + 5$	
$(-5)^2 + 0^2$	25	0^2	$-5 + 5$
$25 + 0$		0	0
25			

For $(4,3)$:

$x^2 + y^2 = 25$		$y^2 = x + 5$	
$4^2 + 3^2$	25	3^2	$4 + 5$
$16 + 9$		9	9
25			

For $(4,-3)$:

$x^2 + y^2 = 25$		$y^2 = x + 5$	
$4^2 + (-3)^2$	25	$(-3)^2$	$4 + 5$
$16 + 9$		9	9
25			

The solutions are $(-5,0)$, $(4,3)$, and $(4,-3)$.

2. $y = x^2$

$x = y^2$

$x = (x^2)^2$

$x = x^4$

$0 = x^4 - x$

$0 = x(x^3 - 1)$

$x = 0 \quad \text{or} \quad x = 1$

$y = 0^2 = 0$

$y = 1^2 = 1$

The solutions $(0,0)$ and $(1,1)$ check.

3. $x^2 + y^2 = 9$,   (1)
    $x^2 - y^2 = 9$ (2)

Here we use the addition method.

$$x^2 + y^2 = 9$$
$$\underline{x^2 - y^2 = 9}$$
$$2x^2 = 18 \quad \text{Adding}$$
$$x^2 = 9$$
$$x = \pm 3$$

If $x = 3$, $x^2 = 9$, and if $x = -3$, $x^2 = 9$, so substituting 3 or -3 in Eq. (1) give us

$$x^2 + y^2 = 9$$
$$9 + y^2 = 9$$
$$y^2 = 0$$
$$y = 0.$$

The possible solutions are $(3,0)$ and $(-3,0)$.

Check:

$x^2 + y^2 = 9$		$x^2 - y^2 = 9$	
$(\pm 3)^2 + (0)^2$	9	$(\pm 3)^2 - (0)^2$	9
$9 + 0$		$9 - 0$	
9			9

The solutions are $(3,0)$ and $(-3,0)$.

4. $y^2 - 4x^2 = 4$,   (1)
    $4x^2 + y^2 = 4$ (2)

$$-4x^2 + y^2 = 4, \quad (1)$$
$$\underline{4x^2 + y^2 = 4} \quad (2)$$
$$2y^2 = 8 \quad \text{Adding}$$
$$y^2 = 4$$
$$y = \pm 2$$

Substitute for y in Eq. (2).

$$4x^2 + 4 = 4$$
$$4x^2 = 0$$
$$x = 0$$

The solutions $(0,2)$ and $(0,-2)$ check.

5. $x^2 + y^2 = 25$,   (1)
    $xy = 12$ (2)

First we solve Eq. (2) for y.

$$xy = 12$$
$$y = \frac{12}{x}$$

Then we substitute $\frac{12}{x}$ for y in Eq. (1) and solve for x.

$$x^2 + y^2 = 25$$
$$x^2 + \left(\frac{12}{x}\right)^2 = 25$$
$$x^2 + \frac{144}{x^2} = 25$$
$$x^4 + 144 = 25x^2 \quad \text{Multiplying by } x^2$$
$$x^4 - 25x^2 + 144 = 0$$

$$u^2 - 25u + 144 = 0 \quad \text{Letting } u = x^2$$
$$(u - 9)(u - 16) = 0$$

$$u = 9 \quad \text{or} \quad u = 16$$

We now substitute x^2 for u and solve for x.

$$x^2 = 9 \quad \text{or} \quad x^2 = 16$$
$$x = \pm 3 \quad \text{or} \quad x = \pm 4$$

Since $y = 12/x$, if $x = 3$, $y = 4$; if $x = -3$, $y = -4$; if $x = 4$, $y = 3$; and if $x = -4$, $y = -3$. The pairs $(3,4)$, $(-3,-4)$, $(4,3)$, $(-4,-3)$ check. They are the solutions.

6. $x^2 - y^2 = 16$,   (1)
    $\underline{x + y^2 = 4}$ (2)
    $x^2 + x = 20 \quad \text{Adding}$

$$x^2 + x - 20 = 0$$
$$(x + 5)(x - 4) = 0$$

$$x = -5 \quad \text{or} \quad x = 4$$

$$y^2 = 4 - x \quad \text{Solving Eq. (2) for } y^2$$
$$y^2 = 4 - (-5) = 9 \text{ and } y = \pm 3$$
$$y^2 = 4 - 4 = 0 \text{ and } y = 0$$

The pairs $(-5,3)$, $(-5,-3)$, and $(4,0)$ check.

7. $x^2 + y^2 = 4$,   (1)
    $16x^2 + 9y^2 = 144$ (2)

$$-9x^2 - 9y^2 = -36 \quad \text{Multiplying (1) by } -9$$
$$\underline{16x^2 + 9y^2 = 144}$$
$$7x^2 = 108 \quad \text{Adding}$$
$$x^2 = \frac{108}{7}$$
$$x = \pm\sqrt{\frac{108}{7}} = \pm 6\sqrt{\frac{3}{7}}$$
$$x = \pm\frac{6\sqrt{21}}{7} \quad \text{Rationalizing the denominator}$$

Substituting $\frac{6\sqrt{21}}{7}$ or $-\frac{6\sqrt{21}}{7}$ for x in Eq. (1) gives us

$$\frac{36 \cdot 21}{49} + y^2 = 4$$
$$y^2 = 4 - \frac{108}{7}$$
$$y^2 = -\frac{80}{7}$$
$$y = \pm\sqrt{-\frac{80}{7}} = \pm 4i\sqrt{\frac{5}{7}}$$
$$y = \pm\frac{4i\sqrt{35}}{7}. \quad \text{Rationalizing the denominator}$$

The pairs $\left(\frac{6\sqrt{21}}{7}, \frac{4i\sqrt{35}}{7}\right)$, $\left(\frac{6\sqrt{21}}{7}, -\frac{4i\sqrt{35}}{7}\right)$, $\left(-\frac{6\sqrt{21}}{7}, \frac{4i\sqrt{35}}{7}\right)$, and $\left(-\frac{6\sqrt{21}}{7}, -\frac{4i\sqrt{35}}{7}\right)$ check. They are the solutions.

8. $x^2 + y^2 = 25,$ (1)

   $25x^2 + 16y^2 = 400$ (2)

   $-16x^2 - 16y^2 = -400$ Multiplying (1) by -16

   $\underline{25x^2 + 16y^2 = 400}$

   $9x^2 = 0$ Adding

        $x = 0$

   $0^2 + y^2 = 25$ Substituting in (1)

        $y = \pm 5$

The pairs $(0,5)$ and $(0,-5)$ check.

9. $x^2 + y^2 = 16,$ $x^2 + y^2 = 16,$ (1)
              or
  $y^2 - 2x^2 = 10$ $-2x^2 + y^2 = 10$ (2)

Here we use the addition method.

   $2x^2 + 2y^2 = 32$ Multiplying (1) by 2

  $\underline{-2x^2 + y^2 = 10}$

        $3y^2 = 42$ Adding

         $y^2 = 14$

          $y = \pm\sqrt{14}$

Substituting $\sqrt{14}$ or $-\sqrt{14}$ for y in Eq. (1) gives us

     $x^2 + 14 = 16$

        $x^2 = 2$

         $x = \pm\sqrt{2}$

The pairs $(-\sqrt{2},-\sqrt{14})$, $(-\sqrt{2},\sqrt{14})$, $(\sqrt{2},-\sqrt{14})$, and $(\sqrt{2},\sqrt{14})$ check. They are the solutions.

10. $x^2 + y^2 = 14,$ (1)

   $\underline{x^2 - y^2 = 4}$ (2)

  $2x^2 = 18$ Adding

      $x^2 = 9$

       $x = \pm 3$

  $9 + y^2 = 14$ Substituting in Eq. (1)

    $y^2 = 5$

     $y = \pm\sqrt{5}$

The pairs $(-3,-\sqrt{5})$, $(-3,\sqrt{5})$, $(3,-\sqrt{5})$, and $(3,\sqrt{5})$ check.

11. $x^2 + y^2 = 5,$ (1)

  $xy = 2$ (2)

First we solve Eq. (2) for y.

  $xy = 2$

  $y = \dfrac{2}{x}$

Then we substitute $\dfrac{2}{x}$ for y in Eq. (1) and solve for x.

    $x^2 + y^2 = 5$

    $x^2 + \left(\dfrac{2}{x}\right)^2 = 5$

    $x^2 + \dfrac{4}{x^2} = 5$

     $x^4 + 4 = 5x^2$ Multiplying by x^2

 $x^4 - 5x^2 + 4 = 0$

  $u^2 - 5u + 4 = 0$ Letting $u = x^2$

 $(u - 4)(u - 1) = 0$

 $u = 4$ or $u = 1$

We now substitute x^2 for u and solve for x.

   $x^2 = 4$ or $x^2 = 1$

    $x = \pm 2$ $x = \pm 1$

Since $y = 2/x$, if $x = 2$, $y = 1$; if $x = -2$, $y = -1$; if $x = 1$, $y = 2$; and if $x = -1$, $y = -2$. The pairs $(2,1)$, $(-2,-1)$, $(1,2)$, $(-1,-2)$ check. They are the solutions.

12. $x^2 + y^2 = 20,$

  $xy = 8$

  $y = \dfrac{8}{x}$

     $x^2 + \left(\dfrac{8}{x}\right)^2 = 20$

     $x^2 + \dfrac{64}{x^2} = 20$

      $x^4 + 64 = 20x^2$

  $x^4 - 20x^2 + 64 = 0$

   $u^2 - 20u + 64 = 0$ Letting $u = x^2$

 $(u - 16)(u - 4) = 0$

  $u = 16$ or $u = 4$

 $x^2 = 16$ or $x^2 = 4$

   $x = \pm 4$ or $x = \pm 2$

$y = 8/x$, so if $x = 4$, $y = 2$; if $x = -4$, $y = -2$; if $x = 2$, $y = 4$; and if $x = -2$, $y = -4$. The pairs $(4,2)$, $(-4,-2)$, $(2,4)$, and $(-2,-4)$ check.

13. $x^2 + y^2 = 13,$ (1)

  $xy = 6$ (2)

First we solve Eq. (2) for y.

  $xy = 6$

  $y = \dfrac{6}{x}$

Then we substitute $\dfrac{6}{x}$ for y in Eq. (1) and solve for x.

    $x^2 + y^2 = 13$

    $x^2 + \left(\dfrac{6}{x}\right)^2 = 13$

    $x^2 + \dfrac{36}{x^2} = 13$

     $x^4 + 36 = 13x^2$ Multiplying by x^2

  $x^4 - 13x^2 + 36 = 0$

$u^2 - 13u + 36 = 0$ Letting $u = x^2$

$(u - 9)(u - 4) = 0$

$u = 9$ or $u = 4$

We now substitute x^2 for u and solve for x.

$x^2 = 9$ or $x^2 = 4$

$x = \pm 3$ $x = \pm 2$

Since $y = 6/x$, if $x = 3$, $y = 2$; if $x = -3$, $y = -2$; if $x = 2$, $y = 3$; and if $x = -2$, $y = -3$. The pairs $(3,2)$, $(-3,-2)$, $(2,3)$, $(-2,-3)$ check. They are the solutions.

14. $x^2 + 4y^2 = 20$,

      $xy = 4$

      $y = \dfrac{4}{x}$

$$x^2 + 4\left(\frac{4}{x}\right)^2 = 20$$

$$x^2 + \frac{64}{x^2} = 20$$

$$x^4 + 64 = 20x^2$$

$$x^4 - 20x^2 + 64 = 0$$

$u^2 - 20u + 64 = 0$ Letting $u = x^2$

$(u - 16)(u - 4) = 0$

$u = 16$ or $u = 4$

$x^2 = 16$ or $x^2 = 4$

$x = \pm 4$ or $x = \pm 2$

$y = 4/x$, so if $x = 4$, $y = 1$; if $x = -4$, $y = -1$; if $x = 2$, $y = 2$; and if $x = -2$, $y = -2$. The pairs $(4,1)$, $(-4,-1)$, $(2,2)$, and $(-2,-2)$ check.

15. $x^2 + y^2 + 6y + 5 = 0$ (1)

      $x^2 + y^2 - 2x - 8 = 0$ (2)

Using the addition method, multiply Eq. (2) by -1 and add the result to Eq. (1).

$x^2 + y^2 + 6y + 5 = 0$ (1)

$\underline{-x^2 - y^2 + 2x + 8 = 0}$ (2)

      $2x + 6y + 13 = 0$ (3)

Solve Eq. (3) for x.

$2x + 6y + 13 = 0$

      $2x = -6y - 13$

        $x = \dfrac{-6y - 13}{2}$

Substitute $\dfrac{-6y - 13}{2}$ for x in Eq. (1) and solve for y.

$$x^2 + y^2 + 6y + 5 = 0$$

$$\left(\frac{-6y - 13}{2}\right)^2 + y^2 + 6y + 5 = 0$$

$$\frac{36y^2 + 156y + 169}{4} + y^2 + 6y + 5 = 0$$

$$36y^2 + 156y + 169 + 4y^2 + 24y + 20 = 0$$

$$40y^2 + 180y + 189 = 0$$

Using the quadratic formula, we find that

$y = \dfrac{-45 \pm 3\sqrt{15}}{20}$. Substitute $\dfrac{-45 \pm 3\sqrt{15}}{20}$ for y in $x = \dfrac{-6y - 13}{2}$ and solve for x.

If $y = \dfrac{-45 + 3\sqrt{15}}{20}$, then $x = \dfrac{-6\left(\dfrac{-45 + 3\sqrt{15}}{20}\right) - 13}{2}$

$$= \frac{5 - 9\sqrt{15}}{20}.$$

If $y = \dfrac{-45 - 3\sqrt{15}}{20}$, then $x = \dfrac{-6\left(\dfrac{-45 - 3\sqrt{15}}{20}\right) - 13}{2}$

$$= \frac{5 + 9\sqrt{15}}{20}.$$

The pairs $\left(\dfrac{5 + 9\sqrt{15}}{20}, \dfrac{-45 - 3\sqrt{15}}{20}\right)$ and $\left(\dfrac{5 - 9\sqrt{15}}{20}, \dfrac{-45 + 3\sqrt{15}}{20}\right)$ check and are the solutions.

16. $2xy + 3y^2 = 7$,   (1)

      $3xy - 2y^2 = 4$ (2)

   $6xy + 9y^2 = 21$ Multiplying (1) by 3

  $\underline{-6xy + 4y^2 = -8}$ Multiplying (2) by -2

       $13y^2 = 13$

         $y^2 = 1$

          $y = \pm 1$

Substitute for y in Eq. (1) and solve for x.

When $y = 1$: $2 \cdot x \cdot 1 + 3 \cdot 1^2 = 7$

               $2x = 4$

                $x = 2$

When $y = -1$: $2 \cdot x \cdot (-1) + 3(-1)^2 = 7$

                $-2x = 4$

                 $x = -2$

The pairs $(2,1)$ and $(-2,-1)$ check.

17. $xy - y^2 = 2$,   (1)

      $2xy - 3y^2 = 0$ (2)

  $-2xy + 2y^2 = -4$ Multiplying (1) by -2

   $\underline{2xy - 3y^2 = 0}$

       $-y^2 = -4$

        $y^2 = 4$

         $y = \pm 2$

We substitute for y in Eq. (1) and solve for x.

When $y = 2$: $x \cdot 2 - 2^2 = 2$

             $2x - 4 = 2$

                $2x = 6$

                 $x = 3$

When $y = -2$: $x(-2) - (-2)^2 = 2$

             $-2x - 4 = 2$

               $-2x = 6$

                $x = -3$

The pairs (3,2) and (-3,-2) check. They are the solutions.

18. $4a^2 - 25b^2 = 0$,   (1)
$2a^2 - 10b^2 = 3b + 4$ (2)

$4a^2 - 25b^2 = 0$
$\underline{-4a^2 + 20b^2 = -6b - 8}$ Multiplying (2) by -2
$-5b^2 = -6b - 8$
$0 = 5b^2 - 6b - 8$
$0 = (5b + 4)(b - 2)$

$b = -\dfrac{4}{5}$ or $b = 2$

Substitute for b in Eq. (1) and solve for a.

When $b = -\dfrac{4}{5}$: $4a^2 - 25\left[-\dfrac{4}{5}\right]^2 = 0$
$4a^2 = 16$
$a^2 = 4$
$a = \pm 2$

When $b = 2$: $4a^2 - 25(2)^2 = 0$
$4a^2 = 100$
$a^2 = 25$
$a = \pm 5$

The pairs $\left[2, -\dfrac{4}{5}\right]$, $\left[-2, -\dfrac{4}{5}\right]$, (5,2) and (-5,2) check.

19. $m^2 - 3mn + n^2 + 1 = 0$,   (1)
$3m^2 - mn + 3n^2 = 13$ (2)

$m^2 - 3mn + n^2 = -1$,   (3)   Rewriting (1)
$3m^2 - mn + 3n^2 = 13$ (2)

$-3m^2 + 9mn - 3n^2 = 3$ Multiplying (3) by -3
$\underline{3m^2 - mn + 3n^2 = 13}$
$8mn = 16$
$mn = 2$
$n = \dfrac{2}{m}$ (4)

Substitute $\dfrac{2}{m}$ for n in Eq. (1) and solve for m.

$m^2 - 3m\left[\dfrac{2}{m}\right] + \left[\dfrac{2}{m}\right]^2 + 1 = 0$
$m^2 - 6 + \dfrac{4}{m^2} + 1 = 0$
$m^2 - 5 + \dfrac{4}{m^2} = 0$
$m^4 - 5m^2 + 4 = 0$ Multiplying by m^2

Substitute u for m^2.
$u^2 - 5u + 4 = 0$
$(u - 4)(u - 1) = 0$

$u = 4$ or $u = 1$
$m^2 = 4$ or $m^2 = 1$
$m = \pm 2$ or $m = \pm 1$

Substitute for m in Eq. (4) and solve for n.
When m = 2, $n = \dfrac{2}{2} = 1$.

When m = -2, $n = \dfrac{2}{-2} = -1$.

When m = 1, $n = \dfrac{2}{1} = 2$.

When m = -1, $n = \dfrac{2}{-1} = -2$.

The pairs (2, 1), (-2, -1), (1, 2), and (-1, -2) check. They are the solutions.

20. $ab - b^2 = -4$,   (1)
$ab - 2b^2 = -6$ (2)

$ab - b^2 = -4$
$\underline{-ab + 2b^2 = 6}$ Multiplying (2) by -1
$b^2 = 2$
$b = \pm\sqrt{2}$

Substitute for b in Eq. (1) and solve for a.

When $b = \sqrt{2}$: $a(\sqrt{2}) - (\sqrt{2})^2 = -4$
$a\sqrt{2} = -2$
$a = -\dfrac{2}{\sqrt{2}} = -\sqrt{2}$

When $b = -\sqrt{2}$: $a(-\sqrt{2}) - (-\sqrt{2})^2 = -4$
$-a\sqrt{2} = -2$
$a = \dfrac{-2}{-\sqrt{2}} = \sqrt{2}$

The pairs $(-\sqrt{2}, \sqrt{2})$ and $(\sqrt{2}, -\sqrt{2})$ check.

21. $a^2 + b^2 = 14$,   (1)
$ab = 3\sqrt{5}$ (2)

Solve Eq. (1) for b.
$b = \dfrac{3\sqrt{5}}{a}$

Substitute $\dfrac{3\sqrt{5}}{a}$ for b in Eq. (1) and solve for a.

$a^2 + \left[\dfrac{3\sqrt{5}}{a}\right]^2 = 14$
$a^2 + \dfrac{45}{a^2} = 14$
$a^4 + 45 = 14a^2$
$a^4 - 14a^2 + 45 = 0$
$u^2 - 14u + 45 = 0$ Letting $u = a^2$
$(u - 9)(u - 5) = 0$

$u = 9$ or $u = 5$
$a^2 = 9$ or $a^2 = 5$
$a = \pm 3$ or $a = \pm\sqrt{5}$

Since $b = 3\sqrt{5}/a$, if a = 3, $b = \sqrt{5}$; if a = -3, $b = -\sqrt{5}$; if $a = \sqrt{5}$, b = 3; and if $a = -\sqrt{5}$, b = -3. The pairs $(3, \sqrt{5})$, $(-3, -\sqrt{5})$, $(\sqrt{5}, 3)$, $(-\sqrt{5}, -3)$ check. They are the solutions.

22. $x^2 + xy = 5$,　　(1)

　　$2x^2 + xy = 2$　　(2)

　　$-x^2 - xy = -5$　Multiplying (1) by -1

　　$\underline{2x^2 + xy = 2}$

　　$x^2 = -3$

　　　　$x = \pm i\sqrt{3}$

Substitute for x in Eq. (1) and solve for y.

When $x = i\sqrt{3}$:　$(i\sqrt{3})^2 + (i\sqrt{3})y = 5$

　　　　　　　　　　　$i\sqrt{3}y = 8$

　　　　　　　　　　　$y = \dfrac{8}{i\sqrt{3}} = -\dfrac{8i\sqrt{3}}{3}$

When $x = -i\sqrt{3}$:　$(-i\sqrt{3})^2 + (-i\sqrt{3})y = 5$

　　　　　　　　　　　$-i\sqrt{3}y = 8$

　　　　　　　　　　　$y = -\dfrac{8}{i\sqrt{3}} =$

　　　　　　　　　　　$\dfrac{8i\sqrt{3}}{3}$

The pairs $\left(i\sqrt{3}, -\dfrac{8i\sqrt{3}}{3}\right)$ and $\left(-i\sqrt{3}, \dfrac{8i\sqrt{3}}{3}\right)$ check.

23. $x^2 + y^2 = 25$,　　(1)

　　$9x^2 + 4y^2 = 36$　　(2)

　　$-4x^2 - 4y^2 = -100$　Multiplying (1) by -4

　　$\underline{9x^2 + 4y^2 = 36}$

　　$5x^2 = -64$

　　　　$x^2 = -\dfrac{64}{5}$

　　　　$x = \pm\sqrt{\dfrac{-64}{5}} = \pm\dfrac{8i}{\sqrt{5}}$

　　　　$x = \pm\dfrac{8i\sqrt{5}}{5}$　Rationalizing the denominator

Substituting $\dfrac{8i\sqrt{5}}{5}$ or $-\dfrac{8i\sqrt{5}}{5}$ for x in Eq. (1) and solving for y gives us

　　$-\dfrac{64}{5} + y^2 = 25$

　　　　$y^2 = \dfrac{189}{5}$

　　　　$y = \pm\sqrt{\dfrac{189}{5}} = \pm3\sqrt{\dfrac{21}{5}}$

　　　　$y = \pm\dfrac{3\sqrt{105}}{5}$.　Rationalizing the denominator

The pairs $\left(\dfrac{8i\sqrt{5}}{5}, \dfrac{3\sqrt{105}}{5}\right)$, $\left(-\dfrac{8i\sqrt{5}}{5}, \dfrac{3\sqrt{105}}{5}\right)$, $\left(\dfrac{8i\sqrt{5}}{5}, -\dfrac{3\sqrt{105}}{5}\right)$, and $\left(-\dfrac{8i\sqrt{5}}{5}, -\dfrac{3\sqrt{105}}{5}\right)$ check. They are the solutions.

24. $x^2 + y^2 = 1$,　　(1)

　　$9x^2 - 16y^2 = 144$　　(2)

　　$16x^2 + 16y^2 = 16$　Multiplying (1) by 16

　　$\underline{9x^2 - 16y^2 = 144}$

　　$25x^2 = 160$

　　　　$x^2 = \dfrac{160}{25}$

　　　　$x = \pm\dfrac{4\sqrt{10}}{5}$

Substituting for x in Eq. (1) and solving for y gives us

　　$\dfrac{160}{25} + y^2 = 1$

　　　　$y^2 = -\dfrac{135}{25}$

　　　　$y = \pm\sqrt{-\dfrac{135}{25}}$

　　　　$y = \pm\dfrac{3i\sqrt{15}}{5}$.

The pairs $\left(\dfrac{4\sqrt{10}}{5}, \dfrac{3i\sqrt{15}}{5}\right)$, $\left(\dfrac{4\sqrt{10}}{5}, -\dfrac{3i\sqrt{15}}{5}\right)$, $\left(-\dfrac{4\sqrt{10}}{5}, \dfrac{3i\sqrt{15}}{5}\right)$, and $\left(-\dfrac{4\sqrt{10}}{5}, -\dfrac{3i\sqrt{15}}{5}\right)$ check.

25. Familiarize: Let x and y represent the numbers. Translate:

　　The product of two numbers is 156.

　　　　$xy = 156$　　(1)

　　The sum of their squares is 313.

　　　　$x^2 + y^2 = 313$　　(2)

Carry out: We solve the system of equations. First solve Eq. (1) for y.

$xy = 156$

$y = \dfrac{156}{x}$

Then we substitute $\dfrac{156}{x}$ for y in Eq. (2) and solve for x.

　　　　$x^2 + y^2 = 313$　　(2)

　　　　$x^2 + \left(\dfrac{156}{x}\right)^2 = 313$

　　　　$x^2 + \dfrac{24,336}{x^2} = 313$

　　　　$x^4 + 24,336 = 313x^2$

　　$x^4 - 313x^2 + 24,336 = 0$

　　$u^2 - 313u + 24,336 = 0$　Letting $u = x^2$

　　$(u - 169)(u - 144) = 0$

　　$u = 169$　or　$u = 144$

We now substitute x^2 for u and solve for x.

　　$x^2 = 169$　or　$x^2 = 144$

　　$x = \pm13$　or　$x = \pm12$

Since $y = 156/x$, if $x = 13$, $y = 12$; if $x = -13$, $y = -12$; if $x = 12$, $y = 13$; and if $x = -12$, $y = -13$. The possible solutions are $(13,12)$, $(-13,-12)$, $(12,13)$, and $(-12,-13)$.

Check: If $x = 13$ and $y = 12$, their product is 156. If $x = -13$ and $y = -12$, their product is 156. The sum of the squares in either case is $(\pm 13)^2 + (\pm 12)^2 = 169 + 144 = 313$. The pairs $(12,13)$ and $(-12,-13)$ do not give us any other solutions.

State: The numbers are 13 and 12 or -13 and -12.

26. Let x and y represent the numbers. Solve the system

$$xy = 60,$$
$$x^2 + y^2 = 136.$$

The solutions are $(6,10)$, $(-6,-10)$, $(10,6)$, and $(-10,-6)$. The numbers are 6 and 10 or -6 and -10.

27. Familiarize: We first make a drawing. Let ℓ = the length and w = the width.

Translate:

Area: $\ell w = \sqrt{3}$ (1)

From the Pythagorean theorem: $\ell^2 + w^2 = 2^2$ (2)

Carry out: We solve the system of equations.

We first solve Eq. (1) for w.

$$\ell w = \sqrt{3}$$
$$w = \frac{\sqrt{3}}{\ell}$$

Then we substitute $\frac{\sqrt{3}}{\ell}$ for w in Eq. (2) and solve for ℓ.

$$\ell^2 + \left[\frac{\sqrt{3}}{\ell}\right]^2 = 4$$
$$\ell^2 + \frac{3}{\ell^2} = 4$$
$$\ell^4 + 3 = 4\ell^2$$
$$\ell^4 - 4\ell^2 + 3 = 0$$
$$u^2 - 4u + 3 = 0 \quad \text{Letting } u = \ell^2$$
$$(u - 3)(u - 1) = 0$$

$$u = 3 \quad \text{or} \quad u = 1$$

We now substitute ℓ^2 for u and solve for ℓ.

$$\ell^2 = 3 \quad \text{or} \quad \ell^2 = 1$$
$$\ell = \pm\sqrt{3} \quad \text{or} \quad \ell = \pm 1$$

Length cannot be negative, so we only need to consider $\ell = \sqrt{3}$ and $\ell = 1$. Since $w = \sqrt{3}/\ell$, if $\ell = \sqrt{3}$, $w = 1$ and if $\ell = 1$, $w = \sqrt{3}$. Length is usually considered to be longer than width, so we have the solution $\ell = \sqrt{3}$ and $w = 1$, or $(\sqrt{3},1)$.

Check: If $\ell = \sqrt{3}$ and $w = 1$, the area is $\sqrt{3} \cdot 1 = \sqrt{3}$. Also $(\sqrt{3})^2 + 1^2 = 3 + 1 = 4 = 2^2$. The numbers check.

State: The length is $\sqrt{3}$ m, and the width is 1 m.

28. Let ℓ = the length and w = the width. Solve the system

$$\ell w = \sqrt{2},$$
$$\ell^2 + w^2 = (\sqrt{3})^2.$$

The solutions are $(\sqrt{2},1)$, $(-\sqrt{2},-1)$, $(1,\sqrt{2})$, and $(-1,-\sqrt{2})$. The pair $(\sqrt{2},1)$ has meaning in this problem. The length is $\sqrt{2}$ m, and the width is 1 m.

29. Familiarize: We let x = the length of a side of one peanut bed and y = the length of a side of the other peanut bed. Make a drawing.

Area: x^2 Area: y^2

Translate:

The sum of the areas is 832 ft².

$$x^2 + y^2 = 832$$

The difference of the areas is 320 ft².

$$x^2 - y^2 = 320$$

Carry out: We solve the system of equations.

$$\begin{aligned}
x^2 + y^2 &= 832 \\
x^2 - y^2 &= 320 \\
\hline
2x^2 &= 1152 \quad \text{Adding} \\
x^2 &= 576 \\
x &= \pm 24
\end{aligned}$$

Since length cannot be negative, we consider only $x = 24$. Substitute 24 for x in the first equation and solve for y.

$$24^2 + y^2 = 832$$
$$576 + y^2 = 832$$
$$y^2 = 256$$
$$y = \pm 16$$

Again, we consider only the positive value, 16. The possible solution is $(24,16)$.

Check: The areas of the peanut beds are 24^2, or 576, and 16^2, or 256. The sum of the areas is $576 + 256$, or 832. The difference of the areas is $576 - 256$, or 320. The values check.

State: The lengths of the beds are 24 ft and 16 ft.

30. Let p = the principal and r = the interest rate. Solve the system

$$pr = 7.5,$$
$$(p + 25)(r - 0.01) = 7.5.$$

The solutions are $(125,0.06)$ and $(-1.50,-0.05)$. Only $(125,0.06)$ has meaning in this problem. The principal was $125 and the interest rate was 0.06, or 6%.

31. $(x - h)^2 + (y - k)^2 = r^2$ (Standard form)

Substitute $(4, 6)$, $(-6, 2)$, and $(1, -3)$ for (x, y).
$(4 - h)^2 + (6 - k)^2 = r^2$ (1)
$(-6 - h)^2 + (2 - k)^2 = r^2$ (2)
$(1 - h)^2 + (-3 - k)^2 = r^2$ (3)

Thus
$(4 - h)^2 + (6 - k)^2 = (-6 - h)^2 + (2 - k)^2$
or $5h + 2k = 3$
$(4 - h)^2 + (6 - k)^2 = (1 - h)^2 + (-3 - k)^2$
or $h + 3k = 7$

We solve the system
$$5h + 2k = 3,$$
$$h + 3k = 7.$$

Solving we get $h = -\frac{5}{13}$ and $k = \frac{32}{13}$. Substituting these values in equation (1), (2), or (3), we find that $r^2 = \frac{5365}{169}$.

The equation of the circle is
$\left(x + \frac{5}{13}\right)^2 + \left(y - \frac{32}{13}\right)^2 = \frac{5365}{169}$.

32. Using $(x - h)^2 + (y - k)^2 = r^2$ and the given points, we have
$(2 - h)^2 + (3 - k)^2 = r^2$ (1)
$(4 - h)^2 + (5 - k)^2 = r^2$ (2)
$(0 - h)^2 + (-3 - k)^2 = r^2$ (3)

Then Eq. (1) - Eq. (2) gives $h + k = 7$ and Eq. (2) - Eq. (3) gives $h + 2k = 4$. We solve the system
$$h + k = 7,$$
$$h + 2k = 4.$$

Then $h = 10$, $k = -3$, $r = 10$ and the circle is $(x - 10)^2 + (y + 3)^2 = 10^2$.

33. Familiarize: Let x and y represent the numbers.
Translate:
The square of a certain number exceeds twice the square of another number by $\frac{1}{8}$.
$$x^2 = 2y^2 + \frac{1}{8}$$
The sum of the squares is $\frac{5}{16}$.
$$x^2 + y^2 = \frac{5}{16}$$

Carry out: We solve the system.
$x^2 - 2y^2 = \frac{1}{8}$,   (1)
$x^2 + y^2 = \frac{5}{16}$ (2)

$x^2 - 2y^2 = \frac{1}{8}$,
$\underline{2x^2 + 2y^2 = \frac{5}{8}}$ Multiplying (2) by 2
$3x^2 \qquad = \frac{6}{8}$
$x^2 = \frac{1}{4}$
$x = \pm \frac{1}{2}$

Substitute $\pm \frac{1}{2}$ for x in (2) and solve for y.
$\left(\pm \frac{1}{2}\right)^2 + y^2 = \frac{5}{16}$
$\frac{1}{4} + y^2 = \frac{5}{16}$
$y^2 = \frac{1}{16}$
$y = \pm \frac{1}{4}$

We get $\left(\frac{1}{2}, \frac{1}{4}\right)$, $\left(-\frac{1}{2}, \frac{1}{4}\right)$, $\left(\frac{1}{2}, -\frac{1}{4}\right)$ and $\left(-\frac{1}{2}, -\frac{1}{4}\right)$.

Check: It is true that $\left(\pm \frac{1}{2}\right)^2$ exceeds twice $\left(\pm \frac{1}{4}\right)^2$ by $\frac{1}{8}$: $\frac{1}{4} = 2\left(\frac{1}{16}\right) + \frac{1}{8}$
Also $\left(\pm \frac{1}{2}\right)^2 + \left(\pm \frac{1}{4}\right)^2 = \frac{5}{16}$. The pairs check.

State: The numbers are $\frac{1}{2}$ and $\frac{1}{4}$ or $-\frac{1}{2}$ and $\frac{1}{4}$ or $\frac{1}{2}$ and $-\frac{1}{4}$ or $-\frac{1}{2}$ and $-\frac{1}{4}$.

34. Make a drawing.

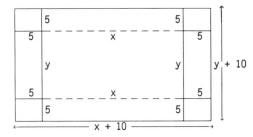

We let x and y represent the length and width of the base of the box, respectively. Then the dimensions of the metal sheet are $x + 10$ and $y + 10$.

Solve the system
$$(x + 10)(y + 10) = 340,$$
$$x \cdot y \cdot 5 = 350.$$

The solutions are $(10,7)$ and $(7,10)$. The dimensions of the box are 10 in. by 7 in. by 5 in.

35. $x^2 + xy = a$,   (1)

    $y^2 + xy = b$ (2)

    Solve Eq. (1) for y.

    $xy = a - x^2$

    $y = \dfrac{a - x^2}{x}$ (3)

    Substitute for y in Eq. (2) and solve for x.

    $\left[\dfrac{a - x^2}{x}\right]^2 + x\left[\dfrac{a - x^2}{x}\right] = b$

    $\dfrac{a^2 - 2ax^2 + x^4}{x^2} + a - x^2 = b$

    $a^2 - 2ax^2 + x^4 + ax^2 - x^4 = bx^2$ Clearing the fraction

    $\qquad\qquad a^2 = ax^2 + bx^2$

    $\qquad\qquad a^2 = x^2(a + b)$

    $\qquad\qquad \dfrac{a^2}{a + b} = x^2$

    $\qquad\pm \dfrac{a}{\sqrt{a + b}} = x$

    $\qquad\pm \dfrac{a\sqrt{a + b}}{a + b} = x$ Rationalizing the denominator

    Substitute for x in Eq. (3) and solve for y.

    When $x = \dfrac{a\sqrt{a + b}}{a + b}$: $y = \dfrac{a - \left[\dfrac{a\sqrt{a + b}}{a + b}\right]^2}{\dfrac{a\sqrt{a + b}}{a + b}} =$

    $\dfrac{a - \dfrac{a^2}{a + b}}{\dfrac{a\sqrt{a + b}}{a + b}} = \dfrac{a^2 + ab - a^2}{a\sqrt{a + b}} = \dfrac{ab}{a\sqrt{a + b}} = \dfrac{b}{\sqrt{a + b}} =$

    $\dfrac{b\sqrt{a + b}}{a + b}$

    When $x = -\dfrac{a\sqrt{a + b}}{a + b}$: $y = \dfrac{a - \left[-\dfrac{a\sqrt{a + b}}{a + b}\right]^2}{-\dfrac{a\sqrt{a + b}}{a + b}} =$

    $\dfrac{a - \dfrac{a^2}{a + b}}{-\dfrac{a\sqrt{a + b}}{a + b}} = \dfrac{a^2 + ab - a^2}{-a\sqrt{a + b}} = \dfrac{ab}{-a\sqrt{a + b}} = -\dfrac{b}{\sqrt{a + b}} =$

    $-\dfrac{b\sqrt{a + b}}{a + b}$

    The pairs $\left[\dfrac{a\sqrt{a + b}}{a + b}, \dfrac{b\sqrt{a + b}}{a + b}\right]$ and

    $\left[-\dfrac{a\sqrt{a + b}}{a + b}, -\dfrac{b\sqrt{a + b}}{a + b}\right]$ check. They are the solutions.

36. $x^2 - y^2 = a^2 - b^2$,   (1)

    $x - y = a - b$ (2)

    Solve Eq. (2) for x.

    $x = y + a - b$ (3)

    Substitute for x in Eq. (1) and solve for y.

    $\qquad (y + a - b)^2 - y^2 = a^2 - b^2$

    $y^2 + 2ay - 2by + a^2 - 2ab + b^2 - y^2 = a^2 - b^2$

    $\qquad\qquad 2ay - 2by = 2ab - 2b^2$

    $\qquad\qquad 2y(a - b) = 2b(a - b)$

    $\qquad\qquad\qquad y = b$

    Substitute for y in Eq. (3) and solve for x.

    $\qquad x = b + a - b = a$

    The pair (a,b) checks.

37. $p^2 + q^2 = 13$ (1)

    $\dfrac{1}{pq} = -\dfrac{1}{6}$ (2)

    Solve Eq. (2) for p.

    $\dfrac{1}{q} = -\dfrac{p}{6}$

    $-\dfrac{6}{q} = p$

    Substitute -6/q for p in Eq. (1) and solve for q.

    $\left[-\dfrac{6}{q}\right]^2 + q^2 = 13$

    $\dfrac{36}{q^2} + q^2 = 13$

    $36 + q^4 = 13q^2$

    $q^4 - 13q^2 + 36 = 0$

    $u^2 - 13u + 36 = 0$ Letting $u = q^2$

    $(u - 9)(u - 4) = 0$

    $u = 9$ or $u = 4$

    $q^2 = 9$ or $q^2 = 4$

    $q = \pm 3$ or $q = \pm 2$

    Since $p = -6/q$, if $q = 3$, $p = -2$; if $q = -3$, $p = 2$; if $q = 2$, $p = -3$, and if $q = -2$, $p = 3$. The pairs (-2,3), (2,-3), (-3,2), and (3,-2) check. They are the solutions.

38. $a + b = \dfrac{5}{6}$,   (1)

    $\dfrac{a}{b} + \dfrac{b}{a} = \dfrac{13}{6}$ (2)

    $b = \dfrac{5}{6} - a = \dfrac{5 - 6a}{6}$

    $\dfrac{a}{\dfrac{5 - 6a}{6}} + \dfrac{\dfrac{5 - 6a}{6}}{a} = \dfrac{13}{6}$

    $\dfrac{6a}{5 - 6a} + \dfrac{5 - 6a}{6a} = \dfrac{13}{6}$

    $36a^2 + 25 - 60a + 36a^2 = 65a - 78a^2$

    $150a^2 - 125a + 25 = 0$

    $6a^2 - 5a + 1 = 0$

    $(3a - 1)(2a - 1) = 0$

$a = \frac{1}{3}$ or $a = \frac{1}{2}$

When $a = \frac{1}{3}$, $b = \frac{5 - 6\left(\frac{1}{3}\right)}{6} = \frac{1}{2}$.

When $a = \frac{1}{2}$, $b = \frac{5 - 6\left(\frac{1}{2}\right)}{6} = \frac{1}{3}$.

The pairs $\left(\frac{1}{3}, \frac{1}{2}\right)$ and $\left(\frac{1}{2}, \frac{1}{3}\right)$ check.

39.
$$x^2 + y^2 = 4, \qquad (1)$$
$$(x - 1)^2 + y^2 = 4 \qquad (2)$$

Solve Eq. (1) for y^2:
$$y^2 = 4 - x^2 \qquad (3)$$

Substitute $4 - x^2$ for y^2 in Eq. (2) and solve for x.

$$(x - 1)^2 + (4 - x^2) = 4$$
$$x^2 - 2x + 1 + 4 - x^2 = 4$$
$$-2x = -1$$
$$x = \frac{1}{2}$$

Substitute $\frac{1}{2}$ for x in Eq. (3) and solve for y.

$$y^2 = 4 - \left(\frac{1}{2}\right)^2$$
$$y^2 = 4 - \frac{1}{4}$$
$$y^2 = \frac{15}{4}$$
$$y = \pm \frac{\sqrt{15}}{2}$$

The pairs $\left(\frac{1}{2}, \frac{\sqrt{15}}{2}\right)$ and $\left(\frac{1}{2}, -\frac{\sqrt{15}}{2}\right)$ check. They are the solutions.

40.
$$a^2b^2 - 2b^2x^2 - a^2y^2 = 0,$$
$$a^2b^2 - b^2x^2 - 2a^2y^2 = 0$$

$$-2a^2b^2 + 4b^2x^2 + 2a^2y^2 = 0,$$
$$\underline{a^2b^2 - b^2x^2 - 2a^2y^2 = 0}$$
$$-a^2b^2 + 3b^2x^2 \qquad = 0$$
$$x^2 = \frac{a^2}{3} \qquad \text{(Assuming } b \neq 0)$$
$$x = \pm \frac{a\sqrt{3}}{3} \qquad \text{(Assuming } a \geqslant 0)$$

$$a^2b^2 - 2b^2\left(\frac{a^2}{3}\right) - a^2y^2 = 0$$
$$y^2 = \frac{b^2}{3} \qquad \text{(Assuming } a \neq 0)$$
$$y = \pm \frac{b\sqrt{3}}{3} \qquad \text{(Assuming } b \geqslant 0)$$

The pairs $\left(\frac{a\sqrt{3}}{3}, \frac{b\sqrt{3}}{3}\right)$, $\left(\frac{a\sqrt{3}}{3}, -\frac{b\sqrt{3}}{3}\right)$, $\left(-\frac{a\sqrt{3}}{3}, \frac{b\sqrt{3}}{3}\right)$ and $\left(-\frac{a\sqrt{3}}{3}, -\frac{b\sqrt{3}}{3}\right)$ where $a > 0$, $b > 0$ check.

41.
$$(x - 2)^4 - (x - 2) = 0, \qquad (1)$$
$$x^2 - kx + k = 0 \qquad (2)$$

In Eq. (1) let $(x - 2) = z$. Then $z^4 - z = 0$, or $z(z - 1)(z^2 + z + 1) = 0$; so that $z = 0, 1, \frac{-1 \pm i\sqrt{3}}{2}$ and then $x = 2, 3, \frac{3 \pm i\sqrt{3}}{2}$.

The roots of Eq. (2) are $\frac{k \pm \sqrt{k^2 - 4k}}{2}$, and comparing this with $\frac{3 \pm i\sqrt{3}}{2}$ we have $k = 3$. [If 2 were a root of Eq. (2) there would be no other common root; likewise for 3.]

42.
$$10x^2 - xy + 4y^2 = 28, \qquad (1)$$
$$2x^2 - 3xy - 2y^2 = 0 \qquad (2)$$

$$10x^2 - xy + 4y^2 = 28$$
$$\underline{4x^2 - 6xy - 4y^2 = 0}$$
$$14x^2 - 7xy \qquad = 28$$
$$14x^2 - 28 = 7xy$$
$$2x - \frac{4}{x} = y$$

Substitute in (2).
$$2x^2 - 3x\left(2x - \frac{4}{x}\right) - 2\left(2x - \frac{4}{x}\right)^2 = 0$$
$$2x^2 - 6x^2 + 12 - 8x^2 + 32 - \frac{32}{x^2} = 0$$
$$-12x^2 + 44 - \frac{32}{x^2} = 0$$
$$3x^4 - 11x^2 + 8 = 0$$

Let $u = x^2$.
$$3u^2 - 11u + 8 = 0$$
$$(3u - 8)(u - 1) = 0$$
$$u = \frac{8}{3} \qquad \text{or} \qquad u = 1$$
$$x = \pm \frac{2\sqrt{6}}{3} \qquad \text{or} \qquad x = \pm 1$$

When $x = \frac{2\sqrt{6}}{3}$, $y = 2\left(\frac{2\sqrt{6}}{3}\right) - \frac{4}{\frac{2\sqrt{6}}{3}} = \frac{4\sqrt{6}}{3} - \sqrt{6}$
$$= \frac{\sqrt{6}}{3}$$

When $x = -\frac{2\sqrt{6}}{3}$, $y = 2\left(-\frac{2\sqrt{6}}{3}\right) - \frac{4}{-\frac{2\sqrt{3}}{3}}$
$$= -\frac{4\sqrt{6}}{3} + \sqrt{6} = -\frac{\sqrt{6}}{3}$$

When $x = 1$, $y = 2 \cdot 1 - \frac{4}{1} = -2$.

When $x = -1$, $y = 2(-1) - \frac{4}{-1} = 2$.

The pairs $\left(\frac{2\sqrt{6}}{3}, \frac{\sqrt{6}}{3}\right)$, $\left(-\frac{2\sqrt{6}}{3}, -\frac{\sqrt{6}}{3}\right)$, $(1, -2)$, and $(-1, 2)$ check.

43. $5^{x+y} = 100$,
$3^{2x-y} = 1000$

$(x + y) \log 5 = 2$, Taking logarithms and
$(2x - y) \log 3 = 3$ simplifying

$x \log 5 + y \log 5 = 2$, (1)
$2x \log 3 - y \log 3 = 3$ (2)

Multiply Eq. (1) by log 3 and Eq. (2) by log 5.

$x \log 3 \cdot \log 5 + y \log 3 \cdot \log 5 = 2 \log 3$
$\underline{2x \log 3 \cdot \log 5 - y \log 3 \cdot \log 5 = 3 \log 5}$
$3x \log 3 \cdot \log 5 \qquad\qquad = 2 \log 3 +$
$\qquad\qquad\qquad\qquad\qquad 3 \log 5$

$$x = \frac{2 \log 3 + 3 \log 5}{3 \log 3 \cdot \log 5}$$

Substitute in (1) to find y.

$$\frac{2 \log 3 + 3 \log 5}{3 \log 3 \cdot \log 5} \cdot \log 5 + y \log 5 = 2$$

$$y \log 5 = 2 - \frac{2 \log 3 + 3 \log 5}{3 \log 3}$$

$$y \log 5 = \frac{6 \log 3 - 2 \log 3 - 3 \log 5}{3 \log 3}$$

$$y \log 5 = \frac{4 \log 3 - 3 \log 5}{3 \log 3}$$

$$y = \frac{4 \log 3 - 3 \log 5}{3 \log 3 \cdot \log 5}$$

The pair $\left(\dfrac{2 \log 3 + 3 \log 5}{3 \log 3 \cdot \log 5}, \dfrac{4 \log 3 - 3 \log 5}{3 \log 3 \cdot \log 5}\right)$
checks. It is the solution.

44. $e^x - e^{x+y} = 0$, (1)
$e^y - e^{x-y} = 0$ (2)

Factor (1): $e^x(1 - e^y) = 0$
$e^x = 0$ or $1 - e^y = 0$
No solution $y = 0$

Substitute in (2).
$e^0 - e^{x-0} = 0$
$1 - e^x = 0$
$x = 0$

The solution is (0, 0).

45. Familiarize: Let x and y represent the numbers.
Let n represent the sum, product and sum of the
squares of the numbers.

Translate: We have a system of equations.
$x + y = n$, (1)
$xy = n$, (2)
$x^2 + y^2 = n$ (3)

Carry out: We solve the system.

Solve Eq. (2) for y: $y = \dfrac{n}{x}$

Substitute in Eq. (1) and solve for n.

$x + \dfrac{n}{x} = n$

$x^2 + n = nx$

$x^2 = nx - n$

$x^2 = n(x - 1)$

$\dfrac{x^2}{x - 1} = n$

Then $y = \dfrac{n}{x} = \dfrac{\frac{x^2}{x-1}}{x} = \dfrac{x}{x - 1}$.

Substitute for y and n in Eq. (3) and solve for x.

$x^2 + \left[\dfrac{x}{x - 1}\right]^2 = \dfrac{x^2}{x - 1}$

$x^2 + \dfrac{x^2}{(x - 1)^2} = \dfrac{x^2}{x - 1}$

$x^2(x - 1)^2 + x^2 = x^2(x - 1)$ Multiplying by
$(x - 1)^2$

$x^4 - 2x^3 + x^2 + x^2 = x^3 - x^2$

$x^4 - 3x^3 + 3x^2 = 0$

$x^2(x^2 - 3x + 3) = 0$

$x^2 = 0$ or $x^2 - 3x + 3 = 0$

Solving $x^2 = 0$, we get $x = 0$.
Solving $x^2 - 3x + 3 = 0$, we get

$$x = \frac{3 \pm \sqrt{9 - 12}}{2} = \frac{3 \pm i\sqrt{3}}{2}.$$

When $x = 0$, $y = \dfrac{0}{0 - 1} = 0$.

When $x = \dfrac{3 + i\sqrt{3}}{2}$, $y = \dfrac{\frac{3 + i\sqrt{3}}{2}}{\frac{3 + i\sqrt{3}}{2} - 1} = \dfrac{3 - i\sqrt{3}}{2}$.

When $x = \dfrac{3 - i\sqrt{3}}{2}$, $y = \dfrac{\frac{3 - i\sqrt{3}}{2}}{\frac{3 - i\sqrt{3}}{2} - 1} = \dfrac{3 + i\sqrt{3}}{2}$.

The pairs (0, 0), $\left(\dfrac{3 + i\sqrt{3}}{2}, \dfrac{3 - i\sqrt{3}}{2}\right)$, and
$\left(\dfrac{3 - i\sqrt{3}}{2}, \dfrac{3 + i\sqrt{3}}{2}\right)$ check. They are the
solutions.

46. (400, 1.43), (400, -1.43), (-400, 1.43),
(-400, -1.43)

47. (-8.53, -2.53), (-8.53, 2.53), (8.53, -2.53),
(8.53, 2.53)

Exercise Set 11.1

1. $a_n = 4n - 1$
   $a_1 = 4 \cdot 1 - 1 = 3$, $a_4 = 4 \cdot 4 - 1 = 15$;
   $a_2 = 4 \cdot 2 - 1 = 7$, $a_{10} = 4 \cdot 10 - 1 = 39$;
   $a_3 = 4 \cdot 3 - 1 = 11$, $a_{15} = 4 \cdot 15 - 1 = 59$

2. $a_1 = (1 - 1)(1 - 2)(1 - 3) = 0$,
   $a_2 = (2 - 1)(2 - 2)(2 - 3) = 0$,
   $a_3 = (3 - 1)(3 - 2)(3 - 3) = 0$,
   $a_4 = (4 - 1)(4 - 2)(4 - 3) = 3 \cdot 2 \cdot 1 = 6$;
   $a_{10} = (10 - 1)(10 - 2)(10 - 3) = 9 \cdot 8 \cdot 7 = 504$;
   $a_{15} = (15 - 1)(15 - 2)(15 - 3) = 14 \cdot 13 \cdot 12 = 2184$

3. $a_n = \dfrac{n}{n - 1}$, $n \geqslant 2$

   The first 4 terms are a_2, a_3, a_4, and a_5:
   $a_2 = \dfrac{2}{2 - 1} = 2$, $a_4 = \dfrac{4}{4 - 1} = \dfrac{4}{3}$,
   $a_3 = \dfrac{3}{3 - 1} = \dfrac{3}{2}$, $a_5 = \dfrac{5}{5 - 1} = \dfrac{5}{4}$.

   $a_{10} = \dfrac{10}{10 - 1} = \dfrac{10}{9}$, $a_{15} = \dfrac{15}{15 - 1} = \dfrac{15}{14}$

4. $a_1 = 1^2 - 1 = 0$ $a_4 = 4^2 - 1 = 15$;
   $a_2 = 2^2 - 1 = 3$, $a_{10} = 10^2 - 1 = 99$,
   $a_3 = 3^2 - 1 = 8$, $a_{15} = 15^2 - 1 = 224$

5. $a_n = n^2 + 2n$
   $a_1 = 1^2 + 2 \cdot 1 = 3$, $a_4 = 4^2 + 2 \cdot 4 = 24$;
   $a_2 = 2^2 + 2 \cdot 2 = 8$, $a_{10} = 10^2 + 2 \cdot 10 = 120$;
   $a_3 = 3^2 + 2 \cdot 3 = 15$, $a_{15} = 15^2 + 2 \cdot 15 = 255$

6. $a_1 = \dfrac{1^2 - 1}{1^2 + 1} = 0$, $a_4 = \dfrac{4^2 - 1}{4^2 + 1} = \dfrac{15}{17}$
   $a_2 = \dfrac{2^2 - 1}{2^2 + 1} = \dfrac{3}{5}$, $a_{10} = \dfrac{10^2 - 1}{10^2 + 1} = \dfrac{99}{101}$;
   $a_3 = \dfrac{3^2 - 1}{3^2 + 1} = \dfrac{8}{10} = \dfrac{4}{5}$ $a_{15} = \dfrac{15^2 - 1}{15^2 + 1} = \dfrac{224}{226} = \dfrac{112}{113}$

7. $a_n = n + \dfrac{1}{n}$

   $a_1 = 1 + \dfrac{1}{1} = 2$, $a_4 = 4 + \dfrac{1}{4} = 4\dfrac{1}{4}$;
   $a_2 = 2 + \dfrac{1}{2} = 2\dfrac{1}{2}$, $a_{10} = 10 + \dfrac{1}{10} = 10\dfrac{1}{10}$;
   $a_3 = 3 + \dfrac{1}{3} = 3\dfrac{1}{3}$, $a_{15} = 15 + \dfrac{1}{15} = 15\dfrac{1}{15}$

8. $a_1 = \left(-\dfrac{1}{2}\right)^{1-1} = 1$, $a_4 = \left(-\dfrac{1}{2}\right)^{4-1} = -\dfrac{1}{8}$;
   $a_2 = \left(-\dfrac{1}{2}\right)^{2-1} = -\dfrac{1}{2}$, $a_{10} = \left(-\dfrac{1}{2}\right)^{10-1} = -\dfrac{1}{512}$,
   $a_3 = \left(-\dfrac{1}{2}\right)^{3-1} = \dfrac{1}{4}$, $a_{15} = \left(-\dfrac{1}{2}\right)^{15-1} = \dfrac{1}{16,384}$

9. $a_n = (-1)^n n^2$
   $a_1 = (-1)^1 1^2 = -1$, $a_4 = (-1)^4 4^2 = 16$;
   $a_2 = (-1)^2 2^2 = 4$, $a_{10} = (-1)^{10} 10^2 = 100$;
   $a_3 = (-1)^3 3^2 = -9$, $a_{15} = (-1)^{15} 15^2 = -225$

10. $a_1 = (-1)^1(1+3) = -4$, $a_4 = (-1)^4(4+3) = 7$;
    $a_2 = (-1)^2(2+3) = 5$, $a_{10} = (-1)^{10}(10+3) = 13$;
    $a_3 = (-1)^3(3+3) = -6$, $a_{15} = (-1)^{15}(15+3) = -18$

11. $a_n = (-1)^{n+1}(3n - 5)$
    $a_1 = (-1)^{1+1}(3 \cdot 1 - 5) = -2$,
    $a_2 = (-1)^{2+1}(3 \cdot 2 - 5) = -1$,
    $a_3 = (-1)^{3+1}(3 \cdot 3 - 5) = 4$,
    $a_4 = (-1)^{4+1}(3 \cdot 4 - 5) = -7$;
    $a_{10} = (-1)^{10+1}(3 \cdot 10 - 5) = -25$;
    $a_{15} = (-1)^{15+1}(3 \cdot 15 - 5) = 40$

12. $a_1 = (-1)^1(1^3-1) = 0$, $a_4 = (-1)^4(4^3-1) = 63$;
    $a_2 = (-1)^2(2^3-1) = 7$, $a_{10} = (-1)^{10}(10^3-1) = 999$;
    $a_3 = (-1)^3(3^3-1) = -26$, $a_{15} = (-1)^{15}(15^3-1) = -3374$

13. $a_n = \dfrac{n + 2}{n + 5}$

    $a_1 = \dfrac{1 + 2}{1 + 5} = \dfrac{3}{6} = \dfrac{1}{2}$, $a_4 = \dfrac{4 + 2}{4 + 5} = \dfrac{6}{9} = \dfrac{2}{3}$;
    $a_2 = \dfrac{2 + 2}{2 + 5} = \dfrac{4}{7}$, $a_{10} = \dfrac{10 + 2}{10 + 5} = \dfrac{12}{15} = \dfrac{4}{5}$;
    $a_3 = \dfrac{3 + 2}{3 + 5} = \dfrac{5}{8}$, $a_{15} = \dfrac{15 + 2}{15 + 5} = \dfrac{17}{20}$

14. $a_1 = \dfrac{2 \cdot 1 - 1}{3 \cdot 1 - 4} = -1$, $a_4 = \dfrac{2 \cdot 4 - 1}{3 \cdot 4 - 4} = \dfrac{7}{8}$;
    $a_2 = \dfrac{2 \cdot 2 - 1}{3 \cdot 2 - 4} = \dfrac{3}{2}$, $a_{10} = \dfrac{2 \cdot 10 - 1}{3 \cdot 10 - 4} = \dfrac{19}{26}$;
    $a_3 = \dfrac{2 \cdot 3 - 1}{3 \cdot 3 - 4} = \dfrac{5}{5} = 1$, $a_{15} = \dfrac{2 \cdot 15 - 1}{3 \cdot 15 - 4} = \dfrac{29}{41}$

15. $a_n = 5n - 6$
    $a_8 = 5 \cdot 8 - 6 = 40 - 6 = 34$

16. $a_9 = 3 \cdot 9 + 10 = 37$

17. $a_n = (3n - 4)(2n + 5)$
    $a_7 = (3 \cdot 7 - 4)(2 \cdot 7 + 5) = 17 \cdot 19 = 323$

18. $a_6 = (2 \cdot 6 - 3)^2 = 81$

19. $a_n = (-1)^{n-1}(4.6n - 18.3)$
    $a_{12} = (-1)^{12-1}[4.6(12) - 18.3] = -36.9$

20. $a_{23} = (-2)^{23-2}[54.76 - 1.3(23)] = -52,135,198.72$

21. $a_n = 5n^2(4n - 100)$
    $a_{11} = 5(11)^2(4 \cdot 11 - 100) = 5(121)(-56) = -33,880$

22. $a_{22} = 4(22)^2(11 \cdot 22 + 31) = 528,528$

23. $a_n = \left(1 + \frac{1}{n}\right)^2$

$a_{20} = \left(1 + \frac{1}{20}\right)^2 = \left(\frac{21}{20}\right)^2 = \frac{441}{400}$

24. $a_{15} = \left(1 - \frac{1}{15}\right)^3 = \left(\frac{14}{15}\right)^3 = \frac{2744}{3375}$

25. $a_n = \log 10^n$

$a_{43} = \log 10^{43} = 43$

26. $a_{67} = \ln e^{67} = 67$

27. $a_n = 1 + \frac{1}{n^2}$

$a_{38} = 1 + \frac{1}{38^2} = 1\frac{1}{1444}$

28. $a_{100} = 2 - \frac{1000}{100} = 2 - 10 = -8$

29. 1, 3, 5, 7, 9, . . .
These are odd integers, so the general term may be 2n - 1.

30. 3^n

31. -2, 6, -18, 54, . . .
We can see a pattern if we write the sequence as
$-1 \cdot 2 \cdot 1,\ 1 \cdot 2 \cdot 3,\ -1 \cdot 2 \cdot 9,\ 1 \cdot 2 \cdot 27,\ . . .$
The general term may be $(-1)^n 2(3)^{n-1}$.

32. 5n - 7

33. $\frac{2}{3}, \frac{3}{4}, \frac{4}{5}, \frac{5}{6}, \frac{6}{7}, . . .$

These are fractions in which the denominator is 1 greater than the numerator. Also, each numerator is 1 greater than the preceding numerator. The general term may be $\frac{n + 1}{n + 2}$.

34. $\sqrt{2n}$

35. $\sqrt{3},\ 3,\ 3\sqrt{3},\ 9,\ 9\sqrt{3},\ . . .$
These are powers of $\sqrt{3}$. The general term may be $(\sqrt{3})^n$, or $3^{n/2}$.

36. n(n + 1)

37. -1, -4, -7, -10, -13, . . .
Each term is 3 less than the preceding term. The general term may be -1 - 3(n - 1). After removing parentheses and simplifying, we can express the general term as -3n + 2, or -(3n - 2).

38. $\log 10^{n-1}$, or n - 1

39. 1, 2, 3, 4, 5, 6, 7, . . .
$S_7 = 1 + 2 + 3 + 4 + 5 + 6 + 7 = 28$

40. $S_8 = 1 - 3 + 5 - 7 + 9 - 11 + 13 - 15 = -8$

41. 2, 4, 6, 8, . . .
$S_5 = 2 + 4 + 6 + 8 + 10 = 30$

42. $S_5 = 1 + \frac{1}{4} + \frac{1}{9} + \frac{1}{16} + \frac{1}{25} = \frac{5269}{3600}$

43. $\displaystyle\sum_{k=1}^{5} \frac{1}{2k} = \frac{1}{2 \cdot 1} + \frac{1}{2 \cdot 2} + \frac{1}{2 \cdot 3} + \frac{1}{2 \cdot 4} + \frac{1}{2 \cdot 5}$

$= \frac{1}{2} + \frac{1}{4} + \frac{1}{6} + \frac{1}{8} + \frac{1}{10}$

$= \frac{60}{120} + \frac{30}{120} + \frac{20}{120} + \frac{15}{120} + \frac{12}{120}$

$= \frac{137}{120}$

44. $\frac{1}{3} + \frac{1}{5} + \frac{1}{7} + \frac{1}{9} + \frac{1}{11} + \frac{1}{13} = \frac{43,024}{45,045}$

45. $\displaystyle\sum_{k=0}^{5} 2^k = 2^0 + 2^1 + 2^2 + 2^3 + 2^4 + 2^5$

$= 1 + 2 + 4 + 8 + 16 + 32$

$= 63$

46. $\sqrt{7} + \sqrt{9} + \sqrt{11} + \sqrt{13} \approx 12.5679$

47. $\displaystyle\sum_{k=7}^{10} \log k = \log 7 + \log 8 + \log 9 + \log 10,$

or $\log (7 \cdot 8 \cdot 9 \cdot 10)$, or $\log 5040$

48. $0 + \pi + 2\pi + 3\pi + 4\pi \approx 31.4159$

49. $\displaystyle\sum_{k=1}^{8} \frac{k}{k + 1} = \frac{1}{1 + 1} + \frac{2}{2 + 1} + \frac{3}{3 + 1} + \frac{4}{4 + 1} +$

$\frac{5}{5 + 1} + \frac{6}{6 + 1} + \frac{7}{7 + 1} + \frac{8}{8 + 1}$

$= \frac{1}{2} + \frac{2}{3} + \frac{3}{4} + \frac{4}{5} + \frac{5}{6} + \frac{6}{7} + \frac{7}{8} + \frac{8}{9}$

$= \frac{15,551}{2520}$

50. $0 + \frac{1}{5} + \frac{1}{3} + \frac{3}{7} = \frac{101}{105}$

51. $\displaystyle\sum_{k=1}^{5} (-1)^k = (-1)^1 + (-1)^2 + (-1)^3 + (-1)^4 + (-1)^5$

$= -1 + 1 - 1 + 1 - 1$

$= -1$

52. 1 - 1 + 1 - 1 + 1 = 1

53. $\sum_{k=1}^{8} (-1)^{k+1}3k = (-1)^{2}3\cdot1 + (-1)^{3}3\cdot2 + (-1)^{4}3\cdot3 +$

$\qquad (-1)^{5}3\cdot4 + (-1)^{6}3\cdot5 + (-1)^{7}3\cdot6 +$

$\qquad (-1)^{8}3\cdot7 + (-1)^{9}3\cdot8$

$\qquad = 3 - 6 + 9 - 12 + 15 - 18 + 21 - 24$

$\qquad = -12$

54. $-4^{2} + 4^{3} - 4^{4} + 4^{5} - 4^{6} + 4^{7} - 4^{8} = -52,432$

55. $\sum_{k=1}^{6} = \dfrac{2}{k^{2}+1} = \dfrac{2}{1^{2}+1} + \dfrac{2}{2^{2}+1} + \dfrac{2}{3^{2}+1} + \dfrac{2}{4^{2}+1} +$

$\qquad \dfrac{2}{5^{2}+1} + \dfrac{2}{6^{2}+1}$

$\qquad = \dfrac{2}{2} + \dfrac{2}{5} + \dfrac{2}{10} + \dfrac{2}{17} + \dfrac{2}{26} + \dfrac{2}{37}$

$\qquad = 1 + \dfrac{2}{5} + \dfrac{1}{5} + \dfrac{2}{17} + \dfrac{1}{13} + \dfrac{2}{37}$

$\qquad = \dfrac{75,581}{40,885}$

56. $1\cdot2 + 2\cdot3 + 3\cdot4 + 4\cdot5 + 5\cdot6 + 6\cdot7 + 7\cdot8 + 8\cdot9 +$

$9\cdot10 + 10\cdot11 = 440$

57. $\sum_{k=0}^{5} (k^{2} - 2k + 3) = (0^{2} - 2\cdot0 + 3) +$

$\qquad (1^{2} - 2\cdot1 + 3) + (2^{2} - 2\cdot2 + 3) +$

$\qquad (3^{2} - 2\cdot3 + 3) + (4^{2} - 2\cdot4 + 3) +$

$\qquad (5^{2} - 2\cdot5 + 3)$

$\qquad = 3 + 2 + 3 + 6 + 11 + 18$

$\qquad = 43$

58. $4 + 2 + 2 + 4 + 8 + 14 = 34$

59. $\sum_{k=1}^{10} \dfrac{1}{k(k+1)} = \dfrac{1}{1(1+1)} + \dfrac{1}{2(2+1)} + \dfrac{1}{3(3+1)} +$

$\qquad \dfrac{1}{4(4+1)} + \dfrac{1}{5(5+1)} + \dfrac{1}{6(6+1)} +$

$\qquad \dfrac{1}{7(7+1)} + \dfrac{1}{8(8+1)} + \dfrac{1}{9(9+1)} +$

$\qquad \dfrac{1}{10(10+1)}$

$\qquad = \dfrac{1}{2} + \dfrac{1}{6} + \dfrac{1}{12} + \dfrac{1}{20} + \dfrac{1}{30} + \dfrac{1}{42} + \dfrac{1}{56} +$

$\qquad \dfrac{1}{72} + \dfrac{1}{90} + \dfrac{1}{110}$

$\qquad = \dfrac{10}{11}$

60. $\dfrac{2}{3} + \dfrac{4}{5} + \dfrac{8}{9} + \dfrac{16}{17} + \dfrac{32}{33} + \dfrac{64}{65} + \dfrac{128}{129} + \dfrac{256}{257} + \dfrac{512}{513} +$

$\dfrac{1024}{1025} \approx 9.2365$

61. $\dfrac{1}{2} + \dfrac{2}{3} + \dfrac{3}{4} + \dfrac{4}{5} + \dfrac{5}{6} + \dfrac{6}{7}$

This is a sum of fractions in which the denominator is one greater than the numerator. Also, each numerator is 1 greater than the preceding numerator. Sigma notation is

$$\sum_{k=1}^{6} \dfrac{k}{k+1}.$$

62. $\sum_{k=1}^{5} 3k$

63. $-2 + 4 - 8 + 16 - 32 + 64$

This is a sum of powers of 2 with alternating signs. Sigma notation is

$$\sum_{k=1}^{6} (-1)^{k}2^{k}, \text{ or } \sum_{k=1}^{6} (-2)^{k}.$$

64. $\sum_{k=1}^{5} \dfrac{1}{k^{2}}$

65. $4 - 9 + 16 - 25 + \ldots + (-1)^{n}n^{2}$

This is a sum of terms of the form $(-1)^{k}k^{2}$, beginning with $k = 2$ and continuing through $k = n$. Sigma notation is

$$\sum_{k=2}^{n} (-1)^{k}k^{2}.$$

66. $\sum_{k=3}^{n} (-1)^{k+1}k^{2}$

67. $5 + 10 + 15 + 20 + 25 + \ldots$

This is a sum of multiples of 5, and it is an infinite series. Sigma notation is

$$\sum_{k=1}^{\infty} 5k.$$

68. $\sum_{k=1}^{\infty} 7k$

69. $\dfrac{1}{1\cdot2} + \dfrac{1}{2\cdot3} + \dfrac{1}{3\cdot4} + \dfrac{1}{4\cdot5} + \ldots$

This is a sum of fractions in which the numerator is 1 and the denominator is a product of two consecutive integers. The larger integer in each product is the smaller integer in the succeeding product. It is an infinite series. Sigma notation is

$$\sum_{k=1}^{\infty} \dfrac{1}{k(k+1)}.$$

70. $\sum_{k=1}^{\infty} \dfrac{1}{k(k+1)^{2}}$

71. $a_1 = 4$ $\qquad a_{k+1} = 1 + \dfrac{1}{a_k}$

$a_2 = 1 + \dfrac{1}{4} = 1\dfrac{1}{4}$

$a_3 = 1 + \dfrac{1}{\frac{5}{4}} = 1 + \dfrac{4}{5} = 1\dfrac{4}{5}$

$a_4 = 1 + \dfrac{1}{\frac{9}{5}} = 1 + \dfrac{5}{9} = 1\dfrac{5}{9}$

72. $a_1 = 256$, $a_2 = \sqrt{256} = 16$, $a_3 = \sqrt{16} = 4$,

$a_4 = \sqrt{4} = 2$

73. $a_1 = 6561$ $\qquad a_{k+1} = (-1)^k \sqrt{a_k}$

$a_2 = (-1)^1 \sqrt{6561} = -81$

$a_3 = (-1)^2 \sqrt{-81} = 9i$

$a_4 = (-1)^3 \sqrt{9i} = -3\sqrt{i}$

74. $a_1 = e^Q$, $a_2 = \ln e^Q = Q$, $a_3 = \ln Q$, $a_4 = \ln(\ln Q)$

75. $a_1 = 2$ $\qquad a_{k+1} = a_k + a_{k-1}$
$a_2 = 3$
$a_3 = 3 + 2 = 5$
$a_4 = 5 + 3 = 8$

76. $a_1 = -10$, $a_2 = 8$, $a_3 = 8 - (-10) = 18$,
$a_4 = 18 - 8 = 10$

77. $a_n = \dfrac{1}{2^n} \log 1000^n$

$a_1 = \dfrac{1}{2} \log 1000 = \dfrac{1}{2} \cdot 3 = \dfrac{3}{2}$

$a_2 = \dfrac{1}{2^2} \log 1000^2 = \dfrac{1}{4} \cdot 6 = \dfrac{3}{2}$

$a_3 = \dfrac{1}{2^3} \log 1000^3 = \dfrac{1}{8} \cdot 9 = \dfrac{9}{8}$

$a_4 = \dfrac{1}{2^4} \log 1000^4 = \dfrac{1}{16} \cdot 12 = \dfrac{3}{4}$

$a_5 = \dfrac{1}{2^5} \log 1000^5 = \dfrac{1}{32} \cdot 15 = \dfrac{15}{32}$

$S_5 = \dfrac{3}{2} + \dfrac{3}{2} + \dfrac{9}{8} + \dfrac{3}{4} + \dfrac{15}{32}$

$= \dfrac{48}{32} + \dfrac{48}{32} + \dfrac{36}{32} + \dfrac{24}{32} + \dfrac{15}{32}$

$= \dfrac{171}{32}$

78. $a_1 = i^1 = i$, $a_2 = i^2 = -1$, $a_3 = i^3 = -i$,
$a_4 = i^4 = 1$, $a_5 = i^5 = i$
$S_5 = i - 1 - i + 1 + i = i$

79. $a_n = \ln(1 \cdot 2 \cdot 3 \cdots n)$

$a_1 = \ln 1 = 0$
$a_2 = \ln(1 \cdot 2) = \ln 2 \approx 0.693$
$a_3 = \ln(1 \cdot 2 \cdot 3) = \ln 6 \approx 1.792$
$a_4 = \ln(1 \cdot 2 \cdot 3 \cdot 4) = \ln 24 \approx 3.178$
$a_5 = \ln(1 \cdot 2 \cdot 3 \cdot 4 \cdot 5) = \ln 120 \approx 4.787$

$S_5 \approx 0 + 0.693 + 1.792 + 3.178 + 4.787 = 10.450$

80. $a_1 = \sin \dfrac{\pi}{2} = 1$, $a_2 = \sin \pi = 0$, $a_3 = \sin \dfrac{3\pi}{2} = -1$,

$a_4 = \sin 2\pi = 0$, $a_5 = \sin \dfrac{5\pi}{2} = 1$

$S_5 = 1 + 0 - 1 + 0 + 1 = 1$

81. $a_n = \cos^{-1}(-1)^n$

$a_1 = \cos^{-1}(-1)^1 = \cos^{-1}(-1) = \pi$
$a_2 = \cos^{-1}(-1)^2 = \cos^{-1} 1 = 0$
$a_3 = \cos^{-1}(-1)^3 = \cos^{-1}(-1) = \pi$
$a_4 = \cos^{-1}(-1)^4 = \cos^{-1} 1 = 0$
$a_5 = \cos^{-1}(-1)^5 = \cos^{-1}(-1) = \pi$

$S_5 = \pi + 0 + \pi + 0 + \pi = 3\pi$

82. $a_1 = |\cos(x + \pi)| = |\cos x|$,
$a_2 = |\cos(x + 2\pi)| = |\cos x|$,
$a_3 = |\cos(x + 3\pi)| = |\cos x|$,
$a_4 = |\cos(x + 4\pi)| = |\cos x|$,
$a_5 = |\cos(x + 5\pi)| = |\cos x|$

$S_5 = |\cos x| + |\cos x| + |\cos x| + |\cos x| + |\cos x| = 5|\cos x|$

83. a) $a_n = n^2 - n + 41$

$a_1 = 1 - 1 + 41 = 41$,
$a_2 = 2^2 - 2 + 41 = 43$,
$a_3 = 3^2 - 3 + 41 = 47$,
$a_4 = 4^2 - 4 + 41 = 53$,
$a_5 = 5^2 - 5 + 41 = 61$,
$a_6 = 6^2 - 6 + 41 = 71$

b) All the terms are prime numbers.

c) $a_{41} = 41^2 - 41 + 41 = 41^2 = 1681$
The pattern does not hold since 1681 is not prime ($1681 = 41 \cdot 41$).

84. 2, 2.25, 2.370370, 2.441406, 2.488320, 2.521626

85. $a_n = \sqrt{n + 1} - \sqrt{n}$

$a_1 = \sqrt{1 + 1} - \sqrt{1} = \sqrt{2} - 1 \approx 0.414214$

$a_2 = \sqrt{2 + 1} - \sqrt{2} = \sqrt{3} - \sqrt{2} \approx 0.317837$

$a_3 = \sqrt{3 + 1} - \sqrt{3} = 2 - \sqrt{3} \approx 0.267949$

$a_4 = \sqrt{4 + 1} - \sqrt{4} = \sqrt{5} - 2 \approx 0.236068$

$a_5 = \sqrt{5 + 1} - \sqrt{5} = \sqrt{6} - \sqrt{5} \approx 0.213422$

$a_6 = \sqrt{6 + 1} - \sqrt{6} = \sqrt{7} - \sqrt{6} \approx 0.196262$

86. 2, 1.553774, 1.498834, 1.491398, 1.490378, 1.490238

87. $a_1 = 2$, $\qquad a_{k+1} = \frac{1}{2}\left(a_k + \frac{2}{a_k}\right)$

$a_2 = \frac{1}{2}\left(2 + \frac{2}{2}\right) = 1.5$

$a_3 = \frac{1}{2}\left(1.5 + \frac{2}{1.5}\right) \approx 1.416667$

$a_4 = \frac{1}{2}\left(1.416667 + \frac{2}{1.416667}\right) \approx 1.414216$

$a_5 = \frac{1}{2}\left(1.414216 + \frac{2}{1.414216}\right) \approx 1.414214$

$a_6 = \frac{1}{2}\left(1.414214 + \frac{2}{1.414214}\right) \approx 1.414214$

88. 2, 4, 8, 16, 32, 64, 128, 256, 512, 1024, 2048, 4096, 8192, 16,384, 32,768, 65,536

89. Find each term by multiplying the preceding term by 0.75:
$3900, $2925, $2193.75, $1645.31, $1233.98, $925.49, $694.12, $520.59, $390.44, $292.83

90. $4.20, $4.35, $4.50, $4.65, $4.80, $4.95, $5.10, $5.25, $5.40, $5.55

91. $S_n = \ln 1 + \ln 2 + \ln 3 + \cdots + \ln n$

$= \ln (1 \cdot 2 \cdot 3 \cdots n) = \ln (n!)$.

92. $S_n = \left(1 - \frac{1}{2}\right) + \left(\frac{1}{2} - \frac{1}{3}\right) + \left(\frac{1}{3} - \frac{1}{4}\right) + \cdots +$

$\left(\frac{1}{n - 1} - \frac{1}{n}\right) + \left(\frac{1}{n} - \frac{1}{n + 1}\right)$

$= 1 - \frac{1}{n + 1} = \frac{n}{n + 1}$

Exercise Set 11.2

1. 3, 8, 13, 18, . . .

$a_1 = 3$

$d = 5$ (8 - 3 = 5, 13 - 8 = 5, 18 - 13 = 5)

2. $a_1 = 1.08$, $d = 0.08$ (1.16 - 1.08 = 0.08)

3. 9, 5, 1, -3, . . .

$a_1 = 9$

$d = -4$ (5 - 9 = -4, 1 - 5 = -4, -3 - 1 = -4)

4. $a_1 = -8$, $d = 3$ (-5 - (-8) = 3)

5. $\frac{3}{2}$, $\frac{9}{4}$, 3, $\frac{15}{4}$, . . .

$a_1 = \frac{3}{2}$

$d = \frac{3}{4}$ $\left(\frac{9}{4} - \frac{3}{2} = \frac{3}{4}, 3 - \frac{9}{4} = \frac{3}{4}\right)$

6. $a_1 = \frac{3}{5}$, $d = -\frac{1}{2}$ $\left(\frac{1}{10} - \frac{3}{5} = -\frac{1}{2}\right)$

7. $1.07, $1.14, $1.21, $1.28, . . .

$a_1 = 1.07

$d = 0.07 ($1.14 - $1.07 = $0.07,
$\qquad\qquad$ $1.21 - $1.14 = $0.07)

8. $a_1 = 316, $d = -$3$ ($313 - $316 = -$3)

9. 2, 6, 10, . . .

$a_1 = 2$, $d = 4$, and $n = 12$

$a_n = a_1 + (n - 1)d$

$a_{12} = 2 + (12 - 1)4 = 2 + 11 \cdot 4 = 2 + 44 = 46$

10. $a_1 = 0.07$, $d = 0.05$, and $n = 11$

$a_{11} = 0.07 + (11 - 1)(0.05) = 0.07 + 0.5 = 0.57$

11. 7, 4, 1, . . .

$a_1 = 7$, $d = -3$, and $n = 17$

$a_n = a_1 + (n - 1)d$

$a_{17} = 7 + (17 - 1)(-3) = 7 + 16(-3) = 7 - 48 = -41$

12. $a_1 = 3$, $d = -\frac{2}{3}$, and $n = 14$

$a_{14} = 3 + (14 - 1)\left(-\frac{2}{3}\right) = 3 - \frac{26}{3} = -\frac{17}{3}$

13. $1200, $964.32, $728.64, . . .

$a_1 = 1200, $d = $964.32 - $1200 = -$235.68$,
$\qquad$ and $n = 13$

$a_n = a_1 + (n - 1)d$

$a_{13} = $1200 + (13 - 1)(-$235.68) =$
$\qquad $1200 + 12(-$235.68) = $1200 - $2828.16 =$
$\qquad -$1628.16$

14. $a_1 = 2345.78, $d = 621.76, and $n = 10$

$a_{10} = $2345.78 + (10 - 1)($621.76) = 7941.62

15. $a_1 = 2$, $d = 4$

$a_n = a_1 + (n - 1)d$

Let $a_n = 106$, and solve for n.

$106 = 2 + (n - 1)(4)$

$106 = 2 + 4n - 4$

$108 = 4n$

$27 = n$

The 27th term is 106.

16. $1.67 = 0.07 + (n - 1)(0.05)$

$1.67 = 0.07 + 0.05n - 0.05$

$1.65 = 0.05n$

$33 = n$

33rd term

17. $a_1 = 7$, $d = -3$

$a_n = a_1 + (n - 1)d$

$-296 = 7 + (n - 1)(-3)$

$-296 = 7 - 3n + 3$

$-306 = -3n$

$102 = n$

The 102nd term is -296.

18. $-27 = 3 + (n - 1)\left(-\frac{2}{3}\right)$

$-81 = 9 + (n - 1)(-2)$

$-81 = 9 - 2n + 2$

$-92 = -2n$

$46 = n$

46th term

19. $a_n = a_1 + (n - 1)d$

$a_{17} = 5 + (17 - 1)6$ Substituting 17 for n, 5 for a_1, and 6 for d

$= 5 + 16 \cdot 6$

$= 5 + 96$

$= 101$

20. $a_{20} = 14 + (20 - 1)(-3) = 14 + 19(-3) = -43$

21. $a_n = a_1 + (n - 1)d$

$33 = a_1 + (8 - 1)4$ Substituting 33 for a_8, 8 for n, and 4 for d

$33 = a_1 + 28$

$5 = a_1$

(Note that this procedure is equivalent to subtracting d from a_8 seven times to get a_1: $33 - 7(4) = 33 - 28 = 5$)

22. $26 = 8 + (11 - 1)d$

$26 = 8 + 10d$

$18 = 10d$

$1.8 = d$

23. $a_n = a_1 + (n - 1)d$

$-76 = 5 + (n - 1)(-3)$ Substituting -76 for a_n, 5 for a_1 and -3 for d

$-76 = 5 - 3n + 3$

$-76 = 8 - 3n$

$-84 = -3n$

$28 = n$

24. $-507 = 25 + (n - 1)(-14)$

$-507 = 25 - 14n + 14$

$-546 = -14n$

$39 = n$

25. We know that $a_{17} = -40$ and $a_{28} = -73$. We would have to add d eleven times to get from a_{17} to a_{28}. That is,

$-40 + 11d = -73$

$11d = -33$

$d = -3.$

Since $a_{17} = -40$, we subtract d sixteen times to get to a_1.

$a_1 = -40 - 16(-3) = -40 + 48 = 8$

We write the first five terms of the sequence:

$8, 5, 2, -1, -4$

26. $\frac{25}{3} + 15d = \frac{95}{6}$

$15d = \frac{45}{6}$

$d = \frac{1}{2}$

$a_1 = \frac{25}{3} - 16\left(\frac{1}{2}\right) = \frac{25}{3} - 8 = \frac{1}{3}$

The first five terms of the sequence are $\frac{1}{3}, \frac{5}{6}, \frac{4}{3}, \frac{11}{6}, \frac{7}{3}$.

27. $5 + 8 + 11 + 14 + \ldots$

Note that $a_1 = 5$, $d = 3$, and $n = 20$. We use the formula of Theorem 3.

$S_n = \frac{n}{2}\left[2a_1 + (n - 1)d\right]$

$S_{20} = \frac{20}{2}[2 \cdot 5 + (20 - 1)3] = 10[10 + 57] = 10 \cdot 67 = 670$

28. $S_{14} = \frac{14}{2}[2 \cdot 11 + (14 - 1)(-4)] = 7[22 - 52] = -210$

29. The sum is $1 + 2 + 3 + \ldots + 299 + 300$. This is the sum of the arithmetic sequence for which $a_1 = 1$, $a_n = 300$, and $n = 300$. We use the formula of Theorem 2.

$S_n = \frac{n}{2}(a_1 + a_n)$

$S_{300} = \frac{300}{2}(1 + 300) = 150(301) = 45,150$

30. $1 + 2 + 3 + \ldots + 399 + 400$

    $S_{400} = \dfrac{400}{2}(1 + 400) = 200(401) = 80{,}200$

31. The sum is $2 + 4 + 6 + \ldots + 98 + 100$. This is the sum of the arithmetic sequence for which $a_1 = 2$, $a_n = 100$, and $n = 50$. We use the formula of Theorem 2.

    $S_n = \dfrac{n}{2}(a_1 + a_n)$

    $S_{50} = \dfrac{50}{2}(2 + 100) = 25(102) = 2550$

32. $1 + 3 + 5 + \ldots + 97 + 99$

    $S_{50} = \dfrac{50}{2}(1 + 99) = 25(100) = 2500$

33. The sum is $7 + 14 + 21 + \ldots + 91 + 98$. This is the sum of the arithmetic sequence for which $a_1 = 7$, $a_n = 98$, and $n = 14$. We use the formula of Theorem 2.

    $S_n = \dfrac{n}{2}(a_1 + a_n)$

    $S_{14} = \dfrac{14}{2}(7 + 98) = 7(105) = 735$

34. $16 + 20 + 24 + \ldots + 516 + 520$

    $S_{127} = \dfrac{127}{2}(16 + 520) = 34{,}036$

35. $S_n = \dfrac{n}{2}\big[2a_1 + (n - 1)d\big]$

    $S_{20} = \dfrac{20}{2}[2 \cdot 2 + (20 - 1)5]$ Substituting 20 for n, 2 for a_1, and 5 for d

    $= 10[4 + 19 \cdot 5]$

    $= 10[4 + 95]$

    $= 10 \cdot 99$

    $= 990$

36. $S_{32} = \dfrac{32}{2}[2 \cdot 7 + (32 - 1)(-3)] = 16(14 - 93) = -1264$

37. We must find the smallest positive term of the sequence 35, 31, 27, ... It is an arithmetic sequence with $a_1 = 35$ and $d = -4$. We find the largest integer x for which $35 + x(-4) > 0$. Then we evaluate the expression $35 - 4x$ for that value of x.

    $35 - 4x > 0$

    $35 > 4x$

    $\dfrac{35}{4} > x$

    $8\dfrac{3}{4} > x$

    The integer we are looking for is 8. Then $35 - 4x = 35 - 4(8) = 3$.

    There will be 3 plants in the last row.

38. $a_{25} = 14 + (25 - 1)(2) = 14 + 24 \cdot 2 = 62$

    $S_{25} = \dfrac{25}{2}(14 + 62) = \dfrac{25}{2}(76) = 950$

39. We go from 50 poles in a row to one pole in the top row, so there must be 50 rows. We want the sum $50 + 49 + 48 + \ldots + 1$. Thus we want the sum of an arithmetic sequence with $a_1 = 50$, $a_n = 1$, and $n = 50$. We will use the formula $S_n = \dfrac{n}{2}(a_1 + a_n)$.

    $S_{50} = \dfrac{50}{2}(50 + 1)$.

    $S_{50} = 25(51) = 1275$

    There will be 1275 poles in the pile.

40. $S_{31} = \dfrac{31}{2}[2 \cdot 10 + (31 - 1)10] = \dfrac{31}{2}[20 + 300] = 4960\text{¢}$, or \$49.60.

41. We want to find the sum of an arithmetic sequence with $a_1 = \$600$, $d = \$100$, and $n = 20$. We will use the formula

    $S_n = \dfrac{n}{2}[2a_1 + (n - 1)d]$.

    $S_{20} = \dfrac{20}{2}[2 \cdot \$600 + (20 - 1)\$100]$.

    $S_{20} = 10(\$3100) = \$31{,}000$

    They save \$31,000 (disregarding interest).

42. $S_{31} = \dfrac{31}{2}[2 \cdot 30 + (31 - 1)20] = \dfrac{31}{2}[60 + 600] = \$10{,}230$.

43. We want to find the sum of an arithmetic sequence with $a_1 = 28$, $d = 4$, and $n = 50$. We will use the formula

    $S_n = \dfrac{n}{2}[2a_1 + (n - 1)d]$.

    $S_{50} = \dfrac{50}{2}[2 \cdot 28 + (50 - 1)4]$.

    $S_{50} = 25(252) = 6300$

    There are 6300 seats.

44. $S_{25} = \dfrac{25}{2}[2 \cdot 5000 + (25 - 1)1125] = \dfrac{25}{2}(10{,}000 + 24 \cdot 1125) = \$462{,}500$

45. $4, m_1, m_2, m_3, m_4, 13$

We look for $m_1, m_2, m_3,$ and m_4 such that $4, m_1, m_2, m_3, m_4, 13$ is an arithmetic sequence. In this case $a_1 = 4$, $n = 6$, and $a_6 = 13$. We use Theorem 1.

$$a_n = a_1 + (n - 1)d$$
$$13 = 4 + (6 - 1)d$$
$$9 = 5d$$
$$1\tfrac{4}{5} = d$$

Thus,

$$m_1 = a_1 + d = 4 + 1\tfrac{4}{5} = 5\tfrac{4}{5}$$

$$m_2 = m_1 + d = 5\tfrac{4}{5} + 1\tfrac{4}{5} = 6\tfrac{8}{5} = 7\tfrac{3}{5}$$

$$m_3 = m_2 + d = 7\tfrac{3}{5} + 1\tfrac{4}{5} = 8\tfrac{7}{5} = 9\tfrac{2}{5}$$

$$m_4 = m_3 + d = 9\tfrac{2}{5} + 1\tfrac{4}{5} = 10\tfrac{6}{5} = 11\tfrac{1}{5}$$

46. $-3, m_1, m_2, m_3, 5$

$a_1 = -3$, $a_n = 5$, $n = 5$

$$a_n = a_1 + (n - 1)d$$
$$5 = -3 + (5 - 1)d$$

$d = 2$; and $m_1 = -3 + 2 = -1$
$$m_2 = -1 + 2 = 1$$
$$m_3 = 1 + 2 = 3.$$

47. $1 + 3 + 5 + 7 + \ldots + n$

$$S_n = \frac{n}{2}[2a_1 + (n - 1)d]$$

Note that $a_1 = 1$ and $d = 2$.

$$S_n = \frac{n}{2}[2 \cdot 1 + (n - 1)2] = \frac{n}{2}(2 + 2n - 2)$$

$$= \frac{n}{2} \cdot 2n$$

$$= n^2$$

48. We find the sum of an arithmetic sequence with $a_1 = 1$, $a_n = n$, and $n = n$. We use the formula

$$S_n = \frac{n}{2}(a_1 + a_n).$$

$$S_n = \frac{n}{2}(1 + n), \text{ or } \frac{n(n + 1)}{2}$$

49. Let x represent the first number in the sequence, and let d represent the common difference. Then the three numbers in the sequence are x, $x + d$, and $x + 2d$.

We write a system of equations:

The sum of the first and third numbers is 10.

$$x + x + 2d \qquad = 10$$

The product of the first and second numbers is 15.

$$x(x + d) \qquad = 15$$

Solving the system of equations we get $x = 3$ and $d = 2$. Thus the numbers are 3, 5, and 7.

50. $10p + q = 40 - 3q + 2d$

$$10p + 4q - 40 = 2d$$

$$5p + 2q - 20 = d$$

$$a_1 = 40 - 3q - (5p + 2q - 20) = -5p - 5q + 60$$

51. $a_1 = \$8760$

$a_2 = \$8760 + (-\$798.23) = \$7961.77$

$a_3 = \$8760 + 2(-\$798.23) = \$7163.54$

$a_4 = \$8760 + 3(-\$798.23) = \$6365.31$

$a_5 = \$8760 + 4(-\$798.23) = \$5567.08$

$a_6 = \$8760 + 5(-\$798.23) = \$4768.85$

$a_7 = \$8760 + 6(-\$798.23) = \$3970.62$

$a_8 = \$8760 + 7(-\$798.23) = \$3172.39$

$a_9 = \$8760 + 8(-\$798.23) = \$2374.16$

$a_{10} = \$8760 + 9(-\$798.23) = \$1575.93$

52. $S_{10} = \dfrac{10}{2}(\$8760 + \$1575.93) = \$51,679.65$

53. $P(x) = x^4 + 4x^3 - 84x^2 - 176x + 640$ has at most 4 zeros because $P(x)$ is of degree 4. By the rational roots theorem, the possible zeros are $\pm 1, \pm 2, \pm 4, \pm 5, \pm 8, \pm 10, \pm 16, \pm 20, \pm 32, \pm 40, \pm 64, \pm 80, \pm 128, \pm 160, \pm 320, \pm 640$

We find two of the zeros using synthetic division.

```
2 | 1    4   -84   -176    640
  |      2    12   -144   -640
    1    6   -72   -320 |    0
```

```
-4 | 1    6   -72   -320
   |     -4    -8    320
     1    2   -80 |    0
```

Also by synthetic division we determine that ± 1 and -2 are not zeros. Therefore we determine that $d = 6$ in the arithmetic sequence.

Possible arithmetic sequences:

a)   -4   2   8   14

b)   -10   -4   2   8

c) -16 -10   -4   2

The solution cannot be a) because 14 is not a possible zero. Checking -16 by synthetic division we find that -16 is not a zero. Thus b) is the only arithmetic sequence which contains all four zeros. The zeros are -10, -4, 2, and 8.

54. $1, 1 + d, 1 + 2d, \ldots, 50$ has n terms.

$a_1 = 1$, $a_n = 50$, $S_n = 459$

$a_n = a_1 + (n - 1)d$
$50 = 1 + (n - 1)d$
$(n - 1)d = 49$

$S_n = \frac{n}{2} [2a_1 + (n - 1)d]$

$459 = \frac{n}{2} [2 \cdot 1 + 49]$

$n = 18$ and $n - 1 = 17$ means $d = \frac{49}{17}$.

55. The sides are a, $a + d$, and $a + 2d$. By the Pythagorean theorem, we get $a^2 + (a + d)^2 = (a + 2d)^2$. Solving for d, we get $d = \frac{a}{3}$. Thus the sides are a, $a + \frac{a}{3}$, and $a + \frac{2a}{3}$, or a, $\frac{4a}{3}$, and $\frac{5a}{3}$ which are in the ratio 3:4:5.

56. a) $a_t = \$5200 - t\left[\frac{\$5200 - \$1100}{8}\right]$

$a_t = \$5200 - \$512.50t$

b) $a_0 = \$5200 - \$512.50(0) = \$5200$
$a_1 = \$5200 - \$512.50(1) = \$4687.50$
$a_2 = \$5200 - \$512.50(2) = \$4175$
$a_3 = \$5200 - \$512.50(3) = \$3662.50$
$a_4 = \$5200 - \$512.50(4) = \$3150$
$a_7 = \$5200 - \$512.50(7) = \$1612.50$
$a_8 = \$5200 - \$512.50(8) = \$1100$

57. $a_n = a_1 + (n - 1)d$

$a_n = f(n) = d \cdot n + (a_1 - d)$ where $f(n)$ is a linear function of n with slope d and y-intercept $(a_1 - d)$.

58.

$m = p + d$
$\underline{m = q - d}$
$2m = p + q$ (Adding)
$m = \frac{p + q}{2}$

Exercise Set 11.3

---

1. $2, 4, 8, 16, \ldots$

$\frac{4}{2} = 2$, $\frac{8}{4} = 2$, $\frac{16}{8} = 2$

$r = 2$

2. $r = \frac{-6}{18} = -\frac{1}{3}$

3. $1, -1, 1, -1, \ldots$

$\frac{-1}{1} = -1$, $\frac{1}{-1} = -1$, $\frac{-1}{1} = -1$

$r = -1$

4. $r = \frac{-0.8}{-8} = 0.1$

5. $\frac{1}{2}, -\frac{1}{4}, \frac{1}{8}, -\frac{1}{16}, \ldots$

$\frac{-\frac{1}{4}}{\frac{1}{2}} = -\frac{1}{4} \cdot \frac{2}{1} = -\frac{2}{4} = -\frac{1}{2}$

$\frac{\frac{1}{8}}{-\frac{1}{4}} = \frac{1}{8} \cdot \left(-\frac{4}{1}\right) = -\frac{4}{8} = -\frac{1}{2}$

$r = -\frac{1}{2}$

6. $r = \frac{-\frac{4}{3}}{\frac{2}{3}} = -2$

7. $75, 15, 3, \frac{3}{5}, \ldots$

$\frac{15}{75} = \frac{1}{5}$, $\frac{3}{15} = \frac{1}{5}$, $\frac{\frac{3}{5}}{3} = \frac{3}{5} \cdot \frac{1}{3} = \frac{1}{5}$

$r = \frac{1}{5}$

8. $r = \frac{0.6275}{6.275} = 0.1$

9. $\frac{1}{x}, \frac{1}{x^2}, \frac{1}{x^3}, \ldots$

$\frac{\frac{1}{x^2}}{\frac{1}{x}} = \frac{1}{x^2} \cdot \frac{x}{1} = \frac{x}{x^2} = \frac{1}{x}$

$\frac{\frac{1}{x^3}}{\frac{1}{x^2}} = \frac{1}{x^3} \cdot \frac{x^2}{1} = \frac{x^2}{x^3} = \frac{1}{x}$

$r = \frac{1}{x}$

10. $r = \frac{\frac{5m}{2}}{5} = \frac{m}{2}$

11. $\$780, \$858, \$943.80, \$1038.18, \ldots$

$\frac{\$858}{\$780} = 1.1$, $\frac{\$943.80}{\$858} = 1.1$,

$\frac{\$1038.18}{\$943.80} = 1.1$

$r = 1.1$

12. $r = \frac{\$5320}{\$5600} = 0.95$

13. 2, 4, 8, 16, . . .

    $a_1 = 2$, $n = 6$, and $r = \frac{4}{2}$, or 2.

    We use the formula $a_n = a_1 r^{n-1}$.

    $a_6 = 2(2)^{6-1} = 2 \cdot 2^5 = 2 \cdot 32 = 64$

14. $a_9 = 2(-5)^{9-1} = 781{,}250$

15. 2, $2\sqrt{3}$, 6, . . .

    $a_1 = 2$, $n = 9$, and $r = \frac{2\sqrt{3}}{2}$, or $\sqrt{3}$

    $a_n = a_1 r^{n-1}$

    $a_9 = 2(\sqrt{3})^{9-1} = 2(\sqrt{3})^8 = 2 \cdot 81 = 162$

16. $a_{57} = 1(-1)^{57-1} = 1$

17. $\frac{8}{243}$, $\frac{8}{81}$, $\frac{8}{27}$, . . .

    $a_1 = \frac{8}{243}$, $n = 10$, and $r = \frac{\frac{8}{81}}{\frac{8}{243}} = \frac{8}{81} \cdot \frac{243}{8} = 3$

    $a_n = a_1 r^{n-1}$

    $a_{10} = \frac{8}{243}(3)^{10-1} = \frac{8}{243}(3)^9 = \frac{8}{243} \cdot 19{,}683 = 648$

18. $a_{23} = \frac{7}{625}(-25)^{23-1} = \frac{7}{625}(-25)^{22} = 7(25)^{20}$

19. $1000, $1080, $1166.40, . . .

    $a_1 = \$1000$, $n = 5$, and $r = \frac{\$1080}{\$1000} = 1.08$

    $a_n = a_1 r^{n-1}$

    $a_5 = \$1000(1.08)^{5-1} \approx \$1360.49$

20. $a_6 = \$1000(1.07)^{6-1} \approx \$1402.55$

21. 1, 3, 9, . . .

    $a_1 = 1$ and $r = \frac{3}{1}$, or 3

    $a_n = a_1 r^{n-1}$

    $a_n = 1(3)^{n-1} = 3^{n-1}$

22. $a_n = 25\left(\frac{1}{5}\right)^{n-1} = \frac{5^2}{5^{n-1}} = 5^{3-n}$

23. 1, -1, 1, -1, . . .

    $a_1 = 1$ and $r = \frac{-1}{1} = -1$

    $a_n = a_1 r^{n-1}$

    $a_n = 1(-1)^{n-1} = (-1)^{n-1}$

24. $a_n = 2(2)^{n-1} = 2^n$

25. $\frac{1}{x}$, $\frac{1}{x^2}$, $\frac{1}{x^3}$, . . .

    $a_1 = \frac{1}{x}$ and $r = \frac{1}{x}$ (see Exercise 9)

    $a_n = a_1 r^{n-1}$

    $a_n = \frac{1}{x}\left(\frac{1}{x}\right)^{n-1} = \frac{1}{x} \cdot \frac{1}{x^{n-1}} = \frac{1}{x^{1+n-1}} = \frac{1}{x^n}$

26. $a_n = 5\left(\frac{m}{2}\right)^{n-1}$

27. 6 + 12 + 24 + . . .

    $a_1 = 6$, $n = 7$, and $r = \frac{12}{6}$, or 2

    $S_n = \frac{a_1(r^n - 1)}{r - 1}$

    $S_7 = \frac{6(2^7 - 1)}{2 - 1} = \frac{6(128 - 1)}{1} = 6 \cdot 127 = 762$

28. $S_6 = \frac{16\left[\left(-\frac{1}{2}\right)^6 - 1\right]}{-\frac{1}{2} - 1} = \frac{16\left[\frac{1}{64} - 1\right]}{-\frac{3}{2}} = \frac{16\left[-\frac{63}{64}\right]}{-\frac{3}{2}} =$

    $\frac{-\frac{63}{4}}{-\frac{3}{2}} = -\frac{63}{4} \cdot \left(-\frac{2}{3}\right) = \frac{21}{2}$, or 10.5

29. $\frac{1}{18} - \frac{1}{6} + \frac{1}{2} - \cdot \cdot \cdot$

    $a_1 = \frac{1}{18}$, $n = 7$, and $r = \frac{-\frac{1}{6}}{\frac{1}{18}} = -\frac{1}{6} \cdot \frac{18}{1} = -3$

    $S_n = \frac{a_1(r^n - 1)}{r - 1}$

    $S_7 = \frac{\frac{1}{18}[(-3)^7 - 1]}{-3 - 1} = \frac{\frac{1}{18}[-2187 - 1]}{-4} = \frac{\frac{1}{18}(-2188)}{-4} =$

    $\frac{1}{18}(-2188)\left(-\frac{1}{4}\right) = \frac{547}{18}$

30. $a_n = a_1 r^{n-1}$

    $-\frac{1}{32} = (-8) \cdot \left(-\frac{1}{2}\right)^{n-1}$

    $n = 9$

    $S_9 = \frac{-8\left[\left(-\frac{1}{2}\right)^9 - 1\right]}{-\frac{1}{2} - 1} = -\frac{171}{32}$

31. $1 + x + x^2 + x^3 + \ldots$

$a_1 = 1$, $n = 8$, and $r = \frac{x}{1}$, or x

$S_n = \frac{a_1(r^n - 1)}{r - 1}$

$S_8 = \frac{1(x^8 - 1)}{x - 1} = \frac{(x^4 + 1)(x^4 - 1)}{x - 1}$

$= \frac{(x^4 + 1)(x^2 + 1)(x^2 - 1)}{x - 1}$

$= \frac{(x^4 + 1)(x^2 + 1)(x + 1)(x - 1)}{x - 1}$

$= (x^4 + 1)(x^2 + 1)(x + 1)$

32. $S_{10} = \frac{1\left[(x^2)^{10} - 1\right]}{x^2 - 1} = \frac{x^{20} - 1}{x^2 - 1}$

33. $\$200$, $\$200(1.06)$, $\$200(1.06)^2$, $\ldots$

$a_1 = \$200$, $n = 16$, and $r = \frac{\$200(1.06)}{\$200} = 1.06$

$S_n = \frac{a_1(r^n - 1)}{r - 1}$

$S_{16} = \frac{\$200(1.06^{16} - 1)}{1.06 - 1} \approx \$5134.51$

34. $S_{23} = \frac{\$1000(1.08^{23} - 1)}{1.08 - 1} \approx \$60,893.30$

35. $\sum\limits_{k=1}^{\infty} \left(\frac{1}{2}\right)^{k-1}$

$a_1 = 1$, $|r| = \left|\frac{1}{2}\right| = \frac{1}{2}$

$\sum\limits_{k=1}^{\infty} \left(\frac{1}{2}\right)^{k-1} = \frac{a_1}{1 - r} = \frac{1}{1 - \frac{1}{2}} = \frac{1}{\frac{1}{2}} = 2$

36. Since $|r| = |2| < 1$, the sum does not exist.

37. $4 + 2 + 1 + \ldots$

$|r| = \left|\frac{2}{4}\right| = \left|\frac{1}{2}\right| = \frac{1}{2}$, and since $|r| < 1$, the series does have a sum.

$S_\infty = \frac{a_1}{1 - r} = \frac{4}{1 - \frac{1}{2}} = \frac{4}{\frac{1}{2}} = 4 \cdot \frac{2}{1} = 8$

38. $|r| = \left|\frac{3}{7}\right| = \frac{3}{7} < 1$, so the series has a sum.

$S_\infty = \frac{7}{1 - \frac{3}{7}} = \frac{7}{\frac{4}{7}} = \frac{49}{4}$

39. $25 + 20 + 16 + \ldots$

$|r| = \left|\frac{20}{25}\right| = \left|\frac{4}{5}\right| = \frac{4}{5}$, and since $|r| < 1$, the series does have a sum.

$S_\infty = \frac{a_1}{1 - r} = \frac{25}{1 - \frac{4}{5}} = \frac{25}{\frac{1}{5}} = 25 \cdot \frac{5}{1} = 125$

40. $|r| = \left|\frac{9}{12}\right| = \left|\frac{3}{4}\right| = \frac{3}{4} < 1$, so the series has a sum.

$S_\infty = \frac{12}{1 - \frac{3}{4}} = \frac{12}{\frac{1}{4}} = 48$

41. $100 - 10 + 1 - \frac{1}{10} + \ldots$

$|r| = \left|\frac{-10}{100}\right| = \left|-\frac{1}{10}\right| = \frac{1}{10}$, and since $|r| < 1$, the series does have a sum.

$S_\infty = \frac{a_1}{1 - r} = \frac{100}{1 - \left(-\frac{1}{10}\right)} = \frac{100}{\frac{11}{10}} = 100 \cdot \frac{10}{11} = \frac{1000}{11}$

42. $|r| = \left|\frac{18}{-6}\right| = |-3| = 3 < 1$, so the series does not have a sum.

43. $8 + 40 + 200 + \ldots$

$|r| = \left|\frac{40}{8}\right| = |5| = 5$, and since $|r| < 1$ the series does not have a sum.

44. $|r| = \left|\frac{3}{-6}\right| = \left|-\frac{1}{2}\right| = \frac{1}{2} < 1$, so the series has a sum.

$S_\infty = \frac{-6}{1 - \left(-\frac{1}{2}\right)} = \frac{-6}{\frac{3}{2}} = -6 \cdot \frac{2}{3} = -4$

45. $0.6 + 0.06 + 0.006 + \ldots$

$|r| = \left|\frac{0.06}{0.6}\right| = |0.1| = 0.1$, and since $|r| < 1$, the series does have a sum.

$S_\infty = \frac{a_1}{1 - r} = \frac{0.6}{1 - 0.1} = \frac{0.6}{0.9} = \frac{6}{9} = \frac{2}{3}$

46. $|r| = \left|\frac{0.0037}{0.37}\right| = |0.01| = 0.01 < 1$, so the series has a sum.

$S_\infty = \frac{0.37}{1 - 0.01} = \frac{0.37}{0.99} = \frac{37}{99}$

47. $\$500(1.11)^{-1} + \$500(1.11)^{-2} + \$500(1.11)^{-3} + \ldots$

$|r| = \left|\frac{\$500(1.11)^{-2}}{\$500(1.11)^{-1}}\right| = |(1.11)^{-1}| = (1.11)^{-1}$, or $\frac{1}{1.11}$, and since $|r| < 1$, the series does have a sum.

$S_\infty = \frac{a_1}{1 - r} = \frac{\$500(1.11)^{-1}}{1 - \left(\frac{1}{1.11}\right)} = \frac{\frac{\$500}{1.11}}{\frac{0.11}{1.11}} =$

$\frac{\$500}{1.11} \cdot \frac{1.11}{0.11} \approx \$4545.45$

48. $1000(1.08)^{-1} + \$1000(1.08)^{-2} +$
$1000(1.08)^{-3} + \cdots$

$|r| = \left|\dfrac{\$1000(1.08)^{-2}}{\$1000(1.08)^{-1}}\right| = |(1.08)^{-1}| = (1.08)^{-1} < 1,$
so the series has a sum.

$S_\infty = \dfrac{\$1000(1.08)^{-1}}{1 - (1.08)^{-1}} = \dfrac{\frac{\$1000}{1.08}}{\frac{0.08}{1.08}} = \$12,500$

49. $\displaystyle\sum_{k=1}^{\infty} 16(0.1)^{k-1}$

$a_1 = 16(0.1)^{1-1} = 16 \cdot 1 = 16$

$a_2 = 16(0.1)^{2-1} = 16(0.1) = 1.6$

$|r| = \left|\dfrac{1.6}{16}\right| = |0.1| = 0.1 < 1,$ so the series has a sum.

$S_\infty = \dfrac{16}{1 - 0.1} = \dfrac{16}{0.9} = \dfrac{160}{9}$

50. $|r| = |0.6| = 0.6 < 1,$ so the series has a sum.

$S_\infty = \dfrac{4}{1 - 0.6} = 10$

51. $\displaystyle\sum_{k=1}^{\infty} \dfrac{1}{2^{k-1}}$

$a_1 = \dfrac{1}{2^{1-1}} = \dfrac{1}{1} = 1$

$a_2 = \dfrac{1}{2^{2-1}} = \dfrac{1}{2^1} = \dfrac{1}{2}$

$|r| = \left|\dfrac{\frac{1}{2}}{1}\right| = \dfrac{1}{2} < 1,$ so the series has a sum.

$S_\infty = \dfrac{1}{1 - \frac{1}{2}} = \dfrac{1}{\frac{1}{2}} = 2$

52. $|r| = \left|\dfrac{1}{2}\right| = \dfrac{1}{2} < 1,$ so the series has a sum.

$S_\infty = \dfrac{\frac{8}{3}}{1 - \frac{1}{2}} = \dfrac{16}{3}$

53. $0.7\overline{7} = 0.7 + 0.07 + 0.007 + 0.0007 + \cdots$

Note that $a_1 = 0.7$ and $r = 0.1$

$S_\infty = \dfrac{a_1}{1 - r}$

$S_\infty = \dfrac{0.7}{1 - 0.1} = \dfrac{0.7}{0.9} = \dfrac{7}{9}$

54. $8.999\overline{9} = 8 + (0.9 + 0.09 + 0.009 + 0.0009 + \cdots)$

$= 8 + \dfrac{0.9}{1 - 0.1}$

$= 8 + 1 = 9$

55. $0.533\overline{3} = 0.5 + 0.033\overline{3}$

First we consider the repeating part:
$0.033\overline{3} = 0.03 + 0.003 + 0.0003 + \cdots$

$a_1 = 0.03$ and $r = 0.1$

$S_\infty = \dfrac{a_1}{1 - r} = \dfrac{0.03}{1 - 0.1} = \dfrac{0.03}{0.9} = \dfrac{3}{90} = \dfrac{1}{30}$

Thus

$0.533\overline{3} = 0.5 + 0.033\overline{3} = \dfrac{1}{2} + \dfrac{1}{30} = \dfrac{16}{30} = \dfrac{8}{15}$

56. $0.644\overline{4} = 0.6 + (0.04 + 0.004 + \cdots)$

$\qquad = \dfrac{3}{5} + \dfrac{0.04}{1 - 0.1}$

$\qquad = \dfrac{3}{5} + \dfrac{4}{90} = \dfrac{29}{45}$

57. $5.1515\overline{15} = 5 + 0.1515\overline{15}$

First we consider the repeating part.
$0.1515\overline{15} = 0.15 + 0.0015 + 0.000015 + \cdots$
$a_1 = 0.15$ and $r = 0.01$

$S_\infty = \dfrac{a_1}{1 - r} = \dfrac{0.15}{1 - 0.01} = \dfrac{0.15}{0.99} = \dfrac{15}{99} = \dfrac{5}{33}$

Thus

$5.1515\overline{15} = 5 + \dfrac{5}{33} = 5\dfrac{5}{33},$ or $\dfrac{170}{33}$

58. $0.4125\overline{125}$

$= 0.4 + (0.0125 + 0.0000125 + \cdots)$

$= \dfrac{4}{10} + \dfrac{0.0125}{1 - 0.001}$

$= \dfrac{4}{10} + \dfrac{125}{9990} = \dfrac{4121}{9990}$

59. The rebound distances form a geometric sequence:

$\dfrac{1}{4} \times 16, \quad \left(\dfrac{1}{4}\right)^2 \times 16, \quad \left(\dfrac{1}{4}\right)^3 \times 16, \ldots,$

or $4, \quad \dfrac{1}{4} \times 4, \quad \left(\dfrac{1}{4}\right)^2 \times 4, \ldots$

The height of the 6th rebound is the 6th term of the sequence.

We will use the formula $a_n = a_1 r^{n-1}$, with $a_1 = 4$, $r = \dfrac{1}{4}$, and $n = 6$:

$a_6 = 4\left(\dfrac{1}{4}\right)^{6-1}$

$a_6 = \dfrac{4}{4^5} = \dfrac{1}{4^4} = \dfrac{1}{256}$

The ball rebounds $\dfrac{1}{256}$ ft the 6th time.

60. $S_\infty = \dfrac{4}{1 - \frac{1}{4}} = \dfrac{4}{\frac{3}{4}} = \dfrac{16}{3}$ ft, or $5\dfrac{1}{3}$ ft

61. In one year, the population will be
$100,000 + 0.03(100,000)$, or $(1.03)100,000$. In two years, the population will be $(1.03)100,000 + 0.03(1.03)100,000$, or $(1.03)^2100,000$. Thus the populations form a geometric sequence:

$$100,000, \quad (1.03)100,000, \quad (1.03)^2100,000, \ldots$$

The population in 15 years will be the 16th term of the sequence.

We will use the formula $a_n = a_1r^{n-1}$ with $a_1 = 100,000$, $r = 1.03$, and $n = 16$:

$$a_{16} = 100,000(1.03)^{16-1}$$
$$a_{16} \approx 155,797$$

In 15 years the population will be about 155,797.

62.
$$200,000 = 100,000(1.03)^{n-1}$$
$$2 = (1.03)^{n-1}$$
$$\ln 2 = (n-1)\ln 1.03$$
$$\frac{\ln 2}{\ln 1.03} = n - 1$$
$$23.4 \approx n - 1$$
$$24.4 \approx n$$

It will take about 24 years for the population to double.

63. The amounts owed at the beginning of successive years form a geometric sequence:

$$\$1200, \quad (1.12)\$1200, \quad (1.12)^2\$1200,$$
$$(1.12)^3\$1200, \ldots$$

The amount to be repaid at the end of 13 years is the amount owed at the beginning of the 14th year.

We use the formula $a_n = a_1r^{n-1}$ with $a_1 = \$1200$, $r = 1.12$, and $n = 14$:

$$a_{14} = \$1200(1.12)^{14-1}$$
$$a_{14} \approx \$5236.19$$

At the end of 13 years, $5236.19 will be repaid.

64. We have a sequence 0.01, $2(0.01)$, $2^2(0.01)$, $2^3(0.01)$, $\ldots$. The thickness after 20 folds is given by the 21st term of the sequence.

$$a_{21} = 0.01(2)^{21-1} = 10,485.76 \text{ in.}$$

65. The lengths of the falls form a geometric sequence:

$$556, \quad \left[\frac{3}{4}\right]556, \quad \left[\frac{3}{4}\right]^2556, \quad \left[\frac{3}{4}\right]^3556, \ldots$$

The total length of the first 6 falls is the sum of the first six terms of this sequence. The heights of the rebounds also form a geometric sequence:

$$\left[\frac{3}{4}\right]556, \quad \left[\frac{3}{4}\right]^2556, \quad \left[\frac{3}{4}\right]^3556, \ldots, \quad \text{or}$$

$$417, \quad \left[\frac{3}{4}\right]417, \quad \left[\frac{3}{4}\right]^2417, \ldots$$

When the ball hits the ground for the 6th time, it will have rebounded 5 times. Thus the total length of the rebounds is the sum of the first five terms of this sequence.

We use the formula $S_n = \frac{a_1(r^n - 1)}{r - 1}$ twice, once with $a_1 = 556$, $r = \frac{3}{4}$, and $n = 6$ and a second time with $a_1 = 417$, $r = \frac{3}{4}$, and $n = 5$.

D = Length of falls + length of rebounds

$$= \frac{556\left[\left[\frac{3}{4}\right]^6 - 1\right]}{\frac{3}{4} - 1} + \frac{417\left[\left[\frac{3}{4}\right]^5 - 1\right]}{\frac{3}{4} - 1}.$$

We use a calculator to obtain $D \approx 3100$.

The ball will have traveled about 3100 ft.

66. We add the sums of the two infinite geometric series in Exercise 65.

$$\frac{556}{1 - \frac{3}{4}} + \frac{417}{1 - \frac{3}{4}} = 3892 \text{ ft}$$

67. The amounts form a geometric series:

$$\$0.01, \quad \$0.01(2), \quad \$0.01(2)^2, \quad \$0.01(2^3) + \ldots + (\$0.01)(2)^{27}$$

We use the formula $S_n = \frac{a_1(r^n - 1)}{r - 1}$ to find the sum of the geometric series with $a_1 = 0.01$, $r = 2$, and $n = 28$:

$$S_{28} = \frac{0.01(2^{28} - 1)}{2 - 1}$$

We use a calculator to obtain $S_{28} \approx \$2,684,355$.

You would earn about $2,684,355.

68. The first $1000, invested for 40 years, will become $1000(1.11)^{40}$. The second $1000, invested for 39 years will become $1000(1.11)^{39}$. The fortieth $1000, invested for only 1 year, will become $1000(1.11)^1$.

We consider the following sequence:

$$\$1000(1.11)^1, \quad \$1000(1.11)^2, \quad \$1000(1.11)^3, \ldots$$

$$S_{40} = \frac{1000(1.11)[(1.11)^{40} - 1]}{1.11 - 1} \approx \$645,826.93$$

69. The total effect on the economy is
$\$13,000,000,000 + \$13,000,000,000(0.85) + \$13,000,000,000(0.85)^2 + \$13,000,000,000(0.85)^3 + \ldots$
which is a geometric series with $a_1 = \$13,000,000,000$ and $r = 0.85$.

$$S_\infty = \frac{a_1}{1 - r}$$
$$S_\infty = \frac{\$13,000,000,000}{1 - 0.85} = \frac{\$13,000,000,000}{0.15}$$
$$\approx \$86,666,666,667$$

70. The total number of people who will buy the product can be expressed as a geometric series.

$5{,}000{,}000(0.4) + 5{,}000{,}000(0.4)^2 +$

$5{,}000{,}000(0.4)^3 + 5{,}000{,}000(0.4)^4 + \ldots$

Note that $a_1 = 5{,}000{,}000(0.4)$ and $r = 0.4$.

$$S_\infty = \frac{a_1}{1 - r}$$

$$S_\infty = \frac{5{,}000{,}000(0.4)}{1 - 0.4} = \frac{2{,}000{,}000}{0.6} \approx 3{,}333{,}333, \text{ or}$$

$3.3\overline{3} \times 10^6$

3,333,333 represents what % of the population?

$3{,}333{,}333 = x \cdot 5{,}000{,}000$

$$\frac{3{,}333{,}333}{5{,}000{,}000} = x$$

$0.666\overline{6} = x$

$66\frac{2}{3}\% = x$

71. See the answer section in the text.

72. a) $x + 7 - (x + 3) = 4x - 2 - (x + 7)$

$$x = \frac{13}{3}$$

The three given terms are $\frac{13}{3} + 3 = \frac{22}{3}$,

$\frac{13}{3} + 7 = \frac{34}{3}$, and $4 \cdot \frac{13}{3} - 2 = \frac{46}{3}$.

Then $d = \frac{12}{3}$, or 4, so the fourth term is

$\frac{46}{3} + \frac{12}{3} = \frac{58}{3}$.

b) $\dfrac{x + 7}{x + 3} = \dfrac{4x - 2}{x + 7}$

$x = -\frac{11}{3}$ or $x = 5$

For $x = -\frac{11}{3}$: The three given terms are

$-\frac{11}{3} + 3 = -\frac{2}{3}$, $-\frac{11}{3} + 7 = \frac{10}{3}$, and

$4\left(-\frac{11}{3}\right) - 2 = -\frac{50}{3}$.

Then $r = -5$, so the fourth term is

$-\frac{50}{3}(-5) = \frac{250}{3}$.

For $x = 5$: The three given terms are $5 + 3 = 8$,

$5 + 7 = 12$, and $4 \cdot 5 - 2 = 18$. Then $r = \frac{3}{2}$,

so the fourth term is $18 \cdot \frac{3}{2} = 27$.

73. $1 + x + x^2 + \ldots$

This is a geometric series with $a_1 = 1$ and $r = x$.

$$S_n = \frac{a_1(r^n - 1)}{r - 1} = \frac{1(x^n - 1)}{x - 1} = \frac{x^n - 1}{x - 1}$$

74. $S_n = \dfrac{x^2[(-x)^n - 1]}{-x - 1}$, or $\dfrac{x^2[1 - (-x)^n]}{x + 1}$

75. See the answer section in the text.

76. $$\frac{a_{n+1}}{a_n} = r$$

$$\ln \frac{a_{n+1}}{a_n} = \ln r$$

$\ln a_{n+1} - \ln a_n = \ln r$

Thus, $\ln a_1$, $\ln a_2$, $\ln a_3$, ... is an arithmetic sequence.

77. $a_{n+1} - a_n = d$ (a_1, a_2, a_3, ... is arithmetic)

$\dfrac{5^{a_{n+1}}}{5^{a_n}} = 5^{a_{n+1} - a_n} = 5^d$, a constant

Hence 5^{a_1}, 5^{a_2}, 5^{a_3}, ... is a geometric sequence.

78. The length of a side of the first square is 16 cm. The length of a side of the next square is the length of the hypotenuse of a right triangle with legs 8 cm and 8 cm, or $8\sqrt{2}$ cm. The length of a side of the next square is the length of the hypotenuse of a right triangle with legs $4\sqrt{2}$ cm and $4\sqrt{2}$ cm, or 8 cm. The areas of the squares form a sequence:

$(16)^2$, $(8\sqrt{2})^2$, $(8)^2$, . . . , or

256, 128, 64, ...

This is a geometric sequence with $a_1 = 256$ and $r = \frac{1}{2}$.

We find the sum of the infinite geometric series $256 + 128 + 64 + \ldots$.

$$S_\infty = \frac{a_1}{1 - r}$$

$$S_\infty = \frac{256}{1 - \frac{1}{2}} = 512$$

The sum of the areas is 512 cm².

Exercise Set 11.4

1. $n^2 < n^3$

$1^2 < 1^3$, $2^2 < 2^3$, $3^2 < 3^3$, $4^2 < 4^3$, $5^2 < 5^3$

2. $1^2 - 1 + 41$ is prime, $2^2 - 2 + 41$ is prime, etc.

3. A polygon of n sides has $\dfrac{n(n - 3)}{2}$ diagonals.

A polygon of 3 sides has $\dfrac{3(3 - 3)}{2}$ diagonals.

A polygon of 4 sides has $\dfrac{4(4 - 3)}{2}$ diagonals., etc.

4. The sum of the angles of a polygon of 3 sides is $(3 - 2) \cdot 180°$., etc.

5. See the answer section in the text.

6. S_n: $4 + 8 + 12 + \ldots + 4n = 2n(n + 1)$

   S_1: $4 = 2 \cdot 1 \cdot (1 + 1)$

   S_k: $4 + 8 + 12 + \ldots + 4k = 2k(k + 1)$

   S_{k+1}: $4 + 8 + 12 + \ldots + 4k + 4(k + 1) =$
   $\qquad 2(k + 1)(k + 2)$

   1) <u>Basis step</u>: Since $2 \cdot 1 \cdot (1 + 1) = 2 \cdot 2 = 4$, S_1 is true.

   2) <u>Induction step</u>: Let k be any natural number. Assume S_k. Deduce S_{k+1}. Starting with the left side of S_{k+1}, we have
   $$4 + 8 + 12 + \ldots + 4k + 4(k + 1)$$
   $$= \quad 2k(k + 1) \quad + 4(k + 1) \quad \text{(By } S_k\text{)}$$
   $$= (k + 1)(2k + 4)$$
   $$= 2(k + 1)(k + 2)$$

7. See the answer section in the text.

8. S_n: $3 + 6 + 9 + \ldots + 3n = \dfrac{3n(n + 1)}{2}$

   S_1: $3 = \dfrac{3(1 + 1)}{2}$

   S_k: $3 + 6 + 9 + \ldots + 3k = \dfrac{3k(k + 1)}{2}$

   S_{k+1}: $3 + 6 + 9 + \ldots + 3k + 3(k + 1) =$
   $$\dfrac{3(k + 1)(k + 2)}{2}$$

   1) <u>Basis step</u>: Since $\dfrac{3(1 + 1)}{2} = \dfrac{3 \cdot 2}{2} = 3$, S_1 is true.

   2) <u>Induction step</u>: Let k be any natural number. Assume S_k. Deduce S_{k+1}. Starting with the left side of S_{k+1}, we have
   $$3 + 6 + 9 + \ldots + 3k + 3(k + 1)$$
   $$= \quad \dfrac{3k(k + 1)}{2} \quad + 3(k + 1) \quad \text{(By } S_k\text{)}$$
   $$= \dfrac{3k(k + 1) + 6(k + 1)}{2}$$
   $$= \dfrac{(k + 1)(3k + 6)}{2}$$
   $$= \dfrac{3(k + 1)(k + 2)}{2}$$

9. See the answer section in the text for S_n, S_1, S_k, and S_{k+1}.

   1) <u>Basis step</u>: Since $\dfrac{1}{1 + 1} = \dfrac{1}{2} = \dfrac{1}{1 \cdot 2}$, S_1 is true.

2) <u>Induction step</u>: Let k be any natural number. Assume S_k. Deduce S_{k+1}.
$$\dfrac{1}{1 \cdot 2} + \dfrac{1}{2 \cdot 3} + \ldots + \dfrac{1}{k(k + 1)} = \dfrac{k}{k + 1} \quad (S_k)$$
$$\dfrac{1}{1 \cdot 2} + \dfrac{1}{2 \cdot 3} + \ldots + \dfrac{1}{k(k+1)} + \dfrac{1}{(k+1)(k+2)} =$$
$$\dfrac{k}{k+1} + \dfrac{1}{(k+1)(k+2)}$$
$$\left[\text{Adding } \dfrac{1}{(k+1)(k+2)} \text{ on both sides}\right]$$
$$= \dfrac{k(k + 2) + 1}{(k + 1)(k + 2)}$$
$$= \dfrac{k^2 + 2k + 1}{(k + 1)(k + 2)}$$
$$= \dfrac{(k + 1)(k + 1)}{(k + 1)(k + 2)}$$
$$= \dfrac{k + 1}{k + 2}$$

10. S_n: $2 + 4 + 8 + \ldots + 2^n = 2(2^n - 1)$

    S_1: $2 = 2(2 - 1)$

    S_k: $2 + 4 + 8 + \ldots + 2^k = 2(2^k - 1)$

    S_{k+1}: $2 + 4 + 8 + \ldots + 2^k + 2^{k+1} = 2(2^{k+1} - 1)$

    1) <u>Basis step</u>: Since $2(2 - 1) = 2 \cdot 1 = 2$, S_1 is true by substitution.

    2) <u>Induction step</u>: Let k be any natural number. Assume S_k. Deduce S_{k+1}. Starting with the left side of S_{k+1}, we have
    $$2 + 4 + 8 + \ldots + 2^k + 2^{k+1}$$
    $$= \quad 2(2^k - 1) \quad + 2^{k+1} \quad \text{(By } S_k\text{)}$$
    $$= 2^{k+1} - 2 + 2^{k+1}$$
    $$= 2 \cdot 2^{k+1} - 2$$
    $$= 2(2^{k+1} - 1)$$

11. S_n: $1^3 + 2^3 + 3^3 + \ldots + n^3 = \dfrac{n^2(n + 1)^2}{4}$

    S_1: $1^3 = \dfrac{1^2(1 + 1)^2}{4}$

    S_k: $1^3 + 2^3 + 3^3 + \ldots + k^3 = \dfrac{k^2(k + 1)^2}{4}$

    S_{k+1}: $1^3 + 2^3 + 3^3 + \ldots + k^3 + (k + 1)^3 =$
    $$\dfrac{(k + 1)^2(k + 2)^2}{4}$$

    1) <u>Basis step</u>: Since $\dfrac{1^2(1 + 1)^2}{4} = \dfrac{1 \cdot 2^2}{4} = \dfrac{1 \cdot 4}{4} = 1 = 1^3$, S_1 is true.

    2) <u>Induction step</u>: Let k be any natural number. Assume S_k. Deduce S_{k+1}. Add $(k + 1)^3$ on both sides of S_k. Then simplify the right side.

$1^3 + 2^2 + 3^3 + \ldots + k^3 + (k + 1)^3$

$= \dfrac{k^2(k + 1)^2}{4} + (k + 1)^3$

$= \dfrac{k^2(k + 1)^2 + 4(k + 1)^3}{4}$

$= \dfrac{(k + 1)^2[k^2 + 4(k + 1)]}{4}$

$= \dfrac{(k + 1)^2(k^2 + 4k + 4)}{4}$

$= \dfrac{(k + 1)^2(k + 2)^2}{4}$

12. S_n: $\dfrac{1}{1 \cdot 2 \cdot 3} + \dfrac{1}{2 \cdot 3 \cdot 4} + \dfrac{1}{3 \cdot 4 \cdot 5} + \cdots + \dfrac{1}{n(n + 1)(n + 2)}$

$= \dfrac{n(n + 3)}{4(n + 1)(n + 2)}$

S_1: $\dfrac{1}{1 \cdot 2 \cdot 3} = \dfrac{1(1 + 3)}{4 \cdot 2 \cdot 3}$

S_k: $\dfrac{1}{1 \cdot 2 \cdot 3} + \dfrac{1}{2 \cdot 3 \cdot 4} + \cdots + \dfrac{1}{k(k + 1)(k + 2)}$

$= \dfrac{k(k + 3)}{4(k + 1)(k + 2)}$

S_{k+1}: $\dfrac{1}{1 \cdot 2 \cdot 3} + \dfrac{1}{2 \cdot 3 \cdot 4} + \cdots + \dfrac{1}{k(k + 1)(k + 2)} +$

$\dfrac{1}{(k + 1)(k + 2)(k + 3)}$

$= \dfrac{(k + 1)(k + 1 + 3)}{4(k + 1 + 1)(k + 1 + 2)} = \dfrac{(k + 1)(k + 4)}{4(k + 2)(k + 3)}$

1)   <u>Basis step</u>:   Since $\dfrac{1}{1 \cdot 2 \cdot 3} = \dfrac{1}{6}$ and $\dfrac{1(1 + 3)}{4 \cdot 2 \cdot 3} =$

$\dfrac{1 \cdot 4}{4 \cdot 2 \cdot 3} = \dfrac{1}{6}$, S_1 is true.

2)   <u>Induction step</u>:   Let k be any natural number.
Assume S_k.   Deduce S_{k+1}.

Add $\dfrac{1}{(k + 1)(k + 2)(k + 3)}$ on both sides of S_k
and simplify the right side.

Only the right side is shown here.

$\dfrac{k(k + 3)}{4(k + 1)(k + 2)} + \dfrac{1}{(k + 1)(k + 2)(k + 3)}$

$= \dfrac{k(k + 3)(k + 3) + 4}{4(k + 1)(k + 2)(k + 3)}$

$= \dfrac{k^3 + 6k^2 + 9k + 4}{4(k + 1)(k + 2)(k + 3)}$

$= \dfrac{(k + 1)^2(k + 4)}{4(k + 1)(k + 2)(k + 3)}$

$= \dfrac{(k + 1)(k + 4)}{4(k + 2)(k + 3)}$

13. S_n: $n < n + 1$

S_1: $1 < 1 + 1$

S_k: $k < k + 1$

S_{k+1}: $k + 1 < k + 2$

1)   <u>Basis step</u>:   Since $1 + 1 = 2$ and $1 < 2$, S_1 is
true.

2)   <u>Induction step</u>:   Let k be any natural number.
Assume S_k.   Deduce S_{k+1}.

   $k < k + 1$ (S_k)

$k + 1 < k + 1 + 1$ (Adding 1)

$k + 1 < k + 2$

14. S_n: $2 \leqslant 2^n$

S_1: $2 \leqslant 2^1$

S_k: $2 \leqslant 2^k$

S_{k+1}: $2 \leqslant 2^{k+1}$

1)   <u>Basis step</u>:   Since $2 \leqslant 2$, S_1 is true.

2)   <u>Induction step</u>:   Let k be any natural number.
Assume S_k.   Deduce S_{k+1}.

    $2 \leqslant 2^k$ (S_k)

   $2 \cdot 2 \leqslant 2^k \cdot 2$ (Multiplying by 2)

$2 < 2 \cdot 2 \leqslant 2^{k+1}$ $(2 < 2 \cdot 2)$

    $2 \leqslant 2^{k+1}$

15. S_n: $3^n < 3^{n+1}$

S_1: $3^1 < 3^{1+1}$

S_k: $3^k < 3^{k+1}$

S_{k+1}: $3^{k+1} < 3^{k+2}$

1)   <u>Basis step</u>:   Since $1 + 1 = 2$ and $3^1 < 3^2$,
S_1 is true.

2)   <u>Induction step</u>:   Let k be any natural number.
Assume S_k.   Deduce S_{k+1}.

   $3^k < 3^{k+1}$ (S_k)

$3^k \cdot 3 < 3^{k+1} \cdot 3$ (Multiplying by 3)

$3^{k+1} < 3^{k+1+1}$

$3^{k+1} < 3^{k+2}$

16. S_n: $2n \leqslant 2^n$

S_1: $2 \cdot 1 \leqslant 2^1$

S_k: $2k \leqslant 2^k$

S_{k+1}: $2(k + 1) \leqslant 2^{k+1}$

1)   <u>Basis step</u>:   Since $2 = 2$, S_1 is true.

2)   <u>Induction step</u>:   Let k be any natural number.
Assume S_k.   Deduce S_{k+1}.

   $2k \leqslant 2^k$ (S_k)

$2 \cdot 2k \leqslant 2 \cdot 2^k$ (Multiplying by 2)

   $4k \leqslant 2^{k+1}$

Since $1 \leqslant k$, $k + 1 \leqslant k + k$, or $k + 1 \leqslant 2k$.
Then $2(k + 1) \leqslant 4k$.

Thus $2(k + 1) \leqslant 4k \leqslant 2^{k+1}$, so $2(k + 1) \leqslant 2^{k+1}$.

17. See the answer section in the text.

18. S_n: $a_1 + (a_1 + d) + \ldots + [a_1 + (n - 1)d] =$

$$\frac{n}{2}[2a_1 + (n - 1)d]$$

S_1: $a_1 = \frac{1}{2}[2a_1 + (1 - 1)d]$

S_k: $a_1 + (a_1 + d) + \ldots + [a_1 + (k - 1)d] =$

$$\frac{k}{2}[2a_1 + (k - 1)d]$$

S_{k+1}: $a_1 + (a_1 + d) + \ldots + [a_1 + (k - 1)d] +$

$$[a_1 + kd] = \frac{k + 1}{2}[2a_1 + kd]$$

1) Basis step: Since $\frac{1}{2}\big[2a_1 + (1 - 1)d\big] =$
$\frac{1}{2} \cdot 2a_1 = a_1$, S_1 is true.

2) Induction step: Let k be any natural number. Assume S_k. Deduce S_{k+1}. Starting with the left side of S_{k+1}, we have

$$\underbrace{a_1 + (a_1 + d) + \ldots + [a_1+(k-1)d]}_{} + [a_1 + kd]$$

$$= \quad \frac{k}{2}[2a_1 + (k - 1)d] \quad + [a_1 + kd]$$
$$\text{(By } S_k\text{)}$$

$$= \frac{k[2a_1 + (k - 1)d]}{2} + \frac{2[a_1 + kd]}{2}$$

$$= \frac{2ka_1 + k(k - 1)d + 2a_1 + 2kd}{2}$$

$$= \frac{2a_1(k + 1) + k(k - 1)d + 2kd}{2}$$

$$= \frac{2a_1(k + 1) + (k - 1 + 2)kd}{2}$$

$$= \frac{2a_1(k + 1) + (k + 1)kd}{2}$$

$$= \frac{k + 1}{2}[2a_1 + kd]$$

19. See the answer section in the text.

20. S_n: $\cos n\pi = (-1)^n$

S_1: $\cos \pi = (-1)^1$

S_k: $\cos k\pi = (-1)^k$

S_{k+1}: $\cos[(k + 1)\pi] = (-1)^{k+1}$

1) Basis step: Since $\cos \pi = -1 = (-1)^1$, S_1 is true.

2) Induction step: Let k be any natural number. Assume S_k. Deduce S_{k+1}. Starting with the left side of S_{k+1}, we have
$$\cos[(k + 1)\pi] = \cos(k\pi + \pi)$$
$$= \cos k\pi \cos \pi - \sin k\pi \sin \pi$$
$$= [\cos k\pi](-1) - [\sin k\pi]\cdot 0$$
$$= (-1)\cos k\pi$$
$$= (-1)(-1)^k \qquad \text{(By } S_k\text{)}$$
$$= (-1)^{k+1}$$

21. See the answer section in the text.

22. S_n: $|\sin(nx)| \leqslant n|\sin x|$

S_1: $|\sin x| \leqslant |\sin x|$

S_k: $|\sin(kx)| \leqslant k|\sin x|$

S_{k+1}: $|\sin(k + 1)x| \leqslant (k + 1)|\sin x|$

1) Basis step: Since $|\sin x| = |\sin x|$, S_1 is true.

2) Induction step: Let k be any natural number. Assume S_k. Deduce S_{k+1}. Starting with the left side of S_{k+1}, we have

$\qquad |\sin(k + 1)x|$

$= |\sin(kx + x)|$

$= |\sin kx \cos x + \cos kx \sin x|$

$\leqslant |\sin kx \cos x| + |\cos kx \sin x|$

$= |\sin kx||\cos x| + |\cos kx||\sin x|$

$\leqslant k|\sin x||\cos x| + |\cos kx||\sin x| \qquad \text{(By } S_k\text{)}$

$= |\sin x|(k|\cos x| + |\cos kx|)$

$\leqslant |\sin x|(k + 1)$,

$\qquad$ since $|\cos x| \leqslant 1$

$\qquad$ and $|\cos kx| \leqslant 1$

23. See the answer section in the text.

24. S_2: $\log_a(b_1 b_2) = \log_a b_1 + \log_a b_2$

S_k: $\log_a(b_1 b_2 \ldots b_k) = \log_a b_1 + \log_a b_2 + \ldots +$
$$\log_a b_k$$

S_{k+1}: $\log_a(b_1 b_2 \ldots b_{k+1}) = \log_a b_1 + \log_a b_2 +$
$$\ldots + \log_a b_{k+1}$$

1) Basis step: S_2 is true by the properties of logarithms.

2) Induction step: Let k be a natural number $k \geqslant 2$. Assume S_k. Deduce S_{k+1}.

$\quad \log_a(b_1 b_2 \ldots b_{k+1}) \qquad$ (Left side of S_{k+1})

$= \log_a(b_1 b_2 \ldots b_k) + \log_a b_{k+1} \qquad$ (By S_2)

$= \log_a b_1 + \log_a b_2 + \ldots + \log_a b_k + \log_a b_{k+1}$

25. See the answer section in the text.

26. S_1 = $\overline{z^1}$ = $\overline{z}^1$

S_k = $\overline{z^k}$ = $\overline{z}^k$

$\overline{z^k} \cdot \overline{z}$ = $\overline{z}^k \cdot \overline{z}$ (Multiplying both sides of S_k by $\overline{z}$)

$\overline{z^k} \cdot \overline{z}$ = $\overline{z}^{k+1}$

$\overline{z^{k+1}}$ = $\overline{z}^{k+1}$

27. See the answer section in the text.

28. S_2: $\overline{z_1 z_2}$ = $\overline{z_1} \cdot \overline{z_2}$

S_k: $\overline{z_1 z_2 \ldots z_k}$ = $\overline{z_1}\,\overline{z_2}\ldots\overline{z_k}$

Starting with the left side of S_{k+1}, we have

$\overline{z_1 z_2 \ldots z_k z_{k+1}}$ = $\overline{z_1 z_2 \ldots z_k} \cdot \overline{z_{k+1}}$ (By S_2)

$= \overline{z_1}\,\overline{z_2}\ldots\overline{z_k} \cdot \overline{z_{k+1}}$ (By S_k)

29. See the answer section in the text.

30. S_1: 3 is a factor of $1^3 + 2 \cdot 1$

S_k: 3 is a factor of $k^3 + 2k$, i.e. $k^3 + 2k = 3 \cdot m$

S_{k+1}: 3 is a factor of $(k + 1)^3 + 2(k + 1)$

Consider:

$(k + 1)^3 + 2(k + 1)$

$= k^3 + 3k^2 + 5k + 3$

$= (k^3 + 2k) + 3k^2 + 3k + 3$

$= 3m + 3(k^2 + k + 1)$ (A multiple of 3)

31. See the answer section in the text.

32. S_1: 5 is a factor of $1^5 - 1$.

S_k: 5 is a factor of $k^5 - k$, i.e., $k^5 - k = 5 \cdot m$

S_{k+1}: 5 is a factor of $(k + 1)^5 - (k + 1)$.

Consider:

$(k + 1)^5 - (k + 1)$

$= (k^5 + 5k^4 + 10k^3 + 10k^2 + 5k + 1) - (k + 1)$

$= (k^5 - k) + 5(k^4 + 2k^3 + 2k^2 + k)$

$= 5 \cdot m + 5(k^4 + 2k^3 + 2k^2 + k)$ (A multiple of 5)

33. See the answer section in the text.

34. S_n: $\dfrac{1}{\sqrt{1}} + \dfrac{1}{\sqrt{2}} + \dfrac{1}{\sqrt{3}} + \cdots + \dfrac{1}{\sqrt{n}} > \sqrt{n}$

S_2: $\dfrac{1}{\sqrt{1}} + \dfrac{1}{\sqrt{2}} > \sqrt{2}$

S_k: $\dfrac{1}{\sqrt{1}} + \dfrac{1}{\sqrt{2}} + \dfrac{1}{\sqrt{3}} + \cdots + \dfrac{1}{\sqrt{k}} > \sqrt{k}$

S_{k+1}: $\dfrac{1}{\sqrt{1}} + \dfrac{1}{\sqrt{2}} + \dfrac{1}{\sqrt{3}} + \cdots + \dfrac{1}{\sqrt{k}} + \dfrac{1}{\sqrt{k + 1}}$

$> \sqrt{k + 1}$

1) Basis Step: $\dfrac{1}{\sqrt{1}} + \dfrac{1}{\sqrt{2}} = 1 + \dfrac{1}{\sqrt{2}}$

$= \dfrac{\sqrt{2} + 1}{\sqrt{2}} > \dfrac{2}{\sqrt{2}} = \sqrt{2}$

(Since $\sqrt{2} > 1$)

2) Induction Step: Let k be a natural number, $k \geqslant 2$. Assume S_k. Deduce S_{k+1}.

$\dfrac{1}{\sqrt{1}} + \dfrac{1}{\sqrt{2}} + \dfrac{1}{\sqrt{3}} + \cdots + \dfrac{1}{\sqrt{k}} > \sqrt{k}$, (by S_k).

Therefore, adding $\dfrac{1}{\sqrt{k + 1}}$,

$\dfrac{1}{\sqrt{1}} + \dfrac{1}{\sqrt{2}} + \dfrac{1}{\sqrt{3}} + \cdots + \dfrac{1}{\sqrt{k}} + \dfrac{1}{\sqrt{k + 1}} >$

$\sqrt{k} + \dfrac{1}{\sqrt{k + 1}}$

Then

$\sqrt{k} + \dfrac{1}{\sqrt{k + 1}} = \dfrac{\sqrt{k} \cdot \sqrt{k + 1} + 1}{\sqrt{k + 1}} > \dfrac{k + 1}{\sqrt{k + 1}}$

$= \sqrt{k + 1}.$

35. See the answer section in the text.

36. S_n: $n = n + 1$

S_1: $1 = 1 + 1$

S_k: $k = k + 1$

S_{k+1}: $k + 1 = (k + 1) + 1$

a) Basis step: $1 = 1 + 1$ cannot be proved.

b) Induction step: Let k be any natural number. Assume S_k. Deduce S_{k+1}.

$k = k + 1$ (S_k)

$k + 1 = (k + 1) + 1$ (Adding 1)

The induction step can be proved.

c) The statement is not true.

37. See the answer section in the text.

38. a) Figure (2):

Number of sides: 12

Perimeter: $12\left[\dfrac{a}{3}\right] = 4a$

Area: $\dfrac{a^2}{4}\sqrt{3} + 3\left[\dfrac{1}{2}\left[\dfrac{a}{3}\right]\left[\dfrac{a}{6}\sqrt{3}\right]\right] = \dfrac{a^2}{3}\sqrt{3} = $

$A_1\left[1 + \dfrac{1}{3}\right]$, where A_1 is the area of Figure (1)

Figure (3):

Number of sides: 48

Perimeter: $48\left[\dfrac{a}{9}\right] = \dfrac{16a}{3}$

Area: $\frac{a^2}{3}\sqrt{3} + 12\left[\frac{1}{2}\left(\frac{a}{9}\right)\left(\frac{a}{18}\sqrt{3}\right)\right] = \frac{10a^2}{27}\sqrt{3} =$

$A_1\left[1 + \frac{1}{3} + \frac{1}{3}\cdot\frac{4}{9}\right]$, where A_1 is the area

of Figure (1)

Figure (4):

Number of sides: 192

Perimeter: $192\left(\frac{a}{27}\right) = \frac{64a}{9}$

Area: $\frac{10a^2}{27}\sqrt{3} + 48\left[\frac{1}{2}\left(\frac{a}{27}\right)\left(\frac{a}{54}\sqrt{3}\right)\right] =$

$\frac{94a^2}{243}\sqrt{3} = A_1\left[1 + \frac{1}{3} + \frac{1}{3}\cdot\frac{4}{9} + \frac{1}{3}\left(\frac{4}{9}\right)^2\right]$,

where A_1 is the area of Figure (1)

b) Let N_n represent the number of sides of the nth figure.

Conjecture: $N_n = 3(4^{n-1})$

S_1: $N_1 = 3(4^{1-1}) = 3$

S_k: $N_k = 3(4^{k-1})$

S_{k+1}: $N_{k+1} = 3(4^k)$

1) Basis step: S_1 is true by part (a).

2) Induction step: Let k be any natural number. Assume S_k. Deduce S_{k+1}.

$N_k = 3(4^{k-1})$

Adding another equilateral triangle to each side creates 4 sides where each side originally was. Then $N_{k+1} = 3(4^{k-1})(4) = 3(4^k)$.

c) Let P_n represent the perimeter of the nth figure.

Conjecture: $P_n = 3a\left(\frac{4}{3}\right)^{n-1}$ $\left[$or $\frac{4^{n-1}a}{3^{n-2}}\right]$

S_1: $P_1 = 3a\left(\frac{4}{3}\right)^{1-1} = 3a$

S_k: $P_k = 3a\left(\frac{4}{3}\right)^{k-1}$

S_{k+1}: $P_{k+1} = 3a\left(\frac{4}{3}\right)^k$

1) Basis step: S_1 is true by part (a).

2) Induction step: Let k be any natural number. Assume S_k. Deduce S_{k+1}.

$P_k = 3a\left(\frac{4}{3}\right)^{k-1}$

Adding another equilateral triangle to each side increases the length of each side by $\frac{1}{3}$, so the new length is $\frac{4}{3}$ of the former length. Then

$P_{k+1} = 3a\left(\frac{4}{3}\right)^{k-1}\left(\frac{4}{3}\right) = 3a\left(\frac{4}{3}\right)^k$.

d) Since Figure (2) has 12 sides, we observe that in going from Figure (2) to Figure (3) we gain 12 additional triangles of side $\frac{a}{3^2}$.

Hence, the additional area is $12\cdot\frac{\left(\frac{a}{9}\right)^2}{4}\sqrt{3}$, or $\frac{1}{3}r\cdot A_1$, where $r = \frac{4}{9}$. In going from Figure (3) to Figure (4) we gain

$48\cdot\frac{\left(\frac{a}{27}\right)^2}{4}\sqrt{3}$, or $\frac{1}{3}r^2\cdot A_1$, and so on.

Let A_n represent the area of the nth figure. Recall that N_n represents the number of sides of the nth figure.

Conjecture:

$A_n = A_1\left[1 + \left[\frac{1}{3} + \frac{1}{3}r + \cdots + \frac{1}{3}r^{n-2}\right]\right]$

$A_n = A_1\left[1 + \left[\frac{1}{3}\cdot\frac{1-r^{n-1}}{1-r}\right]\right]$

$A_n = \frac{a^2\sqrt{3}}{20}(8 - 3r^{n-1})$, $n \geq 1$

S_1: $A_1 = \frac{a^2\sqrt{3}}{20}(8 - 3\cdot1) = \frac{a^2\sqrt{3}}{4}$

S_k: $A_k = \frac{a^2\sqrt{3}}{20}(8 - 3r^{k-1})$, or

$\frac{1}{5}A_1(8 - 3r^{k-1})$

S_{k+1}: $A_{k+1} = \frac{a^2\sqrt{3}}{20}(8 - 3r^k)$

1) Basis step: S_1 is true by part (a).

2) Induction step: Let k be any natural number. Assume S_k. Deduce S_{k+1}.

Adding another equilateral triangle to each side of the kth figure adds the area of N_k equilateral triangles with side of length $\frac{a}{3^k}$. Thus

$A_{k+1} = A_k + N_k\cdot\frac{\left(\frac{a}{3^k}\right)^2}{4}\sqrt{3}$

$= \frac{1}{5}A_1(8 - 3r^{k-1}) + N_k\cdot\frac{1}{9^k}\cdot A_1$

$= A_1\left[\frac{8}{5} - \frac{3}{5}r^{k-1} + 3\cdot4^{k-1}\cdot\frac{1}{9^k}\right]$

$= A_1\left[\frac{8}{5} - \frac{3}{5}r^{k-1} + \frac{3}{4}r^k\right]$

$= \frac{a^2\sqrt{3}}{20}(8 - 3r^k)$

e) $\lim_{n\to\infty} A_n = \frac{a^2\sqrt{3}}{20}\cdot8 = \frac{2}{5}a^2\sqrt{3}$, or $0.4\,a^2\sqrt{3}$

Exercise Set 11.5

1. $_4P_3 = 4\cdot3\cdot2 = 24$ (Theorem 8, Formula 1)

2. $_7P_5 = 7\cdot6\cdot5\cdot4\cdot3 = 2520$

3. $_{10}P_7 = 10 \cdot 9 \cdot 8 \cdot 7 \cdot 6 \cdot 5 \cdot 4 = 604{,}800$ (Theorem 8, Formula 1)

4. $_{10}P_3 = 10 \cdot 9 \cdot 8 = 720$

5. Without repetition: $_5P_5 = 5 \cdot 4 \cdot 3 \cdot 2 \cdot 1 = 120$ (Theorem 7)

With repetition: $5^5 = 3125$ (Theorem 10)

6. a) $_4P_4 = 24$

b) $4^4 = 256$

7. $_5P_5 = 5 \cdot 4 \cdot 3 \cdot 2 \cdot 1 = 120$ (Theorem 7)

8. $_7P_7 = 7! = 5040$

9. DIGIT

There are 2 I's, 1 D, 1 G, and 1 T for a total of 5.

$P = \dfrac{5!}{2! \cdot 1! \cdot 1! \cdot 1!}$ (Theorem 9)

$= \dfrac{5!}{2!} = \dfrac{5 \cdot 4 \cdot 3 \cdot 2!}{2!} = 5 \cdot 4 \cdot 3 = 60$

10. $\dfrac{6!}{2!} = 360$

11. There are only 9 choices for the first digit since 0 is excluded. There are also 9 choices for the second digit since 0 can be included and the first digit cannot be repeated. Because no digit is used more than once there are only 8 choices for the third digit, 7 for the fourth, 6 for the fifth, 5 for the sixth and 4 for the seventh. By the Fundamental Counting Principle the total number of permutations is

$9 \cdot 9 \cdot 8 \cdot 7 \cdot 6 \cdot 5 \cdot 4$, or 544,320.

Thus 544,320 7-digit phone numbers can be formed.

12. $_5P_5 \cdot {_4P_4} = 2880$

13. $a^2 b^3 c^4 = a \cdot a \cdot b \cdot b \cdot b \cdot c \cdot c \cdot c \cdot c$

There are 2 a's, 3 b's, and 4 c's, for a total of 9.

Thus $P = \dfrac{9!}{2! \cdot 3! \cdot 4!}$ (Theorem 9)

$= \dfrac{9 \cdot 8 \cdot 7 \cdot 6 \cdot 5 \cdot 4!}{2 \cdot 1 \cdot 3 \cdot 2 \cdot 1 \cdot 4!} = \dfrac{9 \cdot 8 \cdot 7 \cdot 6 \cdot 5}{2 \cdot 3 \cdot 2} = 1260$

14. $\dfrac{6!}{3! 2!} = 60$

15. a) $_5P_5 = 5!$ (Theorem 7)

$= 5 \cdot 4 \cdot 3 \cdot 2 \cdot 1 = 120$

b) There are 5 choices for the first coin and 2 possibilities (head or tail) for each choice. This results in a total of 10 choices for the first selection.

There are 4 choices (no coin can be used more than once) for the second coin and 2 possibilities (head or tail) for each choice. This results in a total of 8 choices for the second selection.

There are 3 choices for the third coin and 2 possibilities (head or tail) for each choice. This results in a total of 6 choices for the third selection.

Likewise there are 4 choices for the fourth selection and 2 choices for the fifth selection.

Using the Fundamental Counting Principle we know there are

$10 \cdot 8 \cdot 6 \cdot 4 \cdot 2$, or 3840

ways the coins can be lined up.

16. a) $4 \cdot 3 \cdot 2 \cdot 1 = 24$

b) $(4!) \cdot 2^4 = 384$

17. $_{52}P_4 = 52 \cdot 51 \cdot 50 \cdot 49$ (Theorem 8, Formula 1)

$= 6{,}497{,}400$

18. $_{50}P_5 = \dfrac{50!}{45!} = 50 \cdot 49 \cdot 48 \cdot 47 \cdot 46 = 254{,}251{,}200$

19. $P = \dfrac{24!}{3! \cdot 5! \cdot 9! \cdot 4! \cdot 3!}$ (Theorem 9)

$= \dfrac{24 \cdot 23 \cdot 22 \cdot 21 \cdot 20 \cdot 19 \cdot 18 \cdot 17 \cdot 16 \cdot 15 \cdot 14 \cdot 13 \cdot 12 \cdot 11 \cdot 10 \cdot 9!}{3 \cdot 2 \cdot 1 \cdot 5 \cdot 4 \cdot 3 \cdot 2 \cdot 1 \cdot 4 \cdot 3 \cdot 2 \cdot 1 \cdot 3 \cdot 2 \cdot 1 \cdot 9!}$

$= 23 \cdot 11 \cdot 7 \cdot 19 \cdot 17 \cdot 8 \cdot 15 \cdot 14 \cdot 13 \cdot 12 \cdot 11 \cdot 10$ (Simplifying)

$= 16{,}491{,}024{,}950{,}400$

20. $\dfrac{20!}{2! \ 5! \ 8! \ 3! \ 2!} = 20{,}951{,}330{,}400$

21. MATH:

$_4P_4 = 4 \cdot 3 \cdot 2 \cdot 1 = 24$ (Theorem 7)

BUSINESS: 1 B, 1 U, 3 S's, 1 I, 1 N, 1 E, a total of 8.

$P = \dfrac{8!}{1! \cdot 1! \cdot 3! \cdot 1! \cdot 1! \cdot 1!}$ (Theorem 9)

$= \dfrac{8!}{3!} = \dfrac{8 \cdot 7 \cdot 6 \cdot 5 \cdot 4 \cdot 3!}{3!} = 8 \cdot 7 \cdot 6 \cdot 5 \cdot 4 = 6720$

PHILOSOPHICAL: 2 P's, 2 H's, 2 I's, 2 L's, 2 O's, 1 S, 1 C, and 1 A, a total of 13.

$P = \dfrac{13!}{2! \cdot 2! \cdot 2! \cdot 2! \cdot 2! \cdot 1! \cdot 1! \cdot 1!}$ (Theorem 9)

$= \dfrac{13 \cdot 12 \cdot 11 \cdot 10 \cdot 9 \cdot 8 \cdot 7 \cdot 6 \cdot 5 \cdot 4 \cdot 3 \cdot 2 \cdot 1}{2 \cdot 1 \cdot 2 \cdot 1 \cdot 2 \cdot 1 \cdot 2 \cdot 1 \cdot 2 \cdot 1 \cdot 1 \cdot 1 \cdot 1}$

$= 13 \cdot 12 \cdot 11 \cdot 5 \cdot 9 \cdot 4 \cdot 7 \cdot 3 \cdot 5 \cdot 2 \cdot 3$ (Simplifying)

$= 194{,}594{,}400$

22. a) $6! = 720$

    b) $\dfrac{7!}{2!} = 2520$

    c) $\dfrac{11!}{2!\,2!\,2!} = 4{,}989{,}600$

23. There are 80 choices for the number of the county, 26 choices for the letter of the alphabet, and 9999 choices for the number that follows the letter. By the Fundamental Counting Principle we know there are $80 \cdot 26 \cdot 9999$, or 20,797,920 possible license plates.

24. a) $_5P_4 = 120$

    b) $5 \cdot 5 \cdot 5 \cdot 5 = 625$

    c) $1 \cdot {}_4P_3 = 24$

    d) $_3P_2 \cdot 1 = 6$

25. a) We want to find the number of permutations of 10 objects taken 5 at a time with repetition. This is 10^5, or 100,000.

    b) Since there are 100,000 possible zip-codes, there could be 100,000 post offices.

26. a) 10^9, or 1,000,000,000

    b) Yes

27. a) We want to find the number of permutations of 10 objects taken 9 at a time with repetition. This is 10^9, or 1,000,000,000.

    b) Since there are more than 257 million social security numbers, each person can have one.

28. There are 31,557,600 seconds in a year (using 1 yr = 365.25 days).

There are $_{15}P_{15} = 15!$ arrangements.

The time is $\dfrac{15!}{31{,}557{,}600} \approx 41{,}437.7$ yr

29.
$$_nP_5 = 7 \cdot {}_nP_4$$
$$\frac{n!}{(n-5)!} = 7 \cdot \frac{n!}{(n-4)!} \qquad \text{(Theorem 8)}$$
$$\frac{n!}{7(n-5)!} = \frac{n!}{(n-4)!} \qquad \left[\text{Multiplying by } \tfrac{1}{7}\right]$$
$$7(n-5)! = (n-4)! \qquad \begin{array}{l}\text{(The denominators}\\ \text{must be the same.)}\end{array}$$
$$7(n-5)! = (n-4)(n-5)!$$
$$7 = n-4 \qquad \left[\text{Multiplying by } \tfrac{1}{(n-5)!}\right]$$
$$11 = n$$

30.
$$\frac{n!}{(n-4)!} = 8 \cdot \frac{(n-1)!}{(n-4)!}$$
$$n! = 8(n-1)!$$
$$n = 8$$

31.
$$_nP_5 = 9 \cdot {}_{n-1}P_4$$
$$\frac{n!}{(n-5)!} = 9 \cdot \frac{(n-1)!}{(n-5)!} \qquad \text{(Theorem 8)}$$
$$n! = 9(n-1)! \qquad \text{[Multiplying by } (n-5)!]$$
$$\frac{n!}{(n-1)!} = 9 \qquad \left[\text{Multiplying by } \tfrac{1}{(n-1)!}\right]$$
$$\frac{n(n-1)!}{(n-1)!} = 9$$
$$n = 9$$

32.
$$\frac{n!}{(n-4)!} = 8 \cdot \frac{n!}{(n-3)!}$$
$$\frac{1}{(n-4)!} = 8 \cdot \frac{1}{(n-3)!}$$
$$1 = 8 \cdot \frac{1}{n-3}$$
$$n = 11$$

33. There is one losing team per game. In order to leave one tournament winner there must be $n-1$ losers produced in $n-1$ games.

34. 2 losses for each of $(n-1)$ losing teams means $2n-2$ losses. The tournament winner will have lost <u>at most</u> 1 game; thus at most there are $(2n-2)+1$ or $(2n-1)$ losses requiring $2n-1$ games.

Exercise Set 11.6

1. $_{13}C_2 = \dfrac{13 \cdot 12}{2 \cdot 1} = 78$

The 13 tells where to start.

The 2 tells how many factors there are in both numerator and denominator and where to start the denominator.

We used formula (2) from Theorem 11.

2. $_9C_6 = \dfrac{9!}{6!\,3!} = 84$

3. $\dbinom{13}{11} = \dfrac{13!}{11!(13-11)!} = \dfrac{13!}{11!\,2!} = \dfrac{13 \cdot 12 \cdot 11!}{11!\,2!} = \dfrac{13 \cdot 12}{2 \cdot 1} = 78$

We used formula (1) from Theorem 11. Using Theorem 12 we could also have observed that $\dbinom{13}{11} = \dbinom{13}{2}$, giving us 78 as in Exercise 1.

4. $\dbinom{9}{3} = \dbinom{9}{6} = 84$ (See Exercise 2.)

5. $\dbinom{7}{1} = \dfrac{7}{1} = 7$ Formula (2)

6. $\dbinom{8}{8} = \dfrac{8!}{0!\,8!} = 1$

7. $\dfrac{_5P_3}{3!} = {_5}C_3 = \dfrac{5 \cdot 4 \cdot 3}{3 \cdot 2 \cdot 1} = 10$ Formula (2)

8. $\dfrac{_{10}P_5}{5!} = {_{10}}C_5 = \dfrac{10!}{5!5!} = 252$

9. $\dbinom{6}{0} = \dfrac{6!}{0!(6-0)!} = \dfrac{6!}{1 \cdot 6!} = 1$ Formula (1)

10. $\dbinom{6}{1} = \dfrac{6}{1} = 6$

11. $\dbinom{6}{2} = \dfrac{6 \cdot 5}{2 \cdot 1} = 15$ Formula (2)

12. $\dbinom{6}{3} = \dfrac{6!}{3!3!} = 20$

13. ${_{12}}C_{11} = {_{12}}C_1$ Theorem 12

    $= \dfrac{12}{1}$ Formula (2)

    $= 12$

14. ${_{12}}C_{10} = \dfrac{12!}{2!10!} = 66$

15. ${_{12}}C_9 = {_{12}}C_3$ Theorem 12

    $= \dfrac{12 \cdot 11 \cdot 10}{3 \cdot 2 \cdot 1}$ Formula (2)

    $= 220$

16. ${_{12}}C_8 = \dfrac{12!}{4!8!} = 495$

17. $\dbinom{m}{2} = \dfrac{m(m-1)}{2 \cdot 1}$ Formula (2)

    $= \dfrac{m(m-1)}{2}$, or $\dfrac{m^2 - m}{2}$

    Also $\dbinom{m}{2} = \dfrac{m!}{2!(m-2)!}$.   Formula (1)

    This is equivalent to the result using Formula (2).

18. $\dbinom{t}{4} = \dfrac{t!}{4!(t-4)!} = \dfrac{t(t-1)(t-2)(t-3)}{24}$

19. $\dbinom{p}{3} = \dfrac{p(p-1)(p-2)}{3 \cdot 2 \cdot 1}$ Formula (2)

    $= \dfrac{p(p-1)(p-2)}{6}$, or $\dfrac{p^3 - 3p^2 + 2p}{6}$

    Also $\dbinom{p}{3} = \dfrac{p!}{3!(p-3)!}$.   Formula (1)

    This is equivalent to the result using Formula (2).

20. $\dbinom{m}{m} = \dfrac{m!}{0!m!} = 1$

21. By Theorem 12, $\dbinom{n}{r} = \dbinom{n}{n-r}$, so

    $\dbinom{7}{0} + \dbinom{7}{1} + \dbinom{7}{2} + \dbinom{7}{3} + \dbinom{7}{4} + \dbinom{7}{5} + \dbinom{7}{6} + \dbinom{7}{7}$

    $= 2\left[\dbinom{7}{0} + \dbinom{7}{1} + \dbinom{7}{2} + \dbinom{7}{3}\right]$

    $= 2\left[\dfrac{7!}{7!0!} + \dfrac{7!}{6!1!} + \dfrac{7!}{5!2!} + \dfrac{7!}{4!3!}\right]$

    $= 2(1 + 7 + 21 + 35) = 2 \cdot 64 = 128$

22. $\dbinom{6}{0} + \dbinom{6}{1} + \dbinom{6}{2} + \dbinom{6}{3} + \dbinom{6}{4} + \dbinom{6}{5} + \dbinom{6}{6}$

    $= 2\left[\dbinom{6}{0} + \dbinom{6}{1} + \dbinom{6}{2}\right] + \dbinom{6}{3}$

    $= 2(1 + 6 + 15) + 20 = 64$

23. ${_{23}}C_4 = \dbinom{23}{4} = \dfrac{23!}{4!(23-4)!}$ (Theorem 11)

    $= \dfrac{23!}{4! \cdot 19!} = \dfrac{23 \cdot 22 \cdot 21 \cdot 20 \cdot 19!}{4! \cdot 19!}$

    $= \dfrac{23 \cdot 22 \cdot 21 \cdot 20}{4 \cdot 3 \cdot 2 \cdot 1} = 8855$

24. a) ${_9}C_2 = 36$

    b) $2 \cdot {_9}C_2 = 72$

25. ${_{10}}C_6 = \dbinom{10}{6} = \dfrac{10!}{6(10-6)!}$ (Theorem 11)

    $= \dfrac{10!}{6! \cdot 4!} = \dfrac{10 \cdot 9 \cdot 8 \cdot 7 \cdot 6!}{6! \cdot 4!}$

    $= \dfrac{10 \cdot 9 \cdot 8 \cdot 7}{4 \cdot 3 \cdot 2 \cdot 1} = 210$

26. ${_{11}}C_7 = 330$

27. Since two points determine a line and no three of these 8 points are collinear, we need to find out the number of combinations of 8 points taken 2 at a time, ${_8}C_2$.

    $_8C_2 = \dbinom{8}{2} = \dfrac{8!}{2!(8-2)!}$ (Theorem 11)

    $= \dfrac{8 \cdot 7 \cdot 6!}{2 \cdot 1 \cdot 6!}$

    $= \dfrac{8 \cdot 7}{2} = 28$

    Thus 28 lines are determined.

    Since three noncollinear points determine a triangle and no four of these 8 points are coplanar, we need to find out the number of combinations of 8 points taken 3 at a time, ${_8}C_3$.

    $_8C_3 = \dbinom{8}{3} = \dfrac{8!}{3!(8-3)!}$ (Theorem 11)

    $= \dfrac{8 \cdot 7 \cdot 6 \cdot 5!}{3 \cdot 2 \cdot 1 \cdot 5!}$

    $= \dfrac{8 \cdot 7 \cdot 6}{3 \cdot 2} = 56$

    Thus 56 triangles are determined.

28. a) $_7C_2 = 21$

b) $_7C_3 = 35$

29. $_{10}C_7 \cdot {}_5C_3 = \binom{10}{7} \cdot \binom{5}{3}$ (Using the Fundamental Counting Principle)

$= \dfrac{10!}{7!(10-7)!} \cdot \dfrac{5!}{3!(5-3)!}$ (Theorem 11)

$= \dfrac{10 \cdot 9 \cdot 8 \cdot 7!}{7! \cdot 3!} \cdot \dfrac{5 \cdot 4 \cdot 3!}{3! \cdot 2!}$

$= \dfrac{10 \cdot 9 \cdot 8}{3 \cdot 2 \cdot 1} \cdot \dfrac{5 \cdot 4}{2 \cdot 1} = 120 \cdot 10 = 1200$

30. $_8C_6 \cdot {}_4C_3 = 28 \cdot 4 = 112$

31. $_{58}C_6 \cdot {}_{42}C_4$ (Using the Fundamental Counting Principle)

$= \binom{58}{6} \cdot \binom{42}{4}$

32. $\binom{63}{8} \cdot \binom{37}{12}$

33. In a 52-card deck there are 4 aces and 48 cards that are not aces.

$_4C_3 \cdot {}_{48}C_2 = \binom{4}{3}\binom{48}{2}$ (Using the Fundamental Counting Principle)

$= \dfrac{4!}{3!(4-3)!} \cdot \dfrac{48!}{2!(48-2)!}$ (Theorem 11)

$= \dfrac{4!}{3! \cdot 1!} \cdot \dfrac{48!}{2! \cdot 46!}$

$= \dfrac{4 \cdot 3!}{3! \cdot 1!} \cdot \dfrac{48 \cdot 47 \cdot 46!}{2! \cdot 46!}$

$= \dfrac{4}{1} \cdot \dfrac{48 \cdot 47}{2}$

$= 4512$

34. $_4C_2 \cdot {}_{48}C_3 = 103{,}776$

35. a) If order is considered and repetition is not allowed, the number of possible cones is

$_{33}P_3 = 33 \cdot 32 \cdot 31 = 32{,}736.$

b) If order is considered and repetition is allowed, the number of possibilities is

$33^3 = 35{,}937.$

c) If order is not considered and there is no repetition, the number of possibilities is

$_{33}C_3 = \dfrac{33 \cdot 32 \cdot 31}{3 \cdot 2 \cdot 1} = 5456.$

36. a) $_{31}P_2 = 930$

b) $31^2 = 961$

c) $_{31}C_2 = 465$

37. The number of plain pizzas (pizzas with no toppings) is $\binom{12}{0}$. The number of pizzas with 1 topping is $\binom{12}{1}$. The number of pizzas with 2 toppings is $\binom{12}{2}$, and so on. The number of pizzas with all 12 toppings is $\binom{12}{12}$. The total number of pizzas is $\binom{12}{0} + \binom{12}{1} + \binom{12}{2} + \cdots + \binom{12}{12} = 4096.$

38. $3 \cdot 2 \cdot 4096 = 24{,}576$

39. $_{52}C_5 = \binom{52}{5} = \dfrac{52!}{5!(52-5)!}$ (Theorem 11)

$= \dfrac{52!}{5! \cdot 47!}$

$= \dfrac{52 \cdot 51 \cdot 50 \cdot 49 \cdot 48 \cdot 47!}{5! \cdot 47!}$

$= \dfrac{52 \cdot 51 \cdot 50 \cdot 49 \cdot 48}{5 \cdot 4 \cdot 3 \cdot 2 \cdot 1}$

$= 13 \cdot 17 \cdot 10 \cdot 49 \cdot 24$

$= 2{,}598{,}960$

40. $_{52}C_{13} = 635{,}013{,}559{,}600$

41. $_8C_3 = \binom{8}{3} = \dfrac{8!}{3!(8-3)!} = \dfrac{8!}{3! \cdot 5!}$

$= \dfrac{8 \cdot 7 \cdot 6 \cdot 5!}{3 \cdot 2 \cdot 1 \cdot 5!}$

$= 8 \cdot 7 = 56$

42. $\binom{n}{4} = \dfrac{n(n-1)(n-2)(n-3)}{24}$

43. For each parallelogram 2 lines from each group of parallel lines are needed.

Two lines can be selected from the group of 5 parallel lines in $_5C_2$ ways and the other two lines can be selected from the group of 8 parallel lines in $_8C_2$ ways.

Using the Fundamental Counting Principle, it follows that the number of possible parallelograms is

$_5C_2 \cdot {}_8C_2 = \binom{5}{2}\binom{8}{2}$ (Using the Fundamental Counting Principle)

$= \dfrac{5!}{2!(5-2)!} \cdot \dfrac{8!}{2!(8-2)!}$ (Theorem 11)

$= \dfrac{5 \cdot 4 \cdot 3!}{2 \cdot 1 \cdot 3!} \cdot \dfrac{8 \cdot 7 \cdot 6!}{2 \cdot 1 \cdot 6!}$

$= \dfrac{5 \cdot 4}{2} \cdot \dfrac{8 \cdot 7}{2}$

$= 10 \cdot 28 = 280$

Thus 280 parallelograms can be formed.

44. $\binom{n}{r} = \dfrac{n!}{r!(n-r)!} = \dfrac{n!}{(n-r)!r!}$

$= \dfrac{n!}{(n-r)![n-(n-r)]!}$

$= \binom{n}{n-r}$

<u>45.</u> If each team plays each other team once, we have

$$\binom{8}{2} = \frac{8!}{2!6!} = \frac{8 \cdot 7 \cdot 6!}{2 \cdot 1 \cdot 6!} = 28.$$

If each team plays each other team twice, we have

$$2\binom{8}{2} = 2 \cdot 28 = 56.$$

<u>46.</u> $\binom{n}{2} = \frac{n!}{2!(n-2)!} = \frac{n(n-1)}{2};$

$2\binom{n}{2} = 2\left[\frac{n(n-1)}{2}\right] = n(n-1)$

<u>47.</u>
$$\binom{n+1}{3} = 2 \cdot \binom{n}{2}$$

$$\frac{(n+1)!}{3!(n+1-3)!} = 2 \cdot \frac{n!}{2!(n-2)!}$$

(Theorem 11)

$$\frac{(n+1)(n)(n-1)(n-2)!}{3!(n-2)!} = \frac{n(n-1)(n-2)!}{(n-2)!}$$

$$\frac{(n+1)(n)(n-1)}{6} = n(n-1)$$

$$(n+1)(n)(n-1) = 6n(n-1)$$

$$n + 1 = 6$$

$$n = 5$$

<u>48.</u> $\begin{bmatrix} n \\ n-2 \end{bmatrix} = 6$

$$\frac{n!}{(n-2)! \, 2!} = 6$$

$$\frac{n(n-1)}{2} = 6$$

$$n^2 - n - 12 = 0$$

Hence $n = 4$.

<u>49.</u>
$$\binom{n+2}{4} = 6 \cdot \binom{n}{2}$$

$$\frac{(n+2)!}{4!(n+2-4)!} = 6 \cdot \frac{n!}{2!(n-2)!}$$

(Theorem 11)

$$\frac{(n+2)!}{4!(n-2)!} = 6 \cdot \frac{n!}{2!(n-2)!}$$

$$\frac{(n+2)!}{4!} = 6 \cdot \frac{n!}{2!}$$

$$4! \cdot \frac{(n+2)!}{4!} = 4! \cdot 6 \cdot \frac{n!}{2!}$$

$$(n+2)! = 72 \cdot n!$$

$$(n+2)(n+1)n! = 72 \cdot n!$$

$$(n+2)(n+1) = 72$$

$$n^2 + 3n + 2 = 72$$

$$n^2 + 3n - 70 = 0$$

$$(n+10)(n-7) = 0$$

$n + 10 = 0$ or $n - 7 = 0$

$n = -10$ or $n = 7$

The only solution is 7 since we cannot have a set of -10 objects.

<u>50.</u>
$$\begin{bmatrix} n \\ 3 \end{bmatrix} = 2 \cdot \begin{bmatrix} n-1 \\ 2 \end{bmatrix}$$

$$\frac{n!}{3! \, (n-3)!} = 2 \cdot \frac{(n-1)!}{2! \, (n-3)!}$$

$$\frac{n}{3!} = \frac{2}{2!}$$

$$n = 6$$

<u>51.</u> a) $_5C_2 = 10$

b) $_5C_2 - 5 = 5$

<u>52.</u> a) $_6C_2 = 15$

b) $_6C_2 - 6 = 9$

<u>53.</u> a) $_nC_2 = \frac{n(n-1)}{2}$

b) $_nC_2 - n = \frac{n(n-1)}{2} - \frac{2n}{2} = \frac{n(n-3)}{2},$

where $n = 4, 5, 6, \ldots$

c) See the answer section in the text.

<u>54.</u>
$$\begin{bmatrix} n \\ r-1 \end{bmatrix} + \begin{bmatrix} n \\ r \end{bmatrix}$$

$$= \frac{n!}{(r-1)!(n-r+1)!} \cdot \frac{r}{r} + \frac{n!}{r!(n-r)!} \cdot \frac{(n-r+1)}{(n-r+1)}$$

$$= \frac{n![r + (n-r+1)]}{r! \, (n-r+1)!}$$

$$= \frac{(n+1)!}{r! \, (n-r+1)!}$$

$$= \begin{bmatrix} n+1 \\ r \end{bmatrix}$$

Exercise Set 11.7

<u>1.</u> Pascal Method: Expand $(m + n)^5$.

The expansion of $(m + n)^5$ has $5 + 1$, or 6, terms. The sum of the exponents in each term is 5. The exponents of m start with 5 and decrease to 0. The last term has no factor of m. The first term has no factor of n. The exponents of n start in the second term with 1 and increase to 5. We get the coefficients from the 6th row of Pascal's Triangle.

```
              1
           1     1
        1     2     1
     1     3     3     1
   1    4     6     4    1
1    5    10    10    5    1
```

$(m + n)^5 = 1 \cdot m^5 + 5 \cdot m^4 n^1 + 10 \cdot m^3 \cdot n^2 + 10 \cdot m^2 \cdot n^3 + 5 \cdot m \cdot n^4 + 1 \cdot n^5$

$\quad = m^5 + 5m^4 n + 10m^3 n^2 + 10m^2 n^3 + 5mn^4 + n^5$

<u>2.</u> Use the 5th row of Pascal's triangle.

$a^4 - 4a^3 b + 6a^2 b^2 - 4ab^3 + b^4$

3. Pascal Method: Expand $(x - y)^6$.

The expansion of $(x - y)^6$ has $6 + 1$, or 7 terms. The sum of the exponents in each term is 6. The exponents of x start with 6 and decrease to 0. The last term has no factor of x. The first term has no factor of $-y$. The exponents of $-y$ start in the second term with 1 and increase to 6. We get the coefficients from the 7th row of Pascal's Triangle.

$$
\begin{array}{ccccccccccccc}
 & & & & & & 1 & & & & & & \\
 & & & & & 1 & & 1 & & & & & \\
 & & & & 1 & & 2 & & 1 & & & & \\
 & & & 1 & & 3 & & 3 & & 1 & & & \\
 & & 1 & & 4 & & 6 & & 4 & & 1 & & \\
 & 1 & & 5 & & 10 & & 10 & & 5 & & 1 & \\
1 & & 6 & & 15 & & 20 & & 15 & & 6 & & 1
\end{array}
$$

$(x - y)^6 = 1 \cdot x^6 + 6 \cdot x^5 \cdot (-y) + 15 \cdot x^4 \cdot (-y)^2 +$
$\qquad 20 \cdot x^3 \cdot (-y)^3 + 15 \cdot x^2 \cdot (-y)^4 +$
$\qquad 6 \cdot x \cdot (-y)^5 + 1 \cdot (-y)^6$

$\qquad = x^6 - 6x^5y + 15x^4y^2 - 20x^3y^3 + 15x^2y^4 -$
$\qquad\quad 6xy^5 + y^6$

4. Use the 8th row of Pascal's triangle.
$p^7 + 7p^6q + 21p^5q^2 + 35p^4q^3 + 35p^3q^4 + 21p^2q^5 + 7pq^6 + q^7$

5. Pascal Method: Expand $(x^2 - 3y)^5$.

The expansion of $(x^2 - 3y)^5$ has $5 + 1$, or 6, terms. The sum of the exponents in each term is 5. The exponents of x^2 start with 5 and decrease to 0. The last term has no factor of x^2. The first term has no factor of $-3y$. The exponents of $-3y$ start in the second term with 1 and increase to 5. We get the coefficients from the 6th row of Pascal's Triangle.

$$
\begin{array}{ccccccccccc}
 & & & & & 1 & & & & & \\
 & & & & 1 & & 1 & & & & \\
 & & & 1 & & 2 & & 1 & & & \\
 & & 1 & & 3 & & 3 & & 1 & & \\
 & 1 & & 4 & & 6 & & 4 & & 1 & \\
1 & & 5 & & 10 & & 10 & & 5 & & 1
\end{array}
$$

$(x^2 - 3y)^5 = 1 \cdot (x^2)^5 + 5 \cdot (x^2)^4 \cdot (-3y) +$
$\qquad 10 \cdot (x^2)^3 \cdot (-3y)^2 + 10 \cdot (x^2)^2 \cdot (-3y)^3 +$
$\qquad 5 \cdot (x^2) \cdot (-3y)^4 + 1 \cdot (-3y)^5$

$\qquad = x^{10} - 15x^8y + 90x^6y^2 - 270x^4y^3 +$
$\qquad\quad 405x^2y^4 - 243y^5$

6. Use the 8th row of Pascal's triangle.
$(3c - d)^7 = 1 \cdot (3c)^7 + 7(3c)^6(-d) + 21(3c)^5(-d)^2 +$
$35(3c)^4(-d)^3 + 35(3c)^3(-d)^4 + 21(3c)^2(-d)^5 +$
$7 \cdot 3c(-d)^6 + 1 \cdot (-d)^7 = 2187c^7 - 5103c^6d +$
$5103c^5d^2 - 2835c^4d^3 + 945c^3d^4 - 189c^2d^5 +$
$21cd^6 - d^7$

7. Pascal Method: Expand $(3c - d)^6$.

The sum of the exponents in each term is 6. The exponents of 3c start with 6 and decrease to 0. The last term has no factor of 3c. The first term has no factor of $-d$. The exponents of $-d$ start in the second term with 1 and increase to 6. We get the coefficients from the 7th row of Pascal's Triangle. The expansion has $6 + 1$, or 7 terms.

$$
\begin{array}{ccccccccccccc}
 & & & & & & 1 & & & & & & \\
 & & & & & 1 & & 1 & & & & & \\
 & & & & 1 & & 2 & & 1 & & & & \\
 & & & 1 & & 3 & & 3 & & 1 & & & \\
 & & 1 & & 4 & & 6 & & 4 & & 1 & & \\
 & 1 & & 5 & & 10 & & 10 & & 5 & & 1 & \\
1 & & 6 & & 15 & & 20 & & 15 & & 6 & & 1
\end{array}
$$

$(3c - d)^6 = 1 \cdot (3c)^6 + 6 \cdot (3c)^5 \cdot (-d) +$
$\qquad 15 \cdot (3c)^4 \cdot (-d)^2 + 20 \cdot (3c)^3 \cdot (-d)^3 +$
$\qquad 15 \cdot (3c)^2 \cdot (-d)^4 + 6 \cdot (3c) \cdot (-d)^5 +$
$\qquad 1 \cdot (-d)^6$

$\qquad = 3^6c^6 - 6 \cdot 3^5c^5d + 15 \cdot 3^4c^4d^2 -$
$\qquad\quad 20 \cdot 3^3c^3d^3 + 15 \cdot 3^2c^2d^4 - 6 \cdot 3cd^5 + d^6$

$\qquad = 729c^6 - 1458c^5d + 1215c^4d^2 - 540c^3d^3 +$
$\qquad\quad 135c^2d^4 - 18cd^5 + d^6$

8. Use the 7th row of Pascal's triangle.
$(t^{-2} + 2)^6 = 1 \cdot (t^{-2})^6 + 6(t^{-2})^5(2) + 15(t^{-2})^42^2 +$
$\qquad 20(t^{-2})^32^3 + 15(t^{-2})^22^4 + 6(t^{-2})2^5 +$
$\qquad 1 \cdot 2^6$

$\qquad = t^{-12} + 12t^{-10} + 60t^{-8} + 160t^{-6} +$
$\qquad\quad 240t^{-4} + 192t^{-2} + 64$

9. Pascal Method: Expand $(x - y)^3$.

The expansion of $(x - y)^3$ has $3 + 1$, or 4 terms. The sum of the exponents in each term is 3. The exponents of x start with 3 and decrease to 0. The last term has no factor of x. The first term has no factor of $-y$. The exponents of $-y$ start in the second term with 1 and increase to 3. We get the coefficients from the 4th row of Pascal's Triangle.

$$
\begin{array}{ccccccc}
 & & & 1 & & & \\
 & & 1 & & 1 & & \\
 & 1 & & 2 & & 1 & \\
1 & & 3 & & 3 & & 1
\end{array}
$$

$(x - y)^3 = 1 \cdot x^3 + 3 \cdot x^2 \cdot (-y) + 3 \cdot x \cdot (-y)^2 + 1 \cdot (-y)^3$
$\qquad = x^3 - 3x^2y + 3xy^2 - y^3$

10. Use the 6th row of Pascal's triangle.
$(x - y)^5 = 1 \cdot x^5 + 5x^4(-y) + 10x^3(-y)^2 +$
$\qquad 10x^2(-y)^3 + 5x(-y)^4 + 1 \cdot (-y)^5$
$\qquad = x^5 - 5x^4y + 10x^3y^2 - 10x^2y^3 + 5xy^4 - y^5$

11. Binomial Theorem Method: Expand $\left(\frac{1}{x} + y\right)^7$.

Note that $a = \frac{1}{x}$, $b = y$, and $n = 7$.

$$\left(\frac{1}{x} + y\right)^7 = \binom{7}{0}\left(\frac{1}{x}\right)^7 + \binom{7}{1}\left(\frac{1}{x}\right)^6 y + \binom{7}{2}\left(\frac{1}{x}\right)^5 y^2 +$$
$$\binom{7}{3}\left(\frac{1}{x}\right)^4 y^3 + \binom{7}{4}\left(\frac{1}{x}\right)^3 y^4 + \binom{7}{5}\left(\frac{1}{x}\right)^2 y^5 +$$
$$\binom{7}{6}\left(\frac{1}{x}\right) y^6 + \binom{7}{7} y^7$$

$$= \frac{7!}{7!0!}\left(\frac{1}{x}\right)^7 + \frac{7!}{6!1!}\left(\frac{1}{x}\right)^6 y + \frac{7!}{5!2!}\left(\frac{1}{x}\right)^5 y^2 +$$
$$\frac{7!}{4!3!}\left(\frac{1}{x}\right)^4 y^3 + \frac{7!}{3!4!}\left(\frac{1}{x}\right)^3 y^4 +$$
$$\frac{7!}{2!5!}\left(\frac{1}{x}\right)^2 y^5 + \frac{7!}{1!6!}\left(\frac{1}{x}\right) y^6 + \frac{7!}{0!7!} y^7$$

$$= x^{-7} + 7x^{-6}y + 21x^{-5}y^2 + 35x^{-4}y^3 +$$
$$35x^{-3}y^4 + 21x^{-2}y^5 + 7x^{-1}y^6 + y^7$$

12. Use the binomial theorem.

$$(2s - 3t^2)^3 = \binom{3}{0}(2s)^3 + \binom{3}{1}(2s)^2(-3t^2) +$$
$$\binom{3}{2}(2s)(-3t^2)^2 + \binom{3}{3}(-3t^2)^3$$

$$= 8s^3 - 36s^2t^2 + 54st^4 - 27t^6$$

13. $\left(a - \frac{2}{a}\right)^9$

Let $a = a$, $b = -\frac{2}{a}$, and $n = 9$.

Expand using the Binomial Theorem Method.

$$\left(a - \frac{2}{a}\right)^9 = \binom{9}{0}a^9 + \binom{9}{1}a^8\left(-\frac{2}{a}\right) + \binom{9}{2}a^7\left(-\frac{2}{a}\right)^2 +$$
$$\binom{9}{3}a^6\left(-\frac{2}{a}\right)^3 + \binom{9}{4}a^5\left(-\frac{2}{a}\right)^4 +$$
$$\binom{9}{5}a^4\left(-\frac{2}{a}\right)^5 + \binom{9}{6}a^3\left(-\frac{2}{a}\right)^6 +$$
$$\binom{9}{7}a^2\left(-\frac{2}{a}\right)^7 + \binom{9}{8}a\left(-\frac{2}{a}\right)^8 +$$
$$\binom{9}{9}\left(-\frac{2}{a}\right)^9$$

$$= \frac{9!}{9!0!}a^9 + \frac{9!}{8!1!}a^8\left(-\frac{2}{a}\right) + \frac{9!}{7!2!}a^7\left(\frac{4}{a^2}\right) +$$
$$\frac{9!}{6!3!}a^6\left(-\frac{8}{a^3}\right) + \frac{9!}{5!4!}a^5\left(\frac{16}{a^4}\right) +$$
$$\frac{9!}{4!5!}a^4\left(-\frac{32}{a^5}\right) + \frac{9!}{3!6!}a^3\left(\frac{64}{a^6}\right) +$$
$$\frac{9!}{2!7!}a^2\left(-\frac{128}{a^7}\right) + \frac{9!}{1!8!}a\left(\frac{256}{a^8}\right) +$$
$$\frac{9!}{0!9!}\left(-\frac{512}{a^9}\right)$$

$$= a^9 - 9(2a^7) + 36(4a^5) - 84(8a^3) +$$
$$126(16a) - 126(32a^{-1}) + 84(64a^{-3}) -$$
$$36(128a^{-5}) + 9(256a^{-7}) - 512a^{-9}$$

$$= a^9 - 18a^7 + 144a^5 - 672a^3 + 2016a -$$
$$4032a^{-1} + 5376a^{-3} - 4608a^{-5} + 2304a^{-7} -$$
$$512a^{-9}$$

14. Use the binomial theorem.

$$\left(2x + \frac{1}{x}\right)^9 = \binom{9}{0}(2x)^9 + \binom{9}{1}(2x)^8\left(\frac{1}{x}\right) +$$
$$\binom{9}{2}(2x)^7\left(\frac{1}{x}\right)^2 + \binom{9}{3}(2x)^6\left(\frac{1}{x}\right)^3 +$$
$$\binom{9}{4}(2x)^5\left(\frac{1}{x}\right)^4 + \binom{9}{5}(2x)^4\left(\frac{1}{x}\right)^5 +$$
$$\binom{9}{6}(2x)^3\left(\frac{1}{x}\right)^6 + \binom{9}{7}(2x)^2\left(\frac{1}{x}\right)^7 +$$
$$\binom{9}{8}(2x)\left(\frac{1}{x}\right)^8 + \binom{9}{9}\left(\frac{1}{x}\right)^9$$

$$= 512x^9 + 2304x^7 + 4608x^5 + 5376x^3 +$$
$$4032x + 2016x^{-1} + 672x^{-3} + 144x^{-5} +$$
$$18x^{-7} + x^{-9}$$

15. $(1 - 1)^n$

Let $a = 1$ and $b = -1$.

Expand using the Binomial Theorem Method:

$$(1 - 1)^n = \binom{n}{0}1^n + \binom{n}{1}1^{n-1}(-1) + \binom{n}{2}1^{n-2}(-1)^2 +$$
$$\binom{n}{3}1^{n-3}(-1)^3 + \ldots + \binom{n}{n}(-1)^n$$

$$= 1\cdot 1 + n\cdot 1\cdot(-1) + \binom{n}{2}\cdot 1\cdot 1 +$$
$$\binom{n}{3}\cdot 1\cdot(-1) + \ldots + \binom{n}{n}(-1)^n$$

$$= 1 - n + \binom{n}{2} - \binom{n}{3} + \ldots + \binom{n}{n}(-1)^n$$

16. Use the binomial theorem.

$$(1 + 3)^n = \binom{n}{0}1^n + \binom{n}{1}1^{n-1}3 + \binom{n}{2}1^{n-2}3^2 +$$
$$\binom{n}{3}1^{n-3}3^3 + \ldots + \binom{n}{n-2}1^23^{n-2} +$$
$$\binom{n}{n-1}1\cdot 3^{n-1} + \binom{n}{n}3^n$$

$$= 1 + 3n + \binom{n}{2}3^2 + \binom{n}{3}3^3 + \ldots +$$
$$\binom{n}{n-2}3^{n-2} + \binom{n}{n-1}3^{n-1} + 3^n$$

17. $(\sqrt{3} - t)^4$

Let $a = \sqrt{3}$, $b = -t$, and $n = 4$.

Expand using the Binomial Theorem Method.

$$(\sqrt{3} - t)^4 = \binom{4}{0}(\sqrt{3})^4 + \binom{4}{1}(\sqrt{3})^3(-t) +$$
$$\binom{4}{2}(\sqrt{3})^2(-t)^2 + \binom{4}{3}(\sqrt{3})(-t)^3 +$$
$$\binom{4}{4}(-t)^4$$

$$= 1\cdot 9 + 4\cdot 3\sqrt{3}\cdot(-t) + 6\cdot 3\cdot t^2 +$$
$$4\cdot\sqrt{3}\cdot(-t^3) + 1\cdot t^4$$

$$= 9 - 12\sqrt{3}\,t + 18t^2 - 4\sqrt{3}\,t^3 + t^4$$

18. Use the binomial theorem.

$$(\sqrt{5} + t)^6 = \binom{6}{0}(\sqrt{5})^6 + \binom{6}{1}(\sqrt{5})^5 t +$$

$$\binom{6}{2}(\sqrt{5})^4 t^2 + \binom{6}{3}(\sqrt{5})^3 t^3 +$$

$$\binom{6}{4}(\sqrt{5})^2 t^4 + \binom{6}{5}\sqrt{5}\, t^5 + \binom{6}{6} t^6$$

$$= 125 + 150\sqrt{5}\, t + 375 t^2 + 100\sqrt{5}\, t^3 +$$

$$75 t^4 + 6\sqrt{5}\, t^5 + t^6$$

19. $(\sqrt{2} + 1)^6 - (\sqrt{2} - 1)^6$

First, expand $(\sqrt{2} + 1)^6$.

$$(\sqrt{2} + 1)^6 = \binom{6}{0}(\sqrt{2})^6 + \binom{6}{1}(\sqrt{2})^5(1) +$$

$$\binom{6}{2}(\sqrt{2})^4(1)^2 + \binom{6}{3}(\sqrt{2})^3(1)^3 +$$

$$\binom{6}{4}(\sqrt{2})^2(1)^4 + \binom{6}{5}(\sqrt{2})(1)^5 +$$

$$\binom{6}{6}(1)^6$$

$$= \frac{6!}{6!0!} \cdot 8 + \frac{6!}{5!1!} \cdot 4\sqrt{2} + \frac{6!}{4!2!} \cdot 4 +$$

$$\frac{6!}{3!3!} \cdot 2\sqrt{2} + \frac{6!}{2!4!} \cdot 2 + \frac{6!}{1!5!} \cdot \sqrt{2} +$$

$$\frac{6!}{0!6!}$$

$$= 8 + 24\sqrt{2} + 60 + 40\sqrt{2} + 30 +$$

$$6\sqrt{2} + 1$$

$$= 99 + 70\sqrt{2}$$

Next, expand $(\sqrt{2} - 1)^6$.

$$(\sqrt{2} - 1)^6 = \binom{6}{0}(\sqrt{2})^6 + \binom{6}{1}(\sqrt{2})^5(-1) +$$

$$\binom{6}{2}(\sqrt{2})^4(-1)^2 + \binom{6}{3}(\sqrt{2})^3(-1)^3 +$$

$$\binom{6}{4}(\sqrt{2})^2(-1)^4 + \binom{6}{5}(\sqrt{2})(-1)^5 +$$

$$\binom{6}{6}(-1)^6$$

$$= \frac{6!}{6!0!} \cdot 8 - \frac{6!}{5!1!} \cdot 4\sqrt{2} + \frac{6!}{4!2!} \cdot 4 -$$

$$\frac{6!}{3!3!} \cdot 2\sqrt{2} + \frac{6!}{2!4!} \cdot 2 - \frac{6!}{1!5!} \cdot \sqrt{2} +$$

$$\frac{6!}{0!6!}$$

$$= 8 - 24\sqrt{2} + 60 - 40\sqrt{2} + 30 -$$

$$6\sqrt{2} + 1$$

$$= 99 - 70\sqrt{2}$$

$(\sqrt{2} + 1)^6 - (\sqrt{2} - 1)^6 = (99 + 70\sqrt{2}) - (99 - 70\sqrt{2})$

$$= 99 + 70\sqrt{2} - 99 + 70\sqrt{2}$$

$$= 140\sqrt{2}$$

20. $(1 - \sqrt{2})^4 = 1 \cdot 1^4 + 4 \cdot 1^3(-\sqrt{2}) + 6 \cdot 1^2(-\sqrt{2})^2 +$

$$4 \cdot 1 \cdot (-\sqrt{2})^3 + 1 \cdot (-\sqrt{2})^4$$

$$= 1 - 4\sqrt{2} + 12 - 8\sqrt{2} + 4$$

$$= 17 - 12\sqrt{2}$$

$(1 + \sqrt{2})^4 = 1 + 4\sqrt{2} + 12 + 8\sqrt{2} + 4$
(Using the result above)

$$= 17 + 12\sqrt{2}$$

$(1 - \sqrt{2})^4 + (1 + \sqrt{2})^4 = 17 - 12\sqrt{2} + 17 +$

$$12\sqrt{2} = 34$$

21. Expand $(x^{-2} + x^2)^4$ using the binomial theorem.

Note that $a = x^{-2}$, $b = x^2$, and $n = 4$.

$$(x^{-2} + x^2)^4 = \binom{4}{0}(x^{-2})^4 + \binom{4}{1}(x^{-2})^3(x^2) +$$

$$\binom{4}{2}(x^{-2})^2(x^2)^2 + \binom{4}{3}(x^{-2})(x^2)^3 +$$

$$\binom{4}{4}(x^2)^4$$

$$= \frac{4!}{4!0!}(x^{-8}) + \frac{4!}{3!1!}(x^{-6})(x^2) +$$

$$\frac{4!}{2!2!}(x^{-4})(x^4) + \frac{4!}{1!3!}(x^{-2})(x^6) +$$

$$\frac{4!}{0!4!}(x^8)$$

$$= x^{-8} + 4x^{-4} + 6x^0 + 4x^4 + x^8$$

$$= x^{-8} + 4x^{-4} + 6 + 4x^4 + x^8$$

22. $$\left[\frac{1}{\sqrt{x}} - \sqrt{x}\right]^6 = \binom{6}{0}\left[\frac{1}{\sqrt{x}}\right]^6 + \binom{6}{1}\left[\frac{1}{\sqrt{x}}\right]^5(-\sqrt{x}) +$$

$$\binom{6}{2}\left[\frac{1}{\sqrt{x}}\right]^4(-\sqrt{x})^2 + \binom{6}{3}\left[\frac{1}{\sqrt{x}}\right]^3(-\sqrt{x})^3 +$$

$$\binom{6}{4}\left[\frac{1}{\sqrt{x}}\right]^2(-\sqrt{x})^4 + \binom{6}{5}\left[\frac{1}{\sqrt{x}}\right](-\sqrt{x})^5 +$$

$$\binom{6}{6}(-\sqrt{x})^6$$

$$= \frac{1}{x^3} - 6 \cdot \frac{1}{x^2} + 15 \cdot \frac{1}{x} - 20 + 15x -$$

$$6x^2 + x^3, \text{ or}$$

$$x^{-3} - 6x^{-2} + 15x^{-1} - 20 + 15x - 6x^2 + x^3$$

23. Find the 3rd term of $(a + b)^6$.

First, we note that $3 = 2 + 1$, $a = a$, $b = b$, and $n = 6$. Then the 3rd term of the expansion of $(a + b)^6$ is

$$\binom{6}{2}a^{6-2}b^2, \text{ or } \frac{6!}{4!2!}a^4b^2, \text{ or } 15a^4b^2.$$

24. $$\binom{7}{5}x^2y^5 = 21x^2y^5$$

25. Find the 12th term of $(a - 2)^{14}$.

First, we note that $12 = 11 + 1$, $a = a$, $b = -2$, and $n = 14$. Then the 12th term of the expansion of $(a - 2)^{14}$ is

$$\binom{14}{11} a^{14-11} \cdot (-2)^{11} = \frac{14!}{3!11!} a^3(-2048)$$

$$= 364a^3(-2048)$$

$$= -745,472a^3$$

26. $\binom{12}{10} x^2(-3)^{10} = 3,897,234x^2$

27. Find the 5th term of $(2x^3 - \sqrt{y})^8$.

First, we note that $5 = 4 + 1$, $a = 2x^3$, $b = -\sqrt{y}$, and $n = 8$. Then the 5th term of the expansion of $(2x^3 - \sqrt{y})^8$ is

$$\binom{8}{4} (2x^3)^{8-4}(-\sqrt{y})^4$$

$$= \frac{8!}{4!4!} (2x^3)^4(-\sqrt{y})^4$$

$$= 70(16x^{12})(y^2)$$

$$= 1120x^{12}y^2$$

28. $\binom{7}{3}\left[\frac{1}{b^2}\right]^4\left[\frac{b}{3}\right]^3 = \frac{35}{27} b^{-5}$

29. The middle term of the expansion of $(2u - 3v^2)^{10}$ is the 6th term. Note that $6 = 5 + 1$, $a = 2u$, $b = -3v^2$, and $n = 10$. Then the 6th term of the expansion of $(2u - 3v^2)^{10}$ is

$$\binom{10}{5} (2u)^{10-5}(-3v^2)^5$$

$$= \frac{10!}{5!5!} (2u)^5(-3v^2)^5$$

$$= 252(32u^5)(-243v^{10})$$

$$= -1,959,552u^5v^{10}$$

30. Third term: $\binom{5}{2}(\sqrt{x})^3(\sqrt{3})^2 = 30x\sqrt{x}$

Fourth term: $\binom{5}{3}(\sqrt{x})^2(\sqrt{3})^3 = 30x\sqrt{3}$

31. The number of subsets is 2^7, or 128 (Theorem 16).

32. 2^6, or 64

33. The number of subsets is 2^{26}, or 67,108,864 (Theorem 16).

34. 2^{24}, or 16,777,216

35. We use the binomial theorem. Note that $a = \sqrt{2}$, $b = -i$, and $n = 4$.

$$(\sqrt{2} - i)^4 = \binom{4}{0}(\sqrt{2})^4 + \binom{4}{1}(\sqrt{2})^3(-i) +$$

$$\binom{4}{2}(\sqrt{2})^2(-i)^2 + \binom{4}{3}(\sqrt{2})(-i)^3 +$$

$$\binom{4}{4}(-i)^4$$

$$= \frac{4!}{0!4!} (4) + \frac{4!}{1!3!} (2\sqrt{2})(-i) +$$

$$\frac{4!}{2!2!} (2)(-1) + \frac{4!}{3!1!} (\sqrt{2})(i) +$$

$$\frac{4!}{4!0!} (1)$$

$$= 4 - 8\sqrt{2}\, i - 12 + 4\sqrt{2}\, i + 1$$

$$= -7 - 4\sqrt{2}\, i$$

36. $(1 + i)^6 = \binom{6}{0}1^6 + \binom{6}{1}1^5 \cdot i + \binom{6}{2}1^4 \cdot i^2 +$

$$\binom{6}{3}1^3 \cdot i^3 + \binom{6}{4}1^2 \cdot i^4 + \binom{6}{5}1 \cdot i^5 +$$

$$\binom{6}{6}1^6$$

$$= 1 + 6i - 15 - 20i + 15 + 6i - 1$$

$$= -8i$$

37. $(\sin t - \csc t)^7 = \left[\sin t - \frac{1}{\sin t}\right]^7$

$$= \binom{7}{0}\sin^7 t + \binom{7}{1}\sin^6 t\left[-\frac{1}{\sin t}\right] +$$

$$\binom{7}{2}\sin^5 t\left[-\frac{1}{\sin t}\right]^2 + \binom{7}{3}\sin^4 t\left[-\frac{1}{\sin t}\right]^3 +$$

$$\binom{7}{4}\sin^3 t\left[-\frac{1}{\sin t}\right]^4 + \binom{7}{5}\sin^2 t\left[-\frac{1}{\sin t}\right]^5 +$$

$$\binom{7}{6}\sin t\left[-\frac{1}{\sin t}\right]^6 + \binom{7}{7}\left[-\frac{1}{\sin t}\right]^7$$

$$= \sin^7 t - 7\sin^5 t + 21\sin^3 t - 35\sin t +$$

$$35\left[\frac{1}{\sin t}\right] - 21\left[\frac{1}{\sin^3 t}\right] + 7\left[\frac{1}{\sin^5 t}\right] - \frac{1}{\sin^7 t}, \text{ or}$$

$$\sin^7 t - 7\sin^5 t + 21\sin^3 t - 35\sin t +$$

$$35\csc t - 21\csc^3 t + 7\csc^5 t - \csc^7 t$$

38. $(\tan \theta + \cot \theta)^{11} = \binom{11}{0}\tan^{11}\theta +$

$$\binom{11}{1}\tan^{10}\theta \cot \theta + \binom{11}{2}\tan^9\theta \cot^2\theta +$$

$$\binom{11}{3}\tan^8\theta \cot^3\theta + \binom{11}{4}\tan^7\theta \cot^4\theta +$$

$$\binom{11}{5}\tan^6\theta \cot^5\theta + \binom{11}{6}\tan^5\theta \cot^7\theta +$$

$$\binom{11}{7}\tan^4\theta \cot^7\theta + \binom{11}{8}\tan^3\theta \cot^8\theta +$$

$$\binom{11}{9}\tan^2\theta \cot^9\theta + \binom{11}{10}\tan \theta \cot^{10}\theta +$$

$$\binom{11}{11}\cot^{11}\theta$$

$= \tan^{11}\theta + 11\tan^9\theta + 55\tan^7\theta + 165\tan^5\theta +$
$330\tan^3\theta + 462\tan\theta + 462\cot\theta +$
$330\cot^3\theta + 165\cot^5\theta + 55\cot^7\theta +$
$11\cot^9\theta + \cot^{11}\theta$

39. $(a - b)^n = \binom{n}{0}a^n + \binom{n}{1}a^{n-1}(-b) +$

$\binom{n}{2}a^{n-2}(-b)^2 + \cdots + \binom{n}{n}(-b)^n$

$= \binom{n}{0}a^n + \binom{n}{1}(-1)a^{n-1}b +$

$\binom{n}{2}(-1)^2 a^{n-2}b^2 + \cdots + \binom{n}{n}(-1)^n b^n$

$= \sum_{r=0}^{n} \binom{n}{r}(-1)^r a^{n-r}b^r$

40. $\dfrac{(x+h)^n - x^n}{h}$

$= \dfrac{\binom{n}{0}x^n + \binom{n}{1}x^{n-1}h + \binom{n}{2}x^{n-2}h^2 + \cdots + \binom{n}{n}h^n - x^n}{h}$

$= \binom{n}{1}x^{n-1} + \binom{n}{2}x^{n-2}h + \cdots + \binom{n}{n}h^{n-1}$

$= \sum_{r=1}^{n} \binom{n}{r}x^{n-r}h^{r-1}$

41. $\sum_{r=0}^{8} \binom{8}{r}x^{8-r}3^r = 0$

The left side of the equation is sigma notation for the binomial series $(x + 3)^8$, so we have:

$(x + 3)^8 = 0$

$x + 3 = 0$ (Taking the 8th root on both sides)

$x = -3$

42. $\sum_{r=0}^{4} \binom{4}{r} 5^{4-r}x^r = 64$

$(5 + x)^4 = 64$

$5 + x = \pm 2\sqrt{2}$

$x = -5 \pm 2\sqrt{2}$

43. $\sum_{r=0}^{5} \binom{5}{r}(-1)^r x^{5-r}3^r = \sum_{r=0}^{5} \binom{5}{r}x^{5-r}(-3)^r$, so the

left side of the equation is sigma notation for the binomial series $(x - 3)^5$. We have:

$(x - 3)^5 = 32$

$x - 3 = 2$ (Taking the 5th root on both sides)

$x = 5$

44. $\sum_{r=0}^{9} \binom{9}{r}\sin^r x = \sum_{r=0}^{9} 1^{n-r}\sin^r x = (1 + \sin x)^9 = 0$

$1 + \sin x = 0$

$\sin x = -1$

$x = \dfrac{3\pi}{2} + 2k\pi$, k an integer

45. Find the third term of $(0.313 + 0.687)^5$:

$\binom{5}{2}(0.313)^{5-2}(0.687)^2 = \dfrac{5!}{3!2!}(0.313)^3(0.687)^2 \approx$
0.14473

46. $\binom{8}{5}(0.15)^3(0.85)^5 \approx 0.08386$

47. Find and add the 3rd through 6th terms of $(0.313 + 0.687)^5$:

$\binom{5}{2}(0.313)^3(0.687)^2 + \binom{5}{3}(0.313)^2(0.687)^3 +$

$\binom{5}{4}(0.313)(0.687)^4 + \binom{5}{5}(0.687)^5 \approx 0.96403$

48. $\binom{8}{6}(0.15)^2(0.85)^6 + \binom{8}{7}(0.15)(0.85)^7 +$

$\binom{8}{8}(0.85)^8 \approx 0.89479$

49. There are 11 terms in the expression of $(8u + 3v^2)^{10}$, so the 6th term is the middle term.

$\binom{10}{5}(8u)^5(3v^2)^5 = \dfrac{10!}{5!5!}(32,768u^5)(243v^{10}) =$
$2,006,581,248u^5v^{10}$

50. Third term: $\binom{5}{2}(\sqrt{x})^3(-\sqrt{3})^2 = 30x\sqrt{x}$

Fourth term: $\binom{5}{3}(\sqrt{x})^2(-\sqrt{3})^3 = -30x\sqrt{3}$

51. The $(r + 1)$st term of $\left(\dfrac{3x^2}{2} - \dfrac{1}{3x}\right)^{12}$ is

$\binom{12}{r}\left(\dfrac{3x^2}{2}\right)^{12-r}\left(-\dfrac{1}{3x}\right)^r$. In the term which does not contain x, the exponent of x in the numerator is equal to the exponent of x in the denominator.

$2(12 - r) = r$

$24 - 2r = r$

$24 = 3r$

$8 = r$

Find the $(8 + 1)$st, or 9th term:

$\binom{12}{8}\left(\dfrac{3x^2}{2}\right)^4\left(-\dfrac{1}{3x}\right)^8 = \dfrac{12!}{4!8!}\left(\dfrac{3^4 x^8}{2^4}\right)\left(\dfrac{1}{3^8 x^8}\right) = \dfrac{55}{144}$

52. The expansion of $(x^2 - 6y^{3/2})^6$ has 7 terms, so the 4th term is the middle term.

$$\binom{6}{3}(x^2)^3(-6y^{3/2})^3 = \frac{6!}{3!3!}(x^6)(-216y^{9/2}) = -4320x^6 y^{9/2}$$

53. $\dfrac{\binom{5}{3}(p^2)^2\left[-\frac{1}{2}p\sqrt[3]{q}\right]^3}{\binom{5}{2}(p^2)^3\left[-\frac{1}{2}p\sqrt[3]{q}\right]^2} = \dfrac{-\frac{1}{8}p^7 q}{\frac{1}{4}p^8\sqrt[3]{q^2}} = -\dfrac{\sqrt[3]{q}}{2p}$

54. The $(r + 1)$st term of $\left[\sqrt[3]{x} - \frac{1}{\sqrt{x}}\right]^7$ is

$\binom{7}{r}(\sqrt[3]{x})^{7-r}\left[-\frac{1}{\sqrt{x}}\right]^r$. The term containing $\frac{1}{x^{1/6}}$ is the term in which the sum of the exponents is $-1/6$. That is,

$$\left[\frac{1}{3}\right](7 - r) + \left[-\frac{1}{2}\right](r) = -\frac{1}{6}$$
$$\frac{7}{3} - \frac{r}{3} - \frac{r}{2} = -\frac{1}{6}$$
$$-\frac{5r}{6} = -\frac{15}{6}$$
$$r = 3$$

Find the $(3 + 1)$st, or 4th term.

$\binom{7}{3}(\sqrt[3]{x})^4\left[-\frac{1}{\sqrt{x}}\right]^3 = \frac{7!}{4!3!}(x^{4/3})(-x^{-3/2}) = -35x^{-1/6}$,

or $-\dfrac{35}{x^{1/6}}$.

55. The term of highest degree of $(x^5 + 3)^4$ is the first term, or

$\binom{4}{0}(x^5)^{4-0}3^0 = \frac{4!}{4!0!}x^{20} = x^{20}$.

Therefore, the degree of $(x^5 + 3)^4$ is 20.

56. The total number of subsets of a set of 7 bills is 2^7. This includes the empty set. Thus, $2^7 - 1$, or 127, different sums of money can be formed.

57. Familiarize: Let x, $x + 1$, $x + 2$, and $x + 3$ represent the integers.

Translate: We write an equation.
$$x^3 + (x + 1)^3 + (x + 2)^3 = (x + 3)^3$$

Carry out: We solve the equation.
$$x^3 + x^3 + 3x^2 + 3x + 1 + x^3 + 6x^2 + 12x + 8 = x^3 + 9x^2 + 27x + 27$$
$$2x^3 - 12x - 18 = 0$$
$$x^3 - 6x - 9 = 0 \qquad \left[\text{Multiplying by } \tfrac{1}{2}\right]$$

Using the rational roots theorem and synthetic division, we see that 3 is a root of the equation.
$$(x - 3)(x^2 + 3x + 3) = 0$$

The quadratic factor does not have real number zeros, so the only real number solution is 3.

Check: If $x = 3$, then the integers are 3, 4, 5, and 6. It is true that $3^3 + 4^3 + 5^3 = 6^3$. The values check.

State: The integers are 3, 4, 5, and 6.

58. $_{100}C_0 + {_{100}C_1} + \cdots + {_{100}C_{100}}$ is the total number of subsets of a set with 100 members, or 2^{100}.

59. $_nC_0 + {_nC_1} + \cdots + {_nC_n}$ is the total number of subsets of a set with n members, or 2^n (by Theorem 16).

60. $\displaystyle\sum_{r=0}^{23}\binom{23}{r}(\log_a x)^{23-r}(\log_a t)^r =$

$$(\log_a x + \log_a t)^{23} = [\log_a (xt)]^{23}$$

61. $\ln\left[\displaystyle\sum_{r=0}^{15}\binom{15}{r}(\cos t)^{30-2r}(\sin t)^{2r}\right]$

$= \ln\left[\displaystyle\sum_{r=0}^{15}\binom{15}{r}(\cos^2 t)^{15-r}(\sin^2 t)^r\right]$

$= \ln(\cos^2 t + \sin^2 t)^{15} = \ln(1)^{15} = \ln 1 = 0$

62. Basis step: Since $a + b = (a + b)^1$, S_1 is true. Induction step: Let k be any positive integer.

Let S_k be the statement of the binomial theorem with n replaced by k. Multiply both sides of S_k by $(a + b)$ to obtain
$(a + b)^{k+1}$

$= \left[a^k + \cdots + \binom{k}{r-1}a^{k-(r-1)}b^{r-1} + \binom{k}{r}a^{k-r}b^r + \cdots + b^k\right](a + b)$

$= a^{k+1} + \cdots + \left[\binom{k}{r-1} + \binom{k}{r}\right]a^{(k+1)-r}b^r + \cdots + b^{k+1}$

$= a^{k+1} + \cdots + \binom{k+1}{r}a^{(k+1)-r}b^r + \cdots + b^{k+1}$.

This proves S_{k+1}, assuming S_k. Hence S_n is true for $n = 1, 2, 3, \ldots$.

Exercise Set 11.8

1. 100 surveyed
57 wore either glasses or contacts
43 wore neither glasses nor contacts

Using Principle P,

P(wearing either glasses or contacts) $= \dfrac{57}{100}$, or 0.57

P(wearing neither glasses nor contacts) = $\frac{43}{100}$, or

0.43

2. 0.18, 0.24, 0.23, 0.23, 0.12; Opinions might vary, but it would seem that people tend not to pick the first or last numbers.

3. 1044 Total letters in the three paragraphs
   78 A's occurred
   140 E's occurred
   60 I's occurred
   74 O's occurred
   31 U's occurred

   Using Principle P,

   P(the occurrence of letter A) = $\frac{78}{1044} \approx 0.075$

   P(the occurrence of letter E) = $\frac{140}{1044} \approx 0.134$

   P(the occurrence of letter I) = $\frac{60}{1044} \approx 0.057$

   P(the occurrence of letter O) = $\frac{74}{1044} \approx 0.071$

   P(the occurrence of letter U) = $\frac{31}{1044} \approx 0.030$

4. A   78
   E   140
   I   60
   O   74
   U $\underline{31}$
       $383 \div 1044 \approx 0.367$

5. 1044 Total letters
   $-\ 383$ Total vowels   (from Exercise 4)
   $\overline{\ 661}$ Total consonants

   Using Principle P,

   P(the occurrence of a consonant) = $\frac{661}{1044} \approx 0.633$

6. Z; $1 - \frac{1}{1044} \approx 0.999$

7. There are 52 equally likely outcomes.

8. $\frac{4}{52}$, or $\frac{1}{13}$

9. Since there are 52 equally likely outcomes and there are 13 ways to obtain a heart, by Principle P we have

   P(drawing a heart) = $\frac{13}{52} = \frac{1}{4}$.

10. $\frac{13}{52}$, or $\frac{1}{4}$

11. Since there are 52 equally likely outcomes and there are 4 ways to obtain a 4, by Principle P we have

    P(drawing a 4) = $\frac{4}{52} = \frac{1}{13}$.

12. $\frac{26}{52}$, or $\frac{1}{2}$

13. Since there are 52 equally likely outcomes and there are 26 ways to obtain a black card, by Principle P we have

    P(drawing a black card) = $\frac{26}{52} = \frac{1}{2}$.

14. $\frac{4 + 4}{52}$, or $\frac{2}{13}$

15. Since there are 52 equally likely outcomes and there are 8 ways to obtain a 9 or a king (four 9's and four kings), we have, by Principle P,

    P(drawing a 9 or a king) = $\frac{8}{52} = \frac{2}{13}$.

16. $\frac{4}{4 + 10}$, or $\frac{2}{7}$

17. Since there are 14 equally likely ways of selecting a marble from a bag containing 4 red marbles and 10 green marbles, we have, by Principle P,

    P(selecting a green marble) = $\frac{10}{14} = \frac{5}{7}$.

18. 0

19. There are 14 equally likely ways of selecting any marble from a bag containing 4 red marbles and 10 green marbles. Since the bag does not contain any white marbles, there are 0 ways of selecting a white marble. By Principle P, we have

    P(selecting a white marble) = $\frac{0}{14} = 0$.

20. P(4 spades) = $\frac{_{13}C_4}{_{52}C_4} = \frac{11}{4165}$

21. The number of ways of drawing 4 cards from a deck of 52 cards is $_{52}C_4$. Now 13 of the 52 cards are hearts, so the number of ways of drawing 4 hearts is $_{13}C_4$. Thus,

    P(getting 4 hearts) = $\frac{_{13}C_4}{_{52}C_4} = \frac{715}{270{,}725} = \frac{11}{4165}$

22. $\frac{_8C_2 \cdot _6C_2}{_{14}C_4} = \frac{28 \cdot 15}{1001} = \frac{60}{143}$

23. The number of ways of selecting 4 people from a group of 15 is $_{15}C_4$. Two men can be selected in $_8C_2$ ways, and 2 women can be selected in $_7C_2$ ways. By the Fundamental Counting Principle, the number of ways of selecting 2 men and 2 women is $_8C_2 \cdot {}_7C_2$. Thus,

$$P(\text{2 men and 2 women are chosen}) = \frac{_8C_2 \cdot {}_7C_2}{_{15}C_4}$$

$$= \frac{28 \cdot 21}{1365} = \frac{28}{65}$$

24.

1,6	2,6	3,6	4,6	5,6	6,6
1,5	2,5	3,5	4,5	5,5	6,5
1,4	2,4	3,4	4,4	5,4	6,4
1,3	2,3	3,3	4,3	5,3	6,3
1,2	2,2	3,2	4,2	5,2	6,2
1,1	2,1	3,1	4,1	5,1	6,1

$\frac{5}{36}$

25. On each die there are 6 possible outcomes. The outcomes are paired so there are 6·6, or 36 possible ways in which the two can fall. The pairs that total 3 are (1, 2) and (2, 1). Thus there are 2 possible ways of getting a total of 3, so the probability is $\frac{2}{36}$, or $\frac{1}{18}$.

26. $\frac{1}{36}$

27. On each die there are 6 possible outcomes. The outcomes are paired so there are 6·6, or 36 possible ways in which the two can fall. There is only 1 way of getting a total of 12, the pair (6, 6), so the probability is $\frac{1}{36}$.

28. 5 nickels
    8 dimes
    7 quarters
    ────────────
    20 coins

$$\frac{_5C_2 \cdot {}_8C_2 \cdot {}_7C_1}{_{20}C_5} = \frac{10 \cdot 28 \cdot 7}{15,504} = \frac{245}{1938}$$

29. The number of ways of getting 6 coins from a bag containing 20 coins is $_{20}C_6$. Three nickels can be selected in $_6C_3$ ways since the bag contains 6 nickels. Two dimes can be selected in $_{10}C_2$ ways since the bag contains 10 dimes. One quarter can be selected in $_4C_1$ ways since the bag contains 4 quarters. By the Fundamental Counting Principle the number of ways of selecting 3 nickels, 2 dimes, and 1 quarter is $_6C_3 \cdot {}_{10}C_2 \cdot {}_4C_1$. Thus,

$$P(\text{getting 3 nickels, 2 dimes, and 1 quarter})$$

$$= \frac{_6C_3 \cdot {}_{10}C_2 \cdot {}_4C_1}{_{20}C_6} = \frac{20 \cdot 45 \cdot 4}{38,760} = \frac{30}{323}$$

30. $\frac{18}{38}$, or $\frac{9}{19}$

31. The roulette wheel contains 38 equally likely slots. Eighteen of the 38 slots are colored red. Thus, by Principle P,

$$P(\text{the ball falls in a red slot}) = \frac{18}{38} = \frac{9}{19}$$

32. $\frac{36}{38}$, or $\frac{18}{19}$

33. The roulette wheel contains 38 equally likely slots. Only 1 slot is numbered 00. Then, by Principle P,

$$P(\text{the ball falls in the 00 slot}) = \frac{1}{38}.$$

34. $\frac{1}{38}$

35. The roulette wheel contains 38 equally likely slots, 2 of which are numbered 00 and 0. Thus, using Principle P,

$$P\binom{\text{the ball falling in either}}{\text{the 00 or the 0 slot}} = \frac{2}{38} = \frac{1}{19}.$$

36. $\frac{18}{38}$, or $\frac{9}{19}$

37. $_{52}C_5 = 2,598,960$

38. a) 4

   b) $\frac{4}{_{52}C_5} = \frac{4}{2,598,960} \approx 1.54 \times 10^{-6}$

39. Consider a suit

     A K Q J 10 9 8 7 6 5 4 3 2

     A straight flush can be any of the following combinations in the same suit.

       K Q J 10 9
       Q J 10 9 8
       J 10 9 8 7
      10 9 8 7 6
       9 8 7 6 5
       8 7 6 5 4
       7 6 5 4 3
       6 5 4 3 2
       5 4 3 2 A

     Remember a straight flush does not include
     A K Q J 10 which is a royal flush.

     a) Since there are 9 straight flushes per suit, there are 36 straight flushes in all 4 suits.

     b) Since $_{52}C_5$, or 2,598,960 poker hands can be dealt from a standard 52-card deck and 36 of those hands are straight flushes, the probability of getting a straight flush is $\frac{36}{2,598,960}$, or 0.0000139.

40. a) $13 \cdot 48 = 624$; that is, there are 13 ways to pick 4 cards from any one of the 13 denominations. Then there are 48 ways to pick any one of the remaining 48 cards.

     b) $\frac{13 \cdot 48}{_{52}C_5} = \frac{624}{2,598,960} \approx 2.4 \times 10^{-4}$

41. a) $[13 \cdot {}_4C_3] \cdot [12 \cdot {}_4C_2] = 3744$; that is, there are 13 ways to select a denomination. Then from that denomination there are $_4C_3$ ways to pick 3 of the 4 cards in that denomination. Now there are 12 ways to select any one of the remaining 12 denominations and $_4C_2$ ways to pick 2 cards from the 4 cards in that denomination.

     b) $\frac{3744}{_{52}C_5} = \frac{3744}{2,598,960} \approx 0.00144$

42. a) $\left[13 \cdot \begin{bmatrix} 4 \\ 2 \end{bmatrix} \right] \cdot \left[\begin{bmatrix} 12 \\ 3 \end{bmatrix} \cdot \begin{bmatrix} 4 \\ 1 \end{bmatrix} \begin{bmatrix} 4 \\ 1 \end{bmatrix} \begin{bmatrix} 4 \\ 1 \end{bmatrix} \right]$

     $= 1,098,240$

     There are 13 ways to select a denomination and then $\begin{bmatrix} 4 \\ 2 \end{bmatrix}$ ways to pick 2 cards from the 4 cards in this denomination. Now there are $\begin{bmatrix} 12 \\ 3 \end{bmatrix}$ ways to select any 3 of the remaining 12 denominations, and then in each of these 3 denominations there are $\begin{bmatrix} 4 \\ 1 \end{bmatrix}$ ways to pick

1 card from the 4 cards in each of these 3 denominations.

     b) $\frac{1,098,240}{_{52}C_5} = \frac{1,098,240}{2,598,960} \approx 0.423$

43. a) $\left[13 \cdot \begin{bmatrix} 4 \\ 3 \end{bmatrix} \right] \cdot \left[\begin{bmatrix} 48 \\ 2 \end{bmatrix} \right] - 3744 = 54,912.$

     There are 13 ways to select a denomination and then $\begin{bmatrix} 4 \\ 3 \end{bmatrix}$ ways to pick 3 cards from the 4 in this denomination. Now there are $\begin{bmatrix} 48 \\ 2 \end{bmatrix}$ ways to pick 2 cards from the remaining 12 denominations (48 cards); but $13 \begin{bmatrix} 4 \\ 3 \end{bmatrix} \begin{bmatrix} 48 \\ 2 \end{bmatrix}$ includes the 3744 hands (like QQQ-10-10) in a full house. (See Exercise 41.) Subtracting 3744, we have the above result.

     b) $\frac{54,912}{_{52}C_5} = \frac{54,912}{2,598,960} \approx 0.0211$

44. a) $4 \cdot \begin{bmatrix} 13 \\ 5 \end{bmatrix} - 4 - 36 = 5108$

     There are 4 ways to select a suit and then $\begin{bmatrix} 13 \\ 5 \end{bmatrix}$ ways to pick 5 cards from this suit of 13 cards; but $4 \cdot \begin{bmatrix} 13 \\ 5 \end{bmatrix}$ includes hands with all cards in sequence, and so we subtract the 4 royal flushes (Exercise 38) and the 36 straight flushes (Exercise 39) to obtain the above result.

     b) $\frac{5108}{_{52}C_5} = \frac{5108}{2,598,960} \approx 0.00197$

45. a) $\begin{bmatrix} 13 \\ 2 \end{bmatrix} \begin{bmatrix} 4 \\ 2 \end{bmatrix} \begin{bmatrix} 4 \\ 2 \end{bmatrix} \begin{bmatrix} 44 \\ 1 \end{bmatrix} = 123,552$

     There are $\begin{bmatrix} 13 \\ 2 \end{bmatrix}$ ways to select 2 denominations from 13 denominations; then there are $\begin{bmatrix} 4 \\ 2 \end{bmatrix}$ ways to pick 2 of the 4 cards in either of these 2 denominations, and $\begin{bmatrix} 4 \\ 2 \end{bmatrix}$ ways to pick 2 of the 4 cards in the other of these 2 denominations. Finally, there are $\begin{bmatrix} 44 \\ 1 \end{bmatrix}$ ways to select the fifth card from the remaining 44.

     b) $\frac{123,552}{_{52}C_5} = \frac{123,552}{2,598,960} \approx 0.0475$

46. a) $\begin{bmatrix} 10 \\ 1 \end{bmatrix}\begin{bmatrix} 4 \\ 1 \end{bmatrix}\begin{bmatrix} 4 \\ 1 \end{bmatrix}\begin{bmatrix} 4 \\ 1 \end{bmatrix}\begin{bmatrix} 4 \\ 1 \end{bmatrix}\begin{bmatrix} 4 \\ 1 \end{bmatrix} - 4 - 36$

= 10,200

An ace can be high or low. Then there are $\begin{bmatrix} 10 \\ 1 \end{bmatrix}$ ways to select 1 of 10 sets of 5 of 5 consecutive cards:

A K Q J 10
K Q J 10 9
Q J 10 9 8
$\vdots$
5 4 3 2 A

Then in each of these 10 sets there are 4 ways to pick (from 4 suits) each of the 5 cards. Since $10 \cdot 4^5$ includes 4 royal flushes (same suit) and 36 straight flushes (same suit), these numbers are subtracted to give the above result.

b) $\dfrac{10,200}{_{52}C_5} = \dfrac{10,200}{2,598,960} \approx 0.00392$